SOUTH CAROLINA
DEED ABSTRACTS 1719-1772

VOL. III

1755-1768, Books QQ-H-3

Abstracted by

Clara A. Langley

Southern Historical Press, Inc.
Greenville, South Carolina

SOUTHERN HISTORICAL PRESS, INC.
PO BOX 1267
Greenville, SC   29601

ISBN #0-89308-273-2

Printed in the United States of America

To

AGNES LELAND BALDWIN

whose dedicated efforts have made the
sources for South Carolina History and
Genealogy widely available to persons doing
South Carolina Research

SOUTH CAROLINA
COUNTY OUTLINE MAP

WALHALLA

PICKENS

GREENVILLE

SPARTANBURG

GAFFNEY

YORK

UNION

CHESTER

LANCASTER

CHESTERFIELD

BENNETTSVILLE

ANDERSON

LAURENS

WINNSBORO

NEWBERRY

CAMDEN

DARLINGTON

DILLON

MARION

ABBEVILLE

GREENWOOD

SALUDA

COLUMBIA

BISHOPVILLE

FLORENCE

McCORMICK

LEXINGTON

SUMTER

CONWAY

EDGEFIELD

ST. MATTHEWS

MANNING

KINGSTREE

AIKEN

ORANGEBURG

GEORGETOWN

BARNWELL

BAMBERG

ST. GEORGE

MONCKS CORNER

ALLENDALE

WALTERBORO

HAMPTON

CHARLESTON

RIDGELAND

BEAUFORT

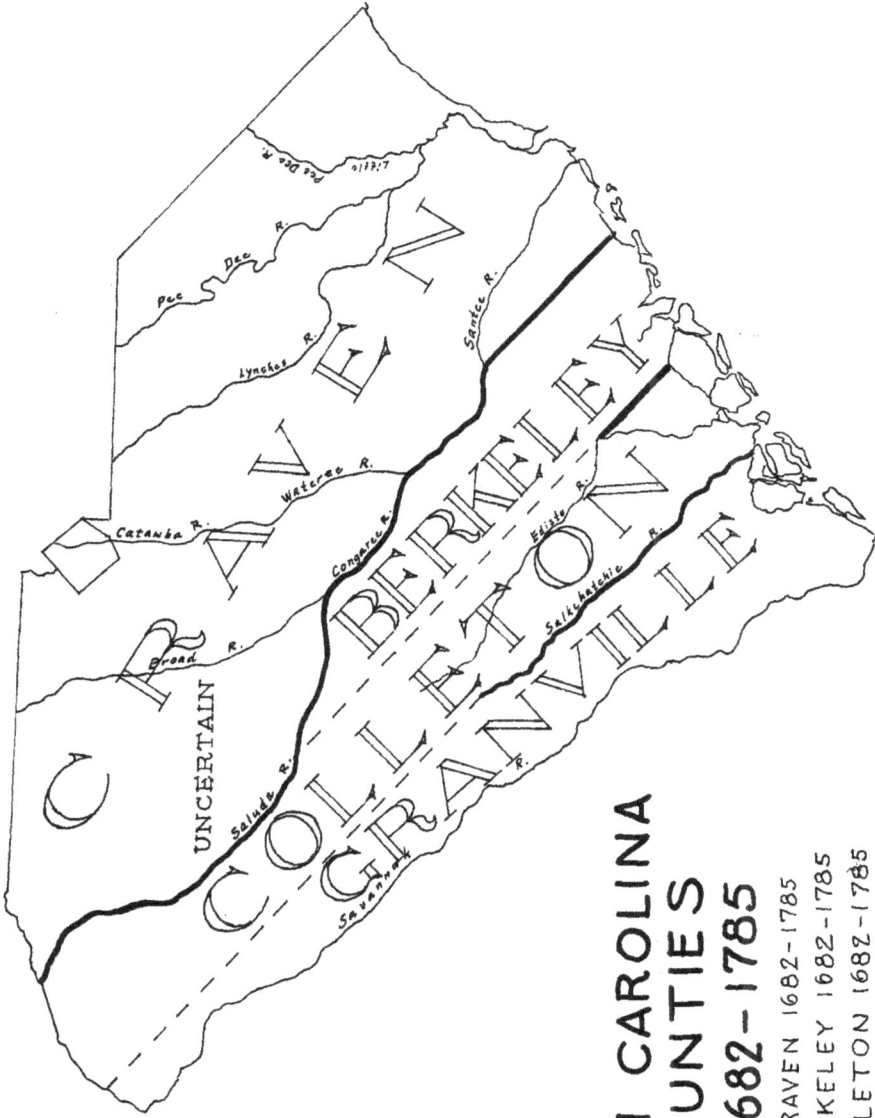

SOUTH CAROLINA COUNTIES 1682-1785

CRAVEN 1682-1785
BERKELEY 1682-1785
COLLETON 1682-1785
GRANVILLE 1710-1785

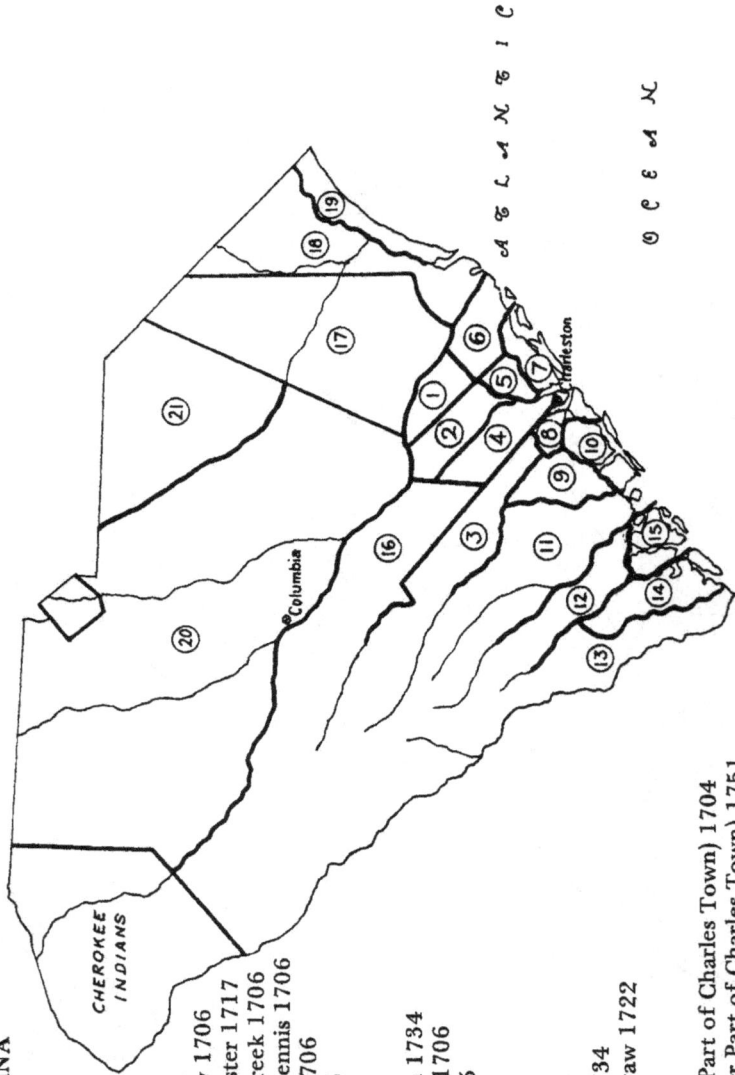

SOUTH CAROLINA
PARISHES

KEY

1. St. Stephen's 1754
2. St. John's, Berkeley 1706
3. St. George, Dorchester 1717
4. St. James, Goose Creek 1706
5. St. Thomas & St. Dennis 1706
6. St. James, Santee 1706
7. Christ Church 1706
8. St. Andrews 1706
9. St. Paul 1706
10. St. John's, Colleton 1734
11. St. Bartholomew's 1706
12. Prince William 1745
13. St. Peter's 1747
14. St. Luke's 1767
15. St. Helena 1712
16. St. Matthew's 1768
17. Prince Frederick 1734
18. Prince George Winyaw 1722
19. All Saints 1767
20. St. Mark's 1757
St. Philip's (Upper Part of Charles Town) 1704
St. Michael's (Lower Part of Charles Town) 1751

By Elmer Oris Parker

INTRODUCTION

Before 1790, land transactions for the entire State of South Carolina were recorded in Charleston. Many of these records are now in the custody of the Charleston County Register of Mesne Conveyance. Between 1936 and 1938 the Works Progress Administration employed Miss Clara A. Langley to prepare abstracts of the earliest seventy-four volumes of conveyances and miscellaneous records that remained in Charleston, and these abstracts are being published here for the first time. Proprietary land records and all Royal grants had earlier been transferred to Columbia, and were not abstracted.

These four volumes of deeds consist largely of abstracts of conveyances or transfers of title to land that had earlier been granted. Conveyances during the Royal period ususally took the form of a "lease and release." Under English law, for an unrestricted conveyance to be made, a buyer had to have possession of a piece of land as a lessor. A separate "lease" for a nominal amount gave him tenancy rights for up to a year. He became eligible to claim possession one day following execution of the lease and thus became entitled to obtain a "release" that gave him absolute and unqualified ownership. These "L. & R." documents contain essentially the same information, and each set was accordingly abstracted as though it were a single record.

Volumes of conveyances were ordinarily used to record only "mesne" or intermediate conveyances. The volumes of "miscellaneous records" that are intermixed in series with them contain any document that a colonist was willing to pay to have registered. Most commonly, these are mortgages and assignments of mortgages, bonds and counterbonds, bills of sale, powers of attorney and revocations of powers of attorney, and apprenticeship agreements. Some other types include bills of exchange, judgments, receipts, petitions, contracts, and purchases of freedom.

The abstracts of all of these records attempt to give every name, relationship, profession, and place mentioned. Only the wording common to every record type was intentionally omitted. Most of this information is accessible only through the indexes prepared for this publication. The names of lessors and lessees was published in 1977 by the Southern Historical Press in *Index to*

Deeds of the Province and State of South Carolina, 1719-1785, and Charleston District, 1785-1800, but this volume did not include the names of adjacent property owners, plantations, and creeks or other information such as professions and Indian names. All of this information has been conscientiously indexed by the indexing staff of Southern Historical Press, and it will be of great assistance in the preparation of local histories and family histories.

Each volume of the records abstracted carries a separate letter designation. The first set was lettered A through Z. The letter B was used twice and so was made B and B-2 (or Ba and Bb). Next, the double letters AA-ZZ were used, and afterwards the letters A through Z again with a 3 added (A3-Z3). The letters U and JJ appear to have been omitted.

Deeds were recorded in roughly chronological order, but some were recorded many years after they were written. For nearly all of the period covered, Charleston was the only place in the Province where deeds could be recorded, and colonists who lived elsewhere had to apply for registration there. Some deeds were never recorded, particularly during the transition from Proprietary to Royal government (1719-1731) and during the period of the American Revolution.

The great majority of conveyances were recorded, though, and they are a tremendously important source of information about most of the 18th Century residents of South Carolina. With no Pre-Revolutionary census and with nearly all early tax records missing, these deeds are the most inclusive set of records available, and they contain the only mention of many individuals in the surviving public records. Only grants and wills are of comparable importance. Very often, a place of residence can be ascertained for an individual and with this knowledge a researcher can turn to local records such as church registers for additional information.

Title searchers who need to exhaust every possibility should consult not only conveyances, grants, and wills, but also collections of plats and memorials in the State Archives. Other significant collections of land records are in the South Caroliniana Library in Columbia and in the Register of Mesne Conveyance and the South Carolina Historical Society in Charleston. For legal purposes, the earliest surviving copies of all of these records should be consulted to minimize the possibility of a transcription error. In the case of the W.P.A. abstracts, Miss Langley first made notes; these were neatly copied in longhand (the second generation copy of the names); the longhand copy was typed with a cloth ribbon and was too indistinct to be reproduced (the third generation copy). All of the information had to be retyped for this publication, which is four generations removed from the certified copies, which themselves were not originals. The typist who prepared the final typescript, Mrs. Pearl Baker, consulted Miss Langley's initial notes whenever questions arose and typed from the handwritten abstracts for the final volumes of deeds that had not previously been typed. She did everything feasible to ensure the accuracy of each entry.

Ideally, the final typescript should have been compared with the copies given to each property owner, but most of these originals have not survived, and even the ones in public collections are widely scattered. The certified copies in the Register of Mesne Conveyance would have been an adequate substitute, but many of them have deteriorated greatly in nearly a half century, and a careful comparison would have required thousands of hours and would have had to be done by a volunteer experienced in reading 18th Century handwriting and knowledgeable of South Carolina names. This too proved unfeasible. As a whole, the present. publication is an amazingly accurate version that is far more useful than the official records themselves because they are much less thoroughly indexed.

Moreover, the publication of these records fills a major gap for genealogists and historians. Even individuals of the Proprietary Period were better known because of Agnes Leland Baldwin's *First Settlers of South Carolina, 1670-1680* and A.S. Sally, Jr.'s *Warrants for Land in South Carolina, 1672-1711*. Mrs. Baldwin's work has been expanded to include every known reference to every individual who settled in South Carolina before 1700, and the publication of this research will be forthcoming. After the Revolution, the Census of 1790 and subsequent national censuses have most Americans represented. It was for the period of Royal Government that we knew the least about South Carolinians, and now Mrs. Baldwin has helped to fill this gap by initiating this publication and by seeing it through.

Gene Waddell,
Director
South Carolina Historical Society

CONTENTS

DEEDS BOOK "Q-Q"
OCT. 1755 - SEPT. 1756

Book Q-Q, p. 1
25 July 1751
L & R

ISAAC GIRARDEAU, planter, & ANN his wife, to
SAMUEL WILKINS, planter, for ₤ 500 SC money,
452 a. in Prince William Parish, Granville Co.,
part of 1000 a. surveyed 8 Apr. 1732 for ISAAC,
JAMES, & RICHARD GIRARDEAU; bounding E on JAMES GIRARDEAU; N on JAMES
GIRARDEAU & MRS. DRAYTON; S on WRAGG'S Barony; W on RICHARD GIRARDEAU.
Witnesses: JOHN BONNEAU, JOSEPH MEGUIRE, PAUL WILKINS. Before STEPHEN
BULL, J.P. WILLIAM HOPTON, Register.

Book Q-Q, p. 8
8 & 9 June 1753
L & R

MATHEW WILSON, & ANN (her mark) his wife, of
the Congaree, to KNOWLENS GILES, planter, of
the Wateree, for ₤ 50 money, 150 a. on N
side Wateree River granted by GEORGE II
through Gov. JAMES GLEN, on 13 Feb. 1753 to MATHEW WILSON, bounding W on
the river; N on land surveyed by authority from NC; E & S on vacant land.
Witnesses: JOHN HAMILTON, WILLIAM BAKER, JOHN BAKER. Before STEPHEN
CRELL, J.P. WILLIAM HOPTON, Register.

Book Q-Q, p. 14
25 Dec. 1753
L & R

KNOWLENS GILES, & MARY (her mark) his wife, of
the Wateree to SAMUEL DUNLAP, planter, of the
Wateree, for ₤ 35 Va. money, 150 a. on N side
of Wateree River granted 13 Feb. 1753 by Gov.
JAMES GLEN to MATHEW WILSON; bounding W on the Wateree River; N on land
surveyed by authority of NC; E & S on vacant land. Witnesses: WILLIAM
BAIRD, ROBERT RAMSAY, RICHARD COUSART. Before JAMES MCGIRTT, J.P. Lease
not proved. WILLIAM HOPTON, Register.

Book Q-Q, p. 20
2 Oct. 1755
L & R

THOMAS POTTS, planter, & SARAH, his wife, to
GEORGE ZANTLER, planter, both of Craven Co.,
for ₤ 62 SC money, 246 a., part of 500 a. on
Jeffry's Creek, in Craven Co., granted to
POTTS; bounding E on JOHN SIMPSON (formerly THOMAS POTTS); S on vacant
land; W by "part of said land"; N on vacant land. Witnesses: JOSEPH HOL-
LAND, SAMUEL CHANDLER. Before TACITUS GAILLARD, J.P. WILLIAM HOPTON,
Register.

Book Q-Q, p. 27
2 Oct. 1755
L & R

THOMAS POTTS, Planter, & SARAH his wife, to
JOSEPH ZANTLER, planter, both of Craven Co.,
for ₤ 125 SC money, 250 a. on Jeffries Creek,
in Craven Co., bounding SW & N on vacant land;
E on part of said tract belonging to GEORGE ZANTLER. Witnesses: JOSEPH
HOLLAND, SAMUEL CHANDLER. Before TACITUS GAILLARD, J.P. WILLIAM HOPTON,
Register.

Book Q-Q, p. 34
28 Nov. 1752
Mortgage

MARY ALBERGOTTI, spinster, of Beaufort, Granville Co., to her mother, PRUDENCE ALBERGOTTI,
widow, of Beaufort, as security on bond of
even date for payment of ₤ 700 currency, with
interest, on 1 Mar. 1754; lot #305 in Beaufort except that part conveyed
by L & R dated 21 & 22 Aug. last, to JOHN DELAGAYE, merchant. Witnesses:
WILLIAM GOUGH, ANTHONY ALBERGOTTI. Before WILLIAM HARVEY, J.P. WILLIAM
HOPTON, Register.

Book Q-Q, p. 36
10 Aug. 1754
Release

JAMES LADSON, planter, & SARAH his wife, to
JOHN MILES, planter, both of St. Pauls Parish,
Colleton Co., for ₤ 850 SC money, 250 a. or
half of a tract of 500 a. in Colleton Co.
Whereas Gov. NATHANIEL JOHNSON & the Lords Proprs. on 5 Mar. 1704 granted
HENRY SAMWAYS 500 a. in Colleton Co., bounding originally NE & SE on JOHN
MILES; other sides on vacant land; & whereas HENRY SAMWAYS on 19 Nov.
1705 for ₤ 5 currency conveyed the tract to JOHN MILES; who, on 1 Aug.
1721, gave the land to his son JEREMIAH MILES; who, by will dated 2 Feb.
1736 devised to his eldest daughter, SARAH, 1000 a. near Horse Savanna,
adjoining his brother THOMAS'S land; the first mentioned 500 a. being
included in the 1000 a.; & whereas JAMES LADSON married said SARAH, the
legatee; now they sell to JOHN MILES the E half of the original tract of

1

500 a. (250) a., bounding W on a line running through the tract at right angles with the N & S lines, dividing the tract into 2 equal parts between JOHN MILES & JOHN MCQUEEN who purchased the W half of the tract, being between this division line & JOHN RAVEN'S line. Witnesses: EDWARD SHIPTON, GEORGE EVANS, THOMAS LADSON. Before J. SKENE, J.P. WILLIAM HOPTON, Register.

Book Q-Q, p. 43
1 & 2 June 1746
L & R

THOMAS ELLIOTT, SR., of Berkeley Co., to MARY CLIFFORD, for ₤ 2000 currency, 436 a. on head of Horse Shoe Creek, Colleton Co., granted THOMAS ELLIOTT 8 Apr. 1736; bounding E on ROGER SANDERS; other sides on vacant land. Witnesses: HENRY HYRNE, GEORGE SAXBY. Before JACOB MOTTE, J.P. WILLIAM HOPTON, Register.

Book Q-Q, p. 49
24 Dec. 1754
L & R of Reversion

ROBERT TURNER, planter, of Colleton Co., to JOSEPH STANYARNE, JOHN FREER, JAMES CARSON, WILLIAM CHAMBERS, HUGH WILSON, & HENRY LIVINGSTON, planters, trustees for ₤ 600 currency, 212 a. on Wadmalaw Island, sold to ROBERT TURNER by HUGH WILSON & ESTHER his wife by L & R dated 22 & 23 Dec. 1749; being part of 664 a. sold to JOHN WILSON & RICHARD PURCEL by HENRY PERONNEAU by L & R dated 1 & 2 Nov. 1733; which was part of 1000 a. formerly belonging to COL. ARTHUR HALL; said 212 a. bounding N on JOHN MCCULLOUGH; E on COL. ARTHUR HALL; S on ROBERT SAMS; W on RICHARD PURCEL; upon trust that said trustees shall permit the minister of the Protestant Presbyterian Church, & Congregation of Christians, who usually assemble for divine worship in their public meeting house on Johns Island, to occupy the 212 a., as tenant. Witnesses: SOLOMON LEGARE, JR., JOHN STANYARNE, JOHN HOLMES. Before ANTHONY MATHEWES, J.P. WILLIAM HOPTON, Register.

Book Q-Q, p. 59
5 Jan. 1747
Sale

RAWLINS LOWNDES, P.M., to CHARLES WRIGHT, ESQ., of Charleston, for ₤ 220 currency, at public auction, 200 a. at Cainhoy, in St. Thomas Parish, Berkeley Co., bounding SE on Wando River; NE on JAMES JAGGERS; NW on WILLIAM SANDERS; SW on HUGH CHIVERS; which land was granted by the Lords Proprs. on 8 Sept. 1697 to DAVID EVANS. Whereas JOHN LINING, Ass't. J. in absence of BENJAMIN WHITAKER, C.J., on 7 July last issued a writ of fieri facias commanding the P.M. to levy a debt of ₤ 414:10:0 on the estate of HUGH CARTWRIGHT, for which THOMAS BOLTON had obtained a judgment; now LOWNDES sells CARTWRIGHT'S land at auction to WRIGHT. Witness: PAUL DOUXSAINT. Before DANIEL CRAWFORD, J.P. WILLIAM HOPTON, Register.

Book Q-Q, p. 61
3 Oct. 1755
Feoffment

ADAM DANIEL, planter, son of JOHN DANIEL, ship carpenter, of Charleston; to JOHN RATTRAY, gentleman, for ₤ 510 currency, part of lot #115 in Charleston, bounding E 32 ft. on King Street; S 100 ft. on a house & lot of THOMAS HOLTON; N on EDWARD VANVELSIN. Witnesses: SAMUEL WAINWRIGHT, GEORGE JACKSON. Before JAMES GRINDLAY, J.P. WILLIAM HOPTON, Register.

Book Q-Q, p. 64
2 & 3 Apr. 1755
L & R

JOHN BAKER, planter, & ANN (her mark) his wife, of Berkeley Co., to EPHRAIM LILES, planter, of Craven Co., for ₤ 20 currency, 100 a. on NE side Broad River; other sides on vacant land. Witnesses: WILLIAM BAKER, GEORGE SUFFS, PHILIP RAILFORD. Before JACOB MOTTE, J.P. WILLIAM HOPTON, Register.

Book Q-Q, p. 69
2 & 3 Apr. 1755
L & R

ANDREW KELLERS, planter, & ANN MARGARET (her mark), his wife, of Berkeley Co., to EPHRAIM LILES, planter, of Craven Co., for ₤ 20 currency, 100 a. on NE side Broad River, bounding NW on ANN LYTHER; other sides on vacant land. Witnesses: GEORGE POOSER, PHILIP RAILFORD. Before JACOB MOTTE, J.P. WILLIAM HOPTON, Register.

Book Q-Q, p. 75
11 June 1745
Feoffment

JOHN GIBBENS, planter, of Christ Church Parish, Berkeley Co., & ELIZABETH his wife, to JAMES OUSLEY, gentleman, of same Parish, for ₤ 1000 currency, 122 a. in said Parish called the JOTHAM GIBBENS tract, adjoining lands belonging to, CAPT. THOMAS BOONE &

others; also 148 a. adjoining above tract, & lands of THOMAS BOONE, THOM-
AS HAMLIN & THOMAS BENNETT; being part of a tract formerly belonging to
BURKE & HAMLIN. ELIZABETH GIBBENS surrenders her dower. Witnesses:
CLEMENT LEMPRIERE, JOHN NELME, JOHN HOLMES. Before ROBERT WILLIAMS, J.P.
WILLIAM HOPTON, Register.

Book Q-Q, p. 78   JOHN MITCHELL, gentleman, & ELEANOR his wife,
8 & 9 Oct. 1754   of Chelsea Park, Middlesex Co., Great Britain,
L & R   to the Rev. MR. ALEXANDER GARDEN, rector of
                         St. Philips Parish, Charleston, for ₺ 1250
currency, part of lot #115 in Charleston, bounding N 66 ft. on Tradd
Street; S on THOMAS HOLTON; E 100 ft. on other part belonging to LEWIS
PASQUEREAU; W on JOHN SMITH; with the house thereon; JOHN & ELEANOR MIT-
CHELL to assure the land to GARDEN through the Court at Westminster.
Witnesses: ANDREW RUTLEDGE, THOMAS SHUBRICK. Before DANIEL CRAWFORD,
J.P. WILLIAM HOPTON, Register.

Book Q-Q, p. 87   FRANCIS HOLMES, merchant, & ELIZABETH his
1 & 2 Aug. 1748   wife, of Charleston, to RICHARD LAMBTON, mer-
L & R in Trust   chant, trustee, as security for payment of
                         HOLMES debts to various people; part of lot
#73 in Charleston, bounding N 30 ft. on Tradd Street; E 99 ft. on JOHN
STONE; S on THOMAS CAPERS; W on FRANCIS HOLMES; also 156 a. in Colleton
Co., bounding N on vacant land; E on JOHN ANDREW; SW on GEORGE MITCHELL;
also 232 a. in Colleton Co., bounding S on GEORGE MITCHELL; W & N on
THOMAS ELLIOTT; E on JOHN ANDREW; also 1/4 undivided part of 11 lots in
Dorchester; also 1/4 undivided part of 500 a. near Dorchester (the titles
now being in the hands of ISAAC HOLMES, merchant, of Charleston); LAMBTON
to sell the above property & divide the proceeds amongst the creditors.
Witnesses: MOSES AUDEBERT, SAMUEL PRIOLEAU, JR. Before JAMES GRINDLAY,
J.P. WILLIAM HOPTON, Register. List of Creditors: JACOB MOTTE, MICHAEL
GELGER, JOHN DART, WILLIAM BANBURY, WRAGG & LAMBTON, JOHN MOVILLE, JR.,
JOSEPH JONES, ISAAC MAZYCK, JOHN MCCALL, SOLOMON ISAACS, ISAAC LADSON,
JOHN SAVAGE & Co., DR. ISAAC MARTIN, JOHN CUTHBERT, JAMES READ, BENJAMIN
ROBERTS, SIMMONS & SMITH, ROBERT COLLIS, WILLIAM HARVEY, THOMAS EBERSON,
TRAPIER & ROMSEY, JOHN MOVILLE, SR., JOHN SCOTT, carpenter, COL. JOHN
BEE, SAMUEL & JAMES WRAGG, EBENEZER SIMMONS, ISAAC HAYNE, STEAD & EVANS,
MR. PETTY, THOMAS BARKSDALE, THOMAS GLIDDELL, WILLIAM WEBB, GEORGE AUS-
TIN, WILLIAM SIMMONS, BENJAMIN PERRY, NICHOLSON & SHUBRICK & Co.: WILLIAM
WOODROPE, ANN BOONE; FISHER, BAKER & GRIFFIN, of Bristol: MRS. GIBBES,
CHILDERMAS CROFT, THOMAS BONNY; POMEROYS & SONS of London; JOHN MCKENZIE,
FRANCIS BAKER, NATHANIEL BROWN, LUKE STOUTENBURGH, MARGARET BARKLEY, JO-
SEPH HARLEY; POMEROYS & SHEATFIELD; WILLIAM SCRIVENS, THOMAS CORKER, JOHN
BEAKMAN, ISAAC HOLMES, JOHN CHAMPNEYS, COL. LAWRENCE SAUNDERS: EDWARD
COYSGARN of London: JOHN RATTRAY, MCCASTLIN & CAMPBELL; PICKERING & SAV-
AGE; THOMAS BLYTH, JAMES BALLENTINE, SAMUEL JONES.

Book Q-Q, p. 98   RICHARD LAMBTON, merchant, of Charleston, as
6 & 7 Nov. 1755   trustee for FRANCIS HOLMES (see p. 87) to JOHN
L & R   LAIRD, planter, of St. Bartholomews Parish,
                         Colleton Co., for ₺ 510 currency, 2 adjoining
plantations; 156 a. in Colleton Co., bounding N on vacant land; E on JOHN
ANDREW; S & W on GEORGE MITCHELL; 232 a. in Colleton Co., bounding S on
GEORGE MITCHELL; W & N on THOMAS ELLIOTT; E on JOHN ANDREW. Witnesses:
JOHN STUART, JAMES GRINDLAY. Before DANIEL CRAWFORD, J.P. WILLIAM HOP-
TON, Register.

Book Q-Q, p. 107   WILLIAM DAWSON, & FRANCES his wife; & WILLIAM
22 Apr. 1754   HODGES & PATIENCE his wife; of Bladen Co., NC,
Sale   to ROBERT WILLIAMS, of Craven Co., for ₺ 25
                         Va. money, all their title (if they have any)
to 200 a. in the WELCH tract in Craven Co., SC, on SW side Great Peedee
River; being part of 250 a. granted EDWARD BOYKIN 22 Jan. 1747; bounding
SE on JOHN WATERS; SW on JACOB BUCHRELSIS (?) vacant land; NW on Cock Run
which divides the 200 a. from 50 a. Witnesses: DAVID LOOPER, GIDEON
ALLEN. Before JOHN CRAWFORD, J.P. WILLIAM HOPTON, Register.

Book Q-Q, p. 110   WILLIAM DAWSON, & FRANCES his wife; & WILLIAM
22 Apr. 1754   HODGES & PATIENCE his wife; of Bladen Co., NC;
Sale   to ROBERT WILLIAMS, of Prince Frederick Parish,

Craven Co., SC, for Ł 25 Va. money; all their title (if they have any) to 200 a. in the WELCH tract in Craven Co., SC, on SW side Great Peedee River; bounding all other sides on vacant land. Witnesses: DAVID LOOPER, GIDEON ALLEN. Before JOHN CRAWFORD, J.P. WILLIAM HOPTON, Register.

Book Q-Q, p. 113
10 Aug. 1754
Release

JAMES LADSON, planter, & SARAH his wife, of St. Pauls Parish, Colleton Co., to JOHN MC-QUEEN, merchant, of Charleston, for Ł 850 currency, the W half of 500 a. (250 a.) extending from JOHN RAVEN'S line to a line intended to be run as a boundary between JOHN MCQUEEN & JOHN MILES & to divide the tract equally. Whereas Gov. NATHANIEL JOHNSON & the Lords Proprs. on 5 Nov. 1704 granted HENRY SAMWAYS 500 a. in Colleton Co., bounding originally NE & SE on JOHN MILES; other sides on vacant land; & whereas SAMWAYS on 19 Nov. 1705 sold the land to JOHN MILES; who on 21 Aug. 1721 gave the tract to his son JEREMIAH MILES; who, by will dated 2 Feb. 1736 devised to his eldest daughter, SARAH, 1000 a. (including said 500 a.) near Horse Shoe Savanna, adjoining his brother THOMAS MILES'S land; & whereas JAMES LADSON married SARAH MILES, the legatee, & became tenant for life; now he & SARAH sell 250 a. half the first tract, to MCQUEEN. Witnesses: EDWARD SHIPTON, THOMAS LADSON, WILLIAM MAINE. Before ALEXANDER STEWART, J.P. WILLIAM HOPTON, Register.

Book Q-Q, p. 120
11 & 12 Nov. 1754
L & R

JANE BOONE, widow, & executrix of MAJ. WILLIAM BOONE, of Charleston, to JOHN LLOYD, ESQ., commander of H.M. Fort Johnson, for Ł 2700 currency, part of lot #73 in Charleston, bounding N 32 ft. on Tradd Street; E 100 ft. on JANE BOONE; S on THOMAS CAPERS; W on JOHN SAVAGE (formerly BENJAMIN SAVAGE). Whereas WILLIAM BOONE by will dated 17 Mar. 1750 authorized his executors to sell his real & personal estate for the benefit of his wife & children & appointed his wife, JANE BOONE & GABRIEL MANIGAULT, ANTHONY MATHEWES, GEORGE AUSTIN, THOMAS SMITH, JR., of Charleston, & THOMAS HANSON & CHARLES ALEXANDER, of Antigua, his executrix & executors; & whereas MANIGAULT, MATHEWES, AUSTIN & SMITH declined to act & JANE became sole executrix; now she sells part of lot #73 to LLOYD. Witnesses: THOMAS FLEMING, WILLIAM BOONE. Before WILLIAM SIMPSON, J.P. WILLIAM HOPTON, Register.

Book Q-Q, p. 128
4 & 5 Feb. 1754
L & R

GEORGE PAWLEY, ESQ., & ANN his wife of Georgetown, to CHRISTOPHER GUIN, planter, of Craven Co., for Ł 600 currency, 300 a. called the boundary house, on NW side Little River, bounding SE on a creek & marsh; NE & SW on WILLIAM WATIES; NW on vacant land. Whereas Gov. ROBERT JOHNSON on 9 Feb. 1732 granted CHARLES HART 300 a., which he sold to WILLIAM WATIES; & whereas WILLIAM WATIES & DOROTHY his wife on 9 Mar. 1734 sold the tract to GEORGE PAWLEY; now PAWLEY sells to GUIN. Witnesses: JOSEPH DUBOURDIEU, JAMES SUMMERS. Before THOMAS HASELL, J.P. WILLIAM HOPTON, Register.

Book Q-Q, p. 133
21 & 22 Oct. 1755
L & R

MARY DICK, planter, of Prince Frederick Parish, Craven Co., to THEODORE GAILLARD, planter, of St. James Santee, for Ł 400 currency, 500 a. on Santee River Swamp, Prince Frederick Parish, granted to RICHARD ALLEN on 6 Sept. 1753 & sold at public auction in Georgetown to MARY DICK; bounding E on ABEL JOHNSON; having been vacant land when laid out. Witnesses: ESTHER BILLING, HANNAH HUNTER, JOHN GAILLARD. Lease not proved. Before WILLIAM BURROWS, J.P. WILLIAM HOPTON, Register.

Book Q-Q, p. 138
10 Aug. 1754
Release

JOHN TOOMER, planter, & ELIZABETH his wife, of St. Helena Island, Granville Co., to THOMAS SNIPES of St. Paul's Parish Colleton Co., for Ł 600 currency, 200 a. in Colleton Co. Whereas Gov. NATHANIEL JOHNSON & the Lords Proprs. on 8 Aug 1704 granted JOHN WILLIAMSON 400 a. in Colleton Co., which he sold on 17 Nov. 1704 to RALPH EMMS, who bequeathed the land to his son, WILLIAM EMMS; who by L & R dated 30 & 31 July 1730 sold the W half, 200 a. adjoining the estate of COL. JOHN SMITH to JOHN TUCKER; & whereas by a resurvey of the 400 a. it was found that 67 a. in the SW corner had been contained within a prior grant to HENRY WILLIAMSON & was accordingly pricked & taken off the plat of the

400 a. was reduced to 333 a.; the said a. bounding on S side of a tract in possession of MR. STANYARNE (formerly of RICHARD CAPERS); W on estate of COL. JOHN SMITH; E on THOMAS SNIPES; being the other part; & whereas JOHN TUCKER by will dated 12 Apr. 1740 bequeathed the use of the 200 a. "at the swamp" to his wife, RUTH TUCKER, during her lifetime & after her death to be divided amongst their grandchildren at her discretion; & whereas at the time of his death JOHN TUCKER had only 1 grand-child, RUTH TOOMER, daughter of JOHN TOOMER & ELIZABETH his wife, who died soon after JOHN TUCKER'S death; & whereas JOHN & ELIZABETH TOOMER had other children during the lifetime of RUTH TUCKER but she had not directed how the 200 a. should be divided among said children, the 200 a. reverted & ascended to ELIZABETH, wife of JOHN TOOMER, as heir to her father JOHN TUCKER; now JOHN & ELIZABETH TOOMER sell the 200 a. to THOMAS SNIPES. Witnesses: WILLIAM CHAPLIN, WILLIAM REYNOLDS, JR., PHILIP SMITH. Before JAMES PARSONS, J.P. WILLIAM HOPTON, Register.

Book Q-Q, p. 146   HENRY MIDDLETON, ESQ., of St. George Parish,
27 Oct. 1755   Berkeley Co., to JACOB MARKLEY, planter, of
Sale   St. Johns Parish, for Ł 400 currency, 552 a.
in Berkeley Co.; 112 a. of the 552 having been part of a tract of 1600 a. granted by JOHN, Lord Granville, Palatine; Gov. NATHANIEL JOHNSON, JAMES MOORE, & NICHOLAS TROTT on 14 July 1705, to the Hon. ARTHUR MIDDLETON, father of HENRY MIDDLETON, the remaining 440 a. being part of 898 a. granted 12 Feb. 1735 by Lt. Gov. THOMAS BROUGHTON to said ARTHUR MIDDLETON. Witnesses: JAMES MCKELVEY, GEORGE NEWMAN. Before JOHN CHEVILLETTE, J.P. Memorial entered in Auditor's office 10 Dec. 1755 in Book B. #4, fol. 117 by JAMES MICHIE, Dep. Aud. WILLIAM HOPTON, Register. Plat given.

Book Q-Q, p. 150   THOMAS MIDDLETON, ESQ., & MARH his wife, to
14 & 15 Nov. 1755   JAMES IRVING, ESQ., both of Charleston, for
L & R   Ł 3000 currency, 4 tracts of land in St. James
Goose Creek Parish; 752 a., called Boochawe; 55-1/2 a.; 340 a. called How Hall; 305 a. called The Pine Lnad; the 4 tracts making 1 plantation of 1452 a. Whereas Gov. JOSEPH MORTON, ARTHUR MIDDLETON, JAMES MOORE, MAURICE MATHEWES, & JOHN GODFREY, commissioners, of WILLIAM, Earl of Craven, Palatine, on 20 Sept. 1683 granted JAMES MOORE, ESQ., 2400 a., English measure, an inland plantation, formerly known by the Indian name of Boochawee & Wampensaw then bounding W & S on ARTHUR MIDDLETON & JOHN FOSTER; other sides on vacant land; & whereas Gov. JOHN ARCHDALE, JOSEPH BLAKE, JOHN BERESFORD, & JOSEPH MORTON, commissioners, on 28 Oct. 1696 by grant reciting that WILLIAM, Earl of Craven, Palatine; JOHN, Earl of Bath; ANTHONY, Lord Ashley; GEORGE, Lord Carteret; SIR JOHN COLLETON, Baronet; & THOMAS AMY, then Lords Proprs., had authorized JOHN ARCHDALE, Gov. of NC, with the consent of 3 of their deputies, to sell lands, etc., & ARCHDALE for Ł 48 currency sold the 2400 a. to JAMES MOORE; & whereas by deed of feoffment dated 17 Oct. 1711 JAMES MOORE, gentleman, son & heir of said JAMES MOORE, for Ł 800 currency, sold DAVID DAVIS, gentleman, of Berkeley Co., 1000 a., part of the 2400 a., bounding S & N on other parts said land; E on DAVID DAVIS; & whereas by deed of feoffment dated 30 Sept. 1712 DAVID DAVIS, for Ł 500 sold the 1000 a., part of 2400 a. called BooChawee (alias Bond Bank) to BENJAMIN SCHENCKINGH; who sold 248 a. of the 1000 a. to _____; & had 752 a. remaining; & whereas by his will dated 21 Feb. 1732, he authorized his executrix. MARGARET SCHENCKINGH, to sell his real & personal estate; & whereas by L & R dated 12 & 13 Apr. 1734, MARGARET SCHENCKINGH, as executrix, sold to ARTHUR MIDDLETON the 752 a., bounding SW on ARTHUR MIDDLETON; NW on CAPT. DRY; N on PAUL MAZYCK; S on JOB HOWES; & whereas by L & R dated 19 & 20 Feb. 1721 BENJAMIN SCHENCKINGH, ESQ., & MARGARET, his wife, sold to ARTHUR MIDDLETON, 55-1/2 a., part of 2 tracts of 1000 a. & 18 a.; bounding N on the 1000 a. sold to BENJAMIN SCHENCKINGH on 30 Sept. 1712 by DAVID DAVIS & ANN his wife; other sides by ARTHUR MIDDLETON; the 18 a. having been conveyed to SCHENCKINGH on 16 May 1717 by COL. JAMES MOORE; the 2 plantations having been bequeathed to THOMAS MIDDLETON by his father ARTHUR MIDDLETON; & whereas by L & R dated 14 & 15 Jan. 1739 RICHARD LAKE, ESQ., of Lake Farm, St. Andrews Parish, & WILLIAM HARE, merchant, of Charleston, attorneys, for THOMAS CHEESMAN, ESQ., of St. James Goose Creek, but then of Island of Babbadoes, sold to THOMAS MIDDLETON (reciting that on 15 Feb. 1738 & on 15 Jan. 1739 owned 340 a., called How Hawl in St. James Goose Creek, bounding N on ARTHUR MIDDLETON (BooChawe)

NE on PAUL MAZYCK; E on Fosters Creek; SE on CHARLES PINCKNEY & ARTHUR MIDDLETON; W on ARTHUR MIDDLETON; also 305 a. called The Pine Land; bounding S & W on PAUL MAZYCK; SE on COL. ALEXANDER PARRIS; other sides on SABINA SMITH or THOMAS TAYLOR; & reciting that CHEESEMAN on 15 Feb. 1738 appointed LAKE & HARE his attorneys with authority to sell his lands, etc.), the 2 tracts of 340 a. & 305 a.; now MIDDLETON sells the 4 tracts to JAMES IRVING. Witnesses: WILLIAM BRANFORD, GEORGE MATHEWES. Before WILLIAM HOPTON, J.P. & Pub. Reg.

Book Q-Q, p. 168   JAMES IRVING, ESQ., & ELIZABETH his wife, of
6 Dec. 1755   Charleston, to RICHARD DUNN LAWRENCE, EST., of
Feoffment   Goose Creek, for ₤ 3000 currency, 752 a.,
                        called Boochawe; 55-1/2 a.; 340 a., called
Hows Hall, & 305 a. called The Pine Land; all in St. James Goose Creek
Parish, Berkeley Co.; & purchased by IRVING from THOMAS MIDDLETON (see p.
150 for details). Witnesses: JAMES LAWRENS, GEORGE WOMBWELL. Before
WILLIAM HOPTON, J.P. & Pub. Reg.

Book Q-Q, p. 172   ARNOLD HARVEY, planter, of Stono, 1 of the
11 & 12 Dec. 1755   sons & devisees of WILLIAM HARVEY, gentleman,
L & R   of Charleston; to ELIZABETH DEDCOTT, widow, of
                        Charleston, for ₤ 1100 currency, his part of
lot #47 near White Point in Charleston, bounding W 155 ft. on King Street;
N 245 ft. on Rivers Street (a 16 ft. lane running from King Street to Old
Church Street, otherwise Meeting Street); E on SAMUEL PERONNEAU; S on
JAMES COCHRAN & ARTHUR HALL. Whereas WILLIAM HARVEY by will dated 21
Sept. 1739 bequeathed to his son, ARNOLD HARVEY, 2 parcels of land E of
King Street, which he had purchased from JOHN RIVERS; now ARNOLD HARVEY
sells 1 of the lots to MRS. DEDCOTT. Witnesses: ALEXANDER PERONNEAU,
THOMAS YEOMANS. Before JAMES MICHIE, J.P. WILLIAM HOPTON, Register.

Book Q-Q, p. 179   ELISHA POINSETT, vintner, & CATHERINE his wife,
21 & 22 Dec. 1755   of Charleston, to CHARLES FAUCHERAUD, of St.
L & R by Mortgage   James Goose Creek, ESAIS BURNETT, & JOHN RAT-
                        TRAY, of Charleston; as security on bond dated
15 Dec. 1755 given FAUCHERAND in penal sum of ₤ 1400 for payment of ₤ 700
currency, with interest, on 15 Dec. 1756; & bond dated 16 Dec. 1755 given
BRUNETT in penal sum of ₤ 4000 for payment of ₤ 2000 currency, with interest, on 16 Dec. 1756; & bond dated 16 Dec. 1755 given RATTRAY in penal
sum of ₤ 2000 for payment of ₤ 1000 currency, with interest, on 16 Dec.
1756; that house & part of lot #27 in Charleston, bounding N on ISAAC
HOLMES & heirs of SAMUEL FLEY; E 88 ft. on JOHN PAGET; S 43 ft. on Middle
Street; W on ATKINS. Witness: GEORGE JACKSON. Before JAMES GRINDLAY,
J.P. WILLIAM HOPTON, Register. On 21 June 1766 ROBERT WILLIAMS, JR., in
behalf of HELEN RATTRAY, widow & executrix of will of JOHN RATTRAY, declared principal & interest due RATTRAY paid. Witness: FENWICKE BULL.
ROBERT JOHNSTON, on behalf of SUSANNAH BLANCHARD, now wife of said ROBERT
JOHNSTON, declared principal & interest due CHARLES FAUCHERAUD & others
paid in full. Witness: FENWICKE BULL.

Book Q-Q, p. 184   ARCHIBALD BAIRD, ESQ., of Georgetown, Craven
22 & 23 Dec. 1755   Co., to WILLIAM STONE, gentleman, of Anson-
L & R by Mortgage   borough, St. Philip's Parish Charleston, as
                        security on 4 bonds dated 1 Feb. lasted in
penal sum of ₤ 400 for payment of 200 currency, to STONE for the use of
JOHN HOPTON, infant son of WILLIAM & SARAH HOPTON of Charleston on 1 Feb.
1756, 1757, 1758 & 1 in penal sum of ₤ 5000 for payment of ₤ 2500 currency to STONE for use of JOHN HOPTON on 1 Feb. 1758; a tract of 127 a. 35
chains on N side Winyaw Bay in Craven Co., bounding E & S on the Bay; W
on Sandpit Creek or Georgetown River & on lots 236, 239, 249, 250, 257,
including half of the 3 last mentioned lots; N on the High Road down to
the Bay; being part of a tract granted to the Hon. JOHN CLELAND, who with
his wife MARY, sold the 127 a. 35 chains to BAIRD by L & R dated 9 & 10
Nov. 1753 (see Book O.O. fol. 138-145); in trust for said JOHN HOPTON.
Witnesses: ANN CLARKE, PETER MONCLAR. Before JOHN CLELAND, J.P. WILLIAM
HOPTON, Register. On 15 Nov. 1756 WILLIAM STONE, at request of WILLIAM
HOPTON, father of JOHN, an infant, declared mortgage discharged. Witness:
WILLIAM HOPTON, Register.

Book Q-Q, p. 193   JOHN (his mark) BUNCH, SR., & MARY (her mark)

15 Dec. 1755   BUNCH, to their child, JOHN BUNCH, for love &
Gift   affection, the NE half of his tract of 350 a.
                    on Santee River, in Amelia Township to be mea-
sured from the river with a parallel line; & half his lot #177 in Amelia
Town; according to plat & grant dated 16 Sept. 1738 signed by Gov. BULL;
son JOHN not to sell the half tract. Witnesses: JOSEPH (his mark) YATES,
planter, of Four Holes; MILES (her mark) JACKSON. Before JOHN FOURQUET,
J.P. WILLIAM HOPTON, Register. On 15 June 1762 JOHN BUNCH, SR., gave
son permission to sell the half given him. Witnesses: AARON LOOCOCK,
WILLIAM HOPTON. This endorsed on deed & recorded at request of JOHN
BUNCH, SR., donor. WILLIAM HOPTON, Register.

Book Q-Q, p. 195   WILLIAM SHACKELFORD, vintner, of Georgetown,
1 & 2 Apr. 1752   to JOHN DUTARQUE, planter, of St. Thomas Par-
L & R by Mortgage   ish, for the use of the children ob NOAH
                    SERRE; as security on bond of even date in pe-
nal sum of Ł 3000 for payment of Ł 1500 currency, with interest, on 1
Apr. 1753; lot #26 in Georgetown, bounding SW 50 ft. on Bay Street, SE
217.9 ft. on lot #27; NW on lot #25. Witness: WILLIAM PARKER. Before
ELIAS FOISSIN, J.P. WILLIAM HOPTON, Register.

Book Q-Q, p. 200   JACOB DE SAURENCY, to JOHN SUTTON, both of
31 July & 1 Aug. 1753 Craven Co., for Ł 14 currency, a tract of 14
L & R   a. 20 rood, part of a tract surveyed by RICH-
                    ARD BARROW, lying in the WELCH tract, in Cra-
ven Co., on NE side Peedee River, beginning at a pine in a valley at the
lower back corner & running upwards a line 66 pole thence W 104 poles to
a hickory on edge of the cane ground, thence back the aforesaid lower
line 78 pole to first station. Plat dated 21 Jan. 1736, certified Aug.
1738. Grant dated 23 Mar. 1744. Witnesses: DAVID HARRY, JEREMIAH PRO-
THRO. Before JOHN CRAWFORD, J.P. WILLIAM HOPTON, Register.

Book Q-Q, p. 204   SAMUEL HOLLINGSWORTH, yeoman, of the WELCH
15 & 16 Apr. 1751   tract, Craven Co., to ANN SUTTON, widow, for
L & R   Ł 100 currency, 145 a. in the WELCH tract,
                    granted by Gov. JAMES GLEN on 29 Nov. 1750 to
said HOLLINGSWORTH. Witnesses: JOHN EVANS, THOMAS JAMES. Before WILLIAM
JAMES, J.P. WILLIAM HOPTON, Register.

Book Q-Q, p. 208   THEORORE TREZEVANT, tailor, & KATHERINE his
29 & 30 Dec. 1755   wife, of Charleston, to the Rev. MR. ALEXANDER
L & R   GARDEN, JR., rector of St. Thomas Parish,
                    Berkeley Co., for Ł 800 currency, 4 tracts of
150, 92, 95, & 92 a.; total 429 a. Whereas WILLIAM, Earl of Craven, Palatine, & the Lords Proprs. granted PETER POITEVINT 300 a., English measure, in Berkeley Co., bounding NE on PETER PAGET; SE on DANIEL TREZEVANT;
NW on DANIEL TREZEVANT & vacant land; SW on vacant land; & whereas PETER
POITEVINT & SUSANNAH his wife on 19 July 1728 sold 150 a., the NW part of
the 300 a., to JOHN SNOW; who, with MARY his wife, SUSANNAH, on 10 June 1729
sold the 150 a. to NICHOLAS BOCHET; who, with MARY his wife, on 24 July
1729 sold the land to THEODORE TREZEVANT; who died intestate, & his eldest son THEODORE, party hereto, inherited; & whereas said THEODORE, party
hereto, inherited through his father another tract of 92 a., part of 530
a. granted by the Lords Proprs. on 7 Dec. 1703 to DANIEL TREZEVANT; sold
by him 17 June 1707 to PETER POITEVINT; who on 9 Oct. 1725 sold to THEO-
DORE TREZEVANT; the 92 a. bounding NW on CORNELIUS PRANPAIN; SW & SE on
PETER POITEVINT; NE on DANIEL TREZEVANT (then JAMES LOUMONNIERE); & whereas said THEODORE TREZEVANT, inherited through his father a tract of 95 a.
in Berkeley Co., bounding W on FRANCIS PAGET; S on PETER JOHNSON; E on
FRANCIS PAGET & PETER POITEVINT; NE on JAMES LOUMONNIERE; being part of
a tract granted by the Lords Proprs. on 5 May 1704 to PETER POITEVINE;
who sold the 92 a. on 9 Oct. 1725 to THEODORE TREZEVANT; & whereas said
THEODORE TREZEVANT inherited through his father 92 a., part of a tract
granted 8 Mar. 1704/5 by the Lords Proprs. to DANIEL TREZEVANT; bounding
NW & SW on PETER POITEVINE; NE on DANIEL TREZEVANT; & by deed of gift
dated 17 June 1707, given to SUSANNAH (DANIEL TREZEVANT'S daughter) & her
husband CORNELIUS PRANPAIN; & whereas CORNELIUS & SUSANNAH died intestate
& without issue, the 92 a. were inherited by THEODORE TREZEVANT; now he
& his wife sell the 4 tracts to GARDEN. Witnesses: WILLIAM WATERS,
GEORGE CUHUN, JAMES BOYDEN. Before WILLIAM HOPTON, J.P. & Pub. Reg.

7

Book Q-Q, p. 218   EZEKIEL BRANFORD, ISAAC BRADWELL, & NATHANIEL
30 Jan. 1750   BRADWELL, executors of will of JACOB BRADWELL,
L & R   planter, of Colleton Co., to JOHN ROBERTS,
                         planter, of PonPon, Colleton Co., for Ł 1300
currency, 500 a. in Colleton Co. Whereas by L & R dated 1 & 2 July 1742
WILLIAM LIVINGSTON, planter, of Colleton Co., only acting executor of
will of ANN LIVINGSTON, widow, & also DANIEL BELL & GEORGE BELL, sons,
residuary legatees & devisees of said ANN LIVINGSTON, sold to JACOB BRAD-
WELL 500 a. formerly granted to JOHN KENNAWAY & by him afterwards (with
another 500 a.) conveyed to WILLIAM LIVINGSTON, gentleman, of Charleston;
the said 500 a. within land then bounding W on the freshes of Edisto River; S on JOSEPH HOLLEY & JOSEPH DEDCOTT; W on an impassable swamp; N on a
swamp & vacant land; E on JOSEPH DEDCOTT; & whereas JACOB BRADWELL, by
will dated 13 Jan. 1744, authorized his executors either to keep & plant
his estate or sell it, the money to be used for his children, & appointed
EZEKIEL BRANFORD & his brothers ISAAC BRADWELL & NATHANIEL BRADWELL his
executors; & they agreed to sell the 500 a. & put the money out at interest; now they sell the 500 a. to ROBERTS. Witnesses: GEORGE LIVING-
STON, DAVID JERVEY. Before CHARLES KNIGHT, J.P. WILLIAM HOPTON, Register.

Book Q-Q, p. 227   DANIEL WELSHUYSEN, gentleman, & CATHERINE his
27 & 28 Mar. 1750   wife, of Charleston, to GEORGE BAGGBY, plant-
L & R   er, of St. James Goose Creek, Berkeley Co.,
                         for Ł 1500 currency, 700 a. in St. James San-
tee Parish, Craven Co., on S side Santee River; bounding E on the river
swamp & MR. GOURDIN; S on DANIEL WELSHUYSEN; W on ISAAC CHILDS, DANIEL
SMART, & the swamp. Witnesses: S. HURST, JOHN BILNEY, WILLIAM BUCHANAN,
WILLIAM KIRK. Lease not proved. Before PETER TAYLOR, J.P. WILLIAM HOP-
TON, Register.

Book Q-Q, p. 233   RAWLINS LOWNDES, P.M., to JOHN GOVAN, at pub-
1 June 1754   lic auction, for Ł 300 currency, 300 a. in
Sale   Prince George Parish, Craven Co., formerly be-
                         longing to WILLIAM WATIES. Whereas HENRY KEN-
NAN & DOUGAL CAMPBELL obtained a judgment against the estate of WILLIAM
WATIES, the executors being ANDREW JOHNSTON & THOMAS WATIES, for a debt
of Ł 195:4:8 currency & costs; & by a writ of fieri facias the P.M. was
directed to recover these sums from the estate; now LOWNDES sells to
GOVAN the 300 a., bounding E on a salt marsh; W & S on JOHN WATIES; N on
ALEXANDER MONTGOMERY. Witnesses: SAMUEL PERKINS, CHARLES LOWNDES. Be-
fore JAMES GRINDLAY, J.P. WILLIAM HOPTON, Register.

Book Q-Q, p. 236   MARY HUGG, of Granville Co., equally to her 2
31 May 1754   daughters, ELIZABETH TOBIAS & ANN ASKEW, for
Sale   love & Ł 150 currency, 250 a. on Port Royal
                         Island, Granville Co., on which she has lived
for many years, being the remaining part of a larger tract, the other
part having been sold; bounding N on salt water creek; SE on COL. JOHN
MULLRINE'S land generally known as Woodward's Oldfield; S on COL. THOMAS
WIGGS; SW on JOHN HOGG. MARY HUGG reserves her residence in the house &
use of pasture during her lifetime. Witnesses: JOHN SHEPPARD, THOMAS
SEARSON. Before STEPHEN BULL, J.P. WILLIAM HOPTON, Register.

Book Q-Q, p. 238   CALEB HOWELL, merchant, of Anson Co., NC, to
26 & 27 Mar. 1755   RODERICK MCIVER, merchant, of Craven Co., SC,
L & R   for Ł 500 currency, 2 tracts in Craven Co.,
                         total 300 a. total; 150 a. on SW side Peedee
River; other sides on vacant land; as by grant to SAMUEL DE SAURENCY dated 22 Jan. 1747; also 150 a., the lower part of a tract of 200 a. in Craven Co., bounding N on JOB EDWARDS; S on SAMUEL DE SAURENCY; W on SAMUEL
DE SAURENCY & vacant land; E on Peedee River; as by grant to JOHN POWELL
dated 22 Jan. 1747. Witnesses: SAMUEL WRAGG, CLAUDIUS PEGUES. Before
GEORGE PAWLEY, J.P. WILLIAM HOPTON, Register. Lease not proved. Plat
certified 19 June 1745 by GEORGE HUNTER, Sur. Gen., made at request of
Gov. JAMES GLEN, dated 4 May 1745, of 150 a. in the WELCH tract on SW
side Peedee River.

Book Q-Q, p. 243   JACOB SUMMARALL, & ANN (her mark) his wife, of
10 Oct. 1755   Granville Co., SC, to WILLIAM WILLIAMS, of

8

L & R   Maryland, for Ḷ 212 SC money, 150 a. in Gran-
                               ville Co., SC, on a branch of Stephens Creek,
bounding on all sides on vacant land, granted by Gov. JAMES GLEN on 13
Mar. 1752 to JOHN SCOTT, who sold to SUMMARALL, who now sells to WILL-
IAMS. Witnesses: ARCHIBALD SMITH, THOMAS JACOBS, JOHN MANER. Before AN-
THONY GROOBS, J.P. WILLIAM HOPTON, Register.

Book Q-Q, p. 248   JOHN (his mark) PERKINS, & MARTHA (her mark)
8 Jan. 1756   his wife, to JOHN LAMAR, both of Granville
L & R   Co., for Ḷ 180 currency, 200 a. in Granville
                               Co., granted 9 Jan. 1755 by Gov. JAMES GLEN to
JOHN PERKINS, bounding NW on Stevens Creek; SW on JAMES MOLLEYBOY (POLLI-
BOE); other sides on vacant land. Witnesses: GEORGE BUSSEY, JACOB BEALL.
Before WILLIAM SIMPSON, J.P. WILLIAM HOPTON, Register.

Book Q-Q, p. 253   THOMAS RED, & SARAH his wife, of the Colony of
28 Jan. 1756   Georgia, to GEORGE BUSSEY, planter, of Gran-
L & R   ville Co., SC, for Ḷ 500 SC money, 600 a. in
                               Granville Co. Whereas 29 Nov. 1750 Gov. JAMES
GLEN granted ALEXANDER MCGRIGOR 600 a. on NE side Savannah River or.
Stephens Creek; bounding on all sides on vacant land; which tract MCGRI-
GOR sold to JOHN SCOTT; who conveyed to THOMAS RED; now RED sells to
BUSSEY. Witnesses: JACOB BEALL, JOHN LAMAR. Before WILLIAM SIMPSCN,
J.P. WILLIAM HOPTON, Register.

Book Q-Q, p. 258   RICHARD GODFREY, planter, of Colleton Co., to
15 & 16 Jan. 1756   JOHN CATTELL, son & executor of will of WIL-
L & R by Mortgage   LIAM CATTELL, as security on bond of even date
                               in penal sum of Ḷ 7848 for payment of Ḷ 3924
currency, with interest, on 16 Feb. 1745; 765 a., part of Seabrooks Island, granted to THOMAS SEABROOKE, who sold to JOHN WOODWARD & JOHN GOD-
FREY, & devised by said JOHN GODFREY to his son JOHN GODFREY, who died
intestate, whereby the Island descended to RICHARD GODFREY, party hereto;
also 960 a. commonly called Godfrey's Savannah, on the Saltketchers, in
Colleton Co., (or Granville Co.); also several Negro slaves. Witnesses:
ROBERT PEIRCE HENDERSON, CHARLES PINCKNEY. Before OTHNIEL BEALE, J.P.
Recorded in Secretary's Book W.W. page 671 by JOHN MURRAY, for Dep. Sec.
WILLIAM HOPTON, Register.

Book Q-Q, p. 266   JAMES (his mark) PRICE, planter, to JAMES
17 May 1755   REID, planter, both of Craven Co., for Ḷ 215
Feoffment   (Ḷ 315 ?) currency, 50 a. on N side Peedee
                               River where PRICE lives, part of 150 a. grant-
ed PRICE on 13 Apr. 1748. Witnesses: JAMES WALL, ROBERT WALL, JAMES RAN-
SOM. Before JOHN WALL, J.P. WILLIAM HOPTON, Register.

Book Q-Q, p. 268   WILLIAM REYNOLDS, JR., planter, & ELEANOR,
7 & 8 Nov. 1750   (her mark) his wife, to WILLIAM GOUGH, scri-
L & R   vener, both of St. Helena Parish , for Ḷ 1200
                               currency, 402-1/2 a. on St. Helena Island,
bounding SE on marsh & a creek; NE on JOHN COWEN; W on ARTHUR DICKS; S on
JOHN CHAPLIN; being part of a tract formerly purchased by JOHN COWEN from
JOHN BEAMOR, & sold by COWEN to JOHN OPHIN (alias FINNY), who sold to
ELEANOR REYNOLDS (she being then widow of JOSEPH SCOTT, of St. Helena Is-
land now wife of said WILLIAM REYNOLDS). Witnesses: ANTHONY ALBERGOTTI,
ANDREW AGNEW. Before ROBERT WILLIAMS, J.P. WILLIAM HOPTON, Register.

Book Q-Q, p. 274   WILLIAM GOUGH, & MAGDALEN, his wife, of Beau-
5 & 6 Feb. 1750   fort, to WILLIAM REYNOLDS, JR., planter, of
L & R   St. Helena Island, for Ḷ 1250 currency, 402-
                               1/2 a. on St. Helena Island, bounding accord-
ing to L & R page 268. Witnesses: ANTHONY ALBERGOTTI, ANDREW AGNEW. Before ROBERT WILLIAMS, J.P. WILLIAM HOPTON, Register.

Book Q-Q, p. 281   JOHN MCBRIDE & ROGER GIBSON, planters, of Wil-
17 & 18 Sept. 1748   liamsburgh Township, Craven Co., to WILLIAM
L & R   MCCALLA, planter, of same Co., for Ḷ 200 cur-
                               rency, 250 a. in Williamsburgh Township, on S
side Black River, bounding SW on ROGER GIBSON; other sides on vacant
land. Witnesses: JOSEPH CHAMBERLIN, SUSANNA MCCULLIS. Before ROGER

GIBSON, J.P.   WILLIAM HOPTON, Register.

Book Q-Q, p. 286   JOHN (his mark) HUGHES, planter, of the WELCH
21 Feb. 1756   tract, Craven Co., to WILLIAM GARDNER, for
L & R   Ł 70 currency, 100 a. on Rhodes Bluff in the
                         WELCH tract, granted by Gov. JAMES GLEN on 6
Nov. 1751 to JOHN HUGHES; bounding W on Peedee River; S on vacant land &
JOHN WESTFIELD; E & N on vacant land. Witnesses: JOSEPH WRIGHT, JACOB
DE SAURENCY. Before JOHN CRAWFORD, J.P.   WILLIAM HOPTON, Register.

Book Q-Q, p. 291   THOMAS WIGG, planter, & ANNE his wife, to JOHN
3 & 4 Feb. 1756   GORDON, merchant, both of Granville Co., for
L & R   Ł 231 currency, 300 a. bounding E & S on
                         creeks & marshes; W on marsh & THOMAS WIGG; N
on JOHN MULLRYNE. Whereas the Lords Proprs. on 10 June 1717 granted
PETER PARMENTER 400 a. on Port Royal Island; & whereas 100 a. were sold
to THOMAS WIGG; & the remaining 300 a. on the death of PETER PARMENTER
were inherited by his eldest son, THOMAS PARMENTER; & whereas he, by L &
R dated 13 & 14 May 1748 sold the 300 a. to HUGH CAMPBELL; who, by L & R
dated 2 & 3 Mar. 1753 sold the tract to THOMAS WIGG; now WIGG sells to
GORDON. Witnesses: FRANCIS STUART, JOHN GRAYSON. Before WILLIAM HARVEY,
J.P.   WILLIAM HOPTON, Register.

Book Q-Q, p. 297   DAVID GIRARDIN, shoemaker, to JOHN LINDER,
18 June 1754   planter, both of St. Peters Parish, Purysburgh
L & R   Township, Granville Co., for Ł 30 currency,
                         250 a. in Purysburgh Township, bounding W on
GEORGE MINGLESDORF; N on DAVID KEFFER; S & E on vacant land; which land
was granted by Lt. Gov. THOMAS BROUGHTON on 17 Mar. 1735 to JOHN, HENRY,
& DAVID GIRARDIN. A knife delivered in lieu of the whole. Witnesses:
GABRIEL RAVOT, JOHN BOURQUIN. Before JOHN BOURQUIN, J.P.   WILLIAM HOP-
TON, Register.

Book Q-Q, p. 303   SAMUEL FULTON, planter, & CHRISTIAN (her mark)
25 & 26 Dec. 1755   his wife, of Williamsburgh Township, to JOHN
L & R   MCDOWELL, planter, of Black Mingo, for Ł 115
                         currency, 250 a. on NW branch of Black River,
in Craven Co., granted to DAVID FULTON by Lt. Gov. THOMAS BROUGHTON on 6
Aug. 1735, then bounding S on MR. SHIPPY; N on JAMES FUTHY; E on vacant
land. Witnesses: THOMAS GEGG, DAVID FULTON. Before JOHN LIVISTON, J.P.
WILLIAM HOPTON, Register.

Book Q-Q, p. 307   GEORGE (his mark) SHOWER (SHOWERS), planter, &
17 & 18 Mar. 1756   MARY (her mark) his wife, to PHILIP SPOOLER,
L & R   planter, both of St. Pauls Parish, Colleton
                         Co., for Ł 1600 currency, 400 a., in Colleton
Co. Whereas the Lords Proprs. on 23 July 1711 granted HENRY TOOMER 400
a. in Colleton Co., bounding N on CAPT. ELLIOTT; & whereas HENRY TOOMER
by will dated 17 Sept. 1737 devised the land to his son SAMUEL, who died
during his father's lifetime; & whereas HENRY TOOMER died without alter-
ing his will & the land was inherited by his eldest son, JOSHUA TOOMER; &
whereas JOSHUA TOOMER & SOPHIA his wife, (she renouncing her dower) sold
the 400 a. to JOHN WATSON, now bounding E on JAMES HARTLEY; N on THOMAS
ELLIOTT; W on THOMAS SANDERS; S on ROBERT MCKEWN; & whereas JOHN WATSON &
ABIGAIL, his wife, by L & R dated 26 & 27 Aug. 1751 sold the tract to
GEORGE SHOWERS; now he sells to SPOOLER. Witnesses: JAMES PENDARVIS,
FREDERICK MERCKLEY. Before WILLIAM HOPTON, J.P. & Pub. Reg. Memorial
entered in Auditor's office 20 Mar. 1756 in Book D #4, page 127, by JAMES
MICHIE, Dep. Aud.

Book Q-Q, p. 315   PHILIP (his mark) SPOOLER, to GEORGE SHOWER,
18 Mar. 1756   planter, both of St. Pauls Parish, Colleton
Mortgage   Co., as security on bond of even date in penal
                         sum of Ł 3200 for payment of Ł 1600 currency,
with interest, on 16 Mar. 1761; the 400 a. sold by SHOWER to SPOOLER (see
page 307); because SHOWER wished to give SPOOLER time to make payment.
Witnesses: JAMES PENDARVIS, FREDERICK MERCKLEY. Before WILLIAM HOPTON,
J.P. & Pub. Reg. On 20 Jan. 1764 EMANUEL GIEGELMAN, planter, of the
Horseshoe, St. Bartholomew Parish, declared that GEORGE SHOWERS died in-
testate, leaving 2 daughters MARGARET & CATHERINE, co-heiresses; that he,

10

GIEGELMAN, married MARGARET; & PHILIP SPOOLER married CATHERINE; that
SPOOLER administered the estate of SHOWER; that SPOOLER paid him half the
principal & interest due of the mortgage, retaining the other half; therefore, this mortgage null & void. Witness: WILLIAM HOPTON, Register.

Book Q-Q, p. 319   NATHAN FRINK, planter, & ELINOR his wife, of
20 Sept. 1755   New Hanover Co., NC, to SOLOMON OGDEN, for
Sale   Ł 200 SC money, 250 a. in Craven Co., N on W
                          branch of Little River; to mouth of a creek
(being IOOR'S or FRINK'S corner); then S to ABBITS to corner; thence
along ABBITS line for the compliment for 250 a.; thence N to river. Witnesses: JOHN BELL, JAMES BELL, WILLIAM ELLIS. Before GEORGE PAWLEY, J.P.
WILLIAM HOPTON, Register.

Book Q-Q, p. 321   JAMES COACHMAN, planter, & HANNAH his wife, of
12 & 13 Jan. 1756   St. James Goose Creek Parish, Berkeley Co., to
L & R   SUSANNAH MAN, widow of Prince Frederick Par-
                          ish, Craven Co., for Ł 1300 currency, 500 a.
in Craven Co., bounding E on Black River; S on JOSEPH POOLE; W on estate
of ANTHONY WHITE; N on JAMES COACHMAN; as by plat by JOHN GREEN. Witnesses: GEORGE PAWLEY, PAUL TRAPIER. Before WILLIAM HOPTON, J.P. & Register.

Book Q-Q, p. 326   WALTER IZARD, ESQ., of St. George Parish,
18 Dec. 1755   Berkeley Co., of 1st part; RALPH IZARD, ESQ.,
Deed of Partition   of same Parish of 2nd part; brothers & devi-
                          sees of THOMAS IZARD, ESQ., of same Parish.
Whereas THOMAS IZARD owned 1000 a. on W side Combahee River in Prince
William Parish, Granville Co., being his share of his father's lands, as
by plat of all the brothers' shares certified by HUGH BRYAN, Dep. Sur.; &
by will dated 24 Dec. 1753 bequeathed to his brothers, WALTER & RALPH,
the 1000 a. to be divided equally between them as they should think fit,
as tenants in common & not as joint tenants; now WALTER & RALPH agree as
follows: WALTER to have a certain inland tupelaw swamp to the NE of a
certain old dam dividing the swamp from a savannah, & continuing the
course of the dam through the swamp to the high land on the SW side (the
dam & line being represented by the line I-K in the plat); the part of
the tupelaw swamp (87 a.) being continued between the red lines, extending from said dam, or line I-K, to the lands of JOSEPH IZARD; & bounding
NW on that part belonging to WALTER IZARD; also all that part situated
between the green line I-H & JOSEPH IZARD'S estate, & the lands of STE-
PHEN BULL, containing 102-1/2 a.; also all that land between the green
lines K.L.M. WALTER IZARD'S land, bounding N on the creek M.N. containing
203 a.; also that part of the river swamp between the creek, the river &
the green line Y.Z. & bounding SW on WALTER IZARD, containing 110 a.;
total 502 a.; that is, it is mutually agreed that a line running along
the center of the old dam & continued through the swamp to the high land
on SW side (K-I) shall be the partition line to divide the swamp & savanna part of the tract & that a line from point I on said SW side of
swamp to SW side & running SE 16° shall be the partition line to divide
that part of the tract on SW side of Tupelaw Swamp; also that the nearest
distance between the angle P (corner of WALTER IZARD'S tract) & the yellow line B-G of RALPH IZARD'S tract equally divided in angle L; & that a
right line extending from said angle to end of dam (bearing SW 28°) &
another extending from angle L to fall on Creek M.Z.N. in point M & bearing NE & SW 4° shall be the partition lines to divide all the land between the savanna & the creek; & also that the river swamp part of the
tract shall be divided by a line on the ground represented by a line Y.Z.
bearing SE & NW 15°; & it is further agreed that RALPH IZARD may occupy
the land to the E, NE, & SE of the partition lines & lying between those
lines & his own tract which fell to his share upon division, of his
father's land amongst the 4 brothers; that is, all that part of the river
swamp NE of line Y.Z. containing 110 a., also that part of high & mixed
line between the yellow lines M.L.K.B.G. & extending from the river &
creek to the savanna, or blue line B.K., containing 203 a.; also that
part called Savanna & Tupelaw Swamp between the blue lines, containing
81-1/2 a.; also that lying on SW side of Savanna, between yellow lines, &
extending to S line of tract, containing in the whole 502-1/2 a.; all as
shown in plat dated 26 May 1755 made & certified by WILLIAM MAINE. Witnesses: BENJAMIN WARING, RICHARD WARING, WILLIAM MAINE. Before BENJAMIN

SMITH, J.P. WILLIAM HOPTON, Register.

Book Q-Q, p. 331   RICHARD LAMBTON, merchant, of Charleston, to
4 & 5 Mar. 1756   JOSEPH ALLSTON, planter, of Prince George Par-
L & R   ish, Craven Co., for Ł 250 currency, 430 a.,
     .   part of 1000 a., in Prince George Parish, on a
neck between the sea & the SW branch of Little River; being that part
which begins at a cedar stake on the bluff, running a SW line 69°. Whereas JOHN ABBOTT, carpenter, & planter, of Craven Co., by L & R dated 15 &
16 Feb. 1736 mortgaged to JOSEPH WRAGG & RICHARD LAMBTON, among other
things, 430 a. he had recently purchased from JONATHAN CALKINS, carpenter; a part of 1000 a.; to be redeemed by payment of Ł 144:15:0 sterling
on 16 Nov. 1736 (see Book R. fol. 219-224); & whereas WRAGG died & no
part of the money was paid to WRAGG or LAMBTON; now LAMBTON sells the
land to ALLSTON. Witnesses: WILLIAM ALLSTON, JOHN REMINGTON. Before
WILLIAM HOPTON, J.P. & Pub. Reg.

Book Q-Q, p. 337   ARCHER SMITH, ESQ., of Goose Creek Parish, to
26 & 27 Mar. 1756   GEORGE PAWLEY, JR., gentleman, for Ł 1620 cur-
L & R   rency, 580 a. in Craven Co., bounding S & N on
                     PERCIVAL PAWLEY; E on sea marsh; W on JONAH
COLLIN'S Creek; also 500 a. in Craven Co., bounding E on the sea marsh;
W on Waccamaw River; S on MR. SIMMONS (now belonging to heirs of the Rev.
MR. DANIEL DWIGHT); N on the 580 a.; which tract of 500 a. is part of
land granted by Lords Proprs. to ROBERT DANIEL with his Landgrave patent;
& sold by ROBERT DANIEL to Landgrave THOMAS SMITH; who on 10 Sept. 1711
sold to CAPT. GEORGE SMITH; who by will (recorded in Philadelphia, Penn.)
devised to ARCHER SMITH, party hereto; who now sells to PAWLEY. Witnesses: BENJAMIN WARING, THOMAS STONE. Before JACOB MOTTE, J.P. WILLIAM
HOPTON, Register.

Book Q-Q, p. 345   BENJAMIN HARVEY, planter, of Stono, to GABRIEL
5 & 6 Mar. 1756   MANIGAULT, ESQ., & SARAH RUTLEDGE, widow, of
L & R   Charleston, for Ł 5750 currency, a brick house
                     & lot on N side Broad Street, inherited from
his father, WILLIAM HARVEY, gentleman, of Charleston, by will dated 21
Sept. 1739; bounding S 154 ft. on Broad Street; W 104 ft. on JOHN HARVEY;
N 154 ft. on JOHN DRAYTON; E 104 ft. on ELIZABETH QUINCY. Witnesses:
CHARLES BRIMBALL, JOHN RUTLEDGE. Before JAMES PARSONS, J.P. WILLIAM
HOPTON, Register.

Book Q-Q, p. 351   BENJAMIN FARLEY, planter, of PonPon, only son
25 Aug. 1753   & 1 of the devisees in will of GEORGE FARLEY,
Foeffment   planter, of PonPon, to JAMES DONNOM, THOMAS
                     CLIFFORD, ANTHONY LAMBRIGHT, & JOSEPH GIBBONS,
planters, of PonPon, trustees of the Presbyterian Congregation in PonPon
for 10 shillings, 4 a. on which the Presbyterian Meeting House now
stands, being part of the 46 a. in St. Bartholomews Parish, on each side
of the Kings High Road leading from the Horseshoe through Jacksonburgh,
which by will, dated 12 Mar. 1740, GEORGE FARLEY bequeathed to his son,
BENJAMIN, party hereto; the 4 a. for a place for christian burial & in
trust for the Rev. MR. JAMES RAYMER, minister at PonPon. FARLEY to have
use of pew #2 free from rent & other charges as long as he & his heirs
continue members of said church. Witnesses: WILLIAM OSWALD, MARY HAYNE,
TOBIAS FORD. Delivery by turf & twig. Before JAMES SKIRVING, J.P. WIL-
LIAM HOPTON, Register. Plat given.

Book Q-Q, p. 355   JOHN PORTMAN, planter, & SARAH (her mark) his
29 & 30 Apr. 1753   wife, to JOHN LILES, planter, both of Berkeley
L & R   Co., for Ł 200 currency, 300 a. at LEA'S FORD,
                     on SW side Broad River, bounding on all sides
on vacant land; as by grant dated 3 Aug. 1753 signed by Gov. JAMES GLEN.
Witnesses: WILLIAM MCCLURE, WILLIAM CRADDOCK, RICHARD KELLY, JOHN FAIR-
CHILD. JOHN & SARAH PORTMAN give bone of Ł 200 proclamation money that
they will sign all necessary papers. Before JOHN CHAVILLETTE, J.P.
WILLIAM HOPTON, Register.

Book Q-Q, p. 360   HENRY SNELL, planter, & BARBARA (her mark) his
16 & 17 May 1748   wife, to ADAM SNELL, planter, both of Orange-
L & R   burg Township, Berkeley Co., for Ł 100

currency, 350 a. in Orangeburg Township, bounding NW & NE on vacant land; SE on HENRY HORGUER; SW on BARTHOLOMEW GARTMAN. BARBARA renounces her claim. Witnesses: JOHN GEISSENDANNER, HEINRICH WURTZER. Before JOHN CHEVILLETTE, J.P. WILLIAM HOPTON, Register.

Book Q-Q, p. 366
24 & 25 Mar. 1756
L & R

HENRY SMITH, gentlemen, & ANN his wife, of Goose Creek, to ELIAS HORRY, gentleman, of Santee, for Ł 2500 currency, 1333-3/4 a. in St. George Parish, Winyaw, Craven Co. Whereas the Lords Proprs. on 12 Aug. 1698 created ROBERT DANIEL a Landgrave with 48,000 a. of land & he surveyed a tract of 12,000 a. in Craven Co., as part of the 48,000 a., bounding N on Winyaw River; other sides on vacant land; according to plat certified by THOMAS BROUGHTON, Sur. Gen., on 4 Apr. 1711; which 12,000 a. were granted by the deputies on 18 June 1711 to ROBERT DANIEL; & whereas ROBERT DANIEL on 19 June 1711 sold THOMAS SMITH, ESQ., of Goose Creek, 2 baronies containing 24,000 a., part of the 48,000 a., of which the first 12,000 a. was a part; & whereas THOMAS SMITH, by will dated 3 May 1738 bequeathed to his sons, HENRY, THOMAS, GEORGE & BENJAMIN, 1000 a. each, to be run off in proportion on the N & S sides of the barony of 12,000 a.; HENRY to have first choice; & should any son die before marrying or coming of age his share to go to his (testator's) wife & surviving children; & whereas son GEORGE died unmarried & under age; & testators wife & daughters made over their shares of GEORGE'S share to HENRY THOMAS, & BENJAMIN; & whereas the 4000 a. has been divided among the 3 brothers, & HENRY chose a tract of 1333-3/4 a. on a place called The Little Mash, bounding SW on Winyaw River; NW on BENJAMIN SMITH; SE on Smith' Town or New Town; now HENRY sells this tract to ELIAS HORRY, free from ANNE'S claim of dower. Witnesses: THOMAS STONE, DANIEL HORR, JR. Before JAMES MICHIE, J.P. WILLIAM HOPTON, Register. Plat certified 10 Dec. 1754 by JOHN HORRY, Dep. Sur.

Book Q-Q, p. 375
8 & 9 June 1748
L & R by Mortgage

JAMES WITHERS, bricklayer, to HENRY PERONNEAU, merchant, both of Charleston, as security on bond of even date in penal sum of Ł 8000 for for payment of Ł 4000 currency, with interest, on 9 June 1749; the house & the N half of the quarter part of lot #19 at the N end of the Bay in Charleston, fronting 29 ft. on the Bay & 120 ft. deep; which N quarter part was formerly occupied by FRANCIS SCAMPTON; bounding E on the Bay; S on HENRY PERONNEAU; W on THOMAS HARDEN (formerly RICHARD GRIMSTONE); N on Queen Street, also, the remaining part of said N quarter part, bounding E 27 ft. on the Bay; W 21-1/2 ft. on THOMAS HARDEN or ISABELLA FINCH; N 120-1/2 ft. on other part herein released; S on part of lot #19 belonging to RICE PRICE. Witnesses: WILLIAM HALL, JOHN REMINGTON. Before WILLIAM PINCKNEY, J.P. WILLIAM HOPTON, Register. On 6 Apr. 1757 HENRY PERONNEAU declared mortgage satisfied. Witness: PETER MONCLAR.

Book Q-Q, p. 382
16 & 17 Oct. 1754
L & R

HANS (his mark) INDERBUIT, planter, & MARGARET (her mark) his wife, to JOHN SOUTHER, bricklayer, both of Orangeburgh Township, Berkeley Co., for Ł 150 currency, 250 a. in Orangeburgh Township, bounding NW & SE on vacant land & on CHRISTIAN TOP; SW on CHRISTIAN ROMPS & ULRICK REBER. MARGARET renounces her claim. Witnesses: CHRISTOPHER MILLER, NICHOLAS (his mark) ZEIGLER. Before JOHN CHEVILLETTE, J.P. WILLIAM HOPTON, Register.

Book Q-Q, p. 389
21 & 22 Aug. 1755
L & R

JOHN SOUTHER, laborer, & MARY CATHERINE his wife, of Berkeley Co., to PETER RHODE, carpenter, for Ł 50 currency, 50 a. in Orangeburgh Township, originally granted to HANS INDERBUIT (see Secretary's Book H.H. fol. 102; 1 Oct. 1736); who on 17 Oct. 1754 sold to JOHN SOUTHER; the 50 a. bounding NW on vacant land; NE on JOHN DEIDRICK, JR., SE on JOHN SOUTHER; SW on PETER RHODE (formerly ULRICH RABER). MARY CATHERINE renounces her claim. Witnesses: HENRY WURTZER, HANS JACOB WEINER, JACOB (his mark) KONEN. Before JOHN CHAVILLETTE, J.P. WILLIAM HOPTON, Register. Plat of 50 a. by PETER FAURE, Dep. Sur. dated 12 Aug. 1755.

Book Q-Q, p. 397
20 Apr. 1756

MICHAEL THOMSON, cooper, to PATRICK LAIRD, cooper, both of Charleston, for Ł 500 currency,

L & R   lot #2 in Charleston, bounding N 61 ft. on
                              Dupuy's Alley; E on ROBERT RAWLINS; W on JOHN
BONHOSTE; S on the back part of a lot fronting Broad Street. Witnesses:
JAMES DAVIDSON, DAVID JERVEY, JAMES ROBERTSON. Before WILLIAM SIMPSON,
J.P. WILLIAM HOPTON, Register.

Book Q-Q, p. 403   JEAN HARLEY (formerly JEAN JACKSON, widow, of
21 & 22 Apr. 1752   CAPT. JOHN JACKSON, of PonPon), & GEORGE JACK-
L & R   SON, executrix & executor of will of CAPT.
                             JOHN JACKSON dated 24 Nov. 1747; to JOHN
SHEARWOOD, tailor, of St. Bartholomew's Parish, Colleton Co., for ₤ 130
currency, lot #15 in Jacksonburgh, bounding 100 ft. front on King Street,
218 ft. deep. Witnesses: CULCHETH GIBBES, WILLIAM BASSFORD. Before
JAMES SKIRVING, J.P. WILLIAM HOPTON, Register.

Book Q-Q, p. 408   LAURENCE COOK, cordwainer, & ROSE his wife, of
9 & 10 Apr. 1755   Granville Co., to FRANCIS STUART, merchant, of
L & R by Mortgage   Beaufort, as security for payment of bond of
                           even date, in penal sum of ₤ 183:7:5 currency,
with interest, on 1 Jan. 1756; 180 a., part of 200 a. surveyed for AN-
THONY ULYSSES ALBERGOTTI, the plat & grant now being in possession of
WILLIAM SPOAD; the 180 a. bounding E on Okatee Creek; N on vacant land; W
on WILLIAM ROBERTS; S on WILLIAM SPOAD & 20 a. leased to THOMAS DAWSON
(being the remaining part of said 200 a.) which land & tenement were made
over to RICHARD HAZZARD; & by him conveyed to WILLIAM SPOAD (SPOOD) who
with his wife by L & R dated 24 & 25 Jan. 1749 conveyed to LAURENCE COOK.
Witnesses: WILLIAM BULLOTT, JOHN BOYD, JR. Before ANDREW VERDIER, J.P.
WILLIAM HOPTON, Register.

Book Q-Q, p. 413   ANDREW AGNEW, vintner, & MARY his wife, joint-
21 Apr. 1756   ly & severally, & PRUDENCE (her mark) ALBER-
Assignment of Bond   GOTTI; to FRANCIS STUART, merchant, all of
& Mortgage   Beaufort, Granville Co. Whereas MARY ALBER-
                           GOTTI (daughter of &LYSSES ALBERGOTTI & PRU-
DENCE, now his widow) now MARY AGNEW, wife of ANDREW AGNEW, on 28 Nov.
1752 mortgaged to her mother, PRUDENCE ALBERGOTTI, lot #305 in Beaufort,
except the part sold to JOHN DELAGAYE, merchant, fronting E on Charles-
Street, W on the half sold to DELAGAYE; giving her mother a bond for
₤ 700 currency, payable with interest on 1 Mar. 1753; & whereas neither
ANDREW nor MARY paid the bond & the lot became the property of PRUDENCE
ALBERGOTTI; & whereas COL. NATHANIEL BARNWELL, COL. THOMAS WIGG, & COL.
JOHN MULLRYNE, as arbitrators for PRUDENCE, ANDREW, & MARY, on 24 Mar.
1756 decided that ANDREW should within 1 month pay PRUDENCE, his mother-
in-law, ₤ 50 sterling with interest from date of bond deducting the in-
terest he has already paid; upon his failure to do this, the house to be
sold at public auction; now PRUDENCE ALBERGOTTI, at the request of ANDREW
& MARY, for ₤ 839:10:11 currency sells to FRANCIS STUART the part of lot
#305 & premises & bond for ₤ 700 & interest & the mortgage, appointing
STUART her attorney to receive payment from ANDREW & MARY. Witnesses:
NATHANIEL BARNWELL, WILLIAM GOUGH. Before WILLIAM HARVEY, J.P. WILLIAM
HOPTON, Register.

Book Q-Q, p. 418   ANN WIGG, of Granville Co., to her eldest
16 Oct. 1753   daughter, ANN, wife of FRANCIS STUART, mer-
Gift   chant, of Beaufort, for love & affection, 2
                           lots in Beaufort, #10 & #138, which she had
purchased from JOHN WATSON of Charleston, & ABIGAIL his wife. Witnesses:
NATHANIEL BARNWELL, MARY BARNWELL. Before WILLIAM HARVEY, J.P. at Beaufort. WILLIAM HOPTON, Register.

Book Q-Q, p. 420   CHARLES BOONE & THOMAS BOONE, ESQRS., both of
27 & 28 May 1755   Berkeley Street, Parish of St. George Hanover
L & R   Square, England only 2 sons of CHARLES BOONE
                           by MARY, his second wife (CHARLES BOONE the
father being a brother of JOSEPH BOONE, merchant, of Charlesetn, SC); to
ANNE WIGG, wife of THOMAS WIGG, ESQ., of Granville Co., SC; for ₤ 3510
SC money, 1170 a. in Port Royal Co. Whereas the Lords Proprs. on 28
Sept. 1702 granted JOSEPH BOONE 1170 a., English measure, in Port Royal
Co., SC, bounding N & NE on St. Helena River; E, SE & S on Datha Creek
separating it from St. Helena Island; W & SW on a creek separating it

from JOHN NORTONS Island; & whereas JOSEPH BOONE by will dated 14 Mar. 1733 left all his land & houses with his wife ANNE (his executrix) to be equally divided amongst the sons of his brother CHARLES & his second wife; & whereas ANNE died & CHARLES & THOMAS came into possession; now they sell the land to ANNE WIGG. Witnesses: WILLIAM JACOB, JOHN CORKRAN, both of Lawrence Poultney Hill, London. Before STEPHEN THEODORE JANSSEN, mayor of London. WILLIAM HOPTON, Register.

Book Q-Q, p. 431 HEZEKIAH EMMS, & WILLIAM EMMS, to THOMAS
28 Jan. 1733/4 ELLIOTT; all of Colleton Co., for Ł 1660 cur-
Sale rency, 100 a. bounding W & S on JOSEPH ELLIOTT;
W on JAMES LAURENS; E on HEZEKIAH EMMS; N on JOHN GODFREY; N on
JAMES MACKEWN; E on HEZEKIAH EMMS; also 220 a. bounding E on THOMAS
ELLIOTT; S on JOSEPH ELLIOTT; N on RICHARD GODFREY & JAMES MACKEWN. Witnesses: THOMAS ELLIOTT, JOSEPH ELLIOTT, SR. Before HENRY HYRNE, J.P. WILLIAM HOPTON, Register.

Book Q-Q, p. 433 GEORGE EVELEIGH, gentleman, of Southampton,
27 & 28 Feb. 1754 Great Britain, by his attorneys SAMUEL EVE-
L & R LEIGH, BENJAMIN STEAD, & SOLOMON MILNER, merchants, of Charleston, SC; to JOHN GIBBES,
ESQ., of Charleston, for Ł 2000 SC money, 303 a. on Johns Island, in Colleton Co., part of 1020 a. granted to CAPT. GEORGE RAYNER; bounding W on BENJAMIN D'HARRIETTE; E & S on Stono River; N & NW on GEORGE SAXBY, WILLIAM HARVEY, & SUSANNA BOSOMWORTH. Whereas the Lords Proprs. on 10 Feb. 1694 granted to CAPT. GEORGE KAYNER, of Colleton Co., 1020 a., English measure, in Colleton Co., which after his death descended to his daughter E. MARY RAYNER; & whereas she married ROGER MOORE, then of Berkeley Co., formerly of Cape Fear, NC, & at her death her only child, GEORGE, inherited, but ROGER MOORE, the father, during the infancy of GEORGE, held the land as tenant for life by the Courtesy; & whereas ROGER MOORE by deed of feoffment dated 2 Nov. 1720 sold the land to ALEXANDER HEXT, ESQ., of Colleton Co., & GEORGE MOORE on 26 July 1737 confirmed the sale (see Book S. fol. 26-28); & whereas ALEXANDER HEXT divided the land by running a line through the S part of the tract, cutting off 303 a. to the S of the line, which by deed of feoffment dated 13 Dec. 1720 he sold to DAVID HEXT, planter, of Colleton Co.; & DAVID HEXT by L & R dated 1 & 2 Feb. 1742 sold the 303 a. to JOHN SEABROOK, planter; who by L & R dated 24 & 25 Apr. 1745 sold to Lt. JOHN PAYNE of H.M.S. The Rose, then in Charleston Harbor; who by L & R dated 10 & 11 May 1749 (by his attorneys BENJAMIN SAVAGE the elder & GABRIEL MANIGAULT, merchants, of Charleston, appointed 29 Dec. 1748) sold to GEORGE EVELEIGH, merchant, of Charleston; & whereas GEORGE EVELEIGH afterwards moved, with his family, to Southampton, Great Britain, & appointed SAMUEL EVELEIGH, BENJAMIN STEAD, & SOLOMON MILNER, his attorneys, to sell the tract, (see Book O.O. fol. 182-187); now they sell to JOHN GIBBES. Witnesses: JAMES LAURENS, CHARLES PINCKNEY. Before WILLIAM HOPTON, J.P. & Pub. Reg.

Book Q-Q, p. 448 ANNE STANYARNE, widow, of THOMAS STANYARNE,
30 & 31 July 1731 painter, of Port Royal, Granville Co., to JOHN
L & R GIBBES, planter, of Stono, Colleton Co., for
Ł 4400 currency, 400 a. on N side Ashepoo, S
on Ashepoo Creek, E on Santelena, W on a marsh between Edisto & Ashepoo; also 220 a. in Colleton Co., bounding N, S & S on marsh of Ashepoo River; W on above land. Whereas RICHARD BENNETT, planter, bequeathed said lands to his wife, HANNAH BENNETT, but the bequest not being put into writing the lands were confirmed to her by a degree of the Court of Chancery; said HANNAH BENNETT being the mother of THOMAS STANYARNE; & whereas THOMAS STANYARNE by will dated 23 Feb. 1730 bequeathed the lands to his wife, ANNE; now she sells to JOHN GIBBES. Witnesses: NATHANIEL BARNWELL, JOHN WOODWARD, ELIZABETH WOODWARD, ANN WATT. Before ANDREW RUTLEDGE, J.P. WILLIAM HOPTON, Register.

Book Q-Q, p. 455 ELIZABETH WOODWARD, widow, of Port Royal,
22 & 23 Jan. 1741 Granville Co., daughter & devisee of JAMES
L & R STANYARNE, planter; to COL. JOHN GIBBES, planter, of St. Johns Parish, Colleton Co., for
Ł 500 currency, 500 a., the W part of 1590 a. Whereas JAMES STANYARNE owned 1590 a. between the 2 branches of Ashepoo River, in Colleton Co., & by will dated 19 Aug. 1703 bequeathed to his son JAMES his whole tract

of 600 a. on Ashley River & his whole tract of 1590 a. to the S between
the 2 branches of Ashepoo River except 500 a. of the W part, which 500 a.
he bequeathed to his daughter ELIZABETH WOODWARD; now she sells this land
to JOHN GIBBES. Witnesses: ELIZABETH FLOWER, WILLIAM PINCKNEY. Before
ROBERT THORPE, J.P. WILLIAM HOPTON, Register.

Book Q-Q, p. 462   JOHN WOODWARD, planter, of Colleton Co., to
4 & 5 Mar. 1741   COL. JOHN GIBBES, planter, of St. Johns Par-
L & R   ish, Colleton Co., several tracts of 644 a.,
       172 a., & 30 a.; also all his Negroes &
slaves, his stock of cattle, horses, & hogs; his carts, carriages & plantation tools; GIBBES to pay WOODWARD L 200 British every year during
WOODWARD'S life, first payment on 25 this Mar. Whereas on 28 Apr. 1733
the King granted JOHN WOODWARD 644 a. on E side Ashepoo River in Colleton
Co., bounding N on MR. BETTERSON & BAGIN; W, E, & S on RICHARD WOODWARD;
& on July 13, 1737 granted WILLIAM PINCKNEY 564 a. adjoining above tract;
& whereas WILLIAM PINCKNEY by L & R dated 7 & 8 Oct. 1737 sold JOHN WOOD-
WARD 170 a., the W part of the 564 a., bounding N, W, & S on JOHN WOOD-
WARD; & whereas JOHN WOODWARD owns a strip of 30 a. taken off the NE side
& N end of a tract sold by JOHN WOODWARD & RICHARD WOODWARD to CHARLES
PINCKNEY, ESQ., bounding S & W on the land sold to CHARLES PINCKNEY; E &
N on said 644 a. belonging to WOODWARD; now JOHN WOODWARD conveys the 3
tracts, his Negroes & his other possessions to COL. JOHN GIBBES. Wit-
nesses: CHARLES PINCKNEY, CULCHETH GOLIGHTLY, MICHAEL JEANES, JOHN BAKER.
Before JACOB MOTTE, J.P. On 1 Apr. 1756 GEORGE SEAMAN, merchant, of
Charleston, testified before CHARLES PINCKNEY, J.P., that as a merchant
he knew WOODWARD had agreed to convey to GIBBES the greater part of his
real & personal estate for which GIBBES was to pay him an annuity of
L 200 sterling; & that he used to receive COL. GIBBES'S crops of rice &
that GIBBES frequently drew on him for larger sums in favor of WOODWARD
on account of said annuity & can produce receipts & believes WOODWARD or
his executors were fully paid. WILLIAM HOPTON, Register.

Book Q-Q, p. 471   WILLIAM SCOTT, shopkeeper, & SUSANNA his wife,
20 June 1732   of Charleston, to HUGH BRYAN, of Colleton Co.,
L & R   for L 180 currency, lot #13 in Beaufort,
       bounding S on the Bay; W on lot #12; E on lot
#14; N on lot #42; also half of lot #42. Witnesses: JAMES FISHER,
CHRISTOPHER SMITH. Before DANIEL GREENE, J.P. WILLIAM HOPTON, Register.

Book Q-Q, p. 477   HUGH BRYAN, planter, & CATHERINE his wife, to
22 & 23 Mar. 1738   RICHARD STEVENS, planter, both of Granville
L & R   Co., for L 315 currency, lot #13 in Beaufort,
       bounding S on the Bay; W on lot #12; E on lot
#14; N on lot #42; also half of lot #42, bounding S on lot #13; W on lot
#39; N on lot #41; E on the other half lot #42. Whereas the Lords
Proprs. granted WILLIAM SCOTT lot #13 in Beaufort, bounding as above;
also lot #42 bounding E on Carteret Street; N on lot #41; W on #39; S
on lot #14 & lot #13; & whereas WILLIAM SCOTT & SUSANNAH his wife, by L &
R dated 20 June 1732 sold to HUGH BRYAN all of lot #13 & half of lot #42;
now BRYAN sells these 1-1/2 lots to STEVENS. Witnesses: JOSEPH EDWARD
FLOWER, AMBROSE REEVES. Before WILLIAM HARVEY, J.P. WILLIAM HOPTON,
Register.

Book Q-Q, p. 484   JOSEPH BRYAN, planter, of St. Pauls Parish,
12 & 13 Aug. 1731   Colleton Co., to JOSEPH SEALY, planter, of
L & R   Edisto Island, for L 750 currency, 500 a. in 2
       tracts. Whereas Gov. ROBERT GIBBES, SAMUEL
EVELEIGH, STEPHEN GIBBES, THOMAS SMITH, & JOHN FENWICKE, Lords Proprs.,
on 6 Nov. 1710 granted DANIEL DICKS 500 a. on St. Helena Island in Granville Co., bounding N on a branch of Port Royal River, other sides on vacant land, which by L & R dated 4 & 5 Aug. 1715 he, & his wife PROVIDENCE,
sold to THOMAS BRUCE, merchant, of Colleton Co.; & whereas said THOMAS
BRUCE, as merchant, of Charleston, & MARY his wife; & WILLIAM SCOTT, merchant, of Charleston & SUSANNA his wife, on 22 Dec. 1716 sold the 500 a.
to BENJAMIN GODIN & BENJAMIN DELA CONSEILLERE, merchants, of Charleston;
who, by L & R dated 27 & 28 Feb. 1723 sold to JOSEPH BRYAN; now he conveys to SEALY. Witnesses: CHARLES ODINSELLS, THOMAS GRIMBALL, JAMES
PARMENTER. Before DANIEL GREENE, J.P. WILLIAM HOPTON, Register.

Book Q-Q, p. 491   JOSEPH SEALY, planter, to RICHARD STEVENS,
27 & 28 Sept. 1747   planter, both of Granville Co., for Ł 1596
L & R   currency, 3 tracts of 798 a. on St. Helena Is-
                          land, St. Helena Parish, Granville Co.; 500 a.
granted by the Lords Proprs. on 6 Nov. 1710 to DANIEL DICKS; who, on 5
Aug. 1715, sold to THOMAS BURCE; who, on 22 Dec. 1716 sold the 500 a.,
with other lands, to GODIN & DELA CONSEILLERE; who, on 8 Feb. 1723, sold
the 500 a. to JOSEPH BRYAN; who, on Aug. 13, 1731, sold to SEALY; 100 a.
of land & marsh bounding W on above tract; N on a branch of Port Royal
River; which 100 a. were granted by the Lords Proprs. on 9 Dec. 1711 to
THOMAS BRUCE, & sold by his co-partner & administrator, WILLIAM SCOTT on
17 Mar. 1723 to JOSEPH BRYAN; who, on 12 Aug. 1731 sold to SEALY & 198 a.
granted SEALY 21 May 1734, bounding N on JOHN JOHNSON; S on first tract;
W on marsh & a branch of Port Royal River. Witnesses: THOMAS GREENE,
THOMAS WIGG. Before WILLIAM HARVEY, J.P. WILLIAM HOPTON, Register.

Book Q-Q, p. 497   DANIEL DICKS, tanner, & PROVIDENCE (her mark)
4 & 5 Aug. 1715   his wife, of Granville Co., to THOMAS BRUCE,
L & R   merchant, of Colleton Co., for Ł 15 currency,
                          500 a. of St. Helena Island, Granville Co.,
bounding W on a branch of Port Royal River; other sides on vacant land.
Witnesses: JOHN GODFREY, DAVID BOURKE. Before THOMAS HEPWORTH, J.P.
WILLIAM HOPTON, Register.

Book Q-Q, p. 502   LUKE STOUTENBURGH, ESQ., to SARAH STOUTENBURGH,
26 & 27 Jan. 1756   gentlewoman, both of Charleston, for Ł 2500
L & R   currency, an undivided half part of 950 a. (or
                          475 a.) in Colleton Co. Whereas by L & R dat-
ed 2 & 3 Jan. 1756 JAMES MATHEWES, ESQ., & CHARLOTTE his wife, of Charleston, for Ł 5000 currency sold to LUKE STOUTENBURGH 950 a. in Colleton Co.,
bounding N, E, & S on vacant land; W on WILLIAM DALTON; according to
grant from the King to NATHANIEL PAYNE, eldest son &heir of EPHRAIM PAYNE;
which by various mesne conveyances became vested in JAMES MATHEWES; &
whereas, before executing the L & R LUKE STOUTENBURGH received Ł 2500,
half the consideration money to be paid MATHEWES, from SARAH STOUTENBURGH;
now LUKE conveys to SARAH half the property purchased. Witnesses: DANIEL
BLAKE, CHARLES PINCKNEY. Before FRANCIS KINLOCH, J.P. WILLIAM HOPTON,
Register.

Book Q-Q, p. 511   RICHARD JACKSON, planter, & MARY (her mark)
20 & 21 Jan. 1747   his wife, to WILLIAM HAY, planter, both of
L & R   Craven Co., for Ł 550 currency, 400 a. in Cra-
                          ven Co., bounding NE on vacant land; SE & SW
on vacant land & JOHN FAIRCHILD (now PHILIP REIFORD, JR.); NW on vacant
land & HUGH MURPHY. Witnesses: STEPHEN CRELL, J.P., BARBARA (her mark)
SCITZ. Before JOHN HAMILTON, J.P. WILLIAM HOPTON, Register.

Book Q-Q, p. 517   HUMPHREY ELLIOTT, planter, of Berkeley Co., &
29 & 30 Apr. 1752   CATHERINE his wife, (lately CATHERINE BOOTH,
L & R   daughter of ROBERT BOOTH, planter, & grand-
                          daughter of WILLIAM ELLIOTT the elder, plant-
er), to THOMAS YOUNG, bricklayer, of Charleston, for Ł 900 currency,
their quarter part of lot #61 on W side Old Church Street in Charleston,
bounding E 25 ft. 6 in. on Old Church Street; N 232 ft. on BENJAMIN SAV-
AGE; W on EBENEZER SIMMONS; S on WILLIAM CATTELL, JR. Whereas WILLIAM
ELLIOTT by various mesne conveyances became owner of a quarter of a lot
in Charleston which, on 9 May 1730, he conveyed to ROBERT BOOTH during
his lifetime & afterwards to CATHERINE BOOTH (now CATHERINE ELLIOTT) his
daughter; & whereas ROBERT BOOTH died & CATHERINE has reached age of 21
years; married HUMPHREY ELLIOTT, & they have had children; now they sell
the quarter lot to YOUNG. Witnesses: JOHN PRUE, BENTLEY STOCKS. Before
WILLIAM SIMPSON, J.P. WILLIAM HOPTON, Register.

Book Q-Q, p. 525   HUMPHREY ELLIOTT, planter, of Berkeley Co., to
30 Apr. 1752   THOMAS YOUNG, bricklayer, of Charleston, in
Bond   penal sum of Ł 1800 currency, to keep agree-
                          ments in above sale (p. 517). Witnesses: JOHN
PRUE, BENTLEY STOCKS. Before WILLIAM SIMPSON, J.P. WILLIAM HOPTON, Register.

17

Book Q-Q, p. 527   WILLIAM ALLEN, planter, & ANNE his wife, to
24 & 25 Mar. 1755   NATHANIEL ADAMS, planter, both of St. Helena
L & R by Mortgage   Island, Granville Co., as security on bond of
                        even date for payment of Ł 600 currency, with
interest, on 25 Mar. 1757; their 1/4 undivided part of 600 a. on St. Helena Island, bounding W on a creek of Port Royal River; N on JOSEPH PAGE;
E on vacant land; S on DANIEL DICKS; which 600 a. were granted by the
Lords Proprs. 15 May 1715 to ARTHUR DICKS; who, on 16 Mar. 1726, conveyed
to JOHN JOHNSON; & he dying intestate on 11 May 1746, the 600 a. descend-
ed to his 4 daughters, MARGARET, SARAH, JANE, & ELIZABETH, as co-heir-
esses. Whereas JANE married JOHN GRADY & with him, by L & R dated 6 & 7
Aug. 1752, conveyed their undivided 1/4 part of the 600 a. & premises to
WILLIAM ALLEN; now he mortgages his share to NATHANIEL ADAMS. Witnesses:
JOHN ELLIS, ELIZABETH BETTISON, DANIEL (his mark) WILLIAMS. Before WIL-
LIAM HARVEY, J.P. WILLIAM HOPTON, Register.

Book Q-Q, p. 533   SAMUEL GREGORY, of Kingston, Jamaica, & MARY
8 Jan. 1750   his wife (formerly MARY DELMASTRE, widow, re-
L & R   siduary legatee & executrix; of will of PETER
                        DELMASTRE, apothecary, of Kingston, Jamaica,
to JOHN GUERARD, merchant, of Charleston, for Ł 860 money, part of lot
#13 in Charleston, bounding N 15-1/2 ft. on Broad Street; E 77 ft. on
DAVID GUERARD; W on part lot #13 belonging to GABRIEL GUIGNARD; S on
ISAAC MAZYCK. Whereas PETER DELMESTRE, formerly of Charleston, bought
part of lot #13 in Charleston from the executor of will of JOHN MCKAY,
planter, & by will dated 19 Nov. 1746 gave his wife, MARY, all his real &
personal estate in Jamaica or Caroline (will proved before EDWARD TRE-
LAWNY, Gov. of Jamaica), & after his death MARY married SAMUEL GREGORY;
now they sell their part of the lot to GUERARD. SAMUEL & MARY GREGORY
made acknowledgement before JOHN HALL. Witness: ISAAC COLCOCK appeared
before JACOB MOTTE, J.P. WILLIAM HOPTON, Register.

Book Q-Q, p. 542   JOHN MCKENZIE, planter, & ELIZABETH his wife
22 & 23 Mar. 1756   (formerly ELIZABETH GREEN), of St. Bartholo-
L & R   mews Parish, to JOHN RATTRAY, ESQ., of Charles-
                        ton, for Ł 3500 currency, 504 a. in St. Bar-
tholomews Parish, bounding N on JAMES FERGUSON; E on heirs of JOHN PARKER;
other sides on heirs of WILLIAM LADSON (formerly JOSHUA SANDERS); as by
grant to JOSHUA GREEN. Whereas Gov. ROBERT JOHNSON on 6 Apr. 1733 granted JOSHUA GREEN 504 a. in Colleton Co. (see grant Book A.A. fol. 11) & he,
by will dated 10 Dec. 1737, after other bequests, devised the remainder &
his estate, real & personal, equally to his nieces ELIZABETH MCKENZIE
(then ELIZABETH GREEN) & her sister SUSANNAH GREEN, now deceased (daughters of JOHN GREEN, planter); & they held the land as tenants in common;
& whereas SUSANNA, by will dated 8 Sept. 1747, bequeathed to RICHARD
BAILEY, her brother, 1/2 of the tract bequeathed to her & ELIZABETH by
their uncle, JOSHUA GREEN, said to be about 2 miles beyong Parkers Ferry
& then in possession of SAMUEL ELMS; & he became tenant in common with
JOHN & ELIZABETH MCKENZIE; & on 16 Mar. 1753 conveyed his half of the
504 a.; now they sell the whole to RATTRAY. Witnesses: JAMES GRINDLAY,
GEORGE JACKSON. Before DANIEL CRAWFORD, J.P. WILLIAM HOPTON, Register.
Plat certified 3 Aug. 1732 by JAMES FERGUSON, Dep. Sur., by warrant from
JAMES ST. JOHN, Sur. Gen., dated 5 Mar. 1731/2. Copy of plat from Sur.
Gen. Office, Book #1, fol. 183, attested 4 Mar. 1756 by WILLIAM DEBRAHM,
Sur. Gen.

Book Q-Q, p. 551   PETER MURER (MURIER), planter, of Berkeley Co.,
2 & 3 Apr. 1756   to LUKE PATRICK, tavern keeper, of Orangeburgh
L & R   Township, for Ł 180 currency, part of a half
                        a. lot #160 in Orangeburgh, bounding NW on a
street; SW on a vacant lot; SE on a vacant lot; NE on a street. Witnesses: SAMUEL LUTHER, HENRY FELDER, HENRICH WURTZER. Before JOHN CHEVIL-
LETTE, J.P. WILLIAM HOPTON, Register.

Book Q-Q, p. 558   HENRY YONGE, planter, formerly of SC, now of
20 July 1750   the Colony of Georgia, & ELIZABETH his wife,
Release   to JOHN KELSALL & ARCHIBALD WILKINS; planters,
                        of SC, for Ł 600 SC money, all their claim to
1000 a. in Granville Co. Whereas Landgrave EDMUND BELLINGER owned several large tracts granted to his father, Landgrave EDMUND BELLINGER, 1st,

18

& by will, dated 21 Feb. 1739, bequeathed to his nephew, WILLIAM BELLIN-
GER, 2000 a. to be allotted at the discretion of his wife & executrix,
ELIZABETH BELLINGER; & whereas WILLIAM BELLINGER died intestate before
allotment was made & the 2000 a. were inherited by his 3 daughters (ELIZ-
ABETH, wife of HENRY YONGE; MARY, the wife of JOHN KELSALL; & ANN, the
wife of ARCHIBALD WILKINS); & whereas ELIZABETH BELLINGER, the executrix,
(now ELIZABETH ELLIOTT) allotted to YONGE, KELSALL, & WILKINS, in right
of their wives, 1000 a. in Granville Co., bounding S on HUGH BRYAN; N on
Purysburgh Road; E on Pocataligo River; now ELIZABETH & HENRY YONGE sell
their share of the 1000 a. to KELSALL & WILKINS. Witnesses: ELIZABETH
BULL, WILLIAM BULL, ELIZABETH WILSON. Before STEPHEN BULL, J.P. WILLIAM
HOPTON, Register.

Book Q-Q, p. 561   WILLIAM WILKINS, gentleman, to ELIZABETH
29 & 30 Mar. 1756   GIBBES, gentlewoman, both of Charleston, as
L & R by Mortgage   security on bond of even date in penal sum of
                          Ƚ 1628:15:0 for payment of, Ƚ 814:7:11 cur-
rency, with interest, on 1 Jan. 1757; a certain house & lot in Charleston, in which WILKINS lived, bounding S 30 ft. on Tradd Street, W 200 ft.
on CHARLES WARHAM; E on JAMES MATHEWES; which house & lot by L & R 2 & 3
Nov. 1752 were sold by JOSEPH MASSEY, gentleman (only son & heir of BEN-
JAMIN MASSEY, gunsmith), to WILLIAM WILKINS. Witnesses: CHARLES PINCK-
NEY, ISAAC JOHNSON. Before OTHNIEL BEALE, J.P. WILLIAM HOPTON, Register. Satisfaction of this mortgage recorded in Book Z.Z. fol. 701-703,
May 2, 1763, by WILLIAM HOPTON, Register.

Book Q-Q, p. 571   WILLIAM FREER, planter, & JEAN his wife, to
29 & 31 Oct. 1746   JOHANAN, joiner, both of St. Johns Parish,
L & R   Colleton Co., for Ƚ 1290 currency, 300 a. on
                          Johns Island, in Parish of St. Johns, bounding
E & N on vacant land; W on Bohicutt Creek; S on COL. WILLIAM DAVIS; being
half of a tract granted by Gov. NATHANIEL JOHNSON in 1703 to WILLIAM
DAVIS, bounding S on another tract belonging to DAVIS. Witnesses: HENRY
YONGE, DAVID BETTISON, SOLOMON FREER. Before ANTHONY MATHEWES, J.P.
WILLIAM HOPTON, Register. Original plat copied 26 Oct. 1746 by HENRY
YONGE, Dep. Sur.

Book Q-Q, p. 577   JOHN BOHANNAN, joiner of St. Johns Parish,
20 Mar. 1755   Colleton Co., of 1st part; THOMAS (his mark)
L & R Tripartite   HUMPHREYS, planter, & ANN (her mark) his wife
                          (lately ANN ARMSTRONG, 1 of the daughters &
devisees of will of CHARLES ARMSTRONG, of James Island, St. Andrews Parish) of 2nd part; JOSEPH STANYARNE, planter, of St. Johns Parish, of 3rd
part. Whereas CHARLES ARMSTRONG owned 600 a. in St. Johns Parish, originally granted by Gov. NATHANIEL JOHNSON in 1703 to WILLIAM DAVIS, then
bounding E & N on vacant land; W on Bohicutt Creek; S on WILLIAM DAVIS; &
by will dated 24 Aug. 1725 bequeathed half (300 a.) to his daughter JANE,
she to have first choice; to his daughter ANN the other half (300 a.); &
whereas JANE married WILLIAM FREER, of St. Johns Parish, now deceased; &
ANN married THOMAS HUMPHRIES; & FREER & HUMPHRIES with consent of their
wives divided the land; WILLIAM & JANE FREER choosing the half now being
sold; & by L & R dated 29 & 31 Oct. 1746 sold their 300 a. to JOHN BOHAN-
NON (p. 571); now JOSEPH BOHANNON for Ƚ 1000 currency, with the consent
of THOMAS HUMPHREYS & ANN his wife, sells to JOSEPH STANYARNE the 300 a.;
now bounding E on THOMAS HEXT; N on WILLIAM ARNOLD; W on Bohicutt Creek;
S on THOMAS & ANN HUMPHREYS. Witnesses: SAMUEL BOONE, WILLIAM WILLIAMS,
JOHN MULL. Before THOMAS FLEMING, J.P. WILLIAM HOPTON, Register.

Book Q-Q, p. 587   JOHN SNOW, planter, of St. James Santee, Cra-
12 & 14 June 1756   ven Co., to JAMES SNOW, planter, of Prince
L & R   Frederick Parish, Craven Co., for Ƚ 100 cur-
                          rency, 40 a. in Craven Co., bounding SE on
JAMES SNOW; other sides on JOHN SNOW. Witnesses: THOMAS PRETTY, GEORGE
SNOW, JOHN FURLONG. Before JOHN LIVISTON, J.P. WILLIAM HOPTON, Register.
Plat of 40 a., part of 500 a. belonging to JOHN SNOW; the 500 a. being
part of 2000 a. originally granted to NATHANIEL SNOW; surveyed 25 May
1756 by JAMES (?) THOMAS, Dep. Sur.

Book Q-Q, p. 591   ABEL EVANS & THOMAS EVANS, planters, of Plum-
26 & 27 May 1756   field, of the WELCH tract, Craven Co., to

L & R WILLIAM KILLINGSWORTH, SR., planter, of same
place, for Ł 200 currency, 125 a. in the WELCH
tract, granted by Gov. JAMES GLEN on 6 Dec. 1744 to THOMAS EVANS, of
Plumfield; bounding S on a vacant swamp; W on Peedee River & vacant land;
N on PHILIP DOUGLAS. Witnesses: DAVID EVANS, PHILIP HOWELL. Before WIL-
LIAM SIMPSON, J.P. WILLIAM HOPTON, Register.

Book Q-Q, p. 596 CHARLES LOWNDES, P.M., to GEORGE SEAMAN, mer-
30 June 1756 chant, of Charleston, at public auction, for
Sale Ł 1000 currency, 1300 a. in Colleton Co.
Whereas Lt. Gov. THOMAS BROUGHTON on 9 Apr.
1736 granted DANIEL WEHSHUYSEN, gentleman, of Charleston, 1300 a. in Colleton Co., bounding N on ROBERT GODFREY; S on vacant land; E on JOHN HILL
(or HILLIARD); W on vacant land; & whereas GEORGE SEAMAN obtained a judgment against WELSHUYSEN to recover Ł 13,709:7:8 currency & costs; &
whereas under writ of fieri facias issued by Justice JOHN LINING on 1
July 1755 the P.M. seized the 1300 a. & offered them for sale at public
auction; SEAMAN being highest bidder; now the P.M. conveys the land to
SEAMAN. Witnesses: WILLIAM LENNOX, WILLIAM READ. Before JACOB MOTTE,
J.P. WILLIAM HOPTON, Register.

Book Q-Q, p. 601 JOHN CREIGHTON, gentleman, of Charleston, to
12 & 13 May 1756 SOLOMON ISAACS, merchant, of Charleston, as
L & R by Mortgage security for payment of 2 certain bonds; 40 a.
& a tenement in Berkeley Co., commonly called
The Quarter House, formerly belonging to JOSEPH HAWKINS; bounding W & S
on RALPH IZARD; E on JOHN BIRD; N on PAUL GRIMBALL. Whereas ISAACS at
CREIGHTON'S request signed CREIGHTON'S bond to WILLIAM GLEN & CHARLES
STEVENSON in trust for estate of PATRICK CLARKE, the bond dated 24 Apr.
last in penal sum of Ł 1200 for payment of Ł 600 currency, with interest;
& whereas CREIGHTON gave ISAACS a bond this date in penal sum of Ł 800
for payment of Ł 400 currency, with interest, on 1 Nov. next; now CREIGH-
TON conveys the Quarter House & 40 a. to secure payment. Witnesses: WIL-
LIAM PINCKNEY, LYONEL CHALMERS. Before WILLIAM HOPTON, J.P. & Pub. Reg.
On 26 July 1748, PETER BACOT, executor of will of SOLOMON ISAACS, declared mortgage satisfied. Witness: WILLIAM HOPTON.

Book Q-Q, p. 609 ELISHA SCREVEN, planter, & HANNAH his wife, of
2 July 1756 Prince Frederick, Winyaw, Craven Co., to
Feoffment CHRISTOPHER GADSDEN, merchant, of Charleston,
for Ł 2500 currency, 4 lots in Georgetown (ex-
cept as excepted); Nos. 33, 34, 65, & 66; lot #33, 50 ft. x 217.9 ft.,
bounding SW on the Bay; NW on Screven Street, NE on lot #65; SE on lot
#34; lot #34, same size, bounding SW on the Bay; NW on #33; NE on #65; SE
on #35; lot #65, 100 ft. x 217.9 ft., bounding SW on #33 & #34; NW on
Screven Street; NE on Prince Street; SE on #66; lot #66, 100 x 217.9 ft.,
bounding NE on Prince Street; NW on #65; SE on #67; SW on #35 & #36; reserving part of lot #66 according to deed of trust dated 15 Jan. 1734
vested in GEORGE PAWLEY, WILLIAM SWINTON, & DANIEL LAROCHE & as said deed
of trust by JOHN CLELAND, & MARY his wife was confirmed by indentures
dated 13 June 1737; the reserved part of lot #66 being contained within
the red lines on the plat lying 130 ft. on (from?) Prince Street down-
wards towards the Bay & 8 ft. wide on Prince Street & same breadth down-
wards for 90 ft., then 24 ft. wide for the remaining 40 ft.; bounding SW
& NW on lot #66; SE on #67; NE on Prince Street. Witnesses: REBECCA
COOKE, THOMAS GODFREY, GEORGE BEDON, JR. Delivery by turf & twig. Before GEORGE PAWLEY, J.P. WILLIAM HOPTON, Register.

Book Q-Q, p. 613 CHARLES MCLANE, planter, of Granville Co., to
28 & 29 Oct. 1755 SAMUEL NASH, blacksmith, of Beaufort, for
L & R Ł 120 currency, lot #347 in Beaufort, bounding
N on #351; E on #348; S on North Street; W on
Harrington Street; which lot #347 was granted ALLEN MCLANE 22 Mar. 1745
(see Secretary's Book E.E. fol. 165-166); & bequeathed by him to his son
CHARLES. Witnesses: WILLIAM GOUGH, THOMAS PARMENTER. Before WILLIAM
HARVEY, J.P. WILLIAM HOPTON, Register.

Book Q-Q, p. 619 MATTHIAS (his mark) SELLER, planter, of Colle-
1 Jan. 1755 ton, to JOSEPH FULLER, of St. Andrews Parish,
Mortgage Berkeley Co., as security on bond of even date

in sum of Ł 1600 currency, to be paid 1 Jan. next; 756 a. in Colleton Co., & 7 Negroes. Witnesses: THOMAS RIVERS, STEPHEN WARREN. Before J. SKENE, J.P. WILLIAM HOPTON, Register.

Book Q-Q, p. 621
29 & 30 Dec. 1755
L & R

REBECCA RACE, widow, of BENJAMIN RACE, of Charleston (& daughter of THOMAS DIXON, bricklayer, of Charleston), to WILLIAM ELLIOTT, ESQ., of Ashley River, for Ł 600 currency, 100 a. in Berkeley Co., (formerly part of 2 tracts) bounding E & N on WILLIAM ELLIOTT; W on JOHN COCKFIELD; S on Ashley River; according to plat dated 22 Jan. 1672/3; which 100 a. were originally granted by the Lords Proprs. to HENRY PRETTY; who conveyed to JOHN SULLIVAN; who conveyed to THOMAS DIXON; who by will dated 30 Mar. 1739 bequeathed to his daughter REBECCA DIXON, party hereto, now REBECCA RACE; who conveys to ELLIOTT. Witnesses: ELIZABETH COSSENS, CHARLES PINCKNEY (attorney). Before JACOB MOTTE, J.P. WILLIAM HOPTON, Register.

Book Q-Q, p. 630
23 June 1756
L & R

WILLIAM CRIPPS, surgeon, of London, by his attorneys, (letter of attorney dated London 8 June 1755), THOMAS SHUBRICK & DANIEL CRAWFORD, merchants, of Charleston, SC; to GEORGE FORD, planter, of Craven Co., for Ł 531:5:0 SC money, 250 a. in Craven Co., bounding S on Greens Creek; E & N on Black River; W & S on WILLIAM HINCKLEY; which 250 a. were granted to PHILIP CHANDLER; who, with his wife, SARAH, by L & R dated 24 & 25 July 1738, sold to WILLIAM CRIPPS. Witnesses: SAMUEL PHILLIPS, ANDREW MARR. Before JACOB MOTTE, J.P. WILLIAM HOPTON, Register.

Book Q-Q, p. 637
3 & 4 July 1755
L & R

BENJAMIN DE ST. JULIEN, planter, of Craven Co., to PETER PORCHER & PHILIP PORCHER, planters, of Craven Co., for Ł 633 currency, 2 tracts of land, in Berkeley Co., total 422 a., English measure; 1 of 332 a. bounding N on CAPT. STEWART (formerly SAMUEL SAUNDERS); E on HENRY DE ST. JULIEN & RENE RAVENEL; S on BENJAMIN DE ST. JULIEN (formerly JAMES DE ST. JULIEN); W on RICHARD HARBIN; the other 90 a., bounding N on the 332 a.; E on RENE RAVENEL; W on estate of GEORGE HAGUE (formerly JOHN RICHBOURGH). Witnesses: JOSEPH PORCHER, BENJAMIN GIGNILLIAT. Before JOHN PAMOR, J.P. WILLIAM HOPTON, Register.

Book Q-Q, p. 644
11 & 12 Feb. 1750/1
L & R

WILLIAM JAMESON, planter, to PETER PORCHER, JR., both of Craven Co., for Ł 1200 currency, 2 plantations in Craven Co., total 800 a., English measure, 1 of 450 a., bounding SE on PETER PORCHER; NW on MR. RAY; N on WILLIAM THOMAS; other sides on vacant land; the other 350 a., bounding S on above 450 a. granted to JAMES SINGLETON, now belonging to WILLIAM JAMESON; E on WILLIAM JAMESON & vacant land. Witnesses: PETER PORCHER, PETER GOURDIN, PHILIP PORCHER. Before JOHN PAMOR, J.P. WILLIAM HOPTON, Register.

Book Q-Q, p. 651
20 & 21 Mary 1756
L & R

HENRY MASHON (MASHOW, MARSHON), of Colleton Co., to JOHN NARNEY (MARNEY), watchmaker, of Charleston, for Ł 1000 currency, 500 a. in 2 tracts of 250 a. each. Whereas the Lords Proprs. on 3 Nov. 1714, by Gov. CHARLES CRAVEN, granted HENRY MASHOW, grandfather of said HENRY, 500 a. in Colleton Co., bounding N on HENRY MASHON; E on WILLIAM EBERSON; S on vacant land; W on OWEN BEGIN & vacant land; & whereas HENRY MASHOW, the grandfather died, intestate & his only son ABRAHAM inherited; & he by will dated 7 Feb. 1734 bequeathed to his daughter, ELIZABETH, 250 a. adjoining JOHN MACCAN (MACCAW ?) & RICHARD DAWSON on W side Horseshoe Savanna; & to his daughter, MARY, 250 a. of same tract; & whereas ELIZABETH died & her share reverted to HENRY MASHON, party hereto, as only son & heir of ABRAHAM; & whereas HENRY MASHOW, the grandfather, also owned 250 a. bounding S & W on said HENRY MASHON; other sides on vacant land; & whereas these 250 a. also descended to HENRY MASHON, party hereto; now he sells both tracts of 250 a. to JOHN NARNEY. Witnesses: JAMES PARSONS, JOHN RUTLEDGE. Before ROBERT WILLIAMS, JR., J.P. WILLIAM HOPTON, Register.

Book Q-Q, p. 659
30 & 31 July 1756

JAMES BEAIRD, planter, of St. Johns Parish, Berkeley Co., to JOHN WARD, JR., merchant, of

L & R   Charleston, as security on bond of even date
                               given by BEAIRD to FRANCIS LEJAU, SR., & FRAN-
CIS LEJAU, JR., executors of will of DANIEL HUGER (which bond JOHN WARD
endorsed at BEAIRD'S request) in penal sum of Ł 2000 for payment of
Ł 1000 currency, with interest, on 30 July 1757; 500 a. in St. Johns Par-
ish, bounding N on Santee River; S on vacant land; E on JAMES KINLOCH; W
on GEORGE BEAIRD; also 650 a. in Craven Co., bounding S on Santee River;
N & E on vacant land; W on GEORGE BEAIRD. Witnesses: JAMES BOX, JOSHUA
WARD. Before WILLIAM BURROWS, J.P. WILLIAM HOPTON, Register.

Book Q-Q, p. 668   SMITH PRENTICE, cooper, formerly of New Eng-
12 & 13 Aug. 1756   land, now of SC, to MARTHA D'HARRIETTE, widow
L & R   of Charleston, for Ł 5 & 6 currency, 394 a. on
                             Beech Hill, St. Pauls Parish, bounding N on
JOHN MOORE; S on WILLIAM & JOHN GRAVES; W on JOHN GRAVES; E on COL. RICH-
ARD BEDON. Witnesses: GEORGE JACKSON, WILLIAM BLAKE. Before JOHN RAT-
TRAY, J.P. WILLIAM HOPTON, Register.

Book Q-Q, p. 672   GABRIEL MANIGAULT, ESQ., & SARAH RUTLEDGE,
24 & 25 Mar. 1756   widow, both of Charleston, to RALPH IZARD,
L & R   ESQ., of St. George Parish, for Ł 6520 curren-
                             cy, a lot in Charleston, bounding S 154 ft. on
Broad Street; W 104 ft. on JOHN HARVEY; N 154 ft. on JOHN DRAYTON; E 104
ft. on ELIZABETH QUINCEY; which lot formerly belonged to BENJAMIN HARVEY,
planter, of Stono (devisee of WILLIAM HARVEY), who conveyed to GABRIEL
MANIGAULT & SARAH RUTLEDGE. Witnesses: WILLIAM MICHIE, JOHN RUTLEDGE.
Before BENJAMIN SMITH, J.P. WILLIAM HOPTON, Register.

Book Q-Q, p. 679   GABRIEL MANIGAULT, ALEXANDER BROUGHTON, &
12 & 13 Apr. 1756   PETER MANIGAULT, executors of will of BENJAMIN
L & R   D'HARRIETTE, merchant, of Charleston; at pub-
                             lic auction, to WALTER IZARD, ESQ., of Dor-
chester, St. George Parish, Berkeley Co., for Ł 5105 currency, the N division of 3 lots in Charleston, bounding N 150 ft. on Queen Street; W
194-1/2 ft. on Meeting House Street, (formerly Old Church Street); E on
JOHN BEE; S on 197 ft. on a private alley (formerly ANTHONY BONNEAU).
Whereas BENJAMIN D'HARRIETTE by will dated 14 Jan. 1756 authorized his
executors to dispose of his real & personal estate, & appointed GABRIEL
MANIGAULT, ALEXANDER BROUGHTON, & PETER MANIGAULT his executors; & whereas at the time of his death, 17 Feb. last, D'HARRIETTE owned the N divi-
sion of 3 lots in Charleston (devised by will of MARY CROSS to her son
WILLIAM BAYLEY & her 2 daughters, MARY BASDEN, & SUSANNAH RAWLINGS); now
the executors sell that portion to IZARD. Witnesses: JOHN CORKER,
CHARLES GRIMBALL, ELIZABETH BANBURY. Before BENJAMIN SMITH, J.P. WIL-
LIAM HOPTON, Register.

Book Q-Q, p. 686   MATHURINE GUERIN, planter, & ELIZABETH his
26 & 27 July 1756   wife, of Berkeley Co., to THOMAS FULLER, ESQ.,
L & R   of St. Andrews Parish, Berkeley Co., for
                             Ł 2800 currency, 56 a. on N side Stono River,
bounding N on JOSEPH FULLER; S & W on MATHURINE GUERIN; E on JOSEPH FUL-
LER & JOSEPH ELLIOTT; being part of 305 a., bounding N on MR. BONNEAU,
BARNARD ELLIOTT, & JOHN TOOMER; E on BARNARD ELLIOTT; JOSHUA TOOMER, &
marsh; S & W & NW on JOSHUA TOOMER; formerly owned by JOSHUA TOOMER, who,
by L & R dated 1 & 2 Oct. 1741 conveyed to MATHURINE TOOMER. Witnesses:
DANIEL BOURQUETT, JAMES VERREE, JOHN GUERIN. Before CHARLES PINCKNEY,
J.P. WILLIAM HOPTON, Register. Plat of 56 a., part of 305 a. formerly
belonging to HENRY TOOMER, later to MATHURINE GUERIN, who sold to JOSEPH
FULLER; the 56 a. now belonging to THOMAS FULLER as heir to JOSEPH; certified 7 May 1756 by ROBERT SCREVEN, Sur.

Book Q-Q, p. 693   JOSEPH WRAGG, merchant, of Richmond, Surry
24 & 25 Sept. 1755   Co., only son & heir of WILLIAM WRAGG, draper,
L & R   formerly of London; WILLIAM BELL, druggist, of
                             Leadenhall Street, London, eldest son & heir &
also devisee in will of BENJAMIN BELL, glover, of London (who married
MERCY, 1 of the daughters of WILLIAM WRAGG, the mother of said WILLIAM
BELL & JAMES PARIS, salter of Southwark, Co. of Surrey, said JAMES PARIS
being surviving devisee in trust named in will of JAMES CHORLEY, soap
merchant, of Southwark, Surry Co., which JAMES CHORLEY married ELIZABETH

22

the other daughter of WILLIAM WRAGG), of 1st part; & THOMAS DRAYTON, ESQ.,
of Charleston, SC, of 2nd part. Whereas JOHN, Lord Carteret, Palatine, &
the Lords Proprs., by grant dated 5 Dec. 1718 & signed by RICHARD SKELTON,
their Secretary, granted JOHN DAWSON, ESQ., merchant, of London, 1 of the
Lords Proprs., 2 Baronies, each of 12,000 a., English measure, on the
Yamasee Land, 1/4 only to lie on the river, the rest backward by a direct
line as near as can be; & whereas the 2 Baronies were surveyed in May
1730 by JOHN FRIPP (or TRIPP) then Sur. Gen., & the 2 Baronies have since
been known as the Southernmost Barony & the Northernmost Barony; & by L &
R dated 29 & 30 Aug. 1722 JOHN DAWSON, as security for payment or debt of
Ŀ 1682:14:6 which DAWSON then owned to WILLIAM WRAGG conveyed to WRAGG
the 2 Baronies; 1 in Craven Co., on Craven River; & a Barony on the River
May; all within the Province of Carolina; to be redeemed by making certain payments at certain times; & whereas by L & R dated 21 & 22 Feb.
1730 between WILLIAM WRAGG, of the 1st part, & JOSEPH WRAGG, BENJAMIN
BELL, JAMES CHORLEY; SAMUEL WRAGG, merchant, of London; & JOSEPH WRAGG,
merchant, of Charleston, of the 2nd part, reciting that the sum of
Ŀ 1682:14:6 had not been paid to said WILLIAM WRAGG the father; now WIL-
LIAM WRAGG, the father for natural love & affection for his son JOSEPH
WRAGG of Richmond, & his sons-in-law BENJAMIN BELL & JAMES CHORLEY, & in
order to enlarge the marriage portions of his daughters MERCY (wife of
BELL) & ELIZABETH (wife of CHORLEY) & for natural love & affection for
natural love & affection for his kinsman WILLIAM WRAGG son of his nephew
said SAMUEL WRAGG, & his kinsman JOHN WRAGG eldest son & his nephew said
JOSEPH WRAGG, merchant, of Charleston, conveys the 2 Baronies to them in
trust; that is, 1 full half part of the 2 Baronies in trust for the use
of said JOSEPH WRAGG of Richmond, BENJAMIN BELL, & JAMES CHORLEY, as tenants in common & not as joint tenants, without benefit or survivorship;
the other half in trust for use of WILLIAM WRAGG (son of SAMUEL WRAGG) &
JOHN WRAGG as follows: 8000 a. (2/3 of the other half of 2 Baronies) in
trust for said WILLIAM WRAGG (son of SAMUEL WRAGG); the remaining third
part (4000 a.) in trust for JOHN WRAGG (son of JOSEPH WRAGG of Charleston), & in order to settle which half should belong to JOSEPH WRAGG of
Richmond, BENJAMIN BELL & JAMES CHORLEY & which to WILLIAM & JOHN WRAGG,
the 2 Baronies are to be surveyed & divided by some proper persons appointed by the major part of them into 2 equal parts & a map made, & the
other parties of the second part decide the allotment as follows: in 1
small scroll of parchment or paper should be written a short description
of 1 part & marked No. 1 on the plan; & on another scroll a description
of the other half & marked off on plat as No. 2; both scrolls to be roll-
ed up & sealed, put in a hat & shuffled; then some indifferent person to
put his hand in & take out 1 scroll & deliver to JOSEPH WRAGG of Richmond, BENJAMIN BELL, & JAMES CHORLEY, or 1 of them; afterwards take out
the other scroll & deliver it to SAMUEL & JOSEPH WRAGG of Charleston; the
scrolls to be immediately opened & read, & their lots to be according to
the scroll received; the scroll delivered to SAMUEL & JOSEPH WRAGG to be
the share of WILLIAM WRAGG (son & SAMUEL) & JOHN WRAGG (son of JOSEPH
of Charleston); the allotment to be final; & whereas the 2 Baronies were
so divided & No. 1 was called the Northernmost Barony & No. 2 the Southernmost Barony; & the Southernmost Barony fell to JOSEPH WRAGG of Richmond, BENJAMIN BELL, & JAMES CHORLEY, & the Northernmost (No. 1) Barony
fell to WILLIAM & JOHN WRAGG; & whereas by deed of partition dated 28
Nov. 1734 between JOSEPH WRAGG of Richmond, BENJAMIN BELL, & JAMES CHOR-
LEY, of 1st part; SAMUEL WRAGG & JOSEPH WRAGG of Charleston, of 2nd part;
& WILLIAM WRAGG (son of SAMUEL) & JOHN WRAGG, of 3rd part; they of the
2nd part, with consent of them of the 3rd part, conveyed to those of the
1st part the Southernmost Barony as tenants in common; & whereas JOHN
DAWSON died intestate, leaving 1 son JOTHAM, & a daughter, BARBARA; &
JOTHAM died intestate without issue, & BARBARA became entitled to the
equity in the mortgage; & whereas BARBARA, by will dated 8 Apr. 1726,
gave the remainder of her real & personal estate equally to MARGARET
MOLLASON & DANIEL DOLLEY & they became entitled to the equity; & whereas
by L & R dated 14 & 15 Jan. 1729 between MARGARET MOLLESON & DANIEL DOL-
LEY of 1st part; MARY DAWSON, widow of JOHN & mother of BARBARA of 2nd
part; & MICHAEL TREPASS, joiner, of Parish of St. Giles Cripple Gate,
London, of 3rd part; MARGARET MOLLESON, DANIEL DOLLEY & MARY DAWSON conveyed, among other things, to MICHAEL TREPPASS the 2 Baronies & all other
lands bequeathed to MARGARET & DANIEL by will of BARBARA DAWSON; & whereas by L & R dated 21 & 22 Jan. 1729 MICHAEL TREPPASS conveyed the Baronies & settlements & all his other lands in Carolina to DANIEL DOLLEY; &

whereas DANIEL DOLLEY died without issue & without disposing of his equity of redemption in said mortgage so that his elder brother & heir,
ROBERT DOLLEY inherited; & whereas by L & R dated 14 & 15 July 1736 ROB-
ERT DOLLEY, grazier, of Souldern, Oxford Co., conveyed his equity in the
3 Baronies to JOSEPH WRAGG (party hereto), BENJAMIN BELL & JAMES CHORLEY,
reciting that the sum of ₺ 1682:14:6 nor any part had been paid by JOHN
DAWSON or any other person but the principle & interest remained due &
reciting that in order to save himself the costs of a suit in equity to
be brought to foreclose his equity, he had agreed to assign to them his
equity in the 3 Baronies; i.e., the Barony on the River May; the Barony
in Craven Co., or Craven River; & the Southernmost Barony on the Yamasee
Land in Granville Co., & whereas JAMES CHORLEY by will dated 21 July 1733
gave BENJAMIN BELL & JAMES PARIS in trust all his real estate to be sold
& the money used for certain purposes, making BELL & PARIS his executors
& they proved the will in the proper ecclesiastical Court of the Archbishop of Canterbury; & whereas BENJAMIN BELL by will dated 28 July 1739
devised his claim to the Baronies to his son WILLIAM BELL in trust, the
lands to be sold & the money used for certain purposes, & appointed his
wife, MERCY, & his sons BENJAMIN & WILLIAM joint executors & they proved
the will in the Prerogative Court of the Archbishop of Canberbury; &
whereas THOMAS DRAYTON has agreed to purchase from JOSEPH WRAGG of Richmond, WILLIAM BELL, & JAMES PARIS the fee simple & inheritance of the
Southernmost Barony (except as excepted) for ₺ 600 British; now they convey to him the 12,000 a. called the Southernmost Barony on the Yamasee
Land in Granville Co., bounding S on land vacant in 1730; E on JOHN BEE &
Cusehatchey Creek; N on Northernmost Barony; W on land vacant in 1730;
subject to the conveyance made by L & R dated 23 & 24 Dec. 1734 by JOSEPH
WRAGG of Richmond, BENJAMIN BELL, & JAMES CHORLEY, to THOMAS OWEN, brewer,
of Millstreet, Parish of St. Mary Magdalen Bermondsaw, Surry Co., Great
Britain, of 1/4 part or share in the Southernmost Barony, & subject to
arrears of taxes. Witnesses: WILLIAM GEORGE FREEMAN, RAWLINS LOWNDES.
Before PETER MANIGAULT, J.P. WILLIAM HOPTON, Register.

Book Q-Q, p. 711   JOHN SMITH, gentlemen, of Charleston, & MARY
12 & 13 Aug. 1756   his wife (formerly MARY BAKER), executrix &
L & R   WILLIAM BRISBANE, merchant, of Charleston, ex-
                          ecutor of will of JAMES BAKER, planter, of St.
George Parish, Dorchester; to WALTER IZARD, ESQ., of St. George Parish;
for ₺ 1200 currency, 298 a. on Ashley River. Whereas CHARLES CANTEY,
planter, of Santee, owned 298 a. on NE side Ashley River in St. George
Parish, bounding SE on WALTER IZARD; NE on PAUL JENYS; SW on a vacant
cedar swamp & a vacant marsh; which on 28 Mar. 1752 he sold for ₺ 1500
currency, to JAMES BAKER; who, by will dated 9 Mar. 1755 authorized his
executors to either keep his real & personal estate or sell, as they
thought fit; appointing his wife MARY executrix & RICHARD BEDON & WILLIAM
BRISBANE, executors of will & guardians, of his children; & whereas after
his death MARY (before her marriage to SMITH) & BRISBANE proved the will
before Gov. JAMES GLEN; now they convey the tract to IZARD. Witnesses:
JOHN RATTRAY, GEORGE JACKSON. Before DOUGAL CAMPBELL, J.P. WILLIAM HOP-
TON, Register.

Book Q-Q, p. 719   JAMES EDMONDS, gentleman, of Charleston, & ANN
1 & 2 Aug. 1756   his wife; CHARLES FAUCHEREAUD, planter, of
L & R   Berkeley Co.; & SARAH HILL, widow, of Berkeley
                          Co.; of 1st part; to PAUL TRAPIER, ESQ., of
Craven Co., for ₺ 61:15:0 SC money, their several third parts or shares
in the undivided plantation of 247 a. in Craven Co., originally granted
to THOMAS SMITH, JR., on 2 May 1717; then bounding N on Peedee River; SE
on THOMAS SMITH; which tract, by various wills & conveyances, became
vested in equal third parts in JAMES EDMONDS, CHARLES FAUCHEREAUD & SARAH
HILL, as tenants in common. Witnesses: MARY FAUCHEREAUD, ELIZABETH
WHITE, WILLIAM HUTSON, RICE PRICE. Before LIONEL CHALMERS, J.P. WILLIAM
HOPTON, Register.

Book Q-Q, p. 728   JAMES EDMONDS, gentleman, of Charleston, to
2 Aug. 1756   PAUL TRAPIER, ESQ., of Craven Co., in penal
Bond   sum of ₺ 11:3:4 currency in token that he will
                          observe the agreements in above conveyance
(p. 719). Witnesses: WILLIAM HUTSON, RICE PRICE. Before WILLIAM HOPTON,
J.P. & Pub. Reg.

Book Q-Q, p. 730   JAMES EDMONDS, gentleman, of Charleston, & ANN
1 & 2 Aug. 1756   his wife; CHARLES FAUCHEREAUD, planter, of
L & R   Berkeley Co., & SARAH his wife; & SARAH HILL,
                          widow, of Berkeley Co., of 1st part; to JOB
ROTHMAHLER, merchant, of Craven Co., for ₤ 120 currency, their several
third parts in the undivided tract of 500 a. in Craven Co., originally
granted to GEORGE SMITH on 16 June 1716, then bounding NW on THOMAS
SMITH, JR., SE on Peedee River; which tract, by various conveyances be-
came vested in equal parts in JAMES EDMONDS, CHARLES FAUCHEREAUD, & SARAH
HILL as tenants in common. Witnesses: MARY FEUCHEREAUD, ELIZABETH WHITE,
WILLIAM HUTSON, RICE PRICE. Before LIONEL CHALMERS, J.P. WILLIAM HOP-
TON, Register.

Book Q-Q, p. 739   JAMES EDMONDS, gentleman, of Charleston, to
2 Aug. 1756   JOB ROTHMAHLER, merchant, of Craven Co., in
Bond   penal sum of ₤ 83:6:8 currency, to keep agree-
                          ments in above conveyance (p. 730). Witness-
es: WILLIAM HUTSON, RICE PRICE. Before WILLIAM HOPTON, J.P. & Pub. Reg.

Book Q.Q., p. 740   THOMAS (his mark) HARRINGTON, planter, of An-
5 & 6 Aug. 1756   son Co., NC, to JAMES JONES, tailor, of Craven
L & R   Co., for ₤ 500 SC money, 350 a. in the WELCH
                          tract, Craven Co., granted by Gov. JAMES GLEN
on 29 Nov. 1750 to THOMAS HARRINGTON. Witnesses: JOHN (his mark) ASHLEY,
JAMES NIVIS. Before WILLIAM HOPTON, J.P. & Pub. Reg.

                          DEEDS BOOK "R-R"
                          SEPT. 1756 - MAY 1757

Book R-R, p. 1   WILLIAM CRIPPS, surgeon, of London, appoints
3 June 1755   THOMAS SHUBRICK & DANIEL CRAWFORD, merchants,
Power of Attorney   of Charleston, SC, his attorneys, to dispose
                          of all his lands, houses, etc., in SC. Wit-
nesses: ALEXANDER MARSHALL, ISAAC MAZYCK, JR. MAZYCK appeared before
JACOB MOTTE, J.P. WILLIAM HOPTON, Register.

Book R-R, p. 3   JOHN STEVENS, planter, & MARY his wife, of
4 & 5 June 1756   Berkeley Co., to GEORGE SMITH & WILLIAM SCOTT,
L & R   merchants, of Charleston, for ₤ 2700 currency,
                          69 a. on N side Ashley River, near Bacon
Bridge, Berkeley Co., bounding W on DR. ROBERT DUNBAR (formerly JOHN
STEVENS) & on HENRY WAY; N on THOMAS NIXON & JOHN COSSENS; E on ISAAC
HOLMES'S land where HOLMES & PERONNEAU kept a store; on which 69 a. stand
the store houses, dwelling houses & other buildings formerly occupied for
several years by JOHN MCQUEEN & Co., now by MAURICE HARVEY & Co., also
18 a. on S side Ashley River, near Bacon Bridge, bounding SE & S on
CHARLES WRIGHT; NE on 2 a. near Bacon Bridge divided into small lots.
Witnesses: SAMUEL STEVENS, SR., SAMUEL STEVENS, JR., JOHN SNELLING. Before CHARLES PINCKNEY, J.P.

Book R-R, p. 11   THOMAS GLEN, ESQ., to ELIZABETH GIBBES, wife
5 & 6 Aug. 1751   of JOHN GIBBES, ESQ., both of Charleston, for
L & R   ₤ 1155 currency, part of lot #197 in Charles-
                          ton. Whereas GABRIEL ESCOTT, merchant, of
Charleston, owned part of lot #197 with its houses, bounding E 35 ft. 5
in. on the Great Street leading from White Point to Ashley River N throu
hrough the Market Place; W on JAMES LAWRENCE (formerly JOHN BAILEY); S on
ALBERT DELMAR; N on JOHN CRAVEN; which property ESCOTT had purchased from
ALBERT DELMAR & CHRISTIAN his wife for ₤ 1200 currency by L & R dated 27
& 28 Aug. 1734; & whereas ESCOTT died intestate in 1740 without children,
brother or sister, & it descended to SARAH HERRING (wife of JOHN HERRING,
gentleman, of St. George Parish, Middlesex; & lately widow of JOHN STAP-
LES, mariner, of London; & first cousin & sole heiress of said GABRIEL
ESCOTT) & whereas in 1742 she appointed CHARLES PINCKNEY of Charleston,
SC, her attorney to take possession in her name; & whereas JOHN HERRING
& SARAH his wife, in the presence of THOMAS BROWN, N.P. & 2 witnesses, by
letter of attorney dated 14 May 1748, before SIR ROBERT SADBROKE, mayor
of London, appointed said CHARLES PINCKNEY their attorney & whereas

PINCKNEY on 14 Feb. 1749, sold the lot to THOMAS GLEN for Ł 165 sterling; now he sells to ELIZABETH GIBBES. Witnesses: RALPH TAYLOR, CHARLES PINCKNEY, JR. Before JACOB MOTTE, J.P. WILLIAM HOPTON, Register.

Book R-R, p. 19   TARLOR (his mark) O'GUIN, & PATTY (her mark)
17 & 18 June 1756   his wife, to NATHAN EVANS, planter, both of
L & R   Craven Co., for Ł 350 SC money, 200 a. in Cra-
                         ven Co., granted 24 May 1745 by Gov. JAMES
GLEN to THOMAS GROOM (Book L.L. fol. 269), who by will in 1747 bequeathed
the land to PATTY O'GUIN; bounding SE on EDMOND ATKIN; NW on PERRY PAW-
LEY; NE on JOHN SANDERS; SW on Peedee River. Witnesses: SAMUEL BUXTON,
CHARLES (his mark) TURBEVILLE, SAMUEL (his mark) TACKMAN (JACKMAN?). Be-
fore ABRAHAM BUCKETTS, J.P. WILLIAM HOPTON, Register.

Book R-R, p. 23   EDMUND ATKIN, ESQ., to ELIZABETH GIBBES, wife
23 & 24 Apr. 1750   of JOHN GIBBES, ESQ., both of Charleston, for
L & R   Ł 968 currency, the S half of lot #36 in
                         Charleston, bounding E 26 ft. on Bedon's Al-
ley; W on MRS. SMITH; S on MR. SWEETING (formerly DR. DALE); N 108 ft. on
other half belonging to EDMUND ATKIN. Whereas JAMES COLLETON, Gov.; PAUL
GRIMBALL & JOHN BERESFORD, deputies of WILLIAM, Earl of Craven, Palatine;
CHRISTOPHER, Duke of Albemarle; ANTHONY, Lord Ashley; GEORGE, Lord Car-
teret; SIR PETER COLLETON, Baronet; SETH SOTHELL, THOMAS ARCHDALE, &
THOMAS AMY, ESQRS.; Lords Proprs.; on 10 Oct. 1689 granted GEORGE BEDON,
SR., lot #36 in Charleston, bounding E on ANDREW PERCIVAL & ROBERT
GIBBES; W on a street parallel with Cooper River & "then by MR. SYMON'S
DOOR"; S on MR. SWEETING; N on MRS. ERPE; & whereas GEORGE BEDON, by will
dated 21 Dec. 1705 gave his tenements & lands in Charleston after the
death of his wife to his son, STEPHEN BEDON; the remainder to his son
HENRY; & whereas STEPHEN had several children (THOMAS, JOHN, STEPHEN,
SARAH, BENJAMIN, REBECCA & GEORGE) & became absolute owner of the proper-
ty bequeathed to him & by L & R dated 15 & 16 Apr. 1736 he conveyed the
land in joint tenancy to JOHN & EDMUND ATKIN, merchants, of Charleston; &
whereas JOHN died & EDMUND inherited his share; now he sells half the lot
#36 to ELIZABETH GIBBES. Witnesses: ANDREW RUTLEDGE, ISAAC HUMPHREYS,
JOHN BASSNETT. Before WILLIAM HOPTON, J.P. & Register.

Book R-R, p. 28   JAMES EDEN, SR., planter, & JANE (her mark)
18 & 19 Nov. 1754   his wife, to SARAH PORTER, widow, both of
L & R   Christ Church Parish, Berkeley Co., for Ł 600
                         currency; 205-1/2 a., English measure, in
Christ Church Parish, bounding SE on WILLIAM BOLLOUGH; NW on WILLIAM
BOLLOUGH & WILLIAM YOUNG. Witnesses: ARCHIBALD MCDOWELL, THOMAS HAMLIN,
JR., ROBERT MURRELL, JR. Before JACOB MOTTE, J.P. WILLIAM HOPTON, Reg-
ister.

Book R-R, p. 34   THOMAS WIGG, planter, to MARY TAILFER, plant-
11 & 12 July 1754   er, both of Port Royal Island, Granville Co.,
L & R   for Ł 1 currency, 39 a., English measure, part
                         of a tract granted to THOMAS GRIMBALL, who
conveyed to WIGG; bounding N on THOMAS PARMENTER; S & W on land & marsh
of MARY TAILFER; E on THOMAS WIGG. Witnesses: JOHN HUTCHISON, JOHN CHAP-
MAN. Before JAMES THOMPSON, J.P. WILLIAM HOPTON, Register.

Book R-R, p. 39   DAVID JERVEY, carpenter, & ANN his wife, to
13 & 14 Sept. 1756   THOMAS OLDFIELD, planter, of St. Bartholomew's
L & R   Parish, Colleton Co., for Ł 325 currency,
                         125 a. (being a fourth part of 500 a. belong-
ing to heirs of THOMAS (JOSEPH?) DEDCOTT on W side PonPon River, & marked
#4 on the plat; bounding N on MR. MATHEWES; E on JOHN PETERS; W on MR.
MATHEWES & MRS. MELVIN (MCLAIN?); S on MRS. MELVIN. Witnesses: GEORGE
JACKSON, WILLIAM BLAKE. Before DAVID GREENE, J.P. WILLIAM HOPTON, Register. Plat given. Whereas ANN JERVEY, ELIZABETH DEDCOTT, MARY MELVIN,
& WILLABLE FAGIN, heirs to estate of said DEDCOTT, agreed to divide the
500 a. into 4 equal lots, & each 1 draw for their share; & lot #4 fell to
ANN JERVEY, therefore WILLIAM MCPHERSON, D.S., surveyed her lot according
to plat certified 10 Nov. 1748.

Book R-R, p. 42   RICHARD BAILEY, planter, & RACHEL his wife, to
11 & 12 May 1756   PATRICK CLARK, both of Colleton Co., for Ł 500

L & R   currency, 198-1/2 a. in Colleton Co., bounding
                               W on MILLER ST. JOHN; S on MADAM BOONE; E on
heirs of MOSES MARTIN; N on JOSEPH GLOVER; being the NW half of 397 a.
granted to SAMUEL SLEIGH; who conveyed to JAMES SKIRVING & MOSES MARTIN;
who by deed of partition allotted the NW half to SKIRVING; who conveyed
to JOSEPH GLOVER; who conveyed to ROBERT HANCOCK; who conveyed to RICHARD
BAILEY. Witnesses: JOSEPH GLOVER, SAMUEL ELMES. Before WILLIAM HOPTON,
J.P. & Pub. Reg.

Book R-R, p. 47   BENJAMIN PARMENTER, planter, & MARTHA his
16 & 17 Oct. 1749   wife, to MARY TAILFER, shopkeeper, both of
L & R   Port Royal Island, for Ł 620 currency, 216 a.,
                            English measure, part of a tract granted JO-
SEPH PARMENTER, SR., by Gov. NATHANIEL JOHNSON in 1706/7; & sold by him
on 6 Dec. 1737 to said BENJAMIN PARMENTER; on Port Royal Island, bounding
S on JOSEPH PARMENTER, JR.; N on THOMAS PARMENTER; W on the Rev. MR. ROB-
ERT ORR; E on JOHN PARMENTER. Witnesses: THOMAS WIGG, JOHN GUINN. Be-
fore JOHN HUTCHINSON, J.P. WILLIAM HOPTON, Register.

Book R-R, p. 52   RAWLINS LOWNDES, P.M., to JOSEPH GLOVER, of
2 Oct. 1753   St. Bartholomews Parish, Colleton Co., at pub-
Sale   lic auction, for Ł 1985 currency, 800 a. in
                            Colleton Co.; also a town lot in Jackson-
borough. Whereas JOHN GODFREY, of St. Bartholomews Parish, at the time
of his death owned 800 a. in Colleton Co., part of 1250 a. granted him by
Lt. Gov. THOMAS BROUGHTON on 16 Jan. 1735, bounding S on vacant land; W
on MRS. CHAMPNEYS; N on JOHN FRAZER; E on THOMAS DRAYTON & COL. TRENCH;
also a lot of half an a. in Jacksonborough where he kept a tan yard; &
whereas JOHN MACKENZIE, MATTHEW ROOCKE, GEORGE JACKSON, & JONATHAN WIT-
TER, after GODFREY died intestate, obtained a judgment against MARY GOD-
FREY, administratrix of GODFREY'S estate, in the amount of Ł 2308:11:0 &
costs, & JAMES GREEME, C.J., issued a writ of fieri facias on 1 Oct. 1751
commanding the P.M. to seize & sell the said estate. Witnesses: DOUGAL
CAMPBELL, WILLIAM READ. Before WILLIAM HOPTON, J.P. & Pub. Reg.

Book R-R, p. 55   ARCHIBALD HAMILTON, planter, of Colleton Co.,
13 & 14 Sept. 1756   to EDWARD FENWICKE, ESQ., of John's Island,
L & R   for Ł 6000 currency, 410 a. in Colleton Co., W
                            of freshes of Edisto River, within land,
bounding N on JOHN KENNEWAY; E on JOSEPH DIDCOTT; S on JOHN ANDREW & va-
cant land; W on vacant land; also 489 a. in Colleton Co., W of freshes of
Edisto River, within land, bounding N on JOHN KENNEWAY; E on JOSEPH DID-
COTT; S on JOHN ANDREW & vacant land; W on vacant land; also 268 a. on W
side PonPon River, bounding W on a creek of Ashpoo River; N on PAUL HAM-
ILTON, the elder; E on PAUL HAMILTON the elder & DANIEL HENDRICK; S on
DANIEL HENDRICK & JOSEPH ANDREW; SW on a Bay swamp. Whereas the Lords
Proprs. on 2 Mar. 1711 granted JOSEPH HARLEY 410 a. in Colleton Co.,
which by will he gave to his son JOSEPH HARLEY, vintner; who, by L & R
dated 1 & 2 Dec. 1749 he sold to BENJAMIN SAVAGE, JR. & JOSEPH PICKERING,
merchants, of Charleston; & by L & R dated 29 & 30 Jan. 1753, sold by JO-
SEPH PICKERING, the surviving partner, to ARCHIBALD HAMILTON; & whereas
the Lords Proprs. on 23 July 1711 granted JAMES COCHRAN, planter, 489 a;
in Colleton Co.; who sold to PAUL HAMILTON the 489 a., then said to be
bounding E on JOSEPH HOLLEY; S on a swamp; W on JOHN CANNAWAY; & by L & R
dated 17 & 18 Feb. 1746, sold by PAUL HAMILTON, planter, eldest son &
heir of said PAUL HAMILTON, to his brother, ARCHIBALD HAMILTON, party
hereto; said release reciting a grant dated 7 Aug. 1735 by Lt. Gov. THOM-
AS BROUGHTON, to PAUL HAMILTON the elder, of 268 a., & reciting that immediately after the death of PAUL HAMILTON the elder the 2 tracts of 489
& 268 a. descended to PAUL, the younger; who sold them to ARCHIBALD HAM-
ILTON, wo now sells to FENWICKE. Witnesses: WILLIAM DRAYTON, JOSEPH
CLAYPOLE, ROBERT CARR. Before PETER MANIGAULT, J.P. WILLIAM HOPTON,
Register.

Book R-R, p. 62   JONATHAN BRYAN, ESQ., of Prince William Par-
29 & 30 Sept. 1756   ish, & MARY his wife, to ANN MATHEWES, widow,
L & R   of ANTHONY MATHEWES of Charleston, for Ł 450
                            currency, 230 a. in Granville Co., near Poco-
talago Neck, between 2 branches of Port Royal River, called Pocotalago
River & Coosawhatchee River, granted 22 Sept. 1733 to WILLIAM TREWIN &

JAMES KILPATRICK, practitioner in physic; & whereas KILPATRICK conveyed
his share to TREWIN; & TREWIN by L & R dated 16 Aug. 1739 sold the tract
to JONATHAN BRYAN; now BRYAN sells to ANN MATHEWES. Witnesses: WILLIAM
MASON, JONATHAN BRYAN, JR. Before STEPHEN BULL, J.P. WILLIAM HOPTON,
Register.

Book R-R, p. 67   THOMAS (his mark) & ELIZABETH (her mark) BEA-
_____ 1754   MOND, to ARTHUR BAXTER, for ₺ 40 currency, lot
Sale   #1 (in _____?) Prince George Parish, on Wac-
                       camaw River, in Craven Co. Witnesses: DAVID
JERDON, JOHN GAUS. Before THOMAS BLYTHE, J.P. WILLIAM HOPTON, Register.

Book R-R, p. 68   GEORGE (his mark) MCKAY, of Amelia Township,
28 & 29 Sept. 1756   to JOHN WISH, yeoman, of Charleston, for ₺ 20
L & R   currency, 50 a. in Amelia Township, bounding N
                       on unknown owner & vacant land; NW on vacant
land & JOHN MORRISON; SE on GARET FITZPATRICK; SW on JOHN MORRISON & vacant land; which land was granted by Gov. JAMES GLEN on 24 Mar. 1756 to
GEORGE MCKAY. Witnesses: JAMES BALLANTINE, WILLIAM (BEAMOR?). Before
WILLIAM HOPTON, J.P. & Pub. Reg.

Book R-R, p. 73   THOMAS COLT, carpenter, of Georgetown, Winyaw,
_____ Oct. 1756   to JOHN FAUER, joiner, of Charleston, & to
Mortgage (broken pages) REBECCA ANNE COLT, as security on 2 bonds ___;
                       lot #222 in Georgetown, 217.9 ft. deep; bound-
ing S on public ground; NW on lot #221; SE on lot #223; also lot #86 in
Georgetown, adjoining the house of MRS. (MARION?) on 1 side; also his
several personal estate (listed but broken). Witnesses: WILLIAM READ,
JAMES LINGARD. WILLIAM HOPTON, Register. Incomplete notation "JOHN
FAURE is now off the Province."

Book R-R, p. 76   ROBERT SCREVEN, planter, of Berkeley Co., &
6 & 7 Oct. 1756   ELIZABETH his wife, to WILLIAM HENDERSON, gen-
L & R   tleman, of Charleston, for ₺ 3750 currency,
                       262 a., part of 379 a. granted in Apr. 1717 by
ROBERT DANIEL, Dep. Gov. to CHARLES ARMSTRONG the elder; who bequeathed
to his son, CHARLES; who by L & R dated 4 & 5 May 1740 (?) sold a part of
the tract to ROBERT SCREVEN; who now sells HENDERSON 262 a. on James Is-
land, St. Andrews Parish, bounding N on Wappoo Creek, E on MR. GLAZE &
MR. SCOTT; S on JAMES SCREVEN; W on WILLIAM HUTSON. Plat by ROBERT SCRE-
VEN dated 29 Sept. 1756. Witnesses: THOMAS LAMBOLL, SR., THOMAS LAMBOLL,
JR. Before WILLIAM HOPTON, J.P. & P.R.

Book R-R, p. 82   ROBERT WILLIAMS, planter, of the WELCH tract
2 & 3 Mar. 1756   in Craven Co., to JAMES BABER, tavern keeper,
L & R   for ₺ 200 currency, 200 a. in on S side Peedee
                       River in Prince Fredericks Parish, Craven Co.,
granted by Gov. JAMES GLEN on 12 Feb. 1755 to ROBERT WILLIAMS; bounding
on all sides on vacant land. Witnesses: WILLIAM SMITH, URIAH (his mark)
MOTT. Before WILLIAM LORD, J.P. WILLIAM HOPTON, Register.

Book R-R, p. 85   WILLIAM TYRREL, cordwainer, of the WELCH
14 Oct. 1756   tract, Craven Co., to JOHN EVANS, planter, 100
L & R   a., bounding on all sides on vacant land;
                       granted by Gov. JAMES GLEN on 9 Oct. 1752 to
TYRREL. Witnesses: JAMES NIVIE, JAMES (his mark) JONES. Before WILLIAM
HOPTON, J.P. & P.R.

Book R-R, p. 88   THOMAS PARMENTER, JR., of Granville Co., &
9 & 10 Nov. 1748   DOROTHY his wife, to JOHN SMITH, merchant, of
L & R   Beaufort, for ₺ 300 currency, lot #16 in Beau-
                       fort, bounding S on the Bay; W on lot #15; N
on lot #45; E on lot #17. Witnesses: WILLIAM GOUGH, EDWARD WIGG. Before
JAMES THOMPSON, J.P. WILLIAM HOPTON, Register.

Book R-R, p. 92   JONATHAN BRYAN, planter, of Granville Co., &
28 & 29 June 1751   MARY his wife, to JOHN SMITH, merchant, of
L & R   Beaufort, for ₺ 260 currency, 52 a. on NW side
                       of Stony Creek, a branch of Pocotaligo River,
in Prince William Parish, Granville Co., bounding NW on JOHN GARNIER

(formerly ANDREW DEVEAUX, JR.); N & NE on High Road from Stony Creek to
Pocotaligo Bridge. Whereas Landgrave EDMUND BELLINGER owned several parcels of land & by will dated 21 Feb. 1739 devised to WILLIAM PALMER 1000
a., & to his son GEORGE 1000 a., & appointed his wife, ELIZABETH sole executrix; & whereas by L & R dated 14 & 15 Feb. 1745 ELIZABETH BELLINGER &
GEORGE BELLINGER sold to WILLIAM PALMER the 1000 a. bequeathed to GEORGE
BELLINGER; & whereas WILLIAM PALMER, & ANN his wife, for Ł 3240 currency,
by L & R dated 1 & 2 July 1748 sold 1049-3/4 a. to JONATHAN BRYAN (the W
part being part of the 1000 a.; the E part being part of the 1000 a. devised to PALMER by Landgrave BELLINGER), bounding E on JAMES DEVEAUX; S
on JONATHAN BRYAN; W on ANDREW DEVEAUX, JR., (formerly BELLINGER estate);
N on part of land devised to PALMER & since sold to ANDREW DEVEAUX, SR.;
now BRYAN sells a part of his land to SMITH. Witnesses: HENRY FEARN,
HENRY BISHOP. Before STEPHEN BULL, J.P. WILLIAM HOPTON, Register. Plat
of 52 a. by HUGH BRYAN, Dep. Sur., dated 12 June 1751.

Book R-R, p. 98   WILLIAM SIMMONS, planter, of Granville Co., to
____ Mar. 1754   JOHN SMITH, merchant, for Ł 300 currency,
Feoffment   184-1/2 square poles, or perches, at Stony
                               Creek, Prince William Parish, bounding NE & W
on said SIMMONS; W on the High Road & said SMITH & includes the house
where SMITH now keeps store. Plat dated 14 Feb. 1754. Delivery by turf
& twig. Witnesses: DAVID CULTON (CULTON); JOSEPH FOX. Before STEPHEN
BULL, J.P. WILLIAM HOPTON, Register.

Book R-R, p. 100   JOHN CROKATT, planter, of Prince William Par-
11 & 12 Oct. 1756   ish, & SUSANNAH his wife, to JOHN MCKENZIE,
L & R   planter, of PonPon, for Ł 1800 currency, 900 a.
                               bounding N & E on JOHN CORKATT in different
tracts; W & S on Pocosaba Creek & marsh. Witnesses: JAMES CUTHBERT, JOHN
MYERS, JOHN PARNHAM, GEORGE JACKSON. Before STEPHEN BULL, J.P. WILLIAM
HOPTON, Register. Plat given.

Book R-R, p. 104   RICHARD DUNN LAWRENCE, planter, to JOHN HAYS,
2 Nov. 1756   both of St. James Goose Creek Parish, for 6
Lease for 6 years.   years, at Ł 100 currency per annum, payable on
                               2 Nov.; 355 a., part of BOUKOY, divided into 2
tracts by a line on the plat, the leaser being wood land; the greater being cleared land; bounding NE on estate of PAUL MAZYCK; S on BOUKOY; W on
Kings High Road. Plat by ROBERT MANNING, Sur., dated 12 Oct. 1756.
HAYES to have certain priviledges. Witnesses: GEORGE JACKSON, WILLIAM
BLAKE. HAYES & LAWRENCE agree that LAURENCE, at any time during said 6
years, shall "reduce" (produce?) a certain title he received (from JA____
VING of Jamaica) whereby LAWRENCE holds the land for life only & procure
a good title so that HAYES can enjoy the land; HAYES promising, in that
case, to pay LAWRENCE Ł 50 a year _____. Before JOHN RATTRAY, J.P. WIL-
LIAM HOPTON, Register.

Book R-R, p. 107   RICHARD DUNN LAURENCE, to JOHN HAYS, plant-
2 Nov. 1756   ers, of St. James Goose Creek, for 6 years, at
Lease for 6 years   12 shillings, 6 d per a. per annum; 26 a. as
                               shown by lines on plat, part of BOUKOY planta-
tion on SW ocrner of certain land now leased by HAYS from LAURENCE; bounding N on a creek; E on estate of PAUL MAZYCK; S on DUNN LAURENCE; W on
land held by LAURENCE, part of which is rented to HAYES. Plat by ROBERT
MANNING, Sur. dated 6 Nov. 1756. Witnesses: GEORGE JACKSON, WILLIAM
BLAKE. Before JOHN RATTRAY, J.P. WILLIAM HOPTON, Register.

Book R-R, p. 108   GEORGE EILAND, planter, to WILLIAM NICHOLS,
1 & 2 Sept. 1755   carpenter, both of Granville Co., for Ł 500
L & R   currency, 350 a. on Noble's Creek, a branch of
                               Stephens Creek, in Granville Co., bounding on
all sides by vacant land; granted by Gov. JAMES GLEN on 8 Mar. 1755 to
GEORGE EILAND. Witnesses: JOB RED, THOMAS PARKER. Before ANTHONY GROOBS,
J.P. WILLIAM HOPTON, Register.

Book R-R, p. 113   HANS (his mark) IMDORFF, planter, & MAGDALEN
18 & 19 Oct. 1756   (her mark) his wife, (lately MAGDALEN PEIRAN,
L & R   widow of JACOB PEIRAN), to HENRY WURTZER,
                               planter, both of Berkeley Co., for Ł 150

currency, 150 a. in Orangeburgh Township, Berkeley Co., bounding NE on
MELCHIOR SACHEVEIL (SACHEVERILLE?); NW on Orangeburgh; SW on PonPon River; SE on JOHN SIMMON & PETER ROHT; which 150 a. formerly belonging to
JACOB PURAN, who died intestate, were inherited by his wife MAGDALEN, who
afterwards married IMDORFF, who was granted letters of administration of
the estate. Witnesses: JOHN GIESSENDANNER, JOHN (his mark) WOLF. Before
CHRISTIAN MINNICK, J.P. WILLIAM HOPTON, Register.

Book R-R, p. 117   JOHN PALMER, planter, to DAVID MURRAY, gentle-
12 & 13 Oct. 1756   man, of Granville Co., for Ł 500 currency,
L & R   500 a. on Camber Island on S side Coosaw Riv-
           er, in Granville Co., bounding W on HENRY
QUINTIN & ELIZABETH BLAKE; S & E on ELIZABETH BLAKE; which land was
granted by the Lords Proprs. on 17 June 1741 to Madam ELIZABETH BLAKE;
who sold to WALTER IZARD; who by L & R dated 9 & 10 Apr. 1725 sold to
DAVID FOX; who on 14 & 15 Mar. 1727/8 reconveyed the 500 a. to WALTER IZ-
ARD; who on 9 & 10 Feb. 1747 sold to WILLIAM PALMER, planter, of Granville Co., who died intestate in Jan. 1754 & his eldest son, JOHN PALMER,
party hereto, inherited. Witnesses: WILLIAM GOUGH, JAMES WILLIAMS. Before JAMES THOMSON, J.P. WILLIAM HOPTON, Register.

Book R-R, p. 123   ARCHIBALD BAIRD, of Georgetown, to THOMAS
5 & 6 Nov. 1756   WATIES, planter, of Craven Co., for Ł 2800 SC
L & R   money, 125 a. in Craven Co., bounding E & S on
           Winyaw Bay; W on Sanpitt Creek or Georgetown
River & lots 237, 238, 249, 250, 257 in Georgetown; N on the High Road to
the Bay; being part of a tract granted JOHN CLELAND. Witnesses: ANDREW
JOHNSTON, ALEXANDER MCDOUALL. Before JAMES GRINDLAY, J.P. WILLIAM HOP-
TON, Register. Plat given.

Book R-R, p. 130   HUGH GRANGE, planter, to BENJAMIN COACHMAN,
3 & 4 Nov. 1756   planter, both of Goose Creek, for Ł 800 cur-
L & R   rency, 600 a. in Berkeley Co., bounding N on
           JOHN GOODBEE; W & SW on BENJAMIN COACHMAN &
WILLIAM COACHMAN (his nephew); SE on MR. WITHERS. Whereas Gov. ROBERT
GIBBES & the Lords Proprs. on 13 Jan. 1710 granted COL. HUGH GRANGE 300
a. in Berkeley Co., then bounding N on vacant land; E on HUGH GRANGE; SW
on MRS. EMPEROUR & Madam GIBBES; & on 23 July 1711 granted COL. HUGH
GRANGE 300 a. in Berkeley Co., then bounding E & N on JOSEPH HOLBRIDGE &
JOHN GOODBY; SE & SW on above tract; W & N on Madam GIBBES; & whereas by
will dated 12 Dec. 1712 HUGH GRANGE bequeathed the 2 plantations to his
sons HUGH GRANTE (father of HUGH, party hereto) & THOMAS GRANGE, directing a division & allotment of the land; & whereas by will dated 21 Mar.
1739 THOMAS GRANGE bequeathed all his real & personal estate to his brother HUGH, under certain conditions; & whereas HUGH GRANGE, by will dated
19 Oft. 1746 bequeathed to his son, HUGH, his dwelling house at St. James
Goose Creek, & 600 a. in 2 tracts, together with 600 a. at the Four Holes;
& whereas HUGH GRANTE, the father, died & the 600 a. in 2 tracts became
vested in his son, HUGH; now he sells to COACHMAN. Witnesses: GEORGE
JACKSON, WILLIAM BLAKE. Before JOHN RATTRAY, J.P. WILLIAM HOPTON, Register. Plat given.

Book R-R, p. 136   JOHN JOOR (IOOR), & MARY his wife, to SAMUEL
22 Nov. 1756   SARVICE, planter, of Prince George Parish, for
Sale   Ł 120 currency, 450 a. on N side Waccamaw Riv-
           er, in Prince George Parish, Craven Co., bound-
ing NE on MICHAEL JANES; SW & SE on vacant land. Witnesses: ROBERT DYMES,
JOHN IOOR. Before JACOB MOTTE, J.P. WILLIAM HOPTON, Register.

Book R-R, p. 137   JUDITH (her mark) WEST, called Free JUDY, of
30 Aug. 1756   Charleston Neck, to JOHN MITCHELL, a free Ne-
Feoffment in Trust gro man, for 5 shillings & other considera-
           tions, 6-1/2 a. on Charleston Neck, bounding
W & S on GEORGE MARSHALL; N on EDWARD BULLARD; E on the Broad Path leading from Charleston to the Quarter House; with all houses thereon; JUDITH
to have the sole use of the property during her lifetime, & after her
death, her daughter, MARTHA NEWTON, to hold the property for her lifetime;
then in trust for JUDITH'S 3 grand children, JOHN HOWELL; ELIZABETH the
daughter of said MARTHA: & JUDITH NEWTON, another daughter of MARTHA.
Witnesses: JAMES SMITH, ANGEL (her mark) SNOW, ANGEL (her mark) HARDING.

Before ALEXANDER STEWART, J.P.

Book R-R, p. 140　　　　　　　MELLER ST. JOHN, gentleman, of Charleston, &
27 & 28 Oct. 1756　　　　　　MARY his wife, to GEORGE LOGAN, gentleman, of
L & R　　　　　　　　　　　　Colleton Co., in fulfilment of an agreement, &
　　　　　　　　　　　　　　　for 10 shillings; 508 a. in Colleton Co.
Whereas THOMAS CATER, planter, of Berkeley Co., purchased from MELLER ST.
JOHN 508 a. in Colleton Co., bounding SE on SAMUEL SLEIGH; SW on THOMAS
BOONE (formerly Madam BOONE); NE on JOHN POSTELL; which 508 a. were granted 12 Apr. 1739 to THOMAS BUTLER & by various mesne conveyances & bequests come to MELLER ST. JOHN; & whereas MELLER ST. JOHN gave his bond
dated 3 Apr. 1751 for Ł 2000 currency that he would give CATER title to
the land by 1 May then next; & whereas CATER died before the conveyance
was made, but had, with ST. JOHN'S consent, taken possession of the land
& had executed his will, in which he directed that as soon as his crop
was sold then the land (with some of his other land) should be sold to
discharge his debts to MELLER ST. JOHN & others, & appointed WILLIAM
MAINE & WALTER IZARD, & NATHANIEL BRADWELL his executors; & whereas WIL-
LIAM MAINE, only acting executor, advertised the tract to be sold at public auction on 5 & 6 June 1753, with notice that said bond from ST. JOHN
to CATER would be assigned to the highest bidder in order that he may receive a complete title from ST. JOHN; & whereas MAINE on 25 Mar. last assigned the tract to GEORGE LOGAN for Ł 1200 currency; & whereas ST. JOHN
agreed to give LOGAN good title to the land; now he carries out his agreement. Witnesses: CHARLES PINCKNEY, WILLIAM MAZYCK. Before JACOB MOTTE,
J.P. WILLIAM HOPTON, Register.

Book R-R, p. 148　　　　　　　TIMOTHY DARGAN, planter, & CATHERINE (her mark)
26 Oct. 1756　　　　　　　　　his wife (1 of the sisters of ANN WATS, widow),
Feoffment　　　　　　　　　　to their son, JOHN DARGAN, for Ł 5 currency,
　　　　　　　　　　　　　　　500 a. in Amelia Township, formerly belonging
to ANN WATTS, bounding W on TIMOTHY DARGAN. Witnesses: ETON MELY,
CHARLES RUSSELL, RICHARD DAVIS. Possession & seizin given by delivery of
a clod of earth & a twig of a tree. Before MOSES THOMSON, J.P. WILLIAM
HOPTON, Register.

Book R-R, p. 151　　　　　　　THOMAS BUTLER, planter, formerly of St. Phil-
5 Apr. 1755　　　　　　　　　ip's Parish, SC, now of Colony of Georgia, to
Release of Equity　　　　　WILLIAM BUTLER, formerly of Stono, St. Pauls
　　　　　　　　　　　　　　　Parish, SC, now of Colony of Georgia, several
tracts. Whereas THOMAS BUTLER on 25 Mar. 1745 (see Book K-3, page 1) for
Ł 7000 SC money sold to WILLIAM BUTLER 759 a. at the Horseshoe, in St.
Bartholomews Parish, SC,; also 840 a. in Island Creek Swamp in said Parish; with a condition of redemption upon payment of several sums; &
whereas the principal & the interest now due are much more than the land
is worth, THOMAS has agreed to convey all his right & equity to WILLIAM;
now he carried out his agreement. Witnesses: DAVID DRUMMOND, mariner;
ELISHA BUTLER, MAURICE DULLEN. Before JAMES PARSONS, J.P. WILLIAM HOP-
TON, Register.

Book R-R, p. 153　　　　　　　BENJAMIN COWEN, planter, of Edisto Island,
25 & 26 Feb. 1756　　　　　　Colleton Co., grandson of JOHN COWEN & son of
L & R　　　　　　　　　　　　BENJAMIN COWEN; & SARAH his wife; of 1st part;
　　　　　　　　　　　　　　　to JOHN FENDIN, planter, of St. Helena, Granville Co., for Ł 1050 currency, 480 a. Whereas Gov. ROBERT GIBBES & the
Lords Proprs. granted JOHN COWEN 640 a. on St. Helena's Island, Granville Co., on NW side of a marsh, bounding on other sides on vacant land;
which land COWEN bequeathed to his son, BENJAMIN; who died intestate &
his son, BENJAMIN, inherited; & now sells a part to FENDEN, leaving 160
a. on NE side, as pricked off on the plat. Witnesses: JOHN FENDIN, JR.,
WILLIAM ADAMS, JACOB COWEN. Before JACOB MOTTE, J.P. WILLIAM HOPTON,
Register.

Book R-R, p. 159　　　　　　　PETER KEIGHLEY, planter, of Peedee River, to
7 Jan. 1754　　　　　　　　　JOEL MCCLENDON, planter, of Craven Co., for
L & R　　　　　　　　　　　　Ł 200 currency, 150 a., being the uppermost
　　　　　　　　　　　　　　　part of 400 a. in the WELCH tract, in Craven
Co., bounding on vacant land & granted 24 May 1745 by Gov. JAMES GLEN to
PETER KEIGHLY (grant Book L.L. fol. 268); beginning at the dividing line
at a pine, thence to a stake a corner; thence to another stake, a corner;

down to the dividing line to a white oak; thence up the dividing line to the first station. Witnesses: DENNIS MCLENDON, JOHN KEIGHLEY. Before SAMUEL JORDAN, J.P. WILLIAM HOPTON, Register.

Book R-R, p. 163　　　　　PETER KEIGHLEY, planter, of Peedee River, to
7 Jan. 1754　　　　　　　DANES (DENNIS) MCCLENDON, planter, of Craven
L & R　　　　　　　　　Co., for ₤ 200 currency, 250 a., the lower
　　　　　　　　　　　　part of 400 a. in the WELCH tract, Craven Co.,
bounding on all sides on vacant land; granted 24 May 1745 by Gov. JAMES GLEN to PETER KEIGHLY (Grant Book L.L. fol. 268); beginning at the dividing line at a pine; thence along a line of marked trees to a black oak, a corner tree; thence to a pine, a corner tree; thence to a white oak a line to the dividing line; then up dividing line to first station. Witnesses: JOEL MCCLENDON, JOHN KEIGHLY. Before SAMUEL JORDAN, J.P. WILLIAM HOPTON, Register.

Book R-R, p. 167　　　　　STEPHEN BULL, planter, son of BURNABY BULL, &
30 & 31 Aug. 1741　　　　ELIZABETH his wife, of Granville Co., to AN-
L & R　　　　　　　　　THONY MATTHEWES, planter, of Colleton Co., for
　　　　　　　　　　　　₤ 2552 currency, 928 a. in Granville Co., in
several tracts; bounding E on Pocotaligo River; S on ANTHONY MATHEWES; W on JAMES ST. JOHN; N on Pocotaligo River & a creek, & on 72 a. sold to HUGH BRYAN & other lands of BURNABY BULL. Whereas GEORGE II by Gov. ROBERT JOHNSTON, on 16 Mar. 1732 granted CAPT. JOHN BULL 500 a. in Granville Co., bounding S on ARTHUR MIDDLETON; W on JAMES ST. JOHN; N on BURNABY BULL & Pocotaligo River; & whereas JOHN BULL, & MARY his wife, by L & R dated 16 & 17 Aug. 1738 sold the 500 a. to STEPHEN BULL; & whereas GEORGE II, by Gov. ROBERT JOHNSTON, on 11 July 1733, granted ARTHUR MIDDLETON 500 a. in Granville Co., bounding N on CAPT. JOHN BULL; E on Poctaligo River; S on CAPT. ANTHONY MATHEWES; W on JAMES ST. JOHN; & whereas ARTHUR MIDDLETON by L & R dated 11 & 12 Apr. 1734 sold his 500 a. to JOHN BULL; & whereas JOHN BULL & MARY his wife by L & R dated 16 & 17 Aug. 1738 sold the 500 a. to STEPHEN BULL; & whereas STEPHEN BULL has already sold to HUGH BRYAN, planter, of Granville Co., 72 a. being the N part of the first mentioned 500 a.; now STEPHEN BULL sells to ANTHONY MATTHEWES, the balance of the 2 tracts. Witnesses: JOSEPH BRYAN, MARY STORY, WILLIAM GRAVES, JONATHAN BRYAN, JOHN MACLANE. Before DAVID GRAEME, J.P. WILLIAM HOPTON, Register.

Book R-R, p. 177　　　　　HUGH BRYAN, planter, to JOSEPH BRYAN, planter,
26 Mar. 1743　　　　　　both of St. Helena Parish, Granville Co., for
Release　　　　　　　　₤ 1280 currency, 740 a. in Granville Co.,
　　　　　　　　　　　　bounding N on CAPT. EDMUND BELLINGER'S Barony;
E on head of Hoospa Creek; S on part of 3140 a. since conveyed to MRS. ELIZABETH BULL; W on 140 a. lately conveyed to JONATHAN BRYAN. Whereas on 24 Nov. 1732 JOSEPH BRYAN, SR., & HUGH BRYAN were granted in jointency, 3140 a. on E side Whale Branch on Pocotaligo River, Granville Co., bounding W on the river; N on CAPT. EDMUND BELLINGER; E on Hoopa Creek; S on HILL CROFT & GEORGE PAWLEY; & whereas on 9 Feb. 1732 JOSEPH BRYAN died intestate & HUGH BRYAN inherited by right of survivorship; now he sells a part to JOSEPH BRYAN. Witnesses: WILLIAM HUTSON, JONATHAN BRYAN. On 21 Dec. 1747 JOSEPH BRYAN acknowledged himself liable for payment of quit-rents on said tract. Witnesses: ISAAC CHANLER, JONATHAN BRYAN, WILLIAM HUTSON. Before STEPHEN BULL, J.P. WILLIAM HOPTON, Register.

Book R-R, p. 182　　　　　HUGH BRYAN, gentleman, to STEPHEN BULL, plant-
15 July 1741　　　　　　er (son of BURNABY BULL, planter), & ELIZABETH
Release　　　　　　　　his wife (daughter of JOSEPH BRYAN, brother of
　　　　　　　　　　　　HUGH BRYAN) for the love & affection he bears
for his niece, said ELIZABETH BULL, (wife of STEPHEN) & other considerations; 900 a. now occupied by STEPHEN & ELIZABETH BULL; being part of 3140 a.; bounding E on branch of Huspa Creek; S on ISAAC MAZYCK & JOSEPH _____ SEY; W & N on other part 3140 a.; with certain limitations in regard to inheritance. Whereas GEORGE II on 24 Nov. 1732, by Gov. ROBERT JOHN-STON, granted JOSEPH BRYAN & HUGH BRYAN (brothers) in jointenancy, 3140 a. in Granville Co., (p. 177), which land HUGH inherited by right of survivorship; now he conveys a part of the tract to his niece ELIZABETH, wife of STEPHEN BULL; STEPHEN promising that ELIZABETH may will the land to whom she pleased. Witnesses: JAMES HOUSTON, JOS. BRYAN, WILLIAM GRAVES. JACOB KIEFFER. Before STEPHEN BULL, J.P. WILLIAM HOPTON, Reg.

32

Book R-R, p. 188   WILLIAM WRAGG, ESQ., to JOHN WRAGG, ESQ., both
29 & 30 Sept. 1755   of Charleston, for Ł 3500 SC money, his 2 un-
L & R   divided third parts of Northern Barony. Where-
                          as WILLIAM WRAGG & JOHN WRAGG owned a Barony
called Northern Barony on the Yamassee Land, in Granville Co., bounding N
on heirs of MR. GIRARDEAU & vacant land; W on vacant land; E on Port Royal River & Cusawhatchee & Chulafinny Creeks; S on the Southern Barony;
now WILLIAM sells his 2 shares to JOHN WRAGG. Witnesses: MARY ROTHMAHLER,
SAMUEL BOWMAN. Before DAVID GRAEME, J.P. WILLIAM HOPTON, Register.

Book R-R, p. 193   JOHN ROGERSON, planter, of Colleton Co., to
27 & 28 Oct. 1756   RALPH IZARD & DANIEL BLAKE, ESQRS., of St.
L & R by Mortgage   George's Dorchester, in trust for MISS ANNE
                          BLAKE, 1 of the daughters & devisees of the
Hon. JOSEPH BLAKE; as security on bond of even date in penal sum of
Ł 2592 for payment of Ł 1296 currency, with interest, on 8 Oct. 1757;
300 a., lately purchased by ROGERSON from STEPHEN BULL, SR., of Granville
Co.; bounding on DANIEL BLAKE & on the Rev. MR. HUDSON; also 5 Negro
slaves. Witnesses: JAMES CLARK, ARCHIBALD CROLL. Before STEPHEN BULL,
J.P. WILLIAM HOPTON, Register.

Book R-R, p. 201   JAMES SNOW, planter, to JOHN BARNS, planter,
14 & 15 May 1755   both of Craven Co., for Ł 300 currency & other
L & R   considerations, 500 a., part of 2000 a., in
                          Craven Co., on N side Black Mingo Swamp,
bounding SW on GEORGE SNOW; NE on JOHN SNOW & HENRY PERONNEAU; SE on PER-
ONNEAU & vacant land; NW on vacant land. Witnesses: GEORGE SNOW, JAMES
CROWLY. Before JOHN LIVISTON, J.P. WILLIAM HOPTON, Register.

Book R-R, p. 204   JOHN SNOW, planter, of St. James Santee, Cra-
15 & 16 June 1756   ven Co., to HENRY O'NEIL, planter, of Prince
L & R   Frederick Parish, Craven Co., for Ł 400 cur-
                          rency, 460 a., part of 2000 a. in Craven Co.,
on N side Black Mingo Swamp, bounding SW on JAMES SNOW (now JOHN BARNS);
SE on HENRY PERONNEAU (now JAMES SNOW) & vacant land; NE & NW on vacant
land. Witnesses: JOHN BARNES, THOMAS DAVISON. Before JOHN LIVISTON,
J.P. WILLIAM HOPTON, Register.

Book R-R, p. 209   SAMUEL TAYLOR, planter, of Williamsburg, & ANN
21 & 22 Nov. 1755   his wife, to JOHN ERVIN, for 5 shillings, 100
L & R   a. in Craven Co., on S side Pudding Swamp, on
                          N side Black River, bounding on all sides on
vacant land; ANN to renounce her claim. Witnesses: ELIZABETH ERVIN, SAM-
UEL (his mark) COBRIN, CHARLES BETTY. Before JOHN LIVISTON, J.P. WIL-
LIAM HOPTON, Register.

Book R-R, p. 217   JAMES WATSON, planter, of Port Royal Island,
10 Dec. 1756   to WILLIAM ELLIOTT, planter, formerly of Ga.,
Release   now of Port Royal Island, for Ł 900 SC money,
                          300 a. Whereas the Lords Proprs. on 4 June
1702 granted JOHN PENNY 1420 a. on Port Royal Island, which descended to
his son, JOHN; who, with his wife, RUTH, on 30 Mar. 1711, sold to JAMES
WATSON a part, or 300 a., bounding W on Penny's Creek; other sides on
said 1420 a. tract; & whereas JAMES WATSON left but 1 daughter, who died
without issue, & the 300 a. became vested in JAMES WATSON, party hereto,
nephew to said JAMES WATSON. Witnesses: FRANCIS STUART, JAMES STEEL.
Before JAMES THOMSON, J.P. WILLIAM HOPTON, Register.

Book R-R, p. 221   GEORGE SNOW, planter, to HUGH ERVIN (ERVING,
15 & 16 Jan. 1756   ERWIN), planter, both of Craven Co., for Ł 460
L & R   currency & other considerations, 500 a. in
                          Craven Co., on N side Black Mingo Swamp being
part of 2000 a. formerly belonging to NATHANIEL SNOW; bounding SW on NA-
THANIEL SNOW; NE on JAMES SNOW (now JOHN BARNES); NW & SE on vacant land.
Witnesses: JOHN BARNS, JOHN ERWIN. Before WILLIAM SIMPSON, J.P. WILLIAM
HOPTON, Register.

Book R-R, p. 224   BENJAMIN COWEN, planter, of Edisto Island, to
26 Feb. 1756   JOHN FENDIN, planter, of St. Helena, Granville
Bond   Co., in penal sum of Ł 2500 currency, to keep

33

agreements of sale. Witnesses: JOHN FENDIN, JR., WILLIAM ADAMS, JACOB COWEN. Before JACOB MOTTE, J.P. WILLIAM HOPTON, Register.

Book R-R, p. 226
16 & 17 July 1756
L & R
OTHNIEL BEALE, ESQ., of Charleston, & CATHER-INE his wife, to ELISHA SCREVEN, SR., planter, of Craven Co., for Ł 1400 currency, 500 a. in Craven Co., bounding NE on Peedee River; NW on OTHNIEL BEALE; other sides on vacant land; also 500 a. adjoining above tract, bounding NE on Peedee River; SE on OTHNIEL BEALE; other sides on vacant land; which 2 tracts were granted to OTHNIEL BEALE by Lt. Gov. THOMAS BROUGHTON on 18 July 1735. Witnesses: DANIEL DWIGHT, THOMAS COW. Before JAMES MICHIE, J.P. Entered in Auditor's Book D-4, fol. 158 on 5 Jan. 1757 by JAMES MICHIE, Dep. Aud. WILLIAM HOPTON, Register.

Book R-R, p. 232
9 & 10 Dec. 1756
L & R
THOMAS WIGG, ESQ., of Granville Co., & ANN his wife, to JOHN CHAPMAN, merchant, of Beaufort, for Ł 750 currency, 200 a., English measure, on Port Royal Island, part of a tract granted to JOSEPH PARMENTER the father in 1706/7 by Gov. NATHANIEL JOHNSTON, & sold by JOSEPH PARMENTER, the son, & JANE his wife, to THOMAS WIGG in 1749; bounding S on estate of SIR NATHANIEL NESBITT; N on MARY TAILFER (now JOHN CHAPMAN); W on the Rev. MR. ROBERT ORR; E on Parmenter's Creek. Witnesses: FRANCIS STUART, LEWIS REEVE. Before JAMES THOMSON, J.P. WILLIAM HOPTON, Register.

Book R-R, p. 238
12 Dec. 1755
Sale
CHARLES LOWNDES, P.M., to JOHN PARKER, plant-er, of St. James Goose Creek Parish, for Ł 1002 currency, 146 a. in St. George Parish, Dorchester. Whereas JOSEPH HASFORT, planter, owned said 146 a., bounding N on JOHN PARKER; S on THOMAS ELMES; W on BENJAMIN CHILD; E on SAMUEL ELMES; & after his death THOMAS SMITH, mer-chant, of Charleston, administrator with will annexed of WILLIAM YEOMANS, merchant, of Charelston, recovered a judgment against CHILDERMAS CROFT & JOHN RATTRAY, executors of will of HUGH CARTWRIGHT, of Charleston, who was executor of will of JOSEPH HASFORT, for Ł 6021:16:10 currency, & costs, & a writ of fieri facias was issued by PETER LEIGH, C.J. on 27 Feb. last directing the P.M. to seize HASFORTS estate & obtain this amount; & whereas on 12 June last the P.M. put the 146 a. up at auction & PARKER was highest bidder; now the conveyance is made. Witnesses: WIL-LIAM READ, JOHN PHELPS. Before CHARLES PINCKNEY, J.P. WILLIAM HOPTON, Register.

Book R-R, p. 242
25 & 26 Mar. 1754
L & R
JACOB SHOEMAKER, planter, of the Congarees, & ANN BARBARA (her mark) his wife, to CONRAD KANSLER, planter, of Broad River, for Ł 65 SC money, 250 a. on N side Broad River, granted by Gov. JAMES GLEN on 2 Jan. 1754, to JACOB SHOEMAKER; bounding NW on MICHAEL KINSEL (misnamed for CONRAD KANSLER); other sides on vacant land. Witnesses: HENRY GALLMAN, JOSEPH CRELLENS. Before STEPHEN CRELL, J.P. WILLIAM HOPTON, Register.

Book R-R, p. 247
19 & 20 Aug. 1755
L & R
MICHAEL (his mark) NEYROOD, & MARGARET (her mark) his wife, of Congarees Fork, to CONRAD KANSLER, planter, of Craven Co., for Ł 60 cur-rency, 250 a. on Lick Creek, a branch of Little Saluda River, bounding SE on JACOB NEYSELLER & vacant land; other sides on vacant land. Witness: MARCY (her mark) KENNERTY. Lease not proved. Before THOMAS KENNERTY, J.P. WILLIAM HOPTON, Register.

Book R-R, p. 252
1 Oct. 1751
Assignment of Power
of Attorney
MICHAEL KINSEL, tailor, to CONRAD KANSLER, planter, of Berkeley Co., for Ł 20 currency, a warrant for 50 a. granted KINSEL by Gov. JAMES GLEN on 2 July 1751, in upper part of Berkeley Co.; & KINSEL appoints ANTHONY STEGG, of Saxe Gotha Township, his attorney, to sign & execute the grant & release. Witnesses: CHRISTIAN SEELMAN, JOHANNA CRELL. Before STEPHEN CREEL, J.P. WILLIAM HOPTON, J.P.

Book R-R, p. 255
1 & 2 Mar. 1754
ANTHONY (his mark) STEG (STEGG), planter, of Saxe Gotha Township, as attorney for MICHAEL

L & R   KINSEL, tailor, to CONRAD KANSLER, planter, of
                                     Broad River, for Ⱡ 20 currency, 50 a. on Cedar
Creek, 1 of the N branches of Broad River. Whereas on 2 Jan. 1754 Gov.
JAMES GLEN granted MICHAEL KINSEL 50 a. on Cedar Creek (surveyed by war-
rant dated 2 July 1751 & prolonged by his order dated 7 Feb. 1753 to JOHN
HUNTER, Sur. Gen.) bounding on all sides on vacant land; & whereas KINSEL,
by assignment with power of attorney (p. 252), conveyed the warrant to
CONRAD KANSLER & appointed ANTHONY STEG his attorney to sign & execute
the conveyance; now STEG conveys to KANSLER. Witnesses: JACOB SELLS,
JOHANNA CRELL. Before STEPHEN CRELL, J.P. WILLIAM HOPTON, Register.

Book R-R, p. 262   FELIX GROSS, planter, of Congarees Fork, to
25 & 26 Oct. 1753   CASPER KANSLER, planter, of Craven Co., for
L & R   Ⱡ 100 currency, 100 a., bounding SW on Broad
                                     Santee River; NW on GILBERT GILDER; with orig-
inal grant to FELIX GROSS (spelled therein FELIX CROUX). Witnesses: PE-
TER HENRY DORSIUS, JOHANNA CRELL. Before STEPHEN CRELL, J.P. WILLIAM
HOPTON, Register.

Book R-R, p. 266   JAMES MCDANIEL, planter, to JOHN HOPE, plant-
10 Dec. 1756   er, both of Craven Co.; as security on bond of
Mortgage   even date in penal sum of Ⱡ 600 for payment of
                                     Ⱡ 300 currency, with interest, within 2 years;
950 a. on a neck called Nisue in Craven Co., on Wateree River, which MC-
DANIEL had purchased from HOPE the day previous. Witnesses: JAMES LIN-
GARD, JAMES ALLEN, SUSANNAH ALLEN. Before SAMUEL BOWMAN, J.P. WILLIAM
HOPTON, Register.

Book R-R, p. 268   BRITON COOPER, gentleman, to THOMAS CORKER,
1 & 2 Oct. 1751   merchant, of Charleston, for Ⱡ 2200 currency,
L & R   half of lot #44 in Charleston, bounding N
                                     217 ft. on a small alley running from Church
Street to Union Street; E on BENJAMIN D'HARRIETTE (formerly JOHN BELL); S
on part same lot belonging GABRIEL MANIGAULT; W 50 ft. on Church Street.
Whereas the Lords Proprs. on 9 May 1694 granted NOAH ROYER, JR., weaver,
of Berkeley Co., lot #44 in Charleston, bounding N on NOAH ROYER, SR.; E
on JOHN BELL; S on PETER BURTTELL; W on Church Street; & whereas NOAH
ROYER, JR., on 6 July 1694, sold the N half of the lot to his father; who,
by will dated 11 Mar. 1694 bequeathed the residue of his real & personal
estate to his wife, MAUDLIN ROYER; & whereas she, on 24 Dec. 1712, sold
the N half to JOHN BRITON, merchant, of Charleston; who, by will dated 3
Oct. 1730 bequeathed the S? part of lot #44 (called #49 in will by error)
to BRITON COOPER, with the 2 tenements thereon now occupied by DR. JAMES
KILPATRICK & DAVID NOBLE; now COOPER sells the N half to CORKER. Witnesses: JAMES MOULTRIE, HUGH ANDERSON. Before JOHN DART, J.P. WILLIAM
HOPTON, Register.

Book R-R, p. 277   Between WILLIAM MOULTRIE, ESQ., of St. Johns
13 Jan. 1757   Parish, Berkeley Co., & DEMARIS ELIZABETH, his
Deed of Partition   (lately DEMARIS ELIZABETH DE ST. JULIEN), &
                                     DANIEL RAVENEL, ESQ., & SARAH his wife (lately
SARAH DE ST. JULIEN). Whereas BENJAMIN DE ST. JULIEN, ESQ., brother of
said DAMARIS ELIZABETH & SARAH, owned several plantations; that is; 60 a.
in Berkeley Co., purchased by JAMES DE ST. JULIEN, gentleman, of Berkeley
Co., from his brother, PAUL DE ST. JULIEN; & devised by said JAMES to
said BENJAMIN DE ST. JULIEN; 740 a., part of 1000 a. in Berkeley Co.,
purchased by the father of said JAMES DE ST. JULIEN from Champernoon
ELLIOTT, & adjoining the 60 a., making a plantation 800 a. called Indian
Fields; likewise devised by JAMES to BENJAMIN (directed by will of JAMES
to be laid out by an E & W line); also 215 a. part of 550 a., formerly
conveyed to PETER DE ST. JULIEN by MARY LAROCHE, widow, of JOHN LAROCHE,
of Charleston, by L & R dated 27 & 28 Nov. 1724; also 1500 a., part of
2000 a., in Craven Co., conveyed to PETER DE ST. JULIEN by JAMES AKIN on
23 May 1722; also 819.3 a., partly in Craven Co., & partly in Berkeley
Co., granted PETER DE ST. JULIEN on 28 Nov. 1735 by Lt. Gov. THOMAS
BROUGHTON; also 755 a. in Berkeley Co., on S side Santee River, granted
PETER DE ST. JULIEN 3 Feb. 1737 by WILLIAM BULL; also 500 a. purchased by
PETER DE ST. JULIEN from WILLIAM WATIES on 1 May 1733; also 600 a. in
Craven Co., granted PETER DE ST. JULIEN on 3 Feb. 1737 by WILLIAM BULL;
also 2000 a., English measure, in Berkeley Co., granted PETER DE ST.

JULIEN (the father) by Gov. NATHANIEL BROUGHTON on 14 Mar. 1704; also
302 a. in Berkeley Co., granted RENÉ RICHBURN, & sold by him to PETER DE
ST. JULIEN; also 500 a. on N side Santee River, in Craven Co., granted
PETER DE ST. JULIEN on 5 July 1740 by WILLIAM BULL, then Lt. Gov.; also
500 a. in Craven Co., called Soho, lately belonging to PETER DE ST. JUL-
IEN; also 1000 a. in Berkeley Co., called Wantoot, granted PETER DE ST.
JULIEN; also 290 a. in Berkeley Co., part of 580 a. granted PETER DE ST.
JULIEN, & adjoining Wantoot; & whereas BENJAMIN DE ST. JULIEN died intes-
tate & without issue on 4 July last past, leaving his 2 sisters, DAMARIS
ELIZABETH MOULTRIE & SARAH RAVENEL, his only nearest of kin, to whom the
plantations descended as coheiresses; & whereas WILLIAM MOULTRIE & DAMAR-
IS ELIZABETH his wife, & DANIEL RAVENEL & SARAH his wife, own the land
jointly & no division has been made; now all of them agree to divide the
land as follows: WILLIAM & DAMARIS ELIZABETH MOULTRIE to have 8 tracts as
follows: the 60 a.; the 740 a.; the W part of the 215 a. (part of 550 a.)
to be divided by the new causeway & a right line from thence produced until it intersects the S boundary line of the 290 a.; also 1500 a. (part
of 2000) in Craven Co.; 819.3 a. in Berkeley & Craven Co.; 755 a. in
Berkeley Co. on S side Santee River; 500 a. formerly belonging to WATIES;
300 a., being the E half of 600 a. in Craven Co., to be divided by a S-N
line from other 300 a. devised by PETER DE ST. JULIEN to his son ALEXAN-
DER; DANIEL & SARAH RAVENEL to have 8 tracts as follows: 2000 a., English
measure, in Berkeley Co.; 302 a. in Berkeley Co.; 500 a. on N side Santee
River, in Craven Co.; 500 a., called Soho; 1000 a., called Wantoot; 290
a., in Berkeley Co., part of 580 a., adjoining Wantoot; 300 a., the W
half of 600 a. in Craven Co.; the E part of 215 a. (part of 550 a.) in
Berkeley Co., formerly belonging to MARY LAROCHES. Witnesses: WILLIAM
ANDERSON, HENRY RAVENEL, JAMES RAVENEL, JR. Before ALEXANDER STUART, J.P.
Whereas the deed does not distinguish the lands that belonged to PETER DE
ST. JULIEN, the father, from those of PETER DE ST. JULIEN, the son, be it
known that those granted by the Crown before 1720 belonged to the father,
those granted after that date to the son. Reacknowledged & redelivered
after 1 erasure in presence of THOMAS CORDES, HENRY RAVENEL, JAMES RAVE-
NEL. Before DAVID GREENE, J.P. WILLIAM HOPTON, Register.

Book R-R, p. 289   JOHN STUART, gentleman, to JOSEPH LADSON,
23 Sept. 1747   planter, both of Colleton Co., for ₤ 665 SC
L & R   money, 535 a. in Colleton Co., formerly grant-
                        ed to EDMUND DUNDON; bounding S on JOHN
NICHOLS; SE on THOMAS DALTON; N on THOMAS STOCK; E & W on Chehaw & Cumbee
Rivers. Witnesses: THOMAS NICHOLLS, JOHN (his mark) MULLINS, SAMUEL
NICHOLLS. Before HENRY HYRNE, J.P. WILLIAM HOPTON, Register.

Book R-R, p. 293   THOMAS LINTHWAITE, tanner, of St. Andrews Par-
4 Dec. 1754   ish, & ANN his wife, to JAMES POSTELL, planter
Mortgage   of St. Bartholomews Parish, as security on
                        bond dated Aug. 1754 (because POSTELL went on
his bond to the SC Society) in penal sum of ₤ 2500 for payment of ₤ 1250
currency, with interest, on 14 Aug. 1755; 2 tanyard lots at Ashley Ferry,
in St. Andrews Parish, Berkeley Co., known in the plat of Shem Town as
Nos. 36 & 37. Witnesses: DAVID GRAEME, WILLIAM WITHERS. Before JOHN
RATTRAY, J.P. WILLIAM HOPTON, Register.

Book R-R, p. 298   ANTHONY POUNCY, planter, & LUCY his wife, to
19 Feb. 1756   ABRAHAM ODAM, planter, both of Craven Co., for
L & R   ₤ 500 currency, 500 a. on S side Wateree River
                        formerly granted by Gov. JAMES GLEN to THOMAS
PAGETT in 2 grants; 1 dated 5 Sept. 1751 for 300 a.; 1 dated 29 Nov. 1750
for 200 a. Witnesses: JOHN WILLIAMS, ABRAHAM (his mark) ODAM, JR., THOM-
AS (his mark) EDWARDS, JOHN (his mark) KELLY, DAVID EDWARDS. Before JOHN
PEARSON, J.P. WILLIAM HOPTON, Register.

Book R-R, p. 305   ABRAHAM (his mark) ODAM, planter, & LIBBY,
26 Mar. 1756   (her mark) his wife, to HENRY TANNAGAN, plant-
L & R   er, both of Craven Co., for ₤ 100 VA. money,
                        300 a. on S side Wateree River granted by Gov.
JAMES GLEN on 5 Sept. 1750 to THOMAS PAGETT. Witnesses: JOHN WILLIAMS,
WILLIAM BOYKIN, EDMUND ONEEL. Before SAMUEL WYLY, J.P. WILLIAM HOPTON.
Register.

36

Book R-R, p. 312   EBENEZER WAY, planter, of Berkeley Co., to
27 Nov. 1722   WILLIAM FISHBURN, for Ŀ 255 currency, 255 a.
Sale   in Colleton Co., purchased 17 Mar. 1717/8 from
                         THOMAS OSGOOD, JR., bounding E on 50 a. pur-
chased from EBENEZER WAY for the Ministry; W on COL. WILLIAM BULL & vacant land; W on WILLIAM BURLEY; N on JOSEPH SUMNER. Witnesses: THOMAS
OSGOOD, JR., URIAH EDWARDS, BARAK NORMAN. Before J. SKENE, J.P. WILLIAM
HOPTON, Register.

Book R-R, p. 314   JAMES WITHERS, planter, & MARY his wife, to
2 & 3 Dec. 1754   WILLIAM COACHMAN & JAMES COACHMAN, all of St.
L & R   James Goose Creek Parish, Berkeley Co., for
                         Ŀ 2100 currency, 700 a. in St. James Goose
Creek, W of a run dividing the 700 a. from the plantation on which JAMES
WITHERS lives; the 700 a. being part of 730 a. lately purchased by JAMES
WITHERS from DR. JOHN MARTINI; the 730 a. bounding E & S on Goose Creek &
HUGH GRANTE; W on PHILIP GIBBES; N on COL. HERBERT'S vista or avenue; the
730 a. having been sold by L & R dated 5 & 6 Aug. 1745 by ALEXANDER MC-
KAY, then of Ireland, by his attorney, ALEXANDER MCGREGOR, gentleman, of
Charleston, to JOHN MARTINI. Witnesses: JOHN MCQUEEN, JAMES SIMPSON.
Before OTHNIEL BEALE, J.P. WILLIAM HOPTON, Register.

Book R-R, p. 321   ADAM DANIEL, son of JOHN DANIEL, of Charleston,
15 Jan. 1757   to JAMES HARTLEY, planter, for Ŀ 650 currency,
Feoffment   part of lot #1 at S end of the Bay in Charles-
                         ton, bounding N on MR. EDMONDS; E 23 ft. on
the Bay; S 144 ft. on other part same lot belonging GEORGE SOMNER; W 21
ft. on JUSTINIUS STULL. Witnesses: JOSEPH BALL, JR., GEORGE JACKSON.
Before JOHN RATTRAY, J.P. WILLIAM HOPTON, Register.

Book R-R, p. 323   PETER HEER, planter, of Broad River Fork, to
5 & 6 Feb. 1756   BENJAMIN APPLY, planter, for Ŀ 40 currency,
L & R   100 a., being the SE half of 200 a. granted by
                         Gov. JAMES GLEN on 14 Nov. 1754 to PETER HEER,
then bounding N on Broad River; SE & SW on vacant land; NW on JOHN REDDY;
the 100 a., on SE half, bounding N on Broad River; SE on CHRISTOPHER
SALTZEN; NW on other half. Witnesses: ANTHONY BACKMAN, JOHANNA CRELL,
PETER CRIM. Before STEPHEN CRELL, J.P. WILLIAM HOPTON, Register.

Book R-R, p. 328   CHARLES LOWNDES, P.M., to ANN WATSON, of
29 Dec. 1756   Charleston, for Ŀ 80 currency, half of lot I
Sale   on Ansonborough near Charleston. Whereas HEN-
                         RY KENNAN, of Charleston, owned an undivided
half part of lot #I, the whole containing 1 a.; in the town of Ansonburgh, near Charleston, bounding SE on lots M & N belonging to MR. DART;
SW on Squirrel Street; NE on lot K belonging to WILLIAM HOPTON; NW on estate of JOSEPH WRAGG; & whereas ANN WATSON recovered a judgment against
HENRY KENNAN & DOUGAL CAMPBELL, merchants, of Charleston, for
Ŀ 10,168:5:10 SC money, & costs, & 2 writs of fieri facias were issued
directing the P.M. to levy this amount against the estates of KENNAN &
CAMPBELL; & therefore LOWNDES on 29 June last put up at public auction
the half of lot I belonging to KENNAN, for which ANNE WATSON was highest
bidder; now the property is conveyed to her. Witnesses: JOHN HARVEY,
WILLIAM READ. Before JAMES GRINDLAY, J.P. WILLIAM HOPTON, Register.

Book R-R, p. 335   ANN WATSON, widow, to WILLIAM HOPTON, merchant,
25 Feb. 1757   both of Charleston, for Ŀ 5 currency, the E
Feoffment   part of lot I, (12 ft. wide) in Ansonborough,
                         St. Philips Parish, bounding E on lot K be-
longing to WILLIAM HOPTON; S on lot M belonging to WILLIAM STONE (formerly JOHN DART); W on part lot I belonging to ANN WATSON; N on marsh
which bounds said lot & Ansonborough. Witnesses: THOMAS HOYLAND, PETER
MONCLAR. Before JOHN CLELAND, J.P. WILLIAM HOPTON, Register.

Book R-R, p. 337   JORDAN ROCHE, gentleman, & REBECCA his wife
10 & 11 Mar. 1746   (daughter & devisee of MILES BREWTON); to JOHN
L & R   PRUE, turner, both of Charleston, for Ŀ 320
                         currency, part of 2 lots, in Charleston,
bounding E 80 ft. on King Street; N 200 ft. on FREDERICK SHUBLE (STRUBLE);
W on MR. PHILIPS; S on THOMAS BINFORD, being the S half of 1-1/2 lots.

Whereas MILES BREWTON, gentleman, owned 2 lots in Charleston, & by will dated 11 Aug. 1743, bequeathed to his daughter, REBECCA ROCHE, 1-1/2 lots S of land owned by JOHN TIPPER & fronting on King Street; now she & her husband sell to PRUE. Witnesses: ESAIS BRUNET, WILLIAM DANDRIDGE, VINCENT SEAY CRAFT. Before WILLIAM PINCKNEY, J.P. WILLIAM HOPTON, Register.

Book R-R, p. 345
5 Mar. 1757
Surrender

The Rev. MR. SAMUEL QUINCY, of Bewly in Hamphire England, by his attorney, JOHN RATTRAY, of Charleston; to JOHN LINING, ESQ., & SARAH his wife, of Charleston, part of lot #160 & 2 plantations. Whereas a release dated 21 Apr. 1747 between SAMUEL QUINCY, clergyman, then of Dorchester, Berkeley Co., SC, of 1st part; ELIZABETH HILL, widow, of Charleston, of 2nd part; & JACOB MOTTE, ESQ., of Charleston, of 3rd part; witnessed that in consideration of an intended marriage between SAMUEL QUINCY & ELIZABETH HILL, she conveyed to JACOB MOTTE, in trust for certain purposes, part of lot #160 in Charleston, bounding 92-1/2 ft. on Broad Street; & 95-1/2 ft. on King Street; with a large dwelling house thereon; which lot had been conveyed by WILLIAM HARVEY & SARAH his wife, to CHARLES HILL & ELIZABETH, his then wife; also a plantation on S side Ashley River, in St. Andrews Parish, Berkeley Co., formerly allotted to BENJAMIN GODFREY, planter, on the division of his father's (CAPT. JOHN GODFREY) land amongst his children, & afterwards sold by MARGARET GODFREY & JANE MONGER, acting executors, of BENJAMIN GODFREY, to RICHARD HILL, who conveys by L & R dated 20 & 21 June 1735 to said ELIZABETH; also 53 a. adjoining said plantation, on Governor's Point, formerly belonging to estate of CHARLES HILL, & purchased by RICHARD HILL, who conveyed to ELIZABETH, & on which she has built a dwelling house; & whereas, after their marriage, QUINCY left SC & resides in England, & during his absence ELIZABETH executed her will & bequeathed to her daughter, SARAH LINING, the plantation on Ashley River; & whereas QUINCY, as survivor has a life interest in the estate; & is willing to dispose of it, & by letter of attorney dated 19 June 1754 appointed JOHN RATTRAY his heir & attorney, to dispose of said interest; & whereas RATTRAY has agreed to convey to JOHN & SARAH LINING on condition that they pay QUINCY L 50 sterling per annum during his lifetime; now QUINCY surrenders his claim. Witnesses: DAVID GUERARD, BENJAMIN GUERARD. Before DAVID GRAEME, J.P. WILLIAM HOPTON, Register.

Book R-R, p. 350
4 & 5 Mar. 1757
L & R

JOHN LINING, ESQ., & SARAH his wife, to JOHN RATTRAY, ESQ., both of Charleston, for L 5000 currency & other considerations, 2 parts of lots 160 & 250 in Charleston. Whereas on 5 Mar. 1728 WILLIAM HARVEY, butcher, of Charleston, & SARAH his wife, sold to CHARLES HILL, merchant, & ELIZABETH his wife, part of lot #160 bounding 92-1/2 ft. on Broad Street, & 95-1/2 ft. on King Street, which by feoffment dated 26 Nov. 1715 had been conveyed to HARBEY by WILLIAM LIVINGSTON & ANN his wife; & whereas CHARLES HILL, by will dated 12 Apr. 1734, bequeathed to his wife ELIZABETH a tenement & lot #160; & whereas ELIZABETH, on 21 Apr. 1747, in consideration of her intended marriage to SAMUEL QUINCY, clergyman, then of Dorchester, SC, conveyed to JACOB MOTTE, in trust for her use, the lot #160 & 2 plantations (see p. 345 for details); & whereas the marriage took place & afterwards QUINCY went to England to live, & ELIZABETH bequeathed the plantation on Ashley River, & all her real estate to her daughter, SARAH LINING; & whereas, after ELIZABETH'S death, QUINCY had a life interest in her estate which he was willing to dispose of & appointed JOHN RATTRAY his attorney for that purpose; & whereas RATTRAY surrendered to SARAH LINING all QUINCY'S interest in lot #160 & the 2 plantations; & whereas SARAH also owns part of lot #250, bounding S ? on THOMAS BOONE; E on JOHN ELLIS; N on MADAM SARAH FENWICK; W ? on King Street; now JOHN & SARAH LINING sell to JOHN RATTRAY their part of lots #160 & 250. Witnesses: DAVID GUERARD, BENJAMIN GUERARD. Before DAVID GRAEME, J.P. WILLIAM HOPTON, Register.

Book R-R, p. 360
1 & 2 Mar. 1757
L & R

BENJAMIN SMITH, gentleman, of Goose Creek, to ELIAS HORRY, gentleman, of Santee, for L 520 currency, 346 a. in Prince George Parish, Winyaw, Craven Co., bounding NE on Winyaw River; SW on JAMES MOORE; SE on HENRY SMITH. Whereas the Lords Proprs. on 12 Aug. 1698 created ROBERT DANIEL a Landgrave, granting him 48,000 a. of

land; & DANIEL ran out 12,000 a. (as part of the 48,000) in Craven Co.,
bounding N on Winyaw River; other sides on vacant land; according to plat
by THOMAS BROUGHTON, Sur. Gen., dated 4 Apr. 1711; which 12,000 was duly
granted him on 18 June 1711; & whereas on 19 June 1711 sold THOMAS SMITh,
ESQ., of Goose Creek, 2 baronies containing 24,000 a., of which said
12,000 a. was a part; & whereas THOMAS SMITH by will dated 3 May 1738 bequeathed to his sons HENRY, THOMAS, GEORGE & BENJAMIN, 1000 a. each, to
be run off in proportion on the N & S sides of said barony, or 12,000 a.,
HENRY to have first choice; directing that should 1 die before marrying
or coming of age such share should go to testators wife; & whereas GEORGE
SMITH died unmarried & under age; & whereas testator's wife & daughters
made over their shares which fell to them by death of said GEORGE to HEN-
RY, THOMAS & BENJAMIN; & whereas the 4000 a. so devised have been divided, & a certain tract of 346 a. was allotted to BENJAMIN; now he sells
that tract to HORRY. Witness: DANIEL HORRY, JR. Before JAMES WRIGHT,
J.P. WILLIAM HOPTON, Register. Plat by JOHN HENRY, Dep. Sur., dated 16
Dec. 1754.

Book R-R, p. 369   THOMAS MOON, planter, & MARY his wife, to WIL-
21 & 22 May 1756   LIAM BOYKIN, planter, both of Craven Co., for
L & R   ₺ 100 currency, 100 a. in Fredericksburg Town-
                          ship, bounding SE on JOSIAH TOMLINSON; NE on
BENJAMIN MCKENNIE; NW & SW on vacant land; according to plat attached to
grant from Gov. JAMES GLEN dated 9 Jan. 1756. Witnesses: ROBERT GRAY,
ISABELLA MARTIN. Before SAMUEL WYLY, J.P. WILLIAM HOPTON, Register.

Book R-R, p. 375   ANN (her mark) SINNIXON, (formerly called ANN
26 Mar. 1756   DUYETT), to WILLIAM BOYKIN, both of Craven
L & R   Co., for ₺ 100 Va. money, 300 a. in Fredericks-
                          burgh Township, on N side Wateree River, bound-
ing NW on MR. MCKINNE; SW on vacant land; according to plat dated 21 Nov.
1746. Deed signed by ANN (her mark) SINNIXON & WILLIAM DUCIT. Witnesses: JOHN BOOK, ABRAHAM ODAM. Receipt signed PETER BUCKHOLT. Before SAM-
UEL WYLY, J.P. WILLIAM HOPTON, Register.

Book R-R, p. 381   JOHN WATSON (WATSONE), merchant, formerly of
10 & 11 Mar. 1757   Charleston, SC, now of London, by his attorn-
L & R   ey, JAMES WRIGHT, ESQ., of Charleston, duly
                          appointed by letter dated 1 July 1752; to
GEORGE SEAMAN, merchant, of Charleston; for ₺ 787 SC money, 2 pieces of
ground in Charleston. Whereas JOHN MCKENZIE, merchant, of Charleston,
owned part of lot #80, bounding N 35 ft. on a street from Cooper River; E
on ANN ELLERY & GEORGE HUNTER; S on another street; W 150 ft. on GEORGE
HUNTER; also another piece of ground bounding N & S 35 ft. on 2 streets;
E 150 ft. on GEORGE HUNTER; W on a street laid out by consent; which 2
lots MCKENZIE had purchased from ANNE ELLERY; & whereas MCKENZIE, by L &
R dated 19 & 20 July 1749, conveyed the lots to JOHN WATSON & KENNETH
MICHIE, as trustees, to sell the lots to the highest bidder & apply the
money as directed; & whereas KENNETH MICHIE died & the trust is not yet
finally executed; now WATSON sells the 2 lots to GEORGE SEAMAN, highest
bidder. Witnesses: DANIEL DWIGHT, DANIEL HORRY, JR. Before DANIEL CRAW-
FORD, J.P. WILLIAM HOPTON, Register.

Book R-R, p. 388   GEORGE HAIG, planter, to JOHN BLEVER, black-
24 & 25 Aug. 1747   smith, both of Saxe Gotha Township, for ₺ 200
L & R   currency, 200 a. near the Congarees, opposite
                          the lower part of Saxe Gotha Township, bound-
ing NW on PHILIP JACKSON (now JAMES MYRICK) & SOLOMON MCGRAW; NE & SE on
vacant land; SW on Santee (Congaree) River. Whereas Gov. JAMES GLEN on
22 Feb. 1745 granted ELIZABETH VERDITTY, widow, of St. John's Parish,
Berkeley Co., 200 a. in Craven Co., which she by L & R dated 1 & 2 Apr.
1746 sold to GEORGE HAIG, along with another tract of 304 a.; now HAIG
sells the 200 a. to BLEVER. Witnesses: WILLIAM BAKER, JOHN JACOB GEIGER.
Before JOHN PEARSON, J.P. WILLIAM HOPTON, Register.

Book R-R, p. 393   WALTER DOWNS, to PHILIP PLEDGER, both of Cra-
14 Dec. 1755   ven Co., for ₺ 400 currency, 200 a. in the
Feoffment   WELCH tract, bounding SW on Peedee River; E on
                         land granted RICHARD BARROW & land granted
SAMUEL SARANCE; N on vacant land; NW on land granted DAVID ROACH & vacant

land. Witnesses: ELISHA JAMES, THOMAS JAMES. Before JOHN WALL (WATT).
WILLIAM HOPTON, Register.

Book R-R, p. 395   JACOB DE SAURENCY, to PHILIP PLEDGER, both of
11 Dec. 1755   Craven Co., for Ł 500 currency, 111 a., part
Feoffment   of 150 a. in Craven Co., granted RICHARD BAR-
                         ROW on 24 May 1745, & conveyed by him to DE
SAURENCY by L & R dated 8 & 9 Feb. 1747; the 111 a. bounding N on SAMUEL
SAURENCY; E on vacant land; S on JOHN SUTTON; W on PHILIP PLEDGER. WIL-
LIAM FITZGERALD, WILLIAM WEBBER, JOHN WINN. Before JOHN CRAWFORD, J.P.
WILLIAM HOPTON, Register.

Book R-R, p. 397   JACOB DE SAURENCY, to PHILIP PLEDGER, both of
9 Sept. 1755   Craven Co., for Ł 300 currency, 100 a. 2 miles
Feoffment   below the Great Charrows on N side Peedee Riv-
                         er in WELCH tract, originally granted on 10
Mar. 1743 to SAMUEL DE SAURENCY; bounding according to plat of grant.
Witnesses: JOHN CHRISTMAS, ROBERT (his mark) CLAREY. Before JOHN CRAW-
FORD, J.P. WILLIAM HOPTON, Register.

Book R-R, p. 399   WILLIAM MOULTRIE, ESQ., & ELIZABETH DAMARIS,
20 & 21 Feb. 1757   his wife, of St. Johns Parish, Berkeley Co.,
L & R   to DAVID GRAEME, attorney-at-law, of Charles-
                         ton, for Ł 1000 currency, 60 a. in Berkeley
Co., formerly bought by JAMES DE ST. JULIEN, gentleman, from his brother
PAUL DE ST. JULIEN, & devised by JAMES to BENJAMIN DE ST. JULIEN, brother
of ELIZABETH DEMARIS MOULTRIE; also 740 a. in Berkeley Co., part of
1000 a. bought by the father of JAMES DE ST. JULIEN from CHAMPERNOON
ELLIOTT, adjoining the 60 a., making 1 plantation of 800 a., called Indian Fields; also the W part of 215 a., part of 550 a. in Berkeley Co.,
conveyed to PETER DE ST. JULIEN by MARY LAROCHES; the W part to be divided from residue of 215 a. by the new causeway & a right line from thence
produced until it intersects the S boundary line of 290 a. belonging to
DANIEL RAVENEL in right of his wife SARAH; also 1500 a., part of 2000 a.
in Craven Co., conveyed to PETER DE ST. JULIEN by JAMES AKIN; also
819.3 a. partly in Craven Co., & partly in Berkeley Co., granted to PETER
DE ST. JULIEN on 28 Nov. 1735 by Lt. Gov. THOMAS BROUGHTON; also 755 a.
in Berkeley Co., on S side Santee River, granted to PETER DE ST. JULIEN;
also 500 a. purchased by PETER DE ST. JULIEN from WILLIAM WATIES; also
300 a., being the E part of 600 a. in Craven Co., granted PETER DE ST.
JULIEN on 3 Feb. 1737 by WILLIAM BULL, then president; the 300 a., divid-
ed from remainder by a N-S line, devised by PETER DE ST. JULIEN to his
son, ALEXANDER; all of which tracts were, by deed of partition dated 13
Jan. last (p. 277) were allotted by DANIEL RAVENEL & SARAH, his wife, to
WILLIAM MOULTRIE, & ELIZABETH DEMARIS, his wife, in her right, (SARAH &
ELIZABETH DEMARIS being co-heiresses of their brother BENJAMIN DE ST.
JULIEN). Witnesses: HENRY RAVENEL, WILLIAM PILLANS. Before JOHN RATTRAY,
J.P. WILLIAM HOPTON, Register.

Book R-R, p. 408   DAVID GRAEME, attorney, of Charleston, to WIL-
25 & 26 Mar. 1757   LIAM MOULTRIE, ESQ., of St. Johns Parish,
L & R   Berkeley Co., for Ł 1000 currency, 60 a.; 800
                         a. in 2 tracts called Indian Fields; W part of
215 a.; 1500 a.; 819.3 a.; 755 a.; 300 a. (see p. 399); which 8 tracts
GRAEME purchased from WILLIAM MOULTRIE. Witnesses: THOMAS ADAM, WILLIAM
PILLAUS (PILLANS). Before JOHN RATTRAY, J.P. WILLIAM HOPTON, Register.

Book R-R, p. 416   CHARLES LOWNDES, P.M., to SOLOMON MILLNER,
28 Dec. 1756   merchant, of Charleston, at public auction,
Sale   for Ł 6000 currency, 1000 a. on Johns Island,
                         Colleton Co. Whereas JAMES TORQUETT, planter,
owned 3 adjacent tracts, making 1 tract of about 1000 a., on Johns Island,
bounding N on WILLIAM ARNOLD & THOMAS HUMPHREYS; E on SOLOMON LEGARE, ANN
MATHEWES & GEORGE HEXT; S on GEORGE HEXT & JAMES MATHEWES; W on JOSEPH
STANYARNE, THOMAS HUMPHREYS, & GEORGE HEXT; & whereas after his death,
GEORGE MATHEWES, executor of will of LOIS MATHEWES, widow, of St. Philip's Parish, obtained a judgement against WILLIAM WILKINS, surviving executor, of will of JAMES TORQUETT, in the sum of Ł 1540 currency, & costs,
& a writ of fieri facias was issued by PETER LEIGH, C.J., commanding the
P.M. to seize TORQUETT'S estate & levy said amounts against the estate; &

40

whereas LOWNDES put said 1000 a. up at auction & MILLNER was highest bidder; now the plantation is conveyed to MILLNER. Witnesses: JOHN GORDON, GEORGE BEDON. Before CHARLES PINCKNEY, J.P. WILLIAM HOPTON, Register.

Book R-R, p. 421   CHARLES JONES, planter, of St. Bartholomews
1 & 2 Apr. 1757   Parish, Colleton Co., to ARCHIBALD SCOTT,
L & R   planter, of James Island, for Ŀ 1200 SC money,
                          213 a. in St. Andrews Parish, Berkeley Co.,
bounding NW on EDMUND BELLINGER; NE on Glebe land & MRS. ELIZABETH FULLER; SW on JOHN MANLEY; SE on marsh of Coppain Creek. Witnesses: JOHN CART, JOHN REMINGTON, JR. Before JOHN REMINGTON, SR., J.P. WILLIAM HOPTON, Register. Plat certified 1 Apr. 1757 by ROBERT SCREVEN, Sur., of 213 a., part of 2 tracts granted FRANCIS FIDLING & others.

Book R-R, p. 427   MARY YEOMANS, widow, of Charleston (formerly
6 & 7 Apr. 1757   MARY LESUEUR, only child & heir of ABRAHAM LA-
L & R   SUEUR, of Charleston who died intestate), to
                          ANN PEACOCK, widow, of St. George Parish, Dor-
chester, for Ŀ 1700 currency, the SW part of lot #37 formerly belonging to ABRAHAM LESUEUR; bounding N 44 ft. on heirs of MR. PORCHER; E 42-1/2 ft. on MARY YEOMANS; S 46-1/2 ft. on heirs of COL. JOHN SMITH; W 43-3/4 ft. on Church Street. Witnesses: JOHN COOPER, JOHN REMINGTON. Before JOHN REMINGTON, SR., J.P. WILLIAM HOPTON, Register. Plat dated 6 Apr. 1757 by WILLIAM WILKINS, Sur.

Book R-R, p. 434   ESAIS BRUNET, carpenter, gave JOHN PRUE, turn-
14 Feb. 1752   er, both of Charleston, a bond in penal sum of
Bond & Satisfaction   Ŀ 1500 currency, that PRUE may peaceably occu-
                          py a certain brick house & other buildings
built & finished by BRUNET on PRUE'S lot; PRUE having this day paid BRUNET Ŀ 600 currency in full for building said houses & fences on the S part of a lot lately leased to BRUNET by PRUE, on W side of King Street, near White Point, where FRANCIS DRAYTON, carpenter, now lives; bounding E 40 ft. on King Street; S 200 ft. on THOMAS BINFORD; W on N on JOHN PRUE, where PRUE now lives, (p. 337). (Note: SUSANNAH, wife of ESAIS BRUNET). Witnesses: LEWIS MIDDLETON, THOMAS LAMBOLL. Before JAMES PARSONS, J.P. WILLIAM HOPTON, Register.

Book R-R, p. 436   GEORGE HEXT, planter, & ELIZABETH his wife, of
14 & 15 Mar. 1757   Johns Island, to SOLOMON MILNER, merchant, of
L & R   Charleston, for Ŀ 1200 currency, 300 a. on
                          Johns Island adjoining land of SOLOMON MILNER
(formerly JAMES TORQUET, p. 416); which land TORQUET purchased from MATTHEW ROCHE, who devised to GEORGE HEXT, party hereto. Witnesses: SOLOMON FREER, THOMAS LEGARE, JR., THOMAS ARNOLD. Before CHARLES PINCKNEY, J.P. WILLIAM HOPTON, Register.

Book R-R, p. 441   CHARLES LOWNDES, P.M., to JOHN SMITH, merchant,
7 Feb. 1757   of Prince William Parish, for Ŀ 628:15:3 cur-
Sale   rency, at public auction, 4883 a. in Granville
                          Co. Whereas HUGH BRYAN, planter, of Prince
William Parish, owned several adjoining tracts of land, making 1 tract of 4883 a. in Granville Co., bounding W on Savannah River & on the Rev. MR. WILLIAM GUY; S on the River & on Town of Purysburgh; E on vacant land; N on THOMAS ELLIOTT & on vacant land; & whereas after HUGH BRYAN'S death, WILLIAM SIMPSON & ELIZABETH his wife, administratrix of will of EDMUND BELLINGER, & WILLIAM BULL, administrator of estate of BARNABY BULL, planter, recovered a judgment against MARY BRYAN, executrix, & JOHN SMITH, executor, of will of HUGH BRYAN, amounting to Ŀ 3484 currency, & costs; & whereas a writ of fieri facias was issued by PETER LEIGH, C.J., commanding the P.M. to seize the estate of HUGH BRYAN; & whereas the P.M. offered the 4883 a. for sale at public auction & SMITH was highest bidder; now the land is conveyed to him. Witnesses: WILLIAM BRISBANE, WILLIAM READ. Before ROBERT WILLIAMS, JR., J.P. WILLIAM HOPTON, Register.

Book R-R, p. 446   JOHN JORDAN, planter, formerly of Peedee, SC,
16 & 17 Jan. 1756   now of NC, to JOB ROTHMAHLER, of Prince George
L & R   Parish, SC, for Ŀ 700 SC money, 5 tracts, to-
                          tal 1150 a.; 450 a., bounding N & E on Peedee
River; S on the lake; N & W on vacant land; also 300 a. bounding NW on

JAMES MAXWELL; NE on JOHN JORDAN'S lake; S on Peedee River; also 200 a. bounding SW & NW on JOSEPH ALLEN; SE on vacant land; NE on Little Peedee River; also 71 a., bounding SE on Peedee & Cypress Rivers; NE on vacant land; SW on THOMAS SMITH; also 229 a. bounding NE on the River Swamp; NW on JOHN JORDAN; other sides on vacant land. Witnesses: JOSEPH RUSS, JOSEPH (his mark) WESTCOAT. Before PAUL TRAPIER, J.P. WILLIAM HOPTON, Register.

Book R-R, p. 450   GEORGE SAXBY, ESQ., & ELIZABETH his wife, of
20 & 21 Jan. 1757   Charleston, to PAUL TRAPIER, ESQ., of Craven
L & R   Co., for Ł.1092 currency, 1940 a. in Prince
                    Frederick Parish, near Peedee, in Craven Co.,
granted by Gov. JAMES GLEN on 1 June 1750 to DANIEL LAROCHE, who by L & R
dated 23 & 24 Jan. 1752 sold to GEORGE SAXBY; bounding N on WILLIAM PEAKE
& on MR. BUCKSTON & on vacant land; E on vacant land & MR. HANDLEN; S on
MR. PAWLEY & JOHN SAUNDERS; W on JOHN WALKER; except 87 a. sold by DANIEL
LAROCHE to STEPHEN PEAKE; also except 182 a. sold by DANIEL LAROCHE to
ALEXANDER CAMPBELL. Witnesses: SUSANNA BOSOMWORTH, MARY GREENE. Before
THOMAS BLYTHE, J.P. WILLIAM HOPTON, Register.

Book R-R, p. 458   JOHN ALLEN, gentleman, of Charleston, eldest
_____ Nov. 1747   son, heir & residuary devisee of will of AN-
Confirmation   DREW ALLEN, merchant, confirmes DAVID HEXT'S
                    title to a certain lot in Charleston. Whereas
ANDREW ALLEN owned a certain lot #274 within a parcel of lots called Ha-
wetts Square in NW part of Charleston, which he sold in 1735 to DAVID
HEXT; & whereas the deeds have become lost or mislaid; now ALLEN confirms
HEXT'S title to the lot, bounding S on Broad Street; W on MR. MAZYCK; N
on THOMAS WEAVER; E on MR. THORPE. Witnesses: BENJAMIN DART, BENJAMIN
BUTLER. Before SAMUEL BOWMAN, J.P. WILLIAM HOPTON, Register.

Book R-R, p. 461   JOHN MCCALL, merchant, & MARTHA his wife; SAM-
25 Sept. 1755   UEL PRIOLEAU, merchant, & PROVIDENCE his wife;
Release   WILLIAM ROPER, merchant, & GRACE his wife;
                    BENJAMIN DART, merchant, & AMELIA his wife; &
ROBERT WILLIAMS, JR., ESQ., & ELIZABETH his wife; all of Charleston;
MARTHA, PROVIDENCE, GRACE, AMELIA & ELIZABETH, 5 daughters of & executors
of will of DAVID HEXT, gentleman; to JEREMIAH THEUS, limner; for Ł 2000
currency; a brick dwelling house on lot #274. Whereas DAVID HEXT owned a
brick dwelling house & lot #274 in Hawetts Square, in NW part of Charleston, bounding S on Broad Street; W on MR. MAZYCK; N on THOMAS WEAVER; E
on ROBERT THORPE; & by will dated 11 May 1751 appointed his 5 daughters
his executors; & bequeathed to them, after the death of his wife, ANN,
the house & lot, to be sold as soon as convenient; & whereas ANN is dead
& THEUS is highest bidder, now the property is conveyed to him. Witnesses: JOHN PRUE, RICHARD MUNCREEF, JAMES VERREE. Before _____. WILLIAM
HOPTON, Register.

Book R-R, p. 469   WILLIAM CHAPMAN, JR., planter, & MARY his wife,
5 Mar. 1754   of James Island, to JAMES VERREE, carpenter,
Release   of Charleston, for Ł 600 currency, a lot on
                    Church Street, in Charleston. Witnesses: WIL-
LIAM GIBBES, RICHARD BAKER, JOHN MCCALL. Before SAMUEL BOWMAN, J.P.
WILLIAM HOPTON, Register.

Book R-R, p. 473   HENRY PERONNEAU, & ELIZABETH his wife; JAMES
29 & 30 Mar. 1750   MICHIE, ESQ., & MARTHA his wife; WILLIAM STEW-
L & R   ART, ESQ., & ANN his wife; & JOHN CATTELL, JR.,
                    eldest son & heir of JOHN CATTELL, SR., & SAR-
AH his wife; all of Charleston; (ELIZABETH, MARTHA, ANN & SARAH being
daughters of COL. ARTHUR HALL & co-heirs of CHRISTOPHER HALL, son & de-
visee of said ARTHUR HALL); of 1st part; to HUGH WILSON, planter, of Wad-
malaw Island, Colleton Co., for Ł 2160 currency; their respective inter-
ests in 864 a. on Wadmalaw Island, commonly called Hall Field, which
CHRISTOPHER HALL inherited from his father; bounding S on THOMAS STAN-
YARNE; N on Wadmalaw River & DR. JAMES WILLIAMS; E on MICAJAH COLE; W on
HUGH WILSON (now occupied by ROBERT TURNER & JOHN MCCULLOCH). Witnesses:
JOHN TROUP, TIMOTHY MORGRIDGE. Before ALEXANDER STEWARD, J.P. WILLIAM
HOPTON, Register.

Book R-R, p. 480   MIKELL SEALY, planter, to FRANCIS PELOT, cler-
25 & 26 Mar. 1757   gyman, both of Granville Co., for ₤ 600 cur-
L & R   rency, 300 a. of Indian land, in Granville
                          Co., where PELOT now lives; bounding E & NE on
Ewhaw Creek; N & W on vacant land; S on marsh land; which 300 a. were
granted on 12 Aug. 1737 to EPHRAIM MIKELL, who sold to JOHN SEALY, who
bequeathed the land to his son MIKELL SEALY. Witnesses: JOHN WILLIAMS,
WILLIAM BETTISON, ALEXANDER LONG. Before ANDREW VERDIER, J.P. WILLIAM
HOPTON, Register.

Book R-R, p. 484   EDMUND BELLINGER, of Berkeley Co., eldest son
26 & 27 Feb. 1756   of Landgrave EDMUND BELLINGER; & MARIE LUCIA,
L & R   his wife; & HENRY HYRNE, JR. (eldest son of
                          HENRY HYRNE, ESQ., of Colleton Co., & SUSANNAH
his wife, 1 of the daughters of Landgrave EDMUND BELLINGER; & heir of
said SUSANNAH his mother); of 1st part; to WILLIAM BRISBANE, merchant, of
Charleston: for ₤ 4000 currency; 2000 a. in Prince William Parish, Granville Co., bounding N on STEPHEN BULL; E on estate of EDMUND BELLINGER; S
on MRS. ELIZABETH BELLINGER; SW on Chuly Phinny Creek; W on THOMAS LAWS
ELLIOTT & CAPT. JAMES MCPHERSON. Whereas EDMUND BELLINGER owned 48,000
a. in Granville Co., granted by the Lords Proprs. to his father; & whereas by will dated 21 Feb. 1739 he devised to his daughter, SUSANNAH, then
wife of HENRY HYRNE, ESQ., 1000 a.; & to his brother, BARNABY BULL, 1000
a.; & directed that all the tracts devised by him should be allotted to
devisees by his wife ELIZABETH as she saw fit; & in case of her death his
son EDMUND to act; except the 1000 a. devised to his nephew WILLIAM PALM-
ER, which were to be allotted to him where he lived; & whereas ELIZABETH
allotted to BURNABY BULL & HENRY HYRNE, SR., (by right of his wife SU-
SANNAH) & HENRY HYRNE, JR., the undivided 2000 a. in Granville Co., to be
held by them in common; & whereas SUSANNAH died without having disposed
of her half, which therefore descended to her son HENRY HYRNE, JR.; &
whereas BURNABY BULL by L & R dated 7 & 8 June 1748, conveyed his half to
EDMUND BELLINGER; & whereas EDMUND BELLINGER & HENRY HYRNE now own the
2000 a. as tenants in common; now they sell the land to BRISBANE. Witnesses: JOHN RATTRAY, GEORGE JACKSON. Before JAMES GRINDLAY, J.P. WIL-
LIAM HOPTON, Register. Plat of 2000 a. certified 7 Feb. 1756.

Book R-R, p. 492   CHARLES LOWNDES, P.M., to WILLIAM BRISBANE,
7 Feb. 1757   practitioner in physic, for ₤ 605 currency, at
Sale   public auction, 1100 a. in several tracts, in
                          Purysburgh Township, Granville Co. Whereas
HUGH BRYAN, planter, of Prince William Parish, owned 6 plantations, namely 1 plantation of 600 a., bounding E on Day's Creek; other sides on vacant land, at time of original grant on 5 July 1736 to SAMUEL AUGSPOUR-
GUES; also 250 a. on W side Day's Creek, bounding N on above tract; E on
MR. COSTES, MR. LAPIER, & on vacant land; S & W on vacant land at time of
grant to JOSEPH BARRAKI dated 16 Dec. 1738; also 100 a., on W side Day's
Creek, bounding S on the AUGSPOURGHER grant; other sides on vacant land
at time of grant to STEPHEN VIGNEAU dated 3 Feb. 1737; also 50 a. bounding N on MR. LAPIER & MR. BARRACKI; S on MR. DESSAUSSAURE & on vacant
land; W on MR. BARRACKI & vacant land at time of original grant to GEORGE
SHONMAN GROBER dated 16 Sept. 1738; also 50 a. W on Day's Creek called
New River, bounding S on DAVID LANCE; E on ANDREW WINCKLER; W on vacant
land at time of grant to JOHN RODOLPH dated 16 Sept. 1738; also 50 a.
bounding on all sides on vacant land at time of grant to DAVID LANCE dated 16 Sept. 1738; total 1100 a.; & whereas after his death WILLIAM SIMP-
SON & ELIZABETH his wife (administratrix of EDMUND BELLINGER), & WILLIAM
BULL (administrator of the goods & chattels of BARNABY BULL, planter),
obtained a judgment against MARY BRYAN, executrix, & JOHN SMITH, executor
of will of HUGH BRYAN, in the amount of ₤ 3484 currency, with costs, & a
writ of fieri facias was issued by PETER LEIGH, C.J., directing the P.M.
to levy this amount against BRYAN'S estate; & whereas no goods or chattels were to be found & the P.M. seized the above lands & offered them
for sale at public auction; now the land is sold to BRISBANE. Witnesses:
JOHN FILBIN, WILLIAM READ. Before JOHN MURRAY, J.P. WILLIAM HOPTON,
Register.

Book R-R, p. 498   JOHN CART, carpenter, & RACHAEL his wife, of
2 Mar. 1757   CHARLESTON, to JOHN DUTARQUE, planter, of
Release   Berkeley Co., for ₤ 550 currency, part of lot

#199 in Charleston, bounding E 43-3/4 ft. on a neighborhood street; S
110 ft. on JOHN REMINGTON; W on JOHN CART; N on THOMAS SMITH, SR., (formerly HENRY MIDDLETON); which part of a lot & other adjacent lands were
devised to HENRY MIDDLETON by his father, ARTHUR MIDDLETON, ESQ., & sold
by HENRY MIDDLETON & MARY his wife on 19 Feb. 1746 to JOHN CART. Witnesses: HUGH ANDERSON, NOAH DUTARQUE. Before JOHN REMINGTON, J.P. WIL-
LIAM HOPTON, Register.

Book R-R, p. 501   FRANCIS KINLOCH, ESQ., & ANN his wife, to
1 & 2 Dec. 1756   GEORGE AUSTIN, ESQ., both of Charleston, 200
L & R   a. being the NE half of the E tract of 400 a.,
                          bounding NW on Santee River; SW on other part
to be conveyed to TACITUS GAILLARD; SE on the half sold to MARGARET
O'NEIL; NE on TRENCH Barony, or vacant land. Whereas the Lords Proprs.
on 5 Sept. 1705 granted JOHN STROUD 3 tracts of 400 a. each at English
Santee, in Craven Co., on S side Santee River; which 3 tracts became the
property of JAMES KINLOCH, ESQ., father of FRANCIS KINLOCH; the 1200 a.
bounding N on Santee River; E & S on TRENCH Barony, called RAPHOE, or vacant land; W on WILLIAM BETTISON; & whereas JAMES KINLOCH conveyed to
MARGARET O'NEIL 200 a. of the E tract (the SE part of 1200 a.); & by L &
R dated 4 & 5 Feb. 1750 granted FRANCIS KINLOCH, his son, the remaining
1000 a., & whereas on 7 Nov. 1753 FRANCIS KINLOCH agreed to sell the
other half of the E tract to JAMES MCKELVAY, planter, of St. Johns Parish,
Berkeley Co., & whereas MCKELVAY died before 1 May 1754 & his representa-
tives & nearest of kin delivered the agreement to GEORGE AUSTIN, having
previously made an agreement with him in regard to the purchase; now to
carry out his agreement, KINLOCH conveys to AUSTIN. Witnesses: JAMES
GRINDLAY, JOHN MAYRANT. Receipt of ₤ 600 currency on 2 Dec. 1756 from
GEORGE AUSTIN acknowledged by JOHN HAMILTON, ANN (her mark) HAMILTON,
JAMES MCKELVEY, & JAMES HAMILTON. Witnesses: ROBERT FLUD, WILLIAM FLUD.
Before DANIEL CRAWFORD, J.P. WILLIAM HOPTON, Register. Plat certified
24 May 1756 by ISAAC PORCHER, Dep. Sur., showing 207 a., part of a tract
JAMES KINLOCH sold to MRS. MARGARET O'NEAL, which 207 a. were surveyed
for WILLIAM FLUD; bounding NW on Santee River; SW on said KINLOCH (now
TACITUS GAILLARD); SE on MRS. O'NEAL; NE on vacant land.

Book R-R, p. 510   BENJAMIN SINGLETON, & REBECCA his wife, of
3 & 4 Dec. 1756   Wassamsaw, to GEORGE AUSTIN, ESQ., of Charles-
L & R   ton, for ₤ 800 currency, 600 a. on N side San-
                          tee River, in Craven Co., bounding SW on JAMES
BEARD; NW & NE on vacant land. Witnesses: SARAH MATHEWES, JOSEPH COX.
Before DANIEL CRAWFORD, J.P. WILLIAM HOPTON, Register.

Book R-R, p. 516   THOMAS (his mark) BASSETT, planter, & ELIZA-
8 & 9 Apr. 1757   BETH his wife, of SC to DANIEL CLARK & LACH-
L & R   LAN MCGILLIVRAY, storekeepers, of GA., for ₤ 5
                          SC money, & other considerations, 450 a. in
New Windsor Township, Granville Co., bounding 1 side on Savannah River; 1
side on impassable swamp; 1 side on EDMOND COSSENS; 1 side on vacant land.
Witnesses: JAMES MCCLELLAN, JOHN WARD. Before CORNELIUS COOK, J.P. WIL-
LIAM HOPTON, Register.

Book R-R, p. 520   The Rt. Hon. GEORGE, Lord ANSON, Baron of So-
26 & 27 Apr. 1757   erton, Co. of Southampton, Great Britain; by
L & R   his attorney RICHARD LAMBTON, ESQ., of Charles-
                          ton, of 1st part; to JOHN RATTRAY, ESQ., of
Charleston; according to agreement, & for ₤ 8350 SC money, part of an
orange grove in St. Philip's Parish, Charleston, being 20 a. of high land
& 20 a. of marsh land, bounding E on Cooper River; W partly on a street
leading from the Bay to Ansonborough, & partly on George Street, partly
on ANSON'S land, & on JOHN WATSON; N on ISAAC MAZYCK; S on MR. SHUBRICK &
on ANSON'S marsh; also all marsh & other land as far as low water mark;
except the wharf & a 35 ft. entrance to the wharf. Whereas Gov. JOHN
ARCHDALE on 14 Oct. 1696 granted ISAAC MAZYCK 90 a., English measure, in
Berkeley Co., & whereas Gov. NATHANIEL JOHNSTON on 1 Feb. 1706 granted
ISAAC MAZYCK 71 a., English measure, in Berkeley Co., & whereas ISAAC
MAZYCK by deed poll dated 9 Apr. 1710, with the consent of MARIAN, his
wife, conveyed to COL. EDWARD TYNTE, then Gov. of SC & NC 63 or 64 a. &
all the marsh land to the E, fronting on Cooper River & running as far N
as the marsh of the back side of the garden; & whereas the 63 or 64 a. by

cancelling the deed poll & sundry conveyances became re-invested in ISAAC
MAZYCK; & whereas ISAAC MAZYCK & MARIANA his wife on 29 Oct. 1720 sold to
THOMAS GADSDEN 63 or 64 a., part of 90 a., & said marsh land, 1 of the
boundaries of the plantation, reserving a right of way through the land
from the Broad Road to the bridge that runs across the marsh to a plantation owned by ISAAC MAZYCK & free liberty to draw & take away water from
the well or spring; & whereas by deed poll dated 29 July 1726 THOMAS
GADSDEN conveyed to FRANCIS LE BRASSEUR, merchant, of Charleston, a certain tract of 63 or 64 a., bounding S 244 ft. on MRS. SARAH RHETT'S pasture land; W & N on THOMAS GADSDEN; E 104 ft. on marsh of Cooper River;
as enclosed by cedar posts & rails about the land; & whereas THOMAS
GADSDEN on 24 Mar. 1726 sold CAPT. GEORGE ANSON, Lord ANSON, then commander of H.M.S. Scarborough, the aforesaid 63 or 64 a., with the marsh
land; excepting above mentioned priviledges for ISAAC MAZYCK; also excepting the land conveyed to LE BRASSEUR, with free passage for LE BRAS-
SEUR; & whereas GEORGE ANSON (as the Rt. Hon. GEORGE, Lord ANSON, Vis-
count Polchester) on 13 Oct. 1747 sold JERMYN WRIGHT 23-1/2 plus a., with
tenements, orange groves, etc., part of said 63 or 64 a., also the marsh;
& other lands as far as low water mark; & whereas JERMYN WRIGHT on 11
Mar. (May?) 1756 reconveyed the land to ANSON; who on a certain date appointed RICHARD LAMBTON his attorney with authority to sell; now LAMBTON
sells RATTRAY as above. Witnesses: GEORGE JACKSON, WILLIAM BLAKE. Before DAVID GRAEME, J.P. WILLIAM HOPTON, Register.

Book R-R, p. 532   JOHN CATTELL, eldest son & heir of JOHN CAT-
18 May 1752   TELL & SARAH his wife (1 of the daughters of
Release & Confirmation   COL. ARTHUR HALL, of Berkeley Co.); for ₤ 540
                          currency, his fourth part of the purchase mon-
ey; confirms HUGH WILSON'S title to 864 a. on Wadmalaw Island. Whereas
JOHN CATTELL, JR. was under age on 30 Mar. 1750 when HENRY PERONNEAU &
ELIZABETH his wife; JAMES MICHIE, & MARTHA his wife; WILLIAM STUART (then
of Charleston) & ANN his wife & said JOHN CATTELL, JR., conveyed to HUGH
WILSON 864 a. on Wadmalaw Island, but came of age on 5 Sept. last; now he
confirms the sale. Witnesses: JAMES MICHIE, JOHN TROUP. Before ALEXAN-
DER STUART, J.P. WILLIAM HOPTON, Register.

Book R-R, p. 535   PHILIP RAIFORD, SR., planter, of Craven Co.,
23 Feb. 1747/8   to his beloved son, WILLIAM HOWELL, 50 a.
Gift   Witnesses: EVEN (his mark) REES, JOHN MYRICK,
                          JOHN HANDYSID. Before STEPHEN CRELL, J.P.
WILLIAM HOPTON, Register. Plat certified by JOHN HAMILTON, Dep. Sur., 10
May 1757, showing 52 a., part of 300 a. in Craven Co., granted to JAMES
CROKATT on 5 June 1742, & since transferred to PHILIP RAILFORD, SR., who
gave to WILLIAM HOWELL.

Book R-R, p. 536   CHARLES WRIGHT, ESQ., of Granville Co., to
3 & 4 May 1757   JAMES WRIGHT, ESQ., of Charleston. Whereas
L & R by Mortgage   JAMES WRIGHT for the debt of CHARLES WRIGHT &
                          JERMYN WRIGHT, ESQRS., of Granville Co., be-
came jointly bound with them, by bond dated 16 Apr. 1756, to WALTER IZARD
& RALPH IZARD, of St. George Dorchester, executors of will of THOMAS
IZARD, in penal sum of ₤ 8000 for payment of ₤ 4000 currency, for the use
of the daughters of JOSEPH IZARD, with interest, on 16 Apr. then next; &
whereas CHARLES WRIGHT gave bond dated 4 this May to JAMES WRIGHT, in penal sum of ₤ 8000, with condition that if CHARLES WRIGHT pay WALTER &
RALPH IZARD said ₤ 4000 & interest due on 1 June next, thereby acquitting
JAMES WRIGHT, this bond to be void; & whereas JAMES WRIGHT, at request of
CHARLES & JERMYN, became bound with them on 4 this May to WALTER & RALPH
IZARD, executors of HENRY IZARD, & for use of HENRY IZARD'S estate in penal sum of ₤ 5138 for payment of ₤ 2569 currency, with interest, on 4 May
next; & whereas CHARLES & JERMYN gave bond of even date to JAMES WRIGHT
in penal sum of ₤ 5138 conditioned on their paying WALTER & RALPH IZARD
said ₤ 2569 & interest, thereby acquitting JAMES; now, to secure payment
of the bonds, CHARLES conveys to JAMES 3450 a. in Granville Co., bounding
SE partly on JERMYN & CHARLES WRIGHT, partly on JAMES GRAEME; SW on vacant swamp & JAMES MICHIE; NW on JAMES MICHIE; N on Purysburgh Township;
which land was granted to CHARLES WRIGHT by Gov. WILLIAM HENRY LYTTLETON
on 14 Mar. last. Witness: DANIEL DWIGHT. Before DAVID GRAEME, J.P.
WILLIAM HOPTON, Register.

Book R-R, p. 546   MAJ. THOMAS LADSON, of Horse Savanna, in St.
5 Apr. 1757   Pauls Parish, to CAPT. JAMES LADSON, of same
Release   place, for Ł 1300 SC money, his half of 300 a.
                     Whereas Gov. CHARLES CRAVEN, & CHARLES HEXT,
ROBERT DANIEL, SAMUEL EVELEIGH, & RALPH IZARD, Lords Proprs. on 23 Nov.
1714 granted ROBERT LADSON, father of said THOMAS & JAMES, 300 a. then in
Berkeley Co., now in Colleton Co., bounding NW & NE on CAPT. THOMAS HEP-
WORTH; SW on JOHN RAVEN; SE on JOHN WARD & vacant land; & whereas by will
dated 19 Dec. 1732 ROBERT LADSON, bequeathed, after the death of his wife,
ANN, the half of the tract on which his house then stood to his son,
JAMES; the other half to THOMAS; now THOMAS sells his share to JAMES.
Witnesses: ANDREW LEITCH, SAMUEL ELLIOTT, JACOB LADSON. Before JAMES
PARSONS, J.P. WILLIAM HOPTON, Register.

                     DEEDS BOOK "S-S"
                     MAY 1757 - APR. 1758

Book S-S, p. 1   GEORGE SAXBY, ESQ., of Charleston; to PETER
9 May 1756   TAYLOR, ESQ., & the Rev. MR. JAMES HARRISON,
L & R by Mortgage   as attorneys for Society for Propagation of
                     the Gospel in Foreign parts, as security on
bond of even date in penal sum of Ł 6000 for payment of Ł 3000 currency,
with interest, on 9 May 1757; 1167 a. on Peedee River in Prince George
Parish, Craven Co., commonly called Bluff Plantation formerly belonging
to THOMAS LAROCHE; bounding E on WILLIAM ALSTON; W on vacant land; S on
MR. WATIES & LUKE STOUTENBURGH (formerly MR. GORDON); N on COL. PAWLEY &
WILLIAM DRAKE; the 1167 a. being in 2 tracts, or 863 a. on W side of river & 304 a. on E side Peedee River. Witnesses: CHARLES PINCKNEY, WILLIAM
MAZYCK. Before JACOB MOTTE, J.P. WILLIAM HOPTON, Register. Plat given.
On 24 Apr. 1766 JAMES HARRISON of Goose Creek notified FENWICKE BULL that
he had received full satisfaction of this mortgage.

Book S-S, p. 6   WILLIAM HAZZARD, planter, of Granville Co., to
30 Sept. 1754   his grandson, WILLIAM HAZZARD WIGG, for love &
                     affection, 500 a., part of 8073 a. formerly
belonging to Gov. ROBERT JOHNSON; bounding E on Port Royal river; S on
Okens Creek; & adjoining 500 a. purchased by L & R dated 5 & 6 July 1754
WILLIAM HAZZARD from GABRIEL MANIGAULT & ROBERT JOHNSON by his attorneys
HECTOR BERINGERDE BEAUFAIN & NATHANIEL BROUGHTON. Witnesses: MARY WIGG,
EDWARD WIGG. Before JOHN MURRAY, J.P. WILLIAM HOPTON, Register.

Book S-S, p. 7   WILLIAM HAZZARD, of Granville Co., to his
30 Apr. 1756   daughter MARY WIGG, for love & affection, lot
Gift   #1 in Old Town, with its brick house & other
                     buildings, wharf, scale house, etc. Witness-
es: RICHARD RICKETTS, JOHN GUINN, JOHN BARNWELL. Before JAMES THOMSON,
J.P. WILLIAM HOPTON, Register.

Book S-S, p. 7   CHARLES LOWNDES, P.M., to ROBERT HARDY, wheel-
30 Apr. 1757   wright, of Charleston, at public auction, for
Sale   Ł 740 currency, lot #254 in Charleston. Where-
                     as THOMAS HAMETT, cabinet maker, owned a part
of lot #254 in the NW part of Charleston, bounding E 45 ft. on King
Street; other sides on other part of said lot; 90 ft. deep; which by deed
of feoffment dated 5 Aug. 1751 was conveyed by JAMES ALLEN of Charleston,
to THOMAS HAMMETT, & also by endorsement on back of deed by JAMES ALLEN
on 26 May 1755; & whereas THOMAS CORKER recovered a judgment against
THOMAS HAMETT in the sum of Ł 1000 & costs & a writ of fieri facias was
issued by PETER LEIGH, C.J., commanding the P.M. to obtain this amount
from HAMETT'S estate; & whereas MOSES MITCHELL obtained a judgment also
against HAMETT for Ł 75:17:11, damages & costs, & another writ of fieri
facias was issued by PETER LEIGH, C.J.; & the P.M. seized the said part
of a lot & offered it for sale at public auction, HARDY being highest
bidder; now the property is conveyed to HARDY. Witnesses: WILLIAM BLAKE,
BENJAMIN GUERARD. Before DAVID GRAEME, J.P. WILLIAM HOPTON, Register.

Book S-S, p. 10   ROBERT HARDY, wheelwright, & MARY his wife, to
4 & 6 June 1757   WILLIAM HOPTON, merchant, & SARAH his wife,

46

L & R by Mortgage   both of Charleston, as security on bond dated
                                     21 Apr. last, in penal sum of Ł 1200 for pay-
ment of Ł 600 currency, with interest, for use of MARY CHRISTIANA HOPTON,
daughter of WILLIAM & SARAH HOPTON, on 21 Apr. 1758; part of lot #254
bounding E 45 ft. on King Street; other sides on other parts said lot,
being 90 ft. deep, & having a dwelling house thereon. Witnesses: JACOB
VIART, GEORGE JACKSON. Before DAVID GRAEME, J.P. WILLIAM HOPTON, Register. On 16 Apr. 1761 WILLIAM HOPTON declared, mortgage paid. Witness:
WILLIAM WILSON.

Book R-R, p. 13   HENRY FOX, planter, of the Wateree River, Cra-
27 & 28 Apr. 1756   ven Co., to HENRY KOLB, planter, of the WELCH
L & R   tract, for Ł 350 currency, 650 a. in Prince
                                     George Parish, Winyaw, Craven Co., granted him
by Gov. WILLIAM BULL on 17 Dec. 1737; bounding NE on MR. HUME; SE on
THOMAS GROOME; SW & NW on vacant land. Witnesses: GEORGE KING, EVAN (his
mark) DAVIS. Before ABRAHAM BUCKHOLTS, J.P. WILLIAM HOPTON, Register.

Book R-R, p. 16   THOMAS BOLTON, gentleman, to ANN ROBERTSON,
2 May 1755   widow, both of Charleston, for Ł 625 SC money,
Release   the N part of lot #218 in Charleston, bounding
                                     S 239-1/4 ft. on heirs of JOSEPH WRAGG (form-
erly JOHN STEEL); W 41 ft. 4 in. on Church Street; E on heirs of JOSEPH
WRAGG (formerly THOMAS MIDDLETON); N on JAMES JORDAN. Whereas THOMAS
HEADY, shipwright, & SUSANNAH his wife, by L & R dated 2 & 3 Oct. 1750,
mortgaged to THOMAS BOLTON, shopkeeper, both of Charleston, to N part of
lot #218 in Charleston; to be redeemed if HEADY paid BOLTON Ł 500 & interest on 27 Feb. 1751 (see Book H.H. p. 234-240); & whereas THOMAS & SU-
SANNAH HEADY by L & R dated 10 & 11 Oct. 1751 sold the same piece of property to EDWARD SWAN, cooper, of Charleston, subject to payment of Ł 500
& interest to BOLTON; & whereas EDWARD SWAN is dead; & neither the principal nor interest has been paid to BOLTON; & whereas BOLTON on 1 May
1755 advertised the property in the SC Gazette No. 1087; & whereas BOLTON
was highest bidder at Ł 600 & took possession; now he sells to ANN ROB-
ERTSON for the amount now due him. Witnesses: HENRY VARNOR, JOHN REM-
INGTON. Before SAMUEL BOWMAN, J.P. WILLIAM HOPTON, Register.

Book R-R, p. 19   CHARLES WRIGHT, ESQ., to SAMUEL WAINWRIGHT,
15 & 16 Mar. 1757   gentleman, both of Charleston, for Ł 1460 SC
L & R   money, 400 a., on Cow Savannah, Berkeley Co.,
                                     at head of Ashley River; being the N part of
942 a. formerly in several tracts, occupied by CHARLES WRIGHT for upwards
of 10 years; the S part of the 942 a., or 542 a. being conveyed, this
date to MARGARET GELZER, widow, of DANIEL GELZER, planter, of St. Pauls
Parish. Witnesses: CHARLES PINCKNEY, WILLIAM MAZYCK, JOHN WAGNER. Before JACOB MOTTE, J.P. WILLIAM HOPTON, Register.

Book R-R, p. 24   PETER TAYLOR, ESQ., attorney for Society for
16 & 17 Mar. 1757   the Propagation of the Gospel in Foreign Parts,
Assignment   to SAMUEL WAINWRIGHT, gentleman, of Charles-
                                     ton. Whereas by L & R & mortgage dated 26 &
27 Apr. 1745 NATHANIEL WICKHAM, ESQ., as security on his bond given the
Society in penal sum of Ł 468 British for payment of Ł 234 British, with
interest, on 27 Apr. 1746, mortgaged to the Society 657 a., part of which
was known as Cow Savannah in Ashley Barony, on S side Ashley River, in
Berkeley Co., bounding NW on the high road leading from Bacons Bridge to
Stono Chapel; S on ROBERT (Black ROBIN) JOHNSTON; E on WILLIAM WALLACE &
ALEXANDER SKENE; & whereas the greater part of said 657 a. by various
mesne conveyances has become vested in SAMUEL WAINWRIGHT, subject to
above mortgage; & whereas there is now due Ł 201:0:2 British; now for
that sum, the Society, through TAYLOR, transfer the property to WAIN-
WRIGHT. Witnesses: CHARLES PINCKNEY, WILLIAM MAZYCK. Before JACOB
MOTTE, J.P. WILLIAM HOPTON, Register.

Book R-R, 28   THOMAS FARR, gentleman, & PHEBE his wife, to
22 & 23 Mar. 1757   SUSANNAH BEE, widow, both of Charleston, for
L & R   Ł 1300 currency, lot #225 in Charleston,
                                     bounding W 105 ft. on Johnson Street; S 288
ft. on lot #240 belonging to JAMES STOBO; E 105 ft. on lot #221 belonging
to ROBERT MCKEWN; N 289-1/2 ft. on lot #224 belonging to SOLOMON LEGARE;

which lot; #225, PETER SHAW & MARTHA, his wife, by L & R dated 28 & 29 Aug. 1741 sold to THOMAS FARR (see Book W. p.120-127). Witnesses: THOMAS EVANCE, BENJAMIN YARNOLD. Before JOHN REMINGTON, J.P. WILLIAM HOPTON, Register.

Book S-S, p. 32 CHARLES WRIGHT, ESQ., to SAMUEL WAINWRIGHT,
16 Mar. 1757 gentleman, both of Charleston, in penal sum of
Bond L 1000 British to keep agreements in L & R
 dated 15 & 16 Mar. 1757. Witnesses: CHARLES
PINCKNEY, WILLIAM MAZYCK, JOHN WAGNER. Before JACOB MOTTE, J.P. WILLIAM HOPTON, Register.

Book S-S, p. 33 EDWARD BULLARD, carpenter, to BENJAMIN ADDI-
28 Feb. & 1 Mar. 1755 SON, saddler, both of Charleston, as security
L & R by Mortgage on bond of even date in penal sum of L 2000
 for payment of L 1000 currency, with interest,
on 1 Mar. 1756; 140 a. on Charleston Neck, known as The Rat Trap; bounding E on the Broad Path, or high road; S on JOHN WATKINS; W on Ashley
River; N on SAMUEL WEST. Witnesses: DAVID REYNOLDS, JOHN REMINGTON. Before WILLIAM SIMPSON, J.P. WILLIAM HOPTON, Register.

Book S-S, p. 36 RALPH BAILEY, planter, & ELIZABETH his wife,
23 & 24 Mar. 1757 to JOHN CALDER, planter, both of St. Johns
L & R Parish, Colleton Co., for L 600 currency, 2
 plantations on Edisto Island; 1 of 180 a.
bounding N on HENRY BAILEY; E & S on vacant land; W on marsh of Edisto
River; according to plat certified 19 Feb. 1705 by JOHN KENEWAY, Dep.
Sur.; the other, 44 a., bounding N on JOHN HAYNES; E on RALPH BAILEY; S
on Givens Creek & marsh; W on JOHN HAYNES Creek; according to plat &
grant dated 23 July 1712; total 224 a. Witnesses: GEORGE FICKLING, ROB-
ERT SEABROOK, JOHN BECKETT. Before SAMUEL BOWMAN, J.P. WILLIAM HOPTON,
Register.

Book S-S, p. 40 · JACOB (his mark) BERRY, planter, of SALUDA
2 & 3 Aug. 1756 (SELUDEY), eldest son & heir of THOMAS BERRY;
L & R to HENRY GALLMAN, planter, of Saxe Gotha Township, Berkeley Co.; for L 150 currency; 150 a.
in Saxe Gotha Township, Berkeley Co., granted by Lt. Gov. THOMAS BROUGH-
TON to THOMAS BERRY on 17 Sept. 1738; bounding NE on Santee River; other
sides on vacant land. Witnesses: JOHN CONRAD GEIGER, HENRY HERTEL. Before STEPHEN CRELL, J.P. WILLIAM HOPTON, Register.

Book S-S, p. 43 ELIJAH PRIOLEAU, planter, to THOMAS ELLIOTT,
25 May 1757 SR., planter, for L 200 currency, his third
Feoffment part, or division, of a certain lot in Charleston. Whereas SAMUEL PRIOLEAU, father of ELI-
JAH, owned a certain piece of land in Charleston measuring 1 a., 1 rood,
2 perches; bounding E on Friend Street; N on Broad Street; NW on lot
#307; W on marsh belonging to JOHN CROKATT; S on THOMAS ELLIOTT; & accord-
ing to plat containing lot #182 or E side of pricked line & chiefly vacant marsh to the W; & whereas by his will dated 25 Oct. 1751 he directed
that the lot should be divided into 3 equal parts & a third given to each
of his sons, PHILIP, SAMUEL, & ELIJAH; & whereas by deed of partition
tripartite dated 5 Apr. 1755 the division was made & that part marked C
on the plat was granted ELIJAH (see Book P.P. p.558-568); bounding E on
Friend Street; S on THOMAS ELLIOTT; W on JOHN CROKATT'S marsh; N on division B assigned to SAMUEL PRIOLEAU. Witnesses: JOHN PRUE, JOSEPH DAN-
DRIDGE. Before JACOB MOTTE, J.P. WILLIAM HOPTON, Register.

Book S-S, p. 45 RAWLINS LOWNDES, P.M., to JOHN CROKATT, mer-
7 June 1754 chant, of Charleston, surviving partner of
Sale firm JOHN CROKATT & KENNETH MICHIE, for L 2050
 currency, several tracts in Granville Co.,
consisting of 640 a., 1269 a., 939 a., 270 a., 78 a., 30 a., 700 a.,
150 a., 300 a., 1000 a., & 222 a. Whereas THOMAS JENYS, merchant, of
Charleston, owned 640 a. bounding S on Pocosaba Creek; W on EDWARD CROFT;
N on ISAAC MAZYCK, SR.; E on FRANCIS TONGE; which 640 a. were originally
granted to JEREMIAH MILNER; who by L & R dated 15 & 16 Apr. 1734 conveyed
to HUGH BRIAN; who by L & R dated 6 & 7 Aug. 1741 sold to THOMAS JENYS;
who also owned 939 a. on E side the Whale branch of Pocotaligo River;

bounding N on a marsh, a creek, & JOSEPH BRIAN; E & S on HILL CROFT, a
marsh, & a creek; which 939 a. were originally granted to ANTHONY MATH-
EWES; who by L & R dated 1 & 2 May 1735 sold to HUGH BRYAN; who by L & R
dated 7 & 8 Aug. 1741 sold to THOMAS JENYS; who also owned 1269 a., bounding E on a branch of Port Royal River, on small creeks & on THOMAS GRAVES;
S & W on HILL CROFT; N on JOSEPH BRIAN & HUGH BRIAN & JOSEPH MASSEY;
which 1269 a. were originally granted to ISAAC MAZYCK, SR.; who by L & R
dated 5 & 6 Nov. 1733 sold to HUGH BRIAN; who by L & R dated 7 & 8 Aug.
1741 sold to THOMAS JENYS; who also owned 270 a., bounding W on MR. LED-
LAND & head of a branch of Pocotaligo River; NE on the 1269 a.; S on ED-
WARD CROFT; which 270 a. were originally granted to JOHN TIPPER; who by
L & R dated 26 & 27 Apr. 1734 sold to HUGH BRIAN; who by L & R dated 7 &
8 Aug. 1741 sold to THOMAS JENYS; who also owned 78 a., bounding S on
marsh & creeks of Port Royal River; N on a branch & marsh of Pocosaba
Creek; which 78 a. were originally granted to ROWLAND SERJANT; who in
1730 sold to HUGH BRIAN; who by L & R dated 7 & 8 Aug. 1741 sold to THOM-
AS JENYS; who also owned 30 a., bounding on all sides on a branch & marsh-
es of Port Royal River; being part of 1300 a. originally granted to GAR-
RAT VANVELSEN; who by L & R dated 1 & 2 Nov. 1733 sold to HUGH BRIAN; who
by L & R dated 7 & 8 Aug. 1741 sold to THOMAS JENYS; who also owned 700
a., bounding E on EDWARD CROFT; S & W on marsh of Pocosaba Creek; N on
JOHN CROFT; which 700 a. were originally granted to EDWARD CROFT; who by
L & R dated 1 & 2 Oct. 1733 sold to HUGH BRIAN; who by L & R dated 7 & 8
Aug. 1741 sold to THOMAS JENYS; who also owned 300 a. on E side Coosa River; bounding E on CAPT. JOHN CROFT; N on JOSEPH BRIAN; W on GEORGE PAWLEY;
which 300 a. were originally granted to HILL CROFT; who by L & R dated 24
& 25 Feb. 1724 sold to RICHARD LUDLAM; who bequeathed the tract to the
Society for the Propagation of the Gospel in Foreign parts; which Society,
by its attorneys, by L & R dated 1 & 2 Feb. 1736 sold to HUGH BRIAN; who
by L & R dated 7 & 8 Aug. 1741 sold to THOMAS JENYS; who also owned 1000
a. near Roses Island; on Port Royal River, being a point of Pocosaba Neck;
which 1000 a. were sold by ALEXANDER TRENCH, (as attorney for JOHN BAYLY
of Ballinaclough, Co. of Tipperary, Ireland, son & heir of JOHN BAYLY) by
L & R dated 9 & 10 Feb. 1729 to FRANCIS YONGE; who with LYDIA his wife by
L & R dated 9 & 10 May 1733 sold to HUGH BRIAN; who, by L & R dated 7 &
8 Aug. 1741 sold to THOMAS JENYS; who also owned the S half of a tract of
300 a. on W side of Tomatly Creek; bounding N on JOHN STONE; S on
CHARLES SHARP; W on MAURICE HARVEY; which 300 a. were originally granted
JOSEPH MASSEY; who with REBECCA his wife, by L & R dated Apr. 1734 sold
to HUGH BRIAN; who by L & R dated 7 & 8 Aug. 1741 sold to THOMAS JENYS;
who also owned 222 a. on S side Combee River; bounding S on COL. JOSEPH
BLAKE & a branch of Combee River; N & E on said river; W on another
branch of said river; which 222 a. were originally granted to ANDREW
ALLEN; whose son & heir JOHN ALLEN, by L & R dated 25 & 26 July 1741 sold
to HUGH BRIAN; who by L & R dated 7 & 8 Aug. 1741 sold to THOMAS JENYS; &
whereas THOMAS JENYS on 13 Mar. 1743 gave bond to JOHN CROKATT & KENNETH
MICKIE in penal sum of Ł 7860 for payment of Ł 3930 currency on 12 July
1744; & whereas THOMAS JENYS died before making payment, & by will had
appointed STEPHEN BEDON, JR., PAUL JENYS, & BRANFIELD EVANS his executors; & whereas CROKATT & MICKIE obtained a judgment against said executors for the amount due them, & costs; & a writ of fieri facias was issued by JOHN LINING, C.J., commanding the P.M. to obtain this amount from
the estate; & the P.M. offered the above named tracts for sale at public
auction, for which JOHN CROKATT was highest bidder; now the 11 tracts are
conveyed to him. Witnesses: DAVID RHIND, JAMES MICKIE. Before JOHN RAT-
TRAY, J.P. WILLIAM HOPTON, Register.

Book S-S, p. 52   ALEXANDER GORDON, son, devisee, & only acting
22 & 23 July 1755   executor of will of ALEXANDER GORDON, ESQ.; &
L & R   FRANCES CHARLOTTE GORDON, spinster, daughter
                         & devisee in will of said ALEXANDER GORDON,
ESQ.; of 1st part; to EGERTON LEIGH, ESQ.; all of Charleston; for Ł 1400
currency, parts of the lots marked H & G in the plan of Ansonburgh.
Whereas the Rt. Hon. Lord GEORGE ANSON, by his attorney BENJAMIN WHITAKER,
of Charleston, by deed of feoffment dated 28 Mar. 1746 conveyed to ALEX-
ANDER GORDON a lot containing 1 a., 2 roods, 20 perches marked H on the
plat of the land now called Ansonbourgh, also right of passage through
the most convenient streets to a landing place on a creek; & whereas
GEORGE HUNTER, by deed of feoffment dated 7 July 1747 conveyed to ALEX-
ANDER GORDON, part of a lot marked G on same plat, bounding W on another

part of lot G at the distance of 410 ft. from the front of said lot on the Broad Road & ranges with the E bounds of LUKE STOUTENBOUGH'S lot; N on JOSEPH WRAGG; E on a marsh (now a pond); S on part of lot H belonging to ALEXANDER GORDON; also right of passage through streets; & whereas ALEXANDER GORDON by will dated 22 Aug. 1754 bequeathed equally to his son ALEXANDER, & to his daughter, FRANCES CHARLOTTE, the said 2 adjacent lots making 1 lot of 2 a., with the house thereon, & appointed said ALEXANDER GORDON & the Hon. HECTOR BERENGER DE BEAUFAIN, his executors; & whereas DE BEAUFAIN renounced the execution; & whereas ALEXANDER & FRANCES CHARLOTTE decided to sell the lots for the benefit of their father's creditors; now they sell the 2 a. to EGERTON LEIGH. Witnesses: SAMUEL CARDY, GEORGE BARKSDALE. Before PETER LEIGH, J.P. WILLIAM HOPTON, Register.

Book S-S, p. 57
9 & 10 Mar. 1757
L & R

ARCHIBALD JOHNSTON, planter, to JOSIAS ALSTON, planter, for Ł 850 currency, 200 a. on Waccamaw Neck Long Bay; 100 a. being part of a tract surveyed by GEORGE BENISON; the other 100 a. being called Woolfs Tract, also part of BENISON'S tract. Witnesses: JOSEPH ALLSTON, ROBERT GIBB. Before CHARLES LEWIS, J.P. WILLIAM HOPTON, Register.

Book S-S, p. 60
8 July 1757
Sale

CHARLES LESSLIE, planter, to WILLIAM FLUD, for Ł 200 currency, 500 a. in Craven Co., bounding NE on Santee River; NW on JOHN HEARNE, according to plat dated 1707 & grant dated 1 June 1709, & deed of gift from his father, CHARLES LESSLIE, recorded 21 Oct. 1728 in Book G. fol. 384-385. Witnesses: WILLIAM MCKELVEY, THOMAS MELL, JR. Before JOHN TROUP, J.P. WILLIAM HOPTON, Regsiter.

Book S-S, p. 62
13 & 14 May 1756
L & R

WILLIAM CRIPSS, surgeon, of London, by his attorneys, THOMAS SHUBRICK & DANIEL CRAWFORD; to JOHN MURRAY, of Georgetown, Winyaw, for Ł 400 SC money, lot #87 in Georgetown, bounding NE 100 ft. on Prince Street; SE on lot #68; SW 217.9 ft. on lots #37 & #38; NW on lot #66. Witnesses: SAMUEL PHILLIPS, ANDREW MARR. Before JACOB MOTTE, J.P. WILLIAM HOPTON, Register.

Book S-S, p. 66
18 & 19 Feb. 1757
L & R

JOHN GEORGE CLEAS, tailor, to FELIX LONG, victualler, both of Charleston, for Ł 25 currency, 50 a. on Indian Field Swamp, in Berkeley Co., bounding SE on PHILIP HOLB & vacant land; NW on WILLIAM BRITCHES & vacant land; SW on JOHN ABERLEY; NE on vacant land. Witnesses: JACOB WARLEY, ANTHONY DEANS. Before ALEXANDER STEWART, J.P. WILLIAM HOPTON, Register.

Book S-S, p. 69
10 & 11 Nov. 1755
L & R

MICHAEL SWARTZ, planter, to ROBERT GOWDIE, Indian trader, for Ł 100 currency, 200 a. on N side Saludie River, bounding SW & NW on the river; NE & SE on vacant land; as granted by Gov. JAMES GLEN on 11 Oct. 1755 to said MICHAEL SWARTZ. Witnesses: GEORGE BRAYTON, CORNELIUS BURCHMEYER. Before JOHN HAMILTON, J.P. WILLIAM HOPTON, Register.

Book S-S, p. 72
9 & 10 Aug. 1756
L & R

ANTHOHY MATHEWES, ESQ., & ANN his wife, to GEORGE SHEED, gentleman, both of Charleston, for Ł 1700 currency, 100 a. in Berkeley Co., bounding S on Newton Creek; W on COL. ARTHUR HALL; E on JOHN WILKINS; N on LAMBRIGHT & WILLIAM WILKINS; which land was granted in May 1699 by the Lords Proprs. to CHRISTOPHER JARRARD, & after several mesne conveyances became the property of ANTHONY MATHEWES. Witnesses: STEPHEN BULL, GEORGE ROUPELL. Before DOUGAL CAMPBELL, J.P. WILLIAM CAMPBELL, Register.

Book S-S, p. 76
21 July 1757
Feoffment

EGERTON LEIGH, ESQ., & MARTHA his wife, to GEORGE SEAMAN, ESQ., both of Charleston; for Ł 800 SC money, 2 lots in Colleton Square, marked E & F on plat; bounding E on Bay Street; N on lot G belonging to heirs of THOMAS ELLERY; W on lot H belonging to JOHN MCKENZIE; S on Hunter Street; also right of passage through convenient streets. Witnesses: JAMES HUNTER, JR., ARCHIBALD BULLOCH. Before

JOHN REMINGTON, J.P. WILLIAM HOPTON, Register.

Book S-S, p. 77   WILLIAM GREEN, planter, to RICHARD GREEN,
30 & 31 July 1754   planter, both of Prince George Parish, Craven
L & R   Co., for ₺ 200 currency, 500 a. on N side
                         Black River in Craven Co., bounding NW on WIL-
LIAM SAXBY; NE on JOHN LEWIS; SE on FLOOD & GLEN; which tract was granted
24 May 1734 by Gov. ROBERT JOHNSON to JOHN GREEN; who bequeathed to RICH-
ARD GREEN; but as the will does not appear authentic or good in law, WIL-
LIAM GREEN as eldest son & heir of JOHN GREEN, conveys to his brother
RICHARD. Witnesses: JOSEPH DUBOURDIEU, MARY DUBOURDIEU. Before THOMAS
BLYTHE, J.P. WILLIAM HOPTON, Register.

Book S-S, p. 80   JACOB EAGNER, planter, of Saxe Gotha Township,
1 July 1757   to WILLIAM BAKER, planter, of same place, as
Mortgages   security on bond of even date in penal sum of
                         ₺ 800 for payment of ₺ 400 currency, with in-
terest, on 1 July 1758; 250 a. in Saxe Gotha Township, bounding NE on
Santee River; SE on PHILIP POOL; also 1 chestnut brown stallion branded
IW; 1 yellow bay gelding branded HM; 1 bay mare branded IE; 1 brown mare
with a blase branded _____ ; 1 black pacing mare branded _____ . Witnesses: STEPHEN CRELL, HENRY GALLMAN. Before JOHN PEARSON, J.P. Note: See
Bk. T.T. p. 515 for assignment of this mortgage to HANS ULRICH BACHMAN
with receipt showing full satisfaction. WILLIAM HOPTON, Register.

Book S-S, p. 81   STEPHEN CRELL, gentleman, & JOHANNA his wife,
29 & 30 June 1757   to JACOB EAGNER, planter, both of Berkeley
L & R   Co., for ₺ 700 currency, 250 a. within the
                         limits of Saxe Gotha Township; bounding NE on
Santee River; SE on PHILIP POOL (formerly JOSEPH CRELL); SW on vacant
land; NW on ANTHONY STEG (formerly RODOLF COPLER); as granted 16 Sept.
1738 by WILLIAM BULL to STEPHEN CRELL. Witnesses: WILLIAM BAKER, HENRY
GALLMAN. Before JOHN PEARSON, J.P. WILLIAM HOPTON, Register.

Book S-S, p. 84   JOHN MYRICK, planter, of Craven Co., SC, to
20 & 21 July 1757   SAMUEL THOMPSON, planter, of Colony of Va.,
L & R   for ₺ 250 SC money, 250 a. on N side Santee
                         River; bounding NW on heirs of PHILIP RAI-
FORD, SR., & vacant land; SE on part of 450 a. belonging to PHILIP RAI-
FORD; other sides on vacant land. . Whereas Lt. Gov. WILLIAM BULL on 7
Sept. 1742 granted PHILIP RAIFORD, SR., 450 a. on N side Santee River;
which he gave to his eldest son, PHILIP RAIFORD, on condition that he
convey to his brother, WILLIAM, 200 a.; which he did by L & R dated 24 &
25 Dec. 1752; the remaining 250 a. of which he & his wife JUDAH sold for
₺ 250 to JOHN MYRICK by L & R dated 20 & 21 Sept. 1757; now MYRICK sells
to THOMPSON. Witnesses: JOHN GEORGE LAPP, CLEMENTS FROM. Before JOHN
PEARSON, J.P. WILLIAM HOPTON, Register.

Book S-S, p. 88   WILLIAM ELLIOTT, of St. Helena, SC; WILLIAM
12 & 13 May 1757   BUTLER, gentleman, of Ga.; & ELIZABETH BUTLER,
L & R   otherwise ELLIOTT, wife of said WILLIAM BUT-
                         LER; of 1st part; to THOMAS ELLIOTT the elder,
gentleman, of St. Pauls Parish, SC; for ₺ 4700 SC money, 570 a. in St.
Pauls Parish, Colleton Co., in 4 tracts; 1 of 300 a. with the house in
which ELISHA BUTLER & ELIZABETH his wife lived, bounding E on marsh
granted to JEREMIAH MILES; S on THOMAS ELLIOTT; W on 100 a. formerly belonging to RALPH EMMES, now 1 of the 4 tracts; N on 1 of the tracts formerly belonging to STEPHEN ELLIOTT; 1 of 70 a. of marshy land; bounding E
on N branch Stono River; W on said 300 a.; 1 of 100 a. bounding NE on
said 300 a.; W on FREDERICK GRIMKE; S on THOMAS ELLIOTT; N on land formerly belonging to STEPHEN ELLIOTT; 1 of 100 a., bounding NE on JOHN DRAY-
TON; NW & S on land formerly belonging to STEPHEN ELLIOTT; E on head of N
branch Stono River. Whereas ELIZABETH BUTLER, formerly wife of ELISHA
BUTLER, gentleman, of Ga., jointly with her husband on 27 Oct. 1738, for
love & affection, give to her son, WILLIAM ELLIOTT, & his heirs, the
plantation of 570 a. on which she & ELISHA then dwelt; & in default of
his having children, then the remainder to ELIZABETH BUTLER (otherwise
ELLIOTT) & MARY ELLIOTT, sisters of said WILLIAM ELLIOTT & whereas MARY
ELLIOTT died a minor, unmarried, & ELIZABETH has sole title to the remainder should WILLIAM die without issue; & whereas WILLIAM BUTLER &

ELIZABETH his wife have agreed to join with WILLIAM ELLIOTT in the sale of the lands to THOMAS ELLIOTT; now the sale is completed. WILLIAM ELLIOTT for Ł 300 SC money, also conveys to THOMAS ELLIOTT, 100 a. being half of 200 a. in St. Pauls Parish, bounding E on THOMAS LAWS ELLIOTT; S & W on THOMAS ELLIOTT; N on STEPHEN NICHOLLS (now ISAAC NICHOLLS). Witnesses: JAMES MACKY, THOMAS GOLDSMITH, JOSEPH BUTLER, JR. Before JAMES PARSONS, J.P. WILLIAM HOPTON, Register.

Book S-S, p. 95
30 June 1757
Release

WILLIAM SPENCER, planter, of Colleton Co., (1 of the sons & devisees of will of WILLIAM SPENCER, the elder, planter, of James Island, Berkeley Co.); & ELIZABETH his wife, to HENRY SAMWAYS, planter, of Berkeley Co., for Ł 812:10:0 currency, 132 a. on W end of James Island, bounding E on ROBERT RIVERS; S on a creek; W on DAVID TAYLOR; N on the Hollowing Island Creek. Whereas the Lords Proprs. on 9 Nov. 1698 granted JOHN ELLIS the younger, 170 a. on W end of James Island; of which land he & his wife, JUDITH, by L & R dated 28 & 29 Jan. 1733 sold 132 a. to WILLIAM SPENCER the elder; who by will dated 19 Feb. 1750 bequeathed to his son WILLIAM; who now sells to SAMWAYS. Witnesses: JOHN RICE, THOMAS LAMBOLL. Before ROBERT PRINGLE, J.P. WILLIAM HOPTON, Register.

Book S-S, p. 99
1 Sept. 1752
Sale

ROBERT MCMURDY, vintner, of Charleston, to GEORGE GALPHIN, Indian trader, for Ł 1000 currency, 400 a. in Granville Co., bounding SE on Condes Cowpen; NE on vacant land; NW on Town Creek; SW on Savannah River; according to plat & grant from Gov. JAMES GLEN dated 6 June 1747. Witnesses: JOHN MCQUEEN, merchant, BENJAMIN FULLER. Before JAMES PARSONS, J.P. WILLIAM HOPTON, Register.

Book S-S, p. 100
7 Feb. 1757
Sale

CHARLES LOWNDES, P.M., to MARY BRYAN, of Prince William Parish, at public auction, for Ł 2000 currency, 2 adjoining tracts of 72 a. & 784 a.; total 856 a. Whereas HUGH BRYAN, planter, of Granville Co., owned 72 a., part of 500 a., bounding E on head of a creek of Pocotaligo River; N on BARNABY BULL; W on JAMES ST. JOHN; S on the remainder of said 500 a. conveyed to HUGH BRYAN by STEPHEN BULL, JR., & ELIZABETH his wife by L & R dated 10 & 11 June 1741; & whereas HUGH BRYAN also owned 784 a. in Granville Co., bounding SE on Pocotaligo River & marsh; NE on CAPT. EDMUND BELLINGER'S Barony; NW on the Barony; & SW on CAPT. JOHN BULL, JAMES ST. JOHN, COL. TRENCH, & MR. BLAND; & whereas after the death of HUGH BRYAN, WILLIAM SIMPSON & ELIZABETH his wife (administratrix of EDMOND BLELINGER) & WILLIAM BULL (administrator of BARNABY BULL, planter) recovered a judgment against MARY BRYAN, executrix, & JOHN SMITH, executor, of will of HUGH BRYAN, for Ł 3484 currency, & costs, & a writ of fieri facias was issued by PETER LEIGH, C.J., commanding the P.M. to levy this amount against HUGH BRYAN'S estate; & whereas the P.M. seized the 2 tracts of land & offered them for sale at public auction; now they are conveyed to MARY BRYAN, the highest bidder. Witnesses: WILLIAM BRISBANE, WILLIAM READ. Before ROBERT WILLIAMS, J.P. WILLIAM HOPTON, Register.

Book S-S, p. 103
1 June 1757
Release of part of
Mortgage

HENRY PERONNEAU, merchant, of Charleston, executor of will of his father HENRY PERONNEAU, acknowledges receipt of Ł 608 currency from DAVID MONGIN, & releases claim to 1 a., 2 roods in Ansonburgh, near Charleston, marked C on the plan of lands of GEORGE ANSON, now Lord ANSON; & to the half of a lot in Ansonburgh containing 1 a., marked R on said plat. (See Book H.H. p. 110-114). Witness: THOMAS BEE. Before JAMES PARSONS, J.P. WILLIAM HOPTON, Register.

Book S-S, p. 103
1 & 2 Mar. 1757
L & R

DANIEL RAVENEL, ESQ., of St. Johns Parish, Berkeley Co., & SARAH his wife, to DAVID GRAEME, attorney, of Charleston, for Ł 1000 currency, 2000 a., English measure, in Berkeley Co., originally granted to PETER DE ST. JULIEN by SIR NATHANIEL BROUGHTON & the Lords Proprs.; also 302 a. in Berkeley Co., originally granted to RENE RICHBURG who sold to PETER DE ST. JULIEN; also 500 a. on N side Santee River, Craven Co., granted 5 July 1740 by Lt. Gov. WILLIAM

BULL to PETER DE ST. JULIEN; also 500 a. called Soho in Craven Co., lately belonging to PETER DE ST. JULIEN; also 1000 a. in Berkeley Co., called
Wantoot, originally granted to PETER DE ST. JULIEN; also 290 a. in Berkeley Co., part of 580 a. adjoining Wantoot, originally granted PETER DE
ST. JULIEN; also 300 a., the W half of 600 a. in Craven Co. granted to
PETER DE ST. JULIEN, to be divided from remaining 300 a. by a N-S line,
devised by PETER DE ST. JULIEN to his son ALEXANDER; also the E part of
215 a., part of 550 a. in Berkeley Co., sold to PETER DE ST. JULIEN by
MARY LAROCHES, to be divided from the residue of said 215 a. by the new
causeway & a right line from thence produced until it shall intersect the
S boundary line of said 290 a.; all of which plantations by deed of par-
tition between DANIEL RAVENEL & SARAH his wife, of 1 part & WILLIAM
MOULTRIE, ESQ., of St. Johns Parish, Berkeley Co., & ELIZABETH DEMARIS
his wife, of other part, dated 13 Jan. last, were assigned to DANIEL &
SARAH RAVENEL, in right of SARAH (SARAH RAVENEL & ELIZABETH DEMARIS MOUL-
TRIE being co-heiresses of their brother BENJAMIN DE ST. JULIEN of St.
Johns Parish); also 500 a., English measure, granted 26 Oct. 1708 by JOHN,
Lord Granville, Palatine, & the Lords Proprs., to GEORGE CHEEL; bounding
W on THOMAS BARKER; S & E on vacant land; N on Santee River. Witnesses:
ISAAC MAZYCK, WILLIAM MOULTRIE. Before PETER MANIGAULT, J.P. WILLIAM
HOPTON, Register.

Book S-S, p. 109   DAVID GRAEME, attorney, of Charleston, recon-
3 & 4 Mar. 1757   veys to DANIEL RAVENEL, ESQ., of St. Johns
L & R   Parish, Berkeley Co., for ₤ 1000 currency, all
                        the tracts of land mentioned on p. 103. Wit-
nesses: THOMAS YEOMANS, GEORGE JACKSON. Before GEORGE SAXBY, J.P. WIL-
LIAM HOPTON, Register.

Book S-S, p. 114   ALEXANDER GORDON, gentleman, only son & heir
9 Sept. 1757   of ALEXANDER GORDON, ESQ., to EGERTON LEIGH,
Feoffment   ESQ., both of Charleston, for ₤ 70 currency,
                        part of lots marked E & F on the plan of Anson-
burgh; 50 ft. X 101 ft.; bounding N on lane leading from high road to lot
H belonging to EGERTON LEIGH (formerly to ALEXANDER GORDON, the father);
E on part of lot H belonging to LUKE STOUTENBURGH; S on part of lot E be-
longing to ELISHA BRUNETT; W on parts of lots E & F. Witness: JAMES HUN-
TER, JR. Before JOHN TROUPE, J.P. WILLIAM HOPTON, Register.

Book S-S, p. 115   WILLIAM PALMER, planter, & ANN his wife, to
1 & 2 July 1748   JONATHAN BRYAN, planter, both of Granville Co.,
L & R   for ₤ 3240 currency, 1059-3/4 a. on Stoney
                        Creek, a branch of Pocotaligo River, in Prince
William Parish, Granville Co., the W part being part of 1000 a. which
WILLIAM PALMER purchased from ELIZABETH BELLINGER & GEORGE BELLINGER; the
E part being part of the 1000 a. devised to WILLIAM PALMER by EDMUND BEL-
LINGER; bounding E on JAMES DEVEAUX; S on JONATHAN BRYAN; W on ANDREW
DEVEAUX, JR. (formerly estate of EDMUND BELLINGER); N on ANDREW DEVEAUX,
SR. (formerly devised by EDMUND BELLINGER to GEORGE BELLINGER & WILLIAM
PALMER); according to plat by HUGH BRYAN, Dep. Sur. Whereas Landgrave
EDMUND BELLINGER, of Berkeley Co., owned several large tracts of land &
by will dated 21 Feb. 1739 gave his nephew, WILLIAM PALMER, 1000 a., &
gave his son, GEORGE BELLINGER, 1000 a., & appointed his wife, ELIZABETH
sole executrix; & whereas by L & R dated 14 & 15 Feb. 1745 ELIZABETH &
GEORGE BELLINGER sold WILLIAM PALMER 1000 a. in Granville Co., bounding
E on said WILLIAM PALMER; SW on JONATHAN BRYAN; NE on JOHN BULL; NW on
EDMUND BELLINGER; now PALMER sells part of his land to BRYAN. Witnesses:
JAMES WILLIAMS, JACOB TURNER. Before ROBERT WILLIAMS, J.P. WILLIAM
HOPTON, Register. Plat of 1059-3/4 a. showing 910 a. sold to WILLIAM
SIMMONS; 52 a. sold to JOHN SMITH; 97-1/2 a. reserved to JONATHAN BRYAN.
The plat of 1059-3/4 by HUGH BRYAN, Dep. Sur., dated 2 Dec. 1747 shows
form & marks as surveyed on Landgrave EDMUND BELLINGERS patent lands,
lately in possession of MAJ. WILLIAM PALMER & JAMES DIXSEE, located on
Stoney Creek, a branch of Pocotaligo River, Prince William Parish, Granville Co., bounding SW on JONATHAN BRYAN; NW on CAPT. ANDREW DEVEAUX; NE
on ANDREW DEVEAUX, SR.; SE on JAMES DEVEAUX. The 59 a. were bought first
from JAMES DIXSEE but title included by PALMER. On 7 Jan. 1747/8 ELIZA-
BETH BELLINGER ELLIOTT (signed also by THOMAS ELLIOTT) certified that the
1059-3/4 a. were laid out to PALMER by HUGH BRYAN by her order, being
part of legacies to WILLIAM PALMER & GEORGE BELLINGER by will of EDMUND

BELLINGER the second Landgrave.

Book S-S, p. 120
21 & 22 Sept. 1757
L & R

JONATHAN BRYAN, ESQ., & MARY his wife, of District of Savannah, Ga., to ANDREW FESCH, ESQ., & PETER GUINAND, ESQ., both of Charleston, for ₤ 4200 SC money, 700 a. in Granville Co.,
bounding N on Stoney Creek, & on·CAPT. EDMUND BELLINGER'S Barony; SE on part of 3140 a. formerly belonging to HUGH BRYAN; W on Pocotaligo River; also 300 a. in Granville Co., bounding W on marsh of Pocotaligo River; N on JONATHAN BRYAN; E & S on part of the 3140 a.; also 97-3/4 a., on Stoney Creek, part of 1059-3/4 a. sold by WILLIAM PALMER & ANN, his wife, to JONATHAN BRYAN, bounding E on JAMES DEVEAUX; S on JONATHAN BRYAN; W on ANDREW DEVEAUX, JR. (formerly estate of EDMUND BELLINGER); N on parts of tracts devised by EDMUND BELLINGER to his son GEORGE BELLINGER & his nephew WILLIAM PALMER. Whereas HUGH BRYAN, planter, of St. Helena, Granville Co., & CATHERINE his wife, by L & R dated 7 & 8 July 1736 sold JONATHAN BRYAN, for ₤ 1400 currency, 700 a., part of 3140 a. granted to JOSEPH BRYAN & HUGH BRYAN in jointenancy (HUGH surviving JOSEPH & becoming sole owner); & whereas HUGH BRYAN, by L & R dated 25 & 26 Mar. 1743, for ₤ 1200 currency, sold JONATHAN BRYAN 300 a., part of the 3140 a. granted JOSEPH & HUGH BRYAN in jointenancy; & whereas by L & R dated 1 & 2 July 1748 WILLIAM PALMER & ANN his wife, for ₤ 3240 currency, sold JONATHAN BRYAN 1059-3/4 a. on Stoney Creek, the W part of which was a part of the 1000 a. which WILLIAM PALMER purchased from ELIZABETH BELLINGER & GEORGE BELLINGER; the E part being part of the 1000 a. devised to WILLIAM PALMER by his uncle EDMUND BELLINGER; now JONATHAN BRYAN sells to FESCH & GUINAND. Witnesses: ELIZABETH SMITH, JOHN SMITH, CHARLES PRYCE, WILLIAM BUCHANAN. Before STEPHEN BULL, J.P. WILLIAM HOPTON, Register.

Book S-S, p. 126
17 & 18 Dec. 1755
L & R

The Rev. MR. ALEXANDER GARDEN, of St. Philips Parish, Charleston, to JONATHAN BADGER, joiner, of Charleston, for ₤ 1100 currency, part of lot #115 in Charleston, bounding N 66 ft.
on Tradd Street, E 100 ft. on PATTUREAU; S on THOMAS HOLTON; W on JOHN SMITH; with the tenement, etc., thereon. Witnesses: THOMAS LAMBOLL, THOMAS LAMBOLL, JR. Before PETER MANIGAULT, J.P. WILLIAM HOPTON, Register.

Book S-S, p. 130
11 & 12 Oct. 1757
L & R

GIBBON WRIGHT, spinster, only daughter of ROBERT WRIGHT, ESQ., by GIBBON his wife, who was only daughter of JOHN CAWOOD; to JOHN BARNWELL, ESQ., both of SC, for ₤ 710 SC money,
250 a. on Port Royal Island, bounding N on heirs of TWEEDIE SOMERVILLE (formerly JAMES PATERSON); W on Port Royal River; S on JACOB BOND (formerly THOMAS BRYAN); E on heirs of MR. WHITMARSH. Whereas the Lords Proprs. on 11 May 1708 granted GEORGE DUCAT 250 a. in Granville Co.; & whereas GEORGE DUCAT & MARTHA his wife, on 3 June 1725 sold the tract to JOHN CAWOOD; who by will dated 7 Oct. 1725 bequeathed to his daughter GIBBON CAWOOD all the residue of his real & personal estate; & whereas she married ROBERT WRIGHT, & they had 1 child, GIBBON, sole heir of her mother; now she sells to BARNWELL. Witnesses: JOHN RATTRAY, JOHN HUME. Before DAVID GRAEME, J.P. WILLIAM HOPTON, Register.

Book S-S, p. 134
12 & 13 Aug. 1757
L & R

GEORGE CUTHBERT, planter, of St. Helena & MARY his wife, to PHILIP BOX, of Beaufort, Port Royal, for ₤ 666:6:8 SC money, his undivided third part of 500 a. in Granville Co., bounding W on marshes, creeks, & sands separating it from a small island; N on Cowan's Creek; other sides on vacant land. Whereas the Lords Proprs. on 14 May 1706 granted JOHN BARNWELL, ESQ., 500 a. in Granville Co.; which by will dated 4 May 1724 he bequeathed to his daughter MARY; who married PAUL GRIMBALL, planter, of Edisto Island; & whereas they had 3 daughters, MARY, party hereto, & CATHERINE, wife of DAVID ADAMS, & ELZIABETH, wife of WILLIAM BAYNARD, both planters, of Edisto; & whereas by the death of their mother, the 3 daughters became co-parceners in fee in the estate; now MARY by & with the advice & consent of her husband, sells her share to PHILIP BOX. Witnesses: FRANCIS STUART, WILLIAM LIVINGSTON. Before JOHN RATTRAY, J.P. WILLIAM HOPTON, Register.

Book S-S, p. 138

PHILIP BOX, of Beaufort, Port Royal, reconveys

15 & 16 Aug. 1757   to GEORGE CUTHBERT, planter, of St. Helena,
L & R   for Ł 666:6:8 currency, the undivided third
                         part of 500 a. mentioned on p. 134. Witness-
es: FRANCIS STUART, JOHN RATTRAY. Before JAMES GRINDLAY, J.P. WILLIAM
HOPTON, Register.

Book S-S, p. 140   JOHN PEARSON, Dep. Sur., executor of will of
28 & 29 Dec. 1756   THOMAS WALLEXELLSON, blacksmith; & attorney
L & R   for PATRICK BROWN & THOMAS CORKER, executors
                         of will of THOMAS BROWN, Indian trader, to
JOHN TAYLOR, planter; all of Craven Co., for Ł 75 Va. money, paid by TAY-
LOR to PEARSON on account of CORKER, surviving executor of THOMAS BROWN;
& to discharge part of a bond & mortgage; 300 a. in Craven Co., bounding
W on Santee River, opposite Saxe Gotha Township; N on GILBERT GIBSON & on
vacant land; E on vacant land; S on JOHN FRAZER & JAMES DENLY. Whereas
on 12 Dec. 1746 Gov. JAMES GLEN granted THOMAS WALLEXELLSON 300 a. in
Craven Co.; & whereas he, by will dated 27 Dec. 1751, approved by Gov.
JAMES GLEN, appointed JOHN PEARSON his sole executor, desiring first that
all his debts be paid & the rest equally divided amongst the legatees
named therein; & whereas THOMAS WALLEXELLSON on 12 July 1746 gave bond to
PATRICK BROWN, THOMAS CORKER, & GEORGE HAIG, executors of THOMAS BROWN,
in penal sum of Ł 641:15:0 for payment of Ł 320:17:6 currency, with interest, on 12 Jan. then next, & for security delivered to BROWN, CROKER,
& HAIG, 1 Negro man, 40 head neat cattle, 100 hogs, 9 horses & mares &
said 300 a. of land (the impost of his real & personal estate), which
mortgage was recorded 23 Sept. 1748; & whereas BROWN & CORKER, surviving
executors, although the money had not been paid, surrendered to PEARSON
(for the uses of WALLEXELLSON'S will) all the mortgage & their interest
in the premises, in order that PEARSON might sell the premises to pay the
bond; now PEARSON sells the property at public auction to JOHN TAYLOR.
Witnesses: JOHN THOMAS, MARTHA BELL, MARY THOMAS. Before JOHN HAMELTON,
J.P. WILLIAM HOPTON, Register.

Book S-S, p. 146   SARAH BROWN, widow, of Berkeley Co., 1 of the
10 & 11 June 1755   daughters & devisees of will of JOSEPH ELLIOTT,
L & R   planter, of Colleton Co., who was 1 of the
                         sons of THOMAS ELLIOTT the elder, planter, of
Berkeley Co., & 1 of the devisees of his will; of 1st part; to MARY ANN
ROSE, wife of FRANCIS ROSE, planter, of Berkeley Co., & sister of SARAH
BROWN; of other part; MARY ANN & SARAH being, by will of their father JO-
SEPH ELLIOTT, joint owners as tenants in common of 664 a. at PonPon in
Colleton Co., now for sisterly love & affection, SARAH conveys her undi-
vided half share to MARY ANN. Witnesses: JEREMIAH SAVAGE, gentleman,
THOMAS ELLIOTT. Before JAMES PARSONS, J.P. WILLIAM HOPTON, Register.

Book S-S, p. 149   WILLIAM BRANFORD, planter, of Berkeley Co., &
22 & 23 May 1754   ELIZABETH his wife (lately ELIZABETH SAVAGE, 1
L & R in Trust   of the devisees of her uncle, BENJAMIN SAVAGE,
                         merchant, of Charleston), to FRANCIS ROSE &
JOHN MILES, planters, of Berkeley Co., as trustees, parts of lots #87 &
#88 in Tradd Street, Charleston. Whereas BENJAMIN SAVAGE owned parts of
2 lots in Charleston, & by his will dated 26 Apr. 1750, bequeathed, among
other things, to ELIZABETH SAVAGE his houses & ground in Charleston which
he had purchased from JOHN ALLEN; & whereas, after his death ELIZABETH
took possession & afterwards married WILLIAM BRANFORD, & they had 2
daughters, ELIZABETH & ANN; now WILLIAM & ELIZABETH convey to ROSE &
MILES, as trustees, for them during their lives, & afterwards as trustees
for the 2 infants, ELIZABETH & ANN, the parts of lots 87 & 88 bounding N
on DANIEL BOURGET; W on ROBERT PRINGLE; S 73 ft. on Tradd Street; E 195
ft. on Old Church Street; with provisoes as to succession. Witnesses:
SAMUEL PERONNEAU, THOMAS LAMBOLL. Before JACOB MOTTE, J.P. WILLIAM HOP-
TON, Register.

Book S-S, p. 154   EDMUND BARNES, planter, & ELIZABETH his wife,
4 & 5 Oct. 1757   to BENJAMIN GARDEN, gentleman, both of Gran-
L & R   ville Co., for Ł 24 currency, 400 a. in Gran-
                         ville Co. Whereas EDWARD LOWREY recovered a
judgment against RICHARD LAMBTON, administrator of will of ROBERT THORPE,
merchant, of Port Royal, for Ł 11,438 & costs, & a writ of fieri facias
was issued on 27 Feb. 1753 by CHARLES PINCKNEY, C.J., directing the P.M.

to seize THORPE'S estate, & in consequence 6323 a. in Granville Co., after being put up at public auction remained unsold for want of purchases; & whereas on 19 Dec. 1754 CHARLES LOWNDES, the P.M., sold EDMUND BARNES 500 a., part of the 6323 a., bounding SE on THOMAS MIDDLETON; NE on JAMES HARTLEY; other sides on ROBERT THORPE; also another 500 a., part of same 6323 a., bounding NE on JAMES HARTLEY; other sides on ROBERT THORPE; now BARNES sells 400 a. of the second 500 a., to GARDEN, as shown on plat. Witnesses: WILLIAM WYATT, JAMES WILLKYE. Before JACOB MOTTE, J.P. WILLIAM HOPTON, Register. Plat shows 400 a. bounding NE on JAMES HARTLEY; SE & SW THOMAS MIDDLETON; NW on EDMUND BARNES.

Book S-S, p. 158
10 & 11 Sept. 1745
L & R

JAMES WITHERS, bricklayer; RICE PRICE, vintner; both of Charleston; & JAMES MACKPHERSON, planter, of Saltketchers; executors of will of JAMES THOMSON, butcher, of Charleston; of 1st part; to PATRICK BROWN, Indian trader, of Charleston; for L 2300 SC money, 6 a. on Charleston Neck. Whereas JOSEPH SHUTE & ANNA his wife, & ISABELL KIMBERLY, by L & R dated 16 & 17 May 1737, sold JAMES THOMSON 6 a. on Charleston Neck, in St. Philips Parish, Berkeley Co., bounding E on the Broad Path leading to Charleston; S on the road to the Free School; W on the Free School land; N on JOSEPH or SAMUEL WRAGG (see Book R. fol. 319); & whereas THOMSON on 7 May last mortgaged the property to THOMAS DRAYTON, planter, for L 730:12:0 currency, payable with interest, on 1 May next (see Book A.A. p. 472-474); & whereas THOMSON by will dated 23 May last authorized his executors to sell the residue of his real & personal estate to pay his debts, & appointed WITHERS, PRICE, & MACKPHERSON his executors; & whereas THOMSON died 15 June last without having satisfied the mortgage & on 2 July last letters testamentary were granted the executors & they paid DRAYTON; now the executors sell the land to BROWN. Witnesses: HENRY GIBBES, WILLIAM GLEN. Before ALEXANDER GORDON, J.P. WILLIAM HOPTON, Register.

Book S-S, p. 162
13 June 1747
Release

PATRICK BROWN, Indian merchant, now sojourning in Charleston, to PETER BENOIST, cooper, of Charleston, for L 3000 SC money, 6 a. on W side of High Road on Charleston Neck, in St. Philips Parish, Charleston, Berkeley Co., bounding N on SAMUEL OR JOSEPH WRAGG; W on Free School land; S on road to Free School. Witnesses: WILLIAM GLEN, JOHN CART. Before ALEXANDER GORDON, J.P. WILLIAM HOPTON, Register. Plat of 13 lots bounding on 1 side 252-1/2 ft. on Broad Road; 1 side 457-1/2 ft. on George Street, a 30 ft. street; 1 side 252-1/2 ft. on St. Phillips Street, a 40 ft. street; lots 1, 2, 3, 4, & 5, fronting the Broad Road being 50-1/2 x 161 ft.; lots 6, 7, & 8, in center, fronting George Street, being 42-1/2 x 252-1/2 ft.; lots 9, 10, 11, 12, 13, fronting on St. Philips Street, varying between 50-1/2 x 158 ft. & 50-1/2 x 170 ft. (in wrong place)?

Book S-S, p. 164
23 & 24 Feb. 1740
L & R

ELIZABETH DILL, widow (formerly ELIZABETH CROSKEYS, daughter of JOHN CROSKEYS, gentleman, of Berkeley Co.), to PETER BENOIST, cooper, of Charleston, for L 1574 currency, part of a lot in Charleston, bounding N 31 ft. 4 in. on Broad Street; E 120 ft. on DANIEL CRAWFORD (formerly PETER GIRARD); S 28 ft. 10 in. on MR. WRAGG (formerly ROBERT GIBBES); W on THOMAS GADSDEN (formerly DR. CHARLES BURNHAM). Whereas JOHN CROSKEYS owned part of a lot in Charleston which by will dated 16 Feb. 1718 he bequeathed to his daughter, ELIZABETH, who later married JOSEPH DILL, mariner, now deceased; now she sells to BENOIST. Witnesses: MARY WYATT, THOMAS LAMBOLL. Before ALEXANDER GORDON, J.P. WILLIAM HOPTON, Register.

Book S-S, p. 169
24 Feb. 1740
Bond

ELIZABETH DILL, widow, of Berkeley Co., gives PETER BENOIST a bond in penal sum of L 3148 currency, that she will keep above covenants (p. 164). Witnesses: MARY WYATT, THOMAS LAMBOLL. Before ALEXANDER GORDON, J.P. WILLIAM HOPTON, Register.

Book S-S, p. 170
7 Jan. 1757
Release

ABRAHAM (his mark) LUNDY, to JOHN CRAWFORD, both of Prince Frederick Parish, Craven Co., for L 10 British; 11 a. on SW side Peedee River, part of 150 a. granted LUNDY on 24 Mar.

1756; beginning at a black oak in WILLIAM HAMSWORTH'S line, running N 57°
E 118 poles to the river; down the water course 40 poles to a stake; then
S 72° W 13 poles to a stake; then N 28° W 13 poles to a stake; then 103
poles to beginning S 72° W. Witnesses: CALEB HOWELL, THOMAS BINGHAM.
Before WILLIAM LORD, J.P. WILLIAM HOPTON, Register.

Book S-S, p. 171   ROBERT EKELLS, planter, & CATHERINE his wife,
21 & 22 June 1757   to WILLIAM BLAKE, for Ł 1600 currency, 219 a.
L & R   Whereas the Lords Proprs. on 13 Jan. 1710
granted MOSES WAY 219 a., then in Berkeley
Co., but now in Colleton Co., bounding NW on STEPHEN DOUSE (now WILLIAM
BLAKE); SE on RICHARD WARING; NE & SE on vacant land; & whereas by will
dated 1 Oct. 1737 he devised 2/3 of all his lands, except a quarter-a.
lot in Dorchester town, to his son PERMENAS WAY, the other 1/3 to his
wife, SARAH during her lifetime, then to PERMENAS (PARMENAS); & whereas
PARMENAS WAY & MARGARET his wife on 24 Feb. 1753 sold the 219 a. to ROB-
ERT EKELLS; now EKELLS sells to BLAKE, the money being paid through RALPH
IZARD. Witnesses: JOHN SNELLING, THOMAS POOLE, WILLIAM BAKER. Before
DAVID GRAEME, J.P. WILLIAM HOPTON, Register.

Book S-S, p. 175   WILLIAM (his mark) BOWEN, planter, to WILLIAM
18 Jan. 1757   TAYLOR, planter, both of Craven Co., for Ł 225
L & R   currency, 100 a. in the WELCH tract in Craven
Co., granted by Gov. JAMES GLEN on 26 Jan.
1741 to THOMAS BOWEN; bounding W on Peedee River; S on JOHN CARTER; other
sides on vacant land. Witnesses: JOHN THOMPSON, THOMAS LIDE, MARY GILLES-
PIE. Before GEORGE HICKS, J.P. WILLIAM HOPTON, Register.

Book S-S, p. 178   THOMAS BOWEN, weaver, of the WELCH tract, in
11 Feb. 1746   Craven Co., gave a bond to SAMUEL HOLLINGS-
Bond   WORTH, yeoman, of the WELCH tract, for Ł 720
SC money, that he would by 2 May 1748 procure
unto HOLLINGSWORTH 100 a. on E side Peedee River, & on N side of JOHN
CARTER'S land (now SAMUEL HOLLINGSWORTH) with plat & grant of said tract.
Witnesses: WALTER DOWNS, ABRAHAM KERSLAKE. Before JOHN CRAWFORD, J.P.
WILLIAM HOPTON, Register.

Book S-S, p. 179   WILLIAM GEORGE FREEMAN, ESQ., & JANE his wife,
7 & 8 July 1748   of Charleston, to JOHN DRAYTON, ESQ., for
L & R   Ł 4000 currency, 52 a. known as Pickpocket
Plantation, on Charleston Neck, bounding NE on
the Broad Road leading from Charleston; SW on THOMAS GADSDEN; NW on part
of same tract sold to CHARLES SHEPHEARD; SE on RICHARD SHUBRICK. Witnesses: JOHN LINING, WILLIAM BURROWS. Before JOHN RATTRAY, J.P. WILLIAM
HOPTON, Register.

Book S-S, p. 182   WILLIAM BAYNARD, planter, of Edisto, & ELIZA-
12 & 14 Nov. 1757   BETH his wife, to GEORGE CUTHBERT, planter, of
L & R   St. Helena, for Ł 666:6:8 SC money, his undivided third part of 500 a. in Granville Co.,
bounding W on marsh, creeks, & sands separating it from a small island; N
on Cowen's Creek; other sides on vacant land. Whereas the Lords Proprs.
on 14 May 1706 granted JOHN BARNWELL 500 a. in Granville Co.; which by
will dated 4 May 1724 he bequeathed to his daughter MARY; who later married PAUL GRIMBALL, planter, of Edisto Island; & whereas they had 3
daughters, MARY, who married GEORGE CUTHBERT; ELIZABETH, party hereto; &
CATHERINE, who married DAVID ADAMS, planter; & whereas after the death of
their parents the 3 daughters became coparceners in the estate; now, ELIZ-
ABETH by & with the consent of her husband, sells her third part to
GEORGE CUTHBERT. Witnesses: JOHN JENKINS, PROVIDENCE JENKINS. Before
JOHN RATTRAY, J.P. WILLIAM HOPTON, Register.

Book S-S, p. 186   ARCHIBALD JOHNSTON, planter, to JOSIAS ALLSTON,
16 & 17 June 1757   planter, for Ł 2300 currency, 952 a. on Wacca-
L & R   maw Neck, Long Bay. Witnesses: THOMAS WATIES,
JOSEPH ALLSTON, JOHN WATIES. Before THOMAS
BLYTHE, J.P. WILLIAM HOPTON, Register. Plat by THOMAS BLYTHE, Dep. Sur.,
dated 28 Jan. 1757 shows resurvey of 952 a. on Long Bay, Prince George
Parish, Craven Co., & "now sold by him to MR. JOHN WATIES," 200 a. of
which were formerly granted to WILLIAM CATCHPOLE; 752 a. being half of

1504 a. granted to CAPT. GEORGE BENNISON; bounding SE on the marsh of
Long Bay; NE & N on other half of BENNISON'S tract (now JOHNSTON'S); SW
partly on land sold to JOSIAS ALLSTON, partly on the 1000 a. tract granted CAPT. BENNISON (now JOHNSTON'S).

Book S-S, p. 190   JOHN DRAYTON, ESQ., & MARGARET his wife, to
14 & 15 Sept. 1757   ANDREW FESCH & PETER GUINAND, gentlemen, of
L & R   Charleston, for ₺ 3000 currency, 52 a. known
                          as Pickpocket Plantation, on Charleston Neck,
bounding NE on the Broad Road leading from Charleston; SW on THOMAS GADS-
DEN; NW on a small part of the tract sold to CHARLES SHEPHEARD; SE on
WILLIAM SMITH & RICHARD SHUBRICK. Witnesses: JAMES GLEN, PETER LEIGH.
Before JOHN RATTRAY, J.P. WILLIAM HOPTON, Register. Plat shows bound-
aries; N on path to CAPT. GADSDEN'S house separating said 52 a. from COL.
JOSEPH BLAKE'S land; NE on Broad Path; SE on DR. GIBSON & WILLIAM SMITH;
SW on CAPT. THOMAS GADSDEN.

Book S-S, p. 193   CHRISTOPHER BEECH, planter, of Prince Fred-
15 & 16 Mar. 1757   erick Parish, Craven Co., to BENJAMIN SIMONS,
L & R   ESQ., of Parish of St. Thomas & St. Dennis,
                          Berkeley Co., for ₺ 150 currency, his undivid-
ed half part of 277 a. in Berkeley Co. Whereas MARY BEECH, widow of
CHRISTOPHER BEECH, planter, of Berkeley Co., some time before her death
purchased from her brother, JOHN BLAKE, 277 a. in the Parish of St. Thomas & St. Dennis, bounding NW on the E branch of Cooper River; NE on JOHN
CUMING (formerly CHRISTOPHER BEECH); SW on heirs of PETER BONNEAU; & by
will dated 28 Mar. 1716 bequeathed the land (called therein 270 a.)
equally to her 2 oldest daughters, GRACE & CHRISTIAN; in case JOSEPH
BEECH, youngest son of CHRISTOPHER & MARY, should inherit the lands left
to RICHARD BEECH, eldest son of CHRISTOPHER & MARY, & by his father's
(CHRISTOPHER'S) will; in case RICHARD should die without issue (which he
did) & accordingly JOSEPH seized the lands & sold them to JOHN CUMING; &
whereas 1/2 part of the 277 a. by the death of CHRISTIAN, who had married
PETER TAMPLET, descended to their son PETER; who sold to BENJAMIN SIMONS,
party hereto; & whereas the other undivided half share descended first to
ANN CUMING (daughter of GRACE BEECH who had married said JOHN CUMING); &
by the death of ANN (then wife of 1 ROCHFORD) without issue then descended to CHRISTOPHER BEECH, party hereto, only brother of JOSEPH BEECH, only brother
of GRACE who left issue behind him; now CHRISTOPHER BEECH, grandson of
MARY BEECH sells his undivided half share to SIMONS, who had purchased
the other half from PETER TAMPLET (see above). Witnesses: JOSEPH DUBOUR-
DIEU, BENJAMIN YOUNG. Before THOMAS BLYTHE, J.P. WILLIAM HOPTON, Register.

Book S-S, p. 197   PETER TAMPLET, joiner, of Charleston, to BEN-
3 Mar. 1749   JAMIN SIMONS, planter, of Parish of St. Thomas,
Feoffment   Berkeley Co., for ₺ 150 currency, his half
                          share of 277 a. in St. Thomas Parish, bounding
NW on E branch of Cooper River; NE on CHRISTOPHER BEECH, husband of said
MARY, (now JOHN CUMING); SW on children of PETER BONNEAU (formerly JOHN
BLAKE); according to plat by GEORGE HUNTER, Sur. Gen. Whereas MARY BEECH,
of Berkeley Co., by will dated 28 Mar. 1716, bequeathed equally to her 2
oldest daughters, GRACE & CHRISTIAN 277 a. (in will called 270 a.) which
she had purchased from her brother, JOHN BLAKE, in case JOSEPH BEECH,
youngest son of CHRISTOPHER & MARY, should inherit the lands left to RICH-
ARD BEECH, eldest son of MARY & CHRISTOPHER, to whom the same was left by
CHRISTOPHER in case RICHARD should die without issue, which he did, &
accordingly JOSEPH seized the lands which he has since sold to JOHN CUM-
ING, of St. Thomas Parish; & whereas CHRISTIAN BEECH married PETER TAM-
PLET, & they had a son, PETER, party hereto, who inherited their half
after the death of his parents; now he sells his share to BENJAMIN SIM-
ONS. Witnesses: JOHN HENTIE, JOHN HASELL. Before FRANCIS LEJAU, J.P.
WILLIAM HOPTON, Register.

Book S-S, p. 200   GEORGE LOGAN, JR., planter, of Berkeley Co., &
17 & 18 Dec. 1753   ELIZABETH his wife; GEORGE LOGAN, SR., gentle-
L & R   man, of NC, & MARTHA his wife, of SC; & LIONEL
                          CHALMERS, chirurgeon, of Charleston, & MARTHA
his wife; all of the 1st part; to WILLIAM VANDERHORST, planter, of Berkeley Co., for ₺ 1950 currency, 620 a., English measure, bounding W & N on

Wando River; E on FRANCIS GRACIA & vacant land; S on THOMAS LYNCH. Whereas the Lords Proprs. on 6 Nov. 1704 by Gov. NATHANIEL JOHNSON, granted THOMAS CARY 620 a. in SC, which by deed of feoffment he conveyed to GEORGE LOGAN the eldest (grandfather of GEORGE, JR.), who by will dated 18 Feb. 1719 devised the land to his eldest son GEORGE, (father of GEORGE, JR.); & whereas GEORGE LOGAN, SR., & MARTHA, his wife, by L & R dated 20 & 21 Feb. 1739, sold the land to LIONAL CHALMERS; & whereas LIONEL CHALMERS, & MARTHA his wife, by L & R dated 4 & 5 Mar. 1746, reconveyed the tract to GEORGE LOGAN, SR., why by letter of attorney dated 22 Jan. 1742 appointed his wife, MARTHA, his attorney with authority to sell any part of the land, & she, by L & R dated 1 & 2 Dec. 1749 conveyed the 620 a. to GEORGE LOGAN, JR., now he, with the consent of the others, conveys to VANDERHORST. Witnesses: CHARLES DEWAR, WILLIAM ELLIS. Before JOHN REMINGTON, J.P. WILLIAM HOPTON, Register.

Book S-S, p. 207   WILLIAM CLEILAND, planter, of Berkeley Co.,
12 & 13 May 1757   (only son & heir of MARGARET CLEILAND, former-
L & R   ly MARGARET MCNABNEY, widow & devisee of JAMES
     MCNABNEY, gentleman, of Charleston); & WILLIAM
VANDERHORST, planter, & MARGARET his wife (only child of JAMES MCNABNEY); of 1st part; to WILLIAM ELLIS, merchant, of Charleston, for Ł 1900 SC money; their respective undivided shares in a house & lot #52 in Charleston. Whereas GEORGE DUCAT, shipwright, of Charleston, owned half of a certain lot in Charleston which, by L & R dated 15 & 16 Apr. 1729, he sold to JAMES MCNABNEY, victualler, of Charleston, & MARGARET his wife (daughter of GEORGE DUCAT); & whereas JAMES MCNABNEY, by will dated 22 July 1731, bequeathed to his wife, MARGARET (only child & heir of her mother MARGARET DUCAT, formerly MARGARET MARSHALL) half his town lot with its house & buildings which he had erected, & bequeathed the other half to his only child his daughter MARGARET (now wife of WILLIAM VANDERHORST); & whereas WILLIAM CLEILAND, now being of age, & WILLIAM VANDERHORST & MARGARET his wife, now also of age, have entered upon their respective shares; now they sell to WILLIAM ELLIS half of lot #52 bounding S 55 ft. on Tradd Street; W 100 ft. on Old Church or Meeting Street; E on the other half lot; N on JEREMIAH MILNER. Witnesses: WILLIAM GUERIN, A. VANDERHORST. Before JOHN REMINGTON, J.P. WILLIAM HOPTON, Register.

Book S-S, p. 213   PERCIVAL PAWLEY, planter, & ANN his wife, to
12 & 13 Jan. 1747   WILLIAM WATIES, planter, both of Craven Co.,
L & R   for Ł 1000 currency, 600 a. in 4 tracts on W
     side Peedee River; 100 a. called Youhaney,
bounding S & W on vacant land; N on a bold creek; 100 a. bounding SW & N on vacant land; 100 a. bounding on vacant land; which 3 tracts of 100 a. each were granted to PERCIVAL PAWLEY by Gov. ROBERT GIBBES on 23 July 1711; & bequeathed by PERCIVAL PAWLEY on 5 June 1722 to his son ANTHONY; who by will dated 22 Apr. 1736 bequeathed to PERCIVAL PAWLEY, party hereto; the other 300 a. being part of 533 a. granted to PERCIVAL PAWLEY, party hereto, by Lt. Gov. THOMAS BROUGHTON on 4 June 1736. Witnesses: AZ. DRING, PERCIVAL PAWLEY, JR., HENRY WARNER. Before WILLIAM POOLE, J.P. WILLIAM HOPTON, Register.

Book S-S, p. 217   MARTHA BONNY, spinster, to WILLIAM HULL, plant-
7 & 8 Oct. 1754   er, both of Prince George Parish, Craven Co.,
L & R   for Ł 750 currency, 2 tracts of 150 a. each,
     being part of 600 a. purchased from PERCIVAL
PAWLEY by WILLIAM WATIES; 150 a. bounding N & W on Peedee River; S on division line between MARTHA BONNY & ANN HULL; E on WILLIAM ALSTON; 150 a. bounding E on Peedee River; N on Youhany Lake; S on division line between MARTHA BONNY & ANN HULL; W on WILLIAM WATSON. Whereas Gov. ROBERT GIBBES on 23 July 1711 granted PERCIVAL PAWLEY 3 tracts of 100 a. each, on W side Peedee River, known as Youhany; 100 a. bounding S & W on vacant land; N on a bold creek; the other 2 tracts surrounded by Peedee River & vacant land; which 3 tracts PERCIVAL PAWLEY on 5 June 1722 bequeathed to his son ANTHONY PAWLEY; who by will dated 22 Apr. 1736 bequeathed them to his son PERCIVAL; & whereas on 4 June 1736 Lt. Gov. THOMAS BROUGHTON granted PERCIVAL PAWLEY, son of ANTHONY, 533 a. on E side Peedee River; & whereas PERCIVAL PAWLEY, son of ANTHONY, on 12 & 13 Jan. 1747 sold 600 a. to WILLIAM WATIES (the 3 tracts of 100 a. each, & part of the 533 a. see p. 213) who bequeathed the land to his wife HANNAH (HANNAH BONNY); who died childless; & her sisters MARTHA BONNY & ANN HULL (alias BONNY, wife

59

of WILLIAM HULL) inherited; & whereas they divided the 600 a., each tak-
ing 150 a. on E side of Peedee River & 150 a. each on W side of Peedee
River, MARTHA taking the upper tracts; now she sells them to WILLIAM HULL.
Witnesses: RICHARD WALKER, JR., ARCHIBALD STARRAT, JOHN MAGEE. Before
THOMAS BLYTHE, J.P. WILLIAM HOPTON, Register. Plat certified 15 May
1754 by ZACHARIAH BRAZIER, Dep. Sur.

Book S-S, p. 221   JOHN PARKER, planter, of Goose Creek, & MARY
17 & 18 Oct. 1757   his wife, to WILLIAM STONE, gentleman, of
L & R   Charleston, for L 1100 currency, the N part of
                          a corner part of lot #14 in Charleston, bound-
ing W 27 ft. on Union Street; N 45 ft. on EDWARD CROFT; S on ADAM DANIEL;
E on CAPT. KING. Witnesses: TIMOTHY PHILLIPS, SAMUEL PERONNEAU, THOMAS
LINTHWAITE, JAMES MCLINCHEE. Before JACOB MOTTE, J.P. WILLIAM HOPTON,
Register.

Book S-S, p. 224   JOSEPH ASH & RICHARD COCHRAN ASH, executors,
17 & 18 Nov. 1757   of will of JOHN DANIEL, planter, of Wando; to
L & R   JOHN ROSE, ship carpenter, of Christ Church
                          Parish, for L 4000 currency, 837 a. on Wando
River. Whereas JOHN DANIEL owned 837 a. on Wando River, in 3 tracts of
600 a., 170 a. & 67 a., formerly belonging to JOSHUA WILKS, bounding N on
creeks & marshes of Wando River; E on CAPT. JACOB BOND; S on ROUSSER'S
Creek & COL. ROBERT BREWTON; W on BREWTON & JAMES ALLEN (ALLIN-ALLING);
NW on ALLEN; & whereas by will dated 12 May 1757 he appointed his brother,
ADAM DANIEL, GEORGE BARKSDALE, RICHARD COCHRAN ASH, & JOSEPH ASH, his
executors with authority to sell; but DANIEL & BARKSDALE refused to act;
now the other executors sell to ROSE. Witnesses: WILLIAM BLAKE, BENJAMIN
GUERARD. Before JOHN RATTRAY, J.P. WILLIAM HOPTON, Register. Plat cer-
tified 14 Nov. 1757 by WILLIAM WILKINS, Sur., shows within hellow lines
600 a. granted JOHN STEVENSON; within black lines 170 a. granted MRS.
MARY MCMARVELL; & within pricked lines 67 a. granted JOSHUA WILKES.

Book S-S, p. 229   THOMAS BARKSDALE, ESQ., to CHARLES BARKSDALE,
3 Feb. 1755   planter, both of Christ Church Parish; for
Feoffment   L 1000 currency, 482 a. in Christ Church Par-
                          ish, formerly belonging to COL. GEORGE BENI-
SON & Lately sold by RAWLINS LOWNDES; bounding W on JOHN BOONE; N on
CHARLES BARKSDALE; S on THOMAS HAMLIN, SR.; E on Cophee Sound. Witness-
es: HANNAH MILLER, ELIZABETH BARKSDALE. Before ROBERT WILLIAMS, J.P.
WILLIAM HOPTON, Register.

Book S-S, p. 230   JOSEPH POOLE, gentleman, to JOHN WATIES, ESQ.,
24 & 25 Nov. 1757   both of Prince George Parish, Craven Co., for
L & R   L 7000 SC money, 5 tracts, total 1177-1/2 a.,
                          on SW side Black River, in Craven Co., bound-
ing SE on the Hon. JOHN CLELAND; SW on ANTHONY WHITE; NW on JOHN GREEN
(now MRS. SUSANNAH MAN). Whereas the Lords Proprs. on 14 Sept. 1705
granted JOHN ABRAHAM MOTTE 200 a. in Craven Co., bounding NE on Waha
Creek; NW & SW on vacant land; SE on Madam ELIZABETH ELLIOTT; which tract
by various conveyances descended to WILLIAM SCREVEN in fee; & whereas
Gov. ROBERT JOHNSON by 2 grants dated 24 May, 1734 gave WILLIAM SCREVEN 2
tracts of 200 a. each in Craven Co., laid out to SAMUEL SCREVEN, father
of said WILLIAM, the grants being made to WILLIAM in accordance with his
fathers will; 1 tract bounding N & S on said SCREVEN; W on vacant land;
the other bounding SE on Black River; S on said SCREVEN; N on JOHN GREEN;
& whereas WILLIAM SCREVEN, & SARAH his wife, by L & R dated 14 & 15 Nov.
1749 sold the 3 tracts, 600 a., to WILLIAM POOLE, the elder who died intestate & JOSEPH, his only surviving son & heir inherited; & whereas Lt.
Gov. THOMAS BROUGHTON on 4 June 1735 granted JOHN GREEN the elder, of
Craven Co., 197-1/2 a. in Craven Co., bounding SW on SAMUEL SCREVEN; SE
on said GREEN; on S side Black River; which land he gave to JOHN GREEN
the younger but did not deliver possession & seizin nor make any particular bequest of the land in his will, so that JOHN GREEN the younger could
not sell the land without the consent of WILLIAM GREEN, his brother as
eldest son & heir of JOHN GREEN the elder; & whereas JOHN & WILLIAM, by
L & R dated 1 & 2 Nov. 1750 sold the 197-1/2 a. for L 1200 SC money to
WILLIAM POOLE the younger; who died intestate in 1751 & JOSEPH POOLE,
party hereto (only surviving son of WILLIAM POOLE the elder, & brother &
heir of WILLIAM POOLE the younger); & whereas Lt. Gov. THOMAS BROUGHTON

on 12 Aug. 1737 granted ANTHONY WHITE 380 a., bounding NW on JOHN GREEN; other sides on WILLIAM SCREVEN; which by will dated 7 Feb. 1746 he bequeathed (with all his real & personal estate) to his executors to be sold to pay his debts; & whereas JOSEPH DUBOURDIEU, executor, by L & R dated 30 & 31 Dec. 1756 sold the 380 a. to JOSEPH POOLE; now JOSEPH POOLE sells the 5 tracts to JOHN WATIES. Witnesses: EDWARD NEWMAN, JOHN MARANT. Before PAUL TRAPIER, J.P. WILLIAM HOPTON, Register.

Book S-S, p. 236   THOMAS (his mark) RUSSELL, planter, to THOMAS
16 & 17 Jan. 1757   BOSHER, planter, both of Craven Co., for Ł 190
L & R   currency, 150 a., in Craven Co., bounding S on
                            Cadoes Lake; other sides on vacant land. Wit-
nesses: BENJAMIN THOMSON, ALEXANDER CAMPBELL, WILLIAM (his mark) LEE.
Before MATTHEW NEILSON, J.P.   WILLIAM HOPTON, Register.

Book S-S, p. 239   THOMAS WALKER, planter, & his wife, to FRANCIS
13 Jan. 1758   LEJAU, SR., & FRANCIS LEJAU, JR., executors of
L & R by Mortgage   will of DANIEL HUGER, as security on bond of
                            even date in penal sum of Ł 4000 for payment
of Ł 2000 currency, with interest, on 13 Jan. 1759; half of 2 tracts,
total 245 a., in St. Thomas Parish, Berkeley Co., purchased by said THOM-
AS WALKER & his brother JOHN WALKER from JACOB WOOLFORD; to wit, half of
105 a. (part of 210 a. granted to COL. ROBERT DANIEL) on Thomas Island,
Berkeley Co., bounding NW on Wattcoe Creek; SW on JOHN DURHAM; SE on
heirs of RICHARD CODNER; NE on other land of heirs of RICHARD CODNER, the
remainder of COL. DANIEL'S 210 a.; also half of 140 a., English measure,
on Thomas Island, bounding S on Wando River; N on JOHN DURHAM; W on ISAAC
LESESNE; E on heirs of RICHARD CODNER; with the dwelling houses, etc., of
the 2 tracts; also 530 a., English measure, on E side Cooper River, in
Berkeley Co., bounding S on Simmon's Creek; SE on Free School land belonging to vestry of St. Thomas Parish; NE on PETER JOHNSON; NW on LEWIS DU-
TARQUE; W on RICHARD GRIFFIN; according to plat of grant dated 27 June
1711 to JOHN WALBANK, father of RUTH BONNY, & sold by THOMAS BONNY & RUTH,
his wife, to THOMAS WALKER; also 70 a. in St. Thomas Parish, on W side
Cooper River, bounding SW on CAPT. JOHN VANDERHORST; NW & SE on JAMES
TAGGERT; being part of 270 a. granted by the Lords Proprs. on 8 Sept.
1690 to JAMES TAGGART, who sold to SARAH MURREL; who sold to THOMAS WALK-
ER. Witnesses: PETER MANIGAULT, THOMAS LAMBOLL, JR.   Before THOMAS MID-
DLETON, J.P.   WILLIAM HOPTON, Register.

Book S-S, p. 244   DANIEL LEGARE, JR., merchant, & ELIZABETH his
17 & 18 Jan. 1758   wife (lately ELIZABETH PAYCOM, only surviving
L & R   niece & heir of JOHN PAYCOM, planter) to BEN-
                            JAMIN DART, merchant; both of Charleston; for
Ł 4500 currency, 835-1/4 a. in 3 tracts on Horse Shoe Savannah, in Colle-
ton Co., bounding N on MR. YOUNG & estate of WILLIAM CATTEL, SR., E on
MR. LOWNDES, DR. SKIRVING, WILLIAM MITCHELL & MR. YOUNG; S on MR. LOWNDES,
& estate of MRS. ELIZABETH GIBBES; W on WILLIAM EVERSON & estate of WIL-
LIAM CATTELL, SR. Whereas JOHN, Lord Granville, Palatine, & the Lords
Proprs. by grant, signed by SIR NATHANIEL JOHNSON, JAMES MORE, & JOB
HOWES, dated 15 Sept. 1706, granted OWEN BAGGIN 500 a., English measure,
in Colleton Co., bounding N on JOHN CATTELL; other sides on vacant land;
& whereas JOHN BAGGIN, only son & heir of OWEN BAGGIN, by deed dated 7
May 1733, reciting that whereas OWEN BAGGIN on 9 Nov. 1710 had conveyed
the land to JOHN PAYCOM (PECOM), but the deed had been accidentally de-
faced, obliterated, & torn, released to PAYCOM his claim to the 500 a.; &
whereas by L & R dated 25 & 26 Mar. 1740, WILLIAM PINCKNEY, gentleman, of
Berkeley Co., & RUTH his wife sold to JOHN PAYCOM 295-1/2 a. in Colleton
Co., bounding N on HENRY JACKSON & JOHN PAYCOM; S on WILLIAM PINCKNEY &
EDWARD NORTH; W on MR. EBERSON & WILLIAM PINCKNEY; E on EDWARD NORTH &
HENRY JACKSON; & whereas 1 JACKSON, planter, sold JOHN PAYCOM 40 a. in
Colleton Co., bounding according to plat; & whereas JOHN PAYCOM died in-
testate & his lands descended to his only surviving niece & heir, ELIZA-
BETH LEGARE (lately ELIZABETH PAYCOM); now she & her husband sell the 3
tracts to DART. Witnesses: JOSIAH SMITH, JR., JOHN LEGARE.   Before ALEX-
ANDER STEWART, J.P. WILLIAM HOPTON, Register. Plat of 858 a. certified
24 Dec. 1757 by WILLIAM WILKINS.

Book S-S, p. 250   ROBERT WILLIAMS, JR., & ELIZABETH his wife, to
6 & 7 Jan. 1758   SAMUEL CARNE, doctor of physic, both of

L & R   Charleston, for Ł 2000 currency & other con-
                               siderations, 1 undivided half of 1000 a. pur-
chased jointly by SAMUEL GARNE & ROBERT WILLIAMS; also 1 undivided half
share of 2 large stills, fixed & annexed to the freehold; also 1 undivided half share of the utensils & implements belonging to the distillery;
reserving to ROBERT WILLIAMS, the father, right of interment on the usual
place of burial on said plantation. Whereas ROBERT WILLIAMS, (father of
ROBERT, JR., party hereto), JOHN COOPER & HENRY KENNAN, gentlemen, of
Charleston, lately owned 4 tracts of 440 a., 90 a., 100 a., & 170 a., in
Christ Church Parish, Berkeley Co., total 800 a., bounding S on Shimee
Creek (now Parris Creek); also 200 a. adjacent to said 4 tracts which had
been conveyed by JOHN RUBERY to ALEXANDER PARRIS; making a total of 1000
a. as possessed by ALEXANDER PARRIS; afterwards by JOHN PARRIS; then by
ALEXANDER PARRIS, who conveyed to ROBERT WILLIAMS, the father, JOHN COOP-
ER & HENRY KENNAN & now known as the Distillery; & whereas WILLIAMS,
COOPER & KENNAN put up a distillery & owned 2 stills & sundry necessary
impletments & utensils; & whereas ANNE WATSON, as executrix of estate of
JOHN WATSON, brought suit against HENRY KENNAN, & by a writ of fieri
facias, CHARLES LOWNDES, the P.M., seized KENNAN'S 1/3 undivided part of
the 1000 a., the stills & implements which he sold at public auction on
27 Feb. 1755 to THOMAS LYNCH, purchaser for SAMUEL CARNE & ROBERT WIL-
LIAMS, JR., to whom he relinquished the property; & whereas WILLIAM MID-
DLETON, attorney for Society for Propagation of the Gospel in Foreign
Parts obtained a writ of fieri facias against JOHN COOPER, HENRY KENNAN &
ROBERT WILLIAMS by which CHARLES LOWNDES, P.M. seized the 2 remaining un-
divided third parts of said 1000 a. stills, implements, etc., which on
30 Mar. 1756 he sold at public auction to SAMUEL CARNE & ROBERT WILLIAMS,
JR., as tenants in common & not as jointenants, for Ł 2266 currency; now
WILLIAMS sells his share to CARNE. Witnesses: EGERTON LEIGH, JOHN RAVEN
BEDON. Before JACOB MOTTE, J.P. WILLIAM HOPTON, Register.

Book S-S, p. 255   JOHN IRWEN, carpenter, & MARY his wife, to
3 & 4 Nov. 1757   DANIEL WILLIAMS, planter, both of Granville
L & R   Co., for Ł 300 currency, 100 a. on Hilton
                              Head, Granville Co., bounding N on DAVID ALEX-
ANDER; S on ALEXANDER TRENCH; W on Scull Creek; being part of 300 a. com-
monly called Trench's Island, sold by ALEXANDER TRENCH to DAVID ALEXAN-
DER, who by L & R dated 21 & 2 Feb. 1737 sold part, or 100 a. to SAMUEL
IRWEN; who bequeathed to JOHN IRWEN. Witnesses: THOMAS WALKER, ANDREW
AGNEW, WILLIAM GOUGH. Before WILLIAM HARVEY, J.P. WILLIAM HOPTON, Reg-
ister.

Book S-S, p. 259   ROBERT RAWLINS, of Charleston Neck, & LYDIA
9 & 10 Jan. 1758   his wife, to WILLIAM LLOYD, merchant, of
L & R by Mortgage   Charleston, as security on bond of even date
                             in penal sum of Ł 4000 for payment of Ł 2000
currency, with interest, on 9 Jan. 1759, that house & land bounding NE
384 ft. on the High Road in St. Philip's Parish leading from Charleston;
NW 35 ft. on HUGH ANDERSON; SE 35 ft. on JOHN GEORGE DALLIBACH; SW 384
ft. on JAMES VOULOUX'S land of 30 ft. wide E & W; which by a codicil of
will of said JAMES VOULOUX was bequeathed to LYDIA his wife, now wife of
ROBERT RAWLINS; also that piece of land which JAMES VOULOUX by a codicil
to his will bequeathed to his wife LYDIA, now LYDIA RAWLINS, at W end of
the other lands bounding W on a certain passageway; being 30 ft. from W
to E; also 300 a. in Amelia Township originally granted to RICHARD JACK-
SON, bounding on all sides on vacant land, & conveyed by JACKSON to THOM-
AS BULLINE; who conveyed to JOHN LLOYD; who conveyed to ROBERT RAWLINS.
Witnesses: NICHOLAS WEST, WILLIAM MASON. Before JACOB MOTTE, J.P. WIL-
LIAM HOPTON, Register. On 6 May 1763 ROBERT RAWLINS declared mortgage
satisfied by BENJAMIN SMITH to whom MARTHA LLOYD, widow of WILLIAM, as-
signed the mortgage. Witness: WILLIAM HOPTON, Register.

Book S-S, p. 264   MARY DICK, widow, to ABEL JOHNSON, planter,
30 June & 1 July 1754   both of Prince Frederick Parish, Craven Co.,
L & R   for Ł 350 currency, 500 a. bounding NW on MARY
                             DICK; other sides on vacant land. Whereas Lt.
Gov. THOMAS BROUGHTON on 6 Sept. 1735 granted RICHARD ALLEIN, ESQ., 500
a. on N side Santee River, bounding NW on RICHARD ALLEIN, other sides on
vacant land, which he bequeathed, with all his real & personal estate, to
MARY DICK; & whereas MARY DICK on 2 June 1752 sold the tract to JOSEPH

DUBOURDIEU who, on 4 June 1752 reconveyed to MARY DICK; now she sells to
JOHNSON. Witnesses: WILLIAM SHACKLEFORD, JR., JOB MARION. Before
OTHNIEL BEALE, J.P. WILLIAM HOPTON, Register.

Book S-S, p. 268 THOMAS (his mark) RUSSELL, to JOSEPH HOWARD,
31 Dec. 1757 saddler, for ₺ 300 currency, 150 a. in Craven
L & R Co., bounding S on Cadoze Lake; N on MR. DE.
ST. JULIEN; other sides on vacant land; which
tract was granted to JAMES MACGIRT; then transferred to JOHN NELSON then
to WILLIAM RUSSELL, father of THOMAS. Witnesses: THOMAS JERNIGAN, PAUL
(his mark) PENDER, JEAN (her mark) JERNIGAN. Before MATTHEW NEILSON,
J.P. WILLIAM HOPTON, Register.

Book S-S, p. 272 Between JAMES AKIN, SR., of Parish of St.
30 July 1752 Thomas & St. Dennis, Berkeley Co., & JAMES
Deed of Partition MARION, planter, of same place, & MARY his
wife. Whereas JAMES BREMAR owned several
plantations not mentioned in his will dated 16 Jan. 1732, viz. 1025 a. in
several tracts in St. Thomas & St. Dennis Parish, Berkeley Co., which he
had purchased from his nephew, FRANCIS BREMAR, by L & R dated 27 & 28
Jan. 1747 (recorded 6 June 1748); 1450 a. on Georgetown River in Prince
George Parish, Craven Co., granted JAMES BREMAR by Lt. Gov. THOMAS BROUGH-
TON on 4 Sept. 1735; 230 a. in St. Thomas & St. Dennis which BREMAR pur-
chased from ANDREW RAMBART by L & R dated 4 & 5 July 1735; 300 a. in same
Parish, purchased by BREMAR from SAMUEL SIMMONS by L & R dated 29 & 30
Mar. 1738; & whereas JAMES BREMAR died 8 Mar. 1749 leaving 2 children,
SARAH the elder, then the wife of JAMES AKIN of Parish of St. Thomas &
St. Dennis, & MARY, since married to JAMES MARION of said Parish; & where-
as said SARAH AKIN died 6 June 1750, leaving several children (the eldest,
JAMES, being in his minority) & in order to divide the land equally among
JAMES AKIN, SR., (by right of his son JAMES, JR.), of the 1 part, & JAMES
MARION & MARY his wife, of the other part, they agree to divide the land
equally in order to cultivate their respective shares, as follows: JAMES
& MARY MARION to have the 230 a. purchased from RAMBART; the 300 a. purchased from SIMMONS; & 247-1/2 a. out of the N part of the land purchased
from FRANCIS BREMAR; said 247-1/2 a. to be in the pineland farthest away
from the cultivated section; also 725 a. being the N half the 1450 a.
granted JAMES BREMAR, & divided by a line run from about the center of
that part bounding on Georgetown River & running S to the W bounds of
said 1450 a., parallel to the 2 side lines; JAMES AKIN, SR., to have the
remaining or S half of the 1025 a. Witnesses: BENJAMIN SIMONS, DANIEL
LESESNE, STEPHEN MILLER. Before SAMUEL THOMAS, J.P. WILLIAM HOPTON,
Register.

Book S-S, p. 277 JAMES MARION, planter, & MARY his wife, to
1 & 2 Aug. 1752 JAMES AKIN, ESQ., both of Parish of St. Thomas
L & R & St. Dennis, Berkeley Co., for ₺ 516:14:6 SC
money, the 247-1/2 a. & 725 a. allotted to
them by deed of partition (see 272). Witnesses: BENJAMIN SIMONS, DAN-
IEL LESESNE, STEPHEN MILLER. Before SAMUEL THOMAS, J.P. WILLIAM HOPTON,
Register.

Book S-S, p. 284 JOHN PURVIS, of Craven Co., to SAMUEL WRAGG &
19 & 20 Mar. 1755 ROTHMAHLER, merchants, of Georgetown, as se-
L & R by Mortgage curity on bond of even date in penal sum of
₺ 420 for payment of ₺ 209:12:0 currency, with
interest; on 20 June next; 250 a. on S side Peedee River, bounding on all
sides on vacant land, with fork of Jefferies Creek running through the
land, which was granted to PURVIS. Witnesses: THOMAS GIBSON, THOMAS FOX.
Before JACOB MOTTE, J.P. WILLIAM HOPTON, Register.

Book S-S, p. 288 PETER ROTH, & AGNES (her mark) his wife, to
21 & 22 Feb. 1757 HENRY WURTZER, both of Berkeley Co., for ₺ 75
L & R currency, 150 a. in Orangeburg Township, grant-
ed ROTH on 17 Sept. 1736; bounding NE on JOHN
SIMMONS; NW on JACOB PIERAN; SW on Ponpon River; SE on CAPT. HUGH PIERCY.
Witnesses: MICHAEL LARRY, ULRICK (his mark) REBER, JOHN GIESSENDANNER.
Before CHRISTIAN MINNICK, J.P. WILLIAM HOPTON, Register.

Book S-S, p. 293 JAMES COACHMAN, JR., planter, of St. James

13 May 1757   Parish, Goose Creek, Berkeley Co., to WILLIAM
Release   COACHMAN, planter, of same place, for Ł 1050
                           currency & other considerations, his claim to
700 a. Whereas on 3 Dec. 1754 JAMES WITHERS, planter, & MARY his wife,
of St. James Goose Creek sold WILLIAM COACHMAN & JAMES COACHMAN, joint
tenants, 700 a. in said Parish to the W of a run dividing the land on
which JAMES then lived (part of 730 a. lately purchased by WITHERS from
DR. JOHN MARTINI), bounding E & S on Goose Creek & HUGH GRANGE; W on
PHILIP GIBBES; N on COL. HERBERT'S vista or avenue; now JAMES sells his
share to WILLIAM. Witnesses: JAMES COACHMAN, BENJAMIN COACHMAN. Before
JOHN REMINGTON, J.P. WILLIAM HOPTON, Register.

Book S-S, p. 294   JAMES HAMILTON & JAMES FLOOD, planters, of
9 & 10 Feb. 1754   Berkeley Co., heirs of their uncle JAMES MC-
L & R   KELVEY the elder, planter; of 1st part; to
                           THOMAS CASITY, planter, of Craven Co., for
Ł 30 currency, 300 a., in Craven Co., bounding S on Jack's Creek; other
sides on vacant land; granted 2 Jan. 1754 to JAMES MCKELVEY the elder.
Witnesses: JOHN HAMILTON, JAMES MCKELVEY, WILLIAM CANTEY, WILLIAM SIMS,
JOHN HOPE. Before RICHARD RICHARDSON, J.P. WILLIAM HOPTON, Register.

Book S-S, p. 299   ISAAC NICHOLES, planter, to MELCHER GARNER,
11 & 12 Mar. 1744   planter, both of St. Pauls Parish, Colleton
L & R   Co., for Ł 880 currency, 350 a., part of 2
                           tracts, at BOB SAVANNAH, St. Pauls Parish,
bounding S on CHARLES FILBEAN, JOHN FILBEAN, & SILAS WELLS; W on JAMES
MCLAUGHLIN & ROBERT GLASS; N on JOSEPH HASFORT & ROBERT GLASS; E on AN-
DREW LIDDLE & JOHN DRAYTON. Whereas the Lords Proprs. on 17 June 1714,
by the Rt. Hon. CHARLES CRAVEN; granted HENRY NICHOLES, father of ISAAC,
500 a. in Colleton Co., bounding E on CAPT. THOMAS DRAYTON; N on JOHN
PRESCOT; other sides on vacant land; & whereas ISAAC, heir apparent, has
authority to dispose of the land; & whereas Gov. ROBERT JOHNSON on 24 May
1734 granted ISAAC NICHOLES 444 a. in Colleton Co., bounding S on SILAS
WELLS & JOHN CATTELL; W on EDWARD NORTH & BENJAMIN PERRY; N on JAMES MC-
LAUGHLIN; E on ISAAC NICHOLES; now ISAAC sells part of both tracts to
GARNER. Witnesses: ANDREW LETCH, PHILIP EVANS, WILLIAM MAINE. Before
WILLIAM MURRAY, J.P. WILLIAM HOPTON, Register. Memorial entered in
Auditors office 13 Nov. 1755 in Book D. 4 fol. 116, by JAMES MICHIE, Dep.
Aud. Plat dated 6 Apr. 1744 by JOHN MILES, Dep. Sur. shows: A 68 a. on W
tract; B 282 a. on E tract; C 350 a. total.

Book S-S, p. 305   THOMAS WRIGHT, ESQ., & MARY his wife, of St.
10 & 11 Nov. 1757   James, Goose Creek, Berkeley Co., to ROBERT
L & R   QUASH, planter, of Parish of St. Thomas & St.
                           Dennis, for Ł 3000 currency, 780 a. called
Fishbrook Plantation, in St. Thoams & St. Dennis Parish, bounding NW & SW
on ROBERT QUASH; SE on GABIREL MANIGAULT; E on CAPT. JOHN HARLESTON.
Whereas CHRISTOPHER ARTHUR, gentleman, of St. Thomas & St. Dennis Parish,
by will dated 24 Oct. 1724 gave BARTHOLOMEW ARTHUR, then of Ireland, now
of SC, half the lands remaining to him of his 1/3 part of a Barony purchased by CHRISTOPHER ARTHUR, DANIEL HUGER, & JOHN GOUGH; which amounted
to about 1860 a. according to a later survey; & whereas BARTHOLOMEW
ARTHUR sold 500 a., part of the 1860 a. to ROBERT QUASH; & the remaining
1360 a. to ROBERT BROWN, surgeon; & whereas ROBERT BROWN, sold to THOMAS
WRIGHT; who, at 2 several times, sold 571 a. part of the 1360 a., to ROB-
ERT QUASH, party hereto; leaving 780 a.; now WRIGHT sells to QUASH. Witnesses: MATTHEW QUASH, GEORGE MCRAE. Before FRANCIS LEJAU, J.P. WILLIAM
HOPTON, Register.

Book S-S, p. 309   JAMES ATKINS, planter, & SARAH his wife, of
10 & 11 Oct. 1757   the Parish of St. Bartholomew, to SAMUEL
L & R   ELLIOTT, planter, of St. Pauls Parish, for
                           Ł 1600 currency, 438 a., in Colleton Co.,
bounding S on WILLIAM HOLMAN (now JAMES ATKINS); W on JOHN HUNT (formerly
COL. FENWICKE); N & E on THOMAS RATCLIFF & MR. EVELEIGH. Witnesses: OWEN
BOWEN, JOHN HUNT, JOHN FERGUSON. Before THOMAS HUTCHINSON, J.P. WILLIAM
HOPTON, Register.

Book S-S, p. 313   DAVID MONGIN, planter, of Granville Co., &
28 & 29 Oct. 1757   ELIZABETH his wife, to JONATHAN BADGER,

L & R   gentleman, of Charleston, for Ⱡ 1600 currency,
                             1 a. & 2 roods, English measure, in Ansonburgh,
near Charleston, marked C on the plan of GEORGE ANSON'S (now Lord ANSON)
land, which, by deed of feoffment dated 8 Apr. 1745, BENJAMIN WHITAKER,
as attorney for ANSON, sold to DAVID MONGIN; also half of a 1 a. lot marked R on said plan, which a. lot, by deed of feoffment dated 20 Feb. 1745,
WHITAKER as attorney, sold to DAVID MONGIN & SAMUEL SMITH & by a deed of
partition dated 29 Oct. 1750 divided equally between MONGIN & SMITH; MON-
GIN'S half bounding S on SMITH'S half; N on a 30 ft. street; E on JOHN
PAGETT; W on DAVID MONGIN'S lot frontint the Broad Path leading from
Charleston, where MONGIN lived, being the first lot named above. Wit-
nesses: ARTHUR CATTELL, HENRY KITTS. Before ANDREW VERDIER, J.P. WIL-
LIAM HOPTON, Register.

Book S-S, p. 319   CATHERINE (her mark) TAYLOR, widow of Berkeley
5 & 6 Dec. 1746   Co., formerly CATHERINE LE NOBLE, daughter &
L & R   devisee of will of CATHERINE LE NOBLE, the
                            elder widow; who was daughter & donee of ELIZ-
ABETH LE SERURIER, widow, of London, Great Britain, of 1st part; to HENRY
BECKMAN, blockmaker, of Charleston; for Ⱡ 530 currency, part of lot #43
in Charleston, bounding E 25 ft. on New Church Street; N on COL. SAMUEL
PRIOLEAU & ISAAC MAZYCK; W on PETER DE ST. JULIEN; S 142 ft. on DEMARIS
DE ST. JULIEN, widow. Whereas ELIZABETH LE SERURIER in London on 7 Sept.
1720 granted CATHERINE LE NOBLE the elder, among other lands, etc., part
of a lot #43 in Charleston, part of the estate devised to her by her husband, JAMES LE SERURIER; & whereas CATHERINE LE NOBLE the elder, by will
dated 25 Jan. 1725, amongst other lands, etc., devised said part of a lot
to her daughter CATHERINE (afterwards CATHERINE TAYLOR, party hereto);
now she sells to BECKMAN. Witnesses: JOSEPH DE ST. JULIEN, DAVID LAFONS.
Before JOHN CHAMPNEYS, J.P. WILLIAM HOPTON, Register.

Book S-S, p. 324   JOSEPH STANYARNE, planter, of Colleton Co.,
25 & 26 May 1742   (grandson & 1 of the devisees in will of WIL-
L & R   LIAM RIVERS, of Berkeley Co.), & ELIZABETH his
                            wife, to THOMAS LAMBOLL, gentleman, of Charles-
ton, for Ⱡ 2000 currency, 300 a. Whereas the Lords Proprs. on 11 Jan.
1694/5 granted WILLIAM RIVERS 300 a., English measure, in Berkeley Co.,
near the Mill Point on James Island; bounding N on Ashley River; S on
marsh & the Sound; E on marsh & WILLIAM RUSSELL; W on DANIEL LACEY, &
WILLIAM COOK, & marsh of Witpeneno Creek (plat & grant registered 1 Apr.
1695); & whereas at the time of his death he owned the above tract as
well as several others & by will dated 3 Oct. 1717 bequeathed all his
real estate to his 2 grandsons, WILLIAM STANYARNE & RIVERS STANYARNE;
that is, to WILLIAM STANYARNE his mansion & half his land; to RIVERS
STANYARNE the other half of the land; with proviso that should either die
before inheriting then grandson JOSEPH STANYARNE to inherit the land of
the 1 dying, & whereas WILLIAM died under age & without issue & JOSEPH
inherited; & whereas JOHN STANYARNE, planter, of Colleton Co., eldest
brother of JOSEPH & RIVERS STANYARNE, in whom the reversion of JOSEPH'S
share of said real estate was supposed to be by the omission of the words
"his heirs forever", by L & R dated 7 & 8 July 1732 confirmed JOSEPH'S
title to the property; & whereas by deed of partition dated 14 Apr. 1737
it was agreed that JOSEPH should have as his share the 300 a. above mentioned; now he sells to LAMBOLL. Witnesses: GEORGE BROWNELL, WILLIAM
HARVEY, JOHN GODFREY. Before JOHN FENWICKE, J.P. Memorial registered in
Auditor's office 25 Sept. 1751 in Bk. 3. fol. 274, by J. WEDDERBURN, Dep.
Aud. WILLIAM HOPTON, Register.

Book S-S, p. 331   LEONARD JURDINE, planter, of Colleton Co.,
6 & 7 Dec. 1757   only son & heir of ANNE JURDINE (formerly ANNE
L & R   STENT, only child of SAMUEL STENT the younger,
                            planter, of James Island; & principal devisee
of his will; who married JOHN JURDINE, planter, father of LEONARD, husband of ANN); ELIZABETH MOULTRIE, executrix of will of JAMES MATTHEWS,
merchant, in behalf of herself & others, executors of JAMES MATTHEWS &
MARY JURDINE, widow of JOHN JURDINE, & administratrix of his goods, etc.,
of 1st part; to THOMAS LAMBOLL, gentleman, of Charleston; for Ⱡ 800 currency, paid to his father & mother, JOHN & ANN JURDINE, by JAMES MAT-
THEWS; & for Ⱡ 65 currency, paid by ELIZABETH MOULTRIE (formerly ELIZA-
BETH MATTHEWES), executrix & others the executors of JAMES MATTHEWS; &

for Ⱡ 100 currency, paid by MARY JURDINE, administratrix of goods, etc.,
of JOHN JURDINE; & of Ⱡ 65 currency, paid to LEONARD JURDINE by LAMBOLL;
100 a., bounding W on RICHARD RIVERS & WILLIAM SCRIVEN; N on JOSEPH STAN-
YARNE & RIVERS STANYARNE; E & S on a creek out of the Sound behind JOHN-
SON'S Fort; except as excepted. Whereas the Lords Proprs. on 14 Oct.
1696, by Gov. JOHN ARCHDALE, granted BENJAMIN LAMBOLL 200 a. on James Island; 100 a. of which by deed poll dated 19 Dec. 1696 he conveyed to SAM-
UEL STENT the elder; being the E part, lying on S side said island, bounding S on a creek & marsh; N on WILLIAM COOK (then JOHN WALKINS); E on vacant land; W on the dividing line; & whereas SAMUEL STENT the elder died
intestate & his eldest son & heir, SAMUEL the younger, inherited; & by
will dated 3 Nov. 1713 gave his brother, DANIEL STENT, 30 of the 100 a.
for the use of said brother & MARY his wife during their lifetime, the
30 a. lying to the E on a branch of a creek; & bequeathed to his unborn
child (ANN who later married JOHN JURDINE) all his real estate (said 100
a. except the use of said 30 a.); & whereas JOHN JURDINE & ANN agreed to
sell the 100 a. to JAMES MATTHEWES, & MATTHEWES actually paid Ⱡ 800 SC
money to JOHN & ANN JURDINE (parents of LEONARD); & whereas JOHN & ANN
JURDINE & JAMES MATTHEWES are all dead; & LEONARD has come of age; now in
order to keep the agreement made by his parents, now he, with the consent
of ELIZABETH MOULTRIE & of MARY JURDINE, sells the tract to LAMBOLL.
Witnesses: SOLOMON FREER, DANIEL HOLMES, THOMAS LEGARE, JR., WILLIAM PIL-
LANS, SOLOMON FREER. Before THOMAS MIDDLETON, J.P. Memorial entered 3
Mar. 1758 in Auditor's Book #4 fol. 207 by JAMES MICKIE, Dep. Aud. WIL-
LIAM HOPTON, Register.

Book S-S, p. 338   KATHERINE (her mark) TAYLOR, of Berkeley Co.,
15 & 16 May 1746   widow (formerly KATHERINE LE NOBLE, daughter &
L & R   devisee of KATHERINE LE NOBLE the elder, who
                      was daughter & donee of ELIZABETH LE SERURIER,
widow, of London); to ISAAC MAZYCK, merchant, of Charleston, for Ⱡ 150
currency, the W part (or 2/3) of the S half of lot #69 in Charleston,
bounding S on KATHERINE TAYLOR'S part of lot #43, on MR. DE ST. JULIEN &
on ISAAC MAZYCK; W 48 ft. on ABRAHAM ROULAIN; N 154-1/2 ft. on part of
lot #69 belonging to MRS. DUPUY, widow; E 48 ft. on part of lot #69 occupied by ELISHA PRIOLEAU (formerly belonging to STEPHEN TAVERON). Whereas
ELIZABETH SERURIER by deed poll dated at London 7 Sept. 1720 gave KATH-
ERINE LE NOBLE the elder, among other lands part of a lot in Charleston,
part of the estate devised to her by her husband, JAMES SERURIER; &
whereas KATHERINE LE NOBLE the elder, by will dated 25 Jan. 1725 devised,
among other lands, etc., the part of a town lot to her daughter KATHERINE
(afterwards KATHERINE TAYLOR); now she sells part of the lot to ISAAC
MAZYCK. Witnesses: DAVID LAFONS, RENE RAVENEL, JR. Before WILLIAM
MOULTRIE, J.P. WILLIAM HOPTON, Register.

Book S-S, p. 343   THOMAS (his mark) POWELL, planter, of the
18 & 19 May 1756 (?) WELCH tract in Craven Co., to WILLIAM SWEET
L & R   (SWETT), planter, for Ⱡ 300 currency, 100 a.,
                      part of 200 a. granted by Gov. JAMES GLEN to
said POWELL on 8 May 1753; bounding SSW on THOMAS POWELL; NNW on WILLIAM
MCGEE; NNE on vacant land; SSE on MR. HUME. Witnesses: THOMAS CHARNOCK,
FRANCIS (his mark) WHITTINGTON. Before ABRAHAM BUCKHOLTZ, J.P. WILLIAM
HOPTON, Register.

Book S-S, p. 346   WILLIAM SWEET (SWETT), planter, & LUCRETIA
12 Jan. 1758   (her mark) his wife, of the WELCH tract, Cra-
L & R   ven Co., to JOHN LEE, planter, for Ⱡ 120 cur-
                      rency, the 100 a. he purchased from THOMAS
POWELL (see p. 343). Witnesses: WALTER FOLEY, BARRETT MONTGOMERY. Before WILLIAM LORD, J.P. WILLIAM HOPTON, Register.

Book S-S, p. 349   WILLIAM ALLSTON, planter, of Winyaw, heir, de-
14 July 1756   visee & executor of will of his father, WIL-
Feoffment   LIAM ALLSTON; to JOSEPH ALLSTON, planter, for
                      Ⱡ 5 currency & other c-nsiderations, the N
half of 1493 a. in Craven Co., bounding N on JOSEPH ALLSTON; W on Waccamaw River; S on JOSIAH ALLSTON; E on marsh & seashore; also an island of
129 a. of swamp land opposite said plantation & surrounded by a creek;
also lot #47 in Georgetown. Witnesses: THOMAS WATIES, JOHN WATIES. Before WILLIAM DRAYTON, J.P. WILLIAM HOPTON, Register.

Book S-S, p. 351   WILLIAM BUSBEE, planter, to JOSEPH CURRY, Dep.
16 & 17 Mar. 1758   Sur., both of Craven Co., for ₤ 100 currency &
L & R   other considerations, 100 a. called the island
                          in the low ground of Santee in Craven Co., op-
posite Mine Hills (Minchells), the dwelling place of CAPT. DANIEL SHYDER,
beginning at a gum 3 x, the SE cor of CHRISTIAN BLIVER'S land, running S
85° W to river; S on WILLIAM MOOR & JAMES WESTON; NE on CHRISTIAN BLIVER;
which tract was granted to BUSBEE by Gov. JAMES GLEN. Witnesses: ANDREW
KIRSCH, JOHN MARTIN FRIDIG. Before PETER CRIM, J.P. WILLIAM HOPTON,
Register. Plat certified 9 Dec. 1757 by JOSEPH CURRY, D.S., showing 100
a. being SW & SE corner of 500 a. originally granted WILLIAM BUSBEE,
bounding N & NW on other part of original tract; N & NE on CHRISTIAN
BLIVER; SE on part of original tract & on WILLIAM MOORE & on JAMES WIL-
SON; SW & S on Santee River.

Book S-S, p. 355   JOHN GOFF to WILLIAM STUART, both of Granville
23 & 24 Feb. 1758   Co., for ₤ 230 currency, 200 a. in Granville
L & R   Co., granted 17 Oct. 1755 to GOFF by Gov.
                          JAMES GLEN, bounding on all sides on vacant
land. Witnesses: THOMAS WALLACE, ROBERT (his mark) KILLEREAS, SR. Before RICHARD WALLACE, J.P. WILLIAM HOPTON, Register.

Book S-S, p. 358   JOSEPH BLACK, bricklayer, & ANN, alias AGNES,
22 & 23 Mar. 1757   (her mark) his wife, to WILLIAM HOPTON, mer-
L & R   chant, both of Charleston, part of lot #80 in
                          Charleston, bounding N 40 ft. on Pinckney
Street; W & S on GABRIEL GUIGNARD; E 75 ft. on GRIFFITH TUBBS. Whereas
BLACK mortgaged the above property to HOPTON & gave bond dated 10 June
1755 in penal sum of ₤ 2000 for payment of ₤ 1000 currency, with interest
at 8% on 10 June 1756; which bond & interest BLAKE had not paid; now HOP-
TON seizes the property, to hold until 10 June 1757. Witnesses: ANN
CLARKE (later ANN SMITH); PETER MONCLAR. Before EGERTON LEIGH. WILLIAM
HOPTON, Register. On 31 Oct. 1765 HOPTON declared mortgage paid. Wit-
ness: OLIVER NOYES.

Book S-S, p. 363   MARY (her mark) SPRY, to her daughter, MARY
19 Sept. 1741   BLISS, both of Parish of Prince Frederick,
Gift   Craven Co., for love & affection, 100 a. on
                          Black River, bounding on DAVID ALLAN'S land,
according to plat by ANTHONY WILLIAMS, Dep. Sur. Witnesses: DAVID ALLAN,
JOHN ALLAN, SAMUEL SPRY. Before JOHN BASSNETT, J.P. WILLIAM HOPTON,
Register.

Book S-S, p. 364   JOHN OSGOOD, cleric, & MARY OSGOOD, of Midway,
____ Dec. 1757   to JOHN EDWARD, of St. George Parish, for
Feoffment   ₤ 150 currency, 2 50 a. lots, bounding W on
                          Minister land; S on Ashley River; E on JOHN
GARTON; N on division line. Delivery by turf & twig. Witnesses: WILLIAM
SMITH, SAMUEL STEVENS, JR., THOMAS STEVENS. Before J. SKENE, J.P. WIL-
LIAM HOPTON, Register.

DEEDS BOOK "T-T"
APR. 1758 - JAN. 1759

Book T-T, p. 1   THOMAS RIVERS, JR., & SARAH his wife, of St.
____ Dec. 1757   Andrews Parish, Berkeley Co., to GEORGE SHEED,
L & R   of St. Philips Parish, Charleston, for ₤ 2000
                          currency, 100 a. on James Island, on N side
Newton Creek, bounding W on GEORGE SHEED; N on WILLIAM WILKINS, SR.; E on
ELIZABETH PERKINS; being part of 500 a. granted by the Lords Proprs. on
31 Mar. 1693 to JAMES DUQUE & by several conveyances became vested in
THOMAS & SARAH RIVERS by the executors & executrix of SAMUEL EVANS in ac-
cordance with the first codicil of EVANS'S will dated 28 Nov. 1749. Wit-
nesses: WILLIAM SCREVEN, JOHN REMINGTON, JR. Before JOHN REMINGTON, J.P.
WILLIAM HOPTON, Register.

Book T-T, p. 7   WILLIAM SIMMONS, planter, of St. Pauls Parish,
13 & 14 Aug. 1751   Colleton Co., to JOHN LAIRD, merchant, of

L & R   Jacksonburg, St. Bartholomews Parish, Colleton
                               Co., for ₤ 900 currency, lot #21 in Jackson-
burg, bounding S 100 ft. on Market Street; 218 ft. deep; which lot by L &
R dated 18 & 19 Jan. 1742 GEORGE JACKSON, planter, of St. Bartholomews
Parish sold to FRANCIS HOLMES & WILLIAM SIMMONS; HOLMES & his wife ELIZA-
BETH selling their half to SIMMONS on 28 July 1748. Witnesses: JAMES
SHARP, HENRY WARNER. Before JAMES BULLOCK, J.P. WILLIAM HOPTON, Regis-
ter.

Book T-T, p. 13   JEAN HARLEY (formerly JEAN JACKSON, widow of
21 & 22 Apr. 1752   CAPT. JOHN JACKSON, of PonPon) & GEORGE JACK-
L & R   SON, executrix & executor of will of JOHN
                              JACKSON, to JOHN LAIRD, merchant, of St. Bar-
tholomews Parish, Colleton Co., for ₤ 93:15:6 currency, lot #24 in Jacksonburgh, bounding S 100 ft. on Market Street; W 218 ft. on Jean Street;
N on ROBERT OSWALD; E on CULTCH GIBBES; also 2 tracts in PonPon, 12-1/2
a. bounding N on CAPT. WILLIAM PETERS (now DAVID HEXT); SW on WILLIAM
HAYNE; SW on public road & lots of Jacksonburgh; 8-1/4 a. bounding SW on
high road to the bridge; NW on Bay Street; NE on Old Road & WILLIAM HAYNE;
SE on PonPon River. Witnesses: JOHN SHARWOOD, WILLIAM BASSFORD. Before
JAMES SHARP, J.P. WILLIAM HOPTON, Register. Plat of 8-1/4 a. dated 1
May 1752 by JOHN STEVENS, Dep. Sur.

Book T-T, p. 20   JEAN HARLEY (formerly JEAN JACKSON, widow of
21 & 22 Apr. 1752   JOHN JACKSON, of PonPon), & GEORGE JACKSON,
L & R   executrix & executor of will of JOHN JACKSON,
                              dated 24 Mar. 1747; to ROBERT OSWALD, planter,
of St. Bartholomews Parish, for ₤ 227:5:0 currency, 4 lots in Jacksonburgh, 16, 8, 41 & 48, each 100 ft. front, 218 ft. deep; also 6 a. bounding NW on Bay Street; SW on JAMES POSTELL; SE on PonPon River; NW on a
dock by the road to the bridge. Witnesses: HENRY WARNER, WILLIAM BASS-
FORD. Before JAMES BULLOCK, J.P. WILLIAM HOPTON, Register.

Book T-T, p. 26   WILLIAM BUSBEY, planter, of the Congarees, to
14 & 15 Sept. 1752   GEORGE RAWLINSON (ROLESSON), planter, of same
L & R   place, for ₤ 50 currency, 200 a. on N side
                              Santee River, nearly opposite lower part of
Saxegotha Township, bounding SE on JOHN BAPTIST MOORE; NE on vacant land
& CHRISTIAN BLAIR; NW on ARTHUR HOWELLS; being part of 500 a. granted
BUSBEY by Gov. JAMES GLEN on 18 May 1751 bounding N on ANTHONY CUTTLER,
ARTHUR HOWELL, CHRISTIAN BLAIR, & vacant land; W on BLAIR; NW on GEORGE
LIX; S on Santee River. Witnesses: RICHARD KIRKLAND, JOHN HAMILTON. Be-
fore JOHN PEARSON, J.P. WILLIAM HOPTON, Register.

Book T-T, p. 32   GEORGE (his mark) RAWLINSON, to JOHN PEARSON,
5 Sept. 1753   D.S., of Craven Co., as security on bond of
Mortgage   even date for payment of ₤ 125 currency, with
                              interest; the above named 200 a. (p. 26).
KATHERINE (her mark) SMITH, JOHN TATE. This mortgage endorsed on fore-
going release. WILLIAM HOPTON, Register.

Book T-T, p. 33   The Hon. JOHN CLELAND, ESQ., of Winyaw, to
17 & 18 Apr. 1758   ARCHIBALD JOHNSON (JOHNSTON), planter, of
L & R   Georgetown, for ₤ 3185 SC money, 737 a. near
                              Georgetown, Winyaw, Craven Co., bounding W on
PAUL TRAPIER; S on Town of Georgetown & on the common; SE on MRS. MARY
LAROCHES; E on Peedee & Black Rivers; N on a creek & on ROBERT WEAVER.
Witnesses: JOHN RATTRAY, WILLIAM BLAKE. Before JAMES GRINDLAY, J.P.
WILLIAM HOPTON, Register. Plat dated 7 Jan. 1758 by THOMAS BLYTHE, Dep.
Sur.

Book T-T, p. 39   WILLIAM GOGGIN, clothier, of Cork, Ireland, &
9 Dec. 1757   ANN (formerly ANN BENNISON) his wife, by their
Release   attorney, WILLIAM GLEN, to ARCHIBALD JOHNSTON,
                              planter, for ₤ 500 SC money, 500 a. in Craven
Co., near Waccamaw, bounding SE on Long Bay; NE on MR. RIVERS & STEPHEN
PEAKE; NW on PEAKE & BOONE; SW on GEORGE BENNISON; being part of 1504 a.
granted GEORGE BENNISON 4 June 1735 (see Book B.B. fol. 400); the 500 a.
having been granted by said GEORGE BENNISON, planter, of Christ Church.
Wando, by L & R dated 16 & 17 Mar. 1743, to his sister ANN GOGGIN;

WILLIAM & ANN GOGGIN, by letter of attorney dated 27 June 1757, having authorized WILLIAM GLEN to sell. Witnesses: WILLIAM MOULTRIE, JAMES PARSONS. Before JAMES GRINDLAY, J.P. WILLIAM HOPTON, Register.

Book T-T, p. 45
27 June 1757
Power of Attorney
WILLIAM GOGGIN (GOGIN), clothier, of Cork, Ireland, & ANN (formerly ANN BENNISON) his wife, appoint WILLIAM GLEN, merchant, of Charleston, SC, their attorney with authority to sell above land (p. 39). Witnesses: DANIEL KENNEDY, JAMES BARRY, EDWARD SCOT YOUNG. KENNEDY appeared before JAMES PARSONS, J.P. WILLIAM HOPTON, Register.

Book T-T, p. 46
10 Apr. 1758
Confirmation
JAMES OSWALD, planter, son of ROBERT OSWALD, of PonPon, ratifies WALTER IZARD'S title to 119 a. (old survey said 100 a.) in PonPon, bounding NW on SAMUEL FARLEY; NE on vacant land; SE & SW on land conveyed to WALTER IZARD by ROBERT OSWALD. Whereas ROBERT OSWALD, held the above tract as tenant by courtesy in right of his former wife, RACHELL, from whom the inheritance descended to her son & heir, JAMES; & whereas ROBERT OSWALD & SUSANNAH his then wife, by L & R dated 6 & 7 May 1754, conveyed the tract to WALTER IZARD; now JAMES OSWALD ratifies the sale. Witnesses: ISAAC MCPHERSON, WILLIAM JACKSON, JOHN LAIRD. WILLIAM HOPTON, Register.

Book T-T, p. 49
28 & 29 July 1757
L & R
CHARLES LESLIE, planter, to WILLIAM YOUNG, planter, both of St. George Parish, for ₤ 50 currency, 100 a., part of 800 a. in Berkeley Co., surveyed in 1736 & granted to CHARLES LESLIE, SR., 13 July 1737; due E on BUCK BRANCH, bounding NE on the remaining 700 a.; other sides on vacant land; according to plat of resurvey by PETER FAURE, Dep. Sur. dated 27 July 1757 & showing Orangeburg main road passing through center of tract. Witnesses: PETER FAURE, SARAH (her mark) FAURE, JOHN BOSWOOD. Before JOHN CHEVILLETTE, J.P. WILLIAM HOPTON, Register.

Book T-T, p. 55
24 Apr. 1758
Mortgage
THOMAS BUER, planter, to JAMES CHRISTIE, surgeon, both of St. Bartholomews Parish, Colleton Co., as security on bond of even date, which CHRISTIE signed for BUER'S debt; given to Lt. WHITE OUTERBRIDGE, in penal sum of ₤ 2000 for payment of ₤ 1000 currency, with interest, on 24 Apr. 1759; 1300 a. in St. Bartholomews Parish, bounding N on MOSES MARTIN; E on JOSHUA SANDERS; S on THOMAS BOONE & JOHN MARTIN; W on WILLIAM MARTIN. Witnesses: JOHN LITTLE, JAMES SIMOND. Before DAVID GREEM, J.P. WILLIAM HOPTON, Register.

Book T-T, p. 60
25 & 26 Mary 1757
L & R
HENRY WOOD, planter, & MARY his wife, of Berkeley Co., to WILLIAM FULLER, planter, of St. Andrews Parish, for ₤ 78 currency, 13 a. in Berkeley Co. granted him by the Lords Proprs. on 20 Aug. 1717. Witnesses: RICHARD BEDON, BENJAMIN FULLER. Before JACOB MOTTE, J.P. WILLIAM HOPTON, Register.

Book T-T, p. 65
27 Apr. 1758
Mortgage
THOMAS BURTIN, storekeeper, of Craven Co., to WILLIAM MASON & MARY MASON, administrator & administratrix of goods, etc., of JOHN JENKINS, shopkeeper, of Charleston, as security on bond of even date in penal sum of ₤ 14,000 for payment of ₤ 7000 currency, on 27 Oct. 1759; 550 a. in Prince Frederick Parish, Craven Co., formerly granted to DANIEL MCDONALD from whom BURTIN purchased the tract, also 4 Negro men, 2 Negro women, & 2 Negro boys. Witnesses: WILLIAM MAZYCK, THOMAS LINTHWAITE. Before JAMES GRINDLAY, J.P. WILLIAM HOPTON, Register.

Book T-T, p. 71
20 & 21 Jan. 1758
L & R
JOHN CROKATT, planter, & SUSANNAH his wife, to JOHN MURRAY & WILLIAM MURRAY, ESQRS., for ₤ 2656 SC money, 1250 a. in Granville Co., bounding N on ALEXANDER FRASER; E on high road to Old Ferry over Port Royal River; W & S on JOHN MCKENZIE, Pocosaba Creek & Whale Branch of Port Royal River; also 78 a. called Rose's Island, on S side said plantation between Pocosaba Creek & Whale Branch. Witnesses: JOHN RATTRAY, WILLIAM LOGAN. Before DAVID GREEME, J.P.

69

WILLIAM HOPTON, Register.   Plat given.

Book T-T, p. 78   JOHN RATTRAY, ESQ., & HELEN his wife, to
18 & 19 Apr. 1758   CHRISTOPHER GADSDEN, ESQ., both of Charleston,
L & R   for Ł 6000 currency, 15 a. of high land & 29 a.
                              marsh land in St. Philip's Parish, Charleston,
bounding E on Cooper River; W on RICHARD LAMBTON (attorney for Lord AN-
SON); N on MR. MAZYCK'S marsh & a small creek; S on JOHN RATTRAY; the
15 a. of high land is bounding W & S by a brick wall; also the brick wall
& the land on which it is built; reserving to RATTRAY 1/2 part of the S
brick wall; also a 30 ft. entry towards bay of Charleston, in a line
fronting the present S gates. Witnesses: JAMES GRINDLAY, WILLIAM MASON.
Before WILLIAM BURROWS, J.P. WILLIAM HOPTON, Register. Plat given.

Book T-T, p. 85   CHARLES LOWNDES, P.M., to CHRISTOPHER GADSDEN,
29 July 1757   merchant, of Charleston, at public auction,
Sale   for Ł 890 currency, 1280 a. on Thompson Creek
                              & Peedee River. Whereas JAMES GILLESPIE, of
Craven Co., owned 1280 a.; & whereas on 16 Mar. 1743 he gave bond to EBE-
NEZER SIMMONS, BENJAMIN SMITH, & JAMES CROKATT, in penal sum of Ł 5782
for payment of Ł 2890:13:10-1/2 currency, with interest, on 1 Jan. 1744;
& whereas GILLESPIE died without having paid the debt & MARY GILLESPIE
was appointed administratrix of his goods, etc.; & whereas SIMMONS, SMITH
& CORKATT obtained a judgment against her & a writ of fieri facias was
issued by PETER LEIGH, C.J. commanding the P.M. to levy this amount
against GILLESPIE'S estate; now the P.M. sells the above tract to GADSDEN.
Witnesses: THOMAS SLAMM, JOSHUA WARD. Before WILLIAM BURROWS, J.P. WIL-
LIAM HOPTON, Register.

Book T-T, p. 89   ISAAC GODIN, gentleman, of St. James Goose
27 Dec. 1757   Creek Parish, to PETER MANIGAULT, barrister-
Feoffment   at-law of Charleston, for Ł 1000 currency,
                              part of a plantation on E side of the Broad
Path bounding NE on Goose Creek; NW on a piece conveyed to PETER MANI-
GAULT; SW on the Broad Road; SE on PETER MANIGAULT (formerly LEWIS LAN-
SAC); also the adjoining piece, bounding W on the Broad Path; SE on above
tract; NE on Goose Creek; N on a creek run & gall crossing the Broad Path.
Whereas by an Act of General Assembly, at Charleston, dated 11 Dec. 1717
the equity of redemption of the heirs of JOHN WRIGHT, gentleman, of
Charleston, to a tract of 896 a. in Goose Creek, Berkeley Co., was foreclosed & vested in SAMUEL WRAGG & JACOB SATUR, merchants, of Charleston
towards satisfying a mortgage of 1000 & interest; & whereas WRAGG & SATUR
by L & R dated 13 & 14 Feb. 1717 sold the 896 a. to EDWARD BROOK, gentleman, of Berkeley Co., who, by L & R dated 22 & 23 Aug. 1718 sold to ED-
WARD SMITH, plasterer, of Berkeley Co., who, by L & R dated 29 & 30 Aug.
1718 to BENJAMIN GODIN, merchant, of Charleston; who bequeathed the land
to his son, ISAAC GODIN, now he sells a part of the tract to MANIGAULT.
Witnesses: CHRISTOPHER JOLLIFFEE, JR., JOHN DENTON, CHRISTOPHER JOLLIFFE,
SR. Before JOHN WRAGG, J.P. WILLIAM HOPTON, Register. Plat given.

Book T-T, p. 93   JOHN WILLSON, eldest son & 1 of devisees' in
13 & 14 June 1757   will of MOSES WILLSON, planter, of Goose Creek,
L & R   to PETER MANIGAULT barrister-at-law, of
                              Charleston, for Ł 650 currency, part of a
plantation of 600 a. & 33 a. of marsh land. Whereas the Lords Proprs. by
Gov. NATHANIEL JOHNSON, for Ł 12 currency, by 2 deeds dated 14 May 1707,
granted LEWIS LANSAC 600 a. in Berkeley Co., bounding E on JOHN PIGHT; N
on Goose Creek; S on CAPT. JONATHAN FITCH; W on JOHN WRIGHT; which LEWIS
LANSAC & SUSANNA his wife, by deed of feoffment dated 20 Dec. 1710 conveyed to JOHN GRANT, mariner, who by will dated 9 May 1713 (after the
death of his wife CATHERINE), gave his son JOHN GRANT & his then unborn
child, equally, all his real & personal estate; & whereas RICHARD FOWLER,
planter, of Berkeley Co., & CATHERINE his wife (the posthumous daughter
of said JOHN GRANT the father) by L & R dated 14 & 15 Apr. 1731, sold
their half of the 600 a. to MOSES WILLSON, planter, of Berkeley Co., &
ISAAC HOLMES, planter, of Charleston; also part of 33 a. of marsh in
Berkeley Co., granted by the Lords Proprs. on 7 June 1711 to JOHN GRANT
the father; bounding NW on JOHN WRIGHT; SW on the 600 a.; SE on JOHN
PIGHT; NE on Goose Creek; & whereas JOHN GRANT, the son, cordwainer, of
Berkeley Co., by L & R dated 22 & 23 Nov. 1732 sold his share of the 600

a. & of the 33 a. of marsh to said MOSES WILLSON & ISAAC HOLMES; & whereas ISAAC HOLMES & SUSANNA his wife, by L & R dated 1 & 2 Oct. 1733 sold
their share to MOSES WILLSON; who became sole owner; & bequeathed to his
son JOHN WILLSON, party hereto, all that part of his plantation at Goose
Creek whereon he lived; lying on NE side of New Broad Path; now JOHN
sells to PETER MANIGAULT. Witnesses: JOHN DENTON, PETER LEGER, JR., THOM-
AS LAMBOLL, JR. Before JOHN WRAGG, J.P. WILLIAM HOPTON, Register.

Book T-T, p. 101   MOSES WILLSON (WILSON), planter, of St. Bar-
14 & 15 Dec. 1757   tholomews Parish, 1 of the sons & devisees of
L & R   MOSES WILSON, of Goose Creek, Berkeley Co., to
                          PETER MANIGAULT, barrister of low, of Charles-
ton, for Ł 450 SC money, the remaining part of his fathers plantation lying on SW side New Broad Path. Whereas the Lords Proprs. for Ł 12 currency, by 2 deeds dated 14 May, 1707, signed by Gov. NATHANIEL JOHNSON,
granted LEWIS LANSAC 600 a. in Berkeley Co., bounding E on JOHN PIGHT; N
on Goose Creek; S on CAPT. JONATHAN FITCH; W on JOHN WRIGHT; & whereas by
deed of feoffment dated 20 Dec. 1710 LEWIS LANSAC & SUSANNA his wife sold
the 600 a. to JOHN GRANT, mariner; who by will dated 9 May 1713 (after
the death of his wife CATHERINE) gave to his son JOHN GRANT & to an unborn child, equally, all his real & personal estate; & whereas RICHARD
FOWLER, planter, of Berkeley Co., & CATHERINE his wife (posthumous daughter of said JOHN GRANT the father) by L & R dated 14 & 15 Apr. 1731 sold
half the 600 a. to MOSES WILLSON, the father, planter, of Berkeley Co., &
ISAAC HOLMES, planter, of Charleston; also part of 33 a. of marsh, bounding NW on JOHN WRIGHT; SW on the 600 a. SE on JOHN PIGHT; NE on Goose
Creek; which 33 a. of marsh land the Lords Proprs. granted to JOHN GRANT,
the father on 7 June 1711; & whereas JOHN GRANT, cordwainer, of Berkeley
Co., by L & R dated 22 & 23 Nov. 1732 sold the other half of the 600 a. &
marsh land to WILSON & HOLMES; & whereas ISAAC HOLMES & SUSANNAH his wife,
by L & R dated 1 & 2 Oct. 1733 sold their half to MOSES WILLSON, the father; who thus became sole owner of the entire tract; & whereas he bequeathed that part of the plantation on which he lived, lying NE of the
New Broad Path to his son JOHN; & the remainder on the SW side to his son
MOSES; now MOSES WILLSON, the son, sells his share to PETER MANIGAULT,
who now becomes sole owner of the entire 600 a. & marsh land. Witnesses:
JOSEPH GLOVER, MARY WILSON. Before THOMAS MIDDLETON, J.P. WILLIAM HOP-
TON, Register.

Book T-T, p. 109   DAVID BROWN, ship carpenter, to PETER MANI-
11 & 12 Oct. 1757   GAULT, barrister-at-law, both of Charleston,
L & R   for Ł 337 currency, part of lot #166 in
                          Charleston, bounding W 30 ft. on the street
leading by the new brick church; S on children of THOMAS STEWART; N on
EXPERIENCE HOWARD; E on JOSEPH WRAGG. Whereas GEORGE BARNETT, the father,
owned part of lot #166 & by will dated 3 June 1715 bequeathed 1/3 his
real & personal estate to his wife ANN, afterwards wife of DAVID HEXT,
planter, of Charleston, & 2/3 equally to his son GEORGE, & his daughter
PHILADELPHIA, & his unborn child (later wife of CHARLES CODNOR); & whereas CHARLES C ODNER, GEORGE BARNETT, & PHILADELPHIA (PHILADOCIA) BARNETT,
by L & R dated 9 & 10 July 1735 sold the lot to DAVID HEXT; who with his
wife, ANN, by L & R dated 9 & 10 Dec. 1735 sold to ICHABOD WENBORN,
planter, of Edisto Island; who with MARY, by L & R dated 6 & 7 Dec. 1736
sold to JAMES JORDAN, mariner, of Charleston; who devised to his wife
MARGERY; who at a later date, before her marriage to 1 ACKLES, a tailor,
of Charleston, by certain articles of marriage reserved the power to dispose of her real & personal estate; & by L & R dated 3 & 4 Mar. 1745 sold
to DAVID BROWN; & whereas JOSEPH BEE sued DAVID BROWN & by writ of fieri
facias CHARLES LOWNDES, P.M. seized the lot & sold it to PETER MANIGAULT
at public auction for Ł 337 currency; now BROWN confirms MANIGAULTS title
to the lot. Witnesses: S. WRAGG, THOMAS LAMBOLL, JR. Before WILLIAM
DRAYTON, J.P. WILLIAM HOPTON, Register.

Book T-T, p. 115   JOHN SANDERS, planter, of Peedee River, SC, &
17 Dec. 1757   ELIZABETH SANDERS, to JOHN SMITH, planter, of
L & R   Craven Co., for Ł 270 SC money, 200 a. in Cra-
                          ven Co., granted by Gov. JAMES GLEN on 29 Nov.
1750 to JOHN SANDERS (Book M.M. fol. 150); bounding on all sides on vacant land; according to plat running SW 45 & 44 chains 80 links to a gum;
NW 45:44 chains 80 links to a black oak; NE 445:44 chains 80 links to a

to a lightwood stump by a hickory. Witnesses: JOHN SCOTT, AGNES (her mark) BUXTON. Before ABRAHAM BUCKHOLTZ, J.P. WILLIAM HOPTON, Register.

Book T-T, p. 121
6 & 7 Jan. 1750/51
L & R

SAMUEL (his mark) BUXTON, planter, of Peedee & SUSANNAH (her mark) BUXTON, to JAMES OWINS, carpenter, of Peedee, in the WELCH tract Craven Co., for Ł 200 currency, 350 a., part of 450 a. in Craven Co., granted by Gov. JAMES GLEN (Book L.L. fol. 257) to SAMUEL BUXTON (who sold a part, 100 a., to STEPHEN PEAK); bounding SE on DANIEL LAROCHE; S on vacant land; NW on land claimed by MICHAEL MURFEE; N on vacant land. Witnesses: ALEXANDER CAMPBELL, JAMES LINGARD. Before LIONEL CHALMERS, J.P. WILLIAM HOPTON, Register.

Book T-T, p. 126
15 & 16 June 1753
L & R

WILLIAM BAKER, shoemaker, & ANN (her mark) his wife, to JOHN JACOB GEIGER, planter, both of Saxegotha Township, for Ł 100 currency, 100 a. in said Township, bounding NE on Santee (Congaree) River; SE on WILLIAM BAKER; SW on vacant land; NW on vacant land & estate of HERMAN GEIGER; which 100 a. was part of 350 a. granted by Gov. JAMES GLEN on 12 Apr. 1744 to RICHARD MEYRICK, bounding NE on Santee (Congaree) River; SE & SW on vacant land; NW on vacant land; & estate of HERMAN GEIGER. Witnesses: JOHN HAMILTON, JOHN BAKER, MARTIN WEZELL. Before STEPHEN CREEL, J.P. WILLIAM HOPTON, Register.

Book T-T, p. 133
5 & 6 May 1758
L & R

THOMAS CAPERS, planter, of Edisto; CHARLES CAPERS his eldest son, planter, of St. Helena; & ANN, wife of CHARLES; of 1st part; to FELIX LONG, of Charleston, for Ł 1500 currency, part of lot #97 in Charleston, bounding N 108 ft. 4 in. on Queen Street, W 96-1/2 ft. on King Street; S 106-1/2 ft. on the Quakers Meeting grounds; E on part same lot. Whereas the Lords Proprs. on 9 May 1695 granted WILLIAM SADLER a half a. lot, English measure, #97 in Charleston, bounding W on a little street leading from Ashley River; N on a street leading from Cooper River; E & S on part of Archdale Square; & whereas WILLIAM SADLER by will dated 12 May 1712 bequeathed all his real & personal estate, except 1 Indian woman, to his daughter, MARY; who later married THOMAS CAPERS; who, since her death, is tenant for life by Courtesy; CHARLES being his mother's heir; now they sell the plot to LONG. Witnesses: JOHN RATTRAY, BENJAMIN GUERARD. Before DAVID GRAEME, J.P. WILLIAM HOPTON, Register.

Book T-T, p. 140
2 & 3 May 1758
L & R

REBECCA ANN COLT, widow, to PAUL TRAPIER, both of Prince George Parish, Winyaw, Craven Co., for Ł 200 SC money, lot #222 in Georgetown, bounding SW on public ground along the river; NW on lot #221; NE 50 ft. on Front Street; SE on lot #223. Whereas ELISHA SCREVEN, gentleman, of Prince George Parish, Winyaw, & HANNAH his wife, by L & R dated 14 & 15 Jan. 1734, conveyed to GEORGE PAWLEY, WILLIAM SWINTON, & DAVID LAROCHE, ESQRS., as trustees, 274-1/2 a. at Sampit, Prince George Parish, Winyaw, bounding SW on Georgetown River; other sides on ELISHA SCREVEN; 174-1/2 a. of which was to be for a town called Georgetown; the trustees to sell lots; 100 a. to be used as a common for the town; & whereas PAWLEY, SWINTON, & LAROCHE, by deed of feoffment dated 25 Feb. 1734 sold lot #222 to JOSIAH SMITH, of Charleston; who, with ELIZABETH his wife, by L & R dated 25 & 26 Oct. 1754, sold the lot to THOMAS RALPH, joiner, of Georgetown; who, by L & R dated 22 & 23 Feb. 1757 sold to REBECCA ANN COLT; now she sells to TRAPIER. Witnesses: DAVID HORRY, WILLIAM PARKER. Before FRANCIS KINLOCH, J.P. WILLIAM HOPTON, Register.

Book T-T, p. 146
14 & 15 Sept. 1757
L & R

DAVID SMELTZLEY, to GILBERT GIBSON, planter, both of the Congaree, for Ł 100 currency, 100 a. on N side Santee (Congaree) River, bounding SE on GILBERT GIBSON; SW on JAMES GARRELL; NW on CHARLES STROTHER & vacant land; NE on vacant land; which tract was granted by Gov. JAMES GLEN on 8 Apr. 1756 to DAVID SMELTZLEY. Witnesses: JAMES DENLEY, HENRY BUEDEKER. Before JOHN HAMELTON, J.P. WILLIAM HOPTON, Register.

Book T-T, p. 151

ISAAC LEGRAND, planter, & MAGDALEN his wife,

27 & 28 Feb. 1758   to GEORGE SIMONS, planter, both of St. James
L & R   Parish, Santee, Craven Co., for ₺ 500 SC mon-
                         ey, 483 a. in St. James, Santee; bounding SE
on Wambaw Creek; E on PETER DE ST. JULIEN; N on ABRAHAM PERDRIAU; W & S
on GEORGE SIMONS; which 483 a. PAUL BRUNEAU sold to ANDREW REMBERT; who
sold to ISAAC LEGRAND. Witnesses: FRANCIS DESCHAMPS, PETER GUERRY, PETER
DESCHAMPS. Before JOHN MAYRANT, J.P. WILLIAM HOPTON, Register.

Book T-T, p. 157   LEGRAND gives SIMONS (see p. 151) bond that he
28 Feb. 1758   will keep said agreement. Witnesses: FRANCIS
Bond of Performance   DESCHAMPS, SR., PETER GUERRY, PETER DESCHAMPS.
                        Before JOHN MAYRANT, J.P. WILLIAM HOPTON,
Register.

Book T-T, p. 158   ROBERT RAWLINS, of Charl-ston, & LYDIA his
22 & 23 May 1758   wife, to SUSANNA GLOUDEY, for ₺ 400 currency,
L & R   the front part of a lot in St. Philip's Parish
                        which RAWLINS purchased from HUGH ROSE by L &
R dated 10 & 11 Oct. 1753; being 25 ft. front & 131 ft. deep from front
division, between said piece of land & MR. WRAGG'S pasture; bounding NE
on the broad path or high road to Charleston; SE on JOSEPH WRAGG; SW & NW
on part smae lot, where ROBERT RAWLINS now lives. Witnesses: JOHN JACOB
LEHRE, JOHN ARMBRISTER. Before ALEXANDER GORDON, J.P. WILLIAM HOPTON,
Register.

Book T-T, p. 165   GEORGE RESTLEY, laborer, & ROSINA (her mark)
12 & 13 June 1754   his wife, to ABRAHAM HEIZENWOOD, laborer, both
L & R   of Berkeley Co., for ₺ 100 currency, 300 a. in
                        Orangeburg Township, Berkeley Co., on Cow
Castle Swamp, bounding on all sides on vacant land. Witnesses: HENRY
FELDER, JOHN (his mark) SIMONS, JACOB RUMPH. Before JAMES TILLY, J.P.
Memorial entered in Auditor's office 25 May 1758 in Book D. 4 by JOHN
BASSNETT, pro. Dep. Aud. WILLIAM HOPTON, Register.

Book T-T, p. 171   MARTIN HASEMEGER, planter, & CATHERINE (her
13 & 14 Dec. 1754   mark) his wife, to GEORGE GLORIF & JOHN SWICOD,
L & R   planters; all of Berkeley Co., for ₺ 190 cur-
                        rency, 250 a. in Berkeley Co., near upper part
of Saxegotha Township, bounding SE on HENRY METZ; SW on Santee (congaree)
River; NW & NE on vacant land. Witnesses: JOHN BICKLEY, MARY (her mark)
KINNERLY. Memorial entered in Auditor's office 25 May 1758 in Book D. 4.
fol. 212, by JOHN BASSNETT, pro Dep. Aud. Before THOMAS KINNERLY, J.P.
WILLIAM HOPTON, Register.

Book T-T, p. 177   EDWARD WIGG, storekeeper, of Beaufort, Gran-
28 & 29 Jan. 1747   ville Co., & MARY his wife, to WILLIAM HAZZARD,
L & R   planter, of Port Royal Island, for ₺ 5000 cur-
                        rency, lot #1 in Beaufort Town, bounding S on
the Bay; W on Charles Street; N on lot #28; E on lot #2. Witnesses: HILL
WIGG, CATHERINE CAMPBELL. Before JOHN HUTCHINSON, J.P. WILLIAM HOPTON,
Register.

Book T-T, p. 182   JOHN MARTINI, practitioner in physic, to JAMES
27 Mar. 1751   WITHERS, bricklayer, both of Charleston, for
Release   ₺ 2000 SC currency, 730 a. in St. James Parish,
                        Goose Creek, bounding E & S on the creek & on
HUGH GRANGE; W on PHILIP GIBBS; N on COL. HERBERTS vista or avenue; which
plantation ALEXANDER MCCAY, then of Ireland, by his attorney ALEXANDER
MCGREGOR, gentleman, of Charleston, sold to MARTINI by L & R dated 5 & 6
Aug. 1745. Witnesses: JOHN TROUP, TIMOTHY MORGRIDGE. Before ALEXANDER
GORDON, J.P. WILLIAM HOPTON, Register.

Book T-T, p. 186   JAMES BROWN, shipwright, to ARCHIBALD BAIRD,
28 & 29 Jan. 1757   ESQ., both of Georgetown, Craven Co., for
L & R   ₺ 125 currency, 250 a. in Queensborough Town-
                        ship, Craven Co., bounding NE on Peedee River;
NW on JACOB BUCKHOLTS; SW on vacant land; SE on WILLIAM WATKINS; which
tract Lt. Gov. WILLIAM BULL on 11 Nov. 1743 granted to SAMUEL BROWN, who
died intestate, & his eldest son, JAMES, party hereto, inherited. Witnesses: JOSEPH DUBOURDIEU, ANTHONY MARTIN WHITE. Before THOMAS BLYTHE,

J.P. WILLIAM HOPTON, Register.

Book T-T, p. 192   ARTHUR MOOR, planter, & MARY (her mark) his
30 & 31 Jan. 1757   wife, to ARCHIBALD BAIRD, ESQ., both of Craven
L & R   Co., for Ł 200 currency, 150 a. in Queens-
                          borough Township, granted MOOR by Gov. WILLIAM
HENRY LYTTLETON on 22 Nov. 1756; bounding NW on SAMUEL BROWN; NE on Pee-
dee River; SE on MARY BUCKOLD; SW on ARTHUR MOOR. Witnesses: JOSEPH DU-
BOURDIEU, WILLIAM BLYTHE, JACOB BUCKHOLT, STEPHEN TAMPLET. Before THOMAS
BLYTHE, J.P. WILLIAM HOPTON, Register.

Book T-T, p. 198   ARTHUR MOOR, planter, & MARY (her mark) his
30 & 31 Jan. 1757   wife, to ARCHIBALD BAIRD, ESQ., both of Craven
L & R   Co., for Ł 300 currency, the 250 a. in Queens-
                          borough Township, Craven Co., granted 22 Nov.
1756 by Gov. WILLIAM HENRY LYTTLETON to ARTHUR MOOR; bounding NE on WIL-
LIAM WATKINS, MARY BUCKHOLTS, & Peedee River; SE on THOMAS LAMBOLL & MARY
BUCKHOLTS; SW on vacant land; NW on vacant land, SAMUEL BROWN, & MARY
BUCKHOLTS. Witnesses: JOSEPH DUBOURDIEU, WILLIAM BLYTHE, JACOB BUCKHOLTS,
STEPHEN TAMPLET. Before THOMAS BLYTHE, J.P. WILLIAM HOPTON, Register.

Book T-T, p. 204   JOSEPH PERRY, gentleman, of St. Pauls Parish,
8 & 9 June 1758   son & heir of RICHARD PERRY; to JOHN MCQUEEN,
L & R   merchant, of Charleston, for Ł 5000 currency,
                          204 a. in 2 tracts; 1 of 1000 a. in Colleton
Co., on GODFREY'S Savannah, granted 26 June 1736 to RICHARD PERRY, then
bounding N on JOHN FENWICKE; E on JOHN HUNT; S on PETER MAY; W on FRANCIS
YONGE & vacant land; the other 1040 a. in Colleton Co., granted 1 June
1738 to RICHARD PERRY; bounding on GODFREY'S Savannah in St. Bartholomew
Parish; S on FRANCIS YONGE; W on ROBERT LADSON, EDWARD PERRY & vacant
land; E on JOHN FENWICKE & RICHARD PERRY; N on vacant land. Witnesses:
THOMAS FERGUSON, JAMES PARSONS, ALEXANDER FYFFE. Before JOHN MURRAY,
J.P. WILLIAM HOPTON, Register.

Book T-T, p. 210   THOMAS GREENE, NATHANIEL GREENE, ANN GREENE, &
22 & 23 Feb. 1758   SUSANNAH GREEN; of Beaufort, Granville Co., to
L & R   GEORGE BLAND, cordwainer, of Beaufort, for
                          Ł 55 currency, lot #141 in Beaufort, bounding
S on the Great PUblic Square; W on Carteret Street, S on lot #140; E on
lot #144; which lot #141 Dep. Gov. ROBERT DANIEL on 12 June 1717 granted
to CAPT. DANIEL GREENE. Witnesses: ROBERT FAIRCHILD, JOHN STORY. Before
WILLIAM HARVEY, J.P. WILLIAM HOPTON, Register.

Book T-T, p. 215   THOMAS SIMPSON, shoemaker, to CHRISTIAN BLEW-
29 & 30 Apr. 1757   ER, planter, & JOHN BLEWER, blacksmith; all of
L & R   Craven Co., for Ł 30 currency, 35 a., bounding
                          N on Raiford Creek; E on PETER HUBER; W on
JAMES BENTLY; S on WILLIAM BUSBY & CHRISTIAN BLEWER. Whereas Gov. JAMES
GLEN on 9 Jan. 1752 granted THOMAS SIMPSON 150 a. opposite Saxegotha
Township, bounding N on THOMAS HODGES; E on PETER HUBER; S on WILLIAM
BUSBY & CHRISTIAN BLEWER; W on JAMES BENTLY; now SIMPSON sells a part of
the land to the BLEWERS. Witnesses: JOHN GEORGE STRAUP, JOHN GEORGE LAPP,
CLEMENTS FROM. Before JOHN PEARSON, J.P. WILLIAM HOPTON, Register.

Book T-T, p. 220   JOSEPH GLOVER, ESQ., of St. Bartholomews Par-
15 & 16 May 1758   ish, & ANN his wife, to JOHN LINING, ESQ., of
L & R   Charleston, for Ł 1375 currency, 2 tracts of
                          500 a. each, total 1000 a., at the root of
Buckhead Branch on Saltcatchers, St. Bartholomew Parish, Colleton Co.,
bounding NE on JAMES SKIRVING & vacant land; NW on vacant land; SW on
JOHN ROBERTS Barony; SE on vacant land. Whereas Gov. JAMES GLEN on 13
May 1756 granted JOSEPH GLOVER 500 a. in Saltcatchers, St. Bartholomews
Parish, bounding NE on JAMES SKIRVING; other sides on vacant land; ac-
cording to plat certified by WILLIAM DEBRAHM, Sur. Gen., & whereas Gov.
WILLIAM HENRY LYTTLETON on 2 May 1758 granted JOSEPH GLOVER 500 a. at the
root of Buckhead Branch on Saltcatchers, bounding NE on vacant land &
JOSEPH GLOVER; NW on vacant land; SW on JOHN ROBERT'S Barony; SE on va-
cant land; according to plat certified by EGERTON LEIGH, Sur. Gen.; now
GLOVER sells both tracts to JOHN LINING. Witnesses: JAMES POSTELL, MOSES
WILSON. Before JAMES SKIRVING, J.P. WILLIAM HOPTON, Register.

Book T-T, p. 225　　　　　GEORGE ANSON, ESQ., by his attorney, BENJAMIN
6 Apr. 1745　　　　　　　WHITAKER, to JOHN WATSON, master & mariner, of
Feoffment　　　　　　　　Charleston, for Ł 1200 currency, 4 a., English
　　　　　　　　　　　　　measure, with the tenements, etc., thereon
erected; being part of ANSON'S plantation. Witnesses: MATHIEU VANALL;
MOSES (his mark) MITCHELL, cordwainer. Before JOHN REMINGTON, J.P. WIL-
LIAM HOPTON, Register.

Book T-T, p. 227　　　　　WILLIAM GLEN & JOHN COOPER, merchants, to JA-
25 & 26 Apr. 1758　　　　COB WARLEY, saddler; all of Charleston; for
L & R　　　　　　　　　　Ł 700 currency, part of lot #105 in Charleston,
　　　　　　　　　　　　　bounding N on other part lately belonging to
JOB ROTHMAHLER (later estate of WILLIAM LINTHWAITE); S on REBECCA FLAVELL;
E on JAMES PAIN; W 13-1/2 ft. on King Street; (incorrectly written 30 ft.
see conveyance Bk. S. fol. 149; DAVID CHRISTINEZ to JACOB JEANNERET); being the same piece of lot which JACOB JEANNERETT by L & R dated 21 & 22
June 1749 sold to JOHN FRANCIS TRIBOUDET; & which TRIBOUDET by L & R dat-
ed 20 & 21 Aug. 1750 (?) sold to GLEN & COOPER. Witnesses: JOHN WAGNER,
JOHN WAGENFELD. Before JOHN RATTRAY, J.P. WILLIAM HOPTON, Register.

Book T-T, p. 231　　　　　JAMES COACHMAN, planter, of Goose Creek, &
2 & 3 Jan. 1756　　　　　HANNAH his wife, to WILLIAM FYFFE, surgeon, of
L & R　　　　　　　　　　Craven Co., for Ł 1400 currency, 500 a. in
　　　　　　　　　　　　　Craven Co., bounding N on CHRISTOPHER GADSDEN;
E on Black River; S on JAMES COACHMAN; W on ANTHONY WHITE. Witnesses:
CHARLES FYFFE, FRANCIS MARION, JOHN WATIES, ALEXANDER FYFFE. Before
GEORGE GABRIEL POWELL, J.P. WILLIAM HOPTON, Register.

Book T-T, p. 235　　　　　FRANCIS JAMES, planter, & ELIZABETH (her mark)
4 & 5 Apr. 1758　　　　　his wife, to ROBERT CARTER, planter, both of
L & R　　　　　　　　　　Craven Co.; for Ł 40 currency, 300 a. on Wa-
　　　　　　　　　　　　　teree River Swamp, in the waters of Santee,
Craven Co., near the high hills, bounding on all sides on vacant land.
Witnesses: JOHN MAXWELL, JOHN EVANS. Before RICHARD RICHARDSON, J.P. of
St. Marks Parish, Craven Co. WILLIAM HOPTON, Register.

Book T-T, p. 241　　　　　JOSEPH FULLER, planter, of Berkeley Co., 1 of
1 & 2 Jan. 1755　　　　　the sons & devisees of will of WILLIAM FULLER
L & R　　　　　　　　　　the elder, planter, of St. Andrews Parish, to
　　　　　　　　　　　　　MATTHIAS SELLER, planter, of Colleton Co., for
Ł 1600 SC money, his half of certain tracts of land, total 756 a., commonly called COBBS'S in St. Pauls Parish, Colleton Co.; bounding SE on
the high road leading from Wiltown to Charleston, & on CRAWFORD'S & on
marsh of Stono River; S on THOMAS FULLER; SW on COL. JOSEPH BLAKE; W on
the high road & on THOMAS FULLER; N on JOHN FARR; NE on CRAWFORD. Whereas WILLIAM FULLER, among other lands, etc., owned 3 tracts called COBBS'S,
in St. Paul's Parish, & by will dated 30 Aug. 1731 bequeathed to his son
JOSEPH, 1/2 of his land on Stono, commonly called COBBS'S, to be allotted
to JOSEPH by the executors according to the value of the land; & bequeathed to his son ZACCHEUS, since deceased, the other half of said tract; &
appointed his kinsman, WILLIAM CATTELL, & his (testator's) son, RICHARD
FULLER, executors; & they proved the will & allotted to JOSEPH FULLER 1/2
(756 a.); now JOSEPH FULLER sells his share to SELLER. Witnesses: JOHN
NEWBULL, THOMAS LAMBOLL. Before JOHN REMINGTON, J.P. WILLIAM HOPTON,
Register. Plat dated 20 June 1749 by JOHN STEVENS.

Book T-T, p. 249　　　　　THOMAS WIGG, planter, to GEORGE DELABERE,
26 June 1758　　　　　　　planter, both of Granville Co., for Ł 700 cur-
Release　　　　　　　　　rency, 266 a. purchased by WIGG from THOMAS
　　　　　　　　　　　　　GRIMBALL, being surplus land within JOSEPH
PALMINTER'S plat, on Port Royal Island, Granville Co., bounding N on
THOMAS PALMETOR (now WILLIAM HARVEY, ESQ.); S on JOSEPH & BENJAMIN PAL-
METOR (now JOHN CHEESMAN) & marsh of Palmetors Creek; E on marshes &
creeks. Witnesses: GEORGE RUSSELL, BENJAMIN GREEN. Before JOHN LINING,
J.P. WILLIAM HOPTON, Register.

Book T-T, p. 253　　　　　JONAH ROBERT, planter, of Craven Co., to JOHN
5 & 6 June 1758　　　　　GRINNAN, of Charleston, for Ł 600 currency,
L & R　　　　　　　　　　490 a. Whereas Lt. Gov. THOMAS BROUGHTON, on
　　　　　　　　　　　　　12 Aug. 1737 granted PETER ROBERTS, planter,

980 a. in Prince Frederick Parish, Craven Co., bounding S on Santee River; W on MR. MORRETT; S on vacant land; E on MR. PHIPPS; N on MR. TEEMOR & on vacant land; & whereas, by will dated 19 Mar. 1731 PETER ROBERTS bequeathed the tract to his son, JONAH; now JONAH sells the W half to GRINNAN. Witnesses: JAMES NORVELL, FREDERICK MERCKLEY. Before JOHN MURRAY, J.P. WILLIAM HOPTON, Register.

Book T-T, p. 258
18 & 19 June 1758
L & R

EDWARD (his mark) MCGRAW, planter, to WILLIAM RAIFORD, planter, both of Craven Co., for ₺ 600 currency, 200 a. in Saxegotha Township, Craven Co., opposite SAVANNAH HUNT BLUFF granted by Gov. JAMES GLEN on 6 Oct. 1752, to EDWARD MCGRAW; bounding S on Congaree River; W on the river & land supposed to belong to PETER PHUL; N on vacant land; E on JAMES JENKINS & JOSEPH HERSMAN. Witnesses: JOSEPH CURRY, JOHN PITTMAN. Before JOHN PEARSON, J.P. WILLIAM HOPTON, Register.

Book T-T, p. 263
30 Nov. 1737
Release

RICHARD CARTWRIGHT, bricklayer, of Berkeley Co., & KEZIA his wife, to JOHN MCKAY, shopkeeper, of Charleston, for ₺ 1850 currency, 730 a. on St. James Parish, Goose Creek, Berkeley Co., bounding E & S on the creek & on HUGH GRANGE; W on PHILIP GIBBES; N on COL. HERBERTS vista or avenue. Witnesses: EDMOND ATKIN, ROBERT BREWTON, JR. Before ALEXANDER STEWART, J.P. WILLIAM HOPTON, Register.

Book T-T, p. 266
29 & 30 Mar. 1755
L & R

The Hon. JOHN CLELAND, to ROBERT WEAVER, carpenter, both of Craven Co., for ₺ 1302 currency, 284 a. in Craven Co., bounding NE on FRANCIS KINLOCH & Black River; other sides on JOHN CLELAND. Witnesses: ARCHIBALD BAIRD, ARCHIBALD JOHNSTON. Before WILLIAM SIMPSON, J.P. WILLIAM HOPTON, Register.

Book T-T, p. 271
23 June 1757
Letter of Attorney

JOHN COLLETON, ESQ., of Conduit Street, Middlesex Co., appoints ZACHARIAH VILLEPONTOUX, ESQ., ROBERT SWAINSTON, & JOSEPH BAIRD, gentlemen, of SC, his attorneys, with authority to handle his plantation affairs & estates in SC, to sell his Negroes & purchase others, handle his accounts in SC, etc., etc. Witnesses: DAVID MITCHELL, CHRISTOPHER BROOKS (master of the ship Fanny). Before BENJAMIN SMITH, J.P. WILLIAM HOPTON, Register.

Book T-T, p. 273
1 & 2 May 1757
L & R by Mortgage

JERMYN WRIGHT & CHARLES WRIGHT, merchants, to FRANCIS LEJAU & FRANCIS LEJAU, JR., executors of will of DANIEL HUGER, ESQ., as security on bond dated 10 aug. 1756 in penal sum of ₺ 6000 for payment of ₺ 3000 currency, with interest, on 9 Aug. 1757; 4 plantations; viz; 480 a. bounding E on PonPon River; N on ELIZABETH CLIFTS & JOHN HUNT; S on JOSEPH BOONE'S Barony; also 80 a., part of ASHLEY Barony or St. Giles, in Berkeley Co., bounding NW on Ashley River & THOMAS BAKER; SW on JOSIAH OSGOOD; SE on ROBERT WRIGHT & Ashley River; also 1000 a. on W side great branch of Forks on head of Salt Catcher River in Granville Co., granted JERMYN WRIGHT 11 May 1739; bounding SE on JOSEPH BUTLER; other sides on vacant land; also 600 a. in Prince Frederick Parish, Craven Co., granted CHARLES WRIGHT 17 Feb. 1736/7; bounding SW on Peedee River; NW on SAMUEL MASTER'S land called Male Bluff; NE on HENRY FOX; SE on vacant land. Witnesses: THOMAS GOLDSMITH, PETER MANIGAULT, THOMAS LAMBOLL, JR. Before JOHN WRAGG, J.P. WILLIAM HOPTON, Register.

Book T-T, p. 278
29 & 30 July 1758
L & R

HENRY CHRISTIE, carpenter, & CATHERINE his wife, to FRANCIS BREMAR, merchant, SAMPSON NEYLE, & ANNE GARDEN, executors & executrix also devises of will of the Rev. MR. ALEXANDER GARDEN, rector of St. Philips Parish, Charleston, for ₺ 750 currency, part of 2 lots in Charleston, #268 & #270, bounding E 140-1/4 ft. on HENRY CHRISTIE; W on WILLIAM PINCKNEY; S 36 ft. on Broad Street; N on an alley or land belonging to JAMES ST. JOHN & ROBERT THORP, ESQ. Whereas by certain Articles of Agreement dated 23 Jan. 1754 JOHN GEURARD, merchant, of Charleston, brother & heir of DAVID GUERARD, agreed to pay ALEXANDER GARDEN, rector of St. Philip's Parish, at a certain date, ₺ 400 proclamation money, according to indorsement dated 27 Jan. 1758 on back

agreement; now the executors purchase a town lot from CHRISTIE. Witnesses: JAMES GRINDLAY, EGERTON‹LEIGH. Before TACITUS GAILLARD, J.P. WIL-
LIAM HOPTON, Register.

Book T-T, p. 284   FRANCIS BREMAR, merchant, of Charleston, ex-
30 & 31 July 1758   ecutor of will of the Rev. MR. ALEXANDER GAR-
L & R Tripartite   DEN, rector of St. Philips Parish; & SAMPSON
                          NEYLE, executor & ANN GARDEN, executrix, of
said will; also devises of said will; of 1st part; HENRY LAURENS & EGER-
TON LEIGH, ESQRS., of 2nd part; BENJAMIN GARDEN, only surviving son of
ALEXANDER GARDEN, of 3rd part. Whereas DAVID GUERARD, merchant, of
Charleston, by will dated 7 Mar. 1725 directed that his brother JOHN,
after reaching age of 21 years, pay his debts, funeral expenses & legacies out of certain rentals; & bequeathed part of a certain town lot &
brick tenement on the bay, with the adjoining brick storehouse & cellars
to his brother JOHN for 6 months upon condition that he pay BENJAMIN GOD-
IN & BENJAMIN DELACONSEILLERE Ł 400 proclamation money to be used for the
purchase of a lot for use of his (testator's) sister, MARTHA GARDEN, during her lifetime; then to her heirs; then to his brother JOHN; or, by default, equally to his cousins DAVID GODIN, son of DAVID GODIN, merchant,
of London, & BENJAMIN GODIN, son of BENJAMIN GODIN, merchant, of Charleston, as tenants in common, not as jointenants; & whereas BENJAMIN GODIN &
BENJAMIN DE LACONSEILLERE, trustees & MARTHA GARDIN, are long since dead;
& whereas by certain Articles of Agreement dated 23 Jan. 1754 JOHN GUER-
ARD, merchant, of Charleston, brother & heir of DAVID GUERARD, agreed to
pay the Rev. MR. ALEXANDER GARDEN, at the end of 4 years from death of
DAVID GUERARD Ł 400 proclamation money to be used for certain purposes;
which sum, according to indorsement on back of agreement, dated 27 Jan.
1758 JOHN GUERARD paid to FRANCIS BREMAR & SAMPSON NEYLE, executors of
GARDEN'S will; & whereas ALEXANDER GARDEN died, leaving 2 children, BEN-
JAMIN & ANN, & by will appointed BREMAR & NEYLE his executors, & ANN GAR-
DEN his executrix; & whereas BENJAMIN GARDEN, being only male heir, is
entitled to Ł 400 proclamation money, to be spent as directed; & whereas
SAMPSON NEYLE, in right of his late wife, MARTHA NEYLE, & said ANN & BEN-
JAMIN GARDEN, surviving children, are entitled to an equal division of
the estate; & whereas said sum is a lien or charge upon the estate, & the
executors & executrix obliged to fulfill the agreement; & whereas by L &
R dated 24 & 25 May 1743 JOHN ALLEN, gentleman, of Charleston, sold HENRY
CHRISTIE, carptner, part of lot #268, 36 ft. x 140-1/2 ft.; which CHRIS-
TIE mortgaged on 23 July 1750 to ALEXANDER GARDEN, & in 1753 gave ALEX-
ANDER a quit claim; & whereas by L & R dated 29 & 30 July 1758 CHRISTIE
conveyed part of 2 lots #268 & 270 to the executors of ALEXANDER GARDEN'S
will; (p. 278); now they, for said Ł 400 proclamation in accordance with
DAVID GUERARD'S will, convey to LAURENS & LEIGH, trustees, parts of lots
#268 & #270 (part of Hewitt's Square, later called Gibbon's & Allens
Square) for the use of BENJAMIN GARDEN & his heirs; or, by default, to
the use of PHILIP NEYLE, only son of SAMPSON NEYLE & MARTHA, his late
wife, 1 of the daughters of ALEXANDER GARDEN; or by default to ANN GAR-
DEN; then JOHN GUERARD, then equally to DAVID GODIN, son of DAVID GODIN,
merchant, of London, & BENJAMIN GODIN, son of BENJAMIN GODIN of Charleston, as tenants in common. Witnesses: PETER GUINAND, JOHN NEYLE. Before
EGERTON LEIGH, J.P. WILLIAM HOPTON, Register.

Book T-T, p. 296   WILLIAM (his mark) BUSBY (BUSBEE), to JOHN
16 & 17 Jan. 1751/2   GEORGE LIX, shoemaker, both of the Congarees,
L & R   for Ł 50 SC money, 100 a. on N side Santee
                          River, bounding W on the river; NE on JOHN
GEORGE LIX; E on ANTHONY CUTLER & ARTHUR HOWELL; S & SW on WILLIAM BUSBY;
being part of 500 a. granted 18 May 1751 by Gov. JAMES GLEN to WILLIAM
BUSBY, bounding N on ANTHONY CUTLER & ARTHUR HOWELL; NW on GEORGE LIX; S
on the river & WILLIAM BUSBY. Witnesses: JOHN HAMILTON, GILBERT GILDER,
FRANCIS HAMILTON. Before ROGER GIBSON, J.P. WILLIAM HOPTON, Register.
Plat certified 15 Jan. 1751 by JOHN HAMILTON, Dep. Sur.

Book T-T, p. 301   BENJAMIN MARION, planter, of Parish of St.
1 & 2 June 1758   Thomas & St. Dennis, Berkeley Co., & ESTHER
L & R   his wife, to SAMUEL BONNEAU, planter, of St.
                          Johns Parish, for Ł 5 currency & the agreement
that BONNEAU shall reconvey the land to MARION; BONNEAU giving bond of
performance; 4 adjoining tracts of 500 a. each, total 2000 a., in Parish

of St. Thomas & St. Dennis, bounding NW on HENRY VIDEAU, estate of THOMAS
ASHBY, & on ROBERT QUASH; NE on EDWARD HARLESTON; SW on estate of THOMAS
ASHBY & on SINGLETARY; SE on SAMUEL THOMAS & said SINGLETARY; also 2
tracts adjoining tracts of 500 a. each, total 1000 a.; in same Parish
bounding N & E on vacant land; S on SAMUEL THOMAS; W on EDWARD HARLESTON.
Whereas BENJAMIN MARION, before his marriage, on 21 Nov. 1752 agreed with
BENJAMIN SIMONS, as trustee for ESTHER his intended wife, that as ESTHER
had 2 sons, then living by a former marriage with PETER BONNEAU, planter,
of same Parish; & her eldest son had no land devised to him by his father
or otherwise, she might be inclined to make a settlement of the lands
formerly belonging to her first husband, in trust of her use during her
lifetime, then to BENJAMIN MARION until her eldest son PETER BONNEAU
should come of age; & whereas BENJAMIN MARION agreed to join his wife in
making such settlement of the lands which descended to her from her late
brother, PETER SIMONS; & whereas ESTHER having lost her second son some
time ago & her eldest son is to inherit PETER BONNEAU'S lands; & believ-
ing it would be better for her son PETER if she were to sell the lands
she received from her brother & invest the money; & BENJAMIN MARION wishing to purchase the land, now they convey the 6 tracts to SAMUEL BONNEAU.
Witnesses: JOHN HENTIE, ANDREW HASELL. Before SAMUEL THOMAS, J.P. WIL-
LIAM HOPTON, Register.

Book T-T, p. 307   SAMUEL BONNEAU, reconveys to BENJAMIN MARION
3 & 5 June 1758   the 6 tracts of land mentioned on p. 301.
L & R   Witnesses: JOHN HENTIE, ANDREW HASELL. Before
                          SAMUEL THOMAS, J.P. WILLIAM HOPTON, Register.

Book T-T, p. 312   ANN MATTHEWS, of Charleston, widow, universal
16 & 17 Dec. 1756   legatee & devisee & executrix of will of AN-
L & R   THONY MATTHEWS the younger, to WILLIAM MURRAY,
                          planter, of St. Bartholomews Parish, Colleton
Co., for Ł 200 currency, 121 a. Whereas Gov. ROBERT JOHNSON on 6 Dec.
1733 granted CAPT. ANTHONY MATTHEWES, SR., 707 a. in said Co., bounding W
on PAUL JENYS; SW on Calf Pen Savannah; E on SAMUEL EVELEIGH; N on GOD-
FREYS Savannah; & whereas by several wills the land descended to ANN
MATTHEWES & an accurate resurvey shows the tract to be only 121 a.; now
she sells to MURRAY. Witnesses: THOMAS LAMBOLL, WILLIAM WILKINS. Before
DANIEL CRAWFORD, J.P. Memorial entered in Auditor's office 18 Dec. 1756
in Book D-f fol. 158 by JAMES MICHIE, Dep. Aud. WILLIAM HOPTON, Register.

Book T-T, p. 318   EDMOND BELLINGER to his brother WILLIAM,
24 Mar. 1757   1000 a. Whereas Landgrave EDMUND BELLINGER
Allotment   II, by will dated 21 Feb. 1739 recited that
                          whereas he was entitled to 48,000 a. by pat-
ent from the Lords Proprs. to his father, Landgrave EDMUND BELLINGER I,
of which 6,000 a. had been taken up by his father & the major part of the
remainder taken up by testator himself, the second Landgrave bequeathed, cum al, to his son WILLIAM 1000 a. of his patent land to be allotted
by his wife ELIZABETH or by his son EDMUND; & whereas ELIZABETH, wife of
EDMOND, 2nd Landgrave, died without having allotted the 1000 a.; & whereas EDMOND, son of 2nd Landgrave, with the consent of the sons & daughters
& devisees of the will, allotted the 1000 a. without obtaining a writ of
partition for ascertaining the respective boundaries; now he gives his
brother WILLIAM 1000 a., bounding according to plat, E on MRS. MARY
ELLIOTT; S on JAMES GIRARDEAU; W on DRAYTON. Witness: JAMES HUNTER, JR.
Before EGERTON LEIGH, J.P. WILLIAM HOPTON, Register.

Book T-T, p. 320   WILLIAM BELLINGER, planter, of St. Bartholo-
25 & 26 Mar. 1757   mews Parish, & ISABELLA his wife, to the Hon.
L & R   JOHN DRAYTON, of St. Andrews Parish, for
                          Ł 2750 currency, 1000 a. in Granville Co.,
bounding E on MRS. MARY ELLIOTT; S on JAMES GIRARDEAU; W on JOHN DRAYTON;
which 1000 a. had been bequeathed to WILLIAM BELLINGER by his father ED-
MUND BELLINGER, 2nd Landgrave (see p. 318). Witnesses: WILLIAM ROPER,
JAMES HUNTER, JR. Before EGERTON LEIGH, J.P. WILLIAM HOPTON, Register.

Book T-T, p. 326   SARAH BEVILL, executrix, & TOBIAS FORD & THOM-
25 May 1753   AS FORD, executors, of will of ABRAHAM COLSON;
Feoffment   to JOHN CRAWFORD; all of Craven Co., for Ł 300

currency, the tract of land on S side Peedee River, in Craven Co., grant-
ed to JEREMIAH ROWELL in Mar. 1743. Witnesses: WILLIAM LITTLE, JOHN
WALL, JR., JOHN CRAWFORD, JR. Before SAMUEL JORDAN, J.P. WILLIAM HOP-
TON, Register.

Book T-T, p. 329   ADAM WOOD, P.M., to JOHN RATTRAY, of Charles-
9 Sept. 1758   ton, at public auction, for Ƚ 5:5:0 currency
Sale   per a., total Ƚ 4499:5:0 SC money, 857 a.,
                         English measure, in Prince William Parish,
Granville Co. Whereas JOHN MCKENZIE, planter, of PonPon, owned 857 a. in
Prince Williams Parish, Granville Co., bounding E on JOHN & WILLIAM MUR-
RAY; N on ALEXANDER FRASER; other sides on marsh of Pocasaba Creek; ac-
cording to plat by WILLIAM MAINE, surveyor; & whereas JOHN MCKENZIE gave
bond dated 1 Oct. 1756 to JOHN RATTRAY, gentleman, of Charleston, in pe-
nal sum of Ƚ 3600 for payment of Ƚ 1800 & interest; & whereas after MC-
KENZIE'S death, RATTRAY obtained a judgment & costs against JAMES GRIND-
LAY, administrator, & PETER LEIGH, C.J., issued a writ of fieri facias
commanding the payment to seize & sell MCKENZIES estate; now he sells to
RATTRAY the 857 a. Witnesses: ROBERT WALL, WILLIAM MASON. Before JAMES
GRINDLAY, J.P. WILLIAM HOPTON, Register. Plat dated 13 July 1758 by
WILLIAM MAINE, Sur.

Book T-T, p. 333   SAMUEL PRIOLEAU, gentleman, of Charleston, &
5 & 6 Sept. 1758   PROVIDENCE, his wife, to THOMAS ELLIOTT,
L & R   planter, of Stono, for Ƚ 1100 currency, house
                         & lot #191 in Charleston, bo-nding E 94 ft. on
Friend Street; N on THOMAS ELLIOTT; W on THOMAS FARR & RICHARD MASON; S
on WILLIAM HARVEY; being 86 ft. in breadth at lower end; & 140 ft. from E
to W. Witnesses: ROBERT WILLIAMS, JR., DANIEL LEGARE, JR. Before JAMES
GRINDLAY, J.P. WILLIAM HOPTON, Register.

Book T-T, p. 338   HENRY LAURENS, & ELEANOR his wife, to EGERTON
13 & 14 Sept. 1758   LEIGH, ESQ., both of Charleston, for Ƚ 5 cur-
L & R   rency, 500 a. on Santee River, in Craven Co.,
                         granted by Gov. WILLIAM HENRY LYTTLETON on 2
May 1758 to HENRY LAURENS; bounding SW on the river; other sides on va-
cant land. Witnesses: MARTHA BREMAR, JAMES HUNTER, JR. Before JOHN MUR-
RAY, J.P. WILLIAM HOPTON, Register.

Book T-T, p. 342   JOHN GRINNAN, of Charleston, to JONAH ROBERTS,
28 Sept. 1758   planter, of Craven Co., for Ƚ 600 currency,
Assignment   the L & R dated 5 & 6 June last by which ROB-
                         ERTS had conveyed to GRINNAN 490 a., being
half of 980 a. in Craven Co., bounding E on JONAH ROBERTS. Witnesses:
JOHN CALVERT, THOMAS YEOMANS. Before JOHN MURRAY, J.P. WILLIAM HOPTON,
Register.

Book T-T, p. 344   JONAH ROBERT, planter, of Amelia Township, to
29 & 30 Sept. 1758   CAPT. JOHN MCDONALD, of the SC Regiment, for
L & R   Ƚ 900 currency, 980 a. in Craven Co., bounding
                         W on MR. MORRILL; S on vacant land; E on MR.
PHIPPS; N on MR. TURNER & on vacant land; which tract was originally
granted by Lt. Gov. THOMAS BROUGHTON to PETER ROBERT, the father, who devised to JONAH. Whereas PETER ROBERT, planter, of St. James Parish, Santee, Craven Co., owned several plantations & by will dated 11 May 1739
gave the choice of the 2 not therein devised to his first son, PETER, &
the 1 remaining to his son JONAH; & whereas PETER ROBERT, the son, made
his choice & JONAH received this tract; now he sells to MCDONALD. Witnesses: JOHN CALVERT, THOMAS YEOMANS. Before JOHN MURRAY, J.P. WILLIAM
HOPTON, Register.

Book T-T, p. 349   ELIAS FOISSIN, ESQ., of Craven Co., to JUDITH
5 & 6 Sept. 1758   WRAGG, widow & executrix of will of JOSEPH
L & R by Mortgage   WRAGG, merchant, of Charleston, as security on
                         bond of even date in penal sum of Ƚ 5400 for
payment of Ƚ 2700 currency, with interest, on 6 Sept. 1759; 700 a. in
Craven Co., bounding SE on Peedee River; SW on WILLIAM SWINTON; NW on
JOHN GREEN; NE on JAMES PAINE. Witnesses: JOHN FOISSIN, ANN ROTHMAHLER.
Before GEORGE PAWLEY, J.P. WILLIAM HOPTON, Register. On 23 Aug. 1770
JOHN WRAGG declared mortgage satisfied. Witness: JAMES KER.

Book T-T, p. 353   JAMES GERRALD, gentleman, to GILBERT GIBSON,
11 & 12 Sept. 1758   planter, both of Craven Co., for Ł 100 curren-
L & R   cy, 31-3/4 a. in Craven Co. opposite Saxegotha
Township, bounding N on THOMAS MCPHERSON; W on
a large lake; S & E on JAMES GERALD. Whereas Gov. JAMES GLEN on 10 Feb.
1749 granted JAMES LESSLEY 300 a. at the Congarees, opposite Saxegotha
Township, bounding S on vacant land & WILLIAM HOWELL; W on the Congaree
River; N on THOMAS MCPHERSON; E on vacant land; & whereas JAMES LESSLEY &
SIBBLE his wife, by L & R dated 19 & 20 Mar. 1749, sold the land for
Ł 300 currency to WILLIAM STROTHER, of Craven Co., & whereas STROTHER
died intestate & his oldest son, CHARLES, inherited; & he by L & R dated
12 & 13 Feb. 1757 sold the tract to JAMES GERRALD for Ł 2000 currency;
now GIBSON sells a part of the land to GIBSON. Witnesses: JOHN EVINS,
GEORGE STROTHER. Before JOHN PEARSON, J.P. WILLIAM HOPTON, Register.

Book T-T, p. 358   JAMES (his mark) BRUNSON, planter, & REBECCA
19 & 20 Dec. 1757   (her mark) his wife, to MATTHEW SHINGLETON,
L & R   carpenter, both of Craven Co., for Ł 200 currency, 200 a. in Craven Co., at the high hills,
bounding SW on MATTHEW SHINGLETON; other sides on vacant land. Witnesses: ISAAC BRUNSON, JAMES BRUNSON. Before WILLIAM BOYKIN, J.P. WILLIAM
HOPTON, Register.

Book T-T, p. 363   JOHN PHILIP (alias CASPAR, his mark) BYERLY,
23 & 24 Oct. 1754   to THOMAS DAVIS, both of Berkeley Co., for
L & R   Ł 50 currency & other considerations, 50 a. on
l of the N branches of Saludy River, called
Reedy River, bounding NE, SE by said river & vacant land; SW & NW on vacant land. Witnesses: ANDREW BROWN, JOHN TURK, CHARLES BANKS. Before
JOHN FRANCIS, J.P. WILLIAM HOPTON, Register.

Book T-T, p. 368   JOHN WILLIAMS, carpenter & planter, of St.
23 & 24 Oct. 1758   James Parish, Santee, Craven Co., to BENJAMIN
L & R   GARDEN, SAMPSON NEYLE, & FRANCIS BREMAR, trustees for ANN STILES (lately married to COPE-
LAND STILES); as security on bond dated 17 July 1750 in the penal sum of
Ł 1800 for payment of Ł 900, currency, with interest, on 17 July 1753,
which bond was given by WILLIAMS to the Rev. ALEXANDER GARDEN, of St.
Philip's Parish, Charleston; & whereas by indenture of same date, 17 July
1750, CHARLES PINCKNEY, ESQ., of Charleston, & ELIZABETH his wife, of 1st
part; JOHN WILLIAMS, joiner & carpenter, then of Charelston, of 2nd part;
& the Rev. ALEXANDER GARDEN, of 3rd part; reciting that PINCKNEY, for
Ł 900, conveyed to GARDEN 2 subdivisions of 4 lots #13 & #14, upon certain trusts & under certain provisoes, redeemed by WILLIAMS on payment of
Ł 900 & intereest; & whereas GARDEN, recently deceased by will appointed
NEYLE & BREMAR his executors & his daughter ANN GARDEN, executrix; &
whereas the devisees & legatees under the will agreed to accept certain
outstanding bonds due the estate as part & share of their claims; &
whereas BREMAR & NEYLE on 31 July last assigned over to ANN GARDEN said
bond as her dividend of her father's estate; & whereas ANN & her husband,
COPELAND STILES, & her trustees wish further security; now WILLIAMS con-
veys to them 400 a. on the seashore near the mouth of the Santee River in
St. James Parish, Santee, bounding SE on the marsh; SW on ROBERT MORRELL;
NW & NE on vacant land lately granted by Gov. WILLIAM HENRY LYTTELTON to
JOHN WILLIAMS. Witnesses: JAMES HUNTER, JR., JOHN NEYLE. Before EGERTON
LEIGH, J.P. WILLIAM HOPTON, Register.

Book T-T, p. 375   WILLIAM KELSEY, planter, of Prince William
18 Oct. 1758   Parish, Granville Co., to JOHN HODSDEN, THOMAS
Mortgage   ELLIS, & BENJAMIN DART, merchants, of Charleston, executors of will of SOLOMON MILNER, mer-
chant, of Charleston; as security on bond of even date in penal sum of
Ł 1893 for payment of Ł 946:10:0 currency, with interest, on 18 Oct.
1759, for the use of MILNER'S estate; 830 a. in Prince William Parish,
adjoining lands of MR. FLOWERS, JAMES ST. JOHN, & the Hoospur Creek; also
delivery 9 Negro slaves. Witnesses: CHARLES PINCKNEY, FRANCIS VANNELSEN.
Before BENJAMIN SMITH, J.P. WILLIAM HOPTON, Register.

Book T-T, p. 380   WILLIAM TYRRELL, planter, & ANN (her mark) his
25 & 26 Nov. 1757   wife, to JOHN BLALOCK, planter, both of the

L & R   WELCH tract, Craven Co., for Ŀ 700 currency,
                               200 a. on Peedee River, in the WELCH tract.
Witnesses: JAMES WENTWORTH, SARAH (her mark) HARRY. Before GEORGE HICKS,
J.P. WILLIAM HOPTON, Register.

Book T-T, p. 384   ABRAHAM (his mark) LUNDY, to JOHN CRAWFORD,
24 & 25 Aug. 1758   both of Craven Co., for Ŀ 20 sterling British,
L & R   150 a. in Craven Co., on SW side Peedee River,
                              bounding SE on JAMES GILLISPIE; SW on vacant
land; NW on WILLIAM HAINSWORTH; which land was granted 24 Mar. 1756 to
LUNDY. Witnesses: THOMAS BINGHAM, DANIEL (his mark) LUNDY, SAMUEL WINDES.
Before WILLIAM LORD, J.P. WILLIAM HOPTON, Register.

Book T-T, p. 390   DAVID EVANS, planter, of Craven Co., heir of
13 & 14 Aug. 1752   MARY EVANS, to JOHN LIDE, planter, for Ŀ 325
L & R   currency, 200 a. in WELCH tract in Craven Co.,
                              granted by Gov. JAMES GLEN on 22 Jan. 1747 to
MARY EVANS, natural mother of DAVID; bounding NE on Peedee River; SE on
ROWELL; SW on vacant land; NW on MR. YOUNG. Witnesses: JOHN HUGHES, ABEL
EVANS, JAMES (his mark) PITMAN. Before WILLIAM JAMES, J.P. WILLIAM HOP-
TON, Register.

Book T-T, p. 394   ELIZABETH STONE & ROBERT RIVERS, of James Is-
12 & 13 June 1758   land, surviving executors of will of BENJAMIN
L & R·   STONE, shipwright, of James Island to MALLORY
                              RIVERS, planter, of James Island, for Ŀ 180
currency, 60 a. on James Island bounding SW & SE on BENJAMIN STILES; NW
on ROBERT RIVERS, son of JEREMIAH; NE on a Savannah; the 60 a. being a
part of 228 a. granted to GEORGE GANTLETT. Whereas BENJAMIN STONE by
will dated 30 Oct. 1751 directed that said 60 a. be sold for the use of
his surviving family; equally, & appointed ELIZABETH STONE & ROBERT RIV-
ERS, executrix & executor, now they carry out his wish. Witnesses: WIL-
LIAM KING, JR., BENJAMIN STONE. Before DANIEL PEPPER, J.P. WILLIAM HOP-
TON, Register.

Book T-T, p. 399   THOMAS STOCKS, cabinet maker, & SARAH (her
1 & 2 Oct. 1758   mark) his wife, to PHILIP MENSING, blacksmith,
L & R   both of Charleston, for Ŀ 660 currency, the SE
                              part of his lot #254 in Charleston, bounding E
45 ft. on King Street; N & W on parts of lot #254; S 90 ft. on lot #252.
Witnesses: STEPHEN TOWNSEND, JAMES HUNTER, JR. Before EGERTON LEIGH,
J.P. WILLIAM HOPTON, Register.

Book T-T, p. 405   JOHN ARMBRISTER, baker, & MARY ELIZABETH his
3 & 4 Nov. 1758   wife, to GABRIEL MANIGAULT, merchant, both of
L & R by Mortgage   Charleston, as security on bond of even date
                              in penal sum of Ŀ 3800 for payment of Ŀ 1900
currency, with interest, on 4 Nov. then next; that lot in Charleston
which by L & R dated 3 & 4 Nov. 1758 he had purchased from HANNAH MCGREG-
OR, widow; bounding E on JAMES ROLLIN & JANE DUPUY; W 43-1/2 ft. on Meeting Street; N 135 ft. on JAMES EADES; S on JOHN LAURENS, STEPHEN MILLER,
& JAMES ROLLIN. Witnesses: JOHN DODD, JAMES HUNTER, JR. Before EGERTON
LEIGH, J.P. WILLIAM HOPTON, Register.

Book T-T, p. 411   CHRISTIAN RUMPH of Berkeley Co., with the con-
19 Oct. 1739   sent of his mother, BARBARA (her mark) RUMPH,
Feoffment   to PETER RHOTE (ROTH), carpenter, for Ŀ 40
                              currency, 50 a. in Orangeburgh Township,
Berkeley Co., bounding NW on PETER INDERHABNOTT; NE & SE on CHRISTIAN
RUMPH; SW on ULRICK REBER. Witnesses: WALTER GORING, PHILIP MORRIS, JOHN
PEARSON. Before CHRISTIAN MOTE, J.P. at Orangeburgh. WILLIAM HOPTON,
Register. Plat given.

Book T-T, p. 414   PETER ROTH, carpenter, to ULRICH BRUNNER, car-
17 & 18 Aug. 1758   penter, both of Orangeburgh Township, for Ŀ 40
L & R   currency, 50 a. in Orangeburgh Township,
                              bounding NW on PETER INHABINETT; NE & SE on
JACOB RUMPH; SW on ULRICH RABER; which land was granted to CHRISTIAN
RUMPH, who on 19 Oct. 1739 sold to ROTH (p. 411). Witnesses: LEWIS GOL-
SAN, JACOB GIESSENDANNER. Before JOHN CHEVILLETTE, J.P. WILLIAM HOPTON,

Book T-T, p. 419   HANNAH MCGREGOR, widow to JOHN ARMBRISTER,
3 & 4 Nov. 1758   baker, both of Charleston, for Ł 1900 paid to
L & R   by ARMBRISTER to GABRIEL MANIGAULT, sole mort-
                    gagee of the lot, in full satisfaction of said
mortgage, & Ł 1000 paid to HANNAH MCGREGOR, a certain lot & premises.
Whereas JOHN LAURENS, merchant, of Charleston, & ELIZABETH his wife, by L
& R dated 23 & 24 Feb. 1746 sold ALEXANDER MCGREGOR, victualer, of
Charleston, husband of HANNAH, a lot in Charleston, bounding W 43-1/2 ft.
on Meeting Street; E on JAMES ROLLIN & JANE DUPUY; S on JOHN LAURENS,
STEPHEN MILLER, & JAMES ROLLIN; N 135 ft. on JAMES EADES; & whereas MC-
GREGOR by will dated 6 Mar. 1755 bequeathed the lot to HANNAH, & she by
L & R dated 3 & 4 June 1755 mortgaged the lot to GABRIEL MANIGAULT for
Ł 1600; now she conveys to ARMBRISTER. Witnesses: JOHN DODD, JAMES HUNT-
ER, JR. Before EGERTON LEIGH, J.P. WILLIAM HOPTON, Register.

Book T-T, p. 425   ROBERT RIVERS, SR., planter, of James Island,
5 & 6 Mar. 1756   & MARY his wife, to MALLORY RIVERS, planter,
L & R   of same place, for Ł 1215:3:6 currency, 85-3/4
                    a., English measure, in St. Andrews Parish; on
S side James Island, part of a tract formerly belonging to his father
GEORGE RIVERS, SR., which 85-3/4 a. by will & other conveyances now in
possession of ROBERT; bounding N on JOHN MATTHEWES; E on CAPT. ROBERT
RIVERS, JR.; S on Lt. ROBERT RIVERS; W on WILLIAM WILKINS & JOHN RIVERS.
Witnesses: THOMAS RIVERS, GEORGE RIVERS, SR., GEORGE RIVERS, JR. Before
ROBERT RIVERS, J.P. WILLIAM HOPTON, Register. Plat of 85-3/4 a. certi-
fied by ROBERT SCREVEN 25 Feb. 1756.

Book T-T, p. 429   JOHN RIVERS, SR., planter, & SARAH (her mark)
28 & 29 June 1756   his wife, to MALLORY RIVERS, planter, both of
L & R   James Island, for Ł 354:2:6 currency, 25 a.,
                    English measure, on S side James Island, part
of a tract formerly belonging to JOHN'S father, GEORGE RIVERS, SR., which
25 a. were allotted to JOHN; bounding N on WILLIAM WILKINS; E on ROBERT
RIVERS, SR.; S on Lt. ROBERT RIVERS'S land called the Savannah; W on DAN-
IEL RIVERS. Witnesses: HENRY SAMWAYS, HANNAH JENKINS, THOMAS COLLINS.
Before ROBERT RIVERS, J.P. Plat of 25 a. certified 8 Mar. 1756 by ROBERT
SCREVEN, Sur. JOHN gave MALLORY bond of performance.

Book T-T, p. 433   JOHN RIVERS, planter, & SARAH (her mark) his
1 & 2 Mar. 1754   wife, to MALLORY RIVERS, planter, both of
L & R   James Island, for Ł 50 currency, 50 a. in
                    Berkeley Co., being an island & marsh on S
side James Island, granted by Gov. JAMES GLEN on 14 May 1752 to JOHN RIV-
ERS. Witnesses: THOMAS RIVERS, GEORGE RIVERS, BENJAMIN STILES. Before
ROBERT RIVERS, J.P. WILLIAM HOPTON, Register.

Book T-T, p. 437   Whereas CAPT. JOHNSON LYNCH, planter, of
30 June 1735   Berkeley Co., some time before his death in
Declaration   Oct. 1709, for Ł 40 currency, sold JOHN (his
                    mark) BLAKE, 100 a. bounding on land belonging
to CHRISTOPHER BEECH; & whereas, sometime after, JOHN BLAKE got 177 a.,
then vacant, run out at the head of said 100 a. & had the 2 tracts of
277 a. granted to him on 23 July 1711; & whereas JOHN BALKE sold the 2
tracts to his sister, MARY BEECH, since descended, & since then they have
become the property of JOHN CUMING, on which he now lives; & whereas on
15 June 1729, being directed by JOHN CUMING that the deed of sale did not
entitle him (JOHN BLAKE) to the 100 a. out of CAPT. JOHNSON LYNCH'S lands,
besides the 277 a. for which he had a grant passed, supposing the 277 a.
were all vacant land, & that if he (BLAKE) would assign JOHNSON LYNCH'S
deed of sale to him (CUMING) he would recover the same, therefore BLAKE
assigned the indenture whereon the assignment was written, etc., to CUM-
ING; now BLAKE, having made himself fully acquainted with the whold matter, certifies that the land on which CUMING lives is the very land sold
BLAKE by LYNCH, & is part of the 277 a. granted BLAKE; that BLAKE has received no money from CUMING, & that the assignment was made through mis-
information. Witnesses: GUILLAUME GALLATIN, JOHN COMBE. Before ELIAS
HORRY, J.P. JOHN COMBE declared before PETER PAGETT, J.P. that he saw
JOHN BLAKE sign said declaration & deliver ti to ANTHONY BONNEAU.

WILLIAM HOPTON, Register.

Book T-T, p. 439   JOHN GIBBES, planter, of Johns Island, son of
8 & 9 Nov. 1758   WILLIAM GIBBES, to WILLIAM GIBBES, merchant,
L & R by Mortgage   of Charleston, as security on bond of even
                         date in penal sum of Ŀ 14,000 for payment of
Ŀ 7000 currency, with interest, on 1 Jan. 1760; 219 a., English measure,
in Christ Church Parish, Berkeley Co., bounding SW on RICHARD FOWLER &
THOMAS BOLTON; NW on CHARLES PINCKNEY & THOMAS WHITESIDE; other sides on
THOMAS WHITESIDE; also 17 a. in Christ Church Parish, bounding SW on NA-
THANIEL POLHILL; NE on THOMAS WHITESIDE & WILLIAM GIBBES; SE on WILLIAM
GIBBES. Witnesses: BARNARD BECKMAN, JOB MILLNER, THOMAS LAMBOLL, JR.
Before PETER MANIGAULT, J.P. WILLIAM HOPTON, Register. On 30 Apr. 1768
WILLIAM GIBBES declared mortgage satisfied. Witness: FELIX WARLEY.

Book T-T, p. 444   MARY RANKIN, widow of JOHN RANKIN, to JOHN
20 Nov. 1758   ELLIS, planter, of St. Helena Island, Gran-
Confirmation   ville Co., for Ŀ 10 currency, 200 a. Whereas
                         JOHN RANKIN & MARY, his wife, by L & R dated
24 & 25 Nov. 1752 sold DANIEL SAVAGE, planter, of Granville Co., 200 a.
on Hilton Head, in Granville Co., bounding N on COL. BARNWELL; W on South
Creek; E & S on ALEXANDER TRENCH, being part of 300 a. sold by TRENCH to
DAVID ALEXANDER; which 200 a. were the right & inheritance of MARY RANKIN
before her marriage with JOHN RANKIN by descent to her on the death of
RICHARD POOR, her father; & whereas DANIEL SAVAGE, & JANE his wife, by L
& R dated 10 & 11 Mar. 1757 sold the 200 a. to JOHN ELLIS; & whereas MARY
RANKIN in first deed did not exclude herself of her inheritance, accord-
ing to law, so that ELLIS'S title is imperfect; now she confirms ELLIS in
his possession. Witnesses: ROBERT WILLIAMS, JR., JOHN MILNER. Before
ALEXANDER GORDON, J.P. WILLIAM HOPTON, Register.

Book T-T, p. 446   JOHN WOODBERRY, planter, to JAMES GERRALD,
9 & 10 Jan. 1756   planter, both of Craven Co., for Ŀ 100 curren-
L & R   cy, 100 a. in Craven Co., bounding E on JONAH
                         COLLINS; N on VAUGHANS Lake; W & S on vacant
land. Witnesses: WILLIAM MATTHEWES, WILLIAM ELVISS, EPHRAIM FRINCK. Before THOMAS BLYTHE, J.P. WILLIAM HOPTON, Register.

Book T-T, p. 449   JOHN WOODBERRY, planter, & MARGARET his wife,
24 & 25 Mar. 1758   to JAMES GERRALD, planter, both of Prince
L & R   George Parish, Craven Co., for Ŀ 100 currency,
                         100 a. on E side Little Peedee, on Vaughans
Lake; bounding NW on EVAN VAUGHAN; SE on land laid out; other sides on
vacant land; which land was granted WOODBERRY on 21 May 1757 by Gov. WIL-
LIAM HENRY LYTTLETON. Witnesses: ANTHONY MARTIN WHITE, WILLIAM ELVISS.
Before THOMAS BLYTHE, J.P. WILLIAM HOPTON, Register.

Book T-T, p. 454   JOB ROTHMAHLER, of Georgetown, to JAMES HAT-
1 & 2 Feb. 1755   CHER, of Port Royal, for Ŀ 300 currency, 200 a.
L & R   on Port Royal Island, Granville Co., bounding
                         S on FRANCIS OLDFIELD; N on Mackey's Creek.
Witnesses: RICE PRICE, WILLIAM PARKER. Before STEPHEN BULL, J.P. WIL-
LIAM HOPTON, Register.

Book T-T, p. 461   THOMAS RIVERS, planter, & MARY (her mark) his
20 & 21 Mar. 1754   wife, to CAPT. ROBERT RIVERS the eldest, plant-
L & R   er, both of James Island, Berkeley Co., for
                         Ŀ 1910 currency, 130 a., English measure, on S
side James Island, being part of 2 tracts formerly belonging to DANIEL
GREATBATCH & GEORGE RIVERS; 1 tract since belonging to THOMAS RIVERS; the
other to the several sons & devisees of will of GEORGE RIVERS; the tract
of 130 a. by wills of DANIEL GREATBATCH & GEORGE RIVERS & by various par-
titions, etc., now being vested in THOMAS RIVERS in fee simple; bounding
N on JOHN WITTER & JOHN RIVERS; E on other parts said 2 tracts belonging
to THOMAS RIVERS; S on marsh; W on part of 1 tract formerly belonging to
GEORGE RIVERS, now to ROBERT RIVERS, 1 of the 2 sons & devisees of GEORGE
RIVERS. Witnesses: ROBERT RIVERS, WILLIAM HOLMES, THOMAS RIVERS, JR.
Before DANIEL PEPPER, J.P. WILLIAM HOPTON, Register. Plat certified 20
Jan. 1754 by ROBERT SCREVEN.

Book T-T, p. 468   GEORGE Lord ANSON, Baron of Soberton, Co. of
1 Sept. 1757   Southampton, Great Britain, appoints RICHARD
Power of Attorney   LAMBTON, merchant, of Charleston, his attorn-
                         ey, to sell his several estates in SC; that
is, his plantation & orange grove of 23-3/4 a. in St. Philips Parish,
Charleston, bounding E on Cooper River; W on ANSON; N on ISAAC MAZYCK; S
on SHUBRICK & Co., also all marsh land & other land around said plantation as far as low water mark; also his half barony (the other half belonging to WILLIAM RUGGE, ESQ.). Witnesses: PHILIP STEVENS, FRANCIS
WELLES (of Boswell Court, Parish of St. Clement Danes, Co. of Middlesex,
gentleman). Before MARSHE DICKINSON, mayor of London, signed by HODGES.
WILLIAM HOPTON, Register.

Book T-T, p. 471   MATHAN EVANS, planter, & ANNE (her mark) his
29 & 30 Aug. 1758   wife, to WADE BLAIR, merchant, both of Craven
L & R   Co., for ₺ 250 currency, 200 a. in Craven Co.,
                         granted 24 May 1745 by Gov. JAMES GLEN to
THOMAS GROOM (see Book L.L. fol. 269); who by will dated 11 Aug. 1747 bequeathed to PATTY O'QUIN; who, with her husband, TAYLOR O'QUIN, by L & R
dated 17 & 18 June 1756 sold to NATHAN EVANS (Book R.R. p. 19); bounding
SE on EDMOND ATKINS; NW on PIERCY PAWLEY; NE on JOHN SAUNDERS; SW on Pee-
dee River. Witnesses: HENRY BERRY, CHARLES PATE, ANDREW (his mark)
BERRY. Before ABRAHAM BUCKHOLTZ, J.P. WILLIAM HOPTON, Register.

Book T-T, p. 475   LAZARUS BROWN, planter, & JANE (JEAN) his
22 & 23 Aug. 1758   wife, to JOSEPH GLOVER, planter, both of St.
L & R   Bartholomew Parish, Colleton Co., for ₺ 1055
                         currency, 400 a. in St. Bartholomew Parish,
bounding N on CULCHETH GIBBES & estate of ISAAC HAINES; E on JOHN JACKSON
& estate of JOHN WILLIAMSON; W on estate of ISAAC HAINES & WALTER IZARD;
N on estate of JOHN WILLIAMSON & JOHN JACKSON; which 400 a. were, by 2
grants of 200 a. each, granted by the Lords Proprs. on 23 July 1711 to
EDWARD FLAHARTY, father of said JANE BROWN, his only child & heir. Witnesses: THOMAS MELVIN, JAMES STOBO, JR. Before JAMES SHARP, J.P. Memorial entered in Auditor's office 27 Nov. 1758 in Book D. #4, p. 234, by
JOHN BASSNETT, Dep. Aud. WILLIAM HOPTON, Register.

Book T-T, p. 479   THOMAS WITTER, planter, of James Island, St.
1 & 2 Nov. 1758   Andrews Parish, Berkeley Co., 1 of the sons &
L & R   devisees of will of JOHN WITTER, the elder,
                         planter, of same place; to WILLIAM SCREVEN,
planter, of same place; for ₺ 1650 currency; his (THOMAS WITTER'S) house
(formerly JAMES SCREVEN'S house); & 1/3 the remaier lands of JOHN WIT-
TER, SR., measuring 165-3/4 a. on James Island, bounding N on the third
allotted to MATTHEW WITTER; E on the Savannah Road; S on the third allotted to JONATHAN WITTER; W on JAMES SCREVEN & land devised by JOHN WITTER
to his grandson, JOHN WITTER, JR., an infant. Whereas JOHN WITTER, by
several grants, wills, etc., owned a certain house & lands; & by will
dated 23 July 1756 bequeathed to his 3 sons, THOMAS, JONATHAN & MATTHEW,
equally, the residue of his lands & appointed his friends HENRY SAMWAYS,
JAMES SCREVEN, & WILLIAM SCREVEN, & his son JONATHAN, his executors; &
whereas after his death his executors divided the residue, or 497-1/4 a.,
equally among the 3 sons; now THOMAS sells his portion to ᵤSCREVEN. Witnesses: THOMAS BALLINE, THOMAS LAMBOLL. Before ROBERT PRINGLE, J.P.

Book T-T, p. 494   JOHN MATTHEWES, gentleman, of Charleston, &
29 & 30 Sept. 1758   SARAH his wife, to GEORGE RIVERS, planter, of
L & R   Berkeley Co., for ₺ 4200 currency, 305-1/2 a.
                         on James Island, on E side Stono River in 2
tracts of 265-1/2 a. purchased from JONATHAN EVANS (eldest son of JONA-
THAN EVANS the elder) & ELIZABETH his wife; & 40 a. purchased from SAM-
UEL EVANS & MARY his wife; the 305-1/2 a. bounding W on the river; N on
DANIEL HEYWARD & JOHN WITTER'S land; E on JAMES SCREVEN & JOHN WITTER'S
land; S on GEORGE RIVERS & WILLIAM WILKINS (son of JOHN WILKINS). Wit-
nesses: THOMAS BALLANTINE, JOSEPH BALL, JR. Before DANIEL CRAWFORD, J.P.
WILLIAM HOPTON, Register.

Book T-T, p. 501   BASTION (his mark) BUSS, planter, & BARBARY
1 & 2 Dec. 1758   (her mark) his wife (formerly BARBARY HUSAR),
L & R   to JOHN JACOB FRIDIG, planter, both of

84

Berkeley Co, for Ł 30 currency, 100 a. granted by Gov. JAMES GLEN on 19
July 1748 to BARBARY HUSAR, 100 a. in Saxegotha Township, bounding on N
corner on JOHN FRIDIG; other sides on vacant land. Witnesses: ULRICH
(his mark) STOOKER, JOHN (his mark) STROUB. Before JOHN PEARSON, J.P.
WILLIAM HOPTON, Register.

Book T-T, p. 506   ALEXANDER ROSE, gentleman, of Charleston, to
12 & 13 Dec. 1757   JOSEPH ALLSTON, planter, of Craven Co., for
L & R   Ł 2250 currency, 2 lots #31 & #32 on the bay
                          of Georgetown, 200 ft. x 217.9 ft., bounding E
on Screven Street; W on lot #30; N on lot #64; S on Front Street down to
low water mark. Witnesses: ARCHIBALD JOHNSON, ANDREW MARR. Before DAN-
IEL CRAWFORD, J.P. WILLIAM HOPTON, Register.

Book T-T, p. 511   STEPHEN CRELL, & JOHANNA his wife, to HANS
17 Oct. 1758   ULRIC BACHMAN, planter, both of Saxegotha Town-
Release   ship, 250 a. in Saxegotha Township bounding NE
                          on Santee River; SE on PHILIP POOL; SW on va-
cant land; NW on RUDY COPLET. Whereas STEPHEN CRELL, by L & R dated 29 &
30 June 1757 (see BB S.S. pages 81-84) sold JACOB EAGNER 250 a. in Saxegotha Township originally granted CRELL on 16 Sept. 173?; & whereas JACOB
EAGNER on July 1, 1757 mortgaged the land to WILLIAM BAKER; & whereas by
L & R dated 29 & 30 Aug. 1757 EAGNER conveyed the land & original grant
to STEPHEN CRELL; & whereas WILLIAM BAKER, for the Ł 400 currency & interest due, assigned the bond & mortgage to HANS ULRIC BACHMAN; now CRELL
releases his claim to BACHMAN with the agreement that CRELL & his wife
JOHANNA be allowed the use of a house during their lifetime; the town lot
mentioned in original grant not being included in said transactions. Witnesses: HENRY GALLMAN, JOHN CONRAD GEIGER. Before PETER GRIM, J.P. WIL-
LIAM HOPTON, Register.

Book T-T, p. 515   WILLIAM BAKER assigns to HANS ULRIC BACHMAN
17 Oct. 1758   (BOUGHMAN) bond & mortgage. See p. 511. See
Assignment of Mortgage   Bk. S.S. page 80. Witnesses: JOHN FREGMOUTH,
                          JOHN CONRAD GEIGER. Before PETER GRIM, J.P.
WILLIAM HOPTON, Register.

Book T-T, p. 516   JONATHAN WITTER, planter, of James Island, St.
5 Sept. 1758   Andrews Parish, Berkeley Co., mortgaged to
Mortgage   JOHN DILL, planter, 160 a. on James Island,
                          with the dwelling house because DILL stood se-
curity for WITTER on 2 bonds; 1 given to JONATHAN RIVERS, ship carpenter;
the other to WILLIAM ELLIS. Witnesses: ISAAC RIVERS, JOHN HEARN. Before
JOHN MURRAY, J.P. WILLIAM HOPTON, Register.

Book T-T, p. 519   ROBERT GODFREY, planter, of Granville Co., &
8 & 9 Feb. 1758   ELIZABETH his wife, to ROBERT SAMS, planter,
L & R   of Colleton Co., for Ł 1200 currency, 500 a.
                          on S side Coosaw River, on Combee Island, Gran-
ville Co., bounding E on WILLIAM HOLMES & ROBERT COCHRAN; S & W on Lady
ELIZABETH BLAKE; which 500 a. were granted 17 June 1714 to Lady BLAKE &
by various conveyances became the property of GEORGE SMITH, gentleman, of
St. Andrews Parish; who died intestate & his daughters ANNE, JANE, & SAR-
AH, inherited. By L & R dated 20 & 21 Nov. 1751 ANNE SMITH, CHARLES
FOUCHERAND & JANE his wife, & SARAH HILL, sold to EDWARD BULLARD,
carpenter, of Charleston; who, by L & R dated 22 & 23 Apr. 1754 sold to
ROBERT GODFREY. Witnesses: WILLIAM GOUGH, JOHN BARNWELL, PHILIP MARTIN-
GAGELE. Before WILLIAM HARVEY, J.P. WILLIAM HOPTON, Register.

Book T-T, p. 525   WILLIAM GIBBONS, planter, of Ga. (1 of the
30 & 31 Mar. 1758   sons & devisees of will of JOSEPH GIBBONS,
L & R   planter, of Wadmalaw Island, Colleton Co.), &
                          SARAH his wife, to ROBERT SAMS, planter, of
Colleton Co., for Ł 2000 currency, 562 a. including a small island of
about 16 a.; bounding N on SAMUEL WINBOURN; NW on marsh & a creek out of
a branch of Bohicket Creek; W on said branch; SW on marsh & said branch;
S on marshes; E on ROBERT SAMS (formerly DAVID FERGUSON). Whereas Lt.
Gov. THOMAS BROUGHTON on 30 Sept. 1736 granted PAUL HAMILTON 1060 a. in
Colleton Co., which HAMILTON by L & R dated 29 & 30 Mar. 1737 sold to
JOSEPH GIBBONS, who divided the tract into 3 parts, marked by 2 black

lines drawn on the plat in the words, JOSEPH'S part; JOHN'S part; WIL-
LIAM'S part; & by will dated 15 Dec. 1750, among other things, bequeathed
to his wife, ANNE, her dwelling on the place where he lived (1065 a.)
during her lifetime; & bequeathed to son WILLIAM, the SE part as indica-
ted on plat, or 562 a. including a small island of 16 a.; now WILLIAM
sells his share to ROBERT SAMS. Witnesses: JOHN JOACHIM ZUBBY, WILLIAM
CLIFTON, JOSEPH GIBBONS. Before JOHN REMINGTON, J.P. WILLIAM HOPTON,
Register.

Book T-T, p. 536   SARAH, wife of WILLIAM GIBBON, renounced her
31 Mar. 1758   title to their share of 1065 a. (562 a.) which
Renunciation of Dower   WILLIAM GIBBONS sold to ROBERT SAMS (p. 525).
                         Before JAMES DEVEAUX, J. of G.C. in Savannah.
WILLIAM HOPTON, Register.

Book T-T, p. 538   JOHN (his mark) YOUNG, shoemaker, of St. James
1 & 2 Sept. 1757   Goose Creek, Berkeley Co., to BENJAMIN FARAR,
L & R   doctor, of Saxegotha Township, for L 300 cur-
                         rency, 250 a. opposite Saxegotha Township,
bounding NW on JOHN FAIRCHILD; E on JOHN FRASER & vacant land; S on vacant land; W on Santee (Congaree River) River; which 250 a. were granted
on 24 May 1745, by Gov. JAMES GLEN to JACOB YOUNG; who died intestate; &
inherited by his eldest son, JOHN. Witnesses: EVAN (his mark) REECE,
JOHN SPARKS. Before JOHN PEARSON, J.P. WILLIAM HOPTON, Register.

Book T-T, p. 545   THOMAS ALLAN, planter, of Berkeley Co., &
20 June 1713   FRANCES his wife (formerly FRANCES NORTHALL),
Feoffment   to WILLIAM GIBBON & ANDREW ALLAN, merchants,
                         of Charleston, for L 130 currency, 3 lots in
Charleston #188, #189, #79, except as accepted; bounding S on a street
leading W from Cooper River by the lands of COL. ROBERT DANIEL, JONATHAN
AMORY, DR. GEORGE FRANKLIN, & DR. JOHN HUTCHINSON; W on a back street,
next the entrenchments, leading to Presbyterian Meeting House; E on DR.
JOHN HUTCHINSON (formerly JOHN HOLLAND); N on Presbyterian Meeting House.
Whereas FRANCES SIMMONS of Charleston owned 3 lots in Charleston, or the
greatest part thereof, 2 of them (#188 & #189) having been granted in 2
grants by the Lords Proprs. to CAPT. HENRY SIMMONS; the other lot, adjoining the other 2, having been granted by the Lords Proprs. to WILLIAM
SADLER; & whereas she had, during her lifetime, settled certain property
in trustees for the use of the Presbyterian Church in Charleston; & whereas she wished to give more of her land to the same use, she, by will dated 6 Dec. 1707 bequeathed "all that plot of garden ground ... adjoining
the E part of the churchyard of the Presbyterian Church" to the same
trustees for the same uses; to her kinsman JOHN HUTCHINSON & NATHANIEL
PARTRIDGE. On 6 May 1756 THOMAS LAMBOLL, gentleman, of Charleston, aged
about 60 years said he well knew HENRY WIGINGTON about 45 years age as an
attorney & eminent conveyancer, then of SC who moved to Great Britain
about 40 years ago & believes he died there 30 years ago; that about 45
years ago deponent was intimately acquainted with DR. JOHN HUTCHINSON
(the most noted physician in town for several years) & NATHANIEL PART-
RIDGE, gentleman, at 1 time P.M., afterwards Clerk of Assembly; that
PARTRIDGE died about 30 odd years ago; that HUTCHINSON died about 20 odd
years ago; that WIGINGTON, PARTRIDGE & HUTCHINSON were good characters &
repute; that deponent was acquainted with their handwriting; & believes
signatures to this deed to be theirs. Before WILLIAM BULL, J.P. WILLIAM
HOPTON, Register.

DEEDS BOOK "V-V"
JAN. 1759 - JULY 1760

Book V-V, p. 1   JONATHAN BRYAN, planter, of Granville Co., &
10 & 11 Apr. 1752   MARY his wife, to WILLIAM SIMMONS, planter, of
L & R   Colleton Co., for L 3600 currency; 910 a. on

86

head of a branch of Pocotalago River called Stony Creek, in Prince Williams Parish, Granville Co., bounding NW on JOHN SMITH & on the high road
leading across the creek, & on ANDREW DEVEAUX, JR.; NE on ANDREW DEVEAUX,
SR.; E on JAMES DEVEAUX; SW on JONATHAN BRYAN & the high road separating
it from JONATHAN BRYAN & from JOHN SMITH. Whereas Landgrave EDMOND BEL-
LINGER of Berkeley Co., owned several large parcels of land, & by will
dated 21 Feb. 1739 devised to his nephew, WILLIAM PALMER, 1000 a. of his
patent land, & to his son, GEORGE BELLINGER, 1000 a., & appointed his
wife, ELIZABETH BELLINGER, his sole executrix; & whereas by L & R 14 & 15
Feb. 1745 ELIZABETH BELLINGER & GEORGE BELLINGER sold WILLIAM PALMER the
1000 a. in Granville Co. devised to GEORGE BELLINGER; bounding E on WIL-
LIAM PALMER; SW on JONATHAN BRYAN; NE on JOHN BULL; NW on estate of ED-
MUND BELLINGER; & whereas by L & R dated 1 & 2 July 1748 WILLIAM PALMER,
& ANNE his wife, sold JONATHAN BRYAN 1059-3/4 a., the W part being the
1000 a. purchased from ELIZABETH & GEORGE BELLINGER, the E part being
part of the 1000 a. devised to WILLIAM PALMER, bounding E on JAMES DE-
VEAUX; S on JONATHAN BRYAN; W on ANDREW DEVEAUX, JR.; N on said 2 tracts
(now ANDREW DEVEAUX, SR.); now BRYAN sells a part to SIMMONS. Witnesses:
WILLIAM BOWER WILLIAMSON, JOHN WILLIAMSON, ANN BRYAN. Before STEPHEN
BULL, J.P. for G. Co. WILLIAM HOPTON, Register. Plat of 27-1/2 a. bounding W on MR. IZARD; S on CAPT. WILLIAM DRY; E on Broad Road from Charleston to Goose Creek. Plat by HUGH BRYAN, D.S., dated 8 Feb. 1752, of
910 a., being the E part of 1059-3/4 a.

Book V-V, p. 6   RICHARD WILLIAMSON, planter, of St. Pauls Par-
1 Nov. 1737   ish, Colleton Co., edlest son & heir of PHEBE
L & R   PETERS, widow, & _____ his wife, to CAPT.
                                 JAMES REED, mariner, of Charleston, for Ł 120
currency, 1400 a. on N side Santee River in Craven Co., granted 13 July
1737 to PHEBE PETERS; bounding N & W on vacant land (except a small part
which buts to the W on JOSEPH CHILD on the Great Savannah). Witnesses:
JOHN TUCKER, BENJAMIN WILLIAMSON, THOMAS FARR. Before PAUL TRAPIER, J.P.
WILLIAM HOPTON, Register.

Book V-V, p. 12   The Rt. Hon. GEORGE, Lord ANSON, Baron of So-
20 Mar. 1758   berton, Co. of Southampton, Great Britain, by
Confirmation   his attorney, RICHARD LAMBTON, ESQ., of
                                 Charleston, SC, to JOHN RATTRAY, ESQ., of
Charleston. Whereas Lord ANSON by deed poll dated 21 May 1756 appointed
LAMBTON his attorney with authority to sell his estates in SC; & whereas
LAMBTON, by L & R dated 26 & 27 Apr. 1757, for Ł 8350 SC money, sold RAT-
TRAY 20 a. of high land & 20 a. of marsh land; & whereas the letter of
attorney was signed by Lord ANSON in England, as witnessed by PHILIP
STEVENS & FRANCIS WELLES, but was not proved to have been executed before
any magistrate in England & could not be proved in Carolina because the
witnesses resided in England, LAMBTON promised RATTRAY to obtain another
letter of attorney from Lord ANSON, executed before the witnesses or before the mayor of London; & whereas LAMBTON has received another letter
of attorney, dated 1 Sept. 1757, proved by WELLES before MARSH DICKINSON,
Lord mayor of London; now he confirms RATTRAY'S title to said land, bounding E on Cooper River; W on a street leading from the Bay to Ansonburgh;
partly on George Street, & partly on ANSON'S land; partly on JOHN WATSON;
N on ISAAC MAZYCK; S on MESSRS. SHUBRICK & ANSON'S marsh; also all marsh
land & other land round about same down to low water mark, except the
wharf reserved to Lord ANSON with an entrance of 35 ft. Witnesses: BEN-
JAMIN GUERARD, BELLAMY CRAWFORD. Before JAMES GRINDLAY, J.P. WILLIAM
HOPTON, Register.

Book V-V, p. 16   JOHN MARTIN MILLER, soldier, of Saxegotha Town-
28 & 29 Sept. 1758   ship, to LEONARD ROOF, planter, for Ł 300 SC
L & R   money, 2 tracts of 25 a. each. Whereas Gov.
                                 JAMES GLEN on 29 May 1747 granted CHRISTIAN
BRABANT 50 a., in Saxegotha Township, bounding NE on Santee River; SE on
CHRISTIAN BRABANT (BRAVANT); S on vacant land; NW on HENRY GALLMAN; &
whereas CHRISTIAN BRABANT, & FROWNICK his wife, by L & R dated 9 & 10
July 1755, sold the 50 a. to JOHN MARTIN MILLER for Ł 100 currency; &
whereas said MILLER owned another tract of 50 a. in said Township on His
Majesty's Bounty, bounding on all sides on vacant land; & whereas MILLER,
by L & R dated 7 & 8 July 1758, for Ł 100 currency, sold JOHN HERRINGSMAN
of said Township 50 a. of land, (that is, 25 a. part of the 50 a. granted

BRABANT, the other 25 a. part of 50 a. granted MILLER, as shown by 3
plats); now MILLER sells the other 2 25 a. tracts to ROOF; 25 a. being
pine land granted MILLER & bounding SE on HERRINGSMAN; other sides on vacant land; & 25 a. bounding NE on HERRINGSMAN; SE on BRABANT & HERRINGS-
MAN; SW on vacant land; NW on HENRY GALLMAN. Witnesses: JACOB GEIGER,
JOHN GEORGE SHLAPPY. Before JOHN PEARSON, J.P. WILLIAM HOPTON, Register. Two plats given.

Book V-V, p. 22   THOMAS JONES, planter, of St. Bartholomews
31 July & 1 Aug. 1758   Parish, & MARY his wife (formerly wife of
L & R in Trust   O'NEAL GOUGH, planter; & formerly wife of WIL-
             LIAM CLIFFORD, planter), to JOHN PARKER,
planter, for ₤ 1000 currency, 96-1/4 a. in St. James Parish, Goose Creek,
bounding N on THOMAS SMITH; W on JEFFREYS Plantation; SW on RALPH IZARD;
E on the Broad Road; also 27-1/2 a. in same Parish, bounding W on RALPH
IZARD; SE on CAPT. WILLIAM DRY; NE on the Broad Road; also 19-1/2 a. in
same Parish, bounding N & S on THOMAS SMITH; E on Broad Road from
Charleston to Goose Creek; W on JEFFREYS Plantation. Whereas WILLIAM
CLIFFORD owned 3 plantations in St. James Parish, Goose Creek, 1 of
94-1/2 a., 1 of 27-1/2 a., 1 of 19-1/2 a.; & by will dated 30 June 1744
bequeathed all his real & personal estate to his wife, MARY; who after
WILLIAM CLIFFORD'S death married O'NEAL GOUGH, whom she also survived; &
she afterwards married THOMAS JONES; now they sell the 3 tracts to PAR-
KER. Witnesses: THOMAS CLIFFORD, MRS. MARY SACHEVERELL, SARAH YOUNG
(YONGE). Before THOMAS SACHEVERELL, J.P. On 19 Sept. 1758 JOHN PARKER
declared that the above release was accepted by him, not for his own
use, but only in trust, to be sold by him & the purchase money applied to
the use of MARY'S children by her former husband, O'NEAL GOUGH, the names
of the children being MARY & JOHN. Witnesses: SAMUEL WALLACE, CHARLES
JONES. WILLIAM HOPTON, Register. Plats of 19-1/2 a. & 96-1/4 a.

Book V-V, p. 29   SARAH RUTLEDGE, widow, of Charleston, quit
31 July 1756   claims to JOACHIM ZUBLY, minister of the Gos-
Release   pel, ARNOLDUS VANDERHORST, JOSEPH SINGLETARY,
             THOMAS BARKSDALE, CHARLES BARKSDALE, GEORGE
BARKSDALE, WILLIAM VANDERHORST, JOHN WHITE, WILLIAM WHITE, RICHARD CAP-
ERS, SR., TIMOTHY CROSBY, NATHANIEL POLHILL, DANIEL LEGARE, ISAAC LEGARE,
NATHAN LEGARE, & WILLIAM CAPERS, planter, of Berkeley Co., for 5 shill-
ings, all her title to 380 a. Whereas SARAH FENWICKE, widow of ROBERT
FENWICKE, planter, of Berkeley Co., owned 380 a., English measure, on E
side Wando River, within land, formerly bounding S on said ROBERT FEN-
WICKE & on JOHN SOVERANCE; E on JOHN HOLLYBUSH; N on JOHN WHITE & JOHN
CROSKEYS; W on ROBERT FENWICKE & JOHN CROSKEYS; according to plat of
original grant dated 8 Oct. 1704, signed by Gov. NATHANIEL JOHNSON & made
to JAMES BASSFORD, planter, of Berkeley Co.; & whereas SARAH FENWICKE by
deed poll dated 16 Jan. 1726 conveyed the tract to JOHN VANDERHORST, ESQ.
& MICHAEL DARBY as a convenient habitation of a dissenting pastor or
teacher, "he or they behaving themselves as becomes the office they bear";
& whereas VANDERHORST & DARBY died without having appointed their successors & doubts & disputes have arisen in regard to such succession, &
SARAH RUTLEDGE desires to settle the question as far as she legally may;
now she conveys the land to the above named men; & whereas under SARAH
FENWICKE'S will certain demands have been made by the minister & congregation against SARAH RUTLEDGE as executrix, of will of ANDREW RUTLEDGE or
as devisee & legatee of SARAH FENWICKE, for obtaining delivery of certain
slaves & plate, & for payment of certain sums of money bequeathed for the
use of said minister & congregation; now to end all such claims the parties of the second part release & discharge SARAH RUTLEDGE as executrix &
devisee from all claims they had against her. Witnesses: WILLIAM BLAKE,
THOMAS YEOMANS. Before DAVID GRAEME, J.P. WILLIAM HOPTON, Register.

Book V-V, p. 32   ROBERT WEAVER, carpenter, of Georgetown, &
8 & 9 Jan. 1759   ELIZABETH his wife, to ARCHIBALD BAIRD, ESQ.,
L & R   for ₤ 2000 currency, the 284 a. purchased by
             L & R dated 29 & 30 Mar. 1755 from the Hon.
JOHN CLELAND, ESQ., bounding NE on FRANCIS KINLOCH, ESQ. & Black River;
other sides on JOHN CLELAND. Witnesses: WILLIAM SHACKLEFORD, JR., ESTHER
SHACKLEFORD. Before THOMAS BLYTHE, J.P. WILLIAM HOPTON, Register.

Book V-V, p. 37   JOHN MOULTRIE, JR., planter, of St. James

19 & 20 Jan. 1759   Parish, Goose Creek, Berkeley Co., to ISAAC
L & R by Mortgage   GODIN, planter, of same Parish, as security on
                           bond of even date in penal sum of Ł 8000 for
payment of Ł 4000 currency, with interest, on 20 Jan. 1760; 1689 a. at
Goose Creek, bounding N on RALPH IZARD; S on JOHN SAUNDERS; W on MRS.
SARAH BARKER, JOHN PARKER, & BENJAMIN MARION; E on Goose Creek. Witness-
es: JOHN AINSLIE, JOHN DENTON. Before PETER MANIGAULT, J.P. WILLIAM
HOPTON, Register.

Book V-V, p. 41   JOSEPH DUBOURDIEU, to PAUL TRAPIER, merchant,
2 & 3 Sept. 1751   both of Georgetown, Craven Co., for Ł 500 cur-
L & R   rency, lot #20 in Georgetown, with right of
                           commonage. Whereas ELISHA SCREVEN & HANNAH,
his wife, on 15 Jan. 1734 conveyed to GEORGE PAWLEY, WILLIAM SWINTON, &
DANIEL LAROCHE, as trustees, a tract of land to be laid out for a town to
be called Georgetown; & whereas said trustees on 27 Feb. 1734 sold AN-
THONY WHITE lot #20, bounding SW 50 ft. on Front Street; NW 217.9 ft. on
lot #19; NE on lot #58; SE on lot #21; with right of commonage in the
common for 1 horse & 1 cow; & whereas ANTHONY WHITE by will dated 7 Feb.
1746 bequeathed his real & personal estate to his executors to be sold to
pay his debts; & whereas JOSEPH DUBOURDIEU, only acting executor, on 3
Mar. 1747 sold the lot to ISAAC TRAPIER; who on 5 Mar. 1747 sold to JO-
SEPH DUBOURDIEU; now DUBOURDIEU sells to PAUL TRAPIER. Witnesses: JOHN
LOWRYMOR, WILLIAM (his mark) GIBSON. Before THOMAS BLYTHE, J.P. WILLIAM
HOPTON, Register.

Book V-V, p. 45   JOSEPH DUBOURDIEU, to PAUL TRAPIER, merchant,
2 & 3 Sept. 1751   both of Georgetown, for Ł 400 currency, 2
L & R   plantations, total 950 a. Whereas Gov. ROBERT
                           JOHNSON on 22 Sept. 1733 granted THEODORA LAWS
650 a. in Craven Co., bounding S on Three Mile Gully; N on DANIEL BRITTON
(or his brother); N on vacant land; W on MR. LANE; E on BENJAMIN LAWS; &
whereas THEODORA LAWS married WILLIAM EDINS & the land became his property, & they on 24 Dec. 1733 sold the 650 a. to ANTHONY WHITE; & whereas
Gov. ROBERT JOHNSON on 22 Sept. 1733 granted BENJAMIN LAWS 1150 a. in
Craven Co., bounding S & W on MR. SOMERHOOF & MRS. THEODORA LAWS; E on
MR. SCRIVEN; N on ANTHONY WHITE; & whereas BENJAMIN LAWS on 14 Dec. 1733
sold 650 a., part of the 1150 a., to ANTHONY WHITE; who, by will dated 7
Feb. 1746 bequeathed his real & personal estate to his executors to be
sold to pay his debts; & whereas JOSEPH DUBOURDIEU, only acting executor,
on 3 Mar. 1747 sold to ISAAC TRAPIER the 650 a. granted to THEORORA LAWS
& 300 a., part of the 650 a. granted to BENJAMIN LAWS total 950 a.; &
ISAAC TRAPIER on 5 Mar. 1747 sold JOSEPH DUBOURDIEU, the 950 a., bounding
S on DANIEL BRITTON; W on ARTHUR FORSTER; N & E on COL. ANTHONY WHITE
(part sold to DANIEL LAROCHE); now DUBOURDIEU sells to PAUL TRAPIER.
Witnesses: JOHN LORIMER, WILLIAM (his mark) GIBSON. Before THOMAS BLYTHE,
J.P. WILLIAM HOPTON, Register.

Book V-V, p. 51   JOACHIM (his mark) PALTHAZAR, bricklayer, of
26 & 27 Sept. 1758   Craven Co., to PAUL TRAPIER, planter, of
L & R by Mortgage   Georgetown, as security on bond of even date
                           in penal sum of Ł 800 for payment of Ł 400
currency, with interest, on 1 Jan. 1759; 2 adjoining plantations, total
400 a. on Sampit Creek, Craven Co., according to original grants. Witnesses: ALEXANDER THOMPSON, JOHN PALTHASAR. Witnesses: THOMAS BLYTHE,
J.P. WILLIAM HOPTON, Register.

Book V-V, p. 57   DANIEL SINCLAIR, mariner, of Charleston, &
20 & 21 Feb. 1759   MARY his wife (lately MARY STEPHENS, daughter
L & R by Mortgage   & heir of EDWARD STEPHENS; & niece & heir of
                           HENRY STEPHENS, gentleman, of Co. of Glouces-
ter, Great Britain), to BERNARD BECKMAN, blockmaker, only acting executor of will of CATHARINE SCURLOCK, widow; as security on 2 bonds; all
their lands, tenements, etc., in Abson, alias Week, & Abson Old Sodbury,
& Iron Action, Co. of Glocester, Great Britain, which formerly belonged
to EDWARD SETPHENS, grandfather of MARY SINCLAIR; also their lands, tenements, etc., in Eastington, Alkerton, Sodbury, Mangorsfield alias Man-
gotsfield, Co. of Gloucester, formerly belonging to HENRY STEPHENS, uncle
of MARY SINCLAIR; that is to say, all those lands, tenement, etc., commonly called the Farther Ground, Middle Ground, Home Ground, Westfield,

the Great Tyning, Church Leaze, the Ox Leaze, Rack Leaze, Nastfield, the
Great Orchard, the upper Orchard, Redstreak Orchard, the Little Mead,
Eastington Mead, the lower mead field, the upper meadfield, Mill End, the
Great Ham, the Lagger Ham, the Lower Grove Leaze, the Upper Grove Leaze,
& Stanleyfield, with the gardens & orchards; in the Parishes of Easting-
ton & Stanley St. Leonards, Co. of Gloucester; also the several meadows,
arable pastures & woodlands belonging therewith; all of which by a decree
of H.M. Court of Chancery in Great Britain dated 6 July 1756 were pro-
nounced vested in MARY SINCLAIR as heir to her uncle HENRY STEPHENS who
was heir of her grandfather EDWARD STEPHENS. However, HENRY STEPHENS,
MARY'S uncle, had mortgaged certain parts of the lands & tenements to
PAUL CASTLEMAN. Witnesses: WILLIAM SLOPER, RICHARD TWINE, JAMES GRINDLAY.
Before DANIEL CRAWFORD, J.P. WILLIAM HOPTON, Register.

Book V-V, p. 70   MARY BOONE, widow, to SAMUEL VERNOR, planter,
12 & 13 Feb. 1759   both of Christ Church Parish, for Ł 900 cur-
L & R   rency, 460 a., part of 500 a., in Christ
                          Church Parish, (360 a. of which were formerly
granted to JOHN SIMS), bounding NW on CHARLES PINCKNEY (formerly ALLEN);
SW on THOMAS WHITESIDES; NE on RICHARD TOOKERMAN; SE on marsh of Cooper-
hee Sound. Witnesses: JOHN BOONE, WILLIAM JOY, WILLIAM BOONE. Before
THOMAS YEOMANS, J.P. WILLIAM HOPTON, Register.

Book V-V, p. 74   Whereas on 1 Jan. 1757 JOHN CORKATT agreed to
11 Feb. 1758   sell JOHN CUTHBERT, planter, formerly of Wil-
Agreement   liamsburgh, now of Indian Land, part of a
                         tract of land formerly belonging to THOMAS
JENNEYS, now to CROKATT, in Prince William Parish; Granville Co., on the
banks of the Cusa River, containing 500 a., for which CUTHBERT agreed to
pay Ł 1000 currency, to commence on 1 Jan. 1757 when he took possession;
& whereas CUTHBERT has received no titles from CROKATT; now CROKATT binds
himself to furnish proper title within 2 years. JOHN MCKENZIE, merchant,
of Charleston, recognized CUTHBERT'S & CROKATT'S handwriting & signatures
before JOHN RATTRAY, J.P. WILLIAM HOPTON, Register.

Book V-V, p. 75   BENJAMIN SINGLETARY, planter, of St. Thomas
27 Sept. 1758   Parish, Berkeley Co., & HANNAH his wife, of
Feoffment   1st part; ELIAS BONNEAU & MARY his wife, of
                         2nd part; JOHN DUTARQUE, SR., of 3rd part.
Whereas SINGLETARY & BONNEAU own a certain plantation in right of their
wives, by descent from MICHAEL DARBY; now the parties of the 1st & 2nd
parts, for Ł 300 currency, sell DUTARQUE 450 a. in Berkeley Co., bounding
S on VINCENT GUERIN; W on ROBERT JOHNSON; N on JOHN MUSGROVE & JAMES
GOODBY; E on JOHN DUTARQUE, JR. Delivery by turf & twig. Witnesses:
PETER GUERIN, NOAH DUTARQUE, ELIZABETH GUERIN, JOHN DUTARQUE, JR. Before
HENRY GREY, Register.

Book V-V, p. 77   JEPHTHAH DUBOSE, planter, of St. Stephens Par-
12 Oct. 1757   ish, to JOHN JORDAN, planter, for Ł 75 curren-
L & R   cy, 75 a. on NE side Santee River, in Prince
                         Frederick Parish, Craven Co., bounding; NE on
THOMAS BOONE; NW on parsonage land of Parish of St. James Santee; SE on
ISAAC DUBOSE. Witnesses: EDWARD JERMAN, JACOB NICHOLAS SCHWARTZKOPFF,
ISAAC DUTART. Before WILLIAM BURROWS, J.P. WILLIAM HOPTON, Register.

Book V-V, p. 83   ISAAC PROCHER, SR., chirurgeon, to CHARLES
29 Oct. 1723   COLLETON, JR., second son of CHARLES COLLETON,
Settlement   SR., both of Berkeley Co., in consideration of
                         the intended marriage between said CHARLES
COLLETON, JR., & SUSANNA PORCHER, youngest daughter of said ISAAC PORCH-
ER; to settle the inheritance of certain lands & tenements on CHARLES,
JR., & SUSANNAH; 300 a. on NE side Wassamsaw Swamp, bounding N on ISAAC
PORCHER, SR.; E on PETER PORCHER; S on ISAAC PORCHER, JR., ROGER GOUGH, &
vacant land; W on vacant land. Witnesses: Rev. RICHARD LUDLAM, JAMES LE-
BASS, JOHN BONNIN. Before H. BUTLER, J.P. WILLIAM HOPTON, Register.

Book V-V, p. 86   JONATHAN WITTER, planter, to BENJAMIN STONE &
19 & 20 Feb. 1759   JONATHAN RIVERS, planters; all of James Is-
L & R by Mortgage   land, Berkeley Co.; as security on bond of
                         even date in penal sum of Ł 4000 for payment

of Ł 2000 currency, with interst, (STONE & RIVERS having gone on WITTER'S bond to THOMAS LAMBOLL & ALEXANDER PERONNEAU, of Charleston, SC, & GEORGE EVELEIGH, gentleman, of Great Britain); 165-3/4 a., English measure, on James Island, bounding N on THOMAS WITTER; NW on JOHN WITTER, JR.; W on GEORGE RIVERS & COL. RIVERS; SE on JOHN RIVERS; E on the high road; which land was devised to JONATHAN by his father, JOHN WITTER. Witnesses: JOHN DILL, ROBERT WILLIAMS, JR. Before JOHN REMINGTON, J.P. WILLIAM HOPTON, Register. On 18 June 1760 JONATHAN RIVERS declared mortgage fully satisfied. Witness: WILLIAM HOPTON. Plat certified 1 Nov. 1758 by WILLIAM WILKINS, Sur., showing said tract, being the part on which JAMES WITTERS dwelling house stood & being 1/3 of JAMES WITTER'S land.

Book V-V, p. 93
6 & 7 Jan. 1759
L & R by Mortgage

WILLIAM TOWNSEND, planter, of John's Island, to GABRIEL MANIGAULT, merchant, of Charleston, as security on bond dated 14 Dec. 1758 in penal sum of Ł 6000 for payment of Ł 3000 currency, with interest, on 14 Dec. 1759; 300 a. on Johns Island, bounding E on DAVID HEXT (formerly FRANCIS HEXT); SW & NW on ABRAHAM WAIGHT; N on Stono River marsh. Witnesses: JAMES MCALPINE, THOMAS LAMBOLL, JR. Before JOHN WRAGG, J.P. WILLIAM HOPTON, Register.

Book V-V, p. 97
15 Nov. 1749
Sale

ANN MASTERS, widow, sole executrix of will of her husband, SAMUEL MASTERS, of Craven Co., to JOHN IOOR & RICHARD BAKER, merchant, for Ł 138 currency, 184 a. in Craven Co., bounding NW on vacant land; NE on IOOR & BAKER; SE on Little River; SW on MR. MASTERS. Witnesses: NATHAN FRINK, MARTHA HAWKINS. Before CHARLES LEWIS, J.P. WILLIAM HOPTON, Register.

Book V-V, p. 99
15 Nov. 1740
Sale

ANN MASTERS, widow, sole executrix of will of her husband, SAMUEL MASTERS, of Craven Co., to JOHN IOOR & RICHARD BAKER, merchant, for Ł 138 currency, 184 a. in Craven Co., bounding NW on vacant land; SW on THOMAS ASH; NE on said MASTERS; SE on Little River. Witnesses: NATHAN FRINK, MARTHA HAWKINS. Before CHARLES LEWIS, J.P. WILLIAM HOPTON, Register.

Book V-V, p. 101
7 & 8 Apr. 1758
L & R

OLIVER (his mark) MAHAFFY, of Craven Co., SC, & PHEOBE (her mark) his wife, to MARTIN FIFER, of Anson Co., NC, for Ł 100 British, 150 a. in Craven Co., on a branch of Wateree River called Granny's Quarter Creek, beginning at a white oak 3, running thence E 38.72 links to a scrub oak 3x, then S 38.72 links to a scrub oak 3 & 1, thence W 38.72 links to hickory 3x, thence N 38.72 links to the beginning white oak; which land was granted to OLIVER MAHAFFY by letters patent dated 6 Mar. 1750. Witnesses: JOHN FROHOCK, DAVID REES. Before NATHANIEL ALEXANDER, J.P. WILLIAM HOPTON, Register.

Book V-V, p. 105
16 & 17 Nov. 1758
L & R

WILLIAM FISHBURN (FISHBOURN), of PonPon, eldest son & heir of WILLIAM FISHBURN, planter, of Colleton Co., to JAMES SMITH, planter, of St. George Parish, Dorchester, for Ł 1200 currency, 260 a. in Beach Hill, Colleton Co., bounding NE on JOHN DRAYTON (formerly the Hon. WILLIAM BULL); SW on JOSEPH SUMNER; SE on JOSEPH WARING; NW on land purchased for the ministry; which 260 a. by will of WILLIAM FISHBURN were devised to WILLIAM, the son, party hereto, but as the will was executed before only 2 witnesses the land descended to WILLIAM, party hereto, as heir. Witnesses: THOMAS MELVIN, ROBERT KEOWIN, JOHN LAIRD. Before JAMES SHARP, J.P. WILLIAM HOPTON, Register.

Book V-V, p. 110
30 May 1752
Release

STEPHEN PENNEL (his mark) BULLOCK, planter, of Berkeley Co., to JAMES ALLEN, planter, of Charleston, for Ł 3500 SC money, the W half of lot #223 in Charleston, bounding E on other part belonging to EBENEZER SIMMONDS; N 127 ft. on Tradd Street; W 102 ft. on King Street. Whereas on 9 May 1694 the Rt. Hon. WILLIAM, Earl of Craven, Palatine, granted PATRICK STEWART, of Berkeley Co., a half a. (English measure) lot, #223, in Charleston; which he, on 24 July 1694, sold to WILLIAM BOLLOUGH; who died intestate; & whereas the lot descended to JOHN BOLLOUGH, only son & heir of said WILLIAM, who also died intestate,

leaving 2 daughters ELIZABETH & MARTHA as co-heiresses; & whereas ELIZA-
BETH, in 1726, married SAMUEL BULLOCK, & MARTHA afterwards married
CHARLES LEWIS, & the lot #223 was divided, SAMUEL & ELIZABETH BULLOCK
getting the @ half, CHARLES & MARTHA LEWIS getting the E half; & whereas
the W half, being on 2 streets, was deemed more valuable, BULLOCK gave
LEWIS a Negro fellow valued at Ⱡ 200; & whereas ELIZABETH died, leaving
said STEPHEN PENNEL BULLOCK, her only son & heir; now he sells to ALLEN.
Witnesses: JOHN REMINGTON, JR., JOHN REMINGTON. Before ALEXANDER STEWART,
J.P. WILLIAM HOPTON, Register.

Book V-V, p. 115   THOMAS HUTCHINSON, cabinet maker, sole execu-
29 & 30 Nov. 1757   tor of will of RIBTON HUTCHINSON, gentleman,
L & R   to LIONEL CHALMERS, chirurgeon; all of
                          Charleston; for Ⱡ 4100 currency, that large
double wooden house & part of lot #85 in Charleston, formerly owned by
RIBTON HUTCHINSON, bounding S 111 ft. on Union Alley running from Union
Street to New Church Street; W 96 ft. 10 in. on ALEXANDER ANDERSON (from
Union Alley to HENRY BATEMAN); N about 100 ft. (?) on HENRY BATEMAN; E
97 ft. 4 in. on JOHN WATSON & estate of RIBTON HUTCHINSON. Whereas by
deed poll dated 18 Feb. 1709 RICHARD BERESFORD, LEWIS PASQUEREAU, & WIL-
LIAM GIBBON, trustees appointed by Act of Assembly, conveyed to LAURENCE
DENNIS, planter, part of a lot in Charleston; & whereas DENNIS owned var-
ous lands & tenements & by will dated 7 Aug. 1733 devised to his wife,
PROVIDENCE DENNIS, among other things, said part of a town lot; & whereas
by a certain marriage settlement, or indenture tripartite, dated 23 Nov.
1734, between RIBTON HUTCHINSON of 1st part; PROVIDENCE DENNIS of 2nd
part; CHARLES PINCKNEY & BENJAMIN D'HARRIETTE of 3rd part; it was agreed
that should the intended marriage between said RIBTON & PROVIDENCE take
place then all the real estate belonging to PROVIDENCE, including said
part of a lot, should be settled in joint tenancy upon RIBTON & PROVI-
DENCE, with the proviso that PROVIDENCE might charge the premises with
any sum not exceeding Ⱡ 2000 Carolina money; & whereas the marriage took
place & she made her will & charged said part of a town lot with Ⱡ 2000
payable as her will directed; & whereas RIBTON survived PROVIDENCE & became sole owner of her lands, with above proviso, & by will dated 11 Aug.
1757, & in order to pay his debts directed his executor, THOMAS HUTCHIN-
SON, to sell his estate, including his slaves, goods & chattels not otherwise bequeathed, at auction, now THOMAS HUTCHINSON sells the part of a
lot to CHALMERS, the highest bidder. Witnesses: GEORGE VANE, EDWARD
NEUFVILLE. Before JOHN REMINGTON, J.P. WILLIAM HOPTON, Register. Plat
given.

Book V-V, p. 126   JACOB DESAURENCY, planter, of the WELCH tract,
26 Nov. 1756   Craven Co., to JAMES OMARR, planter, of same
L & R   Co., for Ⱡ 100 currency, the 67 a. in the
                          WELCH tract granted by Gov. JAMES GLEN on 26
Nov. 1751 to SAMUEL DESAURENCY; bounding S on SAMUEL TAYLOR; E on WILLIAM
GARDINER; W & NW on THOMAS SIMS; N on JACOB DESAURENCY; according to plat
certified 17 Aug. 1751. Witnesses: JOSEPH KING, HENRY BURLINGTON. Before WILLIAM LORD, J.P. WILLIAM HOPTON, Register.

Book V-V, p. 130   HENRY DESAUSSURE, planter, of St. Helens Par-
30 Jan. 1759   ish, Granville Co., & MAGDALENE his wife, to
Sale   JOHN MOORE, planter, of Prince William Parish,
                          Granville Co., for Ⱡ 1000 currency, 584 a.
part of 1150 a., on the head of Days Creek Swamp, between Coasahatchie
& Savannah Rivers, in Granville Co., bounding E on vacant land; S on the
grant line of Township of Purysburgh; W on vacant land; N on other part
of 1150 a.; according to grant dated 6 Oct. 1752 to MORGAN SABB; who sold
to HENRY DESAUSSURE; who now sells to JOHN MOORE. Witnesses: WILLIAM
COACHMAN, PAUL PORCHER, CORNELIUS DUPONT. Before JOHN REMINGTON, J.P.
WILLIAM HOPTON, Register.

Book V-V, p. 133   MARY BRETTON, widow, (formerly MARY GODDARD),
24 & 25 Feb. 1755   of Craven Co., surviving executrix of will of
L & R   FRANCIS GODDARD, innholder, of Charleston, to
                          WILLIAM HUGHES, planter, of Craven Co., for
Ⱡ 763:10:0 currency, 1077 a., a town lot #9, & 450 a. Whereas on 12 Feb.
1736/7 Lt. Gov. THOMAS BROUGHTON granted CAPT. FRANCIS GODDARD 1077 a. in
Williamsburgh Township, Craven Co., bounding SE on vacant land & on

WILLIAM CAMP; NE on vacant land & on WILLIAM CAMP; other sides on vacant land; also lot #9 in said Town; & whereas on 14 Dec. 1739 Lt. Gov. WILLIAM BULL granted CAPT. FRANCIS GODDARD 450 a. in Williamsburgh Township, bounding NW & SW on FRANCIS GODDARD & vacant land; NE on JOHN MCLEVONY; SW on the Township line; which grants are recorded in Book D.D. fols. 136-137; & whereas GODDARD, by will dated 1 Apr. 1741, after devising part of his estate to his wife MARY GODDARD for her lifetime, ordered the rest of his real & personal estate sold, & appointed his wife, MARY, & MARY GODDARD (now MARY BRETTON) his executrixes; now MARY GODDARD being dead, MARY BRETTON sells said 3 parcels of real estate to HUGHES. Witnesses: WILLIAM GODDARD, ALEXANDER SWINTON. Before CHARLES WOODMASON, J.P. WILLIAM HOPTON, Register.

Book V-V, p. 139   RICHARD LAMBTON, merchant, of Charleston, ex-
21 & 22 Feb. 1759   ecutor of will of ROWLAND VAUGHAN, gentleman,
L & R   to MATHURINE GUERINE, planter, of St. Andrews
                          Parish, for Ł 450 currency, that plantation in
St. Andrews Parish, near Ashley Ferry, in Berkeley Co., bounding E on
marsh belonging to JOHN RIVERS; W on other lands of JOHN RIVERS; N on
WILLIAM CLAY; S on WILLIAM ELLIOTT; also 14 a. adjacent to above, bound-
ing S on THOMAS ELLIOTT; W on JOHN RIVERS; N on WILLIAM CLAY; E on above
tract; which 2 tracts by various conveyances became the property of ROW-
LAND VAUGHAN. Witnesses: JOHN MACKENZIE, WILLIAM GRAEME. Before JOHN
RATTRAY, J.P. WILLIAM HOPTON, Register.

Book V-V, p. 144   THOMAS GORDON, wheelwright, & ELIZABETH his
19 Mar. 1759   wife, of Berkeley Co., for good causes & val-
Gift   uable considerations give GOVEN GORDON &
                          GEORGE GORDON, 2 younger brothers of said
THOMAS GORDON, now under the care of their mother, RUTH GORDON, in trust
for them all the claim THOMAS & ELIZABETH might have in the plantation
on which RUTH GORDON now lives, containing 450 a.; also another adjoining
tranct of 50 a. lying highest on N side Collins River, formerly belonging
to JOHN HEIGHLER, who conveyed to JOHN GORDON, deceased; to be divided as
follows: beginning at a hickory the upper corner tree of the 50 a., &
running with the line of the tract until it intersects a line of the 450
a. tract, then with the line of the great tract to a red oak, the back
corner tree of the great tract, thence with the back line of the great
tract to a red oak with 3 notches on each side & a cross over them,
thence with a straight line to a sugar tree marked in like manner standing on river bank; the 50 a. (formerly JOHN HEIGHLER'S) & the upper part
of the 450 a. to be GOVEN GORDON'S; the lower part of the 450 a. with the
improvements & RUTH GORDON'S dwelling house to be GEORGE GORDON'S. Witnesses: SAMUEL AWBREY, ISAAC PENNINGTON, JOHN GORDON. Before JOHN MUR-
RAY, J.P. WILLIAM HOPTON, Register.

Book V-V, p. 146   WALTER DOWNS, planter, of the WELCH tract,
25 & 26 Jan. 1758   Craven Co., to VALENTINE HOLLINGSWORTH, of
L & R   same Co., for Ł 200 currency, 100 a. in the
                          WELCH tract, bounding NE on Peedee River; N on
JOSEPH JELLY; S on JOHN HUGHES. Witnesses: WILLIAM TERRELL, ENOCH THOMP-
SON. Before WILLIAM LORD, J.P. WILLIAM HOPTON, Register.

Book V-V, p. 150   JAMES (his mark) PITTMAN, freeholder, of Cra-
2 Dec. 1758   ven Co., & ELIZABETH (her mark), his wife, for
Gift   good causes & valuable considerations, to his
                          daughter PRISCILLA JAMES (alias PITMAN), wife
of HOWELL JAMES, of Craven Co., a piece of land in the WELCH tract fronting W 11 chains 18 links on Big Peedee River, bounding N on WILLIAM EYNON;
E on vacant land; S 11 chains 18 links from WILLIAM EYNON'S land & continued parallel to EYNON'S line & ending E on vacant land; which piece of
land, or 78 a., was the upper part of 125 a. granted DAVID HENRY (HARRY)
2 Mar. 1743; & sold by HENRY to PITTMAN; bounding, when surveyed, N on
WILLIAM EYNON; W on Big Peedee River; S on other part; E on vacant land.
Should PRISCILLA die without leaving issue then after the death of
PRISCILLA & HOWELL JAMES, the land to revert to JAMES PITTMAN. Plat certified 20 Feb. 1759 by ROBERT EDWARDS, Dep. Sur. Witnesses: ETHELRED
PITTMAN, BENJAMIN JAMES. Before WILLIAM LORD, J.P. WILLIAM HOPTON, Register.

Book V-V, p. 152   JAMES MCCANTS, planter, to ALEXANDER MCKNIGHT,
23 & 24 Mar. 1759   planter, both of Craven Co., for Ł 500 curren-
L & R   cy, 250 a. in Williamsburgh Township, Craven
                          Co., bounding NE on the Township; other sides
on vacant land; also a half-a. lot, #252, in said town; which tract & lot
were granted by Lt. Gov. WILLIAM BULL on 5 July 1740 to DAVID MCCANTS,
SR. Witnesses: ROBERT PAISLEY, JOHN GREGG, ALEXANDER MCMECHAN. Before
JOHN LIVISTON, J.P. Memorial entered in Auditor's office 4 Apr. 1759 by
JAMES MICHIE, Dep. Aud. WILLIAM HOPTON, Registered.

Book V-V, p. 157   BENJAMIN MIKELL, planter, of Granville Co., &
5 & 6 June 1754   REBECCA, (her mark) his wife, to THOMAS DRAY-
L & R   TON, ESQ., of St. Andrews Parish, Berkeley
                          Co., for Ł 350 currency, 350 a. now called
Yeuhau Island (or Uhaws) in Granville Co., granted 9 Sept. 1735 to EPH-
RAIM MIKELL, planter; bounding W on Yehuaw Creek; E on a branch of Yeuhau
Creek; N & S on marsh; & by EPHRAIM MIKELL'S will, dated 2 Sept. 1743 de-
vised to his son, BENJAMIN, party hereto. Witnesses: JOSEPH CLAYPOLE,
GEORGE TRAY. (Note: Not proved). WILLIAM HOPTON, Register.

Book V-V, p. 162   JUDITH PEYRE, widow, of Craven Co., to GEORGE
1 & 2 Nov. 1757   DURAND, planter, of same place, for Ł 200 cur-
L & R   rency, 1100 a. in Craven Co., bounding W on
                          GEORGE HALL; other sides on vacant land. Wit-
nesses: JOHN COMING BALL, JOSEPH PALMER. Before JOHN PAMOR, J.P. Memorial entered in Auditors office 11 Apr. 1759 by JAMES MICHIE, Dep. Aud.
WILLIAM HOPTON, Register.

Book V-V, p. 166   JOB ROTHMAHLER, ESQ., of Peedee, executor, of
30 & 31 Aug. 1757   will of JOB ROTHMAHLER, ESQ., of Charleston,
L & R   to ROBERT BOYD, of Charleston, for Ł 61 cur-
                          rency, 500 a. in Craven Co., bounding on NW
side of a swamp, the head of E branch of Cooper River. Whereas JOB ROTH-
MAHLER, ESQ., owned said 500 a. which by will dated 17 Jan. 1739 authorized his executors to sell the remainder of his real estate, not devised,
& appointed his wife, ANN, executrix, & JOSEPH WRAGG, RICHARD LAMBTON, &
his son JOB, party hereto, his executors; & whereas ANN & WRAGG died, &
LAMBTON declined the office; & whereas the son, JOB, on 26 May 1757 offered the land at public auction & BOYD was highest bidder; now the tract
is conveyed to BOYD. Witnesses: ARTHUR FORBES, JOHN STEWART. Before
WILLIAM BURROWS, J.P. WILLIAM HOPTON, Register.

Book V-V, p. 172   GEORGE LOGAN, ESQ., of Colleton Co., & ELIZA-
7 Apr. 1759   BETH his wife, to RALPH IZARD, ESQ., of St.
Mortgage   George Parish, Dorchester, as security on bond
                          of even date in penal sum of Ł 12,000 for pay-
ment of Ł 6000 currency, with interest, on 7 Apr. 1760; 407 a. on W side
PonPon River, in Colleton Co., bounding N on JOHN BAILLIE; E on COL.
CHARLESWORTH GLOVER; S & W on BRYAN KELLY; according to plat attached to
release dated 10 Aug. 1729 from ALEXANDER TRENCH to JOHN BAILY; & pur-
chased by LOGAN by L & R dated 19 & 20 Mar. 1754 from JOSEPH GLOVER of
St. Bartholomews Parish, Colleton Co.; also 564 a. in Colleton Co.,
bounding N on WILLIAM CRAWL; E on JAMES KELLY & JOHN MUSGROVE; S on JO-
SEPH BOONE; W on JOHN OTTERSON; according to plat of original grant dated
30 Sept. 1736 to MARY CARMICHAEL who by L & R dated 27 & 28 Feb. 1757
conveyed to GEORGE LOGAN; also 508 a. in Colleton Co., bounding SE on
SAMUEL SLEIGH; SW on THOMAS BOONE, ESQ. (formerly Madam BOONE); NE on
JOHN POSTELL; which 508 a. were granted 12 Apr. 1739 to THOMAS BUTLER; &
after belonged to MELLER ST. JOHN, gentleman, of Charleston, who by L & R
dated 27 & 28 Oct. 1756 sold to GEORGE LOGAN; the 3 tracts forming 1
tract of 1479 a.; also all his (43) Negro slaves. Witnesses: JOHN LOGAN,
WILLIAM MAZYCK. Before CHARLES PINCKNEY, J.P. WILLIAM HOPTON, Register.

Book V-V, p. 179   GEORGE NORMAN, planter, of St. James Goose
25 & 26 Apr. 1759   Creek, to JOHN HAYES, planter, of same place,
L & R   for Ł 4000 currency, 800 a. in 2 tracts of
                          500 & 300 a. Whereas the Lords Proprs., by
Gov. CHARLES CRAVEN, & deputies CHARLES HART, ROBERT DANIEL, SAMUEL EVE-
LEIGH & GEORGE LOGAN, by 2 distinct grants dated 21 Mar. 1714/5 granted
DAVID WEBSTER 2 tracts of land; that is, 500 a. in Colleton Co., on E

side S Edisto River, bounding NW on THOMAS WARING; NE on WILLIAM ELLIOTT; SE on vacant land; SW on JOHN PRESCOTT; & 300 a. in Colleton Co., near BOB'S Savannah on E side S Edisto River; bounding N on JOHN PENDARVIS & THOMAS WARING; W on JOHN PENDARVIS; S on THOMAS DRAYTON; & E on JOHN PRESCOTT; & whereas DAVID WEBSTER, by will dated 5 July 1718, bequeathed to his son, WILLIAM, 300 a. of back land on N side PonPon River, part of the 2 tracts; & ordered the rest of his real & personal estate divided equally amongst his wife, MARGARET, & his children, to be divided when daughter MARGARET reached the age of 16; upon his wife's death or re-marriage her share to return to son DAVID; & whereas WILLIAM WEBSTER, son of testator DAVID WEBSTER, left SC 40 years ago & has not since been heard of, nor has GEORGE NORMAN received any notice of his being alize; & whereas it is highly presumable that WILLIAM is dead, whereby DAVID WEBSTER, son of DAVID WEBSTER the testator became his heir & entitled to the 300 a.; & whereas MARGARETT, widow of DAVID WEBSTER, SR., & MARGARETT, his daughter, as also DAVID WEBSTER, JR., being the only surviving children & the remaining 500 a. vested in them equally under the will; & whereas MARGARET, the widow, died & her share descended to son DAVID; & whereas MARGARET, the daughter, married JOSEPH NORMAN, & after the death of MARGARET & JOSEPH, their son, GEORGE NORMAN, became heir to 1/3 said 500 a.; & whereas DAVID WEBSTER died intestate owning 1 tract of 300 a. as heir to his brother WILLIAM; also 1/3 of the 500 a. in right of his mother, MARGARETT; & 1/3 in his own right; so that GEORGE NORMAN by descent & by will of his father, JOSEPH NORMAN, is lawful owner of the 2 tracts; now he sells to HAYES. Witnesses: EDWARD NEUFVILLE, WILLIAM WARD CROSSTHWAITE, JAMES HUNTER, JR. Before EGERTON LEIGH, J.P. WILLIAM HOPTON, Register.

Book V-V, p. 186
25 & 26 Jan. 1759
L & R

GEORGE KEITH & MICHAEL LEITNER, planters, of Saxegotha (formerly Congaree) Township, Berkeley Co., to said MICHAEL LEITNER; for Ⳑ 4:10:0 currency, 50 a., being half of 100 a., in Saxegotha Township, bounding NE on Santee River; NW on JOHN HUBERT & JACOB SPEAL; SE on other half; also a 1/2 a., #21 in Town of Saxegotha. Whereas on 16 Sept. 1738 the Hon. WILLIAM BULL granted JOHN ULRIC MILLER 100 a. in Congaree Township, bounding NE on Santee River; SE on PATRICK BROWN; NW on JOHN HUBERT & JACOB SPEAL; also a 1/2 a. lot #21 in said town; & whereas ANNA MILLER, relict & sole heir of JOHN ULRIC MILLER, jointly with CASPAR FREY, her second husband, by L & R dated 19 & 20 Dec. 1752 sold the 100 a. & lot #21 to CHRISTIAN LEITNER & GEORGE KEITH; CHRISTIAN LEITNER dying intestate & being succeeded by his eldest son & heir, MICHAEL; now KEITH & LEITNER sell to said MICHAEL LEITNER. Witnesses: STEPHEN CREEL, ANDREW KIGLER. Before JOHN HAMILTON, J.P. WILLIAM HOPTON, Register.

Book V-V, p. 191
15 & 16 Mar. 1749
L & R

JOSEPH DUBOURDIEU, executor of will of ANTHONY WHITE of Craven Co., to STEPHEN FORD, planter, of Craven Co., for Ⳑ 205 currency, 820 a., part of 1620 a. Whereas Gov. THOMAS BROUGHTON on 12 Dec. 1735 granted ANTHONY WHITE 1620 a. in Craven Co., bounding N on MEREDITH HUGHES; W on GOUGH & LANE; SE & E on LEACROFT & HAMBLIN; & whereas ANTHONY WHITE, by will dated 6 Feb. 1746 ordered his executors to sell his real & personal estate for the payment of his debts; now DUBOURDIEU sells a part of the real estate to FORD. Witnesses: JOHN ROLLAND, THOMAS TODD, GEORGE PAWLEY, WILLIAM PARKER. Before PAUL TRAPIER, J.P. WILLIAM HOPTON, Register.

Book V-V, p. 195
28 Apr. 1759
Release

WILLIAM GLEN, hatter, & MARGARETT his wife, to THOMAS SMITH, JR., merchant, both of Charleston, for Ⳑ 3800 currency, a lot in Charleston bounding E 59 ft. 2 in. on Union Street; W 57 ft. 2 in. on WALTER IZARD, ESQ.; N 211 ft. 7 in. on GABRIEL MANIGAULT, ESQ.; S on THOMAS SMITH, JAMES CROCKATT, & PAUL TRAPIER; which lot was formerly the estate of WILLIAM BOLLOUGH, blacksmith, of Berkeley Co., afterwards of HENRY SHERIFF, planter, of James Island, by whose will dated 28 Mar. 1750 it was devised to MARGARETT GLEN (lately wife of HENRY SHERIFF). Witnesses: JOHN COOPER, WILLIAM MICHIE. Before BENJAMIN SMITH, J.P. WILLIAM HOPTON, Register. Plat certified 20 Apr. 1759 by WILLIAM WILKINS, Sur.

Book V-V, p. 199   ROBERT FAIRCHILD, joiner, & cabinet maker, &
9 & 10 Mar. 1758   SARAH his wife; JOHN JOYNER, mariner, & ANNE
L & R   his wife; & RICHARD STEVENS, planter, & MARY
                          his wife; all of Granville Co.; of 1st part;
to HENRY TALBOT, bricklayer, of Granville Co.; for Ŀ 70 currency, lot
#110 in Beaufort, bounding S on Port Royal Street; W on new Street; N on
lot #108; E on lot #111; which lot #110 was granted by the Lords Proprs.
on 8 Aug. 1717 to RICHARD WIGG; whose son RICHARD inherited. He died 29
Mar. 1745 & the lot descended to his 3 daughters, SARAH, ANN, & MARY,
parties hereto; now they & their husbands sell to TALBOT. Witnesses:
DANIEL DESAUSSURE, JOHN STORY of Beaufort. Before JAMES THOMPSON, J.P.
WILLIAM HOPTON, Register.

Book V-V, p. 205   ALEXANDER RANTOWLE, merchant, of Charleston, &
9 & 10 May 1759   GERTRUDE his wife, convey to JOHN HALL, black-
L & R   smith, of Charleston, & SARAH his wife, as se-
                          curity that RANTOWLE will pay JOHN & SARAH,
during their joint lives, an annual sum of Ŀ 45 sterling (Ŀ 35 sterling
annually to the survivor); part of lot #66 in Charleston, bounding N on
that part of said lot now used as a cemetery or church yard of St.
Philips Church; E on the part belonging to the heirs of MRS. MULLINGS; S
60 ft. on Queen Street; W 115 ft. on Church Street; also 557 a., being
1/2 of 2 tracts of land & 1 tract of marsh near Stono River, formerly belonging to HENRY TOOMER, bounding S & W on Stono River; N on JOHN HENRY
BONNEAU; E on the other half belonging to JOSHUA TOOMER; JOHN & SARAH
HALL having conveyed the part of town lot to RANTOWLE in consideration of
receiving said annuity. Witnesses: JOHN GOVAN, BENJAMIN GUERARD. Before
JOHN RATTRAY, J.P. WILLIAM HOPTON, Register.

Book V-V, p. 211   GEORGE SAXBY, ESQ., of Charleston, & ELIZABETH
3 & 4 July 1758   his wife, to BENJAMIN YOUNG, merchant, of
L & R   Georgetown, for Ŀ 500 currency, lot #37 in
                          Georgetown, conveyed to SAXBY by DANIEL LA-
ROCHE, merchant, of Georgetown, by L & R dated 22 & 23 Jan. 1752. Wit-
nesses: RICHARD LAMBTON, THOMAS YEOMANS. Before ROBERT WILLIAMS, JR.,
J.P. WILLIAM HOPTON, Register.

Book V-V, p. 215   EDWARD PLOWDEN, planter, & SUSANNAH (her mark)
7 & 8 Aug. 1758   his wife, to JOHN FLEMING, planter; both of
L & R   Williamsburgh, Craven Co., for Ŀ 585 currency,
                          350 a. on N side Black River, in Williamsburgh
Township, on Boggey Swamp, bounding W on JOHN FLEMING; N on ROGER GORDON;
E & S on vacant land. Witnesses: LAURENCE CASEY, JAMES FLEMING, NATHAN-
IEL CATHEEN. Before JOHN LIVISTON, J.P. Memorial entered in Auditor's
office 12 May 1759 by JAMES MICHIE, Dep. Aud. WILLIAM HOPTON, Register.

Book V-V, p. 219   JOHN CUTHBERT, planter, & ESTHER his wife,
15 & 16 Dec. 1756   formerly of Williamsburgh Township, Craven
L & R   Co., to JAMES DICKEY, of said Township, for
                          Ŀ 415 currency, 200 a. in said Township,
bounding N on the common; W on Black River; other sides on vacant land.
Witnesses: LACHLAN MCKINTOSH, HARTLEY FUTHY, HUGH ERVIN. Before JOHN
LIVISTON, J.P. WILLIAM HOPTON, Register.

Book V-V, p. 224   JACOB MARTIN, physician, of Charleston, to
11 & 12 Jan. 1750   NICHOLAS HARLESTON, planter, of St. Johns Par-
L & R   ish, for Ŀ 4000 currency, 560 a. in Berkeley
                          Co., bounding S & SE on E branch of T of Coop-
er River; N & NE on NICHOLAS HARLESTON (formerly RICHARD BLAKE, afterwards JOHN HARLESTON); E on JOHN GUERARD (formerly MAJ. THOMAS BROUGHTON);
also 210 a., part of 420 a., in Berkeley Co., bounding S on E branch of T
of Cooper River; W on other part 420 a.; E on said 560 a.; also 262 a.,
part of 343 a., in Berkeley Co., bounding S on E branch of T of Cooper
River; W on JOHN GUERARD; NE on other part of 343 a.; which lands JACOB
MARTIN had purchased by L & R dated 18 & 19 June 1730 from ANDREW BROUGH-
TON & HANNAH his wife. Witnesses: FRANCIS ROCHE, JAMES PARSONS, JOHN
CLIFFORD. Before D. CAMPBELL, J.P. Memorial entered in Auditors office
12 May 1759 by JAMES MICHIE, Dep. Aud. WILLIAM HOPTON, Register.

Book V-V, p. 230   JOHN SMITH, merchant, & ELIZABETH his wife, to

15 & 16 May 1759   JOHN DELAGAZE, gentleman, both of Charleston,
L & R   for Ŀ 3000 currency, lot #16 in Beaufort, Port
                          Royal Island, Granville Co., bounding S on the
Bay; W on lot #15; N on lot #45; E on lot #17; also lot #45 in Beaufort,
bounding W on Carteret Street; S on lots #15 & #16; E on lot #48; N on
lot #44. Witnesses: MARY HAYNE, ROBERT WILLIAMS, JR. Before WILLIAM
BURROWS, J.P. WILLIAM HOPTON, Register.

Book V-V, p. 235   JOHN KELSALL, planter, & MARY his wife; & AR-
3 & 4 Aug. 1752   CHIBALD WILKINS, planter, & ANN his wife (MARY
L & R   & ANN being sisters & co-heiresses of WILLIAM
                         BELLINGER, 1 of the devisees of will of EDMOND
BELLINGER, 2nd Landgrave); of 1st part; to WILLIAM WILKINS, planter, of
James Island, for Ŀ 1800 SC money, 1000 a. in Granville Co., bounding S
on HUGH BRYAN; N on Purysburgh Road; E on Pocotalego River. Whereas ED-
MOND BELLINGER 2nd Landgrave owned various large tracts of land originally granted to his father, EDMOND BELLINGER, 1st Landgrave; & by will dated 21 Jan. 1739 bequeathed to his nephew, WILLIAM BELLINGER, 2000 a. to
be allotted by his wife, ELIZABETH, as his executrix; & whereas WILLIAM
BELLINGER, by will devised the bulk of his estate to his only child &
daughter (who died in her minority) but made no particular devise of the
2000 a.; & the land was inherited by his sisters, MARY, ANNE, & ELIZA-
BETH; & whereas ELIZABETH BELLINGER, the executrix, laid out 1000 a. for
YONGE, KELSALL & WILKINS, in right of their wives; & whereas HENRY YONGE,
& ELIZABETH his wife, on 20 July 1750 conveyed their share of the 1000 a.
to KELSALL & WILKINS; now they sell the land to WILLIAM WILKINS. Witnesses: THOMAS NOTTAGE, JOHN BULL, JR. Before STEPHEN BULL, J.P. Entered in Auditors office 22 May 1759 by JAMES MICKIE, Dep. Aud. WILLIAM
HOPTON, Register. Plat of 1000 a. given, on which under date of 11 May
1750 ELIZABETH B. ELLIOTT certifies that the 1000 a. were laid out for
HENRY YONGE, late of Pinckney's Island, SC, now of Georgia; JOHN KELLSON
of Woodwards Island; & ARCHIBALD WILKINS, of St. Johns Parish, SC; planters; co-heirs of WILLIAM BELLINGER. Witness to certificate & drawing of
lots; WILLIAM BACKSHELL.

Book V-V, p. 242   WILLIAM WILKINS, planter, of Prince William
2 Feb. 1756   Parish, Granville Co., leases to GEORGE DUNCAN
Lease for 6 Years   & MARY DUNCAN, 1 a., part of the land on which
                        WILKINS lives, near Pocotalego Bridge, adjoin-
ing the highway leading from the bridge to Coosawhatchie, as already
marked; for 6 years at 10 shillings a year; DUNCAN being allowed to erect
houses, etc. Witnesses: JAMES STERLING, JOSHUA MCPHERSON. No probate.
WILLIAM HOPTON, Register.

Book V-V, p. 243   The Hon. EDMUND ATKIN, member of H.M. Council
15 & 16 Sept. 1758   for SC, to THOMAS YOUNGE, bricklayer, of
L & R   Charleston, for Ŀ 780 currency, the N half of
                         lot #36 in Bedon's Alley (Lane), sometimes
called Middle Lane, in Charleston; bounding E 26 ft. on Bedon's Alley; S
107 ft. on other half sold to ELIZABETH GIBBES; N on WILLIAM CARWITHEN,
ISAAC HOLMES, MR. DALTON, & MRS. FIDLING; W on heirs of MRS. ELIZABETH
SMITH, widow. Whereas the Lords Proprs. on 10 Oct. 1689 granted GEORGE
BEDON lot #36 in Charleston; & whereas GEORGE BEDON by will dated 21 Dec.
1705 devised to his son, STEPHEN BEDON, his tenements & land in Charleston after the death of his wife; the remainder to his son HENRY; & whereas said STEPHEN BEDON, carpenter, who claimed lot #36 through his children, THOMAS, JOHN, STEPHEN, SARAH, BENJAMIN, REBECCA, & GEORGE, by L & R
dated 15 & 16 Apr. 1736, sold lot #36 to EDMOND ATKIN & his brother, JOHN
ATKIN, merchants, of Charleston, as joint tenants; & whereas EDMOND ATKIN
survived his brother JOHN & became sole owner & sold the S half of the
lot to ELIZABETH GIBBES; now he sells the N half to YOUNG. Witnesses:
SAMUEL PRIOLEAU, CHARLES PINCKNEY. Before WILLIAM BRISBANE, J.P. WIL-
LIAM HOPTON, Register. Plat of entire lot by GEORGE HUNTER, Sur. Gen.
dated 8 Mar. 1747. Present at survey were THOMAS DALE, ESQ., MRS. FID-
LING, WILLIAM CARWITHEN & COL. ROBERT BREWTON in behalf of MRS. SMITH.

Book V-V, p. 251   SAMUEL VARNOR, of Christ Church Parish, mort-
13 Feb. 1759   gaged to WILLIAM JOY, planter, for Ŀ 500 cur-
Sale by Mortgage   rency, 460 a., bounding NE on MR. TOOKERMAN;
                        NW on MR. PINCKNEY; SW on MR. WHITESIDES;

fronting the seashore opposite Coopehee Sound; formerly the property of
MRS. MARY BOONE; redeemable 13 Feb. next. Witnesses: JOHN GIBBES (son of
WILLIAM); SAMUEL JOY, MOSES JOY. Before ROBERT WILLIAMS, J.P. WILLIAM
HOPTON, Register. On 18 June 1764 SARAH (her mark) HARTMAN acknowledged
satisfaction of sale. Witness: F. BULL.

Book V-V, p. 252   SAMUEL VARNOR, wheelwright, of Christ Church
10 Feb. 1759   Parish, Berkeley Co., gives bond of perform-
Bond   ance to WILLIAM JOY, planter, of said Parish
                         (see p. 251). Same Witnesses; before ROBERT
WILLIAMS, J.P. WILLIAM HOPTON, Register.

Book V-V, p. 253   MRS. SARAH MIDDLETON, widow, of St. James Par-
24 & 25 May 1759   ish, Goose Creek, to JOSEPH BRAILSFORD, ESQ.,
L & R   of St. Pauls Parish, for love & affection,
                         657-1/2 a., part of 3500 a., known in the plat
of a certain resurvey by the letter A; bounding SE on heirs of DR. DAVID
CAW; SW on the part marked by letter C; N on that marked B; NE on vacant
land; also the part marked C containing 657-1/2 a., bounding NW by the
part marked B; NE on the part marked A; SE on land belonging to heirs of
DR. DAVID CAW & on vacant land; SW on part marked D. Whereas Lt. Gov.
THOMAS BROUGHTON on 30 Sept. 1736 granted SARAH MIDDLETON 3500 a. on
Coosawhatchie River Swamp in Granville Co., bounding SE on JOHN CHAMPNEY;
other sides on vacant land; according to plat certified 18 June 1736 by
JAMES ST. JOHN, Sur. Gen.; which land, at SARAH MIDDLETON'S request, was
resurveyed on 5 July 1758 by JAMES MCPHERSON, D.S., & divided into 6 par-
cels, marked on the plat by the letters A, B, C, D, E, & F; now she gives
A & C to JOSEPH BRAILSFORD. Witnesses: Rev. MR. JAMES HARRISON, DR. JOHN
MOULTRIE, JR. Before PETER TAYLOR, J.P. WILLIAM HOPTON, Register.

Book V-V, p. 260   JOHN GEORGE LAPP, carpenter, of Craven Co., to
9 Nov. 1758   HENRY GALLMAN, planter, of Saxegotha Township,
Mortgage   1 bay horse branded on mounting buttock ; 1
                         sorrel mare branded R on mounting buttock; 1
grey mare branded HF on mounting buttock; 3 cows & calves branded H, & 2
yearlings branded H; 12 head hogs marked with an upper keal in each ear;
1 iron bound cart & tackling to it; 30 bushels wheat; 1 saddle & bridle;
also 50 a. in Craven Co., household goods, tools & moveables now thereon;
redeemable by payment of all sums due GALLMAN by 10 Nov. 1759. Witnesses: SAMUEL ROCKER, JOHN CONRAD GEIGER. Before JOHN CHEVILLETTE, J.P.
WILLIAM HOPTON, Register.

Book V-V, p. 262   CHARLES WOODMASON, merchant, of Craven Co., to
10 & 11 May 1759   MOSES AUDIBERT, gentleman, of Charleston, as
L & R by Mortgage   security on bond of even date in penal sum of
                         Ł 700 for payment of Ł 350 currency, with in-
terest, on 11 May 1760; 450 a. on S side Lynch's Creek; in Craven Co.,
bounding NE on vacant land & JOHN CONNOR; NW on JOHN CONNOR & vacant land;
other sides on vacant land. Witnesses: WALTER MANSELL, ROBERT WILLIAMS,
JR. Before WILLIAM BURROWS, J.P. WILLIAM HOPTON, Register.

Book V-V, p. 266   BENJAMIN MCKINNE (MCKENNIE), of Craven Co., &
20 May 1758   MARY MCKINNE, his wife, to his daughter LEMEN-
Gift   DER, wife of JOSEPH KIRKLAND, for love & af-
                         fection, 100 a. adjoining the Wateree in Fred-
ericksburgh Township, being the SW corner of a tract of 400 a. granted
BENJAMIN MCKINNE by Gov. JAMES GLEN on 25 June 1753, to be laid out as
near a square as convenient. Witnesses: EDMUND O'NEIL, ARCHELAUS MC-
KINNE. Before WILLIAM BOYKIN, J.P. Memorial entered in Auditors office
4 June 1759 by JAMES MICHIE, Dep. Aud. WILLIAM HOPTON, Register.

Book V-V, p. 268   SOLOMON (his mark) MCGRAW, planter, & ANNE
25 Apr. 1759   (her mark) his wife, to JAMES LESLIE, black-
Release   smith, both of Craven Co., for Ł 80 currency,
                         100 a. on W side Little River, bounding on
other sides on vacant land; according to grant dated 5 Nov. 1755 from
Gov. JAMES GLEN. Witnesses: JACOB GIBSON, ELIZABETH (her mark) MCGRAW.
Before JACOB GOODOWN, J.P. WILLIAM HOPTON, Register.

Book V-V, p. 271   JAMES COOPER, planter, to JOHN MCFADDEN,

7 Dec. 1758   planter, both of Craven Co., for Ł 120 curren-
Release   cy, 150 a. in Craven Co., bounding on 1 of the
                               S branches of Lynches Lake; other sides on va-
cant land; as granted 16 Dec. 1756 to JAMES COOPER by Gov. WILLIAM HENRY
LYTTELTON. Witnesses: HUGH LORIMER, JOHN WATSON, THOMAS SCOTT. Before
JOHN LIVISTON, J.P. Memorial entered in Auditors office 4 June 1759 by
JAMES MICHIE, Dep. Aud. WILLIAM HOPTON, Register.

Book V-V, p. 274   BENJAMIN STILES, planter, to MALLORY RIVERS,
29 & 30 May 1759   planter, both of James Island, for Ł 1000 cur-
L & R   rency, 125 a. on James Island, in Berkeley Co.,
                              bounding E on estate of JOHN STENT; W on ROB-
ERT RIVERS (son of JEREMIAH RIVERS); N on MALLORY RIVERS; S on marsh of
river. Witnesses: JOHN HOLMES, JOHN SPENCER, DANIEL CLEMENT. Before
WILLIAM BURROWS, J.P. WILLIAM HOPTON, Register.

Book V-V, p. 279   JEAN HARLEY (formerly JEAN JACKSON, widow, of
15 & 16 Mar. 1757   CAPT. JOHN JACKSON, of PonPon), & GEORGE JACK-
L & R   SON, surviving executrix & executor of estate
                              of JOHN JACKSON; to JOHN VINSON, planter, of
St. Bartholomews Parish, Colleton Co., for Ł 242 currency, lot #14 in the
town of Jacksonburgh, bounding 100 ft. on King Street; 218 ft. deep; as
devised by will of CAPT. JOHN JACKSON dated 24 Mar. 1747 giving his executors authority to sell his lots & other lands. Witnesses: JOHN SMITH,
JOHN JACKSON. Before JAMES SHARPE, J.P. WILLIAM HOPTON, Register.

Book V-V, p. 283   ANN WATSON, widow, of Charleston, executrix of
5 June 1759   will of her husband, WILLIAM WATSON; to EDWARD
L & R   DAVIS, merchant, of Charleston, & MARGARET his
                              wife, for Ł 700 currency, that house & part of
lot #88, lately occupied by ANNE SOVERANCE, now by 1 parchable; bounding
N 92 ft. on BERNARD BECKMAN; S on EDWARD DEMPSEY; E 30 ft. on Union
Street. Whereas JOHN WATSON, of Charleston, by will dated 21 Feb. 1754
bequeathed said house & lot to WILLIAM WATSON; who by will dated 24 Sept.
1757 bequeath all his real & personal estate to ANNE; now she sells to
DAVIS. Witnesses: ALEXANDER FYFFE, JAMES ROBERTSON. Before WILLIAM
SIMPSON, J.P. WILLIAM HOPTON, Register.

Book V-V, p. 289   THOMAS MURPHY, planter, & MARY ANN, his wife,
24 Nov. 1753   to PAUL PORCHER, planter, both of Granville
L & R   Co., for Ł 350 currency, 350 a. granted by
                              Gov. JAMES GLEN on 13 Feb. 1753 to THOMAS
MURPHY; lying on head of Days Creek Swamp between Coosawhatchie & Savannah Rivers, in Granville Co., bounding S on DRURY DUNN; other sides on
vacant land. Witnesses: LUKE BLAKELEY, DRURY DUNN. Before A. DUPONT,
J.P. WILLIAM HOPTON, Register.

Book V-V, p. 296   GEORGE SEAMAN, merchant, to DAVID MONGIN,
2 Nov. 1750   watchmaker, both of Charleston, for Ł 1600
Release   currency, 800 a., part of a tract called
                              Rattlesnake Neck, in Granville Co., bounding E
on SAMUEL SMALL; S on a branch of Port Royall River; NW on ARTHUR HALL
(late of James Island); N on another branch of Port Royall River; which
800 a. were sold by HENRY PERONNEAU, merchant, of Charleston, & ELIZABETH
his wife; JAMES MICHIE, & MARTHA his wife; WILLIAM STEWART & ANN his wife;
& JOHN CATTELL, son & heir of SARAH CATTELL, & co-heir with ELIZABETH;
MARTHA & ANN (who were daughters of ARTHUR HALL, ESQ., of James Island);
to GEORGE SEAMAN, by L & R dated 19 & 20 Apr. 1750. Witnesses: TIMOTHY
MORGRIDGE, JOHN TROUP. Before EGERTON LEIGH, J.P. WILLIAM HOPTON, Register.

Book V-V, p. 299   THOMAS LYNCH, planter, & HANNAH his wife; &
8 & 9 July 1757   ANDREW JOHNSTON, planter, & ANN his wife; to
L & R   GEORGE AUSTIN, merchant, of Charleston, for
                              Ł 1200 currency; 200 a. in Craven Co., bound-
ing SE on Peedee River; SW on GEORGE AUSTIN (formerly DANIEL LAROCHE); NW
on JOHN GREEN; NE on THOMAS LYNCH & ANDREW JOHNSTON; also 62-1/2 a.,
bounding SE on a thoroughfare leading to Waccamaw River; NE on THOMAS
LYNCH & ANDREW JOHNSTON; NW on Peedee River; S on DANIEL LAROCHE. Witnesses: ANN WATSON, DOUGAL CAMPBELL. Before WILLIAM BURROWS, J.P.

WILLIAM HOPTON, Register.

Book V-V, p. 304   PETER LEQUEUX, planter, of St. Stephens Par-
17 & 18 Oct. 1758   ish, Craven Co., & MARTHA (her mark) his wife,
L & R   to VALENTINE DARR, planter, of Christ Church
                          Parish, Berkeley Co., for Ł 386:15:0 currency,
182 a. in Christ Church Parish, bounding SE on marsh of Sewee Bay; SW on
MRS. PORTER; NE on ELIZABETH WELDON. Witnesses: DAVID PALMER, JAMES
SINKLER. Before CHARLES CANTEY, J.P. WILLIAM HOPTON, Register. Plat
certified 16 Oct. 1758 by JOHN HENTIE shows 182 a., half of 364 a. divided according to writ of partition dated 4 July 1758; said half being assigned to LEQUEUX & his wife by the referees.

Book V-V, p. 309   THOMAS LYNCH, planter, & HANNAH his wife; &
8 & 9 July 1757   ANDREW JOHNSTON, planter, & ANN his wife; to
L & R   GEORGE GABRIEL POWELL, planter; for Ł 1000 SC
                          money; 200 a. in Craven Co., bounding SE on
Peedee River; SW on GEORGE AUSTIN; NW on JOHN GREEN; NE on GEORGE GABRIEL
POWELL; also 62-1/2 a. bounding SE on a thoroughfare leading to Waccamaw
River; NE on Peedee River; SW on GEORGE AUSTIN. Witnesses: ANN WATSON,
DOUGAL CAMPBELL, JACOB MOTTE, JR. Before JACOB MOTTE, J.P. WILLIAM HOP-
TON, Register.

Book V-V, p. 314   CAPT. PAUL TRAPIER, merchant, of Georgetown,
19 & 20 Feb. 1754   Winyaw, & MAGDALEN his wife, to CLAUDIUS
L & R   PEGUES, of Craven Co., for Ł 700 currency,
                          1000 a. in Craven Co., bounding NE on a lake
on Peedee River; NW on JAMES ABERCROMBIE; SW on vacant land; SE on AARON
HUNSCOMB; as granted to PAUL TRAPIER on 12 Dec. 1746. Witnesses: ELIZA-
BETH FORDYCE, SAMUEL BUTLER. Before JOHN REMINGTON, J.P. WILLIAM HOPTON,
Register. Plat given.

Book V-V, p. 319   WILLIAM (his mark) HEMSWORTH, planter, of Cra-
17 & 18 June 1759   ven Co., & NOEMA (her mark) his wife, to
L & R   CHRISTOPHER GADSDEN, merchant, of Charleston,
                          for Ł 370 currency, 150 a. in Craven Co.,
bounding NE on Peedee River; other sides on vacant land; according to
grant to HEMSWORTH dated 12 June 1751. Witnesses: JOHN GEORGE FRY,
CLAUDIUS PEGUES. Before JOHN WADE, J.P. WILLIAM HOPTON, Register.

Book V-V, p. 323   WILLIAM GREEN, DANIEL MCGINNEY, & SUSANNAH MC-
25 & 26 Nov. 1756   GINNEY (wife of DANIEL), to GEORGE FORD; all
L & R   of Craven Co., for Ł 350 currency, 140 a. on S
                          side Black River, Craven Co., bounding S on
JOHN GREEN; N on Green's Creek. Whereas Lt. Gov. THOMAS BROUGHTON on 13
July 1737 granted JOHN GREEN said 140 a. in Craven Co.; & whereas JOHN
GREEN on 25 May 1741 gave the land to DANIEL MCGINNEY; & whereas JOHN
GREEN did not deliver possession & seizin to MCGINNEY; & whereas GREEN
died without having bequeathed the land; so that it became vested in WIL-
LIAM GREEN, as eldest son & heir; now GREEN & MCGINNEY convey the land to
FORD. Witnesses: JAMES LANE, THOMAS HENNING, SAMUEL BRINDLEY. Before
THOMAS BLYTHE, J.P. WILLIAM HOPTON, Register.

Book V-V, p. 330   GEORGE HICKS, to GEORGE HICKS, JR., both of
31 Mar. 1759   Craven Co., for Ł 1000 currency, 350 a. in the
L & R   WELCH tract in Craven Co., bounding SW on Pee-
                          dee River; other side on vacant land; which
tract was granted JOHN HICKS on 18 Jan. 1745 by Gov. JAMES GLEN; & sold
by JOHN HICKS on 4 June 1748 to GEORGE HICKS, SR. Plat & grant recorded
25 Feb. 1750 in Book P.P. fols. 322-326. Witnesses: HENRY BEDINGFIELD,
ROBERT (his mark) GRAVES. Before THOMAS BLYTHE, J.P. WILLIAM HOPTON,
Register.

Book V-V, p. 334   CAPT. TACITUS GAILLARD, of St. James Santee
31 May 1759   Parish, & ANN his wife, to SARAH STOUTENBURGH,
Mortgage   gentlewoman, of Charleston, as security of
                          bond of even date in penal sum of Ł 10,000 for
payment of Ł 5000 currency, with interest, on 31 May 1760; several plantations; 1800 a. in Berkeley Co., S side Santee River, bounding NW on
JAMES FLOOD, & vacant land; SW on vacant land; SE on EDWARD CORAM, JOHN

PEARCE & ALEXANDER DINGLE & on vacant land; according to plat certified
by EGERTON LEIGH, Sur. Gen. dated 1 Aug. 1758 & grant dated 19 Sept. 1758
to THOMAS LYNCH; who by L & R dated 16 & 17 Mar. last sold to TACITUS
GAILLARD; also 400 a. in Berkeley Co., granted JOHN MOULTRIE, surgeon, of
Charleston, which by various conveyances came to TACITUS GAILLARD; which
400 a. according to plat by EGERTON LEIGH, S.G., are surrounded by the
1800 a. purchased by GAILLARD from WILLIAM MOORE, planter, of Craven Co.,
by L & R dated 18 & 19 Sept. 1754; also half of a tract of 290 a. in Craven Co., bounding E on Wambaw Creek; W on THOMAS EVANCE; S on CHARLES
CANTEY (formerly MRS. MOULTRIE); N on TACITUS GAILLARD; according to plat
dated 14 Oct. 1732 certified by JAMES ST. JOHN, formerly Sur. Gen., originally granted to JOHN GENDRON on 3 Feb. 1737; which half part was by L &
R dated 14 & 15 June 1757 purchased by TACITUS GAILLARD from JOHN BARNETT,
planter, of St. James Santee; also 450 a. originally 500 a. in St. James
Santee Parish, Craven Co., on NW side Wambaw Creek which 500 a. were
bought by GAILLARD from JOHN MAYRANT & ANN his wife by L & R dated 1 & 2
Feb. 1754; GAILLARD having sold to ROBERT PRINGLE, ESQ., of Charleston,
the other 50 a. which adjoined PRINGLE'S land; the 500 a. bounding S on
Wambaw Creek & land bought from BARNETT; W & N on vacant land; E on ROB-
ERT PRINGLE; according to plat on back of release from MAYRANT to GAIL-
LARD; also 40 a. in St. James Santee Parish, bounding W on TACITUS GAIL-
LARD; N on ROBERT PRINGLE; other sides on Wambaw Creek; according to plat
on back of release dated 2 Feb. 1754 from PRINGLE to GAILLARD; & also de-
livers 49 slaves. Witnesses: EDWARD CORAM, WILLIAM (his mark) BUDDIN.
Before CHARLES CANTEY, J.P.   Recorded in Secretary's Book X.X. p. 427 by
WILLIAM MURRAY, pro. Dep. Sec.   WILLIAM DOCKWRAY, Dep. Reg.

Book V-V, p. 343   CAPT. TACITUS GAILLARD of Parish of St. James
8 June 1749   Santee, to ISAAC MAZYCK, THOMAS MIDDLETON &
Mortgage   SAMUEL BRAILSFORD, merchants, of Charleston,
                          as security on bond of even date given MAZYCK
in penal sum of Ł 2428 for payment of Ł 1214 currency, with interest, on
8 June 1760; & another bond of same date given MIDDLETON & BRAILSFORD in
penal sum of Ł 3006:17:4 for payment of Ł 1503:8:8 currency, with interest, on 8 June 1760; several plantations; 1800 a. on S side Santee River
granted 19 Sept. 1758 to THOMAS LYNCH, who conveyed to TACITUS GAILLARD;
400 a. in Berkeley Co., granted THOMAS LYNCH & surrounded by said 1800 a.,
which 400 a. GAILLARD purchased from WILLIAM MOORE, planter, of Craven
Co.; also half of a tract of 290 a. in Craven Co., granted JOHN GENDRON &
purchased by GAILLARD from BARNETT, planter, of St. James Santee Parish;
also 450 a. in St. James Santee, Craven Co., on NW side Wambaw Creek,
originally 500 a., GAILLARD having sold 50 a. adjoining PRINGLE'S land to
ROBERT PRINGLE of Charleston; which 500 a. bounded according to plat on
back of release from JOHN MAYRANT & ANN his wife to GAILLARD also 40 a.
in St. James Santee on NW side Wambaw Creek; bounding according to plat
on back of release from ROBERT PRINGLE to GAILLARD; all of which lands
are described in mortgage to SARAH STOUTENBURGH (p. 334); also 1300 a. on
N & S sides Santee River in 3 tracts which GAILLARD purchased severally
from FRANCIS KINLOCH, JOHN MAYRANT, & BETHELL DEWES; 1 being 500 a., 2
being 400 a. each; also 48 slaves. Witnesses: CHARLES PINCKNEY, WILLIAM
MAZYCK.   Before WILLIAM BURROWS, J.P.   Recorded in Secretary's Book X.X.
fols. 443-449 by WILLIAM MURRAY, Dep. Sec.   WILLIAM DOCKWRAY, Dep. Reg.

Book V-V, p. 351   WILLIAM HART, planter, of Colleton Co., to
12 & 13 July 1759   DAVID STEVENS, planter, of St. Pauls Parish,
L & R   Colleton Co., for Ł 150 currency, 100 a. in
                          the forks of Edisto River on Good Land Swamp,
in Colleton Co., surrounded by vacant land; as granted to HART by Gov.
WILLIAM HENRY LYTTLETON, on 1 Aug. 1758. Witnesses: JACOB STEVENS, JAMES
SMITH, THOMAS POOLE. Before J. SKENE, J.P.   WILLIAM DOCKWRAY, Dep. Reg.

Book V-V, p. 356   JOHN RATTRAY, attorney-at-law, & HELEN his
10 July 1759   wife, to THOMAS SMITH, merchant, both of
Release   Charleston, for Ł 3350 SC money, part of a lot
                          in Charleston, with the messuage thereon oc-
cupied by MESSRS. DEWARR & MARSHALL, bounding S 30 ft. on Broad Street, E
& N on THOMAS SMITH (formerly JOSEPH WRAGG); W 100 ft. on ANN WATSON.
Witnesses: BELLAMY CRAWFORD, BENJAMIN GUERARD.   Before JAMES PARSONS,
J.P.   WILLIAM DOCKWRAY, Dep. Reg.

Book V-V, p. 358   MARY YEOMANS, widow, formerly of Charleston,
9 & 10 July 1759   now of St. Andrews Parish, to WILLIAM GLEN,
L & R   merchant, of Charleston, for Ł 2500 currency,
                      part of lot #37 in Charleston, bounding N on
Eliott Street, MRS. BISSETT, & MRS. REMINGTON; W on part same lot belong-
ing to MRS. BISSETT & part formerly belonging to MARY YEOMANS (now MRS.
PEACOCK); S on heris of WILLIAM SMITH; E on part same lot belonging to
WILLIAM CARWITHEN; measuring 37 ft. 10 in. on Elliott Street, & 83 ft.
6 in. deep. Witnesses: WILLIAM HARVEY, WILLIAM MICHIE. Before JAMES
PARSONS, J.P. WILLIAM DOCKWRAY, Dep. Reg.

Book V-V, p. 363   JOSEPH GLOVER, ESQ., of St. Bartholomews Par-
9 & 10 May 1759   ish, Colleton Co., & ANN his wife, to ELIJAH
L & R   POSTELL, ESQ., of St. George Parish, Dor-
                      chester, for Ł 6500 currency, 800 a. in Colle-
ton Co., part of 1250 a. granted JOHN GODFREY on 16 Jan. 1735, the 1250
a. bounding S on vacant land; W on JOHN CHAMPNEYS; N on JOHN FRASER; E on
THOMAS DRAYTON & COL. TRENCH; which tract of 800 a., on which GODFREY
lived, was sold at public auction by RAWLINS LOWNDES, P.M. on 2 Oct. 1753
to JOSEPH GLOVER for Ł 1985, by writ of fieri facias issued 1 Oct. 1751
at suit of JOHN MCKENZIE, MATTHEW ROCHE, GEORGE JACKSON, & JONATHAN WIT-
TER against GODFREY. Witnesses: JOHN POSTELL, JAMES POSTELL. Before
JAMES SKIRVING, J.P. WILLIAM DOCKWRAY, Dep. Reg.

Book V-V, p. 369   JOSEPH GLOVER gives ELIJAH POSTELL bond for
10 May 1759   Ł 6500 currency for keeping above agreement
Bond   (p. 363). Witnesses: JOHN POSTELL, JAMES POS-
                      TELL. WILLIAM DOCKWRAY, Dep. Reg.

Book V-V, p. 371   WILLIAM (his mark) FINLEY, planter, & HESTER
31 July 1759   his wife (1 of the daughters of JAMES TAYLOR,
Release   planter), to THOMAS HEYWARD, gentleman; all of
                      James Island; for Ł 600 currency, 40 a., bound-
ing N & NW on New Town Cut or the adjoining marsh; E on CHRISTOPHER TAY-
LOR; S on PAUL HAMILTON; W on ELEANOR TAYLOR. Whereas JAMES TAYLOR owned
120 a. on James Island & by will dated 27 May 1755 devised 40 a. to each
of his 3 children, HESTER, ELEANOR, & CHRISTOPHER; & whereas WILLIAM FIN-
LEY married HESTER & became entitled to her third; & whereas a writ of
partition was issued on 15 Nov. 1758 directing THOMAS HEYWARD, THOMAS
RIVERS, SAMUEL HEYWARD, RALPH SANDIFORD & CHARLES JACOB PICHARD to divide
the land into 3 parts, which by their certificate dated 6 Jan. 1759 they
did; now WILLIAM & HESTER FINLEY sell their part to THOMAS HEYWARD. Witnesses: JAMES PARSONS, MACARTAN CAMPBELL (gentlemen), CHRISTOPHER PETER.
Before WILLIAM MURRAY, J.P. WILLIAM DOCKWRAY, Dep. Reg.

Book V-V, p. 375   ISAAC NICHOLES, planter, of St. Pauls Parish,
21 & 22 Dec. 1750   Colleton Co., to JOHN MILES & CHARLES GUY,
L & R   church wardens, & THOMAS LADSON, EDWARD PERRY,
                      JOSEPH BRAILSFORD, JOHN RAILEY, & ANDREW LETCH,
vestrymen of said Parish, in trust for the parishioners of the established Church of England, for Ł 1200 currency, as a parsonage or Glebe land,
444 a. in St. Pauls Parish, part of 1000 a. granted RALPH EMMS by Gov.
NATHANIEL JOHNSTON on 3 Sept. 1709; some part of said land bounding SE on
CALEB TOOMER; W on Caw Caw Swamp; half of the 1000 a. having been be-
queathed by EMMS equally to his 2 sons WILLIAM & HEZEKIAH EMMS. WILLIAM
& HEZEKIAH by 2 deeds of sale, 1 dated 10 June 1725, the other 18 May
1727 sold their halves of said 500 a. to CAPT. HENRY NICHOLES; who by his
will bequeathed several tracts equally to his 2 sons, ISAAC & STEPHEN
NICHOLES; the 500 a. going to STEPHEN NICHOLES; who by his will left to
ISAAC, only surviving executor, the power to sell 444 a. Witnesses:
JAMES LADSON, RACHELL LETCH, WILLIAM COWELL. Before CHARLES LOWNDES,
J.P. WILLIAM DOCKWRAY, Dep. Reg.

Book V-V, p. 383   SAMUEL ASH, planter, & CATHERINE his wife, to
25 & 26 Feb. 1728   BENJAMIN PERRY, planter, both of Berkeley Co.,
L & R in Trustee   for Ł 210 currency, 750 a., English measure,
                      in Colleton Co., bounding S on EDWARD NORTH; N
on WILLIAM LIVINGSTON; W on PonPon River. Whereas the Rev. WILLIAM LEV-
INGSTON, of Charleston, on 21 Mar. 1719 sold THOMAS SMITH, JR., of Berkeley Co., 1750 a. in Colleton Co., being the S part of 4000 a. purchased

by LEVINGSTONE from Landgrave ROBERT DANIEL; the 1750 a. lying on E side
the freshes of Edisto River & nearest the plantation of JAMES RIXOM, &
run off from Edisto River directly backwards to E by a straight line; in
trust for the use of said THOMAS SMITH, JR. & the children of JOHN ASH;
viz.; JOHN, RICHARD, ALGERNOON, SAMUEL, ISABELLA (wife of BENJAMIN BERRY,
shipwright), & THEODORA (wife of JOSEPH LAW, planter); to be divided
equally between SMITH & said children by said SMITH; & whereas all have
agreed that SMITH should give RICHARD ALGERNOON, & SAMUEL ASH, title to
1500 a. (out of the 1750) to be divided by them so that RICHARD may have
300 a. out of the 1750; ALGERNOON 450 a.; & SAMUEL 750 a.; now SAMUEL
sells his share to PERRY. Witnesses: ALGERNOON ASH, JOHN HALE, NATHANIEL
LAW. Before JACOB BOND, J.P. Memorial entered in Auditors office 9 Nov.
1757 in Book D-4, p. 190, by JAMES MICHIE, Dep. Aud. WILLIAM DOCKWRAY,
Dep. Reg.

Book V-V, p. 390   PHILIP (his mark) MURPHY, planter, to PATRICK
3 & 4 Dec. 1756   (his mark) TROY, both of Berkeley Co., for
L & R   Ŀ 75 currency; 50 a. on N side Saludy River,
       on which MURPHY lives, bounding SW on river;
NW on PATRICK KELLY; NE & NW on vacant land. Witnesses: PATRICK WELCH,
JAMES OGILVIE. Before GEORGE MURRAY, J.P. WILLIAM DOCKWRAY, D.R.

Book V-V, p. 395   PATRICK (his mark) TROY, Cherokee trader, for
28 Feb. & 1 Mar. 1759   Ŀ 100 currency assigns above L & R to PATRICK
Assignment   KELTY. Witnesses: THOMAS BICKHAM, CHARLES
       (his mark) ROBINSON. Before JAMES FRANCIS,
J.P. WILLIAM DOCKWRAY, D.R.

Book V-V, p. 396   JOHN (his mark) BENNETT, SR., & JOHN BENNETT,
17 Aug. 1759   JR., yeomen, to THOMAS PHILIPS, planter, all
L & R   of Christ Church Parish, Berkeley Co., for
       Ŀ 130 currency, 100 a., English measure, in
Berkeley Co., bounding E on JOHN WINGOOD; W on THOMAS WHITESIDE & on
THOMAS PHILLIPS (formerly THOMAS PALMER). Witnesses: ALLEN MICKIE,
EPHRAIM (his mark) WINGOOD. Before ROBERT WILLIAMS, J.P. WILLIAM DOCK-
WRAY, D.R.

Book V-V, p. 400   MARY BRYAN, widow of HUGH BRYAN, to THOMAS
17 & 18 Apr. 1758   HUTCHINSON, cabinet maker, of Charleston, for
L & R   Ŀ 1375 currency, part of lots #181 & #198 in
       Charleston, bounding W 117-1/2 ft. on Friend
Street; N 72 ft. 3 in. on part of lot #181; E on RICHARD LAMBTON & CATH-
ERINE GREENLAND; S on part of lot #198; with the tenement erected on S
end. Whereas SAMUEL PRIOLEAU, gentleman, of Charleston, owned part of
lots #181 & #198, bounding W 235 ft. on Friend Street; N 72 ft. 3 in. on
Broad Street; E on RICHARD LAMBTON & CATHERINE GREENLAND; S on part of
lot #198 belonging to GEORGE ROUPELL; with the dwelling house erected on
S end, fronting Friend Street; & by will dated 25 Oct. 1751 bequeathed
the dwelling house & the land N to Broad Street to his daughter MARY BRY-
AN; now she sells the S part of her land to HUTCHINSON. Witnesses: SAM-
UEL PRIOLEAU, ROBERT WILLIAMS, JR. Before WILLIAM BURROWS, J.P. WILLIAM
DOCKWRAY, D.R.

Book V-V, p. 405   MARY BRYAN, widow of HUGH BRYAN, to THOMAS
17 & 18 Apr. 1758   ELFE, cabinet maker, of Charleston, for Ŀ 575
L & R   currency, the N part of lot #181 in Charles-
       ton, bounding W 117-1/2 ft. on Friend Street;
N 72 ft. 3 in. on Broad Street; E on RICHARD LAMBTON; S on other part lot
#181. Whereas SAMUEL PRIOLEAU, gentleman, owned part of lots #181 & #198,
bounding W 235 ft. on Friend Street; N 72 ft. 3 in. on Broad Street; E on
RICHARD LAMBTON & CATHERINE GREENLAND; S on part of lot #198 belonging to
GEORGE ROUPELL; with the dwelling house on S end fronting Friend Street;
& by will dated 25 Oct. 1751 bequeathed the house & the land N of it to
Broad Street to his daughter MARY BRYAN; now she sells the N part of her
land to ELFE. Witnesses: SAMUEL PRIOLEAU, ROBERT WILLIAMS, JR. Before
WILLIAM BURROWS, J.P. WILLIAM DOCKWRAY, D.R.

Book V-V, p. 410   JOHN WATSON (WATSONE), merchant, formerly of
18 Apr. 1758   Charleston, SC, now of London, appoints RAW-
Power of Attorney   LINS LOWNDES, gentleman, of Charleston, his

attorney, to his house in Charleston on Bay Street corner Elliott Street, now occupied by JOHN MCQUEEN; also all his land in SC. Witnesses: CAPT. JAMES RODGER, ANDREW JOHNSTON. JOHNSTON appeared before CHARLES PINCKNEY, J.P. WILLIAM DOCKWRAY, D.R.

Book V-V, p. 412
10 & 11 Sept. 1759
L & R
JOHN WATSONE, merchant, formerly of Charleston, SC, now of London, by his attorney RAWLINS LOWNDES, gentleman, of Charleston, to JOHN MC-QUEEN, merchant, of Charleston, for ₺ 7025 SC money, the tenement & part of lot #13 on the corner of East Bay & Elliott Streets, fronting 33 ft. 6 in. on the Bay from the corner to the tenement & lot belonging to ALEXANDER PETRIE, silversmith; W on Elliott Street, 50 ft. to land belonging to HOPKIN PRICE; & measuring 29 ft. on W; as lately occupied by JOHN MCQUEEN; the property to be free from claim of dower by ABIGAIL, wife of JOHN WATSONE. Whereas BARNARD SCHENKINGH owned several lots in Charleston, in particular, lot #13 on the Bay fronting # 50 ft. on the Bay; S 116 ft. on a neighborhood lane now called Elliott Street; W 72 ft. on DR. JOHN THOMAS; N on ISAAC MAZYCK & Landgrave JAMES COLLETON; & whereas CAPT. BENJAMIN SCHENKINGH, son of BARNARD, after his father's death, claimed the lands as son & heir, but as the grants, deeds & titles to lot #13 & other lots & lands were lost, burned, or worn out & obliterated so as to be of little benefit to him, he petitioned the General Assembly to confirm his estate; which petition was granted; & whereas BENJAMIN SCHENKINGH, & MARGARET his wife, on 14 Feb. 1705 sold part of lot #13 to JOHN BUCKLEY, merchant, of Charleston; who by will, proved before Gov. NATHANIEL JOHNSON on 28 Jan. 1706, bequeathed the property to his wife KATHERINE; who later married FRANCIS LEBRASSEUR, merchant, of Charleston; & whereas FRANCIS & KATHERINE LEBRASSEUR sold the piece of lot on 28 Oct. 1708 to DOMINICK ARTHUR, merchant, of Charleston; who on 29 Feb. 1710 reconveyed to FRANCIS & KATHERINE LEBRASSEUR; & whereas KATHERINE died soon after & FRANCIS became sole heir; & whereas by L & R tripartite dated 28 & 29 Jan. 1730, between FRANCIS LEBRASSEUR of 1st part; THOMAS GADSDEN & JOHN KING, of 2nd part; & ANNE SPLATT, widow of RICHARD SPLATT, of 3rd part; reciting that whereas a marriage was intended between FRANCIS LEBRASSEUR & ANNE SPLATT & LEBRASSEUR conveyed said premises to GADSDEN & KING in trust for FRANCIS & ANNE; which marriage took place; & whereas on 3 Dec. 1736 FRANCIS died at Charleston & ANNE became sole owner; & by L & R dated 22 & 23 Dec. 1740 sold JOHN WATSONE that part of lot #13 bounding E 56 ft. on the Bay; S 100 ft. on Elliott Street; W 71 ft. on part reserved for ANNE; N 112 ft. on JOHN COLLETON; & whereas WATSONE built on the lot 2 large brick tenements fronting the Bay & several other buildings & stores & sold part of the premises fronting on Elliott Street to HOPKIN PRICE, tanner, of Charleston; by L & R dated 18 & 19 Jan. 1750 sold the N tenement & part of lot on the Bay to ALEXANDER PETRIE, silversmith, of Charleston, & dwelt for several years in the S tenement on the corner of the Bay & Elliott Street; & whereas WATSONE by power of attorney dated 18 Apr. 1758 appointed RAWLINS LOWNDES his attorney to sell not only the said house in which he formerly dwelt, then occupied by JOHN MCQUEEN, but also all his plantations, etc., in SC; now LOWNDES sells the house to MCQUEEN. Witnesses: CHARLES PINCKNEY, WILLIAM MAZYCK. Before JACOB MOTTE, J.P. WILLIAM DOCKWRAY, D.R. Plat of lot #13 dated 30 Aug. 1759 by WILLIAM WILKINS, Sur., showing WATSON'S dwelling house, compting house, PRICE'S land, pantry, PETER CALVERT'S property, brick store, estate of GIGNIARD DEASES/ALLEY, JOHN COLLETON'S line, PETRIES house yard & back buildings.

Book V-V, p. 425
11 & 12 Sept. 1759
L & R
JOHN MCQUEEN, merchant, & ANNE his wife, to ALEXANDER PETRIE, silversmith, both of Charleston, for ₺ 7025 currency, that house & lot on corner of the Bay & Elliott Street, purchased from JOHN WATSONE (p. 412), bounding E 36-1/2 ft. on the Bay; S 50 ft. on Elliott Street; W 29 ft. on PETER BOCQUETT (formerly PETER CALVETT); N on ALEXANDER PETRIE & MR. COLLETON. Witnesses: CHARLES PINCKNEY, WILLIAM MAZYCK, ROBERT RAPER. Before JACOB MOTTE, J.P. WILLIAM DOCKWRAY, D.R.

Book V-V, p. 432
28 & 29 Mar. 1757
L & R
JAMES WRIGHT, ESQ., of Charleston, to GEORGE GABRIEL POWELL, ESQ., of Winyaw, for ₺ 1000 currency, 1500 a. in Craven Co., part of 2000 a. on Black River granted COL. WILLIAM RHETT: bounding SW on SAMUEL HUNTER; N on ANTHONY WHITE & JOHN THOMPSON, JR.,

which tract formerly belonged to JOHN THOMPSON, JR., who mortgaged it to DANIEL & THOMAS LAROCHE, of Craven; who assigned the mortgage to JAMES WRIGHT; & sold by WILLIAM PINCKNEY, master of High Court of Chancery, to JAMES WRIGHT by L & R dated 1 & 2 May 1755; SARAH WRIGHT, wife of JAMES, to have no dower claim. Witnesses: DANIEL DWIGHT, DANIEL HORRY, JR., CHARLES WRIGHT. Before WILLIAM MURRAY, J.P. WILLIAM DOCKWRAY, D.R.

Book V-V, p. 438
11 May 1754
Dedimus Potestatem
PETER LEIGH, C.J., at Charleston, commands THOMAS HASELL & PAUL TRAPIER, J.P.'s of Craven Co., to go to ANN JUDITH CUTTINOE, who is unable to travel to Charleston, & receive her acknowledgment of the L & R dated 5 & 6 Apr. 1753 by which her husband JEREMIAH CUTTINOE, of Georgetown, sold to HENRY BOSSARD, SR., planter, of Prince George Parish, half of lot #88 in Georgetown on which a tenement was built, bounding SE 108.9 ft. on Scriven Street; NE on DANIEL BOURGETT'S lot #112; NW on WILLIAM THOMAS'S lot #87; SW 100 ft. on Prince Street. WILLIAM DOCKWRAY, D.R.

Book V-V, p. 439
12 July 1754
Renunciation of Dower
ANNE JUDITH CUTTINOE, wife of JEREMIAH CUTTINOE, gunsmith, of Georgetown, renounces her title, before THOMAS HASELL & PAUL TRAPIER, to the house & part of a lot in Georgetown sold by her husband (p. 438) to HENRY BOSSARD, SR. WILLIAM DOCKWRAY, D.R.

Book V-V, p. 441
24 & 26 Aug. 1754
L & R
HENRY BOSSARD, SR., planter, of Prince George Parish, Winyaw, to GEORGE GABRIEL POWELL, ESQ., for ₤ 820 currency, half of lot #88 in Georgetown, with the tenement thereon, bounding SE 108.9 ft. on Scriven Street; NE 100 ft. on DANIEL BOURGETT'S lot #112; NW on WILLIAM THOMAS'S lot #87; SW on Prince Street. Witness: THOMAS MITCHELL. Before THOMAS HASELL, J.P. WILLIAM DOCKWRAY, D.R.

Book V-V, p. 447
1 & 2 May 1740
L & R
JAMES ST. JOHN, ESQ., of Charleston, to WILLIAM VAUGHAN, merchant, of London, for ₤ 5 SC money, 2 plantations of 1000 a. & 750 a. Whereas GEORGE II on 12 May 1735 granted JAMES ST. JOHN 750 a. in Granville Co., bounding E on CAPT. JOHN BULL, ARTHUR MIDDLETON, & CAPT. MATTHEWS, JR.; S on Chuley Finna Creek; W on RICHARD BLAND; N on BARNABY BULL; & on 9 Apr. 1736 granted JAMES ST. JOHN 1000 a. in Granville Co., bounding N on JOHN PETER PURY; S on JAMES ST. JOHN; W on ROBERT WRIGHT; E on vacant land; now, in pursuance of the direction of a certain award in writing founded on a rule in H.M. Court, Chancery in SC made by JOHN ATKINS & GABRIEL MANIGAULT, ESQRS. & CAPT. OTHNIEL BEALE & JAMES OSMOND, merchants, between said parties on 31 Jan. 1739, ST. JOHN conveys the 2 tracts to VAUGHAN. Witnesses: CHARLES PINCKNEY, JORDAN ROCHE. On 20 Sept. 1759 CHARLES PINCKNEY, ESQ., recognized handwritings of both witnesses before JAMES PARSONS, J.P. WILLIAM DOCKWRAY, D.R.

Book V-V, p. 454
30 Mar. 1759
Power of Attorney
SAMUEL SOUTHOUSE, ironmonger, of Leadenhall Street, London, & JOSEPH NICHOLAS, colourman, of Cornhill, London, surviving assignees of estate & effects of WILLIAM VAUGHAN, broker & chapman, a bankrupt, of Harp Lane Tower Street, London, appoint ROBERT RAPER, ESQ., of Charleston, SC, their attorney, to sell 1750 a. in Granville Co., SC, conveyed to VAUGHAN by JAMES ST. JOHN of SC. Witnesses: Rev. CHARLES GORDON, WILLIAM COOMBES. GORDON appeared before ALEXANDER STEWART, J.P. WILLIAM DOCKWRAY, D.R.

Book V-V, p. 455
20 Sept. 1759
Release
SAMUEL SOUTHOUSE, ironmonger, of Leadenhall Street, London, & JOSEPH NICHOLAS, colourman, of Cornhill, London, assignees of estate & effects of WILLIAM VAUGHAN, broker & CHAPMAN, a bankrupt, of Harp Lane Tower Street, to THOMAS HEYWARD, gentleman, of James Island, SC, for ₤ 1875 SC money, paid to their attorney, ROBERT RAPER, ESQ., of Charleston; 750 a. in Granville Co., granted 12 May 1735 to JAMES ST. JOHN (see p. 447). Witnesses: JAMES PARSONS, CHRISTOPHER PETER, MACARTAN CAMPBELL. Before CHARLES PINCKNEY, J.P. WILLIAM DOCKWRAY, D.R.

Book V-V, p. 461
JAMES CHRISTIE, planter, & practitioner in

22 May 1759   Physick, of St. Pauls Parish, Colleton Co., to
Mortgage   RALPH IZARD, ESQ., of Charleston, surviving
                     executor of will of JOHN IZARD, as security on
bond of even date in penal sum of Ł 5000 for payment of Ł 2500 currency
(borrowed from estate of JOHN IZARD), with interest, on 20 May 1760; 324
a. in St. Pauls Parish, Colleton Co., where CHRISTIE lives; according to
play by JOHN STEPHENS, D.S., dated 26 Oct. 1743; also 10 Negro men, 9
boys, 7 women, 5 girls, 8 riding horses branded F.C. Witnesses: FRED-
ERICK HOLZENDORFF, JOHN LITTLE. Before BENJAMIN SMITH, J.P. Entered in
Secretarys Book X.X. fol. 418-421 by WILLIAM MURRAY, pro Dep. Sec. WIL-
LIAM DOCKWRAY, D.R.

Book V-V, p. 466   WALTER KELLY, SR., cordwainer, of Craven Co.,
2 & 3 Feb. 1759   & ELIZABETH (her mark) his wife, to JOHN PAIN,
L & R   blacksmith, of Fredericksburgh Township, for
                     Ł 150 currency, 150 a. on which KELLY lives,
in Craven Co., on S side Wateree River, bounding NW on land sold by KELLY
to JAMES ADAMSON; SW on vacant land; SE on GEORGE BAREFOOT & vacant land;
which 150 a. & the tract sold to ADAMSON, making 350 a., were granted
KELLY by letters patent dated 9 Jan. 1755 by Gov. JAMES GLEN. (Secretary's Book P.P. p. 275). Witnesses: JOSEPH KERSHAW, (merchant in Fredericksburgh Township), ANDREW ST. JOHN. Before SAMUEL WYLY, J.P. WIL-
LIAM DOCKWRAY, D.P.

Book V-V, p. 473   HANNAH MCGREGOR, widow, to PETER MANIGAULT,
30 Aug. 1759   ESQ., both of Charleston. Whereas THOMAS MC-
Mortgage   KRETH, vintner, of Charleston, & HANNAH MC-
                     GREGOR gave bond this date to PETER MANIGAULT
in penal sum of Ł 1200 for payment of Ł 600 currency with interest on 30
Aug. 1760; & whereas HANNAH on 22 Jan. last became owner of part of lot
#93 in Charleston bounding W 25 ft. on King Street; S on ROBERT HARVEY; E
on MR. BOIGNAND; N on other part lot #93; now she gives the lot to MANI-
GAULT as security. Witnesses: CHARLOTTE WRAGG, JAMES ROBERTSON. Before
JOHN WRAGG, J.P. WILLIAM DOCKWRAY, D.R.

Book V-V, p. 476   JAMES WRIGHT, ESQ., formerly of Charleston,
6 & 7 Mar. 1758   SC, now of London, by his attorneys, SARAH
L & R   WRIGHT, his wife, & BENJAMIN SMITH, ESQ., of
                     Charleston, appointed by letter dated 15 July
1757; of 1st part; to SAMUEL BRAILSFORD, merchant, of Charleston; for
Ł 6300 currency; 508 a. in St. James Parish, Goose Creek, Berkeley Co.,
bounding N on a creek of Cooper River; E on a creek, marsh, & Cooper River; S on land belonging to children of ARTIMAS ELLIOTT & MARY his wife
(formerly to JOSEPH WRAGG) & the old Goose Creek road; W on JAMES MICHIE;
with the capital mansion house, etc. Witnesses: DAVID GREENE, JOHN MAT-
THEWS. Before JAMES PARSONS, J.P. WILLIAM HOPTON, Register.

Book V-V, p. 484   WILLIAM PRING, planter, of Christ Church Par-
30 Oct. 1759   ish, Berkeley Co., & ELIZABETH his wife, to
Feoffment   JOHN DUTARQUE, JR., of St. Thomas Parish,
                     Berkeley Co., for Ł 300 currency, 100 a. in
Berkeley Co., which PRING purchased from WILLIAM PORTER & SARAH his wife;
bounding SE on ROBERT MURRILL, SR.; NE on GEORGE HUGGINS; NW on ROBERT
MURRILL, son of JOHN MURRILL; S on the bay between the mainland & Bull's
Island. Witnesses: STEPHEN MILLER, PAUL TURQUAND, NOAH DUTARQUE. Delivery by turf & twig. Before HENRY GRAY, J.P. WILLIAM HOPTON, Regis-
ter.

Book V-V, p. 486   WILLIAM BAMPFIELD, merchant, to GEORGE CARPEN-
10 & 11 Dec. 1759   TER, carpenter, both of Charleston, for Ł 500
L & R   currency, part of lot #250 bounding S 76 ft.
                     on Queen Street; W 100 ft. on other part lot
#250 (now WILLIAM BAMPFIELD); N on part lot #250 belonging to JOHN CLIF-
FORD; E on part same lot belonging to BENJAMIN BAKER. Witnesses: ROBERT
WILLIAMS, JR., BENJAMIN BAKER. Before WILLIAM BURROWS, J.P. WILLIAM
HOPTON, Register.

Book V-V, p. 490   PHILIP JACKSON, of the Congaree, Craven Co.,
14 & 15 July 1758   & ELIZABETH his wife, to JAMES JENKINS, plant-
L & R   er, of same place, for Ł 200 currency, 125 a.,

known as Greenhill, on N side Santee River. Whereas Lt. Gov. WILLIAM
BULL on 7 Aug. 1741 granted PHILIP JACKSON 250 a. in Craven Co. nearly
opposite Savannah Hunt Bluff, in Saxegotha Township, bounding S on Santee
River; other sides on vacant land; half of which, fronting the river,
AJCKSON sold to JOSEPH HEARSMAN; now he sells the half called Greenhill
to JENKINS. Witnesses: MARTIN WERTZ, WILLIAM MEYER. Before JOHN HAMEL-
TON, J.P. WILLIAM HOPTON, Register.

Book V-V, p. 495   HENRY TOOMER, planter, & SOPHIA, (her mark)
9 & 10 Nov. 1759   his wife, heirs of ISAAC EDWARDS, to JOHN
L & R   TOOMER, planter, both of St. Helena Island,
                         for Ł 1000 currency, 400 a., bounding W on a
creek of Port Royal River; N on the part sold to WILLIAM ALLEN; SE on MR.
REYNOLDS; SW on MR. SEALY; according to plat by JAMES MCPHERSON, D.S.,
dated 22 Oct. 1752. Whereas the Lords Proprs. on 15 May 1715 granted
ARTHUR DICKS of Granville Co., 600 a. on St. Helena Island, bounding W on
a creek of Port Royal River; N on JOSEPH PAGE; E on vacant land; S on
DANIEL DICK; & whereas ARTHUR DICKS on 16 Mar. 1726 sold the 600 a. to
JOHN JOHNSON, planter; who died intestate 11 May 1746; & his 4 daughters,
MARGARET, SARAH (?), JANE, & ELIZABETH inherited, & they divided the 600
a. into 4 equal parts, each receiving 1 part; & whereas 2 of them, MAR-
GARET TOBIAS & ELIZABETH PARMENTER, on 24 Oct. 1752 sold to ISAAC EDWARDS,
planter, their adjoining tracts, bounding W on a creek of Port Royal Riv-
er; N on WILLIAM ALLEN; SE on REYNOLDS; SW on SEALY; according to said
plat; & whereas ISAAC EDWARDS bequeathed the 400 (?) a. to HENRY TOOMER &
SOPHIA his wife; now they sell to JOHN TOOMER 400 a. bounding W on a
creek; N on SARAH FURROW; SE on WILLIAM REYNOLDS; SW on RICHARD STEVENS.
Witnesses: GEORGE SCOTT, THOMAS CHAPLIN, CALEB TOOMER. Before JAMES
THOMPSON, J.P. WILLIAM HOPTON, Register. No plat.

Book V-V, p. 503   THOMAS SHUBRICK, merchant, of Charleston, to
11 & 12 May 1759   SC Society, for Ł 3500 currency, 2 adjoining
L & R   lots in Ansonborough, marked X & Y on the plan
                         recorded in Sur. Gen's. office 14 Feb. 1744,
bounding S on MRS. SARAH TROTT; W on lot A belonging to CAPT. JOHN WAT-
SONE; N on lots W, U, T, & S; E on Anson Street, lot Z; also lot Z,
bounding S on MRS. SARAH TROTT; W on lot Y; N on Centurion Street; W on
land formerly called Petit Versailles, now called the Brewery, formerly
belonging to CHRISTOPHER GADSDEN, now to THOMAS SHUBRICK; which lots, X,
Y, & Z, contain 5 a., 1 rood, 13-3/4 perches; also an adjoining lot, in
St. Phillips Parish, near Charleston, bounding S 240 ft. on MRS. SARAH
TROTT; W on lot Z; N on Centurion Street; E 104 ft. on a road leading
from Charleston through Ansonborough. Witnesses: ROBERT BOYD, WILLIAM
MAZYCK. Before OTHENIEL BEALE, J.P. WILLIAM HOPTON, Register.

Book V-V, p. 510   RICHARD SHUBRICK, merchant, of London, ap-
11 Aug. 1759   points his brother, THOMAS SHUBRICK, merchant,
Power of Attorney   of Charleston, SC, his attorney, to convey to
                         the SC Society his land in St. Philips Parish,
near Charleston, 240 ft. X 100 ft., formerly called Petit Versailles, now
the Brewery, purchased by RICHARD SHUBRICK, by L & R dated 22 & 23 July
1746, from CHRISTOPHER GADSDEN; also 2 adjoining lots in Ansonborough,
near Charleston, marked on plan of Ansonborough, dated 14 Feb. 1744, by
letters X & Y, bounding S on MRS. SARAH TROTT; W on lot A belonging to
CAPT. JOHN WATSON; N on lots W, U, T, & part of S; E on Anson Street &
lot Z; also lot Z, bounding S on MRS. SARAH TROTT; W on lot Y; N on Centurion Street; E on Petit Versailles, now the Brewery; said lots containing 5 a., 1 rood, 13-3/4 perches. Witnesses: JOHN MCKENZIE, SAMUEL
COATES. MACKENZIE appeared before ROBERT PRINGLE, J.P., 31 Dec. 1759.
WILLIAM HOPTON, Register.

Book V-V, p. 512   RICHARD SHUBRICK, merchant, of London, by his
21 & 22 Dec. 1759   attorney his brother THOMAS SHUBRICK (p. 510),
L & R   merchant, of Charleston, SC, to the SC Society
                         (sometimes called the Carolina Society) for
Ł 3500 currency, all his claim to the lots X, Y, & Z in Ansonborough &
the lot known as Petit Versailles, or the Brewery (see pages 503 & 510
for details). Witnesses: JOHN PATIENT, WILLIAM MAZYCK. Before OTHNIEL
BEALE, J.P. WILLIAM HOPTON, Register.

Book V-V, p. 523   JOHN STEVENS, planter, of St. George Parish,
16 Jan. 1754   Berkeley Co., to SAMUEL STEVENS, planter, as
Mortgage   security on 1 bond of even date in penal sum
                         of Ł 9099 for payment of Ł 5049:10:0 currency,
with interest, on 1 Jan. next; & on another bond for Ł 1610:6:6; 32
slaves; also his stock of cattle, horses & hogs, marked in the left ear a
cropt, a hole & a crop & 2 slits in right ear, & branded S; also 475 a.
at Turkey Hill, & 220 a. of Cypress Swamp adjoining MRS. DONNING & JOHN
MOORE; also 60 a. on N side Stevens Bridge; 18 a. on S side; 90 a. pine
land near ROBERT MILLER. Witnesses: ISAAC BRADWELL, JACOB WESTON, ISAAC
HAUSKIN. Before BENJAMIN WARING, J.P. WILLIAM HOPTON, Register.

Book V-V, p. 525   JAMES (his mark) SEWRIGHT, of St. George Par-
4 Sept. 1759   ish, Berkeley Co., to SAMUEL STEVENS, of same
Sale   place, for Ł 20 currency; 5 a. in St. George
                         Parish, bounding W, &, & E on STEVEN'S land; S
on the high road leading from Jacob Creek to Westo Savannah, inclusive,
on S side Ashley River; being part of Ashley Barony. Witnesses: THOMAS
BULLINE, JR., MOSES LINUS. Before BENJAMIN WARING, J.P. WILLIAM HOPTON,
Register.

Book V-V, p. 527   JOSEPH SANDERS, planter, of Colleton Co., &
28 May 1756   ANN his wife, to WILLIAM HAMILTON, periwig
Sale   maker, of Dorchester, for Ł 220 currency, 2 a.
                         bounding N & NE on Bossoe's Creek; SW on MRS.
JUDITH POSTELL; NW on EDWARD VANVELSEY & JAMES RO_____; SE on estate of
GIDEON DOWCE; N on BENJAMIN SUMMER (SUMNER); according to plat certified
by NATHANIEL DEAN, Sur. Whereas JACOB SATUR, merchant, of Berkeley Co.,
on 20 Aug. 1729 sold HUGH MCCOLLUM, tanner, of Berkeley Co., 2 a. in Dorchester, Berkeley Co., known as lot #23; & MCCOLLUM on 1 Jan. 1730 sold
half the lot to WILLIAM WATTS, of Dorchester; & whereas JOHN MCCOLLUM, of
St. Bartholomews Parish, son & heir of said HUGH inherited the other half,
& on 12 July 1738 purchased from MARY CALVERT the half which WILLIAM
WATTS had assigned to her on 9 Jan. 1737; & whereas JOHN MCCOLLUM in 1756
devised the lot (as well as sundry other legacies), to JOSEPH SANDERS;
now SANDERS sells the 2 a. lot to HAMILTON. ANN SANDERS renounces her
dower. Witnesses: JOHN ROBERTS, JR., SAMUEL POSTELL, WILLIAM MAINE
(MAYNE). Before JOHN SKENE, J.P. Delivery by turf & twig. WILLIAM HOP-
TON, Register. (Note: deed says lot #23; plat gives #33). Plat by NA-
THANIEL DEAN, Sur. dated 19 Sept. 1744.

Book V-V, p. 532   The Rev. MR. JOSIAH SMITH, of Charleston, to
17 & 18 Dec. 1759   PAUL TRAPIER, merchant, of Georgetown, for
L & R   Ł 70 currency, lot #223 in Georgetown, bound-
                         ing NE on Front Street; SW on Bay Street; NW
on lot #222; SE on lot #224. Witnesses: JOHN LEGARE, ROBERT WILLIAMS,
JR. Before CHARLES PINCKNEY, J.P. WILLIAM HOPTON, Register.

Book V-V, p. 536   HENRY SMITH, planter, of Berkeley Co., & ANN
14 & 15 Apr. 1758   his wife; & THOMAS SMITH, the youngest, plant-
L & R   er of Berkeley Co., & SUSANNAH his wife (HENRY
                         & THOMAS being 2 of the surviving sons & de-
visees under will of Landgrave THOMAS SMITH); of 1st part; to THOMAS
MITCHELL, planter, of Craven Co., for Ł 1000 SC money, 322-2/3 a., being
the SW part of 605 a.; in Craven Co., bounding SW on ANDREW JOHNSTON; SE
on Waccamaw River; NE on MARY SMITH & BENJAMIN SMITH; NW on Wineau Bay.
Whereas Landgrave THOMAS SMITH owned a piece of Swamp in Craven Co., between Peedee & Waccamaw Rivers, supposed to be about 100 a. but on resurvey found to be 605 a., which by will dated 3 May 1738 gave the land
to be equally divided amongst his wife, MARY, & his sons; & whereas a
division was made after the death of GEORGE SMITH, 1 of the 4 sons, in
his infancy; & the SW part (322-2/3 a.) was allotted to HENRY & THOMAS;
now they sell to MITCHELL. Witnesses: JAMES SCREVEN, THOMAS DIXON, THOM-
AS SCREVEN. Before JOHN REMINGTON, J.P. WILLIAM HOPTON, Register. Plat
of HENRY SMITH'S land certified 19 May 1758 by THOMAS BLYTHE, D.S.

Book V-V, p. 544   JAMES LINGARD, blacksmith, to GEORGE ESMAND,
24 & 25 Jan. 1760   printer, both of Charleston, for Ł 300 curren-
L & R   cy, part of lot #254 in Charleston, bounding N
                         40 ft. on Allen Street; E 90 ft. on ROBERT

HARDY; S on JOSEPH MOODY; W on JAMES LINGARD; lot #254 having been sold to LINGARD by JAMES ALLEN. Witnesses: JOHN HOW, STEPHEN PEAK. Before ROBERT WILLIAMS, JR., J.P. WILLIAM HOPTON, Register.

Book V-V, p. 549　　　　　JOHN DRAYTON, ESQ., of St. Andrews Parish,
21 & 22 Nov. 1758　　　　Berkeley Co., & MARGARET his wife, to JOHN
L & R　　　　　　　　　　MEIK (MECK), baker, of Charleston, for Ł 1600
　　　　　　　　　　　　　currency, that lot in Charleston bounding E
49 ft. on King Street; W on FREDERIC GRIMKE; N 226 ft. on THOMAS DRAYTON; S on JOHN RATTRAY & RALPH IZARD; which lot was bequeathed to JOHN DRAYTON by his mother, ANN DRAYTON. Witnesses: JACOB WARLEY, JOHN WAGNER. Before CHARLES PINCKNEY, J.P. WILLIAM HOPTON, Register.

Book V-V, p. 554　　　　　JOHN MECK (MEIK), baker, of Charleston, & MAR-
17 & 18 Jan. 1760　　　　GARET (her mark) his wife, to RALPH IZARD,
L & R　　　　　　　　　　ESQ., for Ł 1600 currency, part of a lot in
　　　　　　　　　　　　　Charleston, bounding E 49 ft. on JOHN MECK; W
on FREDERIC GRIMKE; on S measuring E 73 ft. as far as the brick coach house erected on RALPH IZARD'S lot; N on THOMAS DRAYTON. Whereas by L & R dated 21 & 22 Nov. 1758 (p. 549) JOHN DRAYTON sold JOHN MECK a lot on King Street, in Charleston; now MECK sells the W end of the lot to IZARD. Witnesses: CHARLES PINCKNEY, JACOB WARLEY. Before ROBERT WILLIAMS, JR., J.P. WILLIAM HOPTON, Register.

Book V-V, p. 562　　　　　GEORGE MONTGOMERY, of Williamsburg Township, &
9 & 10 Mar. 1751/2　　　　JANET his wife, to THOMAS MCCREE, of Craven
L & R　　　　　　　　　　Co., for Ł 187:10:0 currency, 250 a., part of
　　　　　　　　　　　　　1000 a. purchased by MONTGOMERY from JAMES
AKIN, ESQ.; in Williamsburgh Township, bounding SW on THOMAS DOYAL; NE on ALEXANDER MCCREE; other sides on vacant land. Witnesses: HUGH LORIMER, HENRY MONTGOMERY, ALEXANDER MCCREE. Before JOHN LIVISTON, J.P. WILLIAM HOPTON, Register. Plat by JOHN LIVISTON, D.S. dated 3 Sept. 1751.

Book V-V, p. 567　　　　　JOHN HOLLYBUSH, carpenter, to WILLIAM BOLLOUGH,
1 Feb. 1708　　　　　　　planter, both of Christ Church Parish, for
Feoffment　　　　　　　　Ł 10:10:0 currency, 300 a., English measure,
　　　　　　　　　　　　　in Christ Church Parish, bounding E on CAPT.
WILLIAM CAPERS; W on Wando River; N on WILLIAM BOLLOUGH; S on land belonging to BOLLOUGH now in possession of HOLLYBUSH. Deed also signed by ALLISO (her mark) HOLLYBUSH. Witnesses: ANN BARTON, THOMAS BARTON. Witnesses to delivery of possession & seizin: EPHRAIM WINGOOD, WILLIAM WHITE, SAMUEL POSTELL. On 29 Nov. 1758 JOHN MORRALL, planter, of Prince George Parish, Craven Co., testified before JOHN REMINGTON, J.P., that 40 years before he had been intimately acquainted with HOLLYBUSH & was his near neighbor for 6 years before his death, knew his handwriting, etc., & believes this signature genuine. On 30 Jan. 1760 THOMAS LAMBOLL, ESQ., of Charleston, testified before JOHN REMINGTON, J.P., that he knew THOMAS BARTON, gentleman, of Charleston, 40 years previously, had much business with him & believes his signature genuine. WILLIAM HOPTON, Register.

Book V-V, p. 570　　　　　PETER BENOIST, shop keeper, of Charleston, to
15 & 16 July 1756　　　　PAUL TOWNSHEND, gentleman, of Charleston, in
L & R　　　　　　　　　　trust for ABIGAIL BENOIST, PETER'S wife; & for
　　　　　　　　　　　　　ABIGAIL TOWNSHEND, infant daughter & only
child of PAUL TOWNSHEND, & granddaughter of said ABIGAIL, wife of PETER BENOIST; & for said PAUL TOWNSHEND, son of said ABIGAIL, wife of PETER BENOIST; also for his granddaughter, MARY STEVENSON, JR., infant daughter of MARY STEVENSON, wife of CHARLES STEVENSON, merchant; for love & affection, & to settle his house & land; his dwelling house & piece of land in St. Philip's Parish, near Charleston, on E side of the high road leading to Ansonborough; being the SW part of a lot marked F on the general plan, 49-1/2 ft. broad & 200 ft. deep from High Road; bounding N on a common avenue dividing lot F into SW & NE parts; E & S on HUGH ANDERSON; W on High Road; which lot was formerly sold to HUGH ANDERSON; who sold to DAVID CHRISTINA; who sold to GABRIEL GUIGNARD; who sold to PETER BENOIST; including the dwelling house; ABIGAIL BENOIST to hold for her natural life; then ABIGAIL TOWNSHEND, for her natural life; then to her children; if none, then to PAUL TOWNSHEND, for life; then to his children; if none, then to MARY STEVENSON, JR. & her heirs. Witnesses: EDWARD NEUFVILLE, WILLIAM JACKSON HALES. Before ALEXANDER GORDON, J.P. WILLIAM HOPTON,

Register.

Book V-V, p. 577   LEWIS NETMAN (NETTMAN), schoolmaster, of Pur-
8 Nov. 1759   risburgh, to JOHN VAUCHIER, shoemaker, of same
Sale   place, for Ł 50 currency, 200 a. in several
tracts. Witnesses: FRANCIS VAUCHIER, ANTHONY
(his mark) DUPREY, BENJAMIN (his mark) GARDINER. Before WILLIAM HARVEY,
J.P. WILLIAM HOPTON, Register.

Book V-V, p. 577   JOHN MAYRANT, ESQ., eldest son & heir of JAMES
4 & 5 Nov. 1747   NICHOLAS MAYRANT, of Craven Co., to RICHARD
L & R   MONCRIEF, carpenter, of Charleston for Ł 600
currency, part of lot #86 in Charleston, bound-
ing N 36 ft. on Dock Street; E 140 ft. on part sold by JAMES NICHOLAS MAY-
RANT to NOAH SERRE; S on MRS. DOUXSAINT; W on the French churchyard.
Whereas the Lords Proprs. on 23 Mar. 1681 granted FRANCIS GRACIA lot #86
in Charleston; & whereas GRACIA on 30 Oct. 1696 sold the lot to WILLIAM
POPELL; who, on 20 Jan. 1696 conveyed a part of the lot to JONATHAN AMORY,
bounding N 58 ft. on the street leading from Cooper River to Ashley River;
S on JAMES LARDAIN & NOAH ROYER, SR.; W on the French church; E on WIL-
LIAM POPELL; & whereas JONATHAN AMORY died some time afterwards & his eldest son & heir, THOMAS AMORY, merchant, of Boston, New England, inherited;
& whereas on 15 Nov. 1722 he appointed the Hon. ARTHUR MIDDLETON, ESQ.,
of Berkeley Co., & FRANCIS HOLMES, SR., merchant, of Charleston, his attorneys, & they by L & R dated 18 & 19 Mar. 1724, for Ł 350 SC money,
sold the property to JAMES NICHOLAS MAYRANT; who died on 20 Feb. 1727 &
his son JOHN inherited; now he sells a part of the lot to MONCRIEF. Witnesses: THOMAS CORKER, JAMES WRIGHT. Before BENJAMIN SMITH, J.P. WIL-
LIAM HOPTON, Register.

Book V-V, p. 585   SAMUEL BALL, mariner, now of Charleston, to
13 & 14 Jan. 1754   RICHARD MONCRIEF, cabinet maker, of Charleston,
L & R   for Ł 500 currency, the N third part of lot
#51 in Charleston, bounding E 33 ft. 4 in. on
Cooper River; S on middle part formerly belonging to CHRISTOPHER ARTHUR
(now to DAVID BROWN); W 206 ft. on PETER COLLETON'S Square; N on lot #50
belonging to Landgrave COLLETON; free from claim of dower by SARAH BALL,
wife of SAMUEL. Witnesses: WILLIAM SIMPSON, JOHN MENZIES. Before WIL-
LIAM MURRAY, J.P. WILLIAM HOPTON, Register.

Book V-V, p. 591   SAMUEL BRAILSFORD, merchant, & ELIZABETH his
10 & 11 Apr. 1759   wife, to RICHARD MONCRIEF, carpenter, both of
L & R   Charleston, for Ł 2000 currency, part of a lot
in Charleston formerly belonging to THOMAS
AMORY; bounding W 50 ft. on Union Street, including part of Simmon's Al-
ley; E on ISAAC HOLMES; N 106 ft. on JOHN SIMMONS; S on Simmons Alley
leading from Union Street to the Bay; which part of a lot was by L & R
dated 8 & 9 Mar. 1727 sold by THOMAS AMORY, through his attorney, FRANCIS
HOLMES, to ISAAC HOLMES, merchant, of Charleston; whose executor, by L &
R dated 24 & 25 June 1752, sold to SAMUEL BRAILSFORD. Witnesses: CHARLES
PINCKNEY, MORTON BRAILSFORD, EDWARD NEUFVILLE. Before JACOB MOTTE, J.P.
WILLIAM HOPTON, Register.

Book V-V, p. 599   MOSES NORMAN, to URIAH EDWARDS, both of Berke-
24 May 1733   ley Co., for 5 shillings, 2 tracts of land;
Sale   18 a., part of a tract granted by Gov. JOSEPH
BALKE on 8 Sept. 1697 to WILLIAM NORMAN, JR.;
who consigned to MOSES NORMAN; bounding N on JOSEPH BOON; S on the part
belonging to THOMAS WARING, ESQ.; W on the other tract of 28 a. granted
by Gov. ROBERT JOHNSON on 24 May 1733 to MOSES NORMAN; bounding W on the
part now sold to THOMAS WARING; N on land granted to BENJAMIN WARING; S
on the Broad Path; W on said 18 a. Witnesses: THOMAS WARING, STEPHEN
DOWSE, BARAK NORMAN. Before THOMAS WARING, J.P. WILLIAM HOPTON, Register. Plat shows pat of 3 tracts, 18 a., 28 a., & 10 a. for URIAH EDWARDS,
bounding on JOSEPH BOON, MR. NORMAN, MR. SNOW, & broad road to Dorchester
Town.

Book V-V, p. 601   THOMAS WARING, ANDREW SLANN, & ANN SLANN, wife
27 Apr. 1739   of ANDREW; of Berkeley Co., to URIAH EDWARDS,
Sale   of Berkeley Co., for Ł 20 currency, 10 a.,

bounding N on Madam BOON; W on THOMAS WARING; S on URIAH EDWARDS. Witnesses: THOMAS WARING, JR., MELCHIOR GARNER, ROBERT GLASS. Before RICHARD WARING, J.P. WILLIAM HOPTON, Register.

Book V-V, p. 603   THOMAS WARING, planter, & MARY his wife, to
30 Nov. 1750   URIAH EDWARDS, blacksmith, both of Berkeley
Sale   Co., for Ł 100 currency, 100 a. of pine land
                        near head of Ashley River, in St. George Parish, Berkeley Co., bounding E on CAPT. RALPH IZARD; S & W on THOMAS WARING; N on ANN BOON; according to first grant to MAJ. BENJAMIN WARING; the 100 a. being part of a tract of pine land conveyed by ANDREW SLANN, & ANN his wife, to THOMAS WARING by deed of feoffment dated '7 Nov. 1748; MARY to renounce her dower when required. Witnesses: JOSEPH WARING, JOHN EDWARDS, JAMES BOSWOOD. WILLIAM HOPTON, Register. Plat dated 3 July 1750 by JOHN STEVENS.

Book V-V, p. 605   URIAH EDWARDS, blacksmith, to DAVID ALEXANDER,
12 Jan. 1757   shoemaker, both of Berkeley Co., for Ł 250
Sale   currency, several tracts of land, total 156 a.;
                        28 a. & 18 a. purchased from MOSES NORMAN
(p. 599); 10 a. purchased from THOMAS WARING, ANDREW SLANN & ANN SLANN, (p. 601); 100 a. purchased from THOMAS WARING & MARY his wife (p. 603); all in St. George Parish. Witnesses: JOHN GOLLORTHUN, ROBERT RAWLINS. Delivery by turf & twig. WILLIAM HOPTON, Register.

Book V-V, p. 610   DAVID ALEXANDER, shoemaker, of St. Andrews
19 Mar. 1760   Parish, to SAMUEL THOMAS, of St. Pauls Parish,
Sale   for Ł 200 currency, several tracts of land,
                        total 156 a. (see pages 599, 601, 603, 605).
Witnesses: WILLIAM SMITH, WILLIAM PROCTOR. Delivery by turf & twig. WILLIAM HOPTON, Register.

Book V-V, p. 614   MARY BRYAN, widow of HUGH BRYAN, ESQ., of
9 & 10 Oct. 1758   Prince William Parish, Granville Co., of 1st
L & R Tripartite   part; FRANCIS PELOT, gentleman, of St. Helena
                        Parish, of 2nd part; WILLIAM HUTSON, gentleman, of Charleston, of 3rd part. Whereas a marriage is intended between WILLIAM HUTSON & MARY BRYAN; & MARY BRYAN owns a considerable & valuable estate & whereas WILLIAM & MARY have mutually agreed that all her real & personal estate should be conveyed to a trustee for her benefit & to be at her absolute disposal; now MARY BRYAN conveys to FRANCIS PELOT, trustee, 800 a. in said Parish; also all her other lands, tenements, etc., in SC; also 32 slaves; 11 horses & mares; 46 neat or black cattle; 70 sheep; all the books, household & kitchen furniture, plantation implements & utensils, & her other goods & chattels; in trust for her benefit during her lifetime, & that she shall permit her to make use of her estate as she sees fit; should she die intestate, WILLIAM to inherit. Witnesses: JOHN JOACHIM ZUBLY, JOSIAH ROGERSON. Before WILLIAM BURROWS, J.P. WILLIAM HOPTON, Register.

Book V-V, p. 626   JOHN WRAGG, ESQ., of Charleston; SAMUEL WRAGG,
18 & 19 Apr. 1760   merchant, of Winyaw; JUDITH WRAGG the younger;
L & R   MARY WRAGG, ANNE WRAGG, & CHARLOTTE WRAGG,
                        spinsters, of Charleston; PETER MANIGAULT,
ESQ., of Charleston & ELIZABETH his wife; & HENRIETTA WRAGG, spinster, of Charleston; by JOHN WRAGG, their attorney (JOHN, SMAUEL, JUDITH the younger, MARY, ANN, CHARLOTTE & HENRIETTA WRAGG, & ELIZABETH MANIGAULT being sons & daughters of the late the Hon. JOSEPH WRAGG); of 1st part; to THOMAS HUTCHINSON, ESQ., of Parish of St. Bartholomew, Colleton Co., for Ł 450 currency, 500 a. on Chehaw River or Combee Neck, in Colleton Co., granted to JOSEPH WRAGG & PAUL JENYS, being the same tract on which NOAH HURST BLENCOE lived; bounding according to plat of original grant. Whereas NOAH HURST BLENCOE owed JOSEPH WRAGG Ł 799:7:1 currency, with interest, on a bond dated 23 Aug. 1733; & owed PAUL JENYS & JOHN BAKER Ł 654:18:8 currency on bond of same date & as security, BLENCOE & his wife MARY conveyed said tract of 500 a. & died without having executed the mortgage, never having obtained a grant of the same; & whereas WRAGG, JENYS & BAKER agreed to renounce the mortgage in consideration of having the 500 a. granted to WRAGG & JENYS; & whereas Lt. Gov. THOMAS BROUGHTON by a grant dated 19 Aug. 1735, reciting these facts, conveyed the 500 a. to WRAGG &

JENYS; in joint tenancy; & whereas WRAGG survived JENYS & became sole owner & by will dated 6 Sept. 1746 ordered his lands divided amongst all his children; & whereas SAMUEL, JUDITH the younger, MARY, ANN, CHARLOTTE, HENRIETTA (WRAGG) & PETER MANIGAULT & ELIZABETH his wife, by letter dated 30 Dec. 1758, stating that the greater part of the lands had been satisfactorily divided amongst them but because of partnerships it was impossible to divide some parts, the accounts being unsettled, & appointed JOHN WRAGG their attorney to sell the undivided estate; now he sells the 500 a. to HUTCHINSON. Witnesses: JOHN MCCALL, THOMAS STONE, JR. Before WILLIAM BURROWS, J.P. WILLIAM HOPTON, Register.

Book V-V, p. 636
17 & 18 June 1749
L & R

CHARLES FAUCHEREAUD, planter, & JANE his wife (1 of the daughters & co-heirs of GEORGE SMITH), to GIDEON FAUCHEREAUD, planter, for Ł 5000 SC money, 1/3 undivided part of the lands, tenements, etc., in NC & SC, belonging to GEORGE SMITH at the time of his death, & all other lands in NC & SC that have descended to them. Whereas GEORGE SMITH owned divers lands, lots, tenements, etc., in NC & SC, & died intestate, so that his 3 daughters, JANE, SARAH & ANN inherited; now JANE & her husband sell their share of the estate. Witnesses: JOHN NEWMAN OGLETHORPE, GEORGE BODDINGTON, ALEXANDER DEWAR. Before FRANCIS KINLOCH, J.P. WILLIAM HOPTON, Register.

Book V-V, p. 640
5 June 1749
Feoffment

JOHN COACHMAN & WILLIAM WATIES, planters, executors of estate of WILLIAM WATIES, of Craven Co., to SAMUEL BUTLER, scrivener, of Georgetown, for Ł 120 currency, lot #161 in Georgetown, bounding NE 100 ft. on Duke Street; SE 117.9 ft. on lot #162; SW on lot #137; NW on Scriven Street; with right of commonage for 1 horse & 1 cow in the common. Witnesses: JOHN ALRAN, WILLIAM SCHACKLEFORD, JR. Before THOMAS BLYTHE, J.P. WILLIAM HOPTON, Register.

Book V-V, p. 643
20 Oct. 1758
Sale

SAMUEL BUTLER, planter, to CLAUDIUS PEGUES, merchant, both of Craven Co., for Ł 200 currency, lot #161 in Georgetown, bounding NE 100 ft. on Duke Street; SE 117.9 ft. on lot #162; SW on lot #137; NW on Scriven Street; with right of commonage for 1 horse & 1 cow. Witnesses: JOHN ALRAN, JOHN GEORGE FRY. Before THOMAS BLYTHE, J.P. WILLIAM HOPTON, Register.

Book V-V, p. 645
23 & 24 May 1758
L & R

BENJAMIN COACHMAN, planter, & SARAH HILL, widow, to CHARLES FAUCHEREAUD, planter; all of Berkeley Co. Whereas a marriage is intended between BENJAMIN & SARAH (1 of the 3 daughters, co-heirs, of GEORGE SMITH who died intestate; whereby SARAH became entitled to 1 undidided third part of her father's estate) & she has agreed to sell certain lands to FAUCHEREAUD; now for Ł 1600 SC money, she sells him her undivided third part of her father's estate of 970 a. of land & marsh where GEORGE SMITH lived, on NE side of Ashley River, in St. Andrews Parish, bounding SE on RICHARD LAMBTON; W partly on WILLIAM FULLER. Witnesses: JAMES EDMONDS, EDWARD JONES, merchant, of Charleston. Before ROBERT PRINGLE, J.P. WILLIAM HOPTON, Register.

Book V-V, p. 652
27 & 28 Jan. 1757
L & R

JAMES EDMONDS, gentleman, of Charleston & ANN his wife, to CHARLES FAUCHEREAUD, planter, of Berkeley Co., for Ł 1866:13:4 SC money, his undivided 1/3 part of the mansion house & plantation of 970 a. on N & NE sides of Ashley River, lately belonging to GEORGE SMITH, ANN'S father, where SMITH lived. Whereas GEORGE SMITH died intestate & his 3 daughters, JANE, SARAH & ANN inherited his estate in NC & SC, & said third part which descended to ANN has by several measne conveyances become absolutely invested in EDMONDS; now EDMONDS sells to FAUCHEREAUD. Witnesses: JOHN EDWARDS, EDWARD JONES. Before JOHN BASSNETT, J.P. WILLIAM HOPTON, Register.

Book V-V, p. 659
24 Sept. 1759
Feoffment

EDMOND BELLINGER, of St. Andrews Parish, & MARY LUCIA BELLINGER, his wife, to GEORGE SOMMERS, of Charleston, for Ł 870 currency, 580 a. in St. Pauls Parish, Berkeley Co., bounding S on JOHN TUCKER; E on THOMAS FARR; N on MUNROW; W on estate of RIGDON

SMITH (former CHRISTOPHER WIKLINSON). Witnesses: JOHN MCQUEEN, GEORGE WILSON. Before JOHN RATTRAY, J.P. WILLIAM HOPTON, Register. Plat of 860 a. divided into 3 parts; 580 a. on E sold to JOHN MCQUEEN; W of that, 130 a. sold by WILLIAM BELLINGER to RIGDON SMITH'S estate; the W section being 150 a. sold by HENRY HYRNE, JR., to RIGDON SMITH'S estate; certified 24 Aug. 1759 by OWEN BOWEN, Dep. Sur.

Book V-V, p. 662   ELIZABETH WILLIAMSON, widow, of Stono, St.
2 & 3 June 1755   Pauls Parish, Colleton Co., to GEORGE SOMMERS,
L & R   planter, of Charleston, for Ł 300 currency,
                          300 a. in St. Paul's Parish, bounding N on
BENJAMIN HARVEY; W on WILLIAM HARVEY; other sides on THOMAS ELLIOTT &
THOMAS FARR; which land was granted to ELIZABETH WILLIAMSON by Gov. JAMES
GLEN on 10 Feb. 1749. Witnesses: BENJAMIN HARVEY, BENJAMIN ELLIOTT. Before JACOB MOTTE, J.P. WILLIAM HOPTON, Register.

Book V-V, p. 668   ADAM DANIEL, son of JOHN DANIEL, of Charles-
4 Sept. 1755   ton, to GEORGE SOMMERS, gentleman, of Charles-
Feoffment   ton, for Ł 3900 currency, part of lot #1 in
                          Charleston at S end of the Bay; bounding W on
JUSTINUS STULL; N on part same lot; E 47-1/2 ft. on the Bay; S partly on
the brick wall & partly on a small wooden bridge leading W; according to
plat marked A; with the privilege of an eave-drop from the tenement
thereon until a wall shall be built adjoining the N part of said tenement; & in case such wall shall be built higher than or equal in height
to the eave of said tenement then with the privilege of an intervening
spout to carry off the water; also that part of a low water lot bounding
E on Cooper River; N partly on GRANVILLE BASTION & partly on said bridge
& brick wall; S on other low water lots; W on a creek; according to plat
marked B. Witnesses: THOMAS SMITH, HUMPHREYS SUMMERS, JOHN RATTRAY. Before JOHN HUME, J.P. WILLIAM HOPTON, Register. Plats A & G given.

Book V-V, p. 670   GIDEON FAUCHEREAUD, planter, & MARY his wife,
17 & 18 Mar. 1752   to CHARLES FAUCHEREAUD, planter, for Ł 5000 SC
L & R   money, 1 undivided third part of the estate of
                          GEORGE SMITH in NC & SC, which third share was
by L & R dated 17 & 18 June 1749 (see p. 636) conveyed to GIDEON FAUCHER-
EAUD, by said CHARLES FAUCHEREAUD & JANE his wife, 1 of the daughters &
co-heirs of said GEORGE SMITH who died intestate. Witnesses: ANN SMITH
(later MRS. ANNE EDMONDS); FREDERICK HOLZENDORF. Before ROBERT PRINGLE,
J.P. WILLIAM HOPTON, Register.

Book V-V, p. 674   JACOB COLEMAN, planter, to JAMES HOPKINS,
14 & 15 Nov. 1737   planter, both of Saxegotha Township, for Ł 100
L & R   SC money, 150 a., part of 350 a. in the Town-
                          ship at the Congarees, now called Saxegotha
Township; the 150 a. bounding NE on Santee River; NW on PATRICK BROWN &
vacant land; SW on vacant land; SE on vacant land & on JACOB COLEMAN.
Whereas Lt. Gov. THOMAS BROUGHTON on 17 Sept. 1736 granted JACOB COLEMAN
350 a. in the Congarees, bounding NE on Santee River; NW on PATRICK BROWN
& vacant land; SW on vacant land; SE on vacant land & on JOHN GIBSON;
also lot #24; now COLEMAN sells part of the land to HOPKINS. Witnesses:
HARRY COLEMAN, THOMAS BROWN (Indian trader of Craven Co.). Before GEORGE
HAIG, J.P. WILLIAM HOPTON, Register. Plat of 150 a. certified 10 Nov.
1737 by GEORGE HAIG, Dep. Sur.

Book V-V, p. 679   JOSEPH CANTEY, planter, of Craven Co., to JOHN
8 Aug. 1759   MCFADDIAN, planter, of Williamsburg Township,
Release   Craven Co., for Ł 262:10:0 currency, 300 a.,
                          part of 400 a., on a cedar swamp on Black Min-
go Creek in Williamsburg Township, conveyed by WILLIAM SNOW to DAVID
ALLEN; who bequeathed to JOHN ALLEN; who conveyed by mortgage & release
to JOSEPH CANTEY; the 300 a. bounding on lands formerly belonging to WIL-
LIAM JAMES, JOHN HENLING, & other part of said 400 a. occupied by JANE
DICKSON. MARY (her mark) CANTEY, wife of JOSEPH, surrenders her dower
rights. Witnesses: WILLIAM JAMESON, JAMES HARPER, HUGH HARPER. Before
MATTHEW NEILSON, J.P. WILLIAM HOPTON, Register.

Book V-V, p. 682   CHARLES WOODMASON, merchant, to WILLIAM ORR,
31 Dec. 1759   planter, of Craven Co., for Ł 350 currency,

Release   250 a. in Craven Co., on S side Lynch's Lake; bounding on all sides on vacant land. Witnesses: HENRY O'NEIL, ROBERT WARING, NATHANIEL BROWN. Before WILLIAM SIMPSON, J.P. WILLIAM HOPTON, Register.

Book V-V, p. 684   JONATHAN WITTER, planter, 1 of the sons & de-
14 & 15 Feb. 1760   visees of will of JOHN WITTER the elder,
L & R   planter; to JONATHAN RIVERS, planter; all of
                                James Island, in St. Andrews Parish, Berkeley
Co., for Ⱡ 2200 SC money, JONATHAN WITTER'S house (where JAMES WITTER formerly lived) & 1/3 or proportional part of the residue of JOHN WITTER, SR.'S lands; being 165-3/4 a. on James Island, bounding N on the third part allotted to son THOMAS WITTER (now belonging to WILLIAM SCREVEN); E on the Savannah Road; S on GEORGE RIVERS & COL. RIVERS; W on GEORGE RIVERS; NW on part allotted to grandson JOHN WITTER, JR., an infant. Whereas JOHN WITTER owned various lands, tenements, etc., & by will dated 23 July 1756, after other legacies bequeathed the remainder of his lands (597-1/4 a.) equally to his 3 sons, THOMAS, JONATHAN, & MATTHEW; that is, to son JONATHAN the house in which son JAMES (deceased) formerly lived, with a proportionable part of his land; to be delivered to each when arriving at age of 21 years; appointing HENRY SAMWAYS, JAMES SCREVEN, WILLIAM SCREVEN & son JONATHAN WITTER, his executors; now JONATHAN, having reached 21 years & having received his portion, sells his share to RIVERS. Witnesses: JOHN HEARNE, ISAAC RIVERS. Before JEREMIAH SAVAGE, J.P. WILLIAM HOPTON, Register.

Book V-V, p. 693   ANTHONY CUTLAR, cooper to SAMUEL SPYINGER &
3 & 4 Aug. 1757   MAGDALEN HANSER, all of Craven Co., for Ⱡ 100
L & R   currency, 100 a., the E part of 250 a. granted
                                10 Feb. 1749 by Gov. JAMES GLEN to ANTHONY
CUTLAR; the 250 a. being in Craven Co., on N side Congaree River; bounding N on CASPAR COUCH; E on ARTHUR HOWELL & on vacant land; other sides on vacant land; the 100 a. bounding E on ARTHUR HOWELL; N on CASPAR COUCH; W on other part. Witnesses: HENRY BRAWN, MARK (his mark) KELIN, JOHN SPARKS. Before JOHN PEARSON, J.P. WILLIAM HOPTON, Register.

Book V-V, p. 699   HENRY YONGE, ESQ., of the Colony of Georgia, &
22 & 23 Feb. 1759   ELIZABETH his wife; ARCHIBALD WILKINS, plant-
L & R   er, of Granville Co., & ANN his wife; & JOHN
                                KELSALL, planter, of Granville Co., (in behalf
of himself at tenant by Courtesy, & of his heirs, by MARY his late wife, deceased); of 1st part; to CLAUDIA ELLIOTT, widow of THOMAS ELLIOTT, JR.; for Ⱡ 2000 SC money, 535 a. in Colleton Co. Whereas JACOB BEAMER, planter, of SC, owned 535 a. in Colleton Co., & by will dated 6 July 1710 bequeathed all his real & personal estate to his wife, SARAH, as long as she remained his widow, but on her re-marriage, 1/3 only; the residue to remain in her hands for his only son JAMES BEAMER; & whereas SARAH, of Berkeley Co., while his widow, & JAMES, Indian trader, of Berkeley Co., having come of age, by L & R dated 1 & 2 Feb. 1727, sold to WILLIAM BELLINGER, gentleman, of Colleton Co., the 535 a. in Colleton Co., formerly given by MARGARET BEAMER to her son JACOB; bounding W on land formerly given by MARGARET BEAMER, widow, (grandmother of JAMES) to her eldest son, JOHN BEAMER; N on JOHN WILLIAMSON; E & S on Stono River; & whereas WILLIAM BELLINGER died & his son WILLIAM inherited; upon whose death his 3 sisters, ELIZABETH, wife of HENRY YONGE; ANN, wife of ARCHIBALD WILKINS; & MARY, wife of JOHN KELSALL; inherited as copartners in fee; & whereas MARY died, leaving several children, infants; now the father, JOHN, in their behalf joins the other coparceners in conveying to CLAUDIA ELLIOTT. Witnesses: WILLIAM ELLIOTT, JR., JOHN JOYNER, JOHN GORDON, JOHN MULRYNE. Before JAMES THOMPSON, J.P. WILLIAM HOPTON, Register.

Book V-V, p. 706   HENRY YONGE, of Georgia, ARCHIBALD WILKINS, &
23 Feb. 1759   JOHN KELSALL, planters, of Granville Co., SC,
Bond   give bond to CLAUDIA ELLIOTT that they will
                                keep above agreement (p. 699). Witnesses:
WILLIAM ELLIOTT, JR., JOHN JOYNER. WILLIAM HOPTON, Register.

Book V-V, p. 707   RAWLINS LOWNDES, P.M., of SC, to SAMUEL STE-
5 Sept. 1750   VENS, of St. George Parish, at public auction,
Sale   for Ⱡ 20 currency, 509 a. in Colleton Co.,

bounding S & E on JOHN NORMAN; W on PAUL JENYS; N on THOMAS DISTON.
Whereas JOHN BESWICKE, merchant, of Charleston, obtained a judgment
against SAMUEL STEVENS, ISAAC GIRARDEAU, & ANN his wife, administrator &
administratrix of estate of WILLIAM CHAMBERLAIN, planter, of St. Pauls
Parish, in the amount of Ł 350:9:6-1/2 currency, & costs; & a wrif of
fieri facias was issued 2 Jan. 1749 by JAMES GREEME, C.J., directing the
P.M. to levy such sums against CHAMBERLAIN'S estate; now LOWNDES sells
the 509 a. to STEVENS. Witnesses: WILLIAM GREENLAND, WILLIAM BURROWS.
Before ROBERT WILLIAMS, J.P. WILLIAM HOPTON, Register.

Book V-V, p. 709
25 Nov. 1752
Sale

BENJAMIN BAKER, of St. George Parish, Berkeley
Co., to SAMUEL STEVENS, of same Parish, for
Ł 275 currency, 130 a. in said Parish, being a
part of Ashley Barony; bounding NW on SAMUEL
STEVENS; N on Ashley River; E on CHARLES WRIGHT, ESQ.; & DANIEL SLADE; S
on the high road. Witnesses: JOHN OSGOOD, NATHANIEL WAY, FRANCIS LEMON.
Before J. SKENE, J.P. WILLIAM HOPTON, Register.

Book V-V, p. 711
6 & 7 June 1759
L & R

EGERTON LEIGH, ESQ., of Charleston, to EDWARD
GREGG, planter, of Broad River, for Ł 115 SC
money the 300 a. on N side Broad River, bounding on all other sides on vacant land; granted
5 Dec. 1758 by Gov. WILLIAM HENRY LYTTLETON to said EGERTON LEIGH. Witnesses: JAMES HUNTER, JR., WILLIAM WARD CROSSTHWAITE. Before JAMES GRIND-
LAY, J.P. WILLIAM HOPTON, Register.

Book V-V, p. 715
23 Jan. 1738
Lease Tripartite

JOHN HUTCHINSON, gentleman, of SC, of 1st part;
WILLIAM GEORGE FREEMAN, & WILLIAM ROPER, gentleman, of Charleston, of 2nd part; SAMUEL LAV-
INGTON, gentleman, of Island of Antiqua, of
3rd part. HUTCHINSON, for 5 shillings, conveys to FREEMAN & ROPER, 604 a.
on Ashepoo River, in Colleton Co., bounding N & E on JOHN SEABROOK'S Island; S on CAPT. THOMAS FLEMING & JOHN DEAS; which 604 a. is part of 960
a. granted to BENJAMIN WHITAKER; who conveyed to HUTCHINSON. Witnesses:
ISAAC AMYAND, THOMAS HEPWORTH. WILLIAM HOPTON, Register. No probate.
No release.

Book V-V, p. 716
13 & 14 May 1740
L & R

JOHN HUTCHINSON, gentleman, to SAMUEL LAVING-
TON, gentleman, both of Berkeley Co., for
Ł 1963 SC money, 604 a., part of 960 a. in
Colleton Co., bounding N & E on JOHN SEA-
BROOK'S Island; S on CAPT. THOMAS FLEMING & JOHN DEAS. Whereas Lt. Gov.
THOMAS BROUGHTON on 7 Aug. 1735 granted BENJAMIN WHITAKER 960 a. in Col-
leton Co., bounding N on JOHN SEABROOK'S Island; E on Ahsepoo River; S on
CAPT. THOMAS FLEMING & JOHN DEAS; & whereas WHITAKER by L & R dated 2 & 3
June 1736 sold the 960 a. to HUTCHINSON; now he sells a part to LAVING-
TON. Witnesses: JOHN RATTRAY, JAMES WRIGHT. Before JOHN TROUP, J.P.
WILLIAM HOPTON, Register.

Book V-V, p. 723
19 & 20 June 1760
L & R

WILLIAM BLAKE, younger son of the Hon. JOSEPH
BLAKE, ESQ., & ANN his wife, to DANIEL BLAKE,
ESQ., eldest son of said JOSEPH BLAKE, for
Ł 5250 SC money, a lot in Charleston, bounding
S 150 ft. on the Market Square, opposite to the N front of the State
House; W 160 ft. on HENRY LAURENS; N 150 ft. on MRS. HOLLYBUSH; E 160 ft.
on Meeting Street. Whereas JOSEPH BLAKE owned lot #313 in Charleston,
part of Archdale Square, originally granted by the Lords Proprs. to the
Hon. JOSEPH BLAKE, grandfather of WILLIAM & DANIEL; on 28 Oct. 1696; then
bounding S on the Market Place; E on a large street leading from the Mar-
ket Place to the New Church; N on COL. THOMAS CARY, being part of said
Square; W on part of said Square; & whereas JOSEPH BLAKE, father of WIL-
LIAM & DANIEL, by will dated 18 Dec. 1750, amongst several other be-
quests, gave all the residue of his real estate to his 2 sons, DANIEL &
WILLIAM, said lot & premises not being specially devised but included in
the general devise to WILLIAM & DANIEL as jointenants in fee; now WIL-
LIAM sells his share to his brother DANIEL. Witnesses: BELLAMY CRAWFORD,
BENJAMIN GUERARD. Before JAMES GRINDLAY, J.P. WILLIAM HOPTON, Register.

Book V-V, p. 729
1 & 2 Nov. 1759

WILLIAM SNOW, planter, to WILLIAM FLEMING,
planter, of Williamsburgh Township, both of

L & R   Craven Co., for ₺ 350 currency, 400 a. in Cra-
            ven Co., bounding N on Lynch's Lake; SE on
WILLIAM SNOW; SW on vacant land; SE on MR. HUNTER & vacant land. Witnesses: WILLIAM COOPER, GEORGE SNOW, JOHN JAMES, of Prince Frederick Parish. Before CHARLES WOODMASON, J.P. WILLIAM HOPTON, Register.

Book V-V, p. 731   CHARLES FAUCHERAUD, ESQ., to JOHN DRAYTON,
23 & 24 June 1760   ESQ., for ₺ 6000 SC money, 3 adjoining tracts,
L & R   737 a., 200 a., & 33 a., total 970 a., in
            Berkeley Co., on N side Ashley River, bounding
N & NW on WILLIAM FULLER; E & SE on Landgrave THOMAS SMITH (now RICHARD
LAMBTON). Witnesses: BELLAMY CRAWFORD, BENJAMIN GUERARD. Before JOHN
RATTRAY, J.P. WILLIAM HOPTON, Register. Plat of GEORGE SMITH'S 771 a.

DEEDS BOOK "W-W"
JULY 1760 - JULY 1761

Book W-W, p. 1   THOMAS COULLIETTE, gentleman, of Charleston,
7 & 8 July 1760   eldest son & heir of LAWRENCE COULIETTE, gen-
L & R by Mortgage   tleman; to PETER TAYLOR, ESQ., of St. James
            Goose Creek & the Rev. MR. JAMES HARRISON,
rector of said Parish, attorneys for the Society for Propagating the Gospel in Foreign Parts; as security on COULLIETTE'S bond in penal sum of
₺ 1000 for payment of ₺ 500 currency, with interest, on 8 July 1761;
250 a. Whereas BENJAMIN GODFREY, planter, of Berkeley Co., & MARTHA his
wife, by L & R dated 1 & 2 Dec. 1729 sold to LAWRENCE COULLIETTE half of
a tract of 500 a. in Colleton Co., bounding NW on vacant land; other
sides on JOHN WANRIELLS (WANMILLS) Creek or Cypress Swamp; & whereas
LAURENCE COULLIETTE died intestate & his eldest son, THOMAS, inherited;
now he mortgages the land. Witnesses: JOHN SMITH, JR., SARAH READ. Before THOMAS YEOMANS, J.P. WILLIAM HOPTON, Register. On 24 Mar. 1767
JAMES HARRISON declared mortgage satisfied. Witness: FENWICKE BULL.

Book W-W, p. 9   MARY COULLIETTE, widow, of Charleston re-
7 July 1760   nounces her dower in above tract in favor of
Renunciation of Dower THOMAS COULLIETTE. Witnesses: JAMES PRITCHARD,
            MARY COULLIETTE, JR. Before THOMAS YEOMANS,
J.P. WILLIAM HOPTON, Register.

Book W-W, p. 10   CHARLES SPEARS, to EDWARD KIRKLAND, both of
12 Sept. 1755   the Wateree, Craven Co., for ₺ 300 currency,
Release   300 a. in Craven Co., on the Wateree River,
            bounding NE on the river; SE on JOHN GRAY &
vacant land; SW on COL. HENRY FOX; according to grant from Gov. JAMES
GLEN to JOHN GENDRON, ESQ., dated 2 July 1751; who conveyed to SPEARS.
Witnesses: HENRY FOX, WILLIAM HARRISON, ELIZABETH (her mark) THORNTON.
Before SAMUEL WYLY, J.P. WILLIAM HOPTON, Register.

Book W-W, p. 14   ADAM (his mark) STRAIN, planter, of Craven Co.,
22 & 23 Apr. 1757   & MARGARET (her mark) his wife, to SAMUEL
L & R   SCOTT, planter, of Fredericksburg Township,
            Craven Co., for ₺ 200 currency, 200 a. in Fred-
ericksburg Township, bounding SW on Wateree River; NW on ROBERT STUART;
other sides on vacant land. Witnesses: JOHN SCOTT, SAMUEL BURROWS, WIL-
LIAM SCOTT. Before JOHN LIVISTON, J.P. WILLIAM HOPTON, Register.

Book W-W, p. 18   SAMUEL (his amrk) SCOTT, trader, to Lt. JAMES
14 & 15 Nov. 1758   ADAMSON, for ₺ 250 currency, 200 a. in Craven
L & R   Co., in Fredericksburg Township, on N side
            Wateree River, bounding on all other sides on
vacant land; which 200 a. were granted 10 Feb. 1749 by Gov. JAMES GLEN to
ADAM STRAIN (Secretary's Book E.E. fol. 314); who sold to SAMUEL SCOTT on
23 Apr. 1757. Witnesses: TIMOTHY KELLY, JOSEPH KERSHAW. Before SAMUEL
WYLY, J.P. WILLIAM HOPTON, Register.

Book W-W, p. 24   JOHN HUDSON, planter, & ANN his wife, to WIL-
12 & 13 Jan. 1759   LIAM FERRALL, miller, both of Craven Co., for
L & R   ₺ 500 currency, 200 a. in Fredericksburg

116

Township, in Craven Co., on N side Wateree River, bounding SE on JOHN HUD-
SON; other sides on vacant land; also 150 a. half of 300 a. granted to
said JOHN HUDSON, bounding SW on Wateree River; NW on the 200 a.; NE on
vacant land; SE on other half sold by HUDSON to ROBERT BELTON; which 2
tracts were granted 29 Nov. 1750 by Gov. JAMES GLEN to HUDSON. Witnesses: JOSIAH TOMLINSON, WILLIAM DOWNS, weaver. Before SAMUEL WYLY, J.P.
WILLIAM HOPTON, Register.

Book W-W, p. 30   EDWARD (his mark) MOLLOY, planter, & MARY (her
7 & 8 Apr. 1758   mark) his wife, to SAMUEL WYLY, ESQ., both of
L & R   Craven Co., for Ł 230 currency, 150 a. in Cra-
                         ven Co., on N side Pine Tree Creek in Fred-
ericksburg Township, bounding SW on Wateree River; NW on PATRICK MCCOR-
MICK; NE on vacant land; SE on JOHN BLACK; which land was granted to MAL-
LOY 14 June 1751 by Gov. JAMES GLEN. Witnesses: JOHN GRAY, ISABELLE MAR-
TIN, JOHN MARTIN. Before RICHARD RICHARDSON, J.P. WILLIAM HOPTON, Reg-
ister.

Book W-W, p. 35   JOSEPH SHUTE, of Cahrleston, to JONATHAN WIT-
12 & 13 Nov. 1759   TER, planter, of James Island, for Ł 600 cur-
L & R   rency, 170 a. in Colleton Co., bounding N on
                         heirs of RICHARD WOODWARD; SE on W branch of
Ashepoo River; E on COL. HENRY HYRNE; W on MR. MILES; which 170 a. were
granted SHUTE on 24 Apr. 1752. Witnesses: MARY CLEMENT, DANIEL CLEMENT.
Before JOHN REMINGTON, J.P. WILLIAM HOPTON, Register.

Book W-W, p. 40   JOHN DUTARQUE, planter, of Berkeley Co., &
14 & 15 July 1760   MARY his wife, to ROBERT BOYD, merchant, of
L & R   Charleston, for Ł 2105 currency, part of lot
                         #199 in Charleston, bounding E 43-3/4 ft. on a
neighborhood street; S 110 ft. on JOHN REMINGTON, SR.; W on JOHN CART; N
on part same lot sold by HENRY MIDDLETON to THOMAS SMITH, SR. Witnesses:
JOHN DUTARQUE, JR., NOAH DUTARQUE. Before JOHN REMINGTON, J.P. WILLIAM
HOPTON, Register.

Book W-W, p. 45   JOHN LYNN, planter, & NAOMI LYNN, to JOSEPH
4 & 5 Mar. 1760   BURCH, planter, both of Craven Co., for Ł 231
L & R   currency, 50 a. in Craven Co., bounding NW on
                         Peedee River; other sides on vacant land. Wit-
nesses: JOSEPH DUBOURDIEU, WILLIAM BLYTHE. Before THOMAS BLYTHE, J.P.
WILLIAM HOPTON, Register.

Book W-W, p. 51   DR. JOHN LYNN, & NAOMI his wife, to JOSEPH
4 & 5 Mar. 1760   BURCH, planter, both of Craven Co., for Ł 231
L & R   currency, 150 a. in Craven Co., bounding NE on
                         Peedee River; SE & NW on EDWARD HEWSON; SW on
JOSEPH WHITE. Witnesses: JOSEPH DUBOURDIEU, WILLIAM BLYTHE. Before
THOMAS BLYTHE, J.P. WILLIAM HOPTON, Register.

Book W-W, p. 56   EDWARD DANNELLY, planter, of Parish of St.
24 & 26 Mar. 1759   Thomas & St. Dennis, Berkeley Co., to THOMAS
L & R   DEARINGTON, planter, of same Parish, as secur-
                         ity on bond of even date requiring payment of
Ł 500 currency, or 4 Negroes, on 26 Mar. 1760; 200 a. in said Parish, on
E branch of T of Cooper River, bounding SW on LEWIS PICKARD; SE on PETER
JOHNSON; NE on FRANCIS PIGIT & vacant land. Witnesses: JOHN CUMING, JA-
COB BONNEAU, CATHERINE BONNEAU. Before SAMUEL THOMAS, J.P. WILLIAM HOP-
TON, Register.

Book W-W, p. 61   JAMES MCGIRTT & PRISCILLA (her mark) his wife,
17 & 18 Aug. 1759   to NEEDHAM JERNIGAN, both of Craven Co., for
L & R   Ł 200 currency, 200 a. in Craven Co., bounding
                         NE on Wateree River; NW on JOHN & WILLIAM
SCOTT; SW on vacant land; SE on HENRY JERNIGAN; which land was granted 19
Sept. 1758 by Gov. WILLIAM HENRY LYTTLETON to JAMES MCGIRTT. Witnesses:
WILLIAM HUNTER, JR., HENRY (his mark) JERNIGAN, HARDY RICE JERNIGAN. Be-
fore SAMUEL WYLY, J.P. WILLIAM HOPTON, Register.

Book W-W, p. 67   DR. WILLIAM BRISBANE, JAMES FOWLER, & THOMAS
1 & 2 July 1760   LAMBOLL, of Charleston, executors of will of

L & R — MARTHA D'HARRIETTE, widow, of Charleston, to JOHN DRAYTON; for Ⱡ 6100 currency, 3 parts of lot #165 in Charleston, bounding N 94 ft. on Broad Street; W 180 ft. on WILLIAM LOUGHTON; E 132 ft. on JOHN BRAND & PHILIP MASSEY; S 34 ft. on PHILIP MASSEY & 60 ft. on LEWIS TIMOTHY. Whereas JAMES FOWLER, merchant, owned lot #165 in Charleston on S side Broad Street, which, by will dated 27 Apr. 1753, he bequeathed to his wife MARTHA; & whereas she later married BENJAMIN D'HARRIETTE, whom she survived; & by will dated 27 May 1758 directed her executors to sell the residue of her real & personal estate; appointing BRISBANE, FOWLER & LAMBOLL, her executors; & they offered the estate for sale at public auction; now they convey to DRAYTON 3 parts of the lot. Witnesses: FARCHER MCGILLVRAY, JOHN HOW, JOSIAH RUSH. Before JOHN RATTRAY, J.P. WILLIAM HOPTON, Register.

Book W-W, p. 74
10 & 11 July 1760
L & R

The Hon. THOMAS DRAYTON, & MARY his wife, to JAMES SKIRVING, ESQ., for Ⱡ 5000 currency, 78 a., 100 a., 100 a., 500 a., & 931 a. marked A, B, C, D, & E respectively on a certain plat. Whereas the Lords Proprs., on 4 Nov. 1704 granted CHRISTOPHER WILKINSON 178 a. in Colleton Co., in St. Bartholomews Parish, marked A on General Plat; & on 5 Nov. 1704 granted JACOB BEAMER 100 a. in same Parish, marked B on General Plat; & on 5 Nov. 1704 granted JOHN WILLIAMSON 100 a. in same Parish, marked C on General Plat; & on 23 July 1711 granted JOHN WILLIAMSON 500 a. in same Parish, marked D on the General Plan; which 4 tracts are now the property of THOMAS DRAYTON; & whereas Gov. ROBERT JOHNSTON on 11 July 1733 granted JOHN WILLIAMS 931 a. in said Parish, marked E on the General Plan; & whereas JOHN WILLIAMS & MARY his wife by L & R dated 1 & 2 June 1733 sold the 931 a. to THOMAS DRAYTON; now DRAYTON sells SKIRVING the 4 adjoining tracts, total 1809 a., bounding S on MRS. SANDERS & ANTHONY HIATT; N on JOHN REID & ROBERT REID & other land; W on BRYAN KELLY (now MRS. BEATTY) & PETER RUMPH; E on THOMAS DRAYTON; & unknown land; as enclosed by yellow lines on the general plat; also 100 a. originally granted to JOHN WILLIAMSON on 5 Nov. 1704, now belonging to THOMAS DRAYTON, marked F on the plat, bounding NE on MR. GRIMKE; NW on MRS. SANDERS; SW & SE on WILLIAM GLOVER. Witnesses: WILLIAM DRAYTON, GRIZEL MONTFORD. Before WILLIAM BRISBANE, J.P. WILLIAM HOPTON, Register.

Book W-W, p. 83
20 June 1760
Mortgage

JAMES STARNES, perukemaker, & ANN his wife, to CHARLES BROWN, merchant, both of Charleston, for Ⱡ 1019 currency, 550 a. in Williamsburgh Township, Craven Co., bounding SW on Black River; SE on JOSEPH MOODY; other sides on vacant land; also lot #100 in Charleston, originally granted to CHARLES STARNES, father of JAMES; to be redeemed by partial payments. Witnesses: JAMES MOULTRIE, THOMAS MOULTRIE. Before JOHN REMINGTON, J.P. WILLIAM HOPTON, Register.

Book W-W, p. 87
28 & 30 June 1760
Mortgage

WILLIAM HULL, planter, of Prince George Parish, Craven Co., & ANN his wife, to JOHN HARLESTON, NICHOLAS HARLESTON, ELIAS BALL, NATHANIEL BROUGHTON, THOMAS BROUGHTON, THOMAS CORDES & FRANCIS LEJAU, trustees of Childsberry School, for Ⱡ 1200 currency, 600 a.; 100 a. of which lying on W side of Peedee River is called Youhaney, bounding S & W on vacant land; N on a bold creek; another 100 a. of said tract bounding E on Peedee River & vacant land; half the 600 a. (or 300 a.) having been granted originally to PERCIVAL PAWLEY; the other half (300 a.) being part of 533 a. on E side Peedee River opposite Youhaney, originally granted to PERCIVAL PAWLEY, grandson of first named PERCIVAL PAWLEY; who conveyed to WILLIAM WATIES; now vested in ANN, wife of WILLIAM HULL. Date of redemption: 12 Mar. 1761. Witnesses: OLIVER UPSALL, (planter), WILLIAM SMALLWOOD, JOSEPH JOLLEY. Before CHARLES WOODMASON, J.P. WILLIAM HOPTON, Register.

Book W-W, p. 96
17 & 18 Dec. 1758
Mortgage

GEORGE SHEED, schoolmaster, of Charleston, to DANIEL BLAKE & WILLIAM BLAKE, ESQRS., of St. George Parish, Dorchester, as security on bond of even date in penal sum of Ⱡ 9000 for payment of Ⱡ 4500 currency, with interest, on 3 Jan. 1760; 100 a. in Berkeley Co., bo-nding S on Newtown Creek; W on COL. ARTHUR HALL; E on JOHN WILKINS; N on MR. LAMBRIGHT & WILLIAM WILKINS; also 100 a. on James

Island, Berkeley Co., on N side Newtown Creek; bounding W on said 100 a.;
N on WILLIAM WILKINS, SR.; E on ELIZABETH PERKINS; also part of lot #199
in Charleston, bounding S 30 ft. on Queen Street; W 167 ft. on JOHN CART;
N 22-1/2 ft. on the Hon. WILLIAM MIDDLETON; E 167 ft. on a tenement.
Witnesses: WILLIAM HENDERSON, WILLIAM GRAEME. Before WILLIAM MURRAY,
J.P. WILLIAM HOPTON, Register.

Book W-W, p. 103   PETER FAURE, planter, of N Edisto River; near
12 & 13 Dec. 1757   Orangeburgh Township & Berkeley Co., & SARAH
L & R   (her mark) his wife, to JAMES TAYLOR, laborer,
                          of Orangeburgh Township, for ₺ 200 currency,
200 a. in Berkeley Co., bounding on all sides on vacant land. Witnesses:
JOHN TUCKER, JAMES (his mark) FRAZIER, MARY (her mark) FAURE. Before
BENJAMIN WARING, J.P. WILLIAM HOPTON, Register.

Book W-W, p. 109   JAMES (his mark) TAYLOR, planter, & ELIZABETH
2 & 3 Apr. 1760   (her mark) his wife, to HENRY FELDER, planter,
L & R   of Orangeburgh Township, originally granted to
                          PETER FAURE on 8 May 1736 (Book D.D. fol. 74);
who on 13 Dec. 1757 conveyed to TAYLOR; bounding SW on PonPon River;
other sides on vacant land reserved for inhabitants of said Township, not
then laid out. Witnesses: JOHN TUCKER, TOBIAS HARZOG. Before BENJAMIN
WARING, J.P. WILLIAM HOPTON, Register.

Book W-W, p. 116   JOHN MILHOUS, planter, & ABIGAIL his wife, to
18 May 1758   SAMUEL MILHOUS, planter, both of Craven Co.,
L & R   for ₺ 600 currency, 400 a. in Fredericksburgh
                          Township, Craven Co., granted 6 Mar. 1750 by
Gov. JAMES GLEN to GEORGE SENIOR; who conveyed to ROBERT MILHOUS on 5
June 1753 (Book P.P. fol. 128-133); & inherited by his son JOHN MILHOUS;
bounding NW on JOHN COLLINS; SW on Wateree River & a place called Great
Neck; SE on JOHN WILLIAMS (later JAMES MCGIRT); NE on vacant land. Wit-
nesses: STEPHEN TERRY, ISAAC ROSS, DAVID TERRY. Before SMAUEL WYLY, J.P.
WILLIAM HOPTON, Register.

Book W-W, p. 122   SAMUEL MILHOUS, planter, to HENRY MILHOUS,
22 & 23 May 1760   both of Craven Co., for ₺ 300 currency, 300 a.
L & R   in Fredericksburgh Township, Craven Co.;
                          bounding SW on Wateree River & JAMES MICHIE;
NW on land granted GEORGE SENIOR; NE on vacant land; SE on 50 a. sold by
ROBERT MILHOUS to JOHN CANTEY; which 300 a. with CANTEY'S 50 a. were
granted 14 May 1752 to JAMES MCGIRT (Book F.F. fol. 67); & conveyed by
MCGIRT to ROBERT MILHOUS; who bequeathed to SAMUEL MILHOUS. Witnesses:
ROBERT ENGLISH (A Quaker), JOHN WRIGHT, MARY ENGLISH. Before SAMUEL
WYLY, J.P. WILLIAM HOPTON, Register.

Book W-W, p. 128   EDWARD BULLARD, carpenter, of Charleston, to
17 & 18 Sept. 1760   PETER TAYLOR, ESQ., & the Rev. MR. JAMES HAR-
L & R by Mortgage   HARRISON, both of St. James Goose Creek, Par-
                          ish, attorneys for Society for the Propagation
of the Gospel in Foreign Parts; as security on bond of even date in penal
sum of ₺ 3000 for payment of ₺ 1500 currency, with interest, on 18 Sept.
1761; 140 a. on Charleston Neck, commonly called Rat Trap; bounding E on
the broad path, or high road from Charleston; S on JOHN WATKINS; W on
Ashley River; N on heirs of BRANFILL EVANCE (formerly SAMUEL WEST). Witnesses: WILLIAM MAZYCK, JORDAN ROCHE. TAYLOR & HARRISON paid BULLARD
₺ 376:13:4, & paid ₺ 1123:6:8 to HENRY LAURENS, saddler, of Charleston,
attorney for BENJAMIN ADDISON, in full satisfaction of a former mortgage,
making ₺ 1500. Before CHARLES PINCKNEY, J.P. WILLIAM HOPTON, Register.
On 15 Oct. 1767 JAMES HARRISON received full satisfaction of this mortgage from the executors of EDWARD BULLARD. Witness: FENWICKE BULL.

Book W-W, p. 136   JOHN RIVERS, planter, of Colleton Co., to RA-
20 & 21 Aug. 1760   CHAEL DALTON, of same place, for ₺ 805 curren-
L & R   cy, 322 a. in Colleton Co., called 550 a., in
                          original grant dated 16 Mar. 1732 (recorded in
Secretary's office 31 Mar. 1733) from Gov. ROBERT JOHNSON to JOHN RIVERS,
SR., who by will dated 1 Mar. 1738/9 bequeathed to his son JOHN RIVERS;
bounding NW on WILLIAM HOLMAN; SW on NW JOHN WOODWARD; other sides on
vacant land. Witnesses: GABRIEL LY. STOCK, MARY HOLMAN. Before THOMAS

HUTCHINSON, J.P.   WILLIAM HOPTON, Register.

Book W-W, p. 140   CHARLES LOWNDES, P.M., to ADAM COLLIATT, car-
25 Mar. 1757   penter, of St. Bartholomews Parish, at public
Sale   auction, for ₺ 361 currency, lot #48 in Jack-
                         sonburgh & 3 a. in PonPon near said town.
Whereas HENRY WARNER, schoolmaster, of St. Bartholomews Parish, owned
said lot #48 measuring 100 ft. on King Street, & 218 ft. deep; also said
3 a., bounding N on MR. PETERS (now DAVID HEXT); NE on a village lot belonging to estate of HENRY WARNER; S on said lot; SE on MR. LAIRD; fronting the public road; & whereas ABRAHAM HAYNE, recovered a judgment
against MARTHA WARNER, administratrix of HENRY WARNER'S estate; in sum of
₺ 404:16:0 & costs; & a writ of fieri facias was issued by PETER LEIGH,
C.J., commanding the P.M. to levy this amount against said estate; now he
sells part of the estate to COLLIATT. Witnesses: WILLIAM FISHBURN, JAMES
SHARP. Before THOMAS SACHEVERELL, J.P.   WILLIAM HOPTON, Register.

Book W-W, p. 145   JOHN LAIRD, planter, to ADAM CULLIATT, carpen-
5 & 6 May 1757   ter, both of St. Bartholomews Parish, Colleton
L & R   Co., for ₺ 60 currency, 9-1/2 a., part
                         of 12-1/2 a. conveyed by L & R dated 21 &
22 Apr. 1752 by JANE HARLEY & GEORGE JACKSON, executrix & executor of
CAPT. JOHN JACKSON'S estate; bounding N on DAVID HEXT; E on WILLIAM
HAYNES; S on Village of Jacksonburgh; W on HENRY WARNER (now ADAM CUL-
LIATT). Witnesses: ROBERT OSWALD, JR., WILLIAM JACKSON. Before JAMES
SHARP, J.P.   WILLIAM HOPTON, Register.

Book W-W, p. 150   JOHN MARTIN, planter, to ADAM CULLIATT, car-
7 & 8 Apr. 1760   penter, both of Colleton Co., for ₺ 70 curren-
L & R   cy, 70 a.; part of 353 a., in Colleton Co.,
                         formerly belonging to WILLIAM MURRAY, of
Charleston, who by L & R dated 14 & 15 Nov. 1759 conveyed the tract to
JOHN MARTIN; bounding E on Horse Shoe Road; S & W on WALTER IZARD; NW on
Glebe land. Witnesses: JOHN FENDIN, EDWARD BOWER. Before JAMES SHARP,
J.P.   WILLIAM HOPTON, Register.

Book W-W, p. 154   JACOB DESAURENCY, to PHILIP PLEDGER, both of
29 July 1760   Craven Co., for ₺ 500 currency, 100 a., part
Feoffment   of 367 a. in Craven Co., granted SAMUEL DESAU-
                         RENCY 22 Jan. 1744; bounding on WILLIAM CARY'S
land & on Peedee River. Witnesses: JOSEPH KING, JOHN (his mark) LYONS.
Before GEORGE HICKS, J.P.   WILLIAM HOPTON, Register.

Book W-W, p. 156   SAMUEL MILHOUS, JOHN MILHOUS & HENRY MILHOUS,
10 & 11 Nov. 1758   planters, of Fredericksburgh Township, & ABI-
L & R   GAIL, wife of JOHN MILHOUSE, to WILLIAM FER-
                         RALL, for ₺ 277 currency, 3/5 of a tract of
50 a. in said Township & 3/5 of all the houses, etc., bounding NW on PAT-
RICK MCCORMICK; SW on EDWARD MALOY; SE on JOHN PAIN; NE on vacant land;
which tract of 50 a. was granted 14 Mar. 1757 by Gov. WILLIAM HENRY LIT-
TLETON to ROBERT MILHOUS (Bk. F.F. p. 188); who by will dated 23 Oct.
1755 bequeathed to his children, SAMUEL, JOHN, HENRY, ROBERT, & SARAH.
Witnesses: THOMAS ENGLISH, planter, a Quaker, JOHN FURNAS, ROBERT ENGLISH.
Before SAMUEL WYLY, J.P.   WILLIAM HOPTON, Register.

Book W-W, p. 162   BUCKINGHAM (his mark) KEEN, planter, of Prince
16 May 1759   George Parish, Craven Co., to BENJAMIN DAVIS,
L & R   planter, of Prince Frederick Parish, Craven
                         Co., for ₺ 250 currency, 100 a. on NW side
Little Peedee River; also 200 a. on SW Little Peedee River. Witnesses:
FRANCIS GODDARD, MARY BRITTON, WILLIAM RAE (RAY). Before JOSEPH BRITTON,
J.P.   WILLIAM HOPTON, Register.

Book W-W, p. 167   MELCHOIR WERLY, butcher, to JOHN WAGNER, mer-
24 & 25 Sept. 1760   chant, & JEREMIAH THEUS, limner, all of
L & R by Mortgage   Charleston; as security for payment of several
                         sums of ₺ 1000 & ₺ 700 part of lot #134 in
Charleston formerly belonging to JOHN BERESFORD; with a brick tenement
lately erected thereon; bounding W 66-1/2 ft. on King Street; S on other
part same lot belonging to RICHARD BERESFORD; after running 18 in. N from

the corner of a brick tenement lately erected thereon & lately occupied
by CHRISTOPHER EASTON; N on Quakers Meeting House; E on HENRY LAURENS.
Whereas WAGNER & THEUR, at WERLY'S request, went on WERLY'S bond to PETER
MANIGAULT, barrister-at-law; & THEUS went on another of WERLY'S bonds to
RICHARD BERESFORD, ESQ., of Charleston; now WERLY gives security. Wit-
nesses: RICHARD BERESFORD, JAMES GRINDLAY. Before ROBERT WILLIAMS, JR.,
J.P. WILLIAM HOPTON, Register. On 27 Apr. 1772 JOHN WAGNER declared
mortgage satisfied. Witness: GEORGE DAVIDSON.

Book W-W, p. 173   THOMAS ELLIOTT, planter, of St. Andrews Parish,
3 & 4 Oct. 1760   Berkeley Co., to RICHARD MONCREIF, carpenter,
L & R   of Charleston, for ₺ 1600 currency, part of a
                          lot in Charleston now occupied by THOMAS TEW,
tailor; bounding N 23 ft. on Elliott Street (formerly 25 ft. but a 25 ft.
brick building on W side encroached on the lot); E 91 ft. on JOSEPH
ELLIOTT, brother of THOMAS; W on JORDAN ROCHE; S 25 ft. on COL. OTHNIEL
BEALE (formerly RICHARD HILL); which part of a lot was devised to THOMAS
by will of his father, JOSEPH ELLIOTT. Witnesses: WILLIAM MAZYCK, JORDAN
ROCHE. Before CHARLES PINCKNEY, J.P. WILLIAM HOPTON, Register.

Book W-W, p. 180   JAMES DICKEY, planter, to JOHN CANTLEY & HUGH
9 July 1760   ERVIN, all of Williamsburgh Township, Craven
L & R by Mortgage   Co., (because they went on his bond given JOHN
                          CUTHBERT, for ₺ 415 currency); 200 a. in Wil-
liamsburg Township, bounding N on the Commons; W on Black River; other
sides on vacant land. Witnesses: JOHN ERWIN, ROBERT HAMILTON. Before
JOHN LIVISTON, J.P. WILLIAM HOPTON, Register.

Book W-W, p. 184   SAMUEL PERONNEAU, merchant, only son & child
23 Dec. 1758   of ELIZABETH PERONNEAU, who was 1 of the 2
Release   sisters of JAMES COCHRAN the younger; to WIL-
                          LIAM MASON, gentleman, both of Charleston; for
₺ 900 currency; lot #215 in Charleston as originally granted by the Lords
Proprs. on 18 June 1694 to FRANCIS FIDLING; & inherited by his son & heir,
DANIEL FIDLING; who by deed of feoffment, with livery & seizin thereon
indorsed, dated 4 May 1713 conveyed to JAMES COCKRAN; who died intestate;
& the lot was inherited by his only son & heir, JAMES COCKRAN, JR., & by
his will devised equally to the children of his 2 sisters, MARY (wife of
RICHARD ASH) & ELIZABETH (wife of SAMUEL PERONNEAU the elder, & mother of
SAMUEL PERONNEAU, JR.); RICHARD ASH & others being appointed executors of
his will. Witnesses: THOMAS LAMBOLL, THOMAS LAMBOLL, JR. Before JOHN
REMINGTON, J.P. WILLIAM HOPTON, Register.

Book W-W, p. 189   WILLIAM MASON, shop keeper, of Charleston, &
21 Oct. 1760   MARY his wife, to THOMAS BOLTON, planter, of
Mortgage   Christ Church Parish, as security on bond of
                          even date in penal sum of ₺ 2000 for payment
of ₺ 1000 currency, with interest, on 21 Oct. 1761; lot #215 on S side of
White Point in Charleston. Witnesses: THOMAS CAPERS, JOHN REMINGTON.
Before ALEXANDER STEWART, J.P. WILLIAM HOPTON, Register.

Book W-W, p. 193   DAVID HOGGATT, planter, of Granville Co., to
28 Aug. 1760   HECTOR BERINGER DEBEAUFAIN, ESQ., of Charles-
Mortgage   ton, as security on bond of even date in penal
                          sum of ₺ 900 for payment of ₺ 450 currency,
with interest, on 28 Aug. 1762; 150 a., part of the land reserved for the
inhabitants of Purysburgh Township, in Granville Co., bounding W on said
DEBEAUFAIN; N on COL. JOHN PURRY; S on vacant land. Witnesses: STEPHEN
TOWNSEND, JAMES GRINDLAY. Before JOHN RATTRAY, J.P. WILLIAM HOPTON,
Register.

Book W-W, p. 196   THOMAS RALPH, carpenter, to REBECCA ANN COLT,
24 & 25 Oct. 1760   widow, both of Charleston; as security on bond
L & R by Mortgage   of even date in penal sum of ₺ 1286 for pay-
                          ment of ₺ 643 currency, with interest, on 1
Jan. 1761; part of lot #238, fronting E 40 ft. on King Street; & 232 ft.
deep; which lot #238 was sold by CHARLES FAUCHERAUD, planter, & JANE his
wife; SARAH HILL, widow; & ANN SMITH, spinster, of Berkeley Co. (JANE,
SARAH, & ANN co-heiresses of estate of GEORGE SMITH, gentleman, of St.
Andrews Parish); to EDWARD BULLARD, carpenter, of Charleston; who by L &

R dated 1 & 2 Nov. 1759 to THOMAS RALPH. Witnesses: ROBERT ROWAND, SARAH MCLEOD. Before JAMES GRINDLAY, J.P. WILLIAM HOPTON, Register.

Book W-W, p. 202　　　　　　THOMAS (his mark) SMITH, planter, & MARTHA
2 & 3 Mar. 1757　　　　　　(her mark) his wife, to ROBERT HANCOCK, both
L & R　　　　　　　　　　of Craven Co., for ₤ 100 currency, 100 a. on N
　　　　　　　　　　　　side Broad River, in Craven Co., bounding SE
on THOMAS RUTLEDGE; other sides on vacant land. Witnesses: JOSEPH CURRY, JOSEPH CARSON. Before PHILIP RAIFORD, J.P. WILLIAM HOPTON, Register.

Book W-W, p. 206　　　　　　SAMUEL MILHOUS & HENRY MILHOUS, planters, of
1 & 2 May 1759　　　　　　Fredericksburgh Township, to WILLIAM HILLIARD,
L & R　　　　　　　　　　planter, of Craven Co., for ₤ 325 currency,
　　　　　　　　　　　　the 300 a. in Craven Co., on SW side Wateree
River, granted them in 1758 by Gov. WILLIAM HENRY LYTTLETON, bounding NW on ROBERT ROGERS; other sides on vacant land. Witnesses: STEPHEN TERRY, MICAJAH TERRY, JAMES MCCORMICK. Before SAMUEL WYLY, J.P. WILLIAM HOPTON, Register.

Book W-W, p. 212　　　　　　DAVID TAYLOR, shop-keeper, of Charleston, eld-
12 & 13 Apr. 1759　　　　　est son & heir of MARY VANDERWICK, widow; &
L & R　　　　　　　　　　EDITH (her mark) his wife, to WILLIAM KING,
　　　　　　　　　　　　JR., planter, of St. Andrews Parish, Berkeley
Co., for ₤ 813 currency, 100 a., bounding NE on HENRY SAMWAYS; other sides on marsh; also Fendall's Island, of 41 a., bounding W on Stono River; other sides on marsh. Whereas the Lords Proprs. on 9 Nov. 1698 grant-ed JOHN ELLIS, 170 a. on SW part of James Island; & whereas ELLIS died intestate, owning 100 a., part of the 170 a., & his son JOHN, inherited; & he & his wife, JUDITH, by L & R dated 17 & 18 Feb. 1750 sold the 100 a. to MARY VANDERWICK, widow; who also died legally intestate, & her son DAVID TAYLOR, inherited; & whereas Gov. ROBERT JOHNSON on 28 Apr. 1733 granted WILLIAM SPENCER 2 tracts of land, 1 of 41 a. called Fendalls Is-land, on SW part of James Island & E part of Stono River, in Berkeley Co.; & whereas Fendalls Island by various wills & conveyance became the pro-perty of JOHN ELLIS, SR., planter, of Colleton Co., & in 1754 he sold Fendalls Island to DAVID TAYLOR; now TAYLOR sells the 2 tracts to KING. Witnesses: JOHN HEARNE, JOHN SIMMONS, THOMAS HUMPHREYS. Before ROBERT RIVERS, J.P. WILLIAM HOPTON, Register.

Book W-W, p. 222　　　　　　JOHN MAYRANT, ESQ., of Wambaw, St. James San-
7 & 8 Dec. 1753　　　　　　tee Parish, Craven Co., to ROBERT PRINGLE,
L & R　　　　　　　　　　merchant, of Charleston, for ₤ 49 currency,
　　　　　　　　　　　　89 a. in Craven Co., bounding SE on Wambaw
Creek; S on ROBERT PRINGLE; N & NE on JOHN MAYRANT. Witnesses: JOEL HOLMES, PETER MAZYCK. Before ALEXANDER STEWART, J.P. WILLIAM HOPTON, Register. Plat certified 9 Nov. 1759 by ZAH[R]. BRAZIER, Dep. Sur.

Book W-W, p. 226　　　　　　TACITUS GAILLARD, ESQ., of Wambaw, St. James
6 & 7 Feb. 1753　　　　　　Santee, to ROBERT PRINGLE, merchant, of
L & R　　　　　　　　　　Charleston, for ₤ 5 currency, 52 a. in Craven
　　　　　　　　　　　　Co., originally granted by the Lords Proprs.
to DANIEL HUGER, who sold to JAMES NICHOLAS MAYRANT, after whose death his only son & heir, JOHN MAYRANT, inherited; & sold to TACITUS GAILLARD; bounding on ROBERT PRINGLE, TACITUS GAILLARD, & N on vacant land. Wit-nessed: JAMES ROBERT, JOEL HOLMES, PETER MAZYCK. Before ALEXANDER STE-WART, J.P. WILLIAM HOPTON, Register. Plat of 52 a., part of 500 a. sold by JOHN MAYRANT to TACITUS GAILLARD, certified 8 Nov. 1753 by JAH[R]. BRA-ZIER, Dep. Sur.

Book W-W, p. 231　　　　　　GEORGE SAXBY, ESQ., of Charleston, & ELIZABETH
8 & 9 Sept. 1760　　　　　his wife, to WILLIAM LUPTAN, merchant, of
L & R　　　　　　　　　　Georgetown, for ₤ 150 currency, lot #40 in
　　　　　　　　　　　　Georgetown, bounding SW 50 ft. on Front
Street; NW 217.9 ft. on lot #39; NE on lot #68; SE on Queen Street; which lot was sold to SAXBY by DANIEL LAROCHE, merchant, of Georgetown, by L & R dated 22 & 23 Jan. 1752. Witnesses: WILLIAM COATS, DAVID STEPHENS. Before JOHN BASSNETT, J.P. WILLIAM HOPTON, Register.

Book W-W, p. 236　　　　　　JOHN SMELIE, planter, of St. John Bartholomews
14 Aug. 1739　　　　　　　Parish, Colleton Co., gives JAMES STOBO,

Bond   planter, of St. Pauls Parish, Colleton Co., a
                                  bond in sum of ₺ 4000 currency that he will,
by 1 Aug. 1741, give STOBO title to 400 a., called Drum Hall, in Colleton
Co., bounding S on JAMES STOBO; E on COL. JOHN PALMER; N on JAMES COCHRAN
& on Willtown. Witnesses: WILLIAM COCHRAN, HENRY YOUNGE, JOHN NINIAN.
Whereas JOHN SMELIE, sold STOBO the above tract during the minority of
his brother WILLIAM SMELIE, on 11 Jan. 1743 WILLIAM also gave bond of
performance. Witnesses: MARY ANN SAMUELS, ELIZABETH DIDCOTT. HENRY
YOUNGE testified before DAVID GRAEME, J.P. WILLIAM HOPTON, Register.

Book W-W, p. 238   JOSEPH SHUTE, merchant, of Charleston, to
29 Dec. 1759   THOMAS WRIGHT, ESQ., of St. James Goose Creek,
Release   for ₺ 250 currency, the 430 a. in Craven Co.,
                                  bounding S on Little River; E towards the sea;
W on NICHOLAS TRINK which SHUTE, by L & R dated 6 & 7 July 1739, purchased from the attorneys of JOHN ABBOTT, merchant, of Georgetown. Witnesses: CHARLES PINCKNEY, WILLIAM MAZYCK. Before WILLIAM BURROWS, J.P.
WILLIAM HOPTON, Register.

Book W-W, p. 240   DR. JAMES THOMSON, of Beaufort, Port Royal, to
9 & 10 Apr. 1755   ALEXANDER RANROWLE, merchant, of Stono, as se-
L & R   curity on bond dated 5 Oct. 1747 in penal sum
                                  of ₺ 735 for payment of ₺ 367:10:0 currency,
with interest, on 1 Apr. 1756; lot #57 in Beaufort, formerly belonging to
COL. PRIOLEAU. Witness: GEORGE JACKSON. On 27 Nov. 1760 JOHN RATTRAY,
attorney-at-law, of Charleston, recognized JAMES THOMSON'S hand-writing &
also that of GEORGE JACKSON "his late CLARKE who is now in the West
Indies". Before JAMES GRINDLAY, J.P. WILLIAM HOPTON, Register.

Book W-W, p. 244   WILLIAM (his mark) LUCAS, planter, & EDE (her
1 Sept. 1756   mark) his wife, to ABRAHAM ODAM (ODOM), both
L & R   of Craven Co., for ₺ 150 currency, 150 a. on
                                  the Wateree River, bounding NW on ABRAHAM
ODAM; SE on CHARLES SPEARS; as granted 13 Aug. 1756 by Gov. WILLIAM HENRY
LYTTLETON. Witnesses: JOHN WILLIAMS, THOMAS (his mark) EDWARDS, ABRAHAM
(his mark) ODAM, JR. Before SAMUEL WYLY, J.P. WILLIAM HOPTON, Register.

Book W-W, p. 250   CHARLES SPEARS, planter, of Craven Co., execu-
1 & 2 Mar. 1759   tor of will of ROBERT ROGERS, to WILLIAM HUNT-
L & R   er, of Northampton Co., NC, for ₺ 500 curren-
                                  cy, the 350 a. in Craven Co., on S side Wa-
teree River; bounding on other sides on vacant land; granted by Gov.
JAMES GLEN on 3 Sept. 1750 to ROBERT ROGERS. Witnesses: JAMES MCGIRT,
WILLIAM HUNTER, JR. Before WILLIAM BOYKIN, J.P. WILLIAM HOPTON, Register.

Book W-W, p. 255   ABRAHAM (his mark) ODOM, of Craven Co., &
6 & 7 Mar. 1760   SIBBY (her mark) his wife, of Craven Co., SC,
L & R   to WILLIAM HUNTER, of Northampton Co., NC, for
                                  ₺ 665 SC money, 2 plantations in Craven Co.,
on S side of Wateree River; 200 a., surrounded by vacant land, granted by
Gov. JAMES GLEN to THOMAS PAGETT; 150 a., bounding NW on ABRAHAM ODOM; SW
on land laid out; SE on CHARLES SPEARS; granted by Gov. WILLIAM HENRY
LYTTLETON to WILLIAM LUCAS. Witnesses: WILLIAM HUNTER, JR., DAVID ED-
WARDS, HENRY HUNTER. Before SAMUEL WYLY, J.P. WILLIAM HOPTON, Register.

Book W-W, p. 261   ROBERT (his mark) STEWART, planter, of Amelia
2 & 3 Sept. 1760   Township, Berkeley Co., & ANN (her mark) his
L & R   wife, to JAMES ADAMSON, gentleman, of Wateree,
                                  Craven Co., for ₺ 190 currency, 150 a. in
Fredericksburg Township, Craven Co., on N side Wateree River, bounding NW
on SAMUEL WYLY; SE on ADAM STRAIN; other side on vacant land; granted 7
Oct. 1755 by Gov. JAMES GLEN to ROBERT STEWART (Book P.P. p.420). Wit-
nesses: JEREMIAH STROTHER, JOHN FURNAS, HENRY DONGWORTH. Before RICHARD
RICHARDSON, J.P. WILLIAM HOPTON, Register.

Book W-W, p. 267   MARTIN (his mark) JOHNSON, planter, to JOHN
18 Apr. 1759   BONE, planter, both of Craven Co., for ₺ 350
Feoffment   currency, 350 a. on Thomson Creek; granted
                                  MARTIN JOHNSON on 5 Sept. 1750; bounding on

all sides on vacant land. Witnesses to livery & seizin by him & his wife
SARAH JOHNSON, EDWARD BRYAN, THOMAS (his mark) BOATWRIGHT. Delivery by
turf & twig. Before THOMAS BLYTHE, J.P. WILLIAM HOPTON, Register.

Book W-W, p. 270   PHILIP (his mark) JACKSON, & ELIZABETH (her
14 & 15 July 1758   mark) his wife, to JOSEPH HEARSMAN, both of
L & R   Craven Co., for ₺ 200 (₺ 500 ?) currency,
                            125 a. the front half of 250 a. known as Green
Hill. Whereas on 7 Aug. 1741 Lt. Gov. WILLIAM BULL granted PHILIP JACK-
SON 250 a. in Craven Co., opposite a place in Saxegotha Township commonly
called Savannah Hunt Bluff, bounding S on Santee River; other sides on
vacant land; now JACKSON sells half to HEARSMAN. Witnesses: MARTAIN
WERTZ, WILLIAM MEYER. Before JOHN HAMELTON, J.P. WILLIAM HOPTON, Reg-
ister.

Book W-W, p. 274   JOSEPH HUGGINS, planter, to JOHN MCKANTS,
31 May & 1 June 1756   planter, both of Craven Co., for 450 lbs. of
L & R   merchantable indigo, 500 a. in Craven Co.,
                            granted by Lt. Gov. THOMAS BROUGHTON on 12
Dec. 1735 to JOHN BONHOSTE, who, on 3 July 1741 sold the 500 a. for ₺ 40
currency to JOSEPH HUGGINS & JONAH COLLINS; bounding S & E on JONAH COL-
LINS; W on Peedee River. Witnesses: NATHANIEL TREGAGLE, GEORGE APPLEBY.
Before GEORGE PAWLEY, J.P. WILLIAM HOPTON, Register.

Book W-W, p. 279   MARY (her mark) STARLING (STERLING), widow, of
2 & 3 July 1760   JOHN STARLING, to JOHN DILL, planter, both of
L & R   James Island, Berkeley Co., for ₺ 1010 curren-
                            cy, 100 a., English measure, on N side James
Island, formerly belonging to NATHANIEL STARLING, father of said JOHN
STARLING; bounding SW on heirs of MR. SISSIN; NW on heirs of SAMUEL PER-
ONNEAU; SE on New Town Creek. Witnesses: PATRICK KEIR, THOMAS HEYWARD,
WILLIAM HOLMES. Before ROBERT RIVERS, J.P. WILLIAM HOPTON, Register.

Book W-W, p. 285   JOHN DILL, planter, & ELIZABETH his wife, to
2 & 3 Aug. 1760   MARY STARLING, widow of JOHN STARLING, both of
L & R   James Island, Berkeley Co., for ₺ 1015 curren-
                            cy, the 100 a. named in above transfer
(p. 279). Witnesses: PATRICK KEIR, THOMAS HEYWARD, WILLIAM HOLMES. Before ROBERT RIVERS, J.P. WILLIAM HOPTON, Register.

Book W-W, p. 290   EBENEZER SIMMONS, merchant, to CHARLES WARHAM,
1 & 2 Jan. 1740   joiner, both of Charleston, for ₺ 1200 curren-
L & R   cy, that house & lot near middle of N side of
                            Tradd Street; being 1 or more parts of 2 town
lots known as #87 & #88; bounding S 30 ft. on Tradd Street; N on DANIEL
BOURGET; E 200 ft. on BENJAMIN MASSEY; W on ROBERT COLLIS & JAMES TOMSON.
Witnesses: JOHN REMINGTON, THOMAS LAMBOLL. Before JOHN DART, J.P. WIL-
LIAM HOPTON, Register.

Book W-W, p. 296   RENE LEWIS RAVENEL, gentleman, & SUSANNA ELIZ-
11 & 12 Dec. 1760   ABETH, his wife, of Berkeley Co., to ISAAC
L & R   COUTURIER, planter, of Craven Co., for ₺ 150
                            currency, 516 a. in Craven Co., in a place
called Bulltown, bounding NE on GEORGE HALL; other sides on vacant land;
which tract was granted RAVENEL 23 May 1734. Witnesses: DAVID LAFONS,
DANIEL RAVENEL, JAMES RAVENEL. Before PHILIP PORCHER, J.P. WILLIAM HOP-
TON, Register.

Book W-W, p. 302   PETER PORCHER, ESQ., & ELIZABETH his wife, to
1 & 2 Dec. 1760   PHILIP PORCHER, ESQ., both of Craven Co., for
L & R   ₺ 1000 currency, 211 a., being half of 2
                            tracts; 1 of 332 a. in Berkeley Co., bounding
N on SAMUEL SANDERS (later CAPT. JAMES STEWART); E on HENRY DE ST. JULIEN
& RENE RAVENEL; S on JAMES DE ST. JULIEN (later BENJAMIN DE ST. JULIEN);
W on RICHARD HARBIN; originally granted by the Lords Proprs. on 16 Aug.
1698 to JOHN BAYLY, ESQ., & sold by ALEXANDER TRENCH, BAYLY'S attorney,
to PETER DE ST. JULIEN; 1 of the 90 a. in said Co., bounding N on the
332 a.; E on RENE RAVENEL; W on estate of GEORGE HAIG, ESQ. (formerly
JOHN RICHEBOURG); part of 400 a. granted by the Lords Proprs. on 3 June
1714 to PETER DE ST. JULIEN. Witnesses: DAVID LAFONS, I. ELIAS KOCHLER.

MARY (her mark) KOCHLER. Before ISAAC PORCHER, J.P. WILLIAM HOPTON, Register.

Book W-W, p. 310   BENJAMIN COACHMAN, to THOMAS JENKINS, both of
2 Apr. 1757   Craven Co., for Ł 200 currency, 350 a. in Cra-
Sale   ven Co., bounding NW on MR. CORDES; SE & E on
                   vacant land; W on an impassable swamp. Wit-
nesses: ISAAC CHINNERS, WILLIAM COACHMAN, JAMES COACHMAN. Before A. GOR-
DON, J.P. WILLIAM HOPTON, Register.

Book W-W, p. 312   CHARLES ODINGSELL, planter, of Colleton Co., &
22 & 23 Aug. 1759 ESTHER (HESTER) his wife, to JOSEPH GLOVER,
L & R   planter, of St. Bartholomews Parish, Colleton
                   Co., for Ł 1440 currency, 480 a. in Colleton
Co., on S side S Edisto River, opposite Willtown, bounding W on marsh; N
on WILLIAM LIVINGSTON; E on a creek; the 480 a. being part of 500 a.
granted by the Lords Proprs. in 1714 to WILLIAM LIVINGSTON; who devised
to his nephews WILLIAM & HENRY LIVINGSTON in jointenancy; HENRY surviving
WILLIAM; & by L & R dated 8 & 9 June 1754 sold to ODINGSELL. Witnesses:
THOMAS SLANN, WILLIAM BOWER, SAMUEL LAING. Before JAMES STOBO, J.P.
WILLIAM HOPTON, Register.

Book W-W, p. 318   WILLIAM SHACKELFORD, planter, of Georgetown, &
1 & 2 Apr. 1760   ESTHER his wife, to DANIEL HORRY, JR., gentle-
L & R   man, of Craven Co., for Ł 1800 currency, lot
                   #26 in Georgetown. Whereas GEORGE PAWLEY,
WILLIAM SWINTON, & DANIEL LAROCHE, by virtue of certain powers given them
by ELISHA SCREVEN, proprietor of the land on which Georgetown now stands,
on 25 Feb. 1734 sold STEPHEN FORD lot #26 in Georgetown, bounding SW 50
ft. on Front Street; NW 217.9 ft., English measure, on lot #61; SE on lot
#27; with right of commonage for 1 horse & 1 cow on adjoining common; &
FORD, by L & R dated 14 & 15 Apr. 1736, sold the lot to JOSEPH WRAGG &
PETER HORRY, merchants, of Charleston & WILLIAM ROMSEY & PAUL TRAPIER,
merchants, of Georgetown, being copartners; & whereas WRAGG, TRAPIER,
ROMSEY, & HORRY (for WILLIAM ROMSEY & PETER HORRY, their heirs) by their
joint deeds of L & R dated 10 & 11 Apr. 1747 sold the lot to WILLIAM
SHACKELFORD; now he sells to DANIEL HORRY, JR. Witnesses: JOSEPH DU-
BOURDIEU, BENJAMIN PERDRIAU. Before THOMAS BLYTHE, J.P. WILLIAM HOPTON,
Register.

Book W-W, p. 324   The Hon. WILLIAM BULL, EDWARD FENWICKE, ESQRS.,
6 Nov. 1760   & ISAAC MAZYCK, BENJAMIN SMITH, ROBERT PRINGLE,
Feoffment   GEORGE SAXBY, GABRIEL MANIGAULT, & THOMAS MID-
                   DLETON, ESQRS., commissioners for building the
Parish Church of St. Michael, Charleston, to DANIEL HORRY; for Ł 270 cur-
rency, subscribed towards the building of the church; pew #78. Witness-
es: SAMUEL PRIOLEAU, SAMUEL CARDY, architect. Pew delivered by ISAAC
MAZYCK to JOHN HUME for DANIEL HORRY. Before JOHN HUME, J.P. WILLIAM
HOPTON, Register.

Book W-W, p. 325   The Hon. WILLIAM BULL, EDWARD FENWICKE, & OTH-
6 Nov. 1760   NIEL BEALE, ESQRS., & ISAAC MAZYCK, BENJAMIN
Feoffment   SMITH, ROBERT PRINGLE, GEORGE SAXBY, GABRIEL
                   MANIGAULT, & THOMAS MIDDLETON, ESQRS., com-
missioners for building the Parish Church of St. Michael, Charleston; to
JOHN HUME; for Ł 235 currency, subscribed towards the building of the
church; pew #72. Witnesses: SAMUEL PRIOLEAU, SAMUEL CARDY, architect.
Before DANIEL HORRY, JR. WILLIAM HOPTON, Register.

Book W-W, p. 327   THOMAS GADSDEN, merchant, of Charleston; &
30 & 31 Dec. 1760 JAMES GADSDEN, gentleman, of Grace Church
L & R   Street, London, by his attorney, said THOMAS
                   GADSDEN; of 1st part; to JOHN PAUL GRIMKE,
jeweler, of Charleston; for Ł 4106 currency, part of a lot or lots in
Charleston; bounding N 27-1/2 ft. on Broad Street; E on PETER BENOIST; S
on Elliott Street; W on Gadsden's Alley (10 ft. wide); with all buildings
thereon, bricks, stuffs, etc. Whereas THOMAS GADSDEN, father of THOMAS
& JAMES, owned 2 eighth parts of a lot in Charleston & by will dated 20
July 1741 gave all his real & personal estate, except as excepted, to his
2 sons, JAMES & THOMAS; & whereas JAMES, by letter dated 26 Aug. 1760

125

appointed his brother THOMAS his attorney to sell his share, & THOMAS on 23 Dec. 1760 put the property up for sale at public auction, reserving said 10-ft. alley; now the property is transferred to GRIMKE, as highest bidder. Witnesses: WILLIAM BURROWS, JOSHUA WARD. Before ROBERT WILLIAMS, J.P. WILLIAM HOPTON, Register.

Book W-W, p. 335
6 Nov. 1760
Feoffment

The Hon. WILLIAM BULL, EDWARD FENWICKE, & OTH-NIEL BEALE, ESQRS., & ISAAC MAZYCK, BENJAMIN SMITH, ROBERT PRINGLE, GEORGE SAXBY, GABRIEL MANIGAULT, & THOMAS MIDDLETON, ESQRS., commissioners, appointed for building the Parish Church of St. Michael, Charleston; to JOHN PAUL GRIMKE, for Ⱡ 150 currency, subscribed towards the building of the church; pew #74. Witnesses: SAMUEL PRIOLEAU, SAMUEL CARDY, architect. Before WILLIAM BURROWS, J.P. WILLIAM HOPTON, Register.

Book W-W, p. 337
1 Jan. 1759
Confirmation

WILLIAM BOWER WILLIAMSON, planter, to his brother JOHN WILLIAMSON, planter, of Granville Co., for Ⱡ 5 currency, 1 undivided fifth part of the 3 tracts of 100 a., 390 a., & 640 a. Whereas JOHN WILLIAMSON, planter, father of WILLIAM BOWER WILLIAMSON & JOHN WILLIAMSON, owned 1 undivided fifth part in 3 tracts, 1 of 100 a. at Spoons Savannah, in Colleton Co., bounding N & W on JONATHAN FITCH; S & E on vacant land; also in 390 a. at Spoons Savannah, bounding SW on THOMAS DRAYTON; other sides on JONATHAN FITCH; & in 640 a. at Spoons Savannah, bounding N on HENRY COLE; W on JAMES WRIXHAM; E on JOHN WILLIAMSON, the father; other sides on vacant land; & by will dated 4 May 1733 devised his fifth part to his son, JOHN; upon whose death his eldest son, WILLIAM BOWER WILLIAMSON inherited, as heir expectant upon the death of his brother JOHN, who by the father's will had only a life interest in the property; & whereas WILLIAM BOWER WILLIAMSON believed his father had intended to devise his fifth part in the 3 lots to his son, JOHN in fee & not for life, & being willing to release his inheritance to JOHN; now he releases all his claim. Witnesses: BENJAMIN FREEMAN, ROBERT MCLEOD. Before STEPHEN BULL, J.P. WILLIAM HOPTON, Register.

Book W-W, p. 339
8 & 9 Oct. 1760
L & R

JOHN WILLIAMSON, planter, of Granville Co., & MAGDALEN his wife, to JOSEPH PERRY, planter, of Colleton Co., for Ⱡ 2961 currency, 188 a., English measure, at Spoon's Savannah in Colleton Co., part of 390 a., which on a resurvey were found to be 586 a.; bounding NW on other part allotted to THOMAS WILLIAMSON & executors of will of HENRY WILLIAMSON; NE on JOSEPH PERRY; SW & SE on estate of BARNABY REILY. Whereas (see p. 337) JOHN WILLIAMSON became owner of 1 undivded fifth part of 3 tracts of land & by writ of partition was allotted said 188 a.; now he sells his share to PERRY. Witnesses: ROBERT MCLEOD, JOHN BULL, JR., ANDREW THOMSON. Before STEPHEN BULL, J.P. WILLIAM HOPTON, Register.

Book W-W, p. 349
15 Jan. 1761
L & R by Mortgage

ROBERT OSWALD, planter, of St. Bartholomews Parish, Colleton Co., to GEORGE INGLIS, merchant, of Charleston, as security on bond of even date in penal sum of Ⱡ 2661 for payment of Ⱡ 1339:7:0 currency, with interest, on 15 Jan. 1762 (for the executors of JOSEPH PICKERING); 400 a. in St. Bartholomews Parish, bounding W on DR. JAMES SKIRVING; S on JAMES POSTELL; NE on CAPT. WILLIAM SMITH; NW on WILLIAM OSWALD. Witnesses: JAMES GRINDLAY, JOHN COLE. Before JOHN RATTRAY, J.P. WILLIAM HOPTON, Register.

Book W-W, p. 354
26 Feb. 1760
L & R

JACOB (his mark) COONER, to THOMAS BEAMER, planter, late Indian trader, of Berkeley Co., for Ⱡ 500 currency, 200 a. in Amelia Township, Berkeley Co., bounding NE on Santee River; other sides on vacant land. Witnesses: WILLIAM SEWRIGHT, ROBERT (his mark) SEWRIGHT, WILLIAM THOMPSON. Before ANDREW BROWN, J.P. WILLIAM HOPTON, Register.

Book W-W, p. 359
8 & 9 Oct. 1760
L & R

WILLIAM COATS, ESQ., & MARY his wife, to JOHN MCQUEEN, gentleman, for Ⱡ 600 currency, 155-1/2 a., being the S part of 842 a. in

Colleton Co., sold by WILLIAM HARVEY & MARY his wife; GEORGE SAXBY, ESQ.,
& ELIZABETH his wife; & SUSANNA BOSOMWORTH, gentlewoman, all of Charleston, by L & R dated 11 & 12 Feb. 1760 to WILLIAM & MARY COATS; the
155-1/2 a. bounding SW on the part of 842 a. sold to MRS. ANN SMITH;
other sides on GEORGE SOMMERS. Witnesses: GEORGE BEDON, THOMAS YEOMANS.
Before ALEXANDER STEWART, J.P. WILLIAM HOPTON, Register.

Book W-W, p. 365   GEORGE SOMMERS, gentleman, to GEORGE MCQUEEN,
8 & 9 Oct. 1760   (youngest son of JOHN MCQUEEN, merchant, &
L & R   nephew & Godson of GEORGE SOMMERS), all of
                          Charleston, for love & affection & other con-
siderations, 1000 a. in Craven Co., on E side Wateree River in its low
grounds, bounding NW on JOHN POSTELL; other sides on vacant land which
tract was granted SOMMERS on 4 Sept. 1759. Witnesses: JAMES PARSONS,
ALEXANDER FYFFE. Before ALEXANDER STEWART, J.P. WILLIAM HOPTON, Register.

Book W-W, p. 369   JOHN JACKSON, planter, of Prince William Par-
16 & 17 Jan. 1761   ish, Granville Co., to CULCHETH GIBBES, plant-
L & R   er, of Colleton Co., for L 1200 currency, 1
                          undivided half of 728 a. in St. Bartholomews
Parish, Colleton Co., near Jacksonborough, part of 1250 a. devised by
will of JOHN JACKSON, the father, to be equally divided between said JOHN
JACKSON, the son (party hereto) & his sister JANE (formerly JANE BUTLER,
lately the wife of CULCHETH GIBBES; which said JANE left issue); the 728
a. bounding N on heirs of JOSEPH BOONE; SW on CULCHETH GIBBES & EDWARD
FLAHARTY (now JOSEPH GLOVER) & MARY BRYAN (now JOHN MARTIN); E on JOHN
SPLATT. Witnesses: CHARLES PINCKNEY, WILLIAM MAZYCK, JORDAN ROCHE. Before WILLIAM BURROWS, J.P. WILLIAM HOPTON, Register.

Book W-W, p. 375   EDWARD BULLARD, carpenter, to THOMAS RALPH,
1 & 2 Nov. 1759   carpenter, both of Charleston, for L 1200 cur-
L & R   rency, part of lot #238 bounding E 40 ft. on
                          King Street; 232 ft. deep. Whereas CHARLES
FAUCHERAUD, planter, & JANE his wife; SARAH HILL, widow, & ANNE SMITH,
spinster, (JANE, SARAH & ANNE being co-heiresses of GEORGE SMITH, gentle-
man, of St. Andrews Parish) by L & R dated 20 & 21 Nov. 1751 sold EDWARD
BULLARD 2 lots in Charleston, #238 & #239; now BULLARD sells part of lot
#238. Witnesses: JAMES TONGE, JAMES ROBERTSON. Before JOHN REMINGTON,
J.P. WILLIAM HOPTON, Register.

Book W-W, p. 383   BENJAMIN GODIN, merchant, of Charleston, to
9 & 10 June 1735   JOHN MULRYNE, gentleman, formerly of Island of
L & R   Mounserrat, now of Granville Co., for L 1800
                          currency, 1497 a. in Granville Co., bounding N
on Combahee River; S on ROBERT STEEL, the Hon. WILLIAM BULL & THOMAS
LOWNDES; & "lying round a tract" of JOSEPH BRYAN; also 550 a. in Gran-
ville Co., on Combahee River, bounding on all sides on said 1497 a.; to-
tal 2047 a. Whereas Gov. ROBERT JOHNSTON on 22 Sept. 1733 granted COL.
JOSEPH BLAKE 1497 a. in Granville Co., bounding N on Combahee River; S on
ROBERT STEEL, WILLIAM BULL & THOMAS LOWNDES; lying round a tract of JO-
SEPH BRYAN; which 1497 a. JOSEPH BLAKE & SARAH his wife by L & R dated 9
& 10 Oct. 1733 sold to JOSEPH BRYAN; & whereas Gov. NATHANIEL JOHNSTON &
JAMES MOORE & JOB HOWES, Lords Proprs. on 12 Jan. 1705 granted JOSEPH
BRYAN, father of said JOSEPH BRYAN, 550 a., English measure, on Combahee
River, in Granville Co., bounding on all sides on a large cypress swamp;
& being in the middle of the tract granted to BLAKE; & since conveyed by
BLAKE to JOSEPH BRYAN, SR., & inherited by his eldest son JOSEPH; who
conveyed to BENJAMIN GODIN by L & R dated 22 & 23 Oct. 1733 for L 1800;
now GODIN sells both tracts to MULRYNE. Witnesses: RICHARD ALLEIN, DAVID
GODIN, PETER SHAW. On 27 Aug. 1760 the Hon. JOHN GUERARD, merchant, of
Charleston, appeared before WILLIAM SIMPSON, J.P., & recognized the signatures of BENJAMIN GODIN, RICHARD ALLEIN, DAVID GODIN, & PETER SHAW.
WILLIAM HOPTON, Register.

Book W-W, p. 393   JOHN MULLRYNE, gentleman, formerly of Island
17 & 18 June 1735   of Mounserat, now of Granville Co., SC, to
L & R   JAMES FARRILL, gentleman, of Island of Mounse-
                          rat, for L 300 currency of Island of Mounse-
rat; 1/2 of the 2 tracts of 1497 & 550 a. in Granville Co., SC, named on

127

page 383; with 1/2 part of the houses, etc. Witnesses: RICHARD ALLEIN, DAVID GODIN, PETER SHAW. On 27 Aug. 1760 the Hon. JOHN GUERARD, merchant, of Charleston, recognized the signatures of RICHARD ALLEIN, DAVID GODIN, & PETER SHAW. Before WILLIAM SIMPSON, J.P. WILLIAM HOPTON, Register.

Book W-W, p. 403   JAMES FARRILL, ESQ., of Bury St. Edmunds, Co.
10 & 11 Feb. 1761   of Suffolk, Great Briatin, by his attorney
L & R   GABRIEL MANIGAULT, of Charleston, SC, to the
                          Hon. HENRY MIDDLETON, ESQ., of SC, for Ł 1000
British sterling, half his share in the 2 tracts of 1497 & 550 a., in
Granville Co., SC, (see page 393). The Ł 1000 British was paid by HENRY
MIDDLETON through WILLIAM MIDDLETON, ESQ., of Crowfield Hall, Co. of Suf-
folk; & FARRILL by letter of attorney, acknowledging receipt, appointed
ISAAC GODIN, ESQ., of Goose Creek Parish, SC, & GABRIEL MANIGAULT, ESQ.,
his attorneys, jointly & separately. Witnesses: PETER BOUNETHEAU, BEN-
JAMIN GUERARD. Before JOHN RATTRAY, J.P. WILLIAM HOPTON, Register.

Book W-W, p. 415   THOMAS EVANCE, gentleman, to MOSES AUDEBERT,
24 & 25 Jan. 1759   gentleman, both of Charleston, as security on
L & R by Mortgage   bond of even date in penal sum of Ł 4000 for
                          payment of Ł 2000 currency, with interest, on
25 Jan. 1760; 3 tracts of land in St. James Santee Parish, Craven Co.,
263 a. bounding SW & SE on GEORGE SIMONET; NE on BENJAMIN PERDRIAN; NW on
300 a. belonging to EVANCE; also said 300 a., bounding NW & NE on vacant
land; SW on GEORGE SIMONET & vacant land; also 350 a. bounding NW & SE on
vacant land; SW on BENJAMIN PERDRIAN; NE on JOHN MAYRANT. Witnesses:
WALTER MANSELL, JOHN SNELLING. Before ROBERT WILLIAMS, JR., J.P. WIL-
LIAM HOPTON, Register. On 3 May 1768 BENJAMIN DART, executor of mortgage, declared mortgage satisfied. Witness: FENWICKE BULL.

Book W-W, p. 421   SAMUEL MILLER, carpenter & joiner, & MARTHA
21 & 22 June 1751   his wife, to EISEI BRUNETT, joiner, both of
L & R by Mortgage   Charleston, as security on bond dated 20 June
                          1751 in penal sum of Ł 2600 for payment of
Ł 1300 currency, with interest, on 20 June 1752; that part of lot #187 in
Charleston which EBENEZER SIMMONS, of Charleston, purchased from EDWARD
BULLARD & sold to SAMUEL MILLER; bounding E 43 ft. on King Street; S 200
ft. on JOHN STEVENSON; W on ALEXANDER CHISOLME; N on MR. TIMOTHY. Wit-
nesses: JOSEPH LAW, ROBERT RAWLINS. Before JACOB MOTTE, J.P. WILLIAM
HOPTON, Register.

Book W-W, p. 428   STEPHEN BULL, JR., of Sheldon, in Prince Wil-
20 & 21 May 1760   liam Parish, & ELIZABETH his wife (only daugh-
L & R   ter of RICHARD WOODWARD, planter, of Berkeley
                          Co.), to JOHN GOVAN, ESQ., of Prince William
Parish, for Ł 4000 currency, 123 a. in Colleton Co., bounding S on RICH-
ARD WOODWARD; W on a Savanna; N on Cypress Swamp; E on vacant land; also
on an island of 450 a. in Granville Co., adjoining St. Helena, bounding
W on a branch of Port Royal River; N on Cowens Creek; E & SE on marsh & a
creek; also lot #3 in Beaufort, bounding S on the Bay; W on lot #2; N on
lot #29; E on lot #4; also another lot, not described; also Seabrooks
Island, 2080 a., in Colleton Co., on W side Ahsepoo River; also 380 a.
lying back from Ashepoo River, bounding NE on a swamp this & the 2080 a.;
other sides on vacant land; also 200 a. near Beaufort on Pigeon House
Point, being part of the larger tract sold in part to JOHN MULLRYNE &
ROBERT WILLIAMS, & granted by deed of gift to MARY FLOWER; bounding on
other part of said tract & on Beaufort Common; total 3283 a. & 2 town
lots, directed by will of RICHARD WOODWARD to be sold to pay his debts;
also 245 a. near head of Ashepoo River, in Colleton Co., bounding SE, E &
NE on BURRELL HEARN & Ashepoo River; NW on MR. FENWICKE; S, SW, & W on
ELIZABETH BULL; S on JOSEPH SHUTE; also 262 a. in Colleton Co., on head
of W branch of Ashepoo River, bounding NE on MR. FENWICKE & MRS. ELIZA-
BETH WOODWARD; S on JEREMIAH MILES & THOMAS MILES; NW on EDWARD FENWICK &
EDMOND BELLINGER; the last 2 tracts being vested in ELIZABETH BULL in her
own right. Whereas RICHARD WOODWARD by will dated 14 Dec. 1742, ordered
his executors to sell his real estate, except as excepted, & appointed
BENJAMIN GODIN, DAVID GODIN, & ROBERT BRISBANE his executors & his wife
ELIZABETH, executrix; & whereas DAVID GODIN survived BENJAMIN GODIN &
paid WOODWARD'S debts to the amount of over Ł 20,000 currency; & whereas
STEPHEN BULL married ELIZABETH, daughter of RICHARD WOODWARD, & the lands

to be sold became vested in him & his wife; now he sells various pieces
of real estate to GOVAN. Witnesses: BENJAMIN GARDEN, BENJAMIN GUERARD,
BELLAMY CRAWFORD. Before JOHN RATTRAY, J.P. WILLIAM HOPTON, Register.

Book W-W, p. 437   JOHN GOVAN, ESQ., of Prince William Parish, to
30 & 31 July 1760   STEPHEN BULL, of Sheldon, of same Parish, for
L & R   £ 4000 currency, the several tracts of 173 a.,
                          450 a. (an island), lot #3 in Beaufort; an-
other lot in Beaufort, now described, Seabrooks Island (2080 a.), 380 a.,
2000 a., 245 a., 262 a. which he had purchased from BULL (see p. 428).
Witnesses: BENJAMIN GUERARD, BELLAMY CRAWFORD. Before JOHN RATTRAY, J.P.
WILLIAM HOPTON, Register.

Book W-W, p. 443   JOB ROTHMAHLER, of Winyaw, son & heir devisee
14 Feb. 1761   & executor of will of JOB ROTHMAHLER; to WIL-
Release in Trust   LIAM HOPTON, ESQ., of Charleston, for 5 shill-
                          ings, part of lot #105 in Charleston, bounding
S 60 ft. on Broad Street; E 80 ft. on JAMES MICHIE (formerly JAMES
PAINE); W on other part belonging JOHN WAGNER; N on part occupied by
THOMAS HALL (formerly REBECCA FLAVELL). Whereas JOB ROTHMAHLER, the
father, owned the SE part of lot #105 in Charleston which he conveyed to
WILLIAM LINTHWAITE, of Charleston; & whereas WILLIAM HOPTON held the land
in trust by will of ELIANOR SANDWELL, widow, of Charleston, dated 8 Aug.
1749; & also by a certain declaration of turst dated 24 June 1754 between
WILLIAM HOPTON, & SARAH his wife of 1st part, & ANNA MARIA HOYLAND, widow, sole trader of Charleston, of 2nd part; but the deed from ROTHMAHLER
to LINTHWAITE has been burned or lost & not recorded in the register's
office; & whereas JOB ROTHMAHLER, the son, has agreed to secure HOPTON'S
title to the land; now he releases all claim. Witnesses: WILLIAM BUR-
ROWS, JOHN RUTLEDGE. Before JAMES PARSONS, J.P. WILLIAM HOPTON, Register.

Book W-W, p. 447   DR. DAVID CAW, of Charleston, & CATHERINE his
30 & 31 Dec. 1750   wife, to GEORGE HUNTER, ESQ., & JOHN COOPER,
L & R   merchant, of Charleston, in trust for their
                          son THOMAS CAW & any children they might have
later; 1013 a. in several parcels, in St. James Santee, Craven Co., on
Santee River; also 897 a. in several parcels, in St. James Goose Creek;
DAVID & CATHERINE CAW to occupy the 2 tracts during their lifetime; the
1013 a. to go to son THOMAS & the 897 a. to 2nd son, if any; or in case
of default the 2 tracts to go to MARY SERRE & JUDITH SERRE, daughters of
CATHERINE & NOAH SERRE, her former husband; or to NOAH SERRE, son of
CATHERINE & NOAH SERRE; or to WILLIAM CHICKEN & THOMAS CHICKEN, brothers
of said CATHERINE CAW. Whereas CATHERINE CAW owned 3 tracts of land, 2
of them of 200 a. each, the third of 350 a.; total 750 a.; being the
plantation on which ALEXANDER CHOUXVINE lived; bounding NW & SE on estate
of NOAH SERRE; NE on Santee River; SW on vacant land; also 2 adjoining
tracts of 200 a. & 63 a. on Wadbaccaw Island in Santee River, opposite
above plantation; bounding SE & NW on estate of NOAH SERRE; NE on Wadbaccaw Creek; SW on Santee River; all of which tracts she had purchased on 2
Nov. 1745 from ALEXANDER CHOUXVINE; & whereas she also owns another tract
of 100 a. in St. James Goose Creek Parish, Berkeley Co., also an adjoining tract of 1050 a. (except 253 a. sold to JAMES KINLOCH), in St. James
Goose Creek, bounding N on said 100 a. & on EDWARD KEATING, JOB ROTHMAH-
LER, BAGBY SHINGLETON & JAMES KINLOCH; W on WILLIAM ALLEN & JAMES KINLOCH;
S on ROBERT HUME; E on JOSEPH NORMAN; total 897 a.; which were devised to
CATHERINE by her late husband NOAH SERRE; & whereas her oldest son by her
first husband is already provided with excellent lands & she now wishes
to provide for her son THOMAS CAW & her future children; now she appoints
trustees for that purpose. Witnesses: WILLIAM GLEN, WILLIAM MICKIE, merchant. Before JAMES PARSONS, J.P. WILLIAM HOPTON, Register.

Book W-W, p. 457   JOHN CLELAND, to ARCHIBALD JOHNSTON, of George-
22 & 23 Dec. 1758   town, for £ 600 currency, 3 lots in George-
L & R   town, #230, #231 & #232 bounding SE on lot
                          #233; NW on Cannon Street; NE on Front or Bay
Street; SW to low water mark on Georgetown River. Witnesses: ARCHIBALD
BAIRD, THOMAS WATIES. Before WILLIAM SIMPSON, J.P. WILLIAM HOPTON, Reg-
ister.

Book W-W, p. 463   ARCHIBALD JOHNSTON, planter, to ELIAS HORRY,
19 & 20 Dec. 1760   planter, both of Prince George Parish, Craven
L & R   Co., for Ł 700 currency, 3 adjoining lots in
                          Georgetown, #230, #231, & #232, bounding SE on
lot #233; NE on Front Street; NW on Cannon Street; SW to low water mark
of Georgetown River. Witnesses: ANDREW JOHNSTON, JOSEPH DUBOURDIEU. Before THOMAS BLYTHE, J.P. WILLIAM HOPTON, Register.

Book W-W, p. 469   JOSEPH HUNT, planter, of St. Bartholomews Par-
6 & 7 Oct. 1758   ish, to ALEXANDER SHAW, of New Windsor,
L & R   (Georgia ?) for Ł 100 currency, 100 a. in
                          Granville Co., known as Cundeys; bounding SW
on Savannah River; other sides on vacant land. Witnesses: JOHN MCQUEEN,
EDWARD DAVIES. Before JAMES PARSONS, J.P. WILLIAM HOPTON, Register.

Book W-W, p. 473   ALEXANDER SHAW, formerly of New Windsor, now
2 & 3 Dec. 1760   of St. Bartholomews Parish to GEORGE GALPHIN,
L & R   of New Windsor, for Ł 1200 SC money, 500 a. in
                          the District of Augusta, Province of Georgia,
bounding N on Savannah River & granted to him 28 Mar. 1758; also 100 a.
in Granville Co., SC, known as Cundeys; bounding SW on Savannah River;
other sides on vacant land. Witnesses: JOHN MCQUEEN, ALEXANDER FYFFE.
Before JAMES PARSONS, J.P. WILLIAM HOPTON, Register.

Book W-W, p. 477   WILLIAM WILLIAMSON, ESQ., of Charleston, &
26 & 27 Feb. 1761   MARTHA his wife, to WILLIAM BLAKE, gentleman,
L & R   for Ł 3000 currency, 860 a. in St. Bartholo-
                          mews Parish, Colleton Co., bounding NE on WIL-
LIAM BLAKE; SW on BENTLEY COOKE, N on ANNA BLAKE; NW on Combahee or Salt-
catcher River. Witnesses: JOHN RUTLEDGE, BENJAMIN GUERARD. Before JAMES
GRINDLEY, J.P. WILLIAM HOPTON, Register.

Book W-W, p. 484   GABRIEL MANIGAULT, ALEXANDER BROUGHTON, &
22 & 23 Apr. 1756   PETER MANIGAULT, executors of will of BENJAMIN
L & R   D'HARRIETTE, of Charleston; to JOHN LLOYD,
                          ESQ., commander of Fort Johnston, SC, for
Ł 3500 currency, 304 a. on Johns Island, Colleton Co., on GEORGE FROST'S
Creek, bounding S, E, & NW on ROGER MOORE; NW on NATHANIEL NICHOLS; which
304 a. were, by L & R dated 6 & 7 Nov. 1731 sold by THOMAS TOWNSEND,
planter, of Colleton Co., to BENJAMIN D'HARRIETTE, & was part of 400 a.
granted by the Lords Proprs. to MILES BREWTON; also 100 a., part of 200 a.
called FROST'S plantation, on Johns Island, in Colleton Co., granted by
the Lords Proprs., to GEORGE FROST & sold to BENJAMIN D'HARRIETTE by
NATHANIEL NICHOLS, planter, of Colleton Co., & SARAH his wife, by L & R
dated 25 & 26 Feb. 1734; the 100 a. bounding S on Frost's Creek; E on
Madam PETIT; N on MAJ. WILLIAM ALLEN; W on WILLIAM MILLER; also 66 a. on
Johns Island, bounding E on DAVID HEXT; S on marsh of Stono River; W on
BENJAMIN D'HARRIETTE; which 66 a. were sold to D'HARRIETTE by JOHN JOR-
DINE, planter, of Colleton Co., by L & R dated 19 & 20 May 1740, & form-
erly granted by the Lords Proprs. to GEORGE FROST; also 153 a. on Johns
Island, bounding E on BENJAMIN D'HARRIETTE; S on Frost's Creek out of
Stono River; W on 2 other tracts belonging to D'HARRIETTE (formerly to
JOHN WILSON, JOHN PRESCOT & GEORGE FORD); N on land called Allen's Pine
Barren (lately belonging to heirs of THOMAS LADSON); which 153 a. were
formerly 2 tracts of 100 a. & 53 a. sold to D'HARRIETTE by STEPHEN FORD,
planter, of Colleton Co., brother & heir of GEORGE FORD, planter) & MARY
his wife, by L & R dated 28 & 29 June 1734; also their interest in 200 a.,
English measure, on Johns Island, bounding W on JOHN WODEN (lately BEN-
JAMIN D'HARRIETTE); S on JOHN WILKINS; N & E on BENJAMIN D'HARRIETTE;
which interest was quit claimed by STEPHEN FORD to D'HARRIETTE on 29 June
1734; also 200 a. in Colleton Co., granted D'HARRIETTE on 3 Apr. 1735 by
King GEORGE II; bounding N & E on BENJAMIN D'HARRIETTE; S on MR. WILKINS;
W on MR. FLEMING & SAMUEL WODEN; total 1023 a.; which 6 tracts BENJAMIN
D'HARRIETTE by his will dated 14 Jan. last authorized his executors to
sell at auction, which they did after his death on 17 Feb. last. Witnesses: WILLIAM BANBURY, CHARLES GRIMBALL, ELIZABETH BANBURY. Before
ROBERT RIVERS, J.P. WILLIAM HOPTON, Register.

Book W-W, p. 495   WILLIAM CARTWRIGHT, only son & heir of RICHARD
5 & 6 Mar. 1761   CARTWRIGHT, of Charleston, to THOMAS MELL,

L & R   planter, of St. James Goose Creek; for Ł 500
                                currency, 120 a. in St. James Goose Creek,
bounding SW on MRS. ELIZABETH CHANDLER (formerly JOSIAH PENDARVIS); SE on
WILLIAM MELL; NE on JOHN AINSLIE; NW on the Baptist Meeting & THOMAS BA-
KER. Witnesses: WILLIAM BURROWS, JOSHUA WARD. Before ROBERT WILLIAMS,
JR., J.P. WILLIAM HOPTON, Register. Plat of 120 a. certified 12 Oct.
1744, by NATHANIEL DEAN, Sur., measured at request of WILLIAM FOARD for
RICHARD CARTWRIGHT, bounding SE on the Rev. MR. CHANDLER & heirs of BEN-
JAMIN CHILD; SW on CHANDLER & THOMAS BAKER.

Book W-W, p. 502   STEPHEN BULL, SR., planter, eldest son & heir
18 & 19 Feb. 1761   of BARNABY BULL; & ELIZABETH his wife; to the
L & R   Hon. JOHN GUERARD, ESQ., of Charleston; for
                                Ł 5525 currency, 2 adjoining tracts of 605 a.
& 500 a.; total 1105 a. in Prince William Parish; bounding NW on STEPHEN
BULL, JR., of Sheldon; SW on BENJAMIN GARDEN; NE on ALEXANDER FRASER; SE
on THOMAS MIDDLETON & WILLIAM MAIN. Witnesses: ARCHIBALD SIMPSON, WIL-
LIAM MAIN, JOHN WILLIAMSON. Before BENJAMIN GARDEN, J.P. WILLIAM HOP-
TON, Register. Plat given.

Book W-W, p. 508   ADAM CULLIATT, of St. Bartholomews Parish, &
12 & 13 May 1760   MARY his wife, to JOHN MARTIN, for Ł 52 cur-
L & R   rency, that tract of land in PonPon, adjoining
                                the village of Jacksonsburgh, bounding E & SE
on WILLIAM HAYNE; W on ADAM CULLIATT; N on DAVID HEXT; S on Jacksonsburgh;
being 158 ft. front; 840 ft. deep. Witnesses: JOHN FENDIN: JAMES RATTRAY.
Before JAMES SHARP, J.P. WILLIAM HOPTON, Register.

Book W-W, p. 513   JOHN MARTIN, planter, of St. Bartholomews Par-
10 May 1760   ish, Colleton Co., to CATHERINE HOUSER; for
Gift   love & affection; 3 a. in PonPon, for her use,
                                & after her death for the use of husband FRED-
ERICK HOUSER; bounding E & SE on WILLIAM HAYNE; W on ADAM CULLIATT; S on
village of Jacksonsburgh; N on DAVID HEXT. Witnesses: JOHN FENDIN, JAMES
RATTRAY. Before JAMES SHARP, J.P. WILLIAM HOPTON, Register.

Book W-W, p. 514   JOHN RIVERS, carpenter, to JOHN CATTELL, ESQ.,
13 & 14 MAR. 1761   both of St. Andrews Parish, as security on
L & R by Mortgage   bond of even date in penal sum of Ł 770 for
                                payment of Ł 385 currency, with interest, on
14 Mar. 1762; part of lots #216 & #196, bounding W 120 ft. on King Street;
N 212 ft. on part of lot #196 now held by ELIZABETH HUNT; S 212 ft. on
Rivers Street, (a private street); E 120 ft. on lots #142 & #197 now held
by JOHN GIBBES & EDWARD FENWICKE. Witnesses: ROBERT WILLIAMS, JR., PETER
TIMOTHY. Before WILLIAM BURROWS, J.P. WILLIAM HOPTON, Register. On 8
Aug. 1779 BENJAMIN CATTELL, executor of COL. WILLIAM CATTEL, who was executor of JOHN CATTELL the mortgagee, declared mortgage satisfied. Wit-
nesses: GEORGE SHEED.

Book W-W, p. 521   STEPHEN BULL, planter, of Prince William Par-
19 Feb. 1761   ish, eldest son & heir of BARNABY BULL, to the
Bond   Hon. JOHN GUERARD, ESQ., of Charleston, in
                                penal sum of Ł 11,050 currency, for keeping
agreements in release dated 19 Feb. 1761 (see p. 502). Witnesses: WIL-
LIAM MAINE, JOHN WILLIAMSON. Before BENJAMIN GARDEN, J.P. WILLIAM HOP-
TON, Register.

Book W-W, p. 522   JAMES SKIRVING, ESQ., to JAMES HAMILTON, plant-
23 Dec. 1760   er, both of St. Bartholomews Parish, Colleton
Release   Co., for Ł 2000 currency, 419-3/4 a. in St.
                                Bartholomews Parish, bounding N on DAVID FER-
GUSON; NW on JOHN BEATY; S on ROBERT HIETT; E on estate of JOHN ST. JOHN.
Witnesses: JOHN CHAMPNEYS, ARCHIBALD STOBO, JAMES SKIRVING, JR. Before
JAMES SHARP, J.P. WILLIAM HOPTON, Register. Plat showing 9-1/2 a.,
Lords land; 84-1/2 a., Lords land; 325-3/4 King's land; total 419-3/4 a.

Book W-W, p. 526   ROBERT DEANS, carpenter, to JOHN REMINGTON,
6 Feb. 1759   gentleman, both of Charleston, as security on
Mortgage by Release   bond of even date in penal sum of Ł 2800 for
                                payment of Ł 1400 currency, with interest, on

6 Feb. 1760; 2 adjoining lots in Charleston, #119 & #120 of half an a.
each, English measure, conveyed by L & R dated 23 & 24 Oct. 1758 by THOM-
AS BOONE to ROBERT DEANE; bounding E on Archdale Street; S on Queen
Street; W & N on heirs of ISAAC MAZYCK. Witnesses: JOHN CART, ABRAHAM
REMINGTON. Before JACOB MOTTE, J.P. WILLIAM HOPTON, Register.

Book W-W, p. 530   JOHN SAMS, planter, heir & only executor of
21 & 22 Nov. 1760   will of his brother, ROBERT SAMS; to WILLIAM
L & R   WAIGHT, planter, for L 1100 currency, 500 a.,
on Hilton Head Island, bounding N on Port Roy-
al Sound; W on Scull Creek; S on vacant land; E on a creek, marsh & run
adjoining lands of JOHN BARNWELL. Whereas the Lords Proprs. granted JOHN
BARNWELL 500 a. in Granville Co., on Hilton Head; which he bequeathed to
his daughter, BRIDGET; who married ROBERT SAMS & had several children; &
at her death her eldest son, ROBERT SAMS, inherited; now his brother
JOHN, sells the land to WAIGHT. Witnesses: JOHN BARNWELL, ANDREW AGNEW,
JOHN NORTON. Before WILLIAM HARVEY, J.P. A. GORDON, Dep. Reg. On 24
Nov. 1756 ROBERT MANNING, Sur. ran 2 division lines between lands of ROB-
ERT SAMS & DANIEL SAVAGE, on Hilton Head, by agreement of the 2 parties,
the old corner being down, put up a new one in presence of ROBERT GODFREY
& said parties; the old lines not being found. SAMS gives bond that he
will pay any quit rents that may be unpaid. Witness: JOHN NORTON. Before JAMES PARSONS, J.P. A. GORDON, Dep. Register.

Book W-W, p. 537   WILLIAM COATS, merchant, to WILLIAM HARVEY,
23 & 24 Feb. 1761   gentleman, both of Charleston, as security on
L & R by Mortgage   bond in penal sum of L 1500 sterling British
for payment of various bills of exchange; 2 on
GEORGE MACKENZIE & CO., of Cowes, in favor of HARVEY, who indorsed one to
ROBERT MACKENZIE of Charleston; & 1 to GEORGE INGLIS, of Charleston; 2 on
GEORGE & ROBERT UDNY, merchants, of London, in favor of HARVEY, who indorsed 1 to PAUL DROMGOLE, 1 to SAMPSON NEYLE; 60 a. at Morrites Nook
near the head of NW branch of Stono River; in St. Pauls Parish, Colleton
Co., bounding E on CAPT. THOMAS ELLIOTT; S on MR. TUCKER; N & W on 403 a.
formerly belonging to THOMAS ELLIOTT; according to plat certified by WIL-
LIAM BULL, D.S.C., on 8 May 1723; also said 403 a., bounding N on vacant
land; E on said 60 a.; S on MR. TUCKER & HUGH HEXT; W on HUGH HEXT; according to plat certified by WILLIAM BULL, S.D.G., on 9 May 1723; also
175 a. of Pine Barren land, part of 1103 a. granted 24 Apr. 1742 to THOM-
AS FARR, bounding NE on MARY GREEN; E on JOSEPH SMITH; SE on THOMAS SMITH;
W on HUMPHREY SOMMERS; N & NW on THOMAS ROSE; also 500 a., English mea-
sure, between SW & W branches of Stono River, bounding S on THOMAS FARR;
E on JOHN SMITH; N on THOMAS ELLIOTT & HUGH HEXT; W on CHRISTOPHER WIL-
KINSON; total 1138 a., English measure. Witnesses: ROBERT WILLIAMS, JR.,
WILLIAM BULLINE. Before WILLIAM BURROWS, J.P. A. GORDON, Dep. Reg. On
29 Nov. 1771 WILLIAM HARVEY declared mortgage discharged. Witness: J.
BOYNTELL.

Book W-W, p. 552   Rev. MR. JOHN JOAKIN ZUBLY, of Savannah, Ga.,
24 & 25 Sept. 1760   (son & heir of DAVID ZUBLY, of SC), & ANNE his
L & R   wife, to WILLIAM SEALY, planter, of St. Helena
Parish, SC, for L 1200 currency, 600 a. in
Township of Purrysburgh, Granville Co., bounding S on JOSEPH SAGIE, AN-
THONY YATON, & vacant land; other sides on vacant land. Witnesses: JOSH-
UA MCPHERSON, SAMUEL HASTINGS. ANNE signed before DAVID MONTAIGUT, J.P.
HENRY DESAUSSURE, J.P.

Book W-W, p. 558   JONATHAN NORTON, planter, & MARY ANN his wife,
20 & 21 Aug. 1756   to JOHN BARNWELL & JOHN FENDEN, JR., planters,
L & R in Trust   as trustees, & a third person, all of Island
of St. Helena, Granville Co.; 2 a. on St. He-
lena, being the SE part of that 1/9 division of a tract of 960 a., now
vested in JONATHAN NORTON on which are erected the chapel & vestry room
for the public worship of God according to the church of England (but in
the absence of a clergyman of the established church the trustees may
admit a Protestant dissenter of unblemished character, differing not in
the fundamental part of religion as laid down in the confession of the
Faith, he producing his credentials of Ordination). Whereas the Lords
Proprs. on 28 Aug. 1701 granted JOHN NORTON, of Johns Island, 400 a. on
Island of St. Helena & an island of 560 a., separated from first tract by

a creek & marsh; total 960 a.; & whereas JOHN NORTON died intestate in 1705 & his children inherited the 960 a. divided into 9 equal parts; son JONATHAN receiving the S part of the 400 a. on St. Helena Island; & whereas the House of Assembly & several persons contributed money & material for building a chapel & vestry room on said island; now nearly completed; now JONATHAN places the 2 a., buildings & burial ground in the hands of certain trustees & their successors. Witnesses: MAGDELINE GOUGH, WILLIAM GOUGH. Before JAMES THOMPSON, J.P. A. GORDON, D.R.P.

Book W-W, p. 568
27 & 28 Jan. 1761
L & R

ISABELLA (her mark) FINCH, widow of WILLIAM FINCH, mariner, to JAMES KIRKWOOD, cabinet maker, all of Charleston, for Ł 1225 currency, part of lot #18, bounding W 19 ft. on Union Street; E on HOPKIN PRICE; N 124 ft. on RAWLINS LOWNDES (formerly THOMAS HARDIN); S on part lot #18 belonging to ISABELLA FINCH. Witnesses: WILLIAM GLEN, JOHN COLE. Before ALEXANDER STEWART, J.P. WILLIAM HOPTON, Register.

Book W-W, p. 576
28 Jan. 1761
Bond

ISABELLA (her mark) FINCH, gives JAMES KIRKWOOD, bond in sum of Ł 1225 currency that she will perform above agreement (p. 568). Witnesses: WILLIAM GLEN, JOHN COLE. WILLIAM HOPTON, Register.

Book W-W, p. 577
28 & 29 Jan. 1761
L & R by Mortgage

JAMES KIRKWOOD, cabinet-maker, & MARY his wife, to THOMAS SMITH, JR., merchant; all of Charleston; as security on bond of even date in penal sum of Ł 2000 for payment of Ł 1000 currency, with interest, on 1 Jan. 1762; part of lot #18 purchased from ISABELLA FINCH (see p. 568). Witnesses: JOHN COLE, ALEXANDER GORDON. Before ALEXANDER STEWART, J.P. ALEXANDER GORDON, D.P.R.

Book W-W, p. 585
2 & 3 Apr. 1761
L & R by Mortgage

WILLIAM LLOYD, merchant, & MARTHA his wife, to BARNARD ELLIOTT, gentleman, executor of will of BARNARD ELLIOTT; both of Charleston, as security on bond of even date in penal sum of Ł 2800 for payment of Ł 1400 currency, with interest, on 3 Apr. 1762; part of certain lot, conveyed to him by said BARNARD ELLIOTT & others, bounding N 30 ft. on Elliott Street; W 86 ft. on JOHN MCALL; S on WILLIAM ELLIOTT & OTHNIEL BEALE; E on BARNARD ELLIOTT. Witnesses: THOMAS ELLIS, JOHN LEHRE, THOMAS BATTY. Before ALEXANDER STEWART, J.P. A. GORDON, D.P.R. On 28 Apr. 1761 BARNARD ELLIOTT declared mortgage satisfied. Witness: THOMAS YOUNG.

Book W-W, p. 595
19 Jan. 1761
Feoffment

JOHN LAIRD, merchant, of Charleston, to JAMES DONNOM, planter, of St. Bartholomews Parish, Colleton Co., for Ł 100 currency, 8-1/4 a. in Colleton Co., bounding W on the common of Jacksonburgh; E on PonPon River; S on road leading to PonPon Bridge; N on WILLIAM HAYNES. Witnesses: NATHANIEL DOAN, ARCHIBALD STOBO, WILLIAM JACKSON. Possession & seizin given. Before JAMES SHARP, J.P. WILLIAM HOPTON, Register. Plat by JOHN STEVENS, Dep. Sec., dated 1 May 1752 shows NW boundary on Bay Street of said village; NE on old road; SW on new road to bridge.

Book W-W, p. 598
28 Feb. 1757
L & R

MARY CARMICHAEL, widow, of St. James Parish, to GEORGE LOGAN, planter, of St. Bartholomew's Parish, for Ł 1400 currency, 564 a. in Colleton Co., granted by Lt. Gov. THOMAS BROUGHTON on 30 Sept. 1736 to MARY CARMICHAEL, bounding N on WILLIAM CRAWL; E on JAMES KELLY & JOHN MUSGROVE; S on JOSEPH BOONE & vacant land; W on JOHN OTTERSON. Witnesses: CATHERINE CROLL, THOMAS FERGUSON. Before JOSEPH BRAILSFORD, J.P. WILLIAM HOPTON, Register.

Book W-W, p. 607
30 & 31 Mar. 1761
L & R

JOHN LINDER, planter, of St. Bartholomews Parish, Colleton Co., & JANE (her mark) his wife (formerly JANE CROLL, daughter & 1 of the coheiresses of WILLIAM CROLL, planter, of Colleton Co.), to JOHN LOGAN, merchant, of Charleston, for Ł 1500 SC money, 373 a., originally granted to WILLIAM CROLL; bounding NE on vacant land;

E on MR. DRAYTON; S on vacant land; SW on ROGER SANDERS & WILLIAM CLIF-
FORD; N on JOHN COCKRAN & vacant land; also 327 a. granted WILLIAM CROLL,
bounding E on WILLIAM CROLL; S on MR. KELLY; N & W on MR. CHAMPNEY; also
500 a., part of BAYLY'S Barony or Landgravate, formerly bounding on all
sides on vacant land; also 200 a. granted BRYAN KELLY, to the W of the
freshes of Edisto River, within land, near the Round O Savannah, then
bounding on vacant land; total 1400 a. in Colleton Co., also their 2 undivided third parts of 377 a. & houses thereon, bounding on THOMAS PAINE.
Whereas Lt. Gov. THOMAS BROUGHTON granted WILLIAM CROLL 373 a. in Colleton Co. (Secretary's office Book G.G. fol. 211); & on 7 Aug. 1735 granted
WILLIAM CROLL 327 a. (Secretary's office Book C.C. fol. 43); & whereas
JOHN BAYLY of Ballinaclough, Co. of Tipperary, Ireland, son & heir of
JOHN BAYLY, ESQ., of same place, by ALEXANDER TRENCH, his attorney, by
L & R dated 21 & 22 Sept. 1731 sold WILLIAM CROLL & THOMAS MCKEE 500 a.,
but MCKEE dying intestate, CROLL became sole owner; & whereas CROLL by
certain conveyances owned 200 a. originally granted to BRYAN KELLY; total
1400 a. in Colleton Co.; & whereas CROLL also owned 377 a. bounding on
THOMAS PAINE'S land; & by will dated 4 Nov. 1743 devised to JANE CROLL,
now wife of JOHN LINDER, & to MARGARET CROLL, his 2 eldest daughters, his
1527 a. in Colleton Co., bounding on JAMES BOGGS, vacant land, MELLER ST.
JOHN, & on JOHN CARMICHAEL, together with his dwelling house & other tenements; & bequeathed to ELIZABETH CROLL, his youngest daughter, now wife
of JOHN LOGAN, the 377 a. tract; which will was signed by only 2 witnesses & therefore not legally good, & the land descended to his 3 daughters
(JANE & MARGARET, sisters by the same mother; & ELIZABETH by another
"Venter", now wife of JOHN LOGAN), as co-partners; & whereas MARGARET
died in her infancy & JANE, as heiress of the whole blood inherited MAR-
GARET'S third; now JANE & her husband sell their 2/3 to JOHN LOGAN &
ELIZABETH his wife. Witnesses: JAMES KIRKWOOD, JOSEPH SANDERS. KIRKWOOD
testified before JAMES GRINDLAY, J.P. 1 Apr. 1761. Recorded 25 May 1761
by WILLIAM HOPTON, Register.

Book W-W, p. 621   The Hon. WILLIAM BULL, EDWARD FENWICK, OTHNIEL
6 Nov. 1760   BEALE, & ISAAC MAZYCK, BENJAMIN SMITH, ROBERT
Feoffment   PRINGLE, GEORGE SAXBY, GABRIEL MANIGAULT, &
                          THOMAS MIDDLETON, commissioners, for building
the Parish House of St. Michaels, Charleston; to SUSANNA CROKATT; for
L 200 currency, subscribed towards the building the church; Pew No. 70,
forever. Witnesses: SAMUEL PRIOLEAU, SAMUEL CARDY, architect. Possession & seizin given by GABRIEL MANIGAULT. CARDY testified before JAMES
PARSONS, J.P. on 20 Apr. 1761. Recorded 26 May 1761 by WILLIAM HOPTON,
Register.

Book W-W, p. 624   The Hon. WILLIAM BULL, EDWARD FENWICKE, OTH-
6 Nov. 1760   NIEL BEALE, & ISAAC MAZYCK, BENJAMIN SMITH,
Feoffment   ROBERT PRINGLE, GEORGE SAXBY, GABRIEL MANI-
                          GAULT, & THOMAS MIDDLETON, commissioners, for
building Parish Church of St. Michaels, Charleston; to WILLIAM HENDERSON;
for L 150 currency subscribed towards building the church; Pew No. 54,
forever. Witnesses: SAMUEL PRIOLEAU, SAMUEL CARDY, architect. CARDY
testified before ALEXANDER GORDON, J.P. on 1 May 1761. Recorded 27 May
1761 by ALEXANDER GORDON, D.P.R.

Book W-W, p. 626   Between WILLIAM HENDERSON, gentleman, of 1st
13 Apr. 1761   part; & WILLIAM BURROWS, & others of 2nd part,
Declaration of Trust   all of Charleston. Whereas in 1752 the mem-
& Feoffment   bers of Solomons Lodge of F & A Masons in
                          Charleston, desiring to procure title to 2
pews in the new church about to be built, known as St. Michaels, empower-
ed 2 of their members, WILLIAM HENDERSON & MOREAU SARRAZIN, to subcribe
L 150 currency, each, towards the building of the church, to entitle the
members of the lodge to 2 pews; & it was agreed that the titles should be
taken in the names of HENDERSON & SARRAZIN who would afterwards make them
over by deeds of trust to 7 or more lodge members, with certain clauses
included, according to minutes entered in the lodge books on 5 Oct. 1752;
& whereas HENDERSON subscribed for Pew #54 (see p. 624); & the lodge members have appointed WILLIAM BURROWS, DR. SAMUEL CARNE, JOB MILNEW, BAR-
NARD BECKMAN, RICHARD PARK STOBO, THOMAS STONE, & ROBERT WILSON, trustees,
to receive the deed (Minutes book 9 Feb. 1761); now HENDERSON conveys the
deed to the lodge members. Witnesses: SAMUEL CARDY, JAMES GRINDLAY.

134

Possession & seizen given. CARDY testified before ALEXANDER GORDON, J.P. on 1 May 1761. Recorded 27 May 1761 by ALEXANDER GORDON, D.P.R.

Book W-W, p. 633
6 Nov. 1760
Feoffment

The Hon. WILLIAM BULL, EDWARD FENWICKE, OTH-NIEL BEALE, & ISAAC MAZYCK, BENJAMIN SMITH, ROBERT PRINGLE, GEORGE SAXBY, GABRIEL MANI-GAULT, & THOMAS MIDDLETON, commissioners, appointed for building the new Parish Church of St. Michaels, Charleston; to MOREAU SARRAZIN; for Ł 150 currency, Pew No. 55, forever. Witnesses: SAMUEL PRIOLEAU, SAMUEL CARDY, architect. Possession & seizin given. CARDY testified before ALEXANDER GORDON, J.P. on 1 May 1761. Recorded 27 May 1761 by _____.

Book W-W, p. 635
13 Apr. 1761
Declaration of Trust

JONATHAN SARRAZIN, silversmith, of Charleston, son & heir of MOREAU SARRAZIN, silversmith, to WILLIAM BURROWS, SAMUEL CARNE, JOB MILNER, BARNARD BECKMAN, RICHARD PARK STOBO, THOMAS STONE, & ROBERT WILSON, gentlemen, of Charleston, trustees appointed by the members of Solomon's Lodge of F & A Masons to receive the deed; deed to Pew #55 in St. Michael's Church (see p. 626). Witnesses: SAMUEL CARDY, JAMES GRINDLAY. Possession & seizin delivered. CARDY testified before ALEXANDER GORDON, J.P. on 1 May 1761. Recorded 28 May 1761 by ALEXANDER GORDON, D.P.R.

Book W-W, p. 641
6 Nov. 1760
Feoffment

The Hon. WILLIAM BULL, EDWARD FENWICKE, OTH-NIEL BEALE, & ISAAC MAZYCK, BENJAMIN SMITH, ROBERT PRINGLE, GEORGE SAXBY, GABRIEL MANI-GAULT, & THOMAS MIDDLETON, commissioners, appointed for building the new Parish Church of St. Michaels; for Ł 225 currency, subscribed for building said church; Pew No. 13, forever. Witnesses: SAMUEL PRIOLEAU, SAMUEL CARDY, architect. Possession & seizin given by BENJAMIN SMITH to WILLIAM HOPTON, attorney, for WILLIAM STONE. CARDY testified before ALEXANDER GORDON, J.P. on 1 May 1761. Recorded 29 May 1761 by ALEXANDER GORDON, D.P.R.

Book W-W, p. 644
6 Nov. 1760
Feoffment

The Hon. WILLIAM BULL, EDWARD FENWICKE, OTH-NIEL BEALE, & ISAAC MAZYCK, BENJAMIN SMITH, ROBERT PRINGLE, GEORGE SAXBY, GABRIEL MANI-GAULT, & THOMAS MIDDLETON, commissioners, for building the new Parish Church of St. Michaels, Charleston; to WILLIAM HOPTON, for Ł 200 currency, subscribed towards building the new church; Pew No. 87. Witnesses: SAMUEL PRIOLEAU, SAMUEL CARDY, architect. Possession & seizin given. CARDY testified before ALEXANDER GORDON, J.P. on L May 1761. Recorded 29 May 1761 by ALEXANDER GORDON, D.P.R.

Book W-W, p. 647
8 & 9 June 1754
L & R

HENRY LEVINGSTON, planter, of Wadmalaw, to CHALRES ODINGSELLS, planter, of Willtown, St. Pauls Parish, for Ł 200 currency, 480 a., part of 500 a. granted his uncle WILLIAM LEVING-STON, 20 a. of which sold to DR. MITCHELL; which 480 a. were devised to HENRY & his brother WILLIAM in joint tenancy by will of said uncle, WIL-LIAM LEVINGSTON; but WILLIAM, the brother, dying intestate, HENRY inherited; bounding S on MAJ. EVE; W on a marsh; N on said LEVINGSTON; E on a creek of S. Edisto River; lying opposite Willtown. Witnesses: THOMAS WILSON, JAMES PRATT. PRATT testified before WILLIAM BURROWS on 7 Apr. 1761. Recorded 30 May 1761 by WILLIAM HOPTON, Register.

Book W-W, p. 654
4 & 5 May 1761
L & R

SARAH RUTLEDGE, widow, only daughter & devisee of will of HUGH HEXT, to RICHARD DOWNES, merchant, both of Charleston, for Ł 7000 curren-cy, 555 or 556 a. in St. Paul's Parish, Colle-ton Co., bounding N on Cawcaw Swamp; E on ANDREW SMITH; S on ELIJAH PRIO-LEAU & JAMES FITCH; W on FITCH & JOSEPH STANYARNE. Whereas HUGH HEXT, gentleman, of Colleton Co., owned 310 a. near head of NW branch of Stono River, then bounding N on HUGH HEXT; E on THOMAS TUCKER & THOMAS ELLIOTT; S on THOMAS FARR; W on CAPT. WILKINSON; also 400 a. bounding N on a cy-press swamp running into Stono River; W on HENRY TOOMER; S & E on vacant land; & whereas on 10 Jan. 1710/11 HUGH HEXT sold 155 a. (part of 1st tract) to COL. JOHN PALMER, leaving 555 a.; according to resurvey by ROB-ERT MANNING, Dep. Sur.; now his daughter, SARAH RUTLEDGE, sells this land to DOWNES. Witnesses: HUMPHRY SOMMERS, JOHN RUTLEDGE. SOMMERS testified before ALEXANDER GORDON, J.P. on 5 May 1761. Recorded 3 June 1761 by ALEXANDER GORDON, D.P.R. Plat by MANNING dated 27 Apr. 1759.

Book W-W, p. 662   BARNARD ELLIOTT, only son of BARNARD ELLIOTT
1 & 2 Apr. 1761   the elder, & THOMAS LAMBOLL, all gentlemen,
L & R   (ELLIOTT & LAMBOLL being executors of will of
                          BARNARD ELLIOTT the elder); & ELIZABETH ELLI-
OTT, widow of said BARNARD ELLIOTT; of 1st part; to WILLIAM LLOYD, mer-
chant; all of Charleston; for ₤ 1400 currency, part of a lot in Charles-
ton, bounding N 30 ft. on Elliott Street; W 86 ft. on JOHN MCALL; S on
OTHNIEL BEALE & WILLIAM ELLIOTT; E on other part said lot. Whereas BAR-
NARD ELLIOTT the elder owned part of a lot in Charleston on which, by
will dated 16 May 1758, he bequeathed equally to his 4 daughters, ELIZA-
BETH, MARY, AMARENTIA, & CATHERINE, & authorized his executors (LAMBOLL &
ELLIOTT) to sell the property; now they sell to LLOYD. Witnesses: JAMES
MCALPINE, DANIEL CANNON, EDWARD WEYMAN. WEYMAN testified before ALEXAN-
DER GORDON, J.P., On 5 June 1761. Recorded 6 June 1761 by ALEXANDER GOR-
DON, D.P.R.

Book W-W, p. 672   DANIEL REASE (REES), & MARY his wife, to JO-
13 Feb. 1759   SEPH REASE (REES); for ₤ 25 currency, 150 a.
L & R   on E side Little River, in Craven Co., bound-
                          ing on said side of Little River joining part
of said tract belonging to DANIEL REASE; all other sides on vacant land;
according to grant dated 9 Jan. 1750 signed by Gov. JAMES GLEN. Witnesses: WILLIAM NEWMAN, BENJAMIN GREGORY. NEWMAN testified before JACOB
GOODOWN, J.P. on 13 Feb. 1759. Recorded 11 June 1761 by WILLIAM HOPTON,
Register.

Book W-W, p. 678   CHARLES LOWNDES, P.M. of SC, to ISAAC MAZYCK,
27 Dec. 1757   at public auction, for ₤ 220 currency, 2
Sale   tracts in Craven Co., of 500 a. each; also 10
                          lots in Jamestown, Craven Co. Whereas JOHN
GENDRON the elder owned 2 tracts of 500 a. each, in Craven Co., granted
by the Lords Proprs. to his father, PHILIP GENDRON; also 10 lots in
Jamestown, Craven Co., 9 numbered 1, 6, 10, 18, 21, 24, 25, 27, & 36; the
10th, without number, being half an a. near or adjoining #18; total
28-1/2 a., part of 360 a. granted by the Lords Proprs. for a town; &
whereas JOHN GENDRON on 2 Apr. 1747 mortgaged the 2 tracts & 10 lots to
ISAAC MAZYCK & RENE RAVENEL, JR., of Berkeley Co., executors of will of
JAMES DE ST. JULIEN, in penal sum of ₤ 800 currency; & whereas JOHN GEN-
DRON by will appointed his son, JOHN GENDRON, & his son-in-law, JOHN COM-
ING BALL, his executors; & whereas JOHN GENDRON, son of the testator,
died soon after the death of his father, without qualifying as executor,
& JOHN COMING BALL proved the will; & whereas ISAAC MAZYCK, who survived
RENE RAVENEL, JR., obtained a judgment against JOHN COMING BALL, as ex-
ecutor, & a writ of fieri facias was issued by PETER LEIGH, C.J., on 4
Jan. 1757 directing the P.M. to obtain the amount from debtor's estate;
now the property is sold to MAZYCK as highest bidder. Witnesses: CHARLES
PINCKNEY, WILLIAM MAZYCK. MAZYCK testified before ALEXANDER GORDON, J.P.
on _____ May 1761. Recorded 12 June 1761 by WILLIAM HOPTON, Register.

Book W-W, p. 685   ISAAC MAZYCK, ESQ., of Charleston, to JOHN
24 & 25 Apr. 1759   COMING BALL, planter, of St. Johns Parish,
L & R   Berkeley Co., for ₤ 500 currency, 2 adjoining
                          tracts of 500 a. each, granted PHILIP GENDRON
on 24 Jan. 1710, at Savanna Creek, in St. Stephens Parish, Craven Co.,
lately belonging to COL. JOHN GENDRON, of St. James Santee, Craven Co.,
who inherited from his father, said PHILIP GENDRON; & sold by CHARLES
LOWNDES, P.M., to ISAAC MAZYCK for a debt due said ISAAC MAZYCK as executor of will of JAMES DE ST. JULIEN (p. 678), of St. Johns Parish,
Berkeley Co.; the 2 tracts bounding N on JAMES GUERRY (formerly JOHN GEN-
DRON); E on said COMING BALL (formerly JOHN GENDRON). Witnesses: DAVID
LASONS, GEORGE APPLEBY. Memorial entered in Auditor's OFFICE 2 May 1761
in Book D. p. 465 by GEORGE JOHNSTON, D.A. APPLEBY testified before
ALEXANDER GORDON, J.P. Recorded 13 June 1761 by WILLIAM HOPTON, Regis-
ter.

Book W-W, p. 692   ROBERT BOYD, of Charleston, to JOHN COMING

28 & 29 May 1759   BALL, planter, of St. Johns Parish, for ₺ 130
L & R   currency, 500 a. in Craven Co., on NW side of
                          a swamp the head of E branch of Cooper River;
formerly belonging to JOB ROTHMAHLER, ESQ., of Charleston, who by his
will dated 17 Jan. 1739 authorized his executors (his wife, ANN ROTHMAH-
LER, JOSEPH WRAGG, RICHARD LAMBTON, & his son, JOB ROTHMAHLER) to sell
the land; & whereas said testator died on 20 Jan. 1739, & ANN ROTHMAHLER
& JOSEPH WRAGG are since dead, & LAMBTON declined to act, whereby JOB,
the son, became only acting executor. On 30 & 31 Aug. 1757, he sold said
tract at public auction to ROBERT BOYD, who now sells to BALL. Witnesses: JOHN RAVEN, THOMAS LAMBOLL, JR. Memorial entered in Auditor's Office
2 May 1761 in Book D. p. 465 by GEORGE JOHNSTON, Dep. Aud. LAMBOLL testified before ALEXANDER GORDON, J.P. on 11 May 1761. Recorded 16 June
1761 by WILLIAM HOPTON, Register.

Book W-W, p. 701   JOHN SKENE, ESQ., to FRANCIS STUART, merchant,
27 & 28 Sept. 1759   of Beaufort, for ₺ 250 currency, lot #9 in
L & R   Beaufort, Port Royal, bounding W on lot #8; N
                          on lot #36; E on #10. Witnesses: ALEXANDER
FOTHERINGHAM, HENRY STUART. STUART testified before WILLIAM HARVEY,
J.P., on 23 Apr. 1761. Recorded 20 June 1761 by WILLIAM HOPTON, Regis-
ter.

Book W-W, p. 705   SARAH LINING, of Charleston, widow & executrix
18 & 19 May 1761   of will of JOHN LINING, ESQ., to FRANCIS ROSE,
L & R   planter, of St. Andrews Parish, for
                          ₺ 2983:10:0 currency, 306 a. in St. Andrews
Parish, Berkeley Co., devised by JOHN LINING to said SARAH; bounding S on
COL. LUCAS & JOHN RIVERS; W on RIVERS & JOHN GODFREY; N on NATHANIEL
BROWNE, estate of THOMAS GODFREY, & BENJAMIN DART; W on SARAH LINING.
Witnesses: ROBERT DEAN, JOHN RATTRAY. RATTRAY testified before ALEXANDER
GORDON, J.P. on 1 June 1761. Recorded 22 June 1761 by ALEXANDER GORDON,
D.P.R.

Book W-W, p. 713   ABRAHAM PRIOR, cordwainer, & BRIDGET (her
30 & 31 Jan. 1761   mark) his wife, to WILLIAM PORTER, planter,
L & R   both of Craven Co., for ₺ 55 currency, 200 a.,
                          bounding NW on vacant land & MR. CLARK; other
sides on vacant land; according to grant in 1758 from WILLIAM HENRY
LYTTLETON to ABRAHAM PRIOR (Book S.S., p. 442). Witnesses: CHARLES WOOD-
MASON, EDWARD HOYLE. HOYLE testified before JOSEPH BRITTON, J.P. on 9
Apr. 1761. Recorded 22 June 1761 by ALEXANDER GORDON, D.P.R.

Book W-W, p. 719   EDWARD CLARK, of Prince Frederick Parish, Cra-
1 Sept. 1755   en Co., to FRANCIS & JOHN AVANT, of Craven
L & R   Co., for ₺ 600 currency, 450 a. in Queens-
                          borough Township on SW side of Peedee River,
in Craven Co., bounding SE on JAMES GORDON; NW on DAVID HARTIE & on vacant land; also 1 town lot. Witnesses: JOHN RAE, JAMES TOULEE. TOULEE
testified before PAUL TRAPIER, J.P. on 25 Apr. 1761. Recorded 22 June
1761 by ALEXANDER GORDON, D.P.R.

Book W-W, p. 725   FRANCIS KINLOCH, ESQ., son & heir of JAMES
8 & 9 Apr. 1761   KINLOCH, ESQ., of Goose Creek, & ANNE his
L & R   wife, to WILLIAM BLAKE, ESQ., for ₺ 6000 cur-
                          rency, 4 tracts, total 1945 a., bounding N on
RICHARD SINGLETON & MR. FLOOD; E on DR. CAW, MR. CHICKEN, & Flood's Path;
S on GEORGE SEAMAN; W on vacant land; except the quarter a. used for a
burial place, & right of free access for burying members of the family or
erecting tombs. Whereas JAMES KINLOCH owned 4 adjoining tracts in Berke-
ley Co., 1 of 500 a. bounding S on JOSEPH THOROWGOOD; other sides on vacant land; as granted by the Lords Proprs. on 9 Sept. 1796 to JOHN
STROUDE; 1 of 670 a., bounding NW on JOHN FLOOD; E on RICHARD SINGLETON;
S on JOHN STROUDE; as granted by the Lords Proprs. on 14 Mar. 1707 to
THOMAS JONES; 1 of 500 a., bounding SW on RICHARD SINGLETON; NE on THOMAS
SPARKS; as granted by the Lords Proprs. on 23 July 1711 to JOHN WARD; 1
of 275 a., bounding NE & SE on GEORGE CHICKEN; NW & S on JAMES KINLOCH;
as conveyed by GEORGE CHICKEN by L & R dated 2 & 3 Feb. 1740; & whereas
JAMES KINLOCH died intestate & his only son, FRANCIS, inherited; now he
sells to BLAKE. Witnesses: ROBERT HERIOT, GEORGE GAIRDNER. HERIOT

HERIOT testified before JOHN RATTRAY, J.P. on 20 Apr. 1761. Memorial entered in Auditor's office 4 May 1761 in Book D p. 467, by GEORGE JOHNSTON, Dep. Aud. Recorded 23 June 1761 by WILLIAM HOPTON, Register. Memo: 8 Mar. 1763. At request of FRANCIS KINLOCH the record of the original grants were recorded in Secretary's Office in Book W.W., p. 228, because the old Grant Book was much defaced. WILLIAM HOPTON, Register. Witness: FRANCIS KINLOCH.

Book W-W, p. 734
9 Mar. 1761
Sale

DANIEL DOYLEY, P.M. of SC, to RICHARD STEVENS, planter, of Beaufort at public auction, for Ł 740 currency, 2 lots in Beaufort, Nos. 57 & 62; in pursuance of a writ of fieri facias issued 7 Oct. 1760 to DOYLEY directing him to sell said lots belonging to JAMES THOMSON to satisfy a judgment. Witnesses: JOHN WARD, PETER LEGER, JR. LEGER testified before JAMES GRINDLAY, J.P. on 22 May 1761. Recorded 24 June 1761 by WILLIAM HOPTON, Register.

DEEDS BOOK "X-X"
JUNE 1761 - APRIL 1762

Book X-X, p. 1
4 & 5 May 1761
L & R by Mortgage

THOMAS COULLIETTE, gentleman, of Charleston, to PETER TAYLOR, ESQ., of St. James Goose Creek, & the Rev. MR. JAMES HARRISON, rector of the Parish, attorneys, for the Society for the Propagation of the Gospel in Foreign Parts; as security on bond of even date in penal sum of Ł 1000 for payment of Ł 500 currency, with interest, on 5 May 1762; his undivided half part of 500 a. in Colleton Co., bounding NW on vacant land; other sides on JOHN WANNILL'S Creek or Cypress Swamp; as conveyed to THOMAS COULLIETTE by his mother, MARY COULLIETTE by L & R dated 1 & 2 May 1761. Witnesses: WILLIAM MAZYCK, JOHN MATHEWS. MAZYCK testified before CHARLES PINCKNEY, J.P. on 25 May 1761. Recorded 24 June 1761 by WILLIAM HOPTON, Register. On 25 Mar. 1767 JAMES HARRISON declared mortgage satisfied. Witness: FENWICKE BULL.

Book X-X, p. 11
5 Feb. 1761
Feoffment

CHARLES LEWIS, planter, & MARTHA his wife, of 1st part; & DANIEL LEWIS, planter, & MARY his wife, of 2nd part; convey to JOHN DUTARQUE, of 3rd part, for Ł 700 currency, their 3 tracts, in Craven Co., total 770 a., which SUSANNA LYNCH & GEORGE THREADCRAFT conveyed to the father of CHARLES & DANIEL LEWIS; & the titles conveyed to CHARLES LEWIS by ... BUCKINGHAM & MARY his wife; SAMUEL TYLER & LYDY his wife; BENJAMIN SINGALTERY & SARAH his wife; bounding E & S on Owendaw Creek, on N side PETER COTONEAU; W on the Barony; N on vacant land. Witnesses: MATTHEW CROSS, HENRY BONNEAU, JOHN DUTARQUE, JR. Delivery by turf & twig. Witness: FRANCIS DESCHAMP. DUTARQUE testified before BENJAMIN SIMMONS, J.P. on 27 May 1761. Recorded 25 June 1761 by WILLIAM HOPTON, Register.

Book X-X, p. 13
20 & 21 May 1761
L & R

ELIZABETH PACKROW, widow, to her son, JOHN PACKROW, joiner, both of Charleston, for love & affection, part of lot #115 in Charleston, bounding N 20 ft. on Tradd Street; E 66 ft. on ESTHER WRAND; S on LEWIS MIDDLETON; W on PAUL DOUXSAINT (formerly JONATHAN BADGER). Witnesses: ABRAHAM ROULAIN, JOHN SWINHOLL, JOHN EVANS. ROULAIN testified before ALEXANDER GORDON, J.P., on 28 May 1761. Recorded 26 June 1761 by WILLIAM HOPTON, Register.

Book X-X, p. 19
20 & 21 Aug. 1760
L & R

WILLIAM WIDOS, & MARY (her mark) his wife, to WILLIAM FARRELL, both of Craven Co., for Ł 100 currency, 50 a. on S side Wateree River, bounding NW on WILLIAM PAIN; SE on CORNELIUS MELONE & vacant land; SW on vacant land; being part of a tract granted WILLIAM WIDOS on 8 Nov. 1757 by Gov. WILLIAM HENRY LYTTLETON. Witnesses: JOHN HUDSON (of Bevor Creek, Craven Co.), HUGH BENNET. HUDSON testified before SAMUEL WYLY, J.P. on 25 Aug. 1760. Recorded 9 July 1761 by WILLIAM HOPTON, Register.

Book X-X, p. 24

JOHN (his mark) DICKSON, carpenter, &

138

31 Oct. & 1 Nov. 1758   ELIZABETH (her mark) his wife, to WILLIAM
L & R   SLOAN, planter, both of Craven Co., for Ł 200
                         currency, 300 a. on NE side Wateree River, on
Granys Quarter Creek, Craven Co., bounding on all sides on vacant land;
granted 30 Jan. 1756 by Gov. WILLIAM HENRY LYTTLETON to JOHN DICKSON for
Bounty Land. Witnesses: JOHN ALEXANDER, JOHN HEWITT, JOHN GRAY. HEWITT
testified before SAMUEL WYLY, J.P. of Waterees on 1 Nov. 1758. Recorded
10 July 1761 by WILLIAM HOPTON, Register.

Book X-X, p. 32   ISAAC DACOSTA, shopkeeper, to WILLIAM PINCKNEY,
10 Jan. 1754   ESQ., both of Charleston, for Ł 100 currency,
L & R   150 a. opposite Fredericksburgh Township, in
                       Craven Co., bounding SE on Lake Gibson; NE on
Wateree River; NW & SW on vacant land; according to grant dated 3 Sept.
1761 from Gov. JAMES GLEN. Witnesses: SARAH REID, JOHN PATIENT. PATIENT
testified before THOMAS WRIGHT on 10 Jan. 1754. Recorded 11 July 1761 by
WILLIAM HOPTON, Register.

Book X-X, p. 37   MICHAEL BRANHAM, planter, of Craven Co., &
23 & 24 May 1757   SUSANNAH (her mark), to EDWARD FLINN, black-
L & R   smith, of Fredericksburg Township, Craven Co.,
                       for Ł 200 currency, 100 a. in Fredericksburgh
Township; bounding SW on Wateree River; NW on other part; NE on vacant
land; SE on SAMUEL WYLY; being part of 200 a. granted BRANHAM on 22 Feb.
1745 by Gov. JAMES GLEN. Witnesses: SAMUEL MILHOUS, (a Quaker); WILLIAM
SISSON. MILHOUS testified before SAMUEL WYLY on 26 Feb. 1761. Recorded
11 July 1761 by WILLIAM HOPTON, Register.

Book X-X, p. 46   EDWARD RICHARDSON, of Charleston, assignee of
11 & 12 July 1758   ALEXANDER RATTRAY according to several Acts of
L & R   General Assembly for relief of insolvent debt-
                       ors; to WILLIAM BOYKIN, planter, of Freder-
icksburgh Township, for Ł 143 currency, 200 a. in Fredericksburgh Township originally granted 15 May 1751 by Gov. JAMES GLEN to ANN SHELTON,
(Book E.E. fol. 358); bounding SW on Wateree River; NW on JOHN MCCONNELL;
NE on vacant land; SE on CHARLES RATTLIFF. Whereas ALEXANDER RATTRAY
owed EDWARD RICHARDSON various sums of money who brought suit & had RAT-
TRAY arrested; & RATTRAY petitioned for relief & assigned his real & per-
sonal estate to RICHARDSON; now RICHARDSON sells the 200 a. to BOYKIN.
Witnesses: VINCENT SIMMONS, WILLIAM MASON. MASON testified before JAMES
GRINDLAY, J.P. on 12 July 1758. Recorded 13 July 1761 by WILLIAM HOPTON,
Register.

Book X-X, p. 54   JOSEPH EVANS, planter, & ELIZABETH (her mark)
20 & 21 Feb. 1761   his wife, to JOSEPH KERSHAW, ESQ., both of
L & R   Craven Co., for Ł 100 currency, 250 a. on S
                       side Wateree River; bounding NW on TIMOTHY
PUCKETT & ALEXANDER STEWART; SW on STUART & vacant land; SE on vacant
land; which land was granted EVANS on 4 Sept. 1753. Witnesses: JOHN
CANTEY, SAMUEL KELLY. CANTEY testified before SAMUEL WYLY, J.P. Recorded 13 July 1761, by WILLIAM HOPTON, Register.

Book X-X, p. 60   JOSEPH EVANS, planter, & ELIZABETH (her mark)
20 & 21 Feb. 1761   his wife, to JOSEPH KERSHAW, ESQ., both of
L & R   Craven Co., for Ł 150 currency, 400 a. on S
                       side Wateree River, bounding on all sides on
vacant land; according to grant to EVANS dated 4 Sept. 1753 from Gov.
JAMES GLEN. Witnesses: JOHN CANTEY, SAMUEL KELLY. CANTEY testified before SAMUEL WYLY, J.P. Recorded 14 July 1761 by WILLIAM HOPTON, Register.

Book X-X, p. 65   WILLIAM PINCKNEY, ESQ., of Charleston, to
7 & 8 Nov. 1760   ISAAC PIDGEON, planter, of the Waterees, for
L & R   Ł 300 currency, 2 tracts on S side Wateree
                       River, in Craven Co.; 1 of 66 a., bounding NW
on JAMES OUSLEY; SE on ALEXANDER MITCHELL (now WILLIAM PINCKNEY); SW on
vacant land; granted the Hon. CHARLES PINCKNEY 9 Feb. 1749; 1 of 150 a.,
opposite Fredericksburgh Township, in Craven Co., bounding SE on LUKE
GIBSON; NE on Wateree River; NW & SW on vacant land; as granted to ALEX-
ANDER MITCHELL on 6 Aug. 1750. Witnesses: WILLIAM MAZYCK, JORDAN ROCHE.

MAZYCK testified 16 July 1761 before CHARLES PINCKNEY, J.P. Recorded 16 July 1761 by WILLIAM HOPTON, Register.

Book X-X, p. 73
20 May 1761
Confirmation

JOHN RUTLEDGE, II, ESQ., of Charleston, to BENJAMIN CHAPLIN, planter, of St. Helena. Whereas the Lords Proprs. on 20 Jan. 1710 granted EDWARD HEXT & HUGH HEXT 640 a., which by a resurvey were found to be 740 a., on St. Helena Island, Granville Co., bounding N on other lands belonging to EDWARD & HUGH HEXT; W on Port Royal River the less; other parts on broken islands, creeks & marshes of St. Helena Hunting Islands; & whereas HUGH dies & EDWARD became sole owner as surviving joint tenant, & by a certain codicil to his will bequeathed the tract to SARAH, wife of JOHN RUTLEDGE, of Berkeley Co. (mother & father of JOHN RUTLEDGE, party hereto); & whereas, JOHN & SARAH RUTLEDGE, by L & R dated 5 & 6 June, 1746, sold the tract, to JOHN CHAPLIN (father of BENJAMIN) & JOSEPH JENKINS, planters, then of St. Helena; & by a partition between CHAPLIN & JENKINS, CHAPLIN received 370 a., of which he devised to his son, BENJAMIN, 170 a. to the N line & E line towards the Hunting Island; but BENJAMIN wishing to have his title confirmed by JOHN RUTLEDGE, eldest son of JOHN & SARAH; now JOHN releases to BENJAMIN all claim to the 170 a. Witnesses: JOHN PACKROW, HUGH RUTLEDGE. RUTLEDGE testified 8 June 1761 before ALEXANDER GORDON, J.P. Recorded 17 July 1761 by WILLIAM HOPTON, Register.

Book X-X, p. 77
20 May 1761
Confirmation

JOHN RUTLEDGE, ESQ., of Charleston, to JOHN CHAPLIN, planter, of St. Helena. Whereas the Lords Proprs. on 20 Jan. 1710 granted EDWARD HEXT & HUGH HEXT 640 a. (actually 740 a.; see p. 73), of which EDWARD HEXT became sole owner as surviving joint tenant; & by a certain codicil to his will bequeathed the land to SARAH, wife of JOHN RUTLEDGE, of Berkeley Co., (mother & father of JOHN, their eldest son, party hereto); & they on 5 & 6 June 1746 sold the tract to JOHN CHAPLIN (father of JOHN) & JOSEPH JENKINS, planter, then of St. Helena; & whereas by equal partition of the land JOHN CHAPLIN received 370 a. & devised to his son, JOHN, party hereto, 200 a. on the N line, butting on JOHN FINDIN'S land; N on the part devised to his son BENJAMIN CHAPLIN; to the E divided by a N line there from; W on Beaufort River; S on JOSEPH JENKINS; but JOHN CHAPLIN wishing to have his title confirmed by JOHN RUTLEDGE, eldest son of SARAH; now RUTLEDGE releases all his claim to the 200 a. in favor of CHAPLIN. Witnesses: JOHN PACKROW, HUGH RUTLEDGE. RUTLEDGE testified before ALEXANDER GORDON, J.P. 8 June 1761. Recorded 18 July 1761 by WILLIAM HOPTON, Register.

Book X-X, p. 82
20 May 1761
Confirmation

JOHN RUTLEDGE, eldest son of SARAH & JOHN RUTLEDGE, releases to JOSEPH JENKINS, all claim 20 370 a. at St. Helena (see p. 73, 77, for details); bounding N on BENJAMIN CHAPLIN; & JOHN CHAPLIN; W on Beaufort River; E on marsh & St. Philips Hunting Island. Witnesses: JOHN PACKROW, HUGH RUTLEDGE. RUTLEDGE testified before ALEXANDER GORDON, J.P., on 8 June 1761. Recorded 20 July 1761 by WILLIAM HOPTON, Register.

Book X-X, p. 87
23 & 24 May 1755
L & R

JAMES HENDRICK, planter, of Colleton Co., conditional devisee of will of, ROYAL SPRY, planter; & ELIZABETH his wife; to DR. JAMES REID, practitioner in physic, with the consent of SAMUEL SPRY, acting executor; for Ł 1200 currency, 329 a. in Colleton Co., bounding N on SAMUEL LOWLE; W on Penny's Creek; out of PonPon River; S on WILLIAM FERGUSON; E on THOMAS SACHEVEREL. Whereas ROYAL SPRY by will dated 17 Dec. 1746 bequeathed to his nephew, JAMES HENDRICK, 329 a. formerly belonging to DANIEL HENDRICK, father of JAMES, but now belonging to ROYAL SPRY; adjoining N on CASWELL'S lands then in possession of THOMAS SACHEVEREL; W on Penny's Creek; S on FERGUSON; E on DR. MITCHELL; upon the condition that JAMES HENDRICK pay SPRY'S executors Ł 1000 currency; & appointed BARNABY REILY, SAMUEL SPRY, HENRY SPRY, JOHN BEE & THOMAS SACHEVEREL his executors; & whereas JAMES HENDRICK on 10 this inst. May paid SAMUEL SPRY, acting executor, the Ł 1000 currency; now he sells the land to REID. Witnesses: WILLIAM DONNON, SAMUEL SPRY, SAMUEL LOWLE. LOWLE testified before JAMES BULLOCK on 9 Mar. 1757. Recorded 21 July 1761 by WILLIAM HOPTON, Register.

Book X-X, p. 98   THOMAS FORD, planter, of St. Bartholomews Par-
30 Apr. & 1 May 1760   ish, Colleton Co., executor of will of JOHN
L & R   VINSON; to JAMES SHARP, ESQ., of Colleton Co.,
                       for Ł 146 currency, lot #14 in Jacksonburgh;
bounding 100 ft. on King Street; 218 ft. deep; which by L & R dated 5 & 6
Mar. 1757 was sold by JEAN HARTLY & GEORGE JACKSON, executrix & executor
of will of CAPT. JOHN JACKSON to JOHN VINSON; who, by his will dated 9
Apr. 1758, ordered the remainder of his real & personal estate sold by
his executors. Witnesses: JOSEPH GLOVER, JAMES STOBO, JR., JOHN MITCHELL.
STOBO testified before THOMAS SACHEVERELL, J.P. on 18 Aug. 1760. Recorded 22 July 1761 by WILLIAM HOPTON, Register.

Book X-X, p. 104   JAMES NEWTON, planter, of St. Bartholomews
19 & 20 May 1760   Parish, Colleton Co., eldest son of JOHN NEW-
L & R   TON, planter, of Colleton Co., of 1st part;
                       ISAAC NEWTON, planter, of Colleton Co., third
son of JOHN NEWTON, of 2nd part; JAMES SHARP, of same Parish, of 3rd part.
Whereas JOHN NEWTON by will dated 23 Mar. 1744 bequeathed to his second
son, JOSEPH, 300 a. lying S & SW of his plantation & 1/4 his remaining
personal estate, & directed that each son should take possession upon
reaching age of 19; all of his children to live together on the plantation until that age; in case of death of any 1 of them his share to be
equally divided amongst the others; & whereas JOSEPH died before complet-
ing his 21st year & these parties are convinced that testator intended
that the real & personal estate of said deceased child should be divided
amongst the survivors but legally JOSEPH'S 300 a. became vested in JAMES,
ISAAC, & MARY (now wife of JAMES SHARP) as tenants in common for life
only, the reversion to be in (JAMES, the eldest brother); & whereas JAMES
SHARP being in possession of the 300 a. as tenants in common for life by
right of his wife, MARY, has purchased the right & interest of JAMES &
ISAAC in the land; now he pays JAMES & ISAAC NEWTON Ł 450 currency for
the 300 a. in Colleton Co., bounding NW on MOSES MARTIN & JAMES NEWTON;
NE on JAMES NEWTON & heirs of JOSEPH BOONE; SE on WILLIAM LITTLE; SW on
THOMAS ELLIOTT & THOMAS BRADWELL. Witnesses: JOHN ELIAS HUTCHINSON, WIL-
LIAM CARTWRIGHT, WILLIAM JACKSON. JACKSON testified before THOMAS
SACHEVERELL, J.P. Recorded 23 July 1761 by WILLIAM HOPTON, Register.

Book X-X, p. 113   HENRY ELLIOTT FAIRCHILD, to JAMES REID, both
10 & 11 Oct. 1760   of Colleton Co., for Ł 500 currency, 250 a.,
L & R   part of 500 a. which JOHN MCCAW had purchased
                       from ABRAHAM MESHUE & on 15 Dec. 1744 gave
part, or 250 a., to said FAIRCHILD; bounding E on JAMES REID (formerly
HENRY MASHOW); SW on MAURICE WILLIAMS; W on ELIZABETH SNIPE; NE on JAMES
POSTELL. Witnesses: ARCHIBALD STOBO, MOSES DARQUIER, JOHN MITCHELL.
STOBO testified before JAMES SHARP, J.P. Recorded 24 July 1761 by WIL-
LIAM HOPTON, Register.

Book X-X , p. 119   JAMES SKIRVING, ESQ., to DAVID FERGUSON,
22 & 23 Dec. 1760   planter, both of St. Bartholomew's Parish,
L & R   Colleton Co., for Ł 2000 currency, 550-3/4 a.
                       in St. Bartholomew's Parish, bounding W on
TOBIAS FORD; S on JAMES HAMILTON; E on PETER RUMPF; NE on ROBERT REID &
vacant land. Witnesses: JOHN CHAMPNEYS, ARCHIBALD STOBO, JAMES SKIRVING,
JR. STOBO testified before JAMES SHARP, J.P. on 10 Mar. 1761. Recorded
25 July 1761 by WILLIAM HOPTON, Register.

Book X-X, p. 126   ABRAHAM CROUCH, of Charleston, & CATHERINE his
30 & 31 May 1758   wife, to BENJAMIN EVERITT, planter, of the
L & R   Congarees, for Ł 120 currency, 200 a. on N
                       side Santee River (Congaree River); bounding N
W on heirs of JACOB YOUNG; NE & SE on vacant land. Witnesses: ISAAC
PORCHER, JOHN GAILLARD, BARTHOLOMEW GAILLARD. BARTHOLOMEW GAILLARD tes-
tified 23 Jan. 1759 before MOSES THOMPSON, J.P. Recorded 27 July 1761 by
WILLIAM HOPTON, Register.

Book X-X, p. 131   THOMAS SMITH, tavern-keeper, of Johns Island,
5 & 6 June 1761   Colleton Co., to EBENEZER SIMMONS, JR., of
L & R by Mortgage   Charleston, as security on bond of even date
                       in penal sum of Ł 1400 for payment of Ł 700
currency, with interest, on 6 June 1762; 200 a. in St. Johns Parish,

Colleton Co., which he had purchased from GEORGE SCOTT. Witness: JOHN STANYARNE. Before WILLIAM BOONE 9 June 1761. Recorded 28 July 1761 by WILLIAM HOPTON, Register. On 24 Apr. 1762 EBENEZER SIMMONS, JR. declared the 200 a. sold by DANIEL DOLLOY, P.M., & mortgage discharged but not the bond as not enough money was obtained by the sale. Witness: WILLIAM HOPTON.

Book X-X, p. 138   JOSEPH PRINCE, planter, of Prince George Par-
19 Nov. 1755   ish, Craven Co., to JOSEPH CANNON, otherwise
Gift   Prince, natural son of JOSEPH PRINCE by SARAH
                       CANNON, for love & affection, 300 a. in Prince
George Parish, bounding E on the seashore; W on vacant land; N & S on
heirs of CAPT. GEORGE SMITH; granted by Gov. JAMES GLEN on 2 Jan. 1754;
with all houses & buildings, plate, money, household stuff, Negroes & all
his personal estate; upon condition that JOSEPH PRINCE, the elder, have
the use for his natural life; & after the death of JOSEPH, the elder, his
present wife, ELIZABETH MARY, to be paid an annuity of ₤ 300 currency out
of the estate. SUSANNAH the daughter of SARAH (now wife of BENJAMIN
SINGLETARY; lately SARAH LEWIS) & natural daughter of said JOSEPH CANNON,
otherwise PRINCE, by said SARAH, to have a Negro girl named CORSBY either
on her wedding day or 21st birthday. Witnesses: ABEL POOLEY, WILLIAM
TRUSLER, JAMES ALLEN. POOLEY testified before JAMES SKIRVING, J.P. on 21
Nov. 1755. Recorded 29 July 1761 by WILLIAM HOPTON, Register.

Book X-X, p. 143   JAMES REID, ESQ., of Charleston, to JARED NEIL-
12 June 1761   SON, of St. John's Parish, Santee, for ₤ 1250
Release   currency, 6 a. bounding N on GEORGE BEAIRD; E
                       on JAMES REID; W on JARED NEILSON (formerly
JAMES BEAIRD); S on Santee River; being part of 1400 a. originally grant-
ed to PHEBE PETERS in Craven Co. Witnesses: JOHN MAXWELL, MACARTAN CAMP-
BELL, JOHN GLEN. Payment made by hand of JOHN MAXWELL, executor of JAMES
BEAIRD. GLEN testified before JAMES PARSONS, J.P. on 17 June 1761. Re-
corded 30 July 1761 by WILLIAM HOPTON, Register.

Book X-X, p. 147   JOHN MAXWELL, only acting executor of will of
12 June 1761   JAMES BEAIRD, planter, of Santee, to JARED
Release   NEILSON, of St. John's Parish, Santee, Berke-
                       ley Co., for ₤ 5200 currency, 500 a. in St.
John's Parish, Santee, bounding N on Santee River; W & S on vacant land;
E on THOMAS LYNCH (formerly the Hon. JAMES KINLOCH); which 500 a. were
originally granted to MARY BETTESON; who assigned to GEORGE BEAIRD who
devised to his son JAMES BEAIRD; also 50 a., the W part of 200 a., granted 4 Dec. 1735 to GEORGE BEAIRD, bounding N on vacant land; W on 200 a.
lately belonging to JAMES BEAIRD; E on remainder belonging to GEORGE
BEAIRD; S on a small piece granted JAMES BEAIRD; also said 200 a. granted
JAMES BEAIRD on 21 May 1757, bounding N on vacant land; W & S on WILLIAM
JAMIESON; E on said 50 a.; also 8-1/2 a., the W part of 14-1/2 a. granted
on 21 May 1757 to JAMES BEAIRD; bounding N on said 50 a.; E on remainder
of 14-1/2 a. claimed by JAMES REID; W on WILLIAM JAMIESON; S on Santee
River; the last mentioned tracts being in Craven Co.; all of which tracts
JAMES BEAIRD by will dated 23 Apr. 1758 ordered his executors to sell,
appointing as his executors JAMES MAXWELL, SR., JAMES MAXWELL, JR., MAT-
THEW NEILSON, RICHARD RICHARDSON, & JOHN MAXWELL. Witnesses: MACARTAN
CAMPBELL, JOHN GLEN, JAMES REID, JAMES PARSON. GLEN testified 18 June
1761 before ALEXANDER GORDON, J.P. Recorded 1 Aug. 1761 by WILLIAM HOP-
TON, Register.

Book X-X, p. 152   JOHN HALES (HALE), cooper, of Charleston, eld-
1 & 2 June 1761   est son & heir of ELIZABETH HALE, widow, to
L & R   JOSIAS DUPREE, planter, of St. James Santee,
                       for ₤ 425 currency, 500 a. in Craven Co.,
bounding SW on Tibwin Creek; NE on LEWIS MOUZON; NW on vacant land &
STEPHEN SEAVEY; SE on marsh of the seashore. Whereas the Lords Proprs.
on 23 July 1711 granted BENJAMIN WEBB, planter, of Charleston, 500 a. in
Craven Co., then bounding N on CAPT. COLLINGS; which by will dated 5 Oct.
1734 he bequeathed to his grand-daughter ELIZABETH PEIRCEY, who later
married JOHN HALES by whom she had, JOHN HALES the elder, party hereto, &
WILLIAM JACKSON HALES, the younger; & whereas ELIZABETH HALES died intestate, as did her husband in her lifetime, & JOHN inherited; now he sells
to DUPREE. Witnesses: SAMUEL MOUZON, GEORGE MANUELL, JR., HENRY VIDEAU.

VIDEAU testified 18 June 1761 before ALEXANDER GORDON, J.P. Recorded 3 Aug. 1761 by WILLIAM HOPTON, Register.

Book X-X, p. 158   JOHN ARMBRISTER, baker, & MARY ELIZABETH his
15 & 16 June 1761   wife, to JOHN PERDRIAN, saddler, both of
L & R   Charléston, for Ł 3200 currency, part of a lot
in Charleston bounding E ... ft. on JAMES ROL-
LIN & JANE DUPUY; W 43-1/2 ft. on Meeting Street; S on JAMES LAURENS,
STEPHEN MILLER, & JAMES ROLLIN; N 135 ft. on JAMES EDE. Witnesses: JAMES
TONGE, JAMES SIMMONS. SIMMONS testified 20 June 1761 before ALEXANDER
GORDON, J.P. Recorded 6 Aug. 1761 by WILLIAM HOPTON, Register.

Book X-X, p. 164   JOHN PERDRIAU, saddler, & ESTHER his wife, to
15 & 16 June 1761   GABRIEL MANIGAULT, merchant, both of Charles-
L & R by Mortgage   ton, as security on bond of even date in penal
sum of Ł 4400 for payment of Ł 2200 currency,
with interest, on 16 June 1762, the part of the lot to be purchased from
JOHN ARMBRISTER (see p. 158). Witnesses: JAMES TONGE, JAMES SIMMONS.
Recorded 7 Aug. 1761 by WILLIAM HOPTON, Register. On 26 May 1762 MANI-
GAULT declared mortgage satisfied. Witness: WILLIAM DOCKWRAY.

Book X-X, p. 171   ADAM WOOD, P.M., to DR. ALEXANDER FOTHERING-
20 Oct. 1759   HAM, of Dorchester Town, at public auction,
Sale   for Ł 112:12:6 currency, lot #95 & part of lot
#96 in Dorchester. Whereas FREDERICK HOLZEN-
DORF, saddler, owned a 1/4 a. lot #95, & that part of lot #96 adjoining
lot #95 & measuring 20 x 155 ft.; & whereas MAURICE HARVEY & ROBERT
PHILP, merchants, obtained a judgment against HOLZENDORF for Ł 1540:13:6
SC money & costs & a writ of fieri facias was issued by PETER LEIGH, C.J.
on 4 Oct. 1757, directing the P.M. to levy these amounts against HOLZEN-
DORF'S estate; now WOOD sells the 2 lots to FOTHERINGHAM. Witnesses:
SAMUEL HAMLIN, JOHN JACKSON. HAMLIN testified 31 May 1762 before JOHN
IOOR, J.P. Recorded 7 Aug. 1761 by WILLIAM HOPTON, Register.

Book X-X, p. 175   JAMES CHARLES FREDERICK HOLZENDORFF, saddler,
28 & 29 Nov. 1760   of Charleston, & MARY ANNE (her mark) his
L & R   wife, to DR. ALEXANDER FOTHERINGHAM of Dor-
chester, for Ł 240 currency, lots #96 & #97 in
Dorchester; #96 being 44 x 155 ft.; lot #97 being 1/4 a., bounding E on
George Street; S on ELIJAH POSTELL; W on another street; N on ALEXANDER
FOTHERINGHAM & part of lot #96; which 2 1/4 a. lots, #96 & #97, CHARLES
LOWNDES, P.M., sold HOLZENDORFF on 7 Apr. 1755. Witnesses: ARCHIBALD MC-
NEILL, BENJAMIN GUERARD. MCNEILL testified 26 Mar. 1762 before JOHN
SKENE, J.P. Recorded 8 Aug. 1761 by WILLIAM HOPTON, Register.

Book X-X, p. 182   SARAH SIMPSON, widow, of Charleston, to THOMAS
30 & 31 Jan. 1758   FULLER, planter, of St. Andrews Parish, Berke-
L & R by Mortgage   ley Co., administrator of will of WILLIAM FUL-
LER the elder, planter; 550 a. on S side Ash-
ley River which she had purchased by L & R dated 27 & 28 this inst. Jan.;
bounding E & SE on JOHN CATTELL; N & NE on marsh, the high road, & on
BENJAMIN CATTELL; NW, W & S on JOHN ANGIER & the high road; S on BENJAMIN
FULLER. Whereas WILLIAM FULLER, the elder, by will dated 30 Aug. 1731
bequeathed to his daughter SARAH, now SARAH SIMPSON, the use of Ł 750
proclamation money during her lifetime, she giving good security to his
executors, appointing his kinsman, WILLIAM CATTELL, & his son RICHARD
FULLER; & whereas after the death of WILLIAM CATTELL & RICHARD FULLER,
letters of administration were granted THOMAS FULLER, son of said RICHARD,
& eldest grandson of WILLIAM, & he gave SARAH the sum of Ł 750 proclamation money; for which she gives the above property as security. Witnesses: ELIZABETH LANDER, DANIEL HORRY, THOMAS LAMBOLL. Recorded 8 Aug. 1761
by WILLIAM HOPTON, Register.

Book X-X, p. 194   JOHN PACKROW, cabinet-maker, of Charleston,
23 June 1761   gave bond to DAVID BOILLAT, shop-keeper, in
Bond   penal sum of Ł 600 currency, because BOILLAT
went on PACKROW'S bond of even date to THOMAS
CORKER, merchant, for payment of Ł 300 currency, with interest, on 23
June 1762. Witnesses: MATTHEW YUTS, A. GORDON. Recorded 10 Aug. 1761 by
WILLIAM HOPTON, Register.

Book X-X, p. 196   JOHN PACKROW, cabinet-maker, to DAVID BOILLAT,
22 & 23 June 1761   as security on above bond, part of lot #115 in
L & R   Charleston, bounding N 20 ft. on Tradd Street;
                          E 66 ft. on ESTHER WRAND; S on LEWIS MIDDLETON;
W on JONATHAN BADGER (now PAUL DOUXSAINT). Witnesses: MATTHEW YUTZ, A.
GORDON. Recorded 18 Aug. 1761 by WILLIAM HOPTON, Register.

Book X-X, p. 204   WILLIAM TREDWELL BULL, to HUGH HEXT, ESQ.,
4 May 1723   both of St. Pauls Parish, Colleton Co., for
Sale   Ł 1500 currency, 400 a. Whereas the Lords
                          Proprs. by Gov. ROBERT GIBBES on 13 Jan. 1710
or 1711 granted SAMUEL EVANS 400 a.; which SAMUEL EVANS & ANNE his wife,
on 29 Aug. 1712 conveyed to HENRY NICHOLS; who, with HANNAH his wife, on
9 Feb. 1712 (or 1713) sold to THOMAS ROSE; who, with ELIZABETH his wife,
on 31 July 1718 sold to ELIZABETH NAIRNE; who, on 22 Mar. 1718 (1719)
sold to BULL, party hereto. Witnesses: THOMAS JOHN ELLIOTT, WILLIAM
FLECKNOW, JOHN (his mark) FREEMAN. FLECKNOW & FREEMAN testified 6 May
1723 before JOHN FENWICKE, J.P. Recorded 20 Aug. 1761 by WILLIAM HOPTON,
Register.

Book X-X, p. 208   JANE BOONE, widow, to SAMUEL CARSAN, merchant,
11 Mar. 1761   both of Charleston, for 3 years, at Ł 350 cur-
Lease for 3 Years   rency a year, the house on S side Tradd Street,
                          now occupied by CARSON & SWALLOW, merchants,
bounding E on JOHN STONE, block maker (now occupied by THOMAS STONE, the
younger, merchant; W on JACOB MOTTE the younger (now occupied by WILLIAM
BURROWS, ESQ.); S on THOMAS CAPERS the elder. Witnesses: THOMAS VARDELL,
JAMES CARSON (administrator of SAMUEL CARSAN, merchant). On 22 June 1761
JAMES CARSON, administrator, for Ł 5, assigns the lease to NEWMAN SWALLOW,
merchant. Witnesses: THOMAS STONE, JR., THOMAS LISTON. Recorded 20 Aug.
1761 by WILLIAM HOPTON, Register.

Book X-X, p. 212   JOHN WATIES, planter, & ELIZABETH his wife, to
23 & 24 Feb. 1759   JOSEPH ALLSTON, planter, both of Prince George
L & R   Parish, Craven Co., for Ł 300 currency, 500 a.
                          in NC, bounding N on MR. PINSON; E on a branch
of Little River; S on WILLIAM ALLSTON. Witnesses: ANN ROTHMAHLER, SAMUEL
WRAGG. WRAGG testified on 29 June 1761 before GEORGE GABRIEL POWELL,
J.P. Recorded 22 Aug. 1761 by WILLIAM HOPTON, Register.

Book X-X, p. 216   JOHN WATIES, planter, & ELIZABETH his wife, to
23 & 24 Feb. 1759   JOSEPH ALLSTON, planter, both of Prince George
L & R   Parish, Craven Co., for Ł 300 SC money, 300 a.
                          in Craven Co., bounding N on THOMAS WATIES; E
on Waccamaw River; S on MR. BROUGHTON; W on vacant land. Witnesses: ANN
ROTHMAHLER, SAMUEL WRAGG. WRAGG testified on 29 June 1761 before GEORGE
GABRIEL POWELL, J.P. Recorded 22 Aug. 1761 by WILLIAM HOPTON, Register.

Book X-X, p. 220   JOHN WATIES, planter, & ELIZABETH His wife, to
23 & 24 Feb. 1759   JOSEPH ALLSTON, planter, both of Prince George
L & R   Parish, Craven Co., for Ł 2500 SC money, ·1150
                          a. in Craven Co., bequeathed to JOHN WATIES by
his father WILLIAM WATIES; bounding E on salt marsh; S on JOSEPH ALLSTON;
W on Waccamaw River; N on ALEXANDER MONTGOMERY (formerly JOHN GOVAN).
Witnesses: ANN ROTHMAHLER, SAMUEL WRAGG. WRAGG testified 29 June 1761 before GEORGE POWELL, J.P. Recorded 22 Aug. 1761 by WILLIAM HOPTON, Register.

Book X-X, p. 227   CHRISTOPHER WILKINSON, JR., of Colleton Co., &
4 & 5 Apr. 1759   ELIZABETH his wife (heir to MARY HILL, widow,
L & R   to whom the land was granted), to ROBERT PAIS-
                          LEY, SR., for Ł 600 currency, 600 a. in Craven
Co., bounding SW on WILLIAM SNOW; NW on vacant land; NE & NW on RICHARD
SINGLETON, JR., (now ALEXANDER MCNIGHT); NE & SE on vacant land. Wit-
nesses: FRANCIS WILKINSON, DANIEL HOUGH, EDWARD WILKINSON, JR. EDWARD
WILKINSON testified 5 Apr. 1759 before FRANCIS YONGE, J.P. Memorial en-
tered in Auditor's Book D, p. 477 on 6 July 1761 by RICHARD LAMBTON, Dep.
Aud. Recorded 26 Aug. 1761 by WILLIAM HOPTON, Register.

Book X-X, p. 234   ALEXANDER SCOTT, planter, of Craven Co., &

7 & 8 June 1759
L & R
MARGARET (her mark) his wife, to ROBERT PAIS-
LEY, of Prince Frederick Parish, for Ⱡ 100
currency, 100 a. in Craven Co., on S side of
swamp that runs into Lynch's Lake; bounding on all sides on vacant land.
Before JOHN PACKER (PARKER?), ISABEL SCOTT. PACKER testified 20 Oct.
1759 before JOHN LIVISTON, J.P. Memorial entered in Auditor's Book, D,
p. 477, on 6 July 1761 by RICHARD LAMBTON, Dep. Aud. Recorded 27 Aug.
1761 by WILLIAM HOPTON, Register.

Book X-X, p. 240
12 Feb. 1754
Feoffment
WILLIAM ELLIOTT, planter, of Berkeley Co., to
JOSEPH FULLER, planter, for Ⱡ 1896 currency,
237 a., bounding SW on THOMAS DRAYTON; N & NW
on HUMPHREY ELLIOTT; E on public road & WIL-
LIAM ELLIOTT; S on JOSEPH ELLIOTT. Plat given. Witnesses: HUMPHREY
ELLIOTT, WILLIAM BONNEAU. Possession given by turf & twig. BONNEAU tes-
tified 16 Feb. 1760 before JEREMIAH SAVAGE, J.P. Memorial entered in
Auditor's Book D, #4, p. 454, by JOHN PATIENT for JOHN BASNETT, Pro. Dep.
Aud. Recorded 29 Aug. 1761 by ALEXANDER GORDON, D.P.R.

Book X-X, p. 242
18 Oct. 1708
Release
FRANCIS GRACIA, joiner, & ELIZABETH his wife,
to COL. GEORGE LOGAN, ESQ., both of Charles-
ton, for Ⱡ 110 currency, the 460 a., English
measure, in Berkeley Co., on SE side Wando
River, granted 11 May 1699 by WILLIAM, Earl of Craven, Palatine, & the
Lords Proprs. to FRANCIS GRACIA; bounding NE on a creek; SE on a creek; W
& SW on GEORGE LOGAN. Witnesses: JOHN ABRAHAM MOTTE, JOHN HOLLAND, THOM-
AS HEPWORTH. Livery & seizin declared. On 9 July 1761 JACOB MOTTE, son
of said JOHN ABRAHAM MOTTE, recognized his father's signature before
ALEXANDER GORDON, J.P. Recorded 29 Aug. 1761 by WILLIAM HOPTON, Regis-
ter.

Book X-X, p. 248
28 Dec. 1706
Release
THOMAS CARY, to COL. GEORGE LOGAN, of Charleston, for Ⱡ 400 currency, 620 a., English measure, in Berkeley Co., known as Wando Neck,
bounding W & N on Wando River; E on FRANCIS
GRACIA & vacant land; S on THOMAS LYNCH; as granted to CARY by JOHN, Lord
Granville, Palatine, & the Lords Proprs., by Gov. NATHANIEL JOHNSON; also
all buildings, neat cattle, sheep, hogs, plantation tools, carts, plows,
harrows, etc. CARY appoints THOMAS BARTON, gentleman, of Berkeley Co.,
his attorney to execute this deed. Witnesses: JOHN ABRAHAM MOTTE, JAMES
INGERSON, HENRY WIGINGTON. On 3 Nov. 1707 BARTON delivered livery &
seizin. Witnesses: JOHN BOONE, BENJAMIN QUELCH, JOHN ABRAHAM MOTTE, PE-
TER BOWDON, JOHN STRODE. On 9 July 1761 JACOB MOTTE, son of JOHN ABRAHAM
MOTTE, recognized his father's signature before ALEXANDER GORDON, J.P.
Registered in book G. p. 238, on 2 Aug. 1711. Entered in Auditor's
Office 24 May 1733. Recorded 2 Sept. 1761 by WILLIAM HOPTON, Register.

Book X-X, p. 254
11 May 1699
Grant
Whereas WILLIAM, Earl of Craven, Palatine;
JOHN, Earl of Bath; ANTHONY, Lord Ashley;
GEORGE, Lord Carteret; SIR JOHN COLLETON, Bar-
onet; & THOMAS AMY, ESQ., Lords Proprs., on
31 Aug. 1694 impowered Gov. JOHN ARCHDALE & 3 or more deputies, to settle
the method of granting & selling lands; therefore, JOSEPH BLAKE, Gov. of
SC, according to such adopted method, granted FRANCIS GRACIA 460 a., Eng-
lish measure. Signed: EDMUND BELLINGER, JAMES MOORE, JOSEPH BLAKE, JO-
SEPH MORTON. Recorded 2 Sept. 1761 by WILLIAM HOPTON, Register.

Book X-X, p. 256
6 Nov. 1704
Grant
Whereas JOHN, Lord Granville; Palatine; WIL-
LIAM, Lord Craven; JOHN, Lord Carteret: MAU-
RICE ASHLEY, ESQ.; SIR JOHN COLLETON, Baronet;
& the Lords Proprs., on 18 June 1702 impowered
Gov. NATHANIEL JOHNSTON, JAMES MOORE, NICHOLAS TROTT, & JOB HOWES, ESQRS.,
or any 3 of them, to grant lands; now TROTT, JOHNSTON, HOWES, ESQRS., or
any 3 of them, to' grant lands; now TROTT, JOHNSTON, HOWES, & MOORE grant
COL. THOMAS CARY 620 a., English measure, in Berkeley Co. Copy of orig-
inal plat made 10 Sept. 1704 by JOB HOWES, Sur. Gen., showing boundaries;
W & N on Wando River; E on FRANCIS GRACIA & vacant land; S on THOMAS
LYNCH.

Book X-X, p. 257
JOHN CATTELL, planter, (son of PETER) of St.

14 & 15 July 1761   George Parish, Berkeley Co., to SARAH MIDDLE-
L & R   TON, widow of the Hon. ARTHUR MIDDLETON, as
                           security on bond of even date in penal sum of
Ł 5000 for payment of Ł 2500 currency, with interest, on 15 July 1762;
for the use of MORTON WILKINSON (son of FRANCIS), of St. Paul's Parish;
350 a. in Berkeley Co., bounding E on SAMUEL WRAGG; W on RALPH IZARD; N
on CAPT. WILLIAM DOUGLAS; S on WILLIAM CATTELL. Witnesses: CATHERINE
BROWN, ALEXANDER WILSON. CATHERINE BROWN testified 15 July 1761 before
HENRY MIDDLETON, J.P. Recorded 4 Sept. 1761 by WILLIAM HOPTON, Register.

Book X-X, p. 264   SEDGWICK LEWIS, planter, of St. James Goose
18 June 1761   Creek, Berkeley Co., to THOMAS SMITH, mer-
Release   chant, of Charleston, for Ł 2500 SC money,
                           part of lot in Charleston, bounding E 50 ft.
on Church Street; W on WILLIAM ROPER; N 245 ft. on ISAAC GODIN; S on JOHN
MILLER. Witnesses: BENJAMIN WARING, JR., JAMES MOULTRIE. WARING testified before BENJAMIN SMITH, J.P. on 11 July 1761. Recorded 6 Sept. 1761
by WILLIAM HOPTON, Register.

Book X-X, p. 270   GEORGE CHICKEN, planter, to JAMES KINLOCH,
3 Feb. 1740   ESQ., for Ł 1250 currency, 275 a. in St. James
Sale   Goose Creek Parish, part of the tract on which
                           CHICKEN now lives, bounding NE & SE on GEORGE
CHICKEN; NW & S on JAMES KINLOCH. Witnesses: FRANCIS KINLOCH, PHILIP
TOWLER. KINLOCH testified on 4 Apr. 1761 before JOHN RATTRAY, J.P. Recorded 28 Sept. 1761 by WILLIAM HOPTON, Register. Plat certified 4 Jan.
1740/1 by GEORGE HUNTER.

Book X-X, p. 273   ROGER SAUNDERS, planter, of Berkeley Co., &
15 Mar. 1722   ESTHER his wife (lately called ESTHER EDGELL,
Release   widow of RICHARD EDGELL, planter), to JAMES
                           KINLOCH, ESQ., of Berkeley Co., for Ł 1000
currency, 670 a., English measure, in Berkeley Co., bounding NW on JOHN
FLOOD; E on MR. SINGLETON; S on JOHN STRIDE; according to plat dated 14
May 1707; also 500 a., English measure, in Berkeley Co., bounding SW on
MR. SINGLETON; NW on vacant land; NE on THOMAS SPARKS, according to plat
dated 23 July 1707. Whereas Gov. NATHANIEL JOHNSON on 14 Mar. 1707 granted THOMAS JONES 670 a., English measure, in Berkeley Co.; which he, on 14
Mar. 1707, for Ł 120 currency, sold to THOMAS PARKS & ROBERT CHAMBERS;
who, on 8 Oct. 1714, sold to RICHARD EDGELL; who by will dated 10 Dec.
1711, bequeathed the tract to his wife, ESTHER (now wife of ROGER SAUN-
DERS);& whereas Gov. ROBERT GIBBES on 23 July 1711 granted JOHN WARD
500 a., English measure, in Berkeley Co.; which he, & his wife, FRANCES,
on 26 July 1716, for Ł 110 SC money conveyed to ROGER SAUNDERS; now he &
his wife sell the 2 tracts to JAMES KINLOCH. Witnesses: JOHN GOUGH,
JAMES NARINE. Entered in Auditor's Office 2 May 1733. On 21 Sept. 1761
ANNE SCOTT recognized the signature of JOHN GOUGH before FRANCIS KINLOCH,
J.P. Recorded 29 Sept. 1761 by WILLIAM HOPTON, Register.

Book X-X, p. 283   JOHN MARTIN, to WILLIAM MCCANTS, both of Col-
24 & 25 Apr. 1761   leton Co., for Ł 800 currency, 400 a. in Col-
L & R   leton Co., bounding S on the Horseshoe Road; W
                           on land given by MARTIN to the Presbyterian
Congregation at PonPon; N on JOSEPH GLOVER; E on JOHN NORTH. Witnesses:
CHARLES COLLETON, JONAH DAVIES. DAVIES testified before JAMES SHARP,
J.P. on 20 July 1761. Recorded 1 Oct. 1761 by WILLIAM HOPTON, Register.

Book X-X, p. 288   LUKE STOUTENBURGH, gentleman, to EGERTON
27 July 1761   LEIGH, ESQ., both of Charleston, for Ł 1750
Feoffment   currency, a 1 a. lot marked P on the plat of
                           lands belonging to GEORGE ANSON, ESQ., now
called Ansonsborough near Charleston, bounding N on lot marked H; W on
lot marked Q; S on a parth or street marked aaa; E on a path or street
marked ae; also the 1 a. lot marked Q; bounding N on lot H; W on lots E &
D; S on the street marked aaa; E on lot P; as occupied for many years
past by said STOUTENBURGH. Witnesses: THOMAS LINTHWAITE, THOMAS BEALE.
Possession & seizin delivered. LINTHWAITE testified before ALEXANDER
GORDON, J.P., on 28 July 1761. Recorded 7 Oct. 1761 by ALEXANDER GORDON,
Dep. Pub. Reg.

Book X-X, p. 292   THOMAS PACY (PACEY), planter, of Christ Church
25 & 26 June 1761   Parish, & HANNAH his wife, to SAMPSON NEYLE,
L & R   planter, of Charleston, for ₺ 550 currency,
                          350 a. on Wassaw Creek in St. James Parish,
Craven Co., bounding E on CHARLES MAYNE & DANIEL MCGREGOR; SE on unknown
land; SW on JOHN WILLIAMS; N & W on vacant land; which tract was granted
on 16 Jan. 1761 to NATHANIEL CLEVES, who by L & R dated 2 & 3 Mar. 1761
sold to said THOMAS PACEY. Witnesses: EGERTON LEIGH, DAVID BATCHELLER,
JAMES HUNTER, JR. HUNTER testified before ALEXANDER GORDON, J.P., on 12
Aug. 1761. Recorded 20 Oct. 1761 by WILLIAM HOPTON, Register.

Book X-X, p. 300   ELIZABETH BROWN, widow, & RICHARD SINGLETON, &
17 & 18 June 1761   SAMUEL THOMAS, planters, executrix & executors
L & R   of will of DR. ROBERT BROWN, physician of
                          Charleston, to JOHN PAUL GRIMKE, jeweler, of
Charleston, for ₺ 1500 currency, the N part of lot #32 in Charleston,
bounding E (exclusive of width of small alley) 20 ft. on Bay of Charles-
ton; N 195 ft. on other part said lot belonging to estate of ANTHONY
MATHEWES; W on ROBERT DANIEL; S on said alley; which part of a lot ISAAC
HOLMES, merchant, of Charleston (son of ISAAC HOLMES, merchant), on 14
Oct. 1755 sold to DR. ROBERT BROWN; who, by will dated 12 Nov. 1757, ap-
pointed said executrix & executors, giving them authority to sell any of
his real or personal estate. Witnesses: THOMAS YOUNG, WILLIAM GUERIN.
GUERIN testified 18 July 1761 before ALEXANDER GORDON, J.P. Recorded 22
Oct. 1761 by WILLIAM HOPTON, Register.

Book X-X, p. 309   PETER FRANCIS GRENIER, tailor, of Savannah,
25 & 26 June 1756   Georgia, to ADRIAN LOYER, silversmith, of Sa-
L & R   vannah, for 5 shillings sterling 400 a. in
                          Purysburgh Township, Granville Co.; bounding W
on Savannah & Back Rivers; W, E, & S on MAJ. JAMES RICHARD; E on COL.
SAMUEL MONTAGUT; N on vacant land; which 400 a. were granted on 16 Sept.
1738 by Lt. Gov. WILLIAM BULL to JOHN GRENIER, & inherited by his only
son & heir, said PETER FRANCIS GRENIER. Witnesses: WILLIAM JOHNSON, JOHN
PETER GALLASHE, JOHN HATCHER. GALLASHE testified 6 July 1761 before
HENRY YONGE, J.P., of Christ Church Parish, Georgia. Recorded in Register's Office in Georgia in Book C. fols. 582-583 by JOHN TALLEY, Dep.
Reg. Recorded 2 Nov. 1761 by WILLIAM HOPTON, Register.

Book X-X, p. 316   LYDIA DURHAM, widow (formerly widow of WILLIAM
13 & 14 July 1730   BRADLEY, vintner, of Charleston), to JOB ROTH-
L & R   MAHLER, for ₺ 700 currency, lot #105 in
                          Charleston containing half an a. Witnesses:
JOHN OULDFIELD, ISAAC CHILD, MARGARET (her mark) CHILD. On 4 March. 1761
RICHARD SINGLETON, ESQ., of St. James Goose Creek recognized OULDFIELD'S
signature before JAMES GRINDLAY, J.P. Recorded 2 Nov. 1761 by WILLIAM
HOPTON, Register.

Book X-X, p. 319   WILLIAM, Earl of Craven, Palatine; JOHN, Earl
15 May 1694   of Bath; ANTHONY, Lord Ashley; GEORGE, Lord
Grant   Carteret; SIR PETER COLLETON; SETH SOTHEL,
                          THOMAS ARCHDALE, & THOMAS AMY, ESQRS., Lords
Proprs.; to WILLIAM BRADLEY, vintner, of Berkeley Co.; a half a. town
lot, English measure, in Berkeley Co. Signed by the Hon. THOMAS SMITH,
Landgrave & Gov., in presence of JOSEPH BLAKE & PAUL GRIMBALL. In ac-
cordance with warrant issued by THOMAS SMITH, Landgrave & Gov., on 15
Mar. 1693/4, STEPHEN BULL, Sur., laid out lot #105 at Charleston, bound-
ing S on the great street leading from Cooper River to the Market Place;
N on THOMAS ARCHDALE; E on WILLIAM BRADLEY; W on a little street leading
by MRS. BENSON'S door. Plat certified 20 Mar. 1693/4 by STEPHEN BULL.
Recorded 2 Nov. 1761 by WILLIAM HOPTON, Register.

Book X-X, p. 324   DANIEL DOYLEY, P.M., to JOHN BURN, gentleman,
28 July 1761   of Charleston, at public auction, for ₺ 20,500
Sale   currency, several lots & parcels of land.
                          Whereas CHARLES MAYNE, merchant, of Charleston,
owned 1 undivided half part of an undivided half part of lot #15 in
Charleston, bounding E on the Bay; W on Union Street; also 1 undivided
half part of the bridge & wharf & low water lot #333, bounding on the
curtain line before the Bay; N on lot #16; & running E into Cooper River

as far as low water mark; also an undivided half of the half part of said low water lot #16, bounding S on said lot #333; W on the curtain line; N on other half, & running E into Cooper River to low water mark; being 50 ft. wide, as by L & R dated 1 & 2 Dec. 1752 from WILLIAM DRY & MARY JEAN his wife; also that other undivided half part of a half part of lot #15 in Charleston, bounding E on the Bay; W on Union Street; also that undivided half part of the bridge & wharf & low water lot #333, bounding W on the curtain line; N on lot #16, & running E into Cooper River to low water mark; also that undivided half part of low water lot #16, bounding S on low water lot #333; W on the curtain line; N on other half said lot, & running E into Cooper River down to low water mark; being 50 ft. wide, according to L & R dated 17 & 18 May 1753 from THOMAS FRANKLAND, of Great Britain, & SARAH his wife; also that parcel of land in Charleston, fronting part of lot #16 on the Bay, 25 ft. wide, fronting Cooper River, down to low water mark, bounding N on BENJAMIN D'HARRIETTE; S on part same lot belonging to STEPHEN MILLER; also the low water mark before a part of lot #17 25 ft. broad, down to low water mark, bounding W on the curtain line; the 2 pieces of low water land making 1 lot 50 ft. wide, as by L & R from BENJAMIN D'HARRIETTE & ANNE his wife, dated 13 & 14 July 1753; also shoal lot (low water lot) fronting Bay lot #16 & the S quarter part of low water lot fronting #17, belonging to CHARLES MAYNE, as by grant from Gov. JAMES GLEN, dated 12 May 1755; & whereas CHARLES MAYNE, gave JAMES MICHIE & HENRY PERONNEAU, ESQRS., of Charleston, a bond dated 2 Oct. 1755, in penal sum of Ł 8000 British (Ł 56,000 SC money), for payment of Ł 200 British every year to MARTHA MICHIE, the then intended wife of CHARLES MAYNE, during her natural life; & whereas MICHIE & PERONNEAU obtained a judgment against JOHN BURN, gentleman, as administrator of the estate of CHARLES MAYNE, & a writ of fieri facias was issued directing the P.M. to obtain the amount of the judgment & costs from the MAYNE'S estate; now DOYLEY sells the above named lots at auction to JOHN BURN. Witnesses: JAMES PARSONS, JOHN GLEN. On 30 July 1761 GLEN testified before JAMES GRINDLAY, J.P. Recorded 3 Nov. 1761 by WILLIAM HOPTON, Register.

Book X-X, p. 334   JOHN BURN, gentleman, administrator of estate
28 & 29 July 1761   CHARLES MAYNE, merchant, to BENJAMIN SMITH &
L & R by Mortgage   THOMAS SMITH, merchants, all of Charleston; as
                         security on a certain bond; because BENJAMIN &
THOMAS SMITH went on BURN'S bond to HENRY PERONNEAU all the property
listed on p. 324, which DOYLEY conveyed to BURN; the condition of the
bond being that BURN (or BENJAMIN & THOMAS SMITH) shall pay MARTHA HO-
WARTH, wife of HENRY HOWARTH, gentleman, of Charleston, Ł 200 British an-
nually, during her lifetime. Witnesses: JOHN RATTRAY, JAMES GRINDLAY.
GRINDLAY testified 30 July 1761 before JAMES PARSONS, J.P. Recorded 4
Nov. 1761 by ALEXANDER GORDON, Dep. Pub. Reg. On 2 Sept. 1773, BENJAMIN
& THOMAS SMITH declared mortgage & bond void. Signed by THOMAS SMITH for
himself & as executor for BENJAMIN. Witness: WILLIAM RUGELEY.

Book X-X, p. 348   WILLIAM MYDDELTON, planter, of Colleton Co.,
4 & 5 Mar. 1757   to WILLIAM SMITH, planter, of St. Johns Par-
L & R   ish, Colleton Co., for Ł 400 currency, 258 a.
                         in St. Johns Parish, bounding N on Liddenwah
Creek; E on SAMUEL & THOMAS WINBORN; S on JOSEPH PHIPPS; W on marsh of
Liddenwah Creek; which 258 a. WILLIAM NASH purchased at sale of his
father's estate; & sold by him to CHARLES BOWLER; who sold to WILLIAM
MYDDELTON. Witnesses: CHARLES BOWLER, ALEXANDER GORDON. GORDON testi-
fied 15 July 1757 before JOHN TROUP, J.P. Recorded 4 Nov. 1761 by ALEX-
ANDER GORDON, Dep. Pub. Reg.

Book X-X, p. 354   JOSEPH GIBBONS, planter, of Georgia, & HANNAH
16 & 17 Nov. 1757   his wife, to SAMUEL WINBORN, merchant, of
L & R   Charleston, for Ł 500 currency, 222 a. on SW
                         side Wadmalaw Island, in Colleton Co., part of
1060 a. granted PAUL HAMILTON; bounding N on JOHN GIBBONS & SAMUEL WIN-
BORN; E on CAPT. ROBERT SAMS; S on WILLIAM GIBBONS; W on JOSEPH PHIPPS;
according to plat certified by WILLIAM WILKINS, surveyor on 8 Aug. 1757.
Whereas on 30 Sept. 1736 Lt. Gov. THOMAS BROUGHTON granted PAUL HAMILTON
the elder 1060 a. in Colleton Co.; which he, by L & R dated 29 & 30 Mar.
1737 sold to JOSEPH GIBBONS (father of JOSEPH, party hereto), planter;
who by his will dated 15 Dec. 1750, bequeathed to his son JOSEPH the
middle part, or 222 a.; now JOSEPH sells this to WINBORN. Witnesses:

JONATHAN BRYAN, JOHN JOACHIM ZUBLY, WILLIAM CLIFTON. ZUBLY testified before THOMAS YEOMANS, J.P. on 7 Feb. 1758. Entered in Auditor's Book D-4, fol. 208 by JOHN BASSNETT, Pro. Dep. Aud. Plat given. Recorded 5 Nov. 1761 by ALEXANDER GORDON, D.P.R.

Book X-X, p. 366   WILLIAM SMITH, planter, of St. Johns Parish,
30 & 31 Jan. 1761   Colleton Co., to SAMUEL WINBORN, merchant, of
L & R   Charleston; for ₺ 400 currency, 258 a. in said
                          Parish, bounding N on Leadenwah Creek; E on
SAMUEL WINBORN & THOMAS WINBORN; S on JOSEPH PHIPPS; W on marsh of Leadenwah Creek; which tract WILLIAM NASH purchased at sale of his father's estate; & sold by him to CHARLES BOWLER; who sold to WILLIAM MYDDLETON; who by L & R dated 4 & 5 Mar. 1757 sold to WILLIAM SMITH. Witnesses: JOHN GIBBONS, CHARLES FREEMAN, JAMES LITTLE. GIBBONS testified 25 Apr. 1761 before JAMES CARSON, J.P. Entered in Auditor's Book E on 17 Apr. 1761, by GEORGE JOHNSTON, Dep. Aud. Recorded 6 Nov. 1761 by ALEXANDER GORDON, D.P.R.

Book X-X, p. 374   THOMAS MAPLES, planter, & MARY his wife, to
27 & 28 June 1750   HENRY SIMS, both of Craven Co., for ₺ 15 cur-
L & R   rency, 150 a. in Craven Co., bounding NW on
                          WENTWORTH WEBB; other sides on vacant land.
Witnesses: FRANCIS JAMES, MICHAEL BROWN. JAMES testified 28 June 1760 before RICHARD RICHARDSON, J.P. Recorded 6 Nov. 1761 by ALEXANDER GORDON, D.P.R.

Book X-X, p. 381   MARGUERETE CNOC, to DANIEL HUMBERT, planter,
11 & 12 June 1761   both of St. Peter's Parish, SC, for ₺ 100 cur-
L & R   rency, 400 a. in Purisburgh Township, on
                          Aposhey Creek. Witnesses: DAVID GIROUD,
GLOUDE (his mark) CNOC. GIROUD testified 11 June 1761 before ADRIAN MAYER, J.P. Recorded 6 Nov. 1761 by ALEXANDER GORDON, D.P.R.

Book X-X, p. 386   JOHN FREEMAN, tailor, of Charleston, & MARY
15 & 16 Sept. 1757   his wife, to WILLIAM WESTBURY, planter, of
L & R   Wadmalaw Island, for ₺ 300 currency & other
                          considerations, 200 a. on Wadmalaw Island,
bounding N on Wadmalaw River; E on MR. ELLIS; S on THOMAS UPHAM; W on land called Upham's Chimney & JAMES LAROCHE (formerly WILLIAM WILLIAMS); reserving to FREEMAN & his heirs right of burial in the usual place on said tract. Whereas EDWARD CURRANT, father of said MARY FREEMAN, owned 200 a. on St. John's Island, in Colleton Co., between WILLIAM WILLIAMS & THOMAS HARRISON, near the head of Wadmalaw River; & whereas EDWARD CURRANT died intestate in 1731, leaving 4 children; 1 son, GERSHAM, & 3 daughters, JANE, BARSHABA, & MARY, party hereto; & soon afterwards GERSHAM died under age & intestate, leaving only said MARY alive (JANE & BARSHABA having died in his lifetime); now MARY & her husband sell to WESTBURY. Witnesses: WILLIAM WYATT, ALEXANDER GORDON. GORDON testified 25 May 1758 before JOHN TROUP, J.P. Recorded 19 Nov. 1761 by ALEXANDER GORDON, D.P.R.

Book X-X, p. 393   JOHN PAMOR, ESQ., planter, of St. Stephen's
26 Apr. 1760   Parish, Craven Co., & MARIANE his wife, to
Lease   JOHN COUTURIER, 300 a. in Santee River Swamp,
                          St. Stephen's Parish, bounding S on ELIZABETH
COUTURIER; W on PETER COUTURIER; N on vacant land; E on PETER BENOIST. Witnesses: DAVID PAMOR, DANIEL WILLIAMS. Memo: that JOHN PAMOR made previous conveyance to COUTURIER but deed was not to be found. DAVID PAMOR testified before CHARLES CANTEY 3 Aug. 1761. Entered in Auditor's Book D-4, p. 440 by JOHN BASSNETT, Pro. Dep. Aud. Recorded 20 Nov. 1761 by ALEXANDER GORDON, D.P.R.

Book X-X, p. 395   ABRAHAM HAYNE, planter, to HENRY LIVINGSTON,
7 Feb. 1761   planter, both of Colleton Co., for ₺ 1100 cur-
L & R   rency, 200 a. in St. Pauls Parish, bounding S
                          on CHARLES ODINGSELL; N on JOHN PETERS. Wit-
nesses: JOSEPH FABIAN, EDWARD CANDY, JAMES GRAVES. ALEXANDER GORDON, J.P. Recorded 20 Nov. 1761 by ALEXANDER GORDON, D.P.R.

Book X-X, p. 402   DANIEL LAROCHE & WILLIAM FLEMING, gentleman,

1 & 2 Apr. 1748   to FRANCIS FUTHY & ROBERT FUTHY, planters, all
L & R   of Craven Co., for Ł 1000 currency, 1150 a. in
Craven Co., on N branch of Black River, bound-
ing N on vacant land; S on a swamp & on ANTHONY WHITE; W on WILLIAM SWIN-
TON or JOHN THOMSON; E on vacant land (now JASPER KING); also 500 a. on N
branch of Black River, bounding N on ANTHONY WHITE; S on a great swamp; E
on ANTHONY WHITE & MAURICE MURFIE or JASPER KING; W on WILLIAM SWINTON &
ANTHONY WHITE; total 1650 a. Whereas ANTHONY WHITE in his will ordered
all his real estate sold & JOSEPH DUBOURDIEU his executor, on 2 Apr. 1748
sold 2 tracts of 1650 a. to DANIEL LAROCHE & WILLIAM FLEMING, bounding S
on a great swamp; N on vacant land; E on JASPER KING; W on JOHN THOMSON;
now they sell to GRANCIS & ROBERT FUTHY. Witnesses: JOHN OULDFIELD, JO-
SEPH DUBOURDIEU. DUBOURDIEU testified before PAUL TRAPIER, J.P., on 19
May 1752. Recorded 8 Dec. 1761 by WILLIAM HOPTON, Register.

Book X-X, p. 408   Rev. MR. JOHN BAXTER & JAMES MCKEE, of Prince
1 June 1756   Frederick's Parish, in Craven Co., only acting
L & R   executors of will of ROBERT FUTHY; to HENRY
FUTHY, planter, of same Parish, for Ł 452 cur-
rency, 1320 a. on Black Mingo Swamp, in said Parish, bounding SE on ROB-
ERT FUTHY; SW on JOHN BORCKINGTON & JAMES AKIN; NW on WILLIAM THOMSON,
JR.; NE on vacant land. Whereas ROBERT FUTHY by his will ordered his
real estate (except 500 a. on which he lived) sold by his executors & executrix (appointing JOHN MCIVER, JAMES MEKEE, & the Rev. MR. JOHN BAXTER
his executors); & BAXTER & MCKEE on 21 Mar. 1754 offered 1320 a. for sale
at auction; now they convey the land to HENRY FUTHY, the highest bidder.
Witnesses: HENRY O'NEIL, ANTHONY WHITE. WHITE testified 22 Feb. 1757 before JOHN LIVISTON, J.P. Recorded 10 Dec. 1761 by WILLIAM HOPTON, Register.

Book X-X, p. 413   FRANCIS FUTHY, planter, to ROBERT FUTHY,
9 Oct. 1751   planter, both of Craven Co., for Ł 800 curren-
L & R   cy, all his title to 2 tracts of land, total
1650 a. (being half of said tract or 85 a.).
Whereas the will of ANTHONY WHITE ordered all his real estate sold & JO-
SEPH DUBOURDIEU executor, on 2 Apr. 1748 sold 2 tracts, total 1650 a., to
DANIEL LAROCHE & WILLIAM FLEMING, who on 2 Apr. 1748 (p. 402) sold to
FRANCIS & ROBERT FUTHY; now FRANCIS sells his half to ROBERT. Witnesses:
ANTHONY MARTIN WHITE, JOSEPH WHITE. ANTHONY M. WHITE testified 19 June
1752 before ELIAS FOISSIN, J.P. Recorded 12 Dec. 1761 by WILLIAM HOPTON,
Register.

Book X-X, p. 418   HENRY FUTHY, planter, & JANE (her mark) his
16 & 17 May 1757   wife, to MATTHEW NEILSON, planter, both of
L & R   Craven Co., for Ł 1300 currency, 1320 a. (being the identical land conveyed to HENRY FUTHY
by the executor of ROBERT FUTHY by L & R dated 31 May & 1 June 1756) on N
side Black Mingo Creek, Craven Co., bounding SW on JOHN BROCKINGTON &
JAMES AKIN; NW on BROCKINGTON & JOHN THOMSON; due N on land laid out; SE
on land willed to ELIZABETH FUTHY, daughter of ROBERT. Witness: ARCHI-
BALD BAIRD, SAMUEL NELSON, JR., HUGH LORRIMER. LORRIMER testified 17 May
1757 before JOHN LIVISTON, J.P. Recorded 17 Dec. 1761 by WILLIAM HOPTON,
Register. Plat certified 13 Apr. 1757 by JOHN LIVISTON, D.S.

Book X-X, p. 423   THOMAS TUCKER, mariner, of Charleston, & SARAH
20 & 21 July 1761   his wife, to JOSEPH ASH, planter, of Colleton
L & R   Co., for Ł 300 currency, his E half of lot
#46 in Charleston, E of King Street, near
White Point, sold by WILLIAM BRANFORD, planter, of Berkeley Co., & ELIZ-
ABETH his wife, to said TUCKER; bounding W on other half belonging to
FRANCIS ROSE; N on ARNOLD HARVEY (now ELIZABETH DIDCOT); E on JAMES COCH-
RAN; S on S Bay of White Point; except that part on which the Public
Works or Fortifications are erected & also a certain public passage 30
ft. wide, N of the Fortifications & appointed by Act of Assembly dated 7
May 1743 for making satisfaction, etc.; which lot #46 was granted by the
Lords Proprs. on 18 June 1694 to FRANCIS FIDLING & inherited by his eldest son & heir, JOHN; who died intestate; & inherited by his eldest
brother & heir, DANIEL FIDLING; who, with his wife, ELIZABETH, on 4 July
1713 sold to ARTHUR HALL; whose son, CHRISTOPHER, inherited, &, dying intestate, the land descended to his 3 sisters, ELIZABETH PERONNEAU, MARTHA

MICHIE, & ANN STEWART, & his nephew JOHN CATTELL (eldest son of SARAH, another sister); who sold the lot to WILLIAM BRANFORD. Witnesses: GEORGE BEDON, THOMAS LAMBOLL, JR. LAMBOLL testified 15 Aug. 1761 before ALEXANDER GORDON, J.P. Recorded 19 Dec. 1761 by WILLIAM HOPTON, Register.

Book X-X, p. 431
22 & 23 May 1753
L & R

The Hon. CHARLES PINCKNEY, HECTOR BERENGER DEBEAUFAIN, & WILLIAM BULL, JR., ESQ., members of H.M. Honorable Council, & DAVID CAW, GABRIEL MANIGAULT, THOMAS SMITH, JOHN SAVAGE, & RAWLINS LOWNDES, ESQRS., of Charleston, of 1st part; to WILLIAM BANBURY, merchant, of Charleston, for Ⱡ 3010 SC money, part of lot #7 in Charleston, on N side Tradd Street, formerly belonging to ROBERT TRADD, gentleman, & sold by his executors, MILES BREWTON & THOMAS LAMBOLL to JACOB MOTTE; on which lot stands 1 front store occupied by JOHN COOPER & ROBERT WILLIAMS, & 2 back stores. Whereas JACOB MOTTE, Public Treasurer of SC, by L & R dated 29 & 30 Dec. 1752 conveyed to said parties of 1st part, as trustees appointed by an order of the Council & Commons House of Assembly, sundry lands, lots, shoals, wharves, houses, etc., to be sold at public auction within 6 months; the money to be used for making good the sum of Ⱡ 90,000 currency for the use of holders of outstanding tax certificates issued by him in 1746, 1747, 1748, 1749, 1750, & 1751 (Book N. N. fol. 80-86); & whereas ELIZABETH, wife of JACOB MOTTE, was absent from the Province & could not join in conveying the real estate but on 24 Feb. freely acknowledged her satisfaction & renounced her right of dower to them (Office of Common Pleas, Book 5, fol. 574); & whereas CHARLES PINCKNEY is about to leave SC for some considerable time & by letter of attorney dated 28 Mar. 1753 appointed GABRIEL MANIGAULT his attorney to sell said property (Secretary's Book I.I. p. 443); & whereas the trustees on 10 May inst. put part of lot #7 up at auction for which BANBURY was highest bidder; now the trustees convey that part to him. Witnesses: CHARLES GRIMBALL, JOHN REMINGTON. REMINGTON testified 15 Aug. 1761 before ROBERT WILLIAMS, J.P. Recorded 22 Dec. 1761 by WILLIAM HOPTON, Register.

Book X-X, p. 437
2 & 3 July 1759
L & R

WILLIAM BANBURY, merchant, to GABRIEL MANIGAULT, merchant, both of Charleston, for Ⱡ 3010 currency, part of lot #7 in Charleston, on N side Tradd Street, formerly belonging to ROBERT TRADD, gentleman, which is executors, MILES BREWTON & THOMAS LAMBOLL, sold to JACOB MOTTE, & on which there is 1 front store lately occupied by JOHN COOPER & ROBERT WILLIAMS, & 2 back stores occupied by GABRIEL MANIGAULT. Witnesses: BENJAMIN CATON, PETER BOUNETHEAU. BOUNETHEAU testified 7 Aug. 1761 before JOHN REMINGTON, J.P. Recorded 28 Dec. 1761 by WILLIAM HOPTON, Register.

Book X-X, p. 441
29 & 30 Apr. 1757
L & R

ISAAC GODIN, planter, of Goose Creek, Berkeley Co., to GABRIEL MANIGAULT, ESQ., of Charleston, for Ⱡ 5000 currency, part of lot #17 in Charleston, bounding E 25 ft. on the Bay; S on STEPHEN MILLER; W 25 ft. on Union Street; N on other part said lot; also lot #35 bounding E on Union Street; W on JOHN CORKER; S on GABIREL MANIGAULT; N on DENOUS (DENNIS) Alley; formerly bounding E on MRS. CROSS; W on NOAH ROYER, JR.; S on WILLIAM BALLAUGH; N on NOAH ROYER, SR.; which 2 lots were sold by L & R dated 13 & 14 Apr. 1757 to ISAAC GODIN by the executors of BENJAMIN D'HARRIETTE. Witnesses: PETER MANIGAULT, JOSEPH LEVY, THOMAS LAMBOLL, JR. LEVY testified 24 Aug. 1761 before JOHN REMINGTON, J.P. Recorded 30 Dec. 1761 by WILLIAM HOPTON, Register.

Book X-X, p. 446
13 July 1754
Assignment of Mortgage

JOHN DART, OTHNIEL BEALE, JOHN GUERARD, & HENRY LAURENS, as trustees in behalf of themselves & other creditors of JAMES EDES, for Ⱡ 4000 currency, assign to JAMES HUNTER, baker, of Charleston, a certain mortgage (see Book K.K. p. 45-52). Witness: JOSIAH SMITH, JR. Before JACOB MOTTE, J.P. Recorded 30 Dec. 1761 by WILLIAM HOPTON, Register.

Book X-X, p. 447
11 & 12 July 1754
L & R

JAMES EDES, shopkeeper, & PENELOPE his wife, to JAMES HUNTER, baker, both of Charleston, for Ⱡ 4000 currency, the N half of 3 lots in Charleston, #101, #111, & #59, bounding W 63 ft. on Old Church Street; N 132 ft. on ROBERT HUME & SUSANNA

WIGINGTON; S on other part said 3 lots belonging to JOHN LAURENS; which
land JAMES EDES purchased from ANTHONY BONNEAU, HENRY BONNEAU, & PETER
BONNEAU, executors of will of ANTHONY BONNEAU (see L & R dated 25 & 26
Sept. 1746); being part of a lot which ANTHONY BONNEAU purchased from
JOHN LAURENS, & on which RICHARD LAMPERD lived as his tenant. Witnesses:
PAUL VILLEPONTOUX, JAMES GRINDLAY. GRAINDLAY testified 12 Jan. 1757 be-
fore JACOB MOTTE, J.P. Recorded 31 Dec. 1761 by WILLIAM HOPTON, Regis-
ter.

Book X-X, p. 458   ROBERT MACKEWN, planter, of Colleton Co., to
16 & 17 Aug. 1761   THOMAS FERGUSON, planter, of Berkeley Co., for
L & R   •   Ł 1503:15:0 currency, 501-1/4 a. near Spoon
                          Savannah, in St. Paul's Parish, Colleton Co.,
bounding SW on JOSEPH PERRY; NW on JOHN MILES, JOHN REILY, & THOMAS
ELLIOTT; E on JOSHUA TOOMER; SE on ROBERT MACKEWN; which 501-1/4 a. (then
called 550 a.) were granted on 20 June 1754 by Gov. JAMES GLEN to ROBERT
MACKEWN. Witnesses: LAURENCE MAYER, JEHU ELLIOTT, JOSEPH LAW. LAW tes-
tified 18 Aug. 1761 before ANDREW LEITCH, J.P. Recorded 2 Jan. 1762 by
WILLIAM HOPTON, Register.

Book X-X, p. 468   DAVID HUMBERT, planter, & URSULA (her mark)
12 & 13 June 1761   his wife, to ANDREW HENDREE & HUGH BURNS,
L & R   planters, of Georgia, for Ł 800 SC money, 400
                          a. in Purysburgh Township, bounding E on JERI-
MIAH RIMOND (REMOND); W on Apochee Creek; other sides on vacant land.
Witnesses: ADRIAN MAYER, DAVID GIROUD. GIROUD testified 13 June 1761 be-
fore JOHN BAPT. BOURQUIN, J.P., of Granville Co. Recorded 2 Jan. 1762 by
WILLIAM HOPTON, Register.

Book X-X, p. 473   WILLIAM SCREVEN, gentleman, of St. Andrews
16 Apr. 1751   Parish, James Island, to PHILIP JAMES, minis-
Release   ter of the Gospel, of the Welch tract, Craven
                          Co., for Ł 200 currency, 150 a. in the Welch
tract, granted by Gov. JAMES GLEN on 29 Nov. 1750 to WILLIAM SCREVEN.
Witnesses: JUSTINUS STOLL, DOVONALL (DEVONALL). DEVONALL testified 6
Dec. 1754 before GEORGE PAWLEY, J.P. Recorded 4 Jan. 1762 by WILLIAM
HOPTON, Register.

Book X-X, p. 477   ROBERT WRIGHT: ALEXANDER FOTHRINGHAM & ISABEL-
2 & 3 Nov. 1761   LA his wife; & ARCHIBALD MCNEILL & MARY his
L & R   wife; all of St. George Parish, Dorchester
                          (ROBERT WRIGHT, ISABELLA & MARY being only
surviving children of ROBERT WRIGHT); of 1 part; to JOHN THOMSON, merchant, of Dorchester; for Ł 2000 currency, 500 a. in Berkeley Co., on S
side of head of Ashley River, bounding E on ALEXANDER SKENE, ESQ.; S on
JOHN SKENE & SAMUEL WAINWRIGHT, ESQRS.; NE on estate of JOSEPH WRAGG,
ESQ.; NW on JERMYN WRIGHT, ESQ., & estate of RALPH IZARD; which 500 a.
was lately occupied by GIBBON WRIGHT, deceased, sister to ROBERT, ISA-
BELLA, & MARY. Witnesses: THOMAS JONES, ANDREW MCLEAN. MCLEAN testified
3 Nov. 1761 before WILLIAM BURROWS, J.P. Recorded 5 Jan. 1762 by WILLIAM
HOPTON, Register.

Book X-X, p. 486   EDWARD BULLARD, carpenter, & SARAH his wife,
28 & 29 Sept. 1761   to THOMAS CORKER, merchant, both of Charleston,
L & R by Mortgage   as security on bond of even date in penal sum
                          of Ł 2800 for payment of Ł 1400 currency, with
interest, on 29 Sept. 1762; his house & the S part of lot #238 in Charleston, bounding E 60 ft. on King Street; N 232 ft. on other part said lot
belonging to WILLIAM DANDRIDGE; W on S part of lot #239 belonging to ED-
WARD BULLARD; S on the house & part of lot #237 occupied by THOMAS SMITH,
merchant. Witnesses: ELIZABETH FINLAY, THOMAS CORKER, JR. CORKER testified 4 Nov. 1761 before ALEXANDER GORDON, J.P. Recorded 7 Jan. 1762 by
WILLIAM HOPTON, Register. On 28 Sept. 1767 THOMAS CORKER declared mortgage satisfied. Witness: FENWICKE BULL.

Book X-X, p. 497   MARY BRYAN, widow, of Granville Co., to THOMAS
1 & 2 Sept. 1760   CLIFFORD, planter, of Colleton Co., for Ł 2000
L & R   currency, 661 a., English measure, in Colleton
                          Co., part of 1410 a. granted WILLIAM FAIR-
CHILD; bounding S on PHILIP EVANS, ABRAHAM MICHEAU, & part of said

1410 a; W on said part of 1410 a.; N on said part of 1410 a. & on land
granted ANN ELLIOTT; E on ANN ELLIOTT, THOMAS CLIFFORD, & PHILIP EVANS;
also 521 a., English measure, in Colleton Co., part of 650 a. granted ANN
ELLIOTT; bounding N on JOHN WILLIAMSON & THOMAS CLIFFORD; E on THOMAS
CLIFFORD; S on JOHN WILLIAMSON & part of said 1410 a.; W on part said
1410 a.; also 250 a., English measure, in Colleton Co., granted JOHN WIL-
LIAMSON, bounding E on THOMAS CLIFFORD; N on THOMAS CLIFFORD & ANN
ELLIOTT; W & S on ANN ELLIOTT; total 1432 a. Witnesses: JOHN HODSDEN,
JOHN SMITH. HODSDEN testified 8 Oct. 1760 before ROBERT WILLIAMS, JR.,
J.P. Recorded 11 Jan. 1762 by WILLIAM HOPTON, Register.

Book X-X, p. 508   HENRY WOOD, weaver, of Ashley River, in St.
9 Nov. 1761   Andrews Parish, Berkeley Co., to JONATHAN
Mortgage   WOOD, son of JOSEPH WOOD, Charleston, as se-
                    curity on bond of even date in penal sum of
Ł 1200 for payment of Ł 600 currency, with interest, on 1 Dec. next; 60 a.
on Dorchester Road, bounding on WILLIAM FULLER on 1 side & COL. RICHARD
BEATON (part same tract) on another. Witnesses: MARY CROSSWELL, THOMAS
HARVEY. MARY CROSSWELL testified 16 Nov. 1761 before GEORGE MURRAY, J.P.
Recorded 12 Jan. 1762 by WILLIAM HOPTON, Register.

Book X-X, p. 511   BARNARD ELLIOTT, gentleman, of Charleston,
20 & 21 May 1761   only son of BARNARD ELLIOTT, gentleman; &
L & R   THOMAS LAMBOLL, gentleman; executors of will
                    of said BARNARD ELLIOTT; & ELIZABETH ELLIOTT,
his widow; of 1st part; at public auction, to TUNIS TEABOUT, blacksmith,
& BARNARD BEEKMAN, blockmaker; all of Charleston; for Ł 5010 currency,
for the use of RICHARD BOHUN BAKER in right of ELIZABETH his wife, & of
MARY ELLIOTT, AMARANTIA ELLIOTT & CATHERINE ELLIOTT, 3 minor daughters of
said BARNARD ELLIOTT, SR.; part of the E Bay lot, or lots, in or near
Charleston, measuring 250 ft. from the eastern curtain line or brick wall
of the Bay now built there towards Cooper River; & extending 21 ft. N
from N side of a 28 ft. passage laid out on the wharf (which passage BAR-
NARD ELLIOTT & OTHNIEL BEALE had agreed should be left open forever out
of their adjacent lands for the common use, of the wharves & buildings &
for all persons to pass & repass on foot or with horses, carts, & carriages at pleasure, by night or day, according to deed poll dated 26 May
1753). Whereas BARNARD ELLIOTT the elder owned said part of lot, or lots,
with the buildings thereon, & by will dated 16 May 1758 gave to his 4
daughters ELIZABETH, MARY, AMARENTIA, & CATHERINE, equally the remainder
of his real estate not absolutely devised, of which said piece of land
was a part, each to receive her portion on 21st birthday or day of marriage; giving his executors the authority to sell the rest of his real
estate for the better execution of his will; & whereas daughter ELIZABETH
married RICHARD BOHUN BAKER & is now entitled to her fourth part; now the
executors sell said property to TEABOUT & BEEKMAN. Witnesses: EDWARD
BULLARD, WILLIAM GREENLAND, JOHN CALVERT. CALVERT testified 11 June 1761
before BENJAMIN SMITH, J.P. Recorded 27 Jan. 1762 by WILLIAM HOPTON,
Register.

Book X-X, p. 525   TUNES TEABOUT, blacksmith, & BARNARD BEEKMAN,
10 & 11 June 1761   blockmaker, to BENJAMIN SMITH, ESQ.; all of
L & R by Mortgage   Charleston; as security on bond of even date
                         in penal sum of Ł 10,000 for payment of Ł 5000
currency, with interest, on 10 June 1762, for use of estate of PAUL JENYS,
ESQ., of Dorchester; (TEABOUT & BEEKMAN having borrowed the money to pay
for the property mentioned in L & R on page 511); on which land is now
built a long brick building containing shops, stores erected by BARNARD
ELLIOTT the elder. Witnesses: CHARLES ATKINS, THOMAS WARING. ATKINS
testified 11 June 1761 before CHARLES PINCKNEY, J.P. Recorded 1 Feb.
1762 by WILLIAM HOPTON, Register.

Book X-X, p. 536   ARCHIBALD JOHNSTON, planter, of Winyaw, to
11 & 12 Nov. 1761   DANIEL HUGER, planter, of St. Johns Parish,
L & R   for Ł 4500 currency, 737 a. near Georgetown,
                         in Craven Co., bounding W on PAUL TRAPIER; S
on Georgetown Common; SE on MRS. MARY LAROCHE; E on joint waters of Peedee & Black Rivers; N on a creek & on ROBERT WEAVER; which land JOHNSTON
purchased from the Hon. JOHN CLELAND by L & R dated 17 & 18 Apr. 1758.
Witnesses: ELIAS HORRY, WILLIAM LUPTON, JOHN STEWART. LUPTAN testified

13 Nov. 1761 before BENJAMIN YOUNG, J.P.   Recorded 3 Feb. 1762 by WILLIAM
HOPTON, Register.

Book X-X, p. 543   JOHNSTON gives HUGER a bond that he will keep
12 Nov. 1761   above agreements. Same witnesses, etc.
Bond.

Book X-X, p. 544   BARNARD ELLIOTT, gentleman, executor of will
19 Nov. 1761   of BARNARD ELLIOTT the elder, being now 21
Confirmation   years of age, confirms the title of TEABOUT &
                        BEEKMAN in above named property (see p. 511)
as tenants in common & not as joint tenants; 1 undivided half part to
each. Witnesses: MILES BREWTON, RICHARD RODGERS. RODGERS testified 23
Nov. 1761 before D. CAMPBELL, J.P. Recorded 4 Feb. 1762 by WILLIAM HOP-
TON, Register.

Book X-X, p. 548   JAMES SKIRVING, ESQ., to TOBIAS FORD, planter,
22 & 23 Dec. 1760   both of St. Bartholomew's Parish, Colleton
L & R   Co., for Ł 2000 currency, 764-1/4 a. in said
                        Parish, bounding S on JOHN BEATY; E on DAVID
FERGUSON; NW on JOHN REID; SW on vacant land. Witnesses: JOHN CHAMPNEYS,
ARCHIBALD STOBO, JAMES SKIRVING, JR. STOBO testified 27 May 1761 before
JAMES SHARP, J.P. Recorded 9 Feb. 1762 by WILLIAM HOPTON, Register.
Plat showing A-352 a., Lord's land; B-21-1/2 ditto; C-390-3/4 King's
land.

Book X-X, p. 555   JOSEPH SCOTT, gentleman, of Berkeley Co., eld-
11 & 12 Nov. 1761   est son & heir of JOHN SCOTT, shipwright, of
L & R   Charleston, to ANTHONY BOCHETT, planter, of
                        Berkeley Co., for 10 shillings & other consid-
erations, 65 a. on Edward's Island, part of a larger tract sold by NEWEL
EDWARDS to said JOHN SCOTT, bounding N on land called Clowters (now RICH-
ARD BERESFORD); NW on a marsh; other sides on JOHN MOORE; also a piece of
land, part of a plantation called Rhettsbury Point, in Berkeley Co., NW
of the boundary line of Charleston, & on SW side of a certain 20 ft.
street; measuring 100 ft. on NW & SE & 160 ft. on NE & SW; bounding NE on
said street; other sides on different parts of said Rhettsbury Point
Plantation divided into lots; also Pew No. 4 in St. Philip's Church,
Charleston. Whereas JOHN SCOTT owned certain real estate but died intestate inasmuch as his will was not executed or attested by 3 witnesses, so
that his property descended to his eldest son, JOSEPH, who is willing to
carry out his father's intentions towards his younger brother, WILLIAM
SCOTT, of Charleston, infant & son of his mother MARY, now wife of AN-
THONY BOCHETT, party hereto; now JOSEPH conveys the above named property
to BOCHETT in trust for said WILLIAM SCOTT until he comes of age. Witnesses: HENRY GRAY, THOMAS WALKER. GRAY testified 7 Dec. 1761 before
JOHN REMINGTON, J.P. Recorded 10 Feb. 1762 by WILLIAM HOPTON, Register.

Book X-X, p. 564   THOMAS JACKSON, carpenter, to JAMES MAY, car-
8 & 9 Aug. 1757   penter, of Craven Co., for Ł 357 currency,
L & R   357 a., the remainder of 500 a., in Craven
                        Co., on N side Congaree River, bounding N on
WILLIAM HAY & WILLIAM MOORE; W on JOHN EVANS'S part of said 500 a. & on
estate of JAMES MCKELVEY; S on vacant land; E on EDWARD HOLLIS, the other
part of said 500 a. Whereas Gov. JAMES GLEN on 24 Apr. 1752 granted
THOMAS JACKSON 500 a. in Craven Co., on N side Congaree River, bounding
N on WILLIAM HAY, WILLIAM MOORE, & HUGH MURPHY; W on RICHARD JACKSON,
HENRY SNELLING & JAMES MCKELVEY; S & E on vacant land; & whereas THOMAS
JACKSON, for Ł 81 currency, on 17 June 1752, sold EDWARD HOLLIS 81 a.; &
for Ł 60 currency, sold JOHN EVANS 62 a.; now he sells the remainder to
JAMES MAY. Witnesses: JOHN SPARKS, GEORGE (his mark) RAWLINSON. SPARKS
testified before JOHN PEARSON, J.P., on 10 Aug. 1757. Recorded 13 Feb.
1762 by WILLIAM HOPTON, Register.

Book X-X, p. 571   JAMES BRADLEY & AGNES his wife, to THOMAS
26 & 27 Oct. 1761   HOUSE, both of Craven Co., for Ł 200 currency,
L & R   200 a. on N side of Main Swamp of Black River,
                        bounding NW on the swamp & PETER MALETT; E on
JOHN JONES; NE on vacant land. Witnesses: SAMUEL BRADLEY, WILLIAM MCKAY,
ROGER MCGILL. BRADLEY testified 7 Nov. 1761 before HENRY CASSELLS, J.P.

Recorded 16 Feb. 1762 by WILLIAM HOPTON, Register.

Book X-X, p. 576   ELIZABETH COLLIS, widow, to GEORGE GARDNER,
28 June 1760   both of Charleston, for 7 years, for Ł 10 cur-
Lease for 7 Years   rency a year, a lot on W side of King Street,
                       bounding S on JOHN CLIFFORD; N on estate of
THOMAS ROSE; W on BENJAMIN BAKER; GARDNER to build, at his own expense,
before the end of said 7 years & keep in good repair 1 wooden tenement
fronting 15 ft. on King Street; 30 ft. deep; 1 story high, with brick
foundation, with a Dutch roof; 8 ft. from floor to ceiling; 7-1/2 from
the eaves to the pitch of the roof; with a shop & kitchen according to
plan. Witness: JOHN TROUP. Before EGERTON LEIGH, J.P. on Dec. 17, 1761.
Recorded 18 Feb. 1762 by WILLIAM HOPTON, Register. Plat given.

Book X-X, p. 580   GEORGE GARDNER, for Ł 150 currency, assigns
3 Nov. 1761   above lease to HANS ERNEST HOFF, wheelwright,
Assignment   of Charleston, as executor to GEORGE COMMERCIL.
                       Witness: MARK ANTHONY BESSELLEAU. Before ROB-
ERT PRINGLE, J.P., on 15 Dec. 1761. Recorded 18 Feb. 1762 by WILLIAM
HOPTON, Register.

Book X-X, p. 581   SAMUEL CARDY, architect, to ABRAHAM SPITAL,
23 & 24 Feb. 1759   tanner; both of Charleston, for Ł 500 curren-
L & R   cy, the S part of lot #260, bounding W 40 ft.
                       on Archdale Street; S 232 ft. on a lane lead-
ing from Archdale Street to King Street; E 40 ft. on CHRISTOPHER EASTON;
N on other part belonging to SAMUEL CARDY; which lot formerly contained
97 ft. front on Archdale Street, except 9 ft. making part of said lane.
Whereas on 12 June 1694 CAPT. HENRY SYMONDS was granted several lots in
the NW part of Charleston, particularly lot #260, fronting W on Archdale
Street; E on lot #261, granted to HENRY SYMONDS; S on lot #255, also
granted HENRY SYMONDS; N on lot #258, afterwards granted to ROBERT FEN-
WICKE; being 97 ft. wide & extending NE 232 feet; & whereas he bequeathed
lot #260 & all his real & personal estate to his wife FRANCES SYMONDS;
who by her will dated 6 Dec. 1707 bequeathed said lot to her kinswoman,
FRANCES NORTHALL; who married THOMAS ALLEN & had 2 sons, THOMAS the eldest & JAMES the youngest; THOMAS, after her death, dying a minor & unmarried; & JAMES inherited the lot; & by L & R dated 26 & 27 Jan. 1759
conveyed to SAMUEL CARDY; now he sells the S half to SPITAL. Witnesses:
WILLIAM JORDAN, ALEXANDER GORDON. GORDON testified 26 June 1759 before
DAVID OLIPHANT, J.P. Recorded 20 Feb. 1762 by WILLIAM HOPTON, Register.

Book X-X, p. 590   ELIZABETH HAYES, widow, & executrix; JOHN WAR-
18 & 19 May 1761   ING & JOSEPH SMITH, planters, of St. George
L & R   Parish; acting executors of will of JOHN HAYES,
                       planter, of St. Pauls Parish, Colleton Co., of
1st part; at public auction, to BENJAMIN STEAD, merchant, of Charleston,
now of London, Great Britain; for Ł 7065 SC money, paid by STEAD through
his attorney, DANIEL BLAKE; 2 tracts of 500 a., & 300 a.; total 800 a.
Whereas JOHN HAYES owned said 2 tracts in Colleton Co., 500 a. being on E
side S Edisto River, bounding N on THOMAS WARING; NE on WILLIAM ELLIOTT;
SE on vacant land; SW on JOHN PRESCOTT; 300 a. being near Bob's Savannah
on E side S Edisto River, bounding N on JOHN PENDARVIS & THOMAS WARING;
W on JOHN PENDARVIS; S on THOMAS DRAYTON; E on JOHN PRESCOTT; which 2
tracts HAYES purchased by L & R dated 25 & 26 -Apr. 1759 from GEORGE HAR-
MAN, planter, of St. James Goose Creek Parish; & whereas HAYES by his
will dated 4 July 1760 authorized his executors to sell any part of his
real or personal estate for the benefit of his children, MARTHA & ELIZA-
BETH, appointing his wife ELIZABETH, executrix, & his brothers, BENJAMIN
WARING, JOHN WARING, JOSEPH SMITH, JOSEPH WARING, & THOMAS SMITH, JR.,
his executors; now the acting executors sell to STEAD. Witnesses: CATH-
ERINE WARING, AMERENTIA SMITH, ROGER MAKEY. MAKEY testified 2 Nov. 1761
before J. SKENE, J.P. Recorded 3 Mar. 1762 before WILLIAM HOPTON, Register.

Book X-X, p. 600   ELIZABETH HAYES, widow, of JOHN HAYES, re-
19 May 1761   nounces her right of dower in above lands to
Renounciation of Dower BENJAMIN STEAD (p. 590). Same witnesses. Re-
                       corded 4 Mar. 1762 by WILLIAM HOPTON, Regis-
ter.

Book X-X, p. 604   MARTHA LLOYD, widow & executrix of will of
30 Nov. & 1 Dec. 1761   WILLIAM LLOYD, merchant; & HOPKIN PRICE & JOHN
L & R   SCOTT, merchants, executors of said will; to
                          THOMAS YOUNG, bricklayer; all of Charleston;
for Ł 1568 currency, certain town lots. Whereas WILLIAM LLOYD owned,
among other pieces of property part of a certain lot which was part of
the estate of BARNARD ELLIOTT the elder, & sold by BARNARD ELLIOTT the
younger & other executors of will of his father to WILLIAM LLOYD (L & R
dated 1 & 2 Apr. 1761), bounding N 30 ft. on Elliott Street; W 86 ft. on
JOHN MCCALL; S on OTHNIEL BEALE & WILLIAM ELLIOTT; E on estate of BARNARD
ELLIOTT the elder (now FARQUAR MCGILLIVRAY); & whereas WILLIAM LLOYD by
will dated 5 Sept. 1761 ordered the residue of his real & personal estate
sold, appointing said executors; now they sell the lot at public auction
to YOUNG. Witnesses: JOHN SCOTT, THOMAS BATTY, BARNARD ELLIOTT. SCOTT
testified before OTHNIEL BEALE, J.P. on 1 Dec. 1761. Recorded 10 Mar.
1762 by WILLIAM HOPTON, Register.

Book X-X, p. 615   JOHN BONHOSTE, planter, of Christ Church Par-
22 & 23 Mar. 1756   ish, Berkeley Co., & HESTER his wife (1 of the
L & R   daughters & co-heiresses of JANE GROSET), to
                          JAMES HUNBER, baker, of Charleston, for Ł 300
currency, a lot in Charleston, marked #3 on a certain plat, being part of
lot #70. Whereas ANDREW DUPUEY inherited from his father lot #70 in
Charleston; died intestate & without issue; & his sisters (1 of whom was
JANE GROSET) inherited; & whereas lot #70 was divided into 3 parts, 2
parts fronting Church Street & marked A & B on the plat; the 3rd part being bounded on the E by said 2 parts & also divided into 3 parts fronting
Dupuy's Lane; the parts being marked #1, #2, & #3; & whereas JOHN BON-
HOSTE & his wife HESTER are entitled to a share of the N part of said
lot, (or lot #70?) bounding E 49-1/2 ft. on Church Street; N on a 10 ft.
lane called Dupuy's Alley; W on JAMES HUNTER & ALEXANDER MCGREGOR; S on
JAMES ROULAIN, ISAAC MAZYCK & heirs of COL. SAMUEL PRIOLEAU; the lots being divided & allotted by writ of partition recorded in Office of Clerk
of Court of Common Pleas; BONHOSTE & his wife being allotted lot #3,
bounding E on PETER GODFREY; W on JAMES HUNTER; N 60 ft. on Dupuy's Alley; S on JAMES ROULAIN; now BONHOSTE & his wife sell their share to
HUNTER. Witnesses: THOMAS YEOMANS, ROBERT RAWLINGS. On 10 Jan. 1757
RAWLINS testified before JACOB MOTTE, J.P. Recorded 11 Mar. 1762 by
WILLIAM HOPTON, Register.

Book X-X, p. 623   JOHN GOLDING, of St. George Parish, Dorchester,
9 & 10 Apr. 1759   & SARAH his wife, to GEORGE EVANS, planter, of
L & R   St. Bartholomews Parish, for Ł 6800 SC money,
                          471 a. (formerly belonging to his father,
PETER GOLDING, & then supposed to be 400 a.), bounding SW on a road lead-
ing to HENRY IZARD'S plantation; SE on HENRY IZARD & CAPT. WILLIAM SMITH;
NE on CHARLES WRIGHT; (now MICHAEL GEIZER or CIGAR); NW on a road leading
to Bacons Bridge, through Cow Savannah. Witnesses: JAMES SMITH, EDWARD
PERRY, ELIJAH POSTELL. On 2 June 1759 PERRY testified before J. SKENE,
J.P. Recorded 12 Mar. 1762 by WILLIAM HOPTON, Register.

Book X-X, p. 631   JOSEPH ALISON, planter, & SARAH his wife, to
22 Dec. 1761   JOHN HAM, planter, both of Craven Co., for
Release   Ł 300 currency, 300 a. in Craven Co., bounding
                          NE on Peedee River; NW on JOHN KEYTHLEY; SW on
land surveyed by COL. PAWLEY; SE on JOHN PERKINS & on vacant land. Witnesses: ELIZABETH ALISON, JOHN ALRAN. On 31 Dec. 1761 ALRAN testified
before WADE BLAIR, J.P. Recorded 13 Mar. 1762 by WILLIAM HOPTON, Register. Plat given.

Book X-X, p. 637   JOSEPH BUTLER, JR., planter (son of JOSEPH
23 Dec. 1761   BUTLER, of Berkeley Co., & MARY his wife,
Release of Right   formerly MARY LAROCHE, daughter of JAMES LA-
                          ROCHE, for Ł 5 & other considerations, release
to HOPKINS PRICE all his claim to lot #195 in Charleston bounding E on
the great street leading from Ashley River, through the Market Place; W
on ISAAC REEDWOOD; S on WILLIAM YEOMANS; N on a marsh; which lot JOSEPH
BUTLER, the elder, & MARY his wife, by L & R dated 12 & 13 Feb. 1733 conveyed to ROBERT STEEL, tanner, of Charleston; & by several mesne conveyances became vested in HOPKINS PRICE, tanner, of Charleston. Witnesses:

SHEM BUTLER, JACOB BARKLEY. On 30 Dec. 1761 BARKLEY testified before
JOHN REMINGTON, J.P. Recorded 15 Mar. 1762 by WILLIAM HOPTON, Register.

Book X-X, p. 639   JERMYN WRIGHT, ESQ., & ROBERT WRIGHT, gentle-
23 & 24 Oct. 1761   man, to CHARLES WRIGHT, ESQ., for Ł 2000 cur-
L & R   rency, 500 a. in Berkeley Co., on S side of
                          head of Ashley River, bounding E on ALEXANDER
SKENE; S on JOHN SKENE & SAMUEL WAINWRIGHT; NE on estate of JOSEPH WRAGG;
NW on JERMYN WRIGHT & estate of RALPH IZARD; being now the estate of
JERMYN & ROBERT WRIGHT & lately owned by GIBBON WRIGHT. Witnesses: JOHN
CHAMPNEYS, WILLIAM SKIRVING. On 26 Oct. 1761 CHAMPNEYS testified before
JAMES SKIRVING, J.P. Recorded 16 Mar. 1762 by WILLIAM HOPTON, Register.

Book X-X, p. 646   KENOWAY EATON, cordwainer, of Edisto Island,
2 Nov. 1761   to his uncle JOSHUA EATON, for affection &
Gift   other considerations, 120 a., part of 2 tracts
                          surveyed to JOHN BRAYES on 13 June 1694; 1 of
140 a. bounding N on Edisto River & fronting W on said river; E on THOMAS
RAKE; S on HENRY BAYLEY; the other, 100 a., on N side Edisto River,
fronting W on said river; bounding E on KENOWAY EATON; N on AARON RIPP-
ING; S on HENRY BAYLEY. Witnesses: PATRICK JOHNSTON, JACOB DONNOM. On
11 Nov. 1761 JOHNSTON testified before JAMES SHARP, J.P. of Colleton Co.
Recorded 19 Mar. 1762 by WILLIAM HOPTON, Register.

Book X-X, p. 648   JOHN WATSON, carpenter, to JAMES BLAKELEY,
11 & 12 Feb. 1757   planter, both of Craven Co., for Ł 150 curren-
L & R   cy, 150 a. in Williamsburg Township, bounding
                          due E on JOHN SCOTT & JOHN LIVISTON; S on
JAMES BLAKELEY; W on JAMES PETTIGRAU; other sides on vacant land. Wit-
nesses: JOHN SCOTT, SAMUEL BURROWS, JOHN SCOTT, JR. Before JOHN LIVIS-
TON, J.P. Recorded 24 Mar. by WILLIAM HOPTON, Register.

Book X-X, p. 653   ROBERT RIVERS, planter, & REBECCA his wife, to
24 & 25 Aug. 1761   WILLIAM ALLSTON, both of James Island, Berke-
L & R   ley Co., for Ł 500 currency, 854 a. in Craven
                          Co., formerly belonging to ROBERT RIVERS, SR.,
father of ROBERT, party hereto; bounding SW on WILLIAM ARNOLD; other
sides on vacant land. Witnesses: JOHN DENTON, ESTHER BOONE, JAMES BOONE.
On 2 Feb. 1762 DENTON testified before JOHN REMINGTON, J.P. Entered 21
Nov. 1761 in Auditor's Book D. p. 488 by GEORGE JOHNSTON for RICHARD
LAMBTON, Dep. Aud. Recorded 26 Mar. 1762 by WILLIAM HOPTON, Register.

Book X-X, p. 661   JOSIAS DUPREE, planter, of St. James Parish,
10 & 11 Dec. 1761   Santee, & ANN his wife, to SAMUEL MOUZON,
L & R by Mortgage   planter, of Christ Church Parish, as security
                          on bond of even date in penal sum of Ł 767:7:6
(because MOUZON went on DUPREE'S bond to JOHN HALES, cooper of Charleston) for payment of Ł 383:13:8 currency, with interest, on 1 Jan. 1762;
500 a. in Craven Co., bounding SW on Tibwin Creek; NE on LEWIS MOUZON; NW
on vacant land on STEPHEN SEAVEY; SE on marsh of the seashore; which
500 a. were sold by JOHN HALES to JOHN DUPREE by L & R dated 1 & 2 June
last. Witnesses: JOHN SKINNER, LEWIS DUPREE. SKINNER testified 3 Feb.
1762 before WILLIAM BURROWS, J.P. Recorded 30 Mar. 1762 by WILLIAM HOP-
TON, Register.

Book X-X, p. 670   HENRY METZGER, baker, to CHARLES WARHAM, cabi-
20 & 21 Jan. 1762   net maker, both of Charleston, as security on
L & R by Mortgage   bond of even date in penal sum of Ł 2000 for
                          payment of Ł 1000 currency, with interest, on
1 Jan. 1763; a lot in Charleston bounding E 48 ft. on King Street; W on
FREDERICK GRIMKE; N 227 ft. on COL. OTHNIEL BEALE; S on JOHN MICK. Wit-
nesses: THOMAS STONE, JR., THOMAS GRIMBALL, JR. GRIMBALL testified 3
Feb. 1762 before WILLIAM BURROWS, J.P. Recorded 2 Apr. 1762 by WILLIAM
HOPTON, Register. On Apr. 1777 WARHAM declared mortgage paid off by
MICHAEL MUCKENFUSS, JR. Witness: GEORGE SHEED.

Book X-X, p. 678   CHARLES FARRINGTON, gentleman, late of Aghrim,
15 & 16 Jan. 1762   Ireland, to JOHN MCBRIDE, planter, of Craven
L & R   Co., for Ł 375 currency, 650 a. in Williams-
                          burgh Township, bounding on S side of Black

River; NW on DANIEL MUNIE; NE on ANTHONY WILLIAMS. Witnesses: JAMES
FLEMING, JAMES BLEACKLEY, JOHN WATTSON. On 16 Jan. 1762 FLEMING testi-
fied before JOHN LIVISTON, J.P. Recorded 3 Apr. 1762 by WILLIAM HOPTON,
Register.

Book X-X, p. 684   THOMAS BUTLER, planter, of Prince George Par-
29 & 30 Jan. 1762   ish, Craven Co., to CHARLES FYFFE, physician
L & R   of Georgetown, for ₺ 1125 currency, 1/2 part
                          of a part of lot #14 in Charleston, bounding
according to survey 1706/1707 E 18 ft., English measure, on the Bay; S
48 ft. on MR. PETERSON; W on other part same lot; N on MR. DRY. Witnesses: JOSEPH DUBOURDIEU, BENJAMIN PERDRIAU. On 2 Feb. 1762 DUBOURDIEU
testified before BENJAMIN YOUNG, J.P., of Craven Co. Recorded 6 Apr.
1762 by WILLIAM HOPTON, Register.

Book X-X, p. 690   SIMON MALPHURS, planter, to THOMAS KIRTON,
16 & 17 Sept. 1761   planter, both of Craven Co., for ₺ 200 curren-
L & R   cy, 150 a. on Catfish Creek, in Craven Co.,
                          bounding on all sides on vacant land; granted
MALPHURS 22 Jan. 1759 by Gov. WILLIAM HENRY LYTTLETON, (Book T.T. p. 75).
Witnesses: DAVID WILLIAMS, JR., JOHN PHILLIPS, JR. WILLIAMS testified 24
Nov. 1761 before JOSEPH BRITTON, J.P. Recorded 7 Apr. 1762 by WILLIAM
HOPTON, Register.

Book X-X, p. 695   ARCHIBALD JOHNSTON, gentleman, of Prince
18 & 19 July 1761   George Parish, to WILLIAM BELLUNE, planter, of
L & R   Prince Frederick Parish, for ₺ 300 currency,
                          500 a., bounding NW on Peedee River; NE on EB-
ENEZER DUNNAM; SE on vacant land; SW on other 500 a. belonging to ARCHI-
BALD JOHNSTON; the 500 a. being half of a tract of 1000 a., granted JOHN-
STON on 24 Mar. 1756 by Gov. JAMES GLEN, lying in Queensborough Township,
Prince Frederick Parish, & bounding NW on Peedee River; NE on JAMES WED-
DERBURN; SE on vacant land; SW on JOHN GOODWIN. Witnesses: THOMAS PORT,
JOHN FATHERREE, FRANCES PORTE. On 1 Feb. 1762 PORT testified before JO-
SEPH BRITTON, J.P. Recorded 9 Apr. 1762 by WILLIAM HOPTON, Register.

Book X-X, p. 701   SARAH LOWLE, widow, & sole executrix of will
9 & 10 Mar. 1761   of SAMUEL LOWLE, planter, of 1st part; JOHN
L & R. Tripartite by   MITCHELL, school-master, of 2nd part; JAMES
Marriage Settlement   DONNOM, JOHN MARTIN, & SAMUEL SPRY, planters,
                          of 3rd part; all of Colleton Co. Whereas a
marriage is intended between JOHN MITCHELL & SARAH LOWLE; & whereas SARAH
is entitled by SAMUEL LOWLE'S will to all his real estate, being 900 a.
in Colleton Co., bounding W on Penny's Creek; S on DR. JAMES REID; E on
THOMAS SACHEVERELL; N on SARAH CHAMPNEYS; subject to the payment of his
debts & legacies; now SARAH conveys the 900 a. to DONNOM, MARTIN, & SPRY,
in trust, to secure payment of said debts & legacies; for the use of
SARAH until her marriage, then for JOHN & SARAH jointly; then to be disposed of according to her will. Witnesses: SARAH WAY, JONATHAN DONNOM.
DONNOM testified 5 Feb. 1762 before JAMES SHARPE, J.P. Recorded 15 Apr.
1762 by WILLIAM HOPTON, Register.

Book X-X, p. 711   FREDERICK (his mark) RESHTER, planter, of
10 & 11 Aug. 1761   Purysburgh, to SIMEON LEBRAND, (LEIBRAND),
L & R   planter, of Saludy, for ₺ 40 currency, 250 a.
                          on NW side Saludy River, in Berkeley Co.,
formerly belonging to his father JOHN RESHTER; bounding S on FREDERICK
ARNOLD & vacant land; other sides on vacant land. Witnesses: JOHANNA
CRELLY, ANTHONY BACHMAN. BACHMAN testified 13 Aug. 1761 before STEPHEN
CRELL, J.P. Recorded 15 Apr. 1762 by WILLIAM HOPTON, Register.

Book X-X, p. 717   GEORGE ROUPELL, ESQ., & ELIZABETH his wife, 1
14 & 15 Jan. 1762   of the daughters of SAMUEL PRIOLEAU, ESQ., to
L & R   NATHANIEL SCOTT, brewer; all of Charleston;
                          for ₺ 1250 currency, part of lot #198 in
Charleston, 61 ft. wide; with the S tenement of the house built some time
ago on the N part thereof; bounding W 140 ft. on Friend Street; N on the
N tenement of said house (a timber building); E on other part said lot
#198 formerly belonging to MRS. CATHERINE GREENLAND (now THOMAS SMITH,
JR., merchant); S on part same lot belonging to GEORGE ROUPELL &

ELIZABETH his wife. Whereas SAMUEL PRIOLEAU owned parts of 2 lots, & houses erected thereon, on E side of Friend Street, & by will dated 25 Oct. 1751 bequeathed them equally to his 2 daughters, MARY, the wife of HUGH BRYAN, & ELIZABETH PRIOLEAU; the N tenement of the large house & the land to the N to Broad Street, to MARY BRYAN; the S tenement of the large house & the land to the S, to Tradd Street; to ELIZABETH; now the ROU-PELLS sell their part of the house & lot to SCOTT. Witnesses: ROBERT DEANS, JAMES GRINDLAY. GRINDLAY testified 19 Feb. 1762 before WILLIAM BURROWS, J.P. Recorded 16 Apr. 1762 by WILLIAM HOPTON, Register. Plat given.

Book X-X, p. 726   JOHN SHALLER, planter, conveys to MICHAEL
4 Mar. 1762   GEIGER both of St. Paul's Parish, Colleton
Mortgage   Co., because GEIGER became security for SHAL-
                      LER on a bond given ANDREW JOHNSTON of St.
Philip's Parish, Berkeley Co., dated 31 Jan. 1761, for Ł 850 currency;
300 a., part of 3000 a. called Ashley Barony & St. Giles; which 300 a.
was lately in possession of ANDREW JOHNSTON; then bounding NE & SW on
JOHN SKEEN; NW on CHARLES WRIGHT & GIBBON WRIGHT; SE on WILLIAM WRAGG.
Witnesses: A. DELLIEND, JACOB RUSS. RUSS testified 4 Mar. 1762 before
JOHN REMINGTON, J.P. Recorded 17 Apr. 1762 by WILLIAM HOPTON, Register.

Book X-X, p. 728   JAMES FLUD, planter, to WILLIAM FLUDD, both of
12 & 13 Jan. 1762   St. John's Parish, Berkeley Co., as security
L & R by Mortgage   on bond of even date in penal sum of Ł 6948
                      for payment of Ł 3474 currency, with interest,
on 1 Feb. 1762; 800 a. called Pon Bluff, in Berkeley Co., on S side Santee River; bounding NE on THOMAS LYNCH; NW on PETER DUMMAY & JAMES ROB-
ERT; also 400 a. in Berkeley Co. called MR. NICHOLL'S Corner, bounding NW
on THOMAS LYNCH; N on Santee River; other sides on vacant land; also half
of 200 a. at the Congarees, on N side Santee River; bounding SW on HENRY
SNELLING; other sides on vacant land. Witnesses: JOHN LITTLE, JOHN AXSON,
GEORGE MCNICHOLL. MCNICHOLL testified 27 Feb. 1762 before JOHN COLLETON,
J.P. Recorded 21 Apr. 1762 by WILLIAM HOPTON, Register.

Book X-X, p. 733   SIR JOHN COLLETON, of Charleston, Knight &
2 & 3 Mar. 1762   Bart., eldest son & heir of JOHN COLLETON,
L & R   ESQ.; & ANN his wife; to WILLIAM FLUD, of St.
                      John's Parish, Berkeley Co., for Ł 375 curren-
cy, 200 a., bounding N & E on Santee River; other sides on vacant land;
also 75 a. bounding NW on MR. BRUNSTON; SE on MR. NEILSON; SW on vacant
land; NE on Santee River; also 35 a. bounding SE & NW on JOHN COLLETON
(formerly MR. NEILSON); NE on Santee River; also 289 a., bounding SW on
JOHN COLLETON (formerly MR. NEILSON); NE on Santee River; other sides on
vacant land; the 4 adjoining tracts making 1 plantation of 599 a. in
Berkeley Co.; also 126 a. in Craven Co., bounding NE on vacant land; SW
on Santee River; other sides on vacant land. Witnesses: WILLIAM SKIRV-
ING, JAMES HAMILTON, JOSHUA WARD. WARD testified 5 Mar. 1762 before WIL-
LIAM BURROWS, J.P. Recorded 23 Apr. 1762 by WILLIAM HOPTON, Register.

DEEDS BOOK "Y-Y"
APRIL 1762 - SEPT. 1762

Book Y-Y, p. 1   HENRY DURANT, & REBEKAH his wife; & MARY WAR-
18 Feb. 1757   NOCK, spinster; to ELIAS FOISSIN, ESQ.; all of
Feoffment   Prince George Parish, Craven Co., for Ł 225
                      currency, their 1/3 part of 3 tracts in Craven
Co.; 1 of 500 a. on Waccamaw Neck, bounding SE on the sea & marsh; NW on
Waccamaw River; SW on estate of GEORGE THREADCRAFT; NE on second 500 a.;
1 of 500 a. on Waccamaw Neck, bounding SW on 1st tract; NE on PETER AL-
STON; SE on the sea; NW on Waccamaw River; 1 of 124 a. on an island be-
tween Waccamaw & Peedee Rivers; part of 214 a. recently granted ABRAHAM
WARNOCK; the 124 a. bounding SE on Waccamaw River; NW on ELIAS FOISSIN;
NE on other part of said 214 a. sold to PETER ALSTON; SW on JOSEPH LE-
BRUCE; total 1124 a. Witnesses: JOHN GODFREY, JOHN CHEESBOROUGH. Livery
& seizin delivered 18 Feb. 1757. CHEESBOROUGH testified 21 Feb. 1757 before GEORGE PAWLEY, J.P. Recorded 24 Apr. 1762 by WILLIAM HOPTON, Register.

Book Y-Y, p. 7   SARAH JOHNSTON, of Charleston, formerly SARAH
17 & 18 Nov. 1761   COLLINGS, widow & sole executrix of will of
L & R   JONATHAN COLLINGS the elder, mariner, of
                        Charleston of 1st part; to JOHN MCALL, ROBERT
COLLINGS, & ROBERT JOHNSTON, the 3 surviving children of said SARAH JOHN-
STON; & MARIAN COLLINGS & SARAH COLLINGS, the children of her late son
JONATHAN COLLINGS the younger; & MARY FOGARTIE & SARAH FOGARTIE, the
children of her late duaghter, MARY FOGARTIE the elder (heretofore MARY
DOUGLASS), grandchildren of said SARAH JOHNSTON; of 2nd part. Whereas
JONATHAN COLLINGS the elder owned 545 a. granted 1 June 1709 by Gov. NA-
THANIEL JOHNSON to PETER LEGER; near the Orange Quarters, sometimes call-
ed the Bull Head, in Berkeley Co., bounding SE on JOHN DONHOM; & by will
dated 17 Aug. 1727 bequeathed to his wife SARAH COLLINGS (now SARAH JOHN-
STON) the use of the residue of his real & personal estate during her
lifetime, giving her authority to dispose of the property among her chil-
dren; now she gives JOHN MCALL, ROBERT JOHNSTON, MARIAN COLLINGS, SARAH
COLLINGS, MARY FOGARTIE, & SARAH FOGARTIE, each, 1 a. taken out of the NE
part of the 545 a.; the remainder to ROBERT COLLINGS. Witnesses: THOMAS
ADAM, MALCOLM BROWN, THOMAS WRIGHT. BROWN testified 10 Mar. 1762 before
JAMES PARSONS, J.P. Recorded 24 Apr. 1762 by WILLIAM HOPTON, Register.

Book Y-Y, p. 17   JOHN BAXTER, planter, of St. Andrews Parish, &
9 & 10 Mar. 1762   ANN (her mark) his wife, to PETER DOURGONIST,
L & R   planter, of New Windsor Township, for Ł 255
                        currency, 400 a. in New Windsor at a place
called Savannah Town, about 2 miles from his Majesty's Garrison Fort
Moor; bounding SW on Savannah River; which tract was originally granted
on 12 Aug. 1737 to MARTHA MCGILLIVRAY & by various conveyances came to
BAXTER. Witnesses: GEORGE JOHNSTON, JOHANN (his mark) WINCKLER. JOHN-
STON testified 10 Mar. 1762 before JOHN MURRAY, J.P. Recorded 29 Apr.
1762 by WILLIAM HOPTON, Register.

Book Y-Y, p. 23   GEORGE SAXBY, ESQ., & ELIZABETH his wife, to
1 & 2 Feb. 1762   WILLIAM BLAKE, ESQ., both of Charleston, for
L & R   Ł 945 British, & an annuity of Ł 140 British;
                        a lot in Charleston, bounding N 104 ft. on
Queen Street; S on Broad Street; E on MRS. MAGDALEN DEVEAUX & GEORGE SAX-
BY; W 481 ft. on Allen's Street; also a lot bounding S on MRS. MAGDALEN
DEVEAUX; N 48 ft. on Queen Street; E 150 ft. on HENRY MIDDLETON; W on
first lot; also the W half of lot #229 (the whole containing half an a.,
English measure), bounding E on other half; W on proprietors of the Sugar
House; S on marsh of Ashley River; N on Broad Street. Whereas GEORGE
SAXBY gave bond dated 12 Apr. 1754 to ISABELLA GLEN, wife of DR. THOMAS
GLEN, formerly widow of JAMES GREEME, C.J., for Ł 2400 British for pay-
ment of an annuity of Ł 140 British to said ISABELLA GLEN on the Royal
Exchange of London, should she reside in Great Britain, or at her dwell-
ing house in Charleston, should she reside there; giving said lots as se-
curity; & whereas SAXBY has agreed to sell the lots to BLAKE, BLAKE agreeing to pay SAXBY Ł 945 British & to pay ISABELLA the annuity during her
lifetime, now SAXBY conveys the lots to BLAKE. Witnesses: DAVID GREEME,
WILLIAM GREEME. WILLIAM GREEME testified 11 Mar. 1762 before JOHN REM-
INGTON, J.P. Recorded 1 May 1762 by WILLIAM HOPTON, Register.

Book Y-Y, p. 35   SAMUEL (his mark) FRY, planter, of Granville
20 & 21 Aug. 1760   Co., to SUSANNAH PERKINS, of District of Au-
L & R   gusta, St. Paul's Parish, Georgia, for Ł 100
                        British, 100 a. on the Salt Catchers, Gran-
ville Co., SC, where FRY now dwells. Witnesses: ANTHONY GROOBS, JOHN
SALLIS. SALLIS testified 20 Sept. 1760 before WILLIAM DRAKE, J.P. Recorded 1 May 1762 by WILLIAM HOPTON, Register.

Book Y-Y, p. 40   JOSEPH HASFORT, planter, son & heir of JOSEPH
12 & 13 Sept. 1759   HASFORT, to ROBERT BALLINGALL, planter, for
L & R   Ł 1500 SC money, 1000 a. in Berkeley Co.,
                        bounding N on JAMES COACHMAN & vacant land; SE
& NW on vacant land; SW on DAVID MULICE & vacant land; also 2/3 of 400 a.,
bounding NE on Santee River; SE on DONE WILLIAMSON; NW on JOHN STRODE; SW
on vacant land; also 500 a. on E side S Edisto River, near Bob's Savannah, in Colleton Co., bounding E on JOHN PENDARVIS & JOHN PRESCOTT; N on
JOHN PENDARVIS; S on HENRY NICHOLS; also 330 a. in Berkeley Co., bounding

Eon GEORGE CANTEY; N on JOSEPH BLACK; W on JAMES DUNNAHOE; S on HUGH FER-
GUSON; SE on MR. NORWOOD; also 50 a. on N side Ashley River, bounding E
on ELIHU BAKER, SR.; S & W on RICHARD BUTLER; N on JOSEPH HASFORD; also
400 a. in Colleton Co., bounding NE on NW branch of PonPon River; SE & SW
on vacant land; NW on FRANCIS FOSTER. Witnesses: BENJAMIN GUERARD, BEL-
LAMY CRAWFORD. CRAWFORD testified 19 Feb. 1762 before JAMES GRINDLAY,
J.P. Recorded 3 May 1762 by WILLIAM HOPTON, Register.

Book Y-Y, p. 46   ANDREW GOVAN, planter, of Berkeley Co., to
21 & 22 Jan. 1762   HELEN RATTRAY, widow & executrix of will of
L & R by Mortgage   JOHN RATTRAY, ESQ., of Charleston, as security
                         on bond dated 9 Feb. 1760 in penal sum of
Ł 5360 for payment of Ł 2680 SC money, with interest, on 1 July 1763;
721 a. in Berkeley Co., originally granted to JOSEPH HASFORD; bounding NE
& SE on vacant land; SW on CAPT. PETER TAYLOR & DAVID BLACK; NW on JAMES
ANDERSON & JOHN BAKER; also 200 a. adjoining the 721 a., being part of
300 a. granted JAMES ANDERSON, in Colleton Co., bounding SE on said land
granted HASFORT; NE on vacant land; NW on JOHN HARWOOD CRUM; SW on vacant
land. Witnesses: ROBERT WILLIAMS, JR., JAMES GRINDLAY. GRINDLAY testified 19 Feb. 1762 before WILLIAM BURROWS, J.P. Recorded 4 May 1762 by
WILLIAM HOPTON, Register.

Book Y-Y, p. 53   JOHN GOVAN, ESQ., of Prince William Parish,
5 & 6 Feb. 1762   Granville Co., to JAMES GRINDLAY, attorney, of
L & R by Mortgage   Charleston, as security on bond dated 28 Oct.
                         1761 in penal sum of Ł 5330 for payment of
Ł 2665 currency, with interest, on 28 Oct. 1762; 500 a. in Prince William
Parish, lately in possession of JOHN CUTHBERT; bounding N on GEORGE CUTH-
BERT; W on a path leading to Port Royal Old Ferry; S & SE on Coosaw Riv-
er; NE on a creek. Witnesses: ROBERT WILLIAMS, JR., ALEXANDER CORMOCK.
WILLIAMS testified before WILLIAM BURROWS, J.P. on 16 Feb. 1762. Record-
ed 4 May 1762 by WILLIAM HOPTON, Register.

Book Y-Y, p. 59   PAUL DE ST. JULIEN, & MARY his wife, to JAMES
21 July 1741   DE ST. JULIEN, ESQ., both of Berkeley Co., for
Release   Ł 100 currency, 60 a. in Berkeley Co., bound-
                         ing N on JAMES DE ST. JULIEN; E on PETER DE
ST. JULIEN; S on heirs of DANIEL RAVENEL; W on PAUL DE ST. JULIEN; which
60 a. is part of 550 a. granted 6 Oct. 1696 by the Lords Proprs. to JOHN
STEWART. Witnesses: JOSEPH DE ST. JULIEN, DAVID LAFONS, RICHARD BUSK.
LAFONS testified 12 July 1759 before WILLIAM MOULTRIE, J.P. Recorded 5
May 1762 by WILLIAM HOPTON, Register.

Book Y-Y, p. 63   JANE HARLEY (formerly JANE JACKSON, widow, of
15 & 16 Mar. 1757   CAPT. JOHN JACKSON, of PonPon) & GEORGE JACK-
L & R   SON, surviving executrix & executor of estate
                         of CAPT. JOHN JACKSON, to GIDEON DUPONT,
planter, of St. Bartholomew's Parish, Colleton Co., for Ł 773 currency,
299 a. in St. Bartholomew's Parish, adjoining the village of Jacksonburgh
being part of 400 a. granted 28 Aug. 1700 to JOHN JACKSON, out of which
said village was taken; bounding S on THOMAS MELVIN; N on WILLIAM PETERS
& ROBERT OSWALD; W on ROBERT OSWALD; SE on JAMES POSTELL; the 299 a. having been devised to them by CAPT. JACKSON'S will dated 24 Mar. 1747 giving them authority to sell. Witnesses: JOHN SMITH, JOHN JACKSON. SMITH
testified 3 Dec. 1761 before JAMES SHARP, J.P. Recorded 6 May 1762 by
WILLIAM HOPTON, Register. Plat certified 22 May 1752 by JOHN STEVENS,
D.S.

Book Y-Y, p. 69   NATHANIEL TREGAGLY, gentleman, of Molchot
19 & 20 Mar. 1762   Park, in White Parish, Co. of Wilts, Great
L & R   Britain, by his attorney, ARCHIBALD JOHNSTON,
                         planter, of Craven Co., SC, to WILLIAM SMITH,
shopkeeper, of Georgetown, for Ł 1200 SC money, lot #28 in Georgetown,
bounding SW 150 ft. on Front Street; NW 217.9 ft. on lot #27; NE on lot
#62; SE on lot #29. Witnesses: ARCHIBALD BAIRD, JOSEPH DUBOURDIEU. DU-
BOURDIEU testified 20 Mar. 1762 before JOSEPH BROWN, J.P. Recorded 21
May 1762 by WILLIAM HOPTON, Register.

Book Y-Y, p. 78   WILLIAM GREEN, planter, of Prince Frederick
1 & 3 Aug. 1761   Parish, Craven Co., & JANE his wife, to

161

L & R WILLIAM SMITH, planter, of Prince George Parish, Craven Co., for Ł 150 currency, 315-1/2 a. Whereas Lt. Gov. THOMAS BROUGHTON on 12 Dec. 1735 granted ANTHONY WHITE 1620 a. in Prince George Parish; & whereas WHITE by his will gave his executors, authority to sell his real & personal estate, & JOSEPH DUBOURDIEU, acting executor, by L & R dated 1 & 2 Mar. 1748 sold WILLIAM GREEN 400 a., part of the 1620 a.; now GREEN sells a part to SMITH. Witnesses: ALEXANDER DUNN, WILLIAM LUPTAN. DUNN testified 7 Sept. 1761 before THOMAS BLYTHE, J.P. Recorded 26 May 1762 by WILLIAM HOPTON, Register.

Book Y-Y, p. 85
5 & 6 Jan. 1762
L & R by Mortgage

WILLIAM HARVEY, gentleman, & MARY his wife, to THOMAS CORKER, merchant, all of Charleston, as security on 2 bonds, 1 of even date in penal sum of Ł 8000 for payment of Ł 4000 currency, with interest, on 6 Jan. 1763; the other for Ł 1000; the W part of lot #60, formerly the estate of ROBERT TRADD; bounding N 100 ft. 8 in. on Tradd Street; W on Old Church Street; E on heirs of DANIEL TOWNSHEND. Witnesses: ROBERT WILLIAMS, JR., THOMAS CORKER, JR. CORKER testified 28 Jan. 1762 before MOSES THOMSON. Recorded 27 May 1762 by WILLIAM HOPTON, Register. On Jan. 6, 1762 CORKER acknowledged receipt of Ł 1000 in payment of 2nd bond. On 25 June 1770 CORKER acknowledged receipt of Ł 2426:2:8 part payment on 1st bond "on account of that part of the premises wherein GEORGE ABBOTTSTALL being sold to GEORGE SAVAGE, ESQ." Witness: JAMES KER. JOSIAH SMITH, JR., cole executor of CORKER'S will, on 6 Mar. 1772 acknowledged receipt of full satisfaction.

Book Y-Y, p. 93
20 & 21 June 1759
L & R

BENJAMIN DART, gentleman, of Charleston (eldest son & heir of HANNAH DART & JOHN DART), & AMELIA his wife, to THOMAS SACHEVERELL, planter, for Ł 1687:10:0 currency, 562-1/2 a., English measure, near Wiltown, in Colleton Co., bounding SW on WILLIAM LIVINGSTON; NW on HENRY LIVINGSTON; being part of 2250 a. formerly belonging to WILLIAM LIVINGSTON, the elder; the 562-1/2 a. being HANNAH'S inheritance. Whereas upon the death of HANNAH the land descended to BENJAMIN as her heir expectant, but her husband JOHN DART was tenant by the Courtesey of England for his lifetime; & whereas JOHN DART died some time ago, now BENJAMIN may sell. Witnesses: JOHN MILNER, NATHANIEL BULLINE. BULLINE testified 18 July 1750 before ROBERT WILLIAMS, JR., J.P. Recorded 28 May 1762 by WILLIAM HOPTON, Register. Plat given.

Book Y-Y, p. 103
30 Apr. 1759
Feoffment

ANDREAS BOUCH, joiner, of Saxegotha Township, Berkeley Co., to his son, JOHN LEONARD BOUCH, planter, for love & affection & other considerations, 150 a. part of 400 a., in Saxegotha Township granted 22 Feb. 1745 to ANDREAS BOUCH; bounding E on land given HENRY BOUCH, brother of JOHN LEONARD BOUCH by said ANDREAS, his father; N on Saludy River; W on land given to GEORGE MILLER (son-in-law to said ANDREAS BOUCH) by said ANDREAS; S on vacant land. Witnesses: JOHN GEORGE MILLER, ELIZABETH (her mark) REIZTER, HENRY (his mark) BOUCH. ELIZABETH REIZTER testifies 30 Apr. 1759 before JOHN PEARSON, J.P. Recorded 28 May 1762 by WILLIAM HOPTON, Register. Plat certified 29 Mar. 1759 by JOHN PEARSON, D.S.

Book Y-Y, p. 107
30 Apr. 1759
Feoffment

ANDREAS BOUCH, joiner, of Saxegotha Township, Berkeley Co., to his son-in-law, GEORGE MILLAR, shoemaker, for the better support of MARGARET, wife of GEORGE MILLAR & daughter of ANDREAS BOUCH; 50 a. in Saxegotha Township, bounding E on JOHN LEONARD BOUCH; N on Saludy River; W on JOHN GRANGETT & vacant land; S on vacant land. Witnesses: ELIZABETH (her mark) RAIZTER, JOHN LEONARD (his mark) BOUCH, HENRY (his mark) BOUCH. ELIZABETH RAIZTER testified 30 Apr. 1759 before JOHN PEARSON, J.P. Recorded 30 May 1762 before WILLIAM HOPTON, Register. Plat certified 29 Mar. 1759 by JOHN PEARSON, D.S., showing 50 a., part of 400 a. granted ANDREAS BOUCH on 22 Feb. 1745.

Book Y-Y, p. 111
16 & 17 Mar. 1762
L & R

ELIAS FOISSIN, planter, of Prince George Parish, to HENRY PERONNEAU, merchant, of Charleston, executor of will of HENRY PERONNEAU, as security on bond of even date in penal sum of

Ł 6294 for payment of Ł 3147 currency, with interest, on 16 Mar. 1753; &
bond dated 28 Mar. 1752 given HENRY PERONNEAU the elder in penal sum of
Ł 7225:9:0 for payment of Ł 3612:4:6 currency, with interest on 28 Mar.
1753, 700 a. granted ELIAS FOISSIN on 28 Nov. 1735, in Craven Co., bound-
ing SE on Peedee River; SW on WILLIAM SWINTON; NW on JOHN GREEN; NE on
JAMES PAYNE; also 14 Negroes, a penknife delivered. Witnesses: JOHN
CHAMPNEYS, WILLIAM WEBB. WEBB testified 18 Mar. 1762 before DAVID RHIND,
J.P. Recorded 2 June 1762 by WILLIAM HOPTON, Register. On 6 June 1766
PERONNEAU received full satisfaction of mortgage from ROGER PINCKNEY,
P.M. Witness: FENWICKE BULL.

Book Y-Y, p. 120   RICHARD GOUGH, planter, to THOMAS CORDES,
22 Jan. 1753   planter, both of St. Johns Parish, Berkeley
Feoffment   Co., for Ł 800 currency, 200 a. in St. Johns
                         Parish, bounding N on THOMAS CORDES; S on
RICHARD GOUGH; SE on land called Dockum, belonging to JOHN BALL; W on W
branch of T of Cooper River; according to plat dated 18 Jan. 1753 certified by JOHN HENTIE. Witnesses: NICHOLAS HARLESTON, ELIAS BALL, JOHN
COMING BALL. Livery & seizin delivered. HARLESTON testified 1 Mar. 1753
before FRANCIS LEJAU, J.P. Recorded 3 June 1762 by WILLIAM HOPTON, Register. Plat given.

Book Y-Y, p. 125   GEORGE PAWLEY, gentleman, of Craven Co., to
10 & 11 Aug. 1749   THOMAS CORDES, planter, of Berkeley Co., for
L & R   Ł 300 currency, 130 a. in St. Johns Parish,
                         bounding E on THOMAS CORDES; S on GEORGE PAW-
LEY; NW on W branch of Cooper River; N on JAMES CORDES; according to
grant dated 6 Sept. 1711 from Gov. ROBERT GIBBES to PERCIVAL (PAWLEY),
recorded 7 Sept. 1711. ANN PAWLEY, wife of GEORGE, releases her claim.
Witnesses: PERCIVAL PAWLEY, WILLIAM PAWLEY, BENJAMIN (his mark) WEBB.
PERCIVAL PAWLEY testified 17 Nov. 1758 before THOMAS BLYTHE, J.P. Re-
corded 5 June 1762 by WILLIAM HOPTON, Register.

Book Y-Y, p. 134   SAMUEL STEVENS, planter, of Berkeley Co., to
5 Oct. 1751   JAMES SMITH, for Ł 390 currency, 130 a. in St.
Feoffment   George Parish, Berkeley Co., bounding NW on
                         said STEVENS; N on Ashley River; E on CHARLES
WRIGHT & WILLIAM MILES; S on WILLIAM MILES & JAMES SEWRIGHT. Turf & twig
delivered. Witnesses: THOMAS BULLINE, JR., ROBERT MILLER, WILLIAM POOLE.
POOLE testified 10 Mar. 1762 before BENJAMIN WARING, J.P. Recorded 5
June 1762 by WILLIAM HOPTON, Register.

Book Y-Y, p. 136   THOMAS HUTCHINSON, cabinet maker, of Charles-
27 Mar. 1762   ton, sole executor of will of RIBTON HUTCHIN-
Release   SON, gentleman; to JOHN STORY, joiner, of St.
                         Helena Parish, for Ł 75 currency, a lot in
Beaufort. Whereas on 8 Aug. 1717 Dep. Gov. ROBERT DANIEL granted LAW-
RENCE DENNIS lot #79 in Beaufort, 60 ft. x 120 ft., bounding S on lot
#80; W on Scott Street; N on lot #78; E on lot #74; which lot by his will
dated 7 Aug. 1733 DENNIS bequeathed to his wife PROVIDENCE; who later
married RIBTON HUTCHINSON & conveyed the lot to him; & whereas said
HUTCHINSON by his will dated 11 Aug. 1757 directed his executor, THOMAS
HUTCHINSON, to sell the lot; now THOMAS sells to STORY. Witnesses: DAN-
IEL CLEMENT, BENJAMIN LORD. CLEMENT testified 5 Apr. 1762 before HENRY
GRAY, J.P. Recorded 7 June 1762 by WILLIAM HOPTON, Register.

Book Y-Y, p. 140   JOHN RUSHING, planter, to JACOB JOHNSON,
25 Apr. 1759   planter, both of Craven Co., for Ł 300 curren-
Lease   cy, 150 a. on Thompson's Creek, granted JOHN
                         RUSHING 29 Nov. 1750, bounding on all sides on
vacant land. Delivery by turf & twig. Witnesses: MARTIN (his mark)
JOHNSON, PETER (his mark) WALKER. WALKER testified 25 Apr. 1759 before
WILLIAM LORD, J.P. Recorded 7 June 1762 by WILLIAM HOPTON, Register.

Book Y-Y, p. 143   JOHN CRAWFORD, SR., to JOHN LIDE, both of Cra-
19 Feb. 1755   ven Co., for Ł 350 currency, a tract of land
Release   in Craven Co., on S side Peedee River, granted
                         2 Mar. 1743 to JEREMIAH ROWELL, & by various
mesne conveyed became the property of ABRAHAM COLSON, & transferred by
his executrix to JOHN CRAWFORD on 25 May 1753. Witnesses: SAMUEL TAYLOR,

THOMAS BINGHAM, THOMAS CRAWFORD, DURHAM HILLS. TAYLOR testified 24 Feb. 1755 before GEORGE HICKS, J.P. Recorded 8 June 1762 by WILLIAM HOPTON, Register.

Book Y-Y, p. 147   THOMAS ELLERBEE, planter, to THOMAS LIDE,
13 & 14 Sept. 1756   planter, both of Craven Co., for ₤ 850 curren-
L & R   cy, 300 a. in Craven Co., in the Welch tract,
                          granted by Gov. JAMES GLEN on 12 Dec. 1746 to
JOHN BROWN; who by L & R dated 6 & 7 Feb. 1748 sold to JOHN ELLARBEE;
bounding SW on Peedee River; other sides on vacant land. Witnesses:
CLAUDIUS PEGUES, JOHN CRAWFORD, JR. PEGUES testified 12 Sept. 1756 before JOHN WALL, J.P. Recorded 9 June 1762 by WILLIAM HOPTON, Register.

Book Y-Y, p. 153   JOHN PETER, planter, to JOHN PERREMAN (PERRI-
29 Nov. 1742   MAN), both of Colleton Co., for ₤ 600 curren-
Release   cy, 200 a. in Colleton Co., W of the freshes
                          of Edisto; bounding on all sides on vacant
land. Witnesses: ROYAL SPRY, WILLIAM HARVEY, AUSTIN ROBERT LOCKTON.
HARVEY testified 25 Apr. 1761 before JAMES SKIRVING, J.P. Recorded 10
June 1762 by WILLIAM HOPTON, Register.

Book Y-Y, p. 156   RICHARD BERESFORD, ESQ., of Charleston, &
10 Oct. 1761   SARAH his wife, to DANIEL LESESNE, planter, of
Feoffment   St. Thomas Parish, Berkeley Co., for ₤ 3000
                          currency, 70 a., part of 300 a. in St. Thomas
Parish granted EDGAR WELLS & by various mesne conveyances became bested
in BERESFORD. Witnesses: EDWARD NEUFVILLE, HENDRICK KOHLER, HARRIET
BERESFORD, ELIZABETH BERESFORD. Witnesses to delivery of possession &
seizin: ROBERT COLLINS, JOHN DUBOISE, STEPHEN FOGARTIE. NEUFVILLE testified 4 Mar. 1762 before CHARLES PINCKNEY, J.P. Recorded 11 June 1762
by WILLIAM HOPTON, Register. Plat of 70 a. by JOHN HENTIE, dated 18
Sept. 1761, bounding SE on RICHARD BERESFORD; NE on JOHN DUTARQUE; NW on
DANIEL LESESNE & STEPHEN FOGARTIE; SW on RICHARD BERESFORD.

Book Y-Y, p. 162   MARGARET BRUNSON, widow, to DAVID BRUNSON,
27 Feb. 1752   both of Craven Co., for ₤ 50 currency, 300 a.
Feoffment   in Craven Co., bounding NW on Wateree River;
                          SE on CAPT. PATER PORCHER; other sides on va-
cant land. Witnesses: ISAAC BRUNSON, SAMUEL NELSON, JR., GEORGE BRUNSON.
Livery & seizin delivered. MARGARET signed before JAO^DE NEILSON. Recorded 14 June 1762 by WILLIAM HOPTON, Register.

Book Y-Y, p. 166   GEORGE BRUNSON, SR., cordwainer, of Prince
2 & 3 Feb. 1762   Frederick Parish, Craven Co., to ISAAC BRUN-
L & R   SON, SR., planter, of St. Marks Parish, Craven
                          Co., for ₤ 85 currency, 100 a. on N side San-
tee River, in St. Johns Parish, Berkeley Co., bounding on all sides on
vacant land; originally granted to MARGARET BRUNSON. Witnesses: SAMUEL
BENNETT, GEORGE BRUNSON, JR. BENNETT testified 4 Feb. 1762 before RICH-
ARD RICHARDSON, J.P. Recorded 16 June 1762 by WILLIAM HOPTON, Register.

Book Y-Y, p. 174   HENRY YONGE, Sur. Gen., of Georgia, & ELIZA-
4 & 5 Jan. 1760   BETH his wife (formerly ELIZABETH BELLINGER, 1
L & R   of the sisters of WILLIAM BELLINGER, nephew of
                          Landgrave Edmund Bellinger); to ARCHIBALD WIL-
KINS, planter, of Granville Co., & ANN his wife (formerly ANN BELLINGER,
another sister of said WILLIAM BELLINGER); for ₤ 833:6:8 SC money, their
undivided third part of 1000 a. (patent land of Landgrave EDMUND BALLIN-
GER) in Granville Co., on SW side Port Royal River, on the Euhaw (Euhan);
bounding N & E on said EDMUND BELLINGER; W & S on JASPERS Barony. Whereas Landgrave EDMUND BELLINGER by will dated 21 Feb. 1739 gave his wife,
ELIZABETH, & his sons, daughters, nephews & other persons certain lands,
to be allotted by his wife, or his son EDMUND; & whereas WILLIAM BELLIN-
GER, now deceased was entitled to a certain part, & ELIZABETH YOUNG, ANN
WILKINS & the heirs of MARY HELSALL (formerly MARY BELLINGER, another
sister of WILLIAM BELLINGER), became entitled to said WILLIAMS land; &
whereas EDMUND BELLINGER, 2nd, by authority of his father's will, allotted to ELIZABETH, ANN, & the heirs of MARY, 1000 a.; now ELIZABETH & her
husband sell their share to WILKINS. Witnesses: JOHN MULLRYNE, JAMES
EDWARD POWELL. MULRYNE testified 29 Apr. 1760 before JAMES THOMSON, J.P.

Recorded 18 June 1762 by WILLIAM HOPTON, Register. Plat of 1000 a. by OWEN BOWEN, Dep. Sur., dated 24 Aug. 1759. On 30 Aug. 1760 ELIZABETH YONGE renounced her dower to above land before JAMES DEVEAUX, Ass't. Judge of General Court, in Savannah, Georgia. Recorded 18 June 1762 by WILLIAM HOPTON, Register.

Book Y-Y, p. 184   ALEXANDER TAYLOR, tailor, to EGERTON LEIGH,
23 Jan. 1762   ESQ., both of Charleston, for Ŀ 150 currency,
Feoffment   the E part of a lot (the whole being 1 a., 2
                        roods) marked E on the plan of Ansonborough,
containing 9383 S.F., bounding N on GEORGE HUNTER; E on LUKE STOUTENBURGH
(now EGERTON LEIGH); S on heirs of RICHARD WAINWRIGHT; W on other part
same lot. Witnesses: MARTHA BREMAR, JAMES GRINDLAY, JOHN BREMAR. JOHN
BREMAR testified 16 Apr. 1762 before ROBERT WILLIAMS, J.P. Recorded 21
June 1762 by WILLIAM HOPTON, Register. Plat by WILLIAM WILKINS, dated 22
Jan. 1762, showing square marked A 59 x 79, representing 3660 ft., enclosed, belonging to TAYLOR; an oblong marked B representing 5723 S.F.,
59 x 98 (97); the whole lot containing 65,340 S.F.

Book Y-Y, p. 188   JOACHIM HARDSTONE, & ANN (her mark) his wife,
27 June 1761   to JACOB STROUBART, planter, of Purrysburgh,
L & R   St. Peters Parish, Granville Co., for Ŀ 400
                        currency, 200 a. in Purrysburgh Township,
bounding W on DAVID HUMBART; S on GEORGE STROUBART; other sides on HENRY
BOURGUIN. Witnesses: HENRY LEWIS BOURGUIN, MARIANNE BOURGUIN. HENRY
BOURGUIN testified 28 June 1761 before JOHN BAPTIST BOURGUIN, J.P. Recorded 23 June 1762 by WILLIAM HOPTON, Register.

Book Y-Y, p. 196   DAVID GIROUD, carpenter, & ANN MARY, his wife,
20 Aug. 1761   to JACOB STROUBART, planter, both of Purrys-
L & R   burgh, Granville Co., for Ŀ 1125 currency,
                        700 a. in Purrysburgh Township, in 5 adjoining
tracts; 100 a. granted LEWIS KEHL, 16 Sept. 1738; 50 a. granted JOHN
FRANCIS HENRY 14 Dec. 1739; 50 a. granted MARY HENRY 14 Dec. 1739; 350 a.
granted DAVID GIROUD 16 Jan. 1761; 150 a. granted DAVID GIROUD; bounding
S on JOHN PETER PURY & HENRY MAYERHOFFER; W on THERESE DE JEAN & GEORGE
STROUBERT; N on FRANCIS VAUCHIER & PETER LAFFITTE; E on DANIEL PILETT.
Witnesses: JOSEPH MCPHERSON, FRANCIS VAUCHIER, JOHN GEORGE KEHL. KEHL
testified 17 Feb. 1762 before ADRIAN MAYER, J.P. Recorded 28 June 1762
by WILLIAM HOPTON, Register.

Book Y-Y, p. 204   JANE BOONE, widow, only acting executrix, GA-
19 & 20 May 1757   BRIEL MANIGAULT, GEORGE AUSTIN, & THOMAS SMITH,
L & R   JR., merchants, only surviving executors of
                        will of MAJ. WILLIAM BOONE; all of Charleston;
of 1st part; to WILLIAM MATHEWES, planter, of Colleton Co., for
Ŀ 3107:4:6 currency, at public auction, 671 a. (except as excepted) part
of 820 a. on W side Stono River, on John's Island, Colleton Co., bounding
S on OBADIAH WILKINS; being the remaining part of said 820 a. originally
granted by Gov. JOSEPH BLAKE on 17 Aug. 1700 to CAPT. WILLIAM DAVIS, who
died intestate; & inherited by his only daughter & heir, ELIZABETH, then
wife of WILLIAM WILKINS; then inherited by her eldest son & heir, OBADIAH
WILKINS; his father, WILLIAM, having released his interest to him; OBA-
DIAH & his wife ELIZABETH selling 671 a. to WILLIAM BOONE by L & R dated
22 & 23 Oct. 1742; W on MR. WHIPPY (formerly RICHARD WILSON); other sides
on Davis Creek & marsh. Whereas WILLIAM BOONE owned 671 a. & by will
dated 17 Mar. 1750 authorized his executors to sell his real & personal
estate as most beneficial for his wife & children, appointing his wife,
JANE, & GABRIEL MANIGAULT, ANTHONY MATHEWES, GEORGE AUSTIN & THOMAS SMITH,
JR., of Charleston, & THOMAS HANSON & CHARLES ALEXANDER, of Antigua, his
executrix & executors; now they sell the 671 a. to WILLIAM MATHEWES, except 2 a. (marked within 3 yellow lines on a plat) bounding NW on the
creek & extending to the SE; in which ground BOONE was buried & reserved
as a burial place for BOONE'S family & not for MATHEWES or his heirs.
Witnesses: THOMAS LAMBOLL, JOHN FREER. LAMBOLL testified 24 Apr. 1762
before JEREMIAH SAVAGE, J.P. Recorded 5 July 1762 by WILLIAM HOPTON,
Register.

Book Y-Y, p. 218   ANTHONY MATHEWES, ESQ., to WILLIAM MATHEWES,
9 & 10 Nov. 1752   gentleman, both of Charleston, for Ŀ 1300

L & R   currency, 260 a. in Colleton Co. Whereas
                         THOMAS LLOYD, gentleman, of Charleston, owned
260 a. in Colleton Co., bounding N on MAJ. BOONE; S on a marsh of Keewaw
River; W on WILLIAM WHIPPEY; E on Stono River; which by L & R dated 23 &
24 Mar. 1749 he conveyed to ANTHONY MATHEWES in trust for MARY, wife of
said THOMAS LLOYD; & whereas MARY, now aged 22, on 7 this inst. Nov. has
ordered the land sold to WILLIAM MATHEWES; now said trustee conveys the
land as stated. Witnesses: MOSES AUDEBERT, JEREMIAH SAVAGE. AUDEBERT
testified 23 Apr. 1762 before WILLIAM BURROWS, J.P. Recorded 6 July 1762
by WILLIAM HOPTON, Register.

Book Y-Y, p. 228   THOMAS LYNCH, ESQ., of Charleston, eldest son
29 & 30 Mar. 1762   & heir of COL. THOMAS LYNCH; & HANNAH his
L & R   wife; to ISAAC LESESNE, planter, of Daniel's
                        Island, in St. Thomas Parish; for ₤ 5000 SC
money, 633 a. of high land & swamp in Prince George Parish, Craven Co.,
bounding NW on ROBERT HUME; SE on CAPT. WILLIAM MOULTRIE; SW on Santee
River; also 425 a. of swamp or marsh land on an island, bounding NE on
Santee River; NW on ROBERT HUME; SE on CAPT. WILLIAM MOULTRIE & JACOB
MOTTE. Witnesses: DAVID OLIPHANT, WILLIAM PARKER. PARKER testified 21
Apr. 1762 before JAMES MOULTRIE, J.P. Recorded 7 July 1762 by WILLIAM
HOPTON, Register. Plats of 425 a. & 633 a. pricked off from JOHN HORRY'S
maps by WILLIAM WILKINS, Sur., on 1 Apr. 1762.

Book Y-Y, p. 237   Assignment by Mortgage, of feoffment from ROB-
28 Apr. 1762   ERT EKELLS to NATHANIEL RAYMOR, which feoff-
                        ment was ordered not to be recorded. Whereas
ALEXANDER ROSE, merchant, of Charleston, loaned RAYMOR ₤ 630:18:2 SC money, RAYMOR conveyed to ROSE, as security, lot #18 on Union Street, 26 ft.
10 in. by 122 ft., with the tenements thereon. Witness: JAMES MOULTRIE.
Recorded 8 July 1762 by WILLIAM HOPTON, Register. Note: The feoffment
from EKELLS to RAYMOR gave boundaries as follows: N on a messuage &
ground belonging to JAMES KIRKWOOD; E on part same lot; S on part same
lot belonging to MARY HESKEL; partly of HOPKINS PRICE; & partly of MARY
HESKEL; W on Union Street.

Book Y-Y, p. 240   THOMAS BECKETT, butcher, to JOSEPH TOBIAS,
9 Mar. 1759   merchant, both of Charleston, as security on
Mortgage   bond of even date in penal sum of ₤ 377:4:0
                        for payment of ₤ 188:12:0 currency, with int-
erest, on 9 Mar. 1760; a tenement & lot on White Point, in Charleston,
bounding S on THOMAS LAMBOLL. Witnesses: WILLIAM GOWDEY, DAVID OLIVERE
(a Quaker). OLIVERE testified 19 Mar. 1759 before JOHN MURRAY, J.P.
Recorded 8 July 1762 by WILLIAM HOPTON, Register.

Book Y-Y, p. 242   CHARLES PINCKNEY, ESQ., & ELIZABETH his wife,
28 Dec. 1751   to JOSEPH BLACK, bricklayer, both of Charles-
Feoffment   ton, for ₤ 150 currency, part of 4 lots in
                        Charleston, (which PINCKNEY purchased jointly
with HENRY PERONNEAU from the executors of WILLIAM WATIES, & which they
afterwards divided into several smaller lots, & severed the jointenancy
between them), being the N part of subdivision #10, bounding N 30 ft. on
Hunter Street; W on PERONNEAU; E 75 ft. on PINCKNEY; S on other half of
#10 sold by PINCKNEY to CHRISTOPHER BLACK; with all houses thereon. Wit-
nesses: ANN PINCKNEY, ELIZABETH CORNISH. Livery & seizin delivered. ANN
DOYLEY (formerly ANN PINCKNEY) testified 24 June 1760 before JOHN REMING-
TON, J.P. Recorded 9 July 1762 by WILLIAM HOPTON, Register.

Book Y-Y, p. 246   JOHN BARNWELL, planter, & MARTHA his wife, to
21 Oct. 1760   EDWARD ELLIS, planter, both of St. Helena Par-
L & R   ish, Granville Co., for ₤ 1100 currency, 500
                        a., called Fish Hall, on Hilton Head Island,
granted COL. JOHN BARNWELL, who bequeathed to JOHN, party hereto; bounding N on Port Royal Sound; E on the inlet; W on a small creek; S on heirs
of TRENCH. Witnesses: JONATHAN NORTON, JOHN NORTON, ANN BARNWELL, (late
ANN DEVEAUX), SAMUEL GREEN. GREEN testified 23 Apr. 1762 before WILLIAM
HARVEY, J.P. Recorded 9 July 1762 by WILLIAM HOPTON, Register.

Book Y-Y, p. 253   JANE MASSEY, widow, to JANE MASSEY, JR., for
17 & 18 Feb. 1762   ₤ 500 currency, part of lot #164 in Charleston,

L & R   bounding E 60 ft. on King Street; W on JOHN
                               DRAYTON; S on MR. VARAMBEAU; N 142 ft. on es-
tate of JOHN HYCOTT. Witnesses: SARAH BROWN, ELIXABETH BOURQUIN. SARAH
testified before JAMES MOULTRIE, J.P., 2 Mar. 1762. Recorded 10 July
1762 by WILLIAM HOPTON, Register.

Book Y-Y, p. 258   JONAH COLLINS, planter, of Craven Co., to JOHN
28 & 29 Mar. 1753   ATCHESON, planter, of Berkeley Co., for Ł 2925
L & R   SC money, an island plantation of 1580 a.,
                             called Bull's Island, in Berkeley Co.; also
345 a. in Craven Co., adjoining the 500 a. on which JONAH COLLINS now
lives (formerly belonging to MARK SLOMAN); also a settled tract of 500 a.
in Craven Co., at Waccamaw, adjoining a tract of 1000 a. belonging to
JONAH COLLINS; also 500 a. (being half of said 1000 a.) at Waccamaw, next
to the settled 500 a. Witnesses: JACOB MOTTE, JOHN MCCOLL, merchant.
MOTTE & MCCOLL testified 25 May 1749 before THOMAS LAMBOLL, J.P. Recorded 19 July 1762 by WILLIAM HOPTON, Register.

Book Y-Y, p. 268   WILLIAM BUCHANAN, planter, of Santee, to JONAH
8 & 9 Aug. 1750   COLLINS, called the younger, now of Bull's Is-
L & R   land, Craven Co., for Ł 100 currency, 1580 a.
                            called Bull's Island; also 345 a. adjoining
the 500 a. on which JONAH COLLINS, SR., lived & on MARK SLOMAN. Whereas
by L & R dated 26 May 1743 JOHN ATCHISON, planter, of Berkeley Co., conveyed to DANIEL MCGREGOR & WILLIAM BUCHANAN, as jointenants in fee, among
other estates, the 2 tracts above named in trust for JONAH COLLINS, JR.,
an infant; & whereas JONAH COLLINS, SR., & MCGREGOR are both dead, & JON-
AH COLLINS, JR., is now 21 years old; now BUCHANAN delivers the property
to COLLINS. Witnesses: JOSEPH HUGGINS, WILLIAM BELL. On 24 Apr. 1756
BELL testified before PAUL TRAPIER, J.P. Recorded 12 July 1762 by WIL-
LIAM HOPTON, Register.

Book Y-Y, p. 275   JONAH COLLINS, planter, of St. James Santee,
27 & 28 Apr. 1762   to THOMAS SHUBRICK, ESQ., of Charleston, for
L & R   Ł 4250 currency, 1580 a. in Berkeley Co.,
                            called Bull's Island, originally granted to
SAMUEL HARTLEY, afterwards belonging to JONAH COLLINS, of Craven Co., who
by L & R dated 28 & 29 Mar. 1743 conveyed the island to JOHN ATCHESON,
planter, of Berkeley Co.; who by L & R dated 26 & 27 May 1743 conveyed to
DANIEL MCGREGOR & WILLIAM BUCHANAN, in trust, for his infant son, JONAH
COLLINS; BUCHANAN (as survivor of COLLINS the elder & of MCGREGOR) conveying the island to JONAH the younger by L & R dated 8 & 9 Aug. 1750;
who now sells the island to SHUBRICK. Witnesses: ISAAC MAZYCK, JOHN
SNELLING. SNELLING testified 29 Apr. 1762 before JACOB MOTTE, J.P. Recorded 13 July 1762 by WILLIAM HOPTON, Register.

Book Y-Y, p. 284   JOSEPH JENKINS, JR., planter, to ARCHIBALD MC-
11 & 12 May 1762   DONALD, planter, both of St. Helena Parish,
L & R   for Ł 225 currency, 450 a. on N side Santee
                            River, in Prince George Parish, Craven Co.,
bounding on land not laid out. Witnesses: JAMES SIMMONS, ADAM MCDONALD,
DANIEL CANNON. MCDONALD testified 13 May 1762 before RICHARD RICHARDSON,
J.P. Recorded 13 July 1762 by WILLIAM HOPTON, Register.

Book Y-Y, p. 291   ANN SNOW, spinster, to GEORGE SNOW, planter,
16 & 17 Oct. 1761   both of Craven Co., for Ł 500 currency, 500 a.
L & R   in St. James Goose Creek, Berkeley Co., bound-
                            ing NW on NATHANIEL SNOW; SW on JAMES WITHERS;
SE on THOMAS SMITH & MR. WALTERS; NE on marsh of Cooper River. Witnesses: ROBERT WARING, JAMES MCIVER, BENJAMIN PAGE. WARING testified 2 Apr.
1762 before JOHN LIVISTON, J.P. Recorded 14 July 1762 by WILLIAM HOPTON,
Register.

Book Y-Y, p. 295   THOMAS LINTHWAITE, tanner, eldest son & heir
14 & 15 May 1762   of WILLIAM LINTHWAITE; to JAMES PARSONS; all
L & R   of Charleston; for Ł 550 currency, 550 a. on E
                            branch Salt Catcha River Swamp, in Colleton
Co., granted WILLIAM LINTHWAITE on 13 May 1735; bounding S on THOMAS
WEAVER; other sides on vacant land. Witnesses: ROBERT COLLINS, JOHN
GLEN. GLEN testified 14 May 1762 before WILLIAM BURROWS, J.P. Recorded

14 July 1762 by WILLIAM HOPTON, Register.

Book Y-Y, p. 302   JOHN HUTSON, planter, & ANN his wife, to ROB-
31 May & 1 June 1756   ERT BELTON, weaver, both of Craven Co., for
L & R   Ŀ 200 currency, 150 a. being the SE part of
                        300 a.; bounding SW on Wateree River; NW on
JOHN HUTSON; NE on vacant land; SE on JOSIAH TOMLINSON; which 150 a. were
granted 29 Nov. 1750 by Gov. JAMES GLEN to JOHN HUTSIN. Witnesses: JO-
SEPH MICKLE, BENJAMIN DUGARD. MICKLE testified 3 Mar. 1762 before ANDREW
ALLISON, J.P. Recorded 16 July 1762 by WILLIAM HOPTON, Register. Plat
of 150 a. surveyed for LUDWICK HUTSON on 20 Jan. 1756.

Book Y-Y, p. 310   WILLIAM FARRELL (FERRELL) & MARTHA his wife,
23 & 24 June 1760   to SAMUEL REED, both of Craven Co., for Ŀ 500
L & R   currency, 200 a. on N side Wateree River; in
                        Fredericksburg Township, Craven Co., bounding
SE on JOHN HUTSON; other sides on vacant land; also 150 a., (being half
of 300 a. granted JOHN HUTSON) in Fredericksburg Township, bounding SW on
Wateree River; NW on said 200 a.; NE on vacant land; SE on other half of
300 a. sold by HUTSON to ROBERT BELTON; which 200 a. & 150 a. were grant-
ed 29 Nov. 1750 by Gov. JAMES GLEN to JOHN HUTSON; who conveyed & confirmed to WILLIAM FARRELL. Witnesses: THOMAS PRESTWOOD, GEORGE GAIRDNER
(GARDNER). PRESTWOOD testified 24 June 1760 before SAMUEL WYLY, J.P.
Recorded 17 July 1762 by WILLIAM HOPTON, Register.

Book Y-Y, p. 320   MARK (his mark) CATTERTON, planter, & ANNE
30 Apr. & 1 May 1747   (her mark) his wife, to HUGH ANSTISS, planter,
L & R   both of Craven Co., for Ŀ 150 currency, 200 a.
                        in Fredericks Township, Craven Co., bounding
on all sides on vacant land; according to plat dated 10 Feb. 1743 attached to grant. Witnesses: WILLIAM BAKER, THOMAS JACKSON. JACKSON testified 2 May 1747 before STEPHEN CRELL, J.P. Recorded 20 July 1762 by
WILLIAM HOPTON, Register.

Book Y-Y, p. 330   HUGH (his mark) ANSTISS, planter, & HEBSIBETH
22 Oct. 1753   (her mark) his wife, assign to JOHN BELTON,
Assignment   planter, for Ŀ 170 currency, 200 a. in Fred-
                        ericksburgh Township, where ANSTISS lived;
bounding on all sides on vacant land. Witnesses: JOSEPH MICKLE, SAMUEL
KELLY. MICKLE testified 6 Feb. 1762 before ANDREW ALLISON, J.P. Recorded 20 July 1762 by WILLIAM HOPTON, Register.

Book Y-Y, p. 336   ROBERT HARPER, planter, of Craven Co., & MARY
17 Nov. 1761   his wife, to JOHN SELL, planter, of Anson Co.,
Release   NC, for Ŀ 350 SC money, 150 a., part of 300 a.,
                        in Craven Co., on middle branch of Lynch's
Creek, called Flet Creek, beginning at a hickory on S side of Flet Creek,
then N 60 E 54 chains 77 links to a stake; S 30 E 27-28 links to a corner; then S 60 W 54 chains 77 links to a red oak; then NW 60 W 30 E 27.38
to beginning. No witnesses given. Signed 18 Nov. 1761 before THOMAS
SIMPSON, J.P. Recorded 21 July 1762 by WILLIAM HOPTON, Register.

Book Y-Y, p. 342   GOVEE (his mark) BLACK, son & heir of JOHN
28 & 29 Jan. 1762   BLACK, to SAMUEL WYLY, ESQ., both of Craven
L & R   Co., for Ŀ 125 currency, 50 a. on Wateree Riv-
                        er, in Fredericksburgh Township, Craven Co.,
bounding SW on JOHN BENNETT; NW on JOSEPH KERSHAW, merchant; SE on PAT-
RICK MCCORMICK & on vacant land; NE on vacant land; NW on BRYAN O'RARK;
being half of 100 a. granted JOHN BLACK 18 Oct. 1749 by Gov. JAMES GLEN.
Witnesses: JOHN N. OGLETHORPE, JOHN CHESNUT. OGLETHORPE testified 6 Feb.
1762 before ANDREW ALISON, J.P. Recorded 22 July 1762 by WILLIAM HOP-
TON, Register. Plat given.

Book Y-Y, p. 349   MATHIAS SOUTHER, joiner, & ANNE MARY (her
30 & 31 Aug. 1754   mark), his wife, to JAMES OTTERSON, planter,
L & R   both of Berkeley Co., for Ŀ 60 currency, 200
                        a. in Berkeley Co., bounding W on a branch of
Broad River called Woodal or Tiger (Tyger) River; other sides on vacant
land. Witnesses: DANIEL WILLIAMS, JEREMIAH (his mark) WILLIAMS. Signed
before THOMAS KINNERLY, J.P. Recorded 22 July 1762 by WILLIAM HOPTON,

Register.

Book Y-Y, p. 357   ANTHONY (his mark) DEUESTO, planter, to JOSIAH
21 & 22 Dec. 1755   TOMLINSON, planter, both of Craven Co., for
L & R   Ł 600 currency, 300 a. in Craven Co., on N
                          side Wateree River in Fredericksburg Township,
bounding NW on DANIEL BREADY & vacant land; NE on vacant land; SE on MARK
CATTERTON; which 300 a. were granted by Gov. JAMES GLEN on 4 Dec. 1751 to
DEUESTO. Witnesses: DANIEL FERRELL, ARCHIBALD WATSON. WATSON testified
17 Oct. 1757 before SAMUEL WYLY, J.P. Recorded 23 July 1762 by WILLIAM
HOPTON, Register.

Book Y-Y, p. 367   ANTHONY (his mark) DEUESTO, planter, to JOSIAH
22 Dec. 1755   TOMLINSON, planter, both of Craven Co., for
Assignment   Ł 150 currency, 100 a. in Fredericksburg Town-
                          ship where DEUESTO formerly lived, bounding SW
on Wateree River; NW on JOHN HUDSON; NE on vacant land; SE on ANTHONY
DEUESTO; according to plat dated 31 May 1749; which 100 a. DEUESTO pur-
chased from DANIEL BREADY on 20 Jan. 1752. Witnesses: DANIEL FARRELL,
ARCHIBALD WATSON. WATSON testified 17 Oct. 1757 before SAMUEL WYLY, J.P.
Recorded 24 July 1762 by WILLIAM HOPTON, Register.

Book Y-Y, p. 372   MARY WATSON, widow, to WILLIAM ANCRUM, LAMBERT
20 & 21 Apr. 1759   LANCE, & AARON LOCOCK, merchants, all of
L & R   Charleston, as tenants in common & not as
                          joint tenants, for Ł 5500 currency, part of
lot #42 in Charleston, bounding S 67 ft. on Broad Street; E 73 ft. on
Church Street; N on part belonging to MARY WATSON; W on estate of ROBERT
HUME (now JOHN PAUL GRIMKE); according to plat certified by WILLIAM WIL-
KINS, Sur. Witnesses: ROBERT RAPER, GEORGE MILLIGEN, JAMES GRINDLAY.
GRINDLAY testified 23 Apr. 1759 before JOHN MURRAY, J.P. Recorded 26
July 1762 by WILLIAM HOPTON, Register. Plat given.

Book Y-Y, p. 382   SAMUEL WYLY, planter, of Craven Co., & DINAH
3 & 4 May 1762   his wife, to JOSEPH KERSHAW, storekeeper, of
L & R   Pinetree Hill, Craven Co., for Ł 500 currency,
                          497 a., in Fredericksburgh Township, bounding
SE on AARON LOOCOCK & LAMBERT LANCE; other sides on vacant land; being
the E part of 650 a. granted SAMUEL WYLEY 2 Apr. 1761 by Lt. Gov. WILLIAM
BULL. Witnesses: SAMUEL KELLY, JOSHUA ENGLISH, a Quaker. ENGLISH testi-
fied 13 May 1762 before GEORGE JOHNSTON, J.P. Recorded 26 July 1762 by
WILLIAM HOPTON, Register. Plat given.

Book Y-Y, p. 389   JAMES MCGIRT, planter, & PRISCILLA (her mark)
29 & 30 Apr. 1761   his wife, to JOSEPH KERSHAW, merchant, both of
L & R   Craven Co., for Ł 400 currency, 350 a. in
                          Fredericksburgh Township, bounding SW on Wa-
teree River; NW on JOHN BLACK & vacant land; which 350 a. were granted 3
Apr. 1754 by Gov. JAMES GLEN to WILLIAM GRAY; & sold by WILLIAM GRAY &
ELIZABETH, his wife, on 11 Sept. 1754 to JAMES MCGIRT (Book P.P. p. 671).
Witnesses: JOHN CANTEY, ELY KERSHAW. CANTEY testified 6 Apr. 1762 before
ANDREW ALISON, J.P. Recorded 27 July 1762 by WILLIAM HOPTON, Register.

Book Y-Y, p, 398   WILLIAM SERUG, planter, of Craven Co., to JO-
8 Feb. 1762   SEPH KERSHAW, merchant, of Pinetree Hill, Cra-
Assignment   ven Co., for Ł 250 currency, 350 a. in Fred-
                          ericksburgh Township, bounding SW on Wateree
River; NW on JOHN BLACK & vacant land; other sides on vacant land; which
tract was sold 11 Feb. 1755 by WILLIAM GRAY, & ELIZABETH his wife, to
WILLIAM SERUG. Witnesses: SAMUEL KELLY, THOMAS TOBIAS. TOBIAS testified
6 Apr. 1762 before ANDREW ALISON, J.P. Recorded 28 July 1762 by WILLIAM
HOPTON, Register.

Book Y-Y, p. 404   GOVES (his mark) BLACK, son & heir of JOHN
28 & 29 Jan. 1762   BLACK, to JOSEPH KERSHAW, merchant, both of
L & R   Craven Co., for Ł 125 currency, 50 a. on Wa-
                          teree River, in Fredericksburgh Township, Cra-
ven Co., bounding SW on SAMUEL WYLY; SW & NW on vacant land; NW on vacant
land & BRYAN O'RORK; being half of 100 a. granted JOHN BLACK on 18 Oct.
1749 by Gov. JAMES GLEN; the other half having been sold to SAMUEL WYLY.

Witnesses: JOHN N. OGLETHORPE, JOHN CHESNUT. OGLETHORPE testified 6 Feb.
1762 before ANDREW ALLISON, J.P. Recorded 28 July 1762 by WILLIAM HOP-
TON, Register. Plat of 50 a. showing boundaries; NE on WILLIAM ANCRUM;
SE on JAMES SHEALY; SW & NW on SAMUEL WYLY.

Book Y-Y, p. 410   JOSEPH JOYNER, & MILES (her mark) his wife, to
1 & 2 Apr. 1761   JOSEPH KERSHAW, ESQ., both of Craven Co., for
L & R   ₺ 50 currency, 20 a. in the fork of Santee &
                           Wateree Rivers, bounding SW on Santee River;
NE & NW on JOSEPH JOYNER; SE on CAPT. JOHN MCCORD; being part of 300 a.
granted JOSEPH JOYNER 9 Jan. 1752 by Gov. JAMES GLEN. Plat certified 12
Mar. 1761 by JOHN HAMELTON, D.S. Witnesses: JOHN MCCORD, ELY KERSHAW.
KERSHAW testified 15 May 1762 before JAMES MOULTRIE, J.P. Recorded 29
July 1762 by WILLIAM HOPTON, Register.

Book Y-Y, p. 416   ISAAC PIDGEON, planter, of Wateree River, Cra-
17 Feb. 1762   ven Co., & SARAH his wife, to JOSEPH KERSHAW,
Release   merchant, of Pinetree Hill, Craven Co., for
                           ₺ 350 currency, 2 plantations on S side Wa-
teree River; 1 of 66 a. bounding NW on JAMES OUSLY; SE on WILLIAM PINCK-
NEY (now ISAAC PIDGEON); SW on vacant land; according to plat attached to
grant on 8 Feb. 1749 to the Hon. CHARLES PINCKNEY; the other of 150 a.
opposite Fredericksburg Township, bounding SE on LUKE GIBSON; NE on Wateree River; NW & SW on vacant land; according to grant to ALEXANDER MIT-
CHELL dated 6 Aug. 1751. Witnesses: JOHN CANTEY, SAMUEL KELLY. CANTEY
testified 6 Apr. 1762 before ANDREW ALISON, J.P. Recorded 29 July 1762
by WILLIAM HOPTON, Register.

Book Y-Y, p. 420   WILLIAM FARRELL, miller, & MARTHA his wife, to
25 Jan. 1762   JOSEPH KERSHAW, merchant, both of Craven Co.,
Assignment   for ₺ 1700 currency, the 3/4 of 50 a. which
                           SAMUEL MILHOUS, JOHN MILHOUS, & HENRY MILHOUS,
planters of Fredericksburgh Township, & ABIGAIL MILHOUS, wife of JOHN
MILHOUS, sold on 11 Nov. 1758 to WILLIAM FARRELL, miller, lying in Fred-
ericksburgh Township, & bounding NW on PATRICK MCCORMICK; SW on EDWARD
MOLLOY; SE on JOHN PAYNE; NE on vacant land. Witnesses: SAMUEL KELLY,
JOHN CHESNUT. CHESNUTT testified 6 Feb. 1762 before ANDREW ALLISON, J.P.
Recorded 30 July 1762 by WILLIAM HOPTON, Register.

Book Y-Y, p. 426   THOMAS LAMAR, SR., to DANIEL WALLACON, plant-
_____ Jan. 1762   er, both of Granville Co., for ₺ 100 currency,
L & R   150 a. in New Windsor Township, on Savannah
                           River in Granville Co., granted 16 Nov. 1756
by Gov. WILLIAM BULL to THOMAS LAMAR, & surveyed 16 Nov. 1756 for ZACH-
ARIAH LAMAR; bounding W & SW on Savannah River; S & E on vacant land; N
on ULRICH TOBLER. Witnesses: JOHN STUART, THOMAS LAMAR. STUART testi-
fied 14 May 1762 before JOHN REMINGTON, J.P. Recorded 30 July 1762 by
WILLIAM HOPTON, Register.

Book Y-Y, p. 431   MARTIN CAMPBELL, JAMES PARSONS, & WILLIAM
23 Apr. 1762   GUERIN, executors of will of JOHN GORDON, tav-
Release   ern keeper, all of Charleston; to the Hon.
                           JOHN DRAYTON, ESQ., of Drayton Hall, for
₺ 1950 currency, 200 a. in St. Andrews Parish, bounding N on WILLIAM
CATTELL, SR.; E on WILLIAM BRANDFORD; S on BENJAMIN STANYARNE; W on estate of ROBERT LADSON. Whereas by L & R dated 25 & 26 Mar. 1747 BENJAMIN
STANYARNE, planter, sold JOHN GORDON, planter, 200 a.; which by his will
dated 13 Jan. 1762 GORDON bequeathed to his executors; directing them to
sell his real & personal estate to pay his debts; now they sell the 200
a. at auction to DRAYTON. Witnesses: JAMES GRIERSON, JOHN GLEN. GLEN
testified 19 May 1762 before HENRY GRAY, J.P. Recorded 31 July 1762 by
WILLIAM HOPTON, Register.

Book Y-Y, p. 437   ELIZABETH BUTLER, widow, of Georgia, to
3 & 4 May 1762   CHARLES ELLIOTT, gentleman, of St. Pauls Par-
L & R   ish, Colleton Co., SC, for ₺ 3000 currency,
                           250 a. near PonPon River, in St. Paul's Par-
ish, bounding N on MR. BANFORD & THOMAS ELLIOTT; W on JAMES WRIXIM; E on
another tract of 360 a.; also said 360 a. bounding W & S on above tract;
E on CHARLES ELLIOTT (formerly THOMAS ELLIOTT), being part of 610 a., &

pricked off on a plat 46 chains from W corner pine tree with a cross
thereon. Whereas THOMAS ELLIOTT, planter, of Colleton Co., father of
CHARLES ELLIOTT, on 21 Sept. 1738, for love & affection, gave his nieces
ELIZABETH & MARY ELLIOTT, daughters of WILLIAM ELLIOTT, 610 a. near Pon
Pon River in 2 tracts; & whereas MARY died a minor & unmarried; & ELIZA-
BETH (who after the execution of the deed had married WILLIAM BUTLER,
since deceased) inherited; now she sells the 2 tracts to CHARLES ELLIOTT.
Witnesses: SUSANNA PARSONS, JOHN GLEN, JAMES PARSONS. GLEN testified be-
fore BENJAMIN SMITH, J.P. Recorded 31 July 1762 by WILLIAM HOPTON, Reg-
ister.

Book Y-Y, p. 443　　　　　　SAMUEL POITEVINT, planter, now of Cape Fear,
10 & 12 Dec. 1737　　　　　　NC, to ELIAS HORRY, ESQ., of Prince George
L & R　　　　　　　　　　　　Parish, Craven Co., for Ⱡ 200 SC money, 200 a.
　　　　　　　　　　　　　　　in Williamsburgh Township, on head of Black
River, bounding E on JAMES TAYLOR; other sides on vacant land; which
200 a. were granted POITEVINT by Lt. Gov. THOMAS BROUGHTON on 30 Sept.
1736. Witnesses: ROBERT WALKER, JAMES SMALLWOOD. WALKER testified 21
Feb. 1738 before THOMAS LAROCHE, J.P. Recorded 31 July 1762 by WILLIAM
HOPTON, Register.

Book Y-Y, p. 449　　　　　　ELIAS HORRY, planter, of Prince George Parish,
13 Oct. 1755　　　　　　　　to JOHN VERTUE, gunsmith, of Prince Frederick
L & R　　　　　　　　　　　　Parish, for Ⱡ 200 currency, 200 a. in Williams-
　　　　　　　　　　　　　　　burgh Township, on head of Black River, bounding E on JAMES TAYLOR; other sides on vacant land; which 200 a. were
granted 13 Sept. 1736 by Lt. Gov. THOMAS BROUGHTON to ELIAS HORRY. Witnesses: WILLIAM CROOK, WILLIAM DOBIEN. DOBIEN testified 5 May 1760 before JOHN LIVISTON, J.P. Recorded 2 Aug. 1762 by WILLIAM HOPTON, Register.

Book Y-Y, p. 455　　　　　　TUNES TEBOUT (TEABOUT), blacksmith, of Charles-
9 Sept. 1750　　　　　　　　ton, to WOOD FURMAN, yeoman, of St. Mark's
Release　　　　　　　　　　　Parish, Craven Co., for Ⱡ 40 currency, 500 a.
　　　　　　　　　　　　　　　in St. Mark's Parish on NE side of Wateree
River, bounding NW on BERNARD BECKMAN; other sides on vacant land; as
granted by Gov. WILLIAM HENRY LYTTLETON to TEABOUT on 13 Oct. 1759. Witnesses: JOHN HARVEY, BENJAMIN BACKHOUSE. BACKHOUSE testified 28 May 1762
before JOHN REMINGTON, J.P. Recorded 3 Aug. 1762 by WILLIAM HOPTON, Register.

Book Y-Y, p. 461　　　　　　BERNARD BEEKMAN, blockmaker, of Charleston, to
29 Aug. 1760　　　　　　　　WOOD FURMAN, yeoman, of St. Mark's Parish,
Release　　　　　　　　　　　Craven Co., for Ⱡ 50 currency, 550 a. in St.
　　　　　　　　　　　　　　　Mark's Parish, on NW side Wateree River, bounding SE on TUNIS TEBOUT; other sides on vacant land; which tract was granted by Gov. WILLIAM HENRY LYTTLETON on 13 Oct. 1759 to BEEKMAN. Witnesses: JOHN HARVEY, BENJAMIN BACKHOUSE. BACKHOUSE testified 28 May 1762 before JOHN REMINGTON, J.P. Recorded 4 Aug. 1762 by WILLIAM HOPTON, Register.

Book Y-Y, p. 469　　　　　　Whereas JOHN, Lord Carteret, Palatin; the most
26 Aug. 1729　　　　　　　　Noble HENRY, Duke of Beaufort; the Rt. Hon.
Declaration of Trust　　　　WILLIAM, Lord Craven; the Hon. JAMES BERTIE &
　　　　　　　　　　　　　　　HENRY BERTIE, his brother; SIR JOHN COLLETON,
Baronet; & SIR JOHN TYRREL, Baronet; 7 of the Lords Proprs., of SC, on 25
Oct. 1726 granted ISAAC LOWNDES a Barony of 12,000 a., & requiring the
Sur. Gen. of SC within 20 days after notice to set out the Barony in any
place in SC; now ISAAC LOWNDES declares that his name was used in the
grant only as trustee for THOMAS LOWNDES, gentleman, of Parish of St.
John the Evangelist, in City of Westminster; & appoints said THOMAS
LOWNDES his attorney to take possession of the Barony. Witnesses: JAMEM
GUEST, KATHERINE SPONG. No probate. Recorded 5 Aug. 1762 by WILLIAM
HOPTON, Register.

Book Y-Y, p. 472　　　　　　DANIEL DOYLEY, P.M., to the Hon. JOHN GUERARD,
6 Apr. 1762　　　　　　　　of H.M. Council, for Ⱡ 12,600 currency,
Sale　　　　　　　　　　　　9336 a., part of a Barony of 12,000 a. Where-
　　　　　　　　　　　　　　　as ROBERT THORPE, merchant, of Granville Co.,
owned 9000 a. (on re-survey found to be 9336 a.) in Granville Co., at

head of Oketty Creek, a branch of Port Royal River, being part of a Barony of 12,000 a. granted by the Lords Proprs. on 25 Oct. 1726 to ISAAC
LOWNDES, afterwards sold to ROBERT THORPE in fee; laid down to the N of
the division line that runs through the plat; the other lands laid down
to the S of said division line; being other part of said Barony now belonging to MARY DE LA FOUNTAIN, widow, of London, which on a late resurvey was found to contain 3112 a. allotted to her by writ of partition; &
whereas ROBERT THORPE died intestate & RICHARD LAMBTON, merchant, of
Charleston was appointed administrator of his estate on 2 Feb. 1749 by
Gov. JAMES GLEN; & whereas THORPE had given a bond on 11 Aug. 1749 to
JOHN NICHOLSON, RICHARD SHUBRICK, & THOMAS SHUBRICK, merchants, of
Charleston, for payment of Ł 3812 currency, with interest; & whereas
NICHOLSON had died & RICHARD & THOMAS SHUBRICK obtained a judgment
against LAMBTON, as administrator, & several writs of fieri facias were
renewed from time to time, & a certain writ of fieri facias was issued on
9 Feb. last by CHARLES SHINNER, C.J., directing the P.M. to seize the estate; & the P.M. offered the tract of 9336 a. for sale at public auction;
now he conveys the land to GUERARD. Witnesses: JAMES PARSONS, CHARLES
PINCKNEY. PARSONS testified 2 June 1762 before JAMES MAGHLIN, J.P. Recorded 6 Aug. 1762 by WILLIAM HOPTON, Register. Broken plat.

Book Y-Y, p. 479   FRANCIS ROCHE, gentleman, of St. Thomas Parish
21 & 22 May 1762   (being eldest Uncle's eldest son, on father's
L & R   side, of JORDAN ROCHE, JR., a minor, of
                         Charleston, who was only son & heir of JORDAN
ROCHE, SR.); & ANN ROCHE, wife of FRANCIS ROCHE; of 1st part; to ALEXAN-
DER PERONNEAU, gentleman, of Charleston; for Ł 2000 currency, the W part
of the marsh land of Colleton Square, in Charleston, bounding W 60 or
67 ft. on Meeting Street (formerly called Old Church Street); S on lot
#167; E on another part said marsh sold by the Hon. CHARLES PINCKNEY to
PETER LARY; on lot #200; also the S part of lot #200 bounding W 109 ft.
on Meeting Street; S & E on the marsh; the land on which the fence of 2
covered cannon formerly stood; N on the line of the fence of the Fortifications formerly erected on the land side of the town; which part of lot
#200 & the marsh land is shown on a plat annexed to release from CHARLES
PINCKNEY, & ELIZABETH his wife, to MATHEW ROCHE; & recited in deed of
sale from RAWLINS LOWNDES to JORDAN ROCHE; also lot #167, bounding E on
ALEXANDER TEZEE CHASTANEZ; W on Meeting Street; S on SAMUEL PERKINS
(formerly MR. MAZYCK); N on the marsh. Whereas on 16 June 1750 RAWLINS
LOWNDES, P.M., sold JORDON ROCHE, the eldest, several town lots; & whereas said JORDAN ROCHE died intestate on 29 May 1752, leaving JORDAN ROCHE
the younger his only son & heir; & whereas JORDAN ROCHE the younger died
at Charleston, a minor & unmarried, on 18 Aug. 1761; & the property descended to FRANCIS ROCHE as next of kin in the collateral line of the
whole blood of his faterh; now FRANCIS ROCHE sells 3 parcels of land to
PERONNEAU. Witnesses: BENJAMIN SIMMONS, ROBERT QUASH, N. VALOI, THOMAS
LINING. QUASH testified 24 May 1762 before BENJAMIN SIMMONS, J.P. Recorded 7 Aug. 1762 by WILLIAM HOPTON, Register.

Book Y-Y, p. 491   SARAH RAMSAY & MARY ALLAN, widows, of Charles-
17 & 18 May 1762   ton, administrators, of the part of the estate
L & R   of their father MICHAEL JEANES, a blacksmith,
                         left unadministered by their mother MARY
JEANES, deceased, who was sole executrix of her husband's will; to JAMES
LINGARD, blacksmith; for Ł 1500 currency, lots #281 & #282 in Charleston,
70 ft. front x 90 ft. deep, bounding N on a small street leading from
King Street into Old Church, or Meeting Street; W on JOHN CARMICHAEL (now
THOMAS FERGUSON); S on THOMAS ELLIOTT (formerly CHILDERMAS CROFT); E on
BENJAMIN HARVEY (formerly EDWARD WEEKLY); & purchased by MICHAEL JEANES
as follows: 30 ft. in front from JOHN CARMICHAEL; 30 from BRYON RAILEY;
10 ft. from EDWARD WEEKLY; according to deeds executed by CARMICHAEL,
RAILEY & WEEKLY. Witnesses: ANN SMITH, JOHN CHEESEBOROUGH. CHEESE-
BOROUGH testified 22 May 1762 before LIONEL CHALMERS, J.P. Recorded 9
Aug. 1762 by WILLIAM HOPTON, Register.

Book Y-Y, p. 497   JAMES LINGARD, blacksmith, of St. Philip's
19 & 20 May 1762   Parish, Charleston, to SARAH RAMSAY, widow,
L & R   for Ł 1560 currency, lots #281 & #282 in
                         Charleston, 70 ft. front, 90 ft. deep (see
p. 491). Witnesses: MARION DONOVAN, JOHN CHEESBOROUGH. CHEESBOROUGH

testified 26 May 1762 before LIONEL CHALMERS, J.P.   Recorded 9 Aug. 1762
by WILLIAM HOPTON, Register.

Book Y-Y, p. 503   JOSEPH POOLE, planter, & CAROLINE his wife, to
25 & 26 Apr. 1755   GEORGE STARRATT, planter, both of Prince
L & R   George Parish, Craven Co., for Ŀ 4725 curren-
                                    cy, 5 plantations, total 2100 a. in Craven
Co., between Waccamaw River & the sea. Whereas Gov. ROBERT GIBBES on 28
June 1711 granted MILES BREWTON, of Charleston, 2 tracts 500 a. each; &
whereas MILES BREWTON & his wife, SUSANNA, by L & R dated 2 & 3 June 1732
sold the 2 tracts to WILLIAM POOLE, ESQ.; & whereas Gov. ROBERT GIBBES on
15 May 1711 granted THOMAS HEPWORTH, gentleman, of Charleston, 500 a. in
Craven Co.; which by L & R dated 23 &24 Mar. 1738 he sold to WILLIAM
POOLE; & whereas by deed of feoffment dated 7 Jan. 1737 JAMES GORDON &
RACHEL his wife sold to WILLIAM POOLE 100 a., part of 200 a. granted to
GORDON, & whereas GEORGE PAWLEY by L & R dated 20 & 21 Oct. 1743 sold to
WILLIAM POOLE 500 a. in Craven Co.; & whereas WILLIAM POOLE died intes-
tate & his eldest surviving son, JOSEPH, party hereto, inherited his real
estate; now he sells the 5 tracts to STARRATT. Witnesses: ARCHIBALD
BAIRD, JOSEPH DUBOURDIEU. DUBOURDIEU testified 23 Jan. 1762 before JO-
SEPH BROWN, J.P.   Recorded 11 Aug. 1762 by WILLIAM HOPTON, Register.

Book Y-Y, p. 513   JOHN COMING BALL, planter, to HENRY LAURENS,
11 & 12 May 1756   merchant, both of Berkeley Co., for Ŀ 249 cur-
L & R   rency, 1 undivided half part of 1000 a. in
                                    Craven Co., in St. James Santee Parish; part
of Wambaw Swamp; the 1000 a. bounding E, N & S on vacant land; W on JOHN
GENDRON; the 1000 a. being part of 3000 a. purchased by BENJAMIN GODDIN
on 6 Apr. 1727 from ALEXANDER TRENCH, attorney, for JOHN BAYLEY of Ballinaclough, Ireland. Witnesses: JOSEPH KERSHAW, GEORGE APPLEBY. APPLE-
BY testified 28 June 1762 before JACOB MOTTE, J.P. Recorded 11 Aug. 1762
by WILLIAM HOPTON, Register.

Book Y-Y, p. 521   JOHN COMING BALL, planter, of Berkeley Co.,
11 & 12 May 1756   executor of will of JOHN GENDRON, JR., to
L & R   HENRY LAURENS, merchant, of Berkeley Co., for
                                    Ŀ 2500 currency, 1 undivided half of 1500 a.
at Wambaw in St. James Santee, bounding N on ISAAC MAZYCK & vacant land;
S on vacant land; E on vacant land & on COL. THOMAS CORDES; W on PAUL
DOUXSAINT & the children of ISAAC LEGRAND DONERVILLE. Whereas by L & R
dated 17 & 18 July 1749 JOHN GENDRON of St. James Santee sold to his son,
JOHN GENDRON, JR., & JOHN COMING BALL, of St. Johns Parish, Berkeley Co.,
for Ŀ 4000 currency, 1500 a. at Wambaw; 1/2 to each; & whereas JOHN GEN-
DRON, JR., by will dated 6 Oct. 1755, appointed his brother-in-law, the
said JOHN COMING BALL, his executor, with authority to sell his lands;
now BALL sells JOHN GENDRON'S half to LAURENS. Witnesses: JOSEPH KER-
SHAW, GEORGE APPLEBY. APPLEBY testified 28 June 1762 before JACOB MOTTE,
J.P. Recorded 13 Aug. 1762 by WILLIAM HOPTON, REgister.

Book Y-Y, p. 530   WILLIAM HAZZARD, SR., gentleman, of Granville
10 May 1756   Co., to his daughter, ELIZABETH HARVEY, & to
Gift   his grandson, THOMAS ELEAZER HARVEY, for love
                                    & affection, 912-1/2 a. purchased by HAZZARD
from THOMAS PARMENTER of Beaufort by L & R dated 9 & 10 Feb. 1756; which
L & R HAZZARD has delivered to his son-in-law, WILLIAM HARVEY; the
912-1/2 a. being on Port Royal Island, Granville Co., & bounding E on
Parmenters Creek & branches; N on COL. WIGGS & RICHARD RICKETS; W on estate of ROBERT ORR; S on MRS. TELFAIR & COL. WIGGS; the land to be
equally divided between them but ELIZABETH to have the land divided as
she chooses & to choose her half part; also he gives ELIZABETH his large
schooner which carries about 82 barrels of rice; also 4 Negroes. Witnesses: GEORGE WELCH, RICHARD RICKETTS. WELCH & RICKETS testified 29
Mar. 1757 before JOHN HUTCHINSON, J.P. Recorded 13 Aug. 1762 by WILLIAM
HOPTON, Register.

Book Y-Y, p. 532   JOHN WADE, planter, of St. Marks Parish, to
11 & 12 Mar. 1762   THOMAS CRAWFORD, planter, of Prince Frederick
L & R   Parish, for Ŀ 500 currency, 350 a. on Lynch's
                                    Creek, St. Marks Parish, bounding on all sides
on vacant land; which tract was granted 1 Feb. 1758 by Gov. WILLIAM

173

HENRY LYTTLETON to JOHN WADE. Witnesses: DURHAM HILLS, THOMAS LIDE.
LIDE testified 16 June 1762 before ALEXANDER MCINTOSH, J.P. Recorded 14
Aug. 1762 by WILLIAM HOPTON, Register.

Book Y-Y, p. 538   JAMES MCPHERSON, to his son, ISAAC MCPHERSON,
18 June 1762   for love & affection, 500 a. in Granville Co.,
Gift   bounding SW on JAMES MCPHERSON (formerly CAPT.
                         EDMUND BELLINGER); SE on CAPT. JOHN BULL; N on
BENJAMIN WARING; W on WILLIAM KEATING & vacant land. Witnesses: DAVID
TOOMER, JOSEPH PERRY, ANDREW POSTELL, JOHN MCPHERSON. Livery & seizin
made by delivery of turf & twig. PERRY testified 19 June 1762 before
JAMES SHARP, J.P. Recorded 14 Aug. 1762 by WILLIAM HOPTON, Register.

Book Y-Y, p. 541   CHARLES COLLETON, of Colleton Co., to JOHN
15 Mar. 1762   SMITH & SUSANNA SMITH, as security on bond of
Mortgage   even date in penal sum of ₺ 1400 for payment
                        of ₺ 700 currency, with interest, on 1 Aug.; 2
lots in Jacksonborough, #7 & #60, with all houses. Witnesses: BENJAMIN
SINGLETON, WILLIAM JACKSON, EDWARD KEATING. KEATING testified 16 Mar.
1762 before JOHN REMINGTON, J.P. Recorded 14 Aug. 1762 by WILLIAM HOP-
TON, Register.

Book Y-Y, p. 544   CATHERINE (her mark) HOLMES, widow, of
30 Apr. 1761   Charleston, (formerly CATHERINE FOWLER, wife
Release   of RICHARD FOWLER, planter, of Berkeley Co.,;
                        & daughter of JOHN GRANT), to PETER MANIGAULT,
barrister, of Charleston; for ₺ 250 currency; 1/2 part of 600 a.; also
1/2 part of 33 a. of marsh land. Whereas RICHARD FOWLER & CATHERINE, his
wife, by L & R dated 14 & 15 Apr. 1731 sold MOSES WILSON, planter, of
Berkeley Co., & ISAAC HOLMES, gentleman, of Charleston, 1/2 part of 600
a. in Berkeley Co., bounding E on JOHN PIGHT; N on Goose Creek; S on
CAPT. JONATHAN FITCH; W on JOHN WRIGHT; also 1/2 part of 33 a. of marsh
land in Berkeley Co., bounding NW on JOHN WRIGHT; SW on JOHN GRANT; SE on
JOHN PIGHT; NE on Goose Creek; & whereas JOHN GRANT, cordwainer, of
Berkeley Co., son of JOHN GRANT, by L & R dated 22 & 23 Nov. 1732 sold &
confirmed to MOSES WILSON & ISAAC HOLMES the other half of the 2 tracts;
& whereas ISAAC HOLMES, & SUSANNA his wife, by L & R dated 1 & 2 Oct.
1733 sold & confirmed his half of the 2 tracts to MOSES WILSON; who bequeathed to his son, JOHN WILSON, that part at Goose Creek on which he
lived, which lies on NE side of the new Broad Path; & bequeathed to his
son, MOSES WILSON, the remainder of the plantation at Goose Creek, lying
on SW side of New Broad Path; said plantation being the 600 a. of land &
33 a. of marsh; & whereas JOHN WILSON, by L & R dated 13 & 14 June 1757
sold to PETER MANIGAULT hte part on NE side of Broad Path; & MOSES WILSON,
by L & R dated 14 & 15 Dec. 1757 sold the part on the SW side of the
Broad Path to PETER MANIGAULT; & whereas CATHERINE HOLMES was not then of
age; now she releases her claim to half the plantation. Witnesses: WIL-
LIAM MAZYCK, JOHN MATHEWES, WILLIAM MEWHENNEY. MATHEWES testified 30
Apr. 1761 before CHARLES PINCKNEY, J.P. Recorded 16 Aug. 1762 by WILLIAM
HOPTON, Register.

Book Y-Y, p. 549   JOHN BUTLER PIGGOTT, merchant, of Charleston,
1 June 1761   to JOHN CLIFFORD, as security on bond of even
Mortgage   date in penal sum of ₺ 3000 for payment of
                        ₺ 1500 currency, with interest, on 1 June 1762;
lot #210 in Charleston, fronting 35-1/2 ft. on King Street. Witness:
MICHAEL MUCKENFUSS testified 19 July 1762 before JOHN REMINGTON, J.P.
Recorded 16 Aug. 1762 by WILLIAM HOPTON, Register. On 25 Aug. 1762 JOHN
CLIFFORD declared mortgage satisfied. Witness: WILLIAM HOPTON.

Book Y-Y, p. 551   GEORGE KEITH, tanner, & ELIZABETH (her mark)
19 Jan. 1762   his wife, to HENRY GALLMAN, JR., planter, both
Release   of Saxegotha Township, for ₺ 200 currency,
                        125 a. in Saxegotha Township, bounding E on
Santee River; SE on HANS JACOB RIEMERSPERGER; NW on HENRY GALLMAN, JR.;
which land said GALLMAN on 15 Jan. 1759 had conveyed to KEITH in consid-
eration of KEITH'S marriage to ELIZABETH, daughter of said HENRY GALLMAN,
JR. Witnesses: HANS ULRIC (his mark) BACKMAN, JOSEPH (his mark) BACK-
MAN. HANS ULRIC BACKMAN testified 20 Jan. 1762 before STEPHEN CRELL,
J.P. Recorded 17 Aug. 1762 by WILLIAM HOPTON, Register.

174

Book Y-Y, p. 555　　　　　ALEXANDER DUNN, tavern keeper, of Georgetown,
12 & 13 Aug. 1761　　　　to ROBERT WEAVER, carpenter, of St. Mark's
L & R by Mortgage　　　　Parish, as security on bond of even date in
　　　　　　　　　　　　the penal sum of Ł 1200 for payment of Ł 600
currency, with interest, on 13 Aug. 1763; lot #30 in Georgetown, bounding
SW 50 ft. on Front Street; NW 217.9 ft. on lot #29; NE on lot #63; SE on
lot #31. Witnesses: THOMAS WILSON, JOSEPH DUBOURDIEU. DUBOURDIEU testified 24 July 1762 before CHARLES FYFFE, J.P. Recorded 18 Aug. 1762 by
WILLIAM HOPTON, Register. On 20 Oct. 1768 WEAVER declared mortgage satisfied. Witness: FENWICK BULL, Register.

Book Y-Y, p. 562　　　　　WILLIAM (his mark) FROST, planter, & ELIZABETH
30 Mar. & 1 Apr. 1759　　(her mark) his wife, to ABRAHAM ODAM, planter,
L & R　　　　　　　　　　both of Craven Co., for Ł 200 currency, 200 a.
　　　　　　　　　　　　in Craven Co., on S side Wateree River, bounding on other sides on vacant land; granted said WILLIAM FROST 22 Jan.
1759 by Gov. WILLIAM HENRY LYTTLETON. Witnesses: CHARLES SPEARS, WILLIAM
MCGRAW, DAVID EDWARDS. SPEARS testified 10 June 1760 before SAMUEL WYLY,
J.P. Recorded 19 Aug. 1762 by WILLIAM HOPTON, Register.

Book Y-Y, p. 569　　　　　JOHN JACOB FRIDIG, planter, & BARBARY (her
1 & 2 June 1762　　　　　mark) his wife, to HENRY HARTLE, planter, both
L & R　　　　　　　　　　of Saxegotha Township, for Ł 250 currency,
　　　　　　　　　　　　150 a. Whereas on 3 Sept. 1754 Gov. JAMES
GLEN granted MICHAEL SCHOULDER 150 a. on a branch of Edisto River called
Chinkapin, bounding on all sides on vacant land; which SCHOULDER sold by
L & R dated 23 & 24 July 1756 to MARTIN FRIDIG; who died intestate; & his
eldest son JOHN JACOB FRIDIG (party hereto) inherited; now he sells the
land to HARTLE. Witnesses: JOHN FRIDIG, JOHN (his mark) STRUCK. JOHN
FRIDIG testified 2 June 1762 before JOHN PEARSON, J.P. Recorded 20 Aug.
1762 by WILLIAM HOPTON, Register.

Book Y-Y, p. 576　　　　　JOHN (his mark) STRUCK, planter, of Berkeley
1 & 2 June 1762　　　　　Co., & ANN (her mark) his wife, to HENRY
L & R　　　　　　　　　　HARTLE, planter, of Saxegotha Township, for
　　　　　　　　　　　　Ł 300 currency, 350 a. & a town lot #51 in
Saxegotha Township, which on 1 June 1750 Gov. JAMES GLEN granted JOHN
STRUCK; the 350 a. bounging SW on vacant land; NW on vacant land & on
HANS JACOB GEIGER; NE on Santee River; SE on vacant land & on HENRY
SCONE. Witnesses: MARY ANN PEARSON, JOHN FRIDIG. FRIDIG testified 2
June 1762 before JOHN PEARSON, J.P. Entered in Auditor's Book F #6, p.
126, on 26 July 1762 by RICHARD LAMBTON, Dep. Aud. Recorded 21 Aug. 1762
by WILLIAM HOPTON, Register.

Book Y-Y, p. 583　　　　　JACOB CASTELL, of Broad River, SC, & MARGARET
　　　　1760　　　　　　　(her mark) his wife, to JOHN LEE, for Ł 50
L & R　　　　　　　　　　currency, 250 a. on Broad River, on main fork
　　　　　　　　　　　　of Little River, bounding on all sides on vacant land. Witnesses: ROBERT EOLLENS, HUGH MCDONALD, WILLIAM (his mark)
STONE. COLLENS testified 15 Jan. 1762 before THOMAS FLETCHALL, J.P. of
Craven Co. Recorded 24 Aug. 1762 by WILLIAM HOPTON, Register.

Book Y-Y, p. 591　　　　　SUSANNA BOSOMWORTH, widow, to MARY COOPER,
16 & 17 June 1762　　　　widow, both of Charleston, for Ł 2100 curren-
L & R　　　　　　　　　　cy, the W part of lot #103 in Charleston,
　　　　　　　　　　　　formerly belonging to JOHN MARTINI; bounding
N 19 ft. on Broad Street; 106 ft. deep. Witnesses: WILLIAM HARVEY, ANN
COOPER. ANN COOPER testified 5 Aug. 1762 before ROBERT WILLIAMS, JR.,
J.P. Recorded 26 Aug. 1762 by WILLIAM HOPTON, Register.

Book Y-Y, p. 600　　　　　DAVID HUGUENIN, carpenter, of St. Peters Par-
3 & 4 June 1762　　　　　ish, Purysburgh, (for himself & ABRAHAM
L & R　　　　　　　　　　HUGUENIN), to GABRIEL RAVOT, tanner, of same
　　　　　　　　　　　　place, for Ł 98:11:0 SC money, 200 a. in
Purysburgh Township, Granville Co., bounding W on Savannah River; N on
JEAN BAPTISTE BURGUIN; E on MR. LEONARD; S on Church Glebe & DAVID
GIROUD; which land was granted by WILLIAM BULL on 11 Nov. 1743 to DANIEL,
ABRAHAM, & MARGARET HUGUENIN. Witnesses: STEPHEN DRAYTON, HENRY DESAUS-
SURE. A knife delivered. DUSAUSSURE testified 4 June 1752 before THOMAS
DRAYTON, J.P. Entered in Auditor's Book F #6, p. 135 on 9 Aug. 1762 by

RICHARD LAMBTON, Dep. Aud.   Recorded 27 Aug. 1762 by WILLIAM HOPTON, Register.

Book Y-Y, p. 607   WILLIAM MASON, of Charleston, & MARY his wife,
7 Feb. 1759   to RICHARD JENKINS, planter, of Edisto Island,
Feoffment   for Ł 200 currency, part of lot #64 in Charles-
                         ton, 15-1/2 ft. x 48 ft. 9 in., being the part
which ELIZABETH JENKINS on 1 Jan. 1741 gave to MARY JENKINS, & known as
#2 on a certain plat. Witnesses: ROBERT HOG, JOHN CLUNIE, DAVID STOLL.
Livery & seizin delivered. HOG testified 26 July 1762 before WILLIAM
BURROWS, J.P. Recorded 28 Aug. 1762 by WILLIAM HOPTON, Register.

Book Y-Y, p. 610   RICHARD JENKINS, planter, of Edisto Island, &
1 & 2 July 1761   MARTHA his wife, to GEORGE WALKER, SR., vint-
L & R   ner, of Charleston, for Ł 200 currency, that
                         part of a lot #64 in Charleston, marked #2 on
a certain plat; bounding S 48-3/4 ft. on a lane leading from Church
Street to the Bay; W 15-1/2 ft. on part marked #1 belonging to estate of
JOHN JENKINS; E on part #3 belonging to said estate; N on THOMAS CAPERS,
SR. Whereas ELIZABETH JENKINS, widow, owned lot #64 in Charleston bounding W 15 ft. on Church Street; E 16 ft.; N 195 ft. on THOMAS CAPERS; S on
a lane 5 ft. wide & 195 ft. long, left by ELIZABETH JENKINS as a passage
for all people which lot #64 she divided into 4 equal parts called, 1, 2,
3, & 4; & by deed poll dated 1 Jan. 1741 gave #1 to her son DAVID ADAMS;
#4 to her son NATHANIEL ADAMS; #2 to her daughter MARY JENKINS; & #3 to
her daughter HANNAH CAPERS; & whereas, after the death of ELIZABETH JEN-
KINS, MARY married WILLIAM MASON, tanner, of Charleston, & on 7 Feb. 1759
(see p. 607) they sold their part (#2) to RICHARD JENKINS; now he sells
to WALKER. Witnesses: HENRY VIDEAU, ALEXANDER GORDON. VIDEAU testified
21 Apr. 1762 before WILLIAM BURROWS, J.P. Recorded 30 Aug. 1762 by WIL-
LIAM HOPTON, Register.

Book Y-Y, p. 619   DANIEL DOYLEY, P.M., to WILLIAM BEE, planter,
19 Oct. 1761   of James Island, for Ł 1275 currency, 75 a. on
Sale   James Island, part of 539 a. Whereas WILLIAM
                         SCREVEN, planter, owned 539 a., English mea-
sure, on James Island, bounding N on a creek out of New Town Creek & on
parsonage land; E on MATTHEW WITTER & on MR. ATWELL; S on MATTHEW WITTER
& JOHN WITTER; S on THOMAS RIVERS & estate of JAMES SCREVEN; which tract
has been divided into 3 parts; 239 a., 75 a., & 225 a.; & whereas WILLIAM
SCREVEN on 22 May 1758 gave MARY COOPER, widow, of Charleston, a bond in
penal sum of Ł 2000 currency, & whereas MARY COOPER obtained a judgment
against CATHERINE SCREVEN, widow, administratrix of estate of said WIL-
LIAM SCREVEN for the debt & costs, & a writ of fieri facias was issued
commanding the P.M. to obtain the amount from the estate; now the P.M.
sells BEE, at public auction, 75 a., bounding N on a creek out of New
Town Creek; E on MR. ATWELL & MATTHEW WITTER; S on MATTHEW WITTER; W on a
path leading from public landing to the Savannah. Witnesses: JOHN MAT-
THEWES, MARK ANTHONY BESSELEAU. BESSELEAU testified 15 June 1762 before
JOHN REMINGTON, J.P. Recorded 1 Sept. 1762 by WILLIAM HOPTON, Register.
Plat of 539 a. certified 9 Jan. 1760 by WILLIAM WILKINS, Sur. At request
of MRS. CATHERINE SCREVEN, said WILLIAM WILKINS divided the plat of 539
a. into 3 parts on 31 Aug. 1761. The 225 a. is a reserve made for the
Baptist meeting according to survey by PRINGLE HAMILTON at request of
WILLIAM SCREVEN.

Book Y-Y, p. 625   WILLIAM BEE, planter, of James Island, to GA-
10 & 11 June 1762   BRIEL MANIGAULT, merchant, of Charleston, for
L & R   Ł 1275 currency, 75 a., part of 539 a. on
                         James Island, formerly belonging to WILLIAM
SCREVEN (p. 619). Witnesses: WILLIAM BANBURY, PETER BOUNETHEAU.
BOUNETHEAU testified 16 June 1762 before JOHN REMINGTON, J.P. Recorded 1
Sept. 1762 by WILLIAM HOPTON, Register.

Book Y-Y, p. 631   MICHAEL JEANES, glazier, of Charleston, sole
30 & 31 Aug. 1754   executor of will of VIRTUE BAKER, widow; to
L & R   BENJAMIN HARVEY, scrivener, of Charleston,
                         highest bidder, for Ł 605 currency, part of
lot #282 originally granted by the Lords Proprs. to CHARLES BASDEN; being
30 ft. x 100 ft. excepting 10 ft. at N end reserved (as agreed upon by

JOHN CARMICHAEL & BRYAN RYLY) as part of a 20 ft. lane called Little
Street, extending from King Street, to Meeting Street; E 100 ft. on ALEX-
ANDER PERONNEAU; S on THOMAS ELLIOTT, JR.; W on MICHAEL JEANES; with the
houses, etc.; which house & grounds, by various conveyances became the
property of VIRTUE BAKER; who by will, dated 9 Mar. 1754 ordered her real
& personal property sold. Witnesses: JOHN COOPER, CHARLES STEVENSON,
PAUL TOWNSEND. TOWNSEND testified 14 Aug. 1762 before WILLIAM BURROWS,
J.P. Recorded 2 Sept. 1762 by WILLIAM HOPTON, Register.

Book Y-Y, p. 641   ISAAC MAZYCK, gentleman, of Charleston, & MARY
12 & 13 Feb. 1759   his wife, to JOHN COMING BALL, planter, of
L & R   Craven Co., & HENRY LAURENS, merchant, of
                        Charleston, for Ł 1500 currency, 500 a. in
Wambaw Swamp, in Craven Co., bounding NW on vacant land; other sides on
land belonging to said BALL & LAURENS (formerly to JOHN GENDRON); being
part of 3000 a. which JOHN GENDRON purchased from BENJAMIN GODIN; which
500 a. GENDRON sold to MAZYCK. Witnesses: AARON LOOCOCK, BENJAMIN
MAZYCK. LOOCOCK testified 28 June 1762 before J. MURRAY, J.P. Recorded
3 Sept. 1762 by WILLIAM HOPTON, Register.

                        DEEDS BOOK "Z-Z"

Book Z-Z, p. 1   JOHN COLLETON, of St. James Parish, within the
4 & 5 June 1762   Liberty of Westminster, Co. of Middlesex, by
L & R   his attorneys, ROBERT RAPER & ROBERT SWAIN-
                        STONE, of SC, to HENRY LAURENS, merchant, of
Charleston; for Ł 8000 SC money, several plantations in Berkeley Co.;
3000 a. on E side of W branch of the T in Cooper River; 76 a. bounding S
on Cooper River; other sides on JOHN COLLETON; 67 a. bounding E on JOHN
COLLETON; S on Cooper River; W & N on Mepkin Creek. Whereas the Lords
Proprs. on 5 Mar. 1681 granted various tracts known as Watboo, Mepshoo, &
Mepkin, to SIR PETER COLLETON, THOMAS COLLETON, & JAMES COLLETON; & whereas THOMAS COLLETON died & SIR PETER & JAMES COLLETON held the land until
the death of SIR PETER in 1703, when JAMES became owner of Mepkin & by
his will dated 12 Jan. 1706 gave all his estate to his son, JOHN COLLETON;
who by will dated 2 Apr. 1720 devised his lands to his son, JOHN COLLETON,
party hereto; which last will was proved in Prerogative Court of the
Archbishop of Canterbury on 24 Dec. 1755; & whereas JOHN COLLETON by
letter dated London, 11 June, 1760, appointed RAPER & SWAINSTONE his
attorneys to sell all his estate in SC; now they sell 3 plantations to
LAURENS. Witnesses: JOHN RUTLEDGE, HUGH RUTLEDGE. HUGH RUTLEDGE testified 8 June 1762 before EGERTON LEIGH, J.P. Recorded 6 Sept. 1762 by
WILLIAM HOPTON, Register.

Book Z-Z, p. 11   RAWLINS LOWNDES, P.M., to JORDAN ROCHE, ESQ.,
16 June 1750   of Charleston, at public auction, for Ł 710
Sale   currency, the W part of the marsh land of Col-
                        leton Square, bounding W 67 ft. on Old Church
Street; S on lot #167; E on part of said marsh sold by CHARLES PINCKNEY
to PETER LARRY; N on lot #200; also part of lot #200 formerly granted to
PETER GIRARD & sold by CHARLES PINCKNEY & ELIZABETH his wife to MATTHEW
ROCHE, bounding W 109 ft. on Old Church Street; S & E on said marsh & the
fence of 2 covered cannon; N on the fence of the Fortifications lately
erected on the land side of the town; also 10t #167 sold by NATHANIEL
BROUGHTON of St. John's Parish & THOMAS BROUGHTON, his son, to MATTHEW
ROCHE. Whereas by L & R dated 1 & 2 Aug. 1748 CHARLES PINCKNEY & ELIZA-
BETH his wife sold MATTHEW ROCHE the first mentioned 2 lots; & on 1 Oct.
1747 the BROUGHTONS sold him lot #167, bounding E on ALEXANDER JEZEE
CHASTAGNEZ; W on the Great Street leading from the Ashley River to the
Market Place; S on MR. MAZYCK; N on the marsh; which lot was the inheri-
tance of MRS. CHARLOTTA HENRIETTA BROUGHTON (wife of NATHANIEL; mother of
THOMAS) & which NATHANIEL held for life as tenant by the Courtesy of Eng-
land; the reversion being in THOMAS as eldest son & heir of CHARLOTTE
HENRIETTA; & whereas MATTHEW ROCHE on 3 Mar. 1748 gave bond to JORDAN
ROCHE in penal sum of Ł 102,000 for payment of Ł 51,000 SC currency on 7
Mar. 1748; & JORDAN recovered a judgment against MATTHEW for the full
amount & costs; & whereas a writ of execution was issued by JAMES GRAEME,

C.J., commanding the P.M. to obtain the amount out of MATTHEW'S estate; now LOWNDES sells the above property to JORDAN ROCHE. Witnesses: BENJAMIN SMITH, DAVID DEAS. DEAS testified 23 Aug. 1762 before WILLIAM BURROWS, J.P. Recorded 7 Sept. 1762 by WILLIAM HOPTON, Register.

Book Z-Z, p. 20
1 Oct. 1747
Feoffment

NATHANIEL BROUGHTON, ESQ., of St. Johns Parish, Berkeley Co., & THOMAS BROUGHTON, his son, (heir to his mother, CHARLOTTE HENRIETTA, grand-daughter of PETER BURTELL); to MATTHEW ROCHE, merchant, of Charleston; for ₺ 500 currency, lot #167, bounding E on ALEXANDER TEZEE CHASTAGNEZ; W on the Great Street leading from Ashley River to the Market Place; S on MR. MAZYCK; N on the marsh; which lot formerly belonged to said CHARLOTTE HENRIETTA BROUGHTON, after whose death her husband had the use of the lot during his lifetime by Courtesy of England; the reversion being in her (their) son THOMAS. Witnesses: JOHN RATTRAY, HENRY IZARD. On 25 Aug. 1762 JAMES GRINDLAY testified before ROBERT WILLIAMS, JR., J.P., that this feoffment was ingrossed by him while clerk to JOHN RATTRAY, deceased. Recorded 8 Sept. 1762 by WILLIAM HOPTON, Register.

Book Z-Z, p. 24
2 Aug. 1748
Release

CHARLES PINCKNEY, ESQ., & ELIZABETH his wife, to MATTHEW ROCHE, merchant, both of Charleston, for ₺ 300:15:0 currency, for the marsh land; & ₺ 706:3:0 currency for part of lot #200; the W part of the marsh land of Colleton Square, & part of lot #200. Whereas the Lords Proprs. on 5 Mar. 1680 granted SIR PETER COLLETON lot #80 in Charleston, commonly called Colleton Square, containing 9 a., 2 roods, 21 perches, English measure, of dry & marsh land, with a small creek in the marsh land; bounding E on Cooper River, THOMAS COLLETON, & Landgrave JAMES COLLETON; W on a street then unnamed; S on CAPT. WILLIAM WALLEY & 2 lots belonging to CAPT. JAMES ADDIE; N on another lot belonging to THOMAS COLLETON & another small street then unnamed; which Square later became the property of JOHN COLLETON, ESQ., of Fairlawn Barony, in St. John's Parish, Berkeley Co.; & whereas JOHN COLLETON & SUSANNA his wife by L & R dated 13 & 14 July 1736, for ₺ 5000 currency, conveyed the Square to GEORGE HUNTER, gentleman, of Charleston, in trust for CHARLES PINCKNEY & THOMAS ELLERY, since deceased; & whereas by agreement between GEORGE HUNTER, CHARLES PINCKNEY, & ANNE ELLERY, widow of THOMAS ELLERY, the land was laid out in small lots by several streets & lanes; & the W part of the marsh land, bounding W on Old Church Street, with other parts of the Square was allotted to CHARLES PINCKNEY; & whereas the Lords Proprs. on 17 May 1694 granted PETER GIRARD, merchant, of Charleston, lot #200, bounding S & E on the marsh land of the Square (now PINCKNEY'S); N on lot #201, granted to said PETER GIRARD (now PINCKNEY'S); W on Old Church Street; & whereas PETER GIRARD by will dated 3 Aug. 1707 bequeathed the residue of his estate (including lot #200) to his daughter JUDITH, who afterwards married HENRY SIMONDS, planter, of St. John's Parish, Berkeley Co.; & whereas on the death of HENRY & JUDITH lot #200 descended to their eldest son & heir, HENRY SIMONDS the younger; who, by his attorney, (his brother, PETER SIMONDS) on 14 June 1748 sold lot #200 to CHARLES PINCKNEY; now PINCKNEY sells ROCHE the W part of the marsh land, bounding W 67 ft. on Old Church Street; S on lot #167 belonging to MATTHEW ROCHE; E on the part of the marsh sold by PINCKNEY to PETER LARRY; N on lot #200; also that part of lot #200 bounding W 109 ft. on Old Church Street; S & E on the marsh & the fence of 2 covered cannon; N on the ence of the Fortifications lately erected on the land side of the town. Witnesses: MARY PINCKNEY, FRANCES ARTHUR. On 25 Aug. 1762 RUTH PINCKNEY, wife of WILLIAM PINCKNEY, ESQ., recognized the hand-writing of her daughter, MARY PINCKNEY, deceased, before J. RUTLEDGE, J.P. Recorded 9 Sept. 1762 by WILLIAM HOPTON, Register.

Book Z-Z, p. 32
4 & 5 May 1761
L & R

JOHN TOBLER, of New Windsor, SC, & ANNA his wife, to JOHN INABNIT, of Orangeburgh, for ₺ 140 currency, 250 a. on PonPon River, granted ULRICK TOBLER by Lt. Gov. THOMAS BROUGHTON on 17 Sept. 1736; bounding NE on vacant land; NW on HENRY WARSTER; SW on PonPon River; SE on JOHN FUSTER; also lot #267 in Orangeburgh, containing 1/2 a., bounding NE on lot #20 belonging to JOHN STURZENEKER; NW on a street; SW on #264 belonging to SIMON TYSE; SE on the parade of the town. Witnesses: JOHN TOBLER, JR., DAVID ZULBY, JOHN KERNE. KERNE testified 8

June 1761 before JOHN CHEVELLETTE, J.P. Entered in Auditor's Book F #6, p. 137, on 31 Aug. 1762 by RICHARD LAMBTON, Dep. Aud. Recorded 10 Sept. 1762 by WILLIAM HOPTON, Register.

Book Z-Z, p. 38   HENRY SMITH, planter, of Berkeley Co., & ANN
23 & 24 Mar. 1762   his wife, (formerly ANN FILBEN, only surviving
L & R   daughter & child of JOHN FILBEN, planter, of
                       Colleton Co.) to JANE HEXT, widow, of Colleton
Co., for Ł 4410 SC money, ANN'S 509 a. & HENRY'S 226 a., total 735 a. in Colleton Co., bounding N & NE on MELCHOR GARDNER & JOHN DRAYTON; E on 1 Pendarvis; S on PENDARVIS & THOMAS SHUBRICK; W on 1 CATTELL; except a square, 30 ft. x 30 ft. fenced in & reserved for a burial place. Whereas JOHN FILBEN by L & R dated 30 & 31 May 1735 purchased from JOHN CATTELL, planter, of Berkeley Co., & SARAH his wife 509 a. (originally granted 20 May 1734 by Gov. ROBERT JOHNSON to JOHN CATTELL & then called 514 a.) in Colleton Co., & by will dated 27 Dec. 1742 bequeathed the residue of his real & personal estate equally to his 2 daughters, ANNE & SUSANNA; & whereas SUSANNA died in childhood & ANNE later married HENRY SMITH & became sole owner of the 509 a.; & whereas by L & R dated 1 & 2 Feb. 1757 JOHN FILBEN (son of CHARLES FILBEN), planter, of St. James Goose Creek, Berkeley Co., & ELIZABETH his wife, sold HENRY SMITH 226 a. adjoining ANN'S 509 a.; now HENRY & ANNE sell their land to JANE HEXT. Plat of 735 a. certified 3 Nov. 1758 by NATHANIEL DEAN, Dep. Sur., showing resurvey of 514 a., 121 a., & part of 2 tracts granted JOHN PENDERVIS & formerly laid off to MR. CORLILE containing 100 a., in Colleton Co., bounding N on MELCHIOR GARDNER & JOHN DRAYTON; NE on JOHN DRAYTON; S & E on PENDERVIS; S on CAPT. SHUBRICK. Witnesses: HERCULES HALL, REBECCA STOLL, DAVID STOLL. STOLL testified 27 Aug. 1762 before WILLIAM BURROWS, J.P. Recorded 11 Sept. 1762 by WILLIAM HOPTON, Register.

Book Z-Z, p. 53   WILLIAM GUERIN & MATHURIN GUERIN, planters, of
5 & 6 May 1761   Berkeley Co., executors of will of JOHN STONE,
L & R   blockmaker, of Charleston, to MAURICE HARVEY,
                       merchant, for Ł 4235 currency, that house &
part of lot #73 formerly belonging to JOHN STONE, bounding E 99 ft. on a house & part of lot #73 belonging to MR. MCCALL; S on lot #64 granted THOMAS ROSE, (now belonging to CAPERS); W on a house & part of lot #73 formerly belonging to GARRET VAN VELSEN; N 30 ft. on Tradd Street. Whereas JOHN STONE owned a house & part of lot #73 on S side Tradd Street, granted 16 Mar. 1693 to CHARLES BASDEN; which part by deed of feoffment dated 13 Dec. 1717 was sold by MARY BASDEN & others (sisters & coheirs of CHARLES BASDEN, JR. who died in infancy) to JOHN STONE; who by will dated 25 June 1756 bequeathed the residue of his estate, including said house & lot, to his executors, said GUERINS, upon special trust; now they sell the house at auction to HARVEY. Witnesses: EDMUND BELLINGER, THOMAS LAMBOLL. LAMBOLL testified 27 Aug. 1764 before WILLIAM BURROWS, J.P. Recorded 14 Sept. 1762 by WILLIAM HOPTON, Register.

Book Z-Z, p. 66   JOHN BUTLER PIGGOTT, merchant, & SARAH his
23 & 24 Aug. 1762   wife, to NICHOLAS VALOIS, gentleman, for
L & R   Ł 1800 currency, lot #210 bounding E 35-1/2
                       ft. on King Street; 125 ft. deep. Witnesses:
DANIEL MACKENET, JOHN BURGIS, PETER BOCQUET. MACKENET testified 1 Sept. 1762 before HENRY GRAY, J.P. Recorded 14 Sept. 1762 by WILLIAM HOPTON, Register.

Book Z-Z, p. 73   HELEN RATTRAY, of Charleston, widow & execu-
19 & 20 Jan. 1762   trix of will of JOHN RATTRAY, to BELLAMY CRAW-
L & R   FORD, gentleman, of Charleston, for Ł 4285
                       currency, 857 a., English measure, in Prince
William Parish, Granville Co., bounding E on JOHN & WILLIAM MURRAY; N on ALEXANDER FRAZER; other sides on marsh of Pocasaba Creek. Whereas JOHN RATTRAY owned considerable real & personal estate, 3/4 of which he bequeathed by his will dated 2 Dec. 1759 to his wife, HELEN, in lieu of dower; giving the other 1/4 to his sister HELEN, wife of the Rev. MR. PHILIP MORRISON, of Charleston, & authorized his wife to sell the property in order to make a just division; now she sells 857 a. to CRAWFORD. Witnesses: JOHN WAGNER, JACOB WARLEY. WAGNER testified before JAMES GRINDLAY on 30 June 1762. Recorded 15 Sept. 1762 by WILLIAM HOPTON, Register.

179

Book Z-Z, p. 81   JOHN DUNNAM, to JOHN DUTARQUE, planter, for
23 July 1762   Ŀ 100 currency, 500 a. in Berkeley Co., bound-
Feoffment   ing NW on JOHN RUSS; SE on MR. SINGLETARY.
                        Witnesses: DAVID SINGLETARY, JOHN DUTARQUE,
JR. Livery & seizen by turf & twig. DUTURQUE testified 3 Sept. 1762 before JOHN REMINGTON, J.P. Recorded 15 Sept. 1762 by WILLIAM HOPTON, Register.

Book Z-Z, p. 83   ALEXANDER MOON, planter, of Colleton Co., &
24 Sept, 1736   SARAH (her mark) his wife, to ALEXANDER LESS-
L & R   LEY, planter, of Goose Creek, 200 a. in Colle-
                        ton Co., bounding SW on JOSEPH DEADCUTT; NE on
JOHN MARTYNE; other sides on vacant land; & should there be more than
200 a. LESSLEY to pay MOON accordingly. Witnesses: JAMES SKIRVING, JOHN
OTTERSON, SAMUEL RIGGS. SKIRVING testified 8 Sept. 1762 before GEORGE
JOHNSTON, J.P. Recorded 16 Sept. 1762 by WILLIAM HOPTON, Register.

Book Z-Z, p. 89   DANIEL DOYLEY, P.M., to FRANCIS GOTTIER, at
10 Sept. 1762   public auction, for Ŀ 405 SC money, 600 a. in
Sale   Prince Frederick Parish, bounding NW on
                        CHARLES WOODMASON; NE & SW on ABRAHAM STAPLES;
SE on Peedee River. Whereas JOSIAS GARNIER DUPREE, planter, of Prince
Frederick Parish, owned 600 a. in Queensborough Township, which were said
to extend over Clerk's Creek & take in part of Johnstons Island; & whereas DUPREE gave bond dated 16 May 1759 to THOMAS MIDDLETON & SAMUEL BRAILS-
FORD, merchants, of Charleston, in penal sum of Ŀ 339:15:4 for payment of
Ŀ 169:17:8 currency, with interest, on 1 Jan. next; & whereas MIDDLETON &
BRAILSFORD obtained a judgment against DUPREE for the full amount & costs,
& in accordance with a writ of fieri facias, duly issued, the P.M. offered up DUPREE'S real estate for sale at auction; now DOYLEY sells the
tract to GOTTIER. Witnesses: WILLIAM SCOTT, ERSKIN HERON. HERON testified 13 Sept. 1762 before JOHN REMINGTON, J.P. Recorded 16 Sept. 1762 by
WILLIAM HOPTON, Register.

Book Z-Z, p. 94   PETER BOCHET, son & heir of NICHOLAS BOCHET,
5 & 6 Apr. 1762   planter, of Parish of St. Thomas & St. Dennis;
L & R   & FRANCES his wife, to the Rev. MR. JOHN JAMES
                        TISSOT, incumbent of the French Congregation
of that Parish, for Ŀ 80 currency, 100 a., English measure, known as the
French Parsonage, on SE side of E branch of T of Cooper River, bounding
SW on Lynch's Creek; SE on NICHOLAS BOCHET (father of PETER); NE on JOHN-
SON LYNCH; NW on GEORGE JUNE; which land was granted to Gov. JAMES MOORE
on 4 June 1701 to JOSEPH MARBEUFF; who on 22 Jan. 1703/4, for Ŀ 45 cur-
rency, sold to GEDEON & GABRIEL FERRON; & sold by GABRIEL FERRON (heir to
GEDEON) & his wife CATHERINE, on 17 Jan. 1711/12, for Ŀ 44 currency, to
ANDREW DUPREY; who, with JANE, his wife, on 8 Nov. 1716, for Ŀ 80 curren-
cy, sold to the Rev. MR. JOHN LAPIERRE; who, with SUSANNA, his wife, on
28 Nov. 1717 sold to MICHAEL BLACKWELL; who on 15 June 1723 sold to PETER
JOHNSON, SR.; who, for Ŀ 127, by L & R dated 17 & 18 Nov. 1730 sold to
NICHOLAS BOCHET. Witnesses: ROBERT GUERIN, JAMES DUBOIS, VINCENT GUERIN.
ROBERT GUERIN testified 31 May 1762 before BENJAMIN SIMMONS, J.P. Record-
ed 17 Sept. 1762 by WILLIAM HOPTON, Register.

Book Z-Z, p. 106   JAMES SHARP, merchant, of Jacksonborough, WIL-
7 July 1762   LIAM LENNOX, BENJAMIN CATON, & ANDREW HUNTER,
Release   of Charleston, executors of will of PATRICK
                        LAIRD of Charleston; dated 8 Nov. 1761 to WIL-
LIAM MEWHENNEY, dealer, of Charleston; for Ŀ 1345 currency, that part of
lot #70 in Charleston, known as part #2, allotted to PETER GODFREY & JANE
his wife (1 of the daughters of JANE GROSAT, who was 1 of the sisters of
ANDREW DUPREE), bounding N 61 ft. on Duprey's Alley; E on the part allot-
ted to ROBERT RAWLINS & his wife; W on JOHN BONHOSTE; S on a lot fronting
on Broad Street. Witnesses: JAMES PARSONS, JOHN GLEN, THOMAS YOUNG.
PARSONS testified 2 June 1762 before JAMES MAGHLIN, J.P. Recorded 20
Sept. 1762 by WILLIAM HOPTON, Register.

Book Z-Z, p. 110   WILLIAM KILLINGSWORTH, gentleman, to GEORGE
28 & 29 Sept. 1761   DUDLEY, gentleman, both of Amelia Township,
L & R   for Ŀ 200 currency, 125 a. whereas by L & R
                        dated 7 & 8 Jan. 1760 FREDERICK MATHEWS,

tailor, of Charleston, sold KILLINGSWORTH 250 a. in said Township, on S side Santee River, bounding E on SAMUEL JORDAN; SW on SAMUEL JORDAN & vacant land; NW on vacant land; now KILLINGSWORTH sells the upper half to DUDLEY & reserves the lower half for his son JACOB. Witnesses: THOMAS LENNON, JOHN KILLINGSWORTH. LENNON testified 2 Oct. 1761 before MOSES THOMSON, J.P. Recorded 22 Sept. 1762 by WILLIAM HOPTON, Register.

Book Z-Z, p. 118　　　　　　　GEORGE EVANS, planter, of St. George Parish,
2 Dec. 1761　　　　　　　　　　Dorchester, to HENRY MIDDLETON, DANIEL BLAKE,
Mortgage　　　　　　　　　　　　& BENJAMIN SMITH, of Charleston, executors of
　　　　　　　　　　　　　　　　will of RALPH IZARD, ESQ., of St. George, Dorchester; as security on bond of even date in penal sum of Ł 16,000 for
payment of Ł 8000 currency, with interest, on 1 Dec. 1762; 471 a. (formerly called 400 a.) purchased by EVANS from JOHN GOLDING; bounding SW on
a road leading to HENRY IZARD'S plantation; SE on HENRY IZARD & CAPT.
WILLIAM SMITH; NE on MICHAEL GEIGER (formerly CHARLES WRIGHT); NW on a
road leading to Bacons Bridge through Cow Savannah; also 75 Negro slaves.
Witnesses: CHARLES STEPHEN STOCKER, RICHARD ROGERS. STOCKER testified 17
Dec. 1761 before D. CAMPBELL, J.P. Recorded 28 Sept. 1762 by WILLIAM
HOPTON, Register. On 4 Nov. 1777 HENRY MIDDLETON declared mortgage sat-
isfied. Witness: GEORGE SHEED.

Book Z-Z, p. 129　　　　　　　JANE (her mark) MASSEY, spinster, to ROBERT
13 & 14 Sept. 1762　　　　　　ROWAND, merchant, of Charleston, as security
L & R·by Mortgage　　　　　　　on bond of even date in penal sum of Ł 1000
　　　　　　　　　　　　　　　　for payment of Ł 500 currency, with interest,
on 14 Sept. 1763; part of lot #164 in Charleston, bounding E 60 ft. on
King Street; W on JOHN DRAYTON; S on MR. VARAMBEAU; N 142 ft. on estate
of JOHN HYCOTT. Witnesses: JAMES GRINDLAY, MARGARET ESMOND. GRINDLAY
testified 14 Sept. 1762 before ROBERT WILLIAMS, JR., J.P. Recorded 29
Sept. 1762 by WILLIAM HOPTON, Register. On 15 June 1778 ROBERT ROWAND
declared mortgage paid. Witness: GEORGE SHEED.

Book Z-Z, p. 137　　　　　　　RACHAEL DALTON, widow, to THOMAS HOLMAN, both
14 & 15 Aug. 1762　　　　　　　of Colleton Co., for Ł 50 currency, 322 a.
L & R　　　　　　　　　　　　　(formerly called 550 a.). Whereas Gov. ROB-
　　　　　　　　　　　　　　　　ERT JOHNSON on 16 Mar. 1732 granted JOHN RIV-
ERS 550 a. in Colleton Co., bounding NW on WILLIAM HOLMAN; SW & NW on
JOHN WOODWARD; other sides on vacant land; as recorded in Secretary's
office 1 Mar. 1733; which land JOHN RIVERS, SR., by will dated 1 Mar.
1738/9 bequeathed to his son JOHN; who, by L & R dated 20 & 21 Aug. 1760,
who sold the land (by resurvey found to be 322 a.) to RACHEL DALTON; now
she sells to HOLMAN. Witnesses: JOHN RIVERS, ELIZABETH JENINGS. RIVERS
testified 14 Sept. 1762 before THOMAS HUTCHINSON, J.P. Recorded 30 Sept.
1762 by WILLIAM HOPTON, Register.

Book Z-Z, p. 143　　　　　　　MARY (her mark) SPRY, HENRY SPRY, & SAMUEL
14 & 15 May 1758　　　　　　　SPRY, executors of will of PHINEAS SPRY, plant-
L & R　　　　　　　　　　　　　er, of Craven Co.; to CHRISTOPHER JERDON, of
　　　　　　　　　　　　　　　　Craven Co.; for Ł 120 currency, 524 a. in Craven Co., bounding NE on ANTHONY SIMMONS; NW on JOSEPH HUGGINS; S on WIL-
LIAM BUCHANAN; SE on THOMAS LYNCH. Whereas Lt. Gov. THOMAS BROUGHTON on
28 Nov. 1735 granted PHINEAS SPRY 600 a. in Craven Co., which by his will,
dated 7 July 1741, he authorized his executors, to sell; which tract, upon a resurvey made 20 Apr. 1758, by THOMAS BLYTHE was found to be only
524 a.; now the executors sell to JERDON. Witnesses: EBENEZER BAGNALL,
SAMUEL NEILSON, SR., GEORGE BRUNSON, JR. On 9 Sept. 1761 BAGNALL testified before JOHN LIVISTON, J.P. Recorded 5 Oct. 1762 by WILLIAM HOPTON,
Register. Plat given.

Book Z-Z, p. 151　　　　　　　The Rev. MR. PHILIP MORRISON, & HELEN his wife,
6 & 7 Sept. 1762　　　　　　　to HENRY LAURENS, ESQ., both of Charleston,
L & R　　　　　　　　　　　　　for Ł 8000 currency, about 4 a. of high land
　　　　　　　　　　　　　　　　with all the marsh land E of the same, being
part of 20 a. of high land & 20 a. of marsh land in St. Philip's Parish,
Charleston, near Ansonburgh, formerly belonging to Lord GEORGE ANSON,
lately purchased by JOHN RATTRAY from Lord ANSON; bounding E on Cooper
River; W on a street leading from the Bay to Ansonborough; N on CHRISTO-
PHER GADSDEN & WILLIAM ELLIS (formerly GEORGE ANSON); S on a street leading from the Bay to Ansonborough & on marsh land; with the marsh & other

land as far as low water mark; except the wharf reserved to Lord ANSON
with an entry of 35 ft.; also reserving to CHRISTOPHER GADSDEN an entry
of 30 ft. towards the Bay in a line (sign?) fronting his south gates.
Whereas JOHN RATTRAY owned considerable real & personal estate & by will
dated 2 Dec. 1759 gave his wife, HELEN, 3/4 of his real & personal estate
in lieu of dower, & the remaining fourth to his sister, HELEN, wife of
PHILIP MORRISON; authorizing his wife to sell the estate to make a just
division; & by L & R dated 12 & 13 Feb. 1762 she sold the above tract to
PHILIP MORRISON; now he sells to LAURENS. Witnesses: WILLIAM ELLIS, WIL-
LIAM BEE, JAMES GRINDLAY. GRINDLAY testified 9 Sept. 1762 before ROBERT
WILLIAMS, JR., J.P. Recorded 8 Oct. 1762 by WILLIAM HOPTON, Register.
Plat given.

Book Z-Z, p. 162   ROBERT RIVERS, planter, & ANNE his wife, to
20 & 21 June 1754   GEORGE RIVERS, planter, both of James Island,
L & R   Berkeley Co., for Ł 955 currency, his undivid-
                          ed half part of 130 a. (65 a.) on S side James
Island, being part of 2 tracts formerly belonging to DANIEL GREATBATCH &
GEORGE RIVERS, SR.; 1 tract since belonging to THOMAS RIVERS; the other
to the several sons of GEORGE RIVERS, & now to ROBERT RIVERS; bounding N
on JOHN WITTER & JOHN RIVERS; E on the part of the 2 tracts belonging to
THOMAS RIVERS; S on a marsh; W on part of 1 of said tracts formerly belonging to GEORGE RIVERS, SR., now to his son ROBERT; also the undivided
half of the houses, etc. Witnesses: ANN PARROTT, WILLIAM HOLMES, SAMUEL
PICKRING. HOLMES testified 9 Nov. 1758 before DANIEL PEPPER, J.P. Recorded 29 Oct. 1762 by WILLIAM HOPTON, Register.

Book Z-Z, p. 172   JACOB (his mark) STROUBART, planter, & CATH-
6 & 7 July 1761   ERINE (her mark) his wife, to FREDERICK RES-
L & R   TER, planter, both of Purysburgh, Granville
                          Co., for Ł 200 currency, 152 a. in Purysburgh,
bounding N on RALPH NETMAN & HENRY MYERHOVER; W on GEORGE MINGLESDORF &
ANDREW WINKLER; S on DAVID VILLARD; E on GREGORY STEERLY. Witnesses:
GEORGE (his mark) STOUGER, HENRY BOURQUIN. BOURQUIN testified 7 July
1761 before JOHN BAPTIST BOURQUIN, J.P. Recorded 29 Oct. 1762 by WILLIAM
HOPTON, Register.

Book Z-Z, p. 181   WILLIAM COACHMAN, planter, & ELIZABETH his
8 & 9 Oct. 1762   wife, to BENJAMIN COACHMAN, planter, both of
L & R   Berkeley Co., for Ł 3000 currency, 1000 a., &
                          200 a. Whereas Gov. CHARLES CRAVEN on 19 Aug.
1714 granted Landgrave ROBERT DANIELL, as part of his patent for 48,000
a., 1000 a. bounding SE on ANDREW PERCIVALL; SW on RICHARD BEDON; NW on
THOMAS STEARS & vacant land; NE on a cypress swamp; which 1000 a. DANIELL
sold on 20 Aug. 1714 to THOMAS BROUGHTON; who on 31 Oct. 1732 sold to
THOMAS JOHNSON; who sold to JAMES MOORE & JOHN MOORE, brothers, as join-
tenants; & whereas JOHN MOORE died intestate, leaving an only child,
ELIZABETH, wife of WILLIAM COACHMAN; his brother JOHN MOORE being surviv-
ing jointenant; now WILLIAM COACHMAN, with the consent of ELIZABETH &
JOHN, sells the 1000 a. to BENJAMIN COACHMAN. And, whereas Lt. Gov. WIL-
LIAM BULL, on 16 Jan. 1761 granted WILLIAM COACHMAN 200 a. in St. George
Parish, Dorchester, bounding E on WILLIAM DONNING; SW on RICHARD BEDON &
WILLIAM GODFREY; NW on WILLIAM COACHMAN (said 1000 a.); now he sells the
200 a., also, to BENJAMIN COACHMAN. Witnesses: JAMES SANDERS, JOHN MAR-
TIN CAMENER. SANDERS testified 11 Oct. 1762 before BENJAMIN WARING,
J.P. Recorded 8 Nov. 1762 by WILLIAM HOPTON, Register.

Book Z-Z, p. 198   ABRAHAM (his mark) GINDRA, & MARY MARGARET his
9 Feb. 1759   wife; STEPHEN (ETIENNE) VEGNEUR & MARY ANN his
L & R   wife; & CATHERINE MORGIN; planters, of Purys-
                          burgh, Granville Co., of the 1st part; to DR.
JOHN BAPTIST BOURQUIN, of Purysburgh, for 15 shillings, 400 a. in Purysburgh Township, formerly belonging to ABRAHAM FALLET, their father &
father-in-law, bounding W on Back River; S on ABRAHAM EBERARD; other
sides on vacant land. Witnesses: JOHN BOURQUIN, JR., JOHN KEALL. KEALL
testified on 9 Feb. 1759 before CHARLES WRIGHT, J.P. Recorded 11 Nov.
1762 by WILLIAM HOPTON, Register.

Book Z-Z, p. 208   JOHN DRAYTON, ESQ., & MARGARET his wife, to
1 & 2 Sept. 1760   ARCHER SMITH, JR., planter, for Ł 1750

L & R   currency, 500 a. in Berkeley Co., on S side
                               Ashley River; bounding S on WILLIAM BULL; N &
E on WILLIAM ELLIOTT, MOSES WAY, STEPHEN DOWSE & THOMAS OSGOOD. Witness-
es: RICHARD BEDON, WILLIAM FULLER. BEDON testified 1 Dec. 1760 before
BENJAMIN WARING, J.P. Entered in Auditor's Book F #6, p. 116, on 2 Nov.
1762 by RICHARD LAMBTON, Dep. Aud. Recorded 15 Nov. 1762 by WILLIAM HOP-
TON, Register.

Book Z-Z, p. 215   HANS (his mark) WALTER, of Four Holes, Berke-
14 & 15 Dec. 1761   ley Co., to HENRY FELDER, of Orangeburgh Town-
                             ship, for Ŀ 50 currency, 300 a. in Orangeburgh
Township, Berkeley Co., granted 17 Dec. 1736 to HANS WALTER, father of
HANS, party hereto (Secretary's Book H.H., fol. 120); bounding NE on vacant land; NW on vacant land & on PETER FAURE; SE on CHRISTIAN STERVETS.
Witnesses: GAVIN PON, PETER FAURE, ISHAM CLAYTON. FAURE testified 2 Jan.
1762 before GAVIN PON. Recorded 16 Nov. 1762 by WILLIAM HOPTON, Register.

Book Z-Z, p. 233   JOHANNES STENGLI, planter, of Saluda, for love
21 Oct. 1762   & affection for his 2 children, GODFREY & ANN,
Gift in Trust   whom he can no longer maintain, conveys to his
                             friend, GODFREY DREHER, miller of Saxegotha
Township, godfather of his son GODFREY; the 50 a. on John's Creek, Saludee, on which STENGLI lives, bounding E on CHARLES BIRKMELER; W on GEORGE
KEITH; 2 horses branded with his usual mark 𝄢 T; 7 cows marked in both
ears with a slit & an upper & lower keel branded 𝄢 T; & the young cattle; the plantation for sole use of son GODFREY; the horses & stock
equally to son GODFREY & daughter ANNA. Witnesses: HANS ULRIC (his mark)
BACKMAN, & ULRIC (his mark) BACKMAN. On 21 Oct. 1762 HANS ULRIC BACKMAN
testified before STEPHEN CRELL, J.P. Recorded 17 Nov. 1762 before WIL-
LIAM HOPTON, Register.

Book Z-Z, p. 227   JERMYN WRIGHT & CHARLES WRIGHT, of Granville
24 & 25 Oct. 1762   Co., to JAMES POSTELL, ESQ., for Ŀ 400 curren-
L & R   cy, 2 lots, #3 & #19, known as CHARLES
                             WRIGHT'S lots, in Jacksonborough, that is, in
the old field near PonPon Bridge; being 2 of 8 lots which JERMYN WRIGHT
purchased from GEORGE JACKSON; lot #3 being 80 ft. front, next to WILLIAM
EBERSON'S store; lot #19 being opposite MR. WILLIAMS lot & next to the
storehouse of JAMES SHARP & Co. Witnesses: PHILIP SMITH, JOHN STRICK-
LAND. STRICKLAND testified 6 Nov. 1762 before JAMES SKIRVING, J.P. Recorded 19 Nov. 1762 by WILLIAM HOPTON, Register.

Book Z-Z, p. 234   HENRY WOOD, weaver, to JOSEPH WOOD, butcher,
18 & 19 Jan. 1762   both of Charleston, for Ŀ 300 currency,
L & R   61-1/4 a., English measure, on NE side Ashley
                             River, in St. Andrews Parish, Berkeley Co.,
bounding N & W on COL. BEDON; N, E, & S on WILLIAM FULLER. Witnesses:
ROBERT WILLIAMS, JR., STEPHEN TOWNSEND. WILLIAMS testified 5 Nov. 1762
before WILLIAM BURROWS, J.P. Recorded 26 Nov. 1762 by WILLIAM HOPTON,
Register.

Book Z-Z, p. 241   WILLIAM GASCOYNE, planter, & CATHERINE (her
5 & 6 Nov. 1762   mark) his wife, to GEORGE GALPHIN, planter,
L & R   both of Silver Bluff, Granville Co., for
                             Ŀ 1100 currency, 650 a. in Granville Co.,
bounding NE on NICHOLAS ROCHE; SE on vacant land; other sides on Savannah
River; as granted 12 Jan. 1737 to ARCHIBALD NEALE; who on 26 Oct. 1738,
sold to MARTIN CAMPBELL, ALEXANDER WOOD & PATRICK BROWNE; who on 15 Oct.
1744 conveyed to WILLIAM GASCOYNE; also 257-1/2 a. in Granville Co.,
bounding NE on JOSHUA SNOWDEN; SE on vacant land: SW on MARTIN CAMPBELL;
NW on Savannah River; which 257-1/2 a. were granted in 1741 to WILLIAM
GUY, JR., & sold on 2 Mar. 1743 by ROBERT MCMURDY to WILLIAM GASCOYNE.
Witnesses: ANTHONY DEANE, SAMUEL GIBSON. DEANE testified 12 Nov. 1762
before JOHN TOBLER, J.P. Recorded 1 Dec. 1762 by WILLIAM HOPTON, Register.

Book Z-Z, p. 250   ISAAC BRABANT, of St. Peters Parish, to DANIEL
21 & 22 June 1762   DESAUSSURE, of Prince William Parish, for
L & R   Ŀ 100 currency, 500 a. in Purysburgh Township,

Granville Co., bounding N on HENRY BOURGUIN; W on the Town Common; S on
LUDOVICH KEILLS & DAVID CONLIER; E on vacant land; which 500 a. were
granted by Gov. ROBERT JOHNSON to DR. DANIEL BRABANT; who died intestate;
& inherited by his son, ISAAC, party hereto. Witnesses: JOHN BAPTIST
BOURQUIN, ABRAHAM RAVOT. BOURQUIN testified 22 June 1762 before ADRIAN
MAYER, J.P.. Recorded 2 Dec. 1762 by WILLIAM HOPTON, Register.

Book Z-Z, p. 255   THOMAS WAITES, planter, & ANN his wife, to
3 & 4 June 1761   WILLIAM ALLSTON, JR., both of Prince George
L & R   Parish, Craven Co., for ₺ 1500 currency, 200
                          a.; & 150 a.; total 350 a. Whereas WILLIAM
WATIES by will dated 29 Jan. 1742 bequeathed to his son THOMAS, party
hereto, several tracts of land; 1 of 457 a. of swamp land, & part of 2
tracts, fronting W on Peedee River over against the 580 a. & extending E
to Wando Passo Creek, bounding S on MR. ALLSTON, & N to a line run due E
across the river from the lower boundary line of the plantation on which
WATIES then lived & continued to Wando River Creek; 1 of the 150 a. at
JOHN WELSTEADS Bluff near Waccamaw River; now THOMAS WATIES sells 200 a.,
being the E part of the 457 a. bounding N & E on Wando Passo Creek or
Thorofare; S on Long Creek & WILLIAM ALLSTON (sold to THOMAS WATIES); W
on other part 457 a.; also 150 a. on Sandy Island, known as Welsteads
Bluff, bounding S on Waccamaw River; W on Wando Passo Creek or Thorofare;
N on Marions Creek & other part of the tract to which the 150 a. belong-
ed; E on JOHN ALLSTON & vacant land. Witnesses: CHARLES FYFFE, ROBERT
HERIOT. FYFFE testified 22 Nov. 1762 before BENJAMIN YOUNG, J.P. Re-
corded 4 Dec. 1762 by WILLIAM HOPTON, Register. Plat of 200 a. dated 16
Apr. 1760 by THOMAS BLYTHE, Dep. Sur.

Book Z-Z, p. 261   WILLIAM MARTIN, commander H.M.S. The Ipswich,
6 Nov. 1740   appoints his friend, GEORGE ATKINS, ESQ., of
Power of Attorney   the Dock, near Portsmouth, Co. of Hampshire,
                          to receive any money due him. Witnesses:
THOMAS SMITH, WILLIAM HARRIS. On 9 Apr. 1741 GEORGE ATKINS of Portsmouth,
Co. of Hampshire, appeared before SAMUEL MARTYN, N.P. in London, & testi-
fied he had substituted JOHN NICKLESON, RICHARD SHUBRICK, & THOMAS SHU-
BRICK, merchants, of Charleston, as attorneys for MARTIN in his place.
Witnesses: THOMAS SMITH, EDWARD FAULKNER (clerk to SAMUEL MARTIN, N.P.).
THOMAS SMITH, ESQ., of Whitehall, Co. Middlesex, testified 9 Apr. 1741
before DANIEL LAMBERT, mayor of London, as to MARTIN'S signature on 6
Nov. 1740; also as to signature of W. HARRIS, gentleman, of Port Mahon;
also as to ATKINS'S signature on 9 Apr. 1749 by WILLIAM GEORGE FREEMAN,
Dep. Sec. Recorded 6 Dec. 1762 by WILLIAM HOPTON, Register.

Book Z-Z, p. 266   RAWLINS LOWNDES, P.M., to THOMAS SHUBRICK,
9 May 1754   merchant, of Charleston, at public auction,
Sale   for ₺ 2330 currency, lots 245, 246, 95, & 96
                          in Charleston, also 6 a., 1 rood, 12 perches
of land. Whereas BENJAMIN DELA CONSEILLERE, merchant, owned #245 in
Charleston, granted 10 June 1700 to ELIZABETH MARSHALL; bounding N on a
little street leading from Cooper River by MR. TREAD & GEORGE KEALING; S
on a marsh; W on JOSEPH OLDY; E on RALPH MARSHALL: also lot #246, granted
10 June 1701 to CATHERINE MARSHALL, bounding E on HENRY NOBLE; W on said
lot then belonging to JOHN BEE; N on King Street; S on a marsh; also 6 a.,
1 rood, 12 perches of land (called 7 a.) bounding N on lots 96, 59, 245,
& 246 on said lots & 1 marsh lot #130 & on vacant marsh;
S on lot #130 & another #131 on marsh not laid out & on Ashley River; W
on marsh not laid out; originally granted 20 Apr. 1716 to JOHN BEE; which
2 lots (245 & 246) & 7 a. JOHN BEE on 6 Nov. 1717 conveyed to BENJAMIN
DELA CONSEILLERE; & whereas BENJAMIN DELA CONSEILLERE also owned lots 95
& 96, bounding S on Ashley River; W on Holdrings Creek; E on aforesaid
lots; N on a street leading to Holdrings Creek; which lots, 95 & 96, JO-
SEPH HOLDRING, planter, of Granville Co., on 19 Aug. 1718 conveyed to
said CONSEILLERE; & whereas WILLIAM MARTIN obtained a judgement against
BENJAMIN GODIN, executor of CONSEILLERE'S estate for ₺ 1200 English
(₺ 8400 SC money) & costs; & whereas OGDIN, by will, appointed MARY ANNE
GODIN, DAVID GODIN, & JOHN GUERARD, his executrix & executors; & whereas
a writ of fieri facias was issued by CHARLES PINCKNEY, C.J., directing
the P.M. to obtain the money from CONSEILLERE'S estate; now the P.M.
sells the 4 lots & 7 a. to SHUBRICK. Witnesses: DOUGAL CAMPBELL, WILLIAM
READ. CAMPBELL testified 2 Dec. 1762 before WILLIAM SIMPSON, J.P.

Recorded 8 Dec. 1762 by WILLIAM HOPTON, Register. Plat given.

Book Z-Z, p. 272   GIDEON NORTON, shipwright, of Charleston, to
19 & 20 Oct. 1747   WILLIAM SCREVEN, planter, of James Island; for
L & R   Ł 1300 currency, part of lot #92 in Charleston; bounding S 40 ft. on Tradd Street; E 102
or 103 ft. on ROBERT COLLIS; W on SAMUEL EVANS; N on JAMES TOMSON. Witnesses: ROBERT RAPER, JOHN REMINGTON. REMINGTON testified 20 Oct. 1747
before THOMAS DALE, J.P. Recorded 10 Dec. 1762 by WILLIAM HOPTON, Register.

Book Z-Z, p. 278   WILLIAM SCREVEN, planter, of James Island, to
24 & 25 Oct. 1753   ELIZABETH CHANDLER, widow, of Charleston, for
L & R   Ł 1500 currency, part of lot #92 in Charles-
ton, (see p. 272). Witnesses: JUSTINUS STOLL,
WILLIAM SCREVEN, JR., SAMUEL CHANLER. STOLL testified 1 Feb. 1762 before
T (?) Murray, J.P. Recorded 12 Dec. 1762 by WILLIAM HOPTON, Register.

Book Z-Z, p. 284   SARAH MIDDLETON, of Berkeley Co., executrix of
8 Oct. 1756   will of her son JOHN MORTON, ESQ., to BENJAMIN
Feoffment   WARING, for Ł 1300 currency, 694 a. on head of
Ashley River, in St. George Parish; bounding N
on THOMAS WARING (formerly WILLIAM STEAD); E on JOHN WALTERS; S on BENJA-
MIN WARING; W on MR. BETH^L. DEWS. Witnesses: MARY WILKINSON, JOHN MOUL-
TRIE, JR., JOSEPH BRAILSFORD. JOHN MOULTRIE testified 1 Dec. 1762 before
JAMES MOULTRIE, J.P. Entered in Auditor's Book on 5 July by JAMES MICHIE,
Dep. Aud. Recorded 13 Dec. 1762 by WILLIAM HOPTON, Register.

Book Z-Z, p. 286   TOBIAS FORD, planter, of St. Bartholomews Par-
7 & 8 Aug. 1761   ish, Colleton Co., & MARY his wife, to JOSIAH
L & R   PERRY, planter, of St. Pauls Parish, Colleton,
Co., for Ł 4600 currency, 764-1/4 a. in St.
Bartholomews Parish conveyed by JAMES SKIRVING to FORD by L & R dated 22
& 23 Dec. 1760; bounding S on JOHN BEATY; E on DAVID FERGUSON; NW on JOHN
REID; SW on vacant land. Witnesses: GIDEON DUPONT, JR., WILLIAM JACKSON,
THOMAS OSBORN. DUPONT testified 8 Aug. 1761 before JAMES SHARP, J.P.
Recorded 22 Dec. 1762 by WILLIAM HOPTON, Register.

Book Z-Z, p. 293   THOMAS DYALL (DYALL), planter, & CATHERINE
28 & 29 July 1758   (her mark) his wife, to JOHN FRIERSON, both of
L & R   Craven Co., for Ł 400 currency, 400 a. in St.
Mark's Parish, Craven Co., bounding on vacant
land; granted THOMAS DYAL 13 Feb. 1753. Witnesses: CHARLES MACKOY, SAM-
UEL MACKOY, SUSANNA CASSELS. CHARLES MACKOY testified 28 July 1758 before HENRY CASSELS, J.P. Recorded 26 Dec. 1762 by WILLIAM HOPTON, Register.

Book Z-Z, p. 299   CHARLES WRIGHT, ESQ., of Granville Co., to
2 & 3 Aug. 1762   WILLIAM MAZYCK, attorney, of Charleston, as
L & R by Mortgage   security on bond of even date in penal sum of
Ł 2420 currency for payment of Ł 1208:15:0 currency,
with interest, on 3 Aug. 1763; 550 a. in St. Peters Parish, Granville
Co.; bounding SE on Savannah Back River; other sides on JERMYN WRIGHT;
which tract was granted CHARLES WRIGHT on 10 Nov. 1761. Witnesses: ISAAC
MAZYCK, ISAAC MAZYCK, JR. ISAAC MAZYCK, JR. testified 8 Dec. 1762 before
TACITUS GAILLARD, J.P. Recorded 30 Dec. 1762 by WILLIAM HOPTON, Regis-
ter.

Book Z-Z, p. 307   CRONICA (her mark) ZURKUS, lately widow of
9 & 10 Feb. 1756   HENRY FEISLER, planter, of Berkeley Co., to
L & R   JOHANN BARTHOLOMEW SMITH, cordwainer, of
Charleston, for Ł 50 currency, 150 a. in low
grounds of Santee River, opposite lower part of Saxegotha Township,
bounding S on Santee River; W & N on vacant land; E on JOHN PEARSON;
which 150 a. were granted by Gov. JAMES GLEN on 30 Apr. 1748 to HENRY
FEISLER. Witnesses: MARY ANN MACKRETH, FRED MERCKLEY. MARY ANN MACKRETH
testified 3 Mar. 1756 before WILLIAM HOPTON, J.P. Recorded 12 Jan. 1763
by WILLIAM HOPTON, Register.

Book Z-Z, p. 313   JOHN HARVEY, gentleman, & CATHERINE his wife,

26 & 27 Nov. 1762   to WILLIAM HARVEY, gentleman, both of Charles-
L & R by Mortgage   ton, as security on bond in penal sum of
                                Ŀ 17,413:8:6 for payment of Ŀ 8,706:14:3 cur-
rency, with interest, on 1 May 1763; 174 a. in St. Andrews Parish, Berkeley Co., formerly belonging to WILLIAM HARVEY, father of said JOHN & WIL-
LIAM; who purchased the tract from the executors of BENJAMIN GODFREY; &
devised by his father to JOHN HARVEY; also 214 a. in same Parish formerly
belonging to his father, WILLIAM HARVEY, who had purchased from WILLIAM
GIBBES & other trustees & devised to his son BENJAMIN; who, by L & R conveyed to JOHN; also 200 a. in same Parish, formerly belonging to his father, WILLIAM HARVEY, who had purchased from WILLIAM GIBBES & other trustees, & devised to his son ARNOLD HARVEY, who by L & R conveyed to JOHN;
total 588 a., bounding E on Ashley River; N on marsh; NW on WILLIAM HAR-
VEY (formerly FRANCIS YONGE); W on OLIVER JOURDION'S creek & marsh. Witnesses: ROBERT WILLIAMS, JR., RICHARD CATON. WILLIAMS testified 14 Oct.
1762 before LIONEL CHALMERS, J.P. Recorded 20 Jan. 1763 by WILLIAM HOP-
TON, Register. On 19 June 1767 WILLIAM HARVEY received full satisfaction
of mortgage by the hands of ROGER PINCKNEY, ESQ. Witness: FENWICKE BULL.

Book Z-Z, p. 321   WILLIAM AXSON, carpenter, of Charleston, to
3 Jan. 1763   DANIEL DOYLEY, for Ŀ 311 currency, a lease of
Assignment of Lease   4 certain lots in Charleston from RICHARD
                               BERESFORD dated 13 July 1761. Witness: JAMES
GUTHRIE. Before WILLIAM BURROWS, J.P. Recorded 21 Jan. 1763 by WILLIAM
HOPTON, Register.

Book Z-Z, p. 323   LEWIS MOUZON, planter, & ELIZABETH his wife,
27 & 28 Dec. 1762   to GEORGE SMITH, JR., both of St. Thomas Par-
L & R   ish, Berkeley Co., for Ŀ 850 currency, 200 a.
                              in St. Thomas Parish, bounding E on a part of
same tract lately belonging to JOHN MUSGROVE, deceased, who received it
through his wife, MARY KING; W on JOHN GUERIN; S on ALEXANDER VANDERDUS-
SEN; N on land formerly belonging to JOSEPH SINGLETARY (now to ROBERT
DANIELL, JOHN SINGLETARY, or NATHAN TART); which tract (400 a.) was originally granted to ABRAHAM WARNOCK on 1 June 1709, & by him bequeathed to
MARY KING & ANNA KING; the above 200 a. being ANNA KING'S half; which
half she (then ANNA MIMACK) & her husband, JOHN MIMACK, by L & R dated 6
& 7 Oct. 1741 sold to LEWIS MOUZON, JR. Witnesses: JAMES BOURDEAUX, SAM-
UEL BOCHET. BOCHET testified 4 Jan. 1763 before WILLIAM BURROWS, J.P.
Recorded 2 Feb. 1763 before WILLIAM BURROWS, J.P. Recorded 2 Feb. 1763
by WILLIAM HOPTON, Register.

Book Z-Z, p. 333   HENRY O'NEILL, planter, of Black Mingo to JOHN
1 Dec. 1759   JAMES, planter, of Craven Co., for Ŀ 500 cur-
L & R   rency, 460 a. in Craven Co., on S side of
                              Lynch's Lake, bounding SW on JOHN BARNS; SE on
JAMES SNOW; NE on vacant land. Witnesses: ROBERT WEARING, NATHANIEL
BROWN. WEARING testified 22 Dec. 1759 before CHARLES WOODMASON, J.P.
Entered in Book G #7, p. 24, on 21 Jan. 1763 by RICHARD LAMBTON, Dep.
Aud. Recorded 3 Feb. 1763 by WILLIAM HOPTON, Register.

Book Z-Z, p. 337   JOHN CARLIN, of Clouds Creek, a branch of
17 & 18 Nov. 1758   Little Saluda River, & WALBURGIN (her mark)
L & R   his wife, to GEORGE HILES, of same place, for
                              Ŀ 100 currency, 200 a. in Clouds Creek, grant-
ed JOHN CARLIN on 12 Feb. 1755 by Gov. JAMES GLEN; bounding on all sides
on vacant land. Witnesses: WILLIAM WATSON, THOMAS DELOACH, ANDREW (his
mark) SHIPS. DELOACH testified 18 Nov. 1758 before JOHN FAIRCHILD, J.P.
Recorded 5 Feb. 1763 by WILLIAM HOPTON, Register. On 21 Aug. 1762 GEORE
(his mark) HILE assigned his interest to JOHN WATSON. Witnesses: WILLIAM
WATSON, DANIEL AWAYS. WATSON testified before JOHN TOBLER, J.P. Recorded 5 Feb. 1763 by WILLIAM HOPTON, Register.

Book Z-Z, p. 344   JOHN ANDERSON, planter, of Prince Frederick
22 & 23 Jan. 1759   Parish; & JOSEPH & WILLIAM ANDERSON, planters,
L & R   of St. James Santee; to ROBERT HAMBELTON,
                              planter, of Williamsburg Township; for Ŀ 350
currency; 500 a. in Williamsburg Township, Craven Co., bounding SW on
Black River; SE on JOHN HERRON & WILLIAM JAMES; NE on vacant land; NW on
JOHN PORTER & THOMAS HALL. Witnesses: JAMES (his mark) LAW, WILLIAM LAW,

JOHN BURGESS. WILLIAM LAW testified 25 Jan. 1763 before JOHN LIVISTON, J.P. Recorded 8 Feb. 1763 by WILLIAM HOPTON, Register.

Book Z-Z, p. 351
18 & 19 July 1754
L & R
ANDREW DEVEAUX & JAMES DEVEAUX, planters, (sons & executors of will of ANDREW DEVEAUX, gentleman), & JOHN DEVEAUX, another son; of 1st part; to ISAAC LESESNE; for Ł 700 currency; 700 a. in several tracts, in Berkeley Co.; according to grants from Gov. CHARLES CRAVEN dated 14 Feb. 1717; which tracts ANDREW DEVEAUX, by will dated 2 Feb. 1754, devised equally to his 3 sons. Witnesses: JEAN GARNER, JOHN B. GIRARDEAU, ANDREW DEVEAUX, JR. ANDREW DEVEAUX, JR. testified 17 Jan. 1763 before THOMAS MIDDLETON, J.P. Recorded 14 Feb. 1763 by WILLIAM HOPTON, Register.

Book Z-Z, p. 360
10 & 11 Feb. 1763
L & R
BENJAMIN DART, gentleman, & AMELIA his wife, to WILLIAM BRANFORD, gentleman, both of Charleston, for Ł 6500 currency, 3 adjoining tracts of 500, 295-1/4, & 40 a., total 835-1/4 a. on Horse Shoe Savannah, Colleton Co., bounding N on MR. YOUNG & estate of WILLIAM CATTELL, SR.; E on MR. LOWNDES, DR. SKIRVING, WILLIAM MITCHELL, & MR. YOUNG; S on MR. LOWNDES & estate of MRS. ELIZABETH GIBBES; W on WILLIAM EBERSON & estate of WILLIAM CATTELL; which 3 tracts formerly belonged to JOHN PAYCOM, who died intestate, & inherited by his niece, ELIZABETH PAYCOM, who afterwards married DANIEL LEGARE the younger, merchant, of Charleston; & conveyed by DANIEL & ELIZABETH LEGARE by L & R dated 17 & 18 Jan. 1758 to said BENJAMIN DART. Witnesses: FRANCIS ROSE, EDWARD BLAKE. BLAKE testified 11 Feb. 1763 before ROBERT WILLIAMS, JR., J.P. Recorded 15 Feb. 1763 by WILLIAM HOPTON, Register. Plat given.

Book Z-Z, p. 372
23 & 24 July 1729
L & R
JOSEPH WRAGG, merchant, of Charleston, to JOHN BAGBY, planter, of Berkeley Co., for Ł 800 currency, 640 a. in St. James Goose Creek, Berkeley Co., bounding SW & NW on vacant land; NE on ISAAC _____; SE on ROGER SAUNDERS; also 100 a. in Berkeley Co., bounding NE & SW on WILLIAM NORMAN; NW on MR. WILLIAMS; SE on MR. MCDANIEL. Witnesses: ALEXANDER STEWART, PETER HORRY. Entered in Auditor's office 15 May 1733. STEWART testified 2 Nov. 1762 before JOHN REMINGTON, J.P. Recorded 18 Feb. 1763 by WILLIAM HOPTON, Register. N.B.: The greater part of this conveyance said to have been eaten by mice.

Book Z-Z, p. 379
14 & 15 Sept. 1762
L & R
DAVID DAVIS, WILLIAM JAMISON & THEODORE GOURDINE, executors of will of JAMES BAGBY, planter, of St. Stephens Parish; to JAMES LENNOX, merchant, of Charleston, for Ł 2360 currency, 640 a. in St. James Goose Creek, Berkeley Co., bounding (when originally surveyed for STEPHEN MONCK), SW & NW on vacant land; NE on ISAAC LEWIS; SE on ROGER SAUNDERS; also 400 a. in 2 tracts of 100 a. & 300 a.; the 100 a. of which formerly belonged to JOSEPH WRAGG, & the 300 a. to JOSEPH NORMAN, who conveyed to JOHN BAGBY, father of said JAMES BAGBY; the 400 a. bounding E on JAMES LENNOX; W on RICHARD SINGLETON; S on heirs of DR. CAW (formerly NOAH SERRÉ); N on lands late of JOSEPH WRAGG & lands late of JOSEPH NORMAN, now in possession of ANDREW MCMASTERS. Whereas JAMES BAGBY, by the will of his father, JOHN BAGBY, dated 31 Oct. 1738, & as surviving devisee of his father & heir of his brother GEORGE BAGBY, became owner of said lands, & by his will dated 12 Jan. 1761 directed his executors to sell the residue of his real & personal estate; now DAVIES, JAMIESON & GOURDINE sell the land to LENNOX. Witnesses: Rev. MR. LEVI DURAND, EDWARD MORTIMER, DANIEL ROSS. DURAND testified 24 Nov. 1762 before ALEXANDER STEWART, J.P. Recorded 18 Feb. 1763 by WILLIAM HOPTON, Register.

Book Z-Z, p. 387
28 Apr. 1761
Bond
NATHANIEL BLUNDELL, planter, of St. Johns Parish, Johns Island, to DANIEL CANNON, of Charleston, bond of indemnity, because CANNON stood security on BLUNDELL'S bond to MARY WATSON, widow, of Charleston, (p. 389). Witnesses: JAMES SIMMONS, JOHN BRAUND, EDWARD WEYMAN. Before JOHN REMINGTON, J.P. Recorded 26 Feb. 1763 by WILLIAM HOPTON, Register.

Book Z-Z, p. 389
NATHANIEL BLUNDELL, planter, of St. Johns

28 Apr. 1761   Parish, Johns Island, to DANIEL CANNON, of
Mortgage   Charleston, as security on bond of even date
                                in penal sum of ₺ 4000 for payment of ₺ 2000
currency, with interest, on 28 Apr. 1762 (because CANNON stood security
on a bond given by BLUNDELL to MARY WATSON, widow, of Charleston); BLUN-
DELL'S house & land on Meeting Street, Charleston, bounding N on the New
England Meeting; S on JAMES HUNTER. A penknife delivered. Witnesses:
JAMES SIMMONS, JOHN BRAUND, EDWARD WEYMAN. WEYMAN testified 8 Feb. 1763
before JOHN REMINGTON, J.P. Recorded 26 Feb. 1763 by WILLIAM HOPTON,
Register. Mortgage satisfied 27 Apr. 1765. Witness: FENWICKE BULL.

Book Z-Z, p. 393   ANN (her mark) NELSON, & SARAH (her mark)
25 & 26 Jan. 1763   QUASH, widows, to HENRY LAURENS, ESQ., all of
L & R   Charleston, for ₺ 900 currency, a lot in part
                              of a plantation called Rhettsberry Point.
Whereas by L & R dated 24 & 25 Sept. 1731 NICHOLAS TROTT, ESQ., of St.
Phillips Parish, Charleston, & SARAH his wife, for ₺ 150 currency, sold
EXPERIENCE HOWARD, carpenter, part of Rhettsberry Point Plantation, in
St. Philip's Parish, Charleston, bounding NE by E 30 ft., English mea-
sure, on marsh; & going back towards SW by W 200 ft.; that is, from the
front line 40 ft., then leaving 20 ft. for a street; then going further
on the line towards SW by W 160 ft.; bounding NW by N on a lot sold by
NICHOLAS & SARAH TROTT to JOHN SCOTT, shipwright; & whereas EXPERIENCE
HOWARD died intestate in 1739, & his only surviving children, ANN NELSON
& SARAH QUASH, inherited, subject to their mother's (RACHEL HOWARD'S)
right of dower; & whereas RACHEL HOWARD on 24 Jan. last released her
right of dower; now ANN & SARAH sell the lot to LAURENS. Witnesses: JO-
SEPH BRAILSFORD, WILLIAM STOUTENBURGH, JOHN BREMAR. BRAILSFORD testified
14 Feb. 1763 before EGERTON LEIGH, J.P. Recorded 28 Feb. 1763 by WILLIAM
HOPTON, Register.

Book Z-Z, p. 403   THOMAS POOLE, pilot, eldest son & heir of
29 & 30 Sept. 1762   THOMAS POOLE, & MARY his wife, to CHARLES DE-
L & R   WAR, merchant, both of Charleston, for ₺ 3600
                             currency, part of town lot #92, formerly be-
longing to THOMAS POOLE, the father; bounding S 63 ft. 9 in. on Tradd
Street; W 100 ft. on part of lot #92 belonging to SAMUEL WAINWRIGHT; N
61-1/2 ft. on ESTHER SIMMONS; E 100 ft. on part of lot #92 belonging to
GEORGE POWELL; with the dwelling house thereon. Witnesses: JAMES GRIND-
LAY, CHRISTOPHER FITZSIMONS. GRINDLAY testified 31 Dec. 1762 before ROB-
ERT WILLIAMS, JR., J.P. Recorded 2 Mar. 1763 by WILLIAM HOPTON, Regis-
ter.

Book Z-Z, p. 411   CODLIB WEIS, of Charleston, & MARY DOROTHY his
9 & 10 July 1761   wife, to BARTHOLOMEW GARTMAN, planter, of the
L & R   fork of Broad & Saluda Rivers, for ₺ 30 cur-
                             rency, 100 a. on S side Broad River, in Berke-
ley Co., bounding NW on vacant land; SW on GEORGE RESINGESS; SE on GEORGE
MARTIN. Witnesses: DANIEL GARTMAN, JOHN MEEK. GARTMAN testified 5 Mar.
1762 before JOHN REMINGTON, J.P. Recorded 3 Mar. 1763 by WILLIAM HOPTON,
Register.

Book Z-Z, p. 418   WILLIAM MOORE, planter, of Georgia, to MARTIN
18 & 19 Sept. 1759   SHIRER, tailor, of Berkeley Co., for ₺ 200,
L & R   currency, 200 a. on N side Broad River; NW on
                             JOSEPH CURRY, NE on vacant land; SE on CONRAD
KENSLER; which land was granted MOORE on 21 May 1757 by Gov. WILLIAM
HENRY LYTTLETON. Witnesses: THOMAS REESEE, ELIZABETH JOYCE, JOHN (his
mark) LORMAN (LOARMAN). LORMAN testified 26 Sept. 1759 before JOHN PEAR-
SON, J.P. Recorded 4 Mar. 1763 by WILLIAM HOPTON, Register.

Book Z-Z, p. 425   JOHN (his mark) HOLLMAN, planter, of Berkeley
28 & 29 Dec. 1762   Co., to the Rev. MR. JOHN NICHOLAS MARTIN, for
L & R   ₺ 50 currency, 50 a. on Crims Creek, in the
                             fork between Broad & Saluda Rivers, granted by
Gov. JAMES GLEN on 27 Aug. 1751 to JOHN HENRY WELCHER (Book N.N. fol.
120); who, for ₺ 20 currency, sold to PETER CRIM; who, for ₺ 20 currency,
on 8 & 9 Sept. 1756 sold to JOHN HOLLMAN; bounding NW on FRANCIS HALL; NE
on MARGARET KENNER; other sides on vacant land. Witnesses: PHILIP PETER
PEARSON, WILLIAM SMITH. PEARSON testified 29 Dec. 1762 before JOHN

JOHN PEARSON, J.P.   Recorded 7 Mar. 1763 by WILLIAM HOPTON, Register.

Book Z-Z, p. 431   JACOB WITSELL & FREDERICK WITSELL, planters,
15 Oct. 1762   of St. Bartholomews Parish, Colleton Co., to
Mortgage   JAMES SHARP, merchant, of same place, as se-
                         curity for payment of Ł 1000 currency, on 1
Jan. 1763; 300 a. in Colleton Co., bounding NW on MOSES MARTIN & JAMES
NEWTON; NE on JAMES MEWTON & heirs of JOSEPH BOONE; SE on WILLIAM LITTLE;
SW on THOMAS ELLIOTT & THOMAS BRADWELL. Witnesses: GIDEON DUPONT, JR.,
EDWARD HEXT. DUPONT testified 18 Feb. 1763 before BENJAMIN SMITH, J.P.
Recorded 7 Mar. 1763 by WILLIAM HOPTON, Register. Mortgaged satisfied 20
Dec. 1765. Witness: OLIVER NOYES.

Book Z-Z, p. 435   Gov. THOMAS BOONE & CHARLES BOONE, ESQ., of
7 & 8 Mar. 1763   St. George Parish, Hanover Square, Co. of Mid-
L & R   dlesex, London, to JAMES POSTELL, ESQ., of St.
                         Bartholomew Parish, SC, for Ł 4987:10:0 SC
money, 1425 a. in St. Bartholomews Parish, bounding N on GEORGE LOGAN; NE
& E on MRS. HUNTER; S on NEWTON; SW on vacant land; SE on ISHAM ANDREWS &
SARAH SAUNDERS & SAUNDERS Path; which 1425 a. comprise 3 tracts original-
ly granted JOSEPH BOONE; & now owned by said THOMAS & CHARLES BOONE;
CHARLES having appointed THOMAS, on 2 Sept. 1752, his attorney, with
authority to sell the land. Witnesses: WILLIAM SIMPSON, WILLIAM DAVIS.
SIMPSON testified 9 Mar. 1763 before GEORGE JOHNSTON, J.P. Recorded 11
Mar. 1763 by WILLIAM HOPTON, Register.

Book Z-Z, p. 442   JAMES EMPSON, shoemaker, of Liverpool, Co. of
3 & 4 Mar. 1763   Lancaster, Great Britain, executor of will of
L & R   THOMAS CROFT, butcher, of Liverpool, who was
                         brother & heir of JOHN CROFT, ferryman, of
Winyaw, SC; JAMES BUNNELL, butcher, of Liverpool, & MARGARET his wife,
sister of said JOHN CROFT; by their attorney, HENRY LAURENS, ESQ., of
Charleston, SC, of the 1st part; to ARCHIBALD JOHNSTON, planter, of
Georgetown; for Ł 1400 currency; 300 a. in Craven Co., being the remainder of 450 a. sold by ROBERT SCREVEN & SARAH his wife, by L & R dated 11
& 12 Mar. 1752 to JOHN CROFT; bounding NW, N, NE, & SE on Sampit Creek;
SW on ARCHIBALD JOHNSTON (formerly JOHN CROFT); S on heirs of NATHANIEL
WICKAM. Whereas THOMAS CROFT, by will dated 25 July last, bequeathed all
his real & personal estate in SC to JOHN BROWNELL, gentleman, of Liver-
pool & JAMES EMPSON, as trustees, to sell his real & personal estate after his death; BROWNELL declining to act; EMPSON accepting; & whereas
EMPSON, JAMES BUNNELL, & MARGARET BUNNELL, on 7 Dec. 1762 appointed HENRY
LAURENS their attorney with power to sell the land; now LAURENS sells to
JOHNSTON. Witnesses: JOSEPH BRAILSFORD, WILLIAM STOUTENBURGH, JOHN BRE-
MAR. BRAILSFORD testified 7 Mar. 1763 before EGERTON LEIGH, J.P. Re-
corded 14 Mar. 1763 by WILLIAM HOPTON, Register.

Book Z-Z, p. 452   GEORGE SAXBY, of Charleston, & ELIZABETH his
18 & 19 May 1762   wife, to ELIAS FOISSIN, of Craven Co., for Ł 5
L & R   currency, his half of 3 tracts of 1800 a.,
                         2100 a., & 1100 a., on Cat Island, in Winyaw
Bay, Craven Co.; which 3 tracts are held by him & FOISSIN as tenants in
common. Witnesses: SUSANNA BOSOMWORTH, FRANCIS PELOT. SUSANNA testified
10 Mar. 1763 before WILLIAM SIMPSON, J.P. Recorded 15 Mar. 1763 by WIL-
LIAM HOPTON, Register.

Book Z-Z, p. 459   JACOB WERNER, planter, of Berkeley Co., & BAR-
7 & 8 Mar. 1763   BARY (her mark) his wife, to MARTHA LLOYD,
L & R by Mortgage   widow, of Charleston, as security on a certain
                         bond; his N half of the W half of lot #46 in
Charleston; which he purchased from MARTIN BRICKEL & MARY his wife by L
& R dated 4 & 5 Mar. 1763; bounding W on King Street; N 52 ft. on ELIZA-
BETH DIDCOTT; E 112 ft. 9 in. on JOSEPH ASH; S on MR. LORIMER. Whereas
JACOB WERNER, JOHN WERNER, planter, HENRY MEDSKER, baker, MITCHAL MONKIN-
FOOT, blacksmith, & JACOB WERNER, clerk, (for JACOB'S debt) gave bond to
MARTHA LLOYD on 28 Feb. 1763 in penal sum of Ł 2000 for payment of Ł 1000
currency, with interest, on 28 Feb. 1764; now JACOB conveys his town lot
to MARTHA as security. Witnesses: THOMAS LAMBOLL, JACOB WIRTH. WIRTH
testified 12 Mar. 1763 before GEORGE JOHNSTON, J.P. Recorded 16 Mar.
1763 by WILLIAM HOPTON, Register. Mortgage satisfied 10 Apr. 1767.

Witness: PETER MANN.

Book Z-Z, p. 472   JANE MASSEY, widow, testified before GEORGE
12 Mar. 1763   SAXBY, J.P. that a certain L & R dated 17 & 18
Deposition   Feb. 1762 between herself & JANE MASSEY, re-
ferring to part of lot #164 in King Street,
Charleston, was made with the design that it should not take place until
after her death, she at that time having been considered in dying condition; that she never received payment; that the L & R were kept in her
own possession; but that JANE MASSEY the younger took the papers without
her consent to the Register's office & had them recorded but never delivered same to her, nor designed to do so; & further declares the land
should have come to her only if she had died of that illness. Recorded
16 Mar. 1763 by WILLIAM HOPTON, Register.

Book Z-Z, p. 473   WILLIAM COCHRAN, & MARGARET (her mark) his
6 Aug. 1739   wife, to SAMUEL MCQUOID, merchant, both of
L & R   James Island, Berkeley Co., for Ł 50 currency,
100 a. in Craven Co., in Williamsburgh Town-
ship, bounding E on WILLIAM CHAMBERS; N on JOHN FLEMING; W on vacant
land; S on JANE (JEAN) ROSS; which land was granted 12 Dec. 1735 by Lt.
Gov. THOMAS BROUGHTON to WILLIAM & MARGARET COCHRAN. Witnesses: HENRY
SHERIFF, ARCHIBALD SCOTT, MARGARET SHERIFF. MARGARET SHERIFF testified
8 Mar. 1753 before WILLIAM PINCKNEY, J.P. Recorded 17 Mar. 1763 by WIL-
LIAM HOPTON, Register.

Book Z-Z, p. 481   SAMUEL MCQUOID, of Wadmalaw Island, & ABIGAIL
2 Aug. 1743   (her mark) his wife, to JAMES MCCLELLAND,
L & R   planter, of Williamsburgh Township, Craven Co.,
for Ł 60 currency, 100 a. in said Township,
bounding E on WILLIAM CHAMBERS; N on JOHN FLEMING; W on vacant land; S on
JANE ROSS. Witnesses: JOHN JOHNSTON, JOHN COWDON. COWDON testified 12
Oct. 1744 before HENRY GIBBES, J.P. Recorded 17 Mar. 1763 by WILLIAM
HOPTON, Register.

Book Z-Z, p. 487   JANE (her mark) ROSS, of Craven Co., to JAMES
21 & 22 May 1744   MCCLELLAND, of Williamsburgh Township, in Cra-
L & R   ven Co., for Ł 20 currency, 50 a. in Williamsburgh Township, bounding E on MR. MCCLELLAND;
N on WILLIAM COCHRAN; W on vacant land; S on WILLIAM MORGAN. Witnesses:
DAVID WITHERSPOON, JOHN LIVISTON. WITHERSPOON testified 20 Oct. 1744 before WILLIAM FLEMING, J.P. Recorded 18 Mar. 1763 by WILLIAM HOPTON, Register.

Book Z-Z, p. 493   JOHN GODFREY, planter, of Prince Frederick
21 July 1761   Parish, Craven Co., being entitled by the will
Gift   of his father, BENJAMIN GODFREY, to a half a.
lot in Charleston, & being uncertain of its
location, & for love & affection, & for the assistance their father has
promised to give in finding out the location; gives to his nephew, JOHN
CHEESBOROUGH, & to his niece, ELIZABETH CHEESBOROUGH (son & daughter of
his sister ELIZABETH CHEESBOROUGH); 1/2 of the half a. lot, situated
among the lots owned by EDWARD FENWICKE which formerly belonged to ROBERT
GIBBES, & not yet divided therefrom; 1/2 the half a. being firm land, the
other half being marsh land. Witness: JOHN CHEESBOROUGH. Before ELIAS
FOISSIN, J.P. Recorded 18 Mar. 1763 by WILLIAM HOPTON, Register.

Book Z-Z, p. 495   ROBERT WEAVER, carpenter, of St. Marks Parish,
11 & 12 Aug. 1761   Craven Co., & ELIZABETH his wife, to ALEXANDER
L & R   DUNN, tavern-keeper, of Georgetown, for Ł 600
currency, lot #30 in Georgetown, bounding SW
50 ft. on Front Street; NW 217.9 ft. on lot #29; NE on lot #63; SE on lot
#31. Whereas a writ of fieri facias was issued 1 Jan. 1744 by BENJAMIN
WHITAKER, C.J., commanding the P.M. to seize the real estate of THOMAS
HENNING, merchant, to satisfy a judgment obtained by JOHN SIMPSON, JR.,
against BENJAMIN SMITH, JOSEPH SHUTE, ROBERT THORPE, & ALEXANDER WOOD,
administrators of THOMAS HENNING'S estate; & SAMUEL HURST, the P.M.,
seized said lot #30, & a back lot #62, also 500 a. near Sampit Creek;
which lands remained unsold for want of bidders; & whereas RAWLINS
LOWNDES, P.M., successor to SAMUEL HURST, on 20 Feb. 1752 sold lot #30 to

BENJAMIN SMITH for Ł 750 currency; who with ANN his wife by L & R dated 17 & 18 Feb. 1756 sold the lot to ROBERT WEAVER; who now sells to DUNN. Witnesses: THOMAS WILSON, JOSEPH DUBOURDIEU. DUBOURDIEU testified 10 Mar. 1763 before JOSEPH BROWN, J.P. Recorded 21 Mar. 1763 by WILLIAM HOPTON, Register.

Book Z-Z, p. 504   DANIEL BLAKE & WILLIAM BLAKE, ESQRS., of
11 & 12 Oct. 1762   Charleston, to DAVID MCKEE, planter, of St.
L & R   Helena Parish, Granville Co., for Ł 1700 cur-
                    rency, 680 a. on Lady's Island in St. Helena
Parish, being part of several tracts supposed to be 1860 a. but on resurvey found to be 2744 a.; which 680 a. appears to the N of the division
pricked line running through the plat or resurvey, marked A, to RICHARD'S
Landing, marked B; & bounding S on lands sold by DANIEL & WILLIAM BLAKE
to JOSIAH TATNELL; N & E on MR. PALMER; W on DANIEL & WILLIAM BLAKE; the
2744 a. having been originally granted to Lady BLAKE, & inherited by her
son the Hon. JOSEPH BLAKE; who devised to his sons DANIEL & WILLIAM,
parties hereto; the 680 a. being sold free from claim of dower by ELIZA-
BETH, wife of DANIEL BLAKE; & of ANNE, wife of WILLIAM BLAKE. Witnesses:
MILES BREWTON, THOMAS WARING. BREWTON testified 17 Mar. 1763 before DOU-
GAL CAMPBELL, J.P. Recorded 22 Mar. 1763 by WILLIAM HOPTON, Register.
Plat showing 1132 a. sold to JOSIAH TATNALL; 680 a. sold to MEKEE;
ELLIS'S Neck tract; boundaries of ELIZABETH BULL, MR. PALMER, COL. MUL-
RYNE, & estate of THOMAS IZARD; also an island of 13 a. & Turkey Buzzards
Island of 26 a.; MULRYNES landing & WILLIAM RICHARD'S landing.

Book Z-Z, p. 515   PETER MOUZON, planter, of St. James Santee
23 & 24 Oct. 1762   Parish, Craven Co., & JUDITH his wife, to LEW-
L & R   IS MOUZON, planter, of Parish of St. Thomas &
                    St. Dennis, Berkeley Co., for Ł 50 currency,
his undivided half part of the 500 a. on which LEWIS MOUZON, the father,
lived, in Berkeley Co.; whereas LEWIS MOUZON, JR., father of PETER & LEW-
IS, bequeathed equally to his 4 sons, JAMES, PETER, SAMUEL & HENRY, the
500 a. on which he lived; JAMES, the eldest, to have his choice, except
that the part on which were the house & buildings was to be HENRY'S;
should any of the 4 die before reaching his majority, then son LEWIS to
have that son's share; should his wife have a posthumous son he to have
his equal share of the 500 a.; now PETER sells his share to LEWIS. Witnesses: HENRY BOCHET, SAMUEL MOUZON, SUSANNAH LAURENS. BOCHET testified
14 Feb. 1763 before BENJAMIN SIMONDS, J.P. Recorded 24 Mar. 1763 by
WILLIAM HOPTON, Register.

Book Z-Z, p. 521   SAMUEL MOUZON, planter, of St. James Santee
23 & 24 Oct. 1762   Parish, Craven Co., to LEWIS MOUZON, planter,
L & R   of St. Thomas & St. Dennis, Berkeley Co., for
                    Ł 50 currency, his undivided share of 500 a.
(see p. 515). Witnesses: PETER MOUZON, HENRY BOCHET, SUSANNAH LAURENS.
BOCHET testified 14 Feb. 1763 before BENJAMIN SIMONS, J.P. Recorded 26
Mar. 1763 by WILLIAM HOPTON, Register.

Book Z-Z, p. 527   JOHN GILDER, planter, to ANTHONY EARNEST,
16 & 17 Mar. 1763   cooper, both of Berkeley Co., for Ł 150 cur-
L & R   rency, 400 a. in Craven Co., granted 7 June
                    1751 by Gov. JAMES GLEN to GILBERT GILDER; who
died intestate & inherited by his ·eldest son, JOHN; bounding SW on Broad
River; other sides on vacant land. Witnesses: JOHN PEARSON, JR., JOHN
TAMPLET. TAMPLET testified before JOHN PEARSON, J.P. Recorded 28 Mar.
1763 by WILLIAM HOPTON, Register.

Book Z-Z, p. 533   SAMUEL THOMPSON, planter, of Granville Co.,
30 Sept. & 1 Oct. 1762   NC, to JOHN PERSON, of Southampton Co., Colony
L & R   of Virginia for Ł 120 Virginia money, 250 a.
                         on N side Santee River, bounding NW on PHILIP
RAIFORD, SR. & vacant land; SE on WILLIAM RAIFORD; other sides on vacant
land formerly occupied by SAMUEL THOMPSON. Whereas on 17 Sept. 1742 Lt.
Gov. WILLIAM BULL of SC, granted PHILIP RAIFORD, SR. 450 a. on N side
Santee River, bounding NW on other land of PHILIP RAIFORD & on vacant
land; other sides on vacant land; which 450 a. he gave to his eldest son,
PHILIP, upon condition that he convey 200 a. of the tract to his brother
WILLIAM, which he did by L & R dated 24 & 25 Dec. 1751; & whereas PHILIP

RAIFORD, JR., & JUDITH his wife, sold the remaining 250 a. for Ł 250 SC
money, by L & R dated 20 & 21 Sept. 1754 to JOHN MYRICK, planter; &
whereas JOHN MURICK, by L & R dated 20 & 21 July 1757, for Ł 250 SC money, sold the 250 a. to SAMUEL THOMPSON, lately of Virginia; now THOMPSON
sells to PERSON. Witnesses: HOWELL EDMUNDS, ANN (her mark) PERSON, WIL-
LIAM PERSON. EDMUNDS testified 24 Feb. 1763 before JOSEPH CURRY, J.P.
Recorded 29 Mar. 1763 by WILLIAM HOPTON, Register.

Book Z-Z, p. 542   JOHN MOULTRIE, physician, of Charleston, &
1 Jan. 1763   ELIZABETH his wife (lately wife of JAMES MATH-
Lease   EWES, merchant), to JAMES MATHEWES (eldest son
         .   & heir of said JAMES MATHEWES) & JOHN MATH-
EWES, the other son; for 99 years, for Ł 1500 currency, part of lot #6 in
Charleston, with various tenements thereon; formerly occupied by MCKENZIE
& ROCHE, now by ALEXANDER CHISOLME; bounding E 30 ft. on the Bay; N on
JOHN ALLEN, S on ANTHONY MATHEWES. Whereas JAMES MATHEWES, SR. devised
said premises to ELIZABETH during her life; & whereas JOHN MOULTRIE &
ELIZABETH have agreed that ELIZABETH shall relinquish her claim for said
amount; now settlement is made. Witnesses: JAMES MOULTRIE, WILLIAM
MOULTRIE. WILLIAM testified 17 Mar. 1763 before WILLIAM DRAYTON, J.P.
Recorded 29 Mar. 1763 by WILLIAM HOPTON, Register.

Book Z-Z, p. 545   JAMES MATHEWES, planter, of John's Island, &
5 Feb. 1763   CHARLOTTE his wife, to JOHN MATHEWES, gentle-
Mortgage   man, of Charleston, as security on bond of
                          even date in penal sum of Ł 4000 for payment
of Ł 2000 currency; the N half of 568 a., bounding S on JAMES MATHEWES;
N on THOMAS HEXT; W on Bohicket River & MR. GOFF: E & SE on GEORGE HEXT &
WILLIAM WEATHERLY. Whereas JAMES MATHEWES, the father, merchant, of
Charleston, owned 1150 a. on John's Island, in Colleton Co., & by will
dated 30 June 1745 half the land to his son JOHN; he being allotted the N
half by the executors on Jan. 21, 1758; & whereas in 1763 JOHN sold his
half to JAMES; now JAMES mortgages that part to JOHN. Witnesses: WILLIAM
MOULTRIE, JAMES MOULTRIE. WILLIAM testified 26 Mar. 1763 before JAMES
PARSONS, J.P. On 26 Mar. 1763 JOHN MATHEWES assigns his interest over to
WILLIAM MOULTRIE. Witness: BENJAMIN MAZYCK. Recorded 30 Mar. 1763 by
WILLIAM HOPTON. On 25 Feb. 1764 WILLIAM MOULTRIE declared mortgage sat-
isfied. Witness: WILLIAM HOPTON, Register.

Book Z-Z, p. 554   JAMES MATHEWES, planter, of John's Island,
5 Feb. 1763   Colleton Co., (eldest son & heir of JAMES
Release   MATHEWES, merchant), & CHARLOTTE his wife, to
                          JOHN MATHEWES, gentleman, of Charleston,
(another son of JOHN); for Ł 3500 currency, his undivided half part of
lot #6 in Charleston, with the tenements & other buildings thereon; occupied by ALEXANDER CHISOLME; bounding E 30 ft. on the Bay; N on tenement
occupied by ROBERT WELLS (formerly JOHN ALLEN); S on ANTHONY MATHEWES;
with the passage to said lot from Tradd Street fronting 6 ft. on Tradd
Street, 21 ft. deep, which JAMES MATHEWES purchased from ALEXANDER HEXT.
Whereas JAMES MATHEWES, the father, owned a certain lot fronting 30 ft.
on the Bay in Charleston, with several buildings erected thereon, & by
will dated 30 June 1745 gave the property to his wife ELIZABETH (now
ELIZABETH MOULTRIE) during her lifetime, & afterwards to his 2 sons,
JAMES & JOHN; & whereas ELIZABETH & her husband JOHN MOULTRIE assigned
their interest in the lot to JAMES & JOHN; now JAMES sells his share to
JOHN. Witnesses: JAMES MOULTRIE, WILLIAM MOULTRIE. Proved by WILLIAM
MOULTRIE before JAMES PARSONS, J.P. Recorded 31 Mar. 1763 by WILLIAM
HOPTON, Register.

Book Z-Z, p. 560   JOHN MATHEWES, gentleman, to WILLIAM MOULTRIE,
2 Mar. 1763   ESQ., both of Charleston, for Ł 12,000 curren-
                          cy, 2 lots in Charleston; 1 being part of lot
#6 in Charleston, with the house thereon formerly occupied by ALEXANDER
CHISOLME (see p. 554); bounding E 30 ft. on the Bay; N on ROBERT WELLS
(formerly JOHN ALLEN); S on ANTHONY MATTHEWES (now in possession of HOOP-
ER & SWALLOW); with the 6 x 21 ft. alley purchased by JAMES MATTHEWES
from ALEXANDER HEXT; the other a lot on Tradd Street devised to JOHN by
his father; with the house thereon occupied by DR. JOHN CLELAND; bounding
S 22 ft. on Tradd Street; W 75 ft. on ALEXANDER TAYLOR; E on WILLIAM
MATHEWES. Witnesses: PETER MAZYCK, JAMES MOULTRIE. Proved by MAZYCK

before JAMES PARSONS, J.P. Recorded 1 Apr. 1763 by WILLIAM HOPTON, Register.

Book Z-Z, p. 568   THOMAS LYNCH, ESQ., (eldest son & heir of COL.
1 Apr. 1762   THOMAS LYNCH) & HANNAH his wife, to WILLIAM
Release   MOULTRIE, ESQ., both of Charleston, for Ł 4000
SC money, 1140 a. in Prince George Parish,
Craven Co., 300 a. being on an island in Santee River, bounding S on 6
mile creek; SW on Broad Creek; E on Dark Creek & THOMAS LYNCH; W on ROBERT HUME; N on Santee River; & 840 a. bounding W on ROBERT HUME; E on
FRANCIS KINLOCH; N on ALLARD BELLINE; S on Santee River; according to
plats. Witnesses: ANN WATSON, JONATHAN BADGER. Proved by ANN WATSON 11
Feb. 1763 before WILLIAM DRAYTON, J.P. Recorded 2 Apr. 1763 by WILLIAM
HOPTON, Register.

Book Z-Z, p. 574   THOMAS SHUBRICK, merchant, to RAWLINS LOWNDES,
30 Oct. 1762   ESQ., both of Chare-ston, for Ł 7000 currency,
Release   lot #2, bounding N 136 ft. on Tradd Street; E
on lot #3 recently sold by THOMAS SHUBRICK to
JAMES POSTELL, ESQ., of Colleton Co., (lots 1, 2, & 3, being according to
plat of resurvey); S on a branch of Councillaires Creek; said lot being
494-1/2 ft. deep, including 100 ft. of land, beach, or shole land according to course of said branch; also the capital mansion house built thereon; as for many years past owned by THOMAS SHUBRICK. Whereas THOMAS SHUBRICK has owned for many years 4 lots in St. Michaels Parish, Charleston,
at the W end & S side of Tradd Street marked 245, 246, 95 & 96, on original plat; also a piece of land formerly marsh land but for some time past
converted by the tides to a sand beach or shole, containing 6 a., 1 rood,
12 perches, lying S & W of said lots; which lots & shole land formerly
belonged to BENJAMIN DE LA CONSEILLERE, merchant; which property SHUBRICK
had resurveyed & divided into lots marked 1, 2, 3, 4, 5, & 6, on the plat
of the resurvey; & put up at auction 13 Sept. last; LOWNDES being highest
bidder for lot #2; now SHUBRICK conveys to LOWNDES. Witnesses: CHARLES
PINCKNEY, CHARLES MOTTE, JOHN MATHEWES; (MOTTE & MATHEWES being clerks to
PINCKNEY). Proved by PINCKNEY 28 Mar. 1763 before JACOB MOTTE, J.P. Recorded 4 Apr. 1763 by WILLIAM HOPTON, Register.

Book Z-Z, p. 582   ISAAC GODIN, planter, to JOHN GUERARD, merchant, both of Charelston, as security on bond
24 & 25 Apr. 1754   chant, both of Charelston, as security on bond
L & R by Mortgage   of even date in penal sum of Ł 8428 for payment of Ł 4214:7:4 currency, with interest, on
25 Apr. 1755; several tracts, total 1500 a. on Wannells Creek, of Cumbahe
River; according to plats attached to grants; bequeathed to ISAAC by his
father, BENJAMIN GODIN, ESQ. Witnesses: JOHN RATTRAY, GEORGE JACKSON.
On 3 May 1762 JAMES GRINDLAY, gentleman, of Charleston, recognized RATTRAY'S signature, also that of GEORGE JACKSON, clerk to RATTRAY, before
ROBERT WILLIAMS, JR., J.P. Recorded 6 Apr. 1763 by WILLIAM HOPTON, Register.

Book Z-Z, p. 594   WILLIAM WILKINS, gentleman & REBEKAH his wife,
16 & 17 Dec. 1762   to JOHN PAUL GRIMKE, gentleman, both of
L & R   Charleston, for Ł 2105 currency, part of a lot
or lots, bounding S 30 ft. on Tradd Street; W
200 ft. on CHARLES WARHAM; N on DANIEL BOURGETT; E on JAMES GRINDLAY; as
by plat drawn 16 Dec. 1762 by WILLIAM WILKINS, Sur., & as enclosed for 20
years past. Witnesses: TIMOTHY PHILLIPS, WILLIAM WILKINS, JR. Proved by
PHILLIPS 5 Apr. 1763 before WILLIAM BURROWS, J.P. Recorded 6 Apr. 1763
by WILLIAM HOPTON, Register. Plat given.

Book Z-Z, p. 601   JOHN SHUTE, merchant, son of JOSEPH SHUTE, to
8 & 9 Apr. 1763   GEORGE MURRAY, gentleman, both of Charleston,
L & R   for Ł 600 currency, his undivided half part of
a tract of 224 a. of marsh land opposite the E
part of Charleston, in Berkeley Co., bounding E & S on Ashley River; W on
Cooper River; N on Hog Island Creek; which undivided half part was by L &
R dated 19 & 20 May 1752 conveyed to SHUTE by WILLIAM WRAGG, ESQ., of
Charleston. Witnesses: JAMES DONOVAN, MATHIAS PETERS. Proved by DONOVAN
9 Apr. 1763 before T. MURRAY, J.P. Recorded 12 Apr. 1763 by WILLIAM HOPTON, Register.

Book Z-Z, p. 609   GEORGE LEA, carpenter, & ELIZABETH his wife,
2 & 3 July 1744   to DAVID BROWN, shipwright, both of Charles-
L & R   ton, for Ł 325 SC money, part of a lot in
                     Charleston called The Point, bounding W 66 ft.
8 in. on other part belonging to GEORGE LEA, N on the part belonging to
CAPT. HOMER; E on Cooper River; S on DAVID BROWN; & extending from W to E
from back part of GEORGE LEA'S kitchen quite down to low water mark.
Witnesses: JOHN HEYWARD, JOHN REMINGTON. Proved by REMINGTON 7 Apr. 1763
before JAMES GRINDLAY, J.P. Recorded 12 Apr. 1763 by WILLIAM HOPTON,
Register.

Book Z-Z, p. 615   GEORGE LEA, carpenter, to DAVID BROWN, ship-
6 Oct. 1746   wright, both of Charleston, for Ł 400 curren-
Feoffment   cy, part of a lot in Charleston, called The
                     Point, bounding W 66 ft. 8 in. on New Street;
S on DAVID BROWN; E on other part sold by LEA to BROWN; N on part belonging to CAPT. HOMER. Witnesses: HENRY CHRISTIE, JOHN REMINGTON, ROBERT
RAPER. Proved by REMINGTON 7 Apr. 1763 before JAMES GRINDLEY, J.P. Recorded 12 Apr. 1763 by WILLIAM HOPTON, Register.

Book Z-Z, p. 618   DAVID BROWN, shipwright, to DR. ALEXANDER GAR-
29 & 30 Apr. 1762   DEN, physician, both of Charelston, for Ł 4210
L & R   currency, part of Colleton Square known as
                     #80, occupied by DAVID BROWN, & marked D on
the plat of the square; bounding S on plat C belonging to heirs of
CHARLES PINCKNEY; W 50 ft. on a street running from the bridge at N end
of the Bay through lots D & C; N on lot #51 in plan of Charleston, formerly belonging to GEORGE LEA, now to DAVID BROWN; E on Cooper River, running quite down to low water mark; also the piece of land called The
Point, being the S part of lot #51 formerly belonging to GEORGE LEA, now
to DAVID BROWN; bounding W 66 ft. 8 in. on said street; N on part of lot
#51 belonging to RICHARD MONCRIEF (formerly CAPT. HOMER); S on plat C;
down to low water mark; the lots being free from all claim except a mortgage on plat D, given JAMES WRIGHT on 1 Sept. 1752 which is paid out of
the purchase money assigned over to ALEXANDER GARDEN. Witnesses: ANDREW
JOHNSTON, JAMES GRINDLAY. Proved by GRINDLAY 7 Apr. 1763 before ROBERT
WILLIAMS, JR., J.P. Recorded 13 Apr. 1763 by WILLIAM HOPTON, Register.

Book Z-Z, p. 628   BROWN gives DR. GARDEN a bond that he will
30 Apr. 1762   perform above covenant (p. 618). Witnesses:
Bond   ANDREW JOHNSTON, JAMES GRINDLAY. Proved by
                     GRINDLAY before ROBERT WILLIAMS, JR., J.P.
Recorded 13 Apr. 1763 by WILLIAM HOPTON, Register.

Book Z-Z, p. 629   DR. ALEXANDER GARDEN, physician of Charleston,
29 & 30 Mar. 1763   & ELIZABETH his wife, to JOHN ROSE, ship-
L & R   wright, of Berkeley Co., for Ł 4210 currency,
                     part of Colleton Square, marked D on plat;
also part of a lot called The Point (see p. 618). Witnesses: DAVID RHIND,
WILLIAM CHAMPNEYS. Proved by RHIND on 9 Apr. 1763 before JAMES GRINDLAY,
J.P. Recorded 14 Apr. 1763 by WILLIAM HOPTON, Register.

Book Z-Z, p. 639   WILLIAM BOONE, planter, of Craven Co., to the
24 Mar. 1763   Hon. BENJAMIN SMITH, of Charleston, in trust
Mortgage   for estate of JOHN IZARD; as security on bond
                     of even date in penal sum of Ł 10,000 for pay-
ment of Ł 5000 currency, with interest, on 1 Mar. 1764; 550 a. in 3
tracts at head of Georgetown River in Craven Co.; that is, 250 a. granted
to JOHN RUSS & then bounding E on GEORGE SUMMERS; other sides on vacant
land; 150 a. granted to ROBERT STEWART, & then bounding N on vacant land;
S on JOHN RUSS & JOHN STEWART; W on JOHN SUMMERS & vacant land; 150 a.
granted ROBERT STEWART, & then bounding N on JOHN RUSS; W on vacant land;
S & E on CHARLES CODNER; according to plats attached to said grants;
which 3 tracts were conveyed by L & R dated 26 & 27 Aug. 1761, by EBENE-
ZER DUNNAM, planter, of Craven Co., & FRANCES his wife, to WILLIAM BOONE.
As further security BOONE delivers 26 Negro slaves. Witnesses: SARAH
NIGHTINGALE, THOMAS FULLALOVE. Proved by FULLALOVE 30 Mar. 1763 before
GEORGE JOHNSTON, J.P. Recorded in Secretary's Book, Z.Z., p. 343-348 on
30 Mar. 1763 by THOMAS SKOTTOWEE, Secretary. Recorded 18 Apr. 1763 by
WILLIAM HOPTON, Register. Mortgage satisfied 20 Jan. 1778. Signed: JOHN

DAWSON, attorney for ALEXANDER WRIGHT. Witness: GEORGE SHEED.

Book Z-Z, p. 648　　　　　　　MRS. REBECCA ROCHE, to FRANCIS ROCHE. FRANCIS
25 Aug. 1761　　　　　　　　ROCHE, planter, of St. Thomas Parish, Berkeley
Renunciation of Dower　　　Co., cousin & heir of JORDAN ROCHE, gentleman,
　　　　　　　　　　　　　　of Charleston, who died in his minority, & who
was only son & heir of JORDAN ROCHE, ESQ., of Charleston; uncle to said
FRANCIS ROCHE; of 1 part; to REBECCA ROCHE, widow of JORDAN ROCHE, ESQ.,
& mother of JORDAN ROCHE, the minor, of other part. Whereas JORDAN ROCHE,
the father, owned various lots & buildings in Charleston, also plantations, etc., which descended to his son, JORDAN, who died a minor, & his
heir, FRANCIS ROCHE, inherited; & whereas REBECCA ROCHE was entitled to
dower in her husband's real estate & has agreed to accept certain pieces
of property in lieu of dower; now FRANCIS ROCHE conveys to REBECCA for
her lifetime, part of lot #57, with the brick house thereon, occupied by
JACOB MOTTE, public treasurer, bounding E on Church Street; S on the Baptist Meeting; W on part same lot occupied by WILLIAM HARVEY; N on part
owned by REBECCA ROCHE (formerly COL. BREWTONO; also the S part of lot
#63, for several years past occupied by DR. DAVID OLLIPHANT, now by MRS.
SARAH LINING; bounding N 239 ft. on the part occupied by JOHN WARD, tai-
lor; S on BENJAMIN GODIN; W on the tan yard formerly belonging to MRS.
ELEANOR WRIGHT; E 25 ft. on Church Street. Witnesses: CHARLES PINCKNEY,
JOHN MATHEWES, CHARLES MOTTE. Proved by MATHEWES 2 Apr. 1763 before
JAMES CARSON, J.P. Recorded 18 Apr. 1763 by WILLIAM HOPTON, Register.

Book Z-Z, p. 654　　　　　　THOMAS SHUBRICK, merchant, of Charleston, to
29 & 30 Oct. 1762　　　　　GEORGE AUSTIN, EDWARD FENWICK, & EDMUND BEL-
L & R　　　　　　　　　　　LINGER, ESQRS., surviving executors of CUL-
　　　　　　　　　　　　　　CHETH GOLIGHTLY, ESQ., Colleton Co., (COL.
CHARLES PINCKNEY, executor, having died) in trust for estate of CULCHETH
GOLIGHTLY, for Ł 3200 currency, the 2 adjoining lots marked 5 & 6 on the
plat of resurvey; bounding N on Tradd Street; E on lot marked #4 lately
sold to CHARLES PINCKNEY; W on Counellaire (Conseillere) Creek; S on a
branch of said creek; said lots containing high land, marsh land, & sand
beach as shown on plat or resurvey. Whereas THOMAS SHUBRICK for many
years past has owned 4 lots in St. Michaels Parish, at the W end & S side
of Tradd Street, marked 245, 246, 95 & 96, on the original plan of
Charleston; also a certain piece of marsh land (now made a sand beach or
shole by the action of the tide) containing 6 a., 1 rood, 12 perches, adjoining said lots & lying S & W of them; all of which lots formerly belonged to BENJAMIN DE LA CONSEILLERS; & wishing to sell the lots SHUBRICK
had them resurveyed & divided into lots marked 1, 2, 3, 4, 5, & 6 on the
plat of resurvey, & put them up at public auction, HENRY HYRNE being
highest bidder for lots 5 & 6 at Ł 1600 currency, (HYRNE acting only as
agent for executors of CULCHETH GOLIGHTLY). Witnesses: JOHN SNELLING,
GEORGE APPLEBY. Proved by APPLEBY 7 Apr. 1763 before JACOB MOTTE, J.P.
Recorded 19 Apr. 1763 by WILLIAM HOPTON, Register.

Book Z-Z, p. 666　　　　　　ISAAC CODIN, gentleman, of Goose Creek, to
28 & 29 Mar. 1763　　　　　WILLIAM SAVAGE, merchant, of Charleston, for
L & R　　　　　　　　　　　Ł 2100 currency, 1 undivided third part of lot
　　　　　　　　　　　　　　#306 in Charleston, containing half an a.,
English measure, commonly called the Sugar House, bounding N on Broad
Street; W & S on marsh; E on JAMES GRAEME; with 1 undivided third part of
the buildings, materials, furnaces, & utensils, etc., for refining sugar.
Witnesses: ROBERT WILLIAMS, JR., FRANCIS GUERIN. Proved by WILLIAMS 13
Apr. 1763 before JAMES GRINDLAY, J.P. Recorded 20 Apr. 1763 by WILLIAM
HOPTON, Register.

Book Z-Z, p. 674　　　　　　JACOB BUCKHOLTS, SR., planter, to the Rev. MR.
25 & 26 May 1758　　　　　ROBERT WILLIAMS, both of Craven Co., for Ł 230
L & R　　　　　　　　　　　currency, 250 a. in the Welch tract in Craven
　　　　　　　　　　　　　　Co., on Pigeon Creek, on SW side Peedee River;
bounding on all sides on vacant land; which tract was granted to BUCK-
HOLTS 22 Mar. 1745 by Gov. JAMES GLEN. Witnesses: BENJAMIN DUE, THOMAS
(his mark) CRAWFORD. Proved by DUE 5 Feb. 1759 before WILLIAM LORD, J.P.
Recorded 20 Apr. 1763 by WILLIAM HOPTON, Register.

Book Z-Z, p. 680　　　　　　WILLIAM JAMES, ESQ., to the Rev. MR. ROBERT
22 & 23 Nov. 1758　　　　　WILSON, both of Craven Co., for Ł 250 currency,

L & R   250 a. in the Welch tract, on NE side Peedee
River, granted JAMES 12 June 1751 by Gov.
JAMES GLEN; bounding SE on OWEN DAVID; other sides on vacant land (as by
plat of grant). Witnesses: PHILIP DOUGLASS, SAMUEL CARPENTER. Proved by
DOUGLAS 2 Jan. 1759 before WILLIAM LORD, J.P. Recorded 21 Apr. 1763 by
WILLIAM HOPTON, Register.

Book Z-Z, p. 687   TIMOTHY KELLY, planter, of Craven Co., to
3 & 4 Jan. 1757   ABRAHAM ODAM, SR., for Ł 100 currency, 200 a.
L & R   in Craven Co., on Friends Neck, on S side Wateree River; bounding NW on SAMUEL RUSSELL;
other sides on vacant land; as granted KELLY on 6 Oct. 1752 by Gov. JAMES
GLEN. Witnesses: SAMUEL KELLY, JOHN (his mark) ROOK, JOHN KELLY. Proved
by ROOK 11 Jan. 1757 before JOHN HAMILTON, J.P. Recorded 22 Apr. 1763 by
WILLIAM HOPTON, Register.

Book Z-Z, p. 695   RICHARD LAMBTON, asignee of estate of ROBERT
22 & 23 Apr. 1763   AUSTIN; to GEORGE SMITH, planter, of Parish of
L & R   St. Thomas & St. Dennis, Berkeley Co., for
Ł 350 currency, 200 a. in said Parish, bound-
ing W on GEORGE SMITH, JR., or other part same tract belonging to JOHN
MIMACK; E on NATHAN TART; S on ALEXANDER VANDERDUSSEN; N on JOHN SINGLE-
TARY & ROBERT DANIEL; which tract ROBERT AUSTIN conveyed to LAMBTON in
trust for himself & others of AUSTIN'S creditors. Witnesses: JOSIAH
SMITH, JR., MARK ANTHONY BEASELLEU. Proved by SMITH 23 Apr. 1763 before
WILLIAM BURROWS, J.P. Entered in Auditor's Book C #7, p. 61 on 23 Apr.
1763 by RICHARD LAMBTON, Dep. Aud. Recorded 28 Apr. 1763 by WILLIAM HOP-
TON, Register.

Book Z-Z, p. 701   Whereas WILLIAM WILKINS did not pay ELIZABETH
3 Dec. 1762   GIBBES the amount due on a certain mortgage on
Satisfaction of   the due date & the mortgage was therefore for-
Mortgage   feited; & whereas ELIZABETH GIBBES in her will
declared her son, WILLIAM RAVEN, to be the ab-
solute residuary devisee & legatee of her real & personal estate, including said mortgage, & executor, of her will; & whereas WILKINS has this
day paid RAVEN in full; now RAVEN declares mortgage satisfied. Witnesses: JOHN RUTLEDGE, HUGH RUTLEDGE. Proved by JOHN RUTLEDGE 23 Apr. 1763
before JAMES MOULTRIE, J.P. Recorded 2 May 1763 by WILLIAM HOPTON, Register.

Book Z-Z, p. 703   SARAH MIDDLETON, of St. James Goose Creek,
1 Apr. 1763   widow of the Hon. ARTHUR MIDDLETON; to THOMAS
Release   SMITH, merchant, of Charleston, for Ł 325
British sterling, part of a lot with the
house thereon, in Charleston, bequeathed to SARAH by her husband; bound-
ing S 16-1/2 ft. on Broad Street; N on PETER BONNETHEAU; W 106 ft. on
JAMES CROCKATT, merchant, of London; E on a house occupied by THOMAS
BOODEN & built on part same lot. Witnesses: JAMES HARRISON, BENJAMIN
WARING. Money paid in a set of bills on JOHN NUTT of London. Witness:
HENRY MIDDLETON. Proved by WARING 9 Apr. 1763 before BENJAMIN SMITH,
J.P. Recorded 2 May 1763 by WILLIAM HOPTON, Register.

Book Z-Z, p. 705   RICHARD BERESFORD, ESQ., to EBERHARD EHNEY,
29 & 30 Apr. 1763   butcher, both of Charleston, for Ł 600 curren-
L & R   cy, part of lot #257 in St. Philips Parish,
Charleston, bounding E 28 ft. on King Street;
S 124 ft. on land leased by RICHARD BERESFORD to CLEAVE NATHAN; W on land
leased to QUACCO MCQUIRE, a free Negro; N on _____. Witnesses: MARK
ANTHONY BESSELLEU, FREDERICK KOUFFMAN. Proved by BESSELLEU 30 Apr. 1763
before JAMES MOULTRIE, J.P. Recorded 2 May 1763 by WILLIAM HOPTON, Register.

Book Z-Z, p. 713   BERESFORD gives EHNEY bond to secure his per-
30 Apr. 1763   formance of above covenant (p. 705). Witness-
Bond   es: MARK ANTHONY BESSELEU, FREDERICK KOUFFMAN.
Proved by BESSELLEU before MOULTRIE. Recorded
by HOPTON, Register.

Book Z-Z, p. 715   HUGH (his mark) MURPHEY, planter, & MARY (her

25 & 26 Jan. 1763   mark) his wife, to the Rev. MR. JOHN ROWAN,
                                     both of Craven Co., for Ł 1275 currency, 2 ad-
joining tracts, total 400 a.; 1 of 150 a. near the Congarees in Craven
Co., granted 8 Aug. 1741 by Lt. Gov. WILLIAM BULL to HUGH MURPHEY; then
bounding W on CAPT. THOMAS BROWN & RICHARD JACKSON; other sides on vacant
land; the other of 250 a. granted 12 Dec. 1746 by Gov. JAMES GLEN to HUGH
MURPHEY; then bounding N on HUGH MURPHEY & vacant land; E on vacant land
& RICHARD JACKSON; S on RICHARD JACKSON & vacant land, & on HUGH MURPHEY;
W on RICHARD JACKSON, HUGH MURPHEY, & THOMAS BROWN; as by plat of grant.
MARY MURPHEY, being a sole trader, requests that her covenants be made a
rule in His ,Majesty's courts. Witnesses: SIMON HIRONS, WILLIAM MEYER,
ELIZABETH HAMELTON.   Proved by HIRONS 31 Jan. 1763 before JOHN HAMELTON,
J.P.   Entered in Auditor's Book C. #7, p. 59 on 2 May 1763 by RICHARD
LAMBTON, Dep. Aud.   Recorded 3 May 1763 by WILLIAM HOPTON, Register.

Book Z-Z, p. 723   ANNE MARIE BOURQUIN, widow, of _____ VILLARD,
17 Feb. 1744   appeared before JEAN LINDER, J.P., of Gran-
Gift   ville Co., & declared she intended to remarry
                            & wished to give her son, DAVID VILLARD, her
plantation with all it contained; further, she gave to her 3 children, in
equal portions, her movable goods; & appointed her brother, DR. JEAN
BAPTISTE BOURQUIN, their guardian. Witnesses: HENRY BOURQUIN, ALEXANDER
LINDER.   Recorded 3 May 1763 by WILLIAM HOPTON, Register.

Book Z-Z, p. 723   THOMAS MITCHELL, planter, & ESTHER his wife,
21 & 22 Apr. 1763   to FRANCIS KINLOCH, ESQ., both of St. George
L & R   Parish, Craven Co., for Ł 1555 currency, 135
                            a. at the mouth of Peedee & Black Rivers,
granted by Gov. WILLIAM HENRY LYTTLETON, on 19 Sept. 1758, to THOMAS
MITCHELL, bounding NW on said rivers; NE on JOHN CHEESBROUGH; SE on
JAMES AKIN; SW on BENJAMIN SMITH; as by plat to grant. Witnesses: THOMAS
GODFREY, JONAH HORRY.   Proved by GODFREY 22 Apr. 1763 before ARCHIBALD
BAIRD, J.P.   Recorded 4 May 1763 by WILLIAM HOPTON, Register.

                            DEEDS BOOK "A-3"
                            MAY 1763 - MARCH 1764

Book A-3, p. 1   HUGH ANDERSON, carpenter, & ANNE his wife, to
23 Apr. 1751   FRANCIS KINLOCH, ESQ., both of Charleston, for
Release   Ł 1050 currency, the E part of a part of lot
                            #66 in Charleston, bounding S 32 ft. 6-3/4 in
on Queen Street; E on the part belonging to FRANCIS KINLOCH; N 31 ft.
9-3/4 in. on St. Philips churchyard & FRANCIS KINLOCH; W 110 ft. on HUGH
ANDERSON.   Whereas MARY MULLINS Owned part of lot #66, & by will dated 21
Nov. 1730 bequeathed half her household goods, plate, rings, cash, real &
personal estate, etc., not otherwise disposed of to 1 SUSANNAH HADDRELL,
& bequeathed to her niece, SARAH HEXT, wife of HUGH HEXT, the other half;
& after MARY'S death, SUSANNAH & SARAH owned the part of said lot in
jointenancy; & whereas HUGH HEXT died & SARAH married ANDREW RUTLEDGE &
the lot was divided between GEORGE HADDRELL & SUSANNAH his wife & ANDREW
RUTLEDGE & SARAH his wife, the E part being allotted to RUTLEDGE, the W
to HADDRELL; & whereas ANDREW & SARAH RUTLEDGE by L & R dated 12 & 13
Nov. 1733 sold their share to RIBTON HUTCHINSON, merchant, of Charleston,
in trust for said ANDREW RUTLEDGE; & whereas by L & R dated 29 & 30 May
1750 ANDREW RUTLEDGE sold the E part to HUGH ANDERSON; now ANDERSON sells
to KINLOCH.   Witnesses: JAMES MOULTRIE, EDWARD SWAN.   Proved by MOULTRIE
3 May 1763 before ROBERT WILLIAMS, J.P.   Recorded 6 May 1763 by WILLIAM
HOPTON, Register.

Book A-3, p. 7   JOHN CART, carpenter, to FRANCIS KINLOCH,
26 & 26 Apr. 1757   ESQ., both of Charleston, for Ł 650 currency,
L & R   part of a part of 3 lots, #66, #67, & #217 in
                            Charleston, bounding 28 ft. on Queen Street;
purchased by CART from DANIEL LESESNE; bounding S 12 ft. on Queen Street;
N on estate of JOSEPH WRAGG; W on JAMES KINLOCH; E 372 ft. on remaining
part belonging to JOHN CART. Witnesses: ISAAC LESESNE, ROBERT DEANS.
Proved by DEANE 3 May 1763 before ROBERT WILLIAMS, J.P.   Recorded 6 May
1763 by WILLIAM HOPTON, Register.

Book A-3, p. 14   ANTHONY WHITE, planter, of Prince Frederick
16 & 17 Mar. 1762   Parish, Craven Co., & DEBORAH hiw wife, to
L & R   HUGH SWINTON, merchant, of Charleston, for
                         Ł 1600 currency, 500 a. on N branch of Black
River, in Craven Co., granted by Gov. CHARLES CRAVEN on 9 June 1714 to
RICHARD WIGG; bounding on other sides on vacant land; which tract RICHARD
WIGG & SARAH his wife by L & R dated 9 & 10 Nov. 1725 sold to JOHN WHITE;
who by will dated 24 Feb. 1758 ordered his eldest son ANTHONY, to choose
for himself 1 of the tracts belonging to said JOHN WHITE'S estate; now
ANTHONY, having chosen the 500 a., sells to SWINTON. Witnesses: ALEXAN-
DER SWINTON, JOHN WAGENFELD, RICHARD MACON. Proved by WAGENFELD 28 Apr.
1763 before JACOB MOTTE, Register. Recorded 9 May 1763 by WILLIAM HOP-
TON, Register.

Book A-3, p. 21   The Rev. MR. JOHN BAXTER, of Prince Frederick
___ May 1762   Parish, Craven Co., & SARAH his wife, to AN-
L & R   DREW BURNET, for love & affection & 10 shill-
                         ings, 1100 a. in Williamsburg Township, bound-
ing SW on MR. FINLEY; other sides on vacant land; granted by Lt. Gov.
THOMAS BROUGHTON on 12 Aug. 1737 to JOHN BAXTER. Witnesses: THOMAS BAX-
TER, JOHN FRAZER. Proved by BAXTER 2 Apr. 1763 before JOSEPH BRITTON,
J.P. Recorded 9 May 1763 by WILLIAM HOPTON, Register.

Book A-3, p. 26   ALEXANDER TAYLOR, tailor, to HENRY METZGER,
18 & 19 Jan. 1762   baker, both of Charleston, for Ł 1876 curren-
L & R   cy, a lot in Charleston, bounding E 48 ft. on
                         King Street; W on FREDERICK GRIMKE; N 227 ft.
on COL. OTHNIEL BEALE; S on JOHN MICK. Witnesses: JAMES MCLEAN, THOMAS
GRIMBALL, JR. Proved by GRIMBALL 6 May 1763 before WILLIAM BURROWS, J.P.
Recorded 11 May 1763 by WILLIAM HOPTON, Register.

Book A-3, p. 34   JACOB MOTTE, the elder, of Charleston, to GAV-
18 & 19 Nov. 1762   IN POU, planter, of Orangeburgh Township, for
L & R   Ł 500 currency, 500 a. in Colleton Co., bound-
                         ing SW on PonPon River; NW on 20,000 a. laid
out for said township; NE & SE on land reserved for inhabitants of said
township. Witnesses: JAMES LAURENS, JOHN MILLER. Proved by LAURENS 11
May 1763 before WILLIAM HOPTON, Register.

Book A-3, p. 39   NICHOLAS WISE, & MARION WISE, of Orangeburgh
18 May 1762   Township, to their friend JACOB NEBLING, of
Gift   same place, for love & affection, 50 a.,
                         bounding SW on other half of the 100 a. given
them by their friends PETER FAURE & SARAH FAURE on 10 Jan. 1761; NW on
heirs of JOSHUA LOCKWOOD, SR.; other sides on vacant land. Witnesses:
PETER FAURE, JOHN (his mark) VALENTINE, BARBURY (her mark) REEP. Proved
by VALENTINE 15 Mar. 1763 before JOHN CHEVILLETTE, J.P. Recorded 18 May
1763 by WILLIAM HOPTON, Register.

Book A-3, p. 41   WILLIAM HAYNE, planter, & MARY his wife, to
16 & 17 July 1759   EZEKIEL BRANFORD, planter, both of Colleton
L & R   Co., for Ł 2300 currency, 483 a. in St. Pauls
                         Parish, Colleton Co., at head of Bee's Creek;
bounding W on JOHN BEE; N on CHRISTOPHER PETER & WILLIAM HAYNE; E on
JAMES BULLOCK; S on SARAH CHAMPNEYS. Witnesses: SARAH CHAMPNEYS, THOMAS
SACHEVERELL, EDWARD SPLATT. Proved by SACHEVERELL 26 May 1763 before
JAMES PARSONS, J.P. Recorded 27 May 1763 by WILLIAM HOPTON, Register.
Plat certified 12 July 1759 by NATHANIEL DEAN, Dep. Sur., of 483 a. in
3 tracts, including surplus, bounding E on MR. SACHEVERELL, ABRAHAM
HAYNE, & EBENEZER WALCOAT, now WILLIAM HAYNE; N on HAYNE; W on estate of
COL. JOHN BEE; NW on BEE, HEXT & PETERS.

Book A-3, p. 48   Lt. Gov. WILLIAM BULL, to his grandson, WIL-
14 & 15 Mar. 1754   LIAM DRAYTON, son of THOMAS DRAYTON, for love
L & R·   & affection, part of a lot in Charleston, 40
                         ft. wide, bounding W on a 10 ft. lane. Wit-
nesses: GEORGE ACKERMAN, JACOB BOOMER. Proved by ACKERMAN 15 May 1754
before WILLIAM BULL, JR., J.P. Recorded 30 May 1763 by WILLIAM HOPTON,
Register.

Book A-3, p. 54   WILLIAM GASCOIGNE, ESQ., of Parish of St.
5 & 6 Mar. 1760   James Westminster, Co. of Middlesex, eldest
L & R   son & heir of JOHN GASCOIGNE, ESQ., of West-
                         ham, Co. of Essex, & 1 time commander of H.M.S.
The Alborough afterwards of The Torbay; of 1 part; to WILLIAM MIDDLETON,
ESQ., of Crowfield Hall, Co. of Suffolk; for Ł 900 British, 1976 a. in
Granville Co., SC, bounding S on River May; E on PETER COLLETON'S Barony;
N on CAPT. CHARLES ODINSELL; W on Landgrave WILLIAM HODGSON; according
to grand plat; which tract was granted GASCOIGNE 12 Jan. 1733. Witnesses: ELISHA BISCOE, JA[MES] GARTH. On 8 Mar. 1760 GASCOIGNE acknowledged
this deed before the Rt. Hon. SIR THOMAS CHITTY, mayor of London. Entered in & Auditor General's office in Bk. F. #6, p. 59, on 25 Feb. 1762 by
RICHARD LAMBTON, Dep. Aud. Recorded 31 May 1763 by WILLIAM HOPTON, Register.

Book A-3, p. 63   BENJAMIN PERDRIAU, of Craven Co., to PAUL
3 & 4 Jan. 1763   TRAPIER, merchant, of George Town, as security
L & R by Mortgage   on bond of even date in penal sum of Ł 3000
                         for payment of Ł 1500 currency, with interest,
on 1 Jan. 1764; 2 tracts; 1 of 200 a. in St. James Santee, Craven Co.,
bounding NW & W on THOMAS EVANS; SW & S on GEORGE SIMMONS; other sides on
vacant land; 1 of 229 a., part of 289 a. in St. James Santee, bounding SE
on THOMAS EVANS; SW on GEORGE SIMMONS; other sides on vacant land. Witnesses: BENJAMIN TRAPIER, ALEXANDER TRAPIER. Proved by BENJAMIN TRAPIER
31 Jan. 1763 before JOSEPH BROWN, J.P. Recorded 9 June 1763 by WILLIAM
HOPTON, Register.

Book A-3, p. 70   CHARLES WRIGHT, ESQ., of Charleston, to
5 & 16 Mar. 1757   MICHAEL GEIGER, planter, of Colleton Co., for
L & R   Ł 4340 currency, 542 a. on Cow Savannah, in
                         Berkeley Co., at head of Ashley River; being
the S part of several tracts of 942 a. owned by WRIGHT for 10 years past;
the N part, or 400 a., having been sold this date to SAMUEL WAINWRIGHT,
gentleman, of Charleston. Witnesses: CHARLES PINCKNEY, WILLIAM MAZYCK,
JOHN MATTHEWES. Proved by MAZYCK 24 Feb. 1761 before WILLIAM BURROWS,
J.P. Recorded 10 June 1763 by WILLIAM HOPTON, Register.

Book A-3, p. 79   PERCIVAL PAWLEY, planter, of Prince George
9 & 10 Aug. 1762   Parish, Craven Co., to JOSEPH ALLSTON, plant-
L & R by Mortgage   er, of same place, as security on bond of even
                         date in penal sum of Ł 1928 for payment of
Ł 964 currency, with interest, on 10 Aug. 1763; 500 a. on E side Peedee
River, bounding S on COL. WILLIAM WATIES; E on PERCIVAL PAWLEY, SR.; N on
THOMAS SMITH; as by plat of grant. Witnesses: BENJAMIN PERDRIAN, JOHN
ALLSTON. Proved by ALLSTON 17 Feb. 1763 before BENJAMIN YOUNG, J.P. Re-
corded 13 June 1763 by WILLIAM HOPTON, Register.

Book A-3, p. 86   THOMAS FERGUSON & MARY ELLIOTT, executor & ex-
15 Feb. 1762   ecutrix of will of ARTIMUS ELLIOTT, (HUGH FER-
Sale   GUSON having refused to act) to VALENTINE
                         KLAWDY, of Charleston Neck, for Ł 700 curren-
cy, 9 a. 6 perches of land in St. Phillips Parish, bounding N & E on
GEORGE AUSTIN; S on a road or avenue leading from the Broad Road into
GEORGE AUSTIN'S plantation; W on the Broad Road; which land ARTMUS
ELLIOTT purchased 25 Apr. 1750 from GEORGE AUSTIN, merchant, & ANN his
wife; & by will dated 22 Apr. 1760 ordered sold by his executors to pay
his debts; appointing THOMAS FERGUSON, MARY ELLIOTT & HUGH FERGUSON his
executors & executrix. Witnesses: SARAH WILLIAMS, JOHN PARKER. Proved
by PARKER 16 Feb. 1762 before JOHN REMINGTON, J.P. Recorded 22 June 1763
by WILLIAM HOPTON, Register. Plat certified 18 Apr. 1750 by GEORGE HUN-
TER, Sur. Gen.

Book A-3, p. 89   VALENTINE KLAWDY (CLOWDEY), vintner, of St.
1 May 1762   Philips Parish, to SUSANNAH his wife, in trust
Gift   for her son (his son-in-law) TOBIAS MIER, the
                         9 a. 6 perches recently purchased from execu-
tors of ARTIMUS ELLIOTT (see p. 86). Should TOBIAS die without issue,
then SUSANNAH to inherit. Witnesses: THOMAS LINTHWAITE, JOSEPH WIRTH.
Proved by WIRTH 22 June 1763 before GEORGE JOHNSTON, J.P. Recorded 22
June 1733 by WILLIAM HOPTON, Register.

Book A-3, p. 91   ROBERT DEAN, carpenter, to THOMAS BUCKLE, mer-
19 & 20 May 1763   chant, both of Charleston, as further security
L & R by Mortgage   on bond in penal sum of Ł 10,000 for payment
                         of Ł 5000 currency, with interest, on 19 May
1764; 2 adjoining lots 119 & 120 in Charleston, each being 1/2 a., English measure, bounding E on Archdale Street; S on Queen Street; W & N on
heirs of ISAAC MAZYCK. Witnesses: JOHN MARLEY, JOHN WAGNER. Proved by
WAGNER 16 June 1763 before JOHN REMINGTON, J.P. Recorded 23 June 1763 by
WILLIAM HOPTON, Register. On 13 July 1765 BUCKLE declared mortgage satisfied. Witness: FENWICKE BULL.

Book A-3, p. 99   ROBERT JOHNSON, ESQ., of Berks Co., Great
11 & 12 Mar. 1763   Britain, eldest son of Gov. ROBERT JOHNSON of
L & R   SC, by his attorney, HECTOR BERENGER DE BEAU-
                         FAIN; to GABRIEL MANIGAULT, merchant, of
Charleston, for Ł 315 sterling British, 5145 a., part of a barony of
12,000 a. granted SIR NATHANIEL JOHNSON, knight, situated at Awendaw
Berkeley Co.; also 779 a. called the Salt Ponds, part of 2 tracts at See-
wee Bay, in Berkeley Co., 1 of 1100 a., the other of 600 a., granted SIR
JOHNSON; also 250 a., part of 500 a., formerly belonging to EDWARD CRISPE,
bounding W on MR. DUPONT & WILLIAM ADAMS; N on ISAAC PORCHER; other sides
on vacant land; also 100 a., half of 200 a., called the Trial, in St.
James Santee Parish, Craven Co., on S side Hell Hole Swamp; also Pew #3
in the middle aisle of St. Philips Church, Charleston; all of which lands
& pew were the estate of THOMAS JOHNSON, ESQ., of Charleston, youngest
brother of said ROBERT JOHNSON, who died without issue, & inherited by
ROBERT. Witnesses: JOHN REMINGTON, ANDREW HUNTER. Proved by REMINGTON
14 May 1763 before ROBERT WILLIAMS, J.P. Recorded 27 June 1763 by WIL-
LIAM HOPTON, Register.

Book A-3, p. 108   GABRIEL MANIGAULT, PETER MANIGAULT, & ALEXAN-
14 Apr. 1757   DER BROUGHTON, executors of will of BENJAMIN
L & R   D'HARRIETTE, of Charleston, to ISAAC GODWIN,
                         planter, of Goose Creek, Berkeley Co., for
Ł 5730 currency, part of lot #17 in Charleston, bounding E 25 ft. on the
Bay; S on STEPHEN MILLER; W 25 ft. on Union Street; N on other part lot
#17; which lot #17 was granted by WILLIAM, Earl of Craven, Palatine, &
the Lords Proprs., to STEPHEN BULL, gentleman; who, on 25 Aug. 1682, sold
the S half to RICHARD CODNER, mariner; whose son, CHARLES CODNER, plant-
er, of Berkeley Co., inherited; who, with ANNE his wife, by L & R dated 5
& 6 Apr. 1734, sold to BENJAMIN D'HARRIETTE; also lot #35 bounding E on
Union Street; W on JOHN CORKER; S on GABRIEL MANIGAULT; N on Dennis's
Alley; formerly bounding E on MRS. CROSS; W on NOAH ROYER, JR.; S on WIL-
LIAM BALLAUGH; N on NOAH ROYER, SR.; which lot #35 was granted by the
Lords Proprs., to JOHN BULL; who on 29 Sept. 1716 sold to WILLIAM GIB-
BONS, ESQ.; who, by L & R dated 11 & 12 Oct. 1723 sold to LAWRENCE DEN-
NIS; who, with PROVIDENCE his wife, on 31 Dec. 1726 sold to BENJAMIN
D'HARRIETTE; who by will dated 14 Jan. 1756 authorized his executors to
sell the lot. Witnesses: JOHN COWDAN, WILLIAM BANBURY, PETER BONNETHEAU.
Proved by BONNETHEAU 3 Oct. 1760 before JOHN REMINGTON, J.P. Recorded 28
June 1763 by WILLIAM HOPTON, Register.

Book A-3, p. 118   The Hon. HENRY MIDDLETON, ESQ., & MARY HEN-
8 & 9 Dec. 1762   RIETTA, his wife, to GABIREL MANIGAULT, ESQ.,
L & R   both of Charleston, for Ł 3993 currency, half
                         of a lot in Charleston, bounding W 50 ft. on
Church Street; N 215 ft. on GABIREL MANIGAULT; E on THOMAS SMITH; S on
other half now belonging to devisees of PAUL JENYS, the younger; which
half lot by L & R dated 6 & 7 Oct. 1760 was sold to HENRY MIDDLETON by
JOHN DREW, yeoman, of Mountecute, Sommerset Co., Great Britain, & MARY
his wife; JOHN BEATON, butcher, of Stoke under Hamboon, same Co., & ELIZ-
ABETH his wife; & WILLIAM SUGG, lincloth maker, of Beamister Co., of Dor-
set, & GRACE his wife; MARY, ELIZABETH & GRACE being co-heiresses of
GEORGE JENYS, ESQ., of Charleston; who was 1 of the sons, & if living,
would be heir-at-law of PAUL JENYS, the elder, merchant, of Charleston;
also devisee named in will of said PAUL JENYS; said PAUL JENYS being eldest son & heir of PAUL JENYS, of Yeovil, Co. of Somerset Mercer; MARY,
ELIZABETH & GRACE being daughters & only children of ROBERT JENYS, yeoman, of Mountecute; who was 1 of the brothers of PAUL JENYS, the other
brothers having died without issue. Witnesses: DAVID GRAEME, WILLIAM

GRAEME. Proved by WILLIAM GRAEME 24 June 1763 before JOHN REMINGTON, J.P. Recorded 30 June 1763 by WILLIAM HOPTON, Register.

Book A-3, p. 127   EDMUND BELLINGER, gentleman, & MARY LUCIA his
9 & 10 Mar. 1748   wife, to ELIAS BALL, gentleman, both of Colle-
L & R   ton Co., for Ł 988 currency, 416 a. in Colle-
                    ton Co., part of 1100 a. laid out to his
father, Landgrave EDMUND BELLINGER as part of his patent; bounding N on
NATHANIEL PAIN; S on MR. GREEN; W on WILLIAM TOWNSEND & SARAH STEVENS; E
on JOHN HILLIARD. Witnesses: GEORGE AUSTIN, BENJAMIN BUTLER, HENRY
HYRNE, L. BELLINGER. Proved 28 June 1763 before ROBERT WILLIAMS, JR.,
J.P. Recorded 1 July 1763 by WILLIAM HOPTON, Register. Plat of survey
dated 2 Mar. 1748/9.

Book A-3, p. 137   LUKE BLAKELY, schoolmaster, to WILLIAM BRAN-
28 & 29 June 1763   FORD, gentleman, both of Charleston, for Ł 420
L & R   currency, 220 a. in Colleton Co., bounding W
                    on Horse Shoe Savannah; S on JOHN WOODWARD;
other sides on vacant land; which tract was granted 28 Apr. 1733 to JO-
SEPH DINGLE; also 200 a. adjoining above tract, bounding N on WILLIAM
EBERSON; SW on JOHN COOK; SE on MR. BOTTISON; other sides on vacant land;
which 200 a. were granted 13 July 1737 to JOHN MCCAW; according to plats
of both tracts. Witnesses: GEORGE SMITH, ROBERT WILLIAMS, JR. Proved by
WILLIAMS 29 June 1763 before JAMES GRINDLAY, J.P. Recorded 4 July 1763
by WILLIAM HOPTON, Register.

Book A-3, p. 147   HENRY LEWIS PAYEN, carpenter, of Savannah, Ga.,
18 Aug. 1762   to JONATHAN BELTON, planter, for Ł 400 curren-
Release   cy, 200 a. on Savannah River in St. Peters
                    Parish, granted 16 Sept. 1738 by Lt. Gov. WIL-
LIAM BULL to ANTHONY PAYER; bounding N on JEREMIAH REMOND; S on CHRISTO-
PHER RINK; W on JOHN GARNER; E on vacant land; as by plat of grant. Wit-
nesses: ANDREW HENDRIC, MICHAEL STUTZ. Proved by HENDRIC 23 June 1763
before ADRIAN MEYER, J.P., of Granville Co. Recorded 5 July 1763 by WIL-
LIAM HOPTON, Register.

Book A-3, p. 150   ALEXANDER SCHWAB, of Jacksonborough, Colleton
31 May 1763   Co., to ISAAC DA COSTA, merchant, as security
Mortgage   on bond of even date in penal sum of Ł 640 for
                    payment of Ł 320 SC money, with interest, on 1
Jan. 1764; a Negro man named Cuffee; also 8 lots in Market Street, Jacksonborough, Nos. 74, 75, 76, 77, 86, 87, 88, & 89; containing 4 a. Witness: DANIEL PRICE. Proved 18 July 1763 before JOHN REMINGTON, J.P. Recorded 19 July 1763 by WILLIAM HOPTON, Register.

Book A-3, p. 153   GEORGE HAIG, ESQ., to HERMAN GEIGER, planter,
1 & 2 Sept. 1743   both of Saxegotha Township, Berkeley Co., for
L & R   Ł 50 currency, 150 a. in Berkeley Co., bound-
                    ing NE on Santee (Congaree) River; NW on HANS
BASS (now HERMAN GEIGER); SW on vacant land; SE on RICHARD MYRICK; which
tract was granted 4 Aug. 1743 by Lt. Gov. WILLIAM BULL to GEORGE HAIG;
according to plat of grant. Witnesses: ANDREW BROWN, DR. WILLIAM JANE-
WAY. Proved by JANEWAY 12 Mar. 1763 before JOSEPH CURRY, J.P. Recorded
28 July 1763 by WILLIAM HOPTON, Register.

Book A-3, p. 160   FRANCIS BOGGS, planter, of Johns Island, to
1 & 2 June 1763   DR. GEORGE SCOTT, of Wadmalaw Island, as se-
L & R by Mortgage   curity of even date (given SCOTT by BOGGS for
                    DAVID HEXT, planter, of Johns Island) in penal
sum of Ł 1600 for payment of Ł 800 currency, with interest, on 1 Feb.
1764; 593 a. in St. Bartholomews Parish, bounding E & S on MR. CRALL; W
on MR. DRAYTON; N on MR. SULLIVANT. Witnesses: HENRY LIVINGSTON, ALBERT
DUYNMIER. Proved by LIVINGSTON 11 June 1763 before WILLIAM MAXWELL, J.P.
Recorded 3 Aug. 1763 by WILLIAM HOPTON, Register.

Book A-3, p. 167   CHARLES LOWNDES, P.M., to PETER SAUNDERS,
27 Apr. 1756   planter, at public auction, for Ł 421 curren-
Release   cy, 250 a. in St. James Parish, Goose Creek,
                    adjoining COL. CHARLES PINCKNEY & JOHN GOODBE.
Whereas WILLIAM WOODROP & PAUL DOUXSAINT obtained a judgment against

JAMES GOODBE, planter, of St. James, Goose Creek, for Ł 4000 currency &
costs, & a writ of fieri facias was issued by PETER LEIGH, C.J., direct-
ing the P.M. to levy this amount against GOODBE'S property; whereby
LOWNDES seized the above tract; now he conveys to SAUNDERS. Witnesses:
JOEL HOLMES, ANDREW CATHCART. Proved by CATHCART 6 Aug. 1763 before JOHN
REMINGTON, J.P. Recorded 18 Aug. 1763 by WILLIAM HOPTON, Register.

Book A-3, p. 172   PETER SANDERS, planter, of St. James, Goose
21 & 22 July 1763   Creek, & ELIZABETH his wife, to JOSEPH DOB-
L & R   BINS, planter, for Ł 1000 currency, 250 a. in
                          St. James Goose Creek (see p. 167) according
to old survey, but by resurvey found to be 413-3/4 a. Witnesses: JOHN
GOLDING, JACOB REMINGTON. Proved by REMINGTON 15 Aug. 1763 before JOHN
REMINGTON, J.P. Recorded 19 Aug. 1763 by WILLIAM HOPTON, Register. Plat
of resurvey by NATHANIEL BRADWELL, Dep. Sur., dated 18 July 1763 showing
boundaries; E on MRS. ELIZABETH SMITH; S on MR. COACHMAN; W on estate of
CHARLES PINCKNEY; N on Fosters Creek.

Book A-3, p. 179   THOMAS BROWN, Indian trader, of Berkeley Co.,
3 Dec. 1745   to GEORGE HAIG, ESQ., in trust for WILLIAM
Lease   BROWN, now under age, 2 tracts of 175 & 186 a.
                          in Craven Co., (see p. 182). Witnesses: AN-
DREW BROWN, JOHN PEARSON. Proved by PEARSON before STEPHEN CRELL, J.P.
Recorded 19 Aug. 1763 by WILLIAM HOPTON, Register.

Book A-3, p. 182   THOMAS BROWN, Indian trader, for love & affec-
4 Dec. 1745   tion, to his natural son, WILLIAM BROWN, now
Gift   15 years old, born of a free Indian woman of
                          the Catawbas Nation "subject & in amity to &
with this government, brought up to the Christian religion," 2 tracts in
Craven Co., 1 of 175 a., near Saxegotha Township, bounding W on Patricks
Creek; S on RICHARD JACKSON; 1 of 186 a. bounding S on above tract; W on
Patrick's Creek; which tracts were originally granted to MATHEW NELSON &
JAMES CRAWFORD; also 1 Negro boy named JACK; 1 Negro girl called NANNY;
10 cows & their calves; now under the care of JOHN COLBORN; the 2 tracts,
Negroes & cows having been conveyed to GEORGE HAIG, by lease for 1 year,
for the use of THOMAS BROWN, & to remain in HAIG'S possession until WIL-
LIAM comes of age. Witnesses: ROBERT BUNING, JOHN MCCORD. Proved by MC-
CORD 3 July 1746 before STEPHEN CRELL, J.P. Entered in Auditor's Book
G #7, p. 122, on 2 Aug. 1763 by RICHARD LAMBTON, Dep. Aud. Recorded 19
Aug. 1763 by WILLIAM HOPTON, Register.

Book A-3, p. 187   MOSES BUTLER, planter, of Granville Co., to
29 & 30 June 1763   BENJAMIN SMITH & MILES BREWTON, merchants, of
L & R by Mortgage   Charleston, as further security on bond dated
                          16 Oct. 1760 long since due; 300 a. in Gran-
ville Co., bounding S on Wimbee Creek; SE on WILLIAM BULL; NE on N branch
of Wimbee Creek; which tract was granted 10 Jul7 1717 to JOHN BUTLER,
father of MOSES. Witnesses: DANIEL BLAKE, WILLIAM MIDDLETON. Proved by
BLAKE 26 Aug. 1763 before PETER MANIGAULT, J.P. Recorded 5 Sept. 1763 by
WILLIAM HOPTON, Register. On 29 May 1769 MILES BREWTON declared mortgage
satisfied. Witness: WILLIAM VALENTINE.

Book A-3, p. 197   ROBERT FLUD, planter, & MARGARET his wife, to
18 & 19 July 1763   JOHN KESSON, gentleman, both of St. James Par-
L & R by Mortgage   ish, Goose Creek, Berkeley Co., as security on
                          bond of even date in penal sum of Ł 8270:12:0
for payment of Ł 4135:6:0 currency, with interest, on 1 Jan. 1764; 180 a.
in St. James Goose Creek, known as the Ten-Mile House, bounding NE on
Landgrave THOMAS SMITH; SE on JOHN PERRYMAN; W on CHARLES GRADY; NW on
heirs of MR. STEAD. Witness: JOHN TROUP. Proved before GEORGE JOHN-
STONE, J.P. Recorded 9 Sept. 1763 by WILLIAM HOPTON, Register.

Book A-3, p. 204   WILLIAM ROPER, gentleman, of Charleston, &
29 & 30 Nov. 1762   GRACE his wife, to BENJAMIN CHAPLIN, planter,
L & R   of Granville Co., for Ł 4000 currency, 500 a.,
                          English measure, on Port Royal Island, in
Granville Co., granted 23 July 1711 to THOMAS GRIMBALL bounding N on
marsh & on Palmeters Creek; NW on JOSEPH PALMETER; other sides of marsh;
also 106 a., English measure, near above tract, on Port Royal Island,

granted 12 Apr. 1739 to ISAAC GRIMBALL, bounding NW & NE on THOMAS GRIM-
BALL; other sides of marsh & creeks; as by plats of grants; as occupied
by JOHN HUTCHINSON, gentleman, deceased, of Granville Co., & since by
WILLIAM ROPER. Witnesses: ROBERT PHILP, ROBERT WILLIAMS, JR. Proved by
WILLIAMS 30 Nov. 1762 before JAMES GRINDLAY, J.P. Recorded 6 Oct. 1763
by WILLIAM HOPTON, Register.

Book A-3, p. 213 LOUIS DEVILLE, of Purrysbourg, to PETER LA-
9 Aug. 1735 FITTE (LAFFITTE) for Ł 15 currency, a lot in
Sale Purrysburgh. Witness; SAMUEL MONTAGIUT. NO
probate. Recorded 6 Oct. by WILLIAM HOPTON,
Register.

Book A-3, p. 214 (Written under above bill of sale written in
25 Feb. 1743 French) PETER LAFFITTE acknowledges receipt of
Sale Ł 40 currency from JOHN BUSH for 2 lots, 1 be-
ing lot #96; the other being above lot (p.
213) sold LAFFITTE by LOUIS DEVILLE. Witness: JOHN RODOLPHE PURY. On 28
May 1763 PETER LAFFITTE, a son of said COL. PETER LAFFITTE appeared be-
fore ADRIAN MAYER, J.P., & declared above assignment was written by AN-
DREW VERDIER & signed by his father, COL. LAFFITTE; that he was present &
ANDREW VERDIER likewose an eye witness. Recorded 6 Oct. 1763 by WILLIAM
HOPTON, Register.

Book A-3, p. 215 (Endorsed on original grant of said lot dated
25 Feb. 1746 2 Feb. 1735). PETER LAFFITTE assigns to JOHN
Sale BUSH his title to lot #96 in Purrysbourg. On
28 May 1763 PETER LAFFITTE, son of COL. PETER
LAFFITTE, testified before ADRIAN MAYER, J.P., of Granville Co., that the
above assignment was written by ANDREW VERDIER, & signed by his father in
his & VERDIER'S presence. Recorded 6 Oct. 1763 by WILLIAM HOPTON, Register.

Book A-3, p. 215 DANIEL HUGER, ESQ., of Charleston, to DANIEL
6 & 7 June 1763 HORRY, JR., of Craven Co., for Ł 3000 curren-
L & R cy, a piece of ground on Trotts Point, near
Charleston, (formerly in 2 pieces of 35 ft. &
5 ft. front) bounding E 40 ft. on Charles Street; S 75 ft. on Guignard
Street; other sides on GABRIEL GUIGNARD. Witnesses: WILLIAM STOUTEN-
BURGH, JOHN RUTLEDGE. Proved by STOUTENBURGH 23 Sept. 1763 before JOHN
HUME, J.P. Recorded 10 Oct. 1763 by WILLIAM HOPTON, Register.

Book A-3, p. 223 BRYANT (his mark) WHITE, planter, & SUSANNAH
28 & 29 Sept. 1763 (her mark), his wife, to JOHN MARPLE, miller,
L & R both of Craven Co., for Ł 200 currency, 150 a.
on S side of Little River, Craven Co., part of
300 a. granted 9 Jan. 1752 by Gov. JAMES GLEN to DANIEL REASE; bounding N
& SE on vacant land; NE on remaining part of said 300 a. REASE conveyed
150 a. to his son JOSEPH REASE; the said river now being the dividing
line; the above 150 a. having been conveyed by DANIEL REASE to SUSANNA
YOUNG, widow, now wife of BRYANT WHITE; as by plat of grant. Witnesses:
JOSHUA EDWARD, ESTHER (her mark) EDWARD. Proved by JOSHUA 29 Sept. 1763
before JOHN PEARSON, J.P. Recorded 10 Oct. 1763 by WILLIAM HOPTON, Register.

Book A-3, p. 231 SAMUEL FICKLING, planter, to WILLIAM RAVEN,
22 & 23 Sept. 1763 gentleman, of Charleston, for Ł 700 currency,
L & R 2 adjoining tracts of 500 a. & 270 a. in Colleton Co.; total 770 a., commonly called
Watch Island, bounding N on Edisto River; W on Watch Island Creek; E on
the sea; also an island of 38 a. in N Edisto River; as granted to JERE-
MIAH FICKLING, father of SAMUEL. Witnesses: GEORGE THOMSON, ROBERT MAC-
KENZIE, JR. Proved by THOMSON 5 Oct. 1763 before JOHN TROUP, J.P. Recorded 11 Oct. 1763 by WILLIAM HOPTON, Register.

Book A-3, p. 241 JOSEPH LABRUCE, SR., planter, of Waccamaw
7 June 1762 Prince George Parish, Craven Co., to his
Gift daughter, REBECCA LABRUCE, for valuable considerations, 300 a. in Craven Co., bounding N
on JOSEPH LABRUCE; SE on the Barony; S on ROBERT PAWLEY; W on Waccamaw

River. Witnesses: WILLIAM PAWLEY, JOSEPH ALLSTON. Proved by PAWLEY 10 Oct. 1763 before JOSIAS ALLSTON, J.P. Recorded 13 Oct. 1763 by WILLIAM HOPTON, Register.

Book A-3, p. 243
14 & 15 Oct. 1763
L & R

GEORGE LIVINGSTON, gentleman, & ELEANOR his wife, to JOHN GUERARD, merchant, both of Charleston, for Ł 4000 currency, 765 a., being the SE half part of 1530 a. (in 4 tracts of 350 a., 340 a., 500 a., & 340 a.), formerly belonging to WILLIAM LIVING-STON the elder, father of GEORGE, & devised by him to GEORGE; the 765 a. being near Broad River, on W side Port Royal Island, in Granville Co., bounding W & SW on marsh of said river, & on COL. JOHN BEAMOR; S & E on WILLIAM HAZARD; SE on JOHN BEAMOR; N & NW on other half. Witnesses: SAMUEL CARNE, JOHN CHAMPNEYS. Proved by CHAMPNEYS 18 Oct. 1763 before JACOB MOTTE, J.P. Recorded 20 Oct. 1763 by WILLIAM HOPTON, Register.

Book A-3, p. 254
15 Oct. 1763
Bond

Whereas the above SE half of 1530 a. (p. 243) upon resurvey has been found to have a sur-plusage of 235 a., now LIVINGSTON & GUERARD agree that GUERARD will apply for a warrant, plat & grant in order to obtain this surplusage from his majesty's bounty for GUERARD'S use; another survey to be made within a year; then LIVING-STON to pay GUERARD Ł 4 per a. for the surplusage. Witnesses: SAMUEL CARNE, JOHN CHAMPNEYS. Proved by CHAMPNEYS 18 Oct. 1763 before JACOB MOTTE, J.P. Recorded 20 Oct. 1763 by WILLIAM HOPTON, Register.

Book A-3, p. 258
10 & 11 Oct. 1763
L & R

THOMAS TUCKER, mariner & master, & SARAH his wife, to JOSIAH SMITH, the younger, merchant, both of Charleston, for Ł 1200 currency, the S part of a certain lot in Charleston, purchased by TUCKER from ISAAC HOLMES, merchant, & REBECCA his wife, by L & R dated 5 & 6 May 1763; said half lot being near Broughton's Battery at White Point, bounding W 68 ft. on Old Church (Meeting) Street; SE 110 ft. on a passageway leading along the Public Fortifications; W 111 ft. on the house & grounds of JAMES BRISBANE; N 104-3/4 ft. on other half of lot; according to plat certified by WILLIAM WILKINS, Sur., 28 Sept. 1763. Witnesses: CHARLES GRIMBALL, THOMAS LAMBOLL, JR. Proved by GRIMBALL 17 Oct. 1763 before ROBERT WILLIAMS, JR., J.P. Recorded 21 Oct. 1763 by WILLIAM HOPTON, Register.

Book A-3, p. 270
26 & 27 Sept. 1763
L & R

DANIEL MCGREGOR, planter, of St. James Santee Parish, Craven Co., eldest son & heir of DAN-IEL MACGREGOR, planter; to DAVID DEAS, mer-chant, of Charleston, for Ł 175 currency, 50 a. between N side of Washashaw Creek & S side of Santee River, part of the W part of 500 a. granted 4 May 1715, by the Lords Proprs. to DANIEL MCGREG-OR the father; shown by red lines on plat. Witnesses: JAMES BELL, DOROTHY CHICKEN. Proved by BELL 28 Sept. 1763 before DAVID HORRY, J.P. Recorded 2 Nov. 1763 by WILLIAM HOPTON, Register.

Book A-3, p. 277
1 & 2 Sept. 1761
L & R

JOSIAS ALLSTON, planter, of Prince George Par-ish, Craven Co., & ANN his wife, to his broth-er, WILLIAM ALLSTON, JR., planter, of same place, for Ł 1800 currency, 752 a. on the Long Bay in Craven Co., being half of 1504 a. granted GEORGE BENNISON; who conveyed to ARCHIBALD JOHNSTON; who sold said 752 a. to JOSIAS ALLSTON; bounding SE on the seashore marsh of Long Bay; SW on Catchpoles & GEORGE BENNISON; N & NE on other half belonging to ARCHIBALD JOHNSTON. Witness-es: CHARLES LEWIS, HENRY DURANT. Proved by DURANT 20 Oct. 1763 before BENJAMIN YOUNG, J.P. Recorded 3 Nov. 1763 by WILLIAM HOPTON, Register. Plat certified 22 Oct. 1760 by THOMAS BLYTHE.

Book A-3, p. 284
1 & 2 Oct. 1737
L & R

JOB ROTHMAHLER, ESQ., of Berkeley Co., & ANN his wife, to WILLIAM LINTHWAITE, brazier, of Charleston, for Ł 540 currency, part of lot #105 in Charleston, bounding S 100 ft. on PETER BIROT; W 30 ft. on Little Street; N 100 ft. on other part lot #105. Witnesses: LAWRENCE COULLIETTE, PETER BIROTT, WILLIAM WITHERS. On 1 June 1762 RICHARD LAMBTON appeared before GEORGE JOHNSTON, J.P., & recognized signatures of JOB & ANNE ROTHMAHLER. Recorded 22 Nov. 1763 by WILLIAM

Book A-3, p. 288   Notes from will of WILLIAM LINTHWAITE in regard to said part of lot #105 (p. 284) as en-
tered in Secretary's office; I give & devise part of a lot lately bought
of JOB ROTHMAHLER, adjoining DAVID CHRISTIAN'S lot, 30 ft. x 100 ft., to
my executors, to be reconveyed to ROTHMAHLER for debt of Ⱡ 480 due him;
should ROTHMAHLER not accept, the executors to sell & apply the money to
the debt dated 28 Apr. 1739. ROTHMAHLER refused the lot; sued; & was
paid in full by ELEANOR, widow & executrix of LINTHWAITE. The conveyance
from ROTHMAHLER to LINTHWAITE was supposed to have been destroyed by hur-
ricane of Sept. 1752 in office of JAMES GRAEME but was found amongst
GRAEME'S papers in 1762. In meantime JACOB WARLEY fenced in 16-1/2 ft.
of the S part of said lot the whole depth from W to E & built a shop on W
end, pretending he had a right to do so, having bought a tenement to the
S of it from WILLIAM GLEN & JOHN COOPER, fronting 13-1/2 ft. on King
Street, & of same depth; there being a mistake in WARLEY'S title, calling
it 30 ft. instead of 13-1/2 ft. GLEN & COOPER bought it or had a mortgage
from JOHN TRIBOUDET, in which was same mistake. TRIBOUDET bought from
JACOB JEANNERET whose conveyance contained the original error, for JEAN-
NERET'S father bought it from DAVID CHRISTINAZ whose conveyance calls it
13-1/2 ft. DAVID CHRISTINAZ did buy 30 ft. from ROTHMAHLER (see Bk. Q.
p. 54-59) & built a house of 2 tenements on it but sold the S tenement
16-1/2 ft. to REBECCA FLAVELL (Bk. Q. p. 319-324) & had 13-1/2 ft. left.
He sold the N tenement (13-1/2 ft.) to JEANNERETTE (Bk. S. 149-151).
LINTHWAITES executors brought ejectment proceedings against WARLEY in
Nov. 1763 to eject him from the 16-1/2 ft. on which he had built his
shop. The executors won & took possession. Certified 22 Nov. 1763 by
WILLIAM HOPTON, Register. See Bk. A.A. p. 243-250 fro mortgage from
JEANNERETTE to DANIEL HUGER. See Bk. F.F. p. 180-184 for conveyance from
JEANNERETTE to TRIBOUDET. See Bk. T.T. p. 227-237 for conveyances from
GLEN to COOPER to WARLEY.

Book A-3, p. 290   JACOB SATUR, merchant, of Charleston, to JER-
13 & 14 Feb. 1729/30   MYN WRIGHT, ESQ., of St. George Parish, Dor-
L & R   chester, (second son of ROBERT WRIGHT); for
Ⱡ 133 SC money, lots 3, 4, 9, & 10 in Dor-
chester, bounding E on the Broad Path leading to & from the dwelling
house of GILSON CLAPP, merchant, on the Bay in Dorchester; N on lots of
GEORGE CRICHTON, BENJAMIN SUMNER, JOANNA WAY, or STEPHEN DOME; W on the
swamp of Ashley River; S on a street leading from Dorchester to the river; total 8 a. Witness: JOHN BONNIN (illegible name). On 3 Nov. 1763
THOMAS LAMBOLL recognized SATUR'S signature before JAMES GRINDLAY, J.P.
Recorded 22 Nov. 1763 by WILLIAM HOPTON, Register.

Book A-3, p. 297   THOMAS SAVAGE, merchant, to HENRY LAURENS,
23 Sept. 1763   ESQ., both of Charleston, for Ⱡ 5 currency,
Feoffment   200 a. of marsh land, including several small
islands, in Berkeley Co., between Town Creek &
Hobcaw Ferry, bounding W on Town Creek; E on Cooper River opposite Hobcaw. Witnesses: MARK MORRIS, CHARLES MINORS. Proved by MORRIS 29 Sept.
1763 before JACOB MOTTE, J.P. Recorded 23 Nov. 1763 by WILLIAM HOPTON,
Register.

Book A-3, p. 300   ARCHIBALD BAIRD, ESQ., to CHARLES FYFFE, sur-
1 & 2 Sept. 1753   geon, both of Craven Co., for Ⱡ 1700 currency,
L & R   lot marked E in plan of Georgetown, bounding W
on low water mark of Georgetown River; SW on
Cannon Street; NW 217.9 ft. on lot D, NE 50 ft. on Front or Bay Street.
Witnesses: GEORGE DICK, WILLIAM LUPTON. Proved by LUPTON 11 Nov. 1763
before BENJAMIN YOUNG, J.P. Recorded 24 Nov. 1763 by WILLIAM HOPTON,
Register.

Book A-3, p. 308   DANIEL DOYLEY, P.M., to HUGH WINTER, planter,
21 Sept. 1763   of Prince Frederick Parish, for Ⱡ 200 curren-
Release   cy, 500 a. on Lynch Lake Swamp. Whereas the
Rev. MR. JOHN BAXTER, now of Prince Frederick
Parish, owned 500 a. on Lynches Lake Swamp, Prince Frederick Parish,
bounding on all sides on vacant land as granted 6 Apr. 1753 by Gov. JAMES
GLEN; & whereas BAXTER gave DR. ALEXANDER GARDEN 3 bonds in the total sum

of Ł 3376 currency; & whereas GARDEN obtained a judgment against BAXTER
for the full amount & costs, & a writ of fieri facias was issued commanding the P.M. to seize BAXTER'S property & recover the amount due; now
DOYLEY sells the 500 a. at public auction to WINTER; subject, however, to
claim of dower by BAXTER'S wife. Witnesses: WILLIAM BAMPFIELD, JOHN MAR-
TIN. Proved by BAMPFIELD 23 Nov. 1763 before WILLIAM BURROWS, J.P. Recorded 25 Nov. 1763 by WILLIAM HOPTON, Register.

Book A-3, p. 313   JOHN THOMSON, merchant, to ALEXANDER FOTHE-
1 & 2 Jan. 1762   RINGHAM & ARCHIBALD MACNEIL, physician; all of
L & R   St. George Parish, Berkeley Co., as tenansa &
                         not as jointenants; for Ł 2000 currency, 500
a. in Berkeley Co., on S side Ashley River, formerly belonging to GIBBON
WRIGHT; bounding E on ALEXANDER SKENE; S on JOHN SKENE & SAMUEL WAIN-
WRIGHT; NE on estate of JOSEPH WRAGG; NW on JERMYN WRIGHT & estate of
RALPH IZARD. Witnesses: JOHN DRAKE, ROBERT BALLINGALL. Proved by DRAKE
8 Feb. 1762 before J. SKENE, J.P. Recorded 26 Nov. 1763 by WILLIAM HOP-
TON, Register.

Book A-3, p. 320   HENRY BOYD, planter, of Goose Creek Parish,
13 & 14 Jan. 1763   Berkeley Co., to ROBERT WINTER, planter, of
L & R   Prince Frederick Parish, Craven Co., for Ł 100
                         currency, 200 a. on 1 of the branches of
Lynches Lake, in Prince Frederick Parish; granted 3 Apr. 1754 by Gov.
JAMES GLEN to JOHN BOYD, father of HENRY BOYD; bounding on all sides on
vacant land. Witnesses: JOHN GREGG, THOMAS NISBITT, ANN LIVISTON. Prov-
ed by GREGG 14 Jan. 1763 before JOHN LIVISTON, J.P. Entered in Auditor
General's book G. 7, p. 37 on 3 Feb. 1763 by RICHARD LAMBTON, Dep. Aud.
Recorded 26 Nov. 1763 by WILLIAM HOPTON, Register.

Book A-3, p. 327   ISAAC BRABANT, merchant, to ADRIAN MAYER,
16 May 1762   ESQ., both of Purisbourg, SC, for Ł 60 ster-
Release   ling, 2 lots in Purisbourg #17 & #19 of 1 a.
                         each; #17 bounding W on the Bay on Front
Street; E on lot #19; N on a street; S on lot #18; lot #19 bounding W on
lot #17; E on a street; N on a street; W on lot #20. Witnesses: JOHN
BAPTIST BOURQUIN, ABRAHAM RAVOT. Proved by RAVOT 12 July 1762 before
STEPHEN BULL, JR., J.P. Recorded 29 Nov. 1763 by WILLIAM HOPTON, Regis-
ter.

Book A-3, p. 330   WILLIAM MATHEWES, ESQ., of St. Johns Parish,
13 June 1763   Colleton Co., to his eldest son, ANTHONY MATH-
Deed of Surrender   EWES, gentleman, by MARY his former wife, for
                         natural love & affection, part of lot #31 in
Charleston, with the two tenements erected thereon, occupied by JOHN
RODOLPH LEGRAND & ISAAC WALDRON; bounding N 43 ft. on Broad Street; S
37 ft. 1 in. on JOHN HOLMES; E 97-1/2 ft. on BENJAMIN SMITH; W on MRS.
JOHNSON; also half of lot #178, bounding N 50 ft. on Broad Street; E 200
ft. on JOHN DRAYTON; S & W on DR. SAMUEL CARNE; which 2 parts of lots
formerly belonged to MARY, former wife of WILLIAM MATHEWES & held by WIL-
LIAM as tenant for live by courtesy of England; ANTHONY being heir expectant on death of WILLIAM. Witnesses: JOHN BOTTERELL, WILLIAM GRAEME.
Proved by GRAEME 22 Sept. 1763 before DAVID GRAEME, J.P. Recorded 1 Dec.
1763 by WILLIAM HOPTON, Register.

Book A-3, p. 333   NICHOLAS VALOIS, gentleman, to WILLIAM DAN-
21 & 23 Apr. 1763   DRIDGE, gentleman, both of Charleston, for
L & R   Ł 1571:2:6 currency, part of lot #210, bound-
                         ing E 35-1/2 ft. on King; N 125 ft. on JOHN
COLCOCK; W & S on part same lot belonging to CATO ASH. Witnesses: JOSEPH
CREIGHTON, FRANCIS THOMAS GREENE. Proved by GREENE 28 Apr. 1763 before
WILLIAM BURROWS, J.P. Recorded 2 Dec. 1763 by WILLIAM HOPTON, Register.

Book A-3, p. 342   JOSEPH ASH, & RICHARD COCHRAN ASH, planters,
9 & 10 Jan. 1761   of Colleton Co., & CATO ASH, bricklayer, of
L & R   Charleston, executors of will of THEODORE
                         EDINGS, widow; to WILLIAM DANDRIDGE, glazier,
of Charleston, highest bidder, for Ł 2003 currency, a brick house & piece
of ground, part of 1 or more town lots lately belonging to THEODORA ED-
INGS, where she lived, & which by her will dated 19 Jan. 1760 she ordered

her executors to sell; which house & lot were sold to THEODORA EDINGS by
WILLIAM EDINGS & MARGARET MARSHELLA his wife; being the NW part of the N
half of 3 lots, #148, #149, & #150; bounding E 30 ft. on King Street; &
continuing westward 30 ft. in width for 160 ft.; being 70 ft. wide at W
end of NW part of said N half of said 3 lots; 45 ft. long; bounding E on
King Street; & on part said half of 3 lots; S on certain parts of said
half; W on lot #243; N on a small alley, being part of lot #210. Witnesses: JOSEPH BALL, JR., MARK MORRIS, THOMAS LAMBALL. Proved by MORRIS
30 Nov. 1763 before GEORGE MURRAY, J.P. Recorded 5 Dec. 1763 by WILLIAM
HOPTON, Register.

Book A-3, p. 352   DANIEL DOYLEY, P.M., to WILLIAM DANDRIDGE, at
17 Mar. 1760   public auction, for Ł 942 currency, a lot on
Sale   King Street. Whereas a writ of fieri facias
                      was issued for levying the sum of Ł 1600 cur-
rency & costs on the goods & chattels of THOMAS RALPH, house carpenter,
recovered against RALPH by EDWARD BULLARD, of Charleston; & DOYLEY seized
1 lot in St. Philips Parish bounding 40 ft. on King Street; 232 ft. deep;
adjoining EDWARD BULLARD'S lot; & offered the lot at public auction; now
he conveys to DANDRIDGE. Witnesses: JOHN CLIFFORD, ROBERT HARVEY. Proved 30 Nov. 1763 by CLIFFORD before GEORGE MURRAY, J.P. Recorded 5 Dec.
1763 by WILLIAM HOPTON, Register.

Book A-3, p. 354   MALLORY RIVERS, planter, of Berkeley Co., &
22 & 23 May 1761   MARY his wife, to MARK MORRIS, wharfinger, of
L & R   Charleston, for Ł 700 currency, part of lot
                      #210, bounding E 22 ft. on King Street; N 206
ft. on house & grounds of WILLIAM RANDAL (now TUCKER); W on lot 240 belonging to JAMES STOBO; S on house & grounds of JOHN TUCKER; which lot
#210 was granted 12 June 1694 to JOSEPH NEEVES; & by various conveyances
came to GREENWOOD MALLORY, mariner; afterwards to MALLORY RIVERS. Witnesses: JOHN LEHRE, DAVID STOLL. Proved 30 Nov. 1763 by LEHRE before
GEORGE MURRAY, J.P. Recorded 5 Dec. 1763 by WILLIAM HOPTON, Register.

Book A-3, p. 363   JAMES ADAMSON, ESQ., & ELEANOR (her mark) his
3 & 4 Aug. 1759   wife, to THOMAS CONNELY, planter, both of Cra-
L & R   ven Co., for Ł 100 currency, 100 a., part of
                      350 a., on SW side Wateree River in Craven
Co., down to the middle of the tract; bounding SE on WALTER KELLY; NW on
JAMES ADAMSON; SW on vacant land; as by plat; which 100 a. were granted
9 Jan. 1755 by Gov. JAMES GLEN to WALTER KELLY. Witnesses: THOMAS PREST-
WOOD, HENRY MAXWELL. Proved by PRESTWOOD Ł9 Oct. 1759 before SAMUEL
WYLY, J.P. Recorded 8 Dec. 1763 by WILLIAM HOPTON, Register.

Book A-3, p. 371   JUSTINUS STOLL, blacksmith, & MARY (her mark)
31 May & 1 June 1762 his wife, to JOHN EDWARDS, merchant, both of
L & R by Mortgage   Charleston, as security on bond of even date
                      in penal sum of Ł 4000 for payment of Ł 2000
currency, with interest, on 1 Dec. 1763; part of lot #102 in Charleston,
bounding SW on a creek 35 ft. wide; E on GEORGE SOMMERS, JAMES HARTLEY, &
WILLIAM ROPER; N on a private alley leading from Church Street, to the
Bay; W on WILLIAM SCREVEN; as by plat certified by WILLIAM WILKINS & annexed to release dated 2 Apr. 1759 from MARY SMITH to JUSTINUS STOLL.
Witnesses: FRANCIS PELOT, SARAH RIVERS. Proved by SARAH RIVERS 5 Dec.
1763 before ROBERT WILLIAMS, JR., J.P. Recorded 8 Dec. 1763 by WILLIAM
HOPTON, Register. On 21 July 1777 JOHN EDWARDS declared mortgage satis-
fied. Witness: GEORGE SHEED.

Book A-3, p. 378   JOHN (his mark) DOWLAN (DOWLING), yeoman, to
3 & 4 Oct. 1758   WILLIAM KEARLEY, ship carpenter, both of Cra-
L & R   ven Co., for Ł 50 currency, 50 a. in Craven
                      Co., on Half Way Swamp Creek, bounding on all
sides on vacant land, as by plat to grant. Witnesses: HENRY MILHOUSE,
THOMAS ENGLISH, ROBERT MILHOUS. Proved by HENRY MILHOUS, a Quaker, 9
Apr. 1760 before SAMUEL WYLY, J.P. Recorded 8 Dec. 1763 by WILLIAM HOP-
TON, Register.

Book A-3, p. 385   THOMAS MAXWELL, planter, to MARY MAGDALEN
14 & 15 Apr. 1761   GIGNILLIAT, widow, both of Granville Co., for
L & R   Ł 700 currency, 250 a. in the "reserved lands

of Purysburgh", Granville Co., bounding N on MORGAN SABBS land outside
the Township; E on DAVID ZOUBLIE (ZUBLY) & vacant land; S on ZOUBLIE &
vacant land; W on HENRY DESAUSSURE; MARY MAGDALEN GIGNILLIAT already being in actual possession by purchase from MICHAEL SEALY, & grant to the
Rev. FRANCIS PELOT dated 1 June 1757. Witnesses: PAUL PORCHER, CORNELIUS
DUPONT, JOHN DAVID MONGIN. Proved by PORCHER 5 Dec. 1763 before WILLIAM
BURROWS, J.P. Entered in Auditor General's book G-7, p. 151, on 5 Dec.
1763, by RICHARD LAMBTON, Dep. Aud. Recorded 9 Dec. 1763 by WILLIAM HOP-
TON, Register.

Book A-3, p. 391   NATHANIEL SCOTT, brewer, to HOPKIN PRICE, ESQ.,
15 & 16 Nov. 1763   both of Charleston, as security on several
L & R by Mortgage   bonds signed by PRICE at SCOTT'S request; 1
                      payable to ELIZABETH PERONNEAU, widow & execu-
trix of will of SAMUEL PERONNEAU (Ł 900); 1 to THOMAS LAMBOLL & ALEXANDER
PERONNEAU, gentleman (Ł 800); 1 to THOMAS LAMBOLL (Ł 300); part of lot
#198 in Charleston with its S tenement; bounding W 148 ft. on Friend
Street (running from Broad Street to Tradd Street); S 48 ft. on GEORGE
ROUPELLE & ELIZABETH his wife (who lately sold said piece of lot & S ten-
ement thereon to NATHANIEL SCOTT); E on THOMAS SMITH, JR.; N on the N
tenement adjoining said S tenement. Witnesses: BENJAMIN GODFREY, JACOB
BARKLEY. Proved by BARKLEY 9 Dec. 1763 before CHARLES WOODMASON, J.P.
Recorded 12 Dec. 1763 by WILLIAM HOPTON, Register. Mortgage satisfied 14
May 1765. Witness: FENWICKE BULL.

Book A-3, p. 404   THOMAS BOWMAN, planter, of Granville Co., &
17 & 18 Nov. 1763   ANN his wife, to JOHN GUERARD, merchant, of
L & R   Charleston, for Ł 6384 currency, his N half of
                      a certain plantation, consisting originally of
4 adjoining tracts of 350 a., 340 a., 500 a., & 340 a.; the N half of
which was said to contain 765 a., but now 1064 a., near the Broad River
running on W side of Port Royal River, in Granville Co.; bounding SW & W
on marsh; N on COL. NATHANIEL BARNWELL; NE on NATHANIEL BARNWELL & ROBERT
WILKINSON; E on NATHANIEL BARNWELL; SE & S on other half of said plantation. Witnesses: WILLIAM HOPE, OWEN BOWEN, STEPHEN BULL, JR. Proved by
HOPE 9 Dec. 1763 before THOMAS MIDDLETON, J.P. Recorded 14 Dec. 1763 by
WILLIAM HOPTON, Register.

Book A-3, p. 413   DANIEL RICHARDSON, blacksmith, & SARAH (her
13 & 14 Apr. 1763   mark) his wife, to MASON GREENING, carpenter,
L & R   both of Craven Co., for Ł 195 currency, 100 a.
                      in Craven Co., on Potato Creek, on N side San-
tee River; bounding on all sides on vacant land. Witnesses: JOHN CANTEY,
JR., MOSES GREEN, WILLIAM BREACH. Proved by GREEN 12 Dec. 1763 before
RICHARD RICHARDSON, J.P. Recorded 22 Dec. 1763 by WILLIAM HOPTON, Register.

Book A-3, p. 422   DANIEL BURNET, JR., heir of DANIEL BURNETT &
24 & 25 Oct. 1763   MARY (her mark) his wife, to WILLIAM CARSON,
L & R   both of Berkeley Co., for Ł 660 currency, 500
                      a. on Great Saludy, granted 4 July 1749 by
Gov. JAMES GLEN to DANIEL BURNET, SR., bounding on all sides on vacant
land. Witnesses: JOHN BURNET, RICHARD LANG. Proved by BURNET 23 Dec.
1763 before ANDREW BROWN, J.P. Recorded 23 Dec. 1763 by WILLIAM HOPTON,
Register.

Book A-3, p. 428   JOHN MEEK, baker, & MARGARET (her mark) his
3 & 4 Oct. 1763   wife, to JOHN WAGNER, merchant, both of
L & R by Mortgage   Charleston, as security on several bonds sign-
                      ed by WAGNER at MEEK'S request; 1 given to
THOMAS SHIRLEY & EDWARD MARTIN, merchants, of Charleston, on 23 Sept.
1763, for payment of Ł 1058:0:8 currency, with interest, on 23 Sept.
1764; 1 of same date to WILLIAM BANBURY for payment of Ł 463:1:4 on 1
Jan. next; 1 to WAGNER, this date, for payment of Ł 478:18:0 on 4 Oct.
1764; a lot bounding E 49 ft. on King Street; W on FREDERICK GRIMKE; N
226 ft. on THOMAS DRAYTON; S on JOHN RATTRAY & RALPH IZARD. Witnesses:
JACOB WARLEY, JOHN SCOTT. Proved by SCOTT 21 Dec. 1763 before J. RUT-
LEDGE, J.P. Recorded 23 Dec. 1763 by WILLIAM HOPTON, Register.

Book A-3, p. 435   SAMUEL PALMARIN, saddler, of Johns Island, &

5 & 6 Dec. 1763   SARAH his wife (formerly SARAH COLE, daughter
L & R   of ROBERT COLE, planter, of Johns Island),
                          lately the wife of WILLIAM WEATHERLY, deceas-
ed), to EBENEZER SIMMONS, ESQ., of Charleston, for Ⱡ 1600 currency, 150
a., old measure, but resurvey found to be 230 a., formerly belonging to
JOHN JONES, & known as Savannah tract, bounding W on JONATHAN STOCKS (now
DANIEL HOLMES); S on Keiwa River & marsh; S on Savannah or Coles Creek; N
on the creek & JAMES MATHEWS; which tract was divided from ROBERT COLE'S
other land by writ of partition dated 25 Nov. 1757 & allotted to SARAH
when she was SARAH WEATHERLY. Witnesses: JOHN ROBERTS, JOSIAH SMITH, JR.
Proved by ROBERTS 14 Dec. 1763 before WILLIAM MASSEY, J.P. Recorded 28
Dec. 1763 by WILLIAM HOPTON, Register.

Book A-3, p. 445   WILLIAM NEILSON, JR., planter, & ELIZABETH his
25 & 26 Mar. 1762   wife, to JOHN WEBB, planter, both of St. Marks
L & R   Parish, Craven Co., for Ⱡ 130 currency, 200 a.
                          on S side Lynch's Creek, bounding on all sides
on vacant land, granted WILLIAM NEILSON, SR. Witnesses: ROBERT LEWIS,
PETER MALLET, JOHN CAPS. Proved 28 May 1762 by LEWIS & MELLET, before
HENRY CASSELS, J.P. Recorded 2 Jan. 1764 by WILLIAM HOPTON, Register.

Book A-3, p. 451   RICHARD CLARK, clerk (cleric ?) of Hexton,
20 & 21 Dec. 1763   Middlesex Co., & SUSANNAH his wife (formerly
L & R   SUSANNAH CROKATT, widow, of Charleston), by
                          their attorney, JAMES GRINDLAY, gentleman, &
THOMAS SMITH, merchant, of Charleston, SC; to THOMAS BOWMAN, planter, of
Granville Co., SC, for Ⱡ 4300 SC money, 1239 a. in Granville Co., SC.
Whereas THOMAS TREDWAY, glover, of Leadenhall Street, London, acting as
trustee for SUSANNAH CROKATT, & using her money for the transaction, pur-
chased in about 1766 from 1 _____ LOWNDES, P.M., of SC, 1239 a. in Prince
William Parish, Granville Co., SC, called Bray's Island, SUSANNAH having
full power to dispose of the tract; & whereas SUSANNAH afterwards married
RICHARD CLARKE, clerk, of Hexton, Co. of Middlesex; & on 26 Mar. 1762
they appointed GRINDLAY & SMITH, of SC, their attorneys to sell their
property in SC; now GRINDLAY & SMITH sell BOWMAN the 1239 a. on E side
Whale Branch of Pocotaligo River, bounding W on a river, marsh, & creek;
N on a marsh, a creek, & BRYAN'S land (now JAMES GUTHBERT); E on ALEXAN-
DER FRASER (formerly ISAAC MAZYCK); S on creeks, marsh, & BELLAMY CRAW-
FORD. Witnesses: BENJAMIN WARING, DANIEL CROKATT. Proved by CROKATT 24
Dec. 1763 before ROBERT WILLIAMS, JR., J.P. Recorded 3 Jan. 1764 by WIL-
LIAM HOPTON, Register.

Book A-3, p. 464   GEORGE LIVINGSTON, gentleman, of Charleston, &
20 Dec. 1763   ELEANOR his wife (widow & devisee for life of
Lease for Life   the houses & land of her former husband, JOHN
                          BEAMOR, planter, of Granville Co.), as tenants
for live; to THOMAS BOWMAN, planter, of Granville Co., for the residue of
ELEANOR'S natural life & no longer; for Ⱡ 700 currency, 160 a. on Port
Royal Island, bounding S & SW on a creek & marsh; SE on said creek, marsh,
& WILLIAM HAZARD; W & NW on land lately sold by GEORGE LIVINGSTON to JOHN
GUERARD; which tract, among other things, BEAMOR bequeathed to his wife
ELEANOR during her life. Witnesses: JOHN CHAMPNEYS, WILLIAM LIVINGSTON.
Proved by LIVINGSTON 24 Dec. 1763 before ROBERT WILLIAMS, JR., J.P. Re-
corded 4 Jan. 1764 by WILLIAM HOPTON, Register.

Book A-3, p. 468   JAMES BUTLER, JR., planter, of St. Philips
14 & 15 June 1763   Parish, on Great Ogeechie, Georgia, to the
L & R   Rev. MR. ROBERT BARON, rector of St. Bartholo-
                          mews Parish, Colleton Co., SC, for Ⱡ 420 SC
money, 840 a. in St. Bartholomews Parish, on Island Creek Swamp, bounding
on all sides on vacant land as by Sur. Gen's plat. Witnesses: ALICE OS-
WALD, JOHN HARN, JR., ROBERT REID. Proved by HARN 21 Dec. 1763 before
JAMES SKIRVING, J.P. Recorded 17 Jan. 1764 by WILLIAM HOPTON, Register.

Book A-3, p. 477   JOSEPH ALLSTON, planter, & CHARLOTTE his wife,
30 Aug. & 5 Dec. 1763   to WILLIAM PAWLEY, planter, both of Prince
L & R   George Parish, Craven Co., for Ⱡ 1500 curren-
                          cy, 2 tracts; 1 of 300 a. on Waccamaw Neck,
Prince George Parish (for Ⱡ 450), bounding E on the seashore; W on vacant
land; N & S on heirs of CAPT. GEORGE SMITH; as by plat of grant dated 2

Jan. 1754 from Gov. JAMES GLEN; the other 700 a. in said Parish (for
Ł 1050), bounding E on sea marsh; W on Waccamaw River; N on vacant land;
S on CAPT. NEVE; according to L & R dated 15 & 16 Nov. 1757 from ARCHER
SMITH; which 2 tracts, formerly belonging to JOSEPH PRINCE, deceased were
sold by DANIEL DOYLEY, P.M., at public auction, to JOSEPH ALLSTON 7 Dec.
1762. Witnesses: ISAAC MARION, ALEXANDER MCDONALL, ROBERT WARING, JOSIAS
ALLSTON. Proved by WARING 11 Jan. 1764 by MARION 13 Jan. 1764 before JO-
SIAS ALLSTON, J.P. Recorded 17 Jan. 1764 by WILLIAM HOPTON, Register.

Book A-3, p. 487   ALEXANDER SWINTON, planter, & ELIZABETH his
18 & 19 July 1763   wife, to GEORGE BURROWS, planter, both of Cra-
L & R   ven Co., for Ł 310 currency, 300 a. on a place
                          called Turkey Creek, surveyed for SWINTON'S
father but never granted; bounding SE on JOSEPH MCCREE; NW on JOSEPH MC-
CREE & JOHN MCMAHON; other sides on vacant land; as by plat. Witnesses:
JOHN SCOTT, JR., JOHN BURROWS. Proved by BURROWS 16 Jan. 1764 before
JOHN TROUP, J.P. Recorded 18 Jan. 1764 by WILLIAM HOPTON, Register.

Book A-3, p. 493   SAMUEL JONES, planter, of Johns Island, & SU-
20 & 21 Jan. 1753   SANNAH his wife, to EBENEZER SIMMONS, merchant,
L & R   of Charleston, for Ł 6000 currency, 3 tracts;
                          total 2500 a.; in Colleton Co. Whereas Gov.
JOHN ARCHDALE on 21 Aug. 1696 granted Lt. Gen. JOSEPH BLAKE 2200 a., English measure, in Colleton Co., on N side of mouth of Edisto River, bounding W on the river; N on Boheecott Creek; S on the ocean; E on Keewaw
Creek; NE on the Hanlover; as by plat; & whereas BLAKE on 27 Feb. 1696
sold the 2200 a. to THOMAS JONES, of Colleton Co.; & whereas JONES owned
200 a. on NW side Keewaw Creek, near the Hanlover, bounding SE on Keewaw
Creek; NW on Booheckett Creek; SW on JOAN GRICE; NE on vacant land; also
100 a. on a neck of land called the Haulover, bounding SE on marsh; W on
Bohecket Creek; NE on vacant land; & whereas JONES, by will dated 9 Aug.
1711 devised all his houses & lands on Boheckit & Keewaw Creeks to his
son JOHN, except 700 a. on Stono which he devised to his son SAMUEL; &
whereas JOHN JONES, by will dated 2 June 1715 devised 1500 a., part of
the 2800 a., & the 200 a. & 100 a. "the residue of his real estate", to
his brother SAMUEL; & whereas SAMUEL, by his will dated 5 Aug. 1736, devised the 2500 a. (part being Jones Island) to his son, SAMUEL, party
hereto; now he sells the 3 tracts to SIMMONS. Witnesses: JOHN THOMAS,
WILLIAM SCOTT. Proved by SCOTT 15 Nov. 1763 before DAVID GRAEME, J.P.
Recorded 24 Jan. by WILLIAM HOPTON, Register.

Book A-3, p. 504   THOMAS LYNCH, ESQ., of Craven Co., to DAVID
26 & 27 Feb. 1755   DEAS, merchant, of Charleston, for Ł 119 cur-
L & R   rency, 119 a., part of 700 a. granted JOHN
                          BOONE), in Craven Co., bounding NW on part
same tract belonging to LYNCH; SE on GILSON CLAPP (now DAVID DEAS); as by
plat. Witnesses: WILLIAM MOULTRIE, JAMES LENNOX. Proved by LENNOX 21
Jan. 1764 before GEORGE MURRAY, J.P. Recorded 24 Jan. 1764 by WILLIAM
HOPTON, Register.

Book A-3, p. 511   JOHN LLOYD, of Amelia Township, Berkeley Co.,
17 & 18 Jan. 1764   to JOHN PERSON, of Southampton Co., Virginia,
L & R   for Ł 195 SC money, 350 a. in Craven Co., be-
                          tween Wateree & Congaree Rivers; granted LLOYD
9 Jan. 1752; as by plat to grant. Witnesses: MARY GARDNER, JOHN BALLARD,
JR. Proved by BALLARD 24 Jan. 1764 before J. RUTLEDGE, J.P. Recorded 26
Jan. 1764 by WILLIAM HOPTON, Register.

Book A-3, p. 516   ROBERT WILLIAMS, gentleman, only acting execu-
10 & 11 Oct. 1763   tor of will of WILLIAM RANDALL, blacksmith, to
L & R   WILLIAM BLAKE; gentleman; all of Charleston;
                          for Ł 979 currency, 2 adjoining tracts origi-
nally called 600 a. & 300 a. but on resurvey by JOSHUA MCPHERSON, Dep.
Sur., found to be 614 a. & 276 a., on W branch of Salcacha River Swamp,
in Colleton Co. Whereas Lt. Gov. THOMAS BROUGHTON on 12 May 1731 granted
WILLIAM RANDALL 600 a. in Colleton Co., on W branch of Salcacha River
Swamp; bounding E on MR. SACHEVEREL; other sides on vacant land; & on 12
May 1735 granted RANDALL 300 a. in Colleton Co., on W branch of Salcacha
River Swamp; bounding S on MR. SACHEVEREL & on MR. RANDALL; other sides
on vacant land; & whereas RANDALL by will dated 28 Aug. 1755, directed

his executors to sell the above tracts, appointing HOPKIN PRICE & ROBERT WILLIAMS his executors; now WILLIAMS conveys to BLAKE the 890 a., bounding SW on JAMES DONNEN (formerly SACHEVEREL) & on vacant land; other sides on vacant land. Witnesses: ROBERT WILLIAMS, JR., JOSEPH BEE. Proved by WILLIAMS 24 Jan. 1764 before JAMES GRINDLAY, J.P. Recorded 28 Jan. 1764 by WILLIAM HOPTON, Register.

Book A-3, p. 527 RICHARD LAMBTON, gentleman, to WILLIAM BLAKE,
11 Oct. 1763 ESQ., both of Charleston, for Ŀ 718 currency,
Release paid in satisfaction of a judgment, releases
his claim to 890 a. (p. 516). Whereas WILLIAM RANDALL, blacksmith, of Charleston, owned 890 a. in 2 tracts; & after his death LAMBTON obtained a judgment against ROBERT WILLIAMS, executor of RANDALL'S estate, for Ŀ 4410:18:9 & costs, which judgment was acknowledged before PETER LEIGH, C.J.; & the 890 a. were sold at public auction to BLAKE; & whereas WILLIAMS has paid LAMBTON Ŀ 718 on account; now LAMBTON confirms BLAKE'S title to the 2 tracts. Witnesses: ROBERT WILLIAMS, JR., JOSEPH BEE. Proved by WILLIAMS 24 Jan. 1764 before JAMES GRINDLAY, J.P. Recorded 28 Jan. 1764 by WILLIAM HOPTON, Register.

Book A-3, p. 531 FRANCIS YONGE, planter, of Colleton Co., only
21 & 22 Aug. 1761 son & sole executor of will of ROBERT YONGE; &
L & R SARAH his wife, to JOSEPH ASH, planter, of
Colleton Co., for Ŀ 1250 currency, 500 a. in Colleton Co., granted 6 Apr. 1733 by Gov. ROBERT JOHNSON to ROBERT YONGE, lying on S side S Colleton River, fronting a creek over against Wiltown, bounding N on MR. LIVINGSTON; S on JAMES COCHRAN; W on marsh; as by plat; which land ROBERT YONGE by will dated 12 Nov. 1751 devised to his son, said FRANCIS YONGE. Witnesses: THOMAS SACHEVEREL, MARY ANN SAMUELS, RUTH PAGE. Proved by SACHEVEREL 7 Apr. 1762 before ROBERT PRINGLE, J.P. Recorded 31 Jan. 1764 by WILLIAM HOPTON, Register.

Book A-3, p. 544 FRANCIS YONGE gives ASH a bond that he will
22 Aug. 1761 perform above agreement (p. 531). Witness:
Bond THOMAS SACHEVEREL. On 1 Feb. 1764 GEORGE LIV-
INGSTON recognized SACHEVEREL'S signature before CHARLES WOODMASON, J.P. Recorded 1 Feb. 1764 by WILLIAM HOPTON, Register.

Book A-3 JAMES GORDAN, planter, of Black Mingo, Craven
28 & 29 Jan. 1763 Co., to CORNELIUS DONOVAN, for Ŀ 180 currency,
L & R 150 a. in Craven Co., on a N branch of Black
River, bounding SW on HUGH ERVIN; other sides on vacant land. Witnesses: JOHN SCOTT, THOMAS SCOTT, HUGH WINTER. Proved by JOHN SCOTT 15 Feb. 1763 before JOHN LIVISTON, J.P. Entered in Auditor's book G. 7, p. 158, on 26 Jan. 1764 by RICHARD LAMBTON, Dep. Aud. Recorded 6 Feb. 1764 by WILLIAM HOPTON, Register.

Book A-3, p. 550 ROBERT CROFT, planter, of Christ Church Par-
28 & 29 May 1760 ish, to GEORGE FORD, planter, of Prince George
L & R Parish, Craven Co., for Ŀ 700 SC money, an Is-
land of 500 a. called Musketo or South Island, bounding E on the sea; N on Winyaw Bay; W on Musketo Creek. Whereas SARAH TROTT, widow, of Charleston, by L & R dated 22 & 23 Apr. 1745 sold EDWARD CROFT, father of ROBERT CROFT, an island called Musketo on South Island, containing 500 a., & the adjoining marsh, at mouth of Winyaw Bay & Santee River, in Craven Co.; & whereas EDWARD CROFT, by will dated 9 Mar. 1756 bequeathed the island to his son ROBERT; now ROBERT sells to FORD. Witnesses: JOSEPH DUBOURDIEU, WILLIAM SHACKELFORD, JR. Proved 29 May 1760 by SHACKELFORD before THOMAS BLYTHE, J.P. Recorded 8 Feb. 1764 by WILLIAM HOPTON, Register.

Book A-3, p. 557 DANIEL LAROCHE, merchant, to ISAAC CARR,
10 & 11 Dec. 1750 planter, both of Craven Co., for Ŀ 1000 cur-
L & R rency, 500 a. in Craven Co., bounding NE on
Black River; SW on Greens Creek & WILLIAM CRIPPS (formerly PHILIP CHANDLER); W & NW on JOHN WHITE; which land Gov. ROBERT JOHNSON on 22 Sept. 1733 granted WILLIAM HINCKLEY; who by L & R dated 22 & 23 Aug. 1739 sold to DANIEL & THOMAS LAROCHE; as by plat of grant. Witnesses: JOHN HENTIE, ALLEN WELLS. Proved 23 Jan. 1764 by

HENTIE before JOHN MAYRANT, J.P. Recorded 10 Feb. 1764 by WILLIAM HOPTON, Register.

Book A-3, p. 565   ISAAC CARR, planter, to DR. CHARLES FYFFE,
10 June 1763   physician, both of Craven Co., for L 1200 cur-
L & R   rency, the 500 a. he purchased from LAROCHE
                      (p. 557); now bounding NE on Black River; SW
on Greens Creek & GEORGE FORD (formerly PHILIP CHANDLER); W & NW on AN-
THONY WHITE (son of JOHN WHITE). Witnesses: CHARLES MINORS, ANTHONY
BONNEAU. Proved 16 June 1763 by MINORS before ARCHIBALD BAIRD, J.P. Recorded 11 Feb. 1764 by WILLIAM HOPTON, Register.

Book A-3, p. 573   GEORGE PAWLEY, planter, to THOMAS BUTLER,
20 & 21 Jan. 1764   planter, both of Prince George Parish, Craven
L & R   Co., for L 2200 currency, 572 a., part of 3
                      tracts or 1500 a. in Craven Co., between Wac-
camaw River & the ocean, bounding SE on the seashore; SW on DR. ALEXANDER
MCDONALD; other sides on GEORGE PAWLEY; as by plat. Whereas by 2 grants
dated 28 June 1711 the Lords Proprs. granted THOMAS STOCKS 2 adjoining
tracts of 500 a. each, total 1000 a., in Craven Co.; & whereas THOMAS
STOCKS, RACHEL STOCKS, SAMUEL STOCKS, & JONATHAN STOCKS, joint heirs of
said THOMAS STOCKS, by L & R dated 23 & 24 Sept. 1731, wold the 2 tracts
to ANTHONY MATHEWES, merchant, of Charleston; who, with LOIS his wife, on
22 May 1733, sold to GEORGE PAWLEY; & whereas the Lords Proprs. on 13
Jan. 1711 granted 500 a. in Craven Co. to THOMAS CLARK; who on 16 Jan.
1716 sold to WILLIAM CATOR; who by L & R dated 20 & 21 July 1736 sold to
JOSEPH ALLEN; who, with MARY his wife, by L & R dated 11 & 12 Oct. 1743,
sold to GEORGE PAWLEY; now PAWLEY sells a part of the 3 tracts to BUTLER.
Witnesses: WILLIAM JAMESON, ELIAS FOISSIN, JR. Proved by FOISSIN 21 Jan.
1764 before JOSEPH BROWN, J.P. Recorded 11 Feb. 1764 by WILLIAM HOPTON,
Register.

Book A-3, p. 582   JACOB WALDBURGER, planter, of Purisburgh, &
25 & 26 Dec. 1763   CATHERINE his wife, to STEPHEN CATER, planter,
L & R   of Dorchester, for L 1200 currency, 2 tracts,
                      1 of 350 a. granted MICHAEL RORER, the other
50 a. granted JOHN GRUBB; in PUrisburgh Township; & conveyed by grantees
to JOHN ULRICH LONG; who sold to WALDBURGER; bounding E, N, & S on HENRY
JENERET; N & W on HENRY CHIFFELLE; S on JOHN LINDER. Witnesses: HENRY
BOURQUIN, HENRY LEWIS BOURQUIN. Proved by HENRY LEWIS BOURQUIN 4 Jan.
1764 before ADRIAN MAYER, J.P. Recorded 13 Feb. 1764 by WILLIAM HOPTON,
Register.

Book A-3, p. 588   GEORGE INGLIS, merchant, of Charleston, &
12 Oct. 1762   CLAUDIA, his wife, to CHARLES ELLIOTT, gentle-
Release   man, of St. Pauls Parish, for L 1000 currency,
                      part of a lot in Charleston, bounding W on
Bedons Alley; S on part smae lot belonging to THOMAS ELLIOTT, father of
CHARLES; E on a house & part same lot formerly belonging to STEPHEN
ELLIOTT (now in possession of CHOLMONDELAY DERING & ELIZABETH his wife);
N on a house & lot belonging to MRS. IOOR; being 26 ft. by 158-1/2 ft.
Witnesses: JOSEPH YOUNG, ALEXANDER INGLIS. Proved by INGLIS 6 Oct. 1763
before JAMES PARSONS, J.P. Recorded 13 Feb. 1764 by WILLIAM HOPTON, Reg-
ister.

Book A-3, p. 591   CHARLES ELLIOTT, planter, of St. Pauls Parish,
21 & 22 Oct. 1763   Colleton Co., to ELIAS VANDERHORST, gentleman,
L & R   of Charleston, for L 5200 currency, 850 a. in
                      Colleton Co., bounding N on Ashepoo River; S
on Chehaw River; E on St. Helena Sound; W on Witchaw Creek. Witnesses:
CHAMPERNOUN WILLIAMSON, JOSHUA WARD. Proved by WARD 8 Dec. 1763 before
WILLIAM BURROWS, J.P. Recorded 13 Feb. 1764 by WILLIAM HOPTON, Register.

Book A-3, p. 600   ELIAS VANDERHORST, gentleman, of Charleston, &
22 & 23 Dec. 1763   ELIZABETH RAVEN VANDERHORST, his wife, to
L & R   THOMAS HUTCHINSON, ESQ., of Chehaw, for L 5000
                      currency, 850 a. in Colleton Co., bounding N
on Ashepoo River; S on Chehaw River; E on St. Helena Sound; W on Witchaw
Creek. Witnesses: MARY COOPER, JOSHUA WARD. Proved by WARD 9 Feb. 1764
before WILLIAM BURROWS, J.P. Recorded 14 Feb. 1764 by WILLIAM HOPTON,

Register.

Book A-3, p. 608   DANIELY DOYLEY, P.M., to JOSEPH ALLSTON,
7 Dec. 1762   planter, for Ł 1200 currency, 2 tracts on Wac-
Sale   camaw Neck in Prince George Parish, 1 of 300
                          a. granted by Gov. JAMES GLEN 2 Jan. 1754,
bounding E on the seashore; W on vacant land; N & S on heirs of CAPT.
GEORGE SMITH; 1 of 700 a. purchased from ARCHER SMITH by L & R dated 15 &
16 Nov. 1757; bounding E on marsh of sea; W on Waccamaw River; N on vacant land; S on CAPT. NEVE. Whereas JOSEPH PRINCE, planter, of Prince
George Parish, Craven Co., owned said 2 tracts, which he mortgaged to
ARCHER SMITH for Ł 437:10:0; & whereas GEORGE SMITH & ARCHER SMITH, ex-
ecutors of will of ARCHER SMITH, obtained a judgment against SAMUEL
BRAILSFORD, administrator of estate of JOSEPH PRINCE, & a writ of fieri
facias directed the P.M. to obtain the amount of the judgment & costs
from PRINCE'S estate; now DOYLEY sells the 1000 a. at public auction to
ALLSTON. Witnesses: JOHN CHAPMAN, JOHN FORBES, JR. Proved by FORBES 10
Feb. 1764 before WILLIAM BURROWS, J.P. Recorded 15 Feb. 1764 by WILLIAM
HOPTON, Register.

Book A-3, p. 614   WILLIAM HOWELL, planter, of Craven Co., of 1st
3 Feb. 1764   part; ROBERT HOWELL, of 2nd part; MALACHI HO-
Release   WELL, of 3rd part; GRACY HOWELL of 4th part.
                          Whereas THOMAS HOWELL, planter, father of all
said parties, by will dated 13 Mar. 1760, devised to his sons, ROBERT &
MALACHI, & to his daughter, GRACY, several tracts of land, but through a
mistake the lands were not devised to them "in fee" as intended; & whereas THOMAS had an eldest son, named THOMAS, who has since died intestate,
so that WILLIAM, now eldest brother, is heir-at-law to THOMAS the younger, & entitled to a reversion in the land given ROBERT & GRACY after
their deaths; & whereas WILLIAM desires to carry out his father's inten-
tion; now he confirms to ROBERT the plantations called The Hill & Hart-
field, in Craven Co.; & confirms to MALACHI the plantation called "the
Plantation up the Path" where their father lived; & to GRACY "a plantation in the Savannah near Gills Creek." Witnesses: WILLIAM GLEN, THOMAS
HEYWARD. Proved by GLEN, merchant, of Charleston, 11 Feb. 1764, before
ROBERT BRISBANE, J.P. Recorded 17 Feb. 1764 by WILLIAM HOPTON, Register.

Book A-3, p. 619   JOHN MEEK, baker, to THOMAS BUCKLE, merchant,
15 & 16 Feb. 1764   both of Charleston, as security on bond of
L & R by Mortgage   even date in penal sum of Ł 5860 for payment
                          of Ł 2930 currency, with interest, on 16 Aug.
1765; part of a lot in Charleston, bounding E 49 ft. on King Street; W on
FREDERICK GRIMKE; N 153 ft. on THOMAS DRAYTON; S on JOHN RATTRAY & RALPH
IZARD. Witnesses: HUGH RUTLEDGE, JOHN SCOTT. Proved by SCOTT 16 Feb.
1764 before JOHN REMINGTON, J.P. Recorded 20 Feb. 1764 by WILLIAM HOP-
TON, Register. Mortgage satisfied 30 July 1773. Witness: WILLIAM RUGE-
LEY.

Book A-3, p. 625   WILLIAM JONES, planter, of Craven Co., & MARY
23 Dec. 1752   his wife, to JOHN STUART, merchant, of Berke-
Release   ley Co., for Ł 400:3:9 currency, 2 tracts; 1
                          of 309 a. in the Welch Tract, granted by Gov.
JAMES GLEN on 2 Jan. 1747 to WILLIAM JONES, bounding NW on PAUL TRAPIER;
SE on EVAN VAUGHAN; as by plat; the other of 141 a. at Pine Bluff in the
Welch tract granted 19 Dec. 1752 by Gov. JAMES GLEN to WILLIAM JONES;
bounding NE by Peedee; other sides on vacant land. Witnesses: JAMES
MICHIE, JOHN TROUP, HOWELL JAMES, WILLIAM JAMES, JR. Proved 20 Jan. 1753
by HOWELL JAMES before WILLIAM JAMES. Recorded 21 Feb. 1764 by WILLIAM
HOPTON, Register.

Book A-3, p. 635   ISAAC LESESNE & DANIEL LESESNE, brothers, of
19 Oct. 1763   St. Thomas Parish, Berkeley Co., to JAMES
Feoffment   BOURDEAUX, planter, of same Parish, for Ł 700
                          currency, 380 a. in said Parish, bounding N on
SARAH JOHNSON & on LESESNE'S land (formerly ANDREW DEVEAUX); other sides
on parts of 2 tracts, 1 of 640 a., the other of 365 a., total 1005 a.,
out of which the 380 a. were taken; as by plat annexed to bill of sale,
31 Jan. 1723 from PETER BREMAR, son of SOLOMON BREMAR to whom the land
was granted, to DANIEL TRESVANT. Witnesses: GEORGE SMITH, JR., JOHN

WIGFALL. Proved by WIGFALL 4 Feb. 1764 before BENJAMIN SIMONS, J.P. Recorded 23 Feb. 1764 by WILLIAM HOPTON, Register.

Book A-3, p. 640
7 & 8 Feb. 1764
L & R

DANIEL MCGREGOR, planter, of St. James Santee Parish, Craven Co., eldest son & heir of DANIEL MCGREGOR, planter; & PHOEBE his wife; to SAMPSON NEYLE, planter, of Charleston, for L 4000 currency, 550 a. in Craven Co., part of 2 tracts of 500 a. each, granted DANIEL MCGREGOR the father by the Lords Proprs. on 4 May 1715; bounding N on Santee River; SE & S on Washo Creek & SAMPSON NEYLE; W on SAMPSON NEYLE. Witnesses: JOSEPH BRAILSFORD, JOHN BREMAR. Proved by BREMAR 18 Feb. 1764 before EGERTON LEIGH, J.P. Recorded 24 Feb. 1764 by WILLIAM HOPTON, Register. Plat showing boundary on lands of Washo Creek; SAMPSON NEYLE (formerly CLEEVE); JONAH COLLINS (formerly DANIEL MCGREGOR); RICHARD WITHERS (formerly DANIEL MCGREGOR); & Santee River.

Book A-3, p. 648
23 Aug. 1759
Release

THOMAS BROUGHTON, ESQ., of Berkeley Co., eldest son & surviving executor of will of ANDREW BROUGHTON, of Seaton, in St. Johns Parish, Berkeley Co., having taken possession of his father's plantation, called Seaton, containing 1500 a.; his mother, HANNAH BROUGHTON (formerly HANNAH GUERARD) having recently died; & his next youngest brother, ANDREW BROUGHTON, planter, of Berkeley Co., having (with the consent of THOMAS) taken possession of his father's other plantation, called Stafford (?) in Berkeley Co., containing 1046 a., being made up of several tracts according to agreement dated 7 Sept. 1724 between his grandfather, THOMAS BROUGHTON the elder & his grandmother, HANNAH GUERARD the elder, widow, upon the contract of marriage intended between ANDREW BROUGHTON the elder (the father) & HANNAH GUERARD the younger, which took effect soon afterP now THOMAS releases to his brother, ANDREW, all claim to Statford (?). Witnesses: PETER BROUGHTON, ANN BROUGHTON. Proved by PETER on 22 Jan. 1762 before JACOB MOTTE, J.P. Recorded 24 Feb. 1764 by WILLIAM HOPTON, Register.

Book A-3, p. 651
22 & 23 May 1759
L & R

WILLIAM VANDERHORST, gentleman, of Christ Church Parish, & MARGARET his wife, to WILLIAM HOPTON, gentleman, of Charleston, for L 4150 SC money, 2 adjoining tracts of 620 a. & 460 a., English measure, total 1080 a. in Christ Church Parish, on SE side Wando River, bounding N & NW on the river; NE on a creek; SE on said creek; S on WILLIAM CLEILAND (formerly THOMAS LYNCH). Whereas on 6 Nov. 1704 Gov. NATHANIEL JOHNSON granted 620 a., English measure, to THOMAS CARY; who sold to GEORGE LOGAN, the eldest; who in 1719 devised the land to his eldest son & heir GEORGE LOGAN, SR.; who, with his wife MARTHA, by L & R dated 20 & 21 Feb. 1739 sold to LIONEL CHALMERS; who with MARTHA his wife, by L & R dated 4 & 5 Mar. 1746, reconveyed to GEORGE LOGAN, SR.; who on 22 Jan. 1742 appointed his wife, MARTHA his attorney with authority to sell his land in SC; by L & R dated 1 & 2 Dec. 1749, she sold to GEORGE LOGAN, JR.; who with his wife ELIZABETH, (also GEORGE LOGAN, SR., & MARTHA his wife; & LIONEL CHALMERS & MARTHA his wife) by L & R dated 17 & 18 Dec. 1753 sold to WILLIAM VANDERHORST (Book S.S. p. 200-207) the 620 a., then bounding W & N on Wando River; E on FRANCIS GRACIA & vacant land; S on THOMAS LYNCH; & whereas WILLIAM, Earl of Craven, Palatine, on 11 May 1699, by the Hon. JOSEPH BLAKE, granted FRANCIS GRACIA 460 a., English measure, bounding N & NW on Wando River; NE & SE on a creek; W & SW on vacant land; & whereas FRANCIS GRACIA & ELIZABETH his wife on 18 Oct. 1708 sold the 460 a. to GEORGE LOGAN; who by will dated 18 Mar. 1719 bequeathed to his son PATRICK LOGAN (but in case of PATRICK'S death, then to daughter HELEN); & whereas PATRICK died without issue, but by will dated 18 Oct. 1726, bequeathed the residue of his real & personal estate to his niece, MARTHA LOGAN, JR., (now MARTHA CHALMERS), daughter of MARTHA LOGAN; & whereas doubts arose as to the validity of the will of GEORGE LOGAN, grandfather of MARTHA CHALMERS (as to whether it was an absolute devise of the fee simple to PATRICK or only as executory devise, with the remainder to testator's daughter HELEN contingent upon PATRICK'S dying without issue; & consequently whether PATRICK had power to devise to niece MARTHA LOGAN) & to secure the premises to MARTHA the said HELEN (HELEN DANIEL) with her husband ROBERT DANIEL, by L & R dated 31 Jan. & 1 Feb. 1727 conveyed to THOMAS COOPER of Charleston; who by L & R dated 1 & 2 Mar. 1727 for L 500 currency, conveyed to MARTHA

214

LOGAN, spinster (MARTHA CHALMERS), eldest daughter of GEORGE LOGAN; & whereas LIONEL CHALMERS, chirurgeon, & MARTHA (MARTHA LOGAN, niece & devisee of PATRICK LOGAN) his wife, by L & R dated 21 & 22 Jan. 1747 conveyed to ALEXANDER PERONNEAU, merchant, of Charleston, (Book E.E. p. 154-160); who with his wife MARGARET, by L & R dated 30 & 31 Aug. 1757 conveyed the 460 a. to WILLIAM VANDERHORST; now he sells both tracts to HOPTON. Witnesses: JOHN MOORE, ARNULDUS VANDERHORST. Proved by VANDERHORST 25 Feb. 1764 before BENJAMIN SMITH, J.P. Recorded 28 Feb. 1764 by WILLIAM HOPTON, Register. Entered in Auditors Book F. 6 p. 85 & 86 on 1 May 1762 by RICHARD LAMBTON, Dep. Aud.

Book A-3, p. 674
22 Sept. 1760
Sale

DANIEL DOYLEY, P.M., to SAMPSON NEYLE, merchant, of Charleston, at public auction, for L 2472:7:6 currency, 3 plantations, total 1735 a. Whereas on 1 July 1760 a writ of fieri facias was issued by JACOB MOTTE for levying the sum of L 9378:11:4 currency & costs recovered against JOHN BURN, administrator of the goods of CHARLES MAYNE, & the P.M. seized 440 a. in Craven Co., bounding NW on Warhaw Creek; N on Santee River; E & S on Alligator marsh; W on JOHN BENNETT; also 795 a. of marsh land in Craven Co., N of said 440 a., bounding W on marsh of JOHN ATCHISON; S on Alligator Swamp; with several buildings thereon; also 500 a. bounding N on Wasoo Creek; W on COL. THOMAS LYNCH & PHILIP CHIVIES; other sides on vacant land; total 1735 a.; now DOYLE sells to NEYLE. Witnesses: WILLIAM GIBBES, JOHN NEYLE. Proved by NEYLE 27 Feb. 1764 before ROBERT RIVERS, J.P. Entered in Auditor's Office in Bk. F-6, p. 113, on 11 June 1762 by RICHARD LAMBTON, Dep. Aud. Recorded 1 Mar. 1764 by WILLIAM HOPTON, Register.

Book A-3, p. 677
27 & 28 Jan. 1758
L & R

THOMAS FULLER, planter, of Berkeley Co., (only son of RICHARD FULLER, planter, eldest son & heir of WILLIAM FULLER the elder, planter) & LYDIA his wife, to SARAH SIMPSON, widow, of Charleston, for L 5750 currency, 550 a., on S side Ashley River, in St. Andrews Parish, being the N part of 1030 a. & 100 a. (1130 a.); bounding E & S on JOHN CATTELL, son of JOHN CATTELL; N & NE on marsh of Ashley River & on the high road & on BENJAMIN CATTELL; NW & SW on JOHN ANGIER & on high road; S on BENJAMIN FULLER. Whereas WILLIAM FULLER the elder owned 2 plantations, 1 of 1030 a. granted 11 May 1705 by Gov. NATHANIEL JOHNSON; 1 of 100 a. granted to ABRAHAM SMITH, who conveyed to WILLIAM FULLER; & whereas WILLIAM FULLER by will dated 30 Aug. 1731 bequeathed to his son RICHARD 500 a. on which he dwelt, also 50 a. out of the Back Land on S end of son RICHARDS land; & whereas RICHARD FULLER by will dated 13 May 1749 the residue of his real & personal estate, including the 550 a. to his son THOMAS FULLER; now THOMAS sells the 550 a. to SARAH SIMPSON. Witnesses: JOSEPH WILLIAMS, SAMUEL WEST, ANTHONY MCCULLOCH, ELIZABETH LANDER, THOMAS LAMBOLL. Proved by MCCULLOCH 27 Feb. 1764 before GEORGE JOHNSTON, J.P. Recorded 1 Mar. 1764 by WILLIAM HOPTON, Register.

Book A-3, p. 691
23 & 24 Feb. 1763
L & R

JAMES MATHEWES, planter, & CHARLOTTE his wife, to WILLIAM MATHEWES, planter, both of Johns Island, Colleton Co., for L 5500 currency, 1136 a. on Johns Island, bounding N on GEORGE GOFF, GEORGE HEXT, & THOMAS HEXT; E on GEORGE HEXT & MRS. COLL; S & SE on WILLIAM WEATHERLY, MRS. COLL, SOLOMON FREER, ELIZABETH ROBERTS & GEORGE GOFF; W on JAMES WITTER, GEORGE GOFF, Bohick River, & GEORGE HEXT. Whereas JAMES MATHEWES, merchant, of Charleston, by will dated 30 June, 1745 gave said 1136 a. to his 2 sons JAMES & JOHN; & JOHN, by L & R dated 28 & 29 Jan. 1763 sold his share to JAMES; now JAMES sells the whole to WILLIAM MATHEWES. Witnesses: JOSEPH STANYARNE, GEORGE MATHEWES. Proved by MATHEWES 25 Feb. 1764 before WILLIAM MASSEY, J.P. Recorded 3 Mar. 1764 by WILLIAM HOPTON, Register.

Book A-3, p. 698
25 & 26 Mar. 1762
L & R

WILLIAM (his mark) CAMELL, to SARAH SEABRIGHT, both of Berkeley Co., for L 180 currency, 200 a. in Amelia Township, Berkeley Co., on SW side Santee River, granted by Gov. JAMES GLEN on 24 Nov. 1737 to WILLIAM CAMELL, bounding SE on vacant land & MARY HAGGETT; other sides on vacant land; as by plat. Witnesses: WILLIAM SCOTT, JOHN HOBBS. Proved by SCOTT 1 Mar. 1764 before MOSES THOMSON, J.P. Recorded 6 Mar. 1764 by WILLIAM HOPTON, Register.

Book A-3, p. 704   JOHN COCHRAN, planter, of Colleton Co., to
26 Nov. 1737   ALEXANDER KILPATRICK, Indian trader, of Craven
Release   Co., for ₺ 200 SC money, 60 a. in Berkeley
                         Co., bounding N on JOHN HENTIE & vacant land;
E on RICHARD LAMBTON; S on RICHARD LAMBTON & vacant land; W on vacant
land & JOHN HENTIE; as by plat; which 60 a. were granted 30 Sept. 1736 by
Lt. Gov. THOMAS BROUGHTON to JOHN COCHRAN. Witnesses: BENJAMIN DEDCOTT,
RICHARD JOHNSTON. Proved by DEDCOTT 5 Dec. 1737 before GEORGE HAIG, J.P.
Recorded 8 Mar. 1764 by WILLIAM HOPTON, Register.

Book A-3, p. 708   ELIZABETH MOULTRIE, of Charleston, (wife of
17 & 18 Feb. 1764   DR. JOHN MOULTRIE, physician, & widow of JAMES
L & R   MATHEWES, merchant); JAMES MATHEWES (son of
                         said JAMES MATHEWES, deceased); planter, of
Colleton Co., & CHARLOTTE his wife; JOHN MATHEWES (also son of said JAMES
MATHEWES, deceased); gentleman, of Charleston; & ISAAC GODIN, ESQ., of
St. James Goose Creek, & his wife (daughter of said JAMES MATHEWES, de-
ceased); of 1st part; to WILLIAM MATHEWES, planter, of St. Johns Parish,
Colleton Co.; for ₺ 100 currency; part of lot #24 in Tradd Street,
Charleston, bounding 28 ft. on Tradd Street & 16 ft. deep, being part of
a lot 16 ft. wide 120 ft. deep, formerly belonging to DR. BRISBANE; who
with his wife MARGARET sold to JAMES MATHEWES by L & R dated 22 & 23 Mar.
1741; bounding W on WILLIAM MOULTRIE; E on MOSES AUDIBERT; N on JOSEPH
NICHOLSON; S on WILLIAM MATHEWES, party hereto. Witnesses: LAMBERT LANCE,
JAMES COURTONNE. Proved by COURTONNE 3 Mar. 1764 before JOHN TROUP, J.P.
Recorded 9 Mar. 1764 by WILLIAM HOPTON, Register.

Book A-3, p. 715   HENRIETTA (her mark) CAMPBELL, widow, & JOHN
26 & 27 Sept. 1763   (his mark) CAMPBELL, her only son, to MARGARET
L & R   NORDON, shop keeper, all of Charleston, for
                         ₺ 35 currency, 250 a. in Amelia Township,
Berkeley Co., bounding NW on RICHARD JACKSON; SW on MILES JACKSON & va-
cant land; other sides on vacant land. Witnesses: MARK ANTHONY BESSELLEU,
RICHARD RIDEOUT. Proved by BESSELLEU, 5 Mar. 1764 before CHARLES WOOD-
MASON, J.P. Recorded 9 Mar. 1764 by WILLIAM HOPTON, Register.

Book A-3, p. 723   JOHN RATTRAY, ESQ., executor, & MARY CRAWFORD
28 & 29 July 1760   & HELEN CRAWFORD, executrixes, of will of DAN-
L & R   IEL CRAWFORD, of Charleston, to DANIEL LEGARE,
                         planter, of Christ Church Parish, for ₺ 2000
currency, 2 adjoining lots containing 2 a., 4 perches, marked V & W in
the plat of Ansonborough, bounding S on lot X; W on lot II; N on GEORGE
Street; E on Anson Street; with right of passage through convenient
streets & a landing place on the creek of Cooper River. Whereas GEORGE,
Lord Anson, by his attorney BENJAMIN WHITAKER on 25 May 1745 sold to DAN-
IEL CRAWFORD said 2 lots, V & W, as by plan certified & recorded in Sur.
Gen.'s office 14 Feb. 1744, recorded in registers office 21 Aug. 1745; &
CRAWFORD by will dated 30 May 1760 ordered his executors to sell his real
estate in order to make an equal division; & appointed his wife, MARY, &
his daughter, HELEN, his executrixes, & his friend JOHN RATTRAY, execu-
tor; now they sell the lots to LEGARE. Witnesses: JOHN GOVAN, BENJAMIN
GUERARD. Proved by GUERARD 25 May 1761 before JAMES GRINDLAY, J.P. Recorded 12 Mar. 1764 by WILLIAM HOPTON, Register.

Book A-3, p. 731   JAMES MOORE, planter, to WILLIAM COACHMAN,
21 & 22 Nov. 1762   planter, both of Berkeley Co., for ₺ 3000 cur-
L & R   rency, 350 a. in St. Bartholomews Parish, Col-
                         leton Co., granted 12 Jan. 1737 by WILLIAM
BULL, the elder, to JOHN LEAVY; who by L & R dated 19 June 1739 sold to
JOHN FABIAN the younger; who devised to his 2 brothers, JOSEPH & JONATHAN;
who on 14 Sept. 1752 sold to JAMES MOORE; bounding NW on RICHARD (ISA-
BELLE ?) IRELAND; NE on THOMAS TUCKER & JOHN COOK; S & SE on JOSEPH AN-
DREWS & JOHN COOK; SW on DANIEL HENDRICK; as by plat of grant; also 200
a. in Colleton Co., granted 29 Mar. 1700 by the Lords Proprs., to RICHARD
IRELAND; bounding SW on freshes of Edisto River; NE on said river; NW on
GEORGE TUCKER; S & SW on vacant land; as by plat of grant; which 200 a.
belonged to PAUL COLE, SUSANNAH COLE, JOSEPH SCOTT, ELEANOR SCOTT, &
RICHARD HALY; who conveyed to JOHN BURNHAM; who with ELIZABETH his wife
by L & R dated 5 & 6 Mar. 1732 sold to ROBERT (BURNHAM) BROOMHEAD; & later sold by 1 HEZEKIAH ROSE & ELIZABETH, his wife, & REBECCA HILL

216

(formerly widow of ROBERT BROOMHEAD), by L & R dated 18 & 19 July 1754 to
JAMES MOORE. Witnesses: BENJAMIN COACHMAN, JAMES COACHMAN. Proved by
JAMES COACHMAN 30 Aug. 1763 before PETER TAYLOR, J.P. Recorded 20 Mar.
1764 by WILLIAM HOPTON, Register.

Book A-3, p. 745
14 & 15 Apr. 1743
L & R

WILLIAM ELLIOTT, of Berkeley Co., (eldest
brother & heir & 1 of the executors of will of
JOSEPH ELLIOTT, of St. Andrews Parish, Berkeley Co.); THOMAS FARR, planter, of Charleston;
& THOMAS ELLIOTT, planter, of Colleton, the other 2 executors; of 1st
part; to JOHN SHEPPARD, gentleman, of Charleston; for Ł 950 currency,
950 a. on St. Helena Island, in Granville Co., bounding N on St. Helena
River; W on Dawton Creek; S & E on Nairnes Creek; as by plat. Whereas
JOHN STUART & MARY his wife, of Colleton Co., owned said 950 a., which
on 26 June 1730 they sold to JOSEPH ELLIOTT; who by will dated 11 Feb.
1739 ordered his real & personal estate sold, & appointed WILLIAM ELLIOTT,
THOMAS FARR, & THOMAS ELLIOTT, his executors; now they sell the tract to
SHEPPARD. Witnesses: JOSEPH SHUTE, DAVID CRAWFORD, THOMAS LAMBOLL.
Proved by LAMBOLL 5 Mar. 1764 before JAMES GRINDLAY, J.P. Recorded 20
Mar. 1764 by WILLIAM HOPTON, Register.

DEEDS BOOK "B-3"
MARCH 1764 - AUGUST 1764

Book B-3, p. 1
25 & 26 Nov. 1762
L & R

THOMAS FARR the elder, in St. Pauls Parish, &
PHEBE his wife, to JOSEPH JENKINS, the elder,
planter, of St. Helena Parish, for Ł 2559:11:3
currency, 405-1/4 a., part of 950 a., on St.
Helena Island, Granville Co., naturally cut off from the remainder by a
marsh, bounding on Dawton Creek & on a tract of 244-3/4 a., purchased
from said THOMAS FARR by JOHN EVANS of St. Helena Parish, also part of
the 950 a. originally granted JOHN STEWART; other sides on marsh land;
the 950 a. bounding N on St. Helena River; W on Dawton Creek; S & E on
Nairne's Creek; as by plat. Witnesses: NATHANIEL DEAN, JOSEPH SMITH,
JOHN EVANS. Proved by EVANS 29 Feb. 1764 before EGERTON LEIGH, J.P. Recorded 23 Mar. 1764 by WILLIAM HOPTON, Register.

Book B-3, p. 9
15 & 16 Apr. 1743
L & R

JOHN SHEPPARD, gentleman, of Berkeley Co., to
THOMAS FARR, planter, of Charleston, for Ł 955
currency, 950 a., lately belonging to JOSEPH
ELLIOTT, planter, of St. Andrews Parish,
Berkeley Co., deceased, on St. Helena Island, Granville Co., bounding N
on wt. Helena River; W on Dawton Creek; as by plat. Whereas JOSEPH
ELLIOTT by will dated 11 Feb. 1739 ordered his plantation sold, & appointed his brother WILLIAM ELLIOTT; his brother-in-law THOMAS FARR; & his
kinsman THOMAS ELLIOTT; his executors; & his executors by L & R dated 14
& 15 Apr. 1743 sold the tract to JOHN SHEPPARD; now he sells FARR. Witnesses: JOSEPH SHUTE, DAVID CRAWFORD, THOMAS LAMBOLL. Proved by LAMBOLL
5 Mar. 1764 before JAMES GRINDLAY, J.P. Recorded 23 Mar. 1764 by WILLIAM
HOPTON, Register.

Book B-3, p. 17
25 & 26 Nov. 1762
L & R

THOMAS FARR, the elder, planter, of St. Pauls
Parish, & PHEBE his wife, to JOHN EVANS, plant-
er, of St. Helena Parish, for Ł 3440:8:9 cur-
rency, 544-3/4 a., part of 950 a. (see p. 1-9);
on St. Helena Island, Granville Co., bounding N on St. Helena River; W on
Dawton Creek; E & S on Nairnes Creek. Witnesses: NATHANIEL DEAN, JOSEPH
SMITH, JOSEPH JENKINS. Proved by JENKINS 29 Feb. 1764 before EGERTON
LEIGH, J.P. Recorded 23 Mar. 1764 by WILLIAM HOPTON, Register.

Book B-3, p. 25
1 & 2 Feb. 1764
L & R

DR. THOMAS HONOUR, physician, of St. Andrews
Parish, & MARY his wife (formerly wife of SAM-
UEL STOCKS); & WILLIAM BOONE, ESQ., of Johns
Island, & MARTHA his wife (MARY & MARTHA being
lately called MARY & MARTHA WELSBY, only children of WILLIAM WELSBY,
planter, of Johns Island); to JANE BOONE, gentlewoman, of Charleston for
Ł 3000 currency, 2 tracts; 1 of 342 a. on Johns Island on which WELSBY
lived for aobut 20 years, bounding W on JOHN MARSHALL, deceased; S on

MELLER ST. JOHN, deceased; E on JOSEPH STANYARNE; N on JOHN LADSON, deceased; the other of 400 a. in Colleton Co., bounding as by plat certified by STEPHEN BULL, Sur., & annexed to grant from Lords Proprs. to SAMUEL DAVIS dated 28 Aug. 1701. Whereas WELSBY'S will was witnessed by JOSEPH PHIPPS, BENJAMIN WEATHERLY, & 1 SAMUEL STOCKS, planter, deceased, of Wadmalaw; & whereas STOCKS was then husband of MARY HONOUR & greatly interested in testator's estate, whereby the will became void, & the lands passed to MARY & MARTHA as only children of their father; now MARY & MARTHA & their respective husbands sell the 2 tracts to JANE BOONE. Witnesses: JOHN TROUP, DANIEL LEGARE, JR. Proved by LEGARE 19 Mar. 1764 before WILLIAM MAXWELL, J.P. Recorded 27 Mar. 1764 by FENWICKE BULL, Register.

Book B-3, p. 32
10 & 11 Feb. 1764
L & R
JANE BOONE, gentlewoman, of Charleston, to JOSEPH ASH, of Colleton Co., for £ 1500 currency, 400 a. in Colleton Co., formerly belonging to WILLIAM WELSBY (see p. 25). Witnesses: CALEB LLOYD, DANIEL LEGARE, JR., CHRISTOPHER SIMPSON. Proved by LEGARE before WILLIAM MAXWELL, J.P. Recorded 30 Mar. 1764 by FENWICKE BULL, Register.

Book B-3, p. 37
14 Jan. 1764
L & R
THOMAS TIMMONS, SR., planter, of St. Bartholomews Parish, Colleton Co., & MARY (her mark) TIMMONS, to THOMAS CRAWFORD, planter, of Prince William Parish, Granville Co., for £ 50 currency, 104 a. on Timmons's Swamp, in St. Bartholomews Parish, known as Plot #3; bounding E on JOHN TIMMONS; S on THOMAS RATCLIFF; W on THOMAS TIMMONS; N on MARY ANN TIMMONS. Witnesses: ELIJAH HARTEE, WILLIAM DAY. Before ROBERT BRISBANE, J.P. Recorded 2 Apr. 1764 by FENWICKE BULL, Register.

Book B-3, p. 43
29 Feb. 1764
L & R
THOMAS CRAWFORD, planter, & MARY CRAWFORD, to DR. WILLIAM DAY, both of St. Bartholomew's Parish, Colleton Co., for £ 600 currency, 104 a., on Timmons's Swamp in said Parish, known as Plot #3, bounding E on JOHN TIMMONS; S on THOMAS RADCLIFFE; W on THOMAS TIMMONS; N on MARY ANNE TIMMONS. Witnesses: ELIJAH HARTEE, JACOB ZAHLER. Before ROBERT BRISBANE, J.P. Recorded 4 Apr. 1764 by FENWICKE BULL, Register.

Book B-3, p. 49
25 Feb. 1764
Mortgage
JAMES MATHEWES, gentleman, of Johns Island to RAWLINS LOWNDES, ESQ., of Charleston, for £ 1251 currency, several plantations of 220 a., 54 a., & 100 a.; the 220 a. & 54 a., being at Bear Swamp, Berkeley Co., making 1 plantation of 274 a., bounding N on NATHANIEL FULLER (formerly WILLIAM FULLER); E on THOMAS LADSON, JR. (formerly NATHANIEL NICHOLS); W on JOHN AUGER (formerly FRANCIS LADSON); S on THOMAS DRAYTON; the 100 a. being part of 250 a. in St. Andrews Parish, Berkeley Co., bounding N on FRANCIS LADSON; E on CHARLES WEST; S & W on STEPHEN DRAYTON. Date of redemption: 25 Feb. 1765. Witnesses: BENJAMIN YARNOLD, SIMON BARWICK. Before ALEXANDER FRASER, J.P. Recorded 5 Apr. 1764 by FENWICKE BULL, Register.

Book B-3, p. 56
8 July 1761
Power of Attorney
Whereas WILLIAM CHAMBERS, of Johns Island, SC, died without issue, leaving as his only next of kin, JOHN (his mark) CHAMBERS (his natural & lawful brother), former, of Tullynisky, in Parish of Carvaghy, Co. of Down, Ireland, & ELIZABETH (her mark) THOMPSON, spinster, of Aghandurevaren, of Co. of Down; now JOHN & ELIZABETH appoint JOHN REA, merchant, of Augusta, SC, & DAVID REA, malster & farmer, of Parish of Drumbo, Co. of Down, their attorneys, to handle any estate left by WILLIAM CHAMBERS. Signed at Belfast, Co. of Antrim, before JAMES HAMILTON, Sovereign of Borough of Belfast, & J.P. Witnesses: JAMES HAMILTON, ROBERT REA, JAMES HERRAN, HENRY JOY (N.P.). Recorded 5 Apr. 1764 by FENWICKE BULL, J.P. On 8 July 1761 WILLIAM THOMPSON, 60, weaver, of Aghandurevarren, Co. of Down, testified before JAMES HAMILTON, that his son, JAMES THOMPSON, was lawfull husband of JANE CHAMBERS, daughter of ALEXANDER CHAMBERS & ELEANOR CHRISTY, his wife, late of Tullendony, Co. of Down, & that JAMES & JANE had 1 daughter called ELIZABETH; that JANE died in City of Dublin; & that ELIZABETH (his granddaughter) was

single, & the niece of WILLIAM CHAMBERS. Witness: HENRY JOY, Not. Pub. of Belfast. Recorded 5 Apr. 1764 by FENWICKE BULL, J.P. On 31 Dec. 1761 ROBERT REA acknowledged above signature before CHARLES PINCKNEY, J.P., of Charleston, SC.

Book B-3, p. 60 JOHN CHAMBERS, farmer, of Tullynisky, Parish
6 & 7 Mar. 1764 of Garvaghy, Co. of Down, Ireland, (eldest
L & R brother & heir of WILLIAM CHAMBERS, planter, of Johns Island, SC), to DR. JAMES CARSON, of Johns Island, for Ł 1680 SC money, 600 a. called Bugby's Hole, on Wadmalaw Island, Colleton Co., SC, conveyed to WILLIAM CHAMBERS by JAMES MICHIE & MARTHA his wife on 4 Feb. 1743; bounding E on EBENEZER SIMMONS & ISAAC WAIGHT (formerly WILLIAM CHAMBERS & ABRAHAM WAIGHT); W on JAMES CARSON (formerly MRS. JONES); S on JOHN LADSON & the Presbyterian Meeting on Johns Island; N on Wadmalaw River; also 67 a., part of 92 a. granted JAMES MICHIE on 6 Mar. 1741, bounding N & E on ISAAC WAIGHT; S on estate of JOHN LADSON; W on the 600 a. Whereas WILLIAM CHAMBERS died intestate & his lands descended to his eldest brother, JOHN, who on 8 July 1761 appointed JOHN REA of Savannah, Georgia, (formerly of Augusta) & DAVID REA, malster & farmer, of Parish of Drumbo, Co. of Down, Ireland, his joint attorneys; & whereas DAVID REA died, now JOHN REA, as attorney, sells the said 2 tracts for JOHN CHAMBERS to DR. CARSON. Witnesses: PAUL TOWNSEND, JOHN GLEN, THOMAS HEYWARD. Before JAMES PARSONS, J.P. Recorded 6 Apr. 1764 by FENWICKE BULL, J.P.

Book B-3, p. 67 The Rt. Hon. GEORGE, Lord Anson, Baron of Sob-
8 & 9 Dec. 1761 erton, by his attorney, RICHARD LAMBTON, of
L & R Charleston, SC, to JERMYN WRIGHT, ESQ., of Granville Co., SC, for a bond & Ł 10 currency, a wharf with the adjoining marsh & high land east of village of Ansonburgh near Charleston & fronting E partly on land of SC Society (formerly the Shubrick's), which wharf & marsh & high land are the residue of lands mortgaged by JERMYN WRIGHT to said GEORGE, Lord Anson, on 11 May 1756 & not yet conveyed by LAMBTON to JOHN RATTRAY & WILLIAM ELLIS, attorneys for ANSON. Witnesses: JOHN HOLMES, THOMAS HEYWARD. Before GEORGE JOHNSTON, J.P. Recorded 7 Apr. 1764 by FENWICKE BULL, Register.

Book B-3, p. 71 THOMAS WRIGHT, ESQ., & MARY his wife of St.
21 & 22 Feb. 1764 James Goose Creek Parish, to JOHN DRAKE, gen-
L & R tleman, of Parish of St. George Dorchester, for Ł 2850 currency, severay tracts; 40 a. in St. James Santee Parish, Craven Co., on NW side Wambaw Creek; bounding W on TACITUS GAILLARD; N on ROBERT PRINGLE, as by plat on back of release from ROBERT PRINGLE to TACITUS GAILLARD dated 2 Feb. 1754; also 250 a. (half of 500 a. granted by King GEORGE II to JOHN GENDRON; who conveyed to JOHN BARNET; who conveyed to TACITUS GAILLARD; who conveyed to THOMAS WRIGHT) in Craven Co., bounding E on Wambaw Creek; W on THOMAS EVANS; S on MRS. MOULTRIE; N on TACITUS GAILLARD; also 450 a. St. James Santee Parish, bounding S on Wambaw Creek & JOHN BARNET; W & N on vacant land; E on ROBERT PRINGLE, according to plat on back of release from JOHN MAYRANT & ANNE his wife to TACITUS GAILLARD dated 2 Feb. 1754. Witnesses: ELIZABETH HARRAMOND, THOMAS GRIMBALL, JR. Before WILLIAM BURROWS, J.P. Recorded 10 Apr. 1764 by FENWICKE BULL, Register.

Book B-3, p. 80 JOHN (his mark) FRASHER, planter, & ELIZABETH
13 & 14 Jan. 1748 (her mark) his wife, of Craven Co., to JACOB
L & R PENNINGTON, blacksmith, for Ł 200 currency, 99 a. in Craven Co., in low grounds of Santee (Congree) River, opposite Saxegotha Township, granted 20 May 1747 by Gov. JAMES GLEN to JOHN FRASHER; bounding N on THOMAS WALLEXELLSON; W on JAMES DENLY & JACOB YOUNG; S & E on vacant land. Witnesses: ROGER PAGETT, ABRAHAM PENNINGTON, ISAAC (his mark) ARLEDG. Before ISAAC WILLCOCKS, J.P. Recorded 11 Apr. 1764 by FENWICKE BULL, Register.

Book B-3, p. 86 JOHN FAIRCHILD, & RACHEL, his wife, of Saxe-
7 & 8 Oct. 1755 gotha Township, to JACOB PENNINGTON, planter,
L & R of Indian Creek, for Ł 200 currency, 200 a. on NE side Santee River; other sides on vacant land. Witnesses: JOHN BONNETHEAU, WILLIAM STERLAND. Before WILLIAM SIMPSON, J.P. Recorded 12 Apr. 1764 by FENWICKE BULL, Register.

Book B-3, p. 91   JACOB PENNINGTON, blacksmith, & MARY his wife,
1 & 2 Mar. 1758   of Berkeley Co., to JOHN THOMAS, planter, of
L & R   Craven Co., for Ⱡ 150 currency, 99 a. in Cra-
                         ven Co., in low ground of Congree River,
bounding N on THOMAS WALLEXELSON; W on JAMES DENLY & JACOB YOUNG; S & E
on vacant land. Witnesses: BENJAMIN FARAR, JAMES (his mark) RUNELS,
ABRAHAM PENNINGTON. Before JOHN PEARSON, J.P. Recorded 12 Apr. 1764 by
FENWICKE BULL, Register.

Book B-3, p. 97   JACOB PENNINGTON, blacksmith, & MARY his wife,
1 & 2 Mar. 1758   of Berkeley Co., to JOHN THOMAS, planter, of
L & R   Craven Co., for Ⱡ 250 currency, 200 a. on NE
                         side Congaree River; other sides on vacant
land. Witnesses: BENJAMIN FARAR, JAMES (his mark) RUNELS, ABRAHAM PEN-
NINGTON. Before JOHN PEARSON, J.P. Recorded 15 Apr. 1764 by FENWICKE
BULL, Register.

Book B-3, p. 103   JOHN BAYLY, ESQ., of Ballinaclough, Co. of
19 & 20 June 1729   Tipperary, Ireland, by his attorney, ALEXANDER
L & R   TRENCH, merchant, of Charleston, SC, to JAMES
                         MCKEWN, planter, of Colleton Co., for Ⱡ 75
currency, 300 a. in Colleton Co., bounding N on THOMAS ELLIOTT; E on HEN-
RY TOOMER, MARTHA EMES & JOHN GODFREY; S on JONATHAN FITCH; W on RICHARD
TERRY. Whereas JOHN, Earl of Bath, & the Lords Proprs. on 16 Aug. 1698
created JOHN BAYLY (the father) a Landgrave & Cassique of SC, granting
him 48,000 a. in SC; & whereas his son, JOHN BAYLY, on 9 Nov. 1722 ap-
pointed ALEXANDER TRENCH, of SC, his attorney, with authority to sell all
the land for him, except 8000 a.; now TRENCH sells 1 tract to MEKEWN.
Witnesses: JOEL POINSET, RICHARD WIGG, HENRY NICHOLLS. On 15 Mar. 1764,
TRENCH & all the witnesses having been dead many years, ANN RODGERS,
ELISHA POINSET, & ROBERT WILLIAMS, all of Charleston, testified before
ROBERT WILLIAMS, J.R, J.P. as follows: ANN RODGERS, recognized the signa-
ture of TRENCH; ELISHA POINSET, son of JOEL, recognized his father's sig-
nature; ROBERT WILLIAMS, that of RICHARD WIGG. Entered in Auditor's
Office 22 May 1733. Recorded 14 Apr. 1764 by FENWICKE BULL, Register.

Book B-3, p. 111   ISAAC GOURDIN, planter, of St. Johns Parish,
22 & 23 Nov. 1757   Berkeley Co., to THEODORE GOURDIN, planter, of
L & R   Prince Frederick Parish, Craven Co., for Ⱡ 600
                         currency, 465 a. in Prince Frederick Parish,
bounding NW on MR. ALLEN; NE unknown; SE on MR. NEWMAN; SW on Santee River Swamp; which tract was granted LEWIS GOURDIN who devised to his son
ISAAC. Witnesses: PETER GOURDIN, MOSES BUTLER, STEPHEN (his mark) MID-
DLEWOOD. Before JOHN REMINGTON, J.P. Entered in Auditor's Office 2 Dec.
1758 in Book D-4, p. 235, by JOHN BASNETT, for Dep. Aud. Recorded 14
Apr. 1764 by FENWICKE BULL, Register.

Book B-3, p. 119   ABRAHAM MICHAU, planter, of Prince Frederick
17 & 18 July 1761   Parish, Craven Co., to WILLIAM ROBERT NEWMAN,
L & R   for Ⱡ 5 currency, 400 a. in said Parish,
                         bounding SE on SAMUEL NEWMAN; NW on THEODORE
GOURDIN; SW on Santee River Swamp; NE on vacant land. Witnesses: DANIEL
MICHAU, PAUL MICHAU, THEODORE GOURDIN. Before GEORGE JOHNSTON, J.P. Re-
corded 14 Apr. 1764 by FENWICKE BULL, Register.

Book B-3, p. 126   THOMAS TUCKER, mariner & master, & SARAH his
14 & 15 Mar. 1764   wife, to JOSIAH SMITH the younger, merchant,
L & R   all of Charleston, for Ⱡ 700 currency, the re-
                         maining N part of a lot in Charleston sold to
TUCKER by ISAAC HOLMES, merchant, & REBECCA his wife, by L & R dated 5 &
6 May 1763; the piece of land being near Broughtons Battery at White
Point, bounding W 33 ft. on Old Church (Meeting) Street; N 104 ft. 9 in.
on THOMAS TUCKER; E on JAMES BRISBANE; S on the part sold by TUCKER to
JOSIAH SMITH. Witnesses: GEORGE SMITH, WILLIAM MILLER. Before ROBERT
RIVERS, J.P. Recorded 14 Apr. 1764 by FENWICKE BULL, Register.

Book B-3, p. 135   WILLIAM WRAGG (only son & heir of SAMUEL
26 & 27 Dec. 1764   WRAGG) & MARY his wife, to SAMUEL WAINWRIGHT,
L & R   gentleman, all of Charleston, for Ⱡ 4500 cur-
                         rency, 762 a., being the SW part of the

remainder of his 2 inland plantations of 1680 a. & 1026 a. granted by the
Lords Proprs. 23 July 1711 & 23 Feb. 1712/13 to Landgrave ABEL KETELBEY;
afterwards sold by L & R dated 8 & 9 May 1735 by KELTELBY to SAMUEL
WRAGG; the 762 a. in Colleton Co., on SW side Ashley River, bounding NE
on WILLIAM WRAGG; SE on EDWARD PERRY & BERNARD ELLIOTT; S on BERNARD
ELLIOTT, JOSIAH WARING, & MR. BOSWOOD; SW & W on THOMAS FARR; N on WIL-
LIAM ELLIOTT. Witnesses: MARK MORRIS, THOMAS LAMBOLL. Before ROBERT
PRINGLE, J.P. Recorded 17 Apr. 1764 by FENWICKE BULL, Register.

Book B-3, p. 146   THOMAS ROSE, cooper, of Charleston, to THOMAS
25 Apr. 1763   LEGARÉ, factor, as security on bond in penal
Mortgage   sum of Ł 223:12:0 for payment of Ł 111:16:0
                     currency, on 25 Apr. 1764; pew #80 in St.
Michael's Church. Witnesses: WILLIAM BAKER, JAMES SCREVEN. Before JOHN
REMINGTON, J.P. Recorded 28 Apr. 1763 in Secretary's Book   page 16;
certified by GEORGE JOHNSTON. Recorded 17 Apr. 1764 by FENWICKE BULL,
Register.

Book B-3, p. 148   EBERHARD EHNEY, butcher, & CHRISTIANA, his
4 & 5 Apr. 1764   wife, to WILLIAM HOPTON, ESQ., executor of
Mortgage   will of DANIEL HUNT, all of Charleston, as se-
                     curity on bond of even date in penal sum of
Ł 4200 for payment of Ł 2100 currency, with interest, on 5 Apr. 1765;
part of lot #257 in St. Philips.Parish, Charleston, bounding E 28 ft. on
King Street; S 124 ft. on land leased by RICHARD BERESFORD, ESQ., to NA-
THAN CLEAVE; W on land leased to QUACCO MCGUIRE, a free Negro; N on BRUCE
(now in EHNEY'S possession). Witnesses: HUGH RUTLEDGE, JOHN SCOTT, JR.
Before J. RUTLEDGE, J.P. Recorded 18 Apr. 1764 by FENWICKE BULL, Regis-
ter. On 19 Feb. 1773 HOPTON declared mortgage paid. Witness: WILLIAM
RUGELEY.

Book B-3, p. 154   ANDREW HENDRIE & HUGH BURN, planters, of St.
18 Sept. 1763   Peters Parish, to DAVID GEROUD (GIROUD), SR.,
Release   planter, of Purisburgh, for Ł 700 currency,
                     200 a. on Savannah River, St. Peters Parish,
Purisburgh Township, granted 14 Dec. 1739 by Lt. Gov. WILLIAM BULL to
JEREMIAH REMOND, whose son & heir, JOHN LEWIS REMOND conveyed to HENDRIE
& BURN on 7 Aug. 1762, bounding N on SAMUEL MONTAGUE; W on land granted
JOHN GRANIER who conveyed to HENDRIE & BURN; S on HENRY LEWIS PATTONS; E
on vacant land. Witnesses: ABRAHAM VAUCHIER, FRANCIS VAUCHIER, ADRIAN
MAYER, JOHN BUCHE. Before DANIEL PEPPER, J.P. Recorded 18 Apr. 1764 by
FENWICKE BULL, Register. See Secretary's Book && fol. 74.

Book B-3, p. 158   JONATHAN BELTON, planter, of St. Peters Par-
9 Nov. 1763   ish, to DAVID GEROUD, planter, of Purisburgh,
Release   for Ł 700 SC money, 200 a. in Purisburgh Town-
                     ship, Granville Co., bounding S on JEREMIAH
REMOND; N on CHRISTOPHER RUIK; E on JOHN GRANCER; W on vacant land; which
200 a. were granted by GEORGE II on 16 Sept. 1738 to ANTHONY PAYN. Witnesses: ANDREW HENDRIE, DAVID VILLARD. Before ADRIAN MAYER, J.P. Recorded 19 Apr. 1764 by FENWICKE BULL, Register.

Book B-3, p. 162   The Rev. MR. JOHN JOACHIM ZUBLY, & ANNE his
30 Mar. 1764   wife, of Christ Church Parish, Georgia, to
Release   ADRIAN MAYER, of Purisburgh, SC, for Ł 12:12:0
                     currency, 1 a. lot #74 in Purisburgh, bounding
N on lot #73; W on lot #72; E & S on a street. Witnesses: JOHN LINDER,
GEORGE GARDNER. Before ITTOLENGHE, J.P. Recorded 19 Apr. 1764 by FEN-
WICKE BULL, Register.

Book B-3, p. 164   THOMAS ROSE, cooper, to ISAAC MAZYCK, both of
16 Sept. 1763   Charleston, as security on bond dated 10 May
Mortgage   1762 in penal sum of Ł 350 for payment of
                     Ł 175:12:6 currency & interest on 1 May 1763;
pew #80 in St. Michaels Church. Witnesses: THOMAS LEGARÉ, JAMES HENRY
BUTLER. Before WILLIAM ROPER, J.P. Recorded 19 Apr. 1764 by FENWICKE
BULL, Register.

Book B-3, p. 167   RICHARD (his mark) CORKER, planter, to CHRIS-
3 Oct. 1761   TOPHER BARR, planter, both of Granville Co.,

Bond 250 a. in Granville Co., on a branch of Saltcatcher River, bounding on all sides on vacant
land; as granted by Gov. WILLIAM HENRY LYTTLETON 21 May 1757; gives bond
to execute title to BARR when such title shall be "produced to him in
writing"; & ELIZABETH his wife to renounce her dower. Witnesses: ROBERT
MCLEOD, HENRY BISHOP. Recorded 19 Apr. 1764 by FENWICKE BULL, Register.

Book B-3, p. 169   ANTHONY MATHEWES, gentleman, of John's Island,
18 & 19 Sept. 1763   Parish of St. John, Colleton Co., to SAMUEL
L & R   CARNE, ESQ., of Charleston, for L 2500 curren-
                       cy, half of lot #178 in Charleston, with
buildings thereon, bounding N 50 ft. on Broad Street; S & W on SAMUEL
CARNE; E 200 ft. on JOHN DRAYTON; which premises by indenture tripartite
dated 28 Nov. 1740 made between ROBERT BREWTON, gentleman, & MARY (formerly MARY LOUGHTON) his wife, of 1st part; WILLIAM MATHEWES, & MARY
(formerly MARY LOUGHTON) his wife, of 2nd part; & BENJAMIN SMITH, & ANNE
(formerly ANNE LOUGHTON) his wife, of 3rd part; were allotted to WILLIAM
MATHEWES & MARY His wife as her part of the several messuages, lands &
tenements devised by WILLIAM LAUGHTON to said MARY BREWTON, MARY MATHEWES
& ANNE SMITH, in jointenancy, & since the death of MARY MATHEWES held by
WILLIAM MATHEWES as tenant for life by curtesy of England, & surrendered
by said WILLIAM to ANTHONY MATHEWES, only son & heir of MARY MATHEWES.
Witnesses: WILLIAM SAMS, ELIZABETH SAMS. Before JAMES CARSON, J.P. Re-
corded 20 Apr. 1764 by FENWICKE BULL, Register.

Book B-3, p. 177   ALEXANDER CHISOLME, vintner, to DR. SAMUEL
1 & 2 Dec. 1758   CARNE, physician, for L 6000 currency, lot
L & R   #229 & half of lot #178, adjoining each other,
                       making 1 lot fronting on both Broad & Tradd
Streets, & known as the Orange Garden, with all buildings thereon. Whereas by L & R dated 5 & 6 Aug. 1746 WILLIAM HANCOCK, merchant, sold ALEXAN-
DER CHISOLME lot #229 in Charleston containing 1/2 a., English measure,
originally granted by the Lords Proprs. to JOHN ELLIOTT; & whereas by L &
R dated 28 & 29 June 1749 BENJAMIN SMITH, merchant, & ANNE his wife sold
said CHISOLME half of lot #178, with the buildings thereon, bounding N
50 ft. on Broad Street; S on lot #229 belonging to CHISOLME; W 200 ft. on
MARY ELLIS (formerly EDWARD CROFT); E on lot #178 belonging to WILLIAM
MATHEWES; now CHISOLME sells the 2 lots to CARNE. Witnesses: ROBERT WIL-
SON, CHARLES PINCKNEY. Before GEORGE MURRAY, J.P. Recorded 20 Apr. 1764
by FENWICKE BULL, Register.

Book B-3, p. 186   DRURY DUNN, planter, of St. Helena's Parish,
10 July 1761   releases to STEPHEN DRAYTON, planter, all
Release   title to 405 a. purchased from THOMAS DRAYTON,
                       deceased, bounding E & N on Bees Creek; W on
public road leading to the Euhaws; S on barony of THOMAS DRAYTON. Witness: ISAAC OLIVER. Recorded 21 Apr. 1764 by FENWICKE BULL, Register.

Book B-3, p. 187   JAMES LINGARD, blacksmith, & MARY his wife, to
5 & 6 Apr. 1764   JOHN RUTLEDGE, both of Charleston, for L 500
L & R   currency, lot #254, bounding S 42 ft. on Allen
                       Street; N on JOSEPH MOODY; E 90 ft. on GEORGE
ESMAND; W on land of elders of Dutch Church. Witnesses: ELIZABETH
TUGUET, JOHN CHEESBOROUGH. Before ROBERT PRINGLE, J.P. Recorded 21 Apr.
1764 by FENWICKE BULL, Register.

Book B-3, p. 193   JERMYN WRIGHT, to HENRY LAURENS, of Charleston,
24 Mar. 1764   for L 1600 currency, a certain wharf, marsh, &
Feoffment   high land E of the village of Ansonborough,
                       near Charleston, & partly in front E of land
in SC Society (formerly Shubrick's); which premises are the residue of
certain lands conveyed by said JERMYN WRIGHT to GEORGE, Lord Anson, by L
& R dated 10 & 11 May 1756 as security on a bond debt, said debt being
paid. Witnesses: WILLIAM HOPTON, WILLIAM HEST, JOHN BREMAR. Livery &
seizin delivered. Before WILLIAM BURROWS, J.P. Recorded 24 Apr. 1764 by
FENWICKE BULL, Register.

Book B-3, p. 196   THOMAS LOAKE, gentleman, & PRISCILLA (her
7 & 9 Apr. 1764   mark) his wife, only daughter & heir of SAMUEL
L & R   GLESER; & SARAH JOHNSON, widow, of 1st part;

to JAMES GUTHRIE, gentleman; all of Charleston; for ₤ 2500 currency, part of lot #121, bounding N 25 ft. on Broad Street; E 104 ft. on part same lot belonging MRS. COOPER (formerly TUNIS FISHER, later JOHN MARTINI); S on an alley; W on part same lot belonging to COL. BEALE (formerly to RALPH RODDA). Witnesses: JOHN CHEESBOROUGH, ALEXANDER RANTOWLE. Before JOHN REMINGTON, J.P. Recorded 25 Apr. 1764 by FENWICKE BULL, Register.

Book B-3, p. 201 JOHN SCOTT, & SARAH (her mark) his wife, of
30 Nov. 1764 Berkeley Co., to SAMUEL SCOTT, gentleman, of
Release Craven Co., for ₤ 500 currency, the 300 a. on
which in Nov. 1764 WILLIAM DEVEAUE & JEMIMA his wife (daughter & sole heir of WILLIAM PAYNE of Onslow Co., NC) sold to JOHN SCOTT; bounding NE on Wateree River; other sides on vacant land, according to plat dated 6 Nov. 1751. Witnesses: ANN (her mark) SUMMA-RALL, JOHN HOLLIS. Before JOSEPH (JACOB?) SUMMARALL, J.P. Recorded 25 Apr. 1764 by FENWICKE BULL, Register. Plat dated 1 Mar. 1764 of Green Point Tract on Combahee River devised by JAMES HARTLEY to his 2 daughters SARAH HARTLEY & MARY PHILP, a red line showing division; N of red line to SARAH; S to MARY. Signed by JAMES PARSONS, ROBERT PHILP, as executors; present, THOMAS HUTCHINSON, EDWARD BELLINGER, H. HYRNE, W. WEBB, JOHN B. GIRARDEAU. THOMAS HARTLEY testified before JOHN TROUP, J.P., as witness to plat.

Book B-3, p. 205 GEORGE SAXBY, & ELIZABETH his wife, to ALEX-
19 & 20 Mar. 1764 ANDER RIGG, both of Charleston, for ₤ 2000
L & R currency, 200 a. on Johns Island, Colleton
Co., bounding E on Stono River; S on an old high road leading W through a tract of 845 a., of which the 200 a. is part; W on WILLIAM HARVEY & on ABRAHAM BOSOMWORTH when divided (now WILLIAM HARVEY); N on a creek of Stono River. Witnesses: ELEANOR YEOMANS, JAMES SHARP. Before EGERTON LEIGH, J.P. Recorded 25 Apr. 1764 by FENWICKE BULL, Register.

Book B-3, p. 210 ALEXANDER RIGG, to GEORGE SAXBY, both of
30 & 31 Mar. 1764 Charleston, for ₤ 2000 currency, the above
L & R named 200 a. (p. 205). Witnesses: THOMAS SHU-
BRICK, GEORGE TEW. Before JACOB MOTTE, J.P. Recorded 26 Apr. 1764 by FENWICKE BULL, Register.

Book B-3, p. 216 WILLIAM LOWREY, tailor, & SARAH his wife,
27 & 28 Aug. 1761 (only surviving child & heir of WILLIAM STAN-
L & R YARNE, planter), to ROBERT TURNER, planter;
all of Colleton Co.; for ₤ 2000 currency, 400 a., being the E part of 503 a., on Wadmalaw Island, granted by the Lords Proprs. on 10 May 1704 to WILLIAM NASH the elder; which 400 a. were by feoffment dated 7 Mar. 1729 sold by WILLIAM NASH the younger (son & heir of the elder) & PRUDENCE, his wife, to WILLIAM STANYARNE (father of said SARAH LOWREY), who died intestate & descended to his 2 only daughters SARAH & ELIZABETH as co-partners; ELIZABETH dying intestate & without children, SARAH became sole owner; the 400 a. bounding S on Leadenwaw Creek & marsh; W on Landgrave JOSEPH MORTON; N on THOMAS CONN; E on MR. SAMMS (formerly RICHARD UNDERWOOD). Before ROBERT PRINGLE, J.P. Witnesses: THEODORE TREZEVANT, THOM-AS LAMBOLL. Before ROBERT PRINGLE, J.P. Recorded 27 Apr. 1764 by FEN-WICKE BULL, Register.

Book B-3, p. 226 ROBERT TURNER, planter, to WILLIAM LOWREY,
5 & 6 Nov. 1761 tailor, both of Colleton Co., for ₤ 2005 cur-
L & R rency, the above mentioned 400 a. (p. 216).
Witnesses: THEODORE TREZEVANT, THOMAS LAMBOLL. Before ROBERT PRINGLE, J.P. Recorded 28 Apr. 1764 by FENWICKE BULL, Register.

Book B-3, p. 233 Deed of partition of will of JOSEPH WRAGG dat-
20 Dec. 1758 ed 26 Sept. 1746; his wife, JUDITH being ex-
Deed of Partition ecutrix. Appraisers: RICHARD SINGLETON, JON-
ATHAN DRAKE, NATHANIEL SAVINEAU, JOHN MCTEER, WILLIAM BROADBELT, WILLIAM MCTEER, ELIAS FOISSIN, DANIEL LAROCHE, PAUL TRAPIER, JAMES WRIGHT, THOMAS GRIMBALL, HENRY DESAUSSURE, ANDREW JOHN-STON, ARCHIBALD JOHNSTON, ARCHIBALD BAIRD, THOMAS SMITH, SR., JOHN SAV-AGE, & JOHN GUERARD. Partitioners: THOMAS LAMBOLL, ISAAC MAZYCK, & DAVID

CAW. Eight shares, marked A, B, C, D, E, F, G, & H; value Ł 5900 each; having been drawn for, were allotted as follows:

A. to SAMUEL WRAGG, second son. 2000 a. (Ł 250) in St. Helena Parish, on N side Purysburgh Township, bounding N on ROBERT WRIGHT; E on estate of JOSEPH WRAGG & THOMAS OWEN; S & W on vacant land; as by grant dated 9 Apr. 1736; also 336 a. near the Quarter House in several tracts (Ł 3360); 1 tract of 190 a. in Berkeley Co., bounding W on MR. MERREY; N on MR. IZARD & MR. HEWITT; E on Cooper River & marsh; as by grant to SARAH BEAMOR dated 15 June 1716; also 70 a. on Charleston Neck which JOHN CHEVILLETTE & SARAH his wife sold to WRAGG by L & R, dated 9 & 10 Jan. 1735; the 70 a. being in 2 tracts, 1 of 55 a. granted JOHN BIRD, bounding E on a creek & on WILLIAM HAWETT; S on WILLIAM HAWETT; SW on MR. RUBERRY; the other 15 a. bought by SIMON VALENTINE from JOHN KING & JUDITH HOLYBUSH, later owned by JACOB BEAMOR, then by his son JAMES BEAMOR; bounding N on JOHN BIRD; S on CAPT. WILLIAM HAWETT & a marsh (formerly WILLIAM EDWARDS & JOHN ATKINSON, schoolmaster); also 30 a. on Cooper River, sold by L & R dated 20 & 21 June 1728 by THOMAS ELLERY & DANIEL GREENE to JOSEPH WRAGG & JOHN FENWICKE, FENWICKE & his wife later selling to WRAGG; bounding SW on PAUL GRIMBALL; NE on Cooper River marsh; SE & NW on 2 marshes; also 46 a. on Charleston Neck (formerly BENJAMIN DENNIS), sold by RICHARD LAMBTON to WRAGG by L & R dated 11 & 12 Oct. 1737; bounding N on MR. BERESFORD; E on Cooper River marsh; S on JOHN BIRD; W on Broad Path; also DENTON'S house, being a lot & brick house (Ł 1330), marked K on plat, bounding W 68 ft. on Union Street; S 103 ft. on blue house lot; E 64 ft. on WRAGG'S estate; N 103 ft. on a lane; also Orange Garden lot marked H on plat (Ł 1000), deduct Ł 320 for MRS. WRAGG), bounding N on Daniels Creek; S on blue house lot; E on JOSEPH WRAGG & JOHN HARLESTON; W on JOHN ADEE (or bounding E 100 ft. on Union Street; N on lot #7 & JONATHAN SCOTT 193-3/4 ft.; 101 ft. on a marsh; W 191 ft.); also chattels Ł 280.

B. to JOHN WRAGG, eldest son of JOSEPH WRAGG. 2000 a. (Ł 250) on NE side Peedee River, granted 25 June 1736; bounding on all sides on vacant land; also pasture lands (Ł 4000, deduct 1/3 for MRS. WRAGG) consisting of 69 a. on Charleston Neck, purchased from ROGER MOORE by L & R dated 21 & 22 Feb. 1731; bounding N on BENJAMIN SCHENCKINGH (later PHILIP DAWES); E on marsh & ISAAC MAZYCK; W on high road; & 10 a. (half of 20 a.) near Charleston; bounding SE on ISAAC MAZYCK, merchant; SW on Broad Path; NW on other half purchased from EDWARD KEATING by L & R dated 5 & 6 Apr. 1731; & 48 a. marsh land in Berkeley Co., purchased from JOHN BRAND 3 & 4 Mar. 1731; bounding W on My Lady's _____; E on MR. BARLEYCORN; S on MR. SCHENCKINGH; N on MR. GRAY; also the 2 blue wooden tenements & lot (Ł 1800), bounding W 40-1/2 ft. on Union Street; N 93 ft. on Orange Garden; E on WRAGG'S estate; S 93 ft. on a lane; chattels Ł 276:13:4.

C. to JUDITH WRAGG, eldest daughter. 931 a. (Ł 116:7:6) in St. Helena Parish, Purysburgh, granted 9 Apr. 1736; bounding N on JAMES ST. JOHN; E & S on MR. WRIGHT; 1 side on MR. OWENS; 1346 a. (Ł 4000) called Spring Grove, in Parishes of St. James Goose Creek & St. Johns; purchased 17 & 18 Jan. 1727 from ROGER MOORE & CATHARINE his wife; also part of lot #115 (Ł 800); purchased from ELIZABETH HOLMES 1 & 2 Oct. 1750; bounding N 30 ft. on Tradd Street; W 130 ft. on SOLOMON LEGARE; S on THOMAS HOLTEN; E on part same lot; also 262 ft. low water land (Ł 900) E of the E Bay lots, purchased from JOHN DANIEL, THOMAS DANIEL (?), GEORGE LOGAN & MARTHA his wife, ALEXANDER GOODBY & ANNE his wife; chattels Ł 83:12:6.

D. to HENRIETTA WRAGG, youngest daughter. 828 a. (Ł 1656) in St. Helena Parish, granted JAMES KINLOCH, who sold to WRAGG; bounding N on JOHN DAWSON; other sides on vacant land; lot & brick store (Ł 2500 deduct 1/3), marked C on plat, bounding E 57-1/2 ft. on the Bay; S 204 ft. on lot B; W 64 ft. on lot K; N 204 ft. on a lane; 8-1/2 a. part of 10 a. (Ł 1300), the N a. having been sold to JAMES KINLOCH & 60 ft. adjoining to another person; bounding S on Charleston; W on parsonage land; N on THOMAS KIMBERLY; E on Broad Path; also lot #22 in Beaufort (Ł 100) granted WRAGG 8 Aug. 1717; also Smallwoods Island (Ł 250), being 100 a. of land & marsh on E side Cooper River, purchased from ANTHONY WHITE & MARY his wife on 25 & 26 Aug. 1729; bounding W on marsh; E on a creek; N on Wando River; plus Ŀ 494.

                    E. to MARY WRAGG, second daughter. 1000 a.
(Ŀ 500) in St. Helena Parish, granted JAMES KINLOCH, who sold to WRAGG;
bounding W on ROBERT WRIGHT; other sides on vacant land; also S tenement
of brick house (Ŀ 3000), part of D on plat, purchased from GEORGE LOGAN &
MARTHA his wife; bounding E 22 ft. on the Bay; S 145 ft. on a lane; W
22 ft. on an alley; N 145 ft. on N tenement; also 1/3 undivided part of
2960 a. called DOCKON (Ŀ 1666:13:4), in Berkeley Co., purchased from JOB
ROTHMAHLER & ANN his wife; also part of lot (Ŀ 350, deduct 1/3) purchased
from JOHN MILNER & HANNAH his wife; ZACHARIAH CARLISLE, JOHN BEE & MARTHA
his wife; bounding W 40 ft. on New Church Street; E 52 ft. on part same
lot; S 120 ft. on part same lot enclosed in churchyard; N on part lot
#218; also Ŀ 495:6:8.

                    F. to ANNE WRAGG, third daughter, 2000 a.
(Ŀ 2000) on S side Combahee River, called Saltcatcher & Cane Ocean plantations; granted 26 Feb. 1733; bounding S & SE on JAMES FERGUSON; NE on
freshes of Saltcatcher River; NW on MR. WRAGG; SW on vacant land; also a
lot (Ŀ 2250, deduct 1/3), being part of lots 318 & 199, purchased 20 & 21
Feb. 1744 from JOHN STEEL & MARY his wife; bounding W on Church Street; E
on MR. SCOTT & JOSEPH WRAGG; S on HENRY MIDDLETON, JOHN CART, JAMES KIN-
LOCH, & JOSEPH WRAGG; N on MR. NASH & JOSEPH BEE; also a lot with 2 brick
stores & a stable (Ŀ 1490), marked G on plat, bounding S 59 ft. on a
lane; E 94 ft. on an alley; N 61 ft. on JONATHAN SCOTT (formerly HARLES-
TON); W 90 ft. on the Orange Garden & part on JOHN WRAGGS blud wooden
houses; also 69 a. (Ŀ 69) vacant land near PonPon, Colleton Co., granted
26 Feb. 1733; bounding N on MR. CLIFF; S on MR. HIP; E on MR. SANDERS; W
on JOHN HUNT; plus Ŀ 347.

                    G. to ELIZABETH MANIGAULT, 5th daughter, wife
of PETER MANIGAULT, 4000 a. (Ŀ 750) in Craven Co., granted 25 June 1736;
bounding NE on JOSEPH WRAGG & vacant land; NW on JOSEPH WRAGG; S on Peedee River; SE on vacant land; also N tenement of brick house (Ŀ 2500) &
land, marked E on plat; bounding E 25 ft. on the Bay; S 145 ft. on other
tenement; N 146 ft. on estate of JOSEPH WRAGG; W 25 ft. on an alley; also
1/3 undivided part (Ŀ 1000) of unimproved lot #12, bounding S 38 ft. on
Elliott Street; & running 74 ft. northward from front sill of porch towards Broad (Cooper) Street; N on THOMAS CARY; E on BENJAMIN SCHENCKINGH;
W on ROBERT GIBBES; also, 1 undivided third part of an unimproved lot
bounding S 27 ft. on a little (Elliott?) Street, (measured from land
granted RICHARD SEARL, now JOHN THOMAS, to lot of THOMAS ROSE, planter,
occupied by FRANCIS GRACIA); E 72 ft. on JOHN THOMAS; W 72 ft. on THOMAS
ROSE; N 27 ft. on JOHN CROSKEYS; which 2 undivided third parts were purchased from JOB ROTHMAHLER & ANN his wife; also 1 unimproved lot (Ŀ 1500,
deduct 1/3), marked F on plat, E 57 ft. on the Bay; S 146 ft. on N tenement of brick house; W 47 ft. on a lane; N 148 ft. on JONATHAN SCOTT;
also 1 undivided third part (Ŀ 350) of 25 a. in Berkeley Co., between MR.
BENOIST & MR. RATCLIFF, bounding E on Broad Path; S on WEEKLEY; W on a
creek; N on CATHARINE L'APOSTRE; also Ŀ 280.

                    H. to CHARLOTTE WRAGG, 4th daughter, 302 a.
(Ŀ 1000) near Georgetown, in Craven Co., granted 26 June 1736 to ROBERT
WRIGHT, who sold to WRAGG; between Black & Peedee Rivers; bounding NE on
WILLIAM SWINTON; also part of a lot on Bay & Blue house & lot (Ŀ 7500,
deduct 1/3); 1 lot (marked A) between NOAH SERE & the blue house; bound-
ing E 28 ft. 3 in. on Bay; S 210 ft. on MRS. SARAH BLAKEWAY; W on JOHN
SIMONS; N on JOSEPH WRAGG; as purchased from JOHN DANIEL & SARAH his wife
on 7 & 8 Oct. 1741; the blue house & lot bounding E 56 ft. on the Bay; W
68 ft. on Union Street; S 309 ft. on lot A & MR. SCOTT; N 308 ft. on C &
K; also 1000 a. (Ŀ 200 less than nothing, being an expense) on Combahee
River, in Colleton Co., bounding N on vacant land; E on MR. PERRY; W on
Black Creek & JOHN MILES; as by grant 26 Feb. 1733 .

                    Partitioned 18 Mar. 1757 by THOMAS LAMBOLL,
ISAAC MAZYCK, DAVID CAW. Witnesses: ROBERT PRINGLE, THOMAS MIDDLETON,
THOMAS LYNCH, GEORGE LOGAN, JR. Before CHARLES PINCKNEY, J.P. ELIZABETH
& HENRIETTA not then being of age, all signed full approval on 19 Apr.
1759 before WILLIAM BURROWS, J.P. Registered 3 May 1764 by FENWICKE BULL,
Register.

Book B-3, p. 271   JAMES WOOD, planter, & ELIZABETH (her mark)
17 Apr. 1754   his wife, of Williamsburgh, Prince Frederick
L & R   Parish, Craven Co., to PETER LESESNE, for
                         Ł 150 currency, 150 a. on N side Black River,
bounding NE on DOYLIS; NW on vacant land; SW on KEMP; being part of 450
a. granted 6 Nov. 1751 to JOHN MCELVIENE, whose wife, JANE, left 300 a.
of it in trust for their 2 daughters, ELIZABETH being 1. Witnesses:
JAMES CANTEY, CAPT. JOHN MCDONALD. Before JOHN PAMOR, J.P. Recorded 3
May 1764 by FENWICKE BULL, Register.

Book B-3, p. 277   THOMAS LOAKE, gentleman, formerly of Jamaica,
28 Apr. 1764   now of Charleston, grandson & heir of THOMAS
Conveyance   MASTERS, of Parish of St. Dorothy, Jamaica,
                         deceased; & son & heir of RICHARD LOAKE & ANNE
his wife (daughter & heiress of THOMAS MASTERS); of 1st part; to BENJAMIN
HUME, ESQ., of Parish of St. Anne, Co. of Middlesex, Jamaica, & SAMUEL
GORDON, ESQ., of Parish of Kings Town, Co. of Surry, Jamaica, of 2nd
part. Whereas THOMAS MASTERS owned a plantation & sugar works formerly
called the Cocoa Walks, now Master's Plantation, in St. Dorothy Parish;
Jamaica, with the tenements, slaves, cattle, stock, etc.; also certain
peu & peu lands in St. Catherine's Parish, with the tenements, slaves,
cattle, etc.; also an undivided moiety of the plantation & sugar works,
called Sommerset Hall, in St. Dorothy Parish; & half the tenements,
slaves, stock, cattle, etc; also divers other lands, tenements, slaves,
etc., in Jamaica; subject to an annuity of Ł 300 Jamaican, payable to his
widow ELIZABETH (now ELIZABETH HILL, widow); & also subject to his debts
in a large amount; & whereas there is now due ZACHARY BAYLY, ESQ., of
Jamaica (attorney to RICHARD LOAKE & attorney to EDWARD BIGLAND, executor
of will of RICHARD LOAKE) a large sum for disbursements on said estate,
etc., now LOAKE has agreed to sell HUME & GORDON, for Ł 2000 Jamaican,
all his interest in the various plantations, sugar works, slaves, cattle,
etc.; HUME & GORDON to assume all debts. Witnesses: THOMAS SAVAGE, JO-
SEPH CATOR. proved by JOSEPH CATOR, merchant, formerly of Jamaica, now
of Charleston, before Gov. THOMAS BOONE, of SC, by GEORGE JOHNSTON, Dep.
Sec. Recorded 3 May 1764 by FENWICKE BULL, Register.

Book B-3, p. 285   WILLIAM BLAKE, gentleman, of Charleston, to
16 & 17 Feb. 1761   FRANCIS YONGE, ESQ., of Colleton Co., for
L & R   Ł 4500 currency, 1000 a., English measure, on
                          N side of swamp & marsh at head of Stono Riv-
er, in Colleton Co., granted 5 July 1683 to BENJAMIN BLAKE; bounding W &
SW on marsh, a creek of Wadmalaw River & PAWLETT'S plantation; NE on
CAPT. WILLIAM PETTERS; NW on vacant land; also 1090 a. called PAWLETTS,
on N side Wadmalaw River, granted 14 May 1696 to Landgrave JOSEPH BLAKE,
bounding SE on a creek & marsh; SE on a creek, marsh, & vacant land; NE
on said 1000 a. & vacant land; NW on vacant land; also 300 a. in Colleton
Co., granted 12 Oct. 1710 to Lady ELIZABETH BLAKE, bounding NW on said
ELIZABETH BLAKE; S on Wadmalaw River; E on New Cut Creek; NE on Stono
River; also 100 a. on N side Wadmalaw River, granted 25 May 1711, to Lady
ELIZABETH BLAKE, bounding NE on Lady BLAKE; SE on a creek; SW on JAMES
GILBERSON; NW on vacant land; also 230 a. granted 25 May 1711 to Lady
ELIZABETH BLAKE, bounding NE on JAMES GILBERSON; other sides on creeks,
marsh, & Wadmalaw River; also 76 a. on N side Wadmalaw River, granted 25
May 1711 to Lady BLAKE, bounding NE on JAMES GILBERSON; SW on ARCHIBALD
STOBO; NW on vacant land; total 2796 a. Witnesses: ROBERT WILLIAMS, JR.,
JOSHUA WARD. Before ROBERT WILLIAMS, J.P. Recorded 5 May 1764 by FEN-
WICKE BULL, Register.

Book B-3, p. 297   Whereas certain lands were sold at public auc-
16 Apr. 1764   tion to SAMUEL CORN; & whereas JOHN NARNEY,
Agreement   watchmaker, of Charleston, wants to purchase
                         the 2 tracts (450 a.) at the horseshoe, ad-
joining his land; now NARNEY agrees to pay the purchase price to FRANCIS
YONGE & JAMES SHARP, executors of estate of THOMAS SACHEVERALL; CORN
transfers the land to NARNEY. Witnesses: WILLIAM DOCKWRAY, BENJAMIN
WESTERLEY, ROBERT (his mark) GRAY. Before JAMES STOBO, J.P. Recorded 9
May 1764 by FENWICKE BULL, Register.

Book B-3, p. 299   ISAAC (his mark) DROZE, & JANE (her mark) his
30 Apr. 1756   wife, daughter of JANE MCELVINE, of Prince

L & R   Frederick Parish, Craven Co., to PETER LESESNE,
                               for L 200 currency, 150 a. in Craven Co., on N
side Black River, bounding NE on DOYLE; NW on vacant land; SW on CAMP
(KEMP); E on part of 450 a. granted 6 Nov. 1751 to JOHN MCELVIENE. JANE
MCELVIENE, wife of JOHN, laid out 300 of the 450 a. in trust for herself
& her 2 daughters (p. 271). Witnesses: JOHN CONNOR, JOSEPH HOWARD. Before ISAAC PORCHER, J.P. Recorded 9 May 1764 by FENWICKE BULL, Register.

Book B-3, p. 305   CORNELIUS DUPONT & PAUL PORCHER, (executors of
22 Aug. 1763   will of ABRAHAM DUPONT), of Granville Co., to
L & R   WILLIAM COACHMAN, planter, of Berkeley Co.,
                               for L 100 currency, 125 a. in Parish of St.
James Goose Creek, Berkeley Co., bounding N on Fosters Creek; W on JOHN
GOODBIE; E on ALLEN; conveyed by HANNAH GOODBEE on 19 Nov. 1745 to JAMES
COACHMAN, who on 13 Mar. 1752 conveyed to ABRAHAM DUPONT, who by will
dated 21 Jan. 1760 directed his executors to sell. See original grants
to WILLIAM RANNOLDS & JOSEPH THORTON dated 13 & 14 Jan. & Mar. 1701 &
1700. Witnesses: ESTHER PORCHER, ELIZABETH ALLISON, ISAAC GONEAR. Delivery by turf & twig. Before CHARLES WOODMASON, J.P. Recorded 10 May
1764 by FENWICKE BULL, Register.

Book B-3, p. 308   BENJAMIN COACHMAN, planter, & SARAH his wife,
22 & 23 Oct. 1762   to WILLIAM COACHMAN, planter, both of Berkeley
L & R   Co., for L 1200 currency, 428 a., part of 578
                               a. on Sandy Island, Prince George Parish, Cra-
ven Co., granted WILLIAM WATIES the elder; who on 1 Apr. 1738 sold to
JOHN ALSTON (ALLSTON) the elder; planter; whose sons, JOHN & JOSIAS (his
executors) on 14 July 1750 sold to BENJAMIN COACHMAN; the 428 a. bounding
N on JOHN WATIES; S on THOMAS WATIES; W on Wando Passo, a thoroughfare
leading from Peedee to Waccamaw. Witnesses: JOHN THOMSON, JAMES COACH-
MAN. Before JOHN IOOR, J.P. Recorded 10 May 1764 by FENWICKE BULL, Register.

Book B-3, p. 316   ROBERT DEANS, carpenter, to JAMES SKIRVING,
28 & 29 Mar. 1764   ESQ., both of Charleston, for L 3500 currency,
L & R   part of lots 119 & 120; each half an a., Eng-
                               lish measure, the 2 lots bounding E on Arch-
dale Street; S on Queen Street; W & N on heirs of ISAAC MAZYCK; which
lots DEANS purchased from THOMAS BOONE & CHARLES BOONE; the parts now
sold bounding S 36 ft. on Queen Street; E 188 ft. on the part belonging
to the Rev. MR. LORRIMER; other sides on ROBERT DEANS. Witnesses: BEN-
JAMIN BAKER, ELENER FERGUSON. Before RAWLINS LOWNDES, J.P. Recorded 11
May 1764 by FENWICKE BULL, Register.

Book B-3, p. 322   RICHARD CAPERS, planter, of Parish of St. Hel-
25 & 26 Apr. 1763   ena, Granville Co., to JACOB WAIGHT, planter,
L & R   of St. Johns Parish, Colleton Co., for L 3500
                               currency, 435 a. on St. Helena Island, granted
13 Jan. 1710 by Gov. ROBERT GIBBES to RICHARD CAPERS, who died intestate,
& inherited by his grandson, RICHARD, son of JOSEPH CAPERS, only son of
said RICHARD CAPERS the elder; bounding SW on WILLIAM CHAPMAN; W on CHAP-
MAN'S Creek; N & NE on creeks; E on vacant land (now JONATHAN NORTHON).
Witnesses: WILLIAM HARVEY, WILLIAM DEVEAUX. Before WILLIAM HARVEY, J.P.
Recorded 12 May 1764 by FENWICKE BULL, Register.

Book B-3, p. 328   FRANCIS EHRHARDT, cordwainer, of Purysburgh,
17 Feb. 1762   Granville Co., & MARY his wife, to JACOB WALD-
Release   BURGER, planter, for L 100 currency, a 1 a.
                               lot in Purisburgh Township, granted ADAM CUL-
LIST, who conveyed to PETER MAILLIER; who sold to DAVID GODET, who sold
to FRANCIS HENRY, who sold to HENRY CHIFFELLE, who sold to DEPONT, who
sold to FRANCIS EHRHARDT; bounding S on Town Street; E on GABIREL RAVOT;
W on Bay fronting Savannah River. Witnesses: GEDEON MALLET, SUSANNAH
MALLET, DAVID (his mark) WONDERLY. Before JOHN BAPTIST BOURQUIN, J.P.
Recorded 14 May 1764 by FENWICKE BULL, Register.

Book B-3, 331   JONATHAN BRYAN, ESQ., of Savannah, Georgia, &
10 Oct. 1763   MARY his wife, to ANDREW HENDRIE & HUGH BURN,
Release   planters, of SC, for L 95 sterling of Georgia,
                               125 a. in Purisburgh Township, Granville Co.,

bounding E on Oposkee Creek; N on HENDRIE & BURN; W on SAMUEL MONTAGUE; S on vacant land; the 125 a. being part of 300 a. granted 9 Apr. 1743 to DAVID GENDER. Witnesses: JAMES ANDERSON, HUGH BRYAN. Before GEORGE BAILLIE, J.P. for Christ Church Parish, Georgia. Entered in Auditor's Book G-7, page 196 on 2 May 1764 by RICHARD LAMBTON, Dep. Aud. Recorded 15 May 1764 by FENWICKE BULL, Register.

Book B-3, p. 336
28 & 29 May 1759
L & R

PETER GOURDIN, planter, of St. Johns Parish, Berkeley Co., to JOSEPH PORCHER, planter, of St. Stephens, Craven Co., for ₺ 1200 currency, 263 a. in St. Stephens Parish, being part of 2 tracts, or 800 a., formerly belonging to DANIEL WELCHUSSEN, who with CATHERINE his wife, on 13 May 1741 sold to LEWIS GOURDIN; who bequeathed the middle part, or 263 a., to his son PETER GOURDIN, according to plat dated 19 Apr. 1756; the 263 a. bounding NW on THEODORE GOURDIN (now the Rev. MR. ALEXANDER KEITH); SE on WILLIAM GOURDIN (now THEODORE GAILLARD); SW on DANIEL WELCHUSSEN (part now GEORGE BAGBY); NE on vacant land (now THEODORE GAILLARD). Witnesses: GABRIEL MARION, BENJAMIN FARAR, GEORGE KING. Before ISAAC PORCHER, J.P. Recorded 15 May 1764 by FENWICKE BULL, Register.

Book B-3, p. 343
26 & 27 Apr. 1761
L & R

JOSEPH PORCHER, planter, & SUSANNAH his wife, to DR. BENJAMIN FARAR, both of St. Stephens Parish, Craven Co., for ₺ 2000 currency, the 263 a. mentioned above (p. 336). Witnesses: BENJAMIN GIGNILLIAT, GABRIEL MARION. Before ISAAC PORCHER, J.P. Recorded 16 May 1764 by FENWICKE BULL, Register.

Book B-3, p. 350
26 & 27 Aug. 1763
L & R

DR. BENJAMIN FARAR, to JOHN GAILLARD, planter, both of St. Stephens Parish, Craven Co., for ₺ 1200 currency, the above named 263 a. (p. 336, 343). Witnesses: ISAAC PORCHER, JOSEPH PORCHER. Before GEORGE JOHNSTON, J.P. Recorded 18 May 1764 by FENWICKE BULL, Register.

Book B-3, p. 358
12 Apr. 1762
Bill of Sale

STEPHEN BULL, JR., JOHN BULL, JOHN KELSALL, & THOMAS MIDDLETON, commissioners for building Parish Church of Prince William, SC, to STEPHEN DRAYTON, for ₺ 260 currency; pew #3 in said church. Witnesses: BENJAMIN GARDEN, JOHN GOVAN. Recorded 18 May 1764 by FENWICKE BULL, Register.

Book B-3, p. 359
18 & 19 Oct. 1759
L & R

JOHN HEARNE, planter, of Georgia, to JACOB MOTTE, SR., of Charleston, for ₺ 300 currency, 500 a. in Colleton Co., bounding SW on PonPon River. Witnesses: JOSEPH BUTLER, ELISHA BUTLER, WILLIAM BUTLER. Before JAMES MACKAY, J.P. Recorded 19 May 1764 by FENWICKE BULL, Register.

Book B-3, p. 365
15 & 16 Nov. 1763
L & R

ALEXANDER FOTHERINGHAM, & ISABELLA his wife; & ARCHIBALD MACNEILL & MARY his wife; all of St. George Parish, Dorchester; to JAMES POSTELL, ESQ., of PonPon; for ₺ 3000 currency, 500 a. in Berkeley Co., on S side of head of Ashley River lately occupied by GIBBON WRIGHT, bounding E on ALEXANDER SKENE; S on JOHN SKENE & SAMUEL WAINWRIGHT; NE on estate of JOSEPH WRAGG; NW on JERMYN WRIGHT & estate of RALPH IZARD. Witnesses: ELIJAH POSTELL, ROBERT WRIGHT. Before JOHN IOOR, J.P. Recorded 21 May 1764 by FENWICKE BULL, Register.

Book B-3, p. 372
20 & 21 Apr. 1762
L & R

MARK HUGGINS, planter, of Craven Co., & ANNA his wife, to WILLIAM LITTEN RUSS, planter, of Berkeley Co., for ₺ 4500 currency, 500 a. & an island of 400 a. Whereas Gov. NATHANIEL JOHNSON on 14 Mar. 1705 granted JOHN BELL the elder 500 a., English measure, on N side Santee River, in Craven Co., bounding NE on JOHN SOUSO; other sides on vacant land; & on 14 Mar. 1705 granted said JOHN BELL an island of 400 a. in said river; & whereas his younger son, JOHN, inherited, & by L & R dated 25 & 26 June 1725 sold the 2 tracts to SAMUEL BLYTH, planter, of Craven Co.; who, by L & R dated 4 & 5 July 1727 sold to JOHN HUGGINS, planter, of Berkeley Co.; who bequeathed the 2 tracts to his 2 sons

JOSEPH & MARK; & whereas JOSEPH died & MARK inherited; now he sells to
RUSS. Witnesses: WILLIAM MATHEWS, DEBORAH MATHEWS, CHRISTOPHER JORDAN.
Before JOHN MAYRANT, J.P. Recorded 22 May 1764 by FENWICKE BULL, Regis-
ter.

Book B-3, p. 384   HENRY HOWARTH, gentleman, to JAMES PARSONS,
7 & 8 May 1764   ESQ., for Ł 275 currency, 1650 a., S of Alta-
L & R   maha (or Great Satilla) River, bounding N & W
                          on vacant land & swamp; E on MR. BULL & a
swamp; E on MR. BULL & a swamp. Witnesses: ROBERT LADSON, JOHN GLEN.
Before JOHN TROUP, J.P. Recorded by FENWICKE BULL, Register.

Book B-3, p. 390   WILLIAM MACKAY, planter, & CATHARINE (CATRAN)
4 & 6 Sept. 1762   his wife, to ROBERT CARTER, both of St. Marks
L & R   Parish, Craven Co., for Ł 140 SC money, 200 a.
                          in Craven Co., on a N branch of Black River,
surrounded by vacant land; as by plat dated 6 Dec. 1757. Witnesses: DA-
VID ANDERSON, ARTHUR GRINES, ROBERT THOMPSON. Before HENRY CASSELS, J.P.
Recorded 3 May 1764 by FENWICKE BULL, Register.

Book B-3, p. 396   JOHN (his mark) GROBB, planter, to DANIEL HEY-
8 & 10 Jan. 1764   WARD, planter, both of St. Helena Parish, for
L & R   Ł 50 currency, 50 a. in Purysburgh Township,
                          surrounded by vacant land. Witnesses: WILLIAM
BETTISON, RICHARD COLE. Before CHARLES WRIGHT, J.P. Recorded 24 May
1764 by FENWICKE BULL, Register.

Book B-3, p. 402   JOSEPH ALLSTON, planter, of Prince George Par-
2 & 3 May 1764   ish, Craven Co., & CHARLOTTE his wife, to WIL-
L & R   LIAM ALLSTON, JR., son of JOHN ALLSTON, plant-
                          er; for Ł 2500 SC money, 640 a. in Craven Co.,
bounding E on the ocean; S on JOSEPH ALLSTON; W on a creek surrounding
JOSEPH ALLSTON'S island; N on GABIREL MARION & JOSEPH ALLSTON. Witnesses: NATHANIEL DWIGHT; JOHN ALLSTON. Before JOSIAS ALLSTON, J.P. Recorded 25 May 1764 by FENWICKE BULL, Register.

Book B-3, p. 409   HENRY PERONNEAU, merchant, of Charleston, to
14 May 1764   JOHN SHUTTERLING, baker, for Ł 2000 currency,
Feoffment   the NW part of a town lot, being part of a lot
                          sold to PERONNEAU by ADAM DANIEL, son of JOHN
DANIEL; the NW part bounding W 54 ft. on King Street; N 167-1/2 ft. on
DR. JACOB MARTIN; E on other part; S on the part sold by PERONNEAU to
MARTIN MILLER. Witnesses: JAMES ANDREWS, WILLIAM WEBB. Before DAVID
RHIND, J.P. Recorded 26 May 1764 by FENWICKE BULL, Register.

Book B-3, p. 413   HENRY PERONNEAU, merchant, of Charleston, to
14 May 1764   MARTIN MILLER, bricklayer, for Ł 2000 curren-
Feoffment   cy, the SW part of a lot sold to PERONNEAU by
                          ADAM DANIEL, son of JOHN DANIEL; the SW part
bounding W 54 ft. on King Street; S 167-1/2 ft. on ELIZABETH ELLIOTT,
widow; E on PERONNEAU; N on JOHN SHUTTERLING. Witnesses: JAMES ANDREWS,
WILLIAM WEBB. Before DAVID RHIND, J.P. Recorded 26 May 1764 by FENWICKE
BULL, Register.

Book B-3, p. 417   MARTIN MILLER, bricklayer, of Charleston, &
15 & 16 May 1764   ANNA MARIA (her mark) his wife, to HENRY
Mortgage   PERONNEAU, merchant, as security on bond of
                          even date in penal sum of Ł 2000 for payment
of Ł 1000 currency, with interest, on 16 May 1765; his lot purchased from
PERONNEAU (p. 413). Witnesses: FELIX LONG, THOMAS LAMBOLL. Before DAVID
RHIND, J.P. Recorded 28 May 1764 by FENWICKE BULL, Register. On 5 July
1774 PERONNEAU declared mortgage paid. Witness: WILLIAM RUGELEY.

Book B-3,. p. 426   JOHN HARLESTON, SR., planter, of Berkeley Co.,
25 July 1737   to his daughter, ANNE for love & affection,
Gift   lot #34 in Charleston, which he purchased from
                          MARMADUKE DANIELL; bounding 100 ft. on the Bay.
Witnesses: NICHOLAS HARLESTON, RICHARD GOUGH, ANNE GOUGH (later, wife of
NATHANIEL SCOTT). Proved before LIONEL CHALMRES, J.P. on 11 June 1756.
Recorded 28 May 1764 by FENWICKE BULL, Register.

Book B-3, p. 428   JOHN SHUTTERLING, baker, of Charleston, & MARY
15 & 16 May 1764   (her mark) his wife, to HENRY PERONNEAU, mer-
Mortgage   chant, as security on bond of even date in pe-
                          nal sum of Ł 2000 for payment of Ł 1000 cur-
rency, with interest, on 16 May 1765; the lot he purchased from PERONNEAU
(p. 409). Witnesses: FELIX LONG, THOMAS LAMBOLL. Before DAVID RHIND,
J.P. Recorded 28 May 1764 by FENWICKE BULL, Register.

Book B-3, p. 437   ABRAHAM IMER, minister, of Purysburg, SC, in-
2 May 1764   tending shortly to marry ANN MAUROUMET, widow,
Bond   of Charleston, daughter of FRANCIS MORAND, who
                          would bring him a considerable personal estate
as her marriage portion; to secure a maintenance for ANN & their future
children; also for her son JOHN MAUROUMET; gives FRANCIS MORAND, shopkeeper, JONATHAN SCOTT, & JOHN SCOTT, JR., merchants, of Charleston, a
bond for Ł 8400 SC money to assure payment of Ł 600 sterling for ANN'S
use within 6 months after IMER'S decease. Witnesses: ROBERT HOGG, CHIL-
DERMAS HARVEY, DANIEL DUE. Before CHARLES WOODMASON, J.P. Recorded 30
May 1764 by FENWICKE BULL, Register.

Book B-3, p. 440   JOHN FREEMAN, tailor, of Wadmelaw Island,
9 May 1764   leases to GEORGE DAVIS, joiner of Charleston,
Lease for 15 Years   for 15 years, for Ł 20 currency, per annum,
                          the N part of lot #197 in Charleston, bounding
E 15 ft. 3 in. on Meeting Street (now St. Michaels or Church) Street; W
160 ft. on JOHN RIVERS; S on ALBERT DITMAR; N on Lady AXTELL & COL. WIL-
LIAM BULL; which piece of ground was purchased by JOHN GOODWIN, butcher;
who sold to ALBERT DITMAR & CHRISTIAN his wife; who on 9 June 1731 sold
to WILLIAM HALL, who married SARAH LAROCHE, widow. Their daughter, MARY,
married WILLIAM BOWER & died without issue during her mother's lifetime;
therefore, ANN LAROCHE, daughter of SARAH & her first husabnd, JAMES LA-
ROCHE, inherited. ANN married RICHARD FREEMAN. Their son, JOHN, inherited & now leases to DAVIS, who agrees to build a 2-story house, 14 x
25 ft., & fence. Witnesses: THOMAS MCCARTHY, CHARLES WOODMASON. Before
WILLIAM MASSEY, J.P. Recorded 30 May 1764 by FENWICKE BULL, Register.

Book B-3, p. 443   JOHN DEAS, merchant, to his friend ROBERT RA-
11 Oct. 1763   PER, ESQ., both of Charleston, for 5 shillings,
Gift   part of a lot in Colleton Square, purchased
                          from heirs of THOMAS ELLERY, & adjoining the
lot purchased from heirs of GEORGE HUNTER; bounding E 150 ft. on the
HUNTER lot; W on ELLERY lot; N 2 ft. on Hunter Street; S 2 ft. on Ellery
Street. Witnesses: GEORGE SEAMAN, WILL STONE, ELIZABETH DEAS. Before
JACOB MOTTE, J.P. Recorded 30 May 1764 by FENWICKE BULL, Register.

Book B-3, p. 444   WILLIAM WOODDROP, merchant, sole executor of
30 June & 1 July 1762   will of GEORGE HUNTER, gentleman, of 1st part;
L & R Tripartite   ROBERT BRISBANE & WILLIAM BRASBANE, merchants,
                          of 2nd part; ROBERT RAPER, gentleman, of 3rd
part; all of Charleston. Whereas GEORGE HUNTER, owned various islands
plantations, lots, etc.; & by will dated 27 Aug. 1745 appointed WOODDROP
sole executor, to dispose of his lands; & bequeathed to his only sisters,
ELIZABETH DUNLOP & MARGARET MACDERMIT, equally, the residue; & whereas
ELIZABETH HUNTER DUNLOP (wife of WILLIAM DUNLOP, coppersmith in Air), &
MARGARET HUNTER MACDERMIT (widow of ROBERT MACDERMIT, in Air), by letter
of attorney dated 26 Aug. 1756, duly proved before ANDREW SLOWAN, of
Skeldon, Lord Provost of the Burgh of Air, appointed ROBERT BRISBANE &
WILLIAM BRISBANE their attorneys to recover their property from WOODDROP;
& whereas by L & R dated 24 & 25 Jan. 1760, WOODDROP conveyed the unsold
real estate to the BRISBANES, as trustees, & they sold the 2 lots at auction to ROBERT RAPER, the highest bidder, but it was thought best that
WOODDROP should be a party to the conveyance; now WOODDROP (for 10 shillings) & ROBERT BRISBANE & WILLIAM BRISBANE (for Ł 975 currency), sell
the 2 lots marked "P" in the plat of Colleton Square, to RAPER; 1 lot
bounding S 40-2/3 ft. on a street by the marsh; E on a street leading
from said street to Hunters Street; N on Hunters Street; W on lot G; the
other being the parcel of land in the marsh of Colleton Square, marked P,
bounding S & E on 2 streets; N on a street alongside the marsh; W on a
lot "O"; the 2 lots being part of lot #80 & its marshes, purchased by L &
R dated 13 & 14 July 1736 by GEORGE HUNTER from JOHN COLLETON, then of

230

Fairlawn Barony, St. Johns Parish, Berkeley Co., & SUSANNAH his wife.
Witnesses: ANDREW CATHCART, CHARLES SHEPHEARD. Before WILLIAM BURROWS,
J.P. Recorded 30 May 1764 by FENWICKE BULL, Register.

Book B-3, p. 455   JOHN MCCORD & SOPHRONISHA his wife, to JOSEPH
8 Dec. 1761   KERSHAW, storekeeper, both of Craven Co., for
Release   Ł 600 currency, 300 a. in Amelia Township,
                        Berkeley Co., bounding NE on Santee River; SE
on ISAAC WINNINGHAM & vacant land; SW on vacant land; NW on vacant land &
on JAMES MICHIE; according to plat dated 9 June 1736; also a half a. lot
in Amelia Township, #101, bounding NE on Front Street; SE on a street; SW
on lot #105; NW on lot #102; which 300 a. & town lot MCCORD purchased on
31 Aug. 1754 from EDWARD WINNINGHAM, laborer, & MARY JACKSON, his mother.
Witnesses: JAMES PRITCHARD, JOHN RUSSELL. Before JOHN REMINGTON, J.P.
Recorded 4 June 1764 by FENWICKE BULL, Register.

Book B-3, p. 460   THOMAS BROUGHTON, ESQ., & JOHN GUERARD, mer-
7 Feb. 1712/3   chant, surviving trustees, to ISAAC MAZYCK,
Release   merchant, all of Charleston, for Ł 60 curren-
                        cy, 32 a., 2 roods, 20 perches. Whereas JOHN,
Earl of Bath, Palatine, on 8 Oct. 1698 granted the Hon. JAMES MOORE 34
a., 2 roods, & 20 perches of land on Ashley River, bounding N on JOHN
HURLSTONE; S & E on CHARLES TOWN; & whereas by Act of Assembly dated 5
Nov. 1709 COL. THOMAS BROUGHTON, CAPT. LEWIS PASQUEREAU, & JOHN GUERARD,
merchant, were appointed trustees to sell MOORE'S estate to pay his
debts; now BROUGHTON & GUERARD sell a portion to MAZYCK; JAMES MOORE re-
serving 2 a. for his own use. Witnesses: BENJAMIN GODIN, SAMUEL EVE-
LEIGH, BENJAMIN DELA CONSEILLERE. Before JACOB MOTTE, J.P. CAPT. DAVID
DAVIS, as attorney for BROUGHTON & GUERARD delivered possession & seizin
to MAZYCK. Witnesses: JOHN PIGHT, JOHN GENDRON, CHARLES MARCHÉ. Before
JACOB MOTTE, J.P. On 12 Apr. 1715 THOMAS BROUGHTON, as only surviving
trustee, for 5 shillings, sold the 2 a. to said ISAAC MAZYCK; JOHN GEN-
DRON acting as his attorney. Witnesses: PETER DE ST. JULIEN, JAMES DE
ST. JULIEN. Witnesses to delivery: BENJAMIN GODIN, JAMES DE ST. JULIEN.
Before RALPH IZARD, J.P. Recorded 7 June 1764 by FENWICKE BULL, Regis-
ter. Entered in Auditor's Office 8 May 1733.

Book B-3, p. 468   Between ISAAC MAZYCK, ESQ., of Charleston,
18 Dec. 1742   eldest son of ISAAC MAZYCK, merchant, of 1st
Deed of Partition   part; PAUL MAZYCK, gentleman, second son, of
                        2nd part; BENJAMIN MAZYCK, planter, of Berke-
ley Co., third son, of 3rd part; STEPHEN MAZYCK, planter, of Berkeley
Co., fourth son, of the 4th part; BENJAMIN GODIN, merchant, of Charleston,
of 5th part; JOHN GENDRON, ESQ., of Craven Co., of 5th part. Whereas the
Lords Proprs. granted CAPT. JAMES MOORE 34 a., 2 roods, 20 perches in
Berkeley Co., bounding N on CAPT. JOHN CUMMINS; W on Ashley River; E & S
on Charleston; & after his death by Act of Assembly dated 5 Nov. 1709 his
estate was put in the hands of certain trustees to be sold to pay his
debts; & whereas THOMAS BROUGHTON & JOHN GUERARD, surviving trustees, on
7 Feb. 1712/13 sold said land to ISAAC MAZYCK, the elder; who by will
dated 10 Jan. 1735 left to the children of his daughter MARYANN, wife of
BENJAMIN GODIN (M____, JUDITH, CHARLOTTE, AMELIA, CATHRINA) 2 a. of said
land, fronting 100 ft. on the street opposite the street leading to the
highway & adjoining certain lots claimed by MR. DUCKETT; & gave his
daughter ELIZABETH, wife of JOHN GENDRON, (JOHN, MARYAN, CATHRINA, &
ELIZABETH) 2 a. adjoining those of the GODINS, also fronting 100 ft. on
said street; & gave his son-in-law, RICHARD WOODWARD, a lot bounding 60
ft. on Queen Street, & 150 ft. deep; & to his 4 sons, ISAAC, PAUL, BENJA-
MIN & STEPHEN, the residue to be equally divided to them; & whereas the
sons allowed the sisters 400 ft.; including a 20 ft. street between the 2
lots, instead of said 200 ft. they allot to ISAAC the lots marked 4, 5,
12, 13, 20, 23, 28 & 31 on their plat; to PAUL, lots 2, 7, 10, 15, 17,
22, 27, & 29; to BENJAMIN, lots 3, 6, 11, 14, 18, 24, 26, & 30; to
STEPHEN, lots 1, 8, 9, 16, 19, 21, 25, & 32; to daughter GODIN'S children
lots, M & G; to daughter GENDRON'S children, lots E & G; to RICHARD WOOD-
WARD lot on Queen Street marked R & W, 60 ft. on Queen Street & 150 ft.
deep; the streets, lanes & alleys to be for public use. Witnesses: JOHN
ROYER, HENRY DEWICK. Before THOMAS LAMBOLL, J.P. Recorded 7 June 1764
by FENWICKE BULL, Register.

Book B-3, p. 476   WILLIAM YOUNG, planter, & MARY (her mark) his
1 Feb. 1754   wife, to HENRY YOUNG, planter, both of Colle-
Release   ton Co., for Ł 200 currency, 150 a. on N side
                         of S fork of Edisto River; as by plat & grant
dated 9 Jan. 1752. Witnesses: DAVID HALL, LUKE PATRICK, BRAND PENDARVIS.
Before JAMES TILLY, J.P. Recorded 7 June 1764 by FENWICKE BULL, Register.

Book B-3, p. 478   PATRICK (his mark) MCCORMICK, planter, & JO-
27 & 28 Mar. 1764   HANNA (her mark) his wife, to JOHN KIRKLAND,
L & R   planter, both of Craven Co., for Ł 500 curren-
                         cy, 200 a. on SW side Wateree River, bounding
SE on SAMUEL BACOT; SW on vacant land; NW on the Hon. THOMAS MICKIE;
which 200 a. were granted 4 Mar. 1755 by Gov. WILLIAM HENRY LYTTLETON to
JOHN CORNELIUS "as family rights"; who, with his wife, ELIZABETH, conveyed PATRICK LAFORTY; who, with his wife, PRUDENCE, sold to PATRICK MCCOR-
MICK. Witnesses: JESSE MOORE, WILLIAM FARGESON, JEREMIAH GALLAHUE. Before THOMAS WADE, J.P. Recorded 8 June 1764 by FENWICKE BULL, Register.

Book B-3, p. 485   ANTHONY (his mark) DUESTO, to BENJAMIN HART,
7 & 8 Mar. 1763   both of Craven Co., for Ł 900 currency, 2
L & R   plantations on S side Wateree River in Fred-
                         ericksburgh Township; 450 a. surrounded by va-
cant land, granted 7 Oct. 1755 to JOSIAH TOMLINSON; & 100 a. SE of above
tract, granted JOSIAH TOMLINSON 1 May 1757. Witnesses: JOSEPH KERSHAW,
DANIEL GARDNER, WILLIAM HUNTER, JR. Before JACOB MOTTE, J.P. Recorded
9 June 1764 by FENWICKE BULL, Register.

Book B-3, p. 491   JACOB FREE, planter, & MARY (her mark) his
8 Feb. 1763   wife, to ANTHONY DUESTO, both of Craven Co.,
Release   for Ł 130 currency, 100 a. on Cedar Creek, a
                         branch of Broad River, surrounded by vacant
land, according to plat dated 1 Aug. 1758; which land FREE purchased 27
July 1762 from JOHN LEE, planter. Witnesses: JOSEPH KERSHAW, SAMUEL
KELLY. Before JACOB MOTTE, J.P. Recorded 9 June 1764 by FENWICKE BULL,
Register.

Book B-3, p. 495   BELLAMY CRAWFORD, ESQ., of Prince William Par-
31 May 1764   ish, to JOHN MURRAY, ESQ., (formerly of
Mortgage   Charleston, now in Great Britain) & WILLIAM
                         MURRAY, ESQ., of Charleston. Whereas WILLIAM
MURRAY (for himself & as attorney for JOHN MURRAY), for Ł 2000 British,
conveyed to CRAWFORD 1250 a. in Granville Co., bounding N on ALEXANDER
FRASER; E on the high road to the old ferry over Port Royal River; W & S
on JOHN MCKENZIE (later JOHN RATTRAY) & on Pocasabo Creek & Whale Branch;
also 78 a. called Roe's Island, between said creek & branch, which plantation & island were sold by L & R dated 20 & 21 Jan. 1758 by JOHN CRO-
KATT & SUSANNAH his wife to JOHN & WILLIAM MURRAY; also 30 slaves; also
the cattle & all stock, tools, carts, carriages, & crops on the plantation; & whereas no money was paid by CRAWFORD, he gives bond to pay within 7 years. Witnesses: CHARLES MOTTE, JOSEPH BRAILSFORD. Before CHARLES
PINCKNEY, J.P. Recorded in Secretary's Book Z.Z., p. 429-433, on 1 June
1764 by GEORGE JOHNSTON, Dep. Sec. Recorded 11 June 1764 by FENWICKE
BULL, Register.

Book B-3, p. 503   HENRY SPRY, planter, to JAMES HARPER, planter,
2 & 3 Nov. 1761   both of Craven Co., for Ł 20 currency, 100 a.,
L & R   on N side Santee River, being the SW part of
                         200 a. granted on 13 Mar. 1751 by Gov. JAMES
GLEN to JOHN BLISS, who sold to SPRY; bounding SE on BLISS & vacant land;
NE on SPRY & vacant land; other sides on vacant land. Witnesses: JOHN
BLISS, WILLIAM BREACH, SAMUEL HARPER. Before JOHN LIVISTON, J.P. Re-
corded 12 June 1764 by FENWICKE BULL, Register.

Book B-3, p. 511   JAMES HARPER, planter, & PURCHASE HARVEY, to
2 & 3 Nov. 1761   HENRY SPRY, both of Craven Co., for Ł 20 cur-
L & R   rency, 100 a. in Craven Co., on N side Santee
                         River, bounding NE & SE on HENRY SPRY; other
sides on vacant land; granted 4 June 1759 by Gov. WILLIAM HENRY LYTTELTON
to JAMES HARPER. Witnesses: JOHN BLISS, WILLIAM BREACH, SAMUEL HARPER.

Before JOHN LIVISTON, J.P. Recorded 12 June 1764 by FENWICKE BULL, Register.

Book B-3, p. 518   JOHN BLISS, shoemaker, & MARY his wife, to
1 & 2 Jan. 1754   HENRY SPRY, planter, both of Craven Co., for
L & R   ₺ 20 currency, 200 a. in Craven Co., on N side
Santee River, bounding SE on BLISS & vacant
land; NE on HENRY SPRY & vacant land; other sides on vacant land; as
granted 13 Mar. 1751 by Gov. JAMES GLEN to JOHN BLISS. Witnesses: JAMES
HARPER, JOHN HARPER, JEAN SPRY. Before RICHARD RICHARDSON, J.P. Recorded 13 June 1764 by FENWICKE BULL, Register.

Book B-3, p. 526   THOMAS HANSCOMBE (HUNSCOMBE), planter, & ELIZ-
10 & 11 Sept. 1761   BETH his wife, & his brother MOSES HANSCOMBE,
L & R   planter, & MARY his wife (THOMAS & MOSES being
only sons of AARON HUNSCOMBE, planter), to
JOSEPH STANYARNE, planter, all of Colleton Co., for ₺ 250 currency, 41 a.
(except a family burying ground 25 ft. square), being the S part of 106
a. on S side John Island granted 13 May 1735 by Lt. Gov. THOMAS BROUGHTON
to AARON HUNSCOMBE; who by will dated 18 Nov. 1760 bequeathed the 106 a.
equally to his 2 sons; the 41 a. called The Point bounding W on JOSEPH
STANYARNE; other sides on marsh of Polo Creek. Witnesses: JOHN HOLMES,
THOMAS ARNOLD, JOHN JURDINE. Before WILLIAM BOONE, J.P. Entered in
Auditor's Book F-6, p. 77, 16 Apr. 1762 by RICHARD LAMBTON, Dep. Aud.
Recorded 14 June 1764 by FENWICKE BULL, Register.

Book B-3, p. 537   WILLIAM GODFREY, planter, & ANNE (her mark)
31 Dec. & 1 Jan. 1764   his wife, to SAMUEL HAMLIN, planter, both of
L & R   St. Georges Parish, Berkeley Co., for ₺ 2100
currency, 207 a. in St. George Parish, bound-
ing NE on WILLIAM DONNING & THOMAS DISTON; SE on THOMAS DISTON; SW on
WILLIAM WAY; NW on RICHARD BEDON. Witnesses: JAMES SMITH, ARCHIBALD
SMITH, HENRY SALTUS. Before JOHN IOOR, J.P. Recorded 15 June 1764 by
FENWICKE BULL, Register.

Book B-3, p. 542   WILLIAM GODFREY, planter, to SAMUEL HAMLIN,
10 Jan. 1764   planter, both of St. George Parish, Berkeley
Release   Co., for 5 shillings, 218-1/2 a. in St. Paul's
Parish, Colleton Co., bounding W on PAUL JENYS
estate; N on THOMAS DISTON estate; E on JAMES SMITH; S on JOHN NORMAN estate; being part of 656 a. Delivery by turf & twig. Witnesses: HENRY
SALTUS, JAMES SMITH, ARCHIBALD SMITH. Before JOHN IOOR, J.P. Recorded
16 June 1764 by FENWICKE BULL, Register.

Book B-3, p. 546   SAMUEL VARNER, of Christ Church Parish, Berke-
13 Mar. 1764   ley Co., gives SARAH HARTMAN, bond to secure
Bond   payment of ₺ 750 currency, with interest, on
13 Mar. 1767. Witnesses: ALLEN MECKEE, FRAN-
CIS JONES. Before WILLIAM VANDERHORST, J.P. Recorded 19 June 1764 by
FENWICKE BULL, Register.

Book B-3, p. 547   SAMUEL VARNER, of Christ Church Parish, Berke-
13 Mar. 1764   ley Co., to SARAH (her mark) HARTMAN, to se-
Mortgage   cure payment of above bond; 405 a. Witnesses:
ALLEN MECKEE, FRANCIS JONES. Before WILLIAM
VANDERHORST, J.P. Recorded 19 June 1764 by FENWICKE BULL, Register. On
17 Sept. 1765 mortgage declared paid. Witness: OLIVER NOYES.

Book B-3, p. 550   WILLIAM ALLSTON, JR., (son of JOHN ALLSTON),
2 & 3 May 1764   planter, & ANN his wife, to JOSEPH ALLSTON,
L & R   planter, both of Prince George Parish, Craven
Co., for ₺ 2500 SC money, 350 a., known as
Welstead Bluff on Sandy Island, bounding N & E on Wando Passo Creek; S on
Long Creek & THOMAS WATIES & Waccamaw River. Whereas WILLIAM WATIES, by
will dated 29 Jan. 1742/3, bequeathed to his son THOMAS, several tracts
of land, particularly 457 a. of swamp land, part of 2 tracts, bounding W
on Peedee, across from the 580 a. & extending E to Wando Passo Creek; S
on MR. ALLSTON; N to a line to be run due E across the river from the
lower boundary line to Wando Passo Creek; also 150 a. on JOHN WELSTEAD'S
Bluff near Waccamaw River; & whereas THOMAS WATIES & ANN his wife, by L &

R dated 3 & 4 June 1761 sold to WILLIAM ALLSTON 200 a. (part of first tract), bounding N & E on Wando Passo Creek or Thorofare; S on Long Creek & WILLIAM ALLSTON'S land (sold at same time to THOMAS WATIES); W on part of the 457 a.; also the 150 a. on Sandy Island at Welstead's Bluff, bounding S on Waccamaw River; W on Wando Passo; N on Marion's Creek & other part of said 150 a.; making total of 350 a.; now WILLIAM ALLSTON sells the 350 a. to JOSEPH ALLSTON. Witnesses: JOHN ALLSTON, NATHANIEL DWIGHT. Before JOHN REMINGTON, J.P. Recorded 21 June 1764 by FENWICKE BULL, J.P.

Book B-3, p. 558
29 & 30 July 1763
L & R

THOMAS PAGETT, planter, of St. George's Parish, & MARY his wife, to JOSEPH ALLSTON, planter, of Craven Co., for Ⱡ 400 currency, 200 a. on Waccamaw at the ferry to ELIAS FOISSIN'S land; being the NW part of 500 a. formerly belonging to GEORGE THREADcraft, father of GEORGE THREADCRAFT, who sold the 200 a. to PAGETT; bounding NW on Waccamaw River; NE on ABRAHAM WARNOCK (now ELIAS FOISSIN); SW on JONATHAN DRAKE; SE on the part sold by GEORGE THREADCRAFT, the father, to his brother THOMAS THREADCRAFT. Witnesses: ROBERT WARING, ARCHIBALD JOHNSTON. Before BENJAMIN YOUNG, J.P. Recorded 22 June 1764 by FENWICKE BULL, Register.

Book B-3, p. 565
24 Oct. 1758
Release

THOMAS BOONE, ESQ., to ROBERT DEANS, carpenter, both of Charleston, for Ⱡ 1400 currency, 2 adjoining lots, #119 & #120, in Charleston, each half an a., English measure, bounding E on Archdale Street; S on Queen Street; W & N on heirs of ISAAC MAZYCK; which 2 lots were granted 13 Aug. 1695 by the Lords Proprs. to SARAH POWYS, widow, (registered 10 Sept. 1695). Witnesses: BENDIX WAAG, JOHN REMINGTON. Before CHARLES WOODMASON, J.P. Indorsed on back: Proprietary Grants for lots 119 & 120 dated 13 Aug. 1695 to SARAH POWYS - registered. On 6 Sept. 1695 SARAH POWYS conveys said 2 lots to JOSEPH BOONE, merchant, not registered. On 14 Mar. 1733 said JOSEPH BOONE by will, his lands not disposed of by his wife ANN during her life, to be divided between the sons of his brother CHARLES BOONE. Said CHARLES leaves 2 sons, CHARLES & THOMAS. CHARLES the son by letter of attorney 2 Sept. 1752 impowers his brother THOMAS to sell. See Secretary's Book H. fol. 356. Recorded 23 June 1764 by FENWICKE BULL, Register.

Book B-3, p. 570
15 & 16 Dec. 1763
L & R

EZEKIEL ALEXANDER, of Mecklinburg Co., NC, & MARTHA (her mark) his wife, to ARCHIBALD MCDOWELL, of same Co., for Ⱡ 13 currency, 200 a. in Granville Co., SC, at Dividing Ridge, between Savannah River & Long Cane, bounding on all sides on vacant land; beginning at a white oak, runs N 24 W 44.73 to a stake on a hill; N 66 E 44.73 to a black oak; S 24 E 44.73 to a stake; S 66 W 44.73 to first station; granted EZEKIAL ALEXANDER 20 Apr. 1763 by Gov. GEORGE JOHNSTON. Before JAMES WYLY, J.P. Recorded 23 June 1764 by FENWICKE BULL, Register.

Book B-3, p. 574
24 & 25 Feb. 1764
L & R

HENRY (his mark) CARTER, in the fork between Congaree & Wateree Rivers, & ELIZABETH (her mark) his wife, to HENRY WHETSTONE, planter, of Orangeburgh Township, for Ⱡ 200 currency, 400 a., being part of a tract of 500 a. at Ox Creek, in Amelia Township, Berkeley Co., bounding E on JOHN SEAL, other sides on vacant land; granted 14 Feb. 1735 to BENJAMIN CARTER; who died intestate, & inherited by his eldest son HENRY; the other 100 a. having been sold to LEWIS YORK by HENRY CARTER. Witnesses: JOHN MCCORD, JOHN RUSSELL. Before MOSES THOMSON, J.P. Entered in Auditor's Book G-7, p. 195, on 2 May 1764 by RICHARD LAMBTON, Dep. Aud. Recorded 23 June 1764 by FENWICKE BULL, Register.

Book B-3, p. 579
29 & 30 Mar. 1763
L & R

JOSIAH TATTNELL, planter, & MARY his wife, to SAMUEL THORPE, planter, both of Granville Co., for Ⱡ 1000 currency, 500 a. on Combahee Island, on S side Coosaw River, granted 17 July 1714 by Gov. CHARLES CRAVEN to ELIZABETH BLAKE, widow; then bounding N on the river; E on WILLIAM HOLMES & ROBERT COCHRAN; S & W on ELIZABETH BLAKE; which land was devised with her other real estate by ELIZABETH to her (then only) son, JOSEPH BLAKE; who conveyed to GEORGE SMITH; who died intestate, & inherited equally by his 3 daughters, ANN, JANE, & SARAH. ANN, JANE (wife of CHARLES FAUCHERAUD), & SARAH HILL by L & R dated 20 &

21 Nov. 1751 sold the 500 a. to EDWARD BULLARD; who by L & R dated 22 & 23 Apr. 1754 sold to ROBERT GODFREY; who with his wife ELIZABETH, by L & R dated 8 & 9 Feb. 1758 sold to ROBERT SAMS; who, with MARY his wife, by L & R dated 31 Oct. & 1 Nov. 1759 sold to NATHANIEL BARNWELL; who with MARY his wife, sold to JOSIAH TATTNELL. Witnesses: WILLIAM ELLIOTT, JR., JOHN GRAY. Before THOMAS MIDDLETON, J.P. Recorded 25 June 1764 by FEN-WICKE BULL, Register.

Book B-3, p. 589
9 & 10 Dec. 1763
L & R

THOMAS JONES, to PETER MELLETT, both of Craven Co., for Ł 150 currency, 200 a. in Craven Co., on N side Wateree River, in North Britain tract, surrounded by vacant land; granted 6 Nov. 1751 to THOMAS JONES. Witnesses: THOMAS PRESTWOOD, ISAAC BRUNSON, DANIEL BRUNSON. Before HENRY CASSELS, J.P. Recorded 26 June 1764 by FENWICKE BULL, Register.

Book B-3, p. 596
22 & 23 June 1764
L & R

ELIZABETH (her mark) VERNER, widow, of Charleston, to ISAAC BRUNSON, planter, for Ł 30 currency, the 100 a. in Craven Co., granted Landwick VERNER "on bounty"; on N side Santee River at Jack's Creek, surrounded by vacant land. Witnesses: MARK ANTHONY BESSELLEU, EBERHARD EHNY. Before JOHN REMINGTON, J.P. Recorded 27 June 1764 by FENWICKE BULL, Register.

Book B-3, p. 601
5 Feb. 1759
L & R

HENRY (his mark) OVERSTREET, planter, to NIM-ROD KILCREASE, planter, both of Granville Co., for Ł 100 currency, 200 a. on Turkey Creek, a branch of Stephens Creek, Granville Co., granted OVERSTREET by Gov. JAMES GLEN on 11 Oct. 1755; bounding on vacant land. Witnesses: ANTHONY WELLS, WILLIAM ODOM. Before ULRICH TOBLER, J.P. Recorded 3 July 1764 by FENWICKE BULL, Register.

Book B-3, p. 606
4 Aug. 1762
Lease for 1 Year

ROBERT (his mark) KILCREASE (CILCREASE), to NIMROD KILCREASE, for 5 shillings, for 1 year, 200 a. on Turkey Creek, a branch of Stephens Creek, in Granville Co. Witnesses: THOMAS PRICE, JOSEPH OLDHAM. Before JACOB SOMMARRAL, J.P. Recorded 5 July 1764 by FENWICKE BULL, Register.

Book B-3, p. 608
29 June 1764
Release

PETER MONCLAR, gentleman, of Charleston, to DR. ADRIAN MAYER, of Purysburgh, for Ł 75 currency, 50 a. in Purysburgh Township, bounding N on JACOB TANNER & FREDERICK HOLZENDORPH; S on FREDERICK DEJEAN; E on JS. JACOB TANNER; W on JOHN PETER SURY & JOHN CHIVELLETTE; also lot #72 in Purysburgh; bounding S & W on a street; N on lot #71; E on lot #74; which tract & town lot were granted by GEORGE II to ANDREW MONCLAIR, & inherited by his only son PETER. Witnesses: STEPHEN CATER, DANIEL MACKENET. Before ROBERT WILLIAMS, J.P. Recorded 5 July 1764 by FENWICKE BULL, Register.

Book B-3, p. 611
5 Dec. 1712
Grant

Grant of land to St. John's Parish Church. Landgrave JOHN COLLETON, of St. John's Parish, Island of Barbados, by his attorneys, CAPT. JOHN HARLESTON & CAPT. THOMAS GADSDEN; to Gov. CHARLES CRAVEN, CHARLES HART, ROBERT GIBBES, THOMAS BROUGHTON, NICHOLAS TROTT, RICHARD BERESFORD, ARTHUR MIDDLETON, the Rev. MR. GIDEON JOHNSTON (rector of St. Philips, Charleston), the Rev. DR. FRANCIS LEJAU (rector of St. James, Goose Creek), the Rev. MR. ROBERT MAULE (rector of St. John's Parish, Berkeley Co.), COL. WILLIAM RHETT, HENRY NOBLE, COL. GEORGE LOGAN, RALPH IZARD, CAPT. BENJAMIN QUELCH, CAPT. DAVID DAVIS, WILLIAM GIBBON, merchant; CAPT. PETER SLANN; CHARLES HILL, Landgrave JOSEPH MORTON, HUGH HEXT, JOHN WOODWARD, WILLIAM BULL, & PHILIP GENDRON; the commissioners appointed by Act of Assembly dated 13 Nov. 1706 for erecting churches for public worship, etc., etc.; 3 a., English measure, in Berkeley Co., in St. John's Parish, on Tibicops Haw Hill, in barony of Watbo, for a church & cemetery; also 100 a., English measure, on N part of Watbo barony, bounding S on PETER GUERARD & SAMUEL DUBOURDIEU; for the use of the minister; COLLETON to have a pew in the church & a vault in the cemetery; no public house for sale of liquor to be erected in church yard. Witnesses: JOHN MILLS, BURCH HOTHERSALL, JOHN SABB (manager of

Watbo). On 4 Apr. 1764, the witnesses being dead, CAPT. JOHN HARLESTON
of St. Thomas Parish, testified in regard to SABB'S handwriting before
BENJAMIN SIMONS, J.P. Recorded 7 July 1764 by FENWICKE BULL, Register.

Book B-3, p. 621   JOHN MCLEAN, bookbinder, & JANE (her mark) his
1 & 2 Feb. 1764   wife (formerly JANE MASSEY, spinster), to WIL-
Mortgage   LIAM MAXWELL & ROBERT ROWAND, merchants, all
                        of Charleston. Whereas JANE, before her mar-
riage, had mortgaged a certain town lot to ROWAND for Ł 500, & owed MAX-
WELL, & ROWAND, merchants, & copartners, Ł 320 for merchandise; & whereas
ROWAND has advanced MCLEAN Ł 100; now to secure payment of said debts
MCLEAN & his wife convey to MAXWELL & ROWAND part of lot #164 bounding E
60 ft. on King Street; W on JOHN DRAYTON; S 142 ft. on MR. VARAMBEAU; N
on estate of JOHN HYCOTT. Witnesses: JOHN MILLER, PETER BELIN, JOHN
MODDIE. Before JAMES GRINDLAY, J.P. Recorded 9 July 1764 by FENWICKE
BULL, Register. On 15 June 1778 ROWAND declared mortgage paid. Witness:
GEORGE SHEED.

Book B-3, p. 629   JOHN FRAMPTON, & ELIZABETH his wife, to JOSEPH
4 & 5 Feb. 1759   FICKLING, both of Edisto Island, for Ł 1400
L & R   currency, 200 a. on Edisto Island, Colleton
                        Co., bounding NE on JOHN JENKINS; SE on a
creek & marsh; SW on WILLIAM EDINGS; NW on WILLIAM EDINGS & PAUL HAMIL-
TON. Witnesses: WILLIAM BAYNARD (Quaker), RICHARD RIPPON, WILLIAM (his
mark) RUSSELL. Before WILLIAM MAXWELL, J.P. Entered in Auditor's Book
G-7, p. 219, on 19 June 1764, by RICHARD LAMBTON, Dep. Aud. Recorded 12
July 1764 by FENWICKE BULL, Register.

Book B-3, p. 636   JAMES STOBO, ESQ., of Colleton Co., to STEPHEN
25 & 26 Mar. 1763   BULL, ESQ., of Sheldon, Granville Co., for
L & R   Ł 3000 currency, 450 a., bounding SW & NW on
                        Savannah River; SE on PATRICK MACKAY; other
sides on Cowpen, alias Clidsdale, Creek; which 450 a. were inherited by
PATRICK MACKAY, who sold to STOBO. Witnesses: ARCHIBALD STOBO, JOHN
FREER, JR., WILLIAM SKIRVING. Before JACOB MOTTE, J.P. Recorded 14 July
1764 by FENWICKE BULL, Register.

Book B-3, p. 644   JOHN SMITH, merchant, & ELIZABETH his wife, of
7 & 8 May 1764   Charleston, to JOHN JOYNER, planter, of Gran-
L & R   ville Co., for Ł 3285 currency, 730 a. on Port
                        Royal Island, in Granville Co., bounding N on
WILLIAM ELLIOTT & JOHN SMITH; SW on EBENEZER HOLMES; other sides on Port
Royal River. Witnesses: ISAAC HAYNE, ROBERT WILLIAMS, JR. Before GEORGE
JOHNSTON, J.P. Recorded 18 July 1764 by FENWICKE BULL, Register.

Book B-3, p. 652   ISAAC HOLMES, merchant, eldest son & heir of
4 & 5 Aug. 1761   ISAAC HOLMES, gentleman, to JOHN SMITH, mer-
L & R   chant, both of Charleston, for Ł 3000 curren-
                        cy, 980 a. (including 510 a. surplus land), on
W side Port Royal River, in Granville Co., bounding S & SW on MR. WATSON
& heirs of EBENEZER HOLMES; W on MR. WATSON & Palmetors Creek; N on Palmetors Creek & vacant land; as surveyed by JAMES MCPHERSON. Whereas
FRANCIS HOLMES, merchant, of Charleston, owned 1020 a. on Port Royal Island, bounding S on a creek; W on a creek; N on vacant land; being part
of 1420 a. granted by the Lords Proprs. to JOHN PENNY; & whereas by will
dated 4 May 1726 FRANCIS HOLMES gave his son ISAAC, father of ISAAC,
party hereto, 1/2 the 1020 a.; the other half to his son EBENEZER; &
whereas on death of FRANCIS his 2 sons held the undivided estate as tenants in common; & whereas by will dated 9 July 1751 son ISAAC directed
his executors to sell his real & personal estate, the money to be divided
equally amongst his children; & after his death his son ISAAC, party
hereto, obtained a writ of partition, & was allotted 980 a. including
510 a. found to be surplus land within the old lines; now he sells to
SMITH, the highest bidder. Witnesses: THOMAS BALLANTINE, JOHN CHAMPNEYS.
Before ROBERT WILLIAMS, JR., J.P. Entered in Auditor's Book F-6, p. 114,
on 19 June 1762 by RICHARD LAMBTON, Dep. Aud. Recorded 20 July 1764 by
FENWICKE BULL, Register.

Book B-3, p. 565   ISAAC HOLMES, merchant, & REBEKAH his wife, to
12 & 13 Jan. 1762   JOHN SMITH, merchant, both of Charleston, for

236

L & R   ₺ 770 currency, 290 a. (being surplus land of
                              510 a. laid out for EBENEZER HOLMES), on Port
Royal Neck, Granville Co., bounding NE on The Old Fort & ISAAC HOLMES
(now JOHN SMITH); SE on marsh of Port Royal River; SW on the 510 a. tract;
W on Pennys Creek; N on WATSONS land; which 290 a. were granted 10 Nov.
1761 by Lt. Gov. WILLIAM BULL to ISAAC HOLMES. Witnesses: SARAH SKIRV-
ING, JOHN CHAMPNEYS. Before ROBERT WILLIAMS, JR., J.P. Recorded 23 July
1764 by FENWICKE BULL, Register.

Book B-3, p. 671   ANDREW ROBERTSON, merchant, & HELEN his wife
20 & 21 Apr. 1763   (daughter of DANIEL CRAWFORD, ESQ.), to GEORGE
L & R   KINCAID, cooper; all of Charleston; for ₺ 6000
                             currency, part of lot #12, being the eastern-
most brick tenement lately occupied by THOMAS DAY, now by WILLIAM LOOCOCK;
bounding N 18 ft. on Broad Street; E 99 ft. on MARY ELLIS; W on the W
brick tenement & land thereto, devised by DANIEL CRAWFORD to his son BEL-
LAMY CRAWFORD, who sold to ISAAC WALDROON; S on part of lot #12 belonging
to ANDREW ROBERTSON & HELEN his wife (formerly to JOSEPH WRAGG; lately to
DANIEL CRAWFORD); also that part of lot #12 formerly belonging to WRAGG,
now to HELEN ROBERTSON), bounding S 37 ft. 2 in. on Elliott Street; E 75
ft. on MR. CALVERT; N on part of same lot; W on part of same lot occupied
by WILLIAM LOOCOCK. Whereas DANIEL CRAWFORD, by will dated 30 May 1760,
bequeathed to his daughter HELEN ROBERTSON the said eastern brick tenement & the land S to Elliott Street; now she sells both lots to KINCAID.
Witnesses: JOHN POAUG, GEORGE WARDROP. Before JAMES GRINDLAY, J.P. Recorded 24 July 1764 by FENWICKE BULL, Register.

Book B-3, p. 681   LEONARD ROOF, planter, & RACHEL (her mark) his
1 & 2 June 1763   wife, to JOHN MORF, planter, both of Saxegotha
L & R   Township, for ₺ 400 currency, 2 tracts of 25
                             a. each. Whereas Gov. JAMES GLEN on 20 May
1747 granted CHRISTIAN BRABANT 50 a. in Saxegotha Township bounding NE on
Santee River; SE on CHRISTIAN BRABANT; SW on vacant land; NW on HENRY
GALLMAN; & whereas CHRISTIAN BRABANT & FROWNICK, his wife, for ₺ 100 currency, by L & R dated 9 & 10 July 1755 sold the 50 a. to JOHN MARTIN MIL-
LER; & whereas MILLER was entitled to a bounty of another 50 a. in said
Township, bounding on all sides on vacant land; & whereas for ₺ 300 cur-
rency, MILELR sold ROOF 2 tracts of 25 a. each, in Saxegotha Township,
the 25 a. in pine land, granted MILLER, bounding SE on part of said tract
now owned by ROOF; other sides on vacant land; the other 25 a. bounding
NE on ROOF; SE on BRABANT & ROOF; SW on vacant land; NW on HENRY GALLMAN
(see L & R 28 & 29 Sept. 1758). Witnesses: CHRISTIAN THEUS, JOHN CONRAD
GEIGER. Before JOHN HAMILTON, J.P. Recorded 25 July 1764 by FENWICKE
BULL, Register.

Book B-3, p. 689   JOHN SMITH, merchant, of Charleston, & ELIZA-
1 & 2 Feb. 1764   BETH his wife, to ROBERT MACLEOD, merchant, of
L & R   Granville Co., for ₺ 2000 currency 52 a. on NW
                             side of Stony Creek, a branch of Pocotalago
River, in Prince William Parish, Granville Co.; sold to SMITH by JONATHAN
BRYAN & MARY his wife, by L & R dated 28 & 29 June 1751; bounding NW on
JOHN GARNIER; N & NE on high road to Pocotalago Bridge; also 184-1/2 sq.
poles, or perches, near Stony Creek, sold to SMITH by WILLIAM SIMMONS in
1754; bounding E, N, & W on said SIMMONS; SW on the high road & said 52
a. Witnesses: MARY BRYAN, ISAAC HAYNE. Before GEORGE JOHNSTON, J.P.
Recorded 26 July 1764 by FENWICKE BULL, Register.

Book B-3, p. 698   JOHN JENKINS, shopkeeper, of Charleston, &
27 & 28 Feb. 1745   MARY his wife, to JOHN FRAMPTON, planter, of
L & R   Colleton Co., for ₺ 1400 currency, 200 a. on
                             Edisto Island, Colleton Co., bounding NE on
WILLIAM JENKINS; SE on a creek & marsh; SW on JOSEPH RUSSELL; NW on JO-
SEPH RUSSELL & PAUL HAMILTON. Whereas Gov. ROBERT GIBBES on 24 Sept.
1710 granted DOROTHY HAMILTON (afterwards OGLE) 400 a. on Edisto Island,
in Colleton Co., which she, on 4 Nov. 1710, sold to JOHN JENKINS, father
of JOHN, party hereto; bounding N on JOHN HAMILTON; E on JOHN FRAMPTON; S
on a creek; W on HENRY BOWER; & whereas on 17 Jan. 1735 JOHN JENKINS, the
father, sold 200 a., being the SW part of said 400 a., to his son JOHN,
bounding W on JOSEPH RUSSELL; E on his son WILLIAM JENKINS (the other
200 a.); now JOHN JENKINS, the son, sells his part to FRAMPTON.

Witnesses: JOHN TUCKER, HUGH CARTWRIGHT, THOMAS KUNDELL. On 20 July 1764
JAMES GRINDLAY & CHARLES GRIMBALL recognized signatures of CARTWRIGHT, &
JOHN & MARY JENKINS. Before ROBERT WILLIAMS, JR., J.P. Recorded 26 July
1764 by FENWICKE BULL, Register.

Book B-3, p. 707   GEORGE KINCAID, cooper, to BENJAMIN SMITH,
14 July 1764   ESQ., both of Charleston, for ₤ 2500 currency,
Mortgage   the E brick tenement occupied by DR. WILLIAM
                  LOOCOCK, on part of lot #12; bounding N 18 ft.
on Broad Street; E 90 ft. on MARY ELLIS; W on W brick tenement; devised
by DANIEL CRAWFORD to his son BELLAMY; who sold to ISAAC WELDROON; S on
part of #12 formerly belonging to JOSEPH WRAGG, now to GEORGE KINCAID.
Witnesses: JOSEPH BRAILSFORD, CHARLES MOTTE. Before CHARLES PINCKNEY,
J.P. Recorded 27 July 1764 by FENWICKE BULL, Register. On 8 Mar. 1770
BENJAMIN SMITH declared mortgage paid. Witness: JAMES KER.

Book B-3, p. 714   CHARLES FARRINGTON, gentleman, formerly of
8 & 9 Mar. 1762   Moat, Co. of Westmeath, Ireland, now of SC, to
L & R & Bond   THOMAS PERRY, planter, of St. Helena Parish,
                  Granville Co., for ₤ 550 currency, 2 tracts of
200 a. Whereas by L & R dated 25 & 26 Nov. 1728 JOHN BAILY of Ballinaclough, Co. of Tipperary, Ireland, son & heir of JOHN BAILEY of same
place, by his attorney, ALEXANDER TRENCH, merchant, of Charleston, sold
THOMAS FARRINGTON, gentleman, of St. Helena Parish, Granville Co., 100 a.
on Hilton Head Island, St. Helena Parish, bounding NW on Skull Creek; NE
& SE on ALEXANDER TRENCH; & whereas by L & R of same date said JOHN BAIL-
EY, by his attorney, TRENCH, sold PATRICK GILCHRIST, surgeon, of St. Hel-
ena Parish, 100 a. on Hilton Head Island, bounding NE on DANIEL WILLIAMS;
SW on 134 a. belonging ALEXANDER TRENCH; & whereas THOMAS FARRINGTON pur-
chased GILCHREST'S tract & by will dated 1 Feb. 1732 bequeathed all his
real & personal estate to his nephew JOHN FARRINGTON, of Aghram, Co. of
Galloway, Ireland; who bequeathed his estate to his sister JUDITH FAR-
RINGTON, of Aghram, who died unmarried but appointed her brother, CHARLES
SLINGSBY FARRINGTON, merchant, of Aghrain (?) her executor, who as her
executor & as heir of JOHN FARRINGTON became entitled to the estates of
JOHN & JUDITH; & whereas CHARLES died in 1757 & bequeathed his estate in
the West Indies & America to his son, CHARLES, party hereto, now he sells
the 2 tracts to PERRY. Witnesses: WILLIAM O'BRIEN, ANDREW AGGNEW. Before WILLIAM HARVEY, J.P. Recorded 27 July 1764 by FENWICKE BULL, Register.

Book B-3, p. 724   THOMAS PERRY, planter, & MARTHA PHEBY PERRY,
30 July 1763   his wife, to HENRY LADSON, planter, both of
L & R   St. Helena Parish, Granville Co., for ₤ 641
                  currency, the 200 a. he purchased from FAR-
RINGTON (see p. 714). Witnesses: JOSEPH SCOTT, CALEB TOOMER. Before
THOMAS MIDDLETON, J.P. Recorded 28 July 1764 by FENWICKE BULL, Register.

Book B-3, p. 732   THOMAS SHUBRICK, merchant, of Charleston, to
30 Oct. 1762   JAMES POSTELL, of Colleton Co., at public auc-
Release   tion, for ₤ 1600 currency, a lot marked #3 on
                  a certain plat; bounding N 60 ft. on Tradd
Street; E on lot #2 sold to RAWLINS LOWNDES; W on lot #4 sold to CHARLES
PINCKNEY; S on a branch of CONSEILLERE'S Creek; the lot being 515 ft.
deep, including 131 ft. of sand beach or shole land. Whereas SHUBRICK
owned 4 lots in St. Michael's Parish, in Charleston at the W & S side of
Tradd Street, being Nos. 245, 246, 95 & 96; also a sand beach of 6 a., 1
rood, 12 perches, S & W of said lots; all formerly belonging to BENJAMIN
DELA CONSEILLERE, merchant; which lots SHUBRICK had resurveyed & marked
1, 2, 3, 4, 5, & 6 on his plat of the resurvey; now he sells #3 to POS-
TELL. Witnesses: BENJAMIN WARING, JR., ISAAC LESESNE, JR. Recorded 30
July 1764 by FENWICKE BULL, Register.

Book B-3, p. 739   JAMES POSTELL, ESQ., & ANN his wife, of St.
17 Dec. 1762   Bartholomew's Parish, Colleton Co., to THOMAS
Release   FERGUSON, ESQ., of St. Paul's Parish, Colleton
                  Co., for ₤ 1900 currency, the lot #3 of the
resurvey, purchased from SHUBRICK (see p. 732). Witnesses: JAMES SKIRV-
ING, JOHN GLEN. Before JOHN TROUP, J.P. Recorded 30 July 1764 by FEN-
WICKE BULL, Register.

Book B-3, p. 744   JERMYN WRIGHT, gentleman, of Granville Co., to
20 Jan. 1763   HENRY GRAY, gentleman, for Ł 550 currency, 80
                         a. in Berkeley Co., purchased from JOSEPH BA-
CON for Ł 500; bounding NW on Ashley River & THOMAS BAKER; SW on JOSIAH
OSGOOD; SE on ROBERT WRIGHT; also 200 a. in same Co., purchased from JOHN
POSTELL in 1735; bounding N & NE on ISAAC PORCHER; SE & NW on JOHN BOIS-
SEAU; SW on BENJAMIN WARING. Witnesses: THOMAS TUCKER, CHARLES WRIGHT.
Before JAMES PARSONS, J.P. Recorded 31 July 1764 by FENWICKE BULL, Reg-
ister.

Book B-3, p. 748   HENRY GRAY, ESQ., & ANN his wife, to JAMES
3 July 1764   PARSONS, ESQ., for Ł 550 currency, the 2
Release   tracts of 80 a. & 200 a. in Berkeley Co., pur-
                         chased from JERMYN WRIGHT (see p. 744). Wit-
nesses: MARY DUPRE, JOHN GLEN. Before JOHN TROUP, J.P. Recorded 31 July
1764 by FENWICKE BULL, Register.

Book B-3, p. 753   JAMES PARSONS, ESQ., of Charleston, to THOMAS
10 July 1764   FERGUSON, ESQ., of St. Pauls Parish, for Ł 550
Release   currency, the 2 tracts of 80 & 200 a. in Berke-
                         ley Co., purchased from HENRY GRAY (see p. 744
& 748). Witnesses: JOHN CHAPMAN, JOHN GLEN. Before JOHN TROUP, J.P.
Recorded 31 July 1764 by FENWICKE BULL, Register.

Book B-3, p. 756   DANIEL MARETTE, sexton, to ADRIAN MAYER, ESQ.,
13 Jan. 1764   both of Purysburgh, for Ł 5 currency, a 1 a.
Release   lot #77 in Purysburgh, bounding N & E on a
                         street; W on lot #75; S on lot #78. Witness-
es: CHRISTOPHER BAHR, LEWIS (his mark) WINGLAR, planter. Before DANIEL
PEPPER, J.P., at Okatee Creek. Recorded 1 Aug. 1764 by FENWICKE BULL,
Register.

Book B-3, p. 758   JAMES STOBO, ESQ., of Colleton Co., to CAPT.
9 & 10 Sept. 1762   PATRICK MACKAY, ESQ., of Granville Co., for
L & R   Ł 5000 currency, 900 a. in Granville Co.,
                         bounding NW on Glidsdale Creek & JAMES BUL-
LOCK; SW on branch of Savannah River; other sides on PATRICK MACKAY; as
granted 13 July 1737 to the Rev. MR. ARCHIBALD STOBO, & inherited by his
eldest son, said JAMES STOBO; the land to free of claim of dower by ELIZ-
ABETH, wife of JAMES STOBO. Witnesses: CHARLES ODINGSELLS, ARCHIBALD
STOBO. Recorded 2 Aug. 1764 by FENWICKE FULL, Register.

Book B-3, p. 766   PATRICK MACKAY, ESQ., & ISABELLA his wife, of
15 & 16 Sept. 1762   Granville Co., to JOSEPH NUTT, merchant, of
L & R   Charleston, for Ł 4400 SC money, 800 a. in St.
                         Peters Parish, Granville Co., bounding S on N
branch of Savannah River; SE on JOHN SMITH; N on PATRICK MACKAY; NW on
JAMES STOBO, (later STEPHEN BULL, JR.); according to plat; 80 a. being
marked off by a pricked line to run NW 71° parallel to & 6 chains distant
from N boundary on entire plat. Witnesses: WILLIAM MAINE, JOHN SMITH.
Before ROBERT WILLIAMS, JR., J.P. Recorded 2 Aug. 1764 by FENWICKE BULL,
Register.

Book B-3, p. 774   JOSEPH NUTT, merchant, to JOHN SMITH, merchant,
24 & 25 May 1764   both of Charleston, for Ł 23,000 currency, the
L & R   800 a. in St. Peters Parish, Granville Co.,
                         excepting 80 a., as purchased from PATRICK
MACKAY (see p. 766); also 48 Negro slaves; 20 head neat cattle; 5 horses;
all rice in the straw; plantation tools, etc. Witnesses: ROBERT WILLIAMS,
JR., WILLIAM STOUTENBURGH. Before JAMES GRINDLAY, J.P. Recorded 2 Aug.
1764 by FENWICKE BULL, Register.

Book B-3, p. 783   JOHN HOLMES, merchant, eldest son & heir of
27 & 28 July 1764   ISAAC HOLMES, of Church Street, Charleston, to
L & R   ROBERT QUASH, planter, of St. Thomas Parish,
                         for Ł 4100 currency, part of a lot in Charles-
ton, bounding E 18 ft. on Church Street; N 140 ft. on WILLIAM BAMPFIELD;
S on FRANCIS ROCHE; W on WILLIAM BAMPFIELD & a 6 ft. alley; which part of
a lot ISAAC HOLMES purchased from BENJAMIN CLIFFORD & SARAH his wife & by
will dated Nov. 1754 bequeathed to his son JOHN. Witnesses: WILLIAM

BAMPFIELD, THOMAS GRIMBALL, J.P. Before WILLIAM BURROWS, J.P. Recorded
3 Aug. 1764 by FENWICKE BULL, Register.

Book B-3, p. 792   EGERTON LEIGH, attorney-at-law, & MARTHA his
1 & 2 Sept. 1763   wife, of Charleston, to PETER PORCHER, plant-
L & R   er, of St. Stephens Parish, for Ł 5000 curren-
                          cy, a lot of 1 a., 2 roods, 20 perches, marked
H on the plan of the lands of GEORGE, Lord Anson, called Ansonborough,
near Charleston; also part of lot marked G on said plan, which LEIGH purchased from ALEXANDER GORDON & FRANCES CHARLOTTE GORDON by L & R dated
22 & 23 July 1755; bounding W 410 ft. on LUKE STOUTENBURGH; N on JOSEPH
WRAGG; E on a pond; S on part of lot H; also 9383 S.F., being the E part
of a lot containing 1 a., 2 roods, marked E on said plan, purchased by
LEIGH from ALEXANDER TAYLOR by deed of feoffment dated 23 Jan. 1762;
bounding N on part of lot F; E on LUKE STOUTENBURGH; S on heirs of RICH-
ARD WAINWRIGHT; W on part of lot E; also part of lot F, bounding N 62 ft.
on a lane leading from Broad Road; E 42 ft. on lot H; s on part of lot E;
W on part of lot F; which piece of lot F LEIGH purchased from ALEXANDER
GORDON by deed of feoffment dated 9 Sept. 1757; also the W part of lot P,
which LEIGH bought from STOUTENBURGH on 27 July 1761; bounding S 68 ft.
on a street marked & & &; E 318 ft. on other part lot P belonging to
EGERTON LEIGH; N on lot H; W on lot Q. Witnesses: ROBERT WILLIAMS, JR.,
JOSEPH BRAILSFORD. Before JAMES GRINDLAY, J.P. Recorded 6 Aug. 1764 by
FENWICKE BULL, Register.

DEEDS BOOK "C-3"
AUGUST 1764 - APRIL 1765

Book C-3, p. 1   HENRY HOWORTH, gentleman, & MARTHA his wife
19 & 20 Oct. 1763   (daughter of JAMES MICHIE), to WILLIAM MICHIE,
L & R   merchant, both of Charleston, for Ł 10,120
                        currency, their undivided 1/4 part of the res-
idue of JAMES MICHIE'S real estate, which consisted of the following:
half of lot #106 in Charleston, bounding S 74 ft. on Broad Street (leading from Cooper River by the State House & Market Place to Ashley River);
E 221 ft. 10 in. on SOLOMON LEGARE; W on lot occupied by MRS. THOMAS HOY-
LAND, widow, (formerly by MRS. ELEANOR SANWELL, then by WILLIAM BRADLEY);
N on JOHN BERESFORD; also 1165 a. (in 3 tracts, formerly thought to be
1119 a.) in Prince William Parish, Granville Co., bounding NW on STEPHEN
BULL; SW on BELLINGER & BROADBELT; which by L & R dated 12 & 13 Sept.
1753 were sold to JAMES MICHIE by JOSEPH BUTLER, planter, now of Georgia,
then of Prince William Parish; also 1000 a., called Mt. Alexander, on
Combahee River, sold 6 Apr. 1757 by CHARLES LOWNDES, P.M., to JAMES
MICHIE, because of judgment against estate of ALEXANDER MOON; bounding E
on JAMES HARTLEY; W on JOSHUA SANDERS; NW on JOSEPH BUTLER; also 864-1/2
a. in Berkeley Co., formerly WILLIAM DRY; bounding N on JOSEPH HURST; S
on SAMUEL BRAILSFORD (formerly NICHOLAS BURNHAM, lately JAMES WRIGHT); E
on Cooper River; also 86 a. (part of 170 a. formerly owned by THOMAS
DALE) in Berkeley Co., bounding SW on Goose Creek Road; N on the 864-1/2
a. tract; E on part of 170 a. belonging to SAMUEL BRAILSFORD (formerly to
JAMES WRIGHT); also 85 a. of marsh, adjoining last 2 tracts; bounding S
on a creek of Cooper River dividing said marsh from SAMUEL BRAILSFORD'S
(formerly JAMES WRIGHT); N on the 864-1/2 a.; E on Cooper River; as
granted MICHIE 30 Aug. 1755; also several tracts on S side Wateree River,
Craven Co.; 2500 a., bounding SE on WILLIAM & JOHN SCOTT; SW on vacant
land; NW on JAMES MCCRELLESS; as granted MICHIE 12 June 1751; 330 a.,
bounding NW on BRYAN TOLAND; SE on JAMES MCCRELLESS; granted MICHIE 6
Mar. 1750; 135 a., bounding SE on JOHN MCKENZIE; other sides on vacant
land; granted MICHIE 1 June 1750; 200 a., bounding NW on JOHN TOD, JR.;
other sides on vacant land; granted MICHIE 12 June 1751; 250 a. surrounded by vacant land, granted MICHIE 12 June 1751; also 250 a. bounding SE
on NOAH GILES; other sides on vacant land; granted MICHIE 2 July 1751;
200 a., surrounded by vacant land; granted MICHIE 12 June 1751; 266 a.
bounding NW on JAMES MICHIE; other sides on vacant land; granted MICHIE 7
Oct. 1755; 172 a. & 278 a., both surrounded by vacant land; 326 a.,
bounding NW on COL. HENRY FOX; other sides on vacant land; which 3 were
granted JOHN MCKENZIE, merchant, who on 3 & 4 June 1752 sold to MICHIE;
also 100 a. in Amelia Township, Berkeley Co., bounding NW on Santee

240

River; & an a. lot #80 in Town of Amelia, bounding NE on lots 81 & 82; SE
on a street & on JOHN BUNCH; other sides on vacant land; granted MICHIE
25 June 1736; also 669 a. in N Briton tract, Craven Co., surveyed 19 June
1749 for KENNETH MICHIE, deceased, surrounded by vacant land when granted
MICHIE 1 Feb. 1759; also 1000 a. on S side Wackamaw River, Craven Co.,
bounding E on vacant land; W on JESSE BADENHOP; S on BADENHOP & vacant
land; granted 29 May 1736 to ISAAC LESESNE, who on 1 & 2 Mar. 1736 sold
to MICHIE; also, in Fredericksburg Township Craven Co., 290 a., bounding
NW on ROBERT SEAWRIGHT; NE on GEORGE SENIOR & JOHN WILLIAMS; other sides
on Wateree River; granted 15 May 1751 to WILLIAM NEWIT EDWARDS, who, on 2
& 3 Sept. 1751 conveyed to MICHIE; 250 a., bounding SE on ROBERT SEA-
WRIGHT; other sides on Wateree River; granted 5 Sept. 1750 to WILLIAM
SEAWRIGHT, who on 17 & 18 Aug. 1752 conveyed to MICHIE; 50 a., bounding
NW on WILLIAM SEAWRIGHT; NE & SW on Wateree River; SE on GEORGE SENIOR &
WILLIAM NEWIT EDWARDS; granted 5 Sept. 1750 to ROBERT SEAWRIGHT, who on
27 & 28 Aug. 1752 conveyed to MICHIE. Whereas JAMES MICHIE, ESQ., by
will dated 6 May 1758 bequeathed the residue of his estate equally to his
wife, MARTHA, & his daughter MARY; appointing his wife, MARTHA, his
friend DAVID CAW, & WILLIAM MICHIE, party hereto, his executors; & whereas he died in Great Britain some time after, leaving said MARTHA MICHIE,
his widow, & said MARTHA HOWORTH & MARY MICHIE (now wife of CHARLES OGIL-
VIE, merchant, of London) his daughters; & whereas the widow & MARY became entitled to the whole estate as tenants in common, & MARTHA (mother
of MARY & MARTHA) died intestate in Great Britain 27 Apr. 1762 before
partition was made; so that her half share descended equally to MARY &
MARTHA, & MARTHA thus became owner of 1/4 of her father's estate; now she
& her husband sell their fourth part to WILLIAM MICHIE. Witnesses: JOHN
GLEN, THOMAS HEYWARD. Before JAMES PARSONS, J.P. Recorded 10 Aug. 1764
by FENWICKE BULL, Register.

Book C-3, p. 25   JONATHAN DRAKE, planter, to MARY WILLIAMS,
14 & 15 Feb. 1764   spinster, daughter of CAPT. JOHN WILLIAMS,
L & R   mariner, both of St. Johns Parish, Berkeley
                    Co., for ₤ 115 currency, 20 a., part of 3000
a., bounding W on Westberry's Creek & Back River, beginning at a live oak
at Westberry's Landing, running N 78° E 50-1/2 perch to a black oak
stump, thence S 12° 63-1/2 perch E to pine tree marked 3 notches, thence
S 78° W 50-1/2 perch to stake in Back River marsh, thence to beginning N
12° W 63-1/2 perch, as by plat. Witnesses: JOHN WILSON, JAMES WILLIAMS,
JOHN WILLIAMS. Before THOMAS SKOTTOWE, J.P. Recorded 10 Aug. 1764 by
FENWICKE BULL, Register.

Book C-3, p. 30   JOHN LOGAN, merchant, of Charleston, & ELIZA-
1 & 2 Aug. 1764   BETH his wife, to THOMAS FORD, planter, of St.
L & R   Bartholomew's Parish, for ₤ 1500 currency,
                    515 a. (formerly thought 373 a.) in Colleton
Co., bounding SW on BENJAMIN FULLER & THOMAS JONES (formerly ROGER SAN-
DERS & WILLIAM CLIFFORD); NE on THOMAS FORD; SE on FREDERICK GRIMKE.
Whereas on 30 Sept. 1736 the said 373 a. were granted WILLIAM CRAWL, who
by will dated 4 Nov. 1743 devised the land to his daughter, ELIZABETH,
but as the will had only 2 witnesses to it the land legally descended,
with his other lands, to his 3 daughters, (JANE (wife of JOHN LINDER),
MARGARET (her sister by the same mother), & ELIZABETH (by another wife);
& whereas MARGARET died in infancy her third part descended to JANE, her
whole sister & heiress; & whereas JOHN & JANE LINDER by L & R dated 30 &
31 Mar. 1731 conveyed their 2 undivided shares to ELIZABETH & her husband;
now they sell to FORD. Witnesses: PETER BUTLER, JOHN SANDIFORD. Before
JAMES PARSONS, J.P. Recorded 11 Aug. 1764 by FENWICKE BULL, Register.

Book C-3, p. 39   JOHN CATTELL & BENJAMIN CATTELL, sons of BEN-
13 & 14 Oct. 1756   JAMIN CATTELL, of 1st part; RICHARD BEDON &
L & R Tripartite   MARTHA his wife, of 2nd part; BENJAMIN FULLER
                    (1 of the sons of WILLIAM FULLER the younger)
of 3rd part; all planters, of Berkeley Co. Whereas THOMAS ELLIOTT & ROG-
ER SAUNDERS the younger, both planters, of Colleton Co., executors of
will of ROGER SAUNDERS the elder, by L & R dated 17 & 18 June 1751 sold
JOHN & BENJAMIN CATTELL 715 a. in Colleton Co., on head of Horse Shoe
Creek, & surrounded by vacant land, granted ROGER SAUNDERS 17 Mar. 1732
by Gov. ROBERT JOHNSON; & whereas THOMAS ELLIOTT in Mar. 1754, as executor, sold JOHN & BENJAMIN 447 a. in Colleton Co., on NW side Horse Shoe

Savannah, bounding SW on MR. CLIFFORD & on vacant land; as granted ROGER
SAUNDERS 13 July 1737 by Lt. Gov. THOMAS BROUGHTON; & whereas JOHN & BEN-
JAMIN CATTELL in certain deeds of trust dated 18 June 1751 & (?), stated
that the 2 tracts were purchased by RICHARD & MARTHA BEDON in trust for
the use of the children of WILLIAM FULLER the younger, the purchase money
being from 2/3 of WILLIAM FULLER'S personal estate, & that the names of
JOHN & BENJAMIN CATTELL in said L & R were used in trust only; now JOHN &
BENJAMIN CATTELL, at the request of RICHARD & MARTHA BEDON, convey to
BENJAMIN FULLER, for Ł 900 currency (part of his share of his father,
WILLIAM FULLER'S personal estate), 581 a. (or the N half of the 2 tracts
of 715 & 447 a.) bounding NW on MR. JONES; NE on MR. GRIMKÉ; S on other
half; SW on MR. ELLIOTT. Witnesses: WILLIAM FULLER, GEORGE PURKIS. Be-
fore JACOB MOTTE, J.P. Recorded 15 Aug. 1764 by FENWICKE BULL, Register.

Book C-3, p. 50   SARAH WARING, WILLIAM SANDERS, & JAMES SANDERS,
2 & 3 Apr. 1764   acting executors of will of BENJAMIN WARING,
L & R   of St. George Dorchester Parish, Berkeley Co.,
                       to JOHN MACTEER, planter, for Ł 1102:10:0 cur-
rency, 150 a. in Granville Co., bounding SE on CAPT. JAMES MCPHERSON; NE
on JOHN LLOYD; NW & SE on vacant land; which 150 a. BENJAMIN WARING by
his will dated 20 July 1759 directed to be sold by his executors, SARAH
WARING, WILLIAM SANDERS, JAMES SANDERS, JOSEPH WARING, GEORGE SMITH &
THOMAS SMITH, JR. Witnesses: ALEXANDER SANDERSON, ANDREW BROUGHTON, DAN-
IEL SLADE. Before JOHN IOOR, J.P. Recorded 18 Aug. 1764 by FENWICKE
BULL, Register.

Book C-3, p. 56   WILLIAM VANDERHORST, planter, of Berkeley Co.,
26 Mar. 1756   (1 of the sons of JOHN VANDERHORST the elder,
Release   planter), & MARGARET his wife, to THOMAS
                       LYNCH, ESQ., of Craven Co., for Ł 2500 curren-
cy, 390 a. in Craven Co., on N side Santee River, bounding NE & W on Col.
THOMAS LYNCH; granted by Lt. Gov. THOMAS BROUGHTON on 12 May 1735 to JOHN
VANDERHORST who by will dated 29 Nov. 1738 bequeathed the tract to his
son WILLIAM. Witnesses: WILLIAM ELLIS, WILLIAM GUERIN. Before THOMAS
SKOTTOWE, J.P. Recorded 20 Aug. 1764 by FENWICKE BULL, Register.

Book C-3, p. 64   The Rt. Hon. GEORGE, Lord Anson, Baron of Sob-
31 Aug. & 1 Sept. 1761 erton, in Co. of Southampton, Great Britain,
L & R   by his attorney, RICHARD LAMBTON, ESQ., of
                       Charleston, SC, to WILLIAM ELLIS, merchant, of
Charleston, for Ł 2050 currency, 3-1/4 a. in Ansonburgh, near Charleston,
bounding E on CHRISTOPHER GADSDEN; W on Squirrel Street; S on JOHN RAT-
TRAY; N on a marsh of Cooper River. Witnesses: JACOB WARLEY, JOHN RAT-
TRAY. Before JAMES GRINDLAY, J.P. Recorded 21 Aug. 1764 by FENWICKE
BULL, Register.

Book C-3, p. 70   JACOB DATARING, yeoman, of Saxegotha Township,
15 & 16 May 1764   Berkeley Co., to JOHN CONRAD GEIGER, planter,
L & R   of same place, for Ł 750 currency, 100 a. in
                       said Township, granted 16 Sept. 1739 by Lt.
Gov. THOMAS BROUGHTON to HERMAN CHRISTOPHER PORDRICK (alias HERMAN CHRIS-
TOPHER DATARING), who died intestate, & inherited by his eldest son JA-
COB. JACOB reserved for himself the half a. lot, #14, in Saxegotha, men-
tioned in said grant. Witnesses: JOHN GALLMAN, JACOB GEIGER. Before JO-
SEPH CURRY, J.P. Recorded 25 Aug. 1764 by FENWICKE BULL, Register.

Book C-3, p. 77   THOMAS LYNCH, ESQ., of Prince George Parish,
31 Oct. 1760   Craven Co., & HANNAH his wife, to FRANCIS KIN-
Release   LOCH, ESQ., of Charleston, for Ł 4236 curren-
                       cy, 1171 a. in several tracts; viz; 390 a.,
bounding S on Santee River; other sides on THOMAS LYNCH; granted 12 May
1735 to JOHN VANDERHORST, who sold to LYNCH by L & R dated 25 & 26 Mar.
1756; 51 a., bounding E on last tract; N & W on said LYNCH; being part of
500 a. granted 29 Aug. 1718 to COL. THOMAS LYNCH; 492 a., bounding SW on
above 2 tracts; N & E on LYNCH; being part of 500 a. granted 19 Aug. 1718
to COL. THOMAS LYNCH; 238 a., bounding S on last 2 tracts; N on ALARD
BELIN & on LYNCH; other sides on LYNCH; being part of 4500 a. granted 28
Apr. 1733 to COL. THOMAS LYNCH. Plat given. Witnesses: MARY ATCHISON,
ARCHIBALD JOHNSTON. Before CHARLES FYFFE, J.P. Recorded 27 Aug. 1764 by
FENWICKE BULL, Register.

Book C-3, p. 82   ARCHIBALD BAIRD, planter, of Craven Co., to
10 Mar. 1764   FRANCIS KINLOCH, ESQ., for Ŀ 2609:15:0 curren-
Mortgage   cy; payable with interest 10 May 1764; 13
                         Negro slaves; also 282 a. formerly belonging
to JOHN CLELAND, bounding SW on ARCHIBALD BAIRD; NW on WILLIAM SHACKEL-
FORD & PAUL TRAPIER; NE on ANTHONY WHITE; SE on JOHN CLELAND'S land called Wehaw; also 284 a. formerly belonging to ROBERT WEAVER, bounding NE on
FRANCIS KINLOCH & on Black River; SE on MR. HUGER; SW on above tract; NW
on FRANCIS KINLOCH. Witnesses: WALTER SCOTT, WILLIAM BLYTHE. Before
ROBERT HERIOT, J.P. Recorded in Secretary's Book & &, p. 148, on 29 Aug.
1764, by GEORGE JOHNSTON, Dep. Sec. Recorded 1 Sept. 1764 by FENWICKE
BULL, Register.

Book C-3, p. 85   ROBERT BRISBANE & WILLIAM BRISBANE, merchants,
25 & 26 June 1764   to GEORGE SEAMAN, ESQ.; all of Charleston; for
L & R   Ŀ 2220 currency; lot I, part of Colleton
                         Square in Charleston, bounding S on 160 ft. on
Hunters Street; E on lot H; W on lot K; N on another street; being part
of lot #80 purchased by GEORGE HUNTER by L & R dated 13 & 14 July 1736
from JOHN COLLETON, ESQ., & SUSANNAH his wife, of St. John's Parish,
Berkeley Co. Witnesses: NICHOLAS BEDGEGOOD, JAMES BRISBANE. Before
PETER MANIGAULT, J.P. Recorded 1 Sept. 1764 by FENWICKE BULL, Register.

Book C-3, p. 94   JOHN (his mark) MELLEU (MELLEV), wheelwright,
11 May 1758   to GEORGE PENDER, planter, both of New Wind-
L & R   sor, for Ŀ 235 currency, 250 a. in Granville
                         Co., bounding W on Savannah River; E & S on
vacant land; N on TINHORD SHIVIER. Witnesses: JOHN SPEISEGGER, JOSANS
(his mark) TOBLER, JOHN (his mark) NAGEL. Before ULRICH TOBLER, J.P.
Recorded 4 Sept. 1764 by FENWICKE BULL, Register.

Book C-3, p. 100   ANTHONY WELES (WLESH) sells GEORGE PENDER,
18 Dec. 1758   for Ŀ 200 SC money, 100 a. on an island (the
Bond   other part belonging to JOSEPH WILLSON ?) &
                         gives bond that he will deliver firm title.
Witnesses: DANIEL BREOMRR, SANDERS (his mark) COLSON. Before JOHN TOB-
LER, J.P. Recorded 4 Sept. 1764 by FENWICKE BULL, Register.

Book C-3, p. 101   JOHN (his mark) FRASER, planter, & ELIZABETH
4 & 5 Sept. 1761   (her mark) his wife, to GEORGE KEITH, tanner,
L & R   both of Saxegotha Township; for Ŀ 610 curren-
                         cy, 200 a., part of 300 a., in Saxegotha Town-
ship; bounding NE on Santee River; SE on JOHN GALLESER & vacant land; NW
on the remaining 100 a.; also town lot #74 in Saxegotha. Whereas the
300 a. & lot #74 were granted 5 June 1742 by Lt. Gov. WILLIAM BULL to
JACOB REIMERSPERGER; the 300 a. bounding NW on HANNAH MARIA STOLEA; &
whereas upon REIMERSPERGER'S death the land was inherited by his 4 daughters & their respective husbands (JOHN FRASER, FREDERICK HOUX, ULRIC
BUSSER, & JACOB REISTER); & whereas by L & R dated 24 & 25 Aug. 1754 the
4 husbands conveyed to JOHN FRASER (coheir) their several fourth parts of
the 300 a. & the town lot; now he sells to KEITH. Witnesses: JOHN HAMEL-
TON, HENRY (his mark) GALLMAN. Before STEPHEN CRELL, J.P. Entered in
Auditor's Book E, p. 163 on 24 Oct. 1761 by GEORGE JOHNSTON, for RICHARD
LAMBTON, Dep. Aud. Recorded 12 Sept. 1764 by FENWICKE BULL, Register.

Book C-3, p. 108   ISAAC DACOSTA, merchant, of Charleston of 1st
12 & 13 Mar. 1764   part; to JOSHUA HART, IMMANUEL CORTISSOS, JO-
L & R   SEPH DACOSTA & SAMUEL DECOSTA, & members of
                         Beth Elohim Congregation of Charleston; BENJA-
MIN MENDES DACOSTA, JOSEPH SALVADOR, SOLOMON DACOSTA, MOSES FRANCO, & JO-
SHUA MENDES DACOSTA, of City of London, & members of the Portuguese Jew-
ish Congregation known as Sahar Ashamaim; JACOB LOPES TORRES, ISAAC
MENDES FURTADE, BENJAMIN DIAS FERNANDES, ISAAC HENRIQUEZ, & ABRAHAM AGUI-
LAR, members of the Jewish Congregation in Kingstown, Island of Jamaica,
known as Sahar Ashamaim; ISAAC PIAZ, BENJAMIN MESSIAS, DAVID CASTELLO,
DAVID LINDO, & ISAAC PINHEIRS, Members of the Jewish Congregation in
Bridge Town, Island of Barbados, known as Nidhe Ishrael; JACOB FRANKS,
DANIEL GOMES, BENJAMIN GOMES, ISAAC MENDES SEIXAS, & HEYMAN LEVY, of Jew-
ish Congregation known as Seherit Israel, in New York City; MOSES LOPES,
MOSES LEVY, NAPHTALI HART, JACOB RODRIGUES (?) RIVERA, & AARON LOPES, of

the Jewish Congregation of Newport, R.I., known as Yeshuat Israel; BENJA-
MIN SHEFTAL, MORDECAI SHEFTAL, MINIS MINIS, ISAAC DELYON, & LEVY SHEFTAL,
of the Jewish Congregation of Savannah, Georgia, known as Mikve Israel;
of 2nd part. Whereas by L & R tripartite, dated 4 & 5 Apr. 1754 between
PETER TAYLOR, ESQ., surviving executor of will of WILLIAM SMITH, planter,
of St. Philips Parish, Charleston, who was eldest son of WILLIAM SMITH,
merchant, of Charleston, of 1st part; ELIJAH PRIOLEAU, ANDREW SMITH, &
JOSEPH SMITH, executors, & MARGARET SMITH, executrix of will of JOHN
SMITH, planter, of Colleton Co., another son of WILLIAM SMITH, merchant,
of 2nd part; & ISAAC DACOSTA, of 3rd part; said PETER TAYLOR, ELIJAH
PRIOLEAU, ANDREW SMITH, JOSEPH SMITH, & MARGARET SMITH sold ISAAC DACOSTA
1-3/4 a. part of 250 a. on Charleston neck; the 1-3/4 a. adjoining the
Village of Cannonsborough; bounding N on the 250 a. & a road leading to
the Broad Path; E on said road & GABRIEL GUIGNARD'S marsh; S & W on said
marsh & the 250 a.; & whereas DACOSTA bought the land for a private burying ground for his family but finding it a convenient place for a burying
ground for the Jews in SC, now, for Ł 70 currency, he conveys the land to
Beth Elohim Congregation. Witnesses: CHARLES DUDLEY, THOMAS NETHERCLIFT.
Before CHARLES WOODMASON, J.P. Recorded 13 Sept. 1754 by FENWICKE BULL,
Register. Plat by ROBERT K. PAYNE, Sur.

Book C-3, p. 122   ADAM CULLIATT, planter, & carpenter, of Jack-
23 & 24 June 1763   sonborough, PonPon, to JOHN GRAHAM, ESQ., of
L & R   Savannah, Georgia, for Ł 1400 currency, 300 a.
                          in Granville Co., SC, bounding W on Savannah
River; S on ELIAS BARNARD; E & N on vacant land; as granted 16 Sept. 1738
to ADAM CULLIATT (father of ADAM, party hereto) & PETER NETMAN, in jointenancy. NETMAN died, & CULLIATT, the father, inherited. He died intestate & son ADAM inherited. Witnesses: CHARLES MOTTE, JOHN MATHEWES. Before CHARLES PINCKNEY, J.P. Recorded 14 Sept. 1764 by FENWICKE BULL,
Register.

Book C-3, p. 131   WILLIAM MOORE, planter, of St. Peters Parish,
5 Sept. 1764   Granville Co., to JOHN CLUNIE & CHARLES BROWN,
Mortgage   merchant, for Ł 1450 currency; 300 a. & a
                          dwelling house in Ebenezer District, on Rooty
Branch, Georgia, also 200 a. on Black Swamp, adjoining JOHN SMITH; also
250 a. on Cypress Creek, adjoining WILLIAM PARMENTER in Purysburgh; & all
his goods & chattels, etc., in SC & Georgia. Witnesses: BELLAMY CRAW-
FORD, CHARLES DALTON. Before STEPHEN DRAYTON, J.P. Recorded 18 Sept.
1764 by FENWICKE BULL, Register.

Book C-3, p. 134   DAVID FULTON, planter, of Prince Frederick
12 Sept. 1764   Parish, Craven Co., to JOHN PERDRIAU & JOHN
Mortgage   FABRE, for Ł 5268 currency, 289 a. on S side
                          Black Mingo Creek, bounding E on COL. JOHN
WHITE; S on vacant land; W on WILLIAM THOMPSON; also 15 Negroes. Witnesses: JOHN WAGENFELD, JOSEPH ROPER. Before GEORGE JOHNSTON, J.P. Recorded in Secretary's Book V.V., p. 155 on 15 Sept. 1764 by GEORGE JOHN-
STON, Dep. Sec. Recorded 20 Sept. 1764 by FENWICKE BULL, Register.

Book C-3, p. 137   HUMPHRY SOMMERS, gentleman, & SUSANNAH his
12 & 13 Sept. 1764   wife, to WILLIAM WILLIAMSON, ESQ., both of
L & R   Charleston, for Ł 1600 currency, lot #1 on re-
                          survey plat, bounding N 47 ft. on Tradd
Street; W on RAWLINS LOWNDES'S lot #2; S on DELA CONSEILLERE'S Creek; the
lot being 442 ft. S from Tradd Street, including about 12 ft. of sand
beach. Whereas THOMAS SHUBRICK, merchant, owned 4 lots in St. Michael's
Parish at W end of S side of Tradd Street, known as Nos. 245, 246, 95, &
96, also a sand beach of 5 a., 1 rood, 12 perches, S & W of said lots,
formerly belonging to BENJAMIN DELA CONSEILLERE, merchant, which lots he
had resurveyed, platted, & marked 1, 2, 3, 4, 5, & 6; & whereas SHUBRICK
by L & R dated 29 & 30 Oct. 1762 sold lot #1 to SOMMERS; now he sells to
WILLIAMSON. Witnesses: MARY WARING, HUGH RUTLEDGE. Before J. RUTLEDGE,
J.P. Recorded 21 Sept. 1764 by FENWICKE BULL, Register.

Book C-3, p. 145   JACOB MOTTE, JR., & REBECCA his wife, daugh-
17 & 18 Sept. 1764   ter of COL. ROBERT BREWTON; of Charleston; to
L & R   ROBERT QUASH, planter, of Parish of St. Thom-
                          as & St. Dennis, for Ł 3900 currency, part of

lot #73 in St. Michael's Parish, Charleston, bounding N 32 ft. on Tradd Street; E 100 ft. on JANE BOONE; S on THOMAS CAPERS; W on JOHN SAVAGE (formerly BENJAMIN SCOTT); with the brick house. Witnesses: JOSEPH BRAILSFORD, CHARLES MOTTE. Before CHARLES PINCKNEY, J.P. Recorded 23 Sept. 1764 by FENWICKE BULL, Register.

Book C-3, p. 153
8 & 9 Feb. 1764
L & R

JOHN SCHWINT, chirurgeon; FREDERICK SHRADY, cordwainer; PHILIP MINSING, blacksmith; ABRA-HAM SPIDLE, tanner; MELCHOR VARLY, butcher; JOHN MACK, baker; JOHN KELLAY, baker; & ERNST HOUFF, wheelwright; all of Charleston; to DR. JOHN SCHWINT, FREDERICK SHRADY, PHILIP MINSING, ABRAHAM SPIDLE, MELCHER VARLY, JOHN MACK, JOHN KELLAY, ERNST HOUFF, CHRISTIAN DUSE, tailor; JOHN WAGNER, merchant; JACOB BRIGEL, bricklayer; MICHAEL KALTEISON, inn keeper; FREDERICK HOUFF, organist; JOHN CHIRCHAR, laborer; HENRY MAZER, baker; JACOB WIRTE, inn keeper; FREDERICK ENNY, cordwainer; FREDERICK KAUFMAN, musician; DANIEL STROUBLE, butcher; MICHAEL BENDER, cordwainer; CONRAD TATTNER, cooper; CLEMENCE POMGEETNER, stocking knitter; ALEXANDER SAYFRYT, baker, CHRISTOPHER SHEETS, baker; CHRISTIAN KAYL, blacksmith; JONAS BEARD, carpenter; JOHN HOUFF, blacksmith; JOHN SPIDLE, butcher; MATHEW BETER, baker; ABRAHAM WURSHUG, inn keeper; JOHN VERNER, planter; FRANCIS GROUSMAN, carter; JOHN KAYLE, cooper; MICHAEL KELLAR, cordwainer; DANIEL EGLHER, cordwainer; JOHN WICKMAN, cordwainer; CHRISTOPHER PACKER, carpenter; GEORGE YOUNG, butcher; FREDERICK EVERLAY, carpenter; FREDERICK ROWE, weaver; MICHAEL MUNCKFUS, blacksmith; MICHAEL RICKER, laborer; CHRISTIAN CALLER, joiner; ZACHARIAH STIRLING, laborer; JOHN HAINS, carter; ELIAS HOUSER, laborer; JOHN SMITH, cordwainer; FREDERICK MATUZ, tailor; GEORGE ADE, carter; JOHN YEORST, butcher; GEORGE BERGOULT, tinker; JOHN LEHRE, inn keeper; JOHN SCHETTERLE, baker; ADAM SPIDLE, butcher; MARTIN MILLER, bricklayer; & EBERHART ENNY, butcher; all of Berkeley Co.; for ₤ 800 currency, lot #255 & St. John's Church to be used by the German Lutheran Congregation or Society of Christians; a parsonage house to be built thereon for the Lutheran minister. Whereas JAMES ALLEN, planter, of Christ Church Parish, only surviving brother & heir of THOMAS ALLEN the younger (who died in infancy & was eldest of the 2 sons & heir of their mother, FRANCES ALLEN, formerly FRANCES NORTHALL A KINSWOMAN OF FRANCES SIMONDS who was widow of HENRY SIMONDS, original grantee of said lot. FRANCES ALLEN died intestate during the lifetime of her husband, THOMAS ALLEN the elder), by L & R dated 22 & 23 Jan. 1759 sold to parties of 1st part, lot #255, bounding N 232 ft. on lot #260; E 97 ft. on lot #253, then occupied by JOSEPH MOODY; W on Archdale Street; & whereas said Parties leased a part of the lot to certain persons for a term of years & laid out part of the lot for an alley; & whereas the first group (SCHWINT, SHRODY, MINSING, SPIDLE, VARLY, MACK, KELLAY, & HOUFF) with the aid of the second group of men, & other protestants, agreed to appropriate the lot for the building of a German Lutheran Church, parsonage, & burial place; & whereas the lot has been fenced in & a large Meeting House built; now it is turned over to the congregation. Witnesses: The Rev. MR. JOHN NICHOLAS MARTIN, JACOB WARLEY, THOMAS LAMBOLL. Before CHARLES WOODMASON, J.P. Recorded 28 Sept. 1764 by FENWICKE BULL, Register.

Book C-3, p. 173
24 & 25 May 1764
L & R

JOHN BARNWELL, planter, & MARTHA his wife, to GEORGE ROBINSON, mariner; both of Beaufort, St. Helena Parish, Granville Co.; for ₤ 100 currency, lot #75 in Beaufort, granted BARN-WELL 13 Oct. 1759 by Gov. WILLIAM HENRY LYTTELTON; bounding N on lot #74 granted FREDERICK FRENCH; E on Scott Street; S on lot #76 granted JOHN GODFREY; W on lot #70 granted THOMAS WIGG in trust. Witnesses: JOHN GRAYSON, ANDREW AGGNEW. Before THOMAS MIDDLETON, J.P. Recorded 3 Oct. 1764 by FENWICKE BULL, Register.

Book C-3, p. 179
9 & 10 Feb. 1761
L & R

MORRIS MURPHEY, merchant, to JAMES SAUDNERS, planter, both of Craven Co., for ₤ 700 currency, 450 a. in the Welch Tract, in Craven Co., bounding NE on JOHN BROWN; SE & NW on vacant land; SW on Peedee River; as granted 20 May 1747 by Gov. JAMES GLEN to MICHAEL MURPHEY (see Secretary's Book L. L. fol. 328), & inherited by MORRIS MURPHEY. Witnesses: MALACHI MURFEE, NATHANIEL SANDERS, REUBIN WHITE. Before WADE BLAIR, J.P. Recorded 4 Oct. 1764 by FENWICKE BULL, Register.

Book C-3, p. 184   JAMES TAYLOR (his mark) WHITE, planter, of
18 & 19 Nov. 1761   Prince George Parish, Craven Co., to MALACHI
L & R   SAUNDERS, of St. Marks Parish, Craven Co., for
                        Ł 200 currency, 200 a., part of 300 a. in the
Welch Tract granted WHITE on 8 Nov. 1757 by Gov. WILLIAM HENRY LYTTELTON;
the 300 a. bounding N on Salsters marsh; W & SW on unknown land; SE on
vacant land; E on heirs of JAMES GILLISPIE; WHITE having conveyed 100 a.
in the upper corner of 300 a. to ABRAHAM MOORE. Witnesses: MORRIS MUR-
PHEY, REUBIN WHITE, NATHANIEL SANDERS. Before WADE BLAIR, J.P. Recorded
4 Oct. 1764 by FENWICKE BULL, Register.

Book C-3, p. 190   The Rev. MR. JOHN BROWN, & SARAH (her mark)
19 & 20 Nov. 1761   his wife, to JAMES SAUNDERS, planter, both of
L & R   Peedee, Craven Co., for Ł 200 currency, 200 a.
                        granted by Gov. JAMES GLEN on 6 June 1747 to
BROWN; surrounded by vacant land. Witnesses: JOHN MCCANTS, WILLIAM SNOW,
MALACHI MURFEE. Before WADE BLAIR, J.P. Recorded 5 Oct. 1764 by FEN-
WICKE BULL, Register.

Book C-3, p. 197   WILLIAM (his mark) FLETCHER, planter, of JEF-
15 & 16 July 1762   FERYS Creek, to SWINTHEA BIRKITT, of Great
L & R   Peedee River, for Ł 125 SC money, 250 a. grant-
                        ed FLETCHER 8 Nov. 1757 by Gov. WILLIAM HENRY
LYTTELTON; bounding E on Peedee River; W on JOHN LOFTUS & ALEXANDER
THOMPSON; N & S on vacant land. Witnesses: ELIZABETH SANDERS & NATHANIEL
SANDERS (brother & sister). Before CHARLES WOODMASON, J.P. Recorded 6
Oct. 1764 by FENWICKE BULL, Register.

Book C-3, p. 202   MALACHI MURFEE, planter, to NATHANIEL SANDERS,
2 & 3 June 1763   planter, both of St. Marks Parish, Craven Co.,
L & R   for Ł 150 SC money, 550 a. on SW side Black
                        Creek, granted 30 Apr. 1748 by Gov. JAMES GLEN
to said MURFEE; the other sides bounding on vacant land. Witnesses: WIL-
LIAM WATKINS, JOHN ALRAN. Before JOSEPH BRITTON, J.P. Recorded 8 Oct.
1764 by FENWICKE BULL, Register.

Book C-3, p. 208   JOB ROTHMAHLER, merchant, to JOHN BEDINGFIELD,
17 Nov. 1760   planter, both of Peedee, for Ł 487:10:0 cur-
Release   rency, 400 a. in Craven Co., bounding NE on
                        Great Peedee River; NW on ELLERBY & vacant
land; SE on vacant land & JOHN MATHEWS. Witnesses: JOSEPH HOOLE, ALEXAN-
DER SMART, HENRY BEDINGFIELD, GEORGE HICKS. Before JOHN ALRAN, J.P. Recorded 8 Oct. 1764 by FENWICKE BULL, Register.

Book C-3, p. 213   WILLIAM GARDNER, to PHILIP PLEDGER, both of
11 Feb. 1763   Craven Co., for Ł 500 currency, 100 a. in the
Release   Welch Tract, bounding on Crooked Creek & va-
                        cant lands; granted GARDNER 4 Nov. 1762. Wit-
nesses: LEWIS GARDNER, SARAH GARDNER. Before ALEXANDER MCKINTOSH, J.P.
Recorded 11 Oct. 1764 by FENWICKE BULL, Register.

Book C-3, p. 214   THOMAS CARY, to PHILIP PLEDGER, both of Craven
9 May 1763   Co., for Ł 400 currency, 150 a., half of a
Release   tract adjoining PHILIP PLEDGER granted CARY 18
                        Jan. 1743; beginning at the river in the mid-
dle of the front running parallel with the other lines. Witnesses: BEN-
JAMIN HUDSON, THOMAS (his mark) SIMS. Before ALEXANDER MCKINTOSH, J.P.
Recorded 12 Oct. 1764 by FENWICKE BULL, Register.

Book C-3, p. 215   SARAH MIDDLETON, widow of the Hon. ARTHUR MID-
20 & 21 Dec. 1761   DLETON, to JOHN THOMPSON & JAMES HUNTER, mer-
L & R   chants, of Charleston, for Ł 800 currency, a
                        1/4 a. lot #15 in Town of Dorchester, St.
George Parish, bounding E on High Street; S on DR. WILLIAM WHITE; W on
undivided lands; N on MRS. BOONE. Witnesses: SARAH DART, MORTON WILKIN-
SON. Before HENRY MIDDLETON, J.P. Recorded 12 Oct. 1764 by FENWICKE
BULL, Register.

Book C-3, p. 222   ANDREW MAYBANK, planter, & MARTHA his wife, to
10 July 1764   EDWARD SPLATT, planter, of Colleton Co., for

Mortgage   Ł 4000 currency, 402 a. on E side PonPon Riv-
                                            er, granted by Gov. ROBERT JOHNSON on 21 May
1734; to JOHN SPLATT the elder; then bounding E on MR. EAGLES; N & W on
JOHN BEE; S on Penny's Creek; & devised to JOHN SPLATT the younger; who
devised to his brother EDWARD; who conveyed to MAYBANK. Witnesses: GID-
EON DUPONT, JR., WILLIAM EBERSON, DAVID MAYBANK. Recorded 13 Oct. 1764
by FENWICKE BULL, Register. On 2 June 1773 EDWARD SPLATT declared mortgage paid. Witnesses: WILLIAM RUGELEY, JAMES CARSON.

Book C-3, p. 233   PAUL TRAPIER, ESQ., to FRANCIS KINLOCH, ESQ.,
13 Nov. 1761   both of Prince George Parish, Craven Co.
Release by Exchange   Whereas on 14 Sept. 1705 the Lords Proprs.
                              granted JOHN ABRAHAM MOTTE 200 a. in Craven
Co., bounding NE on Wahaw Creek; NW & SW on vacant land; SE on ELIZABETH
ELLIOTT; which land descended to WILLIAM SCREVEN; who, with his wife
SARAH, by L & R dated 14 & 15 Nov. 1749 sold to WILLIAM POOLE; who died
intestate; & inherited by his only surviving son, JOSEPH; who by L & R
dated 24 & 25 Nov. 1757 conveyed to JOHN WATIES; by whose will the land
was sold by his executors, ANDREW JOHNSTON & THOMAS WATIES, by L & R dated 2 & 3 Jan. 1751 sold to TRAPIER; & whereas part of the 200 a. was covered by the waters of the reservoir owned by the heris of FRANCIS KIN-
LOCH, the stooping of which water would be a detriment to said estate;
now TRAPIER & KINLOCH agree to exchange the land covered by the water for
a part of the estate lying between TRAPIER'S land & Wehaw Creek. TRAPIER
gives KINLOCH that land covered by the reservoir & its branches, shown
within yellow lines on plat, reserving the cypress trees & timber. Witnesses: ANN MAYRANT, ARCHIBALD BAIRD. Before JOHN MAYRANT, J.P. Recorded 15 Oct. 1764 by FENWICKE BULL, Register. Plat of part of Wehaw Tract,
formerly belonging to JOHN CLELAND, now to KINLOCH heris; also part of
Windsor Tract belonging to PAUL TRAPIER; showing parts affected by great
reservoir; also part of Wehaw Tract, within green lines, bounding S on
Wehaw Creek; W on a line running NW 22° 26 chains 50 links to N on Windsor Tract; E on Black River; being the land KINLOCH exchanged with TRAP-
IER for the several branches of reservoir, within yellow lines.

Book C-3, p. 238   VALENTINE KLAWDY, planter, of Charleston Neck,
15 & 16 Oct. 1764   in order to make some provision, after his
L & R   death, for his wife SUSANNAH & her son TOBIAS
                             MYER by her former husband, conveys to PHILIP
MENSING, blacksmith, of Charleston, for Ł 500 currency, in behalf of TO-
BIAS MYER, the S half of 9 a. 6 perches in St. Philips Parish, conveyed
to KLAWDY by THOMAS FERGUSON & MARY ELLIOTT, executor & executrix of will
of ARTIMUS ELLIOTT; bounding W on the Broad Path; S on a road leading
from Broad Path to plantation of GEORGE AUSTIN; E on GEORGE AUSTIN; N on
other half lately sold to JOHN KELLY; to be held in trust for SUSANNAH'S
use during her lifetime; then for TOBIAS MYER. Witnesses: JOHN KELLY,
JONAS BEARD. Before CHARLES WOODMASON, J.P. Recorded 17 Oct. 1764 by
FENWICKE BULL, Register.

Book C-3, p. 244   JOSEPH BALL, sugar baker, & ELIZABETH (her
9 & 10 Mar. 1764   mark) his wife, to THOMAS YOUNG, bricklayer,
L & R   of Charleston, for Ł 1600 currency, a piece of
                             marsh land on S side of lot #77 purchased by
BALL from executor of will of JOHN MATHEWES; bounding 64 ft. on Church
Street, & by a line running 154 ft. W from Church Street to part of said
marsh behind high land of JOSEPH BALL; & from W end of said line N 33 ft.
towards NW corner of BALL'S vault or necessary house; then a line from N
to S 76 ft. on back part said marsh to an intended 30 ft. street; then a
line from W to E 130 ft. along said Canal or street to Church Street.
Witnesses: HENRY SLADE, WILLIAM BALL. Before JAMES GRINDLAY, J.P. Recorded 19 Oct. 1764 by FENWICKE BULL, Register.

Book C-3, p. 252   WILLIAM WRAGG, ESQ., of Charleston, to JOHN
17 & 18 Oct. 1764   HORRY, ESQ., of Santee, for Ł 350 currency,
L & R   200 a. in Craven Co., bounding S on ROBERT
                             SUTTON; SW on Santee River; NW on JOHN BELL;
as granted 14 Feb. 1715 (recorded 10 July 1717) to WILLIAM GIBBON; later
conveyed to TWEEDIE SOMERVILLE; then conveyed by RAWLINS LOWNDES, P.M.,
to WILLIAM WRAGG. Witnesses: GEORGE JOHNSTON, JOHN PERKINS. Before
GEORGE MURRAY, J.P. Recorded 20 Oct. 1764 by FENWICKE BULL, Register.

Book C-3, p. 256   CASPER (his mark) FAUST, planter, & AMY (her
3 & 4 Oct. 1764   mark) his wife, of Craven Co., to MOSES KIRK-
L & R   LAND, of Saxegotha Township, Berkeley Co., for
                          ₺ 1000 British; 62-1/2 a. on Saludy River, in
Saxegotha Township, bounding S on unknown land; W on vacant land; N on
CASPER HENSLER; E on the river. Witnesses: JACOB FOOST, BENJAMIN FAAR.
Before JOHN HAMELTON, J.P. Recorded 22 Oct. 1764 by FENWICKE BULL, Reg-
ister.

Book C-3, p. 262   SAMUEL LAMAR, planter, to THOMAS GREEN, plant-
28 Oct. 1761   er, both of Granville Co., for ₺ 200 currency,
L & R   400 a. on Savannah River, in New Windsor Town-
                          ship, Granville Co., granted 16 Nov. 1756 by
Gov. WILLIAM HENRY LYTTELTON to CLEMENTIONS DAVIS; bounding S on the riv-
er & THOMAS LAMAR; W on MICHAEL MYERS & THOMAS GOODALE; E on vacant land
& SARAH LAMAR. Witnesses: THOMAS LAMAR, GEORGE BUBSEY. Before GEORGE
JOHNSTON, J.P. Recorded 23 Oct. 1764 by FENWICKE BULL, Register.

Book C-3, p. 267   RICHARD REYNOLDS, planter, & SARAH his wife,
22 & 23 Dec. 1763   to WILLIAM REYNOLDS, planter, both of St. Hel-
L & R & Bond   ena Parish, Granville Co., for ₺ 1500 curren-
                          cy, 200 a. on St. Helena Island & 295 a. on a
hunting island called Reynolds Island, total 495 a., the 200 a. granted
10 Apr. 1738 by Pres. WILLIAM BULL to JAMES REYNOLDS; then bounding W on
RICHARD REYNOLDS, SR.; NE on JOHN STUART; SW on RALPH BAYLEY; SE on
marsh; the 295 a. bounding N on vacant land; E on Sea Bay; S on an inlet
separating it from Fripp's Island; W on creeks & marshes separating it
from St. Helena Island; which 2 tracts JAMES REYNOLDS devised to his son
RICHARD. Witnesses: JOHN FRIPP, ROBERT OSWALD. Before THOMAS MIDDLETON,
J.P. Recorded 25 Oct. 1764 by FENWICKE BULL, Register. RICHARD gives
bond that SARAH shall not claim her dower rights.

Book C-3, p. 278   JAMES SIMMONS, gentleman, & ANNE his wife, to
24 & 25 Oct. 1764   JOSEPH VEREE, house carpenter, both of Charles-
L & R   ton, for ₺ 900 currency, part of lot #223 in
                          Charleston, bounding N 35 ft. on Tradd Street;
W 102 ft. on CHRISTOPHER FITZSIMMONS; S on WILLIAM CATTELL; E on ROWLAND
EVANCE; formerly belonging to EBENEZER SIMMONS, gentleman, who by will
dated 4 Aug. 1763 devised to his son JAMES. Witnesses: JAMES HUME, JO-
SEPH BALL, JR., sugar baker. Before ROBERT PRINGLE, J.P. Recorded 27
Oct. 1764 by FENWICKE BULL, Register.

Book C-3, p. 285   DANIEL RAVENEL, JR., gentleman, of Berkeley
7 & 8 July 1758   Co., to JOSEPH HOWARD, planter, of Craven Co.,
L & R   for ₺ 600 SC money, 500 a. on N side Santee
                          River, in Craven Co., bounding SE on JAMES MC-
GIRT & vacant land; other sides on vacant land; which 500 a. were granted
5 July 1740 to PETER DE ST. JULIEN. Witnesses: JAMES RAVENEL, ISAAC
MAZYCK, JR., DAVID LAFONS. Before JOHN PAMOR, J.P. Recorded 7 Nov. 1764
by FENWICKE BULL, Register.

Book C-3, p. 292   DR. JOSEPH HOWARD, physician, & SARAH (her
16 & 17 Jan. 1761   mark) his wife, to JOHN CANTEY, both of Craven
L & R   Co., for ₺ 830 SC money, 200 a. in Santee Riv-
                          er Swamp, bounding NW on Cadoes Lake & THOMAS
BOSHER; other sides on vacant land; granted JOSEPH HOWARD 4 Mar. 1760.
Witnesses: JAMES NORVELL, GEORGE COGDELL, JAMES DICKSON. Before MATTHEW
NEILSON, J.P. Recorded 9 Nov. 1764 by FENWICKE BULL, Register.

Book C-3, p. 298   DR. JOSEPH HOWARD, physician, & SARAH (her
15 & 17 Jan. 1761   mark) his wife, to JOSEPH HOWARD, planter,
L & R   both of Craven Co., for ₺ 830 currency, 500 a.
                          on N side Santee River, in Craven Co., bound-
ing SE on JAMES MCGIRT & vacant land; other sides on vacant land; as
granted 1 July 1740 to JAMES DE ST. JULIEN. Witnesses: JOHN NORVELL,
GEORGE COGDELL, JAMES DIXSON. Before MATTHEW MEILSON, J.P. Recorded 12
Nov. 1764 by FENWICKE BULL, Register.

Book C-3, p. 303   RAWLINS LOWNDES, P.M., to THOMAS LYNCH & AN-
21 Mar. 1752   DREW JOHNSTON, planter, of Craven Co., for

Sale   Ł 2525 currency, 5 plantations in Craven Co.;
                              viz., 400 a. bounding SE on Peedee River; SW
on DANIEL LAROCHE; NW on JOHN GREENE; NE on STEPHEN PROCTER (then HUGH
SWINTON); 125 a. bounding SE on Thorofare to Waccamaw River; NE on HUGH
SWINTON; NW on Peedee River; SW on DANIEL LAROCHE; 500 a. bounding N on
George Town River; E on vacant land; SE on ROBERT SCREVENS; W on CAPT.
JAMES (GEORGE ?) SMITH; 130 a. bounding NE on ELIAS FOISSINE; NW on Pee-
dee River; 160 a. bounding SE on Peedee River; NW on vacant land; NE on
JOHN GLEN; SW on JOSEPH WRAGG. Whereas by L & R dated 5 & 6 Jan. 1740
WILLIAM SWINTON, planter, mortgaged to ALEXANDER NISBETT, ESQ., of Berke-
ley Co., for an annuity of Ł 100 during his natural life, said 5 tracts
of land; & whereas WILLIAM SWINTON appointed HANNAH SWINTON, HUGH SWIN-
TON, & WILLIAM FLEMING his executrix & executors, & whereas ALEXANDER
NISBETT obtained a judgment against them & a writ of fieri facias was is-
sued ordered the P.M. to levy the amount against SWINTON'S estate; now he
sells the 5 tracts at public auction. Witnesses: DANIEL BLAKE, EDWARD
WAYMAN. Before WILLIAM MOULTRIE, J.P. Recorded 13 Nov. 1764 by FENWICKE
FULL, Register.

Book C-3, p. 309   JOHN DUTARQUE, JR., planter, to HENRY BONNEAU,
4 Oct. 1764   planter, both of St. Thomas Parish, Berkeley
Release   Co., for Ł 667 SC money, 347 a. in St. Thomas
                           Parish, part of a larger tract lately conveyed
to DUTARQUE by THOMAS ALEXANDER VANDERDUSSEN & HENRY TOOMER & MARY his
wife (THOMAS & MARY being surviving devisees of will of COL. ALEXANDER
VANDERDUSSEN). DUTARQUE gives bond of performance. Witnesses: JOHN EV-
ANS, JAMES CLARKE. Before ROBERT WILLIAMS, JR., J.P. Recorded 13 Nov.
1764 by FENWICKE BULL, Register.

Book C-3, p. 314   EDWARD ELLERBEE, of Anson Co., NC, to WILLIAM
24 Apr. 1759   BLACK, JR., son of NELLE BLACK, daughter of
Release   GEORGE MARTLAN, merchant, of Aberdeen; for
                           Ł 160 proclamation money, 96-1/2 a., part of
650 a. granted 14 Mar. 1745; adjoining ALEXANDER GORDON & MARY LUCAS; &
running with said land N 70° E 302-1/2 poles; 20 E 52.9 poles; S 70° W to
Peedee River; up the river to beginning; 4-1/2 a. of the 100 a. being reserved to EDWARD ELLERBEE & MARY LUCAS. Witnesses: WILLIAM HAMER, ALEX-
ANDER GORDON. Registered 6 Oct. 1764 in Anson Co., NC, by ANTHONY HUT-
CHINS, Register. Recorded 14 Nov. 1764 by FENWICKE BULL, Register.

Book C-3, p. 315   JOHN SEABROKE, (SEABROOK), planter, & MARY his
29 Mar. 1743   wife, to RIVERS STANYARNE, planter, both of
Release   Colleton Co., for Ł 2500 currency, 2 tracts of
                           350 & 103-1/2 a.; total 453-1/2 a. Whereas by
L & R dated 2 & 3 Dec. 1736 SARAH WOODWARD, widow, conveyed to COL. ALEX-
ANDER HEXT 350 a. in St. Pauls Parish, Colleton Co., being the E part of
700 a., part of 1055 a. surveyed by FRANCIS YOUNG, Sur. Gen., for JOHN
GODFREY (derived from BAYLY'S alias TRENCH'S patent); the 350 a. bounding
E on land purchased by HEXT from GODFREY; W on part of said 700 a. belonging to RICHARD WRIGHT; N on MARTHA EMMS; S on land purchased by HEXT
from WILLIAM TREDWELL BULL; & whereas by deed of feoffment dated 20 July
1739 RICHARD WRIGHT & MARY his wife sold HEXT 103-1/2 a. in St. Paul's
Parish, Colleton Co., bounding W on RICHARD WRIGHT; E & S on ALEXANDER
HEXT; N on THOMAS ELLIOTT (formerly RALPH EMMS); & whereas these lands
were not mentioned in HEXT'S will, being acquiring after he had made his
will, they descended to his nephew HUGH HEXT; who by L & R dated 23 & 24
Feb. last sold the 453-1/2 a. to JOHN SEABROKE. Witnesses: JOHN STAN-
YARNE, HUGH HEXT. Before JACOB MOTTE, J.P. Recorded 16 Nov. 1764 by
FENWICKE BULL, Register.

Book C-3, p. 321   JOSEPH SCOTT, planter, of Berkeley Co., eldest
20 & 21 Aug. 1764   son & heir of JOHN SCOTT, shipwright, of St.
L & R   Philips Parish; to ROBERT HUME, ESQ., for
                           Ł 2000 currency, his house & part of his plan-
tation called Rhetts Berry Point, on NE side Charleston Neck; bounding SE
40 ft. on land sold by NICHOLAS TROTT, & SARAH his wife to EXPERIENCE
HOWARD (now GEORGE NODDINS); NE 100 ft. on part said tract (formerly
NICHOLAS TROTT); SW on a 20 ft. street called Trott Street. Whereas
NICHOLAS TROTT & SARAH his wife owned the tract called Rhetts Berry Point
which by L & R dated 24 & 25 Sept. 1731 they sold a part fronting 25 ft.

on marsh & going back 40 ft. to a street; & whereas by L & R dated 29 & 30 June 1732 they sold WILLIAM HENDRICK, planter, among other lands, a piece of land contiguous to above parcel, fronting 75 ft. on said marsh & going back 40 ft.; & whereas by L & R dated 11 & 12 Aug. 1737 HENDRICK sold DOROTHY WEBB, widow, the lot 40 x 75 ft.; which she by L & R dated 5 & 6 Apr. 1744 sold to JOHN SCOTT; who died intestate; now his heir sells the 2 lots, 40 x 100 ft. to HUME. Witnesses: WILLIAM ANCRUM, LAMBERT LANCE, ROBERT ROBERTSON. Before FENWICKE BULL, J.P. Recorded 19 Nov. 1764 by FENWICKE BULL, Register. Plat of a lot 69 x 100 ft., bounding NE on heirs of JAMES HAZEL; SE on marsh; SW on HENRY LAURENS; NW on Trott Street.

Book C-3, p. 332
20 Sept. 1760
Lease

JAMES MCMANUS, planter, & MARY his wife, to SAMUEL CEY, both of Anson Co., NC, for Ь 17:6:8 Virginia money; 100 a. on both sides of Hills Creek, part of 1011 a. granted in 1750; beginning at a pine; then 55 W 124 poles to a black oak; thence N 48 E 125 poles to a white oak; thence S 55 E 124 poles to a black oak; thence S 61 W 127 poles to beginning. Witnesses: FREDERICK GRUMSWIGG, TREQ^D CAMPBELL. Registered in Anson Co., NC, by ROBERT HARRIS, Register, by order of Nov. 1760 Court, JOHN KOHOCK, C.C. Resurvey shows part to lie in Craven Co., SC, on N side of S fork of Lynch's Creek. Entered in Auditor's Book C-7, p. 262, on 13 Nov. 1764 by RICHARD LAMBTON, Dep. Aud. Recorded 19 Nov. 1764 by FENWICKE BULL, Register.

Book C-3, p. 334
23 Oct. 1759
Release

THOMAS LYNCH, ESQ., & HANNAH his wife, to DR. DAVID OLIPHANT, physician, both of Charleston, for Ь 2000 currency, 300 a. in Craven Co., bounding NW on THOMAS LYNCH; SE on DAVID DEAS; SW on Santee River; NE on Lightwood Pine; also 380 a. on an island in Craven Co., bounding NE on THOMAS LYNCH; NW on Six Mile Creek; SE on Santee River. The 300 a. having been purchased by LYNCH from THOMAS BOONE, of Berkeley Co., & MARY his wife, by L & R dated 10 & 11 Feb. 1748; the 380 a. being part of 1400 a. granted by Gov. ROBERT JOHNSTON on 28 Apr. 1733 to THOMAS LYNCH, father of said THOMAS LYNCH. Witnesses: WILLIAM MOULTRIE, JOHN MOTTE. Before FENWICKE BULL, J.P. Entered in Auditor's Book F-6, p. 62 on 31 Mar. 1762 by RICHARD LAMBTON, Dep. Aud. Recorded 20 Nov. 1764 by FENWICKE BULL, Register.

Book C-3, p. 340
26 & 27 Nov. 1763
L & R

JAMES GAMBLE, planter, & MARGARET (her mark) his wife, of Williamsburgh Township, Craven Co., to ARCHIBALD MCDOLE (MCDOWL), of Long Cane, for Ь 10 currency, 250 a. in Granville Co., on Long Cane, a branch of Savannah River; bounding NW on ANDREW PICKEN; other sides on vacant land. Before JOHN GAMBELL, ROBERT HENDERSON, WILLIAM GAMBLE. Before HENRY CASSELS, J.P. Entered in Auditor's Book G-7, p. 199, on 14 May 1764 by RICHARD LAMBTON, Dep. Aud. Recorded 21 Nov. 1764 by FENWICKE BULL, Register.

Book C-3, p. 343
4 & 5 Feb. 1762
L & R

JOHN COLLETON, ESQ., & MARY his wife, of Parish, of St. James, Liberty of Westminster, Co. of Middlesex; by their attorneys, ROBERT RAPER & ROBERT SWANSTOWN (SWAINSTON), gentlemen, of Charleston; to JOHN HODSDEN & THOMAS ELLIS, merchants, of Charleston, as tenants in common & not as joint tenants; for Ь 2000 Britihs, 2 brick tenements, called the Stone House, on the Bay of Charleston; 1 occupied by MESSRS. CHARLES OGILVEY & JOHN FORBES; the other by THOMAS ELLIS & CO. Witnesses: DAVID GRAEME, WILLIAM GRAEME. Before JOHN HUME, J.P. Recorded 22 Nov. 1764 by FENWICKE BULL, Register.

Book C-3, p. 350
25 & 26 Apr. 1763
L & R

WILLIAM BLAKE, ESQ., to JOHN HODSDEN, merchant, both of Charleston, for Ь 1000 currency, 39-1/4 a. in St. Philips Parish, on W side high road from Charleston, bounding N on Lady ANNE ATKIN; W on JOHN HODSDEN; S on ANNE SHEPHERD; which tract formerly belonged to the Hon. JOSEPH BLAKE, father of said WILLIAM. Witnesses: JOHN WILLIAMS, THOMAS BATTY. Before HENRY GRAY, J.P. Recorded 23 Nov. 1764 by FENWICKE BULL, Register.

Book C-3, p. 356

WILLIAM CATTELL, ESQ., to ELIZABETH PATTUROE,

12 Apr. 1739   wife of LEWIS PATUROE, for 5 shillings, during
                                her natural life, & to her children WILLIAM,
JANE, LOUIS, BENJAMIN & JOHN, forever; part of lot #115 in Charleston,
bounding N 20 ft. on Tradd Street; E & W 66 ft. on parts same lot; S on
part of said lot. Witnesses: JOHN RAMSAY, WILLIAM WELLS. Before A.
SKENE, J.P. Recorded 23 Nov. 1764 by FENWICKE BULL, Register.

Book C-3, p. 358   HENRY GRAY, ESQ., & ANN his wife, to MARY EL-
10 & 11 Feb. 1764   LIS, widow, both of Charleston, for Ⱡ 4100
L & R   currency, part of lot #207, bounding N on lot
                               #123 belonging to heirs of SARAH TROTT; E on l
part of lot #207 sold by THOMAS SMITH to PETER SAUNDERS & JOSEPH WARD; S
97 ft. on Guignard Street; W 56 ft. on part lot #207 sold by THOMAS SMITH
to HENRY GRAY; besides 10 ft. given to make half of Guiganrd Street.
Witnesses: PETER MANIGAULT, ANN ROGERSON. Before CHARLES PINCKNEY, J.P.
Recorded 27 Nov. 1764 by FENWICKE BULL, Register.

Book C-3, p. 364   DANIEL DOYLEY, P.M., to JOHN HODSDEN, merchant,
15 Mar. 1764   of Charleston; for Ⱡ 262 currency, 3 tracts of
Sale   land in Berkeley Co., subject to claim of dow-
                               er by the present wife of CHARLES COLLETON.
Whereas CHARLES COLLETON, planter, of St. Bartholomews Parish, Craven (?)
Co., owned 3 tracts of land in Berkeley Co., 1 of 320 a., bounding on va-
cant lands; 1 of 320 a. bounding SW on MAJ. CHARLES COLLETON; other sides
on vacant land; as by 2 grants from Gov. ROBERT JOHNSON dated 9 Oct. 1718;
1 of 382-1/2 a. on E side of Four Hole Swamp, bounding SE on BENJAMIN
SINGLETON; NW on ISAAC PORCHER; as purchased from THOMAS SINGLETON by L &
R dated 25 & 26 Jan. 1750; & whereas COLLETON owed THOMAS & WILLIAM ELLIS
& JOHN HODSDEN Ⱡ 2232:10:8 currency & they obtained a judgment against
him, with costs; under writ of fieri facias the P.M. seized the 3 tracts
& sold them at auction to HODSDEN. Witnesses: JOHN WILLIAMS, THOMAS
GUERIN. Before JOHN HUME, J.P. Recorded 29 Nov. 1764 by FENWICKE BULL,
Register. Received in full, MARK ANTHONY BESSELLEU.

Book C-3, p. 370   JAMES DAVIS, planter, & ANN (her mark) his
12 & 13 Oct. 1764   wife, of Granville Co., to King GEORGE III, by
L & R   Lt. Gov. WILLIAM BULL, for Ⱡ 250 currency,
                               150 a. on Little River, or rather, where the 2
main forks of Long Cane Creek meet; bounding on all sides on land reserved for the use of French Protestants & called New Bourdeaux; as granted DAVIS 2 Aug. 1757. Witnesses: BENJAMIN WATSON, JOSEPH PARKS. Before
PATRICK CALHOUN, J.P. Recorded 30 Nov. 1764 by FENWICKE BULL, Register.

Book C-3, p. 375   J. RUTLEDGE, attorney for King GEORGE III com-
30 Oct. 1764   manded PATRICK CALHOUN, J.P. & WILLIAM CALHOUN,
Renunciation of Dower   J.P., to obtain from said ANN DAVIS (p. 370)
                               renunciation of her dower to be certified be-
fore CHARLES SKINNER, C.J.; which was done. Recorded 1 Dec. 1764 by FEN-
WICKE BULL, Register. Received in full by MARK ANTHONY BESSELLEU.

Book C-3, p. 379   JANE MARGARET (her mark) RHOD to JACOB STROU-
25 & 26 May 1761   BART, both of Purysburgh, for Ⱡ 26 currency, a
L & R   1 a. lot, #22, in Purysburgh, bounding W on
                               Front or Bay Street; N on JOHN BAPTIST BOUR-
QUIN; E on ANDREW WINKLER; S on a street. Witnesses: HENRY LEWIS BOUR-
QUIN, GABRIEL RAVOTT. Before HENRY BOURQUIN, J.P. Recorded 4 Dec. 1764
by FENWICKE BULL, Register.

Book C-3, p. 385   JACOB & GEORGE (his mark) STROBHAR, to NICHO-
29 Sept. 1764   LAS STROBHAR; all of Purysburgh; for Ⱡ 10 cur-
L & R   rency, 50 a., bounding W on JACOB & GEORGE
                               STROBHAR; N on LEONARD REIGNHOWARDS; E & S on
JOHN & JACOB BARRAQUER. Witnesses: JOHN GEORGE STROBHAR, JOHN LINDER.
Before FENWICKE BULL, J.P. & Register.

Book C-3, p. 392   DANIEL MCGREGOR, planter, to RICHARD WITHERS,
5 & 6 Oct. 1761   planter, both of St. James Parish, Santee, for
L & R   Ⱡ 1000 SC money, 200 a. swamp land & 50 a. of
                               high land, in Craven Co., part of 1000 a., be-
ing 2 adjoining tracts of 500 a. each, granted by Gov. CHARLES CRAVEN on

10 May 1714 to DANIEL MCGERGOR; the 1000 a. bounging S on Washow Creek; W
on vacant land; N on Santee River; the 250 a. bounding W on land sold to
JONAH COLLINS; N on Wasshaw Creek; E & S on DANIEL MCGREGOR. Witnesses:
JOHN LEWIS, THOMAS SPENCER. Before THOMAS LYNCH, J.P. Recorded 6 Dec.
1764 by FENWICKE BULL, Register.

Book C-3, p. 397   RICHARD WITHERS, planter, of St. James Parish,
13 & 14 Apr. 1764   Santee, Craven Co., & ELIZABETH (her mark) his
L & R   wife, to SAMPSON NEYLE, gentleman, of Charles-
                      ton, for Ł 2500 currency, 250 a. (part of
1000 a.) & his own 200 a. Whereas Gov. CHARLES CRAVEN on 10 May 1714
granted DANIEL MCGREGOR the elder 2 tracts of 500 a. each, on S side Santee River; which descended to DANIEL MCGREGOR the younger; who by L & R
dated 5 & 6 Oct. 1761 sold to RICHARD WITHERS, (p. 392) 200 a. of swamp
land & 50 a. of high land bounding W on the land sold to JONAH COLLINS; N
on Wasshaw Creek; E on the part remaining to DANIEL MCGREGOR (now SAMPSON
NEYLE); according to plat by JOHN HENTIE, surveyor; & whereas Lt. Gov.
WILLIAM BULL on 10 Nov. 1761 granted WITHERS 200 a. in St. James Santee
Parish, bounding S on NATHAN CLEVES (then SAMPSON NEYLE); W on vacant
land; N on JONAH COLLINS; E on DANIEL MCGREGOR (now SAMPSON NEYLE); now
WITHERS sells both tracts to NEYLE. Witnesses: JONATHAN SARRAZIN, S.
WITHERS. Before FENWICKE BULL, J.P. & Pub. Reg.

Book C-3, p. 407   JAMES CROKATT acknowledge receiving Ł 10 cur-
10 Nov. 1762   rency, part of Ł 1000, the purchase price, for
Receipt   120 a. of river swamp exclusive of any branch-
                      es; bounding NW on JOHN GREEN; SW on Black
River; other sides on JAMES CROKATT; being part of 400 a. granted JOHN
HAMMERTON, ESQ. Witness: FRANCIS KINLOCK. Before JOHN TROUP, J.P. Re-
corded 8 Dec. 1764 by FENWICKE BULL, Register. Received in full by MARK
ANTHONY BESSELEU.

Book C-3, p. 408   THOMAS LYNCH, & HANNAH his wife, to SAMPSON
10 & 11 July 1764   NEYLE, gentleman, both of Charleston, for
L & R   Ł 500 currency, 623 a. in St. James Parish,
                      Santee, bounding W on Wassoe Creek & CHARLES
HILL; S on vacant land; E on Alligator Creek; N on JOHN LINING. Witnesses: LYNCH ROBERTS, WILLIAM MEWHENNY. Before JAMES SIMPSON, J.P. Recorded 10 Dec. 1764 by FENWICKE BULL, Register.

Book C-3, p. 413   JOHN WARING, planter, of Berkeley Co., grand-
8 Feb. 1764   son, of JOHN BEAMOR, planter, of Granville
Lease for Life   Co.; to THOMAS BOWMAN, planter, of Granville
                      Co.; for Ł 200 currency; his life interest in
160 a. on Port Royal Island, Granville Co., bounding S & SW on a creek &
marsh; SE on said creek & marsh & WILLIAM HAZARD; W & NW on JOHN GUERARD;
which 160 a. formerly belonged to JOHN BEAMOR; who bequeathed his houses
& lands to his wife ELEANOR during her lifetime & afterwards to his
grandson, JOHN WARING. ELEANOR later married GEORGE LIVINGSTON, gentleman, & JOHN WARING being tenant for life until the death of ELEANOR,
sells his life interest to BOWMAN. Witnesses: GEORGE LIVINGSTON, THOMAS
LAMBOLL. Before FENWICKE BULL, J.P. & Pub. Reg.

Book C-3, p. 415   JAMES HUNTER, for himself, & as executor of
1 & 2 Nov. 1764   will of JOHN THOMSON, merchant, of Charleston,
L & R   & WILLIAM FAIR, the other executor; to DR.
                      ARCHIBALD MCNEILL, physician, of St. George
Dorchester. Whereas by L & R dated 5 & 6 Apr. 1762 JAMES HUNTER & JOHN
THOMSON purchased from ANN CHARNOCK 2 town lots; in Dorchester; each own-
ing a half share; & whereas by will dated 21 Sept. 1763 THOMSON appointed
HUNTER & FAIR his executors; now, for Ł 260:10:0 currency HUNTER sells
MCNEILL 1 undivided half of lot #12 in Dorchester; & for a further
Ł 260:10:0 the said executors sell the other half of lot #12 to MCNEILL.
Witnesses: ALEXANDER FOTHERINGHAM, GEORGE LIVINGSTON, JR. Before FEN-
WICKE BULL, J.P. & Pub. Reg.

Book C-3, p. 421   WILLIAM HAY, of Craven Co., to his son DAVID
6 June 1764   HAY; 100 a., being a part of 400 a. near the
Gift   Congarees in Craven Co., bounding on all sides
                      on vacant land; granted RICHARD JACKSON 5 June

1750; who sold to HAY; the 100 a. to begin at a stake under the hill near Mill Branch; & run NE 67° to a large red oak on edge of old field bank, marked 3 notches on each side; then NE same course until it hits either the old NE & SE lines of 400 a.; then from 1st stake NW 88° to a second stake 8-1/2 chains; then to 3rd stake SW 18° 9 chains; then to a 4th stake SW 48° 7 chains; then SW 15° until it intersects with old lines; then NE until it strikes first line. WILLIAM HAY reserves not more than 15 of the 400 a. for his own use, a note being inserted in deed to HARDY HAY of even date. Should DAVID die before marriage, his land to go to his brother HARDY. Witnesses: ELIZABETH HAMILTON, JOHN SPARKS. Before JOHN HAMILTON, J.P. Recorded 13 Dec. 1764 by FENWICKE BULL, Register.

Book C-3, p. 424
6 June 1764
Gift

WILLIAM HAY, of Craven Co., to his son HARDY HAY, 100 a., part of 400 a. near the Congarees in Craven Co., bounding on all sides on vacant land; granted RICHARD JACKSON 5 June 1750, who conveyed to HAY; said 100 a. to begin at a stake under the hill near the Mill Branch & run NE 67° to a large red oak on edge of bank & old field marked 3 notches on every side; then NE the same course until it hits either of the old lines the NE or SE of said 400 a.; then from stake before mentioned NW 88° to 2nd stake 8-1/2 chains; then to 3rd stake SW 18° 9 chains; then to 4th stake SW 48° 7 chains; then SW 15° until it intersects the old line; then SW along old line; the lake to be boundary line to a gum with 4 blazes; then NE 37° to small white oak on old line with 4 blazes; the SE to meet 1st line from red oak 3x. Should HARHARDY die before marriage the land to go to DAVID, his brother. WILLIAM HAY reserves 15 of the 400 a. for himself. Witnesses: ELIZABETH HAMILTON, JOHN SPARKS. Before JOHN HAMILTON, J.P. Recorded 13 Dec. 1764 by FENWICKE BULL, Register.

Book C-3, p. 426
12 July 1764
Letter of Attorney

ROBERT DEANS, carpenter, of Charleston, intending to depart from SC for some time, appoints ALEXANDER PETRIE, silversmith, of Charleston, his attorney, to take care of his property, real & personal. Witnesses: ROBERT BRISBANE. Before CHARLES PINCKNEY, J.P. Recorded 14 Dec. 1764 by FENWICKE BULL, Register.

Book C-3, p. 429
23 & 24 Apr. 1756
L & R

WILLIAM GLEN & CHARLES STEVENSON, merchants, of Charleston, executors of will of PATRICK CLARK, innkeeper; to JOHN CREIGHTON, gentleman, of Charleston; for £ 1000 SC money; 40 a. on Charleston Neck in Berkeley Co., with the tenement called the Quarter House, formerly belonging to JOSEPH HAWKINS; bounding W & S on RALPH IZARD; E on JOHN BIRD; N on PAUL GRIMBALL. Whereas PATRICK CLARKE by will dated 7 Feb. 1756 appointed GLEN & STEVENSON his executors, directing them to sell all his real & personal estate; now they sell at auction to CREIGHTON. Witnesses: WILLIAM CARWITHIN, GAVIN NICOLL. Before ROBERT BRISBANE, J.P. Recorded 14 Dec. 1764 by FENWICKE BULL, Register.

Book C-3, p. 435
2 Oct. 1764
L & R

ALEXANDER KILPATRICK (son & heir of ALEXANDER KILPATRICK), & JUDITH his wife, to WILLIAM SCOTT, gentleman, of Beaver Creek, for £ 250 currency, 60 a. in Berkeley Co., bounding N on JOHN HENTIE & vacant land; E on RICHARD LAMBTON; S on RICHARD LAMBTON & vacant land; W on vacant land & JOHN HENTIE; as granted 30 Nov. 1736 by Lt. Gov. THOMAS BROUGHTON to JOHN COCKRAN; who by L & R dated 25 & 26 Nov. 1737 to ALEXANDER KILPATRICK. Witnesses: ELIZABETH (her mark) DUKE, JOHN (his mark) KILPATRICK. Before THOMAS FLETCHALL, J.P. Recorded 17 Dec. 1764 by FENWICKE BULL, Register.

Book C-3, p. 442
15 &16 Oct. 1764
L & R

JOHN WOOLFGANGSHELO (JOHN WOLFGANG SHULEIN), (SEILY, SEALY) blacksmith, of Berkeley Co., to GEORGE PRICE, planter, of Craven Co., for £ 120 currency, 50 a., part of 150 a., granted 1 Oct. 1757 to HENDRICK DENNIS; who sold to WOLFGANGSHILO; the 150 a. lying in low grounds of Santee River between Saxegotha & Amelia Townships, bounding N on the river; E on vacant land; S on JACOB GEIGER; W on NICHOLAS FEDEROLP; the 50 a. bounding N on the river; E on MR. BROWN; S on vacant land & JACOB GEIGER; W on NICHOLAS HIGHLAR. Witnesses: SAMUEL LEBER (WEBER ?), CHRISTOPHER WEAVER, CHRISTIAN FEDEROLPH. Before JOHN

HAMILTON, J.P. Recorded 17 Dec. 1764 by FENWICKE BULL, Register.

Book C-3, p. 448   PETER LANE, planter, (son & heir of JOHN LANE)
23 & 24 Mar. 1763   & SARAH his wife, to WILLIAM STEWART, planter,
L & R   both of Prince Frederick Parish, Craven Co.,
                        for Ł 10 currency, 300 a. in Craven Co.,
bounding SW on a great swamp; SE on ABRAHAM STAPLE; other sides on vacant
land; the 300 a. being part of 24,000 a. granted JOHN MONK, Cassique, on
22 Feb. 1682 by WILLIAM, Lord Craven, Palatine; & sold by STEPHEN MONK
(son & heir of JOHN MONK) to JOHN LANE by L & R dated 17 & 18 May 1727.
Witnesses: JOSEPH BROCKINTON, JAMES LANE, PETER LANE, JR. Before CHARLES
TYFFE, J.P. at George Town 30 Mar. 1763. Recorded 19 Dec. 1764 by FEN-
WICKE BULL, Register.

Book C-3, p. 452   WILLIAM DEWES CARPENTER, to HUMPHREY SOMMERS,
15 Dec. 1764   gentleman, both of Charleston, for Ł 500 cur-
Feoffment   rency, 250 a. at the Cypress in St. George
                        Parish, Berkeley Co., bounding W on DANIEL
DROSE (formerly THOMAS DISTON); NE on estate of JEREMIAH KNOTT; S on
ISAAC BRADWELL (formerly CATER). Witnesses: JAMES NUTT, JAMES MEHENEY.
Before ROBERT WILLIAMS, JR., J.P. Recorded 19 Dec. 1764 by FENWICKE
BULL, Register.

Book C-3, p. 455   JOSEPH PERRY, planter, of St. Pauls Parish,
20 Jan. 1759   Colleton Co., to HUMPHRY SOMMERS, of Charles-
Sale   ton, for Ł 152 currency, 38 a. in said Parish,
                        bounding E & NW on HUMPHRY SOMMERS; NW partly
on JOSEPH PERRY; S on WILLIAM HARVEY. Witnesses: GEORGE SOMEMRS, JAMES
MCCLENACHAN. Possession given by delivery of turf & twig. Recorded 19
Dec. 1764 by FENWICKE BULL, Register.

Book C-3, p. 458   BARNABY BRANDFORD, planter, of St. George Dor-
12 & 13 Nov. 1764   chester, Berkeley Co., to the Hon. DANIEL
L & R   BLAKE, member of Council, for Ł 1300 currency,
                        348 a. on the Great Cypress Swamp, at head of
Ashley River, in St. George Parish, Berkeley Co., bounding N on DANIEL
BLAKE; W & SW on WESSIN & BRADWELL; S on MRS. PAYTON; E & S on unknown
land. Witnesses: FRANCIS BEATTY, ANNE BEATTY, CATHERINE IOOR. Before
JOHN IOOR, J.P. Recorded 20 Dec. 1764 by FENWICKE BULL, Register.

Book C-3, p. 465   JAMES KERR, planter, of Granville Co., SC, to
26 & 27 Nov. 1762   ARCHIBALD HAMILTON, of Rowan Co., NC, for
L & R   Ł 100 currency, 100 a. in Granville Co., grant-
                        ed 24 Mar. 1760 by Gov. WILLIAM HENRY LYTTEL-
TON; on branch of NW fork of Long Cane Creek. Witnesses: ALEXANDER NOBLE,
JAMES NOBLE. Before PATRICK CALHOUN, J.P. Recorded 21 Dec. 1764 by FEN-
WICKE BULL, Register.

Book C-3, p. 471   CHARLES CODNER, planter, of St. Thomas Parish,
3 & 4 Sept. 1746   Berkeley Co., to JOHN SCOTT, ship carpenter,
L & R   of Charleston, for Ł 2101 currency, 2 tracts
                        of 170 a. on Etiwan Island, & 76 a. on a marsh
on Allchecaw Creek, total 246 a. in St. Thomas Parish; the 170 a. granted
by WILLIAM, Earl of Craven, Palatine, on 18 Feb. 1680 to THOMAS WILLIAMS,
sawyer, bounding N on Allchecaw Creek; S on WILLIAM JACKSON; W on Cooper
River; E on TIMOTHY BUSHELL; & sold by WILLIAMS on 21 Feb. 1680 to PAT-
RICK STEWART, planter; who with his wife, MARGARET, on 18 July 1680 sold
to RICHARD CODNER, mariner; the 76 a. granted by WILLIAM, Earl of Craven,
Palatine, on 18 Feb. 1680 to RICHARD CODNER, bounding W on RICHARD COD-
NER; E on JOHN NORTON; S on WILLIAM JACKSON; N on Allchecaw Creek; which
land formerly belonged to TIMOTHY BUSHELL. On death of RICHARD CODNER
his only son, CHARLES, inherited. The burying ground reserved to CODNER.
Witnesses: JOHN RATTRAY, JAMES GRINDLAY. Before ROBERT WILLIAMS, JR.,
J.P. Recorded 27 Dec. 1764 by FENWICKE BULL, Register.

Book C-3, p. 479   JAMES VERRE, carpenter, to ROSAMOND PERRY,
8 & 9 Nov. 1764   widow, both of Charleston, for Ł 2500 curren-
L & R   cy, part of 1 or more lots near Broughtons
                        Battery at White Point on E side New Church
Street, continued to said Battery, being part of land sold VERRE by DAVID

STOLL by L & R dated 21 & 22 Sept. 1761; bounding N 79-1/2 ft. on part sold by VERREE to JAMES BRISBANE; E 9 ft. on JAMES BRISBANE; S 76-1/2 ft. on a 30 ft. alley or street; W 76-1/2 ft. on New Church Street. Witnesses: JOSEPH BALL, JR., THOMAS LAMBOLL. Before FENWICKE BULL, Register. Recorded 29 Dec. 1764 by FENWICKE BULL, Register. Received by MARK ANTHONY BESSELLEU.

Book C-3, p. 487   RICHARD LAMBTON, ESQ., to JERMYN WRIGHT, ESQ.,
25 & 26 July 1763   both of Charleston, for Ł 50 currency, 2
L & R   tracts of 500 a. each, in Granville Co.; 1
                       bounding NW on RICHARD LAMBTON; NE on CHARLES
WRIGHT; SE on JOHN SMITH; SW on an impassable swamp; the other bounding N
E on JAMES MCPHERSON, JR. & CHARLES WRIGHT; SW on RICHARD LAMBTON & an
impassable swamp; SW on swamp; NW on JAMES MICHIE. Witness: The Hon.
JAMES MOULTRIE. Before FENWICKE BULL, J.P. & Pub. Reg., 31 Dec. 1764.

Book C-3, p. 493   RICHARD LAMBTON, ESQ., of Charleston, to JER-
25 & 26 July 1763   MYN WRIGHT, gentleman, of Granville Co., for
L & R   Ł 50 currency, 400 a. in Granville Co., bound-
                       ing NW on JOHN SMITH; NE on CHARLES WRIGHT; SE
on JERMYN WRIGHT; SW on Savannah River; as granted LAMBTON by Gov. WIL-
LIAM HENRY LYTTELTON on 4 Mar. 1760. Witness: The Hon. JAMES MOULTRIE.
Before FENWICKE BULL, J.P. & Pub. Reg., 2 Jan. 1765.

Book C-3, p. 498   REBEKAH HOLMES, widow, & THOMAS BEE, only act-
29 & 30 Nov. 1764   ing executor of will of ISAAC HOLMES, mer-
L & R   chant; all of Charleston; to THOMAS FARR,
                       planter, of St. Pauls Parish, for Ł 2500 cur-
rency, lot #232 in Charleston, bounding E 105 ft. on Little Street running S from Tradd Street to Ashley River; S 270 ft. on WILLIAM HENDERSON;
W on HUMPHRY SOMMERS; N on MR. DE ST. JULIEN. Whereas by L & R dated 13
& 14 Feb. 1760 HENRY RAVENEL, DANIEL RAVENEL, & JAMES RAVENEL, planters,
all of St. Johns Parish, Berkeley Co., only surviving sons of RENE RAVE-
NEL by SUSANNA his wife (formerly SUSANNA NOBLE daughter of CATHERINE LE
NOBLE the elder, wife of HENRY LE NOBLE) also devisees of will of CATH-
ERINE LE NOBLE; of 1st part; sold to ISAAC HOLMES their half a. lot, #232,
granted HENRY LE NOBLE on 9 May 1694; bounding E on a certain new
street; N on RALPH MARSHALL; S on MR. GIGNILLIAT; which lot said RAVENELS
held as joint tenants; & whereas ISAAC HOLMES by will dated 1 Apr. 1763
directed that the residue of his estate be sold, appointing his wife,
REBEKAH, executrix, & his friends SAMUEL BRAILSFORD, HENRY PERONNEAU,
WILLIAM SAVAGE, & THOMAS BEE, executors (BRAILSFORD, PERONNEAU, & SAVAGE
declining); now REBEKAH & THOMAS BEE sell to FARR. Witnesses: HENRY PERO-
NNEAU (merchant), JOHN WEBB. Before FENWICKE BULL, J.P. & P.R. Recorded
4 Jan. 1764.

Book C-3, p. 506   JAMES JOHNSTON & SARAH his wife, to ISAAC RAM-
9 & 10 Dec. 1763   SAY, both of Berkeley Co., for Ł 44:10:0 cur-
L & R   rency, 100 a. in Berkeley Co., on Ninety Six
                       Creek, a branch of Saludy River; bounding on
all sides on vacant land. Witnesses: ROBERT GOWEDY, JOHN SAVAGE, J.P.
Recorded 5 Jan. 1765 by FENWICKE BULL, Register.

Book C-3, p. 511   JOHN MURRAY, ESQ., formerly of Charleston, SC,
28 & 29 May 1764   now in Great Britain, by his attorney, WILLIAM
L & R   MURRAY; & WILLIAM MURRAY, ESQ., in his own be-
                       half; of 1st part; to BELLAMY CRAWFORD, ESQ.,
of Prince William Parish, for Ł 2000 British, 1250 a. in Granville Co.,
bounding N on ALEXANDER FRASER; E on High Road to old ferry over Port
Royal River; W & S on BELLAMY CRAWFORD (formerly JOHN MCKENZIE, then of
JOHN RATTRAY) & on Pocosabo Creek & Whale Branch of Port Royal River;
also 78 a. called Roes Island on S side said plantation between Pocosaba
Creek & Whale Branch; which 2 tracts were sold by JOHN CROKATT & SUSANNAH
his wife, by L & R dated 20 & 21 Jan. 1758 to JOHN & WILLIAM MURRAY; also
all Negro slaves (30), also all cattle, poultry, tools, carts, carriages,
& all crops belonging to said plantation. Witnesses: CHARLES MOTTE, JO-
SEPH BRAILSFORD. Before CHARLES PINCKNEY, J.P. Recorded 8 Jan. 1765 by
FENWICKE BULL, Register.

Book C-3, p. 521   JOHN WOLFGANG SEALY (WOLFGANSHILO, SHULEIN,

1 & 2 Oct. 1762   SEILY), blacksmith, to GEORGE OUSMAN, planter,
L & R   both of Berkeley Co., for Ł 100 currency, 50
                        a. in Berkeley Co., between Saxegotha & Amelia
Townships, in low ground of Santee River above mouth of Beaver Creek,
bounding NE on the river; SE on GEORGE KERLEY; SW on JACOB GEIGER; NW on
part original tract first granted to HENRY DENNIS. Witnesses: TIMOTHY
DARGAN, JAMES GIVEEN. Before JOHN HAMILTON, J.P. Recorded 12 Jan. 1765
by FENWICKE BULL, Register.

Book C-3, p. 526   JOSEPH CURRY, ESQ., of Craven Co.; to BENJAMIN
2 & 3 May 1763   EVERETTE, planter, for Ł 500 currency, 200 a.
L & R   in the forks between Congaree & Wateree Riv-
                        ers, bounding SW on Santee River; W on heirs
of THOMAS HOWELL; E on heirs of JAMES MYRICK. Witnesses: JOHN HANDESEYD,
JOSEPH CURRY, JANE CURRY, JAMES (his mark) GILL, JOHN ELDERS. Before
THOMAS CATER, J.P. Recorded 16 Jan. 1765 by FENWICKE BULL, Register.

Book C-3, p. 531   GABRIEL MANIGAULT, ESQ., to the Charleston
8 Jan. 1765   Library Society, for 10 shillings per annum
Lease for 21 Years   for 21 years, the large room, being the whole
                        top story of that brick building lately erect-
ed by GABRIEL MANIGAULT, on W side Union Street, bounding N on DENNIS'S
alley leading from Union Street W to Church Street; W on GABRIEL MANI-
GAULT; S on a passageway belonging to said brick building, with free liberty of ingress & egress on S side. Sealed & delivered at anniversary
meeting of Society 18 Jan. 1765. Witnesses: WILLIAM BULL, Pres., JOHN
NEUFVILLE, treasurer, WILLIAM MASON, secretary, ROBERT DILLON, RICHARD
KING. Before JOHN TROUP, J.P. Recorded 18 Jan. 1765 by FENWICKE BULL,
Register.

Book C-3, p. 534   WILLIAM BAMPFIELD & JOHN DAWSON, merchants,
24 Dec. 1764   church wardens, & RAWLINS LOWNDES, JAMES PAR-
L & R   SONS, JOHN HUME, JOHN WARD, WILLIAM GIBBES,
                        FREDERICK GRIMKE, & EBENEZER SIMMONS, vestry-
men, of St. Michaels Parish, Charleston; of 1st part; to ROBERT PHILIP,
merchant, of Charleston; for Ł 3300 currency, lot #273 in Charleston,
bounding N 92 ft. on Queen Street; W 240-1/2 ft. on JANE HEXT (formerly
THOMAS WEAVER); S on RAWLINS LOWNDES (formerly ROBERT THORPE); E on MIL-
LER ST. JOHN; which lot was granted WILLIAM HAWETT 12 June 1694 & later
became vested in BENJAMIN SMITH & ISAAC MAZYCK, trustees. Whereas by Act
of Assembly dated 14 June 1751 the Parish of St. Philips was divided &
all that part of Charleston S of middle of Broad Street should be called
St. Michaels & a church by that name be built on or near where old St.
Philip's stood, the parsonage house to be built on part of the old church
yard; & whereas Act of Assembly dated 17 Apr. 1759 recited that if ground
for the parsonage be taken from the church yard the church yard would be
too small & enacted that building commissioners should purchase a lot &
house for a parsonage; & soon afterwards BENJAMIN SMITH & ISAAC MAZYCK,
trustees, purchased a large lot & house at W end of Queen Street for
Ł 1500 for said parsonage; but the lot was outside of St. Michaels Parish
& the house too old & unfit for repair; but could be sold for double the
purchase price; & whereas by Act of Assembly passed 10 Aug. 1764 the
house & lot were vested in St. Michael's, to be sold & they were offered
at public auction; now they sell to PHILP. Witnesses: FRANCIS HARLESTON,
DANIEL ALEXANDER. Before FENWICKE BULL, J.P. & Pub. Reg. Recorded 20
Jan. 1765.

Book C-3, p. 544   HENRY HARTLEY (HIRAH, HARTH), of Saxegotha
9 Sept. 1763   Township, Berkeley Co., to MOSES POWELL, for
Lease for 10 Years   Ł 20 per annum for 10 years; 150 a. on a
                        branch of Cloud Creek leading into Little Sa-
luda River; on which land ANDREW SHIPS lived. Witnesses: LEWIS POWELL,
SANDER WALKER, JOHN FAIRCHILD. Before GILBERT HAY, J.P. of Colleton Co.
Recorded 22 Jan. 1765 by FENWICKE BULL, Register.

Book C-3, p. 545   ROBERT DEANS, carpenter, formerly of Charles-
18 & 19 Dec. 1764   ton, now absent, by his attorney, ALEXANDER
L & R   PETRIE, silversmith, of Charleston, to JOHN
                        WARING, planter, of St. George Dorchester, for
Ł 3000 currency, part of 2 lots, #119 & #120, in Deans Square, St.

Philips Parish, opposite Friend Street in Charleston, bounding S 54 ft. 6 in. on Queen Street; E 190 ft. on part of Deans Square sold by ROBERT DEANS to JAMES SKIRVING, ESQ.; W on part of Deans Square sold to WILLIAM MAZYCK; N on part of Deans Square still belonging to ROBERT DEANS; which 2 lots were granted by the Lords Proprs. to SARAH POWYS; who sold to JOSEPH BOONE, merchant; who devised to 2 sons of his brother CHARLES, viz. CHARLES BOONE & THOMAS BOONE; who conveyed to ROBERT DEANS; who subdivided into lots, selling the greater part to different persons. Witnesses: ROBERT BRISBAND, JOSEPH BRAILSFORD. Before FENWICKE BULL, J.P. & Pub. Reg. Recorded 24 Jan. 1765.

Book C-3, p. 553
22 Oct. 1762
Gift

DR. JOHN MOULTRIE, physician, of Charleston, to his son JAMES MOULTRIE, for natural love & affection, a lot bounding N 40 ft. on Broad Street; E on JOHN HUME; S on JOHN GORDON; W on said DR. JOHN MOULTRIE. Witness: MARK ANTHONY BESSELLEU. Before FENWICKE BULL, J.P. & Pub. Reg. Recorded 26 Jan. 1765

Book C-3, p. 555
15 & 16 Jan. 1765
L & R

ISAAC DACOSTA, merchant, & SARAH his wife, to JOHN PAUL GRIMKE, jeweler, both of Charleston, for ₤ 1800 currency, part of a lot, bounding W 16 ft. 8 in. on Union Street; E on EDWARD CROFT'S storehouse; S 70 ft. on JOHN DANIEL'S house & lot; N on WILLIAM CARNES. Witnesses: DANIEL FARFARA, THOMAS GRIMBALL, JR. Before WILLIAM BURROWS, J.P. Recorded 29 Jan. 1765 by FENWICKE BULL, Register.

Book C-3, p. 561
17 Jan. 1742
Feoffment

CAPT. JOHN ALLEN, ESQ., to DANIEL LESSEINE, carpenter, both of Charleston, for ₤ 425 currency, part of lots 66, 67, & 217, bounding S 28 ft. on Queen Street; N on JOHN STEEL; W 372 ft. on JAMES KINLOCK; E on WILLIAM MIDDLETON & heirs of ARTHUR MIDDLETON. Witnesses: WILLIAM SCOTT, JOHN RATTRAY, ISAAC LESSENE (LESESNE). Before JOHN REMINGTON, J.P. Recorded 6 Feb. 1765 by FENWICKE BULL, Register.

Book C-3, p. 564
12 Feb. 1742
Feoffment

DANIEL LESESNE, carpenter, of Berkeley Co., to JOHN CART, carpenter, of Charleston, for ₤ 425 currency, the above lot (p. 561) now bounding E on JOHN CART. Witnesses: ISAAC LESESNE, HUGH ANDERSON, WILLIAM SMITH. Before JOHN REMINGTON, J.P. Recorded 6 Feb. 1765 by FENWICKE BULL, Register.

Book C-3, p. 567
17 Jan. 1742
Feoffment

CAPT. JOHN ALLEN, to JOHN CART, carpenter, both of Charleston, for ₤ 425 currency, part of lots 66, 67, & 217, bounding S 28 ft. on Queen Street; N on JOHN STEEL or heirs of JOHN STUART; W 372 ft. on the part sold by ALLEN to DANIEL LESESNE; E on WILLIAM MIDDLETON & heirs of ARTHUR MIDDLETON. Witnesses: WILLIAM SCOTT, JR., JOHN RATTRAY, ISAAC LESESNE. Before JOHN REMINGTON, J.P. Recorded 6 May 1765 by FENWICKE BULL, Register.

Book C-3, p. 570
12 Dec. 1746
Lease

THOMAS MOSES, joiner, of Prince George Parish, to THOMAS ELLERBEE, gentleman, for ₤ 25 currency, 220 a. in the Welch Tract on S side Great Peedee River; beginning at a mulberry tree at NICHOLAS RODGERS'S corner, running SW to a sassafras; then to a forked oak to a mark; to a white oak; to a gum; to a red oak; to a stake at corner of vacant land; then SE to a stake on THOMAS ELLERBEE'S land; then NE to a hickory; to a white oak; to a hickory; to a black oak; to a gum on the river at THOMAS ELLERBEE'S upper corner; as granted 8 Dec. 1745. Witnesses: JOHN OYSTON, JOHN BARKSDALE, HENRY BEDINGFIELD. Before GEORGE HICKS, J.P. Recorded 9 Feb. 1765 by FENWICKE BULL, Register.

Book C-3, p. 574
31 Dec. 1760
Lease

SAMUEL (his amrk) GRIFFITH, to JAMES GRIFFITH, SR., both of Craven Co., for ₤ 100 currency, 100 a., part of 400 a., marked A on a certain plat; in the Welch tract, bounding SW on Pee-Dee River; NW on JOHN HICKS; NE on vacant land; SE on DAVID ROACH; which tract Gov. JAMES GLEN ordered for SAMUEL GRIFFITH, eldest son of JAMES GRIFFITH, according to petition of ELIZABETH, widow of JAMES, received 28

Nov. 1747. Witnesses: ALEXANDER TRAPIER, WILLIAM LUPTON. Before BENJA-
MIN YOUNG, J.P. Recorded 9 Feb. 1765 by FENWICKE BULL, Register.

Book C-3, p. 575   JAMES (his mark) GRIFFITH, SR., ELIZABETH (her
31 Dec. 1760   mark) GRIFFITH, JAMES GRIFFITH, JR., & MARY
Feoffment   (her mark) GRIFFITH, of 1st part; to MICHAEL
                         GRIFFITH, for ₤ 500 currency, 300 a. granted
ELIZABETH GRIFFITH, widow, JAMES GRIFFITH, MICHAEL GRIFFITH, & WILLIAM
GRIFFITH, sons of JAMES GRIFFITH, by Gov. JAMES GLEN, on 28 Nov. 1747;
lying in Welch tract, bounding SW on Peedee River; NW on JOHN HICKS; NE
on vacant land. JAMES GRIFFITH, SR., to have 100 a. during his lifetime.
Witnesses: ROBERT HICKS, CHARLES BEDINGFIELD, HENRY BEDINGFIELD. Before
GEORGE HICKS, J.P. Recorded 9 Feb. 1765 by FENWICKE BULL, Register.

Book C-3, p. 578   WILLIAM SANDERS, planter, of St. George Parish,
16 & 17 Apr. 1764   Berkeley Co., & ANN his wife, to JAMES POSTELL,
L & R   ESQ., of St. Bartholomew Parish, Colleton Co.,
                         for ₤ 368:15:0 SC money, 147-1/2 a. in St.
Bartholomews Parish, bounding S on estate of COL. LAURENCE SANDERS; W on
JAMES POSTELL; N on JOSEPH SANDERS; E on WILLIAM DRAYTON. Witnesses:
ELIJAH POSTELL, JAMES SANDERS, ALEXANDER SANDERSON. Before JOHN IOOR,
J.P. Recorded 12 Feb. 1765 by FENWICKE BULL, Register.

Book C-3, p. 585   WILLIAM GLEN, merchant, & MARGARET his wife,
8 & 9 Jan. 1765   to HENRY FUTHY, planter, both of Charleston,
L & R   for ₤ 1250 currency, 850 a. in Prince Fred-
                         ericks Parish, Craven Co., bounding SW on
Black River; SE on said river & DANIEL LAROCHE; NW on the Rev. MR. LEWIS
JONES; NE on vacant land; as granted 27 Aug. 1751 to AMOS SHAW. Witness-
es: ALEXANDER MICHIE, THOMAS MACAULEY. Before FENWICKE BULL, J.P. & Pub.
Reg. Recorded 13 Feb. 1765.

Book C-3, p. 592   ISABELLA FINCH, widow, to her kinsman, WILLIAM
16 June 1742   FINLEYSON, carpenter, both of Charleston, for
Release   natural love & affection, lot #40 in Beaufort,
                         Granville Co., bounding S on lot #41; W on lot
#37; N on Port Royal Street; E on Carteret Street; granted by Gov. ROBERT
JOHNSON to WILLIAM SHERRIFF, tailor, of Charleston. (Recorded 7 Jan.
1733 in Grant Book A. A. fol. 462); who on 26 Nov. 1722 conveyed to ISA-
BELLA his then wife, now ISABELLA FINCH. Witnesses: MARGARET MARSHALL,
JOHN REMINGTON. Before HENRY GIBBES, J.P. On 16 July 1742 FINLEYSON
sold said lot #40 for ₤ 21 currency to JOHN CART, carpenter, of Charles-
ton. Witnesses: FRANCIS CLARK, WILLIAM SMITH. Before HENRY GIBBES, J.P.
Recorded 14 Feb. 1765 by FENWICKE BULL, Register.

Book C-3, p. 595   JOHN BASSNETT, master in Court of Chancery, to
30 Oct. 1759   JOHN GORDON, ESQ., of Beaufort, for ₤ 3500
Sale   currency, RICHARD WRIGHT'S half of 500 a.
                         which by L & R dated 19 & 20 June 1729 were
conveyed by JOHN BAYLY, of Ballinaclough, Ireland, by his attorney ALEX-
ANDER TRENCH of Charleston, to MRS. SARAH WOODWARD, then of Colleton Co.;
who by L & R dated 1 & 2 July 1731 conveyed to JOHN & RICHARD WRIGHT;
bounding NW on RICHARD WOODWARD; NE on a cypress swamp of Wannels Creek;
SE on RICHARD WOODWARD; S on a great savannah; also 500 a. granted on 5
Sept. 1733 to RICHARD WRIGHT, bounding NW on said RICHARD WRIGHT; SE on
JOHN BAKER & COL. JOHN FENWICKE; SW on Duck Creek; NE on Cuckolds Creek
or Wannells Creek; also 500 a. on NE side Combee River granted 16 Jan.
1735 to RICHARD WRIGHT, bounding NW on RICHARD WRIGHT; NW on RICHARD
WRIGHT; SW on Combahee & Duck Creek; E on CAPOUR & STEWARD; all in Colleton Co. Whereas by decree of Court of Chancery dated 1 Apr. 1757 in a
cause between ELEANOR COBLEY (late ELEANOR WRIGHT), JOHN GORDON & ELIZA-
BETH his wife (late ELIZABETH WRIGHT); ELEANOR & ELIZABETH being daughters of JOHN WRIGHT, deceased; & JOHN GORDON & ELEANOR COBLEY administrators of estate of JOHN WRIGHT unadministered by RICHARD WRIGHT, deceased;
& also unadministered by JEMMETT COBLEY, BRANFIL EVANCE, & JOHN COLCOCK;
RICHARD WRIGHT being heretofore administrator of JOHN WRIGHT; & JEMMETT
COBLEY, BRANFIL EVANCE, & JOHN CROKATT, after the death of RICHARD WRIGHT,
being administrators of said JOHN WRIGHT not administered by said RICHARD
WRIGHT; complainants; & THOMAS WRIGHT, ELISHA BUTLER, & WILLIAM ROPER,
only acting executors of will of said RICHARD WRIGHT; defendants; it was

decreed that defendants, as executors, should pay complainants out of assets of said RICHARD WRIGHT, ₺ 2837:11:0 SC money, with costs of suit; further decreed that RICHARD WRIGHT'S estate be sold for that purpose; & whereas said executors did not pay, or sell the estate; therefore the M.C. put the estate up at auction. Witnesses: MAURICE HARVEY, ARCHIBALD STOBO, SAMUEL WAINWRIGHT, WILLIAM ELLIOTT, JR. Before WILLIAM BURROWS, J.P. 10 Jan. 1760. Recorded 15 Feb. 1765 by FENWICKE BULL, Register.

Book C-3, p. 601
30 Nov. 1759
Release

JOHN GORDON, ESQ., of Beaufort, & ELIZABETH his wife (surviving daughter & heir of JOHN WRIGHT, & heir of her sister ELEANOR COBLEY, another daughter of JOHN WRIGHT); to DANIEL HEYWARD, ESQ., of Granville Co., for ₺ 5000 currency, 3 tracts, of 500 a. each, a half share of which ELIZABETH inherited from her father, JOHN WRIGHT; the other half share of which (formerly belonging to her uncle, RICHARD WRIGHT) they purchased on 30 Oct. 1759 (p. 595). Witnesses: JOHN DELAGAYE, THOMAS NETHERCLIFT. Before JAMES THOMPSON, J.P. Entered in Auditor's Book F-6, p. 89, on 4 May 1762 by RICHARD LAMBTON, Dep. Aud. Recorded 15 Feb. 1765 by FENWICKE BULL, Register.

Book C-3, p. 606
3 May 1740
Lease

SAMUEL DUPRÉ, planter, & ANNE his wife, to THOMAS WALLY, planter, both of Craven Co., for ₺ 40 SC money, the land on the Cowper Marsh about 3 miles from NE side Peedee River, in Craven Co., bounding on all sides on vacant land; which tract was granted DUPRÉ 14 Dec. 1739. Witnesses: JOSIAS DUPRÉ, GEORGE PAWLEY, MATHEW DRAKE. Before CHARLES WOODMASON, J.P. Recorded 18 Feb. 1765 by FENWICKE BULL, Register.

Book C-3, p. 609
10 & 11 Mar. 1761
L & R

ROBERT REID & ANNIE his wife, to BRYAN KELLY, both of Colleton Co., for ₺ 2800 currency, 700 a., bounding S on the Round O Savannah; other sides on vacant land; as granted 30 Sept. 1736 (Book G. G. p. 243) to ROBERT BEETH, & inherited by his grandson, ROBERT REID, party hereto. Witnesses: ANTHONY HIETT, ISAAC FORD, ROBERT HIETT. Before GEORGE LOGAN, J.P. Recorded 19 Feb. 1765 by FENWICKE BULL, Register.

Book C-3, p. 615
27 & 28 Nov. 1761
L & R

Before GEORGE LOGAN, J.P.

BRYAN KELLY, planter, to TOBIAS FORD, both of St. Bartholomews Parish, Colleton Co., for ₺ 2400 currency, 700 a. (p. 609). Witnesses: ISAAC FORD, STEPHEN FORD, DAVID FERGUSON. Recorded 20 Feb. 1765 by FENWICKE BULL, Register.

Book C-3, p. 623
5 May 1764
Release

JOSEPH JONES, of St. Bartholomews Parish, & CATHARINE his wife, to the Hon. HENRY MIDDLE-TON, of Charleston, for ₺ 4500 currency, 500 a. in Colleton Co., near GODFREYS Savannah; bounding NW on vacant land; other sides on JOHN WANNILS Creek or Cypress swamp; which land was originally surveyed by FRANCIS YOUNG, Sur. Gen., as by plat dated 18 Nov. 1729, & granted by the Lords Proprs. to JOHN BAYLY of Ireland; a half part of the original land having been sold by SARAH WOODWARD to LAWRENCE COULLIETTE & ELIZABETH his wife; father & mother of THOMAS COULLIETTE, who sold to JONES. Witnesses: THOMAS HEYWARD, JOHN GLEN, WILLIAM RATHAL, ALEXANDER MCMULLEN. Before JOHN TROUP, J.P. & JAMES PARSONS, J.P. Recorded 26 Feb. 1765 by FENWICKE BULL, Register.

Book C-3, p. 628
5 Nov. 1760
Release

JOHN CRAWFORD, to CHARLES BEDINGFIELD, for ₺ 600 currency, 150 a., bounding on JOHN ELLER-BY & on both sides of Phillis Creek, in Craven Co., beginning at a stake 3 x to a pine; to corner stake a white oak; granted 8 Mar. 1755 to JOHN WALL; who conveyed to JOHN CRAWFORD; who conveyed to CHARLES BEDINGFIELD on 6 May 1755 (?). Witnesses: WILLIAM LITTLE, THOMAS CRAWFORD, JAMES BLASINGAME. Before JOHN ALRAN, J.P. Recorded 26 Feb. 1765 by FENWICKE BULL, Register.

Book C-3, p. 631
18 Feb. 1764
Release

JOHN BROCKINTON & SAMUEL NESMITH, executors of will of MARGARET DREW; to ALEXANDER MCCREA, for ₺ 350 currency, 450 a. in Williamsburg,

Craven Co., bounding SE on MR. DYALL; NE on MR. TURBEVILLE; other sides
on vacant land; which land was granted 26 June 1736 by Gov. THOMAS BROUGH-
TON, to said MARGARET (then MARGARET BARR), who later married NATHANIEL
DREW; & by her will dated 2 May 1761 directed her executors to sell the
land. Witnesses: THOMAS MCCREA, WILLIAM HAMILTON, JAMES MCCREA. Before
JOHN LIVISTON, J.P. Entered in Auditor's Book C-7, p. 289 on 26 Feb.
1765 by RICHARD LAMBTON, Dep. Aud. Recorded 27 Feb. 1765 by FENWICKE
BULL, Register.

Book C-3, p. 635   JOHN FRASER, merchant, of Charleston, to ALEX-
31 Oct. 1738   ANDER WOOD, & PATRICK BROWN, Indian trader, &
Release   MARTIN CAMPBELL, storekeeper, all of Granville
Co., for ₺ 25 currency, 314 a. in Granville
Co., granted by WILLIAM BULL, Pres., on 12 Jan. 1707 to JOHN FRASER.
Witnesses: P. GILLESPIE, ROBERT STANSMORE. On 22 Feb. 1765 ALEXANDER
FRASER, ESQ., of Charleston, recognized JOHN FRASER'S signature before
D. DOYLEY, J.P. Recorded 27 Feb. 1765 by FENWICKE BULL, Register.

Book C-3, p. 639   MARTIN CAMPBELL, gentleman, to GEORGE GALPHIN,
15 & 16 Feb. 1765   gentleman, both of Charleston, for 10 shil-
L & R   lings, 314 a. in Granville Co., bounding NW on
ARCHIBALD NEIL; NE on vacant land; SE on JOHN
FRASER'S land. Witnesses: WILLIAM TODD, THOMAS HEYWARD, JR. Before
JAMES PARSONS, J.P. Recorded 28 Feb. 1765 by FENWICKE BULL, Register.

Book C-3, p. 643   SARAH RAVEN, widow, of JOHN RAVEN, ESQ., to
2 Feb. 1765   ALEXANDER MICHIE, merchant, all of Charleston,
Release   for ₺ 3020 currency, 1/2 of a quarter part of
lot #26 in Charleston, bounding N 30 ft., Eng-
lish measure, on Broad Street; W 94 ft. on part belonging to JOHN WARD; S
on WILLIAM GLEN & THOMAS LEE; E on lot #20 belonging to DR. ALEXANDER
GARDEN. Whereas by L & R dated 19 & 20 Mar. 1729 THOMAS HEYWARD, hat
maker, of Berkeley Co., & HESTER his wife, sold JOHN RAVEN, planter, of
Colleton Co., father of JOHN RAVEN, a quarter part of lot #26 in Charleston, bounding N 60 ft. on Broad Street; W 94 ft. on DANIEL HUGER & ELISHA
PRIOLEAU; S on THOMAS HEYWORTH & COL. ARTHUR HALL; & whereas JOHN RAVEN,
the father, died intestate 21 Nov. 1733 & his eldest son, JOHN, inherited; & by will dated 27 July 1763 devised the lot to his wife, SARAH; now
she sells half of her quarter lot to MICHIE. Witnesses: WALTER CONNING-
HAM, JOHN WEBB. Before ROBERT BRISBANE, J.P. Recorded 5 Mar. 1765 by
FENWICKE BULL, Register.

Book C-3, p. 649   CONRAD SHNEES (SHNEER), planter, of Craven
7 & 8 Oct. 1756   Co., & ELIZABETH SHNEES, to JACOB HYLY, of
L & R   Saxegotha Township, for ₺ 45 currency, 50 a.
on N side Santee (Congree) River, bounding W
on GEORGE HAIG; N on ANTHONY CUTTLER; part of 100 a. granted 10 Feb. 1749
by Gov. JAMES GLEN. Witnesses: CHRISTIAN (his mark) BAVER, JOHN GEORGE
GUNSELT. Before J. SKENE, J.P. Recorded 5 Mar. 1765 by FENWICKE BULL,
Register.

Book C-3, p. 654   PETER MARION, planter, to NATHANIEL DEAN,
10 & 11 Dec. 1740   planter, both of Berkeley Co., for ₺ 200 cur-
L & R   rency, 1500 a. in Berkeley Co., on Indian
Field Swamp, a branch of PonPon River; bound-
ing SE on CAPT. FRANCIS LADSON & vacant land; SW on vacant land; NW on
PETER MARION & vacant land; NE on vacant land; as granted 13 July 1737 by
Lt. Gov. THOMAS BROUGHTON to PETER MARION. Witnesses: JAMES MARION,
JAMES GARIN, THOMAS DEAN. Before BENJAMIN SIMONS, J.P. Recorded 6 Mar.
1765 by FENWICKE BULL, Register.

Book C-3, p. 659   JOSEPH BAKER, planter, of Beach Hill, & HANNAH
16 & 17 July 1764   his wife, to WILLIAM MELL, of Goose Creek, for
L & R   ₺ 500 currency, 250 a. at Beach Hill, part of
527 a. granted RICHARD BAKER; bounding N on
ISAAC LADSON & JOHN GEILSER; E on estate of JOSEPH WARING; S on other
part said tract; W on ISAAC LADSON. Witnesses: THOMAS GRIMBALL, JR.,
WILLIAM AIR. Before WILLIAM BURROWS, J.P. Recorded 7 Mar. 1765 by FEN-
WICKE BULL, Register.

Book C-3, p. 667　　　　　ELIZABETH PATUREAU (PATTUREAU, PACKROW), widow,
25 & 26 Feb. 1765　　　　　of LEWIS PATTUREAU, & WILLIAM & JOHN PATTUREAU,
L & R　　　　　　　　　　sons of LEWIS & ELIZABETH; to JOHN RUTLEDGE,
　　　　　　　　　　　　ESQ., both of Charleston, for 10 shillings to
ELIZABETH & JOHN, & Ⱡ 250 currency, to WILLIAM; part of lot #115 in
Charleston, bounding N 32 ft. on Tradd Street; E 66 ft. on ESTHER WRAND;
S on LEWIS MIDDLETON; W on JONATHAN BADGER (possessed by ISABEL MARSHALL).
Whereas on 12 Apr. 1739 WILLIAM CATTELL sold said piece of land, by which
sale ELIZABETH became entitled to the land for her natural life term; &
whereas WILLIAM, as eldest son, & JOHN, will be entitled to possession
immediately upon the death of their mother; now they convey to RUTLEDGE.
Witnesses: JOHN BAKER, ALEXANDER HARVEY. Before FENWICKE BULL, J.P. &
Pub. Reg. Recorded 18 Mar. 1765.

Book C-3, p. 673　　　　　WILLIAM MOULTRIE, ESQ., of St. Johns Parish, &
15 Dec. 1764　　　　　　　ELIZABETH his wife, to FRANCIS KINLOCH, plant-
Release　　　　　　　　　er, for Ⱡ 2800 currency, a house & lot occu-
　　　　　　　　　　　　pied by DR. MURRAY, bounding S 22 ft. on Tradd
Street; W 75 ft. on ALEXANDER TAYLOR; E on WILLIAM MATHEWS; which lot &
buildings formerly belonged to JAMES MATHEWES, merchant, who by will dated 13 June 1745, gave it to his son JOHN; who on 2 Mar. 1763 sold to WIL-
LIAM MOULTRIE. Witnesses: JOHN FRIERSON, JOHN TROUP. Before WILLIAM
BURROWS, J.P. Recorded 12 Mar. 1765 by FENWICKE BULL, Register.

Book C-3, p. 678　　　　　WILLIAM ROBINSON, of Charleston, to JOHN WOLF,
21 & 22 Jan. 1762　　　　　of Orangeburgh Township, for Ⱡ 75 currency,
L & R　　　　　　　　　　125 a. on Bull Swamp above Orangeburgh Town-
　　　　　　　　　　　　ship, surrounded by vacant land; being the
upper half of 250 a. granted JOSEPH ROBINSON 1 Aug. 1758 & inherited by
his son, WILLIAM. Witnesses: JOHN BALTZEGAR, BRAND PENDARVIS, JOSEPH
FISHER. Before GAVIN POU, J.P. Entered in Auditor's Book C-7, p. 307,
on 4 Mar. 1765 by RICHARD LAMBTON, Dep. Aud. Recorded 13 Mar. 1765 by
FENWICKE BULL, Register.

Book C-3, p. 684　　　　　BENJAMIN SMITH, planter, of St. James Parish,
19 Sept. 1764　　　　　　　Berkeley Co., & ELIZABETH ANN his wife; & MARY
Release　　　　　　　　　SMITH, widow, of 1st part; to FRANCIS KINLOCH,
　　　　　　　　　　　　ESQ., of Prince George Parish, Craven Co., for
Ⱡ 2823 currency, 282-1/3 a. in Prince George Parish, bounding N & NW on
Winyaw River; SW on part belonging to HENRY SMITH; SE on Waccamaw River.
Whereas Landgrave THOMAS SMITH owned 1004 a. in Prince George Parish, between Peedee & Waccamaw Rivers; which by will dated 3 May 1738 he devised
equally to his 4 sons (HENRY, THOMAS, GEORGE, & BENJAMIN) & his wife,
said MARY; & whereas soon after the father's death GEORGE died, under 21
years, & his share descended to the others; & whereas they divided the
land according to said will, but a resurvey by THOMAS BLYTHE, Dep. Sur.,
on 7 Dec. 1756, showed the tract to contain only 605 a., so that the part
allotted to BENJAMIN & MARY contained no more than 282-1/3 a.; now they
sell to KINLOCH. Witnesses: JOSEPH DOBBINS, HENRY SMITH, THOMAS NEILSON.
Before JAMES SKIRVING, J.P. Recorded 14 Mar. 1765 by FENWICKE BULL, Register. Plat dated 7 Dec. 1756 by THOMAS BLYTHE, D.S., of 2 tracts of
473 & 531 a., total 1004 a., as granted Landgrave SMITH, but the top line
being 53 chains instead of 118 chains, the correct total being 605 a.

Book C-3, p. 692　　　　　DAVID HEXT, planter, of Johns Island, to NA-
5 & 6 Mar. 1765　　　　　　THANIEL BLUNDELL, merchant, of Wadmelah, for
Mortgage　　　　　　　　　Ⱡ 751:8:0 currency; to be repaid with interest
　　　　　　　　　　　　on 6 Mar. 1766; 300 a. on Johns Island bounding E on DAVID HEXT (formerly FRANCIS HEXT); SW & NW on ABRAHAM WAIGHT; N
on Stono River marsh. Witnesses: THOMAS COLYEAR, FRANCIS BOGGS. Before
ROBERT PRINGLE, J.P. Recorded 15 Mar. 1765 by FENWICKE BULL, Register.

Book C-3, p. 698　　　　　Whereas JOSEPH BUTLER, SR., formerly of Ga.,
21 July 1764　　　　　　　now in Charleston, SC, & MARY his wife (form-
Release　　　　　　　　　erly MARY LAROCHE, daughter of JAMES LAROCHE)
　　　　　　　　　　　　by L & R dated 1 & 2 Aug. 1733 sold to WILLIAM
YEOMANS, of Charleston, lot #278 in Charleston which MARY had inherited
from her father; MARY renouncing her dower before ROBERT WRIGHT, C.J., on
18 Aug. 1733; & whereas YEOMANS conveyed the lot to ISAAC MAZYCK, GABRIEL
MANIGAULT, SAMUEL EVELEIGH, THOMAS SMITH, SR., LUKE STOUTENBURGH, &

BENJAMIN D'HARRIETTE, in trust for themselves & his other creditors; & whereas MARY died, leaving JOSEPH BUTLER, JR., her son & heir; & whereas there is some doubt whether MARY was 21 years of age when she signed the deed; & whereas JOSEPH, the father, received the money & gave bond that his son would confirm the title now for 10 shillings British paid by the trustees, JOSEPH, JR., formerly of St. Andrews Parish, SC, now of Ga. releases all claim to the lot. Witnesses: JONATHAN COCKRAN, JAMES COCKRAN, JAMES BUTLER. Before CHARLES PINCKNEY, J.P. Recorded 18 Mar. 1765 by FENWICKE BULL, Register.

Book C-3, p. 703   HENRY (his mark) STACK, planter, of Orange-
9 & 10 Jan. 1764   burgh Township, to HENRY GALLMAN, planter, of
L & R   Saxegotha Township, for Ł 100 currency, 100 a.
                       Whereas on 16 Sept. 1738 Lt. Gov. THOMAS
BROUGHTON granted ROODIE COPLER 200 a. in Saxegotha Township, Berkeley Co., bounding NE on Santee River; other sides on vacant land; & whereas COPLER died intestate & his wife ANNA inherited & bequeathed the land to HENRY STACK; now he sells GALLMAN the 100 a. on the river. Witnesses: EDWARD JONES, JOHN CONRAD GEIGER. Before JOHN HAMILTON, J.P. Recorded 20 Mar. 1765 by FENWICKE BULL, Register.

Book C-3, p. 709   DERBY PENDERGRASS, shop keeper, to HENRY LAU-
27 & 28 Nov. 1764   RENS, merchant, both of Berkeley Co., for
L & R   Ł 1000 currency, 1200 a. bounding E on HENRY
                       LAURENS; W on DAVID DEAS; S on vacant land &
HENRY LAURENS; N on Altamaha River. Witnesses: GEORGE VAIR, JOHN CAL-
VERT. Witnesses: BENJAMIN PERDRIAU, JOHN HOPTON. Before FENWICKE BULL, J.P. & Pub. Reg. Recorded 22 Mar. 1765.

Book C-3, p. 716   CHARLES LOWNDES, P.M., to SARAH SANDERS, wid-
3 Mar. 1757   ow, of St. Bartholomews Parish, for Ł 512 cur-
Release   rency, 200 a. in Colleton Co., within land, W
                       of the freshes of Edisto River, as granted
WILLIAM PETER. Whereas JOHN PERRIMAN, planter, of St. Bartholomews Par-
ish, Colleton Co., owned said 200 a., then surrounded by vacant land; & by will dated 21 Feb. 1745 appointed his brother, BENJAMIN PERRIMAN, & GEORGE VINSON his executors, & PATIENCE PERRIMAN, his executrix; & whereas JOHN PERRIMAN on 6 Aug. 1745 borrowed Ł 276:4:2 currency from JAMES MATHEWES & CO. (viz. JAMES MATHEWES, JOHN MACKENZIE, MATHEW ROCHE, GEORGE JACKSON, & JONATHAN WITTER), merchants; & after PERRIMANS death MAC-
KENZIE, ROCHE, & JACKSON (surviving obligees) recovered a judgment & costs against BENJAMIN PERRIMAN, executor; & whereas PETER LEIGH, C.J. issued a writ of fieri facias to the P.M. commanding him to obtain the amounts from the residue of JOHN PERRIMAN'S estate; now he sells said land at auction. Witnesses: WILLIAM MIDDLETON, WILLIAM SMITH. On 20 Mar. 1765, LOWNDES, MIDDLETON, & SMITH being dead, JAMES SHARPE recognized signatures of LOWNDES & MIDDLETON before FENWICKE BULL, J.P. & Pub. Reg. Recorded 29 Mar. 1765.

Book C-3, p. 724   JOHN GRAHAM (GRAHAME), ESQ., of Savannah, Ga.,
6 & 7 Oct. 1764   & FRANCES his wife, to MILES BREWTON, ESQ., of
L & R   Charleston, for Ł 10,150 SC money, 300 a. in
                       Granville Co., bounding W on the back channel
of Savannah River; S on ELIAS BARNARD; E & N on vacant land; as granted 16 Sept. 1738 to ADAM CULLIATT & PETER NETMAN in jointenancy; & whereas NETMAN died & CULLIATT became sole owner, died intestate, & his son ADAM inherited; he by L & R dated 23 & 24 June 1763 sold to said JOHN GRAHAM; also all his slaves (24), the crops, tools, boats, carriages, etc. Witnesses: JOSEPH FELTHAM, DANIEL GRATTANS. Signed by FRANCES GRAHAM in Savannah, Ga., on 17 Dec. 1764. Witnesses: JOHN SIMPSON, HENRY PRESTONE. Before FENWICKE BULL, J.P. & P. Register. Recorded 2 Apr. 1765.

Book C-3, p. 734   ISAAC MAZYCK, THOMAS SMITH, SR., & LUKE STOUT-
17 & 18 Jan. 1765   ENBURGH, trustees; to JAMES SIMMONS, gentle-
L & R   man; all of Charleston; for Ł 5250 currency,
                       lot #278 in Charleston. Whereas WILLIAM YEO-
MANS, merchant, of Charleston, by L & R dated 9 & 10 Feb. 1748 conveyed to said trustees & his other creditors lot #278 on W side of the great street leading from White Point to the Old Church yard, thence by the Presbyterian Meeting House (now Meeting Street); bounding W on DANIEL

TOWNSHEND; S on the Hon. WILLIAM BULL; N on lot #195 belonging to HOPKIN
PRICE; which lot #278 YEOMANS had purchased from JOSEPH BUTLER, planter,
of St. Andrews Parish & MARY his wife (daughter of JAMES LAROCHE. See p.
698); & whereas, because of supposed defects, the trustees could not sell
the lot until they obtained a release from JOSEPH BUTLER, JR.; which release has been obtained; now the trustees sell the lot at auction. Witnesses: CHARLES PINCKNEY, JOSEPH BRAILSFORD, CHARLES MOTTE. Before JACOB
MOTTE, J.P. Recorded 3 Apr. 1765 by FENWICKE BULL, Register.

Book C-3, p. 743   JANE (S?) HEXT, widow, to HUGH FERGUSON,
14 & 15 Dec. 1764 planter, both of Colleton Co., for Ł 2000 cur-
L & R   rency, 930 a. on NW side Horse Shoe Savannah,
         on head of Baracada Swamp, in Colleton Co.,
which she purchased on 8 June 1764 from DANIEL DOYLEY, P.M.; bounding SE
on THOMAS ELLIOTT; NE on other part of 2 tracts originally granted ROGER
SAUNDERS, & afterwards sold to CHARLES JONES; NW on vacant lands (according to plat by NATHANIEL DEAN, D.S., dated 25 June 1759); SW on vacant
land & unknown persons. Witnesses: SARAH LOWNDES, JACOB STEVENS, JR.
Before EDWARD PERRY, J.P. Entered in Auditor's Book G-7, p. 316, on 21
Mar. 1765 by RICHARD LAMBTON, Dep. Aud. Recorded 4 Apr. 1765 by FENWICKE
BULL, Register.

Book C-3, p. 750   JACOB WHITSELL, of St. Bartholomew Parish,
____ Dec. 1764   Colleton Co., to JOHN PETER, for Ł 500 curren-
Mortgage   cy; a house & lot #7 in King Street in Jack-
         sonburgh; also 1 Negro man. Witness: CHRIS-
TOPHER WILKINSON. Before JAMES STOBO, J.P. Entered in Secretary's Book
& &, p. 210, on 19 Mar. 1765 by GEORGE JOHNSTON, Dep. Sec. Recorded 5
Apr. 1765 by FENWICKE BULL, Register.

Book C-3, p. 752   EDMUND BELLINGER, ESQ., & MARY LUCIA his wife,
4 & 5 June 1764   of St. Andrews Parish, Berkeley Co., to THOMAS
L & R   SKOTTOWE, ESQ., Sec. of the Province; for
         Ł 2000 currency, 785 a., part of a barony of
12,000 a. surveyed for PETER COLLETON; bounding N on marsh land; S on ED-
MUND BELLINGER; E & W on part of said barony. Witnesses: JAMES SIMPSON,
JOHN STACK. Before GEORGE JOHNSTON, J.P. Recorded 6 Apr. 1765 by FEN-
WICKE BULL, Register.

Book C-3, p. 758   MARY ELLIOTT of Charleston, widow, of ARTEMAS
19 & 20 Mar. 1765 ELLIOTT, gentleman; & executrix of his will;
L & R   to HUGH FERGUSON, planter, of Colleton Co., at
         public auction for Ł 379:16:0 currency, 844 a.
Whereas on 13 July 1737 Lt. Gov. THOMAS BROUGHTON granted JONATHAN FITCH
844 a. in Colleton Co., bounding SW on WILLIAM FAIRCHILD, FRANCES SUREAU,
& vacant land; NW on vacant land; NE on ROGER SAUNDERS; SE on FRANCES
SUREAU & WILLIAM FAIRCHILD; & whereas JONATHAN FITCH & FRANCES his wife,
by L & R dated 4 & 5 June 1742 sold the land to ARTEMAS ELLIOTT; who
willed that the residue of his estate be sold ; now his widow sells to
FERGUSON. Witnesses: JOHN LOGAN, HENRY WEBSTER. Before CHARLES WOOD-
MASON, J.P. Recorded 12 Apr. 1765 by FENWICKE BULL, Register.

Book C-3, p. 765   GEORGE ATKINSON, planter, of Prince Frederick
20 & 21 June 1763 Parish, & MARY his wife, to GEORGE SKINNER,
Release   planter, of Prince George Parish; both in Cra-
         ven Co.; for Ł 400 SC money, 400 a. in Craven
Co., granted by Lt. Gov. THOMAS BROUGHTON on 17 Feb. 1737 to ANDREW COL-
LINS; who, with SARAH his wife, by L & R dated 25 & 26 Aug. 1737 sold to
JOHN PYATT; who, with HANNAH his wife, by L & R dated 3 & 4 Feb. 1747
sold to GEORGE ATKINSON; bounding S on vacant land; E on ANTHONY ATKIN-
SON; N on Peedee River; W on JOHN CONN. Witnesses: JOSEPH DUBOURDIEU,
CHARLES FYFFE. Before BENJAMIN YOUNG, J.P. Recorded 15 Apr. 1765 by
FENWICKE BULL, Register.

Book C-3, p. 770   SARAH MEEK, widow, (formerly SARAH BRICKLES) &
24 & 25 Aug. 1764 her son, THOMAS BRICKLES, to MATHEW WEBB, a
L & R & Bond   free Negro, butcher, all of Charleston, for
         Ł 900 currency, the S part of lot #136 in
Charleston, bounding S 234 ft. on lot #156 formerly belonging to JOHN
BRUCE & measured from partition wall in the house on said land so as to

include half said partition wall; E 27 ft. 6 in. on King Street; N 234 ft. on part of lot #136 belonging to SARAH MEEK & THOMAS BRICKLES. SARAH & THOMAS give bond of performance. Witnesses: WILLIAM LOGAN, PATRICK HINDS. Before CHARLES WOODMASON, J.P. Recorded 16 Apr. 1765 by FENWICKE BULL, Register.

Book C-3, p. 778   NICHOLAS BROADWAY, planter, to JOHN JAMES,
8 & 9 Feb. 1759   planter, both of Craven Co., for Ł 30 curren-
L & R   cy, 200 a. in Craven Co., bounding SW & NW on
                       WILLIAM HARRIS & vacant land; other sides on
vacant land. Witnesses: JAMES MCDONALD, JOHN CANTEY. Before JOHN PICK-
ENS, J.P. Recorded 17 Apr. 1765 by FENWICKE BULL, Register.

Book C-3, p. 784   WILLIAM DAVID, schoolmaster, of St. Philips
5 & 6 Sept. 1757   Parish, Charleston, & CHRISTIANNA (her mark)
L & R   his wife, to JOHN TUCKER, laborer, for Ł 10
                       currency, 100 a. in Berkeley Co., on Cattles
Creek Swamp, bounding SE on land formerly belonging to MRS. REBECCA WOOD;
other sides on vacant land. Witnesses: GEORGE ALRICK, WILLIAM (his mark)
ALRICK, NICHOLAS (his mark) THORPE. Before ALEXANDER STEWART, J.P. En-
tered in Auditor's Book G-7, p. 314 on 20 Mar. 1765 by RICHARD LAMBTON,
Dep. Aud. Recorded 19 Apr. 1765 by FENWICKE BULL, Register.

Book C-3, p. 789   HANS (his mark) BUSS, yeoman, to HERMAN GYGER,
7 & 8 Jan. 1742   yeoman, both of Saxegotha Township, Berkeley
L & R   Co., for Ł 100 currency, 250 a. in Saxegotha
                       Township, bounding NE on Santee River; NW on
ROBERT LANG, JR.; SW on vacant land; SE on vacant land & on CHRISTIAN
YORK (formerly GEORGE HAIG); BUSS reserving to himself the half a. town
lot #10 mentioned in original grant from Lt. Gov. WILLIAM BULL dated 5
June 1742. Witnesses: GEORGE BOESER, GEORGE HAIG. Before JOHN REMING-
TON, J.P. Recorded 20 Apr. 1765 by FENWICKE BULL, Register.

Book C-3, p. 794   JONATHAN DRAKE, planter, of St. Johns Parish,
22 & 25 Feb. 1765   Berkeley Co., to IMANUEL CORTISSOR, store
L & R   keeper, of St. Michaels Parish, Charleston,
                       for Ł 525 currency, lots #9 & #10 in Town of
Strawberry, (or Childsberry) in St. Johns Parish, bounding S 132 ft. on
Front or Bay street; N on Mulberry Street; 660 ft. deepl being 1 a. Wit-
nesses: ABRAHAM DACOSTA, THOMAS DURFFEY. Before FENWICKE BULL, J.P. &
P. Reg. Recorded 20 Apr. 1765.

Book C-3, p. 798   WILLIAM HAYNE, executor of will of JOHN SPLATT,
18 Feb. 1763   planter, of St. Pauls Parish, Colleton Co., to
L & R   DAVID MAYBANK, of St. Bartholomews Parish, for
                       Ł 1500 currency, lot #12 in town of Jackson-
burgh, bounding 100 ft. on King Street; 218 ft. deep; as purchased by
SPLATT from CAPT. JOHN JACKSON BY L & R dated 5 Feb. 1743); which lot
SPLATT, by his will dated 16 Oct. 1749, ordered sold. Witnesses: WILLIAM
SMITH, EDWARD SPLATT. Before JOSEPH GLOVER, J.P. Recorded 26 Apr. 1765
by FENWICKE BULL, Register.

Book C-3, p. 803   JOHN JACKSON, merchant, of Charleston, to
19 & 20 Dec. 1764   PHILIP SPOOLER, planter, of St. Pauls Parish,
L & R   Colleton Co., for Ł 1000 currency, 500 a. in
                       Colleton Co., shown by a re-survey to be 544
a., granted 17 Aug. 1714 by Gov. CHARLES CRAVEN to JOHN JACKSON, shoe
maker, of Charleston, grandfather of said JOHN, bounding N on the Hon.
CHARLES HART & ROGER SUMMERS; E on vacant land; S on JOHN STOCK, JR., &
SAMUEL WEST; W on S Edisto River; which land JOHN JACKSON, the grantee,
by will dated 2 July 1718 bequeathed to his son, JOHN, planter, of Colleton Co.; who, by will dated 5 Dec. 1742 bequeathed to his wife, HELENA,
certain legacies & the residue of his estate (including said 544 a.) to
his son, JOHN, party hereto. Witnesses: JOHN MILES, SR., WILLIAM CRAGGS.
Before ANDREW LEITCH, J.P. Recorded 28 Apr. 1765 by FENWICKE BULL, Register.

Book C-3, p. 809   JETHRO MANNING, planter, of Berkeley Co., &
13 & 14 Feb. 1764   ROSINA (her mark) his wife, to JOHN GODLIP,
L & R   potter, of Craven Co., for Ł 500 currency, 2

adjoining tracts of 150 & 50 a. which 150 a. on N side Santee River, opposite Saxegotha Township Gov. JAMES GLEN granted in Nov. 1750 to PETER
RODE; bounding E on JOHN PILLINGER; W on JOHN BLEWER & vacant land; N on
vacant land; the 50 a. being the SE part of 200 a. granted ELIZABETH VER-
DITY, now owned by JOHN BLEWER. Witnesses: CHRISTIAN THEUS, CHRISTIAN
(his mark) BRAVANT, LEONARD RUFF. Before JOHN HAMILTON, J.P. Recorded
29 Apr. 1765 by FENWICKE BULL, Register.

Book C-3, p. 814   JOHN BLEWER, of Craven Co., & ELIZABETH (her
11 Apr. 1750   mark) his wife, to PETER ROAT, planter, for
Feoffment   Ꝉ 50 currency, 50 a. in Craven Co., opposite
                          the lower part of Saxegotha Township, being
part of 200 a. granted by Gov. JAMES GLEN on 22 Feb. 1745 to ELIZABETH
VERDITY hwo by L & R dated 1 & 2 Apr. 1746, sold to GEORGE HAIG; who by
L & R dated 24 & 25 Aug. 1747 sold to JOHN BLEWER; bounding NW on other
part; NE on vacant land; SE on PETER ROAT; SW on Santee River. Witness-
es: DANIEL HOBBIT, ANDREW (his mark) ROMNY, JOHN PEARSON. Before JOHN
HAMILTON, J.P. Entered in Auditor's Book #5, p. 298, by S. WEDDERBURN,
Dep. Aud. Recorded 30 Apr. 1765 by FENWICKE BULL, Register.

                          DEEDS BOOK "D-3"
                    APRIL 1765 - SEPTEMBER 1765

Book D-3, p. 1   JOHN MCQUEEN, merchant, of Charleston, gives
24 Oct. 1760   bond for Ꝉ 1000 British sterling, that GEORGE
Bond   SOMMERS, planter, of St. Pauls Parish & his
                          wife, HENRIETTA SOMMERS, shall have during the
lifetime of said GEORGE & HENRIETTA the full use of the 155-1/2 a. adjoining the lands of GEORGE SOMMERS, which MCQUEEN recently purchased
from WILLIAM COATS & MARY his wife. Witnesses: CHARLES DUDLEY, GEORGE
PARKER. Before WILLIAM ROPER, J.P. Recorded 26 Apr. 1765 by FENWICKE
BULL, Register.

Book D-3, p. 1   JAMES HAMILTON, planter, of St. Bartholomews
8 & 9 Feb. 1765   Parish, Colleton Co., to JOHN LAMBERT, plant-
L & R by Mortgage   er, of St. Pauls Parish, for Ꝉ 4000 currency,
                          442-1/4 a. in St. Bartholomews Parish, bound-
ing NW on FRANCIS BEATTY; S on ANTHONY HIETT & EDWARD HEXT; E on estate
of PETER RUMPH. Witnesses: THOMAS BUER, MOSES DARQUIER, JOHN LAMBRIGHT.
Before JOSEPH GLOVER, J.P. Recorded 1 May 1765 by FENWICKE BULL, Register.

Book D-3, p. 7   WILLIAM SEALY, JR., planter, of St. Helena
11 Feb. 1765   Parish, & TABITHA his wife, to JOHN HEYWARD,
Release   planter, of same place, for Ꝉ 3000 currency,
                          600 a. in Purysburgh Township, Granville Co.,
bounding S on JOSEPH SAGIE, ANTHONY JATONE, & vacant land; other sides on
vacant land; as granted DAVID ZUBLY; & inherited by his son JOHN JOACHIM
ZUBLY; who by L & R dated 24 & 25 Sept. 1760 sold to WILLIAM SEALY. Witnesses: JOHN GLEN, THOMAS HEYWARD, JR. Before JAMES PARSONS, J.P. Recorded 1 May 1765 by FENWICKE BULL, Register.

Book D-3, p. 11   WILLIAM BELLINGER, gentleman, of St. Bartholo-
7 Feb. 1765   mews Parish, & EDMUND BELLINGER, JR., eldest
Release   son of EDMUND BELLINGER, SR., of Ashley River,
                          & grandson & ELIZABETH ELLIOTT (otherwise
BELLINGER, late wife of THOMAS ELLIOTT, planter, of Stono, Colleton Co.),
of 1st part; to THOMAS HEYWARD, gentleman, of James Island; for Ꝉ 3600
currency, 1000 a. at Chulifinny Creek, Granville Co., bounding N on DR.
BRISBANE & MISS MARY ELLIOTT; E on FRENCH'S land; S on THOMAS WRIGHT; W
on DRAYTON & GIRARDEAU. Whereas ELIZABETH ELLIOTT by authority of a marriage settlement made by her husband THOMAS ELLIOTT dated 10 Apr. 1745 by
her will dated 1 May 1752 bequeathed half the residue of her estate to
her son, WILLIAM, party hereto, & the other half to such of her son ED-
MUND BELLINGER'S children as he should direct; & whereas said EDMUND BEL-
LINGER on 6 Feb. inst. named his eldest son, EDMUND, to receive the other
half; now WILLIAM & EDMUND, JR., as tenants in common, sell to HEYWARD.
Witnesses: JAMES PARSONS, JOHN GLEN. Before JOHN TROUP, J.P. Recorded 2

May 1765 by FENWICKE BULL, Register.

Book D-3, p. 16   PHILOTHEOS CHIFFILLE, gentleman, of Charleston,
19 & 20 Apr. 1765   to DANIEL HEYWARD, gentleman, of St. Helena
L & R   Parish, for Ł 3000 currency, 700 a. in Purys-
burgh Township originally granted to the Rev.
MR. HENRY CHIFFILLE & inherited by his eldest son, said PHILOTHEOS;
bounding N on GEORGE STRAUBALL, DAVID RUMPH, & vacant land; W on HENRY
CHIFFELLE, DAVID RUMPH, & vacant land. Witnesses: ROBERT ROBERTSON,
THOMAS HEYWARD, JR. Before JOHN TROUP, J.P. Recorded 3 May 1765 by FEN-
WICKE BULL, Register.

Book D-3, p. 21   JOHN HUME, merchant, & SUSANNA his wife, to
28 & 29 Mar. 1765   AARON LOOCOCK, merchant, both of Charleston,
L & R   for Ł 3400 currency, the E part of lot #159
formerly belonging to PETER MANIGAULT, who
sold to JOHN HUME; the E part bounding N 34 ft. on Broad Street; E 104 ft.
on heirs of ELIZABETH FLEMING; W on DR. JOHN MOULTRIE; S on JOHN HUME.
Witnesses: JAMES HUME, RICHARD MUNCREIFF, MORD MCFARLAN. Before FENWICKE
BULL, J.P. & P. Reg.

Book D-3, p. 26   THOMAS THREADCRAFT, house carpenter, of St.
30 May 1744   Thomas Parish, to JOSEPH LABRUCE, planter, of
L & R   Prince George Parish, for Ł 300 currency,
300 a. in Craven Co., bounding NE on GEORGE
THREADCRAFT; SW on JAMES LESESNE (now HENRY WARNER); NE on ELIAS FOISSIN
(formerly ABRAHAM WARNOCK); SE on Sea Shore which land was willed to
THOMAS THREADCRAFT by GEORGE THREADCRAFT. Witnesses: THOMAS PAGETT, HEN-
RY WARNER. Before THOMAS BLYTHE, J.P. Recorded 14 May 1765 by FENWICKE
BULL, Register.

Book D-3, p. 33   FARCHER (FARQUHAR) MCGILLIVRAY, of St. Mi-
1 Mar. 1765   chaels Parish, Charleston, to JAMES FOWLER,
Mortgage   shopkeeper, for Ł 2500 currency (to be redeemed 1 Sept. 1766); 2 Negro men, a lot in
Elliott Street purchased from estate of BARNARD ELLIOTT, his account
books, & all his real & personal estate. A pocket book delivered. Witnesses: GEORGE GRAY, ROBERT MCGILLIVRAY. Before GEORGE JOHNSTON, J.P.
Entered in Secretary's Book & &, p. 208 on 9 Mar. 1765 by GEORGE JOHNSTON,
Dep. Sec. Recorded 14 May 1765 by FENWICKE BULL, Register.

Book D-3, p. 35   RICHARD BOHUN BAKER, planter, & ELIZABETH his
19 & 20 Aug. 1761   wife, to ALGERNOON WILSON, planter, for Ł 800
L & R   currency, Division B of lot #147 in Charleston, bounding E 50-1/3 ft., English measure,
on Church Street; S 113 ft. on lot #148; W 49-1/4 ft. on Division H of
same lot; N 117-1/2 ft. on Division C; which lot 147 was divided 8 July
1740 by GEORGE HUNTER, Sur. Gen., amongst the heirs of Landgrave THOMAS
SMITH; also Division C of lot #147, bounding E 50-1/3 ft. on Church
Street; W 49-1/4 ft. on Division H & G; N 122 ft. on Division D; S
117-1/2 ft. on Division B. Witnesses: WALTER GILCHRIST, BARNARD ELLIOTT.
Before CHARLES PINCKNEY, J.P. Recorded 15 May 1765 by FENWICKE BULL,
Register.

Book D-3, p. 43   FREDERICK EHNEY & JOHN SMITH, of Berkeley Co.,
26 Feb. 1765   to PAUL SMYSER & ABRAHAM SPDELL, for Ł 1210
Bond & Mortgage   currency, part of lot #81 in Charleston, bound-
ing E 19 ft. on Union Street; N 104 ft. on the
part occupied by ISAAC DACOSTA; W on THOMAS SMITH, JR.; S on EDWARD NEUF-
VILLE. Date of redemption: 30 July. Witnesses: MICHAEL KALTEISON,
GEORGE SANK. Before CHARLES WOODMASON, J.P. Recorded 16 May 1765 by
FENWICKE BULL, Register.

Book D-3, p. 47   PETER BOUNETHEAU, only son & heir of JOHN
25 & 26 Feb. 1765   BOUNETHEAU, & ANNE his wife, to FREDERICK ANEY
L & R   (EHNEY) & JOHN SMITH, shoemakers, all of
Charleston; for Ł 1510 currency, part of lot
#81 in Charleston, bounding E 19 ft. on Union Street; N 104 ft. on the
part occupied by ISAAC DACOSTA; W on THOMAS SMITH, JR.; S on EDWARD NEUF-
VILLE. Witnesses: SIMS WHITE, PATRICK WALDREN. Before CHARLES

WOODMASON, J.P.   Recorded 17 May 1765 by FENWICKE BULL, Register.

Book D-3, p. 54   JOHN HUME, ESQ., & SUSANNA his wife, to HENRY
3 & 4 May 1765   LAURENS, ESQ., both of Charleston, part of lot
L & R by Mortgage   #159, bounding S 33 ft. on an alley leading
                          from Church Street to Old Church, or Meeting
Street; W 91 ft. on DR. JOHN MOULTRIE; N on AARON LOOCOCK (formerly JOHN
HUME); E on SARAH FLEMING.   Date of redemption: 3 June 1764. Witnesses:
CATHARINE COLCOCK, BENJAMIN PERDRIAU, ALEXANDER (his mark) MCCULLOUGH.
Before FENWICKE BULL, Register & J.P.

Book D-3, p. 62   ROBERT BRISBANE & WILLIAM BRISBANE, merchants,
23 Apr. 1765   to AARON LOOCOCK, merchant, all of Charleston,
Feoffment   for ₤ 600 currency, a low water lot in Colle-
                          ton Square, Charleston, bounding E on Cooper
River; S on CRAVENS BASTION; W on Bay Street; N on a street laid out in
the marsh of Colleton Square by MRS. ANN ELLERY, CHARLES PINCKNEY &
GEORGE HUNTER.   Whereas GEORGE HUNTER, gentleman, by will dated 27 Aug.
1745 appointed WILLIAM WOODDROP, merchant, of Charleston, his sole execu-
tor, with authority to sell his lands in town & country, & by L & R dated
15 & 16 June 1764 WOODDROP sold the unsold part of HUNTER'S estate to
ROBERT & WILLIAM BRISBANE; now they sell 1 lot to LOOCOCK. Witnesses:
PATRICK WALDREN, WILLIAM BRISBANE, JR., RICHARD MUNCRIEFF. Recorded 20
May 1765 by FENWICKE BULL, Register.

Book D-3, p. 64   JAMES SIMMONS, gentleman, & ANNE his wife, to
20 & 21 Mar. 1765   MILES BREWTON, ESQ., both of Charleston, for
L & R   ₤ 4000 currency, the N part of lot #278;
                          bounding E 66 ft. on Meeting Street; W on DAN-
IEL TOWNSEND; S on the Hon. WILLIAM BULL; N on lot #195 now belonging to
HOPKIN PRICE; which lot #278 was conveyed by WILLIAM YEOMANS in his life-
time to ISAAC MAZYCK, THOMAS SMITH, SR., LUKE STOUTENBURGH & his other
creditors; who sold to JAMES SIMMONS. Witnesses: TIMOTHY PHILLIPS, JO-
SEPH PHILLIPS. Before FENWICKE BULL, J.P. & P. Reg.

Book D-3, p. 71   FRANCIS KINLOCK, ESQ., to PETER MANIGAULT,
8 & 9 Apr. 1765   barrister, both of Charleston, for 1500 cur-
L & R   rency, several tracts in Craven Co.; 500 a.
                          bounding NE on Santee River; SE on EDWARD WEBB;
other sides on vacant land; also 400 a. on N side Santee River; other
sides on vacant land; as granted THOMAS PLATT; also 400 a. in Prince
Frederick Parish, bounding SW on Santee River; SE on THOMAS PLATT (now
FRANCIS KINLOCK); NE on vacant land; NW on FRANCIS KINLOCK; as granted
said FRANCIS KINLOCK on 14 Mar. 1757; also 400 a. on NE side Santee River,
opposite lands of FRANCIS KINLOCK; bounding NW on THOMAS PLATT; NE on vacant land; SW on the Hon. JAMES KINLOCK; as granted FRANCIS KINLOCK 2
Aug. 1757. Witnesses: JOHN MAYRANT, WILLIAM MOULTRIE. Before ALEXANDER
FRASER, J.P.   Recorded 22 May 1765 by FENWICKE BULL, Register.

Book D-3, p. 77   SAMUEL PRIOLEAU, & ELIJAH PRIOLEAU, & ELIZA-
4 Feb. 1764   BETH ROUPELL (formerly PRIOLEAU), executors, &
Release   executrix of will of their father, SAMUEL
                          PRIOLEAU, gentleman, of Charleston, to ANDREW
VERDIER, gentleman, of Beaufort, for ₤ 300 currency, parts of several
lots in Beaufort. Whereas SAMUEL PRIOLEAU owned 3 lots in Beaufort #55,
#56, & #59, which by will dated 25 Oct. 1751 he authorized his executors
to sell, & bequeathed the money to his wife MARY MAGDALEN PRIOLEAU, his
sons, PHILIP, said SAMUEL, & ELIJAH, & his daughters MARY BRYAN & ELIZA-
BETH, naming them his executors; & whereas, ELIZABETH married GEORGE ROU-
PELL, MARY BRYAN died, & PHILIP left the Province; now the remaining executors, & GEORGE ROUPELL sell VERDIER lot #59; that part of lot #55
taken off at N end & ascertained by continuing the S boundary line of
said lot in a straight line to Charles Street; also part of lot #56 taken
off at S end & ascertained by continuing the N boundary line to Charles
Street. Witnesses: JOHN BENFIELD, MAURICE JONES (merchant of Charleston). Before JAMES PARSONS, J.P. Recorded 23 May 1765 by FENWICKE BULL,
Register.

Book D-3, p. 82   JOHN & JOEL HOLMES, gentlemen, of Charleston,
26 Feb. 1762   to their sister, SUSANNAH WHITE, for her

Assignment   lifetime, part of a lot in Charleston. Where-
                                     as ISAAC HOLMES, gentleman, father of JOHN &
JOEL, by will dated 20 Nov. 1754 desired his wife, SUSANNAH, to have during her lifetime part of a lot in Charleston bounding E 40 ft. on Church
Street; S on land he had given JOHN; N on land he had given JOEL; W on
estate of JONATHAN COLLINS; with the buildings thereon, then occupied by
himself & JOHN DOBELL (now occupied by MRS. DRYDEN & JOHN HOLMES) & bequeathed the residue of his estate to JOHN & JOEL; & whereas SUSANNA,
widow of said ISAAC, being now in Great Britain, has by letter, requested
her sons to let her daughter SUSANNAH, wife of JOSEPH WHITE, now of White
Haven, Cumberland Co., Great Britain, have the buildings during the lifetime of both SUSANNAH'S, the daughter to receive the rents after the
mother's death; now JOHN & JOEL transfer the property to their sister.
Witnesses: JOHN BRAUND, WILLIAM GLEN, JR., ARCHIBALD SCOTT. Before ROB-
ERT PRINGLE, J.P.   Recorded 24 May 1765 by FENWICKE BULL, Register.

Book D-3, p. 86   ISAAC MAZYCK, ESQ., of Charleston, & STEPHEN
21 & 22 Jan. 1762   MAZYCK, gentleman, of St. Johns Parish, Berke-
L & R   ley Co., executors, of will of PAUL MAZYCK,
                                     ESQ., of Charleston, to JAMES VERREE, carpen-
ter, of Charleston, for ₺ 1600 currency, part of 2 town lots known in
deed of partition as lot #3, bounding S 28 ft. on Tradd Street; E 68 ft.
on BENJAMIN MAZYCK; W on FRANCIS VERAMBEAULT. Whereas by deed of partition tripartite dated 18 Jan. inst. between said ISAAC MAZYCK of 1st
part; BENJAMIN MAZYCK, of 2nd part; STEPHEN MAZYCK, of 3rd part; & ISAAC
& STEPHEN MAZYCK, as executors of will of PAUL MAZYCK, of 4th part; it
was agreed to divide a certain part of 2 lots in Charleston, #24 & #25,
divised by ISAAC MAZYCK the elder to his sons; & whereas part #3 was assigned to ISAAC & STEPHEN as executors of will of PAUL MAZYCK, dated 12
Dec. 1746; now they sell that piece to VERREE. Witnesses: THOMAS DAY,
WILLIAM MAZYCK.   Before HENRY RAVENEL, J.P.   Recorded 25 May 1765 by FEN-
WICKE BULL, Register.

Book D-3, p. 92   THOMAS ALEXANDER VANDERDUSSEN, now an Ensign
13 & 14 Aug. 1764   in H.M. 17th Reg. of Foot, by his attorney,
L & R   JOHN TORRANS, merchant, of Charleston, appoint-
                                     ed by letter dated 22 Feb. 1763; & HENRY TOOM-
ER, of NC, & MARY his wife; of 1st part; to JAMES STANYARNE, of St. Pauls
Parish; for ₺ 7800 currency, 529 a. in St. Pauls Parish, Colleton Co.,
bounding E on THOMAS ELLIOTT; deceased; S on EDMUND BELLINGER; N on JOHN
GODFREY.   Whereas ALEXANDER VANDERDUSSEN, ESQ., of SC, by will dated 4
July 1749 bequeated equally to ELIZABETH & MARY, daughters, & THOMAS ALEX-
ANDER, son of MARY NESBITT, the residue of his real & personal estate, &
appointed JOHN CLELAND, JAMES MICHIE & DANIEL WELSHUYSEN his executors; &
whereas ELIZABETH married THOMAS WALLACE, merchant, formerly of Charles-
ton, now of Philadelphia, & afterwards died; whereby THOMAS ALEXANDER &
MARY are entitled to the whole estate; & whereas MARY married HENRY TOOM-
ER; now they sell STANYARNE the aobve named tract. Witnesses: ROBERT
MACKENZIE, JR., JOHN GLEN.   Entered in Auditor's Book C-7, p. 312, on 7
Mar. 1765 by RICHARD LAMBTON, Dep. Aud.   Before JOHN TROUP, J.P.   Record-
ed 27 May 1765 by FENWICKE BULL, Register.

Book D-3, p. 101   JAMES HUNTER, for himself, & as executor of
8 & 9 July 1764   will of JOHN THOMPSON, merchant, of Charleston;
L & R   & WILLIAM FAIR, the other executor; to JOHN
                                     IOOR, planter, of St. George Parish; for
₺ 125:10:0 currency, 1 undivided half of lot #11 in Dorchester; & for
another ₺ 125:10:0 currency, the other half of lot #11. Whereas by L & R
dated 5 & 6 Apr. 1762 ANN CHARNOCK sold JAMES HUNTER & JOHN THOMPSON 2
lots in Dorchester; & whereas THOMPSON by will dated 21 Sept. 1763 appointed HUNTER & FAIR his executors; now HUNTER sells his own half share,
& HUNTER & FAIR, as executors, sell the other half to IOOR. Witnesses:
RICHARD KING, GEORGE LIVINGSTON, JR.   Before JOHN TROUP, J.P.   Recorded
28 May 1765 by FENWICKE BULL, Register.

Book D-3, p. 107   WILLIAM SANDERS & JAMES SANDERS, planters, of
17 & 18 Apr. 1759   St. George Parish, & SARAH SANDERS, wife of
L & R   said JAMES SANDERS, of 1st part; to JOHN IOOR,
                                     planter, of same place; for ₺ 1000 currency,
600 a. in Berkeley Co., bounding N on WILLIAM & JAMES SANDERS; E on

JOSEPH IZARD; S on WILLIAM SANDERS; W on JAMES DALTON. Witnesses: MAR-
GARET SANDERS, SUSANNA WARING. Before BENJAMIN WARING, J.P. Recorded 29
May 1765 by FENWICKE BULL, Register.

Book D-3, p. 112   THEODORE GAILLARD, planter, of St. James San-
1 Apr. 1760   tee, Craven Co., to THEODORE GOURDIN, planter,
L & R   of Prince Frederick Parish, Craven Co., for
                          L 10 currency, 200 a. in Santee River Swamp,
being the upper part of Little River Island, in Craven Co., granted GAIL-
LARD 13 Aug. 1756 by Gov. WILLIAM HENRY LYTTELTON; said 200 a. bounding S
on Santee River; N on Little River; E on THEODORE GAILLARD. Witnesses:
THEODORE GAILLARD, JR., JOHN GAILLARD, JOHN BARNETT. Entered in Auditor's Book C-7, p. 320, on 23 Apr. 1765 by RICHARD LAMBTON, Dep. Aud.
Before ISAAC PORCHER, J.P. Recorded 29 May 1765 by FENWICKE BULL, Register.

Book D-3, p. 116   JACOB BUCKHOLTS, SR., planter, to BUCKINGHAM
16 Feb. 1765   KEENE, planter, both of Craven Co., for L 700
L & R   currency, 550 a. in 2 tracts in Craven Co., in
                          Queensborough Township, bounding NE on Peedee
River; NW & SW on vacant land; SE on SAMUEL BROWN. Witnesses: PETER
BUCKHOLTS, ELIAS TYLER. Before ROBERT WEAVER, J.P. Recorded 3 June 1765
by FENWICKE BULL, Register.

Book D-3, p. 122   FRANCIS LEJAU, planter, of Berkeley Co., to
4 Apr. 1764   EDWARD HEWSON, of Peedee, Craven Co., for L 60
Feoffment   currency, 60 a., being the lower part of 800
                         a., bounding NW on Peedee River & STEPHEN BE-
DON; NE on vacant land; SW on JOHN HAMMERTON, & vacant land; granted
FRANCIS LEJAU 16 Dec. 1736 & by will dated 12 Apr. 1755 bequeathed to
FRANCIS LEJAU, party hereto. Witnesses: BENJAMIN REEDER, JOSEPH (his
mark) BURCH, MARY (her mark) BURCH. Before ROBERT WEAVER, J.P. Recorded
4 June 1765 by FENWICKE BULL, Register.

Book D-3, p. 124   JOHN ALLSTON, planter, of Prince George Par-
26 & 27 Dec. 1764   ish, Craven Co., & MARY his wife, to his
L & R   brother, JOSEPH ALLSTON, planter, of Waccamaw,
                          in same Parish, for L 1000 currency, 500 a. on
Waccamaw, part of 1000 a. bequeathed by will of his father dated 29 Jan.
1743 to JOHN ALLSTON; bounding N on JOSEPH ALLSTON'S part of said 1000 a.
bequeathed to him by his father; on JOSIAS ALLSTON; W on Waccamaw River. Witnesses: ISAAC MARION, ALEXANDER MONTGOMERY. Before BENJAMIN
YOUNG, J.P. Recorded 4 June 1765 by FENWICKE BULL, Register.

Book D-3, p. 131   WILLIAM WARD CROSTHWAITE, gentleman, only son
17 & 18 May 1765   & heir of THOMAS CROSTHWAITE, merchant, of St.
L & R   Philips Parish; to CHARLES PINCKNEY, ESQ.; all
                          of Charleston; for L 1600 currency, the S part
of lot #79 bounding S 58-1/2 ft. on Queen Street; E 130 ft. on WILLIAM
ROPER & THOMAS SMITH; N 54 ft. on part same lot sold to MARY WITHERS; W
130 ft. on MARY WITHERS; which lot #79 THOMAS CROSTHWAITE owned for 10
years & by will dated 11 May 1756 devised to his son WILLIAM. Witnesses:
JOSEPH BRAILSFORD, CHARLES MOTTE. Before ROBERT WILLIAMS, JR., J.P. Recorded 6 June 1765 by FENWICKE BULL, Register.

Book D-3, p. 139   NATHANIEL SCOTT, brewer, to HOPKIN PRICE, ESQ.,
14 May 1765   both of Charleston, for L 1350 currency (be-
Mortgage   cause PRICE stood security on 3 of SCOTT'S
                         bonds; 1 to ELIZABETH PERONNEAU, widow of SAM-
UEL PERONNEAU, merchant; 1 to THOMAS LAMBOLL & ALEXANDER PERONNEAU, gentleman; & 1 to THOMAS LAMBOLL, ALEXANDER PERONNEAU & GEORGE EVELEIGH);
the part of lot #198 purchased by SCOTT from GEORGE & ELIZABETH ROUPELL;
with a house thereon & other buildings; bounding W 140 ft. on Friend
Street running from Broad to Tradd Streets; S on part same lot occupied
by GEORGE ROUPELL & ELIZABETH his wife; E on part same lot belonging to
THOMAS SMITH, JR.; N 61 ft. on part same lot with a house thereon. Witnesses: JACOB BARKLEY, REES PRIS. Before FENWICKE BULL, J.P. & P. Reg.
On 12 May 1767 HOPKIN PRICE declared mortgage paid. Witness: FENWICKE
BULL.

Book D-3, p. 148   TOBIAS FORD, planter, of Colleton Co., to WIL-
16 & 17 Jan. 1764   LIAM COLSON, for Ł 300 currency, 150 a. in the
L & R   Welch tract in Craven Co., on E side Peedee
                          River, bounding SE on GEORGE HICKS; SW on
ABRAHAM COLLSON; other sides on vacant land; as granted 10 Feb. 1749 to
ISAAC NICHOLES; who by L & R dated 27 & 28 Aug. 1752 sold to TOBIAS FORD.
Witnesses: THOMAS WILLIAMS, GEORGE JACKSON. Before FENWICKE BULL, J.P. &
P. Reg. Recorded 10 June 1765,

Book D-3, p. 151   WILLIAM COLSON, of St. Matthews Parish, Ga.,
10 & 11 May 1765   to THOMAS WILLIAMS of the Welch tract, Craven
L & R   •   Co., on E side Peedee River; for Ł 1200 cur-
                          rency, 2 tracts, 600 & 150 a., total 750 a.;
which 600 a. were granted 24 May 1745 to ABRAHAM COLSON; bounding SW on
Peedee River; NW on PENELOPE DAVIS; SE on vacant land; the 150 a. granted
to ISAAC NICHOLES 10 Feb. 1749, bounding SW on ABRAHAM COLSON; other
sides on vacant land. Plat given. Witnesses: DANIEL DONAVAN, GEORGE
JACKSON, ROBERT BROWN. Before GEORGE LOGAN, J.P. for Colleton Co. Recorded 10 June 1765 by FENWICKE BULL, Register.

Book D-3, p. 156   ISAAC NICHOLES, planter, of St. Pauls Parish,
27 & 28 Aug. 1752   Colleton Co., & ELIZABETH his wife, to TOBIAS
L & R   FORD, planter, of St. Bartholomews Parish, for
                          Ł 300 currency, 150 a. in the Welch tract,
Craven Co., bounding SE on GEORGE HICKS; SW on ABRAHAM COLSON; NW & NE on
vacant land; as granted ISAAC NICHOLES by Gov. JAMES GLEN on 10 Feb.
1752. Witnesses: JOHN ROWAN, ANDREW LETCH, ALGERNOON WILSON. Before
FENWICKE BULL, J.P. & P. Reg.

Book D-3, p. 164   ROBERT PRINGLE & FREDERICK GRIMKE, ESQRS., of
4 May 1765   Charleston, to JAMES MCCANTS, of Williamsburgh
Release   Township, for Ł 150 currency, to PRINGLE &
                          5 shillings to GRIMKE; 350 a. in Williamsburgh,
Craven Co., originally granted WILLIAM TURBEVILLE 26 June 1736; bounding
SE on MARGARET BARRA; other sides on vacant land. Whereas JOHN BASNETT,
storekeeper, of Williamsburgh Township, owned said 350 a., but on 27 July
1744 pleaded bankruptcy & on 1 Sept. 1744 assigned his estate to ROBERT
PRINGLE, FREDERICK GRIMKE & RIBTON HUTCHINSON (HUTCHINSON dying soon
afterwards) as trustees for his creditors; now PRINGLE & GRIMKE sell the
land to MCCANTS. Witnesses: JAMES GRINDLAY, JOSEPH BEE. Before ROBERT
BRISBANE, J.P. Recorded 12 June 1765 by FENWICKE BULL, Register.

Book D-3, p. 169   SARAH ALLEN, widow, of ANDREW ALLEN, merchant,
27 Jan. 1740   of Charleston, to JOHN ALLEN. Whereas ANDREW
Surrender   ALLEN owned the brick tenement on S side of
                          Tradd Street, in Charleston, where MRS. PICK-
ERING (now wife of BENJAMIN SAVAGE, merchant), then lived; bounding E on
another of ANDREW ALLEN'S brick tenements then occupied by ROBERT BO-
HANNON (afterwards by BENJAMIN SAVAGE); with the yard, etc., which tenement ANDREW ALLEN by his will, in accordance with certain marriage articles, devised to his wife SARAH so long as she remained his widow; then
to his son JOHN ALLEN; & whereas said house tenement, & buildings were
destroyed by the late fire; now SARAH, for Ł 160 currency, conveys the
undestroyed parts to JOHN ALLEN. Witnesses: MARGARETT WARDEN, THOMAS
LAMBOLL. Before ROBERT WILLIAMS, JR., J.P. Recorded 13 June 1765 by
FENWICKE BULL, Register.

Book D-3, p. 172   JOHN ALLEN, gentleman, of Berkeley Co., eldest
3 & 4 Feb. 1740   son of ANDREW ALLEN, merchant, of Charleston;
L & R   & ANNE his wife, to DAVID HEXT, gentleman, of
                          Charleston; for Ł 2000 currency, that part of
lot #6 lying W of the other part sold to COL. ALEXANDER HEXT, & E of MR.
HINSON; bounding N 57-1/2 ft. on Tradd Street; E 51-1/2 ft. on COL. ALEX-
ANDER HEXT & JAMES MATHEWS; S on CAPT. ANTHONY MATHEWS; W on MR. HINSON.
Whereas ANDREW ALLEN owned part of lot #6, bounding E on Bay of Cooper
River; W on MR. HINSON; &, in accordance with marriage articles made before his marriage with SARAH LEWIS, bequeathed to said SARAH, so long as
she remained his widow, (then to his son JOHN) the W part; viz. the brick
house & yard where MRS. PICKERING (now wife of BENJAMIN SAVAGE, merchant),
then lived, bounding N on Tradd Street; E on another of his brick

tenements occupied by ROBERT BOHANNON (afterwards by BENJAMIN SAVAGE); & bequeathed the residue of his estate to his son JOHN ALLEN; on death of said ANDREW son JOHN inherited the E part of lot #6, also the reversion of the W part after SARAH'S death or remarriage; & whereas on 27 Jan. 1740 (p. 169) SARAH surrendered the W part of lot #6 to son JOHN; & whereas JOHN ALLEN & his wife ANNE lately sold to COL. ALEXANDER HEXT the part of lot #6 lying between the house lately occupied by BENJAMIN SAVAGE & Cooper River; bounding N 120 ft. on Tradd Street; now he sells the W part of the lot to DAVID HEXT. Witnesses: WILLIAM SCOTT, THOMAS LAMBOLL. Before ROBERT WILLIAMS, JR., J.P. Recorded 14 June 1765 by FENWICKE BULL, Register.

Book D-3, p. 182   DAVID HEXT, gentleman, of Berkeley Co., & ANNE
21 & 22 Apr. 1743   his wife, to JOHN MCCALL, merchant, of Charles-
L & R   ton, for ₺ 4000 currency, that part of lot #6
                    lying W of the part sold to COL. ALEXANDER
HEXT, & E of DAVID HEXT, bounding N 29 ft. on Tradd Street; E 51-1/2 ft. on the part sold to COL. ALEXANDER HEXT & on JAMES MATTHEWS; S on ANTHONY MATHEWS; W on DAVID HEXT (see p.p. 169, 172). Witnesses: HENRY DEWICK, LAMBERT LANCE, ANTHONY DEANE. Before JOHN TROUP, J.P. Recorded 17 June 1765 by FENWICKE BULL, Register.

Book D-3, p. 193   JOHN MCCALL, merchant, & MARTHA his wife, to
15 & 16 Apr. 1765   MAURICE JONES, merchant, both of Charleston,
L & R   for ₺ 5000 currency, part of lot #6 bounding N
                    29 ft. on Tradd Street; E 51-1/2 ft. on an
alley formerly belonging to JAMES MATHEWS, now to ROBERT WELLS, printer; S on DAVID GRAEME; W on SAMUEL PRIOLEAU, merchant. Witnesses: JOSHUA WARD, PETER BOURA. Before WILLIAM BURROWS, J.P. Recorded 18 June 1765 by FENWICKE BULL, Register.

Book D-3, p. 200   MAURICE JONES, merchant, to THOMAS GRIMBALL,
9 & 10 May 1765   JR., gentleman, both of Charleston, for ₺ 4250
                    currency, part of lot #6, bounding N 29 ft. on
Tradd Street; E 51-1/2 ft. on an alley formerly belonging to JAMES MATHEWS, now to ROBERT WELLS, printer; S on DAVID GRAEME; W on SAMUEL PRIOLEAU, merchant. Witnesses: JOHN COLCOCK, JOHN RICHARDSON. Before WILLIAM BURROWS, J.P. Recorded 19 June 1765 by FENWICKE BULL, Register.

Book D-3, p. 208   JAMES CROKATT, merchant, of London, & HESTER
30 Jan. 1765   (ESTER) his wife, to THOMAS SMITH, merchant,
Release   of Charleston, SC, for ₺ 1260 British, the lot
                    of ground & brick house which CROKATT purchas-
ed from SAMUEL WRAGG, of London; bounding S on Broad Street; W on JOSEPH WRAGG, merchant; E on lot & brick house of REBECCA FLAVEL, widow, also that part of a lot purchased by CROKATT from JOSEPH WRAGG, merchant, W of 1st house & lot; with the kitchen, etc. JAMES & HESTER CROKATT appoint BENJAMIN SMITH & MILES BREWTON, merchants, of Charleston, their attorneys. Witnesses: WILLIAM COOMBES, JOHN BARNES. Signed by JAMES & HESTER CRO-KATT before SIR CHARLES PRATT, Knight, Lord C.J. of Court C.P., at West-minster on 30 Jan. 1765. COOMBS testified before BENJAMIN SMITH, J.P. 18 Apr. 1765. Recorded 20 June 1765 by FENWICKE BULL, Register.

Book D-3, p. 215   SAMUEL STEVENS (eldest son & heir) & JOSIAH
6 & 7 May 1762   SMITH the younger, gentlemen, only surviving
L & R   executors of will of DR. SAMUEL STEVENS, prac-
                    titioner in Physic; of Berkeley Co.; to HENRY
SMITH, planter, of St. James Goose Creek; for ₺ 17,615:7:0 currency; 1142 a., English measure, on SW side Ashley River, in St. George Parish, Berkeley Co.; bounding N on RALPH IZARD & DR. JOHN MURRAY; E on JAMES SMITH, URIAH EDWARDS, & RALPH IZARD; S on HENRY IZARD; W on JOHN WARING & JOHN DRAYTON; according to plat certified 14 Apr. last by NATHANIEL BRAD-WELL. Whereas SAMUEL STEVENS owned said 1142 a., which by his will dated 24 July 1759 he directed his executors to sell, appointing his son SAM-UEL, & his son-in-law, JOSIAH SMITH, & his other son THOMAS, his execu-tors (THOMAS dying soon after the will was probated); now SAMUEL & JOSIAH sell at auction to SMITH. Witnesses: GEORGE SMITH, EVAN JONES. Before GEORGE MURRAY, J.P. Recorded 21 June 1765 by FENWICKE BULL, Register.

Book D-3, p. 224   CAPT. ANTHONY WHITE, planter, of Black Mingo,

23 Apr. 1764   Craven Co., (holder of mortgage from HENRY
L & R   O'NAIL, deceased), & MRS. SARAH O'NAIL, execu-
                  trix, to JOHN JAMES, planter, for £ 50 curren-
cy, 200 a. on N side Black Mingo Swamp, first surveyed 2 July 1755 to AN-
DREW MCCARTNEY & granted HENRY O'NAIL; bounding NW on NATHANIEL SNOW;
other sides on vacant land. Witnesses: THOMAS G. SCOTT, BARTLY CLARKE,
WILLIAM WILSON. Before JOSEPH BRITTON, J.P. Recorded 24 June 1765 by
FENWICKE BULL, Register.

Book D-3, p. 228   THOMAS MELLICHAMP, planter, of St. Andrews
29 Apr. 1763   Parish, to RICHARD DOWNES, merchant, of
Release   Charleston, for £ 750 currency, 300 a. in Col-
                     leton Co., part of 638 a.; bounding SE on ED-
MUND BELLINGER; NE on THOMAS MELLICHAMP; NW on THOMAS MELLICHAMP & ARCHI-
BALD STANYARNE; SW on CHRISTOPHER WILKINSON. Witnesses: BENJAMIN ELLIOTT,
RICHARD PARK STOBO. Before ROBERT WILLIAMS, JR., J.P. Recorded 24 June
1765 by FENWICKE BULL, Register.

Book D-3, p. 233   JOHN MITCHELL, planter, & MARTHA his wife, to
25 & 26 May 1758   DR. JOHN COCHRAN, physician, both of St. Bar-
L & R   tholomew Parish, Colleton Co., for £ 1100 cur-
                     rency, 3 adjoining tracts; total 590 a. in
said Parish. Whereas JOHN, Earl of Bath, Palatine, on 10 May 1702 grant-
ed JAMES MITCHELL 150 a., English measure, in Colleton Co., bounding S on
MICHAEL STEVENS; W on JOHN JACKSON; N & E on vacant land; & whereas
GEORGE MITCHELL owned 500 a. in Colleton Co. & on 10 Feb. 1724/5 he con-
veyed to his son, JOHN, 100 a. (part of the 500), bounding E on ISRAEL
ANDREW; W on GEORGE MITCHELL; NE on ROBERT COX; according to plat by JOHN
STEPHENS, Dep. Sur.; dated 6 Apr. 1750; & whereas on 7 Aug. 1735 Lt. Gov.
THOMAS BROUGHTON granted GEORGE MITCHELL 340 a., bounding W on Horse Shoe
Creek; N on THOMAS ELLIOTT & JOHN ANDREWS; E on GEORGE MITCHELL & JOHN
MITCHELL, JR.; now JOHN MITCHELL sells to DR. COCHRAN. Witnesses: JOHN
LAIRD, MARY SHARP, MARTHA MCPHERSON. Before JAMES SHARP, J.P. Recorded
25 June 1765 by FENWICKE BULL, Register.

Book D-3, p. 241   JOSEPH MASSEY, planter, & HANNAH his wife, to
4 & 5 Mar. 1754   DR. JOHN COCHRAN, physician, both of Colleton
L & R   Co., for £ 1100 currency, 3 adjoining tracts,
                     total 590 a., in St. Bartholomews Parish; viz.
150 a. granted JAMES MITCHELL 10 May 1702 by Gov. JAMES MOORE; & sold 11
May 1714 to MICHAEL STEVENS, who, with his wife ELIZABETH sold on 29 July
1714 to ISRAEL ANDREW; who on 31 May 1732 sold to JOHN MITCHELL, of Pon-
Pon; 100 a., part of 500 a. granted GEORGE MITCHELL, who on 6 Apr. 1750
gave the 100 a. to his son JOHN; 340 a. granted GEORGE MITCHELL by Lt.
Gov. THOMAS BROUGHTON on 7 Aug. 1735. Witnesses: JOHN WILKINS, JOHN
LAIRD, HENRY WARNER. Before JAMES SHARP. Recorded 26 June 1765 by FEN-
WICKE BULL, Register.

Book D-3, p. 250   GEORGE CUTHBERT, planter, & MARY his wife, to
1 & 2 Jan. 1762   ISAAC WEATHERLY, planter, both of St. Helena
L & R   Island, for £ 2900 currency, their 2 undivided
                     third parts of 500 a., in Granville Co.,
bounding W on marsh & creeks separating it from a small island; N on Cowan's Creek; other sides on vacant land; as granted 14 May 1706. Witnesses: FRANCIS STUART, PHILIP BOX. Before WILLIAM HARVEY, J.P. Recorded 27
June 1765 by FENWICKE BULL, Register.

Book D-3, p. 255   DAVID ADAMS, planter, of Edisto, & CATHARINE
16 & 17 Apr. 1762   his wife, to ISAAC WESTHERLY, planter, of St.
L & R   Helena, for £ 1050 SC money, 1 undivided third
                     part of 500 a. in Granville Co., bounding W on
marsh, creek, & sands separating it from a small island; N on Cowan's
Creek; other sides on vacant land. Whereas the Lords Proprs. on 14 May
1706 granted JOHN BARNWELL 500 a. in Granville Co., bounding W on marsh,
creeks, & sands; N on Cowan's Creek; other sides on vacant land; which,
by will dated 4 May 1724, he bequeathed to his daughter MARY; who married
PAUL GRIMBALL, planter, of Edisto Island; & whereas they had 3 daughters,
MARY (wife of GEORGE CUTHBERT); ELIZABETH (wife of WILLIAM BAYNARD); &
CATHERINE (wife of DAVID ADAM); who inherited equally; now CATHERINE &
DAVID ADAMS sell their share to WEATHERLY. Witnesses: THOMAS CAPERS,

SR., FRANCIS STUART. Before JAMES GRINDLAY, J.P. Recorded 27 June 1765 by FENWICKE BULL, Register

Book D-3, p. 262   ANN CHARNOCK, spinster, of Great Britain, by
5 & 6 Apr. 1762   her attorney, JOB MILNER, merchant, of
L & R   Charleston, SC, to JOHN THOMPSON & JAMES HUNT-
                          ER (as THOMPSON & HUNTER, partners), merchants,
of Charleston, as tenants in common & not as jointenants; for Ł 350 SC
money, 2 lots, 11 & 12, in Dorchester, with the houses, etc., bounding S
on the street leading to the bridge; W on the Square; E on Bay or Front
Street; N on WILLIAM CATTLE. MILNER gives bond of performance. Witnesses: HUGH SWINTON, ALEXANDER CHOVIN. Before JOHN TROUP, J.P. Recorded 28
June 1765 by FENWICKE BULL, Register.

Book D-3, p. 271   The Rev. MR. ABRAM IMER, minister of St. Pe-
6 July 1763   ters Parish, Granville Co., to JOHN BAPTISTE
Mortgage   BOURQUIN, JOHN LEWIS BOURQUIN, & HENRY LEWIS
                          BOURQUIN, gentlmen, administrators, of JOHN
LEWIS DETHERIDGE, for Ł 250 currency, a lot in Purysburgh. Witnesses:
DAVID GIROUD, JOHN VAUCHIER. Before JOHN L. BOURQUIN, J.P. Recorded 29
June 1765 by FENWICKE BULL, Register.

Book D-3, p. 273   NICHOLAS (his mark) WINKLER, planter, of St.
10 May 1764   Peters Parish, to JOHN LINDER, planter, for
Release   Ł 40 currency, 100 a. in Purysburgh Township,
                          granted 17 Mar. 1735 by Gov. THOMAS BROUGHTON
to ANDREW (ANDEROW) WINKLER, next eldest brother of NICHOLAS; bounding S
on DAVID SOUSE; E on PIERRE GALASHES; N on ADAM QULLIAT; W on JEAN HEIWAY
GARDING. Witnesses: MARY MEISNER, LEWIS (his mark) WINKLER, STEPHEN CA-
TER. Before FENWICKE BULL, J.P. & Register.

Book D-3, p. 276   WILLIAM BULOT (GUILLAUME BULLOT), gentleman,
22 May 1765   to JACOB WALDBURGER, planter, both of St. Pe-
Release   ers Parish, for Ł 50 currency, 50 a. in Purys-
                          burgh Township, granted BULLOT; bounding N on
JOSEPH GIRARDIN; S on HENRY BOURQUIN; W on PIERRE LOUIS RECORDON; E on
vacant land; also lot #48 in Purysburgh, bounding N on lot #47; S on a
street; E on a street; W on lot #46. Witnesses: JOHN LINDER, JANE (her
mark) LINDER. Before FENWICKE BULL, J.P. & Register.

Book D-3, p. 278   JOSEPH KIRKLAND, planter, & LEMENDER KIRKLAND,
21 & 22 Jan. 1762   to ZACHARIAH MOREMAN, planter, both of Fred-
L & R   ericksburgh Township, for Ł 275 currency, 100
                          a. on Wateree River, in Fredericksburgh Town-
ship, granted 3 Apr. 1754 by Gov. JAMES GLEN to PATRICK MCCORMICK; who on
10 Oct. 1754 sold to JOSEPH KIRKLAND; bounding NW on SAMUEL BAXTON; SE on
JEFFERY SUMMERFORD; SW on Wateree River; NE on vacant land. Witnesses:
MICHAEL LIGGET, WILLIAM NEAL, MICHAEL (his mark) MCDANIEL. Before ANDREW
ALISON, J.P. of St. Marks Parish, Craven Co. Recorded 1 July 1765 by
FENWICKE BULL, Register.

Book D-3, p. 283   NATHAN TART, of Berkeley Co., & PRISCILLA his
9 & 10 July 1760   wife, to ALEXANDER THOMPSON, planter, of Cra-
L & R   ven Co., for Ł 220 currency, 400 a. on S side
                          Lynch's Lake, being half of 800 a. granted
WILLIAM MORRALL, now owned by NATHAN TART through his wife, PRISCILLA;
bounding SE on unknown land; NW on other half; other sides on vacant land.
Witnesses: RICHARD KING, RICHARD SINGLETARY, ANTHONY WHITE. Before JOHN
LIVISTON, J.P. Recorded 1 July 1765 by FENWICKE BULL, Register.

Book D-3, p. 289   TACITUS GAILLARD, planter, & ANN his wife, to
18 & 19 Mar. 1765   GEORGE PAWLEY the elder, planter, both of Cra-
L & R   ven Co., for Ł 320 currency, 4 lots in George-
                          town, 45, 46, 71, & A; lot 47 bounding SW on
Bay Street; NW on #44; NE on #71; SE on #46; lot #46 bounding SW on Bay
Street; NW on #45; NE on #71; SE on #47; lot #71 bounding NE on Prince
Street; SE on #72; SW on #45; NW on #70; lot A bounding NE on Bay Street;
SE on lot B; SW on the river; NW on public bay lands. Witnesses: BENJA-
MIN FARAR, GEORGE TATE, JOHN WRIGHT, ISAAC GAILLARD. TATE testified be-
fore JOHN LIVISTON, J.P; GAILLARD before CHARLES FYFFE, J.P. Recorded 1

July 1765 by FENWICKE BULL, Register.

Book D-3, p. 295   ANDREW REMBERT, SR., planter, to JOHN DUTART,
11 & 12 Dec. 1764   planter, both of St. James Santee Parish, Cra-
L & R   ven Co., for Ł 600 currency, 500 a. in Craven
                          Co., bounding N on SENECHEAU & DAWSON; E on
JAMES LEGRAND; S & W on vacant land. Witnesses: MOSES MILES, PAUL LAPEAR,
DANIEL DUPRE. Before DANIEL HORRY, J.P. Entered in Auditor's Book C-7,
p. 347 on 3 June 1765 by GEORGE JOHNSTON, per Dep. Aud. Recorded 2 July
1765 by FENWICKE BULL, Register.

Book D-3, p. 301   WILLIAM KILLINGSWORTH, gentleman, of Amelia
7 Jan. 1762   Township, to AARON REILEY & CHARLES CARSON,
Mortgage   merchants, for Ł 358:15:6 currency, 300 a. on
                          NE side Santee River opposite Amelia Township;
275 a. on NE side Peedee River; 20 head cattle, 3 horses, 2 mares, 2
colts, 4 feather beds, all his pewter & household furniture. Redeemable
1 Mar. next. Witnesses: THOMAS LENNON, THOMAS POND. Before MOSES THOMP-
SON, J.P. See Secretary's Book Z. Z., p. 205 & 206; 5 June 1762. Recorded 2 July 1765 by FENWICKE BULL, Register.

Book D-3, p. 305   CHARLES RUSSELL, to MALACHI WESTON, for Ł 1000
4 & 5 June 1765   currency, 100 a. in Craven Co., N side Wateree
L & R   River, running across a small river; granted
                          RUSSELL 30 Aug. 1762; bounding on all sides on
vacant land; also 450 a. granted MARY RUSSELL, mother of CHARLES, on 29
Nov. 1750; bounding N on vacant land; E on Wateree River; S on Santee
River & vacant land; W on the river & MILES JACKSON. Witnesses: THOMAS
HEYWARD, JR., JOHN GLEN. Before FENWICKE BULL, J.P. & P. Reg. Recorded
2 July 1765.

Book D-3, p. 310   BENJAMIN BURNHAM, eldest son, of BENJAMIN BURN-
7 & 8 June 1765   HAM, to THOMAS ELFE, cabinet-maker, of Charles-
L & R   ton, for Ł 500 currency, 172 a. on Thomas Is-
                          land (Daniel's Island), bounding N & W on Watt-
coe Creek; S & E on ISAAC LESESNE; as by plats of original grants (1 plat
showing 62 a. called Bradys or St. Iago Island). Witnesses: ROBERT WIL-
LIAMS, JR., WILLIAM ROPER, JR. Before WILLIAM BURROWS, J.P. Recorded 2
July 1765 by FENWICKE BULL, Register.

Book D-3, p. 317   THOMAS (his mark) HAVARD, to ARCHIBALD OFFUTT,
4 Aug. 1761   both of Granville Co., for Ł 220 currency,
L & R   300 a. on Savannah River, about 10 miles above
                          the mouth of Long Canes in Granville Co.; be-
tween the river & ROBERT BRIAN. Witnesses: NATHANIEL OFFUTT, THOMAS
HOWLE. Before ADRIAN MAYER, J.P. Recorded 3 July by FENWICKE BULL, Register.

Book D-3, p. 323   THOMAS BOONE, Gov. of SC, for himself & as
3 & 4 Mar. 1763   attorney for CHARLES BOONE; & CHARLES BOONE,
L & R   ESQ., of St. George Parish, Hanover Square,
                          Middlesex Co., London, of 1st part; to SARAH
SAUNDERS, of St. Bartholomews Parish, Colleton Co., SC, for Ł 400 SC money, 200 a. in St. Bartholomews Parish, bounding N on THOMAS BOONE; W on
land sold by Gov. THOMAS BOONE to ISHAM ANDREWS; SE on MRS. PENNY; the
200 a. being part of a tract originally granted JOSEPH BOONE. Witnesses:
JAMES POSTELL, CULCHETH GIBBES. Before JOSEPH GLOVER, J.P. Recorded 4
July 1765 by FENWICKE BULL, Register.

Book D-3, p. 329   ROBERT BRISBANE & WILLIAM BRISBANE, merchants,
2 May 1765   of Charleston, to SAMUEL COOPER, of Prince
Release   Frederick Parish, Craven Co., for Ł 1355:9:6
                          currency, 1749 a. in Craven Co., on head of
Black Mingo Creek; bounding E on the Rev. MR. JOHN BAXTER & JOHN LANE; N
on JOHN LANE; W on heirs of ROBERT YEOMANS; being part of 3249 a. conveyed by L & R dated 5 & 6 July 1737 to JAMES KINLOCH, ESQ., of Berkeley Co.;
who by L & R dated 6 & 7 July 1738 sold to GEORGE HUNTER, gentleman, of
Charleston; who by will dated 27 Aug. 1745 appointed WILLIAM WOODROP,
merchant, of Charleston, his sole executor, with authority to sell his
land; who, by L & R dated 15 & 16 June 1764 sold the residue of HUNTER'S

274

real estate to ROBERT & WILLIAM BRISBANE. Witnesses: JAMES FOWLER, JAMES
JOHNSTON. Before FENWICKE BULL, J.P. & P. Reg. Entered in Auditor's
Book G-7, p. 341, on 4 May 1765 by RICHARD LAMBTON, Dep. Aud.

Book D-3, p. 335   PETER ALBATESTIER MON CLAIR, gentleman, of
8 Sept. 1764   Charleston, to ADRIAN MAYER, of Purysburgh,
Release   for ℔ 120 SC money, the tract of land in Purys-
           burgh Township granted 1 June 1738 by King
GEORGE II to ANDREW ALBATESTIER DE MON CLAIR, father of PETER; bounding N
on CAPT. FREDERIC HOLZENDORF; S on CAPT. FREDERIC DEJEAN; W on JOHN PETER
PURY & JOHN CHEVILESS; E on JACOB TANNER & vacant land; also lot #72 in
Purysburgh granted said ANDREW on 2 Feb. 1735; bounding S & W on a street;
E on lot #74; N on lot #71. Witnesses: FELIX LONG, CHARLES STROTHER.
Before JOHN TROUP, J.P. Entered in Auditor's Book G-7, p. 239, on 10
Sept. 1764 by RICHARD LAMBTON, Dep. Aud. Recorded 5 July 1765 by FEN-
WICKE BULL, Register.

Book D-3, p. 337   JAMES MAYSON, LUCAS HOLT, merchant, of Glasgow
29 Mar. 1765   Plantation, to ROBERT DILLON, tavern keeper,
Mortgage   of Charleston, for ℔ 3000 SC money, 556 a.
           called Glasgow where he resides, with all its
buildings, tools, horses, cattle, hogs, sheep, wagons, plate, furniture,
& 6 Negroes. Date of redemption: 8 Apr. next. Witnesses: FORTON DOBS,
JAMES JONES. Before ISAAC PITCHLYNE, J.P. Entered in Secretary's Book
& &, p. 265 on 31 May 1765 by GEORGE JOHNSTON, Dep. Sec. Recorded 3 July
1765 by FENWICKE BULL, Register.

Book D-3, p. 339   PETER MAZYCK, merchant, of Charleston, to
6 & 7 June 1765   PHILIP PORCHER, planter, of Craven Co., for
L & R   ℔ 2500 currency, 740 a. in 2 tracts; 600 a. in
           St. Johns Parish, Berkeley Co., surveyed 31
Aug. 1728 to JOHN BAYLY, eldest son & heir of JOHN BAYLY of Ballinaclough,
Co. of Tipperary, Ireland, as part of the 48,000 a. granted by the Lords
Proprs. 16 Aug. 1698 to JOHN BAYLY the father, as Landgrave & Cassique,
bounding S on JOSEPH GOODBE & JOSEPH DE ST. JULIEN; E on JOSEPH DE ST.
JULIEN & a tract 140 a.; N on JOHN RICHBOURGH (formerly ROBERT QUARTER-
MAN); W on JOSEPH GOODBE & vacant land; also said 140 a. the N part of
400 a. granted by the Lords Proprs. on 3 June 1714 to PETER DE ST. JULIEN;
bounding S on other part of said tract; E on WILLIAM MOULTRIE; N on part
said 400 a. belonging to PHILIP PORCHER; W on said 600 a. Witnesses:
PETER PORCHER, ISAAC MAZYCK, JR., WILLIAM MAZYCK. Before ISAAC PORCHER,
J.P. Inasmuch as the 140 a. tract has not been surveyed PORCHER accepts
it as 140 a. Witnesses: PETER PORCHER, MARIANE PORCHER. Recorded 4 July
1765 by FENWICKE BULL, Register.

Book D-3, p. 350   WILLIAM CHAPMAN, planter, & MARY his wife, of
17 & 18 June 1765   James Island, to JAMES VERREE, house carpen-
L & R   ter, of Charleston, for ℔ 2000 currency, part
           of lot #78 in Charleston, bounding W 48 ft. on
Church Street; N 198 ft. on JAMES VERREE; E on WILLIAM ROPER & JUSTINUS
STOLL; S on DR. WILLIAM BRISBANE & THOMAS SCREVEN. Witnesses: WILLIAM
MORGAN, JOSHUA WARD. Before WILLIAM BURROWS, J.P. Recorded 5 July 1765
by FENWICKE BULL, Register.

Book D-3, p. 358   JOSEPH SEALY, planter, of Colleton Co., to
29 Feb. & 1 Mar. 1743 WILLIAM SEALY, planter, of Granville Co., for
L & R   ℔ 300 currency, 300 a., English measure, being
           the N part of 1000 a. on W side Port Royall
River, Granville Co.; granted JOSEPH SEALY on 23 Apr. 1735 by Gov. ROBERT
JOHNSON; bounding N on head of Uhaw Creek; E on CHARLES ODINGSELL & va-
cant land; S on COL. HALL & a creek; W on CAPT. GASTON & vacant land; the
300 a. bounding N on head of Uhaw Creek; S on other part of 1000 a.; E on
CHARLES ODINGSELL & vacant land; W on vacant land. Witnesses: HUGH BRYAN,
JAMES WILLIAMS, FRANCIS PELOT. Before WILLIAM HARVEY, J.P. Entered in
Auditor's Book G-7, p. 352 on 24 June 1765, by RICHARD LAMBTON, Dep. Aud.
Recorded 5 July 1765 by FENWICKE BULL, Register.

Book D-3, p. 364   FREDERICK HOLTZENDORF, saddler, of Christ
13 June 1765   Church Parish, Ga., to ADRIAN MAYER, ESQ., of
Release   St. Peters Parish, SC, for ℔ 14:5:9 sterling,

200 a. in Purysburgh Township, bounding N on PETER GARRET VANDERHEYDEN; S on ANDREW ALBATESTIER DE MONCLARE & JOHN CHEVILETTE; E on MELCHIOR GAMPERT & W on COL. JOHN PETER PURY. Signed JAMES CHARLES FREDERICK HOLZENDORF. Witness: EDWARD KEATING, JOSIAH TILLY. Before DAVID MONTAIGUT, J.P., in Savannah. Recorded 6 July 1765 by FENWICKE BULL, Register.

Book D-3, p. 369
6 & 7 Sept. 1764
L & R

DR. ALEXANDER FOTHERINGHAM, physician, & ISABELLA his wife, to THOMAS MACKREATH, gentleman, both of Charleston, for Ł 800 currency, 3 lots in Dorchester, 95, 96, & 97. Whereas ADAM WOOD, P.M., on 20 Oct. 1759, sold to DR. FOTHERINGHAM all of lot #95 being 1/4 a.; & part of lot #96 being 25 x 155 ft. adjoining lot #95; & whereas by L & R dated 28 & 29 Nov. 1760 JAMES CHARLES FREDERICK HOLZENDORFF & MARY ANNE, his wife, sold said FOTHERINGHAM, 2 lots of 1/4 a. each, 1 being part of lot #96 (44 x 155 ft.); the other lot #97 bounding E on George Street; S on ELIJAH POSTELL; W on another street; N on ALEXANDER FOTHERINGHAM & part of lot #96; now the 3 lots are sold to MACKREATH. Witness: JOHN TROUP, J.P. Before FENWICKE BULL, J.P. & P. Reg.

Book D-3, p. 377
25 & 26 June 1765
L & R

THOMAS MACKRETH, gentleman, to WILLIAM HOLIDAY, tavern keeper, both of Charleston, for Ł 760 currency, 3 lots in Dorchester Town, #95, #96, & #97 (see p. 369). Witnesses: PETER HORN, BENNET OLDHAM. Before FENWICKE BULL, J.P. & P. Reg.

Book D-3, p. 386
1 & 2 Oct. 1764
L & R

FRANCIS YOUNGE, planter, & SARAH his wife, to TOBIAS FORD, planter, both of Colleton Co., for Ł 1600 currency, 3 adjoining tracts of 200, 130, & 300 a., total 630 a., on Horse Shoe Savannah, in Colleton Co., bounding N on 171 a. lately sold by YOUNGE to GEORGE AUSTIN, & on WILLIAM WALTER; E on THOMAS ELLIOTT & PHILIP HEXT; S on THOMAS ELLIOTT, PHILIP HEXT, WILLIAM MITCHELL & DANIEL LEGERE; W on DANIEL LEGERE & WILLIAM WALTER. Witnesses: JAMES DONNOM, JOHN MITCHELL, JOHN WEBB. Before JOSEPH GLOVER, J.P. Recorded 8 July 1765 by FENWICKE BULL, Register.

Book D-3, p. 393
18 & 19 Oct. 1764
L & R

DAVID FERGUSON, planter, & MARY his wife; to MARY HUNTER, planter, both of St. Bartholomews Parish, Colleton Co., for Ł 5000 currency, 550-3/4 a. in said Parish, bounding W on TOBIAS FORD (now JOSIAH PERRY); S on JAMES HAMILTON; E on PETER RUMPH; NE on THOMAS FARR (formerly ROBERT REID, then TOBIAS FORD), & on vacant land; as purchased from JAMES SKIRVING. Witnesses: JAMES HAMILTON, ISAAC NEWTON, HUGH THOMSON. Before JOSEPH GLOVER, J.P. Recorded 9 July 1765 by FENWICKE BULL, Register.

Book D-3, p. 401
15 Mar. 1762
L & R

JOHN DRAKEFORD, planter, to JOHN ELKINS, shoemaker, both of Craven Co., for Ł 130 currency, 100 a. on SW side Wateree River, bounding SE on WILLIAM SCOTT & vacant land; SW & NW on vacant land; which Gov. JAMES GLEN on 9 Jan. 1756 granted to DRAKEFORD. Witnesses: ROBERT ELKINS, JOHN (his mark) ELKINS, JR. Before JOHN NEWMAN OGLETHORPE, J.P. Recorded 8 July 1765 by FENWICKE BULL, Register.

Book D-3, p. 407
25 & 26 July 1759
L & R

WILLIAM GARDNER, planter, to JAMES COOPER, planter, both of Craven Co., for Ł 180 currency, 300 a. in Craven Co., bounding SW on Williamsburgh Township line; NW & NE on vacant land; SE on WILLIAM GARDNER. Witnesses: JOHN SCOTT, JAMES BLEACKLY. Before JOHN LIVISTON, J.P. Recorded 9 July 1765 by FENWICKE BULL, Register.

Book D-3, p. 412
25 & 26 July 1759
L & R

WILLIAM GARDNER, planter, to JAMES COOPER, planter, both of Craven Co., for Ł 300 currency, 300 a. in Craven Co., where COOPER has resided for several years (see p. 407). Witnesses: JOHN SCOTT, JAMES BLEACKLY. Before JOHN LIVISTON, J.P. Recorded 9 July 1765 by FENWICKE BULL, Register.

Book D-3, p. 417

DANIEL MOONEY & SARAH his wife, (formerly

26 July 1759   widow of WILLIAM GARDNER) appeared before JOHN
Quitclaim   LIVISTON, J.P., & renounced their claim in 2
            adjoining tracts on NE side Williamsburgh
Township sold by WILLIAM GARDNER (heir to WILLIAM GARDNER) of Prince
Frederick Parish, to JAMES COOPER. Before JOHN LIVISTON, J.P. Recorded
9 July 1765 by FENWICKE BULL, Register.

Book D-3, p. 418   Between JAMES COOPER, of 1st part, & DANIEL
20 June 1764   MOONEY & SARAH his wife, in regard to 2 tracts
Agreement   of land formerly belonging to WILLIAM GARDNER,
            now to SARAH (widow of said GARDNER, now wife
of MOONEY) & WILLIAM GARDNER, her son, an idiot, which all of them (DAN-
IEL, SARAH, & WILLIAM, JR.) have sold to JAMES COOPER; DANIEL & SARAH
give bond that the Negro wench, DINAH, delivered by COOPER as part payment, shall be delivered to WILLIAM MOONEY, JR., at death of SARAH. Witness: JAMES MCCANTS. Recorded 9 July 1765 by FENWICKE BULL, Register.

Book D-3, p. 419   FRANCIS GOTTIER, silversmith, of Charleston, &
29 & 30 Nov. 1764   ISABELLA his wife, to WILLIAM SNOW, planter,
L & R   of Prince Frederick Parish, for Ł 1000 curren-
            cy, 600 a. in Queensborough Township, on SE
side Great Peedee River, in Prince Frederick Parish, Craven Co., bounding
NW on CHARLES WOODMASON; SE & SW on ABRAHAM STAPLES; granted JAMES GORDON,
gentleman, 4 Mar. 1734; later vested in JOSIAS GARNIER DUPREE; from whom
it was seized for debt by DANIEL DOYLEY, P.M.; who sold at public auction
on 10 Sept. 1762 to FRANCIS GOTTIER. Witnesses: CHARLES MOTTE, JAMES
FRASER. Before FENWICKE BULL, J.P. & P. Reg.

Book D-3, p. 427   THOMAS LYDE (LIDE), gentleman, to THOMAS WADE,
11 & 13 Feb. 1764   ESQ., both of St. Marks Parish, Craven Co.,
L & R   for Ł 200 currency, 350 a. on Hanging Rock
            Creek, said Parish, granted 10 Nov. 1761 by
Lt. Gov. WILLIAM BULL to said LYDE; bounding N on WILLIAM MCKEE; other
sides on vacant land. Witnesses: JOHN WADE, JAMES IRVIN. Before JOHN
PICKEN, J.P. Recorded 11 July 1765 by FENWICKE BULL, J.P.

Book D-3, p. 432   DANIEL MARETTE to MAJ. JACQUES RICHARD, of
19 Mar. 1734/5   Purysburgh for 15 shillings sterling, 50 a. in
Assignment   Purysburgh Township. Witnesses: JONAS PELOT,
            STEFAN ABOWESKI. Recorded 11 July 1765 by
FENWICKE BULL, Register, at request of MILES BREWTON, ESQ. No probate.

Book D-3, p. 433   GEORGE SNOW & JAMES SNOW, planters, of Prince
10 & 11 Dec. 1764   Frederick Parish, Craven Co., to WILLIAM
L & R   WITHERS, planter, of St. James Goose Creek,
            for Ł 4000 currency, 650 a. in Berkeley Co.,
bounding N on Forsters Creek adjoining NATHANIEL SNOW & PETER LAMB; E on
CAPT. GILL; S on JOB HOW; W on NATHANIEL SNOW, SR. & JOHN EMPEROR; also
408 a. on Goose Creek Neck, Berkeley Co., bo-nding S & E on NATHANIEL
SNOW; N on Forsters Creek; W on PETER LAMB; originally granted by the
Lords Proprs. to NATHANIEL SNOW, 1st, chirurgeon; also 500 a. in St.
James Goose Creek Parish, Berkeley Co., bounding NW on NATHANIEL SNOW; SW
on JAMES WITHERS; SE on THOMAS SMITH & MR. WALTERS; NE on marsh of Cooper
River; originally granted NATHANIEL SNOW, 2nd; total 1558 a. devised by
NATHANIEL SNOW to his daughter ANNE, who afterwards married FRANCIS GOD-
ARD, planter, of Peedee, Craven Co.; & sold by them to GEORGE & JAMES
SNOW. Witnesses: THOMAS PINCKNEY, ROBERT ROBERTSON, E. HIGGINSON. Be-
fore JOHN REMINGTON, J.P. Recorded 10 July 1765 by FENWICKE BULL, Reg-
ister.

Book D-3, p. 442   JOHN STEWART (STUART), JR., of Granville Co.,
8 & 9 July 1764   to WILLIAM WATSON, of Berkeley Co., for Ł 250
L & R   currency, 200 a. in Granville Co., at Turkey
            Creek; bounding on all sides on vacant land;
granted 7 Oct. 1755 by Gov. JAMES GLEN to JOHN GOFF; who by L & R dated
23 & 24 Feb. 1758 sold to WILLIAM STUART; who, by will dated 28 Mar. 1761
bequeathed to JOHN STUART. Signed by JOHN STEWART, JR. & JOHN STEWART,
SR. Witnesses: SANDERS WALKER, JOHN FURNAS, MOSES POWELL. Before JACOB
SUMMERRALL, J.P. Recorded 11 July 1765 by FENWICKE BULL, Register.

Book D-3, p. 449   FRANCIS GODDARD, planter, of Peedee, Craven
2 & 3 Mar. 1764   Co., & ANN his wife (daughter of NATHANIEL
L & R   SNOW, planter, of St. James Goose Creek Par-
                         ish), to GEORGE SNOW & JAMES SNOW, planters,
of Prince Frederick Parish, for Ł 2200 currency, 650 a. in Berkeley Co.,
bounding N on Fosters Creek adjoining NATHANIEL SNOW & PETER LAMB; E on
CAPT. GILL; S on JOB HOW; W on NATHANIEL SNOW, SR., & JOHN EMPEROR; also
408 a. on Goose Creek Neck, Berkeley Co., bounding S & E on NATHANIEL
SNOW- N on Forsters Creek; W on PETER LAMB; as granted by Lords Proprs.
to NATHANIEL SNOW, 1st, chirurgeon; also 500 a. in St. James Goose Creek
Parish, Berkeley Co., bounding NW on NATHANIEL SNOW; SW on JAMES WITHERS;
SE on THOMAS SMITH & MR. WALTERS; NE on marsh of Cooper River; granted
NATHANIEL SNOW, 2nd; total 1558 a. devised by NATHANIEL SNOW to his
daughter ANNE, now wife of said FRANCIS GODDARD. Witnesses: WALTER MAR-
TIN, WILLIAM SNOW, JOHN PORTER. Before JOSEPH BRITTON, J.P. Recorded
12 July 1765 by FENWICKE BULL, Register.

Book D-3, p. 458   JONATHAN MCMURDY, ROBERT MCMURDY, ANNE MCMURDY,
28 & 29 June 1765   & ELIZABETH MCMURDY, surviving children of
L & R   WILLIAM MCMURDY, farmer, of Carran in the Par-
                         ish, Co., & Diocese of Armagh, Ireland, by
their attorney, WILLIAM GLEN, merchant, of Charleston, SC, to WILLIAM
DRAYTON, ESQ., of St. Andrews Parish, SC, for Ł 500 SC money 207 a. in
Colleton Co., bounding S on WILLIAM DRAYTON & CAPT. WILLIAM BROWN; E on
WILLIAM BROWN; W on PAUL JENYS; devised by will of ROBERT MCMURDY the
elder, planter, of PonPon, SC, dated 13 May 1756, to his brother, WILLIAM
MCMURDY, of Armagh, Ireland, for his lifetime, then equally to said
brother's children. Witnesses: JOHN COOPER, WILLIAM GLEN, JR. Before
ROBERT BRISBANE, J.P. Recorded 13 July 1765 by FENWICKE BULL, Register.

Book D-3, p. 465   GEORGE SMITH, JR., planter, & MARY his wife,
8 & 9 May 1765   to ROBERT DANIEL, planter, both of St. Thomas
L & R   Parish, Berkeley Co., for Ł 1300 currency,
                         400 a. where GEORGE SMITH, JR. now lives, in
St. Thomas Parish, bounding E on NATHAN TART; S on JOHN DUTARQUE, JR.; W
on JOHN GUERIN; N on ROBERT DANIEL & JOHN SINGLETARY. Witnesses: JOHN
SINGLETARY, THOMAS CHADWICK. Before JOHN REMINGTON, J.P. Recorded 12
July 1765 by FENWICKE BULL, Register.

Book D-3, p. 472   CHRISTOPHER GADSDEN, ESQ., of Charleston, &
16 & 17 Apr. 1764   MARY his wife, to THOMAS WADE, ESQ., for
L & R   Ł 1783 currency, 150 a. in Craven Co., on SW
                         side PeeDee River, bounding on all sides on
vacant land. Witnesses: DANIEL DOYLEY, THOMAS GRIMBALL, JR. Before WIL-
LIAM BURROWS, J.P. Recorded 13 July 1765 by FENWICKE BULL, Register.

Book D-3, p. 479   ROBERT WILLIAMS, gentleman, of Charleston, &
2 & 3 Nov. 1761   MARGARET his wife, to JONATHAN BRYAN, ESQ., of
L & R   Savannah, Ga., for Ł 1400 SC money, 300 a. in
                         Purysburgh Township, Granville Co., bounding W
on Savannah River; E on Aposkee Creek (traversing the tract from NE to
SW) & COL. SAMUEL MONTAGUE; N on vacant land; S on JOHN GRENIER, vacant
land, & on a tract of 50 a.; which 300 a. were granted 9 Apr. 1743 to
DAVID GENDER & by various conveyances came to ROBERT WILLIAMS; also said
50 a., called Monmouth Point, in Purysburgh Township, bounding N on said
300 a.; W on Savannah River; S on Back River; which 50 a. were granted
16 Sept. 1738 to DANIEL MERETT. Witnesses: JAMES EDWARD POWELL, WILLIAM
EWEN, JOHN CHAPMAN. Before JAMES EDWARD POWELL, in Savannah, Ga. Recorded 15 July 1765 by FENWICKE BULL, Register.

Book D-3, p. 489   ANDREW HENDRIE, planter, of St. Peters Parish,
22 & 23 Apr. 1765   Granville Co., & HUGH BURN, planter, of Christ
L & R   Church Parish, Ga.; to MILES BREWTON, ESQ., of
                         Charleston, for Ł 2400 currency, to HENDRIE &
10 shillings to BURN; 125 a. in Purysburgh Township, Granville Co.,
bounding E on Apokee Creek; W on Samuel Montague; N on ANDREW HENDRIE &
HUGH BURNE; S on vacant land; being part of 300 a. granted DAVID GENDRE;
also 150 a. in Purysburgh Township, bounding W on Aposkee Creek; E on
JEREMIAH RAYMOND; being part of 400 a. granted JOHN GREMIER. Whereas on
13 June 1761 DAVID HUMBERT, planter, of SC, & URSULA his wife, sold

HENDRIE & BURN 400 a. on E side Apokee Creek; & whereas on 10 Oct. 1763
JONATHAN BRYAN, ESQ., of Savannah, Ga. & MARY his wife, sold HENDRIE &
BURN 125 a. on W side of Aposke Creek; & whereas HENDRIE & BURN agreed to
divide the 2 tracts equally by a line drawn from E to W, to be drawn for
by lot, & the N part consisting of the 125 a. sold them by JONATHAN &
MARY BRYAN, & an adjoining 150 a. (part of 400 a. sold them by DAVID &
URSULA HUMBERT) became HENDRIE'S portion; & the S part (the residue of
the 400 a.) was drawn by BURN; & since HENDRIE has agreed to sell his
part to BREWTON; now, to perfect the title, BURN joins HENDRIE in conveying the N division to BREWTON. Witnesses: JOSEPH FELTHAM, JOHN BREWTON,
CHARLES WATSON, GEORGE JARMAN. Before FENWICKE BULL, J.P. & P. Reg. Recorded 16 July 1765.

Book D-3, p. 496   MARY STEVENS (formerly MARY BADGER) widow, of
16 & 17 Apr. 1755   Colleton Co., & SARAH BADGER, spinster, (MARY
L & R   & SARAH being the only children of GEORGE BAD-
                        GER, planter, who died intestate), with the
consent of MARTHA (her mark) SMITH (formerly MARTHA BADGER, widow of said
GEORGE), of 1st part; to DR. JOHN COCHRAN, physician, for L 400 currency,
120 a. Whereas Gov. NATHANIEL JOHNSON on 1 June 1709 granted ROBERT COX
120 a., within land, W of the freshes in Colleton Co., bounding E & W on
vacant land; S on vacant land & MICHAEL STEVENS; N on JOHN ANDREWS; & at
his death his eldest son, JOHN COX, cordwainer inherited; & on 23 Feb.
1727 sold the 120 a. to GEORGE BADGER; now his 2 daughters & widow sell
to COCHRAN. Witnesses: JACOB STEVENS, JAMES DONNOM, JOHN NORTH. Before
GEORGE JOHNSTON, J.P. Recorded 18 July 1765 by FENWICKE BULL, Register.

Book D-3, p. 506   MAURICE JONES, merchant, to JAMES TWEED, mer-
15 & 16 July 1765   chant, both of Charleston, for L 2400 curren-
L & R   cy, 500 a. in Craven Co., on N branch of Black
                        River; other sides on vacant land; granted by
Gov. CHARLES CRAVEN on 9 June 1714 to RICHARD WIGG; who with SARAH his
wife, on 9 & 10 Nov. 1725 sold to JOHN WHITE; who by will dated 24 Feb.
1758 ordered his oldest son, ANTHONY, to choose 1 of his tracts of land.
Upon division of JOHN WHITE'S estate ANTHONY chose said 500 a., & with
DEBORAH his wife, on 16 & 17 Mar. 1762 sold to HUGH SWINTON. Whereas
PETER MANIGAULT, GEORGE INGLIS, & ANDREW MARR obtained a judgment against
SWINTON, with costs, & by writ of fieri facias ROGER PINCKNEY, P.M., sold
the land at auction to JONES; now he sells to TWEED. Witnesses: JOHN
COLCOCK, JOHN GILES. Before FENWICKE BULL, J.P. & P. Reg.

Book D-3, p. 514   JOSHUA SANDERS, planter, of Colleton Co., &
19 & 20 July 1744   ELIZABETH CLARK, his wife, to BENJAMIN GODIN,
L & R   ESQ., of St. James Goose Creek Parish, for
                        L 765 currency, 255 a. being the W part of
500 a.; bounding E on the Broad Path; N & S on BENJAMIN GODIN; W on vacant land & heirs of JOHN PARKER; as marked A & shaded yellow on plat
certified by GEORGE HUNTER, Sur. Gen. Whereas JOHN SANDERS, planter, of
St. James Goose Creek, father of JOSHUA, was granted on 14 Aug. 1702,
500 a. on S side of Goose Creek, within land, in Berkeley Co., bounding E
on said JOHN SANDERS; N on JACOB ALLEN; S on WILLIAM SANDERS; W on vacant
land; & whereas JOHN SANDERS also owned 260 a. adjoining said 500 a.,
bounding E on Yeomans Creek; S on a branch; N on MR. ALLIN (now BENJAMIN
GODIN); W on WILLIAM SANDERS (now BENJAMIN GODIN); making 1 tract of 750
a.; which by will dated 23 Oct. 1716 said JOHN SANDERS ordered divided
among his 4 sons, JOHN, WILSON, JOSHUA, & WILLIAM; & whereas JOHN SANDERS,
the son, by will dated 4 Sept. 1718 bequeathed all his estate to his
brother, WILSON; & whereas JOSHUA & WILLIAM SANDERS by L & R dated 13 &
14 May 1730 conveyed their shares (190 a. each) to WILSON SANDERS; &
whereas WILSON SANDERS by will dated 23 Oct. 1735 bequeathed to his son,
JOHN, all his lands in St. James Goose Creek except as before bequeathed;
item, to son JOHN SANDERS 1368 a. in St. George Parish, on Captains Creek;
item, to son JOHN, 14 Negroes; but should JOHN die before coming of age,
then the land & Negroes to his (testator's) brother JOSHUA; & whereas
JOHN, son of WILSON SANDERS, died 16 Nov. 1743 under 21 years of age &
said JOSHUA inherited; now he sells a portion of his land to GODIN. Witnesses: WILLIAM BRISBANE, THOMAS HOLMES. Before PETER MANIGAULT, J.P.
Recorded 20 July 1765 by FENWICKE BULL, Register.

Book D-3, p. 524   WILLIAM MOULTRIE, ESQ., to JOHN MATHEWES,

1 & 2 Jan. 1763   gentleman, both of Charleston, for payment of
L & R by Mortgage   an annuity of Ⱡ 1200 currency to MATHEWES dur-
                                  ing his lifetime; 1000 a. called Northampton
in St. Johns Parish, bounding E on RENÉ RAVENEL; W on JOSEPH DE ST.
JULIEN; S on WILLIAM MOULTRIE; N on DANIEL RAVENEL; also 100 Negro
slaves. Witnesses: PETER MAZYCK, JAMES MOULTRIE. Before JOHN HUME, J.P.
Entered in Secretary's Book Z.Z., p. 337-340, on Mar. 3, 1763 by THOMAS
SKOTTOWE, Sec. Recorded 22 July 1765 by FENWICKE BULL, Register. On 9
May 1768 JOHN MATHEWES declared mortgage paid. Witness: FENWICKE BULL.

Book D-3, p. 531   ANN CONAWAY, widow (formerly wife of ALEXANDER
31 May 1763   GOODBEE, planter, of Berkeley Co.), of
Release   Charleston, daughter of the Hon. ROBERT DAN-
                                  IELL & MARTHA his wife; of 1st part; to PETER
MANIGAULT, barrister-at-law, & ANN WRAGG, spinster, of Charleston, of 2nd
part; for Ⱡ 425 currency, part of lots #33 & #34 on Bay of Charleston,
bounding E 78 ft. on Cooper River; S 210 ft. on JOSEPH WRAGG; N on MARMA-
DUKE DANIELL (afterwards CAPT. JOHN HARLESTON, now JONATHAN SCOTT); on
the part bounding 78 ft. on the Bay & 145 ft. deep going to MANIGAULT;
the remainder to ANN WRAGG. Whereas ALEXANDER GOODBEE & said ANN CONAWAY
(then his wife) by L & R dated 4 & 5 Mar. 1727 sold to JOSEPH WRAGG, merchant, the said parts of 2 lots; & whereas JOSEPH WRAGG by will dated 26
Sept. 1746 bequeathed all his estate not bequeathed to his wife equally
to his children; & whereas by deed of partition dated 18 Mar. 1757 a certain part (78 ft. on the Bay & 145 ft. deep) was allotted to ELIZABETH
MANIGAULT, wife of PETER, & the remainder (except an alley of 10 ft.) was
allotted to ANN WRAGG; & whereas PETER & ELIZABETH MANIGAULT by L & R
dated 25 & 26 Aug. 1757 sold their part to JOHN DENTON; who by L & R dated 29 & 30 Aug. 1757 sold to PETER MANIGAULT; & whereas ANN CONAWAY on
delivery of L & R between ALEXANDER & ANN GOODBEE & JOSEPH WRAGG was not
of age & did not renounce her inheritance; now she releases all her claim
to the lots. Witnesses: ANDREW HUNTER, WILLIAM BANBURY, PETER BOUNETHEAU.
Before JOHN REMINGTON, J.P. Recorded 23 July 1765 by FENWICKE BULL,
Register.

Book D-3, p. 535   DANIEL MARETTE (MARRETT) of Purysburgh, SC, to
2 & 3 July 1765   ADRIAN LOYER, gunsmith, of Savannah, Ga; for
                                  Ⱡ 50 Ga. money, being equal to Ⱡ 50 sterling
British; 50 a. in Purysburgh Township, bounding N & W on Savannah River;
S on Back River; other sides on vacant land; as granted MARETTE 16 Sept.
1738. Witnesses: DAVID MONTAIGUT, NICHOLAS HORTON, JOSEPH REYMOND. Before P. MOLENGH, J.P. Entered in Pub. Reg. office in Ga. in Book C. fol.
975-976, on 12 July 1765 by THOMAS MOODIE, Dep. Reg. Recorded 23 July
1765 by FENWICKE BULL, Register.

Book D-3, p. 541   WILLIAM COACHMAN, planter, of Prince George
18 Nov. 1751   Winyaw, Craven Co., to ALEXANDER MONTGUMRY, of
Release   same Parish, for Ⱡ 200 currency, 100 a., part
                                  of 400 a. conveyed by WILLIAM WATIES to the
father of WILLIAM COACHMAN; bounding N on JOHN MURRILL (formerly ANTHONY
MATHIS); S on WILLIAM WATIES; W on JOHN WATIES; E on marsh; running back
80 chains; & 12-1/2 chains in front on the marsh; as pricked off on a
certain plat. Witnesses: BENJAMIN COACHMAN, THOMAS WATIES, JAMES COACH-
MAN. Before JOHN REMINGTON, J.P. Recorded 23 July 1765 by FENWICKE
BULL, Register.

Book D-3, p. 543   JOHN GOVAN, planter, to ALEXANDER MONTGOMERY,
11 & 12 Jan. 1759   of Prince George Parish, for Ⱡ 1200 currency,
L & R   300 a. in said Parish, bounding E on salt
                                  marsh; W & S on JOHN WATIES; N on ALEXANDER
MONTGOMERY. Witnesses: JOHN LESESNE, HENRY PRICE. Before THOMAS BLYTHE,
J.P. Recorded 24 July 1765 by FENWICKE BULL, Register.

Book D-3, p. 547   WILLIAM KNOX, planter, of Rowan Co., NC, &
30 July & 1 Aug. 1763   MARGARET (her mark) his wife, to PATRICK CAL-
L & R   HOUN, ESQ., of Granville Co., SC, for Ⱡ 100 SC
                                  money, 200 a. on NW fork of Long Cane Creek, a
branch of Savannah River (supposed to be in Granville Co.), bounding SE
on JAMES ALEXANDER; other sides on vacant land; as granted KNOX by Gov.
THOMAS BOONE on 4 Nov. 1762; beginning at pine 3 x on ALEXANDER'S line;

then N 45° W 44 chains 73 links to stake 3 x; N 45 E 44 chains 73 links to red oak 3 x; S 45 E 44 chains 73 links to dogwood 3 x; S 45 W 44 chains 73 links to beginning. Witnesses: MATHEW LANG, ROBERT KNOX. Before WILLIAM CALHOUN, J.P. Recorded 29 July 1765 by FENWICKE BULL, Register.

Book D-3, p. 552
23 & 24 Oct. 1759
L & R

THOMAS KELLER, of Charleston, to HENRY BAKER, gunsmith, of Long Cane, SC, for ₤ 200 currency, 200 a. in Granville Co., between forks of Long Cane & Little River, branches of Savannah River, bounding on Indian Camp Creek & vacant land, as by plat of grant. Witnesses: THOMAS LINTHWAITE, ABRAHAM PENNINGTON, ADAM SHACKLE. Before JOHN TROUP, J.P. Recorded 29 July 1765 by FENWICKE BULL, Register.

Book D-3, p. 558
24 July 1765
Mortgage

SUSANNAH STANYARNE & SAMUEL PELTON, of Wadmelah Island, St. Johns Parish, Colleton Co., to JOHN GIBBONS, planter, of Ga., for ₤ 800 currency; 260 a. in said Parish, bounding N on Landeway Creek; E on JOHN FENDEN & JOHN SAMS; S on SAMUEL WINBORN & THOMAS WINBOURNE. Witnesses: GEORGE SCOTT, WILLIAM WILLIAMS. Before CHARLES WOODMASON, J.P. Recorded 30 July 1765 by FENWICKE BULL, Register.

Book D-3, p. 561
22 & 23 Feb. 1760
L & R

REUBEN (his mark) ROBERTS, planter, of Long Canes, to EBENEZER WASCOT (WESTCOTE), planter, of same place, for ₤ 200 currency, 250 a. at Long Canes, a branch of Savannah River, bounding on all sides on vacant land. Witnesses: JOHN FOUGUET, RICHARD RATLIFF. Before JOHN FAIRCHILD, J.P. of Berkeley Co. Recorded 30 July 1765 by FENWICKE BULL, Register.

Book D-3, p. 567
22 July 1765
L & R

EBENEZER WESTCOTE, of Amelia Township, & MOAR ANN (her mark) his wife, to WILLIAM RATLIVE, of Long Canes, for ₤ 300 currency, 250 a. at Long Canes, bounding on all sides on vacant land granted 14 Feb. 1760 by Gov. WILLIAM HENRY LYTTELTON to REUBEN ROBERTS, who sold to WESTCOTE (p. 561). Witnesses: SAMUEL WESCOT. Before JOHN LIVISTON, J.P. Recorded 31 July 1765 by FENWICKE BULL, Register.

Book D-3, p. 573
19 July 1758
Sale

ADAM WOOD, P.M., to DR. JOHN COCHRAN, physician, for ₤ 400 currency, 400 a. in St. Bartholomews Parish, Colleton Co., part of 500 a. granted to 1 MITCHEL & later vested in JOSEPH MITCHELL; bounding E, S, & W on JOHN COCHRAN (formerly JOHN MITCHEL); N on JOHN LAIRD & THOMAS ELLIOTT. Whereas JOSEPH MITCHELL owned said 400 a.; & whereas after his death JOHN MOULTRIE & ELIZABETH his wife (late ELIZABETH MATHEWS, widow), JOHN MATHEWS, WILLIAM MATHEWS, & THOMAS LAMBOLL, executrix, & executors of will of JAMES MATHEWS, merchant) obtained a judgment against THOMAS GRIMBALL & MARTHA his wife (lately MARTHA MITCHELL, executrix, of will of JOSEPH MITCHELL) for ₤ 758 currency, & costs & a writ of fieri facias was issued by PETER LEIGH, C.J. on 4 Apr. 1758 commanding the P.M. to seize the estate of JOSEPH MITCHELL; now he sells the 400 a. at auction to COCHRAN. Witnesses: JOHN MACKENZIE, JAMES GRINDLAY. Before GEORGE JOHNSTON, J.P. Recorded 1 Aug. 1765 by FENWICKE BULL, Register.

Book D-3, p. 579
7 & 8 May 1764
L & R

WILLIAM LENNOX, JAMES SHARP, & PHILIP HEXT, surviving executors of will of JOHN LAIRD, merchant (or factor), of Charleston, to MARGARET COCHRAN, widow of DR. JOHN COCHRAN, of St. Bartholomews Parish; for ₤ 1586:14:0 currency, 387 a. in 3 tracts, in Colleton Co., on W side PonPon River, bounding NW & NE on FRANCIS ROSE, NW on THOMAS ELLIOTT, SW & NW on WILLIAM WESTBURY; E on ANTHONY LAMBRIGHT; SW & SE on MARGARET COCHRAN (formerly JOHN COCHRAN); according to plat certified by NATHANIEL DEAN, Dep. Sur. Whereas JOHN LAIRD owned said 3 tracts, viz: 70 a., part of 156 a. (part of 48,000 a. granted JOHN BAYLEY, Landgrave, of Ireland); 232 a., granted THOMAS SACHEVERELL; & 85 a. granted JOHN LAIRD; & by will dated 28 June 1761 authorized his executors to dispose of his estate for the benefit of his daughter, SARAH LAIRD, & appointed his brother, PATRICK, & his friends WILLIAM LENNOX, JAMES SHARP & PHILIP HEXT, executors; & whereas PATRICK died soon after JOHN; & whereas on 4 Mar. 1762 the executors sold said land to JOHN COCHRAN, now deceased, but the purchase money was not paid, pending a re-survey by NATHANIEL DEAN, D.S.; now the executors sell to COCHRAN'S widow. Witnesses: JAMES GRINDLAY, JOSEPH BEE. Before GEORGE JOHNSTON, J.P. Recorded 1 Aug. 1765 by FENWICKE BULL, Register.

Book D-3, p. 587
30 July 1765
Assignment of Mortgage

DAVID BOILLAT, assigns, to JOHN RUTLEDGE, at Charleston, for L 100 currency, a certain bond & mortgage from JOHN PACKROW in penal sum of L 600 (see Book X.X. p. 198, dated 18 Aug. 1761). Witnesses: GEORGE TEW, ALEXANDER HARVEY. Before FENWICKE BULL, J.P. & P. Reg.

Book D-3, p. 589
6 July 1765
Feoffment

BENJAMIN CUMING, tailor, to BENJAMIN SIMONS, JR., planter, both of St. Thomas Parish, Berkeley Co., for L 420 currency, 100 a. on E side of E branch of the T of Cooper River, inland, bounding NW on BENJAMIN CUMING; SE on FRANCIS SIMONS; NE on 200 a. sold by THOMAS DORRINGTON to BENJAMIN SIMONS (now belonging to his son BENJAMIN SIMONS, JR., party hereto); SW on BENJAMIN SIMONS, ESQ.; so that BENJAMIN SIMONS, JR., now owns the 300 a. granted CHRISTOPHER BEECH, bounding NW on BENJAMIN CUMING; SE on ISAAC & DANIEL LESESNE & FRANCIS SIMONS; NE & SW on BENJAMIN SIMONS, ESQ. Whereas on 8 July 1704 the Lords Proprs. granted CHRISTOPHER BEECH 300 a. on E side of E branch of the T of Cooper River, inland, bounding NW on said BEECH; SW on JOHNSON LYNCH; NE on MR. AMANT & vacant land; SE on vacant land; & whereas THOMAS DORRINGTON, planter, of St. Thomas Parish, became owner of 200 of the 300 a.; & JOHN CUMING, father of BENJAMIN CUMING, party hereto, became owner of the remaining 100 a.; & whereas DORRINGTON sold his 200 a. to BENJAMIN SIMONS, ESQ., who gave the 200 a. to his son, BENJAMIN, JR.; & whereas the 100 a. descended to JOHN CUMING'S only son, BENJAMIN CUMING; now BENJAMIN CUMING sells his part to BENJAMIN SIMONS, JR. Witnesses: EDWARD SIMONS, HENRY BOCHET. Before BENJAMIN SIMONS, ESQ. Recorded 3 Aug. 1765 by FENWICKE BULL, Register.

Book D-3, p. 595
24 & 25 Apr. 1765
L & R

MICHAEL MUCKENFUSS, blacksmith, & CATHARINA his wife, to CHRISTIAN GRUBER, cooper, both of Charleston; for L 1050 currency, part of lot #105 bounding W 32 ft. on King Street; N 98 ft. on part belonging to said MUCKENFUSS; E on heirs of JAMES MICKIE (formerly DR. JOHN MARTINI); S on part belonging to JACOB WARLEY, saddler (formerly to heirs of LINTHWAITE). Whereas JOSEPH BALL, sugar baker, & ELIZABETH his wife, of Charleston, by L & R dated 15 & 16 June 1764 sold MICHAEL MUCKENFUSS the N part of lot #105, bounding W 83-1/2 ft. on King Street; N 96-1/2 ft. on RICHARD BERESFORD; S 98 ft. on heirs of 1 LINTHWAITE, E on heirs of JAMES MICHIE (now DR. JOHN MARTINI); now MUCKENFUSS sells CHRISTIAN GRUBER a part of his lot. Witnesses: JAMES GRINDLAY, JOSEPH BEE. Before FENWICKE BULL, J.P. & P. Reg.

Book D-3, p. 602
4 & 5 May 1765
L & R

JAMES HATCHER, JR., planter, & JANE (JEAN) his wife, to WILLIAM PATTERSON, planter, both of St. Helena Parish, Granville Co., for L 1400 currency, 220 a. (290 a. ?). Whereas on 23 July 1711 Gov. ROBERT GIBBES granted RICHARD HATCHER 290 a., English measure, in St. Helena Parish, Granville Co., bounding S & W on a branch of Dawfuskey Creek; N & E on Watters Creek; & whereas RICHARD HATCHER died intestate, & his eldest son, JAMES, inherited; & whereas JAMES conveyed to his brother THOMAS; who died intestate; & his eldest son, JAMES, JR., inherited; now he sells to PATTERSON. Witnesses: ROBERT MCLEOD, STEPHEN BULL, JR., ULYSSES MCPHERSON. Before STEPHEN BULL, JR., J.P. Recorded 7 Aug. 1765 by FENWICKE BULL, Register.

Book D-3, p. 608
10 & 11 June 1765
L & R

SAMUEL PRIOLEAU & ELIJAH PRIOLEAU, gentleman, & GEORGE ROUPELL & ELIZABETH (PRIOLEAU) his wife, surviving executors & executrix of will of SAMUEL PRIOLEAU, gentleman, their father, of Charleston; to JOHN DELAGAYE, gentleman, of Beaufort for L 500 currency, lot #12 in Beaufort, bounding S on the Bay; W on lot #11; N on lot #39; E on lot #13. Whereas SAMUEL PRIOLEAU by his will dated 25 Oct. 1751 authorized his executors to sell his lots in Beaufort & bequeathed the money arising therefrom to his wife, MARY MAGDALEN, his sons PHILIP, SAMUEL, & ELIJAH, & his daughters MARY BRYAN & ELIZABETH (now ROUPELL), naming them his executors; & whereas MARY BRYAN is dead, & PHILIP has left SC, now the others sell lot 12 to DELAGAYE. Witnesses: SIMS WHITE, JAMES CARSON. Before ROBERT WILLIAMS, JR., J.P. Recorded 8 Aug. 1765 by FENWICKE BULL, Register.

Book D-3, p. 616
10 & 11 June 1765
L & R

GEORGE ROUPELL, of Charleston, & ELIZABETH (nee PRIOLEAU) his wife, of Charleston, to JOHN DELAGAYE, gentleman, of Beaufort, for ₺ 50 currency, the low water lot in front of lot #12 in Beaufort, 60 x 165 ft., granted GEORGE ROUPELL on 27 Aug. 1764. Witnesses: SIMS WHITE, JAMES CARSON. Before ROBERT WILLIAMS, JR., J.P. Recorded 9 Aug. 1765 by FENWICKE BULL, Register.

Book D-3, p. 624
22 & 23 July 1765
L & R

MARTIN SOLOMON, soldier, & ELIZABETH (her mark) his wife, to JOSHUA SNOWDEN, hatter, both of Charleston, for ₺ 50 SC money, 150 a. in St. Johns Parish, Berkeley Co., bounding on all sides on vacant land; as by plat of grant dated 21 June last, recorded in Secretary's Book X.X. p. 176, being Kings bounty. Witnesses: JOHN REMINGTON, JR., JACOB REMINGTON. Before JOHN REMINGTON, J.P. Recorded 9 Aug. 1765 by FENWICKE BULL, Register.

Book D-3, p. 628
8 & 9 June 1764
L & R by Mortgage

CHARLES STROTHERS, & MARY his wife, to MRS. SUSANNAH BOSOMWORTH, widow, both of Charleston, for ₺ 3400 currency; the E tenement & part of lot #103 in Charleston, bounding N on Broad Street; W on part same lot belonging to MRS. MARY COOPER; S on the French Church; E on PETER BOCQUET. Witnesses: WILLIAM STOUTENBURGH, ABRAHAM ROULAIN. Before FENWICKE BULL, J.P. & P. Reg. On 25 May 1767 WILLIAM HARVEY, as attorney for SUSANNAH BOSOMWORTH, declared mortgage satisfied.

Book D-3, p. 635
3 Apr. 1764
L & R

KINDRED WILLIAMS, planter, & ELIZABETH (her mark) his wife, to JOB ROUNTREE, planter, both of Granville Co., for ₺ 200 currency, 150 a. in Granville Co., bounding W on Savannah River; other sides on vacant land; according to plat of grant dated 31 Nov. 1757. Witnesses: JAMES BICKHAM, ZEBULON COCK, JOSEPH (his mark) DUPEE. Before JOHN DICK, J.P. Recorded 13 Aug. 1765 by FENWICKE BULL, Register.

Book D-3, p. 641
30 Aug. 1763
L & R

JOHN NELSON (NEELSON), to EZEKIEL WILLIAMS, for ₺ 100 currency, 100 a. near Point Comfort in Granville Co., bounding S on the river; other sides on vacant land; granted 18 Oct. 1757 by Gov. WILLIAM HENRY LYTTELTON to JOHN NELSON. Witnesses: SAMUEL ALEXANDER, JAMES (his mark) NEELSON, ALEXANDER (his mark) NEELSON. Before JOHN DICK, J.P. Recorded 13 Aug. 1765 by FENWICKE BULL, Register.

Book D-3, p. 646
18 & 19 Sept. 1751
L & R

CHARLES PINCKNEY, speaker of Commons House of Assembly, & GABRIEL MANIGAULT, Pub. Treas. & Receiver of SC, as trustees, to COL. SAMUEL PRIOLEAU, ESQ., of Charleston, for ₺ 111 currency, to be used in paying appropriation orders; lot #66 in Beaufort, Port Royal, Granville Co., bounding S on Port Royall Street; W on lot #61; N on lot #65; E on West Street. Whereas on 2 Mar. 1737 it was resolved in the House of Commons that the estate of ALEXANDER PARRIS was indebted to the province a total sum of ₺ 27,171:4:5:1 (viz. ₺ 22,931 on a/c outstanding appropriation orders; ₺ 800 for crossing & filing orders, not performed; ₺ 1930:18:8:3 tax receipts in 1727, 1731, 1732, 1733; ₺ 1509:5:8-1/2 account of fortifications) & chargeable with any other unpaid sums; & whereas JOHN PARRIS, eldest son & heir of ALEXANDER, by L & R dated 23 & 24 Mar. 1737 conveyed to said PINCKNEY & MANIGAULT, as trustees, the lot which stood the dwelling house fronting the Bay (since burned down) formerly owned by ALEXANDER PARRIS, late by JOHN PARRIS, now held by SEAMAN & CROCKATT; also Three Pine Island, behind JOHNSON'S Fort then owned by JOHN PARRIS; also 552 a. in Craven Co., granted ALEXANDER PARRIS; bounding W on NOAH SERREE; N on vacant land & Black River; S on vacant land; also 500 a. on Winyaw River, in Craven Co., bounding E on

Peedee River; S on MR. DITTON; W & N on vacant land; also 9 lots in Beaufort Nos. 5, 27, 30, 63, 64, 66, 82, 86, & 301; also half of Arthurs Island, near Port Royal Island, in Granville Co., formerly owned by ALEXANDER PARRIS now by JOHN PARRIS, adjoining the other half owned by JOHN DELABERS; now the trustees sell lot #66 to PRIOLEAU at auction. Witnesses: JACOB MOTTE, CHARLES PINCKNEY, JR. Before FENWICKE BULL, J.P. & P. Reg. Recorded 16 Aug. 1765.

Book D-3, p. 657
10 & 11 June 1765
L & R

SAMUEL PRIOLEAU, ELIJAH PRIOLEAU, GEORGE ROUPELL & ELIZABETH (nee PRIOLEAU) his wife, surviving, executors & executrix of will of their father, COL. SAMUEL PRIOLEAU, (see p. 608); to ANDREW DEVEAUX, the younger, gentleman, of Granville Co., for Ł 200 currency, lot #66 in Beaufort, bounding S on Port Royal Street; W on lot #61; N on lot #65; E on West Street. Witnesses: SIMS WHITE, JAMES CARSON. Before ROBERT WILLIAMS, JR., J.P. Recorded 16 Aug. 1765 by FENWICKE BULL, Register.

Book D-3, p. 665
1 Mar. 1754
L & R

THOMAS ELLIOTT, planter, of Colleton Co., only surviving executor of will of ROGER SAUNDERS the elder, planter, of St. Andrews Parish, Berkeley Co., at auction, to JOHN CATTELL & BENJAMIN CATTELL, planters, of Berkeley Co., sons of BENJAMIN CATTELL; for Ł 600 currency, 447 a. in Colleton Co., bounding SE & NW on said SAUNDERS; SW on MR. CLIFFORD & vacant land; granted 13 July 1737 by Lt. Gov. THOMAS BROUGHTON to ROGER SAUNDERS (see Secretary's Book G.G. p. 369); who by will dated 4 Sept. 1741 authorized his executors to sell his lands; meaning his brother-in-law, THOMAS ELLIOTT, & his son-in-law, JOHN CHAMPNEYS, & his son, ROGER, his executors; CHAMPNEYS & ROGER SAUNDERS, the son, now being dead. Witnesses: SAMUEL WEST, RICHARD BEDON, JR. Before WILLIAM BURROWS, J.P. Recorded 19 Aug. 1765 by FENWICKE BULL, Register.

Book D-3, p. 674
14 & 15 Aug. 1765
L & R by Mortgage

WILLIAM MOULTRIE, to JOHN MATHEWS, gentleman, both of Charleston, for Ł 12,000 currency, 1000 a. called Northampton, in St. Johns Parish, bounding E on RENE RAVENEL; W on JOSEPH DE ST. JULIEN; S on WILLIAM MOULTRIE; N on DANIEL RAVENEL; also 100 Negro slaves. Witnesses: JOSEPH LEVY, ROBERT DILLON. Before JAMES PARSONS, J.P. Entered in Secretary's Book Z.Z. p. 548 on 15 Aug. 1765 by THOMAS SKETTOWE, Sec. Recorded 19 Aug. 1765 by FENWICKE BULL, Register.

Book D-3, p. 682
13 & 14 Aug. 1765
L & R

JAMES MCPHERSON, gentleman, of Prince Williams Parish, Granville Co., to his son ISAAC MCPHERSON, of St. Pauls Parish, for love & affection, 500 a. in Prince Williams Parish, bounding E on WILLIAM BRISBANE; W & S on SARAH MCPHERSON; N on JAMES MCPHERSON; being part of 2000 a. purchased from ROBERT COOPER. Witnesses: JAMES PARSONS, JOHN GLEN. Before WILLIAM MASON, J.P. Entered in Auditor's Book G-7, p. 436, on 16 Aug. 1765 by RICHARD LAMBTON, Dep. Aud. Recorded 20 Aug. 1765 by FENWICKE BULL, Register.

Book D-3, p. 686
22 & 23 June 1764
L & R

JOHN MAYRANT, of St. James Santee, Craven Co., & ANN his wife, to DANIEL HUGER, of Charleston, for Ł 3250 currency, 500 a. in Craven Co., on N side Santee River, granted by the Lords Proprs. to JOSEPH SPENCER, then bounding on all sides on vacant land according to plat dated 18 Jan. 1709/10 by THOMAS BROUGHTON, Sur. Gen.; also a tract of 300 a. & an island of 9 a. called Fork Island between N & S branches of Santee River, bounding N on N branch; E on JOSEPH HUGGINS, Island Creek, & ISAAC MAZYCK; W on DANIEL HORRY; S on JOHN MAYRANT; being part of 620 a. granted 7 Aug. 1736 to SUSANNAH MAYRANT, mother of said JOHN, then bounding between N & S branches of Santee River; W on MR. HORRY; E on vacant land as by plat of grant dated 9 Jan. 1733 certified by JAMES ST. JOHN, Sur. Gen. Witnesses: ELIAS HORRY, ELIAS HORRY, JR. Before FRANCIS KINLOCK, J.P. Recorded 22 Aug. 1765 by FENWICKE BULL, Register. Plat dated 9 Mar. 1764 of 300 a. by JOHN HORRY being part of JOHN MAYRANT'S island & a small island of 9 a. called Fork Island between N & S branches of Santee River, bounding E on JOSEPH HUGGINS, Island Creek & ISAAC MAZYCK; W on MISS JUDITH DE ST. JULIEN; S on JOHN

284

MAYRANT.

Book D-3, p. 694   JOHN MAYRANT, of St. James Santee, Craven Co.,
22 & 23 Mar. 1765   & ANN his wife, to ELIAS HORRY, of Prince
L & R   George Parish, for Ł 11,000 currency, 300 a.
                      granted DANIEL HUGER 14 Oct. 1696, bounding NE
on Santee River; S on Wambaw Creek; NW on Wallahan Creek; also 160 a.
granted DANIEL HUGER 2 Feb. 1704, bounding E on DANIEL HUGER; NW on Wallahan Creek; S on Wambaw; also 230 a. granted DANIEL HUGER 14 Sept. 1705,
bounding E on DANIEL HUGER; NW on Wallahan Creek; S on Wambaw Creek; also
the remaining part of a plantation of 500 a. granted DANIEL HUGER 14
Sept. 1714, bounding E on DANIEL HUGER; W on LEWIS GOURDIN; S on Wambaw
Creek; also 320 a., part of 620 a. (the other 300 now belonging to DANIEL
HUGER; see p. 686), on Fork Island, between N & S branches of Santee River, granted SUSANNA MAYRANT 7 Aug. 1736, bounding W on DANIEL HORRY; E on
vacant land. Witnesses: JOHN HORRY, HUGH HORRY. Before THOMAS LYNCH,
J.P. Recorded FENWICKE BULL, Register. Two plats given.

Book D-3, p. 701   HENRY ENDERLY, planter, to ADRIAN MAYER, ESQ.,
21 Feb. 1765   both of Purysburgh, Granville Co., for Ł 50 SC
Release   money, 450 a. in Purysburgh Township, bounding
                      N on BENJAMIN HENRIOU & ABRAHAM MAURON, JACOK
WINKLER & JOHN BAPTIST BOURQUIN; S on ANTHONY TERMIN & ANN BARBARA FRANK;
E on HENRY GIRARDIN. Witnesses: GABRIEL RAVOT, DANIEL MALLET. Before
JOHN LEWIS BOURQUIN, J.P. Recorded 24 Aug. 1765 by FENWICKE BULL, Reg-
ister.

Book D-3, p. 703   WILLIAM DALTON, SR., of St. Bartholomews Par-
6 June 1752   ish, Colleton Co., to his son, DANIEL, for
Gift   valuable considerations, 5 Negroes & 247 a. in
                      said Parish on Worrels Creek. Witnesses:
JAMES ATKINS, FRANCIS (his mark) SMITH. Before HENRY HYRNE, J.P. Enter-
ed in Secretary's Book I.I. fol. 254 on 30 July 1752 by WILLIAM PINCKNEY,
Dep. Sec. Recorded 24 Aug. 1765 by FENWICKE BULL, Register.

Book D-3, p. 705   THOMAS LYNCH, ESQ., to MARTHA LISTON, gentle-
4 Oct. 1763   woman, both of Charleston, for Ł 1400 curren-
Feoffment   cy, the N part of lot #104 near White Point in
                      Charleston, bounding N 222 ft. on Lynch's
Street or Lane; E 37 ft. on the Bay; S 199 ft. on DR. JOHN MURRAY & JO-
SEPH COX; S on MRS. MORTIMER; W 30 ft. on MRS. MORTIMER. Witnesses:
CHARLES MOTTE, JOSEPH COX. Before CHARLES WOODMASON, J.P. Recorded 26
Aug. 1765 by FENWICKE BULL, Register.

Book D-3, p. 708   DR. JOHN MOULTRIE, physician, & ELIZABETH his
24 & 25 June 1765   wife, to MARTHA LISTON, spinster, both of
L & R   Charleston, for Ł 1450 currency, a lot in
                      Charleston, bounding W 19 ft. on King Street;
E on MRS. FRASER; N 240 ft. on JOHN CATTELL; S on JAMES WILKYE. Witnesses: WILLIAM GRAEME, JAMES HUME. Before JAMES SIMPSON, J.P. Recorded
26 Aug. 1765 by FENWICKE BULL, Register.

Book D-3, p. 715   MARTHA LISTON, gentlewoman, of Charleston, to
15 & 16 July 1765   ISAAC COX, of Philadelphia, Pa., for Ł 1400
L & R   currency, the N part of lot #104 in Charles-
                      ton (see p. 705). Witnesses: WILLIAM ROPER,
JR., JOSEPH COX. Before WILLIAM BURROWS, J.P. Recorded 27 Aug. 1765 by
FENWICKE BULL, Register.

Book D-3, p. 724   ISAAC MCPHERSON, gentleman, of St. Pauls Par-
13 & 14 Aug. 1765   ish, Colleton Co., to his father, JAMES MC-
L & R   PHERSON, of Prince William Parish, Granville
                      Co., for love & affection, 500 a. in Prince
William Parish, bounding S on JAMES MCPHERSON; N on JOHN MACTEER; W on
WILLIAM KEATING; E on STEPHEN BULL, SR. Witnesses: JAMES PARSONS, JOHN
GLEN, THOMAS HEYWARD, JR. Before WILLIAM MASON, J.P. Entered in Audi-
tor's Book G-7, p. 436, on 16 Aug. 1765 by RICHARD LAMBTON, Dep. Aud.
Recorded 28 Aug. 1765 by FENWICKE BULL, Register.

Book D-3, p. 726   TACITUS GAILLARD & ANN his wife, to JOHN

RUTLEDGE, of Charleston, for ₤ 3000 currency, 800 a., being the residue of 2 tracts, bounding S & SE on Santee River; SW on other part sold to THOMAS LYNCH; E on JAMES MCKELVEY; N on vacant land; also 1000 a. granted FRANCIS KINLOCH, in St. Johns Parish, Berkeley Co., bounding N on Santee River; E on JAMES MCKELVY (formerly GEORGE BEARD); S on vacant land; W on GEORGE AUSTIN & JAMES MCKELVEY. Whereas on 9 Apr. 1754 JOHN MAYNARD was granted 1000 a. in Prince Frederick Parish, on N side Santee River, bounding NW on FRANCIS YOUNG; SW on GEORGE BEARD; NE on vacant land; & whereas on 22 Nov. 1756 CHARLES CANTEY was granted 1000 a. on N side Santee River, bounding E on JAMES MCKELVEY; SW on TACITUS GAILLARD & BENJAMIN SINGLETON; N on vacant land; & whereas on 22 Nov. 1756 FRANCIS KINLOCK was granted 1000 a. on S side Santee River, in St. Johns Parish, Berkeley Co., bounding SW on WILLIAM FLUD & JAMES MCKELVEY; SE on vacant land; NE on GEORGE BEARD; & whereas TACITUS GAILLARD purchased the first tract from JOHN MAYRANT & became owner also of CANTEY'S tract (but GEORGE AUSTIN claimed 400 a. by a prior title, leaving GAILLARD only 600 of the 1000 a.); & whereas GAILLARD lately sold 800 a. (part of the 600 & part of the 1st tract) to THOMAS LYNCH, retaining 800 a.; & whereas FRANCIS KINLOCK conveyed his tract to TACITUS GAILLARD; now GAILLARD sells the remaining 800 a. to RUTLEDGE. Witnesses: FENWICKE BULL, ALEXANDER HARVEY. Before THOMAS WRIGHT, J.P. Recorded 28 Aug. 1765 by FENWICKE BULL, Register.

Book D-3, p. 735
16 June 1764
Release

WILLIAM WOODROPE, merchant, executor of will of GEORGE HUNTER, gentleman; to ROBERT BRISBANE & WILLIAM BRISBANE, merchants; all of Charleston; for ₤ 639:1:7 currency, paid in lieu of commission; 153 a. in Granville Co., known as Barataria Island, purchased by HUNTER from JAMES KINLOCK, bounding E on Charlestons Island; W on Hilton Head Sound; S on River May; N on Dawfuskee; also 250 a., being half of 500 a., in Granville Co., lying partly on Dawfuskee Island & partly on an island of marsh & small pine islands to the W, granted ELIZABETH PARNOR, who sold to GEORGE HAIG & FREDERICK MAYER, bounding N on JAMES COCHRAN; E on GEORGE HAIG & FREDERICK MAYER (lately HUGH EVANS); S on ANDREW ALLIN; W on W River Marsh & New River; which 250 a. were sold by HAIG to GEORGE HUNTER; also 800 a. in Craven Co., granted JOHN ALLIN, who sold to HUNTER, bounding NW on CAPT. WILLIAM DRY; other sides on vacant land; also 1749 a., part of 3249 a. granted JAMES KINLOCK, who sold to HUNTER, on head of Black Mingo Creek; the 3249 a. bounding E on CAPT. WILLIAM BROCKINGTON; N on ANTHONY WHITE & JOHN LANE; W on patent lands of heirs of ROBERT YEAMANS & on vacant land; also 450 a. on SW side Peedee River, granted WILLIAM LEANDER, perukemaker, who sold to THOMAS CHARNOCK, shopkeeper, of Charleston; who sold to HUNTER; bounding N on ABRAHAM STAPLES, planter; E on the Rev. MR. THOMAS MORRIT; W & S on vacant land; also 820 a. on head of Ox Swamp, in Williamsburgh Township, Craven Co., granted GEORGE HUNTER; bounding S on vacant land; SE on Township line; N on ROBERT WITHERSPOON; NW on WILLIAM MCCORMACK; W on JAMES MCCULLOUGH & JOHN BARNES; also 40 a. in Craven Co., sold by ROBERT SCREVEN & SARAH his wife to GEORGE HUNTER; bounding NW on Saw Pitt Creek; other sides on 450 a. sold by ROBERT & SARAH SCREVEN to JOHN CROFT; also 15 a. in Winyah Bay, Prince George Parish, Craven Co., granted JOSHUA WILKES, who sold to HUNTER; being 2 small islands & some marsh bearing from George Town Point SES about 120 chains distant; bounding W on the Bay & vacant marsh; S on marsh; also a lot of 1 a. 2 roods marked F on GEORGE ANSON'S plat, called Ansonburgh, & right of passage through streets to landing place on a creek of Cooper River, conveyed 9 Apr. 1746 by BENJAMIN WHITAKER, as attorney for GEORGE ANSON, to GEORGE HUNTER; also 1 a. 2 roods, marked G on ANSON'S plat, lately purchased from WHITAKER by THOMAS NIGHTINGALE, who sold to HUNTER; also lot in Colleton Square, marked I on plat, 160 ft. front; bounding E on lot H; S on Hunter Street; W on lot K; N on a street running W from the Bay; also 4 marsh lots, part of Colleton Square; & 1 low water lot on N side Craven's Bastion; said lots being part of lot #80 & lot A & marsh, purchased by HUNTER from JOHN COLLETON, ESQ.; also all goods, chattles, money & personal estate of GEORGE HUNTER; also a judgment with costs obtained against JOHN HAMILTON, of Berkeley Co., for ₤ 600 British. Whereas GEORGE HUNTER owner of sundry lands, plantations, lots, etc., by will dated 27 Aug. 1745 appointed WILLIAM WOODROPE his sole executor; with power to sell such lands, bequeathed to his sisters ELIZABETH DUNLOP & MARGARET MCDERMEIT equally the residue of his estate; & whereas ELIZABETH, wife of WILLIAM DUNLOP, copper-smith, in

Ayr; & MARGARET, widow of ROBERT MCDERMEIT, writer, in Ayr, only sisters german of GEORGE HUNTER, with consent of WILLIAM DUNLOP, by letter of attorney dated 26 Aug. 1756, proved before ANDREW SLOWANE, of Skeldon, Provost of Burgh of Ayr, appointed ROBERT & WILLIAM BRISBANE their attorneys to recover their inheritance from WOODROPE; & whereas 2 of the lots mentioned in said will have been sold & the money paid the BRISBANES, but the residue of the property remains unsold; now WOODROPE conveys the estate to the BRISBANES. Witnesses: JAMES HARVEY, WILLIAM GRAEME. Before ANDREW HUNTER, J.P. Recorded 30 Aug. 1765 by FENWICKE BULL, Register.

Book D-3, p. 748   WILLIAM DONNING, planter, of St. George Par-
26 & 27 Aug. 1765   ish, Dorchester, Berkeley Co., to DANIEL DOY-
L & R   LEY, of Charleston, for Ł 6000 currency, 1400
                        a. in said Parish, being the remaining part of
2400 a. after allotting 1000 a. to FRANCIS DANIEL, an infant; the 1400 a. bounding SE on DANIEL BLAKE & said FRANCIS DANIEL; SW on SAMUEL HAMLIN & COL. RICHARD BEDON; NW on THOMAS BROUGHTON (now BENJAMIN COACHMAN) & heirs of MR. SOMNER; NE on MR. WARING. Whereas FARNCES DONNING, widow, mother of WILLIAM, owned about 2400 a. in St. George Parish known as The Ponds or Weston Hall, on which she lived for many years before her death, & by her will in 1752 devised the land to her son, WILLIAM, & her daughter, FRANCES, since dead (FRANCES receiving 1000 a. called The Ponds; WILLIAM the remainder); & whereas FARNCES, the daughter, married ADAM DANIEL, ESQ., of said Parish, & had 1 daughter, FRANCES, now an infant; & whereas WILLIAM had asked for & has been granted a partition of the property, the SE part (or 1000 a.) being allotted to FRANCES DANIEL, the infant; now WILLIAM sells his share to DOYLEY. Witnesses: JAMES SANDERS, JOHN CALVERT. Before GEORGE JOHNSTON, J.P. Recorded 2 Sept. 1865 by FENWICKE BULL, Register. Plat shows: NATHANIEL BRADWELL, D.S., & JOHN DE GIRARDEAU, D.S., at request of MILES BREWTON, ADAM DANIEL & DANIEL DOYLEY, resurveyed lands granted ANDREW PERCIVAL (now WILLIAM DUNNING) in St. George Parish, Dorchester, bounding SE on ANDREW SLAN, JOHN DRAKE, & DANIEL BLAKE; SW on SAMUEL HAMBLIN & COL. RICHARD BEDON; NW on THOMAS BROUGHTON (now BENJAMIN COACHMAN) & heirs of SOMNER; NE on MR. WARING; beginning at corner of DANIEL BLAKE'S ditch at A (established by lawsuit between COL. JOSEPH BLAKE & MRS. FRANCES DUNNING) & running the distance of resurvey at time of dispute by WILLIAM MAINE to B, the side of the pond, a natural landmark; continuing from B to C they found an old remarkable pine corner blown down, marked 4 x, reputed corner of WILLIAM DUNNING'S land; then the head line from C to D where they found a stake 3 x set up at root of old pine corner blown down on Sumners Run, which MR. WAY had proved some years before to have been upwards of 40 years standing; from D to E the course of Gov. BULL'S resurvey & found no blazed trees or stations; but beginning at A, they ran to F the reputed bay corner of MR. DUNNING'S 2000 a., & found rotten remains of bay stump, which COL. BEDON, being present, said was the reputed corner for many years past; the course & distance answering from CAPT. BLAKE'S ditch at A; then from F to G & found the swamp olive corner (boundary between THOMAS BROUGHTON & MR. DUNNING, mentioned on BROUGHTON'S plat & other resurveys for 50 years past); from G to H found plain old line that all surveyors formerly ran for DUNNING'S 2000 a., although Gov. BULL had marked the several marked trees on the pricked line E H which they actually found on line F G H; running from Bay F to Beach Corner I which COL. BEDON said was reputed corner of DUNNING'S 400 a. for many years & found 2 very old stations on BROUGHTON'S .line, between BROUGHTON & DUNNING, 1 cut down but with marks visible; from I to K agreeable to BEDON'S plat they found several marked trees & his corner at K; from K to L MR. HAMLIN'S line agreeable to his plat to interect line L M an old established line between DANIEL BLAKE & MR. DUNNING, said line agreeable to MR. BLAKE'S plat; the line G F I & Figure 2 representing MR. COACHMAN'S trespass on DUNNING'S 2000 & 400 a. tracts; & I 3 & 2 showing COACHMAN'S encroachment on COL. BEDON'S tract; & in their opinion there is not, nor ever was, any vacant land where MR. COACHMAN presumed to take up vacant land. Certified 1 July 1765.

Book D-3, p. 758   GEORGE ANSON, by his attorney BENJAMIN WHITA-
20 Feb. 1745   KER, to SAMUEL SMITH & DAVID MONGIN, of
Feoffment   Charleston, for Ł 240 currency, 1 a. marked R
                        on the plat of Ansonborough. Witnesses: WIL-
LIAM BURROWS, THOMAS NIGHTINGALE, WILLIAM GLEN. Before FENWICKE BULL,

J.P. & Pub. Reg.

Book D-3, p. 760   ROBERT FLUD, planter, of Craven Co., & MARGRET
7 & 8 Oct. 1761   FLUD, to JOHN COLE, of Amelia Township, for
L & R   Ł 500 currency, 850 a. in Craven Co., opposite
                          Amelia Township, bounding SW on Santee River;
other sides on vacant land; as granted 16 Jan. 1761. Witnesses: RICHARD
DAVIS, JOHN MCNICHOLL, MOSES THOMPSON. Before MOSES THOMPSON, J.P. Recorded 4 Sept. 1765 by FENWICKE BULL, Register.

Book D-3, p. 766   JOHN COLE, planter, & MARY (her mark) his
8 & 9 Aug. 1765   wife, to JOHN CALDWELL, merchant, both of
L & R   Amelia Township, for Ł 300 currency, 850 a. in
                          Craven Co., opposite Amelia Township, bounding
SW on Santee River; other sides on vacant land; granted ROBERT FLUD 16
Jan. 1716 & sold by him to COLE (p. 760). Witnesses: THOMAS SABB, WIL-
LIAM HALL. Before JOHN LIVISTON, J.P. Recorded 5 Sept. 1765 by FENWICKE
BULL, Register.

Book D-3, p. 771   JOHN (his mark) WHITEHOUSE, laborer, of Berke-
12 & 13 Aug. 1765   ley Co., to JAMES SULLIVANT, planter, of Amel-
L & R   ia Township, for Ł 30 currency, 150 a. on E
                          side Savannah River, bounding SE on PETER
TURKNET; NW on JAMES BEEKHAM. Witnesses: JOSHUA JOHNSON, WILLIAM ROWAN.
Before JOHN LIVISTON, J.P. Recorded 5 Sept. 1765 by FENWICKE BULL, Reg-
ister.

Book D-3, p. 776   JAMES (his mark) SULLIVANT, planter, & ELLINOR
15 & 16 Aug. 1765   (her mark) his wife, to JOHN CALDWELL, mer-
L & R   chant, both of Amelia Township, for Ł 45 cur-
                          rency, 150 a. bounding W on Savannah River; SW
on PETER TURKNET; NW on JAMES BEEKMAN; originally granted JOHN WHITEHOUSE
21 June 1765 & sold by him to SULLIVANT (p. 771). Witnesses: WILLIAM
HILL, WILLIAM EASTLAND. Before JOHN LIVISTON, J.P. Recorded 6 Sept.
1765 by FENWICKE BULL, Register.

Book D-3, p. 782   JOHN NORTON (NORDAN), planter, & MARGARET (her
12 & 13 Aug. 1765   mark) his wife, to JOHN CALDWELL, merchant,
L & R   both of Amelia Township, for Ł 150 currency,
                          300 a. in St. Marks Parish, Craven Co., bound-
ing SE on ROBERT FLUD; SW on Santee River; other sides on vacant land.
Witnesses: THOMAS SABB, WILLIAM ROWAN. Before JOHN LIVISTON, J.P. Recorded 7 Sept. 1765 by FENWICKE BULL, Register.

Book D-3, p. 787   THOMAS SABB, gentleman, to JOHN CALDWELL, mer-
8 & 9 July 1765   chant, both of Amelia Township, for Ł 60 cur-
L & R   rency, 69 a. in Amelia Township, being part of
                          100 a. granted SABB 21 May 1757 by Gov. WIL-
LIAM HENRY LYTTELTON; bounding NW on part; NE on ELIZABETH DOGGET; SE &
SW on vacant land. Witnesses: WILLIAM SABB, JOHN MAXWELL, THOMAS SABB,
JR. Before MOSES THOMPSON, J.P. Recorded 7 Sept. 1765 by FENWICKE BULL,
Register.

                         DEEDS BOOK - "E-3"
                    SEPTEMBER 1765 - JULY 1766

Book E-3, p. 1   WILLIAM HARRISON, carpenter, & ANN (NANCY)
23 & 24 Sept. 1753   (her mark) his wife, to JOHN DUKES, carpenter,
L & R   both of Craven Co., for Ł 60 currency, 150 a.
                          in Craven Co., on N side Wateree River, other
sides on vacant land; as granted HARRISON by Gov. JAMES GLEN on 6 Mar.
1749. Witnesses: RICHARD KIRKLAND, ROBERT (his mark) HUMPHRIS, JOSEPH
KIRKLAND. Before JAMES MCGIRT, J.P. Recorded 9 Sept. 1765 by FENWICKE
BULL, Register.

Book E-3, p. 7   HENRY FOSTER, planter, & ELIZABETH (her mark)
9 & 10 Aug. 1763   his wife, to JOSEPH BOX, planter, both of
L & R   Berkeley Co., for Ł 200 currency, 150 a. on N

side Saludy River, granted 8 Mar. 1763 by Gov. THOMAS BOONE to HENRY FOS-
TER; bounding NW on Reedie River; NE & SE on vacant land. Witnesses:
JOHN FOSTER, WILLIAM TURK, ANN (her mark) BOYLES. Before ANDREW BROWN,
J.P. Recorded 10 Sept. 1765 by FENWICKE BULL, Register.

Book E-3, p. 12   WILLIAM SIMPSON, ESQ., of Ga., & ELIZABETH his
23 Aug. 1765   wife, to LACHLAN MACINTOSH, ESQ., of SC, for
Release   Ł 3525 SC money, 300 a. on S end of 349 a., on
                        S side Ashley River, in Berkeley Co., bounding
NW on Ferry Path; SE on THOMAS DYMES, CHARLES JONES, MRS. VINCENT, & MRS.
CLAY; SW on SAMUEL JONES & MRS. CLAY. Witnesses: THOMAS SKOTTOWE, THOMAS
ADAM, MALCOM BROWN. Before JOHN HUME, J.P. Recorded 11 Sept. 1765 by
FENWICKE BULL, Register.

Book E-3, p. 15   STEPHEN (ETIENNE) VIGNEUX (VAIGNEUR), tailor,
15 Aug. 1765   of St. Peters Parish, Granville Co., to ADRIAN
Release   MAYER, ESQ., of Purysburgh, for Ł 50 currency,
                        a 1 a. lot, #75, in Purysburgh, bounding N on
a street; S on lot #76; E on lot #77; W on a street. (Evidently formerly
the property of ABRAHAM MATTHEY who, on 17 Nov. 1751 gave all his possessions to MR. & MRS. VAIGNEUR for their care of him). Witnesses: DAVID
GIROUD, JOHN LINDERS, ABRAM JACOB. Before JOHN LEWIS BOURQUIN, J.P.
Recorded 11 Sept. 1765 by FENWICKE BULL, Register.

Book E-3, p. 17   STEPHEN (ETIENNE) VIGNEUX (VAIGNEUR), tailor,
21 Aug. 1765   of St. Peters Parish, Granville Co., to ADRIAN
Release   MAYER, for Ł 150 currency, 100 a. originally
                        granted RICE PRICE of Purysburgh, bounding N
on PETER GALLACHE; S on the Rev. MR. JOSEPH BUGNON; W on FRANCIS BACHELAR;
E on vacant land; also 200 a. originally granted ABRAHAM MATTEY, bounding
S & W on vacant land; E on 17,000 a. originally laid out to JOHN PETER
PURY & granted to CHARLES PURY. Witnesses: DANIEL MARETTE (sexton, of
Purysburgh), ABRAM JACOB. Before JOHN LEWIS BOURQUIN, J.P. Recorded 11
Sept. 1765 by FENWICKE BULL, Register.

Book E-3, p. 20   LANCELOT BLAND, planter, of Prince William
7 & 8 Apr. 1762   Parish, Granville Co., to MARY MARTINANGELE,
L & R   widow of PHILIP MARTIANAGELE, planter, of Port
                        Royal Island, St. Helena Parish, for Ł 1000
currency, 500 a., being the SW half of 1000 a.; bounding SE on JOHN GOR-
DON; NE on other half sold by BLAND to JOHN SMITH, merchant, of Charleston; other sides on marsh of Dafuskee (Days) Creek; according to plat by
ROBERT MANNING, D.S., dated 12 Nov. last. Whereas Gov. ROBERT GIBBES on
13 Jan. 1710 granted NICHOLAS DAY 400 a. on Dafuskee Island; in Granville
Co., bounding SE on SAMUEL HILDEN; NW & SW on Dafuskee Creek; NE on vacant land; & whereas by will dated 29 Nov. 1711 DAY bequeathed all his
real & personal estate in SC to ANDREW ALLEN, merchant, of Charleston; &
whereas on 16 Mar. 1732 Gov. ROBERT JOHNSON granted said ANDREW ALLEN 600
a. on Dafuskee Island, bounding S on said 400 a.; N on vacant land; E on
HUGH EVANS; W on West River; & whereas by will dated 29 Mar. 1735 ALLEN
bequeathed the residue of his real & personal estate to his son JOHN; who
bequeathed to his wife ANN; who afterwards married JOHN SAVAGE, merchant,
of Charleston; who with ANN, by L & R dated 8 & 9 Sept. 1759 sold the
1000 a. to LANCELOT BLAND; now he sells the SW half to MARY MARTINANEGELE.
Witnesses: FRANCIS STUART, PHILIP BOX. Before FENWICKE BULL, J.P. & P.
Reg.

Book E-3, p. 31   DANIEL BLAKE & WILLIAM BLAKE, of Charleston,
14 & 15 July 1761   sons of the Hon. JOSEPH BLAKE, to FRANCIS
L & R   STUART, merchant, of Beaufort, for Ł 2500 cur-
                        rency, 3 adjoining islands on Port Royal Riv-
er, in St. Helena Parish, Granville Co., known as Farringtons Neck & Cane
Island, containing 302 a., 174 a., & 11 a., which by his will dated 18
Dec. 1750 JOSEPH BLAKE bequeathed to his 2 sons as jointenants in fee.
Witnesses: JACOB WARLEY, JOHN RATTRAY. Entered in Auditor's Book G-7,
p. 191, on 7 Apr. 1764 by RICHARD LAMBTON, Dep. Aud. Before FENWICKE
BULL, J.P. & P. Reg. Recorded 13 Sept. 1765.

Book E-3, p. 39   JOSHUA SANDERS, planter, of St. James Goose
14 & 15 June 1744   Creek, & ELIZABETH CLARK, his wife, to JOHN

L & R   FRASER, gentleman, of Charleston, for ₺ 1500
                              currency, 4 tracts in Berkeley Co.; 200 a.
bound S on Yeoman's Creek; other sides on vacant land; granted 18 June
1678 by the Lords Proprs. to LAURENCE SANDERS; & by the Lords Proprs.
again granted on 5 Aug. 1704 to JOHN SANDERS, son of LAURENCE & father of
JOSHUA; also 245 a., bounding E on BENJAMIN GODIN; N on JACOB ALLEN; S on
WILLIAM SANDERS; granted by Lords Proprs. on 14 Aug. 1702 to JOHN SANDERS,
father of JOSHUA; also 60 a.; bounding N & E on OBADIAH ALLIN; S on JOHN
SANDERS; granted by Lords Proprs. on 18 Apr. 1717 to JOHN SANDERS, father
of JOSHUA; also 40 a. bounding W on said 60 a.; other sides on Goose
Creek; granted 18 Apr. 1717 by Lords Proprs. to JOHN SANDERS, father of
JOSHUA. Witnesses: JOHN RATTRAY, JAMES GRINDLAY. On 10 Sept. 1765 ROB-
ERT WILLIAMS, JR., recognized signatures of RATTRAY & GRINDLAY, attorneys-
at-law, GRINDLAY & WILLIAMS having served as clerks to RATTRAY; before
PETER MANIGAULT, J.P. Recorded 16 Sept. 1765 by FENWICKE BULL, P. Reg.

Book E-3, p. 48   JOHN DRAKE, planter, of St. George Parish, Dor-
17 & 18 Feb. 1764   chester, Berkeley Co., to DR. ARCHIBALD MAC-
L & R   NEILL, physician, of same Parish, for ₺ 700
                         currency, 2 lots in Dorchester Town; each 1/4
a.; #5 & #6, formerly belonging to JOHN DRAKE, shipwright, of Dorchester,
father of said JOHN DRAKE. Witnesses: MAURICE HARVEY, EPHRAIM MIKELL.
Before J. SKENE, J.P. Recorded 17 Sept. 1765 by FENWICKE BULL, Register.

Book E-3, p. 53   WILLIAM PERCY, mariner, formerly of Chareston,
19 & 20 Apr. 1762   now of St. John's Southwark, Great Britain,
L & R   son & heir of HUGH PERCY, planter, of SC, by
                         his attorney JOHN RAPER, ESQ., of Charleston;
to CHRISTOPHER ROWE, planter, for ₺ 400 currency, 850 a. in Berkeley Co.,
part of Orangeburgh Township, on PonPon River, known as #21 in grant plat
of said Township, bounding N & W on vacant land; S on JACOB MOTTE, E on
estate of HENRY WURTZER. Whereas Lt. Gov. THOMAS BROUGHTON on 8 Oct.
1737 granted CAPT. HUGH PERCY said 850 a. in Berkeley Co., then bounding
NW partly on #19 belonging to PETER LETCHER, partly on #20 belonging to
MICHAEL SACKWEELER, partly on #32 belonging to BALTAZER STRONMAN; NW on
#33 belonging to HANS RHOTTE; SE on land laid out for inhabitants of said
Township, partly on JOHN HEARNE; SW on PonPon River; & whereas HUGH PERCY
died intestate & son WILLIAM inherited & by letter of attorney dated 16
June 1757 appointed ROBERT RAPER his attorney with authority to sell the
land; now RAPER sells to ROWE. Witness: JOHN TROUP. Before FENWICKE
BULL, J.P. & P. Reg.

Book E-3, p. 64   JOHN RISE, planter, son of GEORGE FREDERICK
27 & 28 Sept. 1764   RISE, to DORAS NEASSE (NEAFFE ?), planter,
L & R   both of Berkeley Co., for ₺ 350 currency, 150
                         a. on S side Santee River in low ground of
Berkeley Co., on upper side Beaver Creek, bounding W on WILLIAM YORK; S
on JACOB GASPER & ANN SUTER; E on vacant land; N on Congaree River; being
part of 250 a. formerly belonging to GEORGE FREDERICK RISE, 50 a. having
been sold to ROSEANNA SHADROW, & 50 a. to JACOB MOOR. Witnesses: DANIEL
STRWINGER, AVERHART STRWINGER, GEORGE WASTER. Before THOMAS CATON, J.P.
Recorded 20 Sept. 1765 by FENWICKE BULL, Register.

Book E-3, p. 69   ALEXANDER CHOVIN, merchant, of Charleston, to
18 Feb. 1765   JACOB JEANNERTT, planter, of Prince Frederick
Feoffment   Parish, Craven Co., for ₺ 1300 currency, 2 ad-
                         joining tracts of 240 a. & 140 a., total 380
a., in St. James Santee Parish, Craven Co., bounding NE on Santee River;
SE & SW on JOHN DE LIESSELINE; NW on ANDREW REMBERT, SR.; also plat &
grant for 200 a., part of said lands, granted 15 Sept. 1705 to PETER
PHILIPS; also L & R dated 11 & 12 Apr. 1750 from JOHN DE LIESSELINE conveying 240 a. to ALEXANDER CHOVIN, father of ALEXANDER, Party hereto;
also L & R dated 1 & 2 May 1751 from JOHN DE LIESSELINE conveying the
140 a. to ALEXANDER CHOVIN the father. Witnesses: PETER GUERRY, PAUL
JAUDON. Before DANIEL HORRY, J.P. Entered in Auditor's Book G-7, p.
494 on 19 Sept. 1765 by RICHARD LAMBTON, Dep. Aud. FENWICKE BULL, Register.

Book E-3, p. 74   THOMAS WARING, JOHN POSTELL, N. WICKHAM, JO-
5 June 1738   SEPH BLAKE, RICHARD BAKER, J. SKENE, M. IZARD:

Sale of a Pew   church wardens & vestry of St. George Parish
                                       church, Dorchester, sell ROBERT WRIGHT, SR.,
for L 250 currency, Pew #9 in said church. Recorded 23 Sept. 1765 by
FENWICKE BULL, Register.

Book E-3, p. 74   JAMES CRAFORD (CROAFORD), Indian trader, to
16 July 1752   JOHN ANDREWS, tailor, for 5 shillings, 300 a.
L & R   on mouth of Stevens Creek, on Sauney River, in
                                       Granville Co. Witnesses: ROBERT GERMANY, THOM-
AS (his mark) HARBARD, JOSEPH GERMANY. Before JOHN RAE, J.P. of Augusta.
Entered in Secretary's Book J.J., p. 466 by WILLIAM PINCKNEY, Dep. Sec.
On 5 June 1753 JOHN ANDREWS assigned said land to CHARLES WRIGHT. Wit-
ness: CHRISTOPHER JOBBRIGHT (?). Recorded 24 Sept. 1765 by FENWICKE BULL,
Register.

Book E-3, p. 78   GEORGE BARKSDALE, planter, of Berkeley Co., to
2 & 3 Sept. 1765   HENRY PERONNEAU, merchant, of Charleston, for
L & R   L 1100 currency, 246 a. on Parris Creek in
                                       Christ Church Parish, on Wando Neck, formerly
belonging to THOMAS BARKSDALE the elder, father of said GEORGE BARKSDALE;
bounding W on said creek & marsh & on DANIEL LEGARE; N on DANIEL LEGARE;
E on the high road & the other land of THOMAS BARKSDALE the elder; S on
JONATHAN SCOTT. Witnesses: ELIAS VANDERHORST, WILLIAM WEBB. Before JOHN
REMINGTON, J.P. Recorded 26 Sept. 1765 by FENWICKE BULL, Register.

Book E-3, p. 86   JOHN JACOB (his mark) METZKER, & CATHERINE MAR-
19 Mar. 1742   GUERITE his daughter, widow of JOHN HENRY DE-
Feoffment   ROCHE of Purysburgh, to DAVID GIROUD, carpen-
                                       ter, of Purysburgh, Granville Co., for L 50
currency, lot #10, 1 a., in Town of Purysburgh, bounding N on DAVID
GIROUD; E on GOMPER MELKER; W on Savannah River & the Bay; S on a street.
Witnesses: HENRY DESAUSSURE, DAVID SAUSEY, DAVID GODET. Before JOHN
LEWIS BOURQUIN, J.P. Recorded 2 Oct. 1765 by FENWICKE BULL, Register.

Book E-3, p. 89   ISAAC NEWTON, planter, of St. Bartholomews
10 & 11 May 1765   Parish, Colleton Co., to JAMES SHARP, merchant,
L & R   of Charleston, for L 843:15:0 currency, 250 a.
                                       in said Parish, being 1/2 of 500 a. granted
JOHN NEWTON & now divided between ISAAC NEWTON & JAMES SHARP by the death
of their brother JAMES NEWTON; lying near CAPT. THOMAS ELLIOTT, & bound-
ing on all sides on vacant land; reserving the quarter a. burial ground.
Witnesses: WILLIAM JACKSON, BENJAMIN PERRIMAN, GIDEON DUPONT, JR. Before
JOSEPH GLOVER, J.P. Recorded 3 Oct. 1765 by FENWICKE BULL, Register.

Book E-3, p. 95   JOHN GANTLETT, carpenter, of Berkeley Co., to
2 & 3 July 1744   ROBERT RIVERS, planter, of James Island, for
L & R   L 40 currency, 110 a. in Berkeley Co., bound-
                                       ing SE on estate of WILLIAM WILKINS; NW on
Savanna lands fronting GEORGE RIVERS, partly on Savanna land fronting MR.
SAMWAYS; SW on SAMWAYS; NE on vacant land; granted GONTLETT by Gov. JAMES
GLEN on 24 May 1744. Witnesses: DANIEL RIVERS, WILLIAM KING, (a quaker),
JOHN RIVERS. Before DANIEL PEPPER, J.P. Recorded 7 Oct. 1765 by FEN-
WICKE BULL, Register.

Book E-3, p. 101   WILLIAM MCTERE, (MACTEER), planter, of Colle-
26 & 27 Apr. 1764   ton Co., & MARTHA his wife, to MALLORY RIVERS,
L & R   planter, of James Island, for L 2500 currency,
                                       200 a. on James Island, where MALLORY RIVERS
now lives, having been for many years before in possession of DANIEL PEP-
PER; bounding W on Stono River; E on MALLORY RIVERS; S on HENRY SAMWAYS;
N on GEORGE RIVERS; also 50 a. on James Island, being half of 100 a.
granted ROBERT COLE, bounding W on Stono River; S on marsh & ponds; E on
HENRY SAMWAYS (formerly ROBERT COLE); N on other half now belonging to
HENRY SAMWAYS; which 2 tracts of 200 a. & 50 a. formerly belonged to WIL-
LIAM HILL & after his death became vested in his 2 daughters SARAH (who
married WILLIAM WILKINS, planter, of the Indian land), & MARY (who married HENRY SAMWAYS, planter, of James Island, now deceased) & after partition of the land the part hereby sold became the share of SARAH WILKINS,
mother of MARTHA MCTERE, party hereto (MARTHA being heiress to her mother
subject to her father's right during his life as tenant by the Curtesy).

Witnesses: WILLIAM MAINE, JOHN CLUNIE, CHARLES BROWN. Before STEPHEN
BULL, J.P. for Granville Co. On 31 May 1764 WILLIAM WILKINS, planter, of
the Indian Land, father of MARTHA MCTERE, & tenant for life by the Curtesy, of said 2 tracts sold to MALLORY RIVERS, for love & affection for
his daughter, & 10 shillings paid RIVERS, renounces all claim to said
tracts. Same witnesses. Before STEPHEN BULL, J.P. Recorded 8 Oct. 1765
by FENWICKE BULL, Register.

Book E-3, p. 110   ROBERT RIVERS, planter, of James Island, Berke-
7 & 8 Mar. 1763   ley Co., son of GEORGE RIVERS, to MALLORY RIV-
L & R   ERS, planter, of James Island, for L 500 cur-
                          rency, 2 plantations on James Island; 110 a.
bounding SE on estate of JOHN STENT; NW on savanna land fronting MALLORY
RIVERS, & on savanna land fronting HENRY SAMWAYS; SW on SAMWAYS; NE on vacant land; granted by Gov. JAMES GLEN on 24 May 1744 to JOHN GANTLET; who
by L & R dated 2 & 3 July 1744 sold to ROBERT RIVERS; & 45 a., part of
100 a. bequeathed by will dated 11 July 1749 by GEORGE RIVERS to his son,
ROBERT; bounding E on GEORGE RIVERS; N & W on MALLORY RIVERS; S on savanna land. Witnesses: WILLIAM HOLMES, HENRY SAMWAYS, MATHEW WITTER. Before ROBERT RIVERS, J.P. Recorded 10 Oct. 1765 by FENWICKE BULL, Register.

Book E-3, p. 117   ALEXANDER HEXT, gentleman, & JANE his wife, to
27 & 28 Sept. 1765   JOHN EDWARDS, merchant, both of Charleston,
L & R by Mortgage   for L 2722:10:6 currency, 384 a. on Johns Is-
                          land, in Colleton Co., bounding N on DAVID
HEXT; W on FRANCIS BOGGES; S on WILLIAM HEXT; E on ALEXANDER HEXT & JOHN
STANYARN. Witnesses: ROBERT WILLIAMS, JR., WILLIAM STOUTENBURGH. Before
WILLIAM BURROWS, J.P. Recorded 10 Oct. 1765 by FENWICKE BULL, Register.
On 3 Feb. 1769 JOHN EDWARDS & CO. declared mortgage satisfied. Witness:
FENWICKE BULL.

Book E-3, p. 123   JERMYN WRIGHT, ESQ., to CHARLES WRIGHT, ESQ.,
14 & 15 Mar. 1763   for L 1500 currency, 800 a. in Granville Co.,
L & R   bounding N on JAMES GRAEME; E on ROBERT WRIGHT,
                          JR.; S on CHARLES WRIGHT; W on JERMYN WRIGHT &
CHARLES WRIGHT; being part of 2000 a. granted ROBERT WRIGHT by Gov. ROB-
ERT JOHNSON on 11 July 1733; & conveyed to JERMYN WRIGHT by L & R dated
30 Nov. & 1 Dec. 1735. Witnesses: CHARLES SMYTH, WILLIAM BRISBANE, JR.
Before JAMES REID, J.P. Recorded 11 Oct. 1765 by FENWICKE BULL, Regis-
ter.

Book E-3, p. 129   JAMES (his mark) CANE (CAIN), Planter, of
27 & 28 June 1764   Granville Co., & FRANCES (her mark) CANE, his
L & R   wife, to ALEXANDER MCPHERSON, dealer, for
                          L 100 currency, 150 a., part of 300 a. on Sa-
vannah River above the mouth of Long Cane Creek, which 300 a. were granted by Gov. WILLIAM HENRY LYTTELTON on 22 Jan. 1759 to said JAMES CANE,
bounding SW on Savannah River; NW on THOMAS HAVARD; NE on vacant land; SE
on NICHOLAS GUNNELL. Witnesses: ALEXANDER NOBLE, SAMUEL KER. Before
PATRICK CALHOUN, J.P. of Granville Co. Recorded 14 Oct. 1765 by FENWICKE
BULL, Register.

Book E-3, p. 134   HENRY LAURENS, merchant, of Berkeley Co., to
8 & 9 Oct. 1765   LACHLIN MACKINTOSH, of Darien, Ga., for love,
L & R   good-will & L 1000 currency, 1200 a. on Alta-
                          maha River, surveyed by DARBY PENDERGRASS,
bounding E on HENRY LAURENS; W on DAVID DEAS; S on vacant land, HENRY
LAURENS, & DAVID DEAS; N on the river. Witnesses: JOHN HOPTON, JAMES
STEVEN. Before FENWICKE BULL, J.P. & P. Reg.

Book E-3, p. 140   ROBERT RAPER & ROBERT SWAINSTON, gentlemen, of
24 & 25 Dec. 1760   SC, attorneys for JOHN COLLETON, ESQ., of Par-
L & R   ish of St. James within the Liberty of West-
                          minster, Co. of Middlesex, London, of 1st
part; to ALEXANDER RUSSELL, ship carpenter, of Charleston, for L 2000
currency, lot #50 on Trott's Point, New Charleston, bounding W 89 ft. on
Bay Street; S on RICHARD MONCRIEF; E on Cooper River, extending from Bay
Street, down to low water lot; N on Pinckney Street; also the low water
lot, 89 ft. wide, 160 ft. deep. Whereas the Lords Proprs. on 5 Mar. 1680

granted Landgrave JAMES COLLETON lot #50 at New Charleston; & whereas by will dated 12 Jan. 1706 JAMES COLLETON bequeathed all his estate to his son, JOHN; the will being authenticated under the Great Seal of the Island of Barbados; & whereas by will dated 2 Apr. 1728 JOHN COLLETON bequeathed all his land in SC to his son, JOHN, party hereto (which will was proved in Prerogative Court of Archbishop of Canterbury); & whereas Lt. Gov. WILLIAM BULL on 19 Nov. 1760 granted JOHN COLLETON, party hereto, the low water lot on Trotts Point, Charleston, bounding W on high water lot belonging to JOHN COLLETON; N on low water lot of Pinckney Street; E on Cooper River; S on RICHARD MONCRIEF; & whereas by letter of attorney dated 11 June 1760 JOHN COLLETON appointed RAPER & SWAINSTON his attorneys with authority to sell his tenement called The Stone House, & other tenements in Charleston, also Wadboo (Watboo) Barony, & his other lands in SC; now they sell the high & low water lots, #50, to RUSSELL. Witnesses: PETER BOCQUET, JR., JOHN RATTRAY. On 14 Oct. 1765 JOHN WAGNER recognized signatures of BOCQUET & RATTRAY before FENWICKE BULL, J.P. & P. Reg.

Book E-3, p. 148   WILLIAM SMITH, of Charleston, to ALEXANDER MC-
2 Sept. 1765   BRIDE & ANDREW WADDEL, for L 30 currency, 200
L & R   a. in St. Bartholomews Parish, Colleton Co.,
                      in the great fork of Saltcatchers, between NE
& SW branches; bounding NE on JAMES JORDAN; other sides on vacant land; which tract was granted by Lt. Gov. WILLIAM BULL on 5 June 1764. Witnesses: ROBERT WARING, JOHN MCDOUGAL. Before CHARLES WOODMASON, J.P. Recorded 17 Oct. 1765 by FENWICKE BULL, Register.

Book E-3, p. 154   GILBERT (his mark) GIBSON, planter, of Craven
16 & 17 June 1760   Co., & ELZIABETH (her mark) his wife, to DA-
L & R   VID TUCKER, gentleman, of Virginia, for L 100
                      currency, 100 a. opposite Saxegotha Township
granted 1 Aug. 1758 by Gov. WILLIAM HENRY LYTTELTON to GILBERT GIBSON; bounding NW on JAMES GERALD & vacant land; NE on vacant land & SARAH REECE; SE on SARAH REECE & JOHN TAYLOR; SW on vacant land. Witnesses: JOHN HANDASYD (HANDAYSID), BENJAMIN BELL, WILLIAM YOUNG. Before JOSEPH CURRY, J.P. Recorded 17 Oct. 1765 by FENWICKE BULL, Register.

Book E-3, p. 160   ROBERT MILHOUS, planter, & ELIZABETH his wife,
12 May 1753   to JOHN CANTEY, planter, both of Craven Co.,
L & R   for L 33:6:8 currency, 50 a. in Fredericks-
                      burgh Township, Craven Co., part of 350 a.
granted JAMES MCGIRT, who sold to MILHOUS; bounding NW on other part, SW on Wateree River; SE on JOHN CANTEY; NE on vacant land. Witnesses: COL. JAMES MCGIRT, JOSEPH EVANS. Before JOHN H. OGLETHROPE, J.P. Recorded 18 Oct. 1765 by FENWICKE BULL, Register.

Book E-3, p. 166   JOHN HORSKINS, planter, & SARAH (her mark) his
12 & 13 Aug. 1754   wife, to JOHN CANTEY, both of Craven Co., for
L & R   L 200 currency, 100 a., English measure, in
                      Craven Co., bounding on all sides on vacant
land. Witnesses: SAMUEL BACOT, JOSIAH CANTEY, WILLIAM CANTEY. Before RICHARD RICHARDSON, J.P. Recorded 18 Oct. 1765 by FENWICKE BULL, Register.

Book E-3, p. 172   THOMAS MAPLES, planter, & MARY his wife, to
4 & 5 Aug. 1755   JOHN CANTEY, planter, both of Craven Co., for
L & R   L 150 currency, 300 a. in Craven Co. on N side
                      Santee River at Allens Old Field, bounding on
all sides on vacant land. Witnesses: THOMAS CASITY, FRANCIS JAMES. Before RICHARD RICHARDSON, J.P. Recorded 19 Oct. 1765 by FENWICKE BULL, Register.

Book E-3, p. 178   WALTER KELLY, planter, & ELIZABETH (her mark)
13 Feb. 1765   his wife, to JAMES ADAMSON, planter, both of
L & R   Craven Co., for L 200 currency, 200 a. being
                      the NW part of 350 a., on SW side Wateree Riv-
er; bounding SE on WALTER KELLY; NW on counciler MICKEY; SW on vacant land; as granted WALTER KELLY on 9 Jan. 1755 by Gov. JAMES GLEN. Witnesses: HENRY DUNGWORTH, JOHN TATE, MICHAEL BRENAN. Before JOHN NEWMAN OGLETHORPE, J.P. Recorded 21 Oct. 1765 by FENWICKE BULL, Register.

Book E-3, p. 184   SAMUEL WYLY, SR., of St. Marks Parish, to JOHN
25 Jan. 1764   CANTEY, of Pine Tree Hill, St. Marks Parish,
Gift   for love & affection & other considerations,
                         4 a. at Pine Tree Hill, beginning at a small
white oak, a corner tree of WILLIAM ANCORUM & said WYLY, running N 80 W
20 poles, then S 60 W 32 poles, then S 30 E 20 poles, then straight line
to beginning oak. Key of dwelling house thereon delivered to CANTEY.
Witnesses: THOMAS JONES, ELY KERSHAW, JOHN CHEESNUT. Before JOHN NEWMAN
OGLETHORPE, J.P. Recorded 21 Oct. 1765 by FENWICKE BULL, Register.

Book E-3, p. 186   THOMAS (his mark) CONNELLY, planter, of Craven
16 & 17 Sept. 1765   Co., & MARGARETT (her mark) his wife, to JOHN
L & R   PAIN, blacksmith, of Fredericksburgh Township,
                         for L 135 currency, 100 a. Whereas on 9 Jan.
1755 Gov. JAMES GLEN granted WALTER KELLY 350 a. in Craven Co., on SW
side Wateree River, bounding NW on JAMES MICKIE, SW on vacant land; SE on
GEORGE BAREFOOT; & whereas KELLY on 13 Feb. 1756 (see p. 178) sold 200 a.
to JAMES ADAMSON; & whereas ADAMSON on 4 Aug. 1759 sold THOMAS CONNELLY
100 a., being half his tract; bounding NE on Wateree River; NW on other
half; SW on vacant land; SE on the part of 350 a. belonging to JOHN PAIN;
now CONNELLY sells his 100 a. to PAIN. Witnesses: HENRY DONGWORTH, JOHN
(his mark) PAIN, SR., JOHN BRADLY. Before JOHN NEWMAN OGLETHORPE, J.P.
Recorded 21 Oct. 1765 by FENWICKE BULL, Register.

Book E-3, p. 192   ISAAC ROSS, planter, & MARY his wife, to SAM-
1 Oct. 1765   UEL GIPSON (GIBSON), planter, both of St.
Conveyance   Marks Parish, Craven Co., for L 10 shillings,
                        500 a. in Craven Co., on S side Wateree River,
granted ROGER GIBSON on 19 Oct. 1748, then bounding on all sides on vacant land; the line on original grant to be the division line. Witnesses: ROBERT MILHOUS, HANNAH (her mark) OGLETHORPE, THOMAS OGLETHORPE. Before JOHN NEWMAN OGLETHORPE, J.P. Recorded 21 Oct. 1765 by FENWICKE BULL,
Register.

Book E-3, p. 194   SAMUEL GIBSON, planter, to ISAAC ROSS, plant-
1 Oct. 1765   er, both of St. Marks Parish, Craven Co., for
Conveyance   10 shillings, 250 a., half of a 500 a. in Cra-
                       ven Co. on S side Wateree River granted ROGER
GIPSON (GIBSON) 19 Oct. 1748, then bounding NE on said river; other sides
on vacant land; the division line marked on said grant being the dividing
line between GIBSON & ROSS. Witnesses: ROBERT MILHOUS, THOMAS OGLETHORP,
SAMUEL WYLY. Before JOHN NEWMAN OGLETHORPE, J.P. Recorded 22 Oct. 1765
by FENWICKE BULL, Register.

Book E-3, p. 197   ROBERT RIVERS the younger, planter, of James
15 & 16 Oct. 1765   Island, to JOHN EDWARDS, merchant, of Charles-
L & R by Mortgage   ton, for L 170 currency, 1157 a., English mea-
                        sure, on the Long Bay, in Craven Co., bounding
NE on MR. WICKHAM & Long Bay; S on WILLIAM BATTOOM; N on MR. CHARNOCK; W
on vacant land; which land THOMAS RIVERS, planter, of James Island, &
MARY his wife, sold to ROBERT RIVERS by L & R dated 25 & 26 Feb. 1762.
Witnesses: CHARLES GRIMBALL, JAMES BALLANTINE. Before ROBERT WILLIAMS,
JR., J.P. Recorded 23 Oct. 1765 by FENWICKE BULL, Register. On 4 Sept.
1759 JOHN EDWARDS & Co. declared mortgage paid. Witness: WILLIAM VALEN-
TINE.

Book E-3, p. 203   JOHN CREIGHTON, gentleman, of Berkeley Co., to
15 & 16 Oct. 1765   JOHN GILES, merchant, of Charleston, for
L & R by Mortgage   L 2500 currency, 40 a. (late resurvey shows
                        53 a.) with dwelling house, etc., thereon,
known as the Quarter House, formerly belonging to JOSEPH HAWKINS, in
Berkeley Co., bounding W & S on RALPH IZARD; E on JOHN BIRD (now MRS.
WRAGG); N on PAUL GRIMBALL (now JOHN CREIGHTON). Witnesses: CHARLES
BEEKMAN, CHARLES MOTTE. Before CHARLES PINCKNEY, J.P. Recorded 24 Oct.
1765 by FENWICKE BULL, Register. On 2 July 1772 JOHN GILES declared
mortgage paid. Witness: GEORGE DAVIDSON.

Book E-3, p. 212   RICHARD BERESFORD, gentleman, of Upham, in
18 & 19 Feb. 1765   Hampshire, Great Britain, by his attorneys,
L & R   WILLIAM LOGAN & JOHN LOGAN, merchants, of

Charleston (appointed 23 Mar. 1764), to WILLIAM PARKER, gentleman, of
Charleston, for Ł 2500 currency, 400 a. in St. Thomas Parish, Berkeley
Co., being the S part of 600 a. granted by the Lords Proprs. on 28 July
1711 to RICHARD BERESFORD, father of said RICHARD; bounding W & NW on
Cooper River; S on a tract of 100 a. & on SAMUEL BLUNDELL; SE on THOMAS
PAGET; E on RICHARD BERESFORD; N on other part of 600 a. formerly belong-
ing to JOHN DANIEL; also said 100 a. granted by Lords Proprs. on 23 July
1711 to RICHARD CODNER; bounding W on Cooper River; S on SAMUEL BLUNDELL
& JOHN PRIMATE, a free Negro; E on JOHN PRIMATE; N on said 400 a. Witnesses: MAURICE HARVEY, ROBERT WILLIAMS, JR. Before WILLIAM BURROWS,
J.P. Recorded 24 Oct. 1765 by FENWICKE BULL, Register.

Book E-3, p. 223   ELIAS VANDERHORST, planter, of Christ Church
12 & 13 Aug. 1762   Parish, to WILLIAM PARKER, merchant, of
L & R   Charleston, for Ł 1368 currency, the E part of
                          the part of lot #297 in Charleston, near White
Point, allotted, with other lands, to ELIAS VANDERHORST by the executors
of the will of his father JOHN VANDERHORST; bounding S 65 ft. on a 12 ft.
alley called Lynch's Lane; W 147-1/2 ft. on another part same lot allotted to said ELIAS VANDERHORST & sold by him to WILLIAM ELLIS; N 65 ft. &
E 147-1/2 ft. on part said lot allotted to WILLIAM VANDERHORST who sold
to JOHN CLIFFORD; plat of division certified by GEORGE HUNTER, Sur. Gen.,
4 May 1741. Witnesses: BENJAMIN BACKHOUSE, THOMAS NETHERCLIFT, SAMUEL
BACOT. Before CHARLES WOODMASON, J.P. Recorded 25 Oct. 1765 by FENWICKE
BULL, Register.

Book E-3, p. 230   DANIEL DOYLEY, P.M., to JAMES BOLTON, merchant,
23 Apr. 1760   of St. Bartholomews Parish, for Ł 305 currency,
Sale   all the interest ROBERT HILL had in lots 3 &
                          13 in Edmundsbury Township, subject to claim
of dower by HILL'S widow. Whereas WILLIAM GLEN, JOHN COOPER, CHARLES
STEPHENSON & WILLIAM MICKIE in Feb. 1760 obtained a judgment against
JAMES BOLTON, administrator of estate of ROBERT HILL for Ł 35:18:3 &
costs; & whereas a writ of fieri facias was issued, commanding the P.M.
to seize HILL'S estate; now DOYLEY sells at auction to BOLTON the said 2
lots, bounding N on Ashepoo River; E on road from Ashepoo Bridge to Combahee Bridge; which premises WILLIAM BUCHANNON on 3 Sept. 1751 agreed to
sell to ROBERT HILL for Ł 600 currency; & on 27 Aug. 1752 acknowledged
receipt of Ł 450, part payment, from HILL. Witnesses: WILLIAM MAZYCK,
CHARLES PINCKNEY. Before FENWICKE BULL, Register, & J.P.

Book E-3, p. 233   THOMAS BUER, at auction, to MARTHA WOODCRAFT,
19 & 20 June 1761   both of Colleton Co., for Ł 675 currency, 200
L & R   a. in Colleton Co., bounding S on JOSEPH
                          BOONE; NW on part of 286 a. given by THOMAS
BUER to WILLIAM MELVIN; NE on THOMAS BUER & MARTHA WOODCRAFT; other sides
on vacant land. Whereas MOSES MARTIN was granted 286 a. by the Lords
Proprs. on 29 Mar. 1709; which land he sold to THOMAS BUER; now he sells
part to MARTHA WOODCRAFT. Witnesses: MOSES DARQUIER, JONATHAN DAVIES.
Before JAMES SHARP, J.P. Recorded 25 Oct. 1765 by FENWICKE BULL, Regis-
ter.

Book E-3, p. 239   HENRY JEANNERET, planter, of St. Peters Par-
17 & 19 Dec. 1763   ish, Granville Co., & URSULA his wife, to
L & R   STEPHEN CATER, ESQ., of Dorchester, for Ł 1700
                          currency, 700 a. in St. Peters Parish granted
10 Nov. 1761 by Gov. WILLIAM BULL to HENRY JENNERETT; bounding N & E on
vacant land; W on the Rev. MR. HENRY CHIFFELLE; S on HENRY JEANNERET &
MICHAEL BOKRER. Witnesses: HENRY SALTUS, JOHN LINDER, MARY MEISNER. Before J. SKENE, J.P. Recorded 26 Oct. 1765 by FENWICKE BULL, Register.

Book E-3, p. 244   HARDYRICE JERNIGAN & NEEDHAM JERNIGAN, of Cra-
15 May 1764   ven Co., to JOSEPH KERSHAW & CO., merchants,
Mortgage   of Pine Tree Hill, for Ł 595:2:5 currency, 3
                          Negroes belonging to HARDYRICE JERNIGAN, &
200 a. on Jumping Gully conveyed to NEEDHAM JERNIGAN by JAMES MCGIRT.
Date of redemption: 1 July next. Witnesses: JOHN CHESNUT (merchant), ELY
KERSHAW. Before JOHN NEWMAN OGLETHORPE, J.P. Entered in Secretary's
Book & & p. 257 on 25 May 1765 by GEORGE JOHNSTON, Dep. Sec. Recorded
26 Oct. 1765 by FENWICKE BULL, Register.

Book E-3, p. 247   WILLIAM HOPTON, gentleman, & SARAH his wife,
9 & 10 July 1760   of 1st part; ANNA MARIA HOYLAND, widow of
L & R Tripartite   THOMAS HOYLAND, tanner, of 2nd part; JOHN WAG-
                          NER, merchant, of 3rd part; all of Charleston.
WILLIAM & SARAH HOPTON & ANNA MARIA HOYLAND, for Ь 170 currency, sell to
JOHN WAGNER, the W part of lot #105 occupied by ANNA MARIA HOYLAND, bound-
ing S 4 ft. on Broad Street; E 80 ft. on SE part said lot occupied by
ANNA MARIA HOYLAND; N on part of lot #105 formerly belonging to REBECCA
FLAVEL, since occupied by THOMAS HALL; W on part same lot #105 lately belonging to heirs of JOB ROTHMAHLER, now to JOHN WAGNER. Whereas a deed
of trust dated 29 June 1754 between WILLIAM HOPTON & SARAH his wife, of 1
part, & ANNA MARIA HOYLAND, sole trader of other part, recited: (1) that
ANNA MARIA owed the HOPTONS Ь 1000, payable 29 June 1755 for use of MARY
CHRISTINA HOPTON, infant daughter of WILLIAM & SARAH HOPTON; (2) that
said ANNA MARIA HOYLAND owed the HOPTONS Ь 1000 payable 29 June 1755 for
benefit of ALICIA HOPTON, infant daughter of WILLIAM & SARAH HOPTON; (3)
that ANNA MARIA HOYLAND owed the HOPTONS Ь 1000 payable 29 June 1755 for
benefit of SARAH HOPTON, infant daughter of WILLIAM & SARAH HOPTON; &
also recited that THOMAS LINTHWAITE, tanner, of Ashley River, son of
ELEANOR SANDWELL, widow, of Charleston, by L & R dated 28 & 29 June 1754
sold WILLIAM HOPTON, for Ь 1300 currency, his undivided half part of the
large wooden dwelling house & SE part of lot #105 in Charleston, bounding
E on 80 ft. on a tenement belonging to DR. JOHN MARTINI; N 60 ft. on part
lot #105 occupied by THOMAS HALL (formerly belonging to REBECCA FLAVEL);
W on part lot #105 belonging to heirs of JOB ROTHMAHLER; S 60 ft. on
Broad Street; & also recited that DANIEL HUNT, gentleman, of St. Philips
Parish, Berkeley Co., by L & R dated 28 & 29 June 1754, for Ь 1700 currency, sold WILLIAM HOPTON the other (his) undivided half of said large
wooden dwelling house & SE part of lot #105; & recited that the 2 undivided parts were purchased in trust for sole use of ANNA MARIA HOYLAND, without intermeddling of her husband, THOMAS HOYLAND; & stated that the sums
of Ь 1300 & Ь 1700 were paid by her out of her own money; that is the
Ь 3000 borrowed from HOPTON, & the purchases made in name of WILLIAM HOP-
TON in trust only; in case of default in payment by ANNA MARIA HOYLAND
then HOPTON to sell the house & lot at auction; & whereas JOHN WAGNER is
highest bidder for 4 ft. of said property; now they sell that much to
WAGNER. Witnesses: FRANCES BAKER, THOMAS LINTHWAITE. Before FENWICKE
BULL, J.P. & P. Reg.

Book E-3, p. 260   ROBERT DEANS, carpenter, who has left Charles-
21 & 22 Oct. 1765   ton; by his attorney, ALEXANDER PETRIE; to
L & R   CHRISTOPHER HOLSON, of St. Philips Parish,
                          Charleston, for Ь 2100 currency, part of lots
#119 & #120 in Deans Square, St. Philips Parish, in Charleston, with the
house built by DEANS, bounding E on Archdale Street; S 113 ft. on the
Rev. MR. CHARLES LORIMER, JAMES SKIRVING, & JOHN WARING; W 37 ft. on
other lands in Deans Square belonging to ROBERT DEANS; N on heirs of
ISAAC MAZYCK; which 2 lots, now called Deans Square, were granted by the
Lords Proprs. to SARAH POWIS; who sold to JOSEPH BOONE, merchant, of
Charleston; who devised to the sons of his brother, CHARLES BOONE; viz.
CHARLES BOONE & THOMAS BOONE; who conveyed to ROBERT DEANS; who subdivi-
ded into lots & sold to different persons. Witnesses: JOHN HILL, CHARLES
MOTTE. Before CHARLES PINCKNEY, J.P. Recorded 26 Oct. 1765 by FENWICKE
BULL, Register.

Book E-3, p. 268   SAMUEL NEILSON, SR., planter, of Lynch's
28 May 1753   Creek, Craven Co., & ELIZABETH (her mark) his
L & R   wife, to JOHN WITHERSPOON, planter, for Ь 5
                          currency, 400 a. in Fredericksburgh Township,
on N side Wateree River, bounding on all sides on vacant land. Witnesses: WILLIAM GAMBLE, ROBERT REILY, ROBERT HAMILTON. Before HENRY RAVENEL,
J.P. Recorded 28 Oct. 1765 by FENWICKE BULL, Register.

Book E-3, p. 273   CHRISTIAN (his mark) RHETTLESPARGER, planter,
4 Feb. 1759   of Berkeley Co., & ANN (her mark) his wife, to
L & R   MELCHIOR HOFMAN, of Saxegotha Township, for
                          Ь 240 currency, 100 a. in Saxegotha Township,
bounding SE on WILLIAM BAKER & vacant land; SW on vacant land; NW on
RICHARD MYRICK; NE on Santee River; according to plat dated 26 Jan. 1741
signed by Gov. JAMES GLEN. Witnesses: THOMAS BRICKLES, CONRAD SKRAM,

ANDREAS KEGLER. Before JOHN PEARSON, J.P. Entered in Auditor's Book
G-7, p. 147 on 25 Oct. 1763 by RICHARD LAMBTON, Dep. Aud. Recorded 28
Oct. 1765 by FENWICKE BULL, Register.

Book E-3, p. 280   PATRICK (his mark) BRADY, yeoman, of St. Marks
9 & 10 Oct. 1765   Parish, Craven Co., to JOHN CHESNUT & ELY KER-
L & R   SHAW, merchant, of same Parish, for ₤ 50 cur-
                          rency, 250 a. on Cedar Creek on NE side Wa-
teree River, in Craven Co., bounding NE on EDWARD DAVIS; other sides on
vacant land; as granted 10 Sept. 1765 by Gov. WILLIAM BULL to PATRICK
BRADY; recorded in Secretary's Book Z.Z., fol. 422. Witnesses: SAMUEL
BOYKIN, RICHARD THOMPSON, WILLIAM (his mark) SMITH. Before JOHN TROUP,
J.P. Recorded 28 Oct. 1765 by FENWICKE BULL, Register.

Book E-3, p. 285   THOMAS MARTIN SANDERS (SAUNDERS), planter, &
27 May 1765   MARY ANN his wife, to JOHN MARION, planter,
L & R   both of St. Thomas Parish, Berkeley Co., for
                          ₤ 700 currency, 100 a. at KAIN HOY in St.
Thomas Parish, bequeathed to said SANDERS by his father, JOHN SAUNDERS;
beginning on Wando River from a post with 3 notches & a cross standing on
the bank, running N 24° W along land of heirs of JOHN SANDERS, JR., 110
chains to a pine tree marked 3 notches & a cross, thence N 66° E along
ROBERT DANIELS land 13 chains 15 links to stake with 3 notches & a cross,
thence s 24° E along dissenting church congregation's land 70 chains &
some ·links to marsh on creek, then course continued across marsh to bank
on other side; thence to follow the several turnings & windings of said
neck & river to first station. Witnesses: ISAAC LESESNE, JR., FRANCIS
GUERIN. Before FENWICKE BULL, J.P. & P. Reg.

Book E-3, p. 292   DAVID (his mark) WILSON, a free Negro & boat
16 & 17 May 1765   builder, to JOHN MARION, planter, both of St.
L & R by Mortgage   Thomas Parish, Berkeley Co., for ₤ 10 curren-
                          cy, 100 a. in said Parish; beginning at a
large pine tree, now dead, marked 3 notches & a cross at head of a marsh;
thence (by plat of grant dated 1711) N 45° W along heirs of JOHN SANDERS,
JR. & RICHARD BERESFORD & from said tree runs N 25° W on other side along
land of ANDREW WARNOCK, making an angle of 20° at said tree, 74 chains &
some links, crossing the public road; then running S 65° W making right
angle, till it intersects first line, having land of THOMAS MARTIN SAND-
ERS on NW. WILSON to pay MARION ₤ 456:5:11-1/2 on 1 July next, with interest. Witnesses: MARTHA FLEMING, WOOD FURMAN. Before ROBERT PRINGLE,
J.P. Recorded 28 Oct. 1765 by FENWICKE BULL, Register.

Book E-3, p. 299   JOHN WHITE, planter, to his son-in-law, ISAAC
23 & 24 Sept. 1765   LEGARE, planter, both of Christ Church Parish,
L & R   for love & affection & 20 shillings, 400 a. in
                          Craven Co., bounding SE on JAMES ROBERTS
(formerly RALPH IZARD); NE on WILLIAM BOHONON; N on JOHN DUBOSE; S on
Wadbacan Creek; other sides on JOHN DUBOISE. Witnesses: THOMAS HUCHIN-
SON, THOMAS HAMLIN, JR., THOMAS PLAYER, JR. Before WILLIAM VANDERHORST,
J.P. Recorded 28 Oct. 1765 by FENWICKE BULL, Register.

Book E-3, p. 305   JAMES POYAS, merchant, & ELIZABETH his wife,
27 & 28 Feb. 1761   (only child of ANTHONY PORTAL, baker), to
L & R   MICHAEL MUCKENFUSS, blacksmith; all of Charles-
                          ton; for ₤ 600 currency, ELIZABETH'S S half of
lot #103 in Charleston sold by L & R dated 29 & 30 Aug. 1737 by NICHOLAS
MATTHISON & MARY his wife to ANTHONY PORTAL, who by will dated 2 Dec.
1739 gave said part of a lot, with other real estate, to his daughter,
ELIZABETH; bounding W 25 ft. on King Street; S 100 ft. on the French
Church; E on DR. JOHN MARTINI; N on other half lot. Witnesses: GEORGE
CROFT, SAMUEL GAILLARD. Before FENWICKE BULL, J.P. & P. Reg. 31 Oct.
1765.

Book E-3, p. 313   JOSEPH BALL, sugar baker, & ELIZABETH (her
15 & 16 June 1764   mark) his wife, to MICHAEL MUCKENFUSS, black-
L & R   smith, both of Charleston, for ₤ 2100 curren-
                          cy, the N part of lot #105 in Charleston,
bounding W 83-1/2 ft. on King Street; N 96-1/2 ft. on RICHARD BERESFORD;
S 98 ft. on other part said lot belonging to heirs of MR. LINTHWAITE; E

on DR. JOHN MARTINI (now heirs of JAMES MICKIE). Witnesses: JOSEPH BEE, ABRAHAM SPIDEL. Before FENWICK BULL, J.P. & P. Reg. 30 Oct. 1765.

Book E-3, p. 319   MRS. MARY WITHERS, gentlewoman, of Charleston,
28 & 29 Oct. 1765   to her son, FRANCIS WITHERS, planter, of Sam-
L & R   pit Creek, near George Town, for love & affec-
                    tion, 500 a. on Waccomaw Neck, bounding SW on
WILLIAM WITHERS; NE on 700 a. belonging to MARY WITHERS; NW & SE on va-
cant land. Witnesses: JOSEPH BRAILSFORD, CHARLES MOTTE. Before FENWICKE
BULL, J.P. & P. Reg. 31 Oct. 1765.

Book E-3, p. 322   JOHN SHUTTERLING, to PHILIP MYER & DANIEL
31 Oct. 1765   STROBLE, all of Charleston, for Ł 1000 curren-
Mortgage   cy, the piece of land in Charleston recently
                    purchased by SHUTTERLING from HENRY PERONNEAU;
bounding W 54 ft. on King Street; N 167-1/2 ft. on DR. JACOB MARTIN; E on
HENRY PERONNEAU; S on a piece of land belonging to HENRY PERONNEAU which
he has agreed to sell to MARTIN MILLER. Witnesses: JOHN MCILRAITH, OL-
IVER NOYES. Before FENWICKE BULL, J.P. & P. Reg. 31 Oct. 1765. On 24
Oct. 1777 MYER & STROBLE declared mortgage satisfied. Witness: GEORGE
SHEED.

Book E-3, p. 325   PAUL LEPEAR, planter, of Prince George Parish,
28 & 29 Oct. 1765   & SARAH his wife, to ISAAC LEGARE & JOSEPH LE-
L & R   GARE, planters, of Christ Church Parish, for
                    Ł 1500 currency 4 tracts of 286, 250, 150, &
50 a., total 736 a., in Craven Co., bounding as follows: 286 a. on Wadbacan Island, bounding E on JOHN DELESSILINE; S on Santee River, other
sides on Wadbacon Creek; the balance on Mainland; 250 a. bounding SW on
Wadbacan Creek; NW on MRS. WHIELDEN, a widow; the 150 a. bounding NW on
above tract; SW on Wadbacan Creek; SE on CAPERS BOONE; NE on JOHN WHITE
(now ISAAC LEGARE); 50 a. on head of above tracts; being 1/3 of 150 a.
granted to JAMES ROBERT; the 736 a. having been purchased from THOMAS
BOONE, planter, of Prince Frederick Parish, by PAUL LEPEAR, father of
PAUL, party hereto, who was eldest son & heir; 1/2 to ISAAC LEGARE, the
other half to JOSEPH LEGARE, as tenants in common. Witnesses: DANIEL
LEGARE, ADAM MILLER. Before WILLIAM BURROWS, J.P. Recorded 31 Oct. 1765
by FENWICKE BULL, Register.

Book E-3, p. 333   ROGER PINCKNEY, P.M., to MARY CHRISTIANA HOP-
31 Oct. 1765   TON, spinster, of Charleston, for Ł 2005 cur-
Sale   rency, part of lot #80 in Charleston, bounding
                    N 40 ft. on Pinckney Street; W & S on GABRIEL
GUIGNARD; E 75 ft. on GRIFFITH TUBBS. Whereas JOSEPH BLACK, bricklayer,
owned said piece of land (by mortgage dated 22 & 23 Mar. 1757; & on 10
June 1755 became indebted to WILLIAM HOPTON, Merchant, for Ł 1000; &
whereas BLACK died intestate & HOPTON on 23 Sept. 1765 obtained a judgment with costs against WILLIAM NEWHENNY & AGNES his wife (formerly widow
& administratrix of said JOSEPH BLACK), & a writ of fieri facias was issued, commanding the P.M. to obtain the amount from BLACK'S estate; now
the P.M. sells said lot at public auction. Witnesses: JOHN MARTIN, JOHN
WAGNER. Before FENWICKE BULL, J.P. & Pub. Reg.

Book E-3, p. 338   DR. JOHN MOULTRIE, JR., physician, of St.
27 & 28 Nov. 1758   James Goose Creek, Berkeley Co., to PETER MAN-
L & R   IGAULT, attorney-at-law, of Charleston, for
                    Ł 1750 currency, the E part of lot #159 in
Charleston, bounding N 34 ft. on Broad Street; E 194 ft. on MR. FLEMING;
W on DR. JOHN MOULTRIE, SR.: S on heirs of JOHN WRIGHT; which piece of
ground JOHN MOULTRIE inherited from his mother LUCRETIA MOULTRIE as eld-
est son & heir. Witnesses: WILLIAM BLAKE, JAMES SIMMONS. Before FEN-
WICKE BULL, J.P. & P. Reg.

Book E-3, p. 343   PETER MANIGAULT, counsellor-at-law, & ELIZA-
1 & 2 Dec. 1758   BETH his wife, to JOHN HUME, merchant, both of
L & R   Charleston, for Ł 1750 currency, (bond given),
                    part of lot #159 (see p. 338). Witnesses:
CHARLOTTE WRAGG, WILLIAM GRAEME, JOHN CROSS, EDWARD SHREWSBUTY. Before
CHARLES WRIGHT, J.P. Recorded 31 Oct. 1765 by FENWICKE BULL, Register.

Book E-3, p. 350   JERMYN WRIGHT, ESQ., of Granville Co., to DA-
3 & 4 May 1757   VID GRAEME, ESQ., of Charleston, for Ł 1500
L & R by Mortgage   currency, (GRAEME having signed bond given by
                          JERMYN & CHARLES WRIGHT to RALPH IZARD, ESQ.,
of St. George Parish, Dorchester), 500 a. in Granville Co., bounding N &
NE on ROBERT WRIGHT, JR.; other sides on vacant land; granted JERMYN
WRIGHT by Lt. Gov. THOMAS BROUGHTON on 17 Feb. 1736. Witness: WILLIAM
HAWKES. Before JOHN REMINGTON, J.P. Recorded 31 Oct. 1765 by FENWICKE
BULL, Register.

Book E-3, p. 358   WILLIAM HAYNE, planter, of St. Paul's Parish,
1 & 2 Oct. 1763   Colleton Co., (by his attorneys JOHN BULLINE &
L & R   ABRAHAM HAYNE), & MARY his wife, to DAVID
                          GRAEME, ESQ., of Charleston, for Ł 8700 cur-
rency, 694-1/4 a., 15 perches, in St. Pauls Parish, bounding S on ABRAHAM
HAYNE & EZEKIEL BRANDFORD; N on CHRISTOPHER PETERS & JOHN SPLATT; W on
EZEKIEL BRANDFORD & CHRISTOPHER PETERS; E on ABRAHAM HAYNE & JOHN SPLATT.
MARY HAYNE, now absent from SC, will renounce her claim after her return.
Witnesses: DANIEL WHEELER, JOHN COOPER. Before FENWICKE BULL, J.P. & P.
Reg.

Book E-3, p. 365   JOHN WALTER, ESQ., of Farleigh Hill, Parish of
29 & 30 Oct. 1765   Swallow Field, Co. of Berks, Great Britain,
L & R   grandson of JOHN WALTER, by his attorney WIL-
                          LIAM WALTER, ESQ., of St. James Goose Creek;
of 1st part; to WILLIAM WITHERS, planter, of St. James Goose Creek Parish, for Ł 350 British, or value, 400 a. in said Parish, bounding E on
Cooper River; S on MASTER WATIS; W on ROBERT HOW; N on NATHANIEL SNOW,
SR., surgeon; also 400 a. in Berkeley Co., bounding E on Cooper River; N
on Landgrave THOMAS SMITH; W on CAPT. GILL; S on NATHANIEL SNOW; excepting & reserving 75 a. granted NATHANIEL SNOW, JR., planter; also excepting & reserving 8 or 10 a. granted GEORGE SMITH & ROBERT TRADD; total
800 a., known as Red Bank; by 2 grants dated 20 Jan. 1710 conveyed by the
Lords Proprs. to NATHANIEL SNOW; who by will dated 3 Oct. 1728 ordered
the land (except as excepted) sold by his son & executor WILLIAM SNOW;
who by L & R dated 26 & 27 May 1729 conveyed to ALEXANDER NIXBIT, merchant, of Charleston; who by L & R dated 20 & 21 Feb. 1733 sold to JOHN
WALTER (grandfather of JOHN, party hereto); who bequeathed to said grandson; who by letter of attorney dated 10 Mar. 1763 directed WILLIAM WALTER
to sell the 2 tracts. Witnesses: JAMES HARRISON, JOHN CANTLE. Before
CHARLES WOODMASON, J.P. Recorded 31 Oct. 1765 by FENWICKE BULL, Register.

Book E-3, p. 373   WILLIAM GLEN, merchant, of Charleston, admini-
5 & 6 Sept. 1765   strator, of SAMUEL THOMAS, to JOHN SAVAGE,
L & R   storekeeper, of Ninety Six, SC, for Ł 182 cur-
                          rency, 200 a. on Six Mile Branch, a branch of
Ninety Six, bounding NE on WILLIAM THOMPSON & vacant land; other sides on
vacant land; also 150 a. on Ninety Six Creek, the waters of Saludy River,
in Granville Co., bounding on all sides on vacant land. Whereas on 9
Jan. 1756 SAMUEL THOMAS was granted said 200 a., & on 4 June 1759 was
granted said 150 a.; & whereas he died intestate & greatly indebted to
WILLIAM GLEN & others; & whereas on 14 Apr. 1764 GLEN obtained letters of
administration of THOMAS'S estate (the personal estate valued at
Ł 120:1:6 the debt being Ł 2102);. now he sells the 2 plantations at public auction. Witnesses: JOHN GLEN, THOMAS HEYWARD, JR. Entered in Auditor's Book G-7, p. 482, on 6 Sept. 1765 by RICHARD LAMBTON, Dep. Aud.
Before FENWICKE BULL, J.P. & P. Reg.

Book E-3, p. 379   JACOB (his mark) WINGLER, planter, to MELCHIOR
12 Oct. 1765   LEICHTENSTEIGER, planter, both of St. Peters
Feoffment   Parish, Granville Co., for Ł 100 currency,
                          400 a. in Purysburgh Township, bounding N on
RICE PRICE & FRANCIS BACHELAR (now GABRIEL SAUSSI); E on vacant land; S
on ANTHONY BILAU & vacant land; W on MELCHIOR LEICHTENSTEIGER & vacant
land. Witnesses: DAVID SAUSSY, GABRIEL SAUSSY, ADRIAN MAYER. Before
JOHN LEWIS BOURQUIN, J.P. Recorded 31 Oct. 1765 by FENWICKE BULL, P.
Register.

Book E-3, p. 381   LAWRANCE FREE (FRUH), planter, of Craven Co.,

22 Aug. 1763   & MARY (her mark) FRUH, his wife, to their son
Feoffment   & heir, ADAM FREE, for love & affection, 100
                      a., the NE part of 400 a. in Craven Co., grant-
ed LAWRANCE FREE on 5 Dec. 1760 by Lt. Gov. WILLIAM BULL, (see Secretary's Book G.G. fol. 229); bounding NE & SE on vacant land; SW & NW on
other part, according to plat certified by JOHN PEARSON, D.S., 4 May 1763.
Witnesses: JACOB HOUKHOUSE, FREDERICK HENRICK. Before JOHN PEARSON, J.P.
Recorded 31 Oct. 1765 by FENWICKE BULL, Register. Plat of 100 a. given.

Book E-3, p. 383   JOHN COLE, planter, of Amelia Township, to DR.
5 & 6 Apr. 1765   WILLIAM TUCKER, physician, of the Congarees,
L & R   for ₤ 200 currency, 150 a. on N side Santee
                      River, bounding on all sides on vacant land;
also 100 a. bounding S on Santee River; SW on WILLIAM DARGAN; other sides
on vacant land. Whereas on 4 Mar. 1760 Gov. WILLIAM HENRY LYTTELTON
granted WILLIAM DARGAN said 150 a., which he sold to JOHN COLE; & whereas
on 31 Jan. 1761 said 100 a. were granted to ANNA CATHERINE FERLINN, who
sold to JOHN COLE; now COLE sells both tracts to TUCKER. Witnesses: JOHN
HAIG, JOHN HANDYSIDE, DANIEL DWIGHT. Before CHARLES WOODMASON, J.P. Recorded 31 Oct. 1765 by FENWICKE BULL, Register.

Book E-3, p. 389   JAMES SIMPSON, cordwainer, of Berkeley Co., to
30 Sept. 1765   JOHN ALLEN, shipwright, for ₤ 350 currency,
Mortgage   the dwelling house in which ALLEN lives, in
                      Charleston, on part of lot of land & marsh
#166, leased by SIMPSON from MRS. ELIZABETH PINCKNEY, acting executrix of
COL. CHARLES PINCKNEY. Witnesses: LUKE BLAKELY, THOMAS COX. Before
GEORGE JOHNSTON, J.P. Recorded 31 Oct. 1765 by FENWICKE BULL, Register.
On 12 Sept. 1766 ALLEN declared mortgage satisfied. Witness: FENWICKE
BULL, Register.

Book E-3, p. 391   JACOB MOTTE the elder, of 1st part; ROBERT
2 & 3 June 1758   BREWTON of 2nd part; JACOB MOTTE the younger,
L & R Quadripartite   gentleman, eldest son of the elder, & REBECCA
                      BREWTON, spinster, daughter of said ROBERT
BREWTON, of 3rd part; BENJAMIN SMITH & MILES BREWTON, merchants, trustees,
of 4th part; all of Charleston. Whereas a marriage is intended between
JACOB MOTTE, JR. & REBECCA BREWTON, JACOB MOTTE the elder (in addition to
what estate JACOB, JR. may have or expect to receive from ROBERT BREWTON
as a marriage portion) conveys to said trustees the low water lot on the
Bay of Charleston, on which is a wharf or bridge known as Motte's Wharf
or Motte's Bridge, together with said wharf, bounding N on low water land
of heirs of JAMES OSMUND; W on curtain line of the Bay; E on Cooper River;
S on the public lower market & low water lots of JAMES MATHEWS in trust
for JACOB MOTTE, SR. during his natural life; then in trust for JACOB,
JR. & REBECCA his wife during their lives; then to their children; with
provisoes. Witnesses: CHARLES PINCKNEY, JR., FRANCIS VANVELSEN. Before
FENWICKE BULL, J.P. & P. Reg.

Book E-3, p. 400   JOHN BELL, of Little River, Prince George Par-
17 Sept. 1765   ish, Craven Co., to HAILE TURNER, mariner, of
Sale   Bristol, Co. of Bristol, Colony of R.I., for
                      ₤ 250 SC money, 50 a. with a dwelling house &
other buildings on N side Little River, in said Parish, bounding SW on
JOHN YORW; NW on vacant land; NE on WILLIAM ALSTONE. Witnesses: DAVID
THAYER, MICAJAH WILLIAMS. PHEBE (her mark) BELL, wife of JOHN, renounces
her claim. Before FENWICKE BULL, J.P. & P. Reg.

Book E-3, p. 401   CHARLES LOWNDES, P.M., to DR. SAMUEL CARNE,
1 Apr. 1756   physician, & ROBERT WILLIAMS, JR., attorney-
Sale   at-law, of Charleston, for ₤ 2266 currency,
                      100 a., also 2 large stills annexed to the
freehold, the implements & utensils belonging to the distillery lately
owned by JOHN COOPER, HENRY KENNAN, & ROBERT WILLIAMS. Whereas ROBERT
WILLIAMS, SR. (father of ROBERT, JR., party hereto) & JOHN COOPER & HENRY
KENNAN, gentleman, of Charleston, owned 4 tracts of 440 a., 90 a., 100 a.,
& 170 a., in Christ Church Parish, Berkeley Co., total 800 a., bounding S
on Skinnee Creek (now Parris's Creek) also 200 a., adjoining, conveyed by
JOHN RUBERRY to ALEXANDER PARRIS; making 1000 a., known as The Distillery,
formerly belonging to ALEXANDER PARRIS, then to JOHN PARRIS, then to JOHN

ALEXANDER PARRIS, planter, of Craven Co., (nephew of JOHN PARRIS, of Charleston; eldest son of ALEXANDER PARRIS), who, with ELIZABETH his wife by L & R dated 30 & 31 Mar. 1752 sold to WILLIAMS, COOPER & KENNON; & whereas WILLIAMS, COOPER & KENNON afterwards erected a distillery, & later owned 2 large stills fixed to the Freehold, with implements & utensils for distilling; & whereas ANN WATSON, executrix of JOHN WATSON, obtained a judgment against them, with costs, which debt they acknowledged before JAMES GRAEME, C.J., who issued a writ of fieri facias which writ was not carried out; & whereas ANN WATSON sued again & PETER LEIGH, C.J., issued another writ commanding CHARLES LOWNDES, P.M., to seize the estate of KENNAN & CAMPBELL, merchants, of Charleston, & LOWNDES sold KENNAN'S share to THOMAS LYNCH (in behalf of CARNE & WILLIAMS) for Ⱡ 516; & whereas WILLIAM MIDDLETON, attorney for Society for the Propagation of the Gospel in Foreign Parts obtained a judgment against COOPER, KENNAN & WILLIAMS, & WILLIAM BULL, Ass't. J., issued a writ of fieri facias commanding the P.M. to obtain this amount from their estate; now LOWNDES sells the entire property to CARNE & WILLIAMS & both judgments are satisfied. Witnesses: CHARLES PINCKNEY, JACOB VIART. CARNE & WILLIAMS agree not to be joint tenants but tenants in common without benefit of survivorship. Witnesses: ANDREW ROBERTSON, ROBERT WILSON. Entered in Auditor's Book D-4, p. 165 on 9 Mar. 1757 by JOHN BASNET, for Dep. Aud. Before FENWICKE BULL, J.P. & P. Reg.

Book E-3, p. 416   DR. SAMUEL CARNE, physician, & CATHARINE his
3 & 4 July 1763   wife, to GEORGE LIVINGSTON, merchant, both of
L & R   Charleston, for Ⱡ 2800 currency, 795 a., English measure, in Christ Church Parish, Berkeley Co., bounding N on Rose's Creek (formerly Wacondaw Creek), ANDREW QUELCH, JACOB BOND, & CAPT. LAMPRIERE; E on DANIEL LEGARE; SE & S on marsh & Sheem's Creek (now Parris Creek); W on marsh, JOHN COOPER, merchant, & ANDREW QUELCH; according to plat certified by WILLIAM WILKINS; the 795 a. being part of 4 tracts. Agreed that ROBERT WILLIAMS shall have right of interment at usual place on said plantation. Witnesses: EDWARD FREEMAN, JOSIAH SMITH, JR. Before FENWICKE BULL, J.P. & P. Reg.

Book E-3, p. 424   GEORGE LIVINGSTON, gentleman, & ELEANOR his
17 & 18 Sept. 1765   wife, to JOHN TORRANS & JOHN POAUG, merchants,
L & R   all of Charleston, for Ⱡ 3000 currency, 795 a., English measure, in Christ Church Parish, Berkeley Co. (see p. 416); reserving to ROBERT WILLIAMS & his heirs the right of burial in the usual place. Witnesses: CATO ASH, JOSHUA EDEN. Before FENWICKE BULL, J.P. & P. Reg.

Book E-3, p. 431   JOSEPH MOODY, merchant, & CATHARINE his wife,
28 & 29 Sept. 1761   to DANIEL LEGARE, merchant, both of Charleston,
L & R   for Ⱡ 4300 currency, part of a lot in St. Michael's Parish, Charleston, bounding N 18-1/2 ft. on Tradd Street; E 96 ft. on GABIREL MANIGAULT; W on JOHN SAVAGE; S on WILLIAM RAVEN. Witnesses: JOHN EDWARDS, EDWARD JONES, THOMAS WIGG. Before ROBERT WILLIAMS, JR., J.P. Recorded 31 Oct. 1765 by FENWICKE BULL, Register.

Book E-3, p. 437   JOHN HOLMES & JOEL HOLMES, gentlemen, to DAN-
30 & 31 Dec. 1760   IEL LEGARE, JR., merchant, both of Charleston,
L & R   for Ⱡ 1200 currency, a lot in Charleston, bounding S on Tradd Street; N on WILLIAM HOPTON; E on JOHN WATSON; W on MRS. GREENLAND; extending SW 81° 60 ft. 4 in., NE 82° 62 ft. 5 in.; SE 8° 411 ft.; NW 8° 412 ft. Witnesses: ROBERT HOGG, THOMAS LISTON. Before ROBERT WILLIAMS, JR., J.P. Recorded 31 Oct. 1765 by FENWICKE BULL, Register.

Book E-3, p. 443   GILBERT (his mark) GIBSON, planter, to JOHN
1 & 2 Aug. 1744   HERSHINGER, potter, both of Sazegotha Town-
L & R   ship, for Ⱡ 42 currency, 50 a. in said Township, on SW side Santee River, in Berkeley Co., bounding SE on ULRICK BUSSER; SW on vacant land; NW on CASPER GALLASER; granted 5 June 1742 by Lt. Gov. WILLIAM BULL to JOHN GIBSON, who died intestate; & inherited by his eldest son, GILBERT. Witnesses: JOHN ROBINSON, WILLIAM SERAIG. Before STEPHEN CRELL, J.P. Recorded 31 Oct. 1765 by FENWICKE BULL, Register.

Book E-3, p. 449   JOHN WRAGG, of Berkeley Co., to JOAKIM HARTS-
5 & 6 Aug. 1765   TON, near Cypress Creek, in Granville Co., for
L & R   Ł 590 currency, 295 a. in Granville Co., grant-
                          ed 16 Apr. 1736 by Lt. Gov. THOMAS BROUGHTON
to JAMES KINLOCK; who by L & R dated 15 & 16 Aug. 1739, for Ł 500 currency, sold (with other lands) to JOSEPH WRAGG, of Charleston; & inherited
by JOHN WRAGG; bounding N on MRS. JUDITH DUBOURDIEU; W on JAMES ST. JOHN
& THOMAS OWEN; S & E on vacant land. Witnesses: WILLIAM GRAHAM, ANDREW
ALLEN. Entered in Auditor's Book G-7, p. 424, on 7 Aug. 1765 by RICHARD
LAMBTON, Dep. Aud. Before FENWICKE BULL, J.P. & P. Reg.

Book E-3, p. 454   JOHN LOGAN, merchant, & ELIZABETH his wife, to
3 & 5 Aug. 1765   WILLIAM SCOTT, ESQ., both of Charleston, for
L & R   Ł 5 currency, their undivided third part of
                          373 a. in Colleton Co., bounding NE & S on va-
cant land; E on MR. DRAYTON; SW on ROGER SAUNDERS & WILLIAM CLIFFORD; N
on JOHN COCHRAN & vacant land; also of 327 a. in Colleton Co., bounding E
on WILLIAM CROLL; S on MR. KELLY; NW on MR. CHAMPNEY; also of 500 a. in
Colleton Co., part of BOYLY'S Barony; bounding on all sides on vacant
land; also of 200 a. granted BRYAN KELLY, W of the freshes of Edisto River, within land, near the Round O Savannah; bounding on all sides on vacant land; total 1400 a.; also 377 a. bounding on THOMAS PAINE. Whereas
JOHN LOGAN in his own right owned 2/3, & in right of his wife ELIZABETH
owned the remaining third part (see Book W.W. reciting L & R dated 30 &
31 Mar. 1761) from JOHN LINDER, planter, of St. Bartholomews Parish, Colleton Co., & JANE his wife, formerly JANE CROLL, to JOHN LOGAN; now they
sell ELIZABETH'S third part to SCOTT. Witnesses: ELIAS VANDERHORST, HEN-
RY WEBSTER. Before LIONEL CHALMERS, J.P. Recorded 31 Oct. 1765 by FEN-
WICKE BULL, Register.

Book E-3, p. 460   WILLIAM SCOTT, ESQ., to JOHN LOGAN, merchant,
6 & 7 Aug. 1765   both of Charleston, for Ł 5 currency, the un-
L & R   divided third part of several tracts which he
                          purchased from said LOGAN on 3 & 5 Aug. 1765
(see p. 454). Witnesses: ELIAS VANDERHORST, HENRY WEBSTER. Before
LIONEL CHALMERS, J.P. Recorded 31 Oct. 1765 by FENWICKE BULL, Register.

Book E-3, p. 465   WILLIAM STANYARNE, canoe builder, to WILLIAM
30 Oct. 1765   SAMS, planter, both of Wadmalaw Island, Colle-
L & R   ton Co., for Ł 600 currency, 230 a. on Wadma-
                          law Island, part of 500 a. granted 15 Sept.
1765 by the Lords Proprs. to THOMAS STANYARNE, father of THOMAS, & grandfather of WILLIAM, party hereto; bounding E on part of said 500 a. sold
to MR. UPHAM; W on part now belonging to WILLIAM SAMS; N on HENRY LIVING-
STON; S on WILLIAM LOGAN. Witnesses: WILLIAM BRADLEY, RICHARD HOGG,
JAMES (his mark) LAMBERT. Before HUGH WILSON, J.P. Recorded 31 Oct.
1765 by FENWICKE BULL, Register.

Book E-3, p. 472   LACHLAN MCGILLIVRAY, ESQ., of Ga., to PETER
9 & 10 Dec. 1763   TURGUNITZ (TURCKINESS), hatter, of SC, for
L & R   Ł 600 SC money, 450 a. in New Windsor Town-
                          ship, Granville Co., bounding on 1 side on
Savannah River; 1 by impassable swamp; 1 on EDMOND COSSENS; 1 on vacant
land. Witnesses: DAVID MONTAIGUT, MATHIAS ASH. Before W. JONES, J.P.
Recorded 31 Oct. 1765 by FENWICKE BULL, Register.

Book E-3, p. 476   ABRAHAM WAIGHT, executor, & HANNAH RIPPON, ex-
11 & 12 Jan. 1765   ecutrix of will of THOMAS JONES, planter, of
L & R   St. Philips Parish, to THOMAS JONES, of
                          Charleston, for Ł 2100 currency, 700 a. in
Colleton Co., on NE side Combahee River; bounding S on WILLIAM FULLER; W
& N on a cypress swamp; E on vacant land; as granted by the Lords Proprs.
on 1 June 1709 to WILLIAM FULLER; who on 25 Jan. 1726 sold to SAMUEL
JONES; & inherited by his son, THOMAS JONES; who by will dated 22 Dec.
1749 directed that the land be sold by said executors; who now sell to
THOMAS JONES. Witnesses: JOHN HOLMES, JOHN TAYLOR. Before FENWICKE
BULL, J.P. & P. Reg.

Book E-3, p. 483   HARDY HAY & DAVID HAY, of Craven Co., agree to
6 June 1764   pay their father's, WILLIAM HAY'S, present

Agreement   debts within 7 years; WILLIAM HAY agrees to
                             rent to HARDY & DAVID, for 7 years, 7 Negro
slaves (named), his horses, cattle, hogs, sheep, tools, & other stock on
the plantation. Witnesses: ELIZABETH HAMILTON, JOHN SPARKS. Before JOHN
HAMILTON, J.P. Recorded 31 Oct. 1765 by FENWICKE BULL, Register.

Book E-3, p. 484   PETER TURGUINITZ, & CHRISTIAN (her mark) his
25 Feb. 1765   wife, of SC, to WILLIAM ARINTON, of Northamp-
L & R   ton Co., NC, for Ł 1500 SC money, 450 a. in
                            New Windsor Township, Granville Co., SC (see
p. 472). Witnesses: JAMES ROSS, JOHN GREEN. Before JOHN DICK, J.P. Recorded 31 Oct. 1765 by FENWICKE BULL, Register.

Book E-3, p. 489   GEORGE RUSSELL, planter, of James Island, to
29 Oct. 1765   WILLIAM BRISBANE, gentleman, of Charleston,
Mortgage   for Ł 3675 currency, 225 a. on James Island,
                            part of 539 a., bounding N on a branch of New
Town Creek & on parsonage land; E on paid branch & part of said 539 a.
sold to WILLIAM BEE; S on part sold to THOMAS DICKSON; W on THOMAS RIVERS;
reserving 1 square a. on S side where the Meeting House stands; also 6
Negro slaves. Witnesses: JOHN DILL, BENJAMIN STILES. Before JOHN MURRAY,
J.P. Recorded 31 Oct. 1765 by FENWICKE BULL, Register. Later BRISBANE
declared mortgage satisfied.

Book E-3, p. 493   ELIJAH PRIOLEAU, planter, of Colleton Co., &
25 & 26 May 1757   ANN his wife; to BENJAMIN BAKER, joiner, of
L & R   Charleston, Berkeley Co., for Ł 700 currency,
                            a house & piece of ground, consisting of part
of 2 lots #236 & #237, bounding S on Queen Street; E 23 ft. on King
Street; N on JOHN CLIFFORD; which property SAMUEL PRIOLEAU the elder by
will dated 25 Oct. 1751 bequeathed to his son, said ELIJAH. Witnesses:
ANDREW SMITH, JOSEPH SMITH. No probate. Recorded 31 Oct. 1765 by FEN-
WICKE BULL, Register.

Book E-3, p. 500   JOHN RATTRAY, ESQ., & HELEN his wife, to BEN-
2 & 3 Jan. 1759   JAMIN BAKER, carpenter, both of Charleston,
L & R   for Ł 560 currency, the E part of lot #250,
                            bounding N on JOHN CLIFFORD; E on ROBERT
COLLIS & JOHN CLIFFORD & BENJAMIN BAKER; S 80 ft. on Queen Street; W
100 ft. on WILLIAM BAMPFIELD. Witnesses: ROBERT DEANS, JAMES GRINDLAY.
Before CHARLES WOODMASON, J.P. Recorded 31 Oct. 1765 by FENWICKE BULL,
Register.

Book E-3, p. 504   DAVID GUERARD & BENJAMIN GUERARD renounce all
15 Feb. 1765   their claim to a lot on Queen Street in
Quitclaim   Charleston, near Deans Square, now owned by
                            BENJAMIN BAKER, formerly by MRS. ELIZABETH
QUINCEY, on which BAKER has lately erected 2 wooden tenements. Recorded
31 Oct. 1765 by FENWICKE BULL, Register.

Book E-3, p. 505   JOHANNES WILDERMAN, to MARTHA WALKER, of
26 Mar. 1759   Berkeley Co., Ł 40 currency, 150 a., on Hornet
Release   Creek, in Amelia Township, Berkeley Co.,
                            granted by Gov. JAMES GLEN; bounding on all
sides on vacant land. Witnesses: JOHN THOMPSON, CASPAR BROWN, JACOB
BOOK. Before MOSES THOMPSON, J.P. Recorded 31 Oct. 1765 by FENWICKE
BULL, Register.

Book E-3, p. 507   SUSANNAH SCOTT, gentlewoman, daughter of JOHN
13 & 14 June 1764   SIMMONS, long since deceased, JOHN SCOTT, JOHN
L & R   SAVAGE & ANNE his wife (formerly ANNE SCOTT);
                            SUSANNAH JONES (formerly SUSANNAH SCOTT), &
WILLIAM SCOTT, (JOHN, ANNE, SUSANNAH, & WILLIAM being children of SUSAN-
NAH SCOTT, & devisees of JOHN SIMMONS their grandfather); ELIZABETH
HOLMES, gentlewoman, another daughter of said JOHN SIMMONS; & JOHN SIM-
MONS, EBENEZER SIMMONS, & JAMES SIMMONS, sons of EBENEZER SIMMONS, ESQ.,
lately deceased, who was also a son of said JOHN SIMMONS; all of the 1st
part; to RICHARD MONCRIEF, carpenter, of 2nd part; all of Charleston; for
Ł 1300 currency; part of a certain lot in St. Philips Parish, Charleston,
occupied for several years past by MRS. BARKSDALE; bounding N 60 ft. on

Simmons Alley; E 46 ft. on lot #32; S on WILLIAM CROSTHWAITE; W on SU-
SANNAH SCOTT & EBENEZER SIMMONS. Witnesses: HER. HALL, JOSHUA TOOMER.
Before FENWICKE BULL, J.P. & P. Reg. Parties of 1st part give MONCRIEF
bond of performance. Recorded 31 Oct. 1765.

Book E-3, p. 517   ROBERT DANIEL, planter, of St. Thomas Parish,
29 & 30 Mar. 1764   & ELIZABETH his wife, to JOHN LOGAN, merchant,
L & R   of Charleston, for ₤ 5000 currency, 2 planta-
tions, 1 of 500 a., in Prince George Parish,
Craven Co., on N side Santee River, bounding NE on JOHN SOUSO; NW on ?;
the other being an island of 400 a., in Santee River, opposite said 500
a., granted to JOHN BELL; which 2 plantations formerly belonged to WIL-
LIAM LITTEN RUSS, who by his will dated 29 July 1763, bequeathed them to
ELIZABETH DANIEL. Witnesses: ELIAS VANDERHORST, JAMES MOULTRIE. Before
FENWICKE BULL, J.P. & P. Reg. Recorded 8 May 1766.

Book E-3, p. 524   JOHN LOGAN, merchant, of Charleston, & ELIZA-
3 Apr. 1764   BETH his wife, to ROBERT DANIEL, planter, of
Release   St. Thomas Parish, for ₤ 5000 currency, 2
plantations conveyed by ROBERT DANIEL to JOHN
LOGAN (see p. 517). Witnesses: JAMES MOULTRIE, ELIAS VANDERHORST. Before FENWICKE BULL, J.P. & P. Reg. Recorded 9 May 1766.

Book E-3, p. 526   DR. FRANCIS THOMAS RICHARD, physician, & MAR-
1 Oct. 1764   THA his wife, to JACOB COWEN, planter, both of
L & R   Granville Co., for ₤ 1610 currency, 161 a.
Whereas on 11 July 1733 Gov. ROBERT JOHNSON
granted RANDOLPH EVANS 154 a. on St. Helena Island, bounding NE & SE on
RANDOLPH EVANS; NW & SW on COL. WILLIAM BULL; which land descended to his
son, JOHN EVANS; who by L & R dated 11 & 12 Apr. 1743 sold to JOSEPH
ELLICOT CAPERS; who by will dated 29 Nov. 1743 bequeathed to his son WIL-
LIAM CAPERS; who died in infancy; & his eldest brother, RICHARD, inher-
ited; who, with SUSANNAH his wife, by L & R dated 13 & 14 Jan. 1764 sold
to FRANCIS THOMAS RICHARD; who had the land resurveyed by ROBERT MANNING,
Sur. Gen., who found it to contain 7 surplus a.; now he sells to COWEN.
Witnesses: JOHN DELAGAYE, ANDREW AGNEW. Before THOMAS MIDDLETON, J.P.
Recorded 9 May 1766 by FENWICKE BULL, Register.

Book E-3, p. 533   EDWARD YOUNG, & ESTER (her mark) his wife, of
22 June 1765   Bertie (?) Co., NC, to REBECCA LIDE, of Craven
Release   Co., SC, for ₤ 50 sterling 270 a. in the Welch
tract, in Craven Co., SC, being the 4th part
of 1100 a. granted FRANCIS YOUNG & ANDREW JOHNSTON (date cut out) on 18
Nov. 1747. Witnesses: THOMAS YOUNG, WILLIAM RHODES. Before ALEXANDER
MACKINTOSH, J.P. Recorded 12 May 1765 by FENWICKE BULL, Register.

Book E-3, p. 535   JOHN GILES, planter, of Anson Co., NC, & MARY
28 Apr. 1766   his wife, to THOMAS LIDE, of Craven Co., for
Release   ₤ 1400 currency, 200 a. in Craven Co., on SW
side Pee Dee River, beginning at a sycamore
tree opposite GEORGE SEAMOR'S land, thence S 70° W 146 poles to a pine,
thence S 20° E 180 poles to a pine, thence N 70° E 214 poles to an ash on
side river, thence the various courses of said river to beginning; which
land was granted SOLOMON HUGHES on 21 Apr. 1745; & sold by him to MARMA-
DUKE KIMSBOROUGH; who sold to WILLIAM LITTLE, which deed was recorded in
Anson Co. Court; & sold by LITTLE to JOHN GILES. Witnesses: LEONARD DOZ-
ER, THOMAS WADE. Recorded 12 May 1766 by FENWICKE BULL, Register.

Book E-3, p. 540   JOHN STEWART & JOHN STEVENS, planter, of St.
29 Feb. & 1 Mar. 1760   Johns Parish, Georgia, executors, of will of
L & R   JOHN STEVENS; & MARY STEVENS of said Parish,
executrix; of 1st part; to JOHN MILES, plant-
er, of St. Pauls Parish, Colleton Co., SC, for ₤ 660 SC money, 220 a. in
St. George Parish, Berkeley Co., SC, bounding N on JOHN LUPTON; NE on
ROGER SUMNER; SE on THOMAS DONNING; SW on CAPT. THOMAS JOHNSTON (now WIL-
LIAM COACHMAN); NW on BENJAMIN BEDON. Witnesses: JOHN STEWART, RICHARD
BAKER, MOSES WAY. Before JOHN ELLIOTT, J.P. Recorded 14 May 1766 by
FENWICKE BULL, Register.

Book E-3, p. 546   SILAS MILES, to his brother, JOHN MILES,

3 May 1763   planter, of St. Pauls Parish, Colleton Co., SC,
Release   for Ł 3000 currency, 500 a. in St. Bartholo-
                    mews Parish, Colleton Co., part of 1000 a.
granted to THOMAS MILES on 11 July 1733, the 1000 a. bounding S on JERE-
MIAH MILES (now JAMES PARSONS); N on WILLIAM MILES. THOMAS MILES by will
dated 13 Oct. 1750 bequeathed to his son SILAS MILES 500 a. (the other
500 going to his brother JOHN MILES), which SILAS now sells to JOHN;
bounding S on JAMES PARSONS; N on JOHN MILES. Witnesses: ISAAC MCPHERSON,
JOSEPH MILES, WILLIAM DAY. Delivery by turf & twig. Before ANDREW
LEITCH, J.P. Recorded 15 May 1766 by FENWICKE BULL, Register.

Book E-3, p. 549   PHILIP PRIOLEAU, merchant, of Island of Jamai-
1 Feb. 1758   ca, to the Hon. OTHNIEL BEALE, of Charleston,
Release   SC, for Ł 4903:16:0 SC money, 1 undivided
                    third part of a pasture in Charleston, bound-
ing E on Friend Street; N on Broad Street; also 1 undivided third part of
3250 a. in Granville Co., on the branches of Coussaw Hatche & Tulyfinny,
adjoining the lands of WILLIAM FISHBOURN & JONATHAN RUSS; also part of
lot #69 in Charleston. Whereas SAMUEL PRIOLEAU, father of PHILIP, by
will dated 25 Oct. 1751 ordered his pasture on Broad & Friend Streets &
his plantation of 3250 a. divided into 3 parts, each. giving 1/3 of each
to his son PHILIP; & whereas ISAAC MAZYCK, merchant, of Charleston, &
MARY his wife, by L & R dated 17 & 18 Sept. 1755 sold PHILIP PRIOLEAU
part of lot #69 in Charleston, bounding S 54 ft. on lot #43 belonging to
MRS. MARY WATSON; E 48 ft. on COL. SAMUEL PRIOLEAU; N on part of lot #70
belonging to ANDREW DUPEY; W on part lot #69 belonging to BENJAMIN STEAD;
now PHILIP PRIOLEAU sells to BEALE. Whereas SAMUEL PRIOLEAU, father of
PHILIP, in his will, further devised to PHILIP the house & lot on Church
Street (where the father lived) after the death of SAMUEL'S wife; also
his pew in S gallery of St. Philips Church, & 621 a. on Coussaw Hatche
Swamp between his tract of 1000 a. & a tract formerly belonging to JAMES
KERR; now PHILIP includes in the sale to BEALE his claim to the house &
land in Church Street, the pew in St. Philips Church, & the 621 a. Wit-
nesses: ISAAC COLCOCK, JAMES HAY. Before WILLIAM BULL, J.P. Recorded 15
May 1766 by FENWICKE BULL, Register.

Book E-3, p. 556   JAMES SIMPSON, cordwainer, to HOPKIN PRICE,
10 May 1766   ESQ., both of Charleston, to satisfy unpaid
Release   bond of Ł 204 currency, with interest; 600 a.
                    on Savannah River, at mouth of Briery, Branch,
in Granville Co., bounding on all sides on vacant land; also 100 a. on
Savannah River, opposite the long reaches, bounding NW on RICHARD FIELDS;
other sides on vacant land; which 2 tracts were granted SIMPSON on 27
Sept. last (see entry in Auditors Book G-7, on 9 Oct.). Witnesses: JA-
COB REMINGTON, JOHN REMINGTON. Before FENWICKE BULL, J.P. & P. Reg. On
5 Mar. 1777 PRICE declared mortgage satisfied. Witness: GEORGE SHEED.

Book E-3, p. 561   WILLIAM HOPTON, ESQ., & SARAH his wife, ANNA
5 Mar. 1766   MARIA HOYLAND, widow, both of Charleston, ac-
Feoffment   cording to previous agreement; a large wooden
                    dwelling house & SE part of lot #105 in
Charleston, bounding E 80 ft. on DR. JOHN MARTINI; N 56 ft. on other part
of lot #105 occupied by THOMAS HALL (formerly belonging to REBECCA FLA-
VEL); W on part belonging to heirs of JOB ROTHMAHLER; S on Broad Street.
Whereas on 29 June 1754 it was agreed among said parties that said house
& lot were purchased in fee simple by said HOPTONS in trust for MRS. HOY-
LAND & that upon her paying them Ł 3000 & interest they would convey the
premises to her; now she has paid said sum & receives the property. Witnesses: THOMAS ELFE, SARAH CLARKE. Before FENWICKE BULL, J.P. & P. Reg.
16 May 1766.

Book E-3, p. 564   THOMAS (his mark) LAND, of Anson Co., NC, &
23 Oct. 1758   ELINOR (her mark) his wife, to THOMAS NIGHTIN-
Feoffment   GALE, saddler, of Charleston, for Ł 50 NC mon-
                    ey, 496 a. in Anson Co., NC, beginning at a
white oak on E side of Barns Creek, then S 5 E 360 poles to a poplar in a
branch, then S 85 W 182 poles crossing said branch to a white oak, then N
21 W 106 poles to a pine, then N 360 poles to a white oak, then to 1st
station. Witnesses: ROBERT MCCLENACHAN, ARCHIBALD ELLIOTT. Recorded in
clerk's office, Anson Co., July Court 1759; JOHN FROHOCK, C.C., by

WILLIAM CUMMINS. Recorded in Registers Book for said Co., G-7, p. 14 & 15, by ROBERT HARRIS, Pub. Reg. Recorded in Charleston 17 May 1766 by FENWICKE BULL, Register.

Book E-3, p. 567   HENRY HENDERLY, planter, of St. Peters Parish,
31 Oct. 1765   Granville Co., to ADRIAN MAYER, of same Par-
Sale   ish, Ł 1250 currency, 500 a. in Purysburgh
                      Township, bounding N on LEWIS DEVILLE, JOHN
LABORDE, PETER MAILLIER, & DAVID PETER HUMBERT; S on ABRAHAM DUVOISIN,
the Rev. MR. HENRY CHIFFELLE, GEORGE MENGERSDORF, JOHN MICHEL (alias JOHN
MICHEL PIAGER), & HUGH ROSE; W on LEWIS DEVILLE, SAMUEL MONTAIGUT, ABRA-
HAM DUVOISIN, the Rev. MR. HENRY CHIFFELLE, & GEORGE MENGERSDORF; E on
JOHN PETER PEROTET, DAVID PETER HUMBERT, HUGH ROSE, & vacant land. Wit-
nesses: ABRAHAM JACOB, MELCHIOR LEICHTENSTEIGER, GABRIEL SAUSSY. Before
JOHN LEWIS BOURQUIN, J.P. Recorded 21 May 1766 by FENWICKE BULL, Regis-
ter.

Book E-3, p. 569   THOMAS BINFORD, merchant, formerly of Charles-
7 Nov. 1765   ton, SC, now of Exter, Great Britain, of 1st
Deed of Trust Tripartite   part; the Hon. COL. OTHNIEL BEALE, of SC, of
                      2nd part; MILES BREWTON, merchant, of SC, of
3rd part. Whereas by L & R dated 15 & 16 Oct. 1731 MARY SALTUS & ANN
SALTUS, spinsters, of Island of Bermudas, alias Summer Islands, only
daughters & coheirs of BARTHOLOMEW SALTUS, who was eldest brother & heir
of MARTHA JONES, theretofore MARTHA SALTUS, widow of JOHN JONES, gunsmith, of SC, sold THOMAS BINFORD 3 lots in Charleston, Nos. 148, 149, &
150, which by 3 separate grants dated 20 June 1694 had been granted by
the Lords Proprs. to JOHN JONES; & whereas THOMAS BINFORD in Feb. 1731
sold lot #150 & half of lot #149 to MILES BREWTON, grandfather of said
MILES BREWTON; so that BINFORD now owns only the entire lot #148 & half
of lot #149 (the value of the half of lot #149 being estimated at Ł 3300
SC money); equal to Ł 471:8:6 sterling British; & whereas BINFORD has an
affectionate regard for his God-son, MILES BREWTON, & has agreed to
settle the lands on BREWTON for an annuity of Ł 37:14:0 sterling, with
provisoes in regard to survivorship; now BINFORD conveys to BEALE, as
trustee, lot #148 & the unsold half of lot #149, in trust for MILES BREW-
TON. Witnesses: ABRAHAM PEARSE, mariner, of Topsham, Devon; & EDWARD
LEGG, pressman, of Exeter, Great Britain; before JOHN BUSSELL, mayor of
City of Exeter on 7 Nov. 1765. Recorded in Charleston 24 May 1766 by
FENWICKE BULL, Register.

Book E-3, p. 581   GEORGE THREADCRAFT, planter, to ANDREW SHUTE,
7 & 8 Aug. 1763   planter, both of Prince William Parish, Gran-
L & R   ville Co., for Ł 329 currency, 200 a. in St.
                      Andrews Parish, Georgia, granted 4 Dec. 1759
by Gov. HENRY ELLIS, of Georgia, to GEORGE THREADCRAFT; bounding SE on
ABIGAIL MINIS; other sides on vacant land. Witnesses: WILLIAM MAIN, BEN-
JAMIN GIGNILLIAT. Before STEPHEN BULL, JR., J.P. Recorded 26 May 1766
by FENWICKE BULL, Register.

Book E-3, p. 589   AUDLEY MAXWELL, of St. Johns Parish, Georgia,
16 Oct. 1765   appoints his beloved brother, MOSES THOMPSON,
Letter of Attorney   of SC, his attorney, with authority to sell 2
                      tracts on Santee River, in Amelia Township,
SC. Witnesses: BENJAMIN FARAR, of St. Marks Parish, Craven Co., JAMES
MCCLENACHAN. Before TACITUS GAILLARD, J.P. Recorded 27 May 1766 by FEN-
WICKE BULL, Register.

Book E-3, p. 590   COL. MOSES THOMPSON, of Amelia Township, SC,
25 Oct. 1765   as attorney for his borther AUDLEY MAXWELL, of
Release   Georgia; to COL. WILLIAM THOMPSON, planter, of
                      Amelia Township; for Ł 100 currency; 200 a. in
said Township, bounding NE on Santee River; SE on unknown land; SW on vacant land, NW on land formerly belonging to AUDLEY MAXWELL but lately
purchased by the church wardens & vestry of St. Mathews Parish as a glebe
for the incumbent, which tract was originally granted to ALEXANDER TATE
who sold to MAXWELL. Witnesses: THOMAS PLATT, JOHN THOMSON, JAMES (his
mark) WATSON. Before JOHN LIVISTON, J.P. Recorded 27 May 1766 by FEN-
WICKE BULL, Register.

Book E-3, p. 593   CHRISTIAN GRINDLAY, of Charleston, widow of
30 & 31 Oct. 1765   JAMES GRINDLAY, attorney-at-law, to DR. ALEX-
L & R   ANDER FOTHERINGHAM & DR. ARCHIBALD MACNEILL,
     physicians, of Berkeley Co., for Ł 1855 cur-
rency, a lot in Charleston, bounding S 30 ft. on Tradd Street; W 200 ft.
on JOHN PAUL GRIMKE (formerly WILLIAM WILKINS); N on DANIEL BOURGETT; E
on ROBERT PRINGLE. Whereas JAMES GRINDLAY owned said lot & by will dated
6 June 1765 authorized his wife to sell the residue of his estate but did
not make any particular disposition of said lot, which then became part
of the residue, now she sells it at auction. Witnesses: ROBERT WILLIAMS,
JR., WILLIAM STOUTENBURGH. Before FENWICKE BULL, J.P. & P. Reg.

Book E-3, p. 603   WILLIAM BURROWS, master in Chancery, & ELIZA-
14 Aug. 1762   BETH MOULTRIE, wife of DR. JOHN MOULTRIE, phy-
Sale   sician (lately ELIZABETH MATHEWS, widow); THOM-
     AS LAMBOLL, & WILLIAM MATHEWS, gentlemen; sur-
viving executrix, & executors of will of JAMES MATHEWS, merchant; of 1st
part; to JAMES GRINDLAY, attorney; all of Charleston; for Ł 1490 curren-
cy, a lot in Charleston bounding S 30 ft. on Tradd Street; W 200 ft. on
WILLIAM WILKINS; N on DANIEL BOURGETT; E on ROBERT PRINGLE. Whereas
JAMES MATHEWS, of St. Andrews Parish, SC, eldest son of said JAMES
MATHEWS deceased; & ISAAC GODIN, gentleman, of St. James Goose Creek, &
MARTHA his wife (lately MARTHA MATHEWS, 1 of the daughters of said JAMES
MATHEWS, deceased); lately complained in Co. of Chancery against JOHN
MOULTRIE & ELIZABETH his wife; THOMAS LAMBOLL; & WILLIAM MATHEWS; surviving executrix & executors; & against THOMAS LLOYD, & MARY his wife; &
JOHN MATHEWS, an infant; in order to obtain a division or sale of certain
lots & real estate, which JAMES MATHEWS by will dated 30 June 1745 devised according to the complaint; & whereas on 1 July last the Court ordered the lots, etc., sold by WILLIAM BURROWS, M.C., the money to be divided according to decree of Court; now they sell to the highest bidder
at public auction, JAMES GRINDLAY. Witnesses: JAMES MOULTRIE, THOMAS
GRIMBALL, JR., MARK ANTHONY BESSELLEU. Before FENWICKE WULL, J.P. & P.
Reg. Recorded 29 May 1766.

Book E-3, p. 608   The church wardens & vestrymen of St. Bartho-
3 Aug. 1761   mews Parish, Colleton Co., to JOHN COCHRAN,
Sale of a Pew   for Ł 200 currency, pew #38 in the brick chap-
     el recently built at Edmundsbury. Signed:
JAMES SHARP, JAMES POSTELL, WILLIAM WEBB, HENRY HYRNE, JR., PHILIP SMITH,
SAMUEL PORCHER. Witnesses: JAMES ATKINS, JONATHAN DAVIES. Before JAMES
GRINDLAY, J.P. Recorded 30 May 1766 by FENWICKE BULL, Register.

Book E-3, p. 609   JOHN WAGNER, merchant, of 1st part; ANN
15 Apr. 1758   BOCQUETT, spinster, of 2nd part; PETER
Marriage Articles   BOCQUETT, baker, of 3rd part. Whereas a mar-
     riage is intended between JOHN WAGNER & ANN
BOCQUETT now WAGNER conveys to PETER BOCQUETT, in trust for ANN, part of
lot #105 in Charleston, bounding 40 ft. on Broad Street; & 60 ft. on King
Street. Witnesses: JACOB WARLEY, MICHAEL BOOMER. Before FENWICKE BULL,
J.P. & P. Reg.

Book E-3, p. 612   SUSANNAH DAMARIS DE ST. JULIEN acknowledges
3 Mar. 1763   receipt of Ł 7380 currency from JOHN MAYRANT,
Receipt   executor of her father's estate; also acknowl-
     edges receipt of her father's estate; also acknowl-
edges receipt of Ł 500 currency for her title to 100 a., being half of
200 a., on the Fork Island, in St. James Santee Parish, granted to her
grandmother. SUSANNAH MAYRANT. Witness: JANE JOLLY (later MRS. JANE VAIR).
Before FENWICKE BULL, J.P. & P. Reg.

Book E-3,   WILLIAM TRUSLER, butcher, & SARAH his wife, to
27 & 28 Sept. 1765   SIMS WHITE, merchant, both of Charleston, for
L & R   Ł 1300 SC money, 1060 a., part of 2000 a. in
     Queensborough Township, in Craven Co., on NE
side Peedee River; bounding NE, NW, & SW on vacant land; SE on JOSEPH
GRAVES & ABRAHAM GILES. Whereas Lt. Gov. THOMAS BROUGHTON granted JOSEPH
WRAGG said 2000 a. & by will dated 26 Sept. 1746 bequeathed all his real
& personal estate to his 8 children, equally, & said plantation became
the share of his son JOHN WRAGG; who by L & R dated 17 & 18 Feb. sold the

2000 a. to EDWARD TRUSLER; who, by will dated 18 Sept. 1755 bequeathed all his real estate to his son WILLIAM TRUSLER; now he sells 1060 a. to WHITE. Witnesses: DANIEL DWIGHT, FELIX LONG, DAVID DUCKNETT. Before JOHN TROUP, J.P. Recorded 2 June 1766 by FENWICKE BULL, Register.

Book E-3, p. 621
9 & 10 June 1763
L & R

THOMAS ELFE, cabinet maker, & RACHEL his wife, to RICHARD HART, chair maker; both of Charleston; for Ł 700 currency, part of lot #250 in Charleston, bounding S 38 ft. on Queen Street; W 100 ft. on lot #250 owned by JOHN STEVENSON; N on part lot #250 owned by JOHN CLIFFORD; E on the part owned by BENJAMIN BAKER. Witnesses: JOSEPH STORDY, THOMAS BURNHAM. Before FENWICKE BULL, J.P. & P. Reg.

Book E-3, p. 626
30 & 31 May 1766
L & R

FREDERICK DORSEY, of Ann Arundel Co., Maryland, eldest son & heir of JOSHUA DORSEY, to ARCHAR SMITH, planter, of St. George Parish, SC, for Ł 300 SC money, 2 quarter a. lots #19 & #20 in town of Dorchester, SC, between the lot of the estate of JOHN IZARD & the lot on which the Free School is built. Witnesses: RICHARD CHITTCH, WILLIAM ROPER, JR. Before WILLIAM BURROWS, J.P. Recorded 5 June 1766 by FENWICKE BULL, Register.

Book E-3, p. 632
31 May & 1 June 1764
Mortgage

WILLIAM HALL, carpenter, of Charleston, to ANN PEACOCK, widow, of St. George Parish, Berkeley Co., for Ł 2000 currency, part of lot #37 in Charleston, formerly belonging to ABRAHAM LESSURE; bounding N 44 ft. on WILLIAM HALL (formerly MR. PORCHER); E 42-1/2 ft. on other part belonging to MARY YEOMANS & occupied by WILLIAM GLEN; S 46-1/2 ft. on JOHN COOPER, merchant, & MARY his wife (formerly WILLIAM SMITH); W 43-3/4 ft. on Church Street. Witnesses: ALEXANDER CORMACK, JOSEPH BEE. Before JAMES GRINDLAY, J.P. Recorded 5 June 1766 by FENWICKE BULL, Register. On 23 Aug. 1768 ANN PEACOCK declared mortgage satisfied. Witness: FELIX WARLEY, for FENWICKE BULL.

Book E-3, p. 638
12 May 1764
L & R

WILLIAM SEALY, JR., planter, & TABITHA, his wife, to REBEKAH GRIMBALL, planter; both of St. Helena Parish, Granville Co.; for Ł 282 currency, 94 a., part of 1000 a. originally granted to CAPT. CHARLES ODINGSEL; bounding E on JOHN SEALY; S & W on JOSEPH SEALY; N on SAMUEL SEALY. Witnesses: SAMUEL SEALY, JOHN SEALY, JR., DAVID CHEYNEY. Before STEPHEN DRAYTON, J.P. Entered in Auditor's Book H-8, p. 36 on 14 May 1766 by RICHARD LAMBTON, Dep. Aud. Recorded 6 June 1766 by FENWICKE BULL, Register.

Book E-3, p. 644
3 June 1766
Mortgage

ARCHIBALD STOBO the younger, gentleman, of Toogoodoo, to THOMAS HEYWARD, planter, of James Island, for Ł 1300 currency, 790 a. in St. Pauls Parish, Colleton Co., bounding SW on ROBERT YOUNG; NE on JAMES STOBO; other sides on ROBERT YOUNG & JAMES STOBO; also 3 Negroes, 30 black cattle, some marked SS & others marked AS. Witnesses: JOHN GLEN, WILLIAM NEWHENNY. Before JAMES PARSONS, J.P. Recorded 9 June 1766 by FENWICKE BULL, Register.

Book E-3, p. 650
27 & 27 May 1766
L & R

JAMES JOHNSTON, planter, of Granville Co., to AUDEON ST. JOHN & Co., merchants, of Berkeley Co., for Ł 250 currency, 250 a. in Craven Co., on Santee River, opposite Kennerley's Neck, granted 17 Mar. 1760 by Gov. WILLIAM HENRY LYTTELTON to JAMES JOHNSTON, bounding on all sides on vacant swamp (see Secretary's Book 11, fol. 448). Witnesses: RANDOLPH THEUS, DANIEL SHIEDER. Before JOSEPH CURRY, J.P. Recorded 10 June 1766 by FENWICKE BULL, Register.

Book E-3, p. 655
12 July 1763
Feoffment

HENRY LAURENS, ESQ., to the Hon. DANIEL BLAKE; both of Charleston; for Ł 1000 currency, part of a lot near the Stadt House in Broad Street, bounding E 38 ft. 3 in. on DANIEL BLAKE; N 109 ft. 9 in. on SARAH HOLLYBUSH & the Quakers Meeting lot; W 69 ft. on RICHARD BERESFORD; S from W to E 30 ft. 3 in. then turning N 31 ft. then E 79 ft. 6 in.; being partly on MARY ELLIS & part on original lot. Witnesses: MILES BREWTON, JAMES GRAHAM, THOMAS LOTEN SMITH. Before FENWICKE

BULL, J.P. & P. Reg.   Recorded 10 June 1766

Book E-3, p. 658   CHARLES STROTHER, butcher, of Charleston, &
22 June 1765   MARY his wife, to JOHN FISHER, merchant, of
L & R   Orangeburgh Township, for Ł 225 currency, 300
                               a. on the shoals of NW fork of Long Creek, a
branch of Savannah River, formerly bounding on all sides on vacant land,
but since taken into the French township. Witnesses: JOHN GASSER, ALEX-
ANDER CHRISTIE. Before FENWICKE BULL, J.P. & P. Reg.

Book E-3, p. 662   WILLIAM STROTHER, planter, of St. Marks Parish
25 & 26 June 1765   & CATHERINE his wife, to JOHN FISHER, mer-
L & R   chant, of Orangeburgh Township, for Ł 200 cur-
                               rency, 100 a. on a place called the Mill Seat
or Shoals of Long Cane Creek, a branch of Savannah River, bounded on all
sides on vacant land, but since taken into the French township. Witnesses: SAMUEL BOONE, SARAH BOONE. Before JOHN DARGAN, J.P. Recorded 13
June 1766 by FENWICKE BULL, Register.

Book E-3, p. 665   BASIL JORDAN, of Christ Church Parish, Berke-
16 May 1766   ley Co., to GEORGE SMITH, JR., planter, of St.
Mortgage   Thomas Parish, for Ł 800 currency; 100 a.
                               called Wraggs Island, bounding W & N on Wando
River, S on a creek adjoining land of JAMES ALTER; also 4 Negro slaves,
his household goods, & furniture, tools, horses, cattle & hogs. Witnesses: JOHN LESSESNE, MARY ELIZABETH BURNHAM. Before FENWICKE BULL, J.P. &
P. Reg.

Book E-3, p. 668   JONATHAN DRAKE, planter, of St. Johns Parish,
23 May 1766   Berkeley Co., to WILLIAM COACHMAN, planter, of
Mortgage   St. Bartholomews Parish, Colleton Co., (DRAKE
                               & COACHMAN having given bonds to RALPH IZARD &
BENJAMIN WARING, of Berkeley Co.), for Ł 3125 currency, 3000 a. on which
DRAKE lives, known as Coaltaw in St. Johns Parish, bounding E on Cooper
River; W on Back River; N on SIR ALEXANDER NESBIT; S on the point of
Cooper & Back Rivers. Witnesses: MATHEW DRAKE, GEORGE (his mark) NICHOLS.
Before JOHN IOOR, J.P. Recorded 16 June 1766 by FENWICKE BULL, Register.
On 31 July 1766 COACHMAN declared mortgage satisfied. Witness: FENWICKE
BULL.

Book E-3, p. 671   RICHARD BERESFORD, ESQ., to WILLIAM PARKER,
28 & 29 May 1766   merchant, both of Charleston, for Ł 1200 cur-
L & R   rency, 300 a. in St. Thomas Parish, Berkeley
                               Co., being the S & W part of 400 a. granted by
the Lords Proprs. on 14 Apr. 1710 to SAMUEL BLUNDELL; bounding W on marsh
& a creek of Cooper River & on JOHN ASHBY; S on JOHN BERESFORD (formerly
RICHARD BERESFORD) & BENTLEY COOKE; NE on THOMAS PADGETT; E on part said
400 a. belonging to JOHN PRIMATE, a free Negro; N on WILLIAM PARKER
(formerly RICHARD CODNER) & JOHN PRIMATE. Witnesses: CHARLES FYFFE,
SAMUEL BACOT. Before FENWICKE BULL, J.P. & P. Register.

Book E-3, p. 680   ROBERT BRISBANE, merchant, of Charleston, sur-
11 June 1766   viving assignee of effects of JOHN MACKENZIE,
Release   of Charleston, to JONAH WOODBERRY, planter, of
                               Pee Dee, for Ł 350 currency, 300 a. Whereas
by L & R dated 26 & 27 Aug. 1744 JOHN GOODWEYNN, of Craven Co. sold ROD-
ERICK MORRISON, storekeeper, of Kingston, SC, 300 a. in Queensborough
Township, Craven Co., bounding SW on Pee Dee River; SE & NE on THOMAS
CHARNOCK; NW on MR. COOK; & whereas by L & R dated 20 & 21 Mar. 1748/9
MORRISON sold the land to JOHN MACKENZIE of Charleston; & whereas MAC-
KENZIE became indebted to JORDAN ROCHE, gentleman, of Charleston; & after
the death of JORDAN ROCHE his widow, REBECCA, administratrix, bought suit
against MACKENZIE, who surrendered his effects 16 May 1760 to REBECCA
ROCHE (since dead), ROBERT BRISBANE, & DANIEL CRAWFORD (since dead); now
BRISBANE sells the land to WOODBERRY. Witnesses: MARTIN CAMPBELL, JOHN
NEVIN. Before FENWICKE BULL, J.P. & Register.

Book E-3, p. 685   THOMAS PEARSE, ESQ., of Rochester, Co. of
12 & 13 Feb. 1752   Kent, sold to STEPHEN POPHAM, gentleman, of
L & R & Letter of   St. James Parish, Liberty of Westminster, Co.

Attorney of Middlesex, Great Britain, for Ł 200 British
sterling, & other considerations, a lot in
Charleston, SC, & all other real estate in SC formerly owned by 1 LAU-
HARNE, of Charleston, which LAUHARNE bequeathed to his wife REBECCA; who
after married & MR. DOVE & outlived him; & REBECCA dying intestate &
without children, the estate descended to her nephew & heir, THOMAS
PEARSE. Witnesses: WILLIAM STEVENS, THOMAS WOODS KNOLLIS. On 17 Feb.
1752 STEPHEN POPHAM appointed SARAH BLAKEWAY, widow, & DR. LIONEL CHALM-
ERS, physician, both of SC, his attorneys, to sell his property in SC.
Witnesses: RICHARD STABLES & THOMAS WOODS KNOLLIS, gentleman, of Parish
of St. John the Evangelist, City of Westminster. Certified before THOMAS
WINTERBOTTOM, mayor of London. Recorded in Charleston 24 June 1766 by
FENWICKE BULL, Register.

Book E-3, p. 694   STEPHEN POPHAM, gentleman, of Parish of St.
14 & 15 Nov. 1754   James, Liberty of Westminster, Co. of Middle-
L & R   sex, Great Britain, to RICHARD BERESFORD, ESQ.,
                      formerly of SC, now residing in City of London,
for Ł 250 British sterling, the LAUHORNE estate he purchased from THOMAS
PEARSE (p. 685, none of which is listed). Witnesses: JAMES BENTLEY, ED-
MOND MASON, WILLIAM LOGAN. Recorded 25 June 1766 by FENWICKE BULL, Register.

Book E-3, p. 702   ANN BOWMAN, widow, of Gosport, Parish of Alver-
25 & 26 Feb. 1766   stoke, Co. of Southampton, England, the natu-
L & R   ral mother & universal devisee named in will
                      of JOHN HARDING, gentleman, of Gosport, by her
former husband, JAMES HARDING, mariner (JAMES HARDING being eldest brother & heir of THOMAS HARDING, formerly of Gosport, now of Charleston, SC),
of 1st part; to THOMAS NIGHTINGALE, saddler, of Charleston, SC; for Ł 100
British; part of lot #18 in Charleston, bounding W 43 ft. on Union Street;
S on ROBERT RUTHERFORD'S house & lot; E on HOPKINS PRICE; N 136 ft. on
Queen Street. Whereas THOMAS HARDING devised all his real estate to his
wife & later on 12 Jan. 1744, bought a certain lot from RICHARD GRIMSTONE,
gentleman, for Ł 500 SC money, so that this lot descended to his nephew,
JOHN HARDING, eldest son of JAMES HARDING, who was eldest brother of
THOMAS HARDING; & whereas JOHN HARDING by will dated 19 June 1761 devised
to his mother, ANN BOWMAN, all the estate formerly belonging to THOMAS
HARDING, appointing her sole (will proved in Prerogative Court of Archbishop of Canterbury, England, on 9 Aug. 1763); now ANN sells above lot.
Witnesses: RICHARD BOLTON, JOHN GOULDING, & EDMOND JAMES, clerk to WIL-
LIAM BEDFORD, attorney-at-law, of Gosport Hants, England. BOLTON testi-
fied before FENWICKE BULL, J.P. & Register 25 June 1766.

Book E-3, p. 711   JAMES ROULAIN, to NEWMAN SWALLOW, merchant,
12 & 13 June 1766   for Ł 1250 currency, 500 a. on E side of W
L & R   branch of Forks on head of Saltcatcher River,
                      Colleton Co., bounding SW on unknown land; SE
on unknown land & on ZATHADIAH LADSON; NE on NEWMAN SWALLOW & vacant land;
NW on unknown land. Witnesses: WILLIAM ROPER, JR., FRANCIS GREENE. Before FENWICKE BULL, J.P. & P. Reg.

Book E-3, p. 716   WILLIAM LIVINGSTON, merchant, to ZACHARIAH
6 & 7 June 1734   VILLEPONTOUX, planter, both of Berkeley Co.,
L & R   for Ł 1000 currency, 500 a. in St. Johns,
                      bounding N on ZACHARIAH VILLEPONTOUX; W on
FRANCIS LEJOU; S on THOMAS SMITH; E on GABRIEL MARION; also 350 a., bound-
ing E on GABRIEL MARION; W on ZACHARIAH VILLEPONTOUX; S on THOMAS SMITH.
Witnesses: JOHN ELDERS, SAMUEL PRIOLEAU, JR., JONATHAN WESBURY. Before
CHARLES CANTEY, J.P. Recorded 30 June 1766 by FENWICKE BULL, Register.

Book E-3, p. 722   ZACHARIAH VILLEPONTOUX, SR., planter, to
30 Apr. 1763   ZACHARIAH VILLIPONTOUX, JR., planter, for
L & R   Ł 1000 currency, 2 tracts of 500 & 350 a. (see
                      p. 716). Witnesses: JONATHAN DRAKE, SARAH
VILLEPONTOUX. Before CHARLES CANTEY, J.P. Recorded 30 June 1766 by FEN-
WICKE BULL, Register.

Book E-3, p. 728   GRIFFITH JONES, cordwainer, of Craven Co., &
12 & 13 Aug. 1757   ELIZABETH his wife, to WILLIAM FOXWORTH,

L & R   saddler, of same Co., for Ł 40 currency, 50 a.
                             in Craven Co.; beginning at a sweet gum, S to
corner hickory, thence bounded on THOMAS JAMES line, then on GRIFFITH
JONES line to corner white oak, then to a pond, up the pond & back to be-
ginning; being part of a larger tract. Granted GRIFFITH JONES by the
Lords Proprs. Witnesses: THOMAS JAMES, WILLIAM HARRALSON. Before ABRA-
HAM BUCKHOLTS, J.P. Recorded 1 July 1766 by FENWICKE BULL, Register.

Book E-3, p. 730   ABRAHAM FREDERICK DE ROCHE, cordwainer, of St.
21 June 1766   Peters Parish, Granville Co., to DAVID GIROUD,
Sale   planter, of Purysburgh, for Ł 42 currency, lot
                             #10, 1 a., in Purysburgh, bounding N on lot #9;
S on a street; E on lot #12; W on the Bay & River. Witnesses: ADRIAN
MAYER, CONRAD RYSELE (RYSSEL). Before JOHN LEWIS BOURQUIN, J.P. Record-
ed 1 July 1766 by FENWICKE BULL, Register.

Book E-3, p. 735   JOHN MORF, planter, of Saxegotha Township,
10 & 11 Mar. 1763   Berkeley Co., to MICHAEL MOULBARE, planter,
L & R   for Ł 50 currency, 250 a. (half of 500 a.) in
                             Saxegotha Township, on S side Broad River,
bounding SE on other half; other sides on vacant land; being 1/2 of 500 a.
granted 24 Apr. 1752 by Gov. JAMES GLEN to HANS JACOB MORF, bounding SE
on HARMAN GEIGER; other sides on vacant land. HANS JACOB MORF died intestate & his eldest son JOHN, inherited. Witnesses: HENRY GALLMAN, JOHN
CONRAD GEIGER. Before JOHN HAMELTON, J.P. Recorded 2 July 1766 by FEN-
WICKE BULL, Register.

Book E-3, p. 741   JOHN MORF, planter, of Saxegotha Township,
9 & 10 Apr. 1764   Berkeley Co., & SUSANNAH his wife, to JOHN
L & R   GOTTFREY, wheelwright, for Ł 60 currency, 250
                             a., half of 500 a. in Saxegotha Township grant-
ed by Gov. JAMES GLEN on 24 Apr. 1752 to HANS JACOB MORF; who died intestate; & his eldest son JOHN inherited; the 250 a. bounding NE on Broad
River; S on HARMAN GEIGER; NE on other part sold to MICHAEL MAULBARE
(p. 735); other sides on vacant land. Witnesses: FITE (his mark) RISING-
ER, JOHN CONRAD GEIGER. Before JOHN PEARSON, J.P. Recorded 2 July 1766
by FENWICKE BULL, Register.

Book E-3, p. 747   BENJAMIN CUMING, planter, of Craven Co., &
18 & 19 June 1766   JUDITH his wife, to BENJAMIN SIMONS, JR.,
L & R   planter, of St. Thomas Parish, Berkeley Co.,
                             for Ł 2000 currency, 3 adjoining tracts; 170,
100, & 121 a.; in St. Thomas Parish, total 391 a.; bounding NW on E
branch of T of Cooper River; SW & NE on BENJAMIN SIMONS, father of said
BENJAMIN; SE on BENJAMIN SIMONS, JR.; which 3 tracts formerly belonged to
JOHN CUMING, father of BENJAMIN CUMING, his only son & heir. Witnesses:
ROBERT WILLIAMS, JR., WILLIAM STOUTENBURGH. Before FENWICKE BULL, J.P. &
Register.

Book E-3, p. 754   JOHN CART, gentleman, to FRANCIS KINLOCK, ESQ.,
19 & 20 Feb. 1766   both of Charleston, for Ł 1500 currency, the N
L & R   part of lots #66, 67, & 217, in Charleston,
                             bounding S 44 ft. on other part said lots; W
186 ft. on part sold by JOHN CART to FRANCIS KINLOCK; N on JUDITH WRAGG;
E on JUDITH WRAGG, MR. MATHEWS, THOMAS SMITH, MRS. WITHERS, MR. PORCHER,
& JOHN REMINGTON; the 3 lots originally fronting 44 ft. on Queen Street &
372 ft. deep. Witnesses: ISAAC LESESNE, PETER MANIGAULT, RUTH RIVERS.
Before JAMES SKIRVING, J.P. Recorded 3 July 1766 by FENWICKE BULL, Register.

Book E-3, p. 759   BRYAN (his mark) TOLAND, planter, of Craven
30 & 31 Aug. 1763   Co., & JANE his wife, to THOMAS DOUGLASS, gen-
L & R   tleman, of Pennsylvania, for Ł 250 currency,
                             150 a. in Craven Co., on S side Wateree River,
bounding SW on BRYAN TOLAND; NE on BROWN'S land; other sides on vacant
land; granted 7 May 1762 by Gov. THOMAS BOONE to BRYAN TOLAND. Witnesses: JOSEPH KERSHAW, JOHN ALEXANDER, JOHN TOLAND. Before JOHN NEWMAN
OGLETHORPE, J.P. Entered in Auditor's Book, H-8, p. 60, on 5 July 1766
by RICHARD LAMBTON, Dep. Aud. Recorded 7 July 1766 by FENWICKE BULL,
Register.

E-3, p. 766 BRYAN (his mark) TOLAND, planter, of Craven
3 & 4 Apr. 1754 Co., & JANE (her mark) his wife, to THOMAS
L & R DOUGLASS, merchant, of Fredericksburg Township, for £ 350 currency, 300 a. in Craven Co.,
on S side Wateree River; bounding SE on JAMES MICHIE; other sides on vacant land; granted 6 Mar. 1750 by Gov. JAMES GLEN to BRYAN TOLAND. Witnesses: GEORGE SENIOR, JAMES ADAMSON. Before SAMUEL WYLY, J.P. Entered
in Auditor's Book, H-8, p. 60, on 5 July 1766 by RICHARD LAMBTON, Dep.
Aud. Recorded 8 July 1766 by FENWICKE BULL, Register.

Book E-3, p. 773 DANIEL RAVENEL, planter, of St. Johns Parish,
16 & 17 June 1766 & CHARLOTTE his wife, 1 of the daughters of
L & R PAUL MAZYCK, of Charleston; to BENJAMIN
MAZYCK, ESQ., of Charleston, for £ 1000 SC
money, half of lot #31 in Charleston, bounding S 53 ft. on Broad Street;
N on JAMES DUGUE; E on PETER DE ST. JULIEN; W on other half formerly belonging to EDWARD RAWLINS; which lot #31 PAUL MAZYCK had purchased from
ISAAC MAZYCK, of Charleston; also 2 other pieces of land, parts of lots
7 & 15; 1 on W end of Broad Street, measuring 50 x 228 ft.; the other on
Queen Street, 50 x 228; according to deed of partition dated 18 Dec. 1742
amongst ISAAC MAZYCK, PAUL MAZYCK, BENJAMIN MAZYCK, STEPHEN MAZYCK, &
others. Whereas PAUL MAZYCK by will dated 12 Dec. 1746 bequeathed to his
daughter CHARLOTTE the house & lot where he lived, also lots 7 & 15; now
she & her husband sell the 3 lots. Witnesses: WILLIAM MAZYCK, MATHIAS
SMITH, JR. Before WILLIAM BURROWS, J.P. Recorded 9 July 1766 by FEN-
WICKE BULL, Register.

Book E-3, p. 780 JOHN DOUGLASS, of the Wateree, to WILLIAM
7 & 8 Mar. 1766 MITCHELL, planter, for £ 26:10:0 currency, 200
L & R a. on Camp Creek, a branch of Wateree River,
bounding on all sides on vacant land; as
granted 9 Jan. 1755 by Gov. JAMES GLEN to JOHN DOUGLASS. Witnesses:
ROBERT RAMSAY, GEORGE DOUGLASS, PATRICK MCMOERY (MCMOCREY). Before JAMES
MCKOWN, J.P. Recorded 9 July 1766 by FENWICKE BULL, Register.

Book E-3, p. 785 WILLIAM MITCHELL, laborer, of St. Marks Parish,
5 & 6 Apr. 1762 to THOMAS WADE, storekeeper, for £ 225 curren-
L & R cy, 200 a. on both sides of Camp Creek, in St.
Marks Parish, bounding on all sides on vacant
land; granted 9 Jan. 1755 by Gov. JAMES GLEN to JOHN DOUGLASS. Witnesses: THOMAS CHICKEN, FREDERICK KIMBALL. Before THOMAS SIMPSON, J.P. Recorded 10 July by FENWICKE BULL, Register.

Book E-3, p. 790 JOHN PICKENS, ESQ., of St. Marks Parish, to
20 & 21 Feb. 1764 THOMAS WADE, for £ 400 currency, 350 a. on
L & R both sides of Lynches Creek, in St. Marks Parish, bounding on all sides on vacant land;
granted by Lt. Gov. WILLIAM BULL on 5 Dec. 1761 to PICKENS. Witnesses:
JAMES CARR, EDWARD BLACK. Before JAMES SIMPSON, J.P. Recorded 10 July
1766 by FENWICKE BULL, Register.

DEEDS BOOK "F-3"
JULY 10, 1766 - MARCH 12, 1767

Book F-3, p. 1 JOHN MCKEE, farmer, son & heir of WILLIAM MC-
17 & 18 May 1764 KEE, of Macklinburg Co., NC, to THOMAS WADE,
L & R ESQ., of St. Marks Parish, SC, for £ 100 currency, 100 a. on Hanging Rock Creek, St. Marks
Parish, granted 2 Jan. 1754 by Gov. JAMES GLEN to WILLIAM MCKEE. Witnesses: GLASS CASTON, HUMPHREY BARNET. Before JAMES SIMPSON, J.P., of
Craven Co. Recorded 10 July 1766 by FENWICKE BULL, Register.

Book F-3, p. 6 FREDERICK FORD, shopkeeper, of St. Marks Par-
13 & 14 May 1765 ish, SC, to THOMAS WADE, merchant, for £ 500
L & R currency, 100 a. in St. Marks Parish, on Cat-
awba River, granted 17 Apr. 1764 by Gov. THOM-
AS BOONE to FREDERICK FORD; bounding on all sides on vacant land. Witnesses: GLASS CASTON, BENJAMIN FORD. Before JAMES SIMPSON, J.P., of

Craven Co. Recorded 11 July 1766 by FENWICKE BULL, Register.

Book F-3, p. 11   SARAH YOUNG leases to BEDIENCE YOUNG, SR., for
4 Oct. 1755   20 years from date, 400 a.; 200 a. lying out-
Agreement & Assignment side the lake, with the plantation & houses
                        where BEDIENCE now lives; the other 200 a. ad-
joining the river & JOHN LIDE'S land, & the lower line of the land on
which SARAH now lives. Witnesses: WILLIAM RHODES, EDWARD HOMES, FRANCIS
(his mark) WILLIAMSON. Before ALEXANDER MACKINTOSH, J.P., of Craven Co.
On 13 Dec. 1763 WILLIAM RHODES, executor of will of BEDIENCE YOUNG, for
Ƚ 50 sterling, assigns said Articles of Agreement to RICHARD FARR. Witnesses: JOHN MILTON, THOMAS GAMBLE, WILLIAM FARR. Before THOMAS WADE,
J.P. Recorded 14 July 1766 by FENWICKE BULL, Register.

Book F-3, p. 13   EDWARD HOMES, & REBECCA his wife, to JAMES PIT-
21 June 1760   MAN, for Ƚ 200 currency, 100 a., part of a
Feoffment   tract granted FRANCIS YOUNG, on which HOMES
                        now lives; which was given EDWARD HOMES by
ISAM YOUNG. Witnesses: EDWARD YOUNG, ETHELRED PITMAN. Before WILLIAM
LORD, J.P. Recorded 15 July 1766 by FENWICKE BULL, Register.

Book F-3, p. 15   JAMES (his mark) PITMAN, planter, of Anson
___ July 1765   Co., NC, to JONATHAN WILLIAMS, planter, of
Feoffment   Craven Co., for Ƚ 300 SC money, 100 a. part of
                        a tract granted FRANCIS YOUNG, on which JONA-
THAN WILLIAMS now lives (p. 13). Witnesses: SAMUEL PITMAN, JAMES SMITH.
Before THOMAS WADE, J.P. of Craven Co. Recorded 16 July 1766 by FENWICKE
BULL, Register.

Book F-3, p. 17   JONATHAN (his mark) WILLIAMS, planter, & MARY
___ Aug. 1765   (her mark) WILLIAMS, to RICHARD FARR, for
Feoffment   Ƚ _____ British, 100 a., part of a tract
                        granted FRANCIS YOUNG (p. 15), & given by IS-
HAM YOUNG to EDWARD HOMES; on which JONATHAN WILLIAMS now lives. Witness-
es: THOMAS WADE, WILLIAM LITTLE. Before THOMAS WADE, J.P. Recorded 16
July 1766 by FENWICKE BULL, Register.

Book F-3, p. 19   BENJAMIN MAZYCK, of Charleston, to DANIEL RAV-
17 & 18 July 1766   ENEL, planter, of St. Johns Parish, for Ƚ 1000
L & R   currency, half of lot #31 in Charleston,
                        bounding N on JAMES DUGUE; S 53 ft. on Broad
Street; E on PETER DE ST. JULIEN; W on other half belonging to EDWARD
RAWLINGS; which lot #31 was purchased by PAUL MAZYCK from ISAAC MAZYCK;
also lots 7 & 15; both 50 x 228 ft.; 1 at W end of Broad Street; the
other on Queen Street; see plat of 2 lots attached to deed of partition
dated 18 Dec. 1742 between ISAAC MAZYCK, PAUL MAZYCK, BENJAMIN MAZYCK,
STEPHEN MAZYCK, & others. Witnesses: WILLIAM BURROWS, RICHARD CHITTCH.
Before JACOB MOTTE, J.P. Recorded 22 July 1766 by FENWICKE BULL, Register.

Book F-3, p. 26   PAUL DOUXSAINT, gentleman, of Charleston, &
14 & 15 July 1766   MARGARET his wife, daughter of WILLIAM HEN-
L & R   DRICK, planter, of Christ Church Parish, &
                        sister & heiress of WILLIAM HENDRICK the young-
er, of same Parish, in trust to EDWARD JERMAN, planter, of Santee; 2
brick tenements on W side Church Street, bounding N on JOHN MILNER; S on
JOHN HODSDEN; W on DANIEL BADGER; also half an a., part of a lot on S
side Queen Street, extending along N side Dupreys Alley; bounding W on
JOHN IZARD; E on WILLIAM HAWKES; the part on Queen having 1 small brick
tenement & 1 wooden tenement; the other part on Dupreys Alley having 2
brick tenements & 1 wooden tenement. Whereas WILLIAM HENDRICK, the father, owned considerable real estate in SC, & by will dated 7 Nov. 1749
ordered his executors to complete his 2 brick tenements fronting New
Church Street; also all the back buildings & necessary appurtenances;
which buildings he then gave to his wife MARY so long as she remained his
widow, & in case of her re-marriage then equally to WILLIAM, JR., & MAR-
GARET; & devised his unsold part of a lot, which he had purchased from
THOMAS SACHEVERELL, on S side Queen Street; to WILLIAM, JR., & MARGARET,
equally; & appointed ALEXANDER PERONNEAU, JOSEPH VANDERHORST, DANIEL LE-
GARÉ, ARNOLDUS VANDERHORST, & WILLIAM VANDERHORST, his executors; &

313

whereas DANIEL LEGARÉ & ARNOLDUS VANDERHORST, proved the will & completed the buildings on New Church Street; & whereas MARY, the widow, remarried, & her interest ceased; & whereas no division of the property has been made; & whereas WILLIAM HENDRICK, JR., died & his sister, MARGARET, inherited the entire property; now they convey the property to JERMAN, in trust for PAUL & MARGARET DOUXSAINT, with provisoes. Witnesses: SAMUEL MCGILL, ANDRES DAVID, JANE DOUXSAINT. Before WILLIAM BURROWS, J.P. Recorded 24 July 1766 by FENWICKE BULL, Register.

Book F-3, p. 36
3 Nov. 1704
Conveyance

THOMAS CAREY, ESQ., of Berkeley Co., to JOHN HOLLYBUSH, for Ł 40 currency, lot #312, being part of lot #97 known as JOHN ARCHDALE'S Square; bounding E on a street leading from the Market Place to the New Church; S on JOSEPH BLAKE; N on THOMAS CARY; which lot #312 was granted by WILLIAM, Earl of Craven, Palatine, by JOHN ARCHDALE trustee on 28 Oct. 1696 to THOMAS CARY. Witnesses: RICHARD BERESFORD, THOMAS HEPWORTH.

Book F-3, p. 40
27 & 28 June 1766
L & R

PETER BOUNETHEAU, to GABRIEL MANIGAULT, merchant, of Charleston, for Ł 5000 currency, 500 a. in Craven Co., bounding NE on Black River; SE on ALEXANDER SKENE; S W & NW on vacant land. Witnesses: WILLIAM BANBURY, ELIZABETH HASELL. Before FENWICKE BULL, J.P. & P. Register.

Book F-3, p. 46
21 June 1728
Sale

PETER PERRY, planter, of Berkeley Co., & ELIZABETH PERRY, to BENJAMIN PERRY, planter, for Ł 120 currency, 100 a. in Colleton Co., laid out in a square, bounding NW on JOHN RAVEN; NNW on ROBERT LADSON; N on WILLIAM CATTELL; E on PETER PERRY. Witnesses: JACOB LADSON, JOHN (his mark) HARRIS. Proved 7 Apr. 1733 before WILLIAM CATTELL, J.P. Recorded 28 July by FENWICKE BULL, Register.

Book F-3, p. 48
28 May 1766
Release

BENJAMIN PERRY, planter, of St. Pauls Parish, son & heir of BENJAMIN PERRY; & FRANCES his wife; to JAMES PARSONS of Charleston; for Ł 1500 currency, 100 a. in St. Pauls Parish, bounding NW on SAMUEL WAINWRIGHT (formerly JOHN RAVEN); NNW on ROBERT LADSON; N on WILLIAM CATTELL; E on SAMUEL WAINWRIGHT (formerly PETER PERRY). Witnesses: ANTHONY DUYER, JOHN GLEN, EDWARD PERRY, SAMUEL ELLIOTT. Before FENWICKE BULL, J.P. & P. Register.

Book F-3, p. 52
1 Apr. 1766
Release

BENJAMIN RATCLIFFE, purser of H.M. Sloop Speedwell, to DERBY PENDERGRASS, merchant, of Charleston, for Ł 200 currency, 500 a. on Four Hole Swamp & Wilkinsons Swamp, in Berkeley Co., bounding NE on DANIEL DEAN; other sides on vacant land; as granted 4 July 1759 to WILLIAM MURRAY; who by L & R dated 9 & 10 July 1764 sold to BENJAMIN RATCLIFFE. Witnesses: JAMES PARSONS, JOHN GLEN. Before JOHN TROUP, J.P. Recorded 1 Aug. 1766 by FENWICKE BULL, Register.

Book F-3, p. 55
1 & 2 Aug. 1766
L & R & Bond

DANIEL LEGARÉ, JR., merchant, & ELIZABETH his wife, to THOMAS HUTCHINSON, joiner, both of Charleston, for Ł 300 currency, the N part of the W half of lot #228 in Charleston, bounding S 60 ft. on DANIEL LEGARÉ; W 30 ft. on THOMAS HUTCHINSON; N 60 ft. on RICHARD LAMBTON; E 30 ft. on part lot #228 belonging to JOHN WATSON. LEGARÉ gives bond of performance. Witnesses: JOHN PACKROW, FREDERICK SCHRADE. Before FENWICKE BULL, J.P. & P. Register.

Book F-3, p. 63
10 & 11 Oct. 1764
L & R

JOHN SEALY, SR., planter, & SUSANNAH his wife, to REBEKAH GRIMBALL, both of St. Helena Parish, Granville Co., for Ł 275 currency, 100 a., part of 1000 a. granted CAPT. CHARLES ODINGSELLS; bounding E on JOHN SEALY, SR.; W on REBEKAH GRIMBALL; N on WILLIAM SEALY, JR.; S on a branch of Port Royal River. Witnesses: SAMUEL SEALY, JOHN SEALY, JR., ELIZABETH DAWSON, HANNAH BARTON. Before STEPHEN DRAYTON, J.P. Entered in Auditor's Book H-8, p. 46, on 9 June 1766 by RICHARD LAMBTON, Dep. Aud. Recorded 8 Aug. 1766 by FENWICKE BULL, Register.

Book F-3, p. 69   ALEXANDER SHWAB, wheelwright, of St. Bartholo-
25 & 26 Oct. 1764   mews Parish, Colleton Co., to LEWIS STAPF, car-
L & R   penter, of St. Pauls Parish, Colleton Co., for
                         ₺ 450 currency, 8 lots in the village of Jack-
sonborough, Nos. 74, 75, 76, 77, 86, 87, 88, & 89, containing 100 ft.
front on Market Street, 218 ft. deep. Witnesses: JOHN HICKEL, JACOB
WIRTH. Before FENWICKE BULL, J.P. & P. Register. Recorded 8 Aug. 1766.

Book F-3, p. 74   JOHN BULLINS, planter, 1 of the sons & sole
16 & 17 Sept. 1762   executor of will of JOHN BULLINE the elder,
L & R   planter; & THOMAS BULLINE, planter, eldest son
                         & heir of THOMAS BULLINE, planter; all of
Berkeley Co.; of 1st part; to PAUL SMYSER, inn keeper, of Charleston, as
highest bidder, for ₺ 900 currency, 350 a. in several adjoining tracts
which JOHN BULLINE, SR., had owned for 15 years or more; in St. James
Goose Creek, bounding SW on the high road & on 1 BARKER; W on JOHN GLAZE;
N on 1 DE LA PLAIN; NE on the high road & on MATHEW FULMER; E on estate
of JOHN BULLINE, SR.; SE on THOMAS BULLINE, JR.; which 350 a. JOHN BUL-
LINE, SR., by will dated 9 Dec. 1761 ordered sold; & whereas some doubts
have arisin in regard to the validity of the title of JOHN BULLINE, SR.,
to the land because the conveyances from THOMAS BULLINE (former owner) to
JOHN BULLINE, SR., are missing; now JOHN BULLINE, JR., with the consent
of THOMAS BULLINE, JR., conveys the land to SMYSER. Witnesses: NATHANIEL
BRADWELL, JOHN SHEPARD, ELIZABETH BRADWELL. Before JOHN TROUP, J.P. Recorded 11 Aug. 1766 by FENWICKE BULL, Register.

Book F-3, p. 84   ROGER PINCKNEY, P.M., to PAUL SMYSER, tavern
8 Aug. 1765   keeper, of Charleston, for ₺ 500 currency, 272
Sale   a. in Craven Co., in Santee Parish, bounding S
                         on PAUL MAZYCK; N on GEORGE SIMMONS; E on Wam-
baw Creek. Whereas PAUL BRUNEAU, planter, of Craven Co., owned said land,
part of 900 a. given him by DAVID PEYRE; & whereas BRUNEAU owed ISAAC
MAZYCK, of Charleston, ₺ 980 currency, & interest for the use of the
heirs of JAMES DE ST. JULIEN; & whereas ISAAC MAZYCK obtained a judgment,
with costs, against ANN BRUNEAU, widow & administratrix of estate of PAUL
BRUNEAU, & a writ of fieri facias was issued, commanding the P.M. to obtain the amount from said estate; now ROGER PINCKNEY sells the 272 a. at
auction to SMYSER. Witnesses: JOHN MARTIN, HOPSON PINCKNEY. Before FEN-
WICKE BULL, J.P. & P. Register.

Book F-3, p. 88   Whereas by indenture dated 1 Feb. 1759 PETER
31 Oct. 1765   TAYLOR, of St. James Goose Creek, surviving
Assignment   executor of will of WILLIAM SMITH, planter, of
                        St. Philips Parish, Charleston, Berkeley Co.,
of 1st part; JOHN COOPER, merchant, of Charleston, & MARY his wife, sole
trader, of 2nd part; & JAMES PARSONS, ESQ., & WILLIAM GLEN, merchant, of
Charleston, of 3rd part; the said PETER TAYLOR, for ₺ 1600 currency (part
of the separate estate of MARY COOPER & paid by her with her husband's
consent) & for 10 shillings paid by PARSONS & GLEN, at the direction of
MARY COOPER, conveyed to PARSONS & GLEN, trustees, part of lot #36 on E
side of the street from White Point to St. Philips Church (called Church
Street), lately belonging to WILLIAM SMITH, bounding W 50 ft. on Church
Street; N 116 ft. on ANN PEACOCK (formerly WILLIAM YEOMANS); E on part
same lot belonging to MARY COOPER (formerly EDMUND ATKINS) & THOMAS
YOUNG; S on part belonging to SARAH STOUTENBOROUGH; now MARY COOPER au-
thorizes said trustees to sell said lot at auction to satisfy first any
debts incurred by GLEN as administrator or because he gave bond to obtain MARY COOPER a passport or ticket to leave SC; or to satisfy any action brought against her; 2nd, to pay order for ₺ 350 drawn by JOHN SMITH
on MARY in favor of BENJAMIN SMITH; 3rd, to pay order for ₺ 250 drawn by
JOHN SMITH on MARY COOPER, in favor of MESSRS. MAZYCK & MOULTRIE; 4th, to
pay ₺ 150 sterling & interest due PAUL DOUXSAINT; 5th, to pay ₺ 600 sterling owing by MARY to RICHARD & THOMAS SHUBRICK; lastly, the remainder
towards paying JOHN COOPER'S creditors; MARY also transfers all the Negro
slaves, furniture & implements as listed. Witnesses: WILLIAM GLEN, JR.,
THOMAS HEYWARD, JR., RICHARD MASON. List of MARY COOPER'S debtors: RICH-
ARD EATON, THOMAS BURTON, ESQ., "BETTY" at MR. SLADE'S, ALEXANDER SEAMAN,
MRS. TOBIAS, KATHARINE ROBERTSON (at ?), MRS. DEAS, RICHARD NICHOLSON,
JOSEPH PERRY, ELISHA BUTLER, MRS. ASH, JAMES MACKAY, "Adventures to Ber-
mudas ₺ 1218.14.3", MR. HANCOCK, glover; MRS. PROCTER, tailor: FRANCIS

YOUNG, MISS SAUNDERS, THOMAS ROSE, cooper; CAPT. RAYMOND DEMERE, THOMAS
STONE (London), MRS. MORTIMORE, MRS. ORAM, ADAM MCDANIELS, MRS. MCKLEWAIN,
PETER TIMOTHY; ADAM SKEKEL, SAMUEL DICKINSON, GEORGE DICKINSON, NATHANIEL
BARNWELL, DANIEL DWIGHT, MR. BARNET (Santee), MRS. SARAH LLOYD, CAPT.
JOHN LLOYD, WILLIAM BONNAR, MR. PLATT, MRS. CORBIN, MRS. FULLER, CAPT.
CAMPBELL, CAPT. SEATON. Proved before WILLIAM MASON, J.P. Recorded 12
Aug. 1766 by FENWICKE BULL, Register.

Book F-3, p. 94   JOHN TROUP, attorney-at-law, of Charleston, &
22 & 23 July 1766   FRANCES CHARLOTTA his wife, to MATHEW NEILSON,
L & R   planter, of Craven Co., for Ł 5 currency, 150
                         a. in St. Marks Parish, Craven Co., in Santee
River swamp, bounding N on ELIZABETH WILLIAMS & vacant land; E on JAMES
NORVILLE; S on JAMES NORVILLE & vacant land; W on JOHN SMITH; granted
JOHN TROUP on 31 Oct. 1765 by Lt. Gov. WILLIAM BULL. Witnesses: WILLIAM
LOOCOCK, JONATHAN SARRAZIN. Before FENWICKE BULL, J.P. & P. Register.

Book F-3, p. 100   RICHARD BERESFORD, of Parish of St. Thomas &
20 Apr. 1762   St. Dennis, to FREDERICK KAUFFMAN (COFFMAN) of
Lease   Charleston, for 19 years, at Ł 15 currency per
                         annum, part of a lot in Charleston bounding
24-1/2 ft. on Beresford St.; E on a lot leased to THOMAS HOW; W on RICH-
ARD BERESFORD; KAUFFMAN agrees to build, within 2 years, a dwelling house
14 x 20 ft. & to fence in the property. Witnesses: FREDERICK HOFF, JACOB
(his mark) BRIKEL. Before FENWICKE BULL, J.P. & P. Register. Recorded
13 Aug. 1766.

Book F-3, p. 102   THOMAS JONES, merchant, of Charleston, to
4 & 5 Aug. 1766   MICHAEL GEIGER & JACOB GEIGER, planters, of
L & R   Colleton Co., as tenants in common, for Ł 2500
                         currency, 1000 a. in Colleton Co., granted by
the Lords Proprs. on 8 July 1696 to JOHN EDWARDS; bounding W & S on Chehaw River; E on Ashepoo River; N on vacant land; according to plat certified 3 July 1696 by JOHN BERESFORD, Sur. Gen. Witnesses: JOSIAH SMITH,
JR., THOMAS GUERIN. Before JACOB MOTTE, J.P. Entered in Auditor's Book
14 (H?) 8, p. 80, on 5 Aug. 1766 by RICHARD LAMBTON, Dep. Aud. Recorded
14 Aug. 1766 by FENWICKE BULL, Register.

Book F-3, p. 110   At request of PLOWDEN WESTON, administrator of
8 Aug. 1766   estate of JOHN HOLLYBURH & SARAH HOLLYBUSH,
Arbitration   deceased JOSEPH VERREE, THOMAS YOUNG & DANIEL
                         CANNON, appraised a lot on W side of Meeting
Street, Charleston, bounding S on DANIEL BLAKE, N on DOUGHTY & DANIEL
CANNON; W on Quakers Meeting Ground; the lot being divided into 2 equal
parts; & valued the S part measuring 50 ft. on Meeting Street; 225-1/2 ft.
deep; bounding S on DANIEL BLAKE, at Ł 4300 SC money; & the N part,
bounding 50 ft. in front, 229-1/2 deep, 49 ft. at back, N on DOUGHTY &
DANIEL CANNON, at Ł 4200 SC money; the 2 divisions being drawn for, &
ELIZABETH HOLLYBUSH, taking first chance, drew the N part; leaving S part
to PLOWDEN WESTON; he to pay ELIZABETH Ł 50 difference. Witness: THOMAS
LADSON. Note: 20 in. distance from wall of MR. BLAKE'S house so settled
& agreed by BLAKE & WESTON this day. On 26 July 1766 WOOD FURMAN, Dep.
Sur., at request of PLOWDEN WESTON, resurveyed a lot #312, in Charleston
granted by JOHN ARCHDALE on 28 Oct. 1696 to THOMAS CARY, & divided the
lot into 2 equal parts, according to plat. Proved before FENWICKE BULL,
J.P. & P. Register.

Book F-3, p. 112   PETER STONE, planter, of St. Andrews Parish,
18 July 1766   to WILLIAM WALTER, ESQ., of Goose Creek, for
Mortgage   Ł 1422:10:0 currency, 194-1/2 a., part of
                         202-1/2 a. on N side of Ashley River in Berke-
ley Co., bounding SE on RALPH IZARD; NW on Landgrave THOMAS SMITH (form-
erly JOSEPH OLDY); also 90 a., part of 250 a., bounding NE on RALPH IZARD;
SW on above tract; NW on Landgrave THOMAS SMITH; SE on RALPH IZARD. Wit-
Witnesses: THOMAS CORBETT, RICHARD CHITTCH. Before WILLIAM BURROWS, J.P.
Recorded 18 Aug. 1766 by FENWICKE BULL, Register.

Book F-3, p. 116   BENJAMIN WALLS, planter, & ANN his wife, to
22 & 23 July 1766   EDWARD DAVIS (DAVIES), merchant, for Ł 2500
L & R   currency, 4-1/4 a. in Ansonborough, called

Bowling Green, now occupied by DAVIS bounding W on the broad road; E on
SC Society land; S on heirs of SARAH TROTT (occupied by THOMAS LYNCH); N
on EDWARD SMITH; which lot formerly belonged to GEORGE ANSON, who conveyed to JOHN WATSON, father of WILLIAM WATSON, late husband of ANN WALLS;
also a lot on W side Union Street, now occupied by JAMES FELLOWES, barber; bounding W on LIONEL CHALMERS; S on EDWARD DEMPSEY; N on EDWARD
DAVIS; which lot formerly belonged to said JOHN WATSON. Witnesses: ED-
WARD CARLTON, GEORGE MILLIKIN, WILLIAM HARVEY, THOMAS MIDDLETON, JOHN
CHAPMAN. Before FENWICKE BULL, J.P. & P. Register.

Book F-3, p. 122   JOSEPH VANALL, tailor, son & heir of MATHEW
13 Aug. 1766   VANALL, carpenter; to PETER BOCQUET, JR., gen-
Assignment   tleman; all of Charleston; for Ł 600 currency,
                         part of lot #92 in Charleston, bounding W 40
ft. on King Street; E on DANIEL BOURGETT; N on THOMAS LEGARE (formerly
EDWARD SCULL); S on OTHNIEL BEALE (formerly JAMES THOMPSON). Whereas on
1 Oct. 1742 the Rev. MR. FRANCIS GUICHARD, pastor of the French Church &
GABRIEL MANIGAULT, ISAAC MAZYCK, PAUL MAZYCK, JACOB MARTIN, JOHN NEUF-
VILLE, BENJAMIN D'HARRIETTE, & GIDEON FAUCHERAUD, leased to MATHEW VANALL,
(now deceased) said lot, for 50 years, for Ł 4:5:0 sterling per annum;
now JOSEPH VANALL assigns the lease to BOCQUET for the remainder of the
term. Witnesses: GEORGE SANDEMAN, JOHN TROUP. Before FENWICKE BULL, J.P.
& P. Register.

Book F-3, p. 127   JOHN IZARD, ESQ., & ISABELLA his wife, to DR.
30 & 31 July 1766   ALEXANDER FOTHERINGHAM, both of Charleston,
L & R   for Ł 1860 currency, part of lot #124 bounding
                         W 30 ft. 5 in. on Meeting Street; S 106 ft. on
JOHN IZARD; N on AARON LOOCOCK (formerly JOHN IZARD); E on JOHN IZARD.
Witnesses: ISAAC HUGER, JAMES HUME. Before CHARLES WOODMASON, J.P. Re-
corded 21 Aug. 1766 by FENWICKE BULL, Register.

Book F-3, p. 133   JOHN HAMILTON, formerly of Parish of St.
27 & 28 Nov. 1755   George, Hanover Square, Co. of Middlesex, now
L & R   of Charleston, SC, to JOSEPH SALVADOR, mer-
                         chant, of Lime Street, London, for Ł 2000
British sterling, 1000,000 a., being half of 200,000 a. granted WILLIAM
LIVINGSTONE & his associates, near Ninety Six, bounding NE on Saludie
River; SE on the other half belonging to JOHN HAMILTON; other sides on
vacant land. Whereas King GEORGE II on 27 June 1752 granted WILLIAM
LIVINGSTONE & his associates 50,000 a., part of 200,000 a. laid out by 4
grants to said LIVINGSTONE, et al; at a place called Ninety Six, in SC,
(as by grant #3); & whereas the King on same date granted LIVINGSTONE &
others another 50,000 a., part of said 200,000 a., above Ninety Six; (as
by grant #4); & whereas LIVINGSTONE by L & R dated 12 & 13 June 1753 sold
JOHN HAMILTON the 200,000 a., including said 2 tracts of 50,000 a. each
(grants 3 & 4); now HAMILTON sells the 2 tracts of 50,000 a. each to
SALVADOR. Witnesses: JAMES GRINDLAY, GEORGE JACKSON. Proved by OLIVER
NOYES before FENWICKE BULL, J.P. & P. Register. Recorded 23 Aug. 1766.

Book F-3, p. 143   PETER TAYLOR, ESQ., of St. James Goose Creek
31 Jan. & 1 Feb. 1759   Parish, SC, acting executor of will of WILLIAM
L & R in Trust   SMITH, planter, of St. Philips Parish, Charles-
                         ton, who was the eldest son of WILLIAM SMITH,
merchant, of Charleston, of 1st part; JOHN COOPER, merchant, of Charleston, & MARY his wife, sole trader, of 2nd part; JAMES PARSONS, ESQ., &
WILLIAM GLEN, merchant, of 3rd part. Whereas WILLIAM SMITH the elder
owned part of lot #36 with a house thereon, on E side of the street leading from White Point to St. Philips Church; & by will dated 30 Aug. 1710
bequeated his house, then occupied by WILLIAM SANDERS, ESQ., with the
part of the lot as fenced in for a garden for said SANDERS, to his wife
ELIZABETH until his son BENJAMIN SMITH reached 21 years, then to said son
BENJAMIN; & whereas BENJAMIN died in infancy & the house & lot descended
to his brother, WILLIAM SMITH the younger, the house & lot descended to
his brother, WILLIAM SMITH the younger, as heir to his brother & as eldest son of his father; who by will dated 30 Dec. 1741 appointed his wife
ELIZABETH his executrix & his brothers-in-law, said PETER TAYLOR & THOMAS
DALE, ESQ., & his friends WILLIAM ELLIOTT & JOHN STANYARNE, his executors,
& ordered how the residue of his real & personal estate should be divided
& ordered said lot sold which will was proved by TAYLOR & DALE before Lt.

Gov. WILLIAM BULL; & whereas MARY COOPER, with her husband's consent, as a free & sole dealer, agreed to purchase said house & lot for ₺ 1600 currency, out of her own money, to be conveyed to PARSONS & GLEN in trust for certain purposes; now TAYLOR conveys to PARSONS & GLEN that part of lot #36 bounding W 50 ft. on Church Street; N 116 ft. on ANN PEACOCK (formerly WILLIAM YOEMANS); E on part same lot belonging to MARY COOPER (formerly EDMUND ATKINS); S on SARAH STOUTENBURGH. Witnesses: WILLIAM MICHIE, WILLIAM GLEN, JR., WILLIAM POOLE. Before JOHN HUME, J.P. Recorded 26 Aug. 1766 by FENWICKE BULL, Register.

Book F-3, p. 154　　　　JAMES PARSONS, ESQ., & WILLIAM GLEN, merchant,
10 & 11 July 1766　　　 trustees, to JOHN IZARD, the highest bidder,
L & R　　　　　　　　　for ₺ 9999 part of lot #36 Charleston (see
　　　　　　　　　　　　p. 143), MARY COOPER having authorized them
(31 Oct. 1765) to sell at public auction. Witnesses: JOHN HUME, JOHN GLEN, ALEXANDER MOULTRIE. Recorded 28 Aug. 1766 by FENWICKE BULL, Register.

Book F-3, p. 164　　　　RICHARD BERESFORD, ESQ., of Upham, Co. of
13 & 14 Aug. 1764　　　Southampton, & SARAH his wife, to ROBERT
L & R　　　　　　　　　SMITH, merchant, of Charleston, for
　　　　　　　　　　　　₺ 1428:11:5 British; the new dwelling house,
kitchen, & stable lately built on a lot in Charleston bounding E 50 ft. on the Bay; S 119 ft. on THOMAS SMITH; N on MRS. SCOTT; W on land occupied by THOMAS PEARSE (formerly POPPLE). Witnesses: R. RAPER, ISAAC CHEESMAN, B. WARD, ROBERT WILLIAMS, JR., WILLIAM BURROWS. Recorded 2 Sept. 1766 by FENWICKE BULL, J.P. & P. Register.

Book F-3, p. 171　　　　A certain fine, with first proclamation made
24 Apr. 1765　　　　　 12 Feb., was levied before SIR CHARLES PRATT,
Proclamation　　　　　 Knight, EDWARD CLIVE, HENRY BATHURST, HENRY
　　　　　　　　　　　　GOULD, justices, at Westminster, Hilary Term,
as follows: This is final agreement between ROBERT SMITH, plaintiff, & RICHARD BERESFORD, gentleman, & SARAH his wife, deforcients of 2 messuages & 1 a. in Parish of St. Philips, Charleston, SC, in Dartford, whereupon RICHARD & SARAH acknowledge said tenements & appurtenances to belong to ROBERT by gift from RICHARD & SARAH, who release their claim for ₺ 60 sterling to ROBERT. Signed: COLEBROOKS HOWE. Recorded 2 Sept. 1766 by FENWICKE BULL, Register.

Book F-3, p. 173　　　　ALEXANDER MICHIE, merchant, to JAMES PARSONS,
11 & 12 June 1765　　　ESQ., both of Charleston, for ₺ 4000 currency,
L & R by Mortgage　　　half of a quarter part of lot #26 in Charles-
　　　　　　　　　　　　ton, bounding N 30 ft., English measure, on
Broad Street; W 94 ft. on part belonging to JOHN WARD; S on WILLIAM GLEN & THOMAS LEE; E on part belonging to DR. ALEXANDER GARDEN; which 1/8 lot was conveyed by SARAH RAVEN, widow of JOHN RAVEN, to said MICHIE by L & R dated 1 & 2 Feb. last. Witnesses: JOHN GLEN, THOMAS HEYWARD, JR. Before FENWICKE BULL, J.P. & P. Register. Recorded 5 Sept. 1766.

Book F-3, p. 180　　　　JOHN WILSON, planter, of St. Bartholomews Par-
24 June 1755　　　　　 ish, son & heir of MOSES WILSON, to ISAAC
Sale of Pew　　　　　 HOLMES, of Charleston, Pew #10 in middle aisle
　　　　　　　　　　　　of St. Philips Parish Church, Charleston.
Witnesses: ABRAHAM CROUCH, MOSES WILSON. Before ALEXANDER STEWART, J.P. Recorded 5 Sept. 1766 by FENWICKE BULL, Register.

Book F-3, p. 182　　　　THOMAS BINFORD, merchant, formerly of Charles-
7 Nov. 1765　　　　　　ton, SC, now of City of Exeter, Great Britain,
Release in Trust　　　of 1st part; COL. OTHNIEL BEALE, of SC, of 2nd
　　　　　　　　　　　　part; MILES BREWTON, merchant, of SC, of 3rd
part. Whereas by L & R dated 15 & 16 Oct. 1731, MARY SALTUS & ANN SALTUS, spinsters, of Island of Bermuda (alias Summer Islands), only daughters & co-heirs of BARTHOLOMEW SALTUS, eldest brother & heir of MARTHA JONES, (formerly MARTHA SALTUS, widow of JOHN JONES, gunsmith, of SC) sold THOMAS BINFORD 3 lots in Charleston, Nos. 148, 149, & 150, granted by the Lords Proprs. by 3 grants dated 20 June 1694 to JOHN JONES; & whereas THOMAS BINFORD in Feb. 1731 conveyed lot #150 & half of lot #149 to MILES BREWTON, grandfather of said MILES BREWTON; reserving lot #148 & other half of lot #149 valued at ₺ 3300 SC money (equal to ₺ 471:8:6

British sterling); which BINFORD has voluntarily consented to settle on his Godson, the said MILES BREWTON, subject to an annuity to be paid him by BREWTON; now BINFORD conveys the unsold (1-1/2) lots to OTHNIEL BEALE in trust for BREWTON, with provisoes. Witnesses: ABRAHAM PEARSE, mariner, of Hopsham, in Devon; & EDWARD LEGG, pressman, of City of Exeter; before JOHN BUSSELL, mayor of Exeter. Proved by LEGG in SC 4 Sept. 1766 before FENWICKE BULL, J.P. & P. Register.

Book F-3, p. 195
1 & 2 Feb. 1758
L & R

JOHANES WINDEL (his mark) ERNEST, of Craven Co., to ROBERT HANAH, blacksmith, of Berkeley Co., for Ł 100 currency, 150 a. in Berkeley Co., on Little River Creek; bounding on all sides on vacant land. Witnesses: THOMAS LINTHWAITE, ABRAHAM PENNINGTON, ADAM (his mark) SHEFLIET. Proved before JOHN TROUP, J.P., 23 Oct. 1759. Recorded 5 Sept. 1766 by FENWICKE BULL, Register.

Book F-3, p. 199
21 Sept. 1765
L & R

ABRAHAM PENNINGTON, planter, of Berkeley Co., to JAMES HARVEY, planter, for Ł 300 currency, 150 a. on Little River Creek, Berkeley Co., bounding on all sides on vacant land; origi-nally granted to JOHANES WINDEL ERNEST (p. 195). Witnesses: WHITENHALL WARNER, JOHN (his mark) BOX, JOHN (his mark) HELMES. Before BARNABAS ARTHUR, J.P. Recorded 6 Sept. 1766 by FENWICKE BULL, Register.

Book F-3, p. 204
19 & 20 Oct. 1756
L & R

AUGUSTINUS (his mark) WERNER, to JOHN JONES, for Ł 100 currency, 50 a. on a branch of Bush River, between Broad & Saluda Rivers, bounding SE on JOHN JONES & vacant land; other sides on vacant land. Witnesses: THOMAS LINTHWAITE, ABRAHAM PENNINGTON, ADAM (his mark) SHECKEL. Before JOHN TROUP, J.P. Recorded 8 Sept. 1766 by FEN-WICKE BULL, Register.

Book F-3, p. 209
25 June 1766
Feoffment

ABRAM JACOT, planter, of St. Peters Parish, to ADRIAN MAYER, merchant, of Purysburgh, for Ł 50 sterling, 250 a. in Purysburgh Township, bounding N on vacant land; S on PETER NICHOLAS; E on THOMAS CAMBER; W on ANTHONY BILOT & MELCHIOR LEICHTENSTEIGER. Wit-nesses: GEORGE KEALL, FRANCIS VAUCHIER. Before JOHN LEWIS BOURQUIN, J.P. Recorded 15 Sept. 1766 by FENWICKE BULL, Register.

Book F-3, p. 211
11 & 12 Aug. 1766
L & R by Mortgage

ELISHA POINSETT, vintner, & CATHERINE his wife, to GABRIEL MANIGAULT, merchant, both of Charleston, for Ł 3800 currency, part of lot #27 in Charleston, bounding N on THEODORE TREZVANT & ELIZABETH RICHARDSON; E on the Rev. MR. ROBERT SMITH; W 88 ft. on THOMAS LEE; S 43 ft. on Middle Street. Witness: JOEL HOLMES. Before JOHN TROUP, J.P. Recorded 17 Sept. 1766 by FENWICKE BULL, Register. On 29 Aug. 1777 GABRIEL MANIGAULT declared mortgage satisfied. Witness: GEORGE SHEED.

Book F-3, p. 216
3 June 1766
Grant

GEORGE III, by Lt. Gov. WILLIAM BULL, to THEO-DORE GOURDIN, 100 a. on N side Santee River, bounding N on said GOURDIN. Plat certified 9 Sept. 1765 by JOHN TROUP, D.S.G. (Page broken & incomplete). Signed by JAMES SIMPSON, C.G.

Book F-3, p. 219
6 & 7 July 1766
L & R

JOHN IZARD, ESQ., & ISABELLA his wife, to LAM-BERT LANCE, merchant, both of Charleston, for Ł 5570 currency, 2 lots in Charleston, #124 (100 & 24?); 1 bounding W 34 ft. 3 in. on Meeting Street; N 105 ft. on Queen Street; E 38 ft. on AARON LOOCOCK (formerly JOHN IZARD); S on ANDREW CUNNINGHAM (formerly JOHN IZARD); the other bounding N 107 ft. 6 in. on JOHN IZARD; S on Beresford Alley; E on JOHN IZARD; W on Meeting Street. Witnesses: JOHN HUME, JAMES HUME. Be-fore FENWICKE BULL, J.P. & P. Register.

Book F-3, p. 226
2 Apr. 1764
Sale

DANIEL DOYLEY, P.M., to CHARLES PINCKNEY, ESQ., at auction, for Ł 100 currency, 2000 a. Whereas ROBERT OSWALD, planter, of St. Bar-tholomews Parish owned 2000 a. on the branches

of Cosahatchie & Chutapenny Creeks, in Granville Co., bounding NW on JON-
ATHAN RUSS; SE on ROBERT MCKEWN; NE & SW on vacant land; as granted 16
Feb. 1759; & whereas OSWALD died intestate & ALICE OSWALD, his widow, was
appointed administratrix by Gov. THOMAS BOONE; & whereas GEORGE INGLES
brought suit against OSWALD'S estate to recover a bond in penal sum of
Ł 2661 & obtained a judgement, with costs; & whereas CHARLES SKINNER,
C.J., issued a writ of fieri facias, ordering the P.M. to obtain said
amount from OSWALD'S estate; now DOYLEY sells the 2000 a. to PINCKNEY.
Witnesses: JOSEPH BRAILSFORD, CHARLES MOTTE. Before FENWICKE BULL, J.P.
& P. Register. Recorded 27 Sept. 1766.

Book F-3, p. 231   WILLIAM SAVAGE, merchant, & THOMAS BEE, attor-
14 & 15 Aug. 1766   ney-at-law, of 1st part; LUKE STOUTENBURGH,
L & R Tripartite   ESQ., & SARAH his wife (late widow of JOHN
                            RAVEN & sole executrix of RAVEN'S will), of
2nd part; GEORGE SEAMAN, ESQ., of 3rd part; all of Charleston. Whereas
JOHN RAVEN, planter, father of said JOHN RAVEN, owned part of a lot on
Bedon's Alley, & died intestate on 21 Nov. 1733, whereby his eldest son,
JOHN, inherited the lot, & by will dated 27 July 1763 devised the residue
of his real estate, including said lot, to SARAH STOUTENBURGH, party here-
to; who, before her marriage with LUKE STOUTENBURGH (with his consent) by
L & R dated 30 & 31 Oct. 1765 transferred all her real estate to SAVAGE &
BEE in trust for certain purposes; & whereas SARAH finds it necessary to
sell the lot to pay RAVEN'S debts; now her trustees sell to SEAMAN for
Ł 2120 currency, the said lot, bounding W 48 ft. 6 in. on Bedon's Alley;
S 38 ft. on HUMPHREY SOMMERS; E on GEORGE SEAMAN & heirs of JAMES OSMOND;
N on GEORGE SEAMAN. Witnesses: TIMOTHY CROSBY, ANTHONY TOOMER. Before
JACOB MOTTE, J.P. Recorded 30 Sept. 1766 by FENWICKE BULL, Register.

Book F-3, p. 241   JOHN MCCALL, & MARTHA his wife; SAMUEL PRIO-
9 & 10 Feb. 1759   LEAU & PROVIDENCE his wife; WILLIAM ROPER &
L & R   GRACE his wife; BENJAMIN DART & AMELIA his
                            wife; ROBERT WILLIAMS, JR. & ELIZABETH his
wife, of 1st part; to CHARLES PINCKNEY, attorney-at-law; all of Charleston; for Ł 810 currency, 300 a., English measure, within a few miles of
Ashepoo Bridge, in St. Bartholomews Parish, Colleton Co., bounding S on
THOMAS FLEMING; E on BENJAMIN WHITAKER & an island; N on GEORGE AUSTIN; W
on JOHN SEABROOKE. Whereas DAVID HEXT, gentleman, of Charleston, father
of MARTHA, PROVIDENCE, GRACE, AMELIA, & ELIZABETH, owned considerable
real estate, including above tract which he had purchased from RICHARD
GODFREY & which he had settled & enjoyed for many years before his death;
& by will dated 11 May 1751 bequeathed the residue of his estate to his 5
daughters, equally; now the daughters, with their husbands, sell said
tract to PINCKNEY. Witnesses: THOMAS STONE, JR., WILLIAM MAZYCK. Before
BENJAMIN SMITH, J.P. Recorded 2 Oct. 1766 by FENWICKE BULL, Register.

Book F-3, p. 249   BENJAMIN SIMMONS, ESQ., of Charleston, & ANN
29 & 30 Sept. 1766   his wife (lately ANN DEWICK, widow of DR. HEN-
L & R   RY DEWICK, physician, of St. George Parish,
                            Berkeley Co.); & HANNAH DEWICK & ANN DEWICK,
spinsters, daughters of HENRY DWEICK; of 1st part; to DR. ALEXANDER FOTH-
ERINGHAM, physician, of Charleston; for Ł 250 currency, 2 lots in Town of
Dorchester, #108 & #109, containing 1/4 a. each; which DEWICK had purchased from WILLIAM BRISBANE & MARGARET his wife; & which by will dated
25 Dec. 1749 DEWICK bequeathed, with all his estate, to his wife & daughters. Witness: JOHN TROUP. Before FENWICKE BULL, J.P. & P. Register.

Book F-3, p. 258   JOHN (his mark) MATHEWS (MATHIS), planter, of
2 Jan. 1764   Anson Co., NC, to JACOB JOHNSON, planter, of
Sale   same place, for Ł 25, 180 a. in Anson Co., NC,
                            on N side Thompson's Creek; beginning at a
pine N 80 W 155 poles to white oak, then S 10 W to creek, then up creek
to line of JAMES MATHEWS, then N 80 E with MATHEWS line to an oak, then N
10 W 167 poles to a pine, then S 64 E 234 poles to a stake, then a direct
line along row of marked trees to first station; being part of a tract
granted BENJAMIN JACKSON 29 Sept. 1756. Witnesses: BENJAMIN JACKSON,
ISAAC (his mark) JOHNSON, RICHARD (his mark) RUSHING, THOMAS FROHOCK,
C.C. of Anson Co., & ANTHONY HUTCHINS, D.R., of Anson Co., NC, certified
that said deed was recorded in Anson Co. Registers Office in Book G, p.
137-138. Recorded in Charleston 12 Oct. 1766 by FENWICKE BULL, Register.

Book F-3, p. 259
18 & 19 July 1766
L & R

ANDREW BROWN, to FRANCES BLACK, both of Berkeley Co., for Ł 50 currency, 90 a. on S side of Santee (Saludy) River; other sides on vacant land; granted BROWN 2 Oct. 1765 by Lt. Gov.
WILLIAM BULL. Witnesses: JOSEPH THOMAS, CHARLES (his mark) ROBINSON. Before JOSEPH CURRY, J.P. Recorded 13 Oct. 1766 by FENWICKE BULL, Register.

Book F-3, p. 264
24 Sept. 1764
Lease for 19 Years

JOSHUA MORGAN, planter, of Prince William Parish, Granville Co., to WILLIAM O'BRIAN, merchant, of St. Helena Parish, for 19 years, at Ł 150 currency, per annum, 350 a. bounding S on Cosay River; W & N on ANDREW POTTEL; E on WILLIAM BOWERS; MORGAN to repair the dwelling house; O'BRIAN to keep it in repair. Witnesses: JOHN PACKROW, THOMAS WATSON, ANTHONY GARDNER. Before THOMAS MIDDLETON, J.P. of Granville Co. Recorded 14 Oct. 1766 by FENWICKE BULL, Register.

Book F-3, p. 267
28 July 1766
Gift

FRANCES (her mark) BLACK, spinster, to her son, ANDREW BROWN, a minor, for love & affection, 90 a. on S side Saludy (Santee) River; FRANCES to have the use of it during her life (p. 259). Witnesses: JOSEPH THOMAS, CHARLES (his mark) ROBINSON. Before JOSEPH CURRY, J.P. Recorded 14 Oct. 1766 by FENWICKE BULL, Register.

Book F-3, p. 270
25 & 26 Sept. 1766
L & R

PETER (his mark) JENNENS (JENNINGS), JOHN JENNENS, & their mother, MARY (her mark) JENNENS, of St. James Santee, Craven Co., to RICHARD DEARINGTON, planter, of Craven Co., for Ł 700 currency, 400 a. in Craven Co., bounding N & NE on Gov. ROBERT JOHNSON; SE & E on MR. ARTHUR & MR. MAHONE; SW on a deep swamp. Witnesses: ROBERT DEARINGTON, JOHN NICHOLSON, ELIZABETH JENNENS. Before FRANCIS ROCHE, J.P. Recorded 15 Oct. 1766 by FENWICKE BULL, Register.

Book F-3, p. 274
18 Sept. 1766
Mortgage

ELIZABETH GARNE, shopkeeper, of Charleston, to JOHN DUTARQUE, planter, of St. Thomas Parish, for Ł 450 currency, part of lot #80 in Charleston, bounding N 40 ft. on Pinckney Street; W on TIMOTHY CROSBY; S on JOHN RICHMOND GASCOYNE; E 75 ft. on MRS. MINISCH. Witnesses: JACOB REMINGTON, JOHN REMINGTON. Before FENWICKE BULL, J.P. & P. Register.

Book F-3, p. 279
6 Oct. 1766
Mortgage

WILLIAM (his mark) RAGIN, of St. Marks Parish, Craven Co., to JAMES DONOVAN, of Charleston, for Ł 159:11:0 currency, 150 a. in St. Marks Parish, Craven Co., surveyed by WILLIAM LEONARD & afterwards conveyed to RAGIN; bounding on ANGELA HARDEN & ROBERT WHITE; also 1 Negro slave. A penknife delivered. Witnesses: PETER BOCQUET, JR., JOHN WAGNER. Before JOHN BULL, JR., J.P. Recorded in Book AA, p. 2, by THOMAS SCOTTOW, Sec. Recorded 15 Oct. 1766 by FENWICKE BULL, Register.

Book F-3, p. 281
24 Dec. 1763
Confirmation

Whereas by marriage settlement tripartite, dated 12 Sept. 1763, between SARAH PALMERIN (by name of SARAH WEATHERLY, widow, of St. Johns Parish, Colleton Co.); of 1st part; DANIEL HOLMES, of the 2nd part; & SAMUEL PALMERIN (present husband of SARAH), saddler, of 3rd part; all of SARAH'S estate was conveyed to DANIEL HOLMES in trust for certain purposes (Secretary's Book LL, p. 642-648); & whereas SARAH & her husband, SAMUEL, by L & R dated 5 & 6 this Dec., for Ł 1600 currency, sold part of her trust estate to EBENEZER SIMMONS, ESQ., of Charleston, viz., 230 a. on Johns Island; & whereas in said deed of settlement the trust estate was conveyed to HOLMES in trust that he should execute legal conveyances as directed by SARAH; now HOLMES, at the request of SARAH & her husband, confesses himself satisfied, & confirms SIMMONS'S title to said tract. Witnesses: THOMAS LEGARE, JR., CHARLES MOTTE. Before JAMES CARSON, J.P. Recorded 16 Oct. 1766 by FENWICKE BULL, Register.

Book F-3, p. 284
8 & 9 Oct. 1766

JAMES RODGERS, mariner, of Charleston, & MARY (her mark) his wife, to King GEORGE III, for

L & R   Ł 700, an island plantation of 231 a., called
                               Middle Bay Island, bounding NE & SE on the
ocean; SW on the creek N of Folly Island & the creek between Middle Bay
Island & Cummins Island; NW on Cummins Creek & marsh; as granted 13 Apr.
1709 to JONATHAN DRAKE & JOHN HERNE; in accordance with an act passed 11
May 1754 for applying 1/5 part of the tax imposed on first purchasers of
Negroes & other slaves imported, which was applied as a bounty to be giv-
en for the building of ships & as an encouragement to shipwrights &
caulkers to become settlers in SC, & for building a pest house & erecting
a beacon, & for appointing commissioners to execute the same & to purchase land for those purposes, also to purchase land in Charleston for
building another powder magazine; also that the commissioners for regulating the pilotage in Charleston Harbor be appointed for building a pest
erect a beacon, purchasing land for this purpose which should be conveyed
to his majesty. Wherefore JOHN TORRANS, WILLIAM WOODROPE, JAMES READE,
COL. ROBERT RIVERS, HENRY LAURENS, JOHN FORBES, & THOMAS SAVAGE, the commissioners for regulating pilotage purchased this land from RODGERS on
which to erect a pest house & beacon. Witnesses: JOHN POAUG, ALEXANDER
MOULTRIE. Before FENWICKE BULL, J.P. & P. Register.

Book F-3, p. 292   JAMES FABIAN, planter, of Colleton Co., & ANN
15 & 16 Sept. 1766   his wife, to JOHN LOGAN, merchant, of Charles-
L & R   ton, for Ł 390 currency, 187 a., old measure,
                              in Colleton Co., bounding S on JOHN NEWTON &
vacant land; W on vacant land; N on WILLIAM CRAWL & JOHN CARMICHAEL &
BRYAN KELLY; E on vacant land; granted 4 Sept. 1735 to JOHN DENNY; who by
L & R dated 11 & 12 Mar. 1737 sold to JOHN FABIAN, JR.; who devised to
his brother, JAMES, party hereto. Witnesses: TOBIAS FORD, JOSEPH SWIN-
DEL, HENRY WEBSTER. Before JOSEPH GLOVER, J.P. Recorded 20 Oct. 1766 by
FENWICKE BULL, Register.

Book F-3, p. 298   ROBERT BOYD, & ANN his wife; & EDWARD MARTIN,
10 & 11 July 1766   merchant, & ELIZABETH his wife; of 1st part;
L & R by Mortgage   to PETER MANIGAULT, barrister-at-law; all of
                              Charleston; as security on 2 bonds for Ł 2138
& Ł 2387:0:6; that part of Colleton Square in Charleston, bounding E
150 ft. on THOMAS ELLERY; S 70 ft. on Hunter Street; W on Charles Street;
N on Ellery Street; on which land THOMAS WALKER built 2 large brick
houses; also the W part of marsh lot marked "O" on plan of Colleton
Square, bounding N on Ellery Street; S 35 ft. on a canal or creek; E 60
ft. on part of marsh lot belonging to ANN ELLERY; W on marsh lot marked
"N" formerly belonging to GEORGE HUNTER. They also deliver 20 slaves.
Witnesses: JOHN CROSS, SARAH WOODSIDES. Before JOHN WRAGG, J.P. Recorded 22 Oct. 1766 by FENWICKE BULL, Register.

Book F-3, p. 305   BOWMAN CRICHLOW, son & heir of JAMES CRICHLOW,
21 & 23 Jan. 1764   to ANTHONY SWEET, planter, both of Craven Co.,
L & R   for Ł 50 currency, 950 a. in Queensborough
                              Township, Craven Co., bounding NE on JOHN
HAMMERTON; SW on Peedee River; NW on vacant land; SE on unknown land.
Witnesses: TILMAN KOLB, JACOB KOLB. Before JOHN ALRAN, J.P. Recorded 24
Oct. 1766 by FENWICKE BULL, Register.

Book F-3, p. 311   ROBERT RUTHERFORD, of Berkeley Co., to WILLIAM
8 Oct. 1766   LOOCOCK & ALEXANDER RUSSEL, for Ł 1000 curren-
Mortgage   cy, lot #18 in Charleston, with all buildings
                              on the lot; bounding W 19 ft. on Union Street;
E on HOPKIN PRICE; N on THOMAS HARDEN; S 124 ft. on other part. Witness:
THOMAS MACE. Before FENWICKE BULL, J.P. & P. Register.

Book F-3, p. 314   RICHARD PARK STOBO, gentleman, & MARY his
29 Aug. 1764   wife, to WILLIAM HARVEY, gentleman, both of
Mortgage   Charleston, as security for repayment of vari-
                              ous sums to ALEXANDER PERONNEAU, & MRS. MARTIN
LLOYD; 2 tracts of land in St. Andrews Parish, Berkeley Co., by resurvey
found to be 500 a.; 1 of 394 (supposed to be 378) a. conveyed by CHAMPER-
NOON WILLIAMSON to STOBO by L & R dated 2 & 3 Feb. 1762; the other 106 a.
conveyed to STOBO by L & R Tripartite dated 25 & 26 Apr. 1763 executed
between JOHN RIVERS, of 1st part; THOMAS STOCK & ANN his wife, of 2nd
part; & RICHARD PARK STOBO, of 3rd part; bounding NE on WILLIAM BRANFORD

& MATHURINE GUERIN; S & SE on MELLICHAMP; S & W on THOMAS FULLER; SW on
THOMAS FULLER & WILLIAM ELLIOTT; N on JOHN DRAYTON; as by plat of resurvey certified by NATHANIEL DEANE on 8 Feb. 1763. Witnesses: JOHN RUT-
LEDGE, ALEXANDER HARVEY. Before GEORGE JOHNSON, J.P. Recorded 28 Oct.
1766 by FENWICKE BULL, Register.

Book F-3, p. 319   JAMES SHARP, merchant, of St. Bartholomews
3 & 4 July 1766   Parish, Colleton Co., to JOHN VAN MARJENHOFF,
L & R   planter, of St. Pauls Parish, Colleton Co.,
                          for ₺ 1150 currency, 300 a. in Colleton Co.,
bounding NW on MOSES MARTIN & JAMES NEWTON; NE on JAMES NEWTON & heirs of
JOSEPH BOONE; SE on WILLIAM LITTLE; SW on THOMAS ELLIOTT & THOMAS BRAD-
WELL; which tract was devised by JOHN NEWTON to his son, JOSEPH NEWTON; &
sold by JAMES NEWTON & ISAAC NEWTON on 19 May 1760 to JAMES SHARP, & also
held by SHARP as tenant in common in right of his wife, MARY. Witnesses:
JOHN LOGAN, MOSES DARQUIER, WILLSON COOK. Before FENWICKE BULL, J.P. &
P. Register.

Book F-3, p. 325   JOHN TOBLER the elder, gentleman, of New Wind-
16 & 17 Apr. 1762   sor, SC, to JOHN TOBLER, the younger, gentle-
L & R   man, for ₺ 1000 currency, 650 a. in New Wind-
                          sor Township, Granville Co., bounding N on UL-
RICK EGGER, LEONARD ULRICK, & MICHAEL MYERS; E on JACOB BENSIGER; S on
JACOB STURTSINGERE; W on vacant land; provided JOHN, JR. permit JOHN,
SR., & his wife, ANN, to occupy the premises during their life time.
Witnesses: THOMAS LAMAR, JOHN STURZENOGER. Before JOHN SCOTT, J.P. Re-
corded 30 Oct. 1766 by FENWICKE BULL, Register.

Book F-3, p. 329   (See Book G, p. 773 for Lease). HENRIETTA
8 & 9 Oct. 1766   RAVEN, widow, executrix, & GEORGE BEDON, mer-
L & R   chant, executor, of will of WILLIAM RAVEN,
                          gentleman, of Charleston; of 1st part; to
ISAAC LESESNE, planter, of Daniels Island; for ₺ 2301 currency 700 a. on
Daniels Island, Berkeley Co., bounding N on ISAAC LESESNE & the creek
back of the island; E on Wando River; S & W on WILLIAM FREWIN & CHARLES
CODNER (formerly MRS. SARAH DANIEL & RICHARD CODNER). Whereas JOHN DAN-
IEL of Parish of St. Thomas & St. Dennis, Berkeley Co., owned said 700 a.
which by L & R dated 22 & 23 July 1728 he mortgaged to the vestry of said
Parish for ₺ 500; & whereas by L & R dated 21 & 22 Mar. 1739 JOHN DANIEL
& SARAH, his wife, mortgaged the tract to ELIZABETH JENNYS for ₺ 6000
withoug giving her notice of first unpaid mortgage; & she purchased first
mortgage from the vestry on 4 Dec. 1744; & whereas by act of assembly no
person who mortgaged the same land a second time, while first mortgage
was in force, should have any pwoer of redemption in equity or otherwise;
& ELIZABETH advertised the land for sale (no part of the debt being paid)
& SAMUEL SMYTH, butcher, of Charleston, was highest bidder; & whereas
ELIZABETH afterwards married JOHN GIBBES, ESQ., & they by L & R dated 26
& 27 May 1745 conveyed the tract for ₺ 1520 to SMYTH (p. 345); who by L &
R dated 30 & 31 May 1745 conveyed to ELIZABETH GIBBES; who by will dated
25 June 1755 devised the residue of her estate including this tract to
her son, WILLIAM RAVEN; who by will dated 14 Oct. 1765 authorized his ex-
ecutrix & executors (naming HENRIETTA RAVEN, GEORGE BEDON, & THOMAS SMYTH,
SR., merchant, of Broad Street, brother of BENJAMIN SMYTH; also CHRISTO-
PHER GADSDEN & JAMES PARSONS) to sell any part of his estate; & to satisfy his pressing creditors, they offered the tract at auction; now they
convey to LESESNE, highest bidder. Witnesses: SUSANNAH BONNEAU, ANTHONY
TOOMER. Before JAMES PARSONS, J.P. Recorded 31 Oct. 1766 by FENWICKE
BULL, Register.

Book F-3, p. 337   THOMAS DEARINGTON, planter, of St. Thomas Par-
12 & 13 Feb. 1762   ish, Berkeley Co., & PRUDENCE his wife, to BEN-
L & R   JAMIN SIMONS, planter, of same Parish, for
                          ₺ 650 currency, 200 a. in Berkeley Co., on E
side of T. of Cooper River, bounding S & W on JOHN CUMING; E on BENJAMIN
SIMONS; being part of 300 a. granted by the Lords Proprs. 8 July 1704.
Witnesses: JACOB BONNEAU, BERNARD LITZ (BRUNNORY ALICZ). Before FRANCIS
ROCHE, J.P. Recorded 4 Nov. 1766 by FENWICKE BULL, J.P.

Book F-3, p. 342   BENJAMIN SIMONS, to his son, BENJAMIN SIMONS,
1 Aug. 1764   both of Parish of St. Thomas, Berkeley Co.,

Gift   for love & affection, the 200 a. he purchased
(p. 337) from THOMAS DEARINGTON; bounding S &
W on BENJAMIN CUMING (son of JOHN). Witnesses: HENRY BOCHER, BERNARD
LITZ (BRUSAN ALIZ). Before FRANCIS ROCHE, J.P. Recorded 4 Nov. 1766 by
FENWICKE BULL, Register.

Book F-3, p. 344   ALEXANDER FORBES, keeper of the Poor House, of
19 Sept. 1766   New York City, & DR. BEEKMAN VAN BEEIREN, phy-
Affidavit   sician of said Poor House, declared before
GEORGE BREWERTON, alderman of the northward &
J.P. for N.Y. City, declared that DR. HUGH SWINTON, physician, of SC,
died in said Poor House on 26 Dec. 1759. Witness: JOHN SCHERMERHORN. Before FENWICKE BULL, J.P. & P. Register 3 Nov. 1766.

Book F-3, p. 345   JOHN GIBBES, ESQ., & ELIZABETH his wife,
27 May 1745   (formerly ELIZABETH JENYS, widow), to SAMUEL
Release   SMITH (SMYTH), butcher, all of Charleston; for
Ł 1520 currency, 700 a. on Daniels Island (p.
329). Witnesses: THOMAS WRIGHT, HENRY BEDON, JOHN WILKINS, CHARLES
PINCKNEY, GEORGE BEDON. Before JAMES PARSONS, J.P. Recorded 7 Nov. 1766
by FENWICKE BULL, Register.

Book F-3, p. 351   BENJAMIN GUERARD, planter, of Charleston, sole
13 & 14 June 1765   acting executor of will of JOHN GUERARD; to
L & R   THOMAS ELFE, cabinet maker; for Ł 1000 curren-
cy, half of lot #243 in Charleston, which by
his will JOHN GUERARD ordered sold at auction; bounding W 52 ft. 6 in. on
New Street (leading from MR. LEGARE'S corner to Ashley River; N 300 ft.
on other half belonging to RALPH IZARD; E on MILES BREWTON & JOHN PRICE;
S on COPELAND STILES, ESQ., of Island of Bermuda (formerly BENJAMIN GAR-
DEN). Witnesses: FRANCIS GOTTIER, PETER SANDERS. Before FENWICKE BULL,
J.P. & P. Register.

Book F-3, p. 358   JOHN NAIL, planter, of New Windsor, Granville
13 Sept. 1766   Co., to MELCHIOR LEICHTENSTEIGER, planter, of
Conveyance   Purysburgh, for Ł 50 currency, 250 a. in Purys-
burgh Township, St. Peters Parish, Granville
Co., granted JOHN NEILE; bounding N on MELCHIOR LEICHTENSTEIGER & JACOB
WINKLER; S on DAVID ECOLIER & vacant land; E & SE on JACOB WINKLER, va-
cant land, & ADRIAN MAYER; W on JAMES RICHARDS, DAVID ECOLIER, & DANIEL
BROBANT. Witnesses: DAVID ZUBLY, MICHAEL MEYER. Before JOHN DICK, J.P.
Recorded 12 Nov. 1766 by FENWICKE BULL, Register.

Book F-3, p. 360   THOMAS SMITH, merchant, to WILLIAM CHAPMAN,
16 May 1702   tanner, for Ł 5 currency, half of the marsh
Conveyance   land bounding W on town lots #64 & #78; E on
other half of marsh land; S on marsh belonging
to THOMAS SMITH; N on remainder of marsh. Whereas the Lords Proprs. Gov.
JAMES MOORE, Landgrave JOSEPH MORTON, & Landgrave EDMOND BELLINGER on 28
Aug. 1701 granted THOMAS SMITH the marsh land between lots 78, 64, 73, 3,
& 5 in Charleston; now SMITH sells half the marsh land. Witnesses: JO-
SEPH ELLICOTT, JAMES WITTER, SR. Before JOHN BUCKLEY, J.P. Recorded 26
Nov. 1766 by FENWICKE BULL, Register.

Book F-3, p. 363   JOHN DUTARQUE, planter, of Berkeley Co., &
15 & 16 Sept. 1766   MARY his wife, to ELIZABETH CARNE, shopkeeper,
L & R   of Charleston, for Ł 1400 SC money, part of
lot #80 in Charleston bounding N 40 ft. on
Pinckney Street; W 75 ft. on TIMOTHY CROSBY; S on JOHN RICHMOND GASCOYNE;
E on MRS. MINNICH; which part of a lot GABRIEL GUIGNARD & FRANCIS his
wife sold to DUTARQUE by L & R dated 16 & 17 Sept. 1751 (Book J.J., p.
293-297). Witnesses: JACOB REMINGTON, JOHN REMINGTON. Before FENWICKE
BULL, J.P. & P. Register.

Book F-3, p. 369   ELIZABETH CARNE, shopkeeper, of Charleston, to
24 & 25 Nov. 1766   JONATHAN FOWLER, planter, of Moncks Corner,
L & R & Settlement   trustee, part of lot #80 in Charleston. Whereas on 14 Nov. 1765 JANE ELIZABETH CARNE,
daughter of said ELIZABETH, married PATY HOLMES, of Charleston, & was entitled to receive from ROBERT WILSON & others, attorneys for SAMUEL CARNE

who gave the sum, Ł 2100 currency as her own property, which sum it was agreed would be used to buy lands & NEGROES for her sole use, not to be controlled by her husband; (the sum being placed with the mother in trust); part of which she used to buy part of a lot from JOHN DUTARQUE (p. 363), the remainder to buy 3 slaves; now to secure the land & slaves to the daughter, now ELIZABETH conveys them to JONATHAN FOWLER in trust for JANE ELIZABETH during her lifetime. Witnesses: EDWARD BEALL, CHARLES MOTTE. Before FENWICKE BULL, J.P. & P. Register.

Book F-3, p. 376
10 Sept. 1755
L & R
SAMUEL (his mark) GREENWOOD, planter, to THOM-AS ROGERS, planter, both of Craven Co., for Ł 200 currency, 350 a. in the Welch Tract, in Craven Co., bounding W on Peedee River; other sides on vacant land; granted 13 Apr. 1748 by Gov. JAMES GLEN to GREEN-WOOD (see Secretary's Book L.L. fol. 374). Witnesses: JAMES STON, GEORGE WOOD. Before JOHN TROUP, J.P. Recorded 2 Dec. 1766 by FENWICKE BULL, Register.

Book F-3, p. 381
28 Sept. 1766
L & R
JOSEPH JACKSON, planter, & MARY his wife, to ROBERT STUART, weaver & planter, both of Berke-ley Co., for Ł 200 currency, 300 a. in fork of Santee & Wateree Rivers, bounding on all sides on vacant land. Witnesses: RANDAL MCCARTHY, BENJAMIN SCOTT. Before JOHN LIVISTON, J.P. Recorded 3 Dec. 1766 by FENWICKE BULL, Register.

Book F-3, p. 386
2 & 3 June 1766
L & R
JOSEPH ALLSTON, planter, of Prince George Par-ish, Craven Co., & CHARLOTTE his wife, to BEN-JAMIN WARING, ESQ., of St. George Parish, Dor-chester, for Ł 3500 currency, 2 tracts; 1 of 200 a. the E part of 457 a., bounding N & E on Wando Passo Creek or Thorofare; S on Long Creek & THOMAS WATERS (formerly WILLIAM ALLSTON); W on other part said 457 a.; 1 of 150 a. on Sandy Island known as Welsteods Bluff; bounding S on Waccamaw River; W on Wando Passo Creek or Thorofare; Non Marions Creek & other part of the tract to which the 150 a. belonged; E on vacant land (formerly JOHN ALLSTON). Whereas WILLIAM WATERS of Prince George Parish, Craven Co., by will dated 29 Jan. 1742 bequeathed to his son, THOMAS WATERS, planter, 457 a. swamp land said to be part of 2 tracts fronting W on Peedee River & extending E to Wando Passo Creek; bounding S on MR. ALLSTON; N on a line to be run due E across the river from the lower boundary line of the plantation on which WILLIAM WATERS then lived & continued to Wando Passo Creek; also 150 a. at JOHN WEL-STEADS Bluff; & whereas THOMAS WATERS by L & R dated 3 & 4 June 1761 sold part of the 457 a. (i.e., 200 a.) & the 150 a. to WILLIAM ALLSTON, JR., planter; who conveyed to JOSEPH ALLSTON; now JOSEPH ALLSTON sells to BEN-JAMIN WARING. Witnesses: WILLIAM ALLSTON, ISAAC MARION, ANDREW JOHNSTON. Before BENJAMIN YOUNG, J.P. Recorded 6 Dec. 1766 by FENWICKE BULL, Reg-ister.

Book F-3, p. 393
19 & 20 Mar. 1765
L & R
JOHN ANDERSON, planter, of Georgia, to WILLIAM HOWELL, planter, of Craven Co., SC, for Ł 120 SC money, 170 a. on N side Santee or Congaree River, bounding W on vacant land; NE on Rai-fords Creek; as granted ANDERSON by Gov. JAMES GLEN 5 Apr. 1751. Wit-nesses: JOHN HOPKINS, GEORGE (his mark) ROLLINSON, GRIFFIN HUMPHRIES. Before JOHN HAMILTON, J.P. Recorded 8 Dec. 1766 by FENWICKE BULL, Regis-ter.

Book F-3, p. 398
7 & 8 Nov. 1766
L & R
CHARLES GRAVES, planter, & ELIZABETH his wife, to HENRY DESAUSSURE, planter, both of Prince William Parish, Granville Co., for Ł 1500 cur-rency, 410 a. in said Parish, granted 5 Apr. 1734 to THOMAS GRAVES, planter, who died intestate, & inherited by his eldest son THOMAS, who also died intestate, & then inherited by his eld-est brother, said CHARLES; bounding NE & SE on a branch of Port Royal River & a small creek; NW & SW on ISAAC MAZYCK. Witnesses: JOHN GRAVES, JOHN COCHRANE, CHARLES GRAVES. Before STEPHEN BULL, JR., J.P. Recorded 9 Dec. 1766 by FENWICKE BULL, Register.

Book F-3, p. 404
27 & 28 Mar. 1765
JACOB MOORE (MOHR, & CHRISTIANA (her mark) his wife, of The Congarees, to MRS. GRACE RUSSELL,

L & R   a sole dealer, of same place for Ł 100 curren-
                                   cy, 50 a., part of 250 a. on S side Congaree
River, granted 8 Mar. 1755 by Gov. JAMES GLEN to FREDERICK REISS, which
250 a. between Saxegotha & Amelia Townships bounded W on WILLIAM YORK; S
on JACOB GASP & ANN SELERIN; E on vacant land. Whereas FREDERICK REISS
died intestate & his eldest son JOHN inherited, & by L & R dated 29 & 30
May 1764 sold 50 a. to JACOB MOORE; now MOORE sells to GRACE RUSSELL the
50 a., bounding E on JOHN SHEDEROFF'S; N on Congaree River; W & S on
other parts of 250 a. Witnesses: DANIEL DWIGHT, JOHN RUSSELL. Before
JOSEPH CURRY, J.P. Recorded 10 Dec. 1766 by FENWICKE BULL, Register.

Book F-3, p. 407   CONRAD (his mark) REMELEY, of St. Bartholomews
13 & 14 July 1763   Parish, Colleton Co., to JOHN WOOD, of Charles-
L & R   ton, for Ł 200 currency, 200 a. in Berkeley
                          Co., between the forks of Broad & Saludy Riv-
ers, bounding on all sides on vacant land. Witnesses: JOHN ASH, THOMAS
JONES, CHARLES COLLETON. Before WILLIAM MASON, J.P., 20 Nov. 1766. Recorded 11 Dec. 1766 by FENWICKE BULL, Register.

Book F-3, p. 411   JOHN TOBLER, to ANNA & ELIZABETH MEYER, of New
6 Feb. 1762   Windsor Township, Granville Co., for Ł 150
Release   currency, 200 a. in said Township, bounding N
                          on CONRAD LUTZ; W on Savannah; E on ULRIC
EGGER & MICHAEL MAYER; SW on ULRICK SCHONHOLTGER; which land was granted
CONRAD ENGSTER in 1743 (1737) as by special warrant in favor of ULRICK
JOHN TOBLER dated Apr. 1759 directed to ULRICH TOBLER. Witnesses: DANIEL
NEAL (MAGEL), JOHANNES BLOCKLER (GLACKLER). Before JOHN DICK, J.P. Re-
corded 12 Dec. 1766 by FENWICKE BULL, Register.

Book F-3, p. 415   ELIZABETH MEYER, to DAVID ZUBLY, both of New
17 & 18 May 1764   Windsor Township, Granville Co., for Ł 350
L & R   currency, 1/2 of above tract (p. 411). Wit-
                          nesses: LUNZ NAGEL (NEAL), CASPAR NAIL (NEAL).
Before JOHN DICK, J.P., 1 Sept. 1766. Recorded 15 Dec. 1766 by FENWICKE
BULL, Register.

Book F-3, p. 422   JOHN PEARSON, & MARY his wife, to JOSEPH CURRY,
28 & 29 May 1756   both of Craven Co., for Ł 500 currency, 250 a.
L & R   in lower part of Saxegotha Township, Craven
                          Co., granted by Gov. JAMES GLEN on 13 Mar.
1752 to JOHN PEARSON; (see Secretary's Book F.F. fol. 49); bounding S on
Santee River; E on JAMES JENKINS & vacant land; N on HENRY FEIZLER. Witnesses: SIMON HIRONS (HIERONS), EVAN (his mark) REES. Before BARNABAS
ARTHUR, J.P., 15 Jan. 1766. Recorded 16 Dec. 1766 by FENWICKE BULL, Register.

Book F-3, p. 426   COL. JOSEPH CURRY, ESQ., to JOHN HOPKINS,
26 & 27 May 1765   planter, both of Craven Co., for Ł 1000 curren-
L & R   cy, 250 a. in low ground of Santee (Congaree)
                          River, opposite lower part of Saxegotha Town-
ship (p. 422). Witnesses: JOHN THOMAS, SR., JOHN THOMAS, JR., JESSE LUM.
Before JOHN PEARSON, J.P. Recorded 17 Dec. 1766 by FENWICKE BULL, Register.

Book F-3, p. 432   WILLIAM ELLIOTT, JR., gentleman, of Beaufort,
13 Sept. 1758   to GEORGE INGLIS, merchant, of Charleston, for
Conveyance   Ł 1000 currency, part of allot in Charleston,
                          bounding W 26 ft. on Bedon's Alley; S 158-1/2
ft. on the part belonging to THOMAS ELLIOTT, son of THOMAS ELLIOTT, deceased; E on a house & part of said lot belonging to STEPHEN ELLIOTT; N
on house & land belonging to MRS. IOOR; which part of a lot THOMAS
ELLIOTT, planter, of Berkeley Co., by will dated 9 June 1731 bequeathed
to his grandson, said WILLIAM. Witnesses: THOMAS BEE, GEORGE ABBOTT HALL.
Before JAMES PARSONS, J.P., 6 Oct. 1765. Recorded 18 Dec. 1766 by FEN-
WICKE BULL, Register.

Book F-3, p. 435   JAMES SKIRVING, ESQ., of Charleston, & SARAH
20 & 21 Apr. 1764   his wife, to CHARLES ELLIOTT, gentleman, of
L & R   St. Pauls Parish, for Ł 2500 currency, lot
                          #240 in Charleston, bounding W on a new street

leading from White Point by to corner of MR. LEGARE'S lot into Tradd
Street; E on ELIZABETH TUCKER, & MARK MORRIS (formerly WILLIAM FOY; later
in possession of MESSRS. TIPPER, SHUTE & RANDALL); S on lot formerly of
RICHARD PHILIPS, lately of RALPH IZARD, now of his grandson, RALPH IZARD;
N on SUSANNAH BEE (formerly JAMES CLEIVES, later of JAMES KEIR). Whereas
WILLIAM LIVINGSTON, cleric, of Charleston, owned lot #240, lying behind
JOHN TIPPER, which by will dated 17 July 1723 he bequeathed to his son,
GEORGE LIVINGSTON; who by L & R dated 20 & 21 Dec. 1736 sold to JAMES
STOBO; who by L & R dated 24 & 25 Feb. 1763 sold to JAMES SKIRVING; now
he sells to ELLIOTT. Witnesses: JOHN STUART, THOMAS HEYWARD. Before
JAMES PARSONS, J.P. Recorded 20 Dec. 1766 by FENWICKE BULL, Register.

Book F-3, p. 443   WILLIAM (his mark) DALTON, of St. Bartholomews
27 & 28 Nov. 1766   Parish, grandson & heir of WILLIAM DALTON,
L & R   planter; to JAMES PARSONS, ESQ.; of Charleston,
                         for Ł 125 currency, 310 a. in said Parish, be-
ing the N & NE part or half of 2 tracts; 1 of 550 a. purchased by said
WILLIAM DALTON, deceased, on 8 Sept. 1742 from ISAAC GRIMBALL; the other
of 71 a. granted WILLIAM DALTON, deceased, on 13 Mar. 1752. Witnesses:
WILLIAM FIELD, WILLIAM CRABB, CHARLES WAMSLEY. Before JOHN TROUP, J.P.
Recorded 22 Dec. 1766 by FENWICKE BULL, Register.

Book F-3, p. 450   JOHN (JOHAN, his mark) WERNER, planter, of
4 & 5 Dec. 1766   James Island, to JOHN SNELLGROVE, planter, of
L & R   Craven Co., for Ł 100 currency, 100 a. on NE
                         side of Saludy River, in Craven Co., bounding
NW on JOHN STIEL & vacant land; NE on vacant land; SE on ANTHONY BONIN;
as granted JOHN WERNER 11 Oct. 1766. Witnesses: JACOB WIRTH, MICHAEL
DICKETT. Before FENWICKE BULL, J.P. & P. Register. Recorded 26 Dec.
1766.

Book F-3, p. 456   JAMES ST. JOHN, ESQ., of Charleston, to his
10 & 11 July 1740   son, JOHN ST. JOHN, gentleman, for love & af-
L & R   fection, 1750 a. in Granville Co., bounding S
                         on THOMAS OWEN, the Hon. JOSEPH WRAGG, & ROB-
ERT WRIGHT; other sides on vacant land. Witnesses: JONATHAN THOMPSON,
WILLIAM IRVIN. Before JAMES ABERCROMBY, 12 July 1740. Recorded 26 Dec.
1766 by FENWICKE BULL, Register.

Book F-3, p. 462   JANE DUMAY, widow, of St. James Santee, Craven
26 Aug. 1766   Co., to EDWARD JERMAN & PETER GUERRY, gentle-
Feoffment   men, of same Parish, trustees for those inhab-
                         itants who subscribed for the building of a
house on some land near the church of Itchaw, to be used as a shelter
from bad weather on Sundays, holy days, & at assembly of the company of
militia at muster there; a small piece of land about 1/4 a., bounding N
on the church yard; E on road to Charleston; W on MRS. DUMAY. Witnesses:
JOHN HENTIE, BENJAMIN PERDRIAU. Before PAUL DOUXSAINT, J.P. Recorded 27
Dec. 1766 by FENWICKE BULL, Register.

Book F-3, p. 465   JAMES WRIGHT, Gov. of Ga., to EDWARD JERMAN,
1 & 2 July 1766   ESQ., of Parish of St. James Santee, SC, for
L & R   Ł 5000 SC money, 1478 a., called Old Settle-
                         ment, now planted by JAMES WRIGHT, 442 a. was
supposed to be swamp according to survey by JOHN HENTIE; bounding SE on
middle of road & dam leading from the pounding machine on the plantation
lately sold by JAMES WRIGHT to GEORGE PADDON BOND to the NW side of the
swamp where the settlement is on land hereby conveyed; NW on vacant land;
NE & SE on THEODORE GAILLARD. Whereas TACITUS GAILLARD, gentleman, of
Santee, owned several adjoining tracts on Wambaw Swamp, in Craven Co.,
making 1 tract of 2478 a.; which, with ANN his wife, he sold by L & R
dated 5 & 6 Sept. 1753, to said JAMES WRIGHT; now WRIGHT sells to JERMAN.
Witnesses: THOMAS ADAM, CHARLES WRIGHT. Before ROBERT PRINGLE, Ass't. J
of Ct. of C.P. Recorded 30 Dec. 1766 by FENWICKE BULL, Register.

Book F-3, p. 474   WILLIAM GLEN, merchant, of Charleston, only
11 & 12 Dec. 1766   acting executor of will of ROBERT MCMURDY,
L & R   planter, of Pon Pon; to JAMES ST. JOHN, plant-
                         er, for Ł 200 currency, 300 a. in Colleton Co.,
bounding, at time of grant dated 18 Sept. 1754, on all sides on vacant

land. Whereas ROBERT MCCURDY by will dated 13 May 1756 bequeathed all his estate to his executors (WILLIAM GLEN; JOHN BEATY, since deceased; & FRANCIS BEATY) in trust, to sell if necessary to pay his debts; now GLEN sells at auction to ST. JOHN. Witnesses: RICHARD MASON, JOSEPH STANYARNE. Before WILLIAM MASON, J.P. Recorded 31 Dec. 1766 by FENWICKE BULL, Register.

Book F-3, p. 480   WILLIAM COACHMAN & BENJAMIN COACHMAN, to DAN-
10 Dec. 1766   IEL DOYLEY. Whereas WILLIAM COACHMAN, plant-
Assignment   er, by plat & grant dated 15 Sept. 1760 & 16
                      Jan. 1760 obtained a grant for 200 a. in St.
George Parish, Dorchester, on presumption said land was vacant; bounding E on WILLIAM DONNING; SW on RICHARD BEDON & WILLIAM GODFREY; NW on WILLIAM COACHMAN; & after obtaining said grant sold the 200 a. & another tract of 1000 a. in said Parish to BENJAMIN COACHMAN, of Parish of Goose Creek; & whereas DANIEL DOYLEY, of Charleston, purchased a part of the Ponds Plantation, or Winten Hall, belonging to WILLIAM DONNING, which COACHMAN'S 200 a. was said to adjoin; & whereas after DOYLEY purchased from DONNING it was found, upon resurvey, that COACHMAN'S 200 a. were not vacant but actually within DOYLEY'S lines; & claimed by him; & whereas DOYLEY agreed with WILLIAM & BENJAMIN COACHMAN that the 200 a. be determined by 3 persons experienced in surveying, namely, WILLIAM MAINE, PHILIP SMITH & JOHN GIRARDEAU, who later decided that said tract was not vacant when granted to COACHMAN but belonged to DONNING, now to DOYLEY; now WILLIAM & BENJAMIN relinquished their claim. Witnesses: WILLIAM MAINE, PHILIP SMITH, JOHN BOHUN GIRARDEAU. Before JOHN IOOR, J.P. Recorded 1 Jan. 1767 by FENWICKE BULL, Register.

Book F-3, p. 484   PERCIVAL PAWLEY, planter, & ANN his wife, to
20 July 1745   GEORGE PAWLEY & WILLIAM POOLE, trustees; all
Release in Trust   of Craven Co.; for Ł 100 currency, 50 a., part
                      of 500 a. formerly belonging to DR. JOHN HUT-
CHING, now to PAWLEY; bounding W on a creek; E on PERCIVAL PAWLEY; N on JOSEPH ALLIN; to be used for a church (Church of England) by the inhabitants of Waccamaw Neck. Witnesses: PERCIVAL PAWLEY, JR., GEORGE PAWLEY, JR. Before BENJAMIN YOUNG, J.P. on 8 Jan. 1766. Recorded 2 Jan. 1767 by FENWICKE BULL, Register.

Book F-3, p. 487   CHARLES WILLIAMS, of Island of St. Helena, to
19 & 20 June 1764   MARY WILLIAMS, SR., of same place, during her
L & R   lifetime, for Ł 100 SC money, 135 a., being
                      1/2 of 270 a. in Granville Co., bounding N on
Lt. Gov. WILLIAM BULL; W on RICHARD CAPERS; SW on WILLIAM ADAMS; SE on marsh opposite Hunting Islands. Plat dated 27 May 1752. Witnesses: JEREMIAH WELLS, THOMAS GREENE. Before JOHN TROUP, J.P. Recorded 5 Jan. 1767 by FENWICKE BULL, Register.

Book F-3, p. 493   PAUL SMISER, planter, & RACHEL (her mark) his
3 & 4 Dec. 1766   wife, to LAMBERT LANCE, merchant, both of
L & R by Mortgage   Charleston, for Ł 2750 currency, 375 a. in
                      Colleton Co., granted 30 Sept. 1736 to JAMES
ST. JOHN; then bounding E on WILLIAM WESTBURY; S on GEORGE VINCENT; W on SAMUEL SLEIGH; N on JOHN GODFREY; also part of a lot in Charleston, bounding N 25 ft. 10 in. on Broad Street; W 200 ft. on part belonging to JAMES NOLOUX; S on land belonging to French Church; E on MATHURINE GUERIN. Witnesses: WILLIAM ROPER, JR., JOHN DART, JR. Before FENWICKE BULL, J.P. & Register. On 22 Mar. 1770 LANCE declared mortgage paid. Witness: JAMES KER.

Book F-3, p. 501   NATHAN BARR, planter, of Craven Co., to JOSEPH
26 & 27 Oct. 1765   PICKENS, planter, of Granville Co., for Ł 130
L & R   currency, 200 a. in Granville Co., on Calhouns
                      Creek, a branch of NW fork of Long Cane Creek;
bounding on all sides on vacant land; which tract was granted 4 Mar. 1760 by Gov. WILLIAM HENRY LYTTLETON to WILLIAM BARR; who bequeathed to his son, NATHAN. Witnesses: WILLIAM DAVIES, JOHN DAVIES, ANN DAVIES. Before PATRICK CALHOUN, J.P. Recorded 7 Jan. 1767 by FENWICKE BULL, Register.

Book F-3, p. 506   WILLIAM WILLIAMSON, ESQ., & MARTHA his wife,
7 & 8 Jan. 1765   to CHARLES ELLIOTT, planter, both of

L & R   Charleston, for ₤ 15,000 currency, 1900 a. in
                               St. Pauls Parish, Colleton Co., commonly call-
ed Spoons Savannah, made up of several tracts; 100 a. granted 5 Nov. 1704
to JOHN WILLIAMSON, then bounding N & W on JONATHAN FITCH; S & E on vacant land; 250 a. sold by JOHN BAYLEY to WILLIAM WILLIAMSON on 2 May 1727;
then bounding SW & NE on WILLIAM WILLIAMSON; W on JOSEPH PECKHAM; NE on
BRYAN REYLEY; 560 a. granted WILLIAMSON 28 Apr. 1733 bounding SE on
Spoons Mavannah; N on BRIAN REYLEY; W & SW on WILLIAMSON; other sides on
vacant land; 446 a. (by re-survey) granted WILLIAMSON 6 Apr. 1733; bounding N on WILLIAMSON; other sides on vacant land; 161 a. (by re-survey)
granted WILLIAMSON 24 May 1734; bounding S on WILLIAMSON; NW on BRYAN
REYLEY & STEVENSON; E on JOSEPH PACOMB; 260 a. (part of 660 a., according
to re-survey, formerly belonging to JOHN WILLIAMSON) allotted to WILLIAM
WILLIAMSON (the other part being allotted to CHAMPERNOWN WILLIAMSON),
bounding NW on REYLEY & WILLIAM WILLIAMSON; W on MR. SPRY; SE & NE on
WILLIAM WILLIAMSON; 118 granted WILLIAMSON 5 May 1761; bounding NW on estate of BRIAN REYLEY; other sides on WILLIAM WILLIAMSON. Witnesses:
FRANCIS GUERIN, BENJAMIN WILLIAMSON. Entered in Auditor's Book H-8, p.
124-128, on 3 Dec. 1766 by RICHARD LAMBTON, Dep. Aud. Before FENWICKE
BULL, J.P. & P. Register.

Book F-3, p. 513   DANIEL LEGARE, ISAAC LEGARE, & JOHN FULLERTON,
16 Apr. 1761   planters, of Christ Church Parish, to JOSEPH
L & R   MAYBANK, planter, of same place, for ₤ 400 cur-
                             rency, 50 a. in Berkeley Co., bounding N on
JOSEPH MAYBANK; other sides on JOHN HUGGINS; the 50 a. to include the re-
serve, or dam of water; used by his predecessors. Witnesses: ALLEN MCKEE,
RICHARD JOY, GEORGE WHITE. Before WILLIAM VANDERHORST, J.P. Recorded 14
Jan. 1767 by FENWICKE BULL, Register.

Book F-3, p. 519   JOHN DUBOSE, planter, & MARY his wife, to CAPT.
27 Oct. 1764   JOSEPH MAYBANK, both of Christ Church Parish,
L & R   Berkeley Co., for ₤ 1000 currency, 300 a. in
                            said Parish, bounding NE on MAJ. HENRY BONNEAU;
SE on marsh of Sewee Bay; SW on SAMUEL SIMON, SR.; N on vacant land. Wit-
nesses: BENJAMIN SIMONS, HENRY SIMONS, JOHN BASKERFIELD. Before WOOD FUR-
MAN, J.P. Recorded 15 Jan. 1767 by FENWICKE BULL, Register.

Book F-3, p. 524   DAVID MAYBANK & ANDREW MAYBANK, planters, of
30 & 31 Mar. 1764   St. Bartholomew Parish, Colleton Co., to JO-
L & R   SEPH MAYBANK, planter, of Christ Church Parish,
                            for ₤ 600 currency, 2 undivided third parts of
500 a. in Christ Church Parish, adjoining SAMUEL WIGFALL'S & ROBERT JOHN-
STON'S plantations, as owned by their father, JOSEPH MAYBANK & now held
by JOSEPH MAYBANK, & devised by will of said father, dated 23 Apr. 1740,
equally to said sons; the land to be free from claims of dower by HANNAH
(wife of DAVID) & MARTHA (wife of ANDREW). Witnesses: DANIEL CANNON,
HENRY CROUCH, JOHN CALVERT. Before FENWICKE BULL, J.P. & Pub. Register.
Recorded 19 Jan. 1767.

Book F-3, p. 532   WILLIAM HALL, farmer, of Rowan Co., NC, to
15 Dec. 1766   CAPT. JOHN BARKELEY in Washaw Settlement, Cra-
Release   ven Co., SC, ₤ 430 SC money, 300 a. on Gills
                            Creek, beginning at a black oak, running W
280 to a pine, then S 40 W 120 poles to white oak, then S 100 poles to
stake; then N 81 E 350 poles to black oak; then N 140 poles to 1st station; as granted 24 Sept. 1754 by Gov. MATHEW RANN, of NC, to WILLIAM
HALL. Witnesses: JOHN HOWE, SAMUEL DUNLAP, JOHN WHITE. Before JOHN CANT-
ZON, J.P. of Craven Co. Recorded 19 Jan. 1767 by FENWICKE BULL, Register.

Book F-3, p. 535   PATRICK MCCORMICK, planter, & JOANNA (her mark)
11 & 12 Mar. 1766   his wife, to JAMES MCCORMICK, planter, both of
L & R   Craven Co., for ₤ 100 currency, 150 a. in Cra-
                            ven Co., granted 20 Oct. 1763 by Gov. THOMAS
BOONE to PATRICK MCCORMICK; bounding N on Wateree River; E on EDWARD
KIRKLAND; other sides on vacant land. Witnesses: PAUL MCCORMICK, DRURY
HUDSON, JOHN (his mark) MCCORMICK. Before ANDREW ALISON, J.P. Recorded
19 Jan. 1767 by FENWICKE BULL, Register.

Book F-3, p. 541   EDWARD JERMAN, ESQ., of St. James Santee

11 Dec. 1766   Parish, to Gov. JAMES WRIGHT, of Ga., for
Mortgage   Ⴑ 5000 currency, 1478 a. called Old Settlement
                      on Wambaw Swamp, Craven Co., SC, lately sold
by JAMES WRIGHT to EDWARD JERMAN; bounding SE on the center of the road &
dam leading through from the pounding machine on the plantation lately
sold by JAMES WRIGHT to GEORGE PADDON BOND to the NW side of the swamp
where the settlement is on the land sold to EDWARD JERMAN; NW on vacant
land; NE & SE on THEODORE GAILLARD. Witnesses: JOHN HENTIE, BENJAMIN
SMITH. Before JOHN TROUP, J.P. Recorded 20 Jan. 1767 by FENWICKE BULL,
Register. On 12 Oct. 1769 BENJAMIN SMITH, on behalf of Gov. JAMES
WRIGHT, declared mortgage satisfied. Witnesses: WILLIAM VALENTINE.

Book F-3, p. 548   WILLIAM DODGIN, late Corp. to MATHEW NEILSON,
2 & 3 Sept. 1765   planter, both of St. Marks Parish, Craven Co.,
L & R   for Ⴑ 200 currency, 200 a. in Santee River
                       Swamp, on Codoes Lake, St. Marks Parish, grant-
ed on the King's bounty 21 June 1765; bounding NW & NE on MATHEW NEILSON;
NE on vacant land; SE on MATHEW NEILSON & vacant land. Witnesses: JAMES
HOPPER, SOLOMON SLATON, WILLIAM (his mark) JONES. Before JAMES LYNAH,
J.P. Recorded 21 Jan. 1767 by FENWICKE BULL, Register.

Book F-3, p. 553   WILLIAM GASCOIGNE, ESQ., of (London) Parish of
26 July 1765   of St. James Westminster, Co. of Middlesex,
Release   eldest son & heir of ADM. JOHN GASCOIGNE,
                       former CAPT. of H.M.S. The Albrough; to THOMAS
SMITH, ESQ., of Charleston, SC, for Ⴑ 125 British; 500 a., called Apps,
granted by the Lords Proprs. to COL. ALEXANDER TRENCH; on SW part of
Trench's Island (formerly Hilton Head Island) on E side Dawfuskie River,
against mouth of River May, Granville, So., SC, bounding S on ROGER
MOORE; W on marsh & a creek of Dawfuskie River; N on Trench's Island; E
on marsh adjoining Bark Creek; as by plat by FRANCIS YOUNG, Sur. Gen.,
dated 16 Aug. 1730. Witnesses: PETER CALMEL, ELISHA BISCOL, JAMES GADS-
DEN of Cheapside; THOMAS GADSDEN of SC. Proved by GADSDEN before JACOB
MOTTE 3 Jan. 1767. Entered in Aud. Gen. Book H-8, p. 134 on 5 Jan. 1767
by RICHARD LAMBTON, Dep. Aud. Recorded 21 Jan. 1767 by FENWICKE BULL,
Register.

Book F-3, p. 558   JOSEPH CANTEY, planter, of St. Marks Parish,
5 & 6 Dec. 1766   Craven Co., & ANN his wife, to MATHEW NEILSON,
L & R   for Ⴑ 100 currency, 100 a. on Black River
                       Swamp, Craven Co., granted 3 Apr. 1759 by Gov.
WILLIAM HENRY LYTTELTON; bounding on all sides on vacant land. Witness-
es: JAMES NORVEL, SAMUEL GIBSON, JOSIAH NEILSON. Before HENRY CASSELS,
J.P. Recorded 22 Jan. 1767 by FENWICKE BULL, Register.

Book F-3, p. 566   ROBERT RAYLEY, yeoman, of St. Marks Parish,
5 & 6 Dec. 1766   Craven Co., to MATHEW NEILSON, of Craven Co.,
L & R   for Ⴑ 100 currency, 100 a. in Craven Co.,
                       bounding E on BENJAMIN JOHNSON; NW on vacant
land; S on GEORGE EVANS; which tract was granted 2 Oct. 1764 by Lt. Gov.
WILLIAM BULL. Witnesses: SAMUEL GIBSON, EBENEZER BAGNALL, JOHN VERTEE.
Before JAMES LYNAH, J.P. Recorded 23 Jan. 1767 by FENWICKE BULL, Register.

Book F-3, p. 573   JOHN EVANS, SR., planter, of St. Helena, Gran-
12 & 13 Jan. 1767   ville Co., to his son, JOHN EVANS, JR., for
L & R   love & affection, 554 a. in St. Helena Island,
                       originally granted JOHN STEWART; later belong-
ing to THOMAS FARR, planter, who sold to EVANS; bounding on creeks &
marshes; also 26 slaves, & horses, cattle & sheep on said plantation.
Witnesses: JOHN FRIPP, WILLIAM FRIPP. Before FENWICKE BULL, J.P. & P.
Register.

Book F-3, p. 579   ALEXANDER SHARROD, of Craven Co., to JOSEPH
14 & 15 May 1765   BROWN, merchant, of Georgetown, for Ⴑ 1960
L & R by Mortgage   currency, 3 tracts, total 616 a. on Peedee
                       River which he purchased from JAMES THOMPSON
& where he lives & plants. Witnesses: DUNCAN SHAW, JOSEPH HUGGINS. Before CHARLES FYFFE, J.P. Recorded 24 Jan. 1767 by FENWICKE BULL, Register.

Book F-3, p. 584   THOMAS SMITH, merchant, & SARAH his wife, to
14 & 15 Dec. 1763   THOMAS HUTCHINSON, cabinet maker; both of
L & R & Bond   Charleston; for ₺ 300 currency, part of the N
                          part of a lot formerly belonging to CATHARINE
GREENLAND; bounding N 60 ft. on RICHARD LAMBTON; E 30 ft. on DANIEL LE-
GARE, JR.; S on other part belonging to THOMAS SMITH; W on THOMAS HUTCH-
INSON. SMITH gives bond of performance. Witnesses: BENJAMIN WARING, DAN-
IEL CROKATT. Before FENWICKE BULL, J.P. & P. Register.

Book F-3, p. 590   WILLIAM MOSMAN, soldier, in H.M. 60th Reg. of
27 & 28 Aur. 1766   Foot; to RALPH PHILIPS, gentleman, of Charles-
L & R   ton for ₺ 12:10:0 currency, 50 a. in Granville
                          Co., bounding NE on vacant land; SE on land
belonging to the Chickasaws; NW on RALPH PHILIPS (formerly JOHN HANDLEY).
Witnesses: JOHN GLEN, ALEXANDER MOULTRIE. Before JAMES PARSONS, J.P.
Entered in Aud. Gen's. Book H-8, p. 82, on 28 Aug. 1766 by RICHARD LAMB-
TON, Dep. Aud. Recorded 27 Jan. 1767 by FENWICKE BULL, Register.

Book F-3, p. 595   JAMES PARSONS, ESQ., to CAPT. RALPH PHILLIPS,
22 & 23 July 1766   gentleman, both of Charleston, for 10 shil-
L & R   lings currency, 600 a. bounding SW on Savannah
                          River; NW on FREDERICK WEBBER & vacant land;
as granted JAMES PARSONS. Witnesses: JOHN GLEN, ALEXANDER MOULTREE. Before JOHN TROUP, J.P. Entered in Aud. Gen's Book H-8, p. 64, on 23 July
1766 by RICHARD LAMBTON, Dep. Aud. Recorded 27 Jan. 1767 by FENWICKE
BULL, Register.

Book F-3, p. 599   JOHN (his mark) HANDLEY, soldier, in H.M. 60th
23 & 24 Oct. 1766   Reg. of Foot, to RALPH PHILLIPS, gentleman, of
L & R   Charleston, for ₺ 12:10:0 currency, 50 a. in
                          Granville Co., bounding NW on JAMES PARSONS;
NE on vacant land; SE on vacant land & WILLIAM MOSMAN. Witnesses: JOSHUA
HIRST, ALEXANDER MOULTREE. Entered in Aud. Gen's Book H-8, p. 116, on 5
Nov. 1766 by RICHARD LAMBTON, J.P. Recorded 28 Jan. 1767 by FENWICKE
BULL, Register.

Book F-3, p. 605   JOHN TOBY SHOP, freeholder, of St. Peters Par-
20 Dec. 1767   ish, Granville Co., to ADRIAN MAYER, ESQ., of
Conveyance   Purysburgh, for ₺ 40 currency, lot #57 in
                          Purysburgh, 1 a., bounding N on a street; E on
lot #58; S on a street; W on the Bay or Front Street. Witnesses: GEORGE
KEHL (KEAL), MELCHIOR LICHTENSTEIGER. Before JOHN LEWIS BOURQUIN, J.P.
Recorded 29 Jan. 1767 by FENWICKE BULL, Register.

Book F-3, p. 607   JOHN BARNWELL, planter, of Granville Co., &
4 & 5 Aug. 1761   MARTHA his wife, to SARAH CHAPLIN, widow, in
L & R   trust for her youngest son, WILLIAM CHAPLIN;
                          for ₺ 1500 currency, 300 a. in Granville Co.,
bounding W on RICHARD STEVENS; N on WILLIAM CHAPLIN; E on flats & marshes;
S on JOHN TOOMER; which tract was originally granted to JOSEPH WATSON, &
inherited by his nephew & heir, JAMES WATSON; who sold to JOHN BARNWELL
in 1745. Witnesses: FRANCIS STUART, LEWIS REEVE. Before WILLIAM HARVEY,
J.P. Entered in Auditor's Book E, p. 162, on 24 Oct. 1761 by GEORGE
JOHNSTON, Pro. Dep. Aud. Recorded 30 Jan. 1767 by FENWICKE BULL, Register.

Book F-3, p. 614   JOSHUA MORGAN, planter, of Prince William Par-
26 Dec. 1763   ish; WILLIAM O'BRYEN, merchant, of St. Helena
L & R   Parish, & ANN his wife; & RICHARD CAPERS,
                          planter, of Savannah, Ga., & SUSANNAH his
wife; of 1st part; to WILLIAM FRIPP, planter, of St. Helena Parish, SC;
for ₺ 3700 currency, an island of 215 a. in St. Helena Parish granted 11
Oct. 1701 by Gov. JAMES MOORE to ROBERT SEABROOK, planter; bounding S &
SW on St. Helena River; other sides on large tracts of marsh on St. Helena Sound, Coosaw River, & Coosaw Creek; which tract ROBERT SEABROOK devised, with other real estate, to WILLIAM PARROT & ANN his wife; who on 1
Apr. 1722 sold to RICHARD CAPERS; who devised to his daughter, ANN MORGAN,
since deceased. Witnesses: RICHARD STEVENS, JOHN GRAYSON, WILLIAM BOWREY.
Before THOMAS MIDDLETON, J.P. Entered in Aud. Book H-8, p. 129, on 1 Dec.
1766 by RICHARD LAMBTON, Dep. Aud. Recorded 31 Jan. 1767 by FENWICKE

BULL, Register.

Book F-3, p. 623   ANTHONY POUNCEY, of Craven Co., to JOSEPH
1 & 2 Jan. 1767   BROWN, merchant, of Georgetown, for
L & R by Mortgage   Ł 7865:15:9 currency, 3 tracts, total 750 a.
            in St. Marks Parish, Craven Co.; 450 a. grant-
ed JOHN BROWN, who conveyed to POUNCEY; 200 a. NW on above tract; 100 a.
S of said 450 a.; the 450 a. bounding NE on Peedee River; S on JOHN KIM-
BROUGH; N on ANDREW SLANN; SW on vacant land. Witnesses: JOSEPH HUGGINS,
GEORGE BONHOSTE. Before CHARLES FYFFE, J.P. Recorded 31 Jan. 1767 by
FENWICKE BULL, Register.

Book F-3, p. 632   JOSEPH JACKSON, planter, & MARY his wife, to
28 Sept. 1766   ROBERT STUART, weaver & planter, both of
L & R   Berkeley Co., for Ł 200 currency, 300 a. in
            fork of Santee & Wateree Rivers; bounding on
all sides on vacant land. Witnesses: RAND MCCARTHEY, BENJAMIN SCOTT.
Before JOHN LIVISTON, J.P. Recorded 31 Jan. 1767 by FENWICKE BULL, Register.

Book F-3, p. 638   JOHN HAMELTON, ESQ., to ISAAC RAIFORD, plant-
4 & 5 Dec. 1766   er, both of Craven Co., for Ł 40 currency, 40
L & R   a. in Craven Co., bounding NW on vacant land;
            NE on ISAAC RAIFORD; SE & SW on Black Swamp;
being part of 300 a. granted HAMELTON by Gov. JAMES GLEN, on N side San-
tee (Congaree) River, nearly opposite Saxegotha Township, bounding NW on
PHILIP RAIFORD; other sides on vacant land. Witnesses: WILLIAM MEYER,
WILLIAM BUTLER. Certified by JOHN HAMELTON. Recorded 4 Feb. 1767 by
FENWICKE BULL, Register.

Book F-3, p. 643   JAMES LINGARD, blacksmith, & MARY his wife, to
7 Feb. 1767   HOPKIN PRICE, ESQ., both of Charleston (be-
Mortgage   cause PRICE went on LINGARD'S bond to ALEXAN-
            DER PERONNEAU, gentleman, of said Town, for
Ł 3500 currency); the southernmost & northernmost parts of lot #48 on E
side of Church Street, St. Philips Parish, near N end of said street; the
southernmost part bounding W 75 ft. on Church Street; S 347 ft. on THOMAS
BEE; E on JOSEPH WRAGG; N on middle part of said lot lately sold by LIN-
GARD to JOHN RUTLEDGE, ESQ.; the northernmost part bounding W 75 ft. on
Church Street; S 347 ft. on middle part belonging to RUTLEDGE; E on JO-
SEPH WRAGG; N on other land or marsh. Witnesses: JAMES SIMPSON, ANN CAD-
MON. Before FENWICKE BULL, J.P. & P. Register.

Book F-3, p. 650   NATHANIEL SCOTT, brewer, to WILLIAM GLEN & AL-
9 Feb. 1767   EXANDER MICHIE, merchants, all of Charleston,
Release in Trust   2 Negro slaves; also several lots in Charles-
            ton, bounding W 140 ft. on Friend Street; N
120 ft. on MR. HUTCHINSON; S on MR. ROUPELL & THOMAS SMITH; E on DANIEL
LEGARE, JR.; in trust, to sell the land & Negroes & pay SCOTTS creditors.
Witnesses: WILLIAM MORGAN, JOHN FRASER. Before FENWICKE BULL, J.P. & P.
Register.

Book F-3, p. 654   RICHARD SPENCER, planter, to JOHN GLAZE,
5 & 6 Mar. 1749   planter, both of St. George Parish, Berkeley
L & R   Co., for Ł 160 currency, 200 a. in said Parish,
            granted 22 July 1718 by Gov. ROBERT JOHNSON to
GEORGE STERLING; later the property of ANTHONY SPENCER, father of RICHARD;
bounding NE & SE on HENRY IZARD; NW on JOHN GLAZE; SE on JAMES MARION.
Witnesses: ALEXANDER MAGEE, WILLIAM JAMES, WILLIAM MAINE. Before JOHN
IOOR, J.P. Recorded 12 Feb. 1767 by FENWICKE BULL, Register.

Book F-3, p. 661   ROBERT GUERIN, planter, to STEPHEN MILLER,
22 Dec. 1766   planter, both of St. Thomas Parish, Berkeley
L & R   Co., for Ł 400 currency, 166 a. in said Par-
            ish, bounding N on the Rev. MR. ROBERT SMYTH;
E on MRS. MARY ANNE BILBOW; S on STEPHEN MILLER; W on ROBERT JOHNSTON;
which tract GUERIN had purchased from THOMAS WATTS & SUSANNA his wife by
L & R dated 18 & 19 Oct. 1759. Witnesses: JOHN MOURET, JOHN HETHERING-
TON. Before FENWICKE BULL, J.P. & P. Register. Recorded 14 Feb. 1767.

Book F-3, p. 670   JAMES ROULAIN, planter, of Parish of St. Thom-
2 & 3 June 1762   as & St. Dennis, to DANIEL RAVENEL, JR., gen-
L & R   tlemen, of St. Johns Parish, Berkeley Co., for
                          Ł 500 currency, part of lot #98 in Charleston,
inherited from his father JAMES ROULAIN; bounding E 46 ft. on ISAAC
MAZYCK; W on other part said lot; S 68 ft. on DANIEL RAVENEL, JR. (formerly PAUL MAZYCK); N on WILLIAM MCILHENNY (formerly JANE DEPEY; afterwards PATRICK LAIRD). Witnesses: ISAAC MAZYCK, WILLIAM MAZYCK. Before
HENRY RAVENEL 26 June 1762. Recorded 16 Feb. 1767 by FENWICKE BULL, Register.

Book F-3, p. 679   BENJAMIN PERRY, planter, & FRANCES his wife,
25 & 26 May 1766   to JOSIAH PERRY, planter, both of St. Pauls
L & R   Parish, Colleton Co., for Ł 1000 currency,
                          345 a. in said Parish, bounding W on Pon Pon
River; S on THOMAS FERGUSON; N on JOHN MCQUEEN & BENJAMIN ELLIOTT; E on
JOSIAH PERRY. Whereas the Rev. MR. WILLIAM LIVINGSTONE, of Charleston,
purchased from Landgrave ROBERT DANIEL 4000 a. in E side of freshes of
Edisto or Pon Pon River, & on 21 Mar. 1719 sold to THOMAS SMITH a part or
1750 a.; & whereas SMITH sold a part, or 1000 a., to SAMUEL ASH; who by
L & R dated 25 & 26 Feb. 1728 sold the 1000 a. to BENJAMIN PERRY of
Berkeley Co.; now BENJAMIN sells a part of the tract to JOSIAH. Witness-
es: PATRICK TURNBULL, JAMES POSTELL, JR., SUSANNA POSTELL. Before SAMUEL
PORCHER, J.P. Recorded 16 Feb. 1767 by FENWICKE BULL, Register.

Book F-3, p. 687   PETER ROBLIN, of Craven Co., to JOSEPH BROWN,
28 & 29 Oct. 1765   merchant, of Georgetown, for Ł 600 currency,
L & R by Mortgage   300 a. on Roblins Neck, where he lives; bound-
                          ing NE on Peedee River; NW on THOMAS EDWARDS;
SE on ROBERT BLAYER; SW on JOHN BRUCE. Witnesses: FELIX WARLEY, JOSEPH
HUGGINS. Before CHARLES FYFFE, J.P. Recorded 17 Feb. 1767 by FENWICKE
BULL, Register.

Book F-3, p. 693   NATHANIEL BROWN, planter, of Peedee having
21 July 1766   given 3 bonds to JOSEPH BROWN, merchant, of
Mortgage   Georgetown, total Ł 1020 currency, conveys to
                          BROWN, as security, 4 Negroes, his horses,
hogs, cattle, furniture, bedding, etc., also 200 a. in Prince George Parish, Craven Co., adjoining GEORGE PAWLEY, JR. A penknife delivered.
Witnesses: JOSEPH HUGGINS, MARK HUGGINS. Before CHARLES FYFFE, J.P. Recorded 18 Feb. 1767 by FENWICKE BULL, Register.

Book F-3, p. 696   WILLIAM (his mark) OWEN, planter, of Peedee,
20 Jan. 1767   Craven Co., to JOSEPH BROWN, for Ł 1578 cur-
Mortgage   rency, 4 Negroes; also 100 a. on Flat Creek,
                          with all houses, furniture, tools, hogs,
cattle, horses, with mark of a crop & 2 slits in left ear & a flower de
luce on right ear. A penknife delivered. Witnesses: JOSEPH HUGGINS,
GEORGE BONHOSTE. Before CHARLES FYFFE, J.P. Recorded 18 Feb. 1767 by
FENWICKE BULL, Register.

Book F-3, p. 699   BENJAMIN JAMES, of Craven Co., to JOSEPH
30 & 31 Oct. 1765   BROWN, merchant, of Georgetown, for Ł 1200
L & R by Mortgage   currency, 200 a. in the Welch Neck, Craven
                          Co., (taken off the front of 350 a. purchased
from THOMAS JAMES), bounding E on Peedee River; W on other part of
tract; other sides on vacant land. Witnesses: JOSEPH HUGGINS, GEORGE
BONHOSTE. Before CHARLES FYFFE, J.P. Recorded 19 Feb. 1767 by FENWICKE
BULL, Register.

Book F-3, p. 705   EDWARD PERRY, SR., planter, of Colleton Co., &
25 Apr. 1743   ROSAMOND, his wife, to their son, BENJAMIN
Release   PERRY, for Ł 940 currency, 188 a. in Colleton
                          Co., bounding E on RALPH IZARD; NE on PHILIP
EVANS; W on EDWARD PERRY. Witnesses: EDWARD PERRY, JR., JAMES LADSON.
Before ANDREW LEITCH, J.P. Recorded 19 Feb. 1767 by FENWICKE BULL, Reg-
ister.

Book F-3, p. 708   GEORGE PAWLEY, JR., planter, & SARAH his wife,
7 & 8 June 1765   to NATHANIEL DWIGHT, planter, both of Prince

L & R George Parish, Craven Co., for Ł 1000 currency, 311 a. in Craven Co., bounding E on sea
marsh; W on CHRISTOPHER GADSDEN (formerly GEORGE PAWLEY, JR.); N on WIL-
LIAM PAWLEY (formerly JOSEPH PRINCE); S on NATHANIEL DWIGHT; being part
of 2 tracts of 1080 a. purchased by PAWLEY from ARCHER SMITH, of Goose
Creek. Witnesses: ELIAS FOISSIN, JR., JOHN DWIGHT. Before JOSIAS ALL-
STON, J.P. On 14 Feb. 1767 DANIEL DWIGHT wrote CHRISTOPHER GADSDEN, enclosing a note MR. BURROWS, proving that GADSDEN might "with safety" issue a certificate that the land "my brother NATHANIEL purchased from COL.
PAWLEY was by your consent". To which letter GADSDEN replied stating the
tract was sold with his consent while he had a judgment against said PAW-
LEY & the money paid to him in part of said judgment. Recorded 20 Feb.
1767 by FENWICKE BULL, Register.

Book F-3, p. 717 THOMAS VANDERDUSSEN, ensign in H.M. 17th Reg.
16 & 17 Feb. 1767 of Foot, by his attorney, JOHN TORRANS, of
L & R Charleston, & HENRY TOOMER, gentleman, of NC;
of 1st part; to WILLIAM WITHERS, planter, of
Goose Creek, for Ł 2000 currency, 2 tracts of 200 & 500 a., total 700 a.
on Goose Creek; the 200 a. bounding N on Red Bank; E on Cooper River; S
on CAPT. SCHINKING; W on the 500 a.; the 500 a. bounding SW on Goose
Creek; SE on Cooper River; NE on the 200 a. & CAPT. SCHINKING; NW on ROB-
ERT HOW. Whereas ALEXANDER VANDERDUSSEN by will dated 4 July 1749 bequeathed the residue of his estate equally to ELIZABETH & MARY, daughters
of MARY NESBITT, & to THOMAS ALEXANDER VANDERDUSSEN; & whereas ELIZABETH
died a minor; & MARY (the daughter) married HENRY TOOMER, had children, &
died; so that VANDERDUSSON is seized in fee of the estate, HENRY TOOMER
being tenant by "the curtesy"; now they sell to WITHERS. Witnesses: JOHN
GLEN, JOHN CALVERT. Before FENWICKE BULL, J.P. & P. Register.

Book F-3, p. 727 THOMAS ALEXANDER VANDERDUSSEN, Ensign in H.M.
2 Oct. 1765 17th Reg. of Foot, appointed JOHN TORRANS,
Letter of Attorney merchant, of SC, his attorney, with power to
sell certain land. Witnesses: SAMUEL WILLIAMS,
LT. 17th Reg.; PERK. MAGRA, LT. 15th Reg. Recorded 23 Feb. 1767 by FEN-
WICKE BULL, Register.

Book F-3, p. 729 GEORGE II, by Gov. WILLIAM HENRY LYTTLETON, to
4 Mar. 1760 THOMAS JERNIGEN, 200 a. on both sides of Cados
Grant Lake, on N side Santee River, in Craven Co.,
bounding S on vacant swamp; E on JARED NELSON
& vacant land; NW on vacant land; SW on vacant land & JOSEPH HOWARD.
Signed: WILLIAM SIMPSON, C.C. Recorded in Secretary's Book T.T. fol.
375 by WILLIAM MURRAY, for Dep. Sec. Plat of survey of 28 Feb. 1758 by
EGERTON LEIGH, Sur. Gen.; JAMES ROBERT, Dep. Sur. Recorded in Auditor's
Book E, p. 51, on 6 May 1761 by GEORGE JOHNSTON, for Dep. Aud.

Book F-3, p. 731 GLIDWELL (his mark) ORRELL, & SARAH (her mark)
12 Jan. 1767 his wife, of Craven Co., to DERICK MANNAN, for
Assignment & Sale Ł 200 proclamation money; 200 a. on Potato
Creek; also his hogs (marked with poplar leaf,
a hole in 1 ear, slit in other), cattle (branded G O), horses, corn, 1
set blacksmiths tools, 1 desk, 1 chest, & 5 chairs. Witness: WALTER POR-
TER. Before FENWICKE BULL, J.P. & P. Register.

Book F-3, p. 733 THOMAS (his mark) WILLIAMS, planter, of Craven
6 & 7 June 1764 Co., & REBECCA his wife, to GLEDWELL ORRELL,
L & R planter, for Ł 200 currency, 200 a. on N side
Santee River, on both sides Cadoes Lake; bound-
ing S on vacant swamp; E on JARED NELSON & vacant land; NW on vacant land;
SW on vacant land, & JOSEPH HOWARD. Witnesses: JOSEPH JOHNSON, WILLIAM
BYERS, JAMES HOPPER. Before JAMES LYNAH, J.P. Assigned by ORRELL to
MANNAN on 12 Jan. 1767. Recorded 23 Feb. 1767 by FENWICKE BULL, Register.

Book F-3, p. 742 NATHANIEL COTTHEEN, to JOSEPH BROWN, merchant,
12 & 13 Feb. 1767 of Georgetown, for Ł 3580:14:3 currency, 3
L & R by Mortgage tracts of 150 a. each, on Peedee River; total
450 a. on which he lives. Witnesses: JACOB
BRUSE, JOSEPH HUGGINS. Before CHARLES FYFFE, J.P. Recorded 27 Feb. 1767
by FENWICKE BULL, Register.

Book F-3, p. 748   LAMBERT LANCE, merchant, & ANNE MAGDALENA (her
22 & 23 Aug. 1766   mark) his wife, to WILLIAM ANCRUM & AARON LOO-
L & R   COCK, merchants; of Charleston, as tenants in
                          common, for certain considerations, 1 full
third part of that part of lot #42 in Charleston, bounding S 67 ft. on
Broad Street; E 73 ft. on Church Street; N on part belonging to MARY WAT-
SON; W on JOHN PAUL GRIMKE; as conveyed 20 Apr. 1759 by MARY WATSON to
ANCRUM, LANCE, & LOOCOCK; also 1 full fourth part of 25 tracts of land,
total 5898 a.; that is, 350 a. on Pine Tree Creek, granted WILLIAM GRAY
on 3 Apr. 1754; 100 a. on fork of Pine Tree, granted JOSEPH KERSHAW on 5
Dec. 1761; 100 a. at the raft; granted him on 31 Mar. 1761; 150 a. at
Pine Tree Hill granted LANCE on 4 June 1759; 100 a. at same place, grant-
ed LANCE on 5 Dec. 1761; 100 a. at Twenty Five Mile Creek granted him on
31 Mar. 1761; 150 a. at Pine Tree Hill granted LOOCOCK 4 June 1759; 150
a. at same place granted ANCRUM on 19 Sept. 1758; 400 a. & 250 a. at
Wateree Fork, granted JOSEPH EVANS on 4 Sept. 1753; 100 a. at Pine Bluff,
Wateree, granted 4 Sept. 1759 to JOHN WILLIAMS; 200 a. at Fredericksburgh
granted 15 May 1751 to WILLIAM GUESS; 50 a. at Pine Tree Mill granted
ROBERT MILLHOUSE 14 Mar. 1757; 20 a., part of 400 a. called Joyner's
Ferry, at the Congarees, granted 3 Apr. 1761 to JOSEPH JOYNER; 497 a. at
Little Pine Tree Mill, part of 650 a. granted SAMUEL WYLY on 2 Apr. 1761;
300 a. at Amelia, garnted THOMAS WINNINGHAM 16 Sept. 1738; 200 a. at High
Hill on Santee, granted WILLIAM HARRISon 4 July 1749; 200 a. at Twenty
Five Mile Creek granted 7 Oct. 1762 to LANCE; 150 a. at Pine Tree Hill
granted 9 Nov. 1765 to LANCE; 150 a., same place, granted LANCE on 7 Oct.
1765; 1000 a. on Wateree Swamp & 1000 more a. at same place granted 20
Oct. 1763 to ANCRUM, LANCE, LOOCOCK, & JOSEPH KERSHAW; 150 a. on Wateree
Fork granted 4 Mar. 1760 to BRYAN TOLAND; 131 a. in Fredericksburgh Town-
ship, granted 4 Oct. 1749 to JOHN BLACK; 50 a. at Wateree Fork granted
LANCE on 25 Oct. 1764. Witnesses: RICHARD MUNCREIFF, MALCOM BROWN. Before FENWICKE BULL, J.P. & P. Register.

Book F-3, p. 761   GEORGE (his mark) LANGLEY, planter, of Colle-
20 & 21 Feb. 1767   ton Co., to JOHN RUTLEDGE, of Charleston, for
L & R   Ƚ 250 currency, 300 a. in Colleton Co., grant-
                          ed GEORGE LANGLEY on 4 Mar. 1760; bounding NW
on COL. LUCAS; other sides on vacant land. Witnesses: JOHN SCOTT, JR.,
JOHN FRASER. Before FENWICKE BULL, J.P. & P. Register.

Book F-3, p. 766   JOHN SHELL, of Orangeburgh Township, to HENRY
1 & 2 Dec. 1766   WHETSTONE, planter, of Amelia Township, Berke-
L & R   ley Co., for Ƚ 150 currency, 140 a. at Ox
                          Creek, in Amelia Township, bounding W on HENRY
WHETSTONE (formerly HENRY CARTER); other sides on vacant land; which 140
a. were granted in 1735 to JOHN SHELL, who died intestate, & inherited by
his eldest son, JOHN, party hereto. Witnesses: PETER STALEY, JOHN
HERISPERGER, GASPER OTT. Before LEWIS GOLSON, J.P. Recorded 10 Mar.
1767 by FENWICKE BULL, Register.

Book F-3, p. 772   BENJAMIN PERRY, of St. Paul's Parish, son &
18 Feb. 1767   heir of BENJAMIN PERRY, planter, of said Par-
Release   ish; & FRANCES his wife, to JAMES PARSONS,
                          ESQ., of Charleston, for Ƚ 2892 currency, 188
a. in Colleton Co., bounding E & S on RALPH IZARD; NE on GEORGE EVANS
(formerly PHILIP EVANS); W on EDWARD PERRY. Witnesses: JOHN GLEN, ALEX-
ANDER MOULTRIE. Before FENWICKE BULL, J.P. & P. Register.

Book F-3, p. 777   THOMAS PINCKNEY, gentleman, formerly of
6 & 7 Aug. 1761   Charleston, SC, now Lt. in H.M. 3 Batt. of his
L & R   Royal American Regiment at Quebec; by his
                          father, MAJ. WILLIAM PINCKNEY, of Charleston;
of 1st part; to CHARLES PINCKNEY, attorney, (brother of said THOMAS); for
Ƚ 1500 currency, the NE corner of 2 lots, #20 & #73 in Charleston, bounding 50 ft. on Union Street; & 130 ft. on Queen (or Dock) Street. Whereas
by a deed of settlement dated 13 Sept. 1746 between CHARLES PINCKNEY,
since deceased, then of Charleston, uncle of said THOMAS of 1st part;
said THOMAS PINCKNEY, of 2nd part; & MARY PINCKNEY & SARAH PINCKNEY, minors, of 3rd & 4th parts; THOMAS became owner of the NE corner of 2 lots
Nos. 20 & 73 in Charleston (see Book C.C., pp. 188-192); & by letter
from Quebec dated 20 July last directed to his brother, CHARLES, agreed

to sell the said corner lot to CHARLES for Ŀ 1500 & informing CHARLES the (THOMAS) had drawn on him for 289 dollars in favor of CAPT. HARRY CHARTERIS; & on same date wrote his father to sell the land to CHARLES for as much as he could get; now the sale is completed. Witnesses: REBECCA PINCKNEY, ELIAS FOISSIN. Before JOHN REMINGTON, J.P. Recorded 6 Mar. 1767 by FENWICKE BULL, Register. On 20 Apr. 1763 THOMAS being in Charleson, declared the release was executed by his father at his (THOMAS'S) request & the money really paid by brother CHARLES & confirms CHARLES'S title. Witnesses: JOHN MATHEWES, CHARLES MOTTE. Before FENWICKE BULL, J.P. & P. Register.

Book F-3, p. 786
3 & 4 Oct. 1765
L & R

MARY DE LA FONTAINE, widow, of STOKE NOWINGTON, Co. of Middlesex, to THOMAS SHUBRICK, merchant, of London, formerly of Charleston, SC, for Ŀ 330 British, 3000 a., English measure, part of a Barony of 12,000 a. in SC, formerly purchased by BENJAMIN DE LA FONTAINE from ISAAC LOWNDES & THOMAS LOWNDES. MARY declares land free from any claim through her, or through BENJAMIN DE LA FONTAINE or THOMAS DE LA FONTAINE, both deceased. Witnesses in Bury Court, St. Mary, London, by RICHARD BOYFIELD, attorney-at-law, & JOHN JAMES PUDNEY, his clerk, & JOHN MUIR. Proved by MUIR 24 Jan. 1766 before JOHN REMINGTON, J.P. Recorded 7 Mar. 1767 by FENWICKE BULL, Register.

Book F-3, p. 793
23 & 24 Dec. 1754
L & R

JOHN SPITZ, of the Congaree, to THOMAS GARY, of Saludee River, for Ŀ 150 currency, 200 a. on Bush Creek, a branch of Saludee River, granted SPITZ by Gov. JAMES GLEN on 14 Nov. 1754; bounding on all sides on vacant land. Witnesses: JOHN HAMILTON (J.P.), GODFREY DRAYER. Recorded 7 Mar. 1767 by FENWICKE BULL, Register.

Book F-3, p. 799
12 Aug. 1764
L & R

MARY WHITE, to GEORGE FOREMAN, for Ŀ 75 currency, 100 a. in Granville Co., bounding on all sides on vacant land; granted 1 Feb. 1758 by Gov. WILLIAM HENRY LYTTELTON to ANDREW BRUMTON. Witnesses: MARTIN FRYAR, FREDERICK FANFMAN (CALFMAN?) & CHRISTENER CALFMAN. Before JOHN DICK, J.P. 23 Jan. 1767. Recorded 10 Mar. 1767 by FENWICKE BULL, Register.

Book F-3, p. 804
17 & 18 Nov. 1766
L & R

ELIZABETH (her mark) ERLABOUCH, to JOHN TANNER, shoemaker, of Granville Co., for Ŀ 100 currency, 100 a. in Granville Co., bounding E on ELIZABETH ROLLARIN; other sides on vacant land; granted 18 Oct. 1757. Witnesses: THOMAS (his mark) ABBERHAT, GASPERY STROBELL. Before JACOB SUMMERALL, J.P. Recorded 10 Mar. 1767 by FENWICKE BULL, Register.

Book F-3, p. 809
24 Nov. 1766
Mortgage

BARBARA HARRISON, of St. Marks Parish, being jointly bound with the Hon. CHARLES SKINNER to BREWTON & SMITH, for Ŀ 985 currency, conveys to MILES BREWTON & THOMAS LOUGHTON SMITH, merchants, of Charleston, as security, 5 Negro slaves & 400 a. which she had purchased from JOSIAH CANTEY. A penknife delivered. Witness: JOHN BREWTON. Before CHARLES PINCKNEY, J.P. Recorded in Secretary's Book A.A.A., p. 38, by JOHN HALL, Pro. Sec. Recorded 14 Mar. 1767 by FENWICKE BULL, Register.

DEEDS BOOK "G-3"
MARCH 1767 - OCTOBER 1767

Book G-3, p. 1
2 & 3 Mar. 1767
L & R by Mortgage

LEONARD GRAVES, planter, of Charleston Neck, & ELEANOR his wife, to JOSEPH PORCHER, gentleman, of Charleston, for Ŀ 2000 currency, 184-1/2 a. on Charleston Neck, formerly belonging to ANDREW JOHNSTON; bounding W on the Broad Path; N on THOMAS SHUBRICK (formerly JAMES GLEN); S on THOMAS BOONE (formerly JOHN COLLETON); E on Cooper River; also 100 a. of adjoining marsh land to the E, bounding E on Town Creek. Witnesses: WILLIAM GRAVES, WILLIAM MASON. Before DOUGAL CAMPBELL, J.P. Recorded 13 Mar. 1767 by FENWICKE BULL, Register.

Book G-3, p. 9   HOWELL JAMES, of Craven Co., to JOSEPH BROWN,
20 & 21 Feb. 1767   merchant, of Georgetown, for Ꝉ 2338 currency,
L & R by Mortgage   4 tracts, total 600 a., in Craven Co., on 1
                        tract (125 a.) of which he lives; bounding S
on DAVID HARRY; N on JOHN EVANS; W on Peedee River; E on vacant land; 125
a., bounding N on above tract; S on DAVID HARRY; W on Peedee River; E on
vacant land; 50 a. bounding S on SIMON PARSONS; E on JOHN WESTFIELD;
other sides on Peedee River; 300 a., bounding N on Peedee River; opposite
first tract; N on JAMES JONES; other sides on vacant land. Witnesses:
THOMAS EVANS, JOSEPH HUGGINS. Before CHARLES FYFFE, J.P. Recorded 14
Mar. 1767 by FENWICKE BULL, Register.

Book G-3, p. 15   GEORGE SANDERS, planter, to SAMUEL BOONE, both
18 & 19 Feb. 1763   of Craven Co., for Ꝉ 355 currency; 200 a. on N
L & R   side Santee River, bounding N on JAMES MCGIRT;
                        E on THOMAS MAPLES; S on JOHN MOORE; W on va-
cant land; granted by Lt. Gov. THOMAS BROUGHTON in 1735 to THOMAS POWELL;
who conveyed to SANDERS. Witnesses: CHARLES SPEARS, WILLIAM SANDERS.
Before TACITUS GAILLARD, J.P. 30 May 1764. Recorded 16 Mar. 1767 by FEN-
WICKE BULL, Register.

Book G-3, p. 21   FRANCIS EHRHARD, planter, of Purysburgh, St.
27 Feb. 1767   Peters Parish, Granville Co., & MARIE URBÉNE
Release   (URBAINE MARY) his wife, to ADRIAN MAYER, ESQ.,
                        of Purysburgh for Ꝉ 500 currency, 400 a. in
said Township, bounding N on vacant land; E on JACOB TANNER; S on ABRAHAM
MERTS & the Rev. MR. JOHN JOACHIM ZUBLY; W on COL. JOHN PETER PURY. Witnesses: JOHN MEYER, DAVID SAUSSY. Before JOHN LEWIS BOURQUIN, J.P. Recorded 17 Mar. 1767 by FENWICKE BULL, Register.

Book G-3, p. 24   GABRIEL FRANCOIS RAVOT (RAVOUT), tanner, to
2 Mar. 1767   ADRIAN MAYER, ESQ., both of St. Peters Parish,
Release   Granville Co., for Ꝉ 100 currency, 50 a. in
                        Purysburgh Township, bounding N on JOHN RO-
DOLPH NETMAN; S & E on vacant land; W on ABRAHAM LEROY. Witness: DANIEL
MALLET. Before JOHN LEWIS BOURQUIN, J.P. Recorded 18 Mar. 1767 by FEN-
WICKE BULL, Register.

Book G-3, p. 26   FRANCIS KINLOCH, gentleman, of Prince George
4 & 5 Feb. 1767   Parish, Craven Co., to ARCHIBALD BAIRD, gen-
L & R   tleman, for Ꝉ 5 currency, 125-1/3 a. in Prince
                        George Parish, bounding NE on FRANCIS KINLOCH;
N & NW on Peedee River; SW on THOMAS MITCHELL; SE on Waccamaw River; be-
ing 1/3 of a certain tract granted Landgrave THOMAS SMITH & purchased by
KINLOCH from BENJAMIN SMITH; ELIZABETH ANN, his wife; & MARY SMITH, widow.
Witnesses: THOMAS MITCHELL, ANTHONY MITCHELL. Before CHARLES FYFFE, J.P.
Recorded 19 Mar. 1767 by FENWICKE BULL, Register.

Book G-3, p. 33   JOSEPH (his mark) NOBELS, planter, of SC, to
29 & 30 Oct. 1765   LAWRENCE RAMBO, formerly of NC, for Ꝉ 425 cur-
L & R   rency, 200 a. on Toblers Creek, a branch of
                        Stephens Creek, granted 8 Mar. 1755 by Gov.
JAMES GLEN, to JOSEPH NOBLES, father of said JOSEPH; bounding on all
sides on vacant land. Witnesses: DAVID ROBESON, JOHN COCKBURN, REUBEN
RAMBO. Before JOHN FAIRCHILD, J.P. Recorded 20 Mar. 1767 by FENWICKE
BULL, Register.

Book G-3, p. 38   HOWEL JAMES, planter, of Craven Co., to SAMUEL
22 & 23 Feb. 1767   WRAGG, merchant, of Georgetown, for Ꝉ 405:10:0
L & R by Mortgage   currency, 500 a., bounding E on Peedee River;
                        W on vacant land; S on JOHN BOOTH; N on URIAH
MOTTE; granted JAMES by Gov. WILLIAM HENRY LYTTELTON. Witnesses: CHRIS-
TOPHER JORDAN, WILLIAM BARTON, JR. Before ARCHIBALD BAIRD, J.P. Record-
ed 21 Mar. 1767 by FENWICKE BULL, Register.

Book G-3, p. 44   JAMES SKIRVING, of Ashepoo, & JOHN LAIRD, of
_____ 1750   Pon Pon, Colleton Co., executors of will of
Release   DR. GEORGE MITCHELL, physician; of 1st part;
                        to ISAAC HAYNE, of Pon Pon, executor of will
of JOHN HAYNE, planter, of same place, & guardian of person & estate of

ABRAHAM HAYNE, second son of JOHN HAYNE & nephew of said ISAAC HAYNE; in trust for ABRAHAM; for Ŀ 2450 currency, 3 adjoining tracts of 200 a., 435 a., & 200 a.; total 835 a. Whereas GEORGE MITCHELL owned 200 a. at Pon Pon, being 1/2 of 400 a. granted JOHN PENNEY, on S side of a creek of Pon Pon (Edisto) River, bounding N on HENRY JACKSON & on MATHEW BEE'S Creek & on swamp; E on other half & MOSES MARTIN; S on JOHN PETER; W on a large cane swamp; which 200 a. MITCHELL had purchased from ELIZABETH EDWARDS, spinster, daughter of JOHN EDWARDS, by L & R dated 23 & 24 Nov. 1749; & whereas JAMES SKIRVING & JOHN LAIRD, executors, purchased from MATHEW ROCHE, merchant, of Charleston, ISAAC HOLMES, merchant, of Charleston, ISAAC HAYNE & WILLIAM SIMMONS, executors, & SUSANNAH BEE, executrix, of will of JOHN BEE, planter, of Pon Pon, 435 a. on E side Pon Pon River, in Colleton Co., granted WILLIAM LIVINGSTON, cleric, & bounding S on MOSES PRINGRY & WILLIAM LIVINGSTON; E on JOHN HAY & ROBERT PENNY; N on Penny's Creek; also 200 a. on Penny's Creek, granted JOHN ASH (from whom LIVING-STON purchased by L & R dated 2 & 3 Mar. 1749); bounding N on PERCIVAL POWELL; S on MRS. ELIZABETH SCHENCKIN; W on Penny's Creek; & whereas GEORGE MITCHELL, by will dated 3 Dec. last, directed his executors to sell the 2 tracts & all his estate; & SKIRVING & LAIRD advertised MIT-CHELL'S real & personal estate; now sale is completed by leave of Court of Chancery. Witnesses: WILLIAM SIMMONS, JOHN GRAVES. Entered in Auditors Book H-8, p. 138, on 27 Jan. 1767, by RICHARD LAMBTON, Dep. Aud. Recorded 24 Mar. 1767 by FENWICKE BULL, Register.

Book G-3, p. 51   ABRAHAM HAYNE, planter, to ARCHIBALD HAMILTON,
7 Sept. 1757   planter, both of Colleton Co., for Ŀ 3400 cur-
L & R   rency, 330 a. & 200 a., total 530 a.; bounding
                         SW on Pon Pon River, Penny's Creek, & ABRAHAM
HAYNE; W & NW on said river & creek; N on said creek, vacant land, & ED-
WARD FERGUSON; NE & E on vacant land, JOSEPH FABIAN & MR. LIVINGSTON; SE
on LIVINGSTON, ABRAHAM PAYNE, & JOHN PETER; S on the river, ABRAHAM
HAYNE, & JOHN PETER; plat by NATHANIEL DEAN. Whereas on 9 Sept. 1696
Gov. JOHN ARCHDALE granted JOHN PENNY 400 a.; & on 5 Feb. 1714 Gov.
CHARLES CRAVEN granted WILLIAM LIVINGSTONE 435 a.; & whereas the W part
of the 435 a. (330 a.) & the N part of the 400 a. (200 a.) descended to
ABRAHAM HAYNE; now he sells to HAMILTON. Witnesses: DAVID MAYBANK, MOSES
DARQUIER. Before JAMES SHARP, J.P. Recorded by FENWICKE BULL, Register.
Entered in Auditor's Book, H-8, p. 138, on 27 Jan. 1767 by RICHARD LAMB-
TON, Dep. Aud.

Book G-3, p. 61   PAUL HAMILTON, planter, of James Island, St.
4 & 5 Mar. 1767   Andrews Parish, executor of will of ARCHIBALD
L & R   HAMILTON; to CHRISTOPHER WILKINSON, planter,
                         for Ŀ 14,000 currency; 3 adjoining tracts of
330 a., 200 a. (see p. 51), & 72 a., total 602 a. in Colleton Co., bounding SW on Pon Pon River & Penny's Creek; W & NW on said river & creek; N
on said creek, JAMES REID & EDWARD FERGUSON; NE & E on FERGUSON, JOSEPH
FABIAN, & LIVINGSTON; SE & S on LIVINGSTON & JOHN PETER; the 72 a. granted by Gov. WILLIAM HENRY LYTTLETON on 8 Nov. 1757 to ARCHIBALD HAMILTON;
bounding S on ARCHIBALD HAMILTON; W on HAMILTON & Pennys Creek; N on
Pennys Creek, JAMES REID & EDWARD FERGUSON; E on FERGUSON. Whereas ARCH-
IBALD HAMILTON by will, May 1766, appointed CHARLES ODINGSELL, ABRAHAM
HAYNE, & PAUL HAMILTON his executors (PAUL only accepting); now PAUL
sells to WILKINSON. Witnesses: EDWARD WILKINSON, JR., JOSHUA WARD. Before ROBERT WILLIAMS, JR., J.P. Entered in Auditor's Book H-8, p. 165,
on 5 Mar. 1767 by RICHARD LAMBTON, Dep. Aud. & recorded 27 Mar. 1767 by
FENWICKE BULL, Register.

Book G-3, p. 74   CAPT. JOHN CLIFFORD, of H.M. 7th Regt. of
10 & 11 Nov. 1766   Foot, commanded by SIR. DAVID CUNNINGHAM, now
L & R   in garrison at Gibralter; to THOMAS HUTCHINSON,
                         ESQ., of St. Bartholomews Parish, for Ŀ 1500
currency, 800 a. on E side Combahee River, in Colleton Co., bounding N on
SAMUEL NICHOLS & vacant land; S on a creek & swamp running between said
tract & WILLIAM PAGE; E on a swamp. Whereas BENJAMIN CLIFFORD owned said
800 a., which descended to his eldest son & heir, said JOHN; who on 24
Jan. 1760 appointed BENJAMIN CLIFFORD, mariner, formelry of Salem, Co. of
Essex, in Massachusetts Bay Province, New England, now of SC, his attorney, with power to sell the land; now BENJAMIN sells to HUTCHINSON. Witnesses: WILLIAM SCOTT, JOSHUA WARD. Before WILLIAM BURROWS, J.P.

Book G-3, p. 80   JOSEPH (his mark) TILLER (TILER), & PRISCILLA
22 Aug. 1764   (her mark) his wife, to MASON GRENNON, carpen-
L & R   ter, both of Craven Co., for Ł 250 currency,
                     200 a. on N side Santee River, bounding NE on
ANGEL HARDIN; other sides on vacant land; granted 13 Feb. 1753 to SAMUEL
WILLIAMS. Witnesses: ISRAEL PICKENS, JOSEPH MOORE. Before JOHN PICKENS,
J.P. Recorded 31 Mar. 1767 by FENWICKE BULL, Register.

Book G-3, p. 87   HENRY MIDDLETON, ESQ., & MARY HENRIETTA his
23 & 24 Feb. 1767   wife, to EGERTON LEIGH, ESQ., both of Charles-
L & R   ton, for Ł 8200 currency, 533 a. in St. James
                     Goose Creek Parish, Berkeley Co., with the
"Capital Mansion" house. Whereas by L & R dated 27 & 28 Feb. 1765 SAMUEL
BRAILSFORD, merchant, & ELIZABETH his wife, sold MIDDLETON 508 a. in St.
James Goose Creek, bounding N on a creek of Cooper River; E on the creek
& marsh; S on children of ARTEMAS ELLIOTT & MARY his wife; JOSEPH WRAGG,
& old Goose Creek Road; W on JAMES MICHIE; & whereas on 16 July 1765 MID-
DLETON was granted 25 a. on said Parish, bounding S & SE on MR. WRAGG; N
& W on said MIDDLETON; making 533 a.; now MIDDLETON sells the whole to
LEIGH. Witnesses: MARY MIDDLETON, RICHARD LAMBTON. Before J. DERING,
J.P. Entered in Auditor's Book H-8, p. 166, on 12 Mar. 1767 by RICHARD
LAMBTON, Dep. Aud. Recorded 2 Apr. 1767 by FENWICKE BULL, Register.

Book G-3, p. 95   WILLIAM BURROWS, master of H.M. Court of Chan-
24 Dec. 1766   cery, at his house in Tradd Street, to ARTHUR
Sale   MIDDLETON, ESQ., both of Charleston, for
                     Ł 1800 currency, the E part of a lot in
Charleston, formerly belonging to JAMES ST. JOHN, near W end of Broad
Street, bounding N 60 ft. on Broad Street; 211-1/2 ft. on other part; SE
43 ft. on WILLIAM LOGAN; SW 191 ft. on ARTHUR MIDDLETON; NW 109 ft. on
SAMUEL SMITH. Whereas ELIZABETH BEATTY (formerly ELIZABETH ST. JOHN,
widow & executrix of will of JOHN ST. JOHN, planter, of Pon Pon, in Colleton Co., 1 of the sons of JAMES ST. JOHN, ESQ.); JAMES ST. JOHN, a minor, son of JOHN ST. JOHN (by ELIZABETH BEATTY his next friend); BENJAMIN
SINGLETON & ELIZABETH his wife, a minor, daughter of JOHN ST. JOHN (by
her husband, her next friend), on 25 Sept. 1766 brought complaint in said
court against LAMBERT LANCE, surviving executor of MELLER ST. JOHN, who
was executor of JAMES ST. JOHN; & JAMES ST. JOHN, a minor, son of MELLER
ST. JOHN, & a decree was issued, ordering the master to sell at auction
the real estate (listed K in first report); also the household goods,
plate, books, etc., formerly belonging to JAMES ST. JOHN (also listed K
in first report); & pay 2/3 of cost of suit; retain Ł 300 for himself &
assistant; pay 1/2 the residue to LANCE in trust for beneficiaries of
MELLER ST. JOHN'S will; pay LANCE Ł 3652:3:7-1/2 due him as executor from
estate of JOHN ST. JOHN; to the solicitors the remainder of costs of
suit; the overplus to ELIZABETH BEATTY as executrix; in trust for beneficiaries from estate of JOHN ST. JOHN; & should money not be sufficient,
to sell such land in Charleston as not allotted; now the M.C. sells MID-
DLETON part of the land allotted to ELIZABETH BEATTY. Witnesses: WILLIAM
ROPER, JR., JOHN DART, JR. Before JACOB MOTTE, J.P. Recorded 3 Apr.
1767 by FENWICKE BULL, Register.

Book G-3, p. 101   WILLIAM BURROWS, M.C., to ARTHUR MIDDLETON, of
27 Mar. 1767   Charleston (in accordance with court decree,
Sale   see p. 95), for Ł 2230 currency, part of a lot
                     near W end of Broad Street; bounding N 60 ft.
on Broad Street; W 211-1/2 ft. on part sold MIDDLETON (p. 95); E 178-1/2
ft. on another part said lot; S on WILLIAM LOGAN; being part of the land
formerly belonging to JAMES ST. JOHN & afterwards allotted to ELIZABETH
BEATTY (marked 4 on a certain plat). Witnesses: WILLIAM ROPER, JR.,
RICHARD CHITTCH. Before JACOB MOTTE, J.P. Recorded 4 Apr. 1767 by FEN-
WICKE BULL, Register.

Book G-3, p. 109   ELIZABETH PERONNEAU, widow of SAMUEL PERONNEAU
20 & 21 Oct. 1766   the elder, merchant, & executrix of will of
L & R   ALEXANDER PERONNEAU; THOMAS LAMBOLL, gentle-
                     man, & SAMUEL PERONNEAU, merchant, executors
of will of SAMUEL PERONNEAU; of 1st part; to THOMAS SKOTTOWE, ESQ.; all
of Charleston; for Ł 1200 currency, the W part of lot #141, near White
Point, formerly belonging to SAMUEL PERONNEAU, bounding N 70 ft., English

measure, on Rivers Alley (running from Old Church Street, or Meeting
Street, to King Street); W 90 ft. on ELIZABETH DIDCOT, widow; E on part
lot #141; S on a water lot. Whereas SAMUEL PERONNEAU, SR. owned said
part of lot #141 which by will dated 21 Feb. 1753, he desired his executors to sell; appointing his wife, ELIZABETH, his 2 brothers, HENRY
(since deceased) & ALEXANDER, THOMAS LAMBOLL, & his son, SAMUEL (when 21),
his executrix, & executors; now they sell at auction to SKOTTOWE. Witnesses: PHILIP TIDYMAN, WILLIAM SAVAGE. Before JOHN BULL, JR., J.P. Recorded 7 Apr. 1767 by FENWICKE BULL, Register.

Book G-3, p. 117   BENJAMIN STONE & JOHN HEARNE, planters, of
1 & 2 May 1765   James Island, Berkeley Co., acting executors
L & R   of will of DANIEL RIVERS; to JOHN RIVERS,
                          planter, of James Island; for L 1580 currency,
79 a. on SE part of James Island, on a neck called by the Indians "Washo-
peau"; being the E part of 100 a. granted 14 July 1698 to THOMAS FAWCETT;
bounding S on a creek & marsh; E on a creek; N on a creek & marsh; W on
other part belonging to JOHN RIVERS, from which it is separated by a
fence running from marsh to marsh. Whereas DANIEL RIVERS owned said 79
a., which by will dated 18 Feb. he directed his executors to sell; appointed said STONE & HEARNE, his sons THOMAS & GEORGE, & JAMES WITTER,
his executors; now STONE & HEARNE sell to JOHN RIVERS. Witnesses: WIL-
LIAM HOLMES, JOHN HOLMES. Before ROBERT RIVERS, J.P. Recorded 9 Apr.
1767 by FENWICKE BULL, Register.

Book G-3, p. 124   RALPH IZARD, ESQ., (eldest son & heir of HENRY
23 & 24 Mar. 1767   IZARD, ESQ., who was eldest son & heir of
L & R   RALPH IZARD, ESQ., of Berkeley Co.), & MAGDA-
                          LEN ELIZABETH, his wife, to BARNARD ELLIOTT,
ESQ., of Charleston, for L 5000 currency, lot #242 in Charleston, bound-
ing N on MR. LIVINGSTON; W on a new street; E on MILES BREWTON & JOHN
TIPPER; S on lot #243; also half of lot #243; bounding N on lot #242; W
on New Street; E on MILES BREWTON & THOMAS BINFORD; S on part lot #243
belonging to THOMAS ELFE. Witnesses: PETER MANIGAULT, JOHN CROSS, & RUTH
RIVERS. Before JOHN WRAGG, J.P. Recorded 10 Apr. 1767 by FENWICKE BULL,
Register.

Book G-3, p. 131   RALPH IZARD, of Charleston, eldest son & heir
23 & 24 Mar. 1767   of HENRY IZARD, of St. James Goose Creek; to
L & R   PETER MANIGAULT, of Charleston, for L 3675
                          currency, 600 a. near Accabee, in St. Philips
Parish, Berkeley Co., bounding S on Ashley River; W on BERNARD ELLIOTT
(formerly WILLIAM ELLIOTT); N on WILLIAM SCREVIN, JOHN PILKINGTON & CAPT.
HAWETT; E & NE on MR. ODINGSAL & THOMAS PERRYMAN; SE on JOHN PRUE (formerly JOHN LADSON; lately DANIEL DOYLEY); excepting 70-1/2 a. in SW corner
lately sold by IZARD to BENJAMIN SMITH, merchant, of Charleston. Witnesses: JOHN CROSS, RUTH RIVERS. Before JOHN WRAGG, J.P. Recorded 11 Apr.
1767 by FENWICKE BULL, Register.

Book G-3, p. 138   ANN BOYD, widow; & EDWARD MARTIN, merchant, &
24 & 25 Mar. 1767   ELIZABETH his wife, of 1st part; to PETER MAN-
L & R by Mortgage   IGAULT, barrister; all of Charleston; for
                          L 1300 currency, part of Colleton Square, in
Charleston, bounding E on THOMAS ELLERY; S on Hunter Street; W 150 ft. on
Charles Street; N 70 ft. on Ellery Street; on which land THOMAS WALKER
had built 2 large brick houses; also a marsh lot S of said lot; being the
W part of marsh lot marked "O" on plan of Colleton Square; bounding N on
Ellery Street; S 35 ft. on a canal or street; E 100 ft. on part of marsh
lot belonging to ANN ELLERY; W on marsh lot "N" belonging to GEORGE HUNT-
ER. Witnesses: JOHN WRAGG, RUTH RIVERS. Before FENWICKE BULL, Register.

Book G-3, p. 144   ANN BOYD, widow of ROBERT BOYD, to PETER MANI-
25 Mar. 1767   GAULT, barrister, both of Charleston. Whereas
Release   in L & R dated 10 & 11 July 1766, ANN BOYD
                          joined with ROBERT BOYD, & EDWARD MARTIN, mer-
chant, & ELIZABETH his wife, in conveying to PETER MANIGAULT part of a
lot in Colleton Square, 150 ft. deep; also the W part of a marsh lot S of
above lot & marked "O" on plan of Colleton Square; for money advanced by
MANIGAULT to ANN before she married BOYD; now ANN releases her claim to
the lots & delivers 20 slaves to MANIGAULT. Witnesses: JOHN WRAGG, RUTH

RIVERS. Before FENWICKE BULL, J.P. & P. Register.

Book G-3, p. 146   ELIZABETH EBERSON, widow & executrix, & TOBIAS
31 Mar. & 1 Apr. 1767   FORD, executor of will of WILLIAM EBERSON,
L & R   planter, of Horse Shoe Savannah, Colleton Co.,
                          to WILLIAM BRANDFORD, ESQ., of Charleston, for
Ŀ 10,000 currency, 3 tracts, total 501 a. on W side Horse Shoe Savannah,
in St. Bartholomews Parish; reserving the EBERSON family burying ground.
Whereas THOMAS EBERSON, planter, of Colleton Co., father of said WILLIAM,
owned said 3 tracts; viz., 260 a. granted 5 Nov. 1704 to THOMAS FARR; 100
a., part of a tract now belonging to DR. JAMES REID, originally granted
28 JULY 1703 to THOMAS DRAYTON; & 141 a. granted 4 June 1735 to THOMAS
EBERSON; the 501 a. bounding N on JAMES REID; W on WILLIAM BRANDFORD; SW
on WILLIAM MAXWELL; NW on estate of THOMAS EBERSON & JAMES REID; which
501 a. THOMAS, by will dated 20 Nov. 1763, he bequeathed to his son, WIL-
LIAM; who by will dated 18 Jan. 1766 appointed his wife ELIZABETH, executrix, & his brother-in-law TOBIAS FORD his executor, with authority to
sell the land; part of his real estate; now they sell to BRANDFORD. Witnesses: JAMES SKIRVING, ROBERT WILLIAMS, JR. Before FENWICKE BULL, J.P.
& P. Register. Plat of resurvey of 3 tracts certified 5 Mar. 1767 by
PHIL SMITH, Sur.

Book G-3, p. 155   ANTHONY POUNCEY, planter, of St. Marks Parish,
9 Dec. 1762   to JOHN KIMBROUGH, planter, for Ŀ 250 curren-
L & R   cy, 300 a., part of 400 a.; beginning where
                          bounded NE by Peedee River, continuing on said
river to mouth of Mill Creek, up said creek to line adjoining BARTHOLOMEW
BALL'S land, running SE to corner on river. Whereas on 15th May 1751
Gov. JAMES GLEN granted ANTHONY POUNCEY 400 a. in St. Marks Parish, bound-
ing NE on Peedee River; NW on land granted JOHN BROWN, who sold to POUN-
CEY; SW on BARTHOLOMEW BALL & GIDEON ELLIS; now POUNCEY sells a part to
KIMBROUGH. Witnesses: JOHN KEITH, JAMES HEETH, AUSTIN (his mark) WINZOR
(WINSER). Before ALEXANDER MACKINTOSH, J.P, 10 Jan. 1763. Recorded 18
Apr. 1767 by FENWICKE BULL, Register.

Book G-3, p. 161   ISAAC EDWARD (his mark) WELLS, planter, to
3 & 4 July 1765   JAMES RUTLAND, SR., both of Craven Co., for
L & R   Ŀ 25 currency, 100 a. on a branch of Cedar
                          Creek, N side of Broad River, in Craven Co.,
bounding on all sides on vacant land. Witnesses: THOMAS SANDERS, BENJA-
MIN WELLS, PATRICK MORRIS. Before JOHN NEWMAN OGLETHORPE, J.P. Recorded
20 Apr. 1767 by FENWICKE BULL, Register.

Book G-3, p. 168   THOMAS SCOTT, planter, of St. Andrews Parish,
6 & 7 Apr. 1767   to JEREMIAH SAVAGE, ESQ., of Charleston, (be-
L & R by Mortgage   cause SAVAGE went on SCOTT'S bond to ELIZABETH
                          HOLMES, widow of Charleston), for Ŀ 1100 cur-
rency, 213 a. in St. Andrews Parish, Berkeley Co., bounding NW on EDMUND
BELLINGER; NE on Glebe land & ELIZABETH FULLER; SW on JOHN MANLEY; SE on
marsh of Coppin Creek; also 17 Negroes, his stock of cattle & horses.
Witnesses: DAVID FOGARTIE, JOSHUA WARD. Before WILLIAM BURROWS, J.P.
Recorded 23 Apr. 1767 by FENWICKE BULL, Register.

Book G-3, p. 178   JAMES CROKATT, merchant, of London, appointed
22 Oct. 1765   ROBERT WILLIAMS, JR., attorney-at-law, of
Letter of Attorney   Charleston, SC, his attorney, to sell the half
                          part of a front lot, #19, in Charleston, oc-
cupied by BASTIAN HUGOETT; bounding E 93-1/2 ft., English measure, on the
Bay; S 126 ft. on JOHN RAPER (formerly RICHARD CODNER); W on JONATHAN
RUSS (formerly JOHN ASHBY) & GEORGE LEA; N on part same lot belonging to
JOHN HESCOTT (formerly CAPT. JOHN GUPPELL); also that part of a front lot
E of the town walls, in front of said half lot, down to low water mark,
purchased by CROKATT from ELEAZER ALLEN; also to collect any sums due the
late partnership of JAMES & CHARLES CROKATT & Co. Witnesses: JAMES
LAURANS, ALEXANDER HEWET; DAVID EWART, Not. Pub. Proved by LAURENS be-
fore JACOB MOTTE, J.P., 26 Mar. 1767. Recorded 22 Apr. 1767 by FENWICKE
BULL, Register.

Book G-3, p. 182   DAVID HAY, for Ŀ 10 currency, assigns to HARDY
22 Feb. 1766   HAY, in accordance with agreement entered in

Assignment   Book F-3, p. 483; all his claim to said arti-
                                    cle of agreement. Witnesses: WILLIAM ARTHUR,
HANNAH RUTLEDGE. Before JOSEPH CURRY, J.P. of Craven Co. Recorded 24
Apr. 1767 by FENWICKE BULL, Register.

Book G-3, p. 184   WILLIAM HAY, planter, of Craven Co., to his
25 & 26 Sept. 1766   HARDY HAY, planter, for Ⱡ 100 currency, 100 a.
L & R   part of a tract of 400 a. granted 5 June 1750
                                    to RICHARD JACKSON, who conveyed to WILLIAM
HAY; near the Congarees, in Craven Co.; beginning at a stake under the
hill near the Mill branch, running NE 67° to a large red oak on edge of
the bank & old field marked 3 notches on every side; then NE same course
until it hits either of the old lines, the NE or SE of said 400 a.; then
from stake to run NW 88° to second stake 8-1/2 chains, then third stake
SW 18° 9 chains, then to fourth stake SW 48° 7 chains; then SW 15° until
it intersects the old line; then SW along old line until it strikes the
lake; then the lake to be boundary until it comes to a gum with 4 blazes;
then along a line from that gum NE 37° to a small white oak on old line
with 4 blazes; then SE to meet first line from red oak 3 notches, etc.
Witnesses: JAMES MAY, JOSEPH HIRSMAN. Before JOSEPH CURRY, J.P. Recorded 25 Apr. 1767 by FENWICKE BULL, Register.

Book G-3, p. 190   JOSEPH CURRY, planter, to WILLIAM HOWELL,
26 & 27 July 1765   planter, both of Craven Co., for Ⱡ 500 curren-
L & R   cy, 250 a. in Craven Co., known as the Island
                                    or Neck called Cojoes Island; in a nick of
Santee River, opposite the present dwelling of FREDERICK ONEAL; granted
WILLIAM BUSBIE & conveyed to JOSEPH CURRY; resurveyed on a warrant of JA-
COB VERNER; that is, 195 a. in said tract; & conveyed to CURRY by said
JACOB; the whole bounding SW on Santee River; N on WILLIAM TUCKER (part
of BUSBIE'S original tract); E on a large lake & JOHN LOWERMAN; S on San-
tee River & WILLIAM HOWELL. Witnesses: JOHN THOMAS, SR., JOHN THOMAS,
JR., HARDY HAY. Before JOHN HAMILTON, J.P., on 31 May 1766. Recorded 27
Apr. 1767 by FENWICKE BULL, Register.

Book G-3, p. 196   JACOB VERNER, planter, of Craven Co., to
18 & 19 Sept. 1759   JOSEPH CURRY, Dep. Sur., for Ⱡ 50 currency,
L & R   195 a. in Craven Co., in a neck of Santee Riv-
                                    er, bounding NE & E on JOSEPH CURRY & GEORGE
RAWLINSON; other sides on Santee River; found in the surplus land of a
tract of 100 a. belonging to JOSEPH CURRY, granted originally to WILLIAM
BUSBIE in 500 a. Witnesses: STEPHEN CRELL, ANDREW KERSH. Before JOHN
PEARSON, J.P., 8 Oct. 1759. Recorded 28 Apr. 1767 by FENWICKE BULL, Reg-
ister.

Book G-3, p. 202   DAVID (his mark) WEBB, planter, of Saxagotha
6 & 7 Nov. 1766   Township, SC, & ELIZABETH his wife, to HOWELL
L & R   EDMUNDS, planter, of Southampton Co., Va, for
                                    Ⱡ 1200 curre-cy, 400 a. in Craven Co., granted
13 Oct. 1759 by Gov. WILLIAM HENRY LYTTELTON to ELIZABETH MERCIER; bounding SW on Santee River; formerly bounding on all other sides on vacant
land; now adjoining plantation of JAMES JINCKINGS near above GEORGE
LITES'S ferry. Witnesses: JOHN HAIG, JOHN CONRAD GEIGER, JOHN STEWART.
Before WILLIAM TUCKER, J.P. Recorded 1 May 1767 by FENWICKE BULL, Register.

Book G-3, p. 209   Whereas when the L & R dated 18 Oct. 1757 were
6 & 7 Apr. 1767   executed between JOHN & MARY PARKER of 1st
L & R   part; & WILLIAM STONE, said MARY was not of
                                    age, now to confirm STONE'S title, JOHN PARKER,
planter, of Goose Creek, & MARY his wife, for Ⱡ 1100 currency, convey to
WILLIAM STONE, gentleman, of Charleston, the N part of a corner of lot
#14 in Charleston, bounding W 27 ft. on Union Street; N 45 ft. on EDWARD
CROFT; S on JOHN DANIEL; E on CAPT. KING. Witnesses: WILLIAM WILKINS,
EDWARD PIERCE. Before JACOB MOTTE, J.P. Recorded 4 May 1767 by FENWICKE
BULL, Register.

Book G-3, p. 216   DENNIS MAHONEY, of Colleton Co., to JAMES RAM-
11 & 12 July 1766   AGE, for Ⱡ 600 currency, 450 a. Whereas on 23
L & R   May 1734 Gov. ROBERT JOHNSON granted FLORENCE

MAHONEY 100 a.; & on 14 Feb. 1735 Lt. Gov. THOMAS BROUGHTON granted him 350 a. adjoining said 100 a.; the 450 a. being on W side Edisto River, bounding N on RICHARD BEDON; W on WILLIAM DRAYTON; S on GEORGE JACKSON; E on vacant land. Whereas FLORENCE MAHONEY bequeathed to his son, DENNIS, the 350 a., & the 100 a. to his second son, FLORENCE; & whereas said son FLORENCE died intestate & his brother DENNIS inherited; now DENNIS sells the 2 tracts to RAMAGE. Witnesses: THOMAS GRANGE, JOHN (his mark) MORGAN. Before ANDREW LEITCH, J.P. Recorded 5 May 1767 by FENWICKE BULL, Register.

Book G-3, p. 222
10 & 11 Apr. 1767
L & R

DAVID OLIPHANT, ESQ., & HANNAH his wife, to JOHN HUGER, gentleman, both of Charleston, for Ł 12,500 currency, 300 a. in Craven Co., bounding NW on JACOB MOTTE, JR. (formerly THOMAS LYNCH); SE on DAVID DEAS; NE on Santee River; SW on Lightwood Pine; also 380 a. on an island in Craven Co., bounding NW on THOMAS LYNCH; NE on Six Mile Creek; SW on Santee River; also 500 a. on Santee River, adjoining said 300 a. granted OLIPHANT. Witnesses: WILLIAM MOULTRIE, CHARLES MOTTE. Before FENWICKE BULL, J.P. & P. Register.

Book G-3, p. 230
15 Apr. 1767
Mortgage

JOEL HOLMES, merchant, to JAMES POYAS, merchant, both of Charleston, for Ł 850 currency, part of lot #37, now occupied by THOMAS FELL, tailor; bounding N 26 ft. on Elliott Street; E 80 ft. on JANE DALTON; S on JOHN ATKIN, or EDMUND ATKIN; W on part said lot belonging to WILLIAM CARUTHEN. Witnesses: ANDREW ROBERTSON, POTT SHAW. Before FENWICKE BULL, J.P. & P. Register. On 9 Sept. 1771 JOSIAH SMITH, JR., attorney for JAMES POYAS, declared mortgage satisfied. Witness: WILLIAM VALENTINE.

Book G-3, p. 234
18 May 1765
L & R

SAMUEL BURNLEY, & ELIZABETH his wife; THOMAS CHRISTIE & SUSANNAH his wife; T OMAS WAY & MARY his wife; all of Ga.; of 1st part; to JOSEPH WARING, of St. George Parish, Dorchester, a minor, son of JOSEPH WARING, deceased, & MARY his wife; for Ł 1116 currency paid by BENJAMIN WARING, JOHN WARING & GEORGE SMITH in behalf of said JOSEPH WARING; 186 a. on Beach Hill, St. Pauls Parish, SC, bounding N on RICHARD WARING; NE on DAVID SOMNER; SE on JAMES SMITH; SW on CAPT. JAMES LADSON. Witnesses: SAMUEL SALTUS, DANIEL SILLOVANT, STEPHEN CATER. Before WILLIAM BURROWS, J.P. Recorded 9 May 1767 by FENWICKE BULL, Register.

Book G-3, p. 242
22 Apr. 1767
Mortgage

WILLIAM MEWHENNEY, tallow chandler, to BENJAMIN SMITH, both of Charleston, for Ł 2000 currency, 10 slaves; also part of a lot, bounding 61 ft. on Dussreys Alley, sold to MEWHENNY by JAMES SHARP, WILLIAM LENNOX, BENJAMIN CATON, & ANDREW HUNTER, executors of PATRICK LAIRD, by L & R dated 6 & 7 July 1762. A penknife delivered. Witness: JOSEPH FELTHAM. Before CHARLES PINCKNEY, J.P. Entered in Secretary's Book A.A.A., p. 120, by THOMAS HORRY, per Sec'y. Recorded 9 May 1767 by FENWICKE BULL, Register. On 10 Mar. 1778 THOMAS SMITH, executor to BENJAMIN SMITH, declared mortgage satisfied. Witness: G. SHEED.

Book G-3, p. 245
22 & 23 July 1766
L & R

The Rev. MR. ROBERT SMITH, rector of St. Philip's Parish, Charleston, & ELIZABETH his wife, to the Rev. MR. ALEXANDER GARDEN, rector of St. Thomas Parish, Berkeley Co., for Ł 700 currency, 150 a., being the SE half of 300 a. in St. Thomas Parish, now bounding NE on MRS. BILBO; SW on ALEXANDER GARDEN; NW on other half now belonging to ALEXANDER GARDEN; SE on ROBERT JOHNSON, ROBERT GUERIN, & MRS. BILBO. Whereas on 6 Apr. 1703 the Lords Proprs. granted PETER POITEVINE 300 a. inland in St. Thomas Parish, on SE side Cooper River, bounding SE on JONATHAN RUSS; NE & NW on DANIEL TRESVANT & vacant land; NW & SW on vacant land; & whereas POITEVINE on 7 Nov. 1706 sold the SE half (over half) to his brother ANTHONY, being the whole length of the tract & half the breadth; & whereas ANTHONY devised his 150 a. to his son, ANTHONY, & his 2 daughters, MAGDALEN GARNIER & MARGERY POSTELL; & whereas the son, ANTHONY POITEVINE, & JEAN GARNER & his wife, the said MAGDALEN, & JOHN POSTELL & his wife, said MARGERY, by L & R dated 25 & 26 Aug. 1725 sold the SE half of the 300 a. to FRANCIS PAGET, SR.; who devised half to his youngest son, JOHN, but the word "heirs" or its equivalent not being in the will, he could hold only for his own life time, but having only 2 brothers who died during his lifetime, the inheritance descended to him; & whereas he devised the 150 a. to his only child, ELIZABETH, now ELIZA-BETH PAGET; now she & her husband sell to GARDEN. Witnesses: JOHN HENTIE, CHARLOTTE HARTLEY. Before BENJAMIN SIMONS, JR., J.P., 24 Apr. 1767. Recorded 12 May 1767 by FENWICKE BULL, Register.

Book G-3, p. 254   CONRAD KYSSELL, gentleman, to PHILIP BAER,
10 & 11 Apr. 1767   wood factor, both of Charleston, for £ 200
L & R   currency, 100 a. in Purysburgh Township, bound-
                    ing SW on PATRICK GRIFFIN; NW & NE on ADRIAN
MEYER; SE on vacant land. Witnesses: GEORGE RUPPELL, JACOB WURTZER. Before FENWICKE BULL, J.P. & P. Register.

Book G-3, p. 260   PHILIP HOWELL, of Craven Co., to JOSEPH BROWN,
20 Mar. 1765   merchant, of Georgetown, for £ 1174:3:0 cur-
L & R by Mortgage   rency, 3 tracts, total 700 a.; 50 a. on Little
                    Cedar Creek where the old mill stands; 100 a.
on Big Cedar Creek, where his new mill is now being built; 550 a. on Cedar Creek; all on Big Peedee River; with the mills & other buildings.
Witnesses: JOSEPH HUGGINS, ABRAHAM BEVILL. Before CHARLES FYFFE, J.P.,
15 Mar. 1766. Recorded 14 May 1767 by FENWICKE BULL, P. Register.

Book G-3, p. 265   SAMUEL SMITH, butcher, to ELIZABETH GIBBES,
31 May 1745   wife of JOHN GIBBES, both of Charleston, for
Release   £ 1520 currency, 700 a. Whereas JOHN DANIEL,
                    planter, of Parish of St. Thomas & St. Dennis,
Berkeley Co., owned 700 a. on which he lived, on St. Thomas Island, bound-
ing N on ISAAC LASSENE & the creek back of the island; E on Wando River;
S & W on MRS. SARAH DANIEL & RICHARD CODNER (lately of WILLIAM TREWIN &
CHARLES CODNER; which 700 a. he mortgaged to the vestry of St. Thomas
Parish for £ 500 by L & R dated 22 & 23 July 1728; & whereas JOHN DANIEL
& SARAH his wife, by L & R dated 21 & 22 Mar. 1739, mortgaged to ELIZA-
BETH JENYS (ELIZABETH GIBBES) the 700 a. for £ 6000 currency without tell-
ing her of the first undischarged mortgage, & she was obliged to take up
the first mortgage (DANIEL being deprived of his equity by law); later
selling the land to SAMUEL SMITH for £ 1520 currency; now he resells to
her for same amount. Witnesses: THOMAS WRIGHT, HENRY BEDON, (a cooper),
JOHN WILKINS, CHARLES PINCKNEY. Before ALEXANDER GORDON, J.P. Recorded
15 May 1767 by FENWICKE BULL, Register.

Book G-3, p. 273   JOHN GIBSON, planter, to DANIEL MCDANIEL, for
25 Mar. 1754   £ 100 currency, 150 a. in Craven Co., on S
Release   side Wateree River, bounding SE on THOMAS
                    HAYNE; other sides on vacant land. Witnesses:
ISAAC VICK, ROBERT (his mark) STEWART, JOHN (his mark) MADDOX. Before
JOHN HAMELTON, J.P. on 15 Feb. 1755. Recorded 16 May 1767 by FENWICKE
BULL, Register.

Book G-3, p. 276   WILLIAM (his mark) DALTON, of St. Bartholomews
4 & 5 May 1767   Parish, grandson & heir of WILLIAM DALTON,
L & R   planter; to JAMES PARSONS, ESQ., of Charleston,
                    for £ 125 currency, 311 a. in said Parish, be-
ing the S, SW, & part of the W part or half of 2 tracts; 1 of 550 a. purchased by said WILLIAM DALTON, deceased, on 8 Sept. 1742, from ISAAC GRIM-
BALL; & 1 of 71 a. granted WILLIAM DALTON, deceased, on 13 Mar. 1752; the
311 a. bounding N & NE on part of said 2 tracts conveyed by WILLIAM (party hereto) to JAMES PARSONS; W on JOHN TIMONS; E on MARY DALTON; S on
Cuckold's Creek. Witnesses: P. VALTON, ALEXANDER MOULTRIE, ROBERT LAD-
SON, JR. Before JOHN TROUP, J.P. Recorded 18 May 1767 by FENWICKE BULL,
Register.

Book G-3, p. 284   NATHANIEL DEAN, planter, of Berkeley Co., to
5 & 6 Dec. 1764   DAVID RUMPH, planter, for £ 375 currency, 500
L & R   a., part of 1500 a. on Indian Field Swamp
                    granted 13 July 1737 to PETER MARION, who on
11 Dec. 1740 sold to DEAN; bounding SE on CAPT. LADSON & vacant land; SW
on vacant land; NW on part of said 1500 a.; NE on vacant land. Witnesses: MICHAEL DORMAN, GEORGE ACERMAN, MICHAEL BOOMER. Before JOHN TROUP,

J.P., 29 Jan. 1766. Recorded 19 May 1767 by FENWICKE BULL, Register.

Book G-3, p. 290 THOMAS BOSHER, planter, of St. Marks Parish,
15 Apr. 1767 (who with GEORGE COGDALE gave bond to BREWTON
Mortgage & SMITH), to MILES BREWTON & THOMAS LOUGHTON
SMITH, merchants, of Charleston, for
L 4739:8:5 currency, 35 slaves, all his horses, neat cattle & 750 a. (in
4 tracts) on which he lives, 450 a. of which he holds on purchase of DR.
HEWARD, ROBERT MALONE, & JACOB LEWIS. A penknife delivered. Witness:
JOHN BREWTON. Before CHARLES PINCKNEY, J.P. Entered in Secretary's Book
A.A.A., p. 116, by THOMAS HORRY, for Sec. Recorded 20 May 1767 by FEN-
WICKE BULL, Register.

Book G-3, p. 293 GEORGE HUPPACH, of Craven Co., to GODFREY
6 July 1766 DRAYER, miller, of Berkeley Co., for L 600
Mortgage currency, 150 a. in Craven Co., in 2 grants,
bounding SW on Broad River; S on MR. SHINGLE;
other sides on vacant land; also a grist & saw mill known as "HUPPACH'S
mills", with their stores, iron & furniture. Witnesses: BENJAMIN GRUBLY,
RALPH HUMPHREYS. Before JOSEPH CURRY, J.P. Entered in Secretary's Book
A.A.A., p. 132, by THOMAS HORRY. Recorded 20 May 1767 by FENWICKE BULL,
Register.

Book G-3, p. 296 GEORGE DRAYER, of Craven Co., to GOTTFRED
11 Nov. 1767 DRAYER, miller, of Berkeley Co., for L 606 cur-
Mortgage rency, 100 a. in Craven Co. in 1 grant, bounding SW on Elix's Creek; W on MOSES MITCHELL; S
on VICKETT; with a grist mill known as G. DRAYER'S mills, with all stores,
irons, & furniture. Witnesses: J. MICHAEL GABLEE, JOSEPH (his mark)
SPIDELL. Before JOSEPH CURRY, J.P. Recorded 21 May 1767 by FENWICKE
BULL, Register.

Book G-3, p. 299 DAVID GRAEME, ESQ., formerly of SC, now resid-
9 & 10 Oct. 1765 ing in London, & ANN his wife, to PETER POR-
L & R CHER, gentleman, of Charleston, for L 600 SC
money, part of lot #32 in Charleston, bounding
E 23 ft. on Bay Street; S 203 ft. (that is, from E 47 ft. then N 6 in.,
then W 156 ft.) on part lot #32 sold by GRAEME to SAMUEL CORDES; W 22-1/2
ft. on RICHARD MUNCRIEF; N 203 ft. on JOHN DUTARQUE, JR. (formerly NOAH
SERRÉ); also the low water lot E & partly opposite said part of lot &
partly opposite parcel sold to SAMUEL CORDES; 25 ft. wide, & extending to
low water mark; also the brick tenement erected on front or E side said
part of lot #32 as separated by a brick wall from a certain other tenement erected to the S thereof on parcel sold to CORDES. Witnesses: ROB-
ERT WALLIS, gentleman, of City of York, England; & DAVID LAMBERT, gentleman, of City of York; before HENRY RAPER, mayor of said city. Recorded
25 May 1767 by FENWICKE BULL, Register.

Book G-3, p. 310 GEORGE KNAPP, carter, of Savannah, Ga., to
24 Mar. 1767 ADRIAN MAYER, ESQ., of Purysburgh, SC, for 20
Sale shillings sterling, his bench #21 in the Parish Church of St. Peters, Purysburgh. Witness-
es: JOHN KEINIER, JOHN J. ZUBLY. Before FENWICKE BULL, Register.

Book G-3, p. 311 SARAH STOUTENBOROUGH (STOUTENBURGH), widow, of
23 & 24 Mar. 1767 Charleston, to JOHN IZARD, ESQ., for L 2300 SC
L & R money, part of lot #36, bounding W 24-1/2 ft.
on Church Street; N 127 ft. on JOHN IZARD; E &
S on SARAH STOUTENBOROUGH; also part of a lot E of said parcel. Witnesses: JAMES SIMPSON, ALEXANDER MICHIE. Before JOHN HUME, J.P. Recorded by
FENWICKE BULL, Register.

Book G-3, p. 318 NEWMAN SWALLOW, merchant, of Charleston, to
24 & 25 May 1767 JAMES ROULAIN, planter, of St. Thomas Parish,
L & R by Mortgage for L 1000 currency, 500 a. on E side of W
branch of forks on head of Saltcatcher River,
in Colleton Co., bounding SW & NW on unknown land; SE on unknown land; &
ZACHARIAH LADSON; NE on NEWMAN SWALLOW & on vacant land; also 200 a. at
the Saltcatcher, bounding E on said 500 a.; other sides on vacant land;
which 200 a. were granted SWALLOW on 24 May 1766. Witnesses: WILLIAM

ROPER, JR., JOHN DART, JR.   Before WILLIAM BURROWS, J.P.   Recorded by
FENWICKE BULL, Register.

Book G-3, p. 326   CHARLES STROTHER, of Charleston, & MARY his
25 & 26 May 1767   wife, to ROBERT EKELLS, planter, of St. James
L & R by Mortgage   Goose Creek, for Ł 3400 currency, the E tene-
                           ment or part of lot #103 in Charleston, bound-
ing N on Broad Street; W on part belonging to MRS. MARY COOPER; S on land
belonging to the French Church; E on PETER BOCQUET. Witnesses: GEORGE
BEASLEY, FELIX WARLEY. Before FENWICKE BULL, J.P. & P. Register. On 29
Nov. 1771 JAMES SANDERS declared mortgage satisfied. Witness: J. BOYN-
TELL.

Book G-3, p. 332   HENRY FULCKER (FULCHER), blacksmith, of
24 & 25 Apr. 1761   Charleston, & HESTER his wife, to MARTIN
L & R   PRIGGEL (BIRCKEL), laborer, of Berkeley Co.,
                           for Ł 200 currency, the N half of his W half
of lot #46 in Charleston, purchased by FULCHER in 1761, from FRANCIS ROSE,
planter, & SARAH his wife, of Berkeley Co.; bounding N on part of lot #47
belonging to ELIZABETH DIDCOT, widow; E on part lot #46 belonging to THOM-
AS TUCKER; S on HENRY FULCKER; W on King Street. Witnesses: THOMAS LAM-
BOLL, THOMAS LAMBOLL, JR. Before FENWICKE BULL, J.P. & P. Register.

Book G-3, p. 340   ROGER PINCKNEY, P.M., to SAMUEL BRAILSFORD,
11 May 1767   ESQ., of Charleston, for Ł 6975 currency, part
Release   of lot #198 in Charlston, bounding W 140 ft.
                           on Friend Street; S 61 ft. on GEORGE ROUPELL;
E on another part of said lot; N on THOMAS HUTCHINSON; also part of back
land of said lot, between Tradd & Broad Streets, bounding N 60 ft. on
THOMAS HUTCHINSON; S on THOMAS SMITH; W 108 ft. on first part; E on DAN-
IEL LEGARE, JR.; subject to claim of dower of ANN SCOTT, now wife of NA-
THANIEL SCOTT. Whereas NATHANIEL SCOTT, brewer, owned said 2 parts of
lot #198 in Charleston, & on 1 June 1763 became indebted to the Rev. MR.
RICHARD CLARKE & SUSANNAH his wife, of Charleston, formerly of London,
for Ł 1100 currency; & on 11 Dec. 1764 to THOMAS SMITH, merchant, of
Charleston, for Ł 864 currency; & whereas CLARKE (who survived SUSANNAH)
& SMITH in 1766 recovered judgments, & costs, against SCOTT, & 2 writs of
fieri facias were issued commanding the P.M. to obtain the sums from
SCOTT'S estate; whereby the P.M. seized the 2 lots; now he sells at auc-
tion to BRAILSFORD. Witnesses: ROBERT WILLIAM POWELL, HOBSON PINCKNEY.
Before FENWICKE BULL, J.P. & P. Register.

Book G-3, p. 347   MARTIN BRICKEL, planter, & MARY (her mark) his
4 & 5 Mar. 1763   wife, to JACOB WERNER, planter, both of Berke-
L & R   ley Co., for Ł 1150 currency, his N half of
                           the W half of lot #46 in Charleston, bounding
W 109 ft. 6 in. on King Street; E 112 ft. 9 in. on JOSEPH ASH; S 52 ft.
on MR. LORIMER; N on ELIZABETH DIDCOT, widow; which part of lot #46 BRICK-
EL purchased (see p. 332) from HENRY & HESTER FULCHER by L & R dated 24 &
25 Apr. 1761. Witnesses: THOMAS LAMBOLL, VALENTINE CROOK. Before FEN-
WICKE BULL, J.P., on 26 May 1767. Recorded 11 June 1767 by FENWICKE BULL,
Register.

Book G-3, p. 356   CHARLES LORIMER, of London, by his attorney,
18 & 19 Mar. 1767   GEORGE INGLIS, merchant, of Charleston; to ED-
L & R   WARD WILKINSON the younger, gentleman, of
                           Charleston, for Ł 3000 currency, part of lot
#46 in Charleston, bounding W 109 ft. 6 in. on King Street; N 52 ft. on
MARTIN BRICKEL (PRIGGLE); E on THOMAS TUCKER; S 52 ft. on a passage-way
30 ft. wide, near Ashley River reserved (by act of assembly) next to &
within the fortifications erected around said Town. Whereas LORIMER for
some years past has owned said part of lot #46 & on 5 July 1764 appointed
GEORGE INGLIS, WILLIAM WOODROP & ROBERT WILLIAMS the younger, of Charleston, his attorneys (WOODROP & WILLIAMS declining) to sell his lands; now
INGLIS sells to WILKINSON. Witnesses: JOSEPH YOUNG, THOMAS INGLIS. Before ROBERT WILLIAMS, JR., J.P. Recorded 15 June 1767 by FENWICKE BULL,
Register.

Book G-3, p. 366   JACOB WERNER, planter, of Berkeley Co., & ANNA
9 & 10 Apr. 1767   MARIA (her mark) his wife, to EDWARD WILKINSON

L & R   the younger, gentleman, of Charleston, for
                               Ŀ 1900 currency, part of lot #46, bounding W
109 ft. 6 in. on King Street; E 112 ft. 9 in. on JOSEPH ASH, deceased; S
52 ft. on EDWARD WILKINSON. Witnesses: PETER SLANN, JOSHUA WARD. Before
WILLIAM BURROWS, J.P. Recorded 17 June 1767 by FENWICKE BULL, Register.

Book G-3, p. 373   JOHN HAYNSWORTH, planter, of St. Marks Parish,
1 & 2 Oct. 1766   Craven Co., to JOHN CORAM, merchant, of
L & R   Charleston, for Ŀ 350 currency, 24 a., 2 roods,
                               in said Parish, part of 300 a. granted 18 Nov.
1747 to WILLIAM OSBURN; bounding SW & SE on BENJAMIN FARRAR; NE on residue of 300 a. Witnesses: WILLIAM AMORY, EDWARD TRISCOTT, RICHARD BARNARD.
Before FENWICKE BULL, J.P. & P. Register. Plat given.

Book G-3, p. 379   ISAAC DA COSTA, merchant, & SARAH his wife, to
21 & 22 May 1767   ROBERT DILLON, vintner, both of Charleston,
L & R by Mortgage   (because DILLON stood security for DILLON'S
                               bond to WILLIAM PARKER, merchant) for Ŀ 1200
currency, 2 lots Nos. 9 & 10 in Town of Strawberry, or Childberry, in St.
Johns Parish, Berkeley Co., containing 1 a., being 330 ft. long & 132 ft.
wide; bounding S on Front or Bay Street; N 132 ft. on Mulberry Street.
Witnesses: ABRAHAM COHEN, HENRY GERDES. Before FENWICKE BULL, J.P. & P.
Register. On 22 Feb. 1768 ROBERT DILLON declared mortgage satisfied.
Witness: FENWICKE BULL, Register.

Book G-3, p. 385   THOMAS (his mark) MCGICHIE, & MARY (her mark)
1 & 2 Sept. 1766   his wife, to WILLIAM FARGESON, planter, both
L & R   of Craven Co., for Ŀ 150 currency, 350 a. on
                               Shingletons Creek, a branch of Wateree River,
in Craven Co., granted MCGICHIE on 3 June 1766 by Lt. Gov. WILLIAM BULL;
bounding on all sides on vacant land. Witnesses: WILLIAM (his mark)
SUTHERLAND, DAVID (his mark) PARRISH, MARY (her mark) CAMP (CEMP). Before G. CASSTON, J.P. Recorded 23 June 1767 by FENWICKE BULL, Register.

Book G-3, p. 391   JAMES STEWART, planter, to JOSEPH HENNING,
2 & 3 Mar. 1767   planter, both of Prince George Parish, Craven
L & R   Co., for Ŀ 1000 currency, 800 a. in said Par-
                              ish, bounding N on JAMES STEWART; W on JOHN
MUSGROVE; S on Georgetown River; E on Turkey Creek; reserving the burial
place 30 ft. square; granted STEWART 7 Aug. 1735 by Lt. Gov. THOMAS
BROUGHTON. Witnesses: JOHN SKRINE, ISAAC FORDYCE. Before ROBERT HERIOT,
J.P. Recorded 24 June 1767 by FENWICKE BULL, Register.

Book G-3, p. 400   JOHN MACKEY, planter, to BENJAMIN HART, plant-
30 & 31 Dec. 1763   er, both of Craven Co., for Ŀ 1000 currency,
L & R   250 a. in Fredericksburgh Township granted 24
                             May 1742 by Gov. JAMES GLEN to CHARLES RAT-
CLIFF; bounding NW on Wateree River & vacant land; other sides on vacant
land; & by L & R dated 10 & 11 Apr. 1746 conveyed by RATCLIFF to BENJAMIN
MCKINNE (proved before RICHARD RICHARDSON, J.P., of Craven Co.); who by
will dated 24 Aug. 1759 ordered the land sold; MACKEY being highest bidder. Witnesses: JOSEPH KIRKLAND, JAMES (his mark) PERRY, WILLIAM (his
mark) HYE. Before BARNABY POPE, J.P., 2 Aug. 1764. Recorded 25 June
1767 by FENWICKE BULL, Register.

Book G-3, p. 405   JOHN (his mark) ROTTON, of SC, to WILLIAM BAR-
9 & 10 Apr. 1764   ROW, of Halifax Co., Nc, for Ŀ 100 currency,
L & R   200 a. in Craven Co., SC, on a branch of Tur-
                             key Creek, bounding on all sides on vacant
land; granted 2 Mar. 1764 by Gov. THOMAS BOONE to JOHN ROTTON (see Sec.
Book X.X., p. 372). Witnesses: WILLIAM HILL, JOSHUA CHERRY, JOSEPH KIRK-
LAND. Before BARNABY POPE, J.P., 18 Aug. 1764. Recorded 26 June 1767 by
FENWICKE BULL, Register.

Gook G-3, p. 411   ABRAHAM PENNINGTON, planter, of Berkeley Co.,
9 July 1762   to GEORGE FYCKE (because FYCKE was PENNING-
Mortgage   TON'S security to DA COSTA & FARR, merchants,
                              in Charleston, for Ŀ 628:17:10); 1 wagon &
harness; 1 grey horse branded P on shoulder; 1 bay horse branded   on
shoulder & W on near buttock; a roan horse branded on near shoulder &

buttock   ; a bay horse branded W with the off ear slit; a black horse
branded on near shoulder   ; 1 grey horse branded on near buttock   ; his
cattle marked with swallow foot   in right ear & slit in left; 200 a.
where he lately dwelt, at head of Long Branch, a branch of Indian Creek;
100 a. on WILLIAM'S beaver-dam creek. Witnesses: ERASMUS (his mark)
NOBLE, ISSACHAR WILLCOCKS (a Quaker). Recorded 26 June 1767 by FENWICKE
BULL, Register.

Book G-3, p. 412   GEORGE III, by Gov. THOMAS BOONE, to JAMES
16 May 1763   PARSONS, 3550 a. S of the Alatamaha, or Great
Grant   Satilla River; bounding N & S on vacant lands
                          & impassable swamps; W on vacant land; E on
Great Satilla River. Signed: GEORGE JOHNSTON, per C.C. Entered in Sec-
retary's Book X.X., p. 55, by GEORGE JOHNSTON, per Sec.; & in Auditor's
Book G-7, p. 73, on 21 May 1763, by RICHARD LAMBTON, Dep. Aud. Recorded
27 June 1767 by FENWICKE BULL, Register. Plat certified 18 Apr. 1763 by
EGERTON LEIGHT, Sur. Gen. T.P. WEANT, Dep. Sur.

Book G-3, p. 415   WILLIAM BURROWS, master in Chancery, of
4 Dec. 1766   Charleston, to JAMES PARSONS, ESQ., for Ł 185
Sale   currency, 200 a. on Pon Pon River, in Colleton
                          Co., granted 30 Sept. 1736 to GEORGE DOUGLAS,
bounding SW on MRS. WELCH; other sides on vacant land; also 232 a. on S
side Pon Pon River, granted same date to DOUGLASS, bounding S on BRYAN
KELLY; E on unknown land. Whereas ELIZABETH BEATTY (lately widow, & executrix of will, of JOHN ST. JOHN, planter, of Pon Pon, in Colleton Co.,
was 1 of the sons of JAMES ST. JOHN, ESQ.); JAMES ST. JOHN, a minor, son
of said JOHN ST. JOHN (by his next friend ELIZABETH BEATTY); BENJAMIN
SINGLETON & ELIZABETH his wife (daughter of said JOHN ST. JOHN), a minor
(by her next friend, her said husband); complained in said court against
LAMBERT LANCE, surviving executor of will of MELLER ST. JOHN (who was executor of said JAMES ST. JOHN); & JAMES ST. JOHN, a minor (son of said
MELLER ST. JOHN); & the court on 25 Sept. 1766 decreed that the M.C.
should sell at auction the lands, etc., included in schedule K; also the
household goods, furniture, plate, books, etc., formerly belonging to
JAMES ST. JOHN listed in schedule K; & from the purchase money pay 2/3
the costs of said suit; retain Ł 300 for himself & assistant for settling
accounts of LANCE as executor; pay LANCE, as executor of MELLER ST. JOHN
& in trust for any beneficiaries of MELLER ST. JOHN'S will 1/2 the money
remaining; also pay LANCE for like purpose Ł 3652:3:7-1/2 due him as executor from estate of JOHN ST. JOHN; pay solicitors, etc.; the overplus
to ELIZABETH BEATTY, as executrix, in trust for several persons; now BUR-
ROWS sells said 2 tracts to PARSONS. Witnesses: WILLIAM ROPER, JR., JOHN
DART, JR. Before JOHN TROUP, J.P. Recorded 29 June 1767 by FENWICKE
BULL, Register.

Book G-3, p. 421   WILLIAM HOPE, merchant, of Beaufort, SC, &
7 & 8 Apr. 1767   CATHERINE his wife, to HENRY MIDDLETON, ESQ.,
L & R by Mortgage   of Charleston, for Ł 84,500 currency, 400 a.
                          on St. Helena Island, in Granville Co., bound-
ing NE on WILLIAM BULL & JOHN FRIPP; SE on JACOB COWEN; SW on WILLIAM
BULL; NW on WILLIAM HARVEY; also lots 306 & 330 in Beaufort on Port Royal
Island; lot #306 bounding N on Craven Street; E on New Castle Street; S
on Bay Street; W on lot #333 belonging to GEORGE SEAMAN; lot #330 bounding S on WILLIAM HAZZARD; W on JOHN BESWICKE; E & N on 2 unnamed streets.
Witnesses: ROBERT MIDDLETON, JOHN JOYNER, JR. Before FENWICKE BULL, Register.

Book G-3, p. 428   WILLIAM WESBURY, planter, of Colleton Co.,
4 & 5 June 1766   (second son of WILLIAM WESBURY, SR., by SARAH
L & R   his wife, later his widow, now deceased; &
                          only surviving brother of EDWARD WESTBURY, de-
ceased, who was eldest son of WILLIAM, SR.; & only uncle of the whole
blood, & heir to ISAAC WESBURY, also deceased, who was only son & heir of
EDWARD WESBURY, & died intestate); with the consent of BENJAMIN SAMUELS,
planter, (eldest surviving son & heir of MARY ANN SAMUELS, formerly MARY
ANN WESBURY, deceased, who was only daughter & WILLIAM & SARAH WESBURY, &
only sister of EDWARD & WILLIAM, JR.); of first part; to WILLIAM MATHEWES,
ESQ., for Ł 120 currency, 100 a. on Johns Island, formerly belonging to
JONATHAN EVANS; land sold by JONATHAN EVANS to JAMES BURT; NE on WILLIAM

WESBURY (formerly COL. DAVIS); SW on ANTHONY MATHEWES; NW on Bohicket
Creek; other sides on WILLIAM MATHEWES. Witnesses: JAMES LAROCH, JOHN
FREEMAN, JOHN HUMPHREYS. Before HUGH WILSON, J.P., 1 July 1766. Record-
ed 2 July 1767 by FENWICKE BULL, Register.

Book G-3, p. 436   MICHAEL MUCKENFUSS, blacksmith, & KATHARINE
10 & 11 May 1767   his wife, to CHARLES WARHAM, cabinet maker,
L & R by Mortgage   both of Charleston, for Ł 1000 currency, the N
                           part of lot #105, bounding W 51-1/2 ft. on
King Street; N 96-1/2 ft. on RICHARD BERESFORD; S 98 ft. on part sold to
CHRISTIAN GRUBER; E on JAMES MICHIE. Witnesses: JOHN DART, JR., JOHN
WARHAM. Before WILLIAM BURROWS, J.P. Recorded 3 July 1767 by FENWICKE
BULL, Register. On Apr. 1777 WARHAM declared mortgage satisfied. Wit-
ness: GEORGE SHEED.

Book G-3, p. 443   JOSEPH DUBOURDIEU, executor of will of ANTHONY
30 & 31 Dec. 1756   WHITE, of Prince Frederick Parish, Craven Co.,
L & R   to JOSEPH POOLE, planter, of Prince George
                           Parish, for Ł 20 currency, 380 a. in Craven
Co., granted 12 Aug. 1737 by Lt. Gov. THOMAS BROUGHTON to ANTHONY WHITE;
bounding NW on JOHN GREEN; other sides on WILLIAM SCREVEN; which land
WHITE, by will dated 7 Feb. 1746 bequeathed to his executors to be sold
to pay his debts. Witnesses: JOHN SKINE, JOHN CHEESBOROUGH. Before
ARCHIBALD BAIRD, J.P., 1 Mar. 1764. Recorded 4 July 1767 by FENWICKE
BULL, Register.

Book G-3, p. 448   WILLIAM GREEN, planter, (eldest son & heir of
1 & 2 Nov. 1750   JOHN GREEN, planter), & LYDIA his wife, of 1st
L & R Tripartite   part; JOHN GREEN, planter, another son of said
                           JOHN GREEN, of 2nd part; WILLIAM POOLE, mer-
chant, of Georgetown, Winyaw, of 3rd part; all of Craven Co. Whereas Lt.
Gov. THOMAS BROUGHTON on 4 June 1735 granted JOHN GREEN the elder 197-1/2
a. on S side of Black River, bounding SW on SAMUEL SCRIVEN; SE on said
GREEN; according to plat certified 30 May 1734 by JAMES ST. JOHN, Sur.
Gen. (see Secretary's Book B.B., fol 398); which land JOHN GREEN, SR.,
gave to JOHN GREEN, JR.; who has verbally agreed to sell to POOLE; but
whereas JOHN GREEN, SR., did not deliver possession & seizin to JOHN,
JR., & he cannot sell without WILLIAM'S consent; now WILLIAM & JOHN sell
to POOLE for Ł 1200 currency. Witnesses: JOHN HENTIE, WILLIAM PARKER.
Before ARCHIBALD BAIRD, J.P., 23 Feb. 1764. Recorded 7 July 1767 by FEN-
WICKE BULL, Register.

Book G-3, p. 456   WILLIAM BURROWS, master in Chancery, at his
25 May 1765   house in Tradd Street, to EDWARD FENWICKE,
Sale   ESQ., of Charleston, for Ł 5570 currency, part
                           of lot #3 in Charleston, bounding E 35 ft. on
the Bay; S 262 ft. on WILLIAM ROPER; W on marsh land belonging to WILLIAM
CHAPMAN; N on EDWARD FENWICKE. Whereas DR. JOHN MARTINI, chirurgeon,
sued in Chancery Court ROBERT RIVERS & REBECCA his wife (lately REBECCA
LLOYD, executrix) & JOHN FREER (executor of JOHN LLOYD, ESQ., who was ex-
ecutor of SARAH FULLER); REBECCA LLOYD, an infant (only child & heir of
JOHN LLOYD & heir of SARAH LLOYD); NATHANIEL FULLER, a minor (heir of
SARAH FULLER); & THOMAS LLOYD, a minor (contingent devisee of SARAH FUL-
LER); & said Court on 11 July 1764 decreed that the M.C. should settle
amount of mortgage due DR. MARTINI; pay ROBERT & REBECCA RIVERS & JOHN
FREER the balance of SARAH FULLER'S estate, including rents, & interest;
also decreed that JOHN FREER, ROBERT RIVERS & REBECCA RIVERS pay said M.C.
balance in their hands; the M.C., if necessary, to sell certain real estate; also ordered NATHANIEL FULLER & REBECCA LLOYD & others foreclosed
of their equity of redemption in said property; now BURROWS sells part of
lot #3 with its buildings to FENWICKE. Witnesses: THOMAS GRIMBALL, JR.,
WILLIAM ROPER, JR. Before ROBERT WILLIAMS, JR., J.P., 2 Oct. 1765. Recorded 7 July 1767 by FENWICKE BULL, Register.

Book G-3, p. 462   JOHN, Lord Berkeley, Palatine, to JOHN COMING,
17 Apr. 1675   mariner, 133 a., English measure, on Oyster
Grant   Point, bounding W on Ashley River; E on Cooper
                           (alias Ittawan) River. By order of SIR JOHN
YEAMANS, baronet, surveyor of SC, to JOHN SULPEPER, Sur. Gen., who re-
ferred to (name obliterated) plat was made 18 June '72. Grant signed:

STEPHEN BULL, JOSEPH WEN, JOHN GODFREY, MAN MATHEWES, RICHARD CONONT, WILL OWEN. Registered 15 June 1675 by JOSEPH WEN, Register. Recorded 7 July 1767 by FENWICKE BULL, Register.

Book G-3, p. 463   ELIAS FOISSIN, of Prince George Parish, Craven
2 & 3 Feb. 1767   Co., & ELIZABETH his wife; & ABRAHAM WARNOCK,
L & R   of St. Thomas Parish, Berkeley Co., & ELIZA-
                          BETH his wife, planters, to THOMAS BUTLER,
planter, of Prince George Parish, for ₺ 3000 currency (i.e., FOISSIN owning 2/3 for ₺ 2400; WARNOCK owning 1/3 for ₺ 600), 1071 a. partly on Waccamaw Neck, partly on island between Waccamaw & Pedee Rivers, the 1000 a.
bounding SE on the ocean; NW on Waccamaw River; SW on JOSEPH ALLSTON
(formerly GEORGE THREADCRAFT); NE on estate of ALEXANDER MCDOWELL (formerly PETER ALLSTON); the 71 a. on the island bounding SE on Waccamaw River; NW & NE on ELIAS FOISSIN; SW on JOSEPH LEBRUCE. Witnesses: JAMES
HASELL, JR., THOMAS LABRUCE, WILLIAM TOWNSEND, BENJAMIN SINGLETARY. Before CHARLES FYFFE, J.P., 10 Mar. 1767. Before ROBERT JOHNSTON, J.P. 16
Apr. 1767. Recorded 8 July 1767 by FENWICKE BULL, Register.

Book G-3, p. 473   WILLIAM ALLSTON, of Parish of Prince George
29 & 30 Jan. 1767   Winyaw, to JOSEPH ALLSTON, of same Parish, for
L & R   ₺ 2350 currency, 1150 a. in Prince George Par-
                          ish, on a Neck between Little River & the sea;
also 330 a. in said Parish, bounding NE on WILLIAM WATIES; N & NW on vacant land; SE on Little River. Whereas WILLIAM WATIES & DOROTHY his wife
on 21 June 1734 sold JONATHAN CALKINS said 1150 a. (as by certain plat &
deed of sale to WATIES from the Hon. THOMAS SMITH & MARY his wife dated
16 Sept. 1726); which CALKINS by L & R dated 5 & 6 May 1754 sold to WIL-
LIAM ALLSTON; & whereas JACOB ROYALL of Boston, in Suffolk Co., Province
of Massachusetts Bay, & ABIGAIL his wife, by deed of feoffment dated 12
May 1758 sold WILLIAM ALLSTON said 330 a.; now WILLIAM ALLSTON sells both
tracts to JOSEPH ALLSTON. Witnesses: PETER SIMONS, WILLIAM ALLSTON, JR.
Before JOSIAS ALLSTON, J.P., 25 Apr. 1767. Recorded 10 July 1767 by FEN-
WICKE BULL, Register.

Book G-3, p. 481   JAMES POYAS, merchant, of 1st part; ELIZABETH
20 Jan. 1767   his wife, of 2nd part; JOSHUA WARD, ESQ., of
Articles of Separation   3rd part. In accordance with their agreement
Tripartite   in regard to their separation, JAMES POYAS
                         conveys to JOSHUA WARD, in trust, for ELIZA-
BETH, part of lot #103 bounding W 50 ft. on King Street; N 100 ft. on
JOHN GASSER; S on MICHAEL MACKENFOSS; 1 Negro woman; 1 Negro girl; &
goods & chattels listed; ₺ 400 currency a year. Witnesses: POTT SHAW,
JANE MORAND. Before FENWICKE BULL, J.P. & P. Register.

Book G-3, p. 485   MARGARET WEBB, tavern keeper, of Prince George
10 Feb. 1761   Parish, Craven Co., to her daughter, AMEY
Gift   PILKINGTON, for her lifetime, then to her
                         daughter, ANN PILKINGTON, part of lot #120 in
Georgetown, Winyaw; bounding NE 100 ft. on other part of lot #120; SE 90
ft. on Cannon Street; SW on lot #96; NW on lot #119; first granted to
PETER ALLSTON; who on 20 June 1737 conveyed to GEORGE PAWLEY; who on 19
June 1749 sold to RICHARD NEDHAM; & sold 6 Jan. 1751/2 to MARGARET WEBB.
Witnesses: CHARLES FYFFE, PETER HANSON. Before ROBERT HERIOT, J.P. Re-
corded 13 July 1767 by FENWICKE BULL, Register.

Book G-3, p. 488   BENJAMIN YOUNG, planter, & MARTHA his wife, to
30 Oct. 1764   PETER SIMONS, planter, both of Craven Co., for
Feoffment   ₺ 1300 currency, 1 undivided half of 420 a. in
                        Prince George Parish, Craven Co., bounding E
on Peedee River; S on ANTHONY PAWLEY (now JAMES WALKER); N on PETER ALL-
STON (now JOHN ALLSTON); W on vacant land; also 1 undivided half of 100
a. in said Parish, bounding W on Peedee River; S on JAMES WALKER; E on a
thoroughfare from Peedee to Waccamaw River; N on JOHN ALLSTON; also 1 undivided half of 150 a., part of 246 a., between Peedee & Waccamaw Rivers,
bounding W on said 100 a. & on JAMES WALKER; NE on other part said 246 a.;
E on WILLIAM WATIES; which 3 tracts of 420, 100 & 150 a., formerly belonged to JOHN ALLSTON, who by L & R dated 13 & 14 Feb. 1748 sold to JOHN
ALLSTON, JR.; & descended to MARTHA (wife of BENJAMIN YOUNG) & ELEANOR
(wife of PETER SIMONS), only surviving daughters of JOHN ALLSTON the

younger; who now hold as coparceners. Witnesses: RICHARD PROCTOR, AN-
THONY MITCHELL. Before CHARLES FYFFE, J.P., 21 Aug. 1766. Entered in
Aud. Gen. Book H-8, p. 79 on 31 July 1766 by RICHARD LAMBTON, Dep. Aud.
Recorded 14 July 1767 by FENWICKE BULL, Register.

Book G-3, p. 494   ROWLAND EVANS, planter, of Santee, Craven Co.,
4 Aug. 1766   to JOHN DEAS, merchant, of Charleston, for
Mortgage   Ł 1000 currency, his tenement & lot, bounding
                          20 ft. on Tradd Street; 100 ft. deep; being
the western 1 of 2 he has recently built there. Witnesses: GEORGE YOUNG,
EDWARDS PIERCE. Before JACOB MOTTE, J.P., 1 July 1767. Recorded 15 July
1767 by FENWICKE BULL, Register.

Book G-3, p. 497   BENJAMIN BURTON, planter, of Port Royal Island,
13 & 14 May 1757   Granville Co., to his sister, MARY BURTON,
L & R   spinster, for Ł 5 currency, lot #309 in Beau-
                          fort, bounding N on part lot #314; E on New
Castle Street; S on Craven Street; W on lot #308; which lot #309 was
granted 24 Aug. 1743 by Lt. Gov. WILLIAM BULL to THOMAS BURTON; who died
intestate; & inherited by his only surviving son, BENJAMIN. Witnesses:
WILLIAM GOUGH, JOHN SMITH. Before WILLIAM HARVEY, J.P. Recorded 16 July
1767 by FENWICKE BULL, Register.

Book G-3, p. 503   LEWIS MILES, planter, of St. James Santee,
20 June 1767   Craven Co., to EDWARD JERMAN, ESQ., of said
Mortgage   Parish, for several sums of Ł 250 each men-
                          tioned in 10 bonds; 3 tracts in said Parish; 1
of 350 a. of pine lands & ponds, part of 700 a. of pine land; 1 of 60 a.
of pine land, including all the buildings formerly belonging to TACITUS
GAILLARD; & all that land conveyed by THEODORE GAILLARD to JAMES WRIGHT
in exchange for other small pieces of land; 1 of 170 a. in the swamp;
total 590 a.; according to deed of feoffment from EDWARD JERMAN to LEWIS
MILES (JERMAN having a true copy signed by JOHN HENTIE, surveyor); bounding SW on EDWARD JERMAN; SE on THEODORE GAILLARD & EDWARD JERMAN; SW in
the swamp on a dam on a line going along the middle of the dam from end
to end; NE on THEODORE GAILLARD & SAMUEL WIGFALL; NW on vacant land.
Witnesses: JOHN HENTIE, MICHAEL BOINEAU, JR. Livery of seizin made.
Proved before THOMAS EVANS, J.P. Recorded 17 July 1767 by FENWICKE BULL,
Register.

Book G-3, p. 509   MARGARET (her mark) JOHNHENRY, to JOHN ROLPH
29 Oct. 1752   BEUNINGER (BENEGAR), both of Purysburgh, Gran-
L & R   ville Co., for Ł 50 currency, 75 a. in Purys-
                          burgh Township, bounding N on DAVID ZUBLY
(formerly DANIEL MULLIETT); S on MARGARET JOHNHENRY; W on Savannah River;
E on pine barren land; which 75 a. were part of 250 a. granted HENRY GRO-
VENBARGO (KRONENBARGER); & sold by his eldest son, NICHOLAS GROVENBARGO,
to MRS. MARGARET HENRY; resurveyed & plat certified 25 June 1767 by JOHN
LINDAR, D.S. Witnesses: ABRAHAM BOURQUIN, JACOB (his mark) STROUBELER.
Before JOHN BOURQUIN, J.P., 26 Feb. 1753. Recorded 20 July 1767 by FEN-
WICKE BULL, Register.

Book G-3, p. 515   WILLIAM PARKER, merchant, of Charleston; &
17 & 19 June 1767   ROBERT QUASH the younger, & BENJAMIN SMITH,.of
L & R   Goose Creek; executors of will (dated 1 Oct.
                          1766) of ROBERT HUME; of 1st part; to JOSEPH
ALLSTON, planter; for Ł 2100 currency, 1050 a. in Craven Co., bounding
(when granted 9 Feb. 1736 to JAMES MAXWELL) W on Peedee River; S on WAL-
TER IZARD; other sides on vacant land. Witnesses: EDWARD HARLESTON, JOHN
HARLESTON. Before FENWICKE BULL, J.P. & P. Register.

Book G-3, p. 521   CHARLES RUSSELL, of Amelia Township, to WIL-
7 & 8 July 1767   LIAM GLEN, merchant, of Charleston, for Ł 500
L & R   currency, 570 a. granted 14 Mar. 1704 to
                          GEORGE STERLAND; then said to be in Craven
Co., & bounding on all sides on vacant land; but, since the Co. boundaries have been established by law, situate in Amelia Township, Berkeley
Co., & bounding E on ROBERT WHITEFORD (lately JOHN FUQUET); other sides
on land supposed to be vacant; which 570 a. STERLAND devised to his 3
sons, GEORGE, WILLIAM, & JOHN; WILLIAM surviving GEORGE & JOHN,

inheriting; & by L & R conveyed to CHARLES RUSSELL, father of CHARLES, party hereto, who, as eldest son, became heir. Witnesses: JOHN HOUSTOUN, ALEXANDER MOULTRIE. Before JAMES PARSONS, J.P. Recorded 22 July 1767 by FENWICKE BULL, Register.

Book G-3, p. 528
19 & 21 Jan. 1760
L & R
WILLIAM KELSEY, carpenter, & MARY his wife, to ALLEN MACLANE, planter, both of Granville Co., for ₤ 690 currency, 230 a. in Prince William Parish, Granville Co., part of 830 a. purchas-ed from the estate of ROBERT THORPE; bounding NE on WILLIAM MAIN; SE on JAMES ST. JOHN; SW on public road leading to Port Royal ferry & on ALBERT ACKERMAN; NW on ALBERT ACKERMAN & WILLIAM HAZEL. Whereas CHARLES LOWNDES, P.M., by writ of fieri facias issued 3 Jan. 1748 by BENJAMIN WHITAKER, C.J., seized the estate of ROBERT THORP (& that of BENJAMIN LLOYD) to satisfy a judgment awarded RICHARD CROFTON, hatter, of London, particu-larly 830 a. in Granville Co., bounding SW on Marsh & Huspa Creek, a branch of Port Royal River; SE on JAMES ST. JOHN; NE & NW on THORPE'S lands; which 830 a. were sold to KELSEY; now KELSEY sells a part to MAC-LANE. Witnesses: WILLIAM HAZEL, THOMAS MARSHALL, ALEXANDER FLINT. Be-fore STEPHEN BULL, J.P. on 14 July 1761. Recorded 24 July 1767 by FEN-WICKE BULL, Register. Plat dated 11 Nov. 1758.

Book G-3, p. 536
18 & 19 Jan. 1759
L & R
JAMES ALLEN, gentleman, to JAMES LINGARD, blacksmith, both of Charleston, for ₤ 430 cur-rency, the remaining part of lot #254 in Charleston, (part sold to THOMAS HEMMETT & part to ROBERT HARDY); fronting 82 ft. on Allens Street; 90 ft. deep; bounding on JOSEPH MOODY; E on ROBERT HARDY; W on JAMES ALLEN; which lot #254 was granted to CAPT. HENRY SYMONDS; who devised to his wife FRANCIS; who devised to her niece FRANCES NORTHALL (later wife of THOMAS ALLEN); & inherited by her only surviving son, JAMES ALLEN. Witnesses: THOMAS RALPH, PETER BONNETHEAU. Before FENWICKE BULL, J.P. & P. Register.

Book G-3, p. 543
11 & 12 June 1767
L & R
JOHN RUTLEDGE, ESQ., to JAMES LINGARD, both of Charleston, for ₤ 500 currency, part of lot #254 in Charleston; bounding S 42 ft. on Allen's Street; N on JOSEPH MOODY; E 90 ft. on GEORGE ESMAND; W on land of elders of the Dutch Church. Witnesses: ED-WARD RUTLEDGE, JOHN FRASER. Before FENWICKE BULL, J.P. & P. Register.

Book G-3, p. 547
10 July 1767
L & R
JAMES LINGARD, & MARY his wife, to CHRISTOPHER RODGERS, both of Charelston, for ₤ 650 curren-cy, part of lot #254, bounding S 42 ft. on Allen's Street; N on JOSEPH MOODY; E 190 ft. on GEORGE ESMAND; W on land claimed by elders of the Dutch Church. Wit-nesses: WILLIAM KELSEY, ANN CADMON. Before FENWICKE BULL, J.P. & P. Reg-ister.

Book G-3, p. 552
23 Sept. 1752
Release
NICHOLAS (German Script) KRONENBARGER, (CRON-INBERGER), of Ebenezer, in Colony of Ga., to MARGARET JOHNHENRY, of Purysburgh, for ₤ 100 currency, 150 a. in Purysburgh Township, bounding S on NICHOLAS WINKLER; W on Savannah River; N on DAVID ZUBLY; E on ABRAM MEURON. Witnesses: ABRAHAM BOURGUIN, GASPAR (his mark) RHAN, DANIEL MARETTE. Before JOHN BOURQUIN, J.P. Recorded 29 July 1767 by FENWICKE BULL, Register.

Book G-3, p. 557
17 June 1767
Release
MARGARETTA (her mark) HENRY (JOHNHENRY?), planter, to ABRAHAM JACOT, shoemaker, both of Town of Purysburgh, for ₤ 18:2:6 currency, lot #58, containing 1 a., in said town, bounding W on lot #57; N, E, & S on streets. Witnesses: DANIEL MARETTE, DAVID GIROUDE, FRANCOIS PROULLIEW (?). Before JOHN LEWIS BOURQUIN, J.P. Re-corded 30 July 1767 by FENWICKE BULL, Register.

Book G-3, p. 559
7 July 1767
Release
HENRY MEURON, planter, to ADRIAN MAYER, ESQ., both of St. Peters Parish, Granville Co., for ₤ 200 currency, 100 a. in Purysburgh Township, bounding N on JEAN HENRY DEROCHE & ANNE JEANERET; E on BENJAMIN HENRIOUD & DEVAL KEUFFER; S on JACOB WINKLER; W

on HENRY GROVINBURGH (CRONENBERGER; KRONENBARGER). Witnesses: DANIEL MARETTE, ABRAHAM JACOT. Before JOHN LEWIS BOURQUIN, J.P. Recorded 30 July 1767 by FENWICKE BULL, Register.

Book G-3, p. 561
13 & 14 July 1767
L & R

ELIZABETH POYAS, wife of JAMES POYAS, merchant, & JOSHUA WARD, attorney-at-law, to THOMAS ELFE, cabinet maker; all of Charleston; for Ł 1100 currency, part of lot #103 in Charleston, bounding W 50 ft. on King Street; N 100 ft. on JOHN GASSER; S on MICHAEL MUCKENFUSS; which property by articles of agreement dated 20 Jan. 1767, POYAS had conveyed to WARD in trust for ELIZABETH (p. 481). Witnesses: JOHN BUSH, BENJAMIN LORD. Before FENWICKE BULL, J.P. & P. Register.

Book G-3, p. 568
13 & 14 July 1767
L & R

JOHN KEILL, cooper, & SUSANNAH (her mark) his wife, to Hon. JOHN BURN, both of Charleston, for Ł 1000 currency, part of lot #117 on White Point, bounding E 33 ft. 4 in. on Old Church (now Meeting) Street; N 105 ft. part lot #117 lately sold by SAMUEL THORNTON to VALENTINE CROOKE; W on heirs of Landgrave THOMAS SMITH; S on part same lot #117 belonging to SAMUEL THORNTON. Witnesses: EGERTON LEIGH, FRANCIS BREMAR. Before RICHARD LAMBTON, J.P. Recorded 4 Aug. 1767 by FENWICKE BULL, Register.

Book G-3, p. 575
13 June 1767
Feoffment

DANIEL HORRY, ESQ., of Charleston, to JOSEPH BEARMAN, planter, of St. James Santee, Craven Co., for Ł 500 currency, 1000 a. in St. James Santee on E side Wambaw Creek, granted 3 Sept. 1735 by Gov. ROBERT JOHNSON, to DANIEL HUGER, ESQ., of St. Johns Parish, Berkeley Co., bounding N on RICHARD & FRANCIS SPENCER; E on DANIEL & ELIAS HORRY; W & NW on PAUL MAZYCK & Wambaw Creek; SSW on vacant land & ELIAS HORRY; & conveyed by said DANIEL HUGER, by L & R dated 28 & 29 July 1736, to DANIEL HORRY, gentleman, of St. James Santee, father of DANIEL HORRY, party hereto. Witnesses: JOHN HENTIE, JOHN REMBERT, JR. Before THOMAS EVANCE, J.P. Entered in·Auditor's Book H-8, p. 237, on 15 July 1767 by RICHARD LAMBTON, Dep. Aud. Recorded 5 Aug. 1767 by FENWICKE BULL, Register.

Book G-3, p. 579
29 Apr. 1767
L & R

THOMAS CRAWFORD, planter, & ELIZABETH his wife, to THOMAS LIDE, planter, both of St. Marks Parish, Craven Co., for Ł 1500 currency, 150 a. on SW side Peedee River, granted 24 Mar. 1756 by Gov. JAMES GLEN to ABRAHAM LUNDY; who conveyed to JOHN CRAWFORD; who bequeathed to his son, said THOMAS; bounding SW on JAMES GILLESPIE & vacant land; NW on WILLIAM HAINESWORTH. Witnesses: JOHN (his mark) WINTERS, JOHN BOHANNON. Before THOMAS WADE, J.P. Recorded 7 Aug. 1767 by FENWICKE BULL, Register.

Book G-3, p. 584
29 Apr. 1767
L & R

THOMAS CRAWFORD, planter, & ELIZABETH his wife, to THOMAS LIDE, planter, both of St. Marks Parish, Craven Co., for Ł 1500 currency, 165 a., or 1/2 of 335 a. in Prince George County, granted 22 Mar. 1744 by Gov. JAMES GLEN to THOMAS ELLERBEE; the 335 a. bounding SW on Peedee River; NW on JOHN BROWN; SE on ABRAHAM COLSON; & conveyed by ELLERBEE to JOHN CRAWFORD; who bequeathed to his 2 sons, JOHN & THOMAS; the 335 a. being divided by Phils Creek; the upper side going to THOMAS; who now conveyed to THOMAS LIDE. Witnesses: JOHN (his mark) WINTERS, JOHN BOHANNON. Before THOMAS WADE, J.P. Recorded 10 Aug. 1767 by FENWICKE BULL, Register.

Book G-3, p. 590
8 Apr. 1767
Conveyance

THOMAS LIDE to CHARLES BEDINGFIELD, for Ł 200 currency, 75 a., part of a tract originally belonging to JOHN BROWN; who conveyed to JOHN ELLERBEE; who bequeathed it to his son, THOMAS ELLERBEE; who sold to THOMAS LIDE; lying on lower side Phils Creek, & adjoining BEDINGFIELD'S land, extending towards the river to the middle of Medder House Slach as the slach goes from where it joins to THOMAS BINGHAMS upper line, all between said slach & BEDINGFIELDS land the lower side of Phils Creek. Witnesses: CHARLES IRBY, WILLIAM TAYLER, JOHN (his mark) STEWARD. Before JOHN ALRAN, J.P. Recorded 10 Aug. 1767 by

FENWICKE BULL, Register.

Book G-3, p. 592   JOHN WALL, to CHARLES IRBY, for ₺ 130 curren-
18 July 1766   cy, 250 a. on Beaver Dam Swamp, surveyed in
Sale   1765 & granted JOHN WALL, SR., & inherited by
                          JOHN WALL, JR.; bounding SW on Peedee River.
Witnesses: THOMAS LIDE, THOMAS CRAWFORD. Proved 9 Jan. 1767 before THOM-
AS WADE, J.P. Recorded 10 Aug. 1767 by FENWICKE BULL, Register.

Book G-3, p. 595   THOMAS (his mark) SIMS, planter, & REBECCA
20 Dec. 1766   (her mark), his wife, to THOMAS LIDE; both of
L & R   '   Craven Co.; for ₺ 450 currency, 150 a. on SW
                          side Peedee River, bounding NW on EVAN VAUGHAN;
SW on FRANCIS YOUNG; SE on JOHN THOMPSON; which land was granted FRANCIS
YOUNG 24 May 1745. Witnesses: REBECCA LIDE, JOHN HEUSTESS. Before THOM-
AS WADE, J.P. 16 May 1767. Recorded 12 Aug. 1767 by FENWICKE BULL, Reg-
ister.

Book G-3, p. 601   EDWARD ELLERBEE, & ELIZABETH his wife, to
31 Dec. 1766   THOMAS LIDE, both of Craven Co., for ₺ 1200
Release   currency, 175 a. in Craven Co., on N side Pee-
                          dee River, part of 650 a., granted JOHN ELLER-
BEE, SR.; who bequeathed to his son, GEORGE; at whose death it descended
to his brother, EDWARD; the 175 a. beginning at a hackberry tree on river
bank, the lower corner of original tract; running N 70 E 343.72 poles to
a stake the NE corner of said grant; then N 20 W to a line of marked
trees run between said EDWARD ELLERBEE & his brother, JOHN ELLERBEE; then
S 70 W along said line to Peedee River; down the river to beginning. Witnesses: WILLIAM LANKFORD, JOHN ELLERBEE. Before THOMAS WADE, J.P. on 26
Feb. 1767. Recorded 12 Aug. 1767 by FENWICKE BULL, Register.

Book G-3, p. 603   EDWARD HOMES, planter, & REBECCA his wife, to
20 June 1760   MICHAEL ALDERAGE, for ₺ 300 SC money, 150 a.
Sale   in Craven Co., bounding NE on Peedee River; NW
                          on EVAN VAUGHAN; SW on FRANCIS YOUNG; SE on
JOHN THOMPSON, JR. Witnesses: WILLIAM JAMES, JR., WILLIAM RHODES. Be-
fore GEORGE HICKS, 11 Aug. 1760. Recorded 12 Aug. 1767 by FENWICKE BULL,
Register.

Book G-3, p. 605   MICHAEL (his mark) ALDERAGE, planter, to JAMES
14 July 1761   PITMAN, for ₺ 400 currency, 150 a. in Craven
Sale   Cr., (see p. 603). Witnesses: WILLIAM RHODES,
                          ROBERT (his mark) CLARY. Before ALEXANDER
MACKINTOSH, J.P., 21 June 1762. Recorded 12 Aug. 1767 by FENWICKE BULL,
Register.

Book G-3, p. 608   JAMES (his mark) PITMAN, planter, to THOMAS
21 Nov. 1761   SIMS, for ₺ 300 currency, 150 a. in Craven
Sale   Co. (see p. 605). Witnesses: WILLIAM RHODES,
                          HOWELL JAMES. Before ALEXANDER MCKINTOSH,
J.P. 30 May 1763. Recorded 13 Aug. 1767 by FENWICKE BULL, Register.

Book G-3, p. 610   JOHN WRIGHT, planter, of Anson Co., NC, to
15 & 16 July 1767   JAMES GORDON, merchant, of Georgetown, Craven
L & R   Co., for ₺ 1400 currency, 200 a. in Anson Co.,
                          NC, on SW side Great Peedee River; bounding
above on Hackleberry Creek; below by THOMAS TOMKINS; E on Peedee River; W
on vacant land; being part of land granted THOMAS JONES. Witnesses: WIL-
LIAM VAUX, JEHU POSTELL. Before CHARLES FYFFE, J.P. Recorded 14 Aug.
1767 by FENWICKE BULL, Register.

Book G03, p. 617   SARAH STOUTENBURGH, widow, of Charleston, to
23 & 24 Mar. 1767   THOMAS LIND, factor, for ₺ 2100 currency; part
L & R   of lot #36 in Charleston; also part of a lot E
                          of said lot; the part of lot #36 bounding W
24-1/2 ft. on Church Street; N 127 ft. on JOHN IZARD (formerly SARAH
STOUTENBURGH); E on SARAH STOUTENBURGH; S on THOMAS LEGARE. Witnesses:
JAMES SIMPSON, ALEXANDER MICHIE. Before FENWICKE BULL, J.P. & Register.
SARAH gives bond for performance.

Book G-3, p. 624   SARAH RAVEN, widow, of 1st part; LUKE STOUTEN-
30 & 31 Oct. 1765   BURGH, gentleman, of 2nd part; WILLIAM SAVAGE,
L & R Tripartite   merchant, & THOMAS BEE, attorney-at-law, of
                          3rd part; all of Charleston. Whereas a mar-
riage is intended between LUKE & SARAH; & whereas SARAH owns a considerable estate consisting of lands, plantation houses, rents, slaves, cattle,
horses, furniture, plate, jewels, bonds, mortgages, etc. (subject to
debts of estate of her husband, JOHN RAVEN, deceased); & whereas LUKE &
SARAH have agreed that such real & personal estate should be conveyed to
trustees for her benefit; now they convey to SAVAGE & BEE, as trustees,
all such real & personal estate, for use of LUKE & SARAH during their
joint lives; should she die first, LUKE to deliver 6 certain slaves &
L 10,000 to her heirs. Witnesses: JOHN WEBB, BENJAMIN MATHEWES. Before
FENWICKE BULL, J.P. & P. Register.

Book G-3, p. 636   EDWARD DAVIES, merchant, (lately copartner
22 & 23 July 1767   with RICHARD WAYNE, merchant, of Charleston) &
L & R by Mortgage   MARGARET his wife, to ROBERT RAPER & WILLIAM
                          ANCRUM, of Charlston, attorneys for WILLIAM
GREENWOOD & WILLIAM HIGGENSON, merchants, of London; (DAVIES & WAYNE being indebted to GREENWOOD & HIGGENSON for balance due on an account annexed to deed of assignment, this date, in sum of L 5583 sterling, British & be said deed assigned all the estate, debts & effects of said co-
partnership to RAPER & ANCRUM; WAYNE also assigning 2 Negroes & his
household goods & furniture; DAVIES agreeing to mortgage his land in
Ansonborough); a parcel of land bounding W 277 ft. 4 in. on King Street;
N 602 ft. on EDWARD SMITH; S on MRS. SARAH TROTT; E on land of SC Society.
Witnesses: JACOB VALK, WILLIAM HALES. Before FENWICKE BULL, J.P. & Register.

Book G-3, p. 641   HUMPHREY PRIMUS, carpenter, now living in Ga.,
1 & 2 May 1767   son of JOHN PRIMUS of St. Thomas Parish, SC,
L & R   to WILLIAM PARKER, merchant, of Charleston,
                          for L 150 currency, his undivided half part of
100 a. on SE side of Cooper River, in St. Thomas Parish; being the N part
of 400 a. granted by the Lords Proprs. on 14 Apr. 1710 to SAMUEL BLUN-
DELL; bounding W & S on other part of said 400 a.; N & W on WILLIAM PAR-
KER; NE on THOMAS PADGETT; which 100 a. now belong to JAMES PRIMUS & HUM-
PHREY PRIMUS. Witnesses: EDWARD JONES, JOHN WHITAKER, JOHN ROSE. Before
FENWICKE BULL, J.P. & Register.

Book G-3, p. 649   TUNES TEBOUT, blacksmith, to PETER MANIGAULT,
25 & 26 June 1767   barrister-at-law, both of Charleston, for
L & R by Mortgage   L 5200 currency, part of a lot bounding 21 ft.
                          on East Bay, & extending 250 ft. E towards
Cooper River from the E curtain line or brick wall erected on said Bay;
bounding N on a 28 ft. street left by BARNARD ELLIOTT & OTHNIEL BEALE for
the common use of the wharves & buildings thereabouts; on which lot BAR-
NARD ELLIOTT built a long brick building containing many shops & stores
(the land & building having been sold by executors of BARNARD ELLIOTT'S
will to TUNES TEBOUT & BARNARD BEEKMAN); also lot #54 in Beaufort, bounding N on Port Royal Street; E on East Street; S on lots #23 & #24; W on
lots #50 & #53. Witnesses: BENJAMIN COACHMAN, WILLIAM CRABB. Before
WILLIAM CRABB, J.P. Recorded 31 Aug. 1767 by FENWICKE BULL, Register.
On 4 Apr. 1788 JOSEPH MANIGAULT & GABRIEL MANIGAULT, sons of PETER (then
deceased), acknowledged satisfaction of mortgage. Before P. HORRY, WIL-
LIAM YARNOLD.

Book G-3, p. 655   JOSIAH BONNEAU, merchant, eldest son & heir of
22 June 1767   ANTHONY BONNEAU (son of JACOB) planter; to the
Feoffment   Rev. MR. ROBERT SMITH, both of Charleston, for
                          L 600 currency, 102 a., in St. Thomas Parish,
Berkeley Co., part of a tract granted PETER VIDEAU; who gave it to his
son-in-law JACOB BONNEAU; whose eldest son JACOB inherited; & sold to his
brother ANTHONY; bounding SE on estate of JAMES AKINS; NE on JAMES MARION;
NW & SW on ROBERT SMITH (formerly JOHN PAGETT). Witnesses: WILLIAM GLEN,
JR., ANTHONY LAMOTTE. Before FENWICKE BULL, J.P. & P. Register.

Book G-3, p. 657   THOMAS (his mark) GOODALE, planter, & FRANCES
14 & 15 Sept. 1759   his wife, formerly of SC, now of Little

L & R   Ogechy, Ga.; to FRANCIS MACARTAN & MARTIN CAMP-
                                   BELL, merchants, of Charleston, for Ł 200 SC
money, 800 a. on Beech Island, in New Windsor Township, Granville Co.,
granted 13 Feb. 1753 by Gov. JAMES GLEN to THOMAS GOODALE; bounding W on
Savannah River; N on ROBERT MCMURDY & vacant land; E on vacant land; S on
vacant & swamp land. Witnesses: THOMAS MOODIE, LEWIS JOHNSON. Before
JAMES PARSONS, J.P. 1 Nov. 1765. Recorded 3 Sept. 1767 by FENWICKE BULL,
Register.

Book G-3, p. 664   THOMAS CRAWFORD, planter, of Craven Co., to
3 Apr. 1767   MARY MCBRIDE, for Ł 130 SC money, a lot of
Sale   half an a. in Georgetown, which CRAWFORD pur-
                                   chased from STEPHEN COLE; who purchased from
ALEXANDER GORDON; who purchased from EDWARD ELLERBEE; being part of 650
a. granted JOHN ELLERBEE 14 Mar. 1745; beginning at a stake at a corner
of JOHN COLE'S lot on said ALEXANDER GORDON'S line; running N 70° E 3.65
perches; then s 20° E 21.9 perches; then S 70° W 3.65 perches, then to
beginning. Witnesses: ROBERT BLAIR, ALEXANDER GORDON. Before CLAUDIUS
PEGUES, J.P. Recorded 3 Sept. 1767 by FENWICKE BULL, Register.

Book G-3, p. 667   ELIJAH PRIOLEAU, planter, of Prince William
14 & 15 Aug. 1766   Parish, Granville Co., & SARAH his wife, to
L & R   BARNABY BRANFORD, planter, of St. George Par-
                                   ish, Berkeley Co., for Ł 2500 currency, 500 a.
in Prince William Parish, bounding SE on FRANCIS ROCHE; NW on ELIJAH
PRIOLEAU; other sides on vacant land; being part of 2000 a. granted 11
Jan. 1732 to JAMES HASSELL. Witnesses: ROBERT MCLEOD, CHARLES DALTON,
ANDREW POSTELL. Before JOHN GOVAN, J.P., 26 Aug. 1766. Recorded 7 Sept.
1767 by FENWICKE BULL, Register. Plat certified 12 July 1766 by ALEXIUS
MADOR FORSTER, Dep. Sur.

Book G-3, p. 673   JAMES (his mark) WELSH, & MARY CATHARINE (her
19 & 20 June 1767   mark) his wife, of Charleston, to THOMAS HODGE,
L & R   planter, of Craven Co., for Ł 150 currency,
                                   100 a. in Santee River Swamp, on N side Santee
River, in Craven Co., bounding SW on the river; SE on JOHN TAYLOR; which
100 a. were granted MARY CATHARINE (then MARY CATHERINE SMITTEN) on 21
Jan. 1761. Witnesses: ARCHIBALD CRAWFORD, VINCENT SIMMONS. Before FEN-
WICKE BULL, J.P. & P. Register.

Book G-3, p. 679   JOSEPH ALLEN, planter, son & heir of JOSEPH
13 & 14 Oct. 1752   ALLEN, shipwright; to WILLIAM ALLSTON, plant-
L & R   er; all of Prince George Parish, Craven Co.;
                                   for Ł 300 currency, 391 a. (part of 500 a.) in
Craven Co., bounding N & E on WILLIAM ALLSTON (formerly THOMAS HEPWORTH);
S on PERCIVAL PAWLEY (formerly JOHN HUTCHINSON); W on HEPWORTH'S creek;
which 391 a. THOMAS HEPWORTH by L & R dated 22 & 23 Mar. 1737 sold to
JOSEPH ALLEN, SR.; who died intestate. Witnesses: MARGARET WEBB, JOB
ROTHMAHLER. Before CHARLES FYFFE, J.P., 17 Aug. 1767. Recorded 12 Sept.
1767 by FENWICKE BULL, Register.

Book G-3, p. 686   HENRIETTA WRAGG, spinster, to PATRICK HINDS,
30 Jan. 1761   shoemaker, both of Berkeley Co., SC, for Ł 650
Feoffment   currency, 1 a. on Charleston Neck, bounding S
                                   on the town line; W on Glebe land of St.
Philips Parish; N on pasture land belonging to HENRIETTA WRAGG; E on the
broad road. Witnesses: JOHN DENTON, JOHN WRAGG. Before PETER MANIGAULT,
J.P., 26 June 1761. Recorded 14 Sept. 1767 by FENWICKE BULL, Register.

Book G-3, p. 688   JAMES CROKATT, ESQ., of London, by his attor-
28 & 29 May 1767   ney, ROBERT WILLIAMS, JR., attorney-at-law, of
L & R   Charleston, to ISAAC LESESNE, planter, of St.
                                   Thomas Parish, for Ł 1750 currency, part of
half of lot #19 in Charleston, bounding E 17 ft. 10 in. on the Bay; N 67
ft. on other half of said lot lately sold by CROKATT to SUSANNAH WALKER;
W 15 ft. on other part of said half lately sold by CROKATT to ESTHER
RAND, widow; S on other part of said lot still belonging to CROKATT &
about to be sold to WILLIAM PARKER; with the tenement & other houses for
several years past occupied by DAVID HENDERSON, barber. Whereas JAMES
CROKATT for many years past has owned 1/2 of lot #19 in Charleston, & on

22 Oct. 1766 appointed WILLIAMS his attorney to sell the property (Book G-3, p. 178), now WILLIAMS sells a part to LESESNE. Witnesses: TIMOTHY CROSBY, JOHN FULLERTON. Before FENWICKE BULL, J.P. & P. Register. Plat certified 1 June 1767 by NATHANIEL DEAN, Dep. Sur.

Book G-3, p. 697　　　　　JAMES CROKATT, of London, by his attorney,
1 & 2 June 1767　　　　　ROBERT WILLIAMS, JR., attorney-at-law, of
L & R　　　　　　　　　　Charleston, (appointed 22 Oct. 1766), to WIL-
　　　　　　　　　　　　 LIAM PARKER, merchant, of Charleston, for
Ł 1750 currency, part of half of lot #19 in Charleston, bounding E 17 ft. 10 in. on the Bay; N 65 ft. on part lately sold by CROKATT to ISAAC LESESNE; W 16 ft. on part sold to ESTHER RAND; S on part sold to JAMES AMOS TAYLOR; with the tenement; as occupied for several years past by AGNES SCOTT, widow. Witnesses: TIMOTHY CROSBY, JOHN FULLERTON. Before FENWICKE BULL, J.P. & P. Register. Recorded 26 Sept. 1767. Plat certified 1 June 1767 by NATHANIEL DEAN, Dep. Sur.

Book G-3, p. 706　　　　　ANTOINE (his mark) BILLEAU, freeholder, to
20 July 1767　　　　　　　ADRIAN MAYER, ESQ., both of St. Peters Parish,
Release　　　　　　　　　 Granville Co., for Ł 60 currency, 100 a. in
　　　　　　　　　　　　 Purysburgh Township, bounding E on ABRAHAM
JACOT; N on JACOB WINKLER; W & S on vacant land. Witnesses: DANIEL MARETTE, FRANCOIS PROULLIAC. Before JOHN LEWIS BOURQUIN, J.P. Recorded 28 Sept. 1767 by FENWICKE BULL, Register.

Book G-3, p. 708　　　　　ABRAHAM FREDERICK DEROCHE, planter, of Ebene-
10 Aug. 1767　　　　　　　zer, to ADRIAN MAYER, ESQ., of Purysburgh,
Release　　　　　　　　　 Granville Co., for Ł 14 currency, 50 a. in
　　　　　　　　　　　　 Purysburgh Township, bounding E on BENJAMIN
HENRIOU; N on WALLIER CULLIAT; W on ANN JEANERET; S on ABRAM MEURON. Witnesses: DAVID GIROUD, DANIEL MARETTE. Before JOHN LEWIS BOURQUIN, J.P. Recorded 29 Sept. 1767 by FENWICKE BULL, Register.

Book G-3, p. 710　　　　　JOSEPH LEWIS (LOUAYS) REYMOND, with the con-
26 Apr. 1742　　　　　　　sent of his wife, ANNE (late widow of PETER
Release　　　　　　　　　 FOURQUERANT), to DAVID GIROUD, of Purysburgh,
　　　　　　　　　　　　 Granville Co., for Ł 35 currency, lot #11 in
Purysburgh, containing 1 a., bounding S on GAMPER MELKER; N & E on streets; W on DAVID GIROUD; which a. had been granted PETER FOURQUERANT. Witnesses: HENRY MEURON, DAVID GODET, ABRAHAM MEURON. Before JOHN LEWIS BOURQUIN, J.P. on 3 Aug. 1767. Recorded 1 Oct. 1767 by FENWICKE BULL, Register.

Book G-3, p. 713　　　　　JOHN HENRY VAUCHER, shoemaker, to DAVID GIROUD,
4 Jan. 1760　　　　　　　 carpenter, both of Purysburgh, Granville Co.,
Release　　　　　　　　　 for Ł 200 currency, 3 tracts in Purysburgh
　　　　　　　　　　　　 Township; 100 a. granted 14 Sept. 1738 to LEW-
IS KEHL; 50 a. granted 14 Dec. 1739 to JOHN FRANCIS HENRY; 50 a. granted 14 Dec. 1739 to MARIA HENRY. Witnesses: FRANCIS EHRHARDT, GABRIEL RAVOT, JOHN LINDER. Before JOHN LEWIS BOURQUIN, J.P on 3 Aug. 1767. Entered in Auditor's Book, P-4, p. 347, on 27 Mar. 1760 by JOHN BASSNETT. Recorded 2 Oct. 1767 by FENWICKE BULL, Register.

Book G-3, p. 717　　　　　The Rev. MR. JOHN JOACHIM ZUBLY, & ANNE his
23 Dec. 1763　　　　　　　wife, of Christ Church Parish, Ga., to DANIEL
Release　　　　　　　　　 MALLET, planter, of St. Peters Parish, SC, for
　　　　　　　　　　　　 Ł 100 SC money, 100 a. Whereas on 17 Mar.
1735, Lt. Gov. THOMAS BROUGHTON granted HENRY GROVENEMBERG, alias CRONEN-BARGER, 250 a. in Purysburgh Township, bounding N on ANNA JANNERE; E on ABRAHAM MEURON; S on JACOB WINKLER; W on Savannah River; which land was inherited by HENRY'S oldest son, NICHOLAS; who sold portions to various persons; selling the N part, or 100 a., to DAVID ZUBLY, planter, of Purys-burgh; & whereas the 100 a. was inherited by 1 of DAVID'S sons, THOMAS; at whose death JOHN JOACHIM inherited; now he sells to MALLET. Witness-es: ROBERT MCCLATCHIE, HENRY GINDRAW, GABRIEL RAVOT. Before ADRIAN MAYER, J.P. on 27 Aug. 1764. Recorded 3 Oct. 1767 by FENWICKE BULL, Register.

Book G-3, p. 721　　　　　LUDWIG KEHL, planter, to MAJ. JAMES RICHARD,
14 Apr. 1736　　　　　　　planter, both of Purysburgh, Granville Co.,
Release　　　　　　　　　 for Ł 40 currency, 150 a. bounding N on CAPT.

PETER LAFFITTE; S & E on VINCENT DALESCELEA; W on Savannah River. Witness: STEPHEN ALOWEXI. Delivery by turf & twig. Memo: On 3 Jan. 1760 JOHN VAUCHIER, of Purysburgh, sold to DAVID GIROUD for Ь 200 SC money, 100 a. granted LUDWIG KEHL, & 50 a. granted to JOHN FRANCIS HENRY "the thrid of 50 a. granted to MARIA HENRY"; in Purysburgh Township. Witnesses: JOHN LINDER, JOHN BUCHE. Recorded 5 Oct. 1767 by FENWICKE BULL, Register.

Book G-3, p. 724　　　　　　DANIEL (his mark) ROGERS, planter, to JENKIN
30 & 31 Oct. 1765　　　　　HARRIS, planter, for Ь 200 currency, 250 a. on
L & R　　　　　　　　　　　a branch of Stephens Creek in Granville Co.,
　　　　　　　　　　　　　granted 25 Oct. 1764 by Gov. WILLIAM BULL to
DANIEL ROGERS; bounding NE on JENKIN HARRIS & vacant land; E & N on vacant land; SW on NOBELS. Witnesses: DAVID ROBESON, MOSES HARRIS, JOHN FAIRCHILD. Before JACOB SUMMARALL, J.P., 20 Feb. 1766. Recorded 7 Oct. 1767 by FENWICKE BULL, Register.

Book G-3, p. 729　　　　　　ANTHONY MURRELL, planter, eldest son of JON-
11 & 12 Apr. 1755　　　　　ATHAN MURRELL, planter; both of Berkeley Co.,
L & R　　　　　　　　　　　for Ь 325 currency, his undivided half part
　　　　　　　　　　　　　of 300 a. (150 a.) at Seawee Bay, bounding SE
on the Bay; SW on MR. HOLLIBUSH; NW on GEORGE HUGGINS; NE on ROBERT MURRELL. Whereas ROBERT MURRELL, besides other real estate, owned said 300 a., which by will dated 5 Mar. 1711 he bequeathed to his son JONA-THAN; who by will dated 22 Mar. 1743 bequeathed equally to his sons, ANTHONY & WILLIAM; now ANTHONY sells his share to BONNEAU. Witnesses: ELI FRISSEL, WILLIAM ELLIOTT, JR., GEORGE HUGGINS, STEPHEN FORGARTIE, JR. Before HENRY GRAY, J.P. Entered in Auditor's Book H-8, p. 268, on 1 Sept. 1767 by RICHARD LAMBTON, Dep. Aud. Recorded 9 Oct. 1767 by FEN-WICKE BULL, Register.

Book G-3, p. 738　　　　　　DR. ALEXANDER FOTHERINGHAM, physician, of
16 Dec. 1766　　　　　　　　Charleston, & ISABELLA his wife, of 1st part;
Deed of Partition　　　　　DR. ARCHIBALD MCNEILL, physician, of St.
　　　　　　　　　　　　　George Parish, Dorchester, & MARY his wife, of
2nd part. Whereas FOTHERINGHAM & MACNEILL, as tenants in common, own an undivided lot in Charleston with the 2 brick houses thereon, bounding S 30 ft. on Tradd Street; W 200 ft. on JOHN PAUL GRIMKE; N 30 ft. on DANIEL BOURGETT; E 200 ft. on ROBERT PRINGLE; which property they had purchased from CHRISTIAN GRINDLAY, widow of JAMES GRINDLAY, attorney-at-law; now they agree to divide the property, FOTHERINGHAM to have the E half, bounding S 15 ft. on Tradd Street; E on PRINGLE; N on BOURGETT; with the brick house & other buildings thereon; MACNEILL to have the W half, bounding S 15 ft. on Tradd Street; W on JOHN PAUL GRIMKE (formerly WILLIAM WILKINS); N on BOURGETT; with the brick house & other buildings thereon. Witnesses: CHARLES DEWAR, MORDICAI MCFARLAN. Before JOHN HUME, J.P. on 12 Jan. 1767. Recorded 12 Oct. 1767 by FENWICKE BULL, Register.

Book G-3, p. 746　　　　　　WILLIAM MURRELL, cordwainer, 1 of the sons of
5 & 6 Aug. 1757　　　　　　JONATHAN MURRELL, planter, who was 1 of the
L & R　　　　　　　　　　　sons of ROBERT MURRELL, planter; of 1st part;
　　　　　　　　　　　　　to HENRY BONNEAU, planter; all of Berkeley
Co.; for Ь 400 currency, his undivided half part of 300 a. (150 a.) at Seawee Bay, bounding SE on the Bay; SW on MR. HOLLYBUSH; NW on GEORGE HUGGINS; NE on ROBERT MURRELL. Whereas ROBERT MURRELL, besides other real estate, owned said 300 a., which by will dated 5 Mar. 1711 he bequeathed to his son JONATHAN; who by will dated 22 Mar. 1743 bequeathed equally to his 2 sons, ANTHONY & WILLIAM; now WILLIAM sells his share to BONNEAU. Witnesses: STEPHEN FOGARTIE, ELI FRISSELL, WILLIAM FRISSELL. Before HENRY GRAY, J.P., 17 Apr. 1758. Entered in Auditor's Book H-8, p. 268, on 1 Sept. 1767, by RICHARD LAMBTON, Dep. Aud.

Book G-3, p. 750　　　　　　MATTHEW CROSS, cordwainer, of Christ Church
23 & 24 July 1761　　　　　Parish, Berkeley Co., & MARY (her mark) his
L & R　　　　　　　　　　　wife (lately MARY FRISELL, only daughter of
　　　　　　　　　　　　　ALEXANDER FRISSELL, SR.); to SARAH BONNEAU,
widow, of St. Thomas Parish, Berkeley Co., for Ь 1500 currency, 340 a., English measure, which MARY inherited as only sister & heir of WILLIAM FRISELL, (who died intestate), of Christ Church Parish, who was only surviving brother of (& joint tenant with) NATHANIEL FRISELL, ELY FRISSELL,

& ALEXANDER FRISSELL, JR., sons of ALEXANDER FRISELL, SR., (whose will
was dated 9 Mar. 1737); the 340 a. being on upper part of Wando Neck;
bounding N on part of 643 a. now belonging to MR. ALSTON & MR. MOSONG; W
on MR. MOSONG & ELIAS FOISSIN; S on ELIAS FOISSIN; E on MR. ALSTON & JOHN
HUGGINS. Witnesses: THOMAS LAMBOLL, JOHN FULLERTON, THOMAS LAMBOLL, JR. .
Before ROBERT PRINGLE, J.P., 21 Aug. 1767. Entered in Auditor's Book H-8,
p. 268, on 1 Sept. 1767. Plat by WILLIAM SCREVEN, Dep. Sur. certified
10 Dec. 1732, showing 340 a.; 250 of which formerly belonged to PETER
CULLIANDER; the other 90 a. being part of 643 a. formerly belonging to
MR. ALSTON. By RICHARD LAMBTON, Dep. Aud. Recorded 17 Oct. 1767 by FEN-
WICKE BULL, Register.

Book G-3, p. 766   MILES BREWTON & THOMAS LOUGHTON SMITH, mer-
Sept. 1767   chants, of Charleston, to DR. JOHN SWINT, phy-
Assignment of Mortgage   sician. Whereas RICHARD BERESFORD, of Parish
                          of St. Thomas & St. Dennis, on 1 Aug. 1761
leased for 20 years to DR. JOHN SWINT part of a lot in Charleston, bounding N 73-1/2 ft. on Beresford Street; S on CHRISTOPHER EASTON; E 84 ft.
on land leased to JOHN CALVERT, & on RICHARD BERESFORD; W on RICHARD
BERESFORD; at Ł 45 currency per annum; SWINT to pay taxes due & to build
a wooden house 20 x 15 ft. & fence in the property; & whereas RICHARD
BERESFORD on 2 Aug. 1761 leased to FREDERICK HOFF, for 20 years, at Ł 15
per annum, part of a lot bounding N 24-1/2 ft. on Beresford Street; E 84
ft. on land leased to DR. JOHN SWINT; W on RICHARD BERESFORD; S on estate
of CHRISTOPHER EASTON; HOFF to pay the taxes & build a wooden house 20 X
14 ft. & fence in the property; which lease HOFF assigned to SWINT on 20
Nov. 1761; & whereas RICHARD BERESFORD, by his attorney, JOHN LOGAN, on
1 May 1764 leased to said JOHN SWINT for 17 years, part of a lot bounding
S 49 ft. on Beresford Street; E on Free Quacos lot; W on FREDERICK HAUFF-
MAN; at Ł 30 currency per annum; SWINT to pay the taxes & build 2 dwelling houses 14 X 20 ft. each, & fence in the premises; & whereas SWINT is
greatly indebted to BREWTON & SMITH; now as security, SWINT conveys the
3 lots & leases to them. Witnesses: WILLIAM EDWARDS, JOHN JONES. Before
FENWICKE BULL, J.P. & P. Register. BREWTON & SMITH acknowledged satisfaction received.

Book G-3, p. 773   HENRIETTA RAVEN & GEORGE BEDON, executors of
18 Oct. 1766   WILLIAM RAVEN; to ISAAC LESESNE. See F-3, p.
Lease   329.

Gook G-3, p. 779   JANE (her mark) PELOT, widow of JONAS PELOT,
30 Sept. (?) 1767   (last, but before of ELIAS BOURNANT), to
Release   ADRIAN MAYER, ESQ., of Purysburgh, Granville
                          Co., for Ł 100 currency, 100 a. granted to
ELIAS BOURNANT (corruptly called & designed by the name of _____ by the
late Scotch surveyor of Purysburgh HUGH ROSE) in Purysburgh Township;
bounding S on the reserved lands of Purysburgh; W on CASPER MAYER; S on
land laid out to ABRAM LATHOY but not granted; E on vacant land. Witnesses: DANIEL MARETTE, ABRAM JACOT. Before JOHN LEWIS BOURQUIN, J.P., 30
Sept. 1767. Recorded 22 Oct. 1767 by FENWICKE BULL, J.P. & P. Register.

Book G-3, p. 781   GEORGE (his mark) MENGERSDORFF & LEONARD (his
6 Nov. 1760   mark) RHEINAUER, to ANDREW PENCE; all of Purys-
Release   burgh; for Ł 8 currency, lot #92 in Purys-
                          burgh. Witnesses: ADRIAN MAYER, JOHN LAST-
INGER, JOHN RODOLPH BUNINGER. Before JOHN LEWIS BOURQUIN, J.P. on 30
Sept. 1767. Recorded 22 Oct. 1767 by FENWICKE BULL, Register.

Book G-3, p. 783   GEORGE II, by Gov. GABRIEL JOHNSTON, at Bath;
3 Apr. 1752   by JOHN RICE, Dep. Sec.; to THOMAS MCHONNEY,
Grant   300 a. in Anson Co., NC, on N side Cataba Riv-
                          er, on the Cataba branch, including a cabin in
an old field, beginning at a white oak on said branch, & runs S 35 chains
140 poles to a red oak, then S 58 W 320 poles to a stake, then S 35 W
160 poles to a white oak on the Cataba branch, then up to the W side of
Cataba branch to beginning. Entered in Auditor's book on 6 Apr. 1752 by
ALEXANDER MCCULLOCH, Dep. Aud. Recorded 23 Oct. 1767 by FENWICKE BULL,
Register. Plat by FRANCIS MACKELWEAN, Dep. Sur.

Book G-3, p. 785   JOHN LESTER, schoolmaster, & ANN (her mark)

5 Oct. 1765   his wife, to NATHANIEL HAWTHORN, both of
Release   Purysburgh, for Ł 100 currency, lot #92 in
                     Purysburgh. Witnesses: JOHN BUCHE, GOERGE
KEALL. Before JOHN LEWIS BOURQUIN, J.P., 30 Sept. 1767 by FENWICKE BULL,
Register.

Book G-3, p. 786   NATHANIEL HAWTHORN, carpenter, of St. Helena
29 Dec. 1766   Parish, Granville Co., to JOHN BUCHE, inn-keep-
Release   er, of Purysburgh, St. Peters Parish, Gran-
                     ville Co., for Ł 100 currency, lot #92, con-
taining 1 a., in Purysburgh, bounding N & W on streets; E & S on other
lots. Witnesses: HENRY MEURON, GEORGE KEALL. Before JOHN LEWIS BOURQUIN,
J.P., on 30 Sept. 1767. Recorded 24 Oct. 1767 by FENWICKE BULL, Register.

Book G-3, p. 789   GEORGE II, by MATTHEW ROWAN, president of NC;
23 Feb. 1754   by JAMES MURRAY, secretary; to WILLIAM JONES
Grant   "forever as of our manor of E Greenwich in our
                     Co. of Kent in free & common soccage"; 500 a.
in Anson Co., NC, beginning at a white oak on N side of S branch of Fish-
ing Creek, a little below SAMUEL MOORE'S corner, thence S 250 poles to a
white oak; thence # 320 poles to a black oak; thence by direct line to
first station. Entered in Auditor's office on 23 Feb. 1754 by RICHARD
LYON, pro. Aud. Recorded 26 Oct. 1767 by FENWICKE BULL, Register. Plat
by ALEXANDER LEWIS, D.S., dated 15 Dec. 1752.

Book G-3, p. 790   MICHAEL CRAWFORD, planter, to THOMAS CRAWFORD,
22 Sept. 1767   gentleman, both of Craven Co., for Ł 1000 cur-
Release   rency, the plantation on which he lives, on NE
                     side of Peedee River; beginning at a Spanish
oak runs N 45° E 62 chains to a stake corner, then S 45° E 38 chains to a
stake corner, then S 45° W 109 chains & 50 links to Peedee River; then up
bank of river to first station; being 300 a. known as Charraw Bluff;
granted DAVID ROACH 29 Jan. 1742 by Lt. Gov. WILLIAM BULL; & conveyed by
L & R dated 10 & 11 July 1749 by ROACH to JOHN CRAWFORD, SR.; who bequeathed to MICHAEL CRAWFORD. Witnesses: ARTHUR HART, THOMAS WILLIAMS.
Before THOMAS WADE, J.P. Recorded 26 Oct. 1767 by FENWICKE BULL, Register.

Book G-3, p. 793   NICOLAS (German script) FEDEROLPH, & ANNA
2 & 3 June 1766   CATHRINA (her mark) his wife, to JOHN BEAR,
L & R   planter, both of Berkeley Co., for Ł 400 cur-
                     rency, 200 a., part of 300 a. granted 13 Aug.
1756 by Gov. WILLIAM HENRY LYTTELTON to said NICOLAS FEDEROLPH; the 300
a. being in Berkeley Co., on Santee River, between Saxegotha & Amelia
Townships; the 200 a. bounding NE on other part of 300 a.; SE on GEORGE
STAINWINTER; SW on ANDREW BERGINER & CONRAD JUMPARD; NW on Santee River.
Witnesses: GEORGE (his mark) PRICE, CHRISTIN (his mark) KYSER. Before
FENWICKE BULL, J.P. & P. Register. Entered by CATHANNA BEAR in Auditor's
office in Book H-8, p. 267 on 28 Aug. 1767; RICHARD LAMBTON, Dep. Aud.

                    DEEDS BOOK "H-3"
             SEPTEMBER 1767 - MAY 1768

Book H-3, p. 1   JAMES PRIMUS, son of JOHN PRIMUS, of Parish of
21 July 1767   St. Thomas, & MARY (her mark) PRIMUS, to WIL-
L & R   LIAM PARKER, merchant, of Charlston, for Ł 150
                     currency, his undivided half part of 100 a. on
SE side of Cooper River, in said Parish, being the N part of 400 a. granted 14 Apr. 1710 to SAMUEL BLUNDELL; bounding W & S on other part of 400
a.; N & W on WILLIAM PARKER; NE on THOMAS PADGET; which 100 a. now belong
to HUMPHREY PRIMUS, carpenter, of Ga., & said JAMES PRIMUS. Witnesses:
JAMES SMITH, GEORGE THREADCRAFT. Before FENWICKE BULL, J.P. & P. Register. Recorded 1 Sept. 1767.

Book H-3, p. 8   JOHN BURGESS, to ADAM MCELVENE, both of Craven
18 & 19 Oct. 1761   Co., for Ł 400 currency, 450 a., being the
L & R   upper part of a tract purchased from THOMAS
                     LYNCH. Witnesses: LAURENCE CASEY, ROBERT

                         360

LOWRY, ROBERT GARRET. Before JOHN LIVISTON, J.P. on 25 Feb. 1762. Recorded 2 Sept. 1767.

Book H-3, p. 13   THOMAS JONES, merchant, to GEORGE SEAMAN, gen-
29 & 30 Dec. 1766   tleman, both of Charleston, for Ł 6000 curren-
L & R   cy, 393 a. on NE side Combahee River, in Col-
                               leton Co.; 183 a. of which are part of 700 a.
granted 1 June 1709 to WILLIAM FULLER; the 210 a. being part of 1200 a.
granted on 3 Mar. 1731 to FRANCIS YONGE; the 393 a. bounding SW on part
of 700 a. belonging to HANNAH RIPPON, widow; NW on ISAAC GODIN; NE on
GEORGE SEAMAN; SE on JOHN DEAS; also 665 a. on NE side Combahee River, in
Colleton Co., part of said tracts of 700 & 1200 a.; bounding N & E on
said river; NW on Batt's Creek & ISAAC GODIN; NE on HANNAH RIPPON; SE on
JOHN DEAS; S on Combahee Old Cawsey. Witnesses: EDWARDS PIERCE, GEORGE
YOUNG. Before JACOB MOTTE, J.P., 10 Aug. 1767. Recorded 4 Sept. 1767 by
FENWICKE BULL, Register. Two plats certified 12 Sept. 1765 by NATHANIEL
DEAN, Dep. Sur. JONES gives bond of performance.

Book H-3, p. 22   WILLIAM ANCRUM, AARON LOOCOCK, & JOSEPH KER-
26 & 27 May 1767   SHAW, merchants, to JOHN CHESNUT & ELY KER-
L & R   SHAW, merchants, according to an agreement, 2
                               undivided fifth parts of 17 tracts of land,
total 2498 a. Whereas WILLIAM ANCRUM, AARON LOOCOCK, JOSEPH KERSHAW &
LAMBERT LANCE owned various tracts of land as tenants in common; & whereas LANCE & ANNA MAGDALENA his wife, by L & R dated 22 & 23 Aug. 1766 conveyed his fourth part of 25 tracts (5898 a.) to ANCRUM & LOOCOCK (Book
F-3, p. 748-753); so that ANCRUM & LOOCOCK owned 6 parts & JOSEPH KERSHAW
4 parts (the whole being divided into 16 shares) as tenants in common; &
whereas ANCRUM, LOOCOCK & JOSEPH KERSHAW have agreed to sell JOHN CHESNUT
& ELY KERSHAW 2 fifth parts of 17 tracts (part of the 25); now for Ł 3500
paid ANCRUM, Ł 3500 paid LOOCOCK, & Ł 1000 paid to KERSHAW, they convey
to CHESNUT & KERSHAW 2/5 of the following: 350 a. on Pine Tree Creek
purchased from WILLIAM SERUG & JAMES MCGIRTH; granted originally on 3
Apr. 1754 to WILLIAM GRAY; 131 a. in Fredericksburgh Township, part of
400 a. granted JOHN BLACK on 4 Oct. 1749; 50 a. at Pine Tree Mill, granted ROBERT MILLHOUSE on 14 Mar. 1757; 497 a. in Fredericksburgh Township,
part of 650 a. granted SAMUEL WYLY on 2 Apr. 1761; 150 a. on Pine Tree
Hill, granted WILLIAM ANCRUM on 19 Sept. 1758; 20 a., part of 300 a.
called Joyners Ferry, at the Congarees, granted JOSEPH JOYNER on 9 Jan.
1752; 150 a. on S side Wateree River, opposite the Rafts, granted THOMAS
SMITH on 1 Feb. 1758; 100 a. on W side Wateree River, granted JOSEPH KER-
SHAW on 31 Mar. 1761; 100 a. on the fork of Pine Tree Creek, granted JO-
SEPH KERSHAW on 5 Dec. 1761; 150 a. in Fredericksburgh Township, granted
LAMBERT LANCE on 4 June 1759; 100 a. on Little Pine Tree, granted LAMBERT
LANCE on 5 Dec. 1761; 150 a. on Pine Tree Creek, granted LAMBERT LANCE on
9 Nov. 1762; 150 a. in Fredericksburgh Township, granted LAMBERT LANCE on
7 Oct. 1762; 100 a. on Twenty-five Mile Creek, granted LAMBERT LANCE on
31 Mar. 1761; 50 a. on Twenty-five Mile Creek, granted LAMBERT LANCE on 7
Oct. 1762; 100 a. on Twenty-five Mile Creek, granted HENRY DONGWORTH on
10 Nov. 1761, who conveyed to JOSEPH KERSHAW; 150 a. in Fredericksburgh
Township granted AARON LOOCOCK on 4 June 1759. Witnesses: RICHARD MUN-
CREIFF, GEORGE ANCRUM. Before FENWICKE BULL, J.P. & P. Register.

Book H-3, p. 31   LEWIS BONA, brick-layer, only son of JACOB
25 & 26 Mar. 1767   BONA, who died intestate; to ABRAHAM SHECOT,
L & R   bricklayer, both of St. Helena Parish, Granv-
                               ille Co., for Ł 170 currency, lot #204 in
Beaufort, granted by Gov. JAMES GLEN on 14 May 1749 to JACOB BONA; then
bounding N on a passageway to lot #207; E on lot #207, not then granted,
& on lot #209 granted JOHN SMITH; S on King Street; W on Charles Street.
Witnesses: ANDREW AGGNEW, JOHN JOYNER, JR. Before FENWICKE BULL, J.P. &
P. Register. Recorded 11 Sept. 1767.

Book H-3, p. 38   JAMES WRIGHT, ESQ., of Charleston, having
18 Sept. 1753   recently purchased 1042 a. on Santee Creek,
Acknowledgement   from TACITUS GAILLARD & ANN his wife, on which
                               land is the family burying place of ISAAC LE-
GRAND DORMERVILLE, father of said ANN GAILLARD, agrees that said burial
ground of 1/4 a. shall be reserved as such for ANN & her heirs. Witnesses: JOHN MENZIES, DANIEL DWIGHT. Before WILLIAM MASON, J.P., 10 Apr.

Apr. 1767. Recorded 11 Sept. 1767 by FENWICKE BULL, Register.

Book H-3, p. 39   BENJAMIN WEBB, planter, of Ashepoo, Colleton
27 & 28 Aug. 1767   Co., & REBECCA his wife, to THOMAS PIKE, gen-
L & R   tleman, of Charleston, for Ł 6600 currency,
the N half of lot #40 in St. Michaels Parish,
Charleston, bounding E 50 ft. 8 in. on Church Street; S 244 ft. 6 in. on
other half of said lot #40 formerly belonging to ISAAC GODIN, who sold to
some persons in trust for the Free Masons; W on heirs of DAVID HEXT; N on
FRANCIS ROCHE; which N half formerly belonged to DAVID GODIN, who bequeathed to BENJAMIN WEBB, who after reaching 21 years of age received
the rents from JAMES LENOX, the tenant. Witnesses: RUTH PINCKNEY, THOMAS
PINCKNEY. Before CHARLES PINCKNEY, J.P. Recorded 29 Sept. 1767 by FEN-
WICKE BULL, Register.

Book H-3, p. 46   DAVID MALLET, planter, to FRANCIS GABRIEL RA-
30 May 1767   VOT, tanner, both of St. Peters Parish, Gran-
Release   ville Co., for Ł 200 currency, 2 tracts in
Purysburgh Township; 100 a. formerly belonging
to JOSEPH LAYE, bounding on all sides on vacant land; 50 a., formerly belonging to ANTHONY JATON, bounding W on JOSEPH LAYE; other sides on vacant land. Witnesses: JOHN BUCHE, MATHIAS AVENSON. Before JOHN LEWIS
BOURQUIN, J.P. Recorded 3 Oct. 1767 by FENWICKE BULL, Register.

Book H-3, p. 48   ANTHONY GILLMORE, to ROBERT HARRISON, mariner,
27 Aug. 1767   both of Charleston, for Ł 40 currency, 150 a.
L & R   in St. Marks Parish, Craven Co., bounding SE
on LEWIS BUCKINGHAM & vacant land; SW on San-
tee River; other sides on vacant land; also 50 a. in Craven Co., on NE
side Wateree River, bounding SE on BENJAMIN DUKES; other sides on vacant
land. Witnesses: M. LUCULLUS RYALL, JOHN NEVIN. Before FENWICKE BULL,
J.P. & P. Register.

Book H-3, p. 54   CONRAD (his mark) SHIROR (SHIREA), planter, to
27 & 28 Feb. 1767   CASPER PHILIP BYERLEY, planter, both of Craven
L & R   Co., for Ł 100 currency, 100 a., the SW part
of 250 a. in the fork between Broad & Saludy
Rivers, granted 27 Aug. 1751 by Gov. JAMES GLEN to CONRAD SHIROR; bounding on all sides on vacant land (see Secretary's Book N.N., fol. 130);
the 100 a. bounding NE part of original tract; NW on JACOB FRY; SW on
KETSINGER & on MARTIN KINER; SE on KINER & on CASPER PHILIP BYERLEY.
Witnesses: JOHANNES VOLMER, JOHN REINHART. Before THOMAS BOND, J.P., 7
Mar. 1767. Recorded 9 Oct. 1767 by FENWICKE BULL, Register. Plat certified 31 Jan. 1767 by PHILIP PEARSON, Dep. Sur.

Book H-3, p. 59   HENRY REEVES, mariner, formerly of Charleston,
30 & 31 May 1766   SC, now of Bur Street, Co. of Middlesex (Great
L & R by Mortgage   Britain), to SAMUEL ROBINSON, merchant, of
Houndsditch, London, for value of Ł 7200 re-
ceived; 3 tenements on Queen & Elliott Streets, in St. Philips Parish,
Charleston, now occupied by HENRY REEVES'S undertenants; also 600 a.
called Pondepond, in Parish of Pond de Pond, occupied by REEVES'S undertenants; 600 a. called the Ac, in St. Philips Parish; also the Negroes &
other slaves; the horses, mules, cattle, stock, implements & utensils;
with various provisoes. Witnesses: JOHN RAINCOCK, gentleman, of Bear-
binder Lane, London; WILLIAM BOLTON of same place. Sworn at Mansion
House 20 June 1766 before GEORGE NELSON, mayor of London. Signed HODGES.
Recorded 14 Oct. 1767 by FENWICKE BULL, Register.

Book H-3, p. 68   SIR JOHN COLLETON, baronet, & LADY ANN COLLE-
14 & 15 Sept. 1767   TON, his wife, of Fairlawn, Berkeley Co., to
L & R   SEDGWICK LEWIS, planter, of St. James Parish,
for Ł 7000 currency, 1000 a. in St. Johns Par-
ish, Berkeley Co., bounding W on the Broad Road leading from Moncks Corner to Charleston; S on MRS. MARY BROUGHTON; E on Cooper River; N on SIR
JOHN COLLETON. Witnesses: JOHN DAWSON, ALEXANDER MOULTRIE. Before FEN-
WICKE BULL, J.P. & P. Register. Plat of resurvey of 1000 a., 174 of
which is River Swamp, known as Little Landing (?), certified 1 Sept. 1767
by JOHN HAIG, D.S.

Book H-3, p. 74   FRANCIS KINLOCH, ESQ., to WILLIAM MOULTRIE,
7 & 8 Feb. 1765   ESQ., both of Charleston, for L 5 currency,
L & R   53 a. in Prince George Parish, Winyaw. Wit-
                        nesses: GAVIN COCHRANE, JAMES MCALPINE. Be-
fore THOMAS LYNCH, J.P., 22 Sept. 1767. Recorded 20 Oct. 1767 by FEN-
WICKE BULL, Register. Plat given.

Book H-3, p. 78   EDWARD DAVIES, merchant, of Charleston, & MAR-
28 & 29 Sept. 1767   GARET his wife, to THOMAS ELFE, cabinet maker,
L & R   of same place, for L 3600 currency, a lot
                        lately occupied by JAMES FELLOWS, barber;
bounding E 21 ft. 4 in. on Union Street; W on DR. LIONEL CHALMERS; S on
EDWARD DEMPSEY; N 92 ft. on EDWARD & MARGARET DAVIES; which lot formerly
belonged to JOHN WATSON, mariner; also part of lot #88 formerly belonging
to said JOHN WATSON, adjoining first lot; bounding E 30 ft. 2 in. on
Union Street; N 92 ft. on MOSES MITCHELL (formerly occupied by BARNARD
BEEKMAN); S of first lot; W on DR. LIONEL CHALMERS. Witnesses: JOHN WAG-
NER, JOHN DODD. Before FENWICKE BULL, J.P. & P. Register. Recorded 21
Oct. 1767.

Book H-3, p. 85   ROBERT COCHRAN, planter, owner of the brigan-
1 Oct. 1767   tine the Prince George, 97-1/2 tons, commanded
Sale   by DAVID WATSON; to JAMES DRUMMOND, of
                        Charleston, for L 225 sterling British, 1/2
said brigantine, complete according to accustomed method of ship building
in SC. Witness: JOHN POOLEY. Before FENWICKE BULL, J.P. & P. Register.

Book H-3, p. 86   Between JAMES DRUMMOND, merchant, & ROBERT
1 Oct. 1767   COCHRAN, planter, both of Charleston; each of
Agreement   whom now owns 1/2 the brigantine Prince George
                        (p. 85). Upon arrival of the Prince George in
London, if MESSRS. ROBINSON & SMITH approve the purchase of COCHRAN'S
half of the boat they are to pay L 250 sterling. If sold COCHRAN will be
entitled to 1/2 the purchase money (no matter what price). If the boat
sells for less than amount DRUMMOND paid, with half her freight included,
COCHRAN to make up the deficiency. If sold for more than L 450 sterling
it will be COCHRAN'S. Witness: JOHN POOLEY. Before FENWICKE BULL, J.P.
& P. Register.

Book H-3, p. 87   GEORGE (his mark) DUCKER (TOOKER), butcher, of
30 Sept. 1767   Christ Church Parish, Ga., to ADRIAN MAYER, of
Release   St. Peters Parish, Granville Co., for L 70
                        currency, 100 a. in Purysburgh Township,
bounding SW on PATRICK GRIFFIN; NW & NE on ADRIAN MAYER; SE on vacant
land. Witnesses: GEORGE KEALL, MELCHOR LEICHTENSTEIGER. Before JOHN
LEWIS BOURQUIN, J.P. Recorded 22 Oct. 1767 by FENWICKE BULL, Register.

Book H-3, p. 89   ANDREW (German script) PENCE, blacksmith, &
6 Nov. 1760   ANNE MARY (his wife), to JOHN LESTER, school-
Release   master, both of Purysburgh for L 100 currency,
                        lot #92 in Purysburgh. Witnesses: ADRIAN MAY-
OR, J.P.; DAVID SAUSSY. Before JOHN LEWIS BOURQUIN, J.P., 30 Sept. 1767.
Recorded 22 Oct. 1767 by FENWICKE BULL, Register.

Book H-3, p. 90   Between WILLIAM ELLIS, gentleman, & CHRISTO-
23 Oct. 1767   PHER GADSDEN, ESQ., both of Ansonburgh. Where-
Agreement   as GADSDEN owns certain lands in Ansonburgh
                        bounding W on ELLIS & is entitled to a street
30 ft. wide from that part of the wall enclosing GADSDEN'S land on the W
side in which is a gate through ELLIS'S land leading to George Street in
Ansonburgh which passage way is plainly shown in plat annexed to release
from GEORGE, Lord ANSON, by his attorney, RICHARD LAMBTON, to JOHN RAT-
TRAY (recorded in Register's Book R.R., 520-532) & is also shown in plat
hereto annexed; but the foundation of GADSDEN'S right was only lately
discovered; & whereas it would be injurious to ELLIS if GADSDEN should
insist on his legal right to the street because ELLIS'S dwelling house
was built on said land; so GADSDEN proposed to accept, instead, 2 streets
or passages from his land through ELLIS'S land into Anson & Scarborough
Streets; 1 30 ft. wide from the W side of the wall on GADSDEN'S land on S
side of ELLIS'S land adjoining HENRY LAURENS into Anson Street; the other

on N side of ELLIS'S land into Scarborough Street, from the wall on GADS-
DEN'S land, to contain 30 ft. in width high land clear of marsh; to which
ELLIS agrees; said street to remain open forever. Witnesses: WILLIAM
ROPER, JR., JOHN DART, JR. Before WILLIAM BURROWS, J.P. Recorded 24
Oct. 1767 by FENWICKE BULL, Register. Plat given.

Book H-3, p. 94   SAMUEL PELTON, planter, of Wadmalaw Island,
10 Aug. 1767   Colleton Co., & SUSANNA his wife, (lately
Assignment   SUSANNAH STANYARNE), who before their marriage
                       gave a certain mortgage dated 24 July 1765 to
JOHN GIBBONS, planter, then of Ga., to secure a payment of Ł 800 SC money,
which payment has not been made; surrender to GIBBONS the 260 a. mentioned in said mortgage. Witnesses: WILLIAM LOWREY, WILLIAM BURNS, CATHRINE
(her mark) PELTON. Before HUGH WILSON, J.P. Recorded 12 Aug. 1767 by
FENWICKE BULL, Register.

Book H-3, p. 96   JAMES JOHNSTON, & MARY (her mark) his wife, of
2 May 1767   St. Marks Parish, Craven Co., to JAMES MC-
Release   ELKENE & WILLIAM MCELKENE, for Ł 200 currency,
                       500 a. on Fishing Creek, which by L & R dated
21 & 22 June 1754   JOHNSTON purchased from WILLIAM JONES; beginning at a white oak on N side of S branch of said creek, a little below
SAMUEL MOOR'S corner; then S 250 poles to a white oak; then E 320 poles
to a black oak; then N 250 poles to a white oak; then direct to first
station; as by plat of original grant enrolled in Auditor General's
Office in NC. Witnesses: THOMAS MCELKENE, JANE (her mark) MCELKENE,
CATHERINE (her mark) MCADOOE. Before JAMES SIMPSON, J.P., 4 May 1767.
Recorded 26 Oct. 1767 by FENWICKE BULL, Register.

Book H-3, p. 99   ANDREW CUNNINGHAM, merchant, of Charleston, &
6 & 7 Oct. 1767   MARGARET his wife, (lately MARGARET COCHRAN,
L & R   widow, of St. Bartholomews Parish), to MOSES
                       DARQUIER, merchant, of St. Bartholomews Par-
ish. Whereas by marriage agreement dated 27 Dec. 1766, among MARGARET,
of 1st part; ANDREW, of 2nd part; & DARQUIER of 3rd part; MARGARET then
1500 a., 33 Negro slaves, Ł 2000 currency; & other effects; it was agreed
that ANDREW should have no right to any part of 1 full half part of the
income or profits from said land, Negroes, monies, or effects listed in
the schedule; said half to continue MARGARETS; & to make the agreement
effectual ANDREW promised DARQUIER said half should be reckoned separately from ANDREW'S estate & all necessary business transacted in DAR-
QUIER'S name in trust for her; but whereas, previous to said marriage, it
was intended that half of said real & personal estate should be vested in
ANDREW; now in order to avoid misunderstanding the estate is to be divided between ANDREW & MARGARET; they convey to DARQUIER 1688 a. (not 1500
as above), the Negroes, & all said estate, DARQUIER within 10 days to
convey to ANDREW the E half of the land (844 a.) & the slaves (half)
listed in Schedule A. No. 1; DARQUIER to retain the remainder (844 a.) of
the land & the slaves (half) named in Schedule B. No. 2, & of the monies,
in trust for MARGARET. Witnesses: JAMES REID, JAMES SHARP, JAMES CARSON.
Before FENWICKE BULL, J.P. & P. Register. Plat of several tracts in St.
Bartholomews Parish, total 1688 a, formerly belonging to DR. JOHN COCHRAN,
then to MARGARET, his widow, now MARGARET CUNNINGHAM; bounding N on THOM-
AS ELLIOTT; E on JOHN ANDREW; S on GEORGE MITCHELL, JR.; W on JOHN JACK-
SON; MICHAEL STEVEN & Horse Shoe Creek; by ARCHIBALD CRAWFORD, Dep. Sur.,
the plat showing 85 a. patented 14 Mar. 1757 by JOHN LAIRD; 232 a. patented 4 June 1735 by THOMAS SACHEVEREL, part said to be covered by THOMAS
ELLIOTT; 156 a. granted JOHN BAYLEY; 500 a. granted 15 Sept. 1705 to
GEORGE MITCHELL; 100 (?) a. granted 1 June 1709 to (broken out); 2 pieces
surplus land; 156 a. granted 7 May 1702 to JAMES MITCHELL; 540 (?) patented 7 Aug. 1735 by GEORGE MITCHELL, SR. Schedules A-1 & B-2 given;
drawn 29 Sept. 1767 before JAMES SHARP.

Book H-3, p. 109   MOSES DARQUIER delivers to ANDREW CUNNINGHAM
9 & 10 Oct. 1767   (p. 99) his share of MARGARET'S estate; being
L & R   844 a. & 17 slaves, valued at Ł 3930 a. in
                       Schedule A. No. 1. Witnesses: JAMES REID,
JAMES SHARP, JAMES CARSON. Before FENWICKE BULL, J.P. & P. Register.

Book H-3, p. 114   ANDREW CUNNINGHAM, merchant, of 1st part;

10 Oct. 1767   MARGARET CUNNINGHAM (lately MARGARET COCHRAN),
Mortgage   wife of ANDREW, of 2nd part; & BENJAMIN SMITH,
                      ESQ., of 3rd part; all of Charleston. Whereas
on this date JAMES CREIGHTON, merchant, of Charleston, & ANDREW CUNNING-
HAM as his security, jointly gave bond to SMITH for Ⱡ 1200 currency on
this condition: that whereas SMITH, at request of CREIGHTON & CUNNINGHAM,
has given CREIGHTON a letter of credit on his agent, JOHN NUTT, merchant,
in London, directing NUTT to pay CREIGHTON Ⱡ 600 British, to be repaid in
Great Britain to SMITH upon request; CREIGHTON & CUNNINGHAM to pay SMITH
with 12 months Ⱡ 600 British with 8% interest; & whereas ANDREW & MARGA-
RET as further security agree to mortgage certain lands (1688 a.) &
slaves (each owning 1 half) (see pages 99 & 109). Witnesses: ALEXANDER
HEWAT, JOHN SIMPSON. Before FENWICKE BULL, J.P. & P. Register.

Book H-3, p. 119   JOSHUA LOCKWOOD, watch maker, of Charleston,
3 May 1764   (eldest son & heir of JOSHUA LOCKWOOD, trader,
Release   of Orangeburgh Township), & MARY his wife, to
                     MELCHOR SMITH, planter, of Orangeburgh Town-
ship, for Ⱡ 100 SC money, 200 a. in said Township, Berkeley Co., granted
9 Apr. 1736, & then bounding SE on PETER FAUCE & JOSHUA LOCKWOOD, SR.;
other sides on vacant land. Witnesses: ARTHUR DOWNES, WILLIAM LEE, FELIX
LONG. Grant recorded in Secretary's Book F.F. fol. 23 on 24 Apr. 1736.
Entered in Auditor's Book H-8, p. 137, on 22 Jan. 1767 by RICHARD LAMB-
TON, Dep. Aud. Before FENWICKE BULL, J.P. & P. Register.

Book H-3, p. 123   JOHN PARKER, ESQ., & MARY his wife, to JOHN
15 & 16 Apr. 1767   LAMBERT, a free Negro, for Ⱡ 1700 currency,
L & R   part of several adjoining lots sold to PARKER
                     by HENRY PERONNEAU by L & R dated 25 & 26 Jan.
1765; bounding W 35 ft. on Church Street; N 150 ft. on Hunter Street; S &
E on JOHN PARKER. Witnesses: BARNARD ELLIOTT, WILLIAM WARD CROSTHWAITE,
JOHN FRASER. Before FENWICKE BULL, J.P. & P. Register, 14 Oct. 1767.
Recorded 7 Nov. 1767.

Book H-3, p. 128   ISAAC PERRY, to HUGH MIDDLETON, planter, both
21 & 22 Nov. 1764   of Granville Co., for Ⱡ 70 currency, 96 a. in
L & R   Granville Co., bounding NW on WALTER VAUGH; NE
                     on vacant land; SE on JOSEPH NELSON; SW on
Savannah River; granted 20 June 1764. Witnesses: CLEMENTIUS DAVIS,
ZACHARIAH LAMAR. Before JACOB SUMMERALL, J.P., on 2 Oct. 1766. Recorded
9 Nov. 1767 by FENWICKE BULL, Register.

Book H-3, p. 133   GEORGE INGLIS, merchant, of Charleston, &
5 & 6 Nov. 1766   CLAUDIA his wife, to EMANUEL GEIGELMAN, plant-
L & R   er, of St. Bartholomews Parish, Colleton Co.,
                     for Ⱡ 1800 currency, 400 a. in said Parish,
bounding W on DR. JAMES SKIRVING; S on JAMES POSTELL; NE on CAPT. WILLIAM
SMITH; NW on WILLIAM OSWALD; formerly belonging to ROBERT OSWALD; & conveyed by virtue of an execution on 31 Mar. 1764 by DANIEL DOYLEY, P.M.,
to GEORGE INGLIS. Witnesses: JOSEPH YOUNG, THOMAS INGLIS. Before FEN-
WICKE BULL, J.P. & P. Register. INGLIS gives bond of performance.

Book H-3, p. 142   WILLIAM WITHERS, planter, of St. James Parish,
21 & 22 May 1767   Goose Creek, to the Rev. MR. JAMES HARRISON,
L & R by Mortgage   attorney for the Society for Propagating the
                     Gospel in Foreign Parts, for Ⱡ 3821:7:10 cur-
rency, 650 a. in Berkeley Co., bounding N on Forsters Creek, NATHANIEL
SNOW, & PETER LAMB; E on CAPT. GILL; S on JOB HOW; W on NATHANIEL SNOW,
SR., & JOHN EMPEROR; also 408 a. on Goose Creek Neck, Berkeley Co.,
bounding S & E on NATHANIEL SNOW; N on Forsters Creek; W on PETER LAMB;
which tract was granted NATHANIEL SNOW; also 500 a. in said Parish & Co.,
bounding NW on NATHANIEL SNOW; SW on JAMES WITHERS; SE on THOMAS SMITH &
MCWALTERS; NE on marsh of Cooper River; granted NATHANIEL SNOW; the 3
gracts making 1 plantation of 1558 a.; also 2 other tracts, 200 & 500 a.,
total 700 a., on Goose Creek; the 200 a. bounding N on Red Bank; E on
Cooper River; S on CAPT. SCHINCKING; W on the 500 a.; the 500 a. bounding
SW on Goose Creek; SE on Cooper River; NE on the 200 a. & CAPT. SCHINCK-
ING; NW on ROBERT HOW. Witnesses: WILLIAM ROPER, JR., JOHN DART, JR.
Before WILLIAM BURROWS, J.P. Recorded 14 Nov. 1767 by FENWICKE BULL,
Register.

Book H-3, p. 152   JAMES BARR, & SARAH his wife, of Mecklinburg
12 & 13 Aug. 1765   Co., NC, to JOHN MCCALPIN, of Granville Co.,
L & R   SC, for Ł 40 SC money, 100 a. on NW part of
                          Long Cane Creek, a branch of Savannah River;
bounding NE on JOHN MCCALPIN; other sides on vacant land; granted JAMES
BARR 17 Mar. 1760. Witnesses: WILLIAM DRENNAN, JAMES HOLLAND. Before
NATHANIEL ALEXANDER, J.P. Proved by DRENNON 24 Oct. 1767 before FENWICKE
BULL, J.P. & P. Register.

Book H-3, p. 157   SAMUEL (his mark) JONES, planter, of Sanput,
3 Aug. 1765   in St. George Parish, to THOMAS BALLOW, of
Feoffment   Craven Co., for Ł 300 SC money, 768 a. at head
                          of Sanput Creek, at Winyaw, Craven Co., bound-
ing N on MR. HODDY; E on CAPT. BONNIS; W on JOSIAH SMITH & HODDY; S on
NATHANIEL FORDE. Witnesses: HANNAH SINGLETARY, ALEXANDER ANDERSON. Before PAUL TRAPIER, J.P., 3 Oct. 1767. Recorded 17 Nov. 1767 by FENWICKE
BULL, Register.

Book H-3, p. 160   ROGER PINCKNEY, P.M., to JOHN MARTIN, of
11 June 1766   Charleston, for Ł 650 currency, 174 a. in St.
Conveyance   Pauls Parish, Colleton Co., bounding N on
                          THOMAS MELLICHAMP; S on JOSEPH BLAKE; E on
THOMAS FARR; W on JOHN HINDS. Whereas ARNOLD HARVEY, planter, of Stono,
Granville Co., owned said 174 a., which on 18 Mar. 1763 (with turf & twig
delivered) he had purchased from THOMAS FARR; & whereas HARVEY on 7 July
1763 became indebted (with 1 WILLIAM HARVEY) to THOMAS CORKER, merchant,
of Charleston, for Ł 2770:18:4; & whereas CORKER recovered a judgment
against SOPHIA HARVEY, executrix of ARNOLD'S will, for the debt & costs &
a writ of fieri facias was issued, commanding the P.M. to seize the estate of ARNOLD HARVEY & satisfy the judgment; now the P.M. sells the land
at auction to MARTIN. Witnesses: HOPSON PINCKNEY, EDWARD RUTLEDGE. Before FENWICKE BULL, on 9 Nov. 1767. Recorded 19 Nov. 1767.

Book H-3, p. 164   JOHN MARTIN, to ROGER PINCKNEY, ESQ., both of
15 & 17 June 1766   Charleston, for Ł 650 currency, 174 a. in St.
L & R   Pauls Parish, Colleton Co., (see p. 160) form-
                          erly belonging to ARNOLD HARVEY; bounding N on
THOMAS MELLICHAMP; S on JOSEPH BLAKE; E on THOMAS FARR; W on JOHN HINDS.
Witnesses: HOPSON PINCKNEY, EDWARD RUTLEDGE. Before FENWICKE BULL, J.P.
& P. Register. Recorded 20 Nov. 1767.

Book H-3, p. 169   ZACHARY ISBELL, of Craven Co., & ELIZABETH
31 Dec. 1766   (her mark) his wife, to AMOS TIMMS, for Ł 500
L & R   currency, 100 a. on Rockay Run, in Craven Co.,
                          bounding on all sides on vacant land; granted
10 Sept. 1765 by Gov. WILLIAM BULL to ISBELL. Witnesses: JOSEPH TIMMS,
WALTER TIMMS. Before THOMAS FLETCHALL, J.P., 24 Oct. 1767. Recorded 23
Nov. 1767 by FENWICKE BULL, Register.

Book H-3, p. 174   CHRISTOPHER MILLER, of Amelia Township, & IN-
19 & 20 July 1759   GELLACA (her mark) his wife, to EDWARD MUS-
L & R   GROVE, Dep. Sur., of Berkeley Co., for Ł 500
                          currency, 200 a. between Broad & Cultaby Riv-
ers, in Craven Co., on Sandy River, a branch of Broad River, & crosses
the wagon road about 4 miles from the fish dams in Broad River at the
ford; bounding on all sides on vacant land. Witnesses: WILLIAM SEWRIGHT,
JAMES CARNEY, FREDERICK (his mark) O'NEAL. Before ABRAHAM CARRADINE on
20 Jan. 1764. Recorded 25 Nov. 1767 by FENWICKE BULL, Register.

Book H-3, p. 181   EDWARD MUSGROVE, ESQ., & HANNAH (her mark) his
6 & 7 Feb. 1764   wife, of Berkeley Co., to THOMAS FLETCHALL,
L & R   ESQ., of Craven Co., for Ł 100 currency, 200
                          a., on Sandy River (see p. 174). Witnesses:
THOMAS LENNON, KEZZIA (his mark) FOWLER, JOHN (his mark) RANDY. Before
ABRAHAM CARRADINE on 13 Feb. 1764. Recorded 27 Nov. 1767 by FENWICKE
BULL, Register.

Book H-3, p. 187   JOHN FOSTER, planter, & AGNESS (her mark) his
16 & 17 Oct. 1767   wife, to JOHN SAVAGE, storekeeper, for Ł 100
L & R   currency, 100 a. in Berkeley Co., granted 17

Apr. 1764 by Gov. THOMAS BOONE to CATHERINE MILLER (recorded in Secretary's Book X.X., p. 452, by GEORGE JOHNSTON, Dep. Sec.); bounding SE on unknown & vacant land; N & NE on Saludy River; other sides on vacant land; which land was conveyed by CATHERINE MILLER on 6 June 1764 to FOSTER. Witnesses: WILLIAM CHRISTIE, JAMES (his mark) WELSH. Before THOMAS BELL, J.P. Recorded 1 Dec. 1767 by FENWICKE BULL, Register.

Book H-3, p. 192
14 & 15 Sept. 1767
L & R
SARAH BULLARD, executrix, & JOHN REMINGTON, executor, of will of EDWARD BULLARD, carpenter, to GEORGE KINCAID, cooper; all of Charleston; for Ł 1405 currency, the SW part of lot #239, bounding N & E on other parts of same lot; S 189 ft. on lot #251; W 50 ft. on Archdale Street. Whereas EDWARD BULLARD by will dated 14 Jan. last authorized his executors to sell his lot in Charleston, bounding 100 ft. on Archdale Street & about 190 ft. deep, being the W part of lot #239; now the executors sell a part of the lot to KINCAID. Witnesses: ELIZABETH CAMPBELL, DARBY PENDERGRASS. Memo: Proprietary grant of lot 239 to NIC. MARSDEN, 18 May 1694; MARSDEN 26 Jan. 1696/7 devised to his wife ELIZABETH; 2 Sept. 1699 ELIZABETH devised all her estate to Landgrave EDMOND BELLINGER; 20 Oct. 1705 BELLINGER conveyed to FRANCIS FIDLING; 7 Aug. 1706 FIDLING devised to his son DANIEL; 11 May 1713 DANIEL FIDLING conveyed to JOHN CARLETON; 31 Aug. 1717 CHARLETON conveyed (Book K., p. 169) to GEORGE SMITH; who died intestate, leaving 3 daughters, ANN, JANE & SARAH, coheiresses; 21 Nov. 1751 they conveyed to EDWARD BULLARD. Proved by PENDERGRASS before FENWICKE BULL, J.P. & P. Register. Recorded 2 Dec. 1767.

Book H-3, p. 198
10 & 11 Jan. 1764
L & R
PETER EASTER, planter, & MARY (her mark) his wife, to WILLIAM MORGAN, planter, both of Craven Co., for Ł 16 currency, 150 a., being the S side of 300 a. on Mill Creek, in Craven Co., granted 11 Jan. 1762 by Gov. THOMAS BOONE to EASTER; then bounding on vacant land; the 150 a. bounding S on MICHAEL DOMPERT; N on a line drawn from E to W through the middle of the 300 a.; E & W on vacant land. Witnesses: WILLIAM HENRY, GEORGE KITTS, FREDERICK HENRY. Proved 10 Feb. 1764 before THOMAS FLETCHALL, J.P. Recorded 4 Dec. 1767 by FENWICKE BULL, Register.

Book H-3, p. 203
2 Oct. 1767
Release
MARGARITHA (her mark) HENRY, planter, to ADRIAN MAYER, ESQ., both of Purysburgh, for Ł 100 currency, 100 a. in Purysburgh Township, granted her late husband JEAN FRANCOIS HENRY, bounding N on ELIAS BOURNANT; W on HECTOR BERINGER DE BEAUFAIN; E on HENRY DESAUSSURE; S on HENRY BOURQUIN. Witnesses: JOHN RODOLPH BENINGER, MELCHIOR LEICHTENSTEIGER. Before JOHN LEWIS BOURQUIN, J.P. Recorded 4 Dec. 1767 by FENWICKE BULL, Register.

Book H-3, p. 205
9 & 10 Nov. 1767
L & R
JOSEPH BULL, sugar baker, & ELIZABETH (her mark) his wife, to JOSEPH VERREE, carpenter, both of Charleston, for Ł 3000 currency, the S part of lot #77, bounding E 85 ft. 10 in., English measure, on Church Street; S 150 ft. 6 in. on THOMAS YOUNG; W 42 ft. on THOMAS YOUNG; N 142 ft. on other part of BALL'S land; also the brick house on the S part. Witnesses: THOMAS YOUNG, BENJAMIN WILKINS. Before FENWICKE BULL, J.P. & P. Register. Recorded 8 Dec. 1767.

Book H-3, p. 213
9 & 10 Nov. 1767
L & R in Trust
DANIEL MUNRO (MUNROW), of Charleston, & SARAH his wife, to JOHN CREIGHTON, of the Quarter House, for Ł 500 currency, a town lot & a certain house called The Crown Inn, fronting E on broad path leading into King Street, bounding N on MICHAEL BOOMER; S on a free Negro called MATT; W on land adjoining the parsonage land in St. Philips Parish, Charleston; DANIEL & SARAH to occupy the premises during their lives, then their heirs. Witnesses: MICHAEL BOOMER, ALEXANDER MOULTRIE. Before FENWICKE BULL, J.P. & P. Register.

Book H-3, p. 218
13 & 14 Aug. 1767
L & R
JACOB (his mark) HURGER, & LOUISA (her mark) his wife; HENRY FELDER, VALENTINE YUZY, & JEREMIAH THEUS, heirs of estate of JOHN SHOUMLEFEL, of Orangeburgh Township, Berkeley Co., of

1st part; to JACOB STROMAN, of said Township, for ₺ 250 currency, 550 a.
in said Township, granted SHOUMLEFEL 10 Mar. 1743/4, bounding NE on JAMES
TILLY & vacant land; SW on vacant land & LEWIS LORIMER; SW & NW on vacant
land; also a half a. lot, #257, in Orangeburgh. Witnesses: WILLIAM
HOUSEEL, JACOB STROWMAN, JR. Before JOHN TROUP, J.P. Recorded 19 Oct.
1767 by FENWICKE BULL, Register.

Book H-3, p. 226   CHARLES PURRY, storekeeper, of Granville Co.,
4 & 5 Mar. 1744   administrator of estate of his father, JOHN
L & R   PETER PURRY, of Purysburgh, to PETER SIMOND,
                          merchant, of London, Great Britain, for ₺ 300
sterling British, 12,350 a. in Granville Co., in the reserved lands of
Purysburgh Township, bounding SW, N & E on vacant land; E & S on ABRAHAM
CHEWDONELL; S & W on Dayes Creek (called New River); S, N & E on River
May. Witnesses: JOHN GARVEY, JOHN DELAGAYE. Proved by DELAGAYE, 26 Oct.
1758 before JOHN REMINGTON, J.P. Recorded 15 Dec. 1767 by FENWICKE BULL,
Register. This conveyance was delivered by MR. SAVAGE about 24 July 1755
to (REMINGTON ?) who "signed a receipt for it written in MR. PURY'S hand
which at the widow's desire I dated before his decease, Viz. 1 July 1754."

Book H-3, p. 232   JOHN SKRINE, planter, of Prince George Parish,
8 & 9 Sept. 1766   Craven Co., to JOHN MARION, planter, of St.
L & R   James Parish, Santee, for ₺ 432 currency, 400
                          a. known as SKRINE'S Ferry, in St. James Par-
tee; beginning at a Cypress tree marked with 3 notches & a cross on Santee River at the dividing line between the premises & FRANCIS KINLOCH, to
run from thence S 27° W 19-1/2 chains; then S 6° W 80 chains 80 links;
then N 84° W 10 chains; then S 6° W 47 chains; then N 82° W 30 chains 30
links; then N 6° E 44 chains 50 links; then S 84° E 15 chains; then N 6°
E to Santee River; then to 1st station as the river runs; bounding E on
FRANCIS KINLOCK; S on JOHN GAILLARD; W on ROBERT JONES or JAMES GAILLARD;
N on Santee River; which land is 1/2 the land bequeathed by BARTHOLOMEW
GAILLARD to his wife, ELIZABETH, during her lifetime, then to his eldest
son FREDERICK GAILLARD; which entire tract FREDERICK sold on 20 Apr. 1736
to JONATHAN SKRINE (father of JOHN); who gave 1/2 to JOHN & 1/2 to his
daughter, MARY, now wife of ISAAC PORCHER, possession to take effect
after the death of JONATHAN & said ELIZABETH "with whom the said ELIZA-
BETH intermarried". On division of the tract between JOHN SKRINE & MARY
PORCHER, after the death of JONATHAN & ELIZABETH, the half above mentioned was allotted to JOHN. Witnesses: ISAAC FORDYCE, WILLIAM SMITH. Before CHARLES FYFFE, J.P. Recorded 18 Dec. 1767 by FENWICKE BULL, Register.

Book H-3, p. 240   ROBERT REAGH, gunsmith, & SARAH his wife; of
7 & 8 Jan. 1767   the Long Canes Settlement, to JOHN MORRIS,
L & R   planter, of the settlement, for ₺ 150 curren-
                          cy, 200 a. in said settlement, granted 4 Mar.
1760 by Gov. WILLIAM HENRY LYTTELTON to ARTHUR DONALDSON, bounding NW on
JOSEPH SWEARINGAIN; beginning at a black oak 3 X, running s 36° W 44
chains 73 links to an elm sappling 3 X; S 54° E 44 chains 73 links to a
stake 3 X pr hickory; N 36° E 44 chains 73 links to a stake 3 X pr black
oak; N 54° W 44 chains 73 links to beginning; which land was sold by
DONALDSON on 18 Jan. 1763 to REAGH. Witnesses: JAMES SIMSON, GILES (his
mark) WILLIAMS. Before PATRICK CALHOUN, J.P. Recorded 19 Dec. 1767 by
FENWICKE BULL, Register.

Book H-3, p. 244   NICHOLAS (his mark) GUNNELL, of Granville Co.,
24 & 25 June 1764   to his son, DANIEL GUNNELL, for ₺ 200 curren-
L & R   cy, 200 a. in Granville Co., granted by Gov.
                          JAMES GLEN on 9 Apr. 1755 to NICHOLAS GUNNELL,
bounding NE on Stephens Creek; other sides on vacant land. Witnesses:
NATHAN DAVIS, JOSHUA (his mark) SANDERS, JOHN MANER. Before JACOB SUM-
MERRALL, J.P. Recorded 22 Dec. 1767 by FENWICKE BULL, Register.

Book H-3, p. 248   NICHOLAS (his mark) GUNNELL, to JOSHUA SANDERS,
25 June 1764   both of Granville Co., for ₺ 200 currency, 200
L & R   a. in Granville Co., granted by Gov. WILLIAM
                          HENRY LYTTLETON on 5 Oct. 1756 to NICHOLAS
GUNNELL, bounding SW on Savannah River; SE on JOSEPH CHATWAN; other sides
on vacant land. Witnesses: NATHAN DAVIS, DANIEL GUNNELL, JOHN MANER.

Before JACOB SUMMERRALL, J.P. Recorded 23 Dec. 1767 by FENWICKE BULL, Register.

Book H-3, p. 253
19 & 20 Nov. 1764
L & R

HENRY SEITHMAN, tailor, to JOHN IZZELLY (IZZELLE), farmer, both of Craven Co., for Ł 100 currency, 100 a. in the fork between Broad & Saludy Rivers near a branch of Cannon Creek, granted 7 Oct. 1762 by Gov. THOMAS BOONE to SEITHMAN, bounding N on GEORGE MICHAEL STEARL; E on JOHN ADAM WILT & JACOB LONG; S on vacant land; W on JOHN DOMINIC & JOHN STOUDEMYER (see Secretary's Book W.W., p. 117). Witnesses: SARAH RAIFORD, MARTHA PEARSON. Before JOHN PEARSON, J.P., 20 Nov. 1764. Recorded 24 Dec. 1767 by FENWICKE BULL, Register.

Book H-3, p. 257
3 & 4 Oct. 1765
L & R

JOHN WOLFGANG SHULEIN, blacksmith, of Berkeley Co., to JOSEPH MARTAIN, planter, of Craven Co., for Ł 200 currency, 150 a. in the fork of Santee & Wateree Rivers, bounding on all sides on vacant land, granted 13 Aug. 1756 by Gov. WILLIAM HENRY LYTTELTON to SHULEIN. Witnesses: PELEGREW (his mark) SALSBERY, JOHN EASON. Before JOHN HAMELTON, J.P., 11 Oct. 1765. Recorded 22 Jan. 1768 by FENWICKE BULL, Register.

Book H-3, p. 262
6 & 7 Sept. 1764
L & R

JEREMIAH WARRIN, planter, to ZEBULON GAUNT, millwright, both of Berkeley Co., for Ł 50 currency, 100 a. on N side Saluda River, on Palmetto Branch, bounding on all sides on vacant land; granted by Gov. WILLIAM HENRY LYTTELTON to JEREMIAH WILLIAMS (?). Witnesses: STEPHEN ELMORE, JAMES COATE. Before ANDREW BROWN, 8 Oct. 1764. Recorded 25 Jan. 1768 by FENWICKE BULL, Register.

Book H-3, p. 266
18 Mar. 1763
Assignment

JOSEPH KERSHAW, merchant, of Pine Tree Hill, Craven Co., to ZEBULON GAUNT, carpenter, of Craven Co., for Ł 350 currency, 2 tracts on S side of Wateree River, in Craven Co., 66 a. bounding NW on JAMES OUSLEY; NE on the river; SE on JOSEPH KERSHAW; SW on vacant land; granted 9 Feb. 1749 to the Hon. CHARLES PINCKNEY; 150 a., opposite Fredericksburgh Township, bounding SE on LUKE GIBBON; NE on Wateree River; NW & SW on vacant land; granted 6 Aug. 1751 to ALEXANDER MITCHELL; which 2 tracts now belong to KERSHAW. Witnesses: JOSHUA ENGLISH, THOMAS SIMMONS. Before SAMUEL WYLEY, J.P., 30 May 1764. Recorded 26 Jan. 1768 by FENWICKE BULL, Register.

Book H-3, p. 268
10 & 11 June 1762
L & R by Mortgage

JOHN FILBIN, planter, of St. James Parish, Goose Creek, to GABIREL MANIGAULT, merchant, of Charleston, for Ł 2500 currency, (4 bonds), 365 a. on Cooper River, in Parish of St. James Goose Creek; which land WILLIAM MAINE, executor of will of RICHARD BAKER, sold on 23 Dec. 1755 to ROBERT HUME; who sold to FILBIN; also 344 a., on which FILBIN lives, adjoining the 365 a., devised to FILBIN by his father, CHARLES FILBIN. Witnesses: WILLIAM WITHERS, PETER BOUNETHEAU. Before FENWICKE BULL, J.P. & P. Register. Recorded 29 Jan. 1768. On 29 July 1779 MANIGAULT declared mortgage satisfied. Witness: GEORGE SHEED.

Book H-3, p. 277
25 & 26 June 1765
L & R

WILLIAM DEWES, carpenter & joiner, & MARY ANN (her mark) his wife; to MICHAEL BOMMER, butcher; both of Charleston, for Ł 400 currency, lot #135 in Charleston, bounding E 36 ft. on the Kings Highway; N 160 ft. on PATRICK HINDS, shoemaker; S on MICHAEL BOMMER, where he lives. Witnesses: GEORGE VAIR, EDWARD COLE. Before JOHN TROUP, J.P., 31 Oct. 1765. Recorded 30 Jan. 1768 by FENWICKE BULL, Register. WILLIAM DEWES & GEORGE SHEED, merchants, give BOMMER bond of performance. Witnesses: EDMUND HIGGINSON, GEORGE VAIR.

Book H-3, p. 283
25 & 26 Sept. 1767
L & R

BENJAMIN GARDEN, ESQ., of Prince William Parish, Granville Co., & AMELIA his wife, to MILES BREWTON, ESQ., of Charleston, for Ł 2000 SC money, already paid by BREWTON at GARDENS request to COPELAND STYLES, merchant, of Bermuda, who was lately in SC; lot #244 in Charleston, granted RICHARD PHILLIPS but now owned by GARDEN; bounding N on lot #243; E on MILES BREWTON (formerly belonging to COL.

MILES BREWTON, deceased, & THOMAS BINFORD); S on marsh land; W on a street running from Ashley River, N & S fronting land of GEORGE ROUPELL, ESQ., formerly called Legare's Street; also the marsh land S of said lot, fronting 92 ft. on Legare Street from corner of lot #244 measured S to a stake & from thence by a line running parallel to Tradd Street; as by plat annexed to release dated 21 Dec. 1736 from the late Hon. WILLIAM BULL to ALEXANDER GARDEN & MARTHA his wife, the father & mother of BENJA-MIN GARDEN, party hereto; said marsh land bounding W on Legare Street; S on marsh land belonging to heirs of WILLIAM BULL, & is part of a tract of marsh land granted WILLIAM BULL on 9 Mar. 1736. Witnesses: SARAH GUERARD, BENJAMIN GUERARD. Before CHARLES PINCKNEY, J.P. Recorded 2 Feb. 1768 by FENWICKE BULL, Register.

Book H-3, p. 291
23 Apr. 1737
Sale

JOHN MACKEY, planter, of Colleton Co., to THOMAS CLIFFORD, planter, for ₤ 225 currency, 100 a. in Colleton Co., near Pecums Point, part of a tract he had purchased from his brother, JOSEPH, bounding NE (W?) on EDWARD NORTH; SW on THOMAS CLIFFORD; other sides on JOHN MACKEY. Witnesses: ROGER SAUNDERS, THOMAS EBERSON, NATHANIEL PAYNE. Delivery by turf & twig. Before CULCHETH GOLIGHTLY, J.P. Recorded 4 Feb. 1768 by FENWICKE BULL, Register.

Book H-3, p. 293
23 July 1767
L & R

NATHANIEL (his mark) SHEPARD, of St. Marks Parish, Craven Co., & RACHEL (her mark) his wife, to NATHANIEL BIBBY, of same Parish, for ₤ 125 currency, 100 a. on a ridge between the heads of 2 branches of Lynch's Creek, 1 called Flat Creek, the other WILLIAMS Creek, bounding on all sides on vacant land. Witnesses: HENRY FOSTER, BENJAMIN BEAVIN. Before JOHN CANTZON, J.P. Recorded 5 Feb. 1768 by FENWICKE BULL, Register.

Book H-3, p. 297
22 & 23 Feb. 1767
L & R

THOMAS JONES, planter, son & heir of JOHN JONES, of the Welch Tract, Prince George Par-ish, Winyaw; Craven Co., to ABEL WILDS, plant-er, for ₤ 100 currency, 100 a. in the Welch Tract, granted 6 Dec. 1744 by Gov. JAMES GLEN to JOHN JONES; bounding W on Peedee River; N on JOHN JONES; other sides on vacant land. Witnesses: JOHN JONES, JAMES SMART. Before CLAUDIUS PEGUES, J.P., 28 Mar. 1767. Recorded 5 Feb. 1768 by FENWICKE BULL, Register.

Book H-3, p. 301
22 & 23 Feb. 1767
L & R

THOMAS JONES, planter, son & heir of JOHN JONES, of the Welch Tract, Prince George Par-ish, Winyaw, Craven Co., to ABEL WILDS, plant-er, for ₤ 500 currency, 250 a. in said tract, granted by Gov. JAMES GLEN on 10 Mar. 1743 to JOHN JONES; bounding W on Peedee River; other sides on vacant land. Witnesses: JOHN JONES, JAMES SMART. Before CLAUDIUS PEGUES, J.P., 28 Mar. 1767. Recorded 8 Feb. 1768 by FENWICKE BULL, Register.

Book H-3, p. 305
28 July 1756
Gift

WILLIAM DALTON, SR., to his son, DARIUS DAL-TON, (when 21), both of St. Bartholomews Par-ish, Colleton Co., for good causes & valuable considerations; 7 Negroes (named), & 311 a. on Wanells Neck, bounding on Folly Creek, part of 621 a.; should DARIUS die before reaching 21 years, then the land & slaves to be equally divided amongst his other children. Witnesses: SARAH (her mark) SMITH, ANDREW MCCULLOUGH, ELEAZER (his mark) ANDREW. Before WILLIAM BOONE, J.P., 12 May 1758. Entered in Secretary's Book L.L., p. 35, by JOHN MURRAY, Dep. Sec. Entered in Auditor's Book F-6, p. 133, on 6 Aug. 1762, by RICHARD LAMBTON, Dep. Aud. Recorded 8 Feb. 1768 by FENWICKE BULL, Register.

Book H-3, p. 307
20 & 21 Jan. 1768
L & R

DARIUS DALTON, planter, of St. Bartholomews Parish, to JAMES PARSONS, ESQ., of Charleston, for ₤ 400 currency, 311 a. on Wanilla Neck, in said Parish, being the S, SW, & part of the W part or half of 621 a., which consisted of 2 tracts, 1 of 550 a. pur-chased 8 Dec. 1742 by WILLIAM DALTON from ISAAC GRIMBALL; 1 of 71 a. granted WILLIAM DALTON on 13 Mar. 1752; the 311 a. bounding N & NE on other half of 621 a. conveyed by WILLIAM DALTON, the grandson, to JAMES PARSONS; W on JOHN TIMMONS; E on MARY DALTON; S on Folly Creek (Cuckold's

Creek). Whereas WILLIAM DALTON, SR., on 28 July 1756 (see p. 305) gave his son, DARIUS, 311 a., to be delivered to DARIUS by his attorneys (DANIEL DALTON & JOHN WARREN) with the proviso that the premises should remain with the rest of his (WILLIAM'S) interest until his decease; & whereas DANIEL DALTON died before livery seizin was made & for various reasons the deed became defective in law, & the premises descended to WILLIAM DALTON, grandson of said WILLIAM; & whereas WILLIAM, the grandson, by L & R dated 4 & 5 May 1767 conveyed the premises to PARSONS; now to remove all defects, & in order not to let DARIUS suffer by any defect, PARSONS agrees to pay DARIUS full value for his interest in the premises. Witnesses: JOSEPH MILES, JOHN HOUSTOUN. Before FENWICKE BULL, J.P. & P. Register. Recorded 9 Feb. 1768.

Book H-3, p. 313   WILLIAM HAMILTON, to MICHAEL PEAGET, both of
2 Mar. 1743/4   Purysburgh, Granville Co., for ₤ 100 currency,
Release   lot #71 in Purysburgh, containing 1 a., bound-
                   ing E on vacant land; N & W on streets; S on
ALBALESTIER DE MON CLAIR; which lot #71 had been granted CAPT. FREDERICK
DEJEAN; also lot #75, containing 1 a., granted JACOB METZKER, who sold to
HAMILTON. Receipt also signed by ANN HAMILTON. Witnesses: JOHN CHEVIL-
LETTE, DAVID GIROUD. Before JOHN LEWIS BOURQUIN, J.P. on 4 Jan. 1768.
Recorded 10 Feb. 1768 by FENWICKE BULL, Register.

Book H-3, p. 316   EBENEZER SIMMONS, ESQ., of Charleston, & JANE
17 & 18 Oct. 1766 his wife, to JAMES WITTER, planter, of James
L & R   Island, for ₤ 2500 currency, 150 a., old mea-
                   sure, on Johns Island, but on resurvey found
to be 230 a.; known as the Savannah tract; formerly belonging to JOHN
JONES; afterwards to SAMUEL PALMERINE & SARAH his wife; bounding W on
DANIEL HOLMES (formerly JONATHAN STOCKS); S on Kawah River & marsh; E on
Savannah or Cole's Creek; N on the creek & JAMES MATHEWES. Witnesses:
ANN MCQUEEN, WILLIAM MILLER. Before JEREMIAH SAVAGE, J.P., 22 Jan. 1768.
Recorded 12 Feb. 1768 by FENWICKE BULL, Register.

Book H-3, p. 322   ROGER PINCKNEY, P.M., to FELIX LONG & DANIEL
22 July 1767   STROBLE, of Charleston, as tenants in common;
Sale   for ₤ 303:15:0 currency, 450 a. in Craven Co.,
                   bounding N on vacant land; E on Wateree River;
S on Santee River & vacant land; W on the river & MILES JACKSON. Whereas
MALACHI WESTON, planter, of Craven Co., who owned the above tract, granted MARY RUSSELL on 29 Nov. 1750 (L & R from CHARLES RUSSELL dated 4 & 5
June 1765), was indebted to WILLIAM GLEN, merchant, of Charleston, for
₤ 2000 currency & interest from 1 Mar. 1765; & whereas GLEN obtained a
judgment, with costs, against WESTON, & a writ of fieri facias was issued
to the P.M. commanding him to seize WESTON'S estate & obtain the necessary amount; now the P.M. sells the 450 a. at auction to LONG & STROBLE;
subject to claim of dower by the wife of WESTON should she survive him.
Witnesses: HOPSON PINCKNEY, JOHN MARTIN. Entered in Auditor's Book H-8,
p. 378, on 19 Jan. 1768 by RICHARD LAMBTON, Dep. Aud. Before FENWICKE
BULL, J.P. & P. Register, 8 Feb. 1768.

Book H-3, p. 327   ROWLAND EVANS, glazier, of Charleston, & ELIZ-
16 & 17 Sept. 1767 ABETH his wife, to REBECCA SINGLETON, for
L & R   ₤ 1650 currency, the W part of lot #223 in
                   Charleston, bounding N 24 ft. on Tradd Street;
E 103 ft. on part sold by EVANS to MRS. ANN TIMARLY; S on WILLIAM CAT-
TELL; W on JOSEPH VERREE; which part of lot #223 was sold by JAMES SIM-
MONS & ANN his wife by L & R dated 12 & 13 Feb. 1764 to EVANS. Witness-
es: DAVID DEAS, EDWARD PIERCE. Before HENRY PERONNEAU 30 Jan. 1768. Re-
corded 16 Feb. 1768 by FENWICKE BULL, Register.

Book H-3, p. 332   JOHN DUTARQUE, planter, of Parish of St. Thom-
2 & 3 Oct. 1767   as, Berkeley Co., & MARY his wife, to RICHARD
L & R   BLAKE, planter, of Parish of St. James, Santee,
                   Craven Co., for ₤ 1600 currency, 3 tracts of
land, total 893 a.; 500 a. on N side Santee River granted PETER ROBERT on
9 June 1714, bounding W on JOHN GAILLARD; E on PETER ROBERTS; NW on vacant land; 200 a. on S side Santee River, nearly opposite 1st tract,
granted HENRY AUGUSTUS CHASTAIGNIER & ALEXANDER THEREE CHASTAIGNIER on 12
Mar. 1698/9; bounding E on PAUL BRUNNEAU; S on vacant land: E on JAMES

BOYD; 200 a. in Parish of St. James, Santee except 7 a. sold by JOHN ROB-
ERT to ISAAC LEGRAND; granted PETER COULIANDAU on 15 Sept. 1705; bounding
N on JOHN BOYD & PETER ROBERT; E on NICHOLAS LANUD; W on MOSES CARION.
Witnesses: JOSEPH FRIZER, MARTHA DUTARQUE, ANDRES DAVID. Before BENJAMIN
MARION, J.P., on 28 Jan. 1767. Recorded 18 Feb. 1768 by FENWICKE BULL,
Register.

Book H-3, p. 338   CHRISTOPHER (German script) SHERP, planter, of
14 & 15 Feb. 1756   Berkeley Co., & ANNA MARIA (German script) his
L & R   wife, to PETER CRIM, JR., for ₺ 200 currency,
                      an island of 145 a. in Broad River, granted 7
Oct. 1755' by Gov. JAMES GLEN to SHERP. Witnesses: JACOB FRIDAY, HANS
GEORGE WERSING, PETER CRIM, ESQ. Before JOHN PEARSON, J.P., on 20 Jan.
1767. Recorded 18 Feb. 1768 by FENWICKE BULL, Register.

Book H-3, p. 343   GEORGE (his mark) CORNELL, planter, of St.
12 & 13 Jan. 1768   Pauls Parish, GEORGIA, & MARGARET his wife; &
L & R   MARY ANN COOK, his mother-in-law; to BENJAMIN
                      TUTT, merchant, of Colleton Co., for ₺ 1500
currency, 500 a. in 2 tracts in Granville Co., SC. Whereas on 26 June
1738 Gov. WILLIAM BULL granted ROBERT VAUGHAN 200 a. in New Windsor Township, bounding S on ROBERT MCMURDY; W on Savannah River; N on the Fort; E
on the town line; & whereas on 23 Aug. 1743 ROBERT VAUGHAN & ARBELA his
wife sold the 200 a. to ROWLAND PRITCHARD; also lot #48 in New Windsor;
which land & lot on 3 Jan. 1743/4 PRITCHETT sold to JAMES PARIS & WILLIAM
MCCARTEY; & whereas 12 Sept. 1741 Gov. WILLIAM BULL granted ROBERT MC-
MURDY 300 a. in New Windsor Township, bounding SE on MARTHA MCGILVERY; N
on the town line & ROBERT VAUGHAN; S on Savannah River; which 300 a. MC-
MURDY sold to ROWLAND PRITCHETT; who on 29 June 1744 sold to WILLIAM MC-
CARTEY & JAMES PARIS; & whereas on 19 Sept. 1748 PARIS transferred his
share in the 500 a. & lot #48 to his partner, MCCARTEY; & whereas MARGA-
RET MCCARTEY, daughter & heir of WILLIAM, married GEORGE CORNELL, & COR-
NELL thus became co-proprietor with his mother-in-law, MARY ANN, widow of
MCCARTEY; now they sell the 500 a. & lot #48 to TUTT. Witnesses: DAVID
ZUBLEY, MATHIAS (his mark) ARDIS. Before JOHN DICK, J.P. Recorded 20
Feb. 1768 by FENWICKE BULL, Register.

Book H-3, p. 350   BENJAMIN TUTT, merchant, of Colleton Co., &
14 & 16 Jan. 1768   BARBARA (her mark) his wife, to MATHIAS ARDIS,
L & R   SR., planter, of Granville Co., for ₺ 1250
                      currency, 350 a. in New Windsor Township,
Granville Co., SC, bounding SE on MARTHA MCGILVERY; SW on Savannah River;
N by a line of marked trees beginning at a Mulberry tree marked on the
Savannah River, thence a straight course to a black oak also marked in
the back line of said tract; 300 a. of which were granted ROBERT MCMURDY
(p. 343); who conveyed to PRITCHETT; who conveyed to MCCARTEY & PARIS;
became vested in CORNELL; who conveyed to TUTT. Witnesses: JOHN GRAY,
JAMES ROSS. Before JOHN DICK, J.P. Recorded 23 Feb. 1768 by FENWICKE
BULL, Register.

Book H-3, p. 356   JOHN STUART, ESQ., & SARAH his wife, to ALEX-
4 & 5 Feb. 1768   PETRIE, gentleman, both of Charleston, for
L & R by Mortgage   ₺ 2800 currency, a small part of Orange Garden
                      in Charleston, which Garden extended from
Broad to Tradd Street & was purchased by PETRIE from SAMUEL CARNE, merchant, of London, & divided into small parcels, leaving an open street 20
ft. wide on the E side, called Orange Street; 1 division #11 being sold
by ALEXANDER PETRIE & ELIZABETH his wife to JOHN STUART by L & R dated 22
& 23 Dec. last; bounding S 55 ft. on Tradd Street; E 153 ft. on Orange
Street; W on 2 small lots, 12 & 10, still belonging to PETRIE. Witnesses: ROBERT BRISBANE, CHARLES PINCKNEY. Before D. CAMPBELL, J.P. Recorded 26 Feb. 1768 by FENWICKE BULL, Register.

Book H-3, p. 362   THOMAS LEE, & MARGERY his wife, to THOMAS
25 & 26 July 1753   WRIGHT, for ₺ 20 Virginia currency, 134 a. on
L & R   both sides of Bear Creek, a fork of cane
                      creek, in Anson Co., NC, beginning at a white
oak, running S 28 W 18 chains to a black oak, then S 47 W 27 chains to a
hickory, then S 15 E 34 chains to a white oak, then N 35 E 25 chains to a
white oak, then NE 10 chains to a white oak, then to first station.

Witnesses: ANDREW PICKENS, MATTHEW PATTON. Proved by PICKENS in Anson
Co., Jan. Court 1754; HENRY HENDRY, clerk ct. Registered in Anson Co.,
NC, Book B, fol. 365-367 by JOHN DUNN, Register. Recorded 27 Feb. 1768
by FENWICKE BULL, Register.

Book H-3, p. 367   THOMAS (his mark) WRIGHT, & MARTHA (her mark)
5 & 6 May 1760   his wife, to DAVID ADAMS, for ₤ 53 proclama-
L & R   tion money of NC, 134 a. on both sides Bear
          Creek, Anson Co., NC, (p. 362). Witnesses:
WILLIAM BARR, JAMES GAMBEL, JOHN BUNTEN. Execution of L & R proved in
Oct. 1767 term of court in Mecklenburgh Co., NC; ROBERT HARRIS, C.C. En-
tered in Register's Office of said Co. 25 Jan. 1768 by ROBERT HARRIS,
Register. Recorded 27 Feb. 1768 by FENWICKE BULL, Register.

Book H-3, p. 371   JOHN MOURDAG of Charleston, & MARGARET, (her
1 Oct. 1767   mark) MOURTAG called "PEGGY", appoint DENNIS
Power of Attorney FEARIS of same place, their attorney; to re-
          cover (Auditor's Office) & sell 350 a. near
Boonsborough Township. Witness: JOHN GEORGE BRUCE (German script).
Proved before FENWICKE BULL, J.P. & P. Register on 17 Dec. 1767. Record-
ed 1 Mar. 1768.

Book H-3, p. 371   AGNES STITT, widow, formerly of Parish of
12 & 13 Feb. 1768 Annahitt, Co. of Antrim, Ireland, now of Cra-
L & R   ven Co., sister & devisee of WILLIAM JAMIESON,
          planter, of Craven Co., to her son, WILLIAM
STITT, planter, of Craven Co., for ₤ 4000 currency, 500 a. in Craven Co.,
granted 24 May 1734 to JOHN GREEN; bounding SW on Black River; NW on WIL-
LIAM SAXBY; NE on JOHN LEWIS; SE on FORD & GLEN; also 35 a., granted 20
June 1764 to WILLIAM JAMIESON, bounding SE on Black River; NW on JOHN
GREEN; NE on JOHN MAMERTON; SE on DANIEL CRAWFORD; (excepting however 120
a. of river swamp, bounding NW on JOHN GREEN; SW on Black River; other
sides on JAMES CROCKATT; being part of 400 a. granted JOHN HAMERTON,
which part was sold by JAMES CROCKATT to WILLIAM JAMIESON on 10 Nov.
1762); also 2000 a. on NE side of Black River on Peters Creek Swamp,
bounding NE on ELIAS FOISSIN; NW on FOISSIN & vacant land; SW on SAMUEL
WRAGG; SE on vacant land; granted WILLIAM JAMIESON 25 Oct. 1764; total
1655 a.; all of which land WILLIAM JAMIESON by will dated 8 Jan. 1766 bequeathed to his sister, AGNES STITT. Witnesses: JAMES PARSONS, JOHN
HOUSTOUN. Before FENWICKE BULL, J.P. & P. Register. Recorded 2 Mar.
1768.

Book H-3, p. 377   JOSEPH BARNETT, of Berkeley Co., to JOHN MUR-
17 & 18 Feb. 1768 RAY, ESQ., of Charleston, for ₤ 7000 currency,
L & R by Mortgage 18,050 a. above Ninety Six, SC, bounding NE on
          Saludy River & BENJAMIN WALKER; SE on JAMES
MASON & vacant land; SW on WILLIAM MURRAY; NW on WILLIAM SIMPSON; which
18,050 a. BARNETT purchased recently from MURRAY. Witnesses: PETER BOC-
QUET, JR., JAMES JOHNSTON. Before DAVID RHIND, J.P. Recorded 3 Mar.
1768 by FENWICKE BULL, Register.

Book H-3, p. 382   DANIEL CANNON, carpenter, & MARY his wife, to
22 & 23 Feb. 1768 JOHN PAUL GRIMKE, jeweler, both of Charleston,
L & R   for ₤ 12,600 currency, the NW part of lot #311
          in Archdale Square, bounding N 180 ft. on
Queen Street; W 116 ft. 4 in. on SIR ALEXANDER NISBETT; then running from
SW corner towards E 55 ft. 8 in, then N 50 ft. 3 in; then E 120 ft.;
bounding S on JOHN HOLLYBUSH messuage of THOMAS DOUGHTY, another part of
lot #311; E on THOMAS DOUGHTY (50 ft.) & 80 ft. on old Church or Meeting
Street. Witnesses: EDMOND EGAN, WILLIAM ROPER, JR. Before WILLIAM BUR-
ROWS, J.P. Recorded 4 Mar. 1768 by FENWICKE BULL, Register.

Book H-3, p. 388   JAMES HENDERSON, tallow chandler, & MARY his
25 & 26 Dec. 1767 wife, to PETER BOCQUET, baker, & PAUL SMISER,
L & R by Mortgage shopkeeper; all of Charleston; because BOCQUET
          & SMISER had stood security for HENDERSON on
bonds given by HENDERSON to MRS. ELIZABETH PERONNEAU, widow & executrix
of will of SAMUEL PERONNEAU, for ₤ 700 & ₤ 450 currency; the N part of
lot #212 in Charleston, with the houses & improvements bounding W 42-1/2
ft. on King Street & the whole depth of the lot; being all he has left of

lot #212 which he purchased from RAWLINS LOWNDES & MARY his wife by L & R dated 7 & 8 Jan. 1762. Witnesses: PETER BOCQUET, JR., MARY EASTON. Before ROBERT RAWLINS, J.P., 13 Jan. 1768. Recorded 5 Mar. 1768 by FENWICKE BULL, Register. On 9 Sept. 1773 PETER BOCQUET declared mortgage paid by 1 W. GEORGE HAGG, executor of HENDERSON. Witness: WILLIAM RUGELEY.

Book H-3, p. 394
26 & 27 Sept. 1766
L & R
PHILLIPINNA (her mark) HOOFMAN, gentlewoman, of Charleston, to JOHN MITCHELL, Dep. Sur., of Amelia Township, for Ł 200 currency, 100 a. in St. Marks Parish, Craven Co., on the fork between Broad & Wateree Rivers; bounding NW on EPHRAIM MITCHELL; SW on Santee River; other sides on vacant land; granted her on 25 Sept. 1766 by Gov. CHARLES GREVILLE Lord MONTAGU (see Secretary's Book, A.A.A., p. 138). Witnesses: THOMAS PLATT, JAMES WRIGHT, MARTIN LENARD. Before TACITUS GAILLARD, J.P., on 23 Apr. 1767. Recorded 8 Mar. 1768 by FENWICKE BULL, Register.

Book H-3, p. 399
9 & 10 Oct. 1767
L & R
DANIEL (his mark) BUTLER, planter, of Craven Co., to JOHN MITCHELL, Dep. Sur., of Matthews Parish, Berkeley Co., for Ł 150 currency, 150 a. in St. Matthews Parish, bounding NW on WILLIAM MITCHELL; SW on NATHAN JOYNER; SE on vacant land; NE on Santee River; granted BUTLER on 16 Dec. 1766 by Gov. CHARLES GREVILLE Lord MONTAGU (see Secretary's Book, A.A.A., p. 211). Witnesses: CHARLES O'NEAL, JAMES MCKELVEY, THOMAS POWELL. Before JAMES LYNCH on 10 Nov. 1767. Recorded 9 Mar. 1768 by FENWICKE BULL, Register.

Book H-3, p. 405
16 & 17 Mar. 1767
L & R
JAMES MCKELVEY, planter, of St. Johns Parish, Berkeley Co., to JOHN MITCHELL, Dep. Sur., of St. Matthews Parish, for Ł 200 currency, 200 a., in Craven Co., bounding W on WILLIAM TUCKER & BOUGHARD BROWN; S on WILLIAM KELLY & EPHRAIM MITCHELL; E on EPHRAIM MITCHELL & MITCHELL SULLIVAN; N on vacant land; granted MCKELVEY 17 Feb. 1767 by CHARLES GREVILLE Lord MONTAGU as recorded in Book A.A.A., p. 316. Witnesses: ROBERT COLLETT, CHARLES O'NEAL, HUGH PHILLIPS. Before JOSEPH CURRY, J.P., on 24 Mar. 1767. Recorded 10 Mar. 1768 by FENWICKE BULL, Register.

Book H-3, p. 410
11 & 12 Feb. 1760
L & R
WILLIAM HARVEY, gentleman, & MARY (formerly MARY SEABROOK) his wife; GEORGE SAXBY, ESQ., & ELIZABETH (formerly ELIZABETH SEABROOK) his wife; & SUSANNA BOSOMWORTH (formerly SUSANNA SEABROOK) gentlewoman; all of Charleston; MARY, ELIZABETH & SUSANNA being devisees & legatees under the will of ALEXANDER HEXT, planter, of Johns Island, Colleton Co.; of 1st. part; to WILLIAM COATS, gentleman, of Charleston, & MARY his wife (formerly MARY GREEN); for love & affection & to settle all disputes; 842 a. on S side of Cawcaw Swamp. Whereas said land on Cawcaw Swamp had been granted the Rev. MR. ALEXANDER GARDEN, late rector of St. Philips Parish, Charleston, on 23 Nov. 1732; & MR. GARDEN by L & R dated 10 & 11 Jan. 1733 sold to ALEXANDER HEXT; who by will dated 16 July 1736, among the other devises, bequeathed to his friends, SAMUEL JONES, planter, of said Co., BENJAMIN D'HARRIETTE, merchant, of Charleston, OTHNIEL BEALE, merchant, of Charleston, & CHARLES PINCKNEY, gentleman, of same place; as trustees; that is, all his plantations & houses on S side of Cawcaw Swamp; in trust for SARAH GREEN, wife of DANIEL GREEN, JR., of Charleston, the eldest daughter of MARY SEABROOK (DANIEL & SARAH GREEN being father & mother of MARY COATS, party hereto), subject to certain limitations; & whereas SARAH GREEN died in the lifetime of ALEXANDER HEXT, & doubts arose as to whether the land reverted to HEXT; & after his death to JONES, D'HARRIETTE, BEALE, PINCKNEY, as trustees for MARY HARVEY, ELIZABETH SAXBY, & SUSANNA BOSOMWORTH; now, to settle all doubts the parties of the 1st part release all their rights to WILLIAM & MARY COATS & their heirs. Witnesses: MARY YEOMANS, SARAH YEOMANS, ELENER YEOMANS. Proved by MARY YEOMANS on 2 Mar. 1768 before FENWICKE BULL, J.P., her daughter SARAH & ELENER, the other witnesses, being then dead. Recorded 11 Mar. 1768 by FENWICKE BULL, Register.

Book H-3, p. 418
22 & 23 Oct. 1764
ELIZABETH BEATTY, planter, of St. Bartholomews Parish, Colleton Co., to JAMES HAMILTON,

L & R   planter, of same place, for Ŀ 625 currency,
                         238-1/2 a. (except the old burial place of
1/4 a.) in said Parish, bounding N on THOMAS BUER & DAVID FERGUSON (form-
erly JAMES HAMILTON); W on ROBERT HIETT; S on EDWARD HEXT; E on PETER
RUMPH. Witnesses: THOMAS GRANGE, SAMUEL BEATTY, ROBERT LITTLE. Before
GEORGE LOGAN, J.P., on 7 Jan. 1768. Recorded 16 Mar. 1768 by FENWICKE
BULL, Register. Plat of 238-1/2 a., part of 437 a. granted in 1731 to
BRYAN KELLY, certified 19 June 1767 by ALEXIUS MADOR FORSTER, D.S.

Book H-3, p. 424   WILLIAM BELLINGER, ESQ., of Ashepoo, to HENRY
14 & 15 Mar. 1768   MIDDLETON, DANIEL BLAKE, & BENJAMIN SMITH,
L & R by Mortgage   ESQ., in trust for the use of the estate of
                         RALPH IZARD. Whereas BELLINGER became indebt-
ed to said trustees for Ŀ 3500 currency, now as security he conveys to
them 977 a. in St. Bartholomews Parish, Colleton Co., formerly belonging
to his father; & BELLINGER delivers to the trustees 50 Negro slaves.
Witnesses: ROGER SAUNDERS, CHARLES PINCKNEY. Before FENWICKE BULL, J.P.
& P. Register. Recorded 29 Mar. 1768. Plat given inscribed "whereas the
will of EDMUND ye 2d LA: BELLINGER his younger children was to be entitled to an equal division of the surplus Ocatey lands to be divided to
them by his executrix. Now we do hereby witness that the plats for the
said surplus lands was laid before us by his said executrix & that we
have equal chance drawn the same between 3 younger children & that this
plat No. 9 was drawn to the said Landgraves son, WILLIAM, an infant, as
witness our hands. ROBERT MACKEWN, JUN., STEPHEN FITCH, WM. BACKSHELL,
WILM. MCPHERSON, Dept. Surv." On 7 Oct. 1779 HENRY MIDDLETON declared
mortgage satisfied. Witness: GEORGE SHEED.

Book H-3, p. 434   JACOB FRIDIG (FRIDAY), & BARBARA (her mark)
11 & 12 Aug. 1767   his wife, of Saxegotha Township, Berkeley Co.,
L & R   to JOHN CASPER LEIBHART, of Saludu River, in
                         Craven Co., for Ŀ 75 currency, 50 a. Whereas
on 5 Oct. 1753 Gov. JAMES GLEN granted RACHEL MATHYS 150 a. opposite
Saxegotha Township, bounding S on Congaree River; W on JOHN JACOB FRIDIG;
N on vacant land; E on ULRICK STOCKER; & whereas RACHEL MATHYS by L & R
dated 16 & 17 Jan. 1756, for Ŀ 50 currency, sold 50 a. of the 150 a.;
bounding S on the Congaree River; E on ULRIC STOCKER; N on vacant land; W
on original tract; to SEBASTIAN BUES; who bequeathed to his wife BARBARA,
who, after his death, married FRIDIG; now she & her husband sell the 50
a. to LEIBHART. Witnesses: ABRAHAM (German script) GEIGER, JOHN CONRAD
GEIGER. Before JOSEPH CURRY, J.P., on 7 Dec. 1767. Recorded 2 Apr. 1768
by FENWICKE BULL, Register.

Book H-3, p. 440   ISAAC STAPLES, planter, of Craven Co., to ALEX-
14 & 15 Feb. 1768   ANDER MCINTOSH, planter, of the Welch tract,
L & R   Craven Co., for Ŀ 200 currency, 150 a. in the
                         Welch tract, granted by Gov. JAMES GLEN on 22
Jan. 1747 to ABRAHAM STAPLES; bounding SW on Pedee River; NW on JOHN
EVANS, PHILIP DOUGLASS & vacant land; NE on vacant land; SE on WILLIAM
JAMES. Witnesses: CHARLES ATKINS, WILLIAM MAXWELL, FRANCIS LADSON. Be-
fore FENWICKE BULL, J.P. & P. Register. Recorded 11 Apr. 1768.

Book H-3, p. 444   MARTHA (her mark) COMBE, of Charleston, widow
22 Mar. 1768   & executrix of will of PHILLIP COMBE, planter,
R & Assignment   to her son, JOHN COMBE, for love & affection &
                         Ŀ 50 currency, all her claim to 130 a., Eng-
lish measure, on SE side of E branch of T of Cooper River, which by his
will dated 22 Feb. 1734 PHILLIP had bequeathed to his wife, MARTHA, during her lifetime, then to his youngest son, JAMES, since deceased, whereby the reversion became vested in JOHN, now only son & heir. Witnesses:
EDWARD SIMONS, FREDERICK ROSSBERG. Before JOHN REMINGTON, J.P. Recorded
12 Apr. 1768 by FENWICKE BULL, Register.

Book H-3, p. 446   JOHN COMBE, planter, of St. Thomas Parish,
30 & 31 Mar. 1768   Berkeley Co., only son & heir of PHILIP COMBE,
L & R   to JOHN LIPES, planter, of same Co., for Ŀ 300
                         currency, 130 a. on SE side of E branch of T
of Cooper River; bounding SW on Lynch's Creek; S on GEORGE JUNE; NE & NW
on JOHNSON LYNCH; originally granted 1 Sept. 1697 to ABEL BOUSHET; who on
17 July 1701 sold to LEWIS MOUZON in fee; who on 4 Aug. 1705 sold to

JOSIAS DU PRÉ; who on 14 Jan. 1712/3 sold to JAMES & PETER BENOIST; JAMES
BENOIST & MARY his wife on 20 Jan. 1723/4 selling their interest to
PETER; who, with JANE his wife, by L & R dated 14 & 15 Feb. 1728/9 sold
to PHILIP COMBE (see Register's Book K, p. 68-71). Witnesses: THOMAS
AKIN, JACOB REMINGTON. Before JOHN REMINGTON, J.P. Recorded 12 Apr.
1768 by FENWICKE BULL, Register.

Book H-3, p. 452   JOHN JAMES, SR., planter, of St. Marks Parish,
4 & 5 Oct. 1765   to JOHN MCINTOSH, planter, for £ 100 currency,
L & R   50 a. in Craven Co., originally granted on
                          bounty to DENNIS HAGIN, on NE side Wateree
River near High Hills, bounding on all sides on vacant land. Witnesses:
JAMES FREEMAN, EDWARD (his mark) LAIN (LANE). Receipt signed by JOHN
JAMES, SR., & SHER^D. JAMES, SR. Before BARNABY POPE, J.P., on 9 Oct.
1765. Recorded 15 Apr. 1768 by FENWICKE BULL, Register.

Book H-3, p. 456   THOMAS FORSTER, planter, to WILLIAM WILLIAMSON,
4 & 5 Apr. 1768   ESQ., for £ 250 currency, 840 a. on Black
L & R   Swamp, the waters of Savannah, granted FOR-
                          STER 3 June 1765; as by plat dated 9 Mar. 1765
by JOHN TROUP, Dep. Sur. Witnesses: ANTHONY GARDNER, WILLIAM ROBERTS,
ALEXIUS M. FORSTER. Recorded 19 Apr. 1768 by FENWICKE BULL, Register.

Book H-3, p. 460   CHARLES ODINGSELLS, ESQ., & SARAH his wife, to
22 & 23 Jan. 1768   MORTON WILKINSON, ESQ., for £ 17,000 currency,
L & R   748 a. in several adjoining tracts in Colleton
                          Co., on E side freshes of Edisto River; 200 a.
granted 18 Sept. 1703 to GEORGE KNATCHBULL; then bounding N on GIDEON
POWELL; E & S on vacant land; 200 a. granted 1 Feb. 1696/7 to JOHN ASH;
then bounding W on a swamp; other sides on JOHN ASH; 100 a. granted ELIZ-
ABETH SCHENKINGH, on 15 July 1697; then bounding S on ELIZABETH SCHEN-
KINGH; N on SAMUEL LOWELL; E on vacant land; 100 a. granted 11 May 1696
to ELIZABETH SCHINKINGH; bounding W on a small creek; NE & S on vacant
land; 125 a.. on N side of S Colleton (or New London) River, granted 25
Feb. 1714/5 to WILLIAM LIVINGSTON; then bounding E on JOHN ASH; S & N on
vacant land; 21 a. in St. Pauls Parish, Colleton Co., granted CHARLES
ODINGSELLS on 6 Apr. 1753, then bounding NW on Pon Pon River; N on ODING-
SELLS; E on ODINGSELLS & RICHARD ASH; S on Willtown. Witnesses: THOMAS
SLANN, JOHN PETER, CHRISTOPHER WILKINSON. Before JAMES DONNOM, J.P., 1
Feb. 1768. Recorded 21 Apr. 1768 by FENWICKE BULL, Register. Plat given.

Book H-3, p. 467   WILLIAM MOULTRIE, ESQ., & ELIZABETH DAMARIS
13 & 14 Apr. 1764   his wife, to ROBERT WELLS, gentleman, both of
L & R   Charleston, for £ 7600 currency, part of lot
                          #6 in Charleston, bounding E 30 ft. on the
Bay; N 124 ft. on house & lot occupied by ROBERT WELLS (formerly belonging to JOHN ALLEN); S on house & lot belonging to HOOPER & SWALLOW (formerly ANTHONY MATHEWES); with the dwelling house thereon lately occupied
by ALEXANDER CHISOLM, now in possession of ROBERT WELLS; also the passage
way, fronting N 6 ft. on Tradd Street, 21 ft. deep, bounding S on said
part of lot; E on ROBERT WELLS (formerly JOHN ALLEN; then later DAVID
HEXT); W on LISTON & BENFIELD (formerly DAVID HEXT). MOULTRIE gives bond
of performance. Witnesses: ISAAC MAZYCK, JR., WILLIAM MAZYCK. Before
FENWICKE BULL, J.P. & P. Register. Recorded 23 Apr. 1768.

Book H-3, p. 475   ANNA MARIA (her mark) HAVENNER, of Craven Co.,
2 & 3 June 1767   to BARTHOLOMEW AUSTIN, planter, for £ 500 cur-
L & R   rency, 100 a. on N side Broad River, in Craven
                          Co., bounding on all sides on vacant land;
granted by Lt. Gov. WILLIAM BULL to ANNA MARIA HAVENNER. Witnesses:
FREDERICK (German script) HENRY, WILLIAM POWELL. Before JOSEPH CURRY,
J.P., on 27 July 1767. Recorded 25 Apr. 1768 by FENWICKE BULL, Register.

Book H-3, p. 480   ROBERT WILLIAMS the younger, attorney-at-law,
15 & 16 Jan. 1768   & ELIZABETH his wife, to THOMAS PIKE, gentle-
L & R   man, both of Charleston, for £ 2000 currency,
                          80 a. on Charleston Neck, in St. Philips Par-
ish, Berkeley Co., bounding E on the high road leading from Charleston to
the Quarter House; N on ROBERT WILLIAMS & heirs of JOHN EYCOTT; S on
heirs of EYCOTT. Witnesses: WILLIAM ROPER, JR., JOHN DART, JR. Before

FENWICKE BULL, J.P. & P. Register. Recorded 26 Apr. 1768. Plat of re-survey dated 16 Jan. 1768 by NATHANIEL BRADWELL, D.S.

Book H-3, p. 486   ALEXANDER PETRIE, gentleman, of Charleston, &
15 & 16 Jan. 1768   ELIZABETH his wife, to THOMAS HEYWARD, gentle-
L & R   man, of James Island, for Ⱡ 3000 currency, the
                      SW part of lot #229 in Charleston, with the
house in which THOMAS PIKE, dancing master, lately lived; bounding S 56
ft. on Tradd Street; W on 1 WATSON, now occupied by a Negro wench named
FREE AMY; N on part belonging to ALEXANDER PETRIE; E 153 ft. on part purchased by JOHN STUART. Whereas PETRIE, by L & R dated 7 & 8 Oct. 1767
purchased from DR. SAMUEL CARNE, physician, formerly of Charleston, now a
merchant, in London, all of lot #229 (see Register's Book J-3, p. 3), now
he sells a part to HEYWARD. Witnesses: ANDREW ROBERTSON, JOHN HOUSTOUN.
Before FENWICKE BULL, J.P. & P. Register. Recorded 28 Apr. 1768.

Book H-3, p. 492   ADRIAN MAYER, ESQ., of Purysburgh, Granville
13 Feb. 1764   Co., & BARBARA (N.B. signature is ANNA), his
Release   wife, to GEORGE KEHL, carpenter, for Ⱡ 50 cur-
                      rency, lot #35 in Purysburgh, containing 1 a.,
bounding N & E on streets; S on lot #36; W on #33. Witnesses: MELCHIOR
(German script) LEICHTENSTEIGER, DAVID SAUSSEY. Before DANIEL PEPPER,
J.P., on 7 July 1764. Recorded 29 Apr. 1768 by FENWICKE BULL, Register.

Book H-3, p. 494   JOSEPH REYMOND, retailer, of Savannah, Ga., to
31 Mar. 1767   GEORGE KEAL (KEHL), tanner, of Purysburgh,
Sale   Granville Co., for 25 shillings, Ga. money,
                      (sterling), Pew #16 in the Church of Purys-
burgh. Witnesses: GEORGE (his mark) TUCKER of Savannah, MATHEW ASH. Before JOHN LEWIS BOURQUIN, J.P., 4 May 1767. Recorded 29 Apr. 1767 by
FENWICKE BULL, P. Register.

Book H-3, p. 495   MARTIN (German script) KAWATCH, planter, to
15 Apr. 1768   GEORGE KEHL, tanner, both of Purysburgh, for
Conveyance   Ⱡ 50 currency, 150 a. on Byng's Branch, Salt-
                      catchers, in Prince William Parish, Granville
Co., bounding NW on GEORGE PHILIP PAACHE & vacant land; other sides on
vacant land. Witnesses: JACOB WALDBURGER, CATHERINE WALDBURGER. Before
JOHN LEWIS BOURQUIN, J.P. Recorded 29 Apr. 1768 by FENWICKE BULL, Register.

Book H-3, p. 497   THOMAS FERGUSON, ESQ., of St. Pauls Parish, &
19 & 20 Apr. 1768   MARTHA his wife, to JOHN HORLBACK & PETER
L & R   HORLBACH, of Charleston, for Ⱡ 4000 currency,
                      lot #282 in Charleston, bounding W 98 ft. on
King Street; E on ALEXANDER PERONNEAU; N 200 ft. on MICHAEL KALTEISEN; S
on a street leading from Old Church Street to King Street. Witnesses:
JOHN AINSLIE, ALEXANDER MOULTRIE. Before FENWICKE BULL, J.P. & P. Register. Recorded 2 May 1768.

Book H-3, p. 503   The Rev. MR. ROBERT SMITH, of Charleston, &
9 & 10 Jan. 1767   ELIZABETH his wife, to JOHN MOORE, planter, of
L & R   St. Thomas Parish, for Ⱡ 1400 currency, 400 a.
                      in Berkeley Co., bounding S on Simmon's Creek,
a branch of Cooper River; E on JOHN WALBANK; N on JOHN CORREAR; granted
11 Jan. 1700 to RICHARD GRIFFEN. Witnesses: PATRICK HINDS, ANN GIBBES.
Before FENWICKE BULL, J.P. & P. Register, on 25 Apr. 1768. Recorded 3
May 1768.

Book H-3, p. 508   RICHARD WOODWARD FLOWER, to STEPHEN BULL, of
20 & 21 Nov. 1767   Sheldon, in Parish of Prince William, for
L & R   Ⱡ 4000 currency, 1100 a. on E & W sides of
                      Fish Ponds, commonly called Ashepoo River, in
Colleton Co., granted 16 Mar. 1732 by Gov. ROBERT JOHNSON to THOMAS &
ELIZABETH WOODWARD, jointly, bounding NE on JAMES ST. JOHN; SE on MRS.
ELIZABETH WOODWARD; SW on MR. BELLINGER & unknown land. Whereas THOMAS
died in his minority before division was made, ELIZABETH inherited his
share as surviving joint tenant; at her death her only son, said RICHARD
WOODWARD FLOWER, inherited. Witnesses: JOSIAH PENDARVIS, GODIN GUARARD,
PETER HOE. Before ANDREW LEITCH, J.P. Recorded 4 May 1768 by FENWICKE

BULL, Register.

Book H-3, p. 512 HENRY MIDDLETON, JOHN NEUFVILLE, GABRIEL MANI-
28 Apr. 1768 GAULT, & JOHN SAVAGE, freeholders, appointed
Appraisal by commissioners named in act passed 18 Apr.
1767, an act for granting the King Ŀ 60,000
for building an Exchange & Custom House & new Watch House, in Charleston,
& by EBENEZER SIMMONS & RICHARD BERESFORD, on whose lands part of the
Exchange & Custom House is to be built, also 30 ft. for a street to the
S, E & N of the walls of said building, certify that they have appraised
SIMMONS'S land at Ŀ 5500 currency, & BERESFORD'S land at Ŀ 650 currency.
Before JACOB MOTTE, J.P. Recorded 4 May 1768 by FENWICKE BULL, Register.

Book H-3, p. 513 JOHN RUTLEDGE, ESQ., to JAMES PARSONS, ESQ.,
17 & 18 Feb. 1768 both of Charleston, for Ŀ 800 currency, the N
L & R half of 400 a., being 200 a., in Purysburgh
Township, bounding W on Back River, the NE
branch of Savannah River; N on JOHN LEWIS BOURQUIN; E on unknown land;
the 400 a. bounding N on BOURQUIN; W on Back River; S on ABRAHAM ERHARD;
E on unknown land. Witnesses: JOHN SCOTT, JR., EDWARD RUTLEDGE. Before
D. CAMPBELL, J.P., on 27 Feb. 1768. Recorded 5 May 1768 by FENWICKE BULL,
Register.

Book H-3, p. 517 WILLIAM SIMPSON, ESQ., of Ga., & ELIZABETH his
24 & 25 Mar. 1768 wife, to WILLIAM MIDDLETON, ESQ., of Crowfield
L & R Hall, Great Britain, for Ŀ 50 Ga. money (sterling, 2 tracts of 1200 a. & 100 a. Whereas
GEORGE III under the Great Seal of Ga., on 4 Aug. 1767 granted WILLIAM
SIMPSON 1200 a. in St. Thomas Parish, Ga., bounding N on HENRY MIDDLETON;
SE on marsh of Crow Creek; NE on marsh of White Oak Creek; & on same date
granted SIMPSON 100 a. in said Parish, bounding SW on HENRY MIDDLETON;
other sides on vacant land; now SIMPSON sells to WILLIAM MIDDLETON. Witnesses: BARBARA SIMPSON, JAMES SIMPSON. Before JOHN DRAYTON, J.P. Recorded 6 May 1768 by FENWICKE BULL, Register.

Book H-3, p. 525 CHARLES CAPERS, planter, of Island of St.
6 & 7 Apr. 1768 Helena, Granville Co., & ANN his wife, to
L & R JOSEPH KIMMEL, baker, of Charleston, for
Ŀ 3670 currency, part of lot #97 in Archdale
Square, Charleston, bounding N 88 ft. 2 in. on Queen Street; E 97 ft.
6 in. on part belonging to JOHN WARD; S 91 ft. 9 in. on land on which
Quaker Meeting House now stands; W 97 ft. 6 in on part belonging to FELIX
LONG. Whereas WILLIAM SADLER owned lot #97 in Archdale Square, & by will
dated 12 May 1712 gave all his estate to his daughter, MARY SADLER, who
later married THOMAS CAPERS; & whereas MARY died intestate & her eldest
son & heir, said CHARLES, inherited; his father, however, being entitled
to the land during his lifetime by Courtesy of England; now the father
having died, CHARLES takes possession & sells a part of the lot. Witnesses: JOHN EDWARDS, CHARLES GRIMBALL. Before ROBERT WILLIAMS, JR., J.P.
Recorded 9 May 1768 by FENWICKE BULL, Register. Plat dated 24 Feb. 1768
by RIGBY NAYLOR.

Book H-3, p. 532 WILLIAM TURK, planter, to JOHN SAVAGE, store-
5 & 6 Apr. 1768 keeper, of Ninety-Six, SC, for Ŀ 200 currency,
L & R 450 a. on S branch of Santee River called
Saluda River, bounding E on DANIEL BURNET
(called Saluda Old Town); S & W on vacant land; granted 12 June 1751 to
JOHN TURK, father of WILLIAM, who bequeathed the land to WILLIAM. Wit-
nesses: WILLIAM CHRISTIE, JAMES JEFFRIES, THOMAS JEFFRIES. Before JAMES
MAYSON, J.P. Recorded 10 May 1768 by FENWICKE BULL, Register.

BOYFIELD, Richard 336
BOYKIN, -- 139
  Edward 3
  Samuel 297
  William 36, 39, 80, 98,
    123, 139
BOYLES, Ann 289
BOYNTELL, J. 132, 346
BRABANT, Christian 87, 88,
  237
  Daniel 184
  Frownick 87, 237
  Isaac 183, 184, 206
BRADLEY, Agnes 154
  James 154
  Lydia 149
  Samuel 154
  William 147, 240, 302
BRADLY, John 294
BRADWELL, Elizabeth 315
  Isaac 8, 108, 254
  Jacob 8
  Nathaniel 8, 31, 202,
    271, 287, 315, 377
BRADWELL, Thomas 141, 189,
  323
BRADY, Patrick 297
BRAILSFORD, Elizabeth 110,
  .339
  Joseph 98, 102, 133,
    185, 189, 214, 232,
    238, 240, 245, 255,
    257, 263, 269, 298,
    320
  Morton 110
  Samuel 101, 106, 110,
    180, 213, 240, 255,
    339, 346
BRANCH, Buck 69
BRAND, John 118, 224
BRANDFORD, Barnaby 254
  Ezekiel 299
  William 151, 170, 341
BRANFORD, Ann 55
  Barnaby 356
  Elizabeth 55, 150, 198
  Ezekiel 8
  William 6, 55, 150,
    187, 322
BRANHAM, Michael 139
  Susannah 139
BRAUND, John 187, 188,
  268
BRAVANT, Christian 265
BRAWN, Henry 114
BRAYES, John 157
BRAYTON, George 50
BRAZIER, Zachariah 60,
  222
BREACH, William 208, 232
BREADY, Daniel 169
BREMAR, Francis 63, 76,
  77, 80, 353
  James 63
  John 165, 188, 189,
    214, 222
  Martha 79, 165
  Peter 213
  Solomon 213
BRENAN, Michael 293
BREOMRR, Daniel 243
BRETTON, Mary 92, 93
BREWERTON, George 324
BREWTON, John 279, 336,
  345
  Mary 222
  Miles 37, 38, 130,
    151, 154, 173, 191,
    202, 262, 267, 271,
    277, 278, 279, 287,
    300, 306, 308, 318,
    319, 324, 336, 340,
    345, 359, 369, 370

BREWTON (cont.)
  Rebecca 300
  Robert 60, 76, 97,
    222, 244, 300
  Susanna 173
BREWTONO, Col. -- 195
BRIAN, Hugh 48, 49
  Joseph 49
  Robert 274
BRICKEL, Martin 189, 346
  Mary 189, 346
BRICKLES, Sarah 263
  Thomas 263, 264, 296
BRIGEL, John 245
BRIKEL, Jacob 316
BRIMBALL, Charles 12
BRINDLEY, Samuel 100
BRISBANE, -- 118
  Elizabeth 128
  James 204, 220, 243,
    255
  Margaret 216, 320
  Robert 130, 213, 218,
    230, 243, 253, 257,
    260, 267, 270, 274,
    275, 278, 287, 309,
    372
  William 24, 41, 43, 52,
    97, 117, 118, 216,
    230, 243, 267, 274,
    275, 279, 284, 286,
    287, 292, 303, 320
BRITCHES, William 50
BRITON, John 35
BRITTON, Daniel 89
  Joseph 120, 137, 158,
    246, 271, 278
  Mary 120
BROADBELT, Mr. -- 240
  William 223
BROADWAY, Nicholas 264
BROBANT, Daniel 324
BROCKINTON, John 259
  Joseph 254
BROKINGTON, William 286
BROOK, Edward 70
BROOKS, Christopher 76
BROOMHEAD, Robert 216,
  217
  Mrs. Robert 216, 217
BROUGHTON, Alexander 22,
  130, 200
  Andrew 96, 214, 242
  Ann 214
  Charlotta Henrietta
    177, 178
  Mrs. Hannah 214
  Mary 362
  Nathaniel 46, 52, 177,
    178
  Peter 214
  Thomas 5. 10, 13, 20,
    27, 34, 35, 36, 38,
    40, 48, 59, 60, 62,
    63, 75, 79, 85, 92,
    95, 98, 100, 111,
    113, 115, 118, 124,
    133, 134, 148, 162,
    171, 177, 178, 181,
    182, 190, 198, 210,
    214, 216, 231, 233,
    235, 241, 242, 253,
    260, 262, 263, 272,
    273, 284, 287, 290,
    299, 302, 307, 337,
    343, 347, 349, 357
BROWN, Andrew 80, 126,
  201, 208, 289, 321,
  369
  Boughard 374
  Catherine 146
  Casper 303
  Charles 118, 244, 292

BROWN (cont.)
  David 71, 110, 194
  Elizabeth 147
  James 73
  Jane (Jean) 84
  John 164, 245, 246,
    332, 341, 353
  Joseph 161, 173, 191,
    199, 212, 330, 332,
    333, 334, 337, 344
  Lazarus 84
  Malcom 160, 289, 335
  Michael 149
  Nathaniel 3, 114, 186,
    333
  Patrick 55, 56, 95,
    113, 260
  Robert 64, 147, 270
  Samuel 73, 74, 269
  Sarah 55, 167, 246
  Thomas 25, 55, 113,
    197, 202
  William 202, 278
BROWNE, Patrick 183
BROWNELL, George 65
  John 189
BRUCE, John 263, 333, 373
  Mary 16
  Thomas 16, 17
BRUMTON, Andrew 336
BRUNEAU, Ann 315
  Paul 73, 315, 371
BRUNETT, Eisei 128
  Elisha 53
BRUNNER, Ulrich 81
BRUNSON, Daniel 235
  David 164
  George, Jr. 164, 181
  George, Sr. 164
  Isaac 80, 164, 235
  Isaac, Sr. 164
  James 80
  Margaret 164
  Rebecca 80
BRUSE, Jacob 334
BRYAN, -- 209
  Ann 87
  Catherine 16, 54
  Edward 124
  Hugh 11, 16, 19, 29,
    32, 41, 43, 52,
    53, 54, 89, 97, 103,
    111, 159, 228, 275
  Jonathan 27, 28, 29,
    32, 53, 54, 86, 149,
    227, 237, 278, 279
  Joseph 16, 17, 32, 54,
    87, 127
  Joseph, Sr. 127
  Mary 27, 41, 43, 52,
    54, 86, 103, 111,
    127, 152, 159, 227,
    237, 267, 279, 283
  Providence 16
  Thomas 54
BUBSEY, George 248
BUCHANAN, William 8, 54,
  167, 181
BUCHANNON, William 295
BUCHE, John 221, 358, 360,
  362
BUCHRELSIS, Jacob 3
BUCKETTS, Abraham 26
BUCKHOLT, Peter 39, 269
BUCKHOLTS, Abraham 47, 311
  Jacob 73, 74, 269
  Jacob, Sr. 95
BUCKHOLTZ, Abraham 66, 71,
  84
BUCKINGHAM, -- 138
  Lewis 362
  Mary 138
BUCKLE, Thomas 200

DICKSON (cont.)
John 138, 139
Thomas 303
DIDCOT, Elizabeth 150,
340, 346
DIDCOTT, Elizabeth 123,
189
Joseph 27
DILL, Elizabeth 56
John 85, 91, 124, 303
Joseph 56
DILLON, Robert 256, 275,
284, 347
DINGLE, Joseph 201
DISTON, Thomas 115, 233,
254
DITMAR, Albert 230
Christian 230
DIXON, Rebecca 21
Thomas 21, 108
DIXSEE, James 53
DIXSON, James 248
DOAN, Nathaniel 133
DOBBINS, Joseph 202, 261
DOBELL, John 268
DOBIEN, William 171
DOBS, Forton 275
DOCKWRAY, William 101,
102, 103, 104, 105,
106, 143, 226
DODD, John 81, 82, 363
DODGIN, William 330
DOGGET, Elizabeth 288
DOLLEY, Daniel 23, 24
DOLLOY, P.M., Daniel 142
DOME, Stephen 205
DOMINIC, John 369
DOMPERT, Michael 367
DONALDSON, Arthur 368
DONAVAN, Daniel 270
DONERVILLE, Isaac Ligrand
173
DONGWORTH, Henry 123, 294,
361
DONHOM, John 160
DONNEN, James 211
DONNING, Frances 287
Thomas 304
William 182, 233, 287,
328
DONNOM, Jacob 157
James 12, 133, 158,
276, 279, 376
Jonathan 158
DONNON, William 140
DONOVAN, Cornelius 211
James 193, 321
Marion 172
DORMAN, Michael 344
DORMERVILLE, Isaac
Legrand 361
DORRINGTON, Thomas 282
DORSEY, Fredrick 308
Joshua 308
DORSIUS, Peter Henry 35
DOUGHTY, Thomas 373
DOUGLAS, John 312
Philip 20
Capt. William 146
DOUGLASS, George 312, 348
Mary 160
Philip 196, 375
Thomas 311, 312
DOURGONIST, Peter 160
DOUSE, Stephen 57
DOUXSAINT, Mrs. -- 110
Jane 314, 325
Margaret 313, 314
Paul 2, 138, 144, 173,
201, 313, 314, 315,
327
DOUCE, Gideon 108
DOWLAN, John 207

DOWLING, John 207
DOWNES, -- 136
Arthur 365
Richard 135, 272
DOWNS, Walter 39, 57, 93
William 117
DOWSE, Stephen 110, 183
DOYLEY, -- 148
Ann 166
Daniel 138, 147, 171,
176, 180, 186, 205,
207, 210, 213, 215,
251, 260, 263, 277,
278, 287, 295, 319,
328, 340, 365
DOYLIS, Mr. 226
DOZER, Leonard 304
DRAKE, John 206, 219,
287, 290
Jonathan 223, 233,
241, 264, 309, 310,
322
Mathew 259, 309
William 46, 160
DRAKEFORD, John 276
DRAYER, George 345
Godfrey 336, 345
DRAYTON, -- 23, 24, 27,
56, 64, 94, 95
Mr. -- 134, 201
Ann 109
Francis 41
John 12, 22, 51, 57,
58, 64, 78, 91,
109, 116, 118, 167,
170, 179, 182, 181,
206, 222, 236, 271,
323, 378
Margaret 58, 109, 182
Mrs. Mary 118
Stephen 175, 218, 222,
228, 244, 302, 308,
314
Thomas 102, 103, 104,
105, 106, 107, 108,
109, 118, 126, 145,
155, 175, 198, 208,
213, 218, 222, 341
William 27, 66, 71,
118, 192, 193, 198,
258, 278, 343
DREHER, Godfrey 183
DRENNAN, William 366
DREW, John 200
Margaret 259
Mary
Nathaniel 260
DRING, Az 59
DROMGOLE, Paul 132
DROSE, Daniel 254
DROZE, Jane 226
Isaac 226
DRUMMOND, David 31
James 363
DRY, Mary Jean 148
William 87, 88, 148,
240, 286
DRYDEN, -- 268
DUBOIS, James 180
John 164
DUBOSE, Isaac 90
Jephthah 90
John 297, 329
Mary 329
DUBOURDIEU, Joseph 4, 51,
58, 61, 62, 73, 74,
89, 95, 117, 125,
130, 150, 158, 161,
162, 173, 175, 191,
211 263, 349
Judith 302
Samuel 235
DUBQURDIEU, Mary 51

DUCAT, George 54, 59
Martha 54
DUCIT, William 39
DUCKER, (TOOKER) George
363
DUCKETT, Mr. -- 231
Elizabeth 231
David 308
DUDLEY, Charles 244, 265
George 180, 181
DUE, Benjamin 195
Daniel 230
DUESTO, Anthony 232
DUGARD, Benjamin 168
DUGUE, James 313
DUKE, Elizabeth 253
DUKES, Benjamin 362
John 288
DULARQUE, Noah 44
DULLEN, Maurice 31
DUMAY, Jane 327
DUMMAY, Peter 159
DUNBAR, Robert 25
DUNCAN, George 97
Mary 97
DUNDON, Edmund 36
DUNGWORTH, Henry 293
DUNHAM, Ebenezer 194
DUNLAP, Samuel 1, 329
DUNLOP, Elizabeth 230,
286
Elizabeth Hunter 230
William 230, 286, 287
DUNN, -- 191
Alexander 162, 175,
190
Drury 99, 222
John 373
DUNNAHOE, James 161
DUNNAM, Ebenezer 158
Frances 194
John 180
DUNNING, Frances 287
William 287
DUPEE, Joseph 283
DUPEY, Andrew 156, 305
DU PONT, Mr. -- 200
DUPONT, A. 99
Abraham 227
Cornelius 92, 208, 227
Gideon 161, 291
Gideon, Jr. 185, 189,
247
DYMES, Thomas 289
DUPRE, Daniel 274
Josiah 376
Mary 239
Samuel 259
DUPREE, Andrew 180
Ann 157, 259
John 157
Josias 142, 157, 259,
277
Josias Garnier 180
Lewis 157
DUPREY, Andrew 180
Anthony 110
Jane 180
DUPUY, Jane 81, 82, 143
DUQUE, James 67
DURAND, George 94
Levi 187
DURANT, Henry 159, 204
Rebekah 159
DURFFEY, Thomas 264
DURHAM, John 61
Lydia 147
DUSE, Christian 245
DUTARQUE, Elizabeth 325
John 7, 43, 90, 117,
138, 164, 180, 278,
321, 324, 325, 345,
371

www.ingramcontent.com/pod-product-compliance
Lightning Source LLC
Chambersburg PA
CBHW021843020426
42334CB00013B/168